THE CAMBRIDGE

History of the Book in Britain

The history of the book offers a distinctive form of access to the ways in which human beings have sought to give meaning to their own and others' lives. Our knowledge of the past derives mainly from texts. Landscape, architecture, sculpture, painting and the decorative arts have their stories to tell and may themselves be construed as texts; but oral traditions, manuscripts, printed books, and those other forms of inscription and incision such as maps, music and graphic images, have a power to report even more directly on human experience and the events and thoughts which shaped it.

In principle, any history of the book should help to explain how these particular texts were created, why they took the form they did, their relations with other media, especially in the twentieth century, and what influence they had on the minds and actions of those who heard, read or viewed them. Its range, too – in time, place and the great diversity of the conditions of text production, including reception – challenges any attempt to define its limits and give an account adequate to its complexity. It addresses, whether by period, country, genre or technology, widely disparate fields of enquiry, each of which demands and attracts its own forms of scholarship.

The Cambridge History of the Book in Britain, planned in seven volumes, seeks to represent much of that variety, and to encourage new work, based on knowledge of the creation, material production, dissemination and reception of texts. Inevitably its emphases will differ from volume to volume, partly because the definitions of Britain vary significantly over the centuries, partly because of the varieties of evidence extant for each period, and partly because of the present uneven state of knowledge. Tentative in so many ways as the project necessarily is, it offers the first comprehensive account of the book in Britain over one and a half millennia.

JOHN BARNARD · D. J. MCKITTERICK · I. R. WILLISON
General Editors

Frontispiece: Robert Seymour, 'The March of Intellect', 1829. Courtesy of The Lewis Walpole Library, Yale University.

THE CAMBRIDGE

History of the Book in Britain

*

VOLUME V

1695–1830

*

Edited by

MICHAEL F. SUAREZ, S.J.

and

MICHAEL L. TURNER

CAMBRIDGE
UNIVERSITY PRESS

University Printing House, Cambridge CB2 8BS, United Kingdom

Cambridge University Press is part of the University of Cambridge.

It furthers the University's mission by disseminating knowledge in the pursuit of education, learning and research at the highest international levels of excellence.

www.cambridge.org
Information on this title: www.cambridge.org/9781107626805

First published 2009
First paperback edition 2014

Printed by CPI Group (UK) Ltd, Croydon CRO 4YY

A catalogue record for this publication is available from the British Library

ISBN 978-0-521-81017-3 Hardback
ISBN 978-1-107-62680-5 Paperback

In Memoriam
Hugh Amory
Don McKenzie
Michael Treadwell
manet opera homines moriuntur

Contents

II · LITERATURE AND THE CULTURE OF LETTERS 631

III · SPECIALIST BOOKS AND MARKETS 711

Illustrations

Plates

Figures

Tables

Contributors

NICOLAS BARKER is Editor of *The Book Collector*.

IAIN BEAVAN is a Senior Curator in Historic Collections, University of Aberdeen.

MAUREEN BELL is Honorary Reader in English Literature at the University of Birmingham and is Director of the *British Book Trade Index* on the Web project.

CHARLES BENSON is Keeper of Early Printed Books at Trinity College Dublin.

JOHN BIDWELL is Astor Curator of Printed Books and Bindings at the Pierpont Morgan Library, New York.

THOMAS F. BONNELL is Professor of English at Saint Mary's College, Notre Dame, Indiana.

ASA BRIGGS is Chairman of the Editorial Advisory Board for *The Cambridge History of the Book in Britain*.

JAMES J. CAUDLE is the Associate Editor of the Yale Boswell Editions at Yale University.

TIM CLAYTON is the author of *The English print, 1688–1802* (1997), *Hogarth* (2007), *Caricatures* (2007), and other works.

BERNHARD FABIAN is Professor Emeritus of English Literature and Bibliography at the University of Münster.

C.Y. FERDINAND is Fellow Librarian at Magdalen College, Oxford.

ANTONIA FORSTER is Professor of English at the University of Akron.

JAMES N. GREEN is Librarian of the Library Company of Philadelphia and on the editorial board of the *History of the Book in America*.

DUSTIN GRIFFIN is Professor of English at New York University.

ISOBEL GRUNDY is Professor Emerita of the University of Alberta and is currently one of the Orlando Project team.

MICHAEL HARRIS is Reader in Media History at Birkbeck College, University of London.

JOHN HINKS was Research Fellow on the *British Book Trade Index* project at the University of Birmingham and is now an Honorary Visiting Fellow at the Centre for Urban History, University of Leicester.

YOLANDE HODSON, formerly of the Military Survey and the British Library Map Room, is an independent map historian currently completing a catalogue raisonné of King George III's military maps in the Royal Collection at Windsor Castle.

P.G. HOFTIJZER is Professor of the History of the Book at the University of Leyden.

DAVID HUNTER is Music Librarian at the University of Texas, Austin.

ANDREA IMMEL is Curator of the Cotsen Children's Library at the Princeton University Library.

RICHARD LANDON is Director of the Thomas Fisher Rare Book Library and Professor of English at the University of Toronto.

O.S. LANKHORST is Librarian at the Centre of Dutch Monastic Life in the monastery of St Agatha (near Nijmegen).

JOHN MCCUSKER is Ewing Halsell Distinguished Professor of American History and Professor of Economics at Trinity University in San Antonio, Texas.

WARREN MCDOUGALL is an honorary fellow at the Centre for the History of the Book, Edinburgh University, and co-editor of vol. II (1707–1800) of the Edinburgh History of the Book in Scotland project.

B.J. MCMULLIN is an Honorary Research Associate in the Centre for the Book at Monash University.

Brian Maidment is Professor of English and Associate Director of the Centre for Literary and Cultural Studies at the University of Salford.

Scott Mandelbrote is a Fellow and Director of Studies in History at Peterhouse, Cambridge, and a Fellow of All Souls College, Oxford.

Keith Maslen is the author of *Samuel Richardson of London, printer* (2001), and an Honorary Fellow of the English Department, University of Otago.

James Mosley, formerly Librarian of the St Bride Printing Library, London, is Visiting Professor in the Department of Typography and Graphic Communication, University of Reading.

Robin Myers is Archivist Emerita to the Worshipful Company of Stationers.

Nicholas Pickwoad is a Visiting Professor at the University of the Arts, London and adviser on book conservation to the National Trust.

Wilfrid Prest is Professorial Fellow in History and Law at the University of Adelaide.

John Valdimir Price is the author of books on David Hume and is one of the General Editors of *The dictionary of eighteenth-century British philosophers* (1999).

James Raven is Professor of Modern History at the University of Essex.

Isabel Rivers in Professor of Eighteenth-Century English Literature and Culture at Queen Mary, University of London.

Shef Rogers is Senior Lecturer in English at the University of Otago.

Mark Rose is Professor of English and Associate Vice Chancellor at the University of California, Santa Barbara.

Graham Shaw is Head, Asia, Pacific and Africa Collections at the British Library, London.

Marie-Luise Spieckermann teaches English Literature at the University of Münster.

Michael F. Suarez, S.J., Director of the Rare Book School at the University of Virginia, is also University Professor and Professor of English.

Kathryn Sutherland is Professor of Bibliography and Textual Criticism at the University of Oxford.

JAMES TIERNEY is Professor Emeritus in the English Department at the University of Missouri-St Louis.

JONATHAN R. TOPHAM is Lecturer in the History of Science, University of Leeds.

MICHAEL L. TURNER was formerly Head of Preservation Services at the Bodleian Library, Oxford, and Lecturer in the History of Printing at the University of Oxford.

MICHAEL TWYMAN is Professor Emeritus of Typography and Graphic Communication at the University of Reading.

MARCUS WALSH is Kenneth Allott Professor of English Literature at the University of Liverpool.

ALICE WALTERS is Associate Dean at St Francis University, Loretto, Pennsylvania.

MARCUS WOOD is Professor of English at the University of Sussex.

Acknowledgements

We are indebted to many who have helped us bring this project to fruition, most especially to our team of contributors - forty-seven strong and hailing from eight countries - who together have produced a book that no one individual could have written: *plurimi pertransibunt, et multiplex erit scientia*.

John Barnard, David McKitterick and Ian Willison, General Editors of the project, have offered encouragement, expertise and good counsel at every turn. In the midst of the many difficulties and small victories attendant upon such an undertaking, they have invariably brought a capacious and humane perspective to our endeavours. All three have generously extended themselves far beyond their remits from Cambridge University Press.

Each of the three dedicatees of this volume, each a friend and much-admired colleague, deserves special mention. Don McKenzie, chief begetter of *The Cambridge History of the Book in Britain*, died while co-editing Volume IV with John Barnard. He was both mentor and example to us. Hugh Amory, co-editor of the first volume of *The History of the Book in America*, was to have written a central chapter on the workings of the book trade for this volume, before death prevented him from undertaking that difficult commission. Michael Treadwell, author of the final chapter in Volume IV, generously intended to begin Volume V with a companion study, a design he had planned to fulfil as co-editor of this book. The volume you now read would have been much the better were it not for the untimely loss of these estimable scholars.

Much of the research in this volume would have been impossible without the *English Short-Title Catalogue* (*ESTC*); accordingly, we wish to acknowledge the Herculean labours of the *ESTC* teams at Riverside, California, and at the British Library. Thanks too are due to the agencies that funded the project over many years, including the Andrew W. Mellon Foundation, the National Endowment for the Humanities, the British Library, the United States Department of Education, the Rockefeller Foundation, the H.W. Wilson Foundation, the

National Endowment for the Humanities, the Carl and Lily Pforzheimer Foundation, the Gladys Krieble Delmas Foundation, the American Council of Learned Societies, the Ahmanson Foundation and the Pew Charitable Trusts. More than any other recent development, the *ESTC* has changed many of the ways in which we conduct book-historical and bibliographical research.

At Cambridge University Press, Caroline Bundy and Linda Bree have sustained us with their kindness, advice and encouragement; Maartje Scheltens has handled technical matters with patient forbearance. During the production process, we have received help from a legion of others too numerous to mention.

Michael Suarez would like to acknowledge the excellent help he has received from Kathleen Urda, Rebecca Stark Gendrano and Megan Burke Witzleben during their time as graduate students at Fordham University. Mark Meredith and Isaias Noel Gendrano III provided expert statistical assistance. Thanks too – for the gifts of time and financial support – are due to the American Council of Learned Societies; the National Endowment for the Humanities; the Radcliffe Institute for Advanced Study, Harvard University; Fordham University; and Campion Hall, Oxford. In addition to the General Editors, a number of colleagues have offered advice and encouragement, including Lesley Higgins, Isabel Rivers, Shef Rogers, Keith Maslen, James McLaverty, Roger Lonsdale, Bruce Redford, Stuart Sherman, Stephen Fix, Sarah Zimmerman, Peter D. McDonald, Robert Darnton, Suzanne Aspden, Adam Budd, William St Clair, David Vander Meulen, Thomas Bonnell, William Zachs, Rick Sher, Stephen Parks, Vincent Giroud, Henry Snyder, Kristian Jensen, Maureen Bell, Ian Gadd, Henry Woudhuysen, Andrew McNeillie, Richard Ovendon, Nick and Pam Coote, William Proctor Williams, Alvaro Ribeiro, Gerard Reedy, Jeffrey von Arx, Brian Dunkle, Gerard Hughes, Joseph McShane, Howard Weinbrot, Stephen Karian, Christine Ferdinand, Tim Clayton, Marcus Walsh, Jim Tierney, Robert DeMaria, James Raven, Anna Battigelli, G. Thomas Tanselle, Martin Maw, Stephen Tabor, Jan Palmowski, Tore Rem, Lukas Erne, John Bidwell, Daniel Traister, Stephen Weissman, John Richetti, Bart Van Es, Simon Eliot, Leslie Howsam, Arthur Cash, Giles Mandelbrote; the Jesuit communities of Campion Hall, Oxford, and Spellman Hall at Fordham University; the late Vincent Bywater, W. Speed Hill and Harold Love. Thanks too to the library staffs of the Bodleian Library (especially the Fantastic Four of the Upper Reading Room) and the British Library. Finally, I'd like to express deep gratitude to my best teachers, Felix and Toni Suarez.

Michael Turner writes:

In addition to the acknowledgements that Michael Suarez has already made, I would particularly like to thank the Bodleian Library which, in giving me employment, provided me with a lifetime surrounded by the raw materials that are the subject of this book. It also provided colleagues who set standards and generously shared their knowledge. I would like to thank my first 'Keeper' – Lars Hanson, who first encouraged me into research – and my three colleagues of those early days – Desmond Neil, David Rogers and Paul Morgan, who taught me so much.

Working in the Bodleian, and travelling under its auspices, also allowed me to meet and learn from so many of the world's leading bibliographers and historians of the book. Many of those already mentioned by Michael Suarez would be included, but I must pay my own respects to Don McKenzie and Michael Treadwell whose work was closest to my own interests and who were the most generous and supportive friends one could have. There is no doubt that my own work largely stems from the influence of Graham Pollard, whom I was privileged to know in his later years and who shared his knowledge and experience in the most entertaining way – usually over tea in the Bodleian canteen, often in the Sorbonne restaurant in Oxford, and on occasion at Blackheath. Other scholars in the field who have influenced and helped me should be acknowledged: Jim and Patience Barnes, Terry Belanger, David Foxon, Louis James, John Johnson (whom I never met, but whose wonderful collections – which taught me so much – I was privileged to curate), Marcus McCorison, Robin Myers, Ray Nash, Simon Nowell-Smith, Roy Stokes, Bob Rosenthal, Bill Todd, Edwin Wolf.

The Bodleian continues in its generous way to extend to me its hospitality and much practical help.

Another project of the Chairman of our Editorial Advisory Board, Lord Briggs – 'The History of Longmans' – provided over a number of years a series of important seminars in Worcester College. Organised by Annabel Jones and sponsored by Tim Rix – two people whose enthusiasm for the subject has proved to be of significant importance over the years – the seminars brought academics into contact with senior and significant members of the 'trade', much to the benefit of the academics. To them we are especially grateful.

Finally, endless thanks to my wife, Elizabeth, for her patience and 'listening'!

Jacob Tonson once sent John Dryden two melons to encourage and sustain him in his labours. For the many kinds of sustenance and encouragement we have received – from those mentioned here and many others – we humbly give thanks.

Michael F. Suarez, S.J.
and
Michael L. Turner

Introduction

MICHAEL F. SUAREZ, S.J.

The worldliness of print

This is a book about the worldliness of print in Britain from the final lapse of the Printing Act in 1695 to the thoroughgoing development of publishing as a specialist commercial undertaking and the industrialization of the book in 1830. The collective aim of the forty-nine contributors to this volume is 'the intrusion of more history' into the study of books and readers, copyrights and profits, censorship and advertising, technologies and trades – the manifold particulars that condition the pluriform ways in which meanings are made.[1]

This is a book about the history of 'the book', a shorthand for any recorded text: catechisms and commodity price currents, encyclopaedias and children's ABCs, manuscripts and mezzotints, serials and playbills. Just as 'there cannot be a history of ideas without a history of objects', so too is there no authentic history of objects without a dedicated effort to recover their makers.[2] And if such a history does not attend to the ever-developing circumstances of production and distribution, to the fugitive testimonies of consumption, then how may it claim a degree of historical legitimacy? Produced and distributed by networks of workers from authors to hawkers, 'the book' – and the concomitant cultures forged by its consumers – proved a powerful agent for the construction of communities and corporate identities. Nor was this constitutive power of print limited to the literate: many unlettered persons could listen to a single reader.

Observing that contemporary treatments of texts are too often 'worldless', Edward Said diagnosed that a fundamental weakness of textual theory and practice in our time is that it has routinely 'isolated textuality from the circumstances, the events, the physical senses that made it possible and render it intelligible as the result of human work'.[3] Yet, no printer, no book, no reader,

1 McKenzie 1988, Lecture 1, 'Textual Evidence', 3.
2 Tanselle 1995, 271.
3 Said 1991, 4.

no scholar is free from the conditions of material existence. When the working practices of the printer are more imagined than historically accurate, when the critic prescinds from the relationship between materiality and meaning, when the reader is an ideal construct formed from the historian's desires rather than years of working in the archive, then the enterprises of book history are seriously compromised. To the condition of textual unworldliness, this book attempts a form of redress.

The history of the book is capacious in its remit and hospitable to multidisciplinary approaches. Books are the products of social processes and they participate in the formation and reproduction of social practices far beyond those directly associated with the creation and transmission of texts. Hence, we must cultivate an understanding of how the performances and institutions of publication, distribution and reception are imbedded in and informed by larger economic, social and political structures.

The chapters in this collection deploy many different strategies of inquiry – from analytic and enumerative bibliography to economic and social history – in order to investigate how the book and its histories are shaped and understood by the contingencies and complexities of being in the world. The main story that this volume has to tell is the efflorescence of a comprehensive 'print culture' in Britain,[4] a phenomenon that had profound effects on 'the forging of the nation' – on politics and commerce, on literature and cultural identity, on education and the dissemination of knowledge, and on the conduct of everyday life.[5] When read together, the contributions in this history not only chronicle the proliferation of print and the rise of what Samuel Johnson called 'the common reader';[6] they also delineate the commercial, social and intellectual relationships of production and consumption determining and, in part, determined by the world of print. This book about books may thus be read as a step towards constructing a geography of knowledge, as it describes and analyses the technologies, institutions, locales and substantive practices that ultimately lead to the worldly exchanges between the reader and the printed page.

In their range of subjects and methods of examination, these chapters reflect something of the extensive interests and notably various disciplinary – and interdisciplinary – ways of conducting book-historical studies. No orthodoxies have been imposed by the editors, nor have they made any attempt to resolve

4 The concept of print culture should not be taken to diminish the ongoing importance of the oral, aural and scribal transmission of ideas. Studies testifying to the continuing vitality of manuscript culture in the period include Havens 2001, 81–97 and N. Smith 2008. See also McKitterick 2003. For a survey of various models of print culture, see Love 2003.

5 See Colley 1994; Hoppit 2000; Prest 1998; and Langford 1989.

6 See Johnson 2006, I, 334–6.

conflicting viewpoints among the contributors. Writing on Bible imports and parliamentary reports, maps and music, newspapers and antiquarian treasures, the authors of this corporate history strive to make creative and responsible use of the available evidence.

For all this collection's limitations, *The Cambridge history of the book in Britain* is a celebration of what survives, a study whose chapters conduce towards the recovery of human labour and human leisure.[7] It is this contact with publishers, writers, patrons and artisans from the past, and our awareness of the communal processes of creation, that calls us to a humble respect and humane regard for our forebears whose lives have been sustained, like ours, by the making of books.

England: people and cities

The period 1695–1830 saw dramatic changes in the demography of Britain.[8] At the close of the seventeenth century, the population was static – births and deaths in equilibrium – but during the first thirty years of the nineteenth century, Great Britain was growing 'more rapidly than at any earlier or later period'.[9] The mandatory recording of Anglican baptisms, marriages and burials in England (from 1538 onward) allows demographers to document and analyse the population history of England reasonably well, despite deficiencies in the original data.[10] Regrettably, this is not the case for Wales or Scotland.[11]

In 1696, the population of England was approximately 5,118,000; in 1756, it had risen to 6,149,000, a gain of about 17 per cent over sixty years. Twenty-five years later, in 1781, England had some 7,206,000 inhabitants, a rise of 15 per cent in two-fifths of the earlier interval. Thereafter, population growth accelerated even more rapidly: there were 8,671,000 residents in 1801; 10,628,000 just fifteen years after that; and an astonishing 13,254,000 in 1831.[12] Between 1791 and 1831, the population rose at an annual rate of 1.32 per cent, as compared with a sluggish 0.2 per cent for the period 1681–1741. In other

7 For some of the historiographical problems and possibilities raised by book history and national histories of the book, see Suarez 2003–4 (2006).

8 On the demography of Wales, see D.W. Howell 2000; see also B.E. Howell 1973. On the Irish population, see Connell 1950; and Daultrey, Dickson and Ó Gráda 1981.

9 Wrigley 2004, 58; I am indebted to Wrigley, Britain's greatest demographer, for most of what follows on this subject.

10 *Pace* Flinn 1970, 20; cf. Wrigley and Schofield 1981, chaps. 3–5.

11 On Scottish demography, see below. Hunter, chap. 41, below, considers families and their incomes in England and Wales, 1698–1803.

12 Wrigley *et al.* 1997, table A9.1, 614–15.

words, the number of potential book buyers in England was increasing more than six times faster at the end of our period than at the beginning.[13]

The growth in the market for print was not merely a function of a larger citizenry, however; among the most important factors contributing to the tremendous rise in the production and consumption of print is the remarkable economic development that ran in tandem with the population increase.[14] Between 1680 and 1820, the population of Great Britain increased by 140 per cent.[15] The British Gross Domestic Product (GDP), or total value of goods produced and services provided, rose approximately 246 per cent, as compared with an increase of approximately 80 per cent among Britain's continental rivals.[16] One economist estimates that in 1820 the GDP per capita in Britain was 36 per cent larger than in the Netherlands and 44 per cent larger than in France.[17] Because England was significantly more prosperous than Wales or Scotland, the differences between England and its continental counterparts would have been even greater.[18]

By 1800, England had the lowest percentage of its workforce engaged in agriculture in all of Europe except the Low Countries: whereas some 55 per cent were working on the land in 1700, only about 40 per cent were doing so in 1800.[19] It was this transformation in agricultural productivity as much as any other factor that drove England's rise in population and widespread prosperity.

Between 1695 and 1830, a significant fall in infant mortality,[20] relative stasis in childhood mortality and an impressive decline in adult mortality – including maternal mortality[21] – combined with higher fertility rates[22] to produce enormous population gains from the 1780s onward.[23] The net effect of these phenomena was that – after recovering from the demographic consequences of the late 1720s, when epidemic disease resulted in England's 'last peacetime quinquennium in which there were more deaths than births'[24] – England experienced accelerating population growth, especially from 1750 onwards.

13 See 'Literacy', below.
14 See Twyman, chap. 2, below, for the increasing predominance of print as a feature of everyday life in Britain.
15 Wrigley 2004, 93.
16 Wrigley 2004, 93.
17 Maddison 1982, table 1.4, 8 and 167; cited in Wrigley 2004, 93.
18 Wrigley 2000, 118–19.
19 Wrigley 1987, 170–2; Wrigley 1986, table 11.12, 332.
20 Wrigley 1998, table 6, 454.
21 Wrigley 2004, 82.
22 Wrigley *et al.* 1997, table 5.3, 134; Wrigley 2004, 74.
23 See also Wrigley 2004, 75, and Wrigley *et al.* 1997, 422.
24 Wrigley 2004, 65; Wrigley and Schofield 1981, table A3.3, 531–5.

Along with this growth came an unprecedented rise in England's urban population. In 1700, 17 per cent of all residents, about 870,000 people, were living in towns with 5,000 or more inhabitants; by 1750, the figure was 21 per cent (the total population had risen by more than a million). In 1800, 28 per cent were urban dwellers[25] – a figure in excess of 2,427,000, or roughly 2.8 times the total for 1700. To put this surge of urbanization into perspective, Wrigley observes that 'England alone accounted for 57 per cent of the net gain in the urban population in western Europe as a whole in the first half of the eighteenth century and as much as 70 per cent in the second half.'[26]

In 1701, approximately 200,000 English people lived in urban settings outside London; by the beginning of the nineteenth century, that figure was rapidly approaching 1.5 million. In 1801, England had six cities with populations greater than 50,000: London (959,000), Manchester (89,000), Liverpool (83,000), Birmingham (74,000), Bristol (60,000) and Leeds (53,000). Following closely behind were Sheffield (46,000), Plymouth (43,000) and Newcastle (42,000). Norwich, the tenth most populous city in England, had 36,000 citizens.[27] To the north, Edinburgh (83,000) was about the same size as Liverpool; Glasgow (77,000) was the fifth largest city in Great Britain and growing rapidly.[28]

London did not grow much faster than the country as a whole: in 1700, Londoners comprised roughly 9 per cent of the nation, as against about 11 per cent in 1801. In marked contrast, however, other urban centres came to a new prominence, rising from just 4 per cent of the national populace in 1700 to 16.5 per cent in 1801.[29] Thus, there were more urban dwellers in England residing outside of the capital than in London itself. The implications for the book trade of this demographic shift were far-reaching indeed.

Scotland: population and trade

Scotland's demographic history is less clear than England's because there are fewer extant records. In 1695, the population of Scotland numbered a little more than one million inhabitants, with some 88 per cent living in the countryside or in towns with fewer than 2,000 citizens.[30] Aberdeen and Dundee each had about 10,000 residents. Glasgow, situated to the west, was half again as

25 Wrigley 1987, table 7.2 on 162; Wrigley 2004, table 3.11, 88.
26 Wrigley 2004, 90; cf. Wrigley 1987, 177–80.
27 Wrigley 2004, 90; Wrigley 1987, table 7.2, 162; cf. Langton 2000, 473, table 14.1.
28 See Scotland, below.
29 Cf. Wrigley 1987, 162.
30 Devine 2000, 151–64; Smout 1987, 204; cf. Houston and Whyte 1989; Houston 1985.

large, with a population of around 15,000, but was growing in size and importance – in part because of its burgeoning trade with Ireland and the Atlantic economy,[31] a connection that would in time become essential for the export of Scottish books. Edinburgh was twice as large as Glasgow, boasting approximately 30,000 souls, a population roughly 5 per cent that of London.

The Bank of Scotland, founded 1695, eventually became a great boon to manufacturing and trade, but many of its more immediate salutary effects were vitiated by the 'Lean Years' (1693–7), a sequence of crop failures causing famine and consequent population loss by emigration and death of some 15 per cent. The Union of 1707 would in the long run also invigorate production and exports, though its bringing together of two economies at very different stages in their development inevitably produced an asymmetrical relationship that, in its first four decades, was often not to Scotland's advantage. Yet, the Union gave Scottish vessels the protection of the British Navy, and made possible legal trade with American markets for such valuable commodities as sugar, rum, indigo and – most lucrative of all – tobacco. In many respects, Scotland's thriving book trade with the American colonies would come to ride the coat tails of the traffic in these goods, which ensured regular, reliable and affordable shipping, and directly led to improvements in overseas finance, marine insurance and cargo handling.[32]

Throughout the first half of the century, the Scottish economy was chiefly agricultural; subsistence farming was more the rule than the exception. During the early decades of the 1700s, a mere 25 per cent of farmers were producing goods chiefly for sale.[33] A number of factors – including war with France (1689–97, 1701–13), the demographic challenges brought on by five years of famine, and competition with financially more developed English markets – help to account for the slow rate of growth in the Scottish economy – and, hence, the book trades – during the first half of the century.[34]

Atlantic trade and exports to Ulster and northern England were helping to animate the Scottish economy, but its structure in 1750 was largely the same as it had been in 1700. Although the towns had grown, about 88 per cent of the population was living in the countryside or in communities with fewer than 4,000 citizens; hence, the economy continued to be predominately agricultural.[35] Moreover, the workforce remained relatively small; the estimated

31 Smout 1963, 194–236; *vide* Lynch 1989, 85–117; Devine 2000, 151–64. Cf. Benson, chap. 17, and Green, chap. 28, both below.

32 Cf. Beavan and McDougall, chap. 16 and Green, chap. 28, both below.

33 Dodgshon 1981, 243; cf. Devine 1994, 15–16.

34 Devine 2004.

35 Crafts 1985.

population had increased since 1700 by a mere 260,000. How then did Scotland come to play such an important role in the printing and publishing trades? In the 1760s, England's northern neighbour began to experience economic growth hitherto unprecedented in Europe.[36]

Industrial development included coal mining, iron, brewing and distilling, and – significantly for the book trades – papermaking, which grew rapidly between 1779 and 1790 and again post-1824.[37] It was in textiles, however, that Scotland came to excel: cotton, linen, wool and silk (in that order) became the nation's most important products. By the beginning of the nineteenth century, the textile industry 'accounted for nearly 90 per cent of all Scottish manufacturing employment'.[38] Another key factor in Scotland's fiscal growth was the tobacco trade. By 1760, Scotland was routinely exceeding England in the annual value of its tobacco imports, with Glasgow holding pre-eminence among all the cities of western Europe in this respect.[39] Scotland's well-developed banking structure nourished these commercial enterprises and was, in turn, strengthened by them.

A government programme of land enclosure (1760–1815) consolidated many smaller holdings, resulting in greater agricultural yields and, hence, higher revenues for the landed classes. The population increased by more than 250,000 between mid-century and 1800 (at a modest growth rate of 0.6 per cent per annum, about half that of England for the same period); a greater proportion of the populace lived in cities and towns, engaging in commercial activity. Of vital importance to the book trades was the fact that, although most Scottish wages remained significantly below those in England,[40] the professional and wealthy mercantile classes were growing both in size and in disposable income.

In 1750, only 10 to 15 per cent of Scotland's still-small urban population belonged to the middle class; by 1830, this important group of consumers constituted 20 to 25 per cent of its burgeoning towns and cities.[41] Cotton manufacturers, lawyers and advocates, and merchants in overseas trade were among the members of this class that increased most rapidly. Because books were luxury goods,[42] the local market was predominantly confined to the landed establishment, the rising commercial elites and their aspiring lesser

36 Crafts 1985; Smout 1987; Mokyr 1993.
37 Thomson 1974, 77, 192. Cf. Bidwell, chap. 8, below.
38 Devine 2004 relating the observation of Sir John Sinclair; on Sinclair, see *ODNB*.
39 Devine 1995.
40 Hunt 1986; cf. Gibson and Smout 1995.
41 Nenadic 1988, 115.
42 See Raven, chap. 3, below.

colleagues, and members of the three traditional professions (doctors, lawyers and the clergy). The Scottish middle class was proportionately smaller than England's; Glasgow and Dundee lacked substantial numbers of professionals, though Edinburgh and Aberdeen were more favourable in this respect.[43] Scotland's trading ties with Atlantic markets, its paper mills, lower wage scales for compositors and pressmen,[44] and inexpensive commercial transport to London, Ulster and the north of England, all made it a particularly attractive centre of the reprint trade.[45]

Figures from the Census of 1841, the first systematic accounting of the Scottish workforce, provide a rough estimate of employment statistics for 1830. In Edinburgh, 3.88 per cent of all workers were engaged in the printing and publishing trades – a higher percentage than were labouring in shipbuilding, coachbuilding, furniture and woodworking, chemicals, or 'general labouring'. Glasgow's printing and publishing workers comprised 1.12 per cent of the total workforce, followed by Aberdeen with 0.91 and Dundee with 0.56 per cent.[46] Although the census results are far from exact for 1841, much less a decade earlier, they nonetheless indicate the Scottish book trade's relative importance.

One reason for the robustness of Scotland's print culture in 1830 was the tremendous urbanization that had taken place during the previous seventy years. According to the 1841 Census, 52 per cent of Scots now inhabited urban-industrial parishes, a remarkable rise of about 40 per cent from the 1750 figure. By 1800, Glasgow and Edinburgh alone accounted for 60 per cent of all Scotland's citizens dwelling in cities and towns. Edinburgh invariably led the way, but between 1800 and 1830 the population of Glasgow was growing faster than that of any other European town of comparable size.[47]

Education and literacy

Literacy in England at the beginning of the eighteenth century was sufficiently high that nearly all those in occupations in which 'literacy was likely to have been of considerable functional value' were able to read and write.[48] At the time of Queen Anne's death, literacy rates in England – calculated from the

43 Nenadic 1988, 111.

44 See Beavan and McDougall, chap. 16 below; cf. Gibson and Smout 1995; Hunt 1986. In contrast, the rate of pay for compositors in Dublin was on a par with their London counterparts, and the wages of Dublin pressmen were only marginally lower than those in London; M. Pollard 1989, 124–6.

45 See Bonnell, chap. 37, below.

46 Rodger 1985.

47 De Vries 1984, 39–48; Devine and Jackson 1995.

48 Mitch 2004, 354; cf. Graff 1987, 234, 242–3.

ability of individuals to sign their names in marriage registers – were approximately 45 per cent for men and 25 per cent for women.[49] The use of signature rates as an index of literacy is sometimes contested, but a number of studies have found that, over time, trends in literacy are positively correlated with signature data.[50] Such figures are best understood as estimates, however, and do not take into account significant variations by region, class or occupation – factors of which the importance has increasingly been recognized.[51]

Many children, even those from labouring-class families, were schooled long enough to acquire basic reading ability.[52] Teaching at home by parents and/or private tutors 'was more important than any group of schools',[53] but the large number of independent, single-teacher schools also had a significant educational impact.[54] Home learning was particularly important for girls. Charity schools too were highly influential in developing literate citizens: in 1723, the Society for Promoting Christian Knowledge (SPCK),[55] which ran the majority of such institutions, had 23,421 students in 1,329 schools. Bibles, catechisms and edifying tracts were, of course, distributed to these institutions, and to many others from the 'lower' classes.[56] Other religious groups and, to a lesser degree, secular benevolent organizations also sponsored schools (e.g. the public grammar schools), but only about 3 or 4 per cent of the school-age population pursued any post-primary formal education.[57]

In Wales, gains in literacy were closely allied to the growth of Methodism, though the Welsh Trust, SPCK and their charity schools were also influential.[58] Although reliable data about literacy levels in Wales are unavailable for our period, general inferences can be made from the growth of printing. In 1718, Wales had one printer (Shrewsbury printers dominating what market there was); by 1820 more than fifty printers were at work, an indication of how much the demand for print – and the market for matter in Welsh and English – had expanded.[59] Although English and Welsh charity schools appear to have

49 Cressy 1980, 176.

50 Schofield 1973; Houston 1988; Reay 1991; cf. Cressy 1980, 53–61. On the limitations of signature data, see Houston 1982, 82 n 8; Graff 1987, 34, 435 n 2.

51 Sanderson 1972; Schofield 1973; Laqueur 1974; Cressy 1977; Houston 1982, 1985; Stephens 1987, 1998, 31–5; Withrington 1988.

52 M. G. Jones 1938, 73–84; Hans 1950; Schofield 1968, 317; J. Simon 1968; Lawson and Silver 1973, 192–5; O'Day 1982; Mitch 1993a, 1993b. Cf. Immel, chap. 40, below, for children's books and school-books.

53 Hans 1951, 22.

54 Lawson and Silver 1973, 202–9.

55 Founded 1698.

56 M. G. Jones 1938, 24; cf. O'Day 1982, 252–5; Lawson and Silver 1973, 181–9, 238–9. Cf. Rivers, chap. 30, McMullin, chap. 31; and Mandelbrote, chap. 32, all below.

57 Roach 1986; Stephens 1998, 40–7; Lawson and Silver 1973, 195–202, 250–6.

58 Jenkins 1998, 113–16.

59 Rees 1998, 132. See also *BBTI*. Cf. Myers, chap. 39, below, for Welsh almanac printing.

declined in importance as the decades progressed,[60] Sunday schools and week-day schools on the monitorial system rose to prominence late in the century.[61] By 1830, there were more students in Sunday schools than in day schools.[62] The resurgent effort to educate the poor in the early nineteenth century was by no means limited to Sunday schools, however.[63] In 1818, there were an estimated 18,500 day schools in England and Wales, with some 644,000 pupils.[64]

Secondary education made no major gains either in enrolments or in curricular development during the century.[65] Much the same could be said for Oxford and Cambridge, though Gibbon's account of his alma mater – probably the most famous assessment of eighteenth-century higher education in England – should not be taken wholly at face value.[66] A sign of the vibrancy of the Scottish universities – in Glasgow, Edinburgh, St Andrews and Aberdeen – is that their enrolments nearly tripled during the eighteenth century.[67] By around 1800, there were more young men studying in the Scottish universities than the combined total number at Oxford, Cambridge and Trinity College, Dublin.[68]

Dissenting academies, though small in number, generally maintained high standards in training ministers and men of commerce.[69] Apprenticeships grew shorter over the century,[70] and the Statute of Artificers had already become largely inoperative before its repeal in 1814.[71] Except in a few circumstances, this decline in formal training probably did not have a significant effect on literacy rates, however.

Throughout the century, literacy continued to rise, with rates for women improving faster than those for men.[72] In most schools, 'instruction itself consisted mainly of spelling, word recognition, and practice reading in the New Testament'.[73] Examining the signatures of grooms in marriage registers,

60 J. Simon 1968.
61 Lawson and Silver 1973, 239–50.
62 See M. G. Jones 1938, 26; Laqueur 1976; Dick 1980; O'Day 1982, 255–8; Mitch 1992; Snell 1999.
63 Lawson and Silver 1973, 239–50.
64 Jones 1938, 27.
65 Lawson and Silver 1973, 177–80; O'Day 1982, 196–216.
66 Stephens 1998, 50–2; O'Day 1982, 258–70; Lawson and Silver 1973, 209–18, 256–8.
67 Stephens 1998, 51.
68 Whatley 1997, 49; O'Day 1982, 275–9.
69 McLachlan 1931; Lawson and Silver 1973, 205–6; O'Day 1982, 212–15; Mercer 2001.
70 Snell 1985; McKenzie 1978 and Turner, chap. 14, below, for book-trade apprenticeships in the eighteenth century.
71 Dunlop and Denman 1912, 240ff.; Derry 1930. See Shaw, chap. 29, below, for young men escaping apprenticeships by going to India.
72 See Grundy, chap. 6, below, for women readers and the growing print markets for them.
73 R. S. Thompson 1971, 21.

Lawrence Stone estimates that, for the period 1754–62, the rate of adult male literacy was 74 per cent in Oxford and Northampton, 66 per cent in Bristol, and 64 per cent in the rural East Riding of Yorkshire.[74] Victor E. Neuburg's reading of the parish register of St Mary, Islington, documenting whether children were able to read or not, provides similar results by a different method.[75] The figures offered by Stone and Neuburg accord reasonably well with R.S. Schofield's more extensive signature research in English marriage registers, indicating that adult male literacy remained stable at around 60 per cent until 1795, rising very modestly to about 66 per cent in 1830. Women made greater strides, however, improving from around 40 per cent possessing reading skills at the mid-eighteenth century to approximately 50 per cent in 1830.[76] As Schofield observes, 'For the early nineteenth century ... a measure based on the ability to sign probably overestimates the number able to write, underestimates the number able to read at an elementary level, and gives a fair indication of the number able to read fluently.'[77]

Correlating these numbers with population statistics accounts for the remarkable growth of the English reading public. Taking into account the changing population and shifting age structure of that population over time, as well as varying literacy rates by gender, we may arrive at the following rough estimates. In 1700, the English reading public aged fifteen and above consisted of approximately 1,267,000 individuals (approximately 815,000 males and 452,000 females).[78] In 1750, the total number of adults able to read was around 1,894,000 (approximately 1,136,000 males and 758,000 females), an increase of nearly 50 per cent. During the following five decades, the rise in the numbers of readers was even more remarkable: the 2,928,000 literate citizens (1,681,000 males and 1,247,000 females)[79] in 1800 constitute a surge approaching 55 per cent. By 1830, there were some 4,287,000 adult readers (2,461,000 males and 1,826,000 females) in England, more than a 46 per cent increase in just three decades. The confluence of an expanding population, especially from 1760 onwards, and improvements in literacy rates, most notably among women,

74 Stone 1969, 104; cf. Schofield 1973.

75 Neuburg 1971, 170–3.

76 Schofield 1973, fig. 2, 445, 446.

77 Schofield 1968, 324; 1973, 440–1.

78 I have not made allowance for the deterioration of literacy with advancing age, a possibility discussed in Cressy 1977, 11–12, who found senescence to be a significant factor only in those over sixty. Those unable to read at the upper end of the age structure would be more than compensated for by readers aged ten to fourteen not counted in this study.

79 For simplicity's sake, I have assumed a sex ratio of 100 (1:1) throughout, when in fact in 1801 it was .974735; Wrigley and Schofield 1981, 594, table A6.6.

produced an adult reading public in England that grew by more than 3 million (approximately 3,020,000) – 238.4 per cent – from 1700 to 1830.

Hazarding a similar analysis for Scotland is fraught with even greater difficulty and, hence, uncertainty. The best calculations I have been able to make must be treated as highly tentative, not least because the historical record is incomplete; I have therefore been obliged to extrapolate from what is known, to make informed assumptions and to rely on estimates.[80] Very roughly then, in 1700 Scotland had about 200,000 readers over the age of fifteen; in 1750, perhaps some 315,000 adults could read, an increase of 57.5 per cent. In 1801, significant increases in population and in female literacy produced a reading public numbering approximately 485,000, a 54 per cent rise. By 1831, that number appears to have grown by some 48.5 per cent to about 720,000, largely for the same reasons.[81] Thus, if such crude demography is to be countenanced, in Scotland there were perhaps 520,000 more adult readers in 1830 than in 1700, an increase of 260 per cent. These estimates for Scotland are less reliable than those calculated for England, but if we combine the final numbers, we may find that some 3,740,000 more readers aged fifteen and over were living in England and Scotland in 1830 than in 1700.[82]

Transportation networks

Improvements in transport networks were essential to the growth of the book trades in our period, not least because increased business was not built so much on selling more books to the same individuals, as it was on selling approximately the same numbers of books to more individuals. Hence, broader and deeper geographic coverage was fundamental. Overland transportation, by far the most common means used to deliver printed materials (whether by mail or private carrier), became faster and more reliable, largely because hundreds of turnpike trusts made substantial investments in improving road quality. By

80 Figures based on Houston 1982; Houston 1985; Flinn 1977; Devine 2000; Houston and Whyte 1989.

81 This figure takes into account the rapidly shifting age structure of the population as well as the findings of Nicholas and Nicholas 1992 on 'deskilling'.

82 Although we may roughly estimate the number of readers in England and Scotland at various intervals between 1700 and 1830, there remains considerable debate about the production, pricing and availability of various kinds of print. In particular, a number of scholars have taken issue with the evidence and arguments marshalled in St Clair 2004, namely, his characterization of readers' habits and access to literature, trade practices, the reprinting and consumption of the 'old canon', and the impact of the 1774 Lords' decision against perpetual copyright on the reprint trade. See Sher 2006, Fergus 2006a, Bonnell 2005–6 (2008) and Bonnell 2008. A number of these, while acknowledging the importance of St Clair's study, have expressed concern about the inaccuracies and omissions besetting his otherwise groundbreaking work. Regrettably, for many contributors to this volume, most of the works here adduced were not published until after their chapters were completed.

1830, approximately 20,000 miles of roads, about one-fifth of the nation's total, were maintained by local entrepreneurs or improvement commissions;[83] the construction and maintenance of bridges was similarly aided by municipal commercial interests.[84] Over time, road surfaces became smoother, more durable and better drained; particularly from the 1750s onward, gradients were engineered to accommodate the transportation of heavy goods.[85] Between 1751 and 1772, virtually every route between the English provincial towns and London was substantially improved, and communication between the provinces could rely on a fairly well-integrated network of roads.[86]

The replacement of pack-horses by wagons, the breeding of more reliable carriage horses (particularly Cleveland Bays), and advances in coach and wagon design also made overland carriage more economical, dependable and faster.[87] Yet, improved overland shipping was also a consequence of better logistical organization and corporate finance – the efficient running of a reliable transportation network over long distances required innovation in both these areas.[88] Between 1695 and 1830, carriers moving goods from London vastly increased their capacity. In 1705, carriers made 453 journeys per week to towns and cities more than twenty miles from London; by 1826, there were 1,025 services, an increase of more than 225 per cent.[89]

Allied to this expansion in services was an even greater rise in productivity: the number of ton-miles hauled expanded between 1.0 and 2.8 per cent with each year.[90] This growth in the number and capacity of carriage services available to the bookseller was accompanied by a concomitant rise in the quality: between 1750 and 1830 average travel times declined by 20 to 30 per cent.[91] In 1750, it took forty hours for the fast coach from London to reach Bristol, 114 miles distant; in 1818, the journey took less than twelve hours.[92] Best of all, increased competition caused charges for overland carriage to fall as much as 33 per cent between 1750 and 1830.[93]

83 Barker and Gerhold 1993, 37–8; cf. Albert 1983.

84 Ginarlis and Pollard 1988, 208–12; Harrison 1992, 246, 259–60.

85 See the *ODNB* for the careers of roadbuilders John Metcalfe and John McAdam.

86 Pawson 1977. These developments were increasingly reflected in British domestic cartography. See Hodson, chap. 42, below.

87 Gerhold 1996.

88 Barker and Gerhold 1993, 23; Daunton 1995, 286. This material and organizational network in turn facilitated the flow of commercial information. See McCusker, chap. 22, below.

89 Gerhold 1988.

90 Ville 2004, 298.

91 Jackman 1916, 335–6.

92 Pawson 1977, 290–1.

93 Pawson 1977, 297; Albert 1983, 55–6; Barker and Gerhold 1993, 40–3.

The net effect of these developments was that books, newspapers and periodicals sent from London to the provinces were arriving more quickly, at a lower cost, and quite possibly in better condition.[94] Greater efficiencies of road transport enabled the London bookseller's premises effectively to become the warehouse of the provincial shop, allowing the provincial bookseller to reduce his stocks while speedily and reliably satisfying local customers' needs.[95] Fewer resources were tied up and opportunity costs were reduced; capital risk was lowered, and the turnover of assets was typically faster because a much higher proportion of inventory passing through the shop was specially ordered rather than purchased on the speculation of future sale.

For the London bookseller, transaction costs were reduced – most immediately in lowered outlays for the delivery of goods, and, perhaps, in more reliable credit arrangements with provincial booksellers who, for the reasons discussed above, could benefit from greater liquidity. In addition, frequent and less expensive overland carriage made consignment arrangements between London and the provinces more convenient and economical, a further stimulus to thoroughgoing market integration. The traffic between provincial consumers and book manufacturers in the capital was not merely amplified, but genuinely transformed.

The market integration made possible by this infrastructure was by no means restricted to transactions involving London, however. By the early 1770s, virtually every city in England was connected to its neighbours by reasonably well-maintained and efficient routes for the conveyance of passengers and goods.[96] Overland transportation from Scotland's principal cities into population centres in northern England had also substantially improved.[97] This augmented network greatly facilitated the conveyance of print *c.*1780–1830 in ways that entirely bypassed the London trade. Books printed in Edinburgh, Glasgow and Aberdeen had ready conduits for circulation in Newcastle, Manchester, Liverpool, York and Leeds; as these cities themselves developed substantial printing industries, their wares could find accessible regional markets. The reach of print was commercially driven, enabled by the co-operation of agents in multiple locations, and made possible by dependable and affordable transport. Stage coaches, heavy goods wagons, hackney carriages, mail coaches, cabriolets, hawkers, runners, porters, costermongers and barrow-men all played their part in the transport and local distribution of books and serials.

94 See Harris, chap. 20; Ferdinand, chap. 21; Tierney, chap. 24; and Maidment, chap. 25, all below.
95 See Ferdinand, chap. 21 and Turner, chap. 23, both below.
96 Pawson 1977.
97 Pawson 1977.

From mid-century onwards, canals and navigable rivers became an increasingly significant part of Britain's infrastructure. Between 1760 and 1830, England and Wales saw the distance covered by inland waterways more than triple to 3,876 miles.[98] In Scotland, three major canals – the Forth and Clyde, the Monkland, and the Union – became vital arteries.[99] In some regions, these watercourses were used for the bulk shipment of paper or books.[100] Britain's ever-growing commercial shipping fleet was also thus employed; seafaring vessels routinely carried books. The British shipping industry was the dominant commercial conduit for bringing British books to India, North America, the Caribbean, continental Europe and Ireland.[101] The port cities of western Scotland played an increasing role in supplying North America with printed matter, for example, while would-be readers of British books and newspapers in India relied almost entirely on cargoes carried by the East India Company's ships.[102] Canal and coastal shipping appears not to have played a significant role in the domestic distribution of print, with the notable exception, from the late 1700s onwards, of Scottish printers using coasters to transport books to London.[103]

The first commercially successful steam locomotives were designed in 1812 for the Middleton Colliery Railway. The Stockton and Darlington Railway, built in 1825 to carry coal from the South Durham coalfield to the port at Stockton-on-Tees, definitively established the superiority of the locomotive over teams of horses for hauling heavy goods. With the construction in 1830 of the Liverpool and Manchester Railway – designed for passengers and freight and powered by George Stephenson's 'Rocket' locomotive – the Railway Age had truly begun.[104]

Newspapers and the Post Office

The growth of the Post Office during the eighteenth century depended upon the improved and expanded transportation network.[105] Ralph Allen of Bath, for example, famously developed cross-posts, extending delivery to regions

98 Duckham 1983, 109.

99 Devine 2004, 404.

100 On the transport of seven cartloads of used books and MSS by river from Norwich to Oxford in Dec. 1731, see the *GM*, 2 (1732), 583. A number of provincial printers were able to serve London thanks to water: Hamilton at Weybridge in the very early nineteeth century is perhaps the most important example. Papermakers in Kent similarly depended upon water transport.

101 The Navigation Acts were relaxed only in the 1820s and were not repealed until 1849. See Beavan and McDougall, chap. 16; Benson, chap. 17; Fabian and Spieckermann, chap. 27; Green, chap. 28; and Shaw, chap. 29, all below. On continental imports, see Hoftijzer and Lankhorst, chap. 26, and McMullin, chap. 31, both below.

102 See Shaw, chap. 29, below.

103 Worthy vessels also carried goods, including books, from Glasgow and points west to Ulster.

104 Gourvish 1988, 57.

105 K. Ellis 1958; Joyce 1893; Hemmeon 1912; Staff 1964; Austen 1978.

well beyond the six principal post roads radiating from London. John Palmer's introduction of mail coaches in 1784 – quickly superseding mounted post boys on main routes – added efficiency and speed. Less generally recognized, however, are the vital importance of the franking system and the role played by the Clerks of the Roads in the distribution of print, especially newspapers.[106]

From the Restoration, the six Clerks of the Roads (officially, 'Clerks of the Inland Office') enjoyed the privilege of franking – sending postage free – as many newspapers as they wished from London to local postmasters throughout the country. The Clerks were paid by the postmasters *2d.* for each newspaper received (in addition to whatever emoluments came from the newspaper publishers); the postmasters, in turn, were entitled to sell or otherwise circulate the newspapers for their own gain. Thus, the Post Office functioned like a newsagent on a national scale. Members of Parliament too could and did frank letters and newspapers, a privilege intended to assist them in conducting business with their constituencies, but in practice used far more liberally.

The numbers of newspapers sent in the early years are not available, but in 1717 the Postmaster General complained that the 'Clerks' ... privilege in franking newspapers ... had grown to such an extent that it was impossible to check the account of them.'[107] Under Walpole, the administration used official state franks in the 1730s to send into the 'country' some 1,400 pro-government newspapers each week to promote its interests (much as Pitt's government would in the 1790s).[108] Within the provinces, distribution was usually handled by local carriers; *Sam. Farley's Bristol Post Man* (published weekly, 1715–25) advertised that it was 'deliver'd to any publick or private house in this city for three half-pence a paper; and seal'd and deliver'd for the country at two pence'.[109]

In 1715, the estimated value of all franks used was £23,000, just 19 per cent of the revenue from pay letters (£121,800). By 1764, the situation had radically changed, largely owing to the growth of newspapers and their readerships outside London: franks were valued at £186,500, with pay letters earning £170,700. The value of postage-free franks now represented 109 per cent of paid-for mail moving through the post; in an interval of less than fifty years, pay letters had increased by half, while franking had risen sevenfold.[110] In the early 1760s, when approximately 9.5 million newspaper stamps were sold annually,

106 What follows is largely taken from Ellis 1958, with supplemental information from Greenwood 1971.
107 Greenwood 1971.
108 See M. Harris 1987; Barker 1998.
109 *ESTC* P3294. See Ferdinand, chap. 21, below.
110 Ellis 1958, 40.

Members of Parliament (including peers) were franking about a quarter of the slightly more than one million newspapers sent through the General Post Office.[111] The remainder were almost entirely franked by the Clerks of the Roads. In addition, the Controller of the Inland Office franked newspapers and other matter to (and from) America and the West Indies, and the Controller and clerks of the Foreign Office to and from the Continent.[112]

By the start of the 1770s, however, newspapers and other printed matter began coming through the Post Office without the need to pay the Clerks. After 1769, when Members' privileges were extended to franking in bulk, they began sending sizeable orders to the Post Office for booksellers and printers.[113] In 1782, when the government sold more than 14 million newspaper stamps, Members' orders accounted for some 60 per cent of the 3 million newspapers sent out of London.[114]

Between 1765 and 1783, Members' franks increased from £34,735 to £97,335 per annum, largely because of bulk circulation orders for newspapers and other forms of print.[115] The creation of a special newspaper sorting office in 1787 helped the Post Office deal with this tide of print – in 1782, for instance, 80,000 newspapers per week were being handled (78,000 going from London and 2,000 coming into the capital). Many of these, especially from 1786 onward, were evening papers created for the provinces – printed late in the day and sent through the mails while still wet. (Customers complained that the damp newspapers frequently spoiled the ordinary letters they came in contact with; the Post Office objected to their weight: sixteen or fewer to the pound.)

By 1792, the abuse of franks for sending newspapers had become so widespread that the need for franking was abandoned; all newspapers could be sent post free. Yet, the Clerks continued to be paid by a number of newspaper publishers because they enjoyed the advantage of strong connections with the nearly five hundred Country Deputies (local postmasters), who were still the main provincial distributors and had authentic and commercially useful local networks. New regulations (1794) also helped the Clerks' business. By 1811, the Clerks were annually sending from London nearly two million newspapers,

111 Ellis 1958, 51. On the government's use of newspaper stamp duties, the 'taxes on knowledge' and regulation of the press, see Rose, chap. 4, and Wood, chap. 48, both below.

112 Ellis 1958, 47. See Green, chap. 28; Hoftijzer and Lankhorst, chap. 26; and Fabian and Spieckermann, chap. 27, all below.

113 Ellis 1958, 52, 158–9.

114 Ellis 1958, 52. This trend threatened the viability of the Inland Office: 75 per cent of the salaries were funded by the Clerks' newspaper revenues.

115 Ellis 1958, 42.

about half of which were evening papers. Yet, by 1829, just 10 per cent of the 11,862,706 newspapers sent from London were conveyed by the Clerks of the Roads. Publishers had their own network of agents, and the extra expense of effectively employing the local postmasters as distributors was, for most, no longer justifiable. In 1834, the newspaper franking privilege for Clerks was terminated.[116]

Even after the free posting of newspapers came into effect, franking privileges continued to have a great impact on the circulation of print. In 1790, Members were franking some 1.6 million items; by 1810, that number had reached 2 million.[117] The movement of printed matter through the post – pamphlets, advertisements, magazines, catalogues – was a major factor in this increase. Politicians of all parties had long recognized the advantages of currying favour with printers, booksellers and publishers. In 1840, however, franking was abolished altogether and a major episode in print distribution was brought to an end.

Chapmen, agents and other networks of distribution

The role played by chapmen in the distribution of print during our period, though impossible to document thoroughly, should not be underestimated.[118] In 1696–7, Parliament passed an Act requiring that all pedlars, hawkers and petty chapmen be licensed; in the first year of registration alone, more than 2,500 men paid the considerable sum of £4 in order to ply their trade legally. About one-fifth of these were in London – where 'the trade publisher supplied the mercuries, the mercuries supplied the hawkers, and the hawkers supplied the public';[119] the rest were widely dispersed over England and Wales. Slightly more than half of those licensed were operating in market towns, where many would have had stalls.[120] A typical chapman's pattern was to purchase local goods in the provinces, selling them en route to the capital; once in London, he bought cheap printed matter – chapbooks, ballads, songbooks, spelling books, woodcut prints, jest books – as well as such goods as combs, pins and needles,

116 Ellis 1958, 125.
117 Ellis 1958, 43.
118 See Turner, chap. 23, below, for a case study on distribution. On distribution in Scotland, Ireland and Wales, see (respectively) Brown and McDougall forthcoming; Gillespie and Hadfield 2006; and Jones and Rees 1998.
119 Treadwell 1982a, 123. Despite their importance, these agents of distribution seldom appear in Stationers' Company records. See Turner, chap. 14, below.
120 Spufford 1981, 116, 118, 120–1.

fabrics and patterns to vend on the return journey.[121] Chapbook wholesalers congregated in Holborn and the Strand and on London Bridge – areas that were well populated with small goods and textile wholesalers as well.[122]

Nor was this extensive network for the distribution of cheap print limited to the capital: a run of chapbooks from 1775 to the 1820s carry the imprint 'Falkirk: printed, where travelling chapmen may be served with histories, catechisms, spelling books, writing paper, &c. as cheap as in Edinburgh or Glasgow',[123] while a Northampton imprint advertises 'ballads, broadsheets, histories, &c. ... much better printed, and cheaper than in any other place in England'.[124] Continued operation of the chapman's trade is testified to both anecdotally – by the reminiscences of an itinerant bookseller travelling through the north-west Highlands to Lochboom in 1820 – and systematically, by the continued prosperity of the printers who catered to this market.[125] Although the survival rates of chapmen's printed wares must be very low indeed,[126] the extant traces of this trade indicate that the market was vigorous, extensive and competitive. The highly effective distribution of the *Cheap repository tracts* (1795–8), and, subsequently, the publications of the Religious Tract Society, in vast numbers by chapmen throughout the country further attests to the vitality of the chapmen's network well into the nineteenth century.[127]

Other networks, including religious groups,[128] also played a prominent role in the spread of print. Imprints document the importance of chapels and vestries as places of distribution and sale in England, Scotland and Wales; to a lesser degree, hospitals were similarly employed, especially for medical and religious tracts. Additionally, the considerable number of books printed for the burgeoning number of clubs and for societies had their own networks of internal distribution and external sales.[129]

Provincial newsagents were another significant means of distributing print. In 1742, the ever-enterprising Benjamin Collins listed ten such representatives from Gloucester to the Isle of Wight in the imprint of the *Salisbury Journal*,

121 On the sale of books by chapmen and pedlars, see Spufford 1981, 111–28; Spufford 1984, 6, 9, 42, 43, 54, 56, 57, 62, 66, 80, 85–6, 89, 145, 154, 163, 204; Rogers 1984 offers a particularly interesting case.
122 Spufford 1981, 111–15; Spufford 1984, 16. On the topography of the print trades in London, see Raven, chap. 13, below.
123 See, for example, *ESTC* T165197, T179560, T177711, T182998, etc. On the Scottish chapbook, see Roy 1974.
124 *ESTC* N70856.
125 Spufford 1981, 124, 128 n 34, 126.
126 For a discussion of survival rates of printed matter, see Suarez, chap. 1, below.
127 See Spinney 1939; Howse 1953, 101–5; Neuburg 1972; Schöwerling 1980; More 2002; Stott 2003, 168–90.
128 See Rivers, chap. 30, and Mandlebrote, chap. 32, both below; Rivers 2007.
129 Clark 2000a. See Topham, chap. 47, below, for the publication and consumption of print by scientific societies. Walters, chap. 46, below, emphasizes the amateur market for scientific and medical books.

which in its first fifty years of circulation (1736–85) had 172 named agents, about 55 per cent of whom were directly affiliated with the book trades.[130] One of these, John Newbery, established a network of forty-three agents to promote and vend the *Reading Mercury*. Such networks became a common feature of regional newspaper dissemination in both England and Scotland, just as London periodicals routinely employed provincial agents.[131]

The strategic use of agents in fixed locations and of travelling representatives was by no means limited to the periodical press, however. Operating from the centre of the book trade at Stationers' Court, Benjamin Crosby (active 1794–1814) sedulously cultivated the provincial market for his books, personally travelling through the provinces to hire agents and establish contacts.[132] Other firms employed travelling salesmen to get their wares into the provinces. An 1806 catalogue for Sabine and Son, just off Fleet Street, explains that 'New and entertaining Histories, Novels, &c.' may be 'had of the Person who leaves this Catalogue, and who will call again with the BOOKS', modestly priced between 6*d.* and 1*s.*[133]

Provincial publishers of books in parts, or numbers, relied almost entirely on travelling representatives for retail sales.[134] Many firms – such as Davies and Booth 'at the Stanhope Press ... Leeds' (with agents in London, Birmingham, Newcastle and Hull); Nuttall, Fisher, Dixon and Gibson's Old-Established Cheap Periodical Publication Warehouses, Liverpool and London; and Cummings's Publication Warehouse in Briggate, Leeds – advertised that subscriptions for books in parts were 'received by the Person who delivers this Bill'. Through the agents of such enterprises, the reach of print was both geographically and socio-economically extensive.

Coffee houses and the book trades

Much has been made of the rise and importance of the bourgeois 'public sphere' in eighteenth-century Britain, and the role that coffee houses played in providing a venue in which newspapers, reviews and the latest political pamphlets were readily available and widely discussed.[135] Yet, coffee houses

130 Ferdinand 1997, 39, 77.
131 See, for example, Bodleian – G. Pamph. 2920, fol. 18; see also an 1809 handbill for *Drakard's Stamford News, and General Advertiser*, fol. 26.
132 Mandal 2006.
133 Bodleian – G. Pamph. 2920, fol. 14.
134 See Benson, chap. 17, below. See Harris, chap. 20, below; Wiles 1957; and Handrea 1978 for books in parts or numbers.
135 Harris 1975. See Forster, chap. 33, below, for the reviews and book reviewing. For a list of coffee houses and inns that had libraries, see *LHD* – Coffee House and Inn Libraries. On coffee houses and allied institutions in Scotland and Ireland as locations for the distribution and consumption of print, see (respectively) Brown and McDougall forthcoming; and Gillespie and Hadfield 2006.

were not only sites of reading and reception; they were also places of promotion, distribution, production and sale. Whether one endorses or disagrees with the highly influential, but much-contested theories of Habermas regarding the coffee house as an arena in which meanings were articulated, negotiated and dispersed,[136] it is clear that a considerable body of bibliographical data testifies to the several roles these establishments played at nearly every stage in the communications circuit.[137]

The *ESTC* lists more than five hundred instances of imprints with 'coffee house' or its variants between 1695 and 1800. Although many of these are merely geographical markers – pointing out that a bookseller's shop is 'over against', 'opposite', 'under', 'next to', 'above' or 'near' a particular gathering place – a substantial number indicate how significant coffee houses were to the conduct of the book trade. Book proposals were frequently distributed, and book subscriptions solicited, at coffee houses, particularly when a specialist clientele (for example, Masons, insurance men, silk traders, antiquaries, Whigs, solicitors) was well matched to a future publication.[138] Evidence from imprints also reveals that published books, especially those printed for the author,[139] were sometimes advertised for sale in coffee houses that catered to groups most likely to buy them – a form of targeted marketing not ordinarily considered in studies of the book trade. A translator of *The liturgy, according to Spanish and Portuguese Jews* (1773), for example, sold his work 'at Sam's Coffee-House, near the Great Synagogue, near Aldgate', London's first Ashkenazic synagogue. Publications undertaken to raise funds for charitable purposes were similarly targeted at specific coffee-house audiences, especially when the author or beneficiary had a personal connection with a particular establishment.[140]

Outside London, authors also helped to ensure the success of their investment by arranging for publications to be sold at the most promising venues: *A guide to the turf* (1786) was principally available 'at Mr Weatherby's coffee-house, New-market', where the likelihood of finding interested consumers was a good bet. The author of a 1735 assize sermon in Rochester used three

136 For 'the public sphere' (*Öffentlichkeit*) see, in addition to Habermas 1989, Melton 2001; and Blanning 2002. See also Warner 1990 and Gross 2002.

137 For the 'communications circuit' in various manifestations, see Darnton 1982; Darnton 1987; and Adams and Barker 1993. Cf. Wolff 1981.

138 The *Public Ledger* for 22 Sept. 1761, for example, advertises that 'a Book for Subscriptions is opened at the Jamaica Coffee-house in St Michael's Alley' for W. Wallace and J. Simpson's *Exact survey of the island of Jamaica, in four maps*.

139 Using evidence from the Bowyer Ledgers, Maslen 1972 finds that, in 1731, about one-third of the number of sheets composed for booksellers were set for authors; approximately 7 per cent of total sheets printed were undertaken at the author's own expense.

140 See, for example, *ESTC* T117082, T12562 and T74560.

locations in Kent to vend his text: the premises of T. Edlin, at the time a bookseller at Maidstone; 'the Star Coffee-House in Chatham'; and 'the Coffee House in Rochester'. Sometimes, when no particular arrangements had been made, an author might resort to the formula 'to be sold at all the coffee-houses in town', such as is found in *The geography and history of Lile* (Edinburgh, 1708), or more generally still, 'to be had of the booksellers, and at the Coffee-Houses, and principal Inns of Edinburgh and Glasgow', as we read in a 1784 imprint.[141]

Occasionally, imprints offer a glimpse into how transactions may have taken place: a volume of continental travels (1742) was 'sold ... at the bar of Old Slaughter's Coffee-house'.[142] A sixteenmo (sextodecimo) pocket book of interest tables (1712) was 'printed for the author, and ... sold at his office in Garaway's Coffee-House'[143] – 'office' more likely denoting 'the place in which a person is usually to be found' than 'a place of business',[144] though both meanings may apply. A number of printer-booksellers had their premises 'at' (next to) or 'at the back of' (behind) coffee houses; their proximity to groups of readers with time, money (or credit) and leisure may well have bolstered sales.

Perhaps the most far-reaching book-trade activity associated with coffee-house culture was the sale of copyright shares among the more important booksellers of the day.[145] The London Coffee House, Ludgate Hill, because of its proximity to Stationers' Hall (just two minutes' walk), was frequently used for sales of copies (copyrights) and stock. Most memorably, the first part of the great Rawlinson sale was held at St Paul's Coffee House in 1722.[146] In the late eighteenth century, trade sales were held at the Horn Tavern, also in Doctors' Commons. The most important institution in this regard, however, was clearly the Chapter Coffee House on the corner of Paul's Alley and Paternoster Row, which grew to be the chief gathering place for members of the trade and the principal centre for the sale of book shares. 'The conversation here naturally turns upon the newest publications, but their criticisms are somewhat singular', observed Bonnell Thornton. 'When they say a *good* book they do not mean to praise the style or sentiment, but the quick and extensive sale of it. That book is best which sells most.'[147]

141 *ESTC* N67860.
142 *ESTC* N67424.
143 *ESTC* T98057.
144 *OED*.
145 See Besterman 1938, 158–60; Blagden 1951; Belanger 1970, 1975; Amory 1984.
146 See Landon, chap. 38, below.
147 *The Connoisseur*, no. 1, 31 Jan. 1754.

The Chapter Coffee House famously took in advertisements for the provincial newspapers; it is less generally recognized that, throughout the eighteenth century, a number of coffee houses in London and Edinburgh were performing a similar function for the local press. In addition, some newspapers used coffee houses to take in 'essays, letters, and articles of intelligence'. The *General Advertiser*[148] gave notice that 'advertisements, letters and essays' would be received at 'Seagoe's and Owle's coffee-houses, Holborn'.[149] In the functions it performed for provincial newspapers, the Chapter Coffee House was preeminent, but by no means unique: the *Salisbury and Winchester Journal*[150] listed its agents in the capital 'where advertisements, articles of intelligence, &c. are taken in' at 'the London, Chapter, Guildhall and Peele's Coffee-Houses'.[151] In addition, many such establishments not only subscribed to a wide variety of newspapers and periodicals, but also were sites of their distribution and sale.

The *Evening Post*[152] advertised that 'This Paper comes out every Post Night at Six a Clock ... [and] is sold by the booksellers and at the following Coffee-Houses, *viz.*: Union in Cornhill, Amsterdam and John's in Swithin's Alley near the Royal Exchange, Boiden's in Tower Street, St James's, Oliver's at Westminster-Hall-Gate, Will's and Tom's in Covent Garden, the Grecian and Tom's in Devereux Court, Nando's, and the Temple-Change in Fleet Street, Squire's, Will's and John's in Fulwood's Rents in Holbourn [near Gray's Inn].' Although we do not know the exact nature of such commercial arrangements, this distribution network – involving more than a dozen coffee houses appealing to a variety of clienteles and with broad geographical range – obviously contributed to the success of London's first evening newspaper.

Yet, the *Evening Post* was not the first paper to make use of the coffee house as a locus for distribution and sale. In a fascinating mix of print and scribal culture, both the *Post Boy* and the *Post Man* at the end of the seventeenth century were issuing handwritten supplements to accompany the printed newspaper when important, late-breaking news required such a measure: 'This is to give Notice that the Post Boy, with a Written Postscript ... of the ... News that arrives after the Printing of the said Post Boy, is to be had only of Mr John Shank, at Nandoe's Coffee House, between the two Temple Gates; and at Mr Abel Roper's [a bookseller] at the Black Boy ... in Fleet Street.'[153]

148 Published Monday to Saturday, 1790–?
149 See *ESTC* P1817, P1837, P1831, P1813 and P469185, respectively.
150 Published weekly, 1772–83.
151 See *ESTC* P87.
152 No. 69, 19–21 Jan. 1710.
153 Quoted in Lillywhite 1963, 382; *c.*1695.

Coffee houses were indispensable to provincial newspapers in a similar way: virtually all printers of papers outside London acknowledged that they relied heavily on handwritten newsletters for their copy, and often advertised that they were printing the latest foreign and/or domestic intelligences 'From X's letter', or 'From Y's and other Letters', or even 'From the Written Letter'. Many such letters either originated from coffee houses, or came from news services that used coffee houses as networks to gather the most up-to-date information, a practice that lasted into the first decades of the nineteenth century.[154]

Commercially valuable news flowed into the capital as well and was collected at particular inns[155] and coffee houses – the most celebrated example being the letters sent to Lloyd's in Lombard Street to compile the all-important shipping news.[156] *Lloyd's List* employed correspondents in all the nation's major ports, and many foreign ones as well. Eventually, by a special arrangement with the Post Office, the letters travelled post free and were accorded priority handling to get them through the post in time for publication.[157] A notice heading the *List* announced that subscriptions were 'taken in ... at the Bar of *Lloyd*'s Coffee-House'.

From the 1670s, coffee houses were important sites for auctions, most especially of artworks and books,[158] a trend that continued until at least mid-century. In many cases, auctioneers began their careers by holding sales in the upper rooms of such establishments and, if successful, went on to occupy premises of their own.

As sites of reading and commercial transactions, coffee houses were especially well suited for the dissemination of book-auction catalogues – which served as both advertisements and inventories – most obviously in the place where the auction was to be conducted. Even when sales were held elsewhere, however, coffee houses proved useful for the distribution of printed catalogues.[159] It may be more than a coincidence that 'Honest' Tom Payne – antiquarian bookseller and most probably the first to issue regular catalogues of his stock – called his premises in Charing Cross the Literary Coffee House as it was meant to be a meeting place for collectors and authors.

154 See the Legh family collection of English newsletters, which spans some 150 years; Legh 1925, 105.
155 London's inns, the termini of the stage-coach and carrying trades, were essential for gathering the most current news from the provinces: see Chartres 1977.
156 The efflorescence of the London marine insurance industry is thoroughly associated with the coffee house.
157 McCusker 1991; Straus 1937, 64–5. See McCusker, chap. 22, below.
158 Cowan 2005, 132–45. See Landon, chap. 38, below, for the importance of book auctions.
159 See, for example, *ESTC* R184613, R218484, R230631, R216287 and R230644.

Finally, many clubs and associations – literary, business, scientific, political, educational – that convened in coffee houses contributed significantly to the production and consumption of print from the quotidian newspaper to the fine-press limited edition.[160] Most famously, the Roxburghe Club was founded in 1812 at a dinner held in St Alban's Tavern and Coffee House (Pall Mall) during the days of the Roxburghe sale.[161] A different elite of leading booksellers – among them Cadell, Davies, Evans, James Dodsley, Lockyer, Longman and Tom Payne – met weekly (at the Devil's Tavern, Temple Bar, and, then, the Grecian Coffee House in Devereux Court), for both recreation and business: many of their joint productions were initiated at these gatherings. Well into the nineteenth century, at London and provincial coffee houses, the traffic in print, commerce and sociability were inextricably linked.

Money, banking and credit

The years 1694 to 1830 saw a revolution in Britain's financial infrastructure – money and banking, credit, insurance, and capital markets – which developed from a rudimentary state to European pre-eminence.[162] A bookseller could make and receive payments by coin, bill of exchange, bank transfer (via deposit banking), banknote and cheque. Even with the Bank of England's 'Great Recoinage' of 1696–9, however, specie was in chronically short supply.[163] Most retail customers relied on credit for purchases, documented with either promissory notes or, more commonly, entries in vendors' daybooks and ledgers.[164] Because accounts receivable were illiquid, and most often slow to become liquid assets, a bookseller's accounts payable might well require external borrowing if sufficient cash reserves were not on hand. When the preferred method of obtaining loans from circles of association[165] was not available, the bookseller might draw a bill of exchange – a loan with a fixed time span – and then sell it at a discount for cash; this was the principal means of obtaining liquid commercial credit in the eighteenth and early nineteenth centuries.[166] A bill of exchange for £100 due in three months might typically be sold (or 'discounted') for £98, which seems a modest enough cost of conducting

160 Ellis 1956; Clark 2000a.
161 See Landon, chap. 38, below.
162 Neal 2000; Quinn 2004; Dickson 1993 (1967); cf. Van der Wee 1977.
163 Li 1963. Recognizing that its coinage was inadequate, especially for small coins, the government allowed traders to mint their own tokens in 1787–97 and 1811–17. The bookseller James Lackington, who ran a cash-only business, was among those who did so; see Dalton and Hamer 1910–18.
164 Kerridge 1988.
165 Hudson 1986, 211; Edwards 1967, 214–15.
166 Van der Wee 1977.

business, but that £2 over three months translates into an annual interest rate of 8.2 per cent.[167]

One consequential development was the banknote, which – because it depended on the bank's pledge to pay and not an individual's reputation – was generally a more secure instrument (the failure of country banks notwithstanding) than promissory notes or bills of exchange. Because the bank had final responsibility to pay, no matter who the bearer was, banknotes had distinct advantages over bills of exchange: their transfer did not entail a series of unsettled credits until the bill was finally paid. Thus, banknotes payable by bearer increased the transferability of funds without increasing liability.[168]

The Bank of England, founded in 1694, was the largest note issuer in the country, but until it opened branches in 1826, these were only payable in London, limiting their utility outside the capital (where they were redeemed at a discount). Having such a giant in their midst, most private London banks operated primarily through deposit banking and bills of exchange. Instead of banknotes, they offered chequing accounts (often with overdraft facilities), which proved so popular that thirty-one City firms established the London Bankers Clearing House in 1773 to speed and reduce the cost of processing cheques.[169] English provincial banks were able to issue notes, but were limited by their reserves; they often acted as de facto branches of London banks by offering remittance services to the capital and these links often proved vital to the conduct of the provincial book trade. Provincial banks also established correspondent relationships with London financial houses, which enabled provincial clients to make investments in the London stock and money markets, developments that in time helped invigorate provincial economies. Unlike the 'country banks', the Bank of Scotland and the Royal Bank of Scotland in Edinburgh (formed in 1695 and 1727, respectively) became important issuers of notes, and by 1771 were the central clearing houses for the Scottish note market. They too were closely linked with London; funds routinely moved between these two banking centres via bills of exchange. In Edinburgh alone there were twenty-one banks by 1772, with an additional ten in other Scottish cities.[170]

Banking in provincial England was slow to develop – there were only about a dozen such firms at mid-century – but then grew with such strength and speed that there were 119 in 1784, 370 in 1800 and 439 in 1830.[171] Similarly, the

167 Daunton 1995, 248.
168 Quinn 2004, 154.
169 Joslin 1954.
170 Checkland 1975, 135.
171 Pressnell 1956, 4, 11.

number of London banks rose from 25 in 1725 to 70 in 1800.[172] The growth of securities trading and the building of the Stock Exchange (1773) also added to the financial network.[173] The establishment of discount houses to deepen the secondary market for bills of exchange, and the development of the London money market to provide robust and ready sources of liquidity to support that market, further stabilized Britain's financial infrastructure.[174]

Savings banks – which allowed consumers to receive a reasonable rate of return on deposits while still preserving their liquidity – began in 1810; by late 1818, there were some 465 operating in the British Isles.[175] British banking was further strengthened when the Bank of England began opening up branches in 1826; by 1829, it had established eleven satellites – in Birmingham, Bristol, Exeter, Gloucester, Hull, Leeds, Liverpool, Manchester, Newcastle, Norwich and Swansea.[176] In addition, from 1826 onward banks more than sixty-five miles from London were allowed to become joint-stock companies of seven or more partners. This too fostered corporate banking and investment.[177]

These institutions made funds accessible to businessmen by discounting bills of exchange, offering mortgages to property owners, and, importantly, by providing overdraft facilities to ease cash-flow problems and supply ready credit. Insurance companies also made capital available, chiefly by lending on the security of life policies. Britain's burgeoning financial infrastructure benefited the book trades not only by providing funds for the operation of their businesses, but also, and often more importantly, by 'improv[ing] the ability of people to get money – liquidity taken in a general sense', a vital factor in the production and sale of luxury goods.[178] In addition, for both wholesale and retail transactions, payment arrangements became both more convenient and more secure. Yet, as regional economies became increasingly tied to the national economy in the last several decades of the eighteenth century, commerce became more susceptible to the volatility of business cycles and financial depressions, a trend that is all too evident in the fortunes of the book trades between 1800 and 1830.[179]

172 Collins 1990; cf. Clapham 1944, 165: 'the number of private banks in London approximately doubled between the sixties and the end of the century'.
173 Mitchie 1999.
174 Neal 2000; Cameron 1967, 58–9.
175 Horne 1947, 43, 81.
176 Neal 1998, 72, cited in Quinn 2004, 174.
177 Cottrel and Newton 1999, 84.
178 Quinn 2004, 150.
179 Daunton 1995; Duffy 1985; Hoppit 1987; Neal 1994; cf. Hoppit 1986; Kent 1994.

Economic historians of the eighteenth and nineteenth centuries have tended to focus on sources of investment in fixed capital (factory buildings and machines), but 'circulating capital and credit ... were at the heart of the economy between 1700 and 1850'.[180] In his study of the contemporary cotton trade, M. M. Edwards emphasizes that when large amounts of fixed capital were not required (as is generally the case with eighteenth-century bookselling, though not with post-1780 publishing), entrepreneurs 'probably seldom needed to have recourse to "professional" investors, such as merchants or attorneys', but instead 'could raise small loans from local business, or social contacts, and relatives'. Accordingly, the key to understanding such businesses is by attending to how inventory was sold, 'the credit mechanism', 'methods of settling debts' and paying wages, as well as 'improvements in marketing and distribution'.[181]

Like many other businesses, the book trades were financed by a chain of credits, both retail and wholesale.[182] The extended credit terms that booksellers routinely offered to retail customers were effectively a means of purchasing a market for their wares, a cost of doing business in luxury commodities that had an inflated price structure.[183] Ledger credit from six to eighteen months was routinely offered to customers,[184] with an anticipated default rate of approximately 2 per cent of trading capital per annum.[185] In the typical retail billing cycle, accounts were resolved once a year, around Christmas time, when rents were also payable.

In light of the many problems germane to retail purchasing on account, James Lackington's controversial expedient of refusing credit to all and running a strictly cash-and-carry retail business makes eminent sense, though Lackington himself reports that his fellow tradesmen believed his plan could never work. To compensate consumers for cash transactions, Lackington's prices were lower than his competitors' (most often, the books were remainders); he certainly depended on a high turnover to make up for his lower margin, but his transaction costs were also significantly reduced.[186]

Credit periods on the production side were necessarily long: printing was a high-volume, relatively high-margin business, so printers could afford to

180 Daunton 1995, 247.

181 Edwards 1967, 214–15, 237; see also 255–6.

182 Finn 2003.

183 The fees and percentages that contemporary retailers pay to credit card companies are a similar, if more secure, means of incurring a business expense that enables customers to make purchases.

184 See, for example, Fergus and Portner 1987, 163 n 9.

185 Vanderlint 1734, 142.

186 Lackington 1792.

extend credit for extended periods. The Bowyer Ledgers show that accounts were ordinarily settled in three to eighteen months, with a six to twelve month interval being the most common.[187] The Strahan Ledgers evince a similar pattern.[188] The Bowyers almost invariably required that the paper be paid for by the bookseller, who could either buy it himself from the papermaker, or arrange for the Bowyers to make the purchase on his behalf.[189] Papermakers routinely complained about the credit terms they were obliged to extend – three to twelve months, with six to nine months most typical – as they paid cash for raw materials and wages.[190]

Almost inevitably, there was a tension between optimizing economies of scale in production and the projected time in which an edition would sell a sufficient number of copies to start making money – very roughly, after half the copies had been sold. Inevitably, the point at which income from sales shifted from covering costs to yielding genuine profits depended on many factors, among them the relationship of production and marketing costs to the book's price, and the number of books retailed to the public at full price versus the quantity sold to the trade at discount rates. Concerted investment in advertising could possibly shorten that interval to profitability, but, if unsuccessful, would delay profitability as it added to post-production costs – Strahan's printing of 104,000 octavo proposals for Rapin's *History of England* in parts (numbers) being an especially noteworthy example.[191]

After paying for paper, composition, printing, warehousing and advertising, the publisher[192] had invested substantial capital in inventory that was slow in yielding a return. If the customer credit extended to retail and trade purchasers was roughly of the same duration as the credit that papermakers and printers gave to publishing booksellers, *and* a given edition sold with sufficient speed to recoup costs in a timely fashion, then all these transactions based on ledger credit should have cost the publishing booksellers nothing (except perhaps the opportunity cost of tying up one's capital in this project, rather than another). Difficulties arose, however, when production debts needed to be paid and real sales income (as opposed to payments due recorded in the ledger) fell short. In practice, if production-side credit was roughly one year, and over the course of

187 See, for example, Maslen and Lancaster 1991, microfilm A184–5, A196, A296 and B407. See Maslen, chap. 9, below, for the Bowyers.
188 Hernlund 1967, 93.
189 Maslen and Lancaster 1991, xxviii, xxxii; cf. Hernlund 1969.
190 Personal communication from John Bidwell. See Bidwell, chap. 8, below, for the cost of paper and the changing scales of production.
191 Hernlund 1967, 95.
192 Book imprints often do not reveal their financial undertakers; see Foxon 1991, 1–8.

that year an edition sold steadily – say, two-thirds of its print run – then the booksellers would still most likely not have sufficient cash in hand *from that edition* to pay their debts because more than half the money owing to them would still only exist as receivables. These might reasonably be accounted as assets (with some allowance for default), but they provided no liquidity (or transferability) to meet production debts.

Several observations reasonably follow. First, the intervals involved in the cycle of credit are one of the major reasons why the overwhelming majority of book printing was in modest edition sizes: Strahan's most common press run was 500, followed by 1,000 and 750; Peter Garside observes that 'a one-off run of 500–750 copies remained the norm for all but exceptional works'.[193] Second, it is easy to understand why booksellers sometimes offered customers discounts for paying cash or for short periods of credit. Third, congers and the share-book system not only enabled publishing booksellers to spread their risk by investing in multiple books, but these financial expedients also helped maintain a steady stream of real income as different books entered the market at varying times, sold at varying rates and had their production costs come due at varying intervals.[194] Finally, the reprint trade was so appealing in part because it added a measure of predictability to a fairly inconstant market.[195] In practice, given the combination of high production costs, uncertain rates of sale (to say nothing of unforeseeable total sales) and long retail credit periods, a publishing bookseller would necessarily plan to pay for one edition with the income from an earlier title. To expect an edition to pay for itself within the credit cycle for meeting production costs – about eighteen months at most – was overly optimistic, if not naive.

External credit was expensive; many booksellers raised money from friends and relatives in order to avoid incurring such additional costs. Yet, as the century progressed and publishing required very large sums of capital, firms depended upon investment from other commercial sources.[196] This was

193 Hernlund 1967, 104; Garside, Raven and Schöwerling 2000, II, 39; cf. Chard 1977, 144; Altick 1998 (1957), 18–19; Besterman 1938, xxxi.

194 A wholesaling conger was a cartel that agreed to a predetermined hierarchy of book prices governing every transaction along the commercial pathway from the producer to the retail purchaser. An association of copyright-owning booksellers who were both wholesalers and retailers, the conger purchased all or part of an edition from a publisher at favourable terms and then sold it to others in the trade at a predetermined price. Similarly, members of printing congers pooled their resources to buy and print copies, also controlling the terms of trade. The share-book system too had an element of the joint-stock company, but was based on ad hoc arrangements rather than more-or-less stable associations. Confusingly, the word 'conger' was also used for these more occasional consortiums. See Hodgson and Blagden 1956, 67–100; H. G. Pollard 1978; Belanger 1975.

195 See Bonnell, chap. 37, below, for the reprint trade.

196 Earlier in the century, the share-book system was especially important in enabling high-investment undertakings, most notably large editions and reference works. In 1746, for example, Samuel Johnson signed a contract with five leading bookselling firms to produce his *Dictionary* for the considerable fee

obviously true of the Longmans, the Rivingtons, Strahan, Cadell and Robinson, but it also applied to many other concerns that are now less well remembered. A representative example is the firm of Nuttall, Fisher and Dixon, which operated chiefly out of the Caxton Buildings, Liverpool, and, to a lesser extent, in Bartholomew Close, London. An engraving, of the kind commonly used on trade cards or billheads of the period, adorns their catalogue (*c.*1816): a factory building of five storeys, each eleven substantial windows across. This 'West View of the Caxton Printing-Office' indicates the considerable size of the premises, which was chiefly a stereotyping factory, but seems to have included more conventional letterpress printing as well.[197] The firm – active 1806–18 as printers, publishers, booksellers and even newsagents – operated on a considerable scale.[198] It is difficult to imagine the existence of such an enterprise in the absence of large sources of commercial capital.

Throughout our period, banks (and individuals acting as banks) proved crucial to nearly all these aspects in the operation of the print trades by supplying businesses with working capital through short-term loans, overdraft provision and bills of exchange.[199] The several Fleet Street banks and goldsmith-financiers – Child's, Gosling's, Hoare's, Praed's, Fowle and Wotton's, Peirson's, Heriot's, Palton's – would have been especially well situated to meet the particular needs of printers and booksellers. Bookseller-bankers such as Robert and Francis Gosling, Benjamin Collins, William Jackson, William Fletcher, Champion Constable Wetton and Thomas Fowler were particularly knowledgeable about the capital needs and credit cycles germane to the trade.[200] Samuel Richardson, for example, invariably entrusted 'the Management of ... Money-Matters' to Francis Gosling,[201] whose other book-trade clients included Bowyer, Innys, the Knaptons, Nichols, Osborne, Rivington, the Tonsons, Woodfall and the Stationers' Company itself.[202] On a more informal basis, William Strahan and William Bowyer the younger took in deposits, made investments and performed other banking services for clients, associates and friends.[203]

of £1,575, a sum that did not include production costs for the two folios. The booksellers paid him over the course of nine years before receiving the manuscript. On eighteenth-century reference books, see Yeo 2001; and Kafker 1981, 1994.

197 See Mosley, chap. 7, below, for developments in printing technologies during the period.

198 See their catalogue *c.*1816: Bodleian – G. Pamph. 2920, fol. 89; cf. Perkin 1987a.

199 Joslin 1954.

200 On the Goslings, see Melton 1985, 7; Joslin 1954, 177–8.

201 Eaves and Kimpel 1971, 160.

202 Fleeman 1975, 224.

203 Maslen and Lancaster 1991, lxvi; Fleeman 1975.

As the examples of Strahan and Bowyer show, even in London, financial intermediaries other than banks were of great importance; in Scotland and the provinces, local capital markets also played a vital role.[204] In a world in which credit frequently depended on personal reputation, and was routinely extended on the promise to pay (without securing collateral), the private provision of capital through kinship groups and circles of acquaintance was almost certainly of more consequence for the book trade and its adjunct business than were banks.[205] Throughout the eighteenth and early nineteenth centuries, the supply of capital was various and, most often, investment was local.[206] Some contemporary evidence suggests that a retailer starting in business was generally extended credit equal to a little more than double his net worth.[207]

The 23-year-old Charles Rivington was able to buy the premises and bookselling business of Richard Chiswell in St Paul's Churchyard in 1711, in part because the recent death of his elder brother in 1710 made more family capital available to him as the (new) eldest son. Similarly, Thomas Longman bought William Taylor's establishment and some of his copyrights in 1724 with his inheritance (in the form of West Country properties, which he sold for ready money).[208] With the profits from his afterpiece, *The toy-shop* (1735), and £100 from Alexander Pope, Robert Dodsley began trading in Pall Mall. Thomas Davies and his wife, Susanna Yarrow, invested the money they had earned as actors in the Drury Lane Company to start a bookselling business (1762), while a loan from two of his former professors at the University of Edinburgh helped William Smellie to establish the first business in which he was the master printer. John Murray I used the whole of his wife's dowry and £300 borrowed from friends to purchase the Fleet Street bookselling business of William Sandby in 1768. James Lackington's great enterprise famously began (in 1774) with a small collection of books and a modest, interest-free loan from his fellow Methodists. Setting up business in 1795, Archibald Constable had the benefit of a loan (£150) from two friends and £300 worth of books from his father-in-law to use in exchange for others.[209] William Pickering established his own bookshop (1820) at Lincoln's Inn Fields with capital provided by an older fellow apprentice, John Joseph Thornthwaite, on whom he also subsequently relied for credit. Again and again, the social capital of 'connection to networks of association, obligation, and support' translated into economic capital.[210]

204 Cairncross 1963, 257–8.
205 See Anon. 1750, 1 (*ESTC* T71157); see also Wrightson 2002, 292.
206 Crouzet 1972, 53.
207 Earle 1989, 112.
208 See Briggs, chap. 19, below.
209 See Beavan and McDougall, chap. 16, below.
210 Wrightson 2002, 290, 294.

Whether lending was external (from banks) or internal (from family, business or religious affiliates), such funds – by securing relatively short-term liquidity requirements – enabled booksellers to maintain smaller cash reserves, which freed more money for investment. Instead of being held over to maintain a buffer against future payables and unforeseen liabilities,[211] the profits from earlier editions could be directed towards new projects, albeit not without the attendant risks of the venture and the added expenses of borrowing. Yet, for some enterprising booksellers at least, the opportunity cost of tying up liquid assets was greater than the costs of borrowing. Although rates varied, estimates of nominal and real interest rates for government bonds and other kinds of capital investments typically averaged between 3 and 7 per cent during our period; external loans might ordinarily come due at roughly 7 to 10 per cent per annum, while internal loans were expected to yield the lender not less than 5 per cent.

The London tradesman (1747) estimated that it would cost a would-be bookseller between £500 and £5,000 to set up shop in London.[212] The range Campbell proposes is very broad; the actual expenses a new bookseller might initially incur depended on the location and size of his premises,[213] the number of titles he was prepared to invest in – purchasing shares in copies from the trade, paying authors copy money[214] and making capital outlays for production costs (paper, composition, printing) – stock on hand, warehousing arrangements, cash reserves for extending credit, and, perhaps, expenses for apprentices and/or journeymen. The greater one's cash reserves, the more one could afford to have many customers (most of whom would make purchases on credit) and, hence, have a greater opportunity for making a profit.

Campbell's figures accord reasonably well with data from booksellers' fire insurance policies held with the Sun Fire Office and the Royal Exchange Assurance between 1775 and 1778. The median value of property insured was £800; the average (or mean) value was £1,064, while the top of the third quartile was £1,400.[215] Based on these figures, booksellers ranked as the fifth

211 Ellis 1998, 104.

212 Campbell 1747, 331, cited in Schwarz 1982, 62; in the third edition of 1757, Campbell's estimates are identical. See also Anon. 1747, which sets a bookseller's minimum initial investment at £500–£1,000. Collyer 1761 suggests that a small retail shop could be established for £100–£200, a maximum of approximately £26,500 in today's currency.

213 Although new booksellers were almost invariably men, the number of women (chiefly wives and widows) active in the print trades – especially in binding, colouring illustrations, distribution (mercuries, hawkers), library proprietorship and bookselling – was considerable. See McDowell 1999; Grundy, chap. 6, below; and *LBT*.

214 See Rose, chap. 4; Griffin, chap. 5; Grundy, chap. 6; Suarez, chap. 34; and Sutherland, chap. 35, all below for copyrights and authors' remuneration.

215 Schwarz 1982, 65.

highest group among all types of business in London (behind mercers, drapers, merchants (overseas traders) and distillers), indicating how capital intensive their profession was.[216] Booksellers paid for policies covering such substantial amounts because they had to keep considerable inventories of costly goods.

Bankruptcy was a common feature of the trade.[217] Booksellers could be particularly vulnerable at the start of their businesses – substantial capital investments and slow returns frequently meant that notes on borrowed funds could easily come due before sufficient profits had accrued. Then, as now, interest on loans added significantly to the cost of trade. Many would-be booksellers simply underestimated the investment required. Thomas Tegg, for example, invested a legacy of £200 in a partnership with Joseph Dalton Dewick (whose financial contribution is unknown) and began trading in Aldgate in 1799. Within approximately a year, however, the firm was dissolved and Tegg was on the verge of bankruptcy. Although he went on to enjoy a successful publishing career, Tegg's false start is typical of many who fared less well.[218] The fall of Archibald Constable and Co., James Ballantyne and Co., and their star author Walter Scott in 1826, though far from typical, is but the best known of many cases of financial ruin in the book trade.[219] Although there were many factors involved, Scott himself believed that the cost of borrowing capital to finance the day-to-day conduct of the firm was a major factor: 'Constable's business seems unintelligible. No man thought the house worth less than £150,000 – Constable told me when he was making his will that he was worth £80,000 ... No bad speculations ... No doubt trading almost entirely on accomodation [*sic*] is dreadfully expensive.'[220]

Many a bookseller found himself in dire financial straits, not only because it took so long to recoup his investment in an edition – as is commonly reported – but also because credit cycles were so long. The effect of such infrequent payments did more than create problems of liquidity, however. Because the chain of credit obligations extended so far, deferral of payment and, worse still, default were fairly common occurrences. Hence, although non-payment is typically overlooked in the modern reckoning of booksellers' profits, such losses were necessarily anticipated in the calculations of the financially astute. Even in the early decades of the nineteenth century (and indeed beyond), the extension of credit to customers whose worth could be judged solely on

216 Schwarz 1982, 65.

217 Hernlund 1994; Ferdinand 2001; Mandelbrote 2003. See Raven, chap. 3, below.

218 Barnes and Barnes, 2000; cf. Tegg 1870.

219 Millgate 1987; J.A. Sutherland 1987; 1995, 281–98; and B. Bell 1998, 123. See Beavan and McDougall, chap. 16, and Sutherland, chap. 35, both below.

220 Scott 1972, 71.

personal appearance, reputation and involvement in a network of social relations was a necessary condition of conducting business, especially when that business involved the retail sale of luxury commodities, as books undoubtedly were.[221] The extension of credit was a calculated risk – and an often poorly calculated one at that – an uninsurable hazard that had to be factored into the cost of doing business. Hence, deferred payments and unpaid debts accounted for a portion of the price of every book sold, both at wholesale and at retail.

Although the fiscal conduct of the book trades was not especially innovative, it was most often characterized by an admirable degree of resourcefulness. The development of Britain's financial infrastructure strengthened the London print market and was essential to the expansion of its productive capacity. Better financial networks made possible the revolutionary development of the provincial trade, and enabled the transformation from bookselling to publishing as a specialist, capital-intensive commercial endeavour. By the end of our period, the age of print as a mass-market commodity had finally arrived.

221 Finn 2003, 21, 288; cf. Williams 1977, 82.

PART I THE QUANTITY AND NATURE OF PRINTED MATTER

1

Towards a bibliometric analysis of the surviving record, 1701–1800

MICHAEL F. SUAREZ, S.J.

Introduction

In the pages that follow, I tender a preliminary analysis of the surviving record of eighteenth-century imprints in Britain and Ireland based on an ordered sampling of the *English short-title catalogue* (*ESTC*, formerly the *Eighteenth-century short-title catalogue*).[1] Hence, this investigation is subject to both the remarkable possibilities and the limitations afforded by the *ESTC*.[2] Like other union catalogues, the *ESTC* was not designed to be used as a statistical tool;[3] yet, the availability of such a wealth of data has made such studies – for all their difficulties and shortcomings – an important feature of book-historical and bibliographical scholarship in recent decades.[4] Among the problems one encounters in using the *ESTC* for data collection and analysis is that it is not a stable database, but rather is constantly growing and changing as it is updated and subject to improvements, additions and corrections.[5] The data in this study were collected between 2002 and 2004; while every effort has been made to control for the shifting nature of the database, such accommodations have not always been possible, especially since neither corrections nor

1 See http://estc.bl.uk. For a conspectus of the eighteenth-century *STC* cataloguing rules, see Zeeman 1991; the Anglo-American Cataloguing Rules (AACR2) (see www.aacr2.org/index.html); and the Library of Congress *Rules of Descriptive Cataloging of Rare Books* (Washington, DC, various edns).

2 See May 1984, 2001; Williams and Baker 2001.

3 Veylit 1994, 34–5, 40–4, 60–1, *et infra*; Stoker 1995, 12; Amory 2001, 7; Bell 2001, 15, 20. I am grateful to Henry Snyder for his encouragement and for bringing Veylit to my attention.

4 For an impressive earlier attempt to use the *ESTC* as a database for a comprehensive statistical analysis, see Veylit 1994. Although his study employs a different methodology and examines the *ESTC* at an earlier stage in its development, Veylit's data are congruent with the findings presented here. Other studies presenting quantitative analyses based on bibliographic records in union catalogues include Tanselle 1980; Mitchell 1987; Bell and Barnard 1992, 1998; Stoker 1995; Bland 1999; Dugas 2001; Gants 2002; and Raven 2007. See also Barnard and Bell 2002b. The more qualitative studies of McKenzie 1974a and 1992, based on *Wing* listings, are also worthy of note; McKenzie 1974a includes a statistical appendix.

5 See John Lancaster's discussion of the problem in Maslen and Lancaster 1991, xi–xii. Raven 2007, 406–7 n. 19, presents some salutary cautions regarding the collection and interpretation of data from *ESTC* searches.

additions to the *ESTC* are marked as new.[6] (At times, one may feel rather like Walter Shandy compiling the Tristapaedia.) Nevertheless, although a significant number of periodicals were added to the database during this period (and since then as well), the basic trends in the data and their analysis appear to be largely reliable.[7]

Regrettably, although this volume of *The Cambridge history of the book in Britain* ends in 1830, it is not possible to perform a similarly comprehensive analysis for the first decades of the nineteenth century because we have no equivalent bibliographical control for this period. *The nineteenth century short-title catalogue* is based on the holdings of a far more limited number of libraries than is the *ESTC*, and is especially weak in provincial publishing at a time when such publications were increasingly important to local and regional markets.[8] Even adding records from Copac® and the Online Computer Library Centre's WorldCat would not produce a bibliography with coverage comparable to the *ESTC*. Other attempts at providing a more thorough conspectus of imprints for the nineteenth century, although valuable, similarly do not have the comprehensive qualities of the *ESTC*.[9]

One crucial caveat should be considered at the outset: the *Eighteenth-century short-title catalogue*, as it was, and the *English short-title catalogue*, as it is now – coverage having been extended retrospectively to the mid-fifteenth century – only records bibliographic information about surviving books.[10] After a careful study of book advertisements, inventories and bibliographies, it seems to this investigator that, excluding jobbing and newspaper printing, as much as 10 per cent of the printed record from 1701–1800 has not been incorporated into the *ESTC*.[11] In other words, for up to 10 per cent of the editions printed in the eighteenth century, not a single copy is known to survive.[12] The question of

6 In studying bibliographical formats for 1783, for example, I should have counted 3,025 records, but find that I have actually counted 3,037; the database was moving (as records were being added) and there was no way to 'freeze' it in time to derive my sample from a fixed dataset.

7 Some significant exceptions are noted below. Throughout this investigation, I have asked not only, 'Can we reasonably believe the data?', but also, 'What can we reasonably believe about the data?'

8 *NSTC* Series 1 (1801–15) records holdings at just six libraries, albeit important ones; *NSTC* Series 2 (1816–70) records holdings from eight libraries. For a discussion of the difficulties inherent in using the *NSTC* for quantitative analysis, see Eliot 1997–8, 80–6.

9 The best attempt at the bibliometric analysis of nineteenth-century British books is Eliot 1994, supplemented and extended by Eliot 1997–8. On the possibilities and limitations of quantitative analysis in book history, see Amory 2000b, 2001; Eliot 2002.

10 On the history of the *ESTC*, see Snyder and Smith 2003; cf. Alston 2004. See also McCorison 1991.

11 Adams and Barker 1993, 38, usefully point out that survival should be construed not merely as the existence of a book, but whether that book is known to exist. In most cases missing editions failed to survive long enough to make it into any union catalogue; in some instances, however, an edition is represented by a surviving copy or copies, but is not (yet) in the *ESTC*.

12 Maslen 1993 tentatively estimates – on the basis of works found in the Bowyer Ledgers, but not known to have survived – that the figure might be roughly 5 per cent (3). Hugh Amory's detailed counts for colonial America and the early United States lead him to conclude, 'it seems unlikely that

survival rates is of vital importance for almost any cumulative accounting in bibliography, and will be discussed at greater length below. Yet, the details of differential survival – varying according to format, genre and other factors – notwithstanding, it is clear that, if we employ the *ESTC* as a tool for conducting bibliographical and book-historical research into eighteenth-century imprints, then it is salutary to calibrate the instrument we are using. Thus, we need to know something about the numbers and kinds of books most likely to be represented in the surviving record – and most likely not to be.[13]

As of this writing, the *ESTC* includes nearly 335,000 records for the period 1701–1800. These cover all imprints and significant bibliographical variants of books published in the British Isles and Great Britain's colonial territories (with the addition of the United States of America, 1776–1800) in any language; books published in English, Irish, Gaelic or Welsh elsewhere in the world (for example, the Low Countries, France, Germany); and any imprint falsely claiming to be from London. Lacking the resources to conduct a detailed analysis of the entire *ESTC* from 1701 to 1800, I have resorted to sampling. Electing to examine all eighteenth-century records that appear in years ending in three – 1703, 1713, 1723 and so on – I have sought to avoid a number of cohort effects, most especially the cumulation of indeterminate records into years ending in '0' or '1' and, to a lesser degree, '5'.[14] A weakness of many statistical studies of union catalogues is that they do not take this problem into account; one investigation found that nearly one-fifth of all imprints grouped in a given year, 1701, were assigned either by 'estimation'

more than 10 per cent of the books printed in America have perished without a trace'; Amory 2000a, 504, 514 (graphs in between); elsewhere, he writes of 'estimating the number of titles that have been lost – about 10% of American production, I believe'; see Amory 2001, 12. May 2001, 289, believes 'one would find *ESTC* missing 10%' of British and Irish imprints for a given year, but he speculates that 'over half those titles would be found extant [but unrecorded] in libraries'. May's estimate is congruent with Jacobs and Forster 1995, who compare fiction titles listed in circulating library catalogues with records in *ESTC* and the *National Union Catalogue* (*NUC*). The exhaustive search for novels, 1770–99, conducted by Raven and Forster found that between 9 and 10 per cent of all editions known to have been published were no longer represented by a single surviving copy. At the time their bibliography was published, 13 per cent of all confirmed editions were not in the *ESTC* (Garside, Raven and Schöwerling 2000, I, 20 and my calculation from data presented I, 125–807).

13 Cf. Jacobs and Forster 1995, 262: 'The rich opportunities offered by the *ESTC* may tempt us to dismiss books that we no longer have as historically and culturally insignificant ephemera, but surely the growing evidence we have that our historical record . . . is rife with accident . . . should make us wary of the assumption that the books our libraries now hold sufficiently represent the bibliographical past.' We should also bear in mind that the *ESTC* itself, dependent as it is on the holdings of libraries – each with its own (often changing) acquisition, preservation and retention policies – cannot be regarded as providing a value-neutral (nor entirely random) representation of the eighteenth-century printed record.

14 I had intended to examine years ending in '8' as well, but as it required more than three years to complete my scrutiny of years ending in '3', I was unable to do so. I do plan to continue the project, however, because adding more sample years will make the data more reliable.

or by 'internal evidence' – that is, without the year appearing in an imprint.[15] *ESTC* lumps undated items into the nearest year ending in '0' or '5', so that 'the peaks in production in such years are therefore to some extent the result of cataloguing practice, rather than increased *real* output'.[16]

In order to determine the number of relevant imprints for analysis, the protocol for this study has been to examine every record in a given year, first sifting out all records that are geographically irrelevant – those coming from the Continent and the American colonies, for example. I have counted in my sample all those records originating in England, Scotland, Wales and, perhaps controversially, Ireland. Although the Act of Union did not incorporate Ireland into the British domain until 1801, I have included Ireland in this analysis because Dublin and, to a lesser degree, its provincial satellites constituted an important market that had a significant impact on the eighteenth-century Scottish and English book trades.[17] The Irish trade was publishing its own books, importing and reprinting English books, and – especially as the century progressed – exporting books to England, Scotland and America.[18] Although considerably more work needs to be done on the circulation of Irish books and books of Irish manufacture in Scotland and England, most especially in England's northern region, it seemed clear that the sequestering of Irish books from this study would effectively ignore important realities of the market.[19]

After eliminating geographical 'undesirables', some 4,286 records in all, I then scrutinized each *ESTC* record, eliminating those that were merely bibliographical variants and did not, in fact, represent different editions.[20] Understandably, such a procedure is fraught with problems. Unless noted by *ESTC* cataloguers, false imprints may well have slipped my notice and been countenanced as being from locations they were fraudulently meant to represent, rather than the place of their true origin. Similarly, unless records

15 Stoker 1995, 13.

16 Bell and Barnard 1992, 56 (emphasis in original). *NSTC* follows the same protocol.

17 See Benson, chap. 17, below. For a discussion of the Dublin trade's extensive relationships with London and Scottish booksellers, see Phillips 1998, 106–25, and more broadly, 125–47; see also Cole 1986, 1–39, 87–147, *et infra*; and Pollard 1989. On the extent of eighteenth-century bookselling networks, see Turner, chap. 23; Beavan and McDougall, chap. 16; Ferdinand, chap. 21; Green, chap. 28; and Shaw, chap. 29, all below.

18 See, for example, Cole 1986; Pollard 1989; McDougall 1997; Phillips 1998; and Lennon 2006.

19 Precedents for including Ireland in eighteenth-century 'British Isles' bibliographies may be found, for example, in Foxon 1975a, Raven 1987 and Garside, Raven and Schöwerling 2000, vol. I.

20 Cf. Amory 2001, 4, 'Only by downloading the entire response and examining it record by record can we arrive at reliable counts.' Cf. Veylit 1994, 88–9, 94–7. Inspecting and hand-counting individual records has the advantage of allowing the bibliographer to make careful discriminations, even as it introduces a degree of subjectivity (to say nothing of human error) and, hence, guarantees the irreproducibility of exact results.

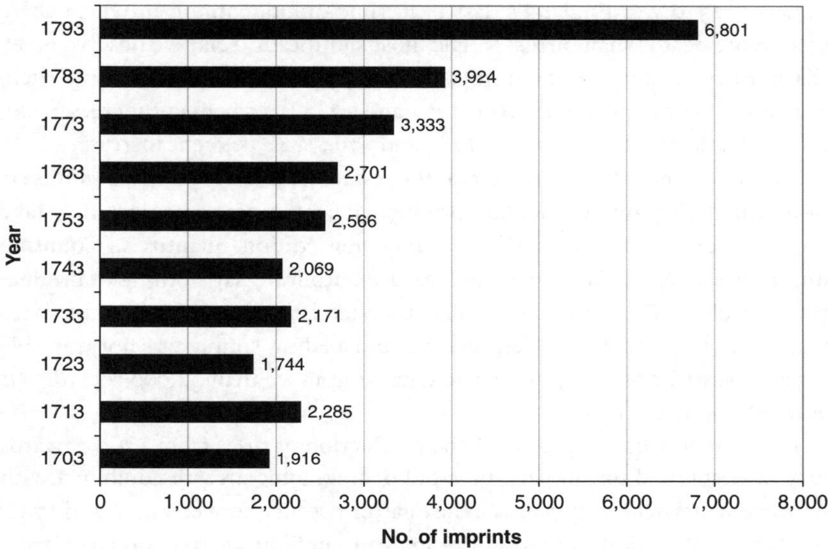

Figure 1.1 Total imprints for England, Scotland, Wales and Ireland, 1701–93 (minus variants)

specifically identified reissues, I have not always been able to detect and separate these false 'hits' from among the data. In all, I examined 34,335 records, partitioned the non-Britain and non-Ireland imprints, leaving 29,510 records, and recorded 134,732 data points. The results of this sorting appear in Figure 1.1.

Immediately we perceive that the number of titles per annum exhibits a remarkable rise from a low of 1,744 per annum in 1723 to 6,801 in 1793, an increase of 390 per cent.[21] Perhaps surprisingly, the year with the fewest number of imprints is not 1703 but 1723, a fact most probably accounted for by the volatility and instability of financial markets in London, and indeed elsewhere, following the South Sea Bubble financial crisis of 1720.[22] (Given England's ongoing dependence on continental paper in this period – despite protectionist tariffs – we might also note that the fall of the Mississippi company in Paris in 1720–1 cannot have been an encouraging development.[23]) It is surprising that the number of imprints for 1733 is so large since the

21 These data are compatible with data presented in Raven 2007, 8, fig. 1.1 (see also 131) and in Veylit 1994, 269, fig. 1, and 270, fig. 2.

22 The fluctuations and trends in the surviving printed output discussed here may usefully be compared with Mitchell 1985 and Veylit 1994, especially, 272, figs. 3 and 4. The all-century low in 1723 exactly matches Veylit's data, despite our somewhat different methodologies.

23 See Neal 1990, 62–117; Carswell 1993; and Dickson 1993 (1967), 90–156.

period 1725–9 was England's 'last peacetime quinquennium in which there were more deaths than births'.[24] The most significant trend we observe is the sharp rise in the number of imprints in 1763–93. Between 1763 and 1773, there is a 19 per cent increase; between 1773 and 1783, a 15 per cent increase; and, most remarkably of all, between 1783 and 1793, a 42 per cent increase.

It is important to bear in mind that these statistics merely represent numbers of imprints; they do not measure productive output per se because they take into consideration neither sheet counts nor edition quantities. Counting imprints is a deeply flawed way to measure output (to say nothing of productive capacity). The only way, really, to establish an accurate picture is to undertake a sheet count.[25] Yet, such a grand analysis simply was not tractable for an investigation using aggregate data from more than 34,000 records – *le mieux est l'ennemi du bien*.[26]

The markedly upward trend in the production of titles from 1763 onwards may be accounted for, in part, by rapid demographic growth combined with improvements in literacy rates. In the quarter-century between 1756 and 1781, England's population increased by more than a million, an exceptional enlargement of 15 per cent. Thereafter, population growth accelerated even more rapidly: there were 8,671,000 residents in England by 1801, a rise of more than 1.4 million in twenty years.[27] Even according to conservative estimates, by the century's end, approximately 60 per cent of adult males and 45 per cent of females were able to read.[28] Although the market for books would come to be notably impeded by the inflationary pressures consequent upon the Napoleonic wars, this burgeoning growth is carried well into the early decades of the nineteenth century.[29]

Altogether, the 34,335 records scrutinized yielded some 134,732 items of data. This information was acquired by examining every record for information pertinent to five principal categories: (1) genre, (2) place of publication, (3) bibliographical format, (4) length (in sheets) and (5) reprints and/or repeat publications. Although sets of protocols for each of these categories were

24 Wrigley 2004, 65; Wrigley and Schofield 1981, table A3.3, 531–5. For a more thoroughgoing discussion of population trends, see Suarez, Introduction, above.

25 See Gants 2002 for an analysis of the London trade's productive output, 1614–18, based on sheet counts. Suarez and Zimmerman 2006 use sheet counts to analyse the business decisions and investments of John Taylor and James Hessey in 1820 and 1821. The sheet counts for 1668 in McKenzie 1974a are especially revealing about the gap between the productive capacity of the London trade and what is now extant in book and pamphlet form.

26 Cf. Bell 2001.

27 Wrigley *et al.* 1997, table A9.1, 614–15.

28 Schofield 1973, fig. 2, 445, and 446; see also 440–1 and Schofield 1968, 324. For a more detailed discussion of literacy rates, see Suarez, Introduction, above.

29 Eliot 1994, 15–20; 1997–8, table A, 87, *et infra*.

developed and strictly adhered to, there still is an inescapable element of subjective judgement in this study. In formulating and carrying out this investigation's design, I have tried to eliminate arbitrariness wherever possible. In the case of genre, for example, where a definitive category could not be determined, the record simply was not counted, rather than make an arbitrary judgement.[30] So too, with respect to bibliographical format: if the information available would not allow for a definitive determination, then no entry for that record was tabulated in the format category.[31] Nevertheless, such protocols do not free an investigation such as this from the fact that many decisions are perforce made subjectively – and that thousands of such judgements are required. Thus, the results of this study are repeatable, but not exactly so. A good case in point is the matter of genre. In Table 1.1, 'Genre', we find various categories: almanacs and practical matters; biography, letters and personal writings; business and finance; and so on. Yet, the very classifications themselves reflect a series of assessments as to how eighteenth-century books might most meaningfully be grouped together for statistical scrutiny.[32] It is to the analysis of books by genre that we now turn.

Analysis by genre

In classifying eighteenth-century books according to eleven categories for analysis, I have been mindful that such disciplinary demarcations may shape our understandings by opening up certain perspectives while foreclosing others. Because the categories identify and delimit a broad spectrum of intellectual and cultural domains, I have endeavoured to fashion them in ways that would have been both intelligible to the eighteenth-century 'common reader'

30 In addition, no single-sheet publications, nor any newspapers or periodicals, were included in the census. After factoring out these and indeterminate (often mixed-genre) items, 23,879 records in all were categorized.

31 Data were recorded for 24,138 records out of a possible population of 29,510. The *ESTC* does not enable comprehensive searching of its eighteenth-century records by format or genre. A book's bibliographical format is often, but not always, part of its *ESTC* record. When formats were not given, I attempted to use pagination statements to calculate them, but this was not always possible. Seven generic categories – advertisements, directories, periodicals/journals, newspapers, prospectuses and proposals for printing, songs and single-sheet verse, and almanacs – are available in the eighteenth-century portion of the *ESTC* database; when applicable, I used these to check my own classification and counting according to the protocols I had earlier established.

32 Feather 1986, for example, used a different set of categories in his subject analysis of eighteenth-century British publishing because his data source, *Eighteenth-century British books* (1979), was organized according to the Dewey Decimal System. Cf. Eliot 1997–8, 83–5, 72–4 on the use of Dewey Decimal categories for the nineteenth century. Veylit 1994, 158–68, *et infra*, uses a classification system involving thirteen subject classes and twenty genre categories; see his figs. XX–XXI (283–4) and XXXVI–LIX (301–24). The Utrecht research group for the history of reading uses a ten-category scheme; see Kruif 2001, 434.

Table 1.1 *Genre of books published between 1703 and 1793*

	1703	1713	1723	1733	1743	1753	1763	1773	1783	1793
Agriculture, almanacs and other practical matters	35	34	27	58	56	54	59	84	78	108
Biography, letters and personal writings	81	114	124	90	104	172	142	143	205	323
Business and finance	146	138	84	117	80	121	169	268	352	821
Education and children's books	30	46	32	39	40	50	72	75	114	117
Entertainment, leisure and travel	26	7	6	10	30	31	32	53	69	204
History, geography and military affairs	77	68	70	52	87	86	76	111	128	206
Literature, classics and belles-lettres	215	320	241	402	275	348	436	523	422	604
Medicine, mathematics and science	70	49	90	98	99	131	131	170	210	223
Music and the visual arts	43	40	23	93	61	73	144	87	189	320
Politics, government and law	370	540	362	467	377	598	589	610	791	1,298
Religion, philosophy and ethics	573	699	436	469	416	532	444	483	449	815
Total	1,666	2,055	1,495	1,895	1,625	2,196	2,294	2,607	3,007	5,039

(a phrase coined by Samuel Johnson) and commercially sensible to the contemporary bookseller. Examining the category 'politics, government and law', we observe that it begins in 1703 with 370 records, each representing an individual title or a new edition of a title. By 1793, such books amount to 1,298 records. In other words, the number of titles more than triples from 1703 to 1793, but stays essentially the same in terms of its ratio to the whole for each year. Such is the boom in print that, throughout the period, this category's relation to the whole – the genre's representation within the total number of books published for each year – remains reasonably constant at approximately 25 per cent of the total. In fact, among the categories I have examined, politics, government and law is the most consistent.

The 'medicine, mathematics and science' group is represented by fewer than 50 titles in 1713 (70 titles in 1703); these numbers comprise approximately 2 per cent of the total productive output of the book trade. By 1783, however, that number has increased to 210, or 7 per cent of all records for that year. The 223 titles in 1793 represent a decrease to about 4.4 per cent of the total, but this is probably because of a sharp increase in provincial publishing, which is less likely to produce scientific and mathematical books that often require detailed illustrations and/or complex typesetting. An upward trend in medicine, mathematics and science publications is clear, and felicitously in accord with our notions about the Enlightenment and its consequent dissemination of scientific ideas.[33]

Just as the eighteenth century is a period of intellectual revolution, so too – and indeed no less – is it a time when the financial infrastructure of England and Scotland radically changes.[34] It is somewhat surprising, therefore, to note a slight downward trend in the ratio of 'business and finance' books to the total output of the trade 1703–53, during which time such titles comprise just 5 per cent of the total. Yet, this trend is markedly reversed from 1763 to 1793, years that exhibit steady rises in both the number and proportion of titles – culminating in 16 per cent of the total recorded for 1793 – and concomitant growth in provincial and London banking, the London stock and money markets, turnpike and other local trusts, joint-stock companies, and industrial investment.[35]

By far the most important publishing category at the start of the century is 'religion, philosophy and ethics'. In 1703, 34 per cent of all titles published belonged to this group. Perhaps surprisingly – considering England's Erastian state and the importance of books and publishing to religious culture in England, Scotland and Wales more generally – this class of titles exhibits a significant downward trend throughout the century, ending with just 16 per cent of the whole, despite a significant increase in the number of publications in the last decade of our sample. Of course, the number of published titles does

33 See, for example, Dickson 1993 (1967); and Sher 2006.
34 See Suarez, Introduction, above.
35 See Suarez, Introduction, above.

not decrease, but it declines as a proportion of the total. That business and finance publications should in the last decade of the century represent the same proportion of publications as religion, philosophy and ethics is highly surprising and may give credence to then-contemporary worries about growing secularization and the need to effect a religious revival. Nevertheless, as John Barnard has established, such numbers cannot be taken wholly at face value because survival rates for certain kinds of religious publications are remarkably low.[36]

The eighteenth century is, famously, the era of 'the rise of the novel'. We know, for example, that *Robinson Crusoe* went through six editions of 1,000 copies each in just four months, that *Pamela* sold approximately 20,000 copies in fourteen months, and that 6,500 copies of *Roderick Random* came on the market in less than two years.[37] Nevertheless, when we examine the numbers of titles published – taking no account of edition sizes – we realize what a small portion of the market fiction actually occupied.[38] During the period 1703–53, fiction of all kinds never constitutes as much as 2 per cent of the market (by editions published, not numbers of copies). Even at its height in the eighteenth century, fiction publishing represents slightly less than 3.5 per cent of all surviving titles. This fact may lead some bibliographers and book historians to question the emphasis on fiction publishing that characterizes so much of the work in our field. When viewing fiction as a percentage of the broader category 'literature, classics and belles-lettres', throughout the century, novel publishing never makes up more than a quarter of this category and, in 1743, is only around 10 per cent of the total.

Similarly, the classification literature, classics and belles-lettres is never more than about 20 per cent of the total; it starts and ends the century at approximately 11 per cent. Within this category, drama publishing fluctuates between 2 and 5 per cent of the overall output, whereas poetry publications – in all languages, and including translations – comprise between about 4.5 and 10.5 per cent (again, in numbers of titles), although the data are fairly noisy.

Because their survival rates are so notoriously poor, 'education and children's books' are especially problematic categories for bibliometric analysis.

36 Barnard 1999. Cf. I. Green 1996, 2000. On the ephemeral nature of certain types of business publications, such as commodity price currents, see McCusker, chap. 22, below.

37 Maslen 1969; Keymer and Sabor 2005, 17; Knapp 1932, 284. For discussions of fiction publishing, see Suarez, chap. 34, and Sutherland, chap. 35, below.

38 For fiction 1770–99, the average edition size was 500 or fewer; most never reached a second edition – see Garside, Raven and Schöwerling 2000, I, 35, *et infra*; see also Raven 1987. Cf. the observation in Watt 1957, that the novel 'was not, strictly speaking, a popular literary form' (42).

We know, for example, that three-quarters of the titles that Edward Homan Turpin (1742–91) is known to have published for children no longer exist in a single copy.[39] Similarly, the Ackers Ledgers reveal that, during the sixteen years from 1733 to 1748, Thomas Dyche's *Guide to the English Tongue* was printed in thirty-three editions comprising 275,000 copies. Five books from three editions are known to exist today.[40] It seems highly implausible, especially in the last two decades of the eighteenth century, that education and children's books should never exceed more than 120 per annum, or a high of approximately 3.75 per cent of the total annual output. Although it is true that sometimes the most interesting and important results in an investigation are counter-intuitive, in this instance our knowledge about survival rates strongly suggests that the data for this publishing category are so far off the mark as to be almost completely unreliable.[41]

In much the same vein, when we examine the group of titles belonging to 'agriculture, almanacs and practical matters', it seems almost impossible to believe that such books, even if we are only counting titles and not edition quantities, never reached as much as 3.5 per cent of the total annual output, and were so constrained as never to exceed more than 108 editions per annum. Again, the answer lies in the fact that, like school-books and children's books, the editions in this category are more than usually subject to stochastic processes. We know, for example, how vibrant the almanac trade was during the Restoration and eighteenth century, how covetously the Stationers' Company protected its almanac monopoly, and how sedulously it fought against those who threatened it.[42] Yet, evidence from the Ackers Ledger makes it clear that, for most of the years during which the publication of *Goldsmith's Almanack* was firmly documented by the printer's records, not a single copy survives. Hence, very few are recorded in the *ESTC*. From 1736 to 1758, Ackers printed *Goldsmith's Almanack* (the editions for 1737–59) for the Stationers' Company. During this same interval, the *ESTC* lists surviving examples in six out of twenty-three years.[43] Ackers records print runs of between 5,000 and 6,500 for editions dated 1737–47 (after which we have no records), making a total of

39 See Immel, chap. 40, below.

40 McKenzie and Ross 1968, 249–52. See *ESTC* T113323, T186254 and N66049. See also Barnard 1999 on the loss rates of ABCs and primers.

41 In addition to the likelihood that most school-books and children's books were used until they were used up, we might also consider that the research libraries on which the *ESTC* primarily depends were, in most instances, inhospitable to such titles for many decades.

42 See Blagden 1958, 1960a, 1960b; Harris 1980; Howe 1981; and Myers, chapter 39, below.

43 1741, 1747, 1752, 1754, 1757 and 1759. McKenzie and Ross 1968, 299 (item 271) note that a copy of the 1739 edition was sold at auction in 1966; it is not recorded in the *ESTC*.

64,000 copies of which only two – one each in 1741 and 1747 – are represented in *ESTC*, a survival rate of 1:32,000. Part of the English Stock, this popular work was a single 24mo sheet, making a small pamphlet of forty-eight pages. Obviously, each almanac's size and the expiration of its serviceableness are primary factors in the extraordinarily high loss rate of this title. As with education and children's books, the results adduced from our sample for this category appear to be wholly unreliable.

Place of publication

It may prove a consolation, therefore, that studying the *ESTC* eighteenth-century records by place of publication seems a significantly more reliable undertaking (see Table 1.2a). Yet, even here there is room for misperception and miscalculation. Unless *ESTC* has identified an imprint as false, I have taken the place of publication as recorded in imprints at face value, despite the fact that some of these (albeit a small percentage most probably) are as yet undetected false imprints of various kinds. A provincial publication may have masqueraded as a London imprint in order to gain greater status, or a book financed and printed in London may have advertised itself as a provincial production in order to win local custom. As David Foxon and Michael Treadwell have variously taught us, imprints are by no means as transparent

Table 1.2a *Place of publication of books published between 1703 and 1793*

	1703	1713	1723	1733	1743	1753	1763	1773	1783	1793
London and the home counties	1,271	1,684	1,156	1,766	1,221	1,551	1,643	1,866	2,254	2,755
South	0	0	0	1	0	2	1	5	11	15
South-west	9	8	9	7	27	27	30	45	63	144
East Anglia	22	24	5	13	24	27	41	47	46	89
West Midlands	0	5	2	8	9	15	22	52	57	144
East Midlands	0	9	3	4	14	5	6	9	28	90
North-east	0	7	1	3	25	20	20	41	75	271
North-west	2	9	4	10	7	10	13	24	52	106
Ireland	145	148	138	120	146	281	227	233	259	406
Scotland	209	195	169	123	187	283	330	298	269	712
Wales	0	0	0	0	0	0	3	14	11	13
Total	1,658	2,089	1,487	2,055	1,660	2,221	2,336	2,634	3,125	4,745

as they may seem.[44] Such difficulties notwithstanding, however, the results of analysis by place of publication do seem comfortingly trustworthy.[45]

The approximately 34,000 editions examined came from 198 different locations. London and the home counties, not surprisingly, dominate the market throughout the century. Yet, at the start of our period, London imprints only constitute about 76 per cent of all the records surveyed, which the reader will recall includes both Scotland and Ireland (although the Act of Union would not be passed for nearly another century). The general trend remains fairly consistent: imprints from London and the surrounding area – those from the near satellites of the capital are few in number – fluctuate between a high of around 82 per cent and a low of around 69 per cent.[46] In general, the ratio of London output remains fairly constant, even in the wake of the increased productive capacity of provincial trade.[47] Examining the numbers of London imprints, we may discern that, roughly speaking, the capacity and output of the London-based trade nearly keeps pace to maintain superiority of about 70 per cent in relation to the rest of the British Isles. Because we are counting titles (editions) rather than sheets, the data are especially crude.[48] Provincial publications tend to be shorter and in smaller press runs than editions originating in the capital. Book work was still mostly undertaken in London, especially for larger publications (where several presses would routinely have been used). For example, we know that, of the 315 novels with imprints in the 1770s, 97 per cent were published in London; in the 1780s, 94.5 per cent of all novels were initially London publications.[49]

In the final decade of our investigation, however, we may observe the beginning of a trend that is carried into the nineteenth century: the efflorescence of provincial printing on a grand scale. The sample for 1793 reveals a rise in the number of London imprints from 2,254 to 2,755, but the ratio of London imprints to the whole declines slightly more than 10 per cent.[50] In

44 Foxon 1991, 1–8; Treadwell 1989. See also Chapman 1931; Hazen 1951; Shaaber 1944; Maslen 1972; and Feather 1985, 59–62, 110–11.

45 Where no information about place of publication was given, none was recorded; 24,010 records were categorized in the census. On the distribution of publications by place, see Veylit 1994, 278–81, figs. 11–17.

46 Cf. Veylit 1994, 278, figs. 11–12, which accord well with the data presented here when North American imprints are removed from the census he represents.

47 On the spread of provincial printing, see Mitchell 1985, 1987; Feather 1985; See also Veylit 1994, 280, figs. 15–16, and 374, table E.

48 Cf. Raven 2007, 7–8.

49 Garside, Raven and Schöwerling 2000, I, 71.

50 Even if we allow for the inflation of the number of London imprints recorded in *ESTC* through the cataloguing of ephemera, it is difficult to reconcile this steady rise in London publications to 2,755 in 1793 with the observation of A. G. Goede that 'upward of eight hundred new publications are annually ushered into the world from the London shops' in 1803; see Goede 1808, cited in St Clair 2004, 457.

both the capital and the provinces, improved financial arrangements – for credit, risk conveyance, negotiable instruments and the like – made the *business* of publishing and bookselling potentially more robust and viable. (Yet, bankruptcies persisted, not least because such arrangements concomitantly made competition keener and risk-taking more possible.) We also know that the improved infrastructure for efficient and affordable transportation of goods, both locally and across the nation, improved tremendously during the century.[51]

Figures for Scottish imprints suggest a more volatile market, though here, as elsewhere, the data would be considerably more reliable if ten more sample sets were part of the study (for example, years ending in '8'). In the absence of any distinctly prevailing trend, it is difficult to ascertain what may be an isolated cohort effect and, hence, a skewed result.[52] Generally speaking, between 1703 and 1783, Scottish imprints fluctuated between approximately 200 and 300 imprints per annum, comprising some 6 to 12 per cent of the total market. The result for 1733, just 123 imprints, is suspiciously low and ought to be regarded as an outlier. In 1793, there are 712 imprints, a spike in the data that raises Scotland's proportion of imprints from around 6 per cent to about 15 per cent. Obviously, more study and analysis are required.

Bearing in mind the salutary caution to consider trends rather than specific numbers, we must also acknowledge that, in the decade 1763–73, Scottish imprints decline by about 10 per cent. Remarkably, between 1773 and 1783, we observe further decline of another 10 per cent. This downward trend in Scottish imprints from 1763 to 1783, combined with the fact that the output for the samples in 1773 and 1783 are very close to the 283 recorded for 1753, together cast some doubt on the idea that – following the *Donaldson* v. *Becket* decision in the House of Lords overturning perpetual copyright – Scottish publishers widely reprinted the so-called 'old canon' of English literature in unprecedented numbers. We should bear in mind, however, that a number of books printed in Scotland bore false London imprints and, if undetected, will not have been counted according to their true origin. Granted, the data in this study exhibit material limitations; yet, it would seem (for now at least) that assertions about a surge in Scottish reprinting might best be treated with some caution.[53]

In contrast to the volatility exhibited in the Scottish market, throughout the century, Irish imprints constitute approximately 8.5 per cent of all titles (as a

51 See Jackman 1916, 335–6; Pawson 1977, 297; Albert 1983, 55–6; Gerhold 1988; Barker and Gerhold 1993, 40–3; and, more generally, Suarez, Introduction, above.

52 Cf. Veylit 1994, figs. 14–16.

53 On the impact of the Lords' decision, see St Clair 2004, especially 109–39. Sher 2006, Fergus 2006a, Bonnell 2005–6 (2008) and Bonnell 2008 all contest St Clair's view, marshalling new information in support of their arguments. On the publishing of British literary works in the years after 1774, see Sutherland, chap. 35, below.

Table 1.2b *Place of publication, by region, of books published between 1703 and 1793*

	1703	1713	1723	1733	1743	1753	1763	1773	1783	1793
UK south and middle	1,302	1,721	1,172	1,795	1,281	1,622	1,740	2,029	2,442	3,160
UK north	356	368	315	260	379	599	596	605	683	1,585
English provincial	33	62	24	46	106	106	133	223	332	859

Notes: UK south and middle includes London and the home counties, the south, south-west, East Anglia, West Midlands and Wales. UK north includes the east Midlands, the north-east, north-west, Ireland and Scotland. English provincial includes all regions of England other than London and the home counties.

linear regression indicates).[54] Understandably, Dublin is very much the centre of the trade, but Belfast and other small cities become increasingly important as the century progresses.[55]

The north of England, an area that includes rapidly growing major metropolitan centres, exhibits a clear trend of growth in the book trade and in many other areas of industry and commerce as well (see Table 1.2b). Here, as elsewhere, the impact of changes in demographics, infrastructure and finance help to account for the markedly upward trend from the early decades of the century to a production total of 6.5 per cent by the century's end.[56] In the early decades of the nineteenth century, this region would become more influential still.

In examining figures for provincial England – that is, all regions of England other than London and the home counties – it is notable that for the first five decades of the century, production in the provinces comprises less than 3 per cent per annum. In 1773, that number is slightly above 4 per cent; a decade later, it more or less doubles, and between 1783 and 1793, it nearly triples to reach almost 17 per cent.[57] Yet, we must ask why the numbers for the whole of provincial England are still relatively low until the final decade of the century.[58] No one explanation can adequately account for this phenomenon, but we would do well to recall that economies of scale made book work more

54 The peak we observe in 1753 may well be an artefact in the data. Cf. Veylit 1994, fig. 17.

55 See Pollard 1989; and Lennon 2006, 75–8.

56 On the growth of northern England – its population, transportation networks and banking – see Suarez, Introduction, above.

57 These numbers are congruent with John Feather's analysis of the development of the provincial trade in England; see Feather 1985, 12–31. Cf. Mitchell 1987; Stoker 1995.

58 The West Midlands, for example, show a steadily increasing trend, but it is very small indeed, going from 0 to 3 per cent over the course of ninety years.

profitable in the capital and transportation networks made the delivery of print economically viable.[59] Moreover, despite the burgeoning growth of England's other principal metropolitan centres – Manchester, Liverpool, Birmingham, Bristol and Leeds all had more than 50,000 inhabitants by the end of the century – London remained far and away the largest population centre in England, and by 1801 was the most populous city in western Europe, having nearly 1.5 million residents.[60]

Thinking about the dominance of London over the provincial trade, we might also consider the nature of the database from which these findings have come. Although my evidence is merely anecdotal, and hence unsystematic, an examination of newspaper advertisements, lists of booksellers' wares at the back of provincially published books, and catalogues of booksellers operating outside the capital suggests that provincial printing is underrepresented in the *ESTC* – even more so than imprints from the capital. One reason for this supposition is that, generally speaking, books produced in the provinces had smaller markets and, hence, smaller press runs than those produced in London.[61] Moreover, provincial books tended to be in smaller formats, and hence had lower survival rates.[62] In addition, we might further consider that, broadly speaking, many regions in provincial England lacked the density of cultural institutions that would, in the nineteenth and early twentieth centuries, have led to the preservation of locally produced eighteenth-century works.[63] Finally, to some extent the underrepresentation of provincial publishing is an artefact of *ESTC* cataloguing practices: when a book was published both in London and provincially, the provincial imprint was not always included; these omitted locations are being gradually added to the appropriate records.

Taking provincial England, Scotland and Wales together, we may observe that, from 1743 to 1783, these 'non-London' publication sites comprise around 20 per cent of the total output of titles in the kingdom. Not surprisingly, a sharp rise in the data for 1793 raises that total to about 34 per cent. Clearly this is an area that merits further investigation. The south and middle of Britain may usefully be considered as a loosely constructed market for books, especially as the century continues. Scrutinizing, therefore, the broad region that includes London and the Home Counties, the south, the south-west, East

59 See Mosley, chap. 7, and Ferdinand, chap. 21, below. See also Suarez, Introduction, above.

60 Wrigley 1987, 162 and table 7.2.

61 Obviously, small press runs are not invariably associated with low survivorship, nor – as the loss rates among school-books and almanacs clearly reveal – are large edition quantities a guarantee of survival; see Willard 1942; Barnard 1999; and Gingerich 2004, 121, 126–9.

62 See May 2001, 298.

63 See Perkin 1984.

Anglia, the West Midlands and Wales, we may observe (with the help of linear regression analysis) that this broad area quite consistently accounts for between 75 and 80 per cent of the trade's total output.

How are we to explain the fact that 1793 exhibits a notable downturn, to approximately 65 per cent of that output, even though more than five hundred additional titles were produced in this category in 1793 than in 1783? The tremendous surge in publications originating in northern Britain and Ireland is responsible. The northern market appears to be more viable than the south, but in general accounts for some 20 per cent of total output between 1703 and 1783. By 1793, however, that number is nearly 35 per cent and northern Britain, along with its Hibernian neighbour, clearly constitutes a viable and more-or-less independent market.[64] Accounting for this emerging market, we would do well to remember that by 1800, six of the ten most populous cities in Britain (that is, not counting Dublin) were located in the north.[65] In addition, from 1770 onwards, the northern transportation infrastructure not only had excellent links between major metropolitan centres and the capital, but also exhibited significant networks of good roads both between cities and within the regions of most market towns.[66]

Finally, if we consider all the publishing centres that comprise the large emporium for print in the British Isles outside London – provincial England, Scotland, Wales and Ireland – we observe that for most of the century, the 'non-London' publishing world accounts for between 20 and 30 per cent of the total market. In 1793, however, that number jumps to more than 40 per cent, a statistic that is largely consonant with the boom in provincial publishing towards the century's end.

Analysis according to format

A book's format signalled something of its contents and hospitability to its readers. Writing to her sister, Jane Austen remarked scornfully on 'those enormous great stupid thick quarto volumes', further confiding 'I detest a Quarto' and castigating those who would 'not understand a man who

64 On this peak in the Irish trade, see Pollard 1989, 143–9; Veylit 1994, 281, fig. 17; and Phillips 1998, table 2, 120. See also Lennon 2006, 86–7; and Cole 1986, 191–2. The high numbers for 1793 in Ireland may well have been in part boosted by the publication of the second *Dublin catalogue of books* in 1791, which undoubtedly augmented foreign sales. In 1794, Britain was at war with France and exports to the Continent from Ireland, Scotland and England were minimal, although it is not clear to what extent this may have curtailed production.

65 Wrigley 2004, 90; see also Wrigley 1987, table 7.2 on 162.

66 Pawson 1977.

Table 1.3 *Principal formats of books published between 1703 and 1793*

	1703	1713	1723	1733	1743	1753	1763	1773	1783	1793
12*	158	207	187	244	252	455	477	526	575	867
8*	469	999	741	939	820	1,045	845	1,070	1,324	2,081
4*	465	261	136	162	194	242	457	426	361	532
2*	182	238	306	387	267	359	312	462	418	540
Total in these formats	1,274	1,705	1,370	1,732	1,533	2,101	2,091	2,484	2,678	4,020
Percentage of total published output	75.5	82.8	89.4	91.4	93.0	94.4	90.4	95.0	88.5	78.3

condenses his thoughts into an octavo', a format that betokened greater accessibility, portability (and, hence, sociability), authorial restraint and unpretentiousness. Her observations, made in 1813, reflect a shift in sensibility more than a century in the making.[67]

The principal bibliographical formats – folio, quarto, octavo and duodecimo – dominated the book market. Between 1713 and 1783, they make up between 70 and 80 per cent of the surviving printed output (see Table 1.3).[68] Intriguingly, the proportion of main formats represented in the samples for 1703 and 1793 is lower, less than 70 per cent in both cases. This phenomenon is accounted for by the higher number of surviving single-sheet publications in these two decades – attributable to the collections from which many such items entered the database (see below).

Looking at Figure 1.2, we see that folios comprised between approximately 10 and 20 per cent of the market (and accounted for approximately 12 to 22 per cent among the four main formats, exclusive of single-sheet publications). In his diary for January 1790, Boswell recorded a conversation with Edmond Malone in which the aspiring biographer revealed his ambition to publish *The Life of Johnson* in folio. Malone, who was attuned to the ways of the London trade, explained that his friend 'might as well throw it into the Thames' because 'a folio would not now be read'.[69] How are we to reconcile this observation with

67 To Cassandra Austen, 9 Feb. 1813; Austen 1995, 206.

68 Cf. Veylit 1994, 287–8, figs. XXIV–XXV; 295, fig. XXX; 297, fig. XXXII; and 375, table F. Additional data, correlating formats with subjects and genres, are represented at 289–94, figs. XXVI–XXIXb.

69 13 January 1790; Boswell 1989, 32–3. In the same vein, John Wesley, writing in the *Armenian Magazine* 4 (1781), iv, remarked, 'I believe if Angels were to write books, we should have very few Folios.' Of course, when thinking about the formats of eighteenth-century books, it is important to remember that there were significant changes in taste and paper size as the century progressed; see Pollard 1941.

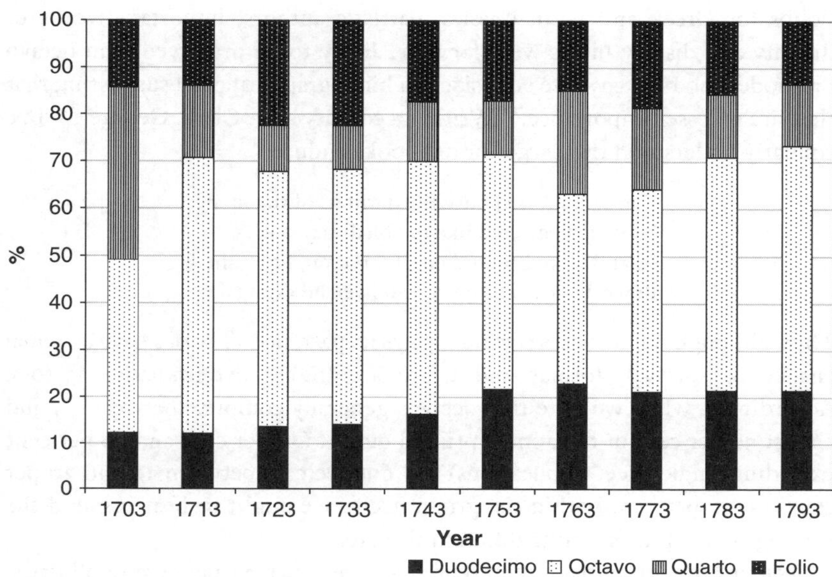

Figure 1.2 Main formats of imprints, 1701–93 (per cent of group)

the approximately 10–15 per cent publication rate of folios we routinely observe in the data? The answer lies, in part, in the disproportionately high survival rates of large-format books. As Roger Stoddard's Law reminds us, 'Bigger books linger longer; little books last least.'[70] Folios and, to a lesser extent, quartos tend to persist; octavos and duodecimos – not only because of their size, but also because of the ways they are read and used – commonly perish.

It was for this very reason that the nonconformist minister Samuel Clark justified the publication of his collection of *Lives of Sundry Eminent Persons* in folio, even though many of the individual biographies had already been published in smaller formats:

> I judge it necessary thus to print them again. For I have observed, that being generally Printed in little Volumes, few of them come to a second Impression, but after a little time, are thrown aside and forgotten; whereas, when many excellent Lives are collected into one or more Volumes, they do continue, and will so do, till Printing shall be no more . . .[71]

70 Gingerich 2004, 127. Cf. Willard 1942, 175.
71 Clark 1683, 1. (Thanks to Isabel Rivers for this reference.)

Folios for Greek and Latin classics, patristic authors, important works of divinity and display bibles were far more likely to be preserved than octavo or duodecimo books whose very size is a bibliographical code suggesting that they are of lesser importance.[72] Writing a century after Clark, George Crabbe similarly understood that large-format books endure:

> Yon Folio's, [*sic*] once the darlings of the mode,
> Now lie neglected like the birth-day ode . . .
> Chain'd like Prometheus, lo! the mighty train
> Brave Time's fell tooth, and live and die again.[73]

Thus, although randomness certainly plays its part, not all books have an equal chance of survival; format and genre are highly determinative factors. Accordingly, when we note that octavos generally comprise between 35 and almost 50 per cent of the annual printed output (40 per cent and 60 per cent excluding single-sheet publications) and duodecimos between 10 and 20 per cent (12–22 per cent within the group itself), we ought to bear in mind the varying survival rates among different formats.

Quartos, though initially represented in more than 25 per cent of all titles, mostly hover between 10 and 15 per cent for much of the century (10 and 38 per cent within the group). One reason for the decline in quartos is the increase in the size of the sheet, making smaller formats more viable;[74] another cause is the shift – during the 1710s and 1720s – from quarto to octavo or even duodecimo as the preferred format for reprinting dramatic texts.[75] During the first half of the century, however, quartos became increasingly popular in a closely allied sector of the market. Many works of poetry, especially separately printed original works and translations that would have formerly been published as folios early in the century, came more and more to be issued as quartos.[76] In general, we may observe a trend, among literary works at least, for genres to move from larger to smaller formats, even for initial publication, so that what formally would have been folios were printed as quartos or even large octavos; quartos became octavos; and the kinds of books one would have thought of as octavos were issued as duodecimos. All the early unabridged editions of *Moll Flanders* (1722), for example, were octavos; *Pamela* (1740), *Evelina* (1778) and *Caleb Williams* (1794) were all first issued as duodecimos.

72 See McGann 1991, 13–16, 52–8.
73 Crabbe 1781, lines 73–4, 76–8.
74 Pollard 1941.
75 McMullin 1993; see Suarez, chap. 34, below.
76 The chronological index in Foxon 1975a is especially useful for tracing this shift.

The difficulties of adjusting our figures to account for the lower survival rates among octavos and duodecimos notwithstanding, it seems prudent to presume that the 40–50 per cent proportion of octavos reflects a lower number than the reality, and that the 12–20 per cent duodecimos would require an even greater adjustment upwards. Yet, in the absence of a reliable algorithm for estimating loss rates, we must remain uncertain as to what the actual figures may have been.

When we consider one-sheet formats – that is, both unfolded publications such as broadsides in their several manifestations and single-sheet pamphlets – we should be even more troubled by the inherent uncertainties introduced both by the ephemerality of such forms and by the cataloguing practices of the *ESTC*. Obviously, these are the kinds of publication for which the loss rates will be the highest – and about which we know the least regarding survivorship. Even more than books, single-sheet publications were especially subject to stochastic processes materially affecting their survival. Although books were certainly used for waste paper, broadsides and other ephemera of one sheet or less were particularly susceptible to become 'Martyrs of Pies, and Reliques of the Bum'.[77] Oddly, the largest proportion of one-sheet publications appears in our sample in the first and last decades of the century.[78] This seems to be explicable by two principal factors: for many years the *ESTC* was very unsystematic in its gathering and cataloguing of single-sheet publications, and several collections of ephemera included in the *ESTC* have particularly strong coverage (both in the British Library and in the John Johnson collection in the Bodleian Library, Oxford) at the beginning and the end of the century. The greater survival through collection and preservation at these two ends of our timeline leads us to recall that one-sheet formats almost certainly comprised the majority of all publishing activity. Yet, even the figures we have for 1703 and 1793 surely fall well below the numbers of one-sheet publications actually produced.

Analysis by length (in sheets)

The vagaries of survival rates and the varying representations of different formats in the extant record necessitate a consideration of publications by

77 John Dryden, *Mac Flecknoe* (1682), line 101.

78 Veylit 1994, 376, table G, also finds the largest proportion of single-sheet publications in the last decade of the century, with high proportions in the early decades and a trough in the middle years. Differences between his data and mine (Veylit represents the 1730s as having the second highest proportion of single-sheet publications among the surviving printed output) may perhaps be accounted for by the fact that his census is not restricted to England, Wales, Scotland and Ireland.

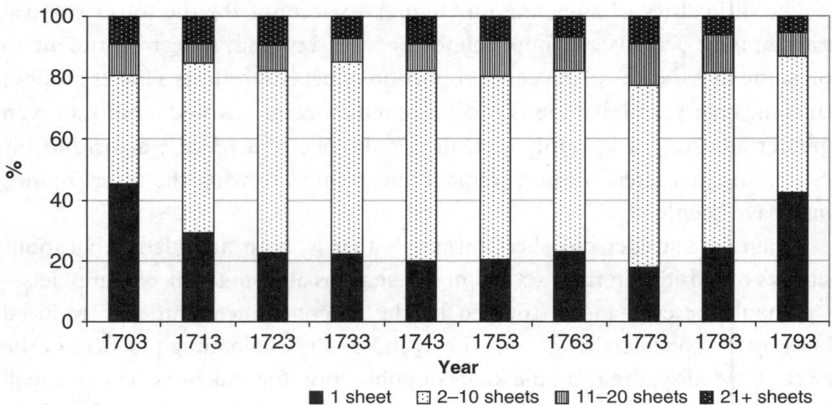

Figure 1.3 Length of imprints, 1701–93

their length.[79] Reviewing Figure 1.3, we observe that, throughout the century, more than 80 per cent of surviving titles are between one and ten sheets long regardless of format, with two to ten sheets being most common.[80] Publications of eleven to twenty sheets and of more than twenty sheets comprise less than 20 per cent of the century's extant record, although one may reasonably expect that such larger publications would have higher survival rates. 'Bigger books linger longer' with respect to both their format and the number of sheets they contain. Given the investment required and the slow return on capital that typified the publishing of most substantial books, it should come as no surprise that publications of ten sheets or fewer should so thoroughly dominate the market. Longer books required more capital and higher press runs to create an economy of scale, and were slower to return their investment. Hence, longer books and bigger publishing projects more typically paved the way to bankruptcy than did more modest productions.[81]

As Figure 1.3 indicates, between 1713 and 1783, longer books of eleven to twenty sheets increase from around 7 to around 12 per cent, a finding accounted for both by the increased use of smaller formats and perhaps by better capitalization in financing the trade. Yet, books of twenty-one sheets or more appear to decline as a percentage of total output (or, rather, of surviving

79 In all, 25,103 records were classified and counted, as against 24,138 for the category of bibliographical format. No determination was possible for 4,407 records.

80 Although the data are not strictly comparable because of the presence of North American (and other) records in Veylit's results, cf. Veylit 1994, 296, fig. XXI, for counts of single-sheet publications.

81 See Hernlund 1994; Ferdinand 2001; Mandelbrote 2003; see also Raven, chap. 3, below.

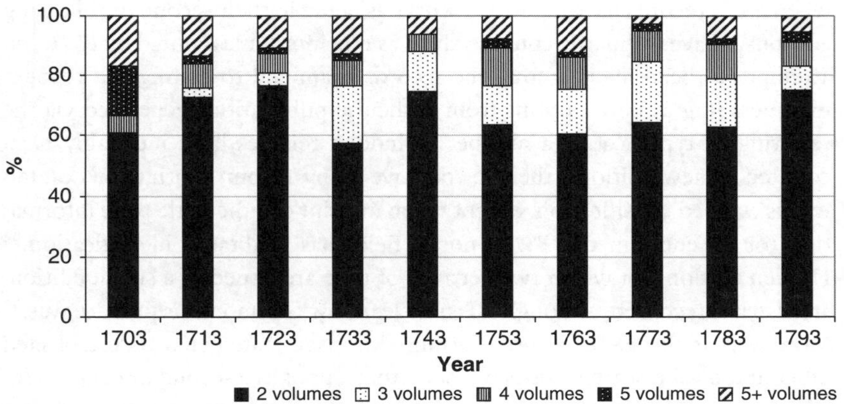

Figure 1.4 Multiple volumes, 1701–93

copies) from roughly 10 to 5 per cent. This downward trend may tentatively be explained by the publication of more multi-volume works, not least to satisfy the needs of the circulating libraries (see Figure 1.4).[82] Pursuing this line of inquiry, we may perceive a distinct trend, albeit on a small scale, in which the number of titles of between two and five volumes rises from about 15 in 1703 to some 250 in 1793, an overall increase of slightly less than 5 per cent in relation to the whole. Considering these categories as a percentage of the multiple-volumes group, we may observe that two-volume works predominate with consistently more than 60 per cent of multi-volume works, and two- and three-volume titles together comprising about 80 per cent.

Analysis of reprints

Reprinting titles that had proved to be successful was an essential feature of the book trade in an era when, according to the highly successful bookseller Andrew Millar, very few books actually made a profit.[83] Thus, collecting and analysing the numbers of repeat publications in our sample is useful, if not entirely unproblematic. Although title page edition statements should often be treated more as marketing stratagems than as bibliographical pronouncements,

82 See Hamlyn 1947; Kaufman 1967; Varma 1972; Fergus 1984; and Jacobs 2003.

83 Samuel Kenrick to James Wodrow, 13 Feb. 1788 (letter no. 135 in the Wodrow–Kenrick correspondence in Dr Williams's Library, London): 'I remember . . . [Millar] told me that he lost by twenty books where he gained by one.' (My thanks to Richard Sher for this reference.) On the literary reprint trade, see Bonnell, chap. 37, below, and Bonnell 2008.

when *ESTC* records have identified works as being in their second or following editions, I have ordinarily counted them as reprints. Unless noted by *ESTC*, no attempt has been made among the records examined to distinguish reissues masquerading as new editions from authentic publications generated via the resetting of type. Yet, if a number of hidden reissues have inevitably been counted as new editions, then so too have many Dublin reprints of London works escaped classification, except when imprint or other title page information (or an entry in the *ESTC* 'notes' field) has facilitated identification.[84] Hidden editions, in which two settings of type are issued as a single edition, are also not recorded, although it is not clear how common this practice was.[85] Moreover, if the *ESTC* record – using title page statements or established bibliographical research – does not state that a book is a second or subsequent edition, then I have not been able to identify it as a reprint, and this is almost certainly the most significant source of under-counting. Nevertheless, we also need to remember that entire editions of many often-reprinted books did not survive and, hence, are not represented in *ESTC*. As noted above in our analysis of publishing output by genre, among the books most likely to perish were educational and children's books, and certain classes of religious works. It is important to bear in mind too that reprints were likely to be published in smaller formats than first editions, increasingly so as the century progressed, and that these 'little books last least'.

In 1703, about 190 surviving titles were identifiable as repeat publications; by 1793, that number was in excess of 550 (see Figure 1.5). Yet, because of the increased productivity of the book trade, both figures represent almost exactly 10 per cent of the total output in each of their respective sample years. Oddly enough, between 1763 and 1793, the proportion of repeat publications, which one might expect to rise in the aftermath of *Donaldson* v. *Becket*, appears to decline from 14 per cent to 10 per cent.[86] Complicating this picture, however, is the fact that many reprints, especially when undertaken by a bookseller-publisher who did not originally own the copy, do not signal their status, either via edition statements or by supplying other indicative title page information. Although fairly consistent, the 10 per cent figure considerably underestimates the number of reprinted editions in the eighteenth century.[87] Yet again,

84 On the importance of Dublin as a centre of reprinting, see Benson, chap. 17, below; Cole 1986; Pollard 1989, 66–164; Phillips 1998; Sher 2006, 443–502; and Lennon 2006.

85 See Todd 1952 and Suarez 1997.

86 On the history of intellectual property and the Lords' ruling against the idea of perpetual copyright, see Rose, chap. 4, below. On the impact of the Lords' decision, see note 53, above.

87 In an analysis of data from the Term Catalogues, Barnard and Bell 2002a, 788, table 4, find that, of all books registered between 1688 and1709, an average of 26.9 per cent were reprints. This figure does not

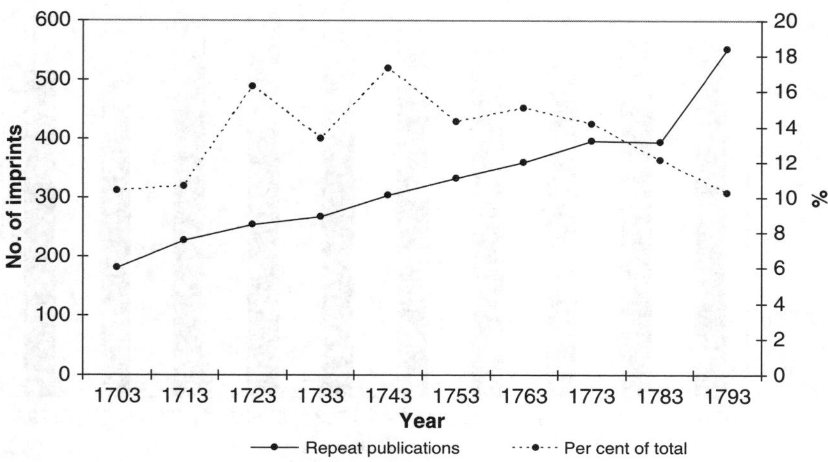

Figure 1.5 Repeat publications, 1701–93

problems associated with classifying and counting records for bibliometric analysis are not easily remedied.

Considering different kinds of repeat publications as a portion of the group, we may observe that second to fifth editions make up between 65 and 81 per cent of all reprints (see Figure 1.6). In every year, however, sixth to tenth editions and titles in more than the tenth edition – if their title pages are to be believed – constitute more than 20 per cent of all repeat publications (and in some decades, more than 30 per cent). The eighteenth-century reprint trade was a vital source of reliable income, both for copy owners and for opportunistic (and sometimes unscrupulous) booksellers alike.

Critiquing his own analytic study of compositorial practices in a Cambridge edition of Beaumont's *Psyche* (1702), Don McKenzie (one of the dedicatees of this volume) wryly observed, 'The statistics are impeccable; the assumptions, and therefore the inferences, are nonsense.'[88] Hugh Amory (also a dedicatee)

include Bibles, Testaments, the Book of Common Prayer, ABCs, catechisms, and other works printed by exclusive privilege and, hence, not requiring registration in the Catalogues. It would be useful to know what percentage of the registered reprints are represented in the *ESTC*, but I have not yet undertaken such an investigation. Although there may well have been a greater financial incentive to register (and so protect) reprinted works because of their proven value, one might also imagine that busy publishing booksellers might have been disinclined to register a reprinted edition, either because an earlier registration was understood as sufficient or because previous editions had already reasonably established ownership according to the custom of the trade. See G. Mandelbrote 1997 for many examples of reprinted texts not in the Stationers' Register.

88 McKenzie 1984, 114.

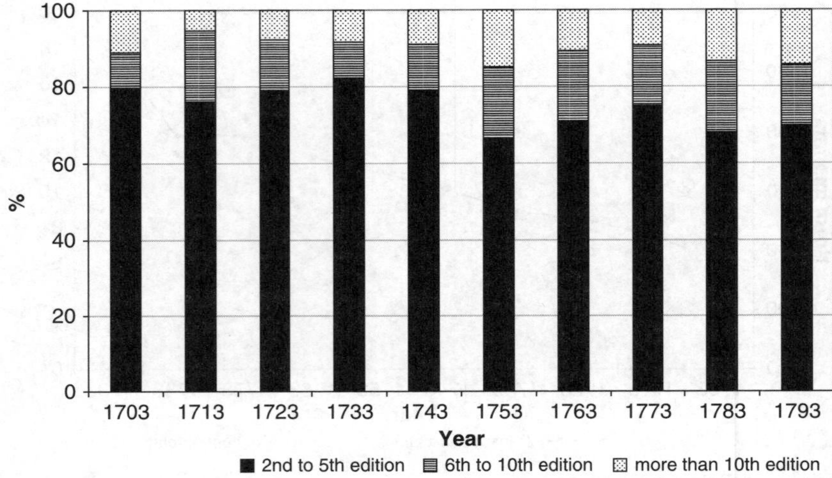

Figure 1.6 Repeat publications, 1701–93 (per cent of group)

similarly cautioned that the seeming precision of statistical treatments 'should not be mistaken for accuracy'.[89] Both bibliographers understood that statistics – apparently proffering 'scientific' truths – could be enticing, and both were wary.[90]

In addition to the shortcomings of my investigation already noted, would-be users of these statistics will do well to keep certain admonitions before them. This study neglects the kinds of printing that chiefly occupied the presses and personnel of most London and provincial printing offices.[91] It does not tell us about financial losses and gains, although the printing, publishing, marketing and vending of books were almost always commercial enterprises. It pays no attention whatsoever to manuscripts, the production and circulation of which remained consequential throughout the century.[92] It tells us neither what was actually read, nor by whom, nor how.[93] I think of this study as a series of hand-drawn maps, surveys – made from a great distance and in fading light – of a vast and complex terrain in which local knowledge of the whole is not genuinely

89 Amory 2000a, 515. See also Blayney 2007.

90 For an exemplary instance of statistical analysis in the service of book history, see Kruif 1999.

91 See Twyman, chap. 2, below. On the importance of jobbing printing, see (by way of an *inclusio*) Johnson 1937 and Stallybrass 2007.

92 See, for example, Havens 2001, 81–97; McKitterick 2003; Fairer 2003, 1–20; and N. Smith 2008.

93 On eighteenth-century reading, see Engelsing 1969, 1971; Darnton 1984; 1990, 154–87, esp. 165–6; Chartier 1987, 222, 224–5, 231–3; and Brewer 1996. Chartier 1995 and Price 2004 provide excellent surveys of reading as a subject of inquiry. Scepticism about documenting reading practices and the nature of such evidence features in Fowler 1975; Hadfield 2004; Price 2004; and Suarez 2003–4 (2006).

possible. They have taken years to produce, so that even the slow turning of the world has affected their clarity and contributed to their imprecision. Undertaken in the hope that they might prove useful for other scholars' explorations, they are most reliable when charting general trends and delineating relationships (typically expressed in percentages), and much less trustworthy when providing what the casual tourist might mistake for exact measurements of particular geographical features. I look forward to the day when these surveys will be superseded by better, more accurate representations. Meanwhile, perhaps they will suggest some routes into the tremendous amount of work that is yet to be done.

2

Printed ephemera

MICHAEL TWYMAN

Two terms are commonly applied to the category of work discussed in this chapter: jobbing printing and ephemera. The first, which strictly speaking relates to work printed on a single sheet, is a printer's term and focuses on the means of production; the second, which puts emphasis on the brief life such documents were designed or likely to have, tends to be used retrospectively. Both are more easily defined than applied, and they are used somewhat loosely here. In a publication concerned with the history of the book it might have made more sense to call this chapter 'non-book printing'. But this too is far from ideal, since newspapers, journals, maps and music are considered elsewhere in this volume. Even without such categories, however, this chapter is wide enough in scope to embrace scores of different kinds of printed documents.

Seen from the point of view of book production, the period covered by this volume is broadly one of continuity and consolidation, but when we turn to ephemera this is less obviously the case. Though most routine work of this kind was printed from type matter in the eighteenth century and followed the conventions and typographic style of books, this was to change significantly in the early nineteenth century. At this point several innovations left their mark on the design and production of ephemera, which had the gradual and long-term effect of distancing them from book printing.

All kinds of printing establishments produced ephemera. Some were large letterpress firms that also printed books and newspapers; others were small letterpress houses for which large-scale book production would have presented a real challenge; yet others were intaglio workshops that had as much to do with printmaking as printing. Ephemera may also have been produced in workshops with both letterpress and intaglio facilities, and in the nineteenth century by firms using lithography, either separately or alongside the older processes.

Until the mid-eighteenth century, ephemera may not have figured prominently in the output of the printing and printmaking trades, though such is the paucity of recorded material that even this is not certain. What we can surmise is that by the end of our period ephemera formed a major part of the output of many printing houses. The evidence we have for this is twofold: the appearance of new kinds of documents, and a gradual shift from manuscript to print production in others. Although *ESTC* has identified numerous items of ephemera, the rarity of surviving material makes it extremely difficult to form any clear idea of the scale of ephemera production before the nineteenth century. The danger of drawing conclusions from surviving items alone is underlined by a document known as a king's evil certificate. We learn from an announcement in the *London Gazette* for 18/21 November 1672 that those wishing to be 'touched' by the king in the hope of being cured of the king's evil (scrofula) needed to bring with them a 'certificate' signed by the minister or churchwarden of their parish. Charles II (r.1660–85) is recorded as having 'touched' some 90,000 of his subjects, all of whom would, presumably, have required certificates; yet not one such certificate is known to have survived.[1]

Additional evidence for the low survival rate of ephemera comes from the closing decades of our period. The difficulty of finding further copies of items of jobbing work held in printing archives suggests that what has come down to us is not simply a matter of chance. Unless a printing house kept its own records (usually in an album or on a spike), or its products were incidentally filed by other parties at the time (among business, family, estate or solicitors' papers), they are not likely to have survived long after their initial use. Lottery ephemera illustrate this point well: it has been estimated that more than twenty-five million lottery tickets and shares must have been produced between 1694 and 1826, though early examples are now very rare.[2] What is available for study is therefore only a tiny fraction of an enormous body of jobbing printing, nearly all of which has been lost or, if not actually lost in the sense of destroyed, cannot easily be located. Interpretation of this aspect of printing history is therefore fraught with difficulties.

Nevertheless, ephemera that survive from the eighteenth century – however fragmentary and unrepresentative they may be – suggest a general opening up of printing to ordinary people on an unprecedented scale. The relationship between this and the thorny issue of the growth of literacy is difficult to establish. The production of a document – whether a poor-law form, a royal proclamation or even a sales notice – does not mean that all its intended readers would have been able to understand it. The evidence of numerous documents signed with a cross testifies to this. What we might surmise, however, is that the

1 Rickards 2000, 188.
2 Grant 2001, 9.

design and wording of ephemera, particularly early nineteenth-century advertising, changed in response to the rise of literacy and the existence of a large semi-literate public.[3]

New demands and opportunities

The proliferation of printed ephemera in the period covered by this volume reflects several changes in society. Perhaps the most direct was the growth of bureaucracy, which can be seen both as an inevitable consequence of the increasing complexity of society and as an instrument of control. It existed at national and local levels of government, and also in some large organizations, particularly the army and the church. Categories of ephemera that mark this development include forms, certificates, proclamations, taxation documents and passports, all of which played a significant role in our period. One provincial printer, J. Tymbs, who printed the *Worcester Journal*, issued an advertisement in 1780 in which he named eighty-five different forms, including burial affidavits, exchequer writs, land tax receipts, orders of removal, parish certificates and petitions for insolvents.[4] Surviving work of the Ulverston printer John Soulby (junior) dating from the period 1819 to 1827 includes a good range of legal forms of this kind, most of which were printed, and reprinted regularly, for the local attorneys.[5] The development of trade and industry in the late eighteenth century resulted in the growth of large towns which, by their very scale, created a demand for ephemera. The oral tradition of the marketplace gradually gave way to written and, later, printed advertising, and an increase in the scale of production opened up markets beyond the immediate locality. Selling at a distance also meant that commodities and services needed to be described and transactions recorded. Trade cards, in particular, highlight the changing methods of those selling products, and it is no accident that they were among the first categories of ephemera to be taken seriously by scholars.[6] Along with billheads, window bills, trade lists, price lists, invoices, receipts, bills of lading, cheques and money orders, they provide us with an invaluable record of commercial practices.

Other printed documents reflect leisure activities, and especially the increasing role entertainment played in society.[7] Probably the earliest such ephemera

3 Cf. Altick 1998.
4 Twyman 1998b, fig. 1.
5 Twyman 1966, 43, 49–53, fig. 56.
6 Heal 1968.
7 Plumb 1972.

were popular ballads and broadsheets of the kind already being collected in large numbers in the seventeenth century by Samuel Pepys (1633–1703). Throughout the century illustrated broadsheets, the precursors of our tabloid press, provided a rich assortment of sensational material – scandals, murders, portents, disasters, monsters and prodigies – for popular consumption. In addition, London theatres commissioned ephemera on a regular basis from the late seventeenth century. Normally called playbills,[8] such documents doubled up as advertisements and programmes. They seem to have been preserved more consistently than any other category of ephemera, and good runs of eighteenth-century examples survive in the British Library for several London theatres (Covent Garden, Drury Lane, Haymarket). Even provincial theatres were issuing playbills regularly before the end of the eighteenth century. Similar bills were produced for popular spectacles, such as balloon ascents, freak shows, circuses and, in London, for the great pleasure gardens. Sporting events, mainly horse racing, but prize fights and cricket matches too, were also advertised through printing.

The spread of printing to small country towns in the late eighteenth century, though a response to changes in society, also helped to bring about change by facilitating communication. By the end of the century, categories of ephemera that had previously been available only in the capital, and perhaps a few other large towns, were in common use by provincial tradesmen and were being posted on church boards and in marketplaces throughout the country.

Finally, among the forces that influenced ephemera production, there were the technological changes that took place within the printing trade.[9] At the beginning of our period printing technology was relatively stable. Type manufacture and letterpress printing had hardly changed in two hundred and fifty years and were geared primarily to the production of books. As the term implies, letterpress printing put a premium on words: it catered for illustrations as best it could, usually by incorporating relatively crude woodcut images alongside text. When quality was required, illustrations were usually printed from intaglio plates on the letterpress-printed sheets of a book, or were inserted as separate leaves in the course of binding. Such work was undertaken by copper engravers and etchers and often had to be put out by letterpress printers to specialist intaglio workshops. This arrangement had served the book trade reasonably well from the early sixteenth century, but appears not to have been widely followed for the production of ephemera.

8 *OED*, first use 1673.
9 See Mosley, chap. 7, below.

The intaglio trade, which at the end of the seventeenth century was mainly concerned with a combination of line engraving and etching on copper, had likewise changed little over the years. The main innovation was the introduction of a hard varnish and new tools that allowed the etcher to imitate the marks of the line engraver, and hence reduce origination costs. Even so, intaglio printing remained an expensive process. What is more, it favoured pictorial work: if words were needed, they had to be produced individually, character by character, by the etcher or engraver. This meant that the intaglio trade tended to specialize in refined pictorial and decorative ephemera, such as bookplates, trade cards and prestigious invitations, whereas the letterpress printer of ephemera focused on run-of-the-mill work. These essential differences remained, and were perhaps accentuated, with the development of the tonal intaglio processes of mezzotint in the mid-seventeenth century and aquatint in the last decades of the eighteenth century, though neither made any real inroads into ephemeral printing.

This general pattern was to change in the decades around the turn of the eighteenth and nineteenth centuries. In this period several technical developments took place that revolutionized jobbing printing, along with some branches of the book trade. First, and most significantly for the long term, was the invention of lithography, a new process of printing that depended not on physical differences of relief between printing and non-printing areas, but on chemical principles. It was introduced to Britain from Germany in 1801, though its commercial development in Britain was delayed until around 1820.

The second development took the form of refinements made by Thomas Bewick to engraving on wood around 1780 that gave letterpress printers the opportunity to include delicate images alongside type for printing at one pass through the press. This process – called wood-engraving to distinguish it from its cruder precursor, woodcut – had an immediate impact on book illustration. It influenced jobbing printing too, but principally through metal casts taken from wood-engravings, known as stock blocks.[10] This, the third significant advance to be referred to here, meant that improvements to engraving on wood at the more expensive end of the market found their way into low-level jobbing printing. Stock blocks were sold by type founders (occasionally by wood-engravers), and for the first time 'ready-made' pictures of reasonable quality became available to the letterpress printer.

The fourth of the innovations to affect the jobbing printer was the iron platen press, the first being the Stanhope press, which dates from the very early

10 See Mosley, chap. 7, below.

nineteenth century.[11] This was followed by the Columbian, introduced from America around 1819, and its British rival, the Albion, of around 1822. The greater efficiency of these iron presses, compared with the common press, allowed for the printing of larger formats and work with a higher ink to paper ratio. They made possible the first radical departure of letterpress ephemera from book conventions: the introduction of large, bold and visually arresting typefaces. After 1815, or thereabouts, all the leading type founders issued such types, which were designed specifically to attract attention in advertising. They were soon taken up by printers throughout the country and for more than a century had a profound effect on the design of printing intended for public display.

The producers of ephemera

With the relaxation of control over the setting up of printing houses in Britain, we see a gradual spread of printing beyond London and the universities of Oxford and Cambridge to the rest of the country. Initially it was the major centres of population that attracted printing, and by the middle of the eighteenth century most large towns would have had at least one printer. Later in the century the spread of printing to smaller market towns had the effect of bringing printing to rural communities, where most people then lived.

London letterpress printers who specialized in jobbing work, or undertook it on a regular basis, are more difficult to identify than provincial ones until we get to the nineteenth century. There are two main reasons for this. First, coherent collections of work by individual London jobbing printers do not seem to have survived as they have for some provincial printers. Second, leaving aside proclamations, it was by no means common for imprints to be included on single-sheet work until the 'Seditious Societies Act' of 1799[12] made this compulsory; and even then the letter of the law was not consistently followed.

The number of letterpress printers working in London in the earlier part of our period is difficult to establish, but in its final decades it more than doubled from 124 in 1785[13] to 316 in 1824.[14] The collective output of jobbing printing by so many letterpress firms must have been considerable. It seems that all but the most dedicated book printers would have taken on some work of this kind, and that many would have specialized in it. This was certainly the case with

11 See Mosley, chap. 7, below.
12 See Wood , chap. 48, below.
13 Pendred 1955.
14 Johnson 1824, II, 649–51.

Catnach, Pitts and other early nineteenth-century printers of popular street literature who worked in the Seven Dials area of London, where execution broadsheets in particular were produced in vast quantities.[15]

London retained control of the book trade, but not of jobbing printing, which played a major part in the growth of the provincial press in the course of the eighteenth century. The local newspaper often provided a focal point for this development, advertising products and services over a wide area, and thus encouraging the use of other forms of printed communication. Most provincial newspaper houses offered jobbing printing as one of their services, which must have helped to keep their presses busy in slack periods of the week. Until 1814, when *The Times* pioneered the use of powered cylinder machines, newspaper and jobbing work would have been produced on the same sorts of presses; and for some decades after this most newspaper houses would still have been in a position to switch from running sheets of their paper to printing broadsides, advertisements, forms or billheads without any difficulty.

Though we lack an overall picture of the growth of the provincial printing trade, a few detailed studies of particular printing houses of the late eighteenth and early nineteenth centuries give some indication of the output of presses that provided the rural community with ephemera. These include John Cheney, who founded a press in Banbury around 1767 that continued to be run as a family firm for a couple of centuries;[16] Jasper Sprange, who ran a press in Tunbridge Wells from the early 1770s to the early 1820s;[17] William Davison, who set up in business in Alnwick as a pharmacist early in the nineteenth century, and also worked as a printer between 1807 and 1858;[18] George Gitton of Bridgnorth, who established a press there in 1788 that was continued by his son, George Robert, well into the second half of the nineteenth century;[19] and the two John Soulbys of Ulverston, whose separate firms span the period from about 1796 to 1827.[20]

These printers' own designations of the trades they conducted give an idea of the scope of their businesses: Cheney referred to himself as 'Printer, bookseller and stationer'; Sprange as 'Printer, Bookseller, Bookbinder and Stationer, at his Circulating Library'; Davison as 'Chemist & druggist, printer, bookseller, bookbinder, stationer, &c'; George Gitton as 'Printer, Book Seller, Stationer, Binder, Music-Seller and General Stamp Distributor'; and the

15 Hindley 1966, 159.
16 Cheney and Cheney 1936.
17 Knott 1973–4, 7–8.
18 Isaac 1968.
19 Mackarill 2002.
20 Twyman 1966.

Soulbys as 'Bookseller, printer, stationer, etc', and 'Printer, bookbinder, etc'. But the range of products and services offered ranged even more widely than this: printers functioned much as village post offices were to do much later. All the printers mentioned above were involved with the production of books (William Davison more than the others), and all worked as binders too; but in each case jobbing work seems to have formed a substantial if not major part of their printing output. It helped to put them at the heart of their community, where printers in country towns were normally located.

Substantial collections of jobbing printing from all these presses survive: in the case of Soulby junior, 500 items of ephemera from a nine-year period, including as many as two items a week for 1826. Together, therefore, such collections give us a good idea of the products of printers in market towns towards the end of our period. Some also provide an indication of the size of print runs through manuscript additions to what must have been file copies. In the 1820s it was not unusual for Soulby junior to print 50 or 100 copies of an auction bill or form, and 500 or 1,000 copies of a billhead or inn tally, or for Gitton to print 100 copies of a 'reward' or other notice, 500 copies of an election bill, and up to 1,000 copies of a playbill or race card.

Davison and both Soulbys advertised their facilities for copperplate printing, though there is little evidence that the Soulbys undertook much work of this kind. In general, copperplate engravers and printers carried on their businesses as specialists, quite separately from letterpress printers. Some provincial craftsmen, among them the Beilby family who worked in Newcastle mainly in the late eighteenth century, are known to have specialized in what might be called jobbing engraving.[21] Such craftsmen were accustomed to working the right way round on glass, silverware or brass (for doorplates and coffin plates), but also in reverse on printing plates. They provided a service for local gentry and tradesmen by engraving and printing a range of decorative and lettered ephemera, including bookplates, visiting cards, invitations, trade cards and billheads.

The new process of lithography, which competed with intaglio engraving in some fields of jobbing printing, was slow to take root in the provinces. Apart from an atypical early flurry in Bath, where it attracted the attention of a few artists and amateurs in the years 1813–14, it was not until the mid-1820s that lithography began to find its way into a few large British towns (Bristol, Edinburgh, Glasgow and Manchester). Even in such places, however, its impact on jobbing printing appears to have been negligible.

21 Tattersfield 1999.

Major categories of ephemera in the eighteenth century

Many kinds of ephemera in existence at the end of the seventeenth century had to do with administration in one way or another, and they continued throughout the following century. Among them were proclamations, bills of mortality, indentures, licences, certificates, lighthouse dues papers, bills and receipts for public lotteries, and single-sheet almanacs. Some were aimed at the community at large; others were more directly targeted at particular groups.

First in significance among the former was the proclamation. Typically, this instrument of government was a broadside measuring about 15×12 in (380×305 mm); at its top was the royal coat of arms, followed by a heading in which the word 'proclamation' figured prominently. Its text, usually opening with a drop initial letter, consisted of a preamble giving the reasons for the legislation, followed by a brief outline of the legislation itself. Its closely fitting lines were often set to a wide measure and, in their disregard for legibility, provide a foretaste of the 'small print' of today. Proclamations confirmed a message that had already been delivered by the town crier and provided indisputable evidence that the public had been informed of a particular piece of legislation. Early examples were set in black-letter type, while antiqua types became the norm in the course of the eighteenth century. But apart from this, and some other responses to prevailing typographic tastes, proclamations retained much of their early graphic form into the nineteenth century. They were the prerogative of the printers to the king, and among imprints on them are those of John Baskett and his successors (in the early eighteenth century) and of Charles Eyre & Andrew Strahan and George Eyre & Andrew Strahan (in the late eighteenth and early nineteenth centuries).

Numerous examples of administrative ephemera had to do with family or individual affairs. Today, many would be described generically as forms, though on the documents themselves they might be referred to as a 'licence', 'certificate' or 'indenture'. What they have in common is that they were intended to elicit or present information in an orderly way, and that they usually involved two or more parties: a producer and respondents. Early examples were handwritten throughout, a practice that continued into the eighteenth century, but by the end of the century most were printed. Unambiguous language and utility of design were paramount, and because of this early printed forms tend to look similar, regardless of what they were actually called. A typical example left gaps of varying sizes according to what had to be filled in, the structure of the language serving as a prompt to the writer. Until the nineteenth century, it was rare for a form to include any printed guides (such as lines or leader dots) to make the user's task easier. As with proclamations, book conventions were followed in almost every respect: drop initial letters were commonly used for the first letter of the text, and sometimes the whole of its first word was set in capitals. Invariably, the text was justified, which had the effect of emphasizing any unfilled gaps and, when completed by hand, any ill-fitting written parts. Official forms frequently declared their origins by carrying a royal or City of London coat of arms at their head. Similarly, indentures can be identified by their opening words – 'This Indenture' – which were usually set in black-letter type somewhat larger than the rest of the text. The wording and design of forms appear to have changed little over the centuries, and since forms aimed to cover most eventualities (different sovereigns, dates, localities, people and occupations) those surviving without manuscript additions or coats of arms are often difficult to date.

Other partially printed administrative documents with a long history include orders to attend (issued, for example, by the Masters and Wardens of Trinity House), receipts for lighthouse dues, and burial in woollen affidavits. This last category came into being with an Act of 1667 (18, 19 Charles II.c.4); it stipulated that corpses had to be wrapped in wool before burial, and it remained in force until 1815.[22] Some versions of the burial in woollen affidavit were written throughout by hand, but most were printed, often with woodcut surrounds depicting or symbolizing death.

Early trade ephemera are not nearly as commonly found as administrative ephemera, which by their nature are more likely to have survived. From the late seventeenth century we have trade cards, and perhaps a few billheads, though there is little to support the view that such items were common at the time. Products that needed to be wrapped for practical reasons, such as tobacco and playing cards, led to the production of printed packaging. And in the case of tobacco wrappers – which incorporated imagery and sometimes a reference to a point of sale – there is an echo of the trade card. Other trade-related ephemera already available at the end of the seventeenth century include notices of sailings of vessels, some of which display delicate engravings of ships.

Little seems to have been recorded about public entertainment ephemera of the late seventeenth century, though surviving broadsides advertise a range of events, such as freak shows, firework displays and theatrical performances. Particularly intriguing are the keepsakes that were printed on presses installed on ice when the Thames froze over, as it did, for example, in the winter of 1683–4, and again in 1730 and 1814. Yet, by far the most widespread category of

22 Rickards 2000, 65–6.

entertainment ephemera from at least the early eighteenth century was the playbill. Typically, eighteenth-century examples are about the size of an octavo book, printed in black only, and have their major lines in capitals no larger than 12mm high. By 1770, however, some bills were being printed in red and black that were four times as large (in area) as the earlier ones and have capitals 34mm high. The theatre bills of the eighteenth century rarely show imprints, but in the opening decades of the following century many were printed at the press of Charles Lowndes (for a time Lowndes & Hobb[e]s) in Drury Lane, and some at the theatre itself. Provincial theatres normally used their local printer who, not infrequently, sold tickets for them as well. In Ulverston, for example, during the Theatre Royal's 1810 season, George Ashburner and John Soulby senior – both of whom sold tickets for all performances – alternated as printers of the playbills.[23] In addition, playbills served as programmes; in the early nineteenth century they seem to have been printed two to a sheet (perhaps by the work and turn method), which may help to explain their characteristic slim format.

The commissioning of ephemera for personal or family use was also well established by the beginning of our period. The most obvious products of this kind are book labels and bookplates, both of which had their origins in the sixteenth century. Though only marginally considered ephemera on several accounts, it is appropriate to refer to them at this point since the letterpress book label and its relative, the intaglio-printed bookplate (distinguished by its armorial and other decorative and pictorial work), must have helped to establish a link between the individual customer and the printer. Originally, customers would have been limited to the nobility and gentry, though later on tradesmen too commissioned bookplates. It can be assumed that many of those who ordered book labels and bookplates would have turned to their local engravers and printers for other kinds of personal ephemera. Intaglio-printed dinner invitations of the late seventeenth century in the Pepys Library (Magdelene College, Cambridge) give some idea of the effort that went into decorative work of this kind, as do invitations to other private leisure events of the eighteenth century. Funeral invitations, perhaps the most common examples of personal and family ephemera, seem to have been produced for a wider social range. Beginning with such chilling words as 'you are desired to accompany the corps of...' and, like the burial in woollen affidavit, often depicting the emblems of death, they are, with bills of mortality, among the most poignant ephemera of their age.

23 Twyman 1966, 27.

Printed almanacs, particularly sheet almanacs, served both a public and private purpose and were produced throughout Europe well before our period begins. Until 1775, the Stationers' Company and the universities of Oxford and Cambridge had the exclusive right to publish them in Britain.[24] Sheet almanacs, with their calendars organized in tabular form, and often printed in small type in red and black, would have presented one of the most demanding tasks for the jobbing printer, and this may well account for the survival of what was essentially the same design idea over many years.

The trade card which, as we have seen, had its roots in the seventeenth century, came into its own in the eighteenth, along with its related trade document, the billhead.[25] These two items of stationery served similar functions, though the trade card was the more elaborate and general in its use, and prepared the way for the billhead. Both advertised a tradesman's wares or services, often with the help of illustrations. The billhead can nearly always be distinguished from the trade card by the inclusion of 'Bot of', 'Dr to' and similar wording; but the same intaglio plate was sometimes used for both items, and occasionally a trade card itself served as a billhead. When trade directories began to include sections of advertisements, the same plate was often used for this purpose too.

Though generally called trade cards, most were printed on paper until the closing years of the eighteenth century, when pasteboard (known as Bristol board) was introduced. The largest were about the size of a large sheet of notepaper, the smallest no bigger than a domestic visiting card. Generally, those of the early nineteenth century were small, which may be a consequence of the change from paper to card. Typically, elaborate trade cards were printed intaglio from the second half of the eighteenth century onwards, though humbler trade cards continued to be printed from type matter, sometimes with a woodcut or wood-engraved image. The more utilitarian billhead was even more likely to have been a letterpress production, presumably because of the greater number of copies needed.

The trade card was among the most inventive and prestigious items of eighteenth-century ephemera, particularly when engraved and printed intaglio. Initially it featured the tradesman's shop sign, but this changed when hanging signs were prohibited in London streets on grounds of safety in the early 1760s. Thereafter, the trade card became more elaborate and included – increasingly with a street number – pictures of products, tradesmen at work

24 See Myers, chap. 39, below.
25 Lambert 2001.

and premises. Like the bookplate and formal invitation, decorative trade cards of the eighteenth century reflect the prevailing baroque and rococo styles of ornamentation, only to give way to neo-classicism in the new century.[26] London trade cards were often unsigned, though when London engravers produced similar work for the provinces they were less reticent. One prolific engraver of trade cards was William Newman of Bishopsgate in London.[27] He is credited with more than a hundred examples from the first quarter of the nineteenth century, some of them for tradesmen in the provinces. Among the few leading artist-engravers who produced trade cards were Bartolozzi, Bewick and Hogarth.[28]

The ephemera that probably made the most impact on the general public were letterpress-printed bills (public notices and advertising) that were posted in prominent places in villages and towns throughout the land. By 1820 they began to be recorded in town views, usually haphazardly posted on walls, and in at least one case, beside the injunction 'Stick no bills'. The public notice, which owes something to the proclamation, seems to have emerged as a category of ephemera in the late eighteenth century, and was soon to be widespread. The issuing body may have been the Lord Mayor, a mayor or a local constable; reward notices (a particularly popular category) were often issued by local associations concerned with public order, and 'missing' notices by the police or even a bereft relative.

'For sale' and 'To let' bills also began to make a major impact on the output of jobbing printers from the late eighteenth century, though their origins were earlier. They were printed to advertise all kinds of properties, from the most modest cottage through to large estates; the status of the property usually influenced the size of the bill, the largest in the 1820s measuring about 20×16 in (510×407mm). Allied to property bills were auction bills for furniture, books, prints and other possessions. Similar bills were also printed for the sale of local produce, such as timber, wheat, butter and turnip seeds; such bills, often no larger than a sheet of notepaper, seem to have been designed for display in windows or shop interiors.

Political propaganda emerged as an increasingly noticeable category of ephemera in the late eighteenth century. As contested elections became more common, local printers almost inevitably found themselves involved in the rough and tumble of political debate. Witty and hard-hitting though the texts of such messages often were in the eighteenth century, they usually took the

26 See Barker, chap. 11 below.
27 Lambert 2001, 135–8.
28 See BL, Heal Collection and Bodleian, John Johnson Collection.

form of typographically bland addresses, with such headings as 'To the worthy electors of...' and 'To the independent burgesses or freeholders of...'. At this stage, electoral propaganda made no use of the striking typographic effects of the kind seen in the early nineteenth century when candidate and printer must have worked hand in glove, sometimes responding to the opposition's claims and counter-claims on a daily basis. Among coherent sets of provincial electoral bills are those for campaigns in Newcastle in 1777 and 1784 (BL 8135.g.5), Nottingham in 1797 (BL 1888.c.18), Shrewsbury from 1768 (BL L.23.b.18) and Westminster (BL 807.h.23). Events unfolding in France fuelled British political ephemera in the closing decades of the century.[29] Though constrained by the 'Seditious Societies Act' of 1799, republican sympathizers continued to use printing to promote their ideas – as did supporters of the Crown in countering them. Much of the republican material must have been seized and destroyed at the time, but some records of those supporting the crown have survived.

1800–1830: innovation

Items of jobbing printing designed for display in public places began to show a marked change in style around 1815. The conventions of book typography, which had governed most eighteenth-century work of this kind, gave way in a remarkably short time to typography that drew attention to its message visually as well as textually.[30] This typographic change set the pattern for the letterpress poster for the rest of the century and beyond. It involved displaying a few key lines or words in large sizes of the new types that were coming on the market. When a printer did not have such types, he cut a few letters in wood,[31] and a couple of surviving bills for the Westminster election of 1818, printed by James Roach (BL 1888.c.19), have fat-face woodcut letters measuring 60mm and, on one line, 80mm high. A bill of June 1818 in the same volume refers to a 'posting bill', in contrast, presumably, to a handbill, thus drawing attention to the more public methods of display that were coming into fashion.[32] Decisions about the design of this new kind of bill would generally have been taken by the printer – though clients may well have played their part too – and it would have been remarkably difficult for either to resist the new graphic styles of the day.

Just as noticeable in the early nineteenth century, though not nearly as common, was the use of colour in advertising. With a few exceptions,

29 See Wood, chap. 48, below.
30 See Barker, chap. 11, below.
31 Chambers 1882, 28.
32 *OED*, 'handbill', first use 1753; 'poster', first use 1838.

ephemera were printed in black before then, just as utilitarian ephemera continued to be for many decades to come. Yet, some categories of advertising, particularly those associated with leisure and entertainment, increasingly made use of colour – colour-printing, coloured papers (usually stained) or hand-colouring.

In the closing decades of the eighteenth century some playbills for the Theatre Royal, Drury Lane, were printed in red and black; in the provinces, as in London, others were printed in black on coloured paper. But the most enterprising commissioners of coloured advertising were undoubtedly the contractors for the public lotteries (which ended, temporarily, in 1826). Many contractors issued colour-printed bills before 1820, and Evans & Ruffy printed some for the contractor Thomas Bish (senior) as early as 1806. Red and black was the dominant two-colour combination, and a third colour, normally ochre, was occasionally added. Some bills were printed in red only; others had some colour added by hand. Thomas Bish (junior) and Carroll appear to have been the contractors who used colour-printing most regularly, though even with these firms a single black working remained the rule.

Three leading London lottery printers produced extra-large, colourful bills for the draw held on 21 January 1817, using red and black for their type matter, but otherwise adopting very different means of attracting attention (BL 74/1887.c.15). Evans & Ruffy printed a bill in three colours (yellow being added to red and black workings on its elaborate architectural surround); Gye & Balne enclosed their type matter within a patterned, woodcut border, printed in black; and Thorowgood included a large hand-coloured woodcut vignette at the head of his sheet. Thereafter the proprietors of Vauxhall Gardens (one of them being Frederick Gye) became regular users of colour-printed advertising, employing as their printers Gye & Balne and later, in the 1830s, members of the Balne family.

Interest in colour-printing at the time would have been stimulated by the publication of William Savage's book *Practical hints on decorative printing* (London, 1819–22), which included ambitious examples of colour-printing, and by a national investigation, begun in 1818, to find ways of producing forgery-proof banknotes. One of those who submitted ideas for banknote printing was William Congreve, better known as the inventor of the rocket, who proposed a colour-printing process he called compound-plate printing.[33] It involved making a relief-printing surface that could be divided into parts, inked in different colours, and then brought together for printing at one pass

33 Harris 1968–70, 55–66.

through the press. Security was enhanced by engraving intricate patterns across the joins of the composite plate. Though Congreve's idea was rejected, his process was given a prestigious airing at the coronation of George IV in 1821. The tickets for Westminster Abbey were printed in red and blue; those for Westminster Hall in red, blue and black; and both were set within a blind-embossed border by Dobbs, whose firm specialized in such work.

Congreve's printing was done for him by Branston & Whiting, who acquired the rights to use the compound-plate process around 1824. Whiting's firm (under a variety of business styles) produced some effective and stylish ephemera by such means, mainly ream labels, lottery bills and other items that were loosely associated with security. It also specialized in cameo work, which involved embossing and printing at the same time to produce a white image against a coloured ground. Some of the most elegant invitations, tickets and trade cards of the 1820s were produced in this way – or simply with blind embossing – often picking up on classical features of ornamentation made popular by the stucco work of Robert Adam.

The final decades of our period also saw the initial impact on ephemera of two new printing methods: lithography and steel-engraving.[34] The first effectively created a new category of ephemera: the multiplied handwritten document.[35] The process essentially undermined copper-engraving at the cheaper end of the market by enabling craftsmen to write directly on stone in reverse or, even more conveniently, the right way round on specially prepared paper for transferring to stone. When short runs were required it proved to be more economical than both letterpress and intaglio printing. It had further advantages over letterpress printing because it could combine pictures and text with ease, give a personalized look to a document, and cope with complex arrangements of material. When used in such ways lithography took on some of the characteristics of a duplicating process, its main applications being circulars, plans, tables, genealogies and other documents that were difficult and expensive for a letterpress printer to set in type.

Many early London lithographers undertook work of this kind, and one of them, Charles M. Willich, specialized in it. Among his surviving ephemera from around 1820 are several sheets showing complicated financial tables, all written out by hand and organized with the help of ruled lines.[36] Lithography was also used in the 1820s for a variety of other short-run printing, including billheads, tickets and small advertisements, but the field which it made its own

34 See Mosley, chap. 7, below.
35 Twyman 2001, 7–8, 84–9, 144–73.
36 Twyman 2001, 145, fig. 102.

within a very short time was the illustrated sheet-music cover. All the leading London lithographic printers of the time – William Day, Engelmann, Graf Coindet and Co., Charles Hullmandel and Joseph Netherclift – undertook such work, which typically included a crayon-drawn vignette.

Steel-engraving catered for very different markets. Invented by Jacob Perkins in America in the first decade of the nineteenth century, and developed by him commercially in England from 1819, it was the first printing process to be imported from the New World.[37] In its simplest form it offered much longer print runs and greater refinement of mark-making than copper-engraving, and for these reasons alone provided new opportunities in the field of illustration. Perkins also made use of recently developed methods of hardening and softening steel to replicate any kind of image many times over on the same plate. He saw the value of these methods for security printing and submitted them to the committee that had been set up to investigate such matters. As was the case with Congreve, his proposals were not accepted, but his process (which he called siderography) was soon taken up for the production of banknotes, cheques and, a couple of decades later, the first postage stamps.

The innovations referred to above – emphatic typographic display, colour-printing, lithography and steel-engraving – prepared the way for changes in the appearance of ephemera in the early nineteenth century. Among other things, these new approaches to design and production helped to characterize different market sectors: monochrome and often robust letterpress printing catered for routine work; coloured and refined designs for the tastes of a leisured class. This distinction may not have been entirely new, but it was one that must have become increasingly evident from the 1820s. Even more significantly, however, these graphic and technical innovations paved the way for the explosion of ephemera later in the century.

37 Harris 1968–70, 66–74.

PART II ECONOMIC, LEGAL AND CULTURAL CONTEXTS

3
The book as a commodity

JAMES RAVEN

Print and consumption

Commercial ingenuity dominates the history of printing and publishing in Britain in the eighteenth and early nineteenth centuries, and in many ways booksellers – but also authors and readers – came to treat the various products of the printing press more as market commodities, more as goods directed to specific audiences. Such promotional developments must be evaluated, however, against a continuing production regime characterized by the extreme variability of the size and price of the printed text, by multiple but modestly sized reprintings of successful titles (instead of ambitious single print runs), and by the manufacture of many non-commercial books (in the sense that full costs were not always recovered from sale). Above all, the price of new and reprinted books was modulated for much of the period by the effective cartelization of the trade in which booksellers' protection of reprinting rights maintained monopoly prices in England (although not in Ireland and only ineffectively in Scotland, where booksellers led the challenge against English claims to perpetual copyright).[1] With increasing effect before the momentous legal challenges of the 1770s (but also residually thereafter), leading bookseller-publishers maintained prices, and hence the primary determinant of access to new literature, by the successful assertion of their property rights.[2]

Book 'commodification' certainly did not automatically mean cheap print. Much popular literature was reduced in price by the mass production and reprinting of books and magazines in the late eighteenth century, and even more notably after the advent of steam-powered printing in the early nineteenth century, but many bookseller-publishers continued to prosper under the protection of jealously guarded reproduction monopolies (even if many of them were now technically legally unenforceable). Other consumer goods

1 See Rose, chap. 4 and Bonnell, chap. 37, both below.

2 St Clair 2004, chap. 1.

besides books and print were, of course, eagerly taxed by government but none, before at least 1774, were so subject to state-protected price fixing. This, it has been argued, even encouraged the rationing of supply to the market.[3] In effect, such practices positioned books as both consumer and luxury goods; many books promoted as typical products of the eighteenth-century consumer revolution were grossly overpriced. Many publications, reliant not just on literary content but on design and modishness, also created great fortunes for the most successful of their commercial producers. The other, most obvious feature of this publishing regime was that those who might be deemed the original manufacturers, the authors, largely failed to benefit from the market boom.[4]

Economic conditions before the late seventeenth century ensured that (with eccentric exceptions) only the very wealthiest commanded sufficient disposable income to spend regularly and systematically on inessential goods such as books and print. Both the level and the elasticity of domestic demand remained severely limited. The changes during the 1690s and even more clearly after the 1740s are chronicled by diaries and inventories recording increased possession of books and other print, as well as by the gradual private accumulation of libraries and print collections. Book demand grew fastest among the middling, propertied classes, for whom the possession of luxury goods was also a certain sign of status.[5]

In its increasingly commercial gearing, the eighteenth-century publishing industry updated and extended popular print. New productions notably included newspapers, serial publications, novels, playbooks, instructional books and books for children,[6] but booksellers also pursued new marketing techniques that accentuated product familiarity, fashion and emulative buying. As the volume and diversity of publication increased markedly after the mid-eighteenth century (but without any inclination to reduce prices), most publishers introduced competitive packaging devices. These included recognizable title page and typographical styles (often reproduced in advertisements for the same publications) and the pre-retail binding of books in a house design. By the final third of the eighteenth century, many publishers expertly practised what today would be called product branding. Presentational strategies, together with innovative advertising techniques, played a critical part in encouraging demand – both from those already accustomed to acquiring literature and also

3 Raven 2007, chaps. 6–8.
4 See Griffin chap. 5, below.
5 See, for example, Myers and Harris 1982; Earle 1989; Isaac and McKay 1997; Clayton 1997; Raven 1998.
6 See Harris, chap. 20, Ferdinand, chap. 21, Suarez, chap. 34, and Immel, chap. 40, all below.

from those new to the purchase of print, or at least unfamiliar with books other than the penny chapbook, church bible or prayerbook. As early as 1766, the *Monthly Review* observed that 'we seem to live in an age when retailers of every kind of ware aspire to be the original manufacturers, and particularly in literature'.[7]

In the history of book manufacture it is manifest that the technological base and productive capacity of publishing were transformed by the introduction of steam power to papermaking (from about 1807) and then to printing itself (from 1814). New technology revolutionized a centuries-old trade regime of low productivity rates and high labour intensity, but the shift post-dated the eighteenth-century commercial revolution in the trade. Technological changes also took some decades to reach the country towns. The printer of the *Salisbury Journal*, for example, did not abandon his wooden hand-press until 1852.[8] We have, then, to emphasize that it was during the final hundred years or so of the dominance of the manual printing and rolling presses that booksellers reacted with speed and effectiveness to unprecedented market demands, publishing specialist works in response both to new professional interests and to new vogues in entertainment and instruction. Key supporting agencies ranged from commercial libraries and subscription book clubs to debating societies and the recommendations of the periodical reviews.[9] Publication rates soared, and for those who could afford it, access to print became both easier and more diverse. The Post Office carried a massively increased volume of print, while many more publications were available from expanded retail operations. By the beginning of the nineteenth century, the literate were engaged with a sophisticated, expansive and highly commercial print culture, and yet the most remarkable thing – especially in comparison with other early consumer industries – was that the transformation of the book trade into a contemporary consumer industry had been achieved within the technological constraints of the hand-press. Booksellers, in John Britton's words, had become the 'manufacturers of literature'.[10]

From early in the eighteenth century, the book trade assumed particular distinction in the bustling commercial and urban expansion of Hanoverian Britain. London, the site of hundreds of trades and industries, also comprised a vast consumer's market that dominated the British economy. In 1660 up to 100,000 people lived within the walls of London, but between then and 1750

7 *Monthly Reveiw* (*MR*), 34, 480 (June 1766).
8 Raven 2007, 326.
9 See Suarez, chap. 34 and Forster, chap. 33, both below.
10 Rees and Britton 1896, 9.

the city's population increased by not much more than 3,000. In the second half of the eighteenth century, however, London was transformed. Greater London's population reached 900,000 by 1800 and nearly 2 million by 1830. Its main rival, Paris, boasted the largest urban population in Christian Europe at the beginning of the eighteenth century; a hundred years later, London was at least a third larger than the French capital and dwarfed all other European cities.[11]

The London literary market developed close to the centres of book production and distribution and enjoyed a particular affluence, notably in the parliamentary season. The structural concentration of the trade in London greatly assisted both the stimulation of demand and the optimism of those commencing publishing that they might confound the general perception (not confined to the book trade) that if the market was limited, profit margins could never be high. Just as marked, however, was what has been called the British 'urban renaissance' and the growth of the 'leisure town'.[12] By 1750, London's population matched that of all country towns put together, but by 1801 this combined total was almost double that of the capital. In the first census returns of 1801, forty-eight towns claimed populations of more than 10,000, fifteen of which were in excess of 20,000. Between 1801 and 1831, the total population of Great Britain and Ireland soared from some 16 million to nearly 25 million. By 1821, Birmingham, Liverpool and Manchester all boasted populations of more than 100,000 – and Glasgow (200,000 inhabitants by 1830) was firmly established as the second city of the empire.[13]

This vast expansion in population was both supported by and further boosted a commercial and industrial transformation fully underway during the final third of the eighteenth century. Between 1760 and 1785, 10 per cent more patents were registered than for the entire period 1617–1760.[14] Domestic demand soared. During the three decades after 1750, modest price inflation and low taxation combined to boost the fortunes of the propertied. Families with incomes between £40 and £400 increased from about 15 per cent to about 25 per cent of the population.[15] These were the formative years in the market for home-finished silks, cottons, calicoes, fine woollens and English porcelain. The manufacture of 'toy' goods (many centred in Birmingham), of buckles, buttons and much else besides, accompanied the importation of new consumer luxuries such as tea, mahogany, and foreign porcelains and silks.

11 Wrigley and Schofield 1981; Mathias 1969, 26, 451; Mitchell and Deane 1962, 8–10, 19, 24–7.
12 Borsay 1977; McInnes 1988; Borsay and McInnes 1990; Sweet 1999.
13 Corfield 1982; Mitchell and Deane 1962, 19, 24–7.
14 Langford 1989, 655.
15 McKendrick 1982, 24.

Print notably contributed to this conspicuous consumption. Book-trade entrepreneurs like Samuel Richardson, Thomas Longman, Charles Rivington, William Strahan, Thomas Cadell and George Robinson rank with Hogarth, Boulton, Watt and Wedgwood as the promoters and beneficiaries of an evolving 'consumer society'.[16] It was not simply that printed advertisements and other promotional publications advanced a great range of consumer goods (as has been much noted),[17] but books, magazines and prints themselves became prominent exemplars of the new decencies and conveniences gracing the homes of the middling sort. The products of the print shop took their place in the community of consumers and consumption addressed in Smith's *Wealth of nations*.[18] Additionally, print proved a decisive conduit for the pursuit of politeness and social advancement fostered by the expanding economy. The book trade dominated the commodification of culture and the extension of the leisure market in which the consumption of often very expensive texts occurred as both private reception and social occasion.[19] Commercial considerations effectively determined the public impact of literature – broadcasting social standards and notions of refinement and deviance, fixing a 'middle-class' culture, and defining and legitimizing new class relationships. Books became not only the products of a newly affluent society, but also the guides to and critics of conduct within it.[20] Nor was this a solely English development; in many ways the social penetration of print in Scotland and the much smaller but fast-developed domestic market for books and newspapers in eighteenth-century Ireland are the more remarkable.[21]

The evaluation of print consumption in relation to other consumer industries offers a valuable comparative perspective, albeit with important cautions. In a sense, of course, the book had always been an exchangeable or marketable commodity and a progressive commercialization is observable in the bookselling practices of Tudor and Stuart Britain. In limited scope, indeed, it was evident in the career of Caxton and his stationer predecessors.[22] Mechanization and stereotyping led the transformation of the trade in the nineteenth century, but even in the age of the manual printing press certain critical turning-points can be identified – most notably perhaps, the 1680s and

16 Jones 1973; McKendrick 1982; Lippincott 1983.
17 Alden 1952; McKendrick 1982, 32, 81–2, 157–74; Lippincott 1983.
18 Cf. Langford 1989, 68–71.
19 Cf. Paulson 1995; Brewer 1995, 346–58.
20 Raven 1992, 83–263; Bellamy 1998.
21 McDougall 1974; Pollard 1989; Ó Ciosáin 1997. See Beavan and McDougall, chap. 16 and Benson, chap. 17, both below.
22 See, for example, Christianson 1999; Green and Peters 2002, 88–93; Raven 2002a, 571–2, 574–8, 582; Raven 2007, chaps. 1–2.

1690s, the 1740s, and the 1770s when particular entrepreneurship, syndicate regime change and new commercial strategies are clearly observable. From the very beginning of the period, retailing and allied services more obviously expanded according to the changing commercial potential of the audience. Elite support for specialist literature was nurtured by subscription collection and by specialist publishers directing their output to specific clients, professions, interest groups, and even regions.[23] Much of the direct retailing centred on the active (but often overlooked) second-hand market as well as on the sales of lesser productions, notably the thousands of almanacs, pamphlets and chapbooks peddled by chapmen and general traders. Auctions and fixed-price catalogue sales with set times nurtured the crucial second-hand market.[24]

The fundamental change in the technological base of printing in the early nineteenth century, together with distribution improvements, further transformed productivity, reducing manufacturing costs, allowing new marketing strategies, enticing new investments and hugely extending the price reductions launched by the reprinting entrepreneurs from the mid-1770s.[25] As adopted from the first decade of the nineteenth century, and spreading gradually thereafter, stereotyped plates avoided the time and cost of recomposition. A technology in use on the Continent since the late seventeenth century, stereotyping has some claim to be the most significant advance largely neglected by the syndicate-led, quality-obsessed London trade of the eighteenth century. Various experiments with iron presses during the 1810s introduced improvements that allowed double-platen presses from the late 1820s. The manufacture of paper by machine effectively dates from a decade after the Fourdrinier patent registration of 1804, and by 1825 more than half of all English paper was mechanically produced.[26] Most dramatic of all was the application of steam power to printing itself, enabling the bookseller Charles Knight to declare that 'what the printing press did for the instruction of the masses in the fifteenth century, the printing machine is doing for the nineteenth'.[27] However, these major technological changes did not introduce, but further extended the commercial revolution in the book and print trade. From the 1740s the growing demand for books that culminated in the challenge to the cartelization of the trade was stimulated by successive developments in entrepreneurial publishing methods, and it was these that created the

23 See chaps. 30–48 below.
24 Cf. Pollard and Ehrman 1965; Myers 1982, 2001; and Suarez 1999a. Cf. also Landon, chap. 38, below.
25 See Bonnell, chap. 37, below.
26 See Bidwell, chap. 8, below.
27 Weedon 2003, 64–76 (70 cites Knight 1834).

conditions for technological innovation. By catalogues, reviews, advertisements and a variety of ingenious puffs, print itself was instrumental in promoting print across a range of prices and formats as a commodity.[28]

In highlighting consumerism in the British book trade of the eighteenth century, we are not imposing a concept unfamiliar to contemporaries. Quite the contrary. Terms such as emulative spending, loss leaders, pyramid selling, product differentiation, special offers, market research and inertia-selling campaigns might all be modern, but all were well understood by eighteenth- and early nineteenth-century book promoters – and their effects were debated widely. The adaptation of publishing to a consumer society found colourful contemporary expression. Consumption was compared to digestion, and critics (who on one occasion described themselves as 'caterers for the Public'[29]) wrote of the literary appetite, of books 'going down', of printed 'delicacies', of a diet of this or a taste for that, of nourishment, swallowing, gorging, devouring, feasting, and much more besides.[30] Especially shrill by the end of the eighteenth century were accusations that quickly produced literature was a common merchandise that devalued literary merit, invited derision, and tempted nervous agitation and mental derangement, particularly among women, servants and the labouring poor.[31] As one of the more temperate commentators put it, 'a fashionable writer makes a fashionable book, and creates a number of fashionable readers – readers, who pay more attention to the fashion of the writer, than to the fashion of the book'.[32] In the words of another reviewer, new book promotions were nothing less than 'insidious attempts at the purses of the Public'.[33]

Commercial developments

The first, most obvious characteristic of commercial change in the book trade was one of scale. A growing number of printers and booksellers encouraged and profited from advances in the range and methods of distribution, and output increased (not only by the number of titles but also, in the case of proven successes, by the size of editions). Books, just like textiles, china, cutlery, furniture and other consumer goods, were manufactured in

28 See Forster, chap. 33, Tierney, chap. 24, Maidment, chap. 25, Harris, chap. 20, and Ferdinand, chap. 21, all below.
29 See Raven 2000a, 118.
30 Typically *MR*, 52, 187 (Feb. 1775); cf. Raven 2000a, 117–19.
31 Gallaway 1940; Taylor 1943; Raven 1998, 282; 2000b, 110–21; Pearson 1999.
32 Paterson 1772, 41.
33 *Biographical and Imperial Magazine*, 3 (1790), 113.

unprecedented quantity and quality. Before 1700, up to about 1,800 different printed titles (including the most minor items) were produced annually; by 1830, up to 6,000.[34] A crude measure of numbers of titles (including different editions of the same title) suggests an average publication growth rate of just over 2 per cent per annum for the years between 1740 and 1800.[35] The sharply rising title production curve from the watershed decade of the 1740s, with a particular spurt in the 1780s,[36] hides the largely unknown increases in edition sizes for popular works, an increase that escalated during the 1820s.[37] This certainly affects the way that printed items might be viewed as commodities. The multiplication of magazine titles in the 1780s and 1790s, for example, included many very short-lived publications at the very time that booksellers requested mammoth printings of assured sellers such as popular school-books, hymn books and dictionaries.[38]

In most cases, the labour costs of composition and presswork made it unviable to print very small editions, while the risks of high capital expenditure and storage made it unwise to print large editions. Most book editions therefore remained at about 750 copies. The clear exceptions to this were the monster and repeatedly reprinted editions of school and service books. Playbooks might reach editions of 2,000 copies or more, and histories, with proven appeal, might in some cases be issued in 4,000-copy editions; but these pall before the huge printings commissioned, for example, by Thomas Longman II for staple titles like Watts's *Hymns*, Johnson's *Dictionary* in quarto, and numerous instruction books, such as an 18,000-copy edition of Fenning's spelling manual. Even so, the question of risk had to be measured carefully. All remembered the sorry history of Andrew Millar's first 1751–2 edition of Fielding's *Amelia*, issued in two impressions totalling 8,000 copies. Millar had hoped to emulate the runaway success of *Tom Jones* (10,000 copies printed between 1749 and 1750), but was left embarrassed, with copies still for sale ten years later.[39]

Another measure of commercial expansion, but with quantification problems of its own,[40] is the use of statistics charting the increasing foreign concerns and specialisms of London and other British publishers. Britain first

34 *ESTC*; Eliot 1994.
35 See Suarez, chap. 1, above.
36 An average annual growth rate by number of titles, 1740–80, of 1.5 per cent, but increasing to nearly 3.5 per cent, 1780–1800.
37 Weedon 2003, 45–52.
38 St Clair 2004. Cf. Tierney, chap. 24 and Maidment, chap. 25, both below.
39 Further examples given in Raven 2000a, 93–5.
40 Methodological problems discussed in Raven 1997b, 33–9; and Barber 1976.

became a net exporter of books sometime in the 1740s, after three centuries of high dependency on imported paper and books. To an increasing degree during the second half of the eighteenth century, almost every leading London publishing and bookselling house (and many shrewd Glasgow, Edinburgh, Dublin and Belfast printers and booksellers[41]) engaged in trade to foreign customers (notably in British North America, the Caribbean and India[42]), but the real take-off both in worldwide and in European exports came during the 1820s. It was an export boom that seems to have happily engaged with (rather than suffered from) the coming-of-age of American publishing in the early nineteenth century and the forging of new relationships between British and American (and other foreign) publishers. After 1818, for example, Constable and Longman regularly sent pre-publication sheets of Scott's novels across the Atlantic to Carey and Lea of Philadelphia, itself a monopoly agreement, but one resulting in almost immediate, widespread and cut-price American reprinting.[43]

Whether destined for the domestic or the colonial market, the increased volume of publication was based on a broadly changing business structure. The rise in publication totals from the 1740s onwards reflected the expansion of the country newspaper and book distribution network,[44] increased individual and institutional demand, and new productivity based on financial and organizational innovation. New entrants to both the London and provincial trade oversaw improved productivity and flexibility advanced by new and greater capitalization and by the challenge to official and unofficial restrictive practices.[45] Book-trade profits and monies reinvested in publishing in Britain from the mid-eighteenth century resulted not only from greater diversification of trade, but also from the deepening of money markets and the expansion of the financial infrastructure available. Leading booksellers and printers like Strahan, Cadell and Longman in London and, later, Blackwood and Constable in Edinburgh, drew capital from new and diverse sources. In addition, a more flexible use of assets was ensured by new means of gaining access to capital and limiting risk. Inflows of capital from increased mercantile activity sustained the expanding London, Glasgow and Edinburgh money markets – with freer availability of monies to trading partners by the readier discounting of bills of exchange. This enabled the extension of credit chains, encouraging greater risks, but also inducing greater failures. Bankruptcies were common, especially in the 1790s

41 See Beavan and McDougall, chap. 16 and Benson, chap. 17, both below.
42 See Green, chap. 28 and Shaw, chap. 29, both below.
43 Barnes 1983; Raven 2001b; Weedon 2003, 38–45, 157; Garside 2000, 99; cf. Green, chap. 28, below.
44 See Ferdinand, chap. 21, below.
45 Raven 2001a; 2007, chaps. 5–7.

(and again in the 1820s), and a very large proportion of new magazine and newspaper titles ceased publication within a few years of their launch.[46]

From fragile and limited beginnings in the late seventeenth century, banking and insurance services came to reduce risk on stock, buildings, shipping and other transportation (although fire insurance remained the most valued safeguard). Credit and insurance availability lowered book-trade transaction costs, even though such developments were markedly variable. Until at least the mid-nineteenth century (and in certain respects thereafter), banking operations remained based primarily on the relative respectability and credit reputation of the operators. This meant that those in the book trade who had prospered most from new financial mechanisms and opportunities were well-resourced printer- and bookseller-publishers such as the Strahans, the Rivingtons, the Longmans, the Robinsons and the Murrays. All were able to demonstrate the respect and trust of a far-flung business elite. More provocative booksellers – such as William Lane, John Bell, John Cooke, J. F. Hughes and C. Whittingham – all benefited from the commercial developments, but could not take advantage of the sort of reductions in long-term capital tie-up and risk acceptance available to the richest and most eminent in their profession. While the humblest operators struggled to cope with credit and risk conveyance, the grandest publishers invested more diversely in property, annuities, and a broader range of commercial and banking activities. Increasingly in the nineteenth century, these included investments overseas and in the colonial trades.[47]

By the 1820s, leading firms such as those of the second John Murray and the third Thomas Longman dominated the British publishing industry by a variant form of copyright purchase and cartelization practised by earlier book-trade elites. What is quite clear, however (and embodied in the different relationships between prominent authors and prominent publishers), is that by 1830 manifold developments left the publishing house working largely in the image of its publisher, a firm centred on the businessman and his particular tastes. Nor could any firm escape one other result of this development: the sensitivity of credit brokering, insurance services and economic confidence to external commercial pressures. In one way or another, the charts of book-trade output and bankruptcies register the crisis years of the American war in the 1770s, the Revolutionary wars of the 1790s and the ensuing Napoleonic shortages, the 1826 crash, and the 1839–42 trade depression.[48]

46 Anderson 1969, 1970; Mathias 1979, chap. 5; Maxted 1977, table 14; and further references in Raven 1997a. See Harris, chap. 20 and Maidment, chap. 25, both below.

47 See Raven 2001a; 2002b, esp. ch. 8. Cf. Green, chap. 28 and Shaw, chap. 29, both below.

48 Maxted 1977.

Distribution

The changing mechanics of distribution proved a pivotal feature of this commerce. In England, a transportation network radiating outwards from London characterized book-trade organization. By the early nineteenth century some 90 per cent of all British titles were still published in London and the mushrooming numbers of provincial booksellers served not as publishers of new titles, but mostly as book distribution agents and sometimes as newspaper printers (the newspapers themselves acting as advertising platforms for the London publishers).[49] Nevertheless, with the advance after mid-century of publishing in Edinburgh and Glasgow and, after 1800, increasing book and magazine publication in Manchester, Liverpool, Aberdeen, Perth, Newcastle, Leeds and other cities, the status of London in both book distribution and manufacture was changed for the first time since the Restoration Licensing Laws, and, arguably, since the invention of printing.[50] A generation after Scots such as Millar, Strahan and Murray made their fortunes in the London book trade, cross-border partnerships flourished. The first two John Murrays co-operated with Creech and Eliot and later Blackwood in Edinburgh. Scottish branch shops were established in London, like that of Blackwood itself.[51]

Above all, given the way in which changes in distributive networks stimulated demand and serviced the effective oligopolies of London booksellers' cartels, the role both of the Post Office and of new transport routes should not be underestimated. Postmasters remained principal distribution agents, especially for the circulation of newspapers and advertisers. During the eighteenth century, the cost of newspaper distribution had been lowered by the activity of groups with Post Office franking privileges.[52] The turnpike mania beginning in the 1750s resulted in some 20,000 miles of road maintained by trusts by the end of the third decade of the nineteenth century.[53] Improvements in transport routes and distance times encouraged the development of discount systems to promote greater retail distribution in the country. Transportation costs had always been a significant add-on, and with many booksellers' business calculations allowing little scope for the major tie-up of capital in printed and warehoused stock, the efficiency of distribution was critical. Nevertheless, economic historians have also stressed the limits to growth in this area,

49 See Harris, chap. 20 and Ferdinand, chap. 21, both below.
50 See Turner, chap. 23, below.
51 Finkelstein 2002. See Beavan and McDougall, chap. 16, below.
52 See Raven 2001a, 24–6; Tierney, chap. 24, below.
53 Albert 1972.

particularly emphasizing the deplorable state of the roads; the railways were to be the major breakthrough.

The market and book prices

The expansion in literary commerce – supported by widened distribution – turned, like all other domestic industries, on the attractiveness of the product. The fundamental determinant of the market for new publications was price, and although it is extremely perilous to do so, we should try to establish the course of the relative price of new books. Pricing by publishers was not only a very variable science, but historical measures of an average price are almost impossible to calculate. In the first place, the idea of the book as a commodity applied primarily to new publications in Britain – to the fashionable and the freshly minted. The full market, however, clearly incorporated sales of antiquarian and second-hand books (despite some bookseller-publishers' attempts to rein in this market)[54] and complete and broken-up libraries as well as the continued importation of books from the Continent, notably France. Even more central to the transformation of general manufacturing profiles from the late eighteenth century was the multiplication of reprinted titles, reinvigorated from the 1820s by the new capacities of mechanized printing. Back lists remained prominent, the most commonly reprinted works ranging most obviously from the patent-protected Bibles, Testaments, prayer books and psalms, to primers, ABCs, school-books and almanacs.[55] To this extent, the expanding market from the mid-eighteenth century was also a more segregated market in which literary commodities, including the new 'novel', the periodical 'review' and the 'magazine', were increasingly demarcated by both genre and audience.[56]

The further difficulty in analysing price is that what counts as a 'book' and also what counts as an 'edition' are so diverse. Not only was there an enormous price range, but there was wild variation in the proportion of expensive folios to duodecimos and other sizes.[57] Existing estimates of production based on counts of titles (and almost always new titles at that) also fail to capture the fluctuations in edition size and hence the total volume of publication. Both issues distort calculations and make any 'average' retail price for all books a

54 St Clair 2004, chaps. 5 and 12. Cf. Landon, chap. 38, below.

55 See Bonnell, chap. 37 and Myers, chap. 39, both below; cf. *CHBB* IV 788, table 4.

56 See Walsh 2001, esp. 213; O'Brien 2001. See Suarez, chap. 34, Sutherland, chap. 35, Forster, chap. 33, Tierney, chap. 24, and Maidment, chap. 25, all below.

57 J. A. Sutherland 1987 acknowledges but cannot wholly overcome this problem. See Suarez, chap. 1, above.

very artificial figure, one skewed according to the distribution of different types of publication in each year. What is at least clear is that book publishers looked to a highly stratified market, where there was certainly overlap between consumer interests, but also great differentiation in the price and quality of products.

In a crude attempt to estimate average retail prices of new publications, annual totals of the advertised price of bound books within different size or format categories can be derived from the monthly listings of the *Monthly Review* (from 1749) and *Critical Review* (from 1756) until about 1810 (when reviewing coverage changes).[58] Many of the new titles were published in two or more volumes. Obviously a crude overall average of volume price can be computed from the total price of all titles reviewed in each year divided by the total number of volumes per title listed.[59] It is this, however, which is misleadingly distorted by format and edition size distribution (and, more broadly, by the reprinting rates of both new and old titles).[60] Calculations of average edition sizes and reprinting rates currently require much more research, but we can at least create a general index of the average price of new-title volumes within each format multiplied by a weighting calculated by dividing the number of volumes in that format by the total number of all volumes across all format groups. From the sum of the result gained for each format group, annual averages can be calculated and then reincorporated into a five-yearly moving average in a weighted index of the average advertised retail price of new-title, bound publications. This index gives a per volume value of 2 in 1750, 2.2 in 1755, 2.54 in 1760, 2.83 in 1765 and 3.5 in 1770. After significant dips in the 1780s, the index reaches 3.6 in 1790, 5.5 in 1795, 5.9 in 1800 and 6.3 in 1810.[61] The artificially reckoned 'average volume' for a new publication of 1810, therefore, was priced some three times higher than its equivalent of fifty years earlier. Such price rises also reflect late eighteenth-century general price inflation, but still constitute a significant increase.[62]

A more accurate assessment of market stratification requires the relation of the pricing of books to the broader economic context. A price index of books, with a further index of the movement in real purchasing power to buy books,

58 See Forster, chap. 33, below.

59 By volumes here is meant the number (usually one, two or three) of volumes comprising a complete work or 'title' and not (the often unknowable) number of copies (or in one sense 'volumes') per edition.

60 J. A. Sutherland 1987 has categorization difficulties, where price is not weighted in an index.

61 Changes to periodical review listings prevent the continuation of these calculations much beyond 1810; for thoroughgoing calculation of price structures after 1836, see Weedon 2003.

62 The index also revises much-cited estimates that the price of quarto, octavo and duodecimo volumes nearly doubled between 1750 and 1800; Knight 1854, 238.

can be constructed from the estimates already given for average retail prices of books during this period. From the calculations of the average advertised retail prices of books, a derivative index with base value of 100 in 1750 reaches 297 by the turn of the century. Annual values taken from a money wage index, historically problematic as this is,[63] can be divided by the equivalent annual values from the index of book prices to provide a further index of the real purchasing power to buy books. From a base of 1.2 in 1750 this index falls slowly to 1770 (0.68), recovers up until 1785 (0.76) and then falls away to 0.415 by 1800. In other words, the purchasing power for books for someone receiving the estimated average money wage is only a third in 1800 of what it was in 1750. This trend can be compared with the equivalent index for real wages, where the index is just over one-half in 1800 of what it was in 1750. The index offers limited support for the popular view that after the Thomas Carnan and Alexander Donaldson copyright victories 'in real terms, the price of books probably fell under the stimulus of competition'.[64] But it was a short-term reprieve. Notwithstanding the cheapening of certain out-of-copyright books in the 1770s, for most people new books became more, not less, of a luxury item by 1800.

The crudity of this index of real prices before 1810 must be emphasized, just as we must be clear that any analysis of the book market as a whole should take account of the second-hand market as well as the continuing variations in edition sizes.[65] The market as a whole was also swollen by the extraordinary increase in reprinting after 1774 and by the development of successive reprint series and cheaper editions that in due time further supplied the stalls of old books.[66] Nevertheless, the conclusion that new publications, at least, became comparatively more expensive during the eighteenth century accords pleasingly with contemporary observation. Whatever the interest in back lists or the going rate for the second-hand book – and, as today, every auction hosted its winners and losers, its obsessive bibliophiles and its cheerful bargain hunters[67] – it was the price of new publications that stole contemporary attention and increasingly brought complaints about overpricing. In the early nineteenth century, John Aikin wrote of 'typographical luxury which, joined to the necessary increase of expence in printing, has so much enhanced the price of new books as to be a material obstacle to the indulgence of a laudable and reasonable curiosity by the reading Publick'.[68]

63 Mitchell and Deane 1962, 346–9.
64 Feather 1988a, 117.
65 See Landon, chap. 38, below.
66 See Bonnell, chap. 37, below.
67 See Myers, Harris and Mandelbrote 2001.
68 Aikin in Nichols 1812–16, III, 464.

One further way of testing the proposition that book prices steadily rose is to construct a simple demand equation to measure the extent to which sales of new books were a function of independent variables such as income, literacy, taste, the price of new books, and the price of non-luxury alternatives to new books (including reprints and second-hand books).[69] In this exercise, data were given for sixty-one annual observations from 1750 to 1810, with the dependent variable (the number of new books demanded) based on *ESTC* title counts (and, for specific categories of literature demanded, on bibliographical surveys of economic and imaginative publications).[70] The other variables included estimates of imported books,[71] GNP,[72] real wages,[73] an index of the price of alternative goods,[74] retail price of books,[75] similar price indices for specific sizes of books, and estimated male and female literacy rates.[76] There are, of course, major weaknesses in such a procedure. The independent variables and indices taken to represent them are based on often seriously flawed selection judgements, all limited by the evidence available. If there had been an acceptable measurement of transportation costs, for example, it should certainly have been included.[77] With all its imperfections, the model attempts to determine the extent to which movements in the relationship between various independent variables affect changes in the number of books demanded.

What the exercise does at least suggest is a strong relationship over these sixty years between increases in GNP and an encouragement to import books. With the average price of all books increasing, the tendency to import also paralleled increased demand for domestic books, supporting the theory of a separate but still important market for specialist, luxury texts. The greater the demand, it seems, the greater the real price of books, again implying that certain books were such a luxury good that supply could also be determined by the costliness of the product. That, after all, is the basis of decisions by specialist manufacturers to produce fewer goods when the price is too low and, conversely, for their encouragement of exclusivity by a generous dose of

69 Raven 1988.

70 Higgs 1935; Hanson 1963; Raven 1992, figs. 5, 6; and listings in Raven 1987 and 2000a.

71 Data from Barber 1982, 102; Raven 1997b, 1999.

72 Tables in Feinstein 1981.

73 Real wage series from Wrigley and Schofield 1981, table A9.2, based on Phelps-Brown and Hopkins wage and price data.

74 Basket of non-foodstuffs ('consumables other than cereals'), Mitchell and Deane 1962, XVI, table 1, 468–9.

75 Five-year moving average retail price index per volume of all advertised books 1750–1800, weighted for annual variations in size and format, as above.

76 Bedfordshire data from Schofield 1973.

77 The model also requires compensations for in-built but ahistorical assumptions that one year's results (for example, income data) do not bear any relationship to the next year's figures (autocorrelation), and that there is no direct relationship between the independent variables (multicollinearity).

overpricing. The model suggests in particular, however, that movements in real wages and movements in literacy rates did not have a significant effect on the demand for books. By contrast, changes in the resources of rent, income and land, to which the fortunes of the propertied were all tied, do seem to be correlated to changing book demand. The modelling further indicates that the changing values of alternative goods had no significance in the demand for books, suggesting that purchasers of books bought non-essential consumables as well as books, rather than having to choose between them. The model, with all its limitations, supports the contention that rapid increase in late eighteenth-century book production was directed to a literate and wealthy section of the population. Changes in real wages and literacy have no significant effect upon changes in book demand. The 'widening circle'[78] of readership for new books appears largely restricted to those of extensive income.[79]

Consumer demand

This characterization of late eighteenth-century book demand and production suggests also that the increasing number of new books sold represented a notable expansion of the numbers of books bought by and for an already book-reading section of the population, rather than simply a great expansion in book purchasing among those of small income. Such a demand profile certainly underpins the marked advance of book buying in the late 1780s. James Lackington noted the increase in demand after the end of the American war in 1784, and the same trend is confirmed by George Miller, a bookseller who described himself as belonging to 'the wooden-ladle class'.[80] The boom was supported in the main by increased incomes for the professional and trading classes, even though it was also at this time that the new challengers to the bookselling cartels launched more modestly priced publications and reprints. Nevertheless, in revising conservative estimates of the book sales of one leading country bookseller, John Clay of Daventry, Rugby, Lutterworth and Warwick, Jan Fergus and Ruth Portner still show that the volumes he sold were usually substantial books, certainly costing more than 1*s*. and up to 5*s*. and more.[81] The consequence of this for the publishing directions of the London wholesale booksellers is supported by a further study of Samuel

78 Korshin 1976.

79 Further econometric modelling should focus on particular formats, subjects and prices of books, to determine, for example, how demand for cheap books only (and as compared with other categories) is affected by movements in real wages or GNP or literacy.

80 Raven 1994, 5, 16.

81 Fergus and Portner 1987, replying to Feather 1984.

Clay's bookshop in Warwick in the early 1770s. Clay's records confirm not only extensive middle-class support for his business, but also that tradesmen and artisans bought very few books.[82] Clay could not have survived on the trade of the lesser middling sort alone.

Such studies further reject suggestions of exceptionally increased demand in the second half of the eighteenth century for traditional almanacs and chapbooks. These maintained a steady sale, and stalwart older titles from *Jack of Newbury* to *Fair Rosamond* were supported by new tracts, often 24-page versions of selected modern imaginative literature. As Pat Rogers has demonstrated, penny versions of Bunyan and *Robinson Crusoe* were popular sellers, along with chapbook versions of *Moll Flanders*, *Pamela* and *Tom Jones*.[83] This, however, was about the limit to cheap versions of new works, and although such titles went through dozens of editions, they represented a narrow base for the expansion of penny tracts. The promotion of cheap children's literature does seem to have been more successful. John and Francis Newbery's innovative publications, priced between 2*d*. and 6*d*., were presented as an affordable luxury to customers of limited income.[84]

It is clear, however, that for those of modest means, book buying was increasingly concentrated on a few prized purchases – perhaps a three-shilling professional instruction manual or a recommended work of improvement or biblical commentary – rather than diversified on many cheap chapbooks and small antiquated books. The obvious exceptions were new publications by instalment, which distributed the purchaser's outlay over a longer period. From the mid-eighteenth century, part-books proved a profitable and popular venture for many London booksellers,[85] but again custom was drawn from the wealthier ranks of the propertied. Weekly payments might lessen the burden of payment, but this was no compensation for those whose income was seasonal or erratic. Significantly, in Clay's country bookshop and market stalls during the third quarter of the eighteenth century, purchases of part-number books actually declined, whereas the sales of magazines (many aimed at the upper-income fashionable market) increased fivefold.[86] Circulating libraries and booksellers' lending services were already widening literary access for the 'middling sort', and most notably after the rupture of the 'high monopoly period',[87] modestly priced 'classic' or collectable pocket editions accompanied

82 Fergus 1984, 188, notably supplemented by Fergus 1996.
83 Rogers 1972, 1985.
84 Roscoe 1973; Jackson 2003. Cf. Immel, chap. 40, below.
85 See Harris, chap. 20, below.
86 Fegus and Portner 1987.
87 The phrase of St Clair 2004 (and see his table 3.1).

a new range of works superior to the chapbook, but cheaper than the quality octavos or quartos that they imitated.[88]

We can conclude, then, that in real terms most printed matter became more expensive in the decades before the technological innovations of the 1810s, and that a certain commodification of the book – based on monopoly pricing for new literature but also increased publication and then reprinting rates – was supported by a rising, propertied group of consumers. This continued to be so despite the remodelling of the early nineteenth-century publishing industry, propelled by cheaper popular literature (such as John Murray's *Family library*, first issued in 1829), and despite recurrent economic depressions such as those of 1817–21 and 1839–42. It was increased custom from the propertied classes that was responsible from the mid-eighteenth century for transforming the retailing of books, before the extension of cheap print and a new working-class market that by the mid-nineteenth century was quite distinct from the older chapbook and ballad readership of the previous two centuries.[89]

Production expenses and profits

If this is the case, then we need to ask why new publications were so expensive in this burgeoning market, sustained by rising incomes. Changing production costs, and notably the relative price of paper, have been credited with much responsibility for pricing policy, especially given that retail mark-ups also seem to have varied widely. Much reliance has been placed on a suggestion that the average retail price of books in this period was about five times the cost of production.[90] The most common observation in production estimates is how the publishing sector was especially handicapped by the requirement to have so much capital tied up in a particular item of production (an edition) before any part of this could be sold to realize returns.

On the basis of the constituent format price averages already calculated from the *Monthly* and *Critical* listings, the retail price per sheet can be assessed for new books of known format. In 1750 the average *advertised* retail price per sheet for a new octavo title seems to have been about 2*s*. 8*d*. In 1790 it was 3*s*. 3*d*., and in 1800, 3*s*. 6*d*. The average retail price per sheet for a quarto title was 4*s*. 3*d*. in 1750, 5*s*. 6*d*. in 1795 and 6*s*. 5*d*. in 1800. Such estimates, however, disguise enormous fluctuations in the pricing of constituent formats. Of new octavo titles published in 1790, for example, the average retail price per sheet

88 See Bonnell, chap. 37, below.
89 Eliot 1994.
90 Gaskell 1972, 179.

for books sold at *6d.* was *3s. 8d.*; *1s.*, *4s.8d.*; at *2s. 6d.*, *3s. 6d.*; at *7s.*, *2s. 7d.*; and at *8s.*, *3s. 4d.* Although the trends in this and other format sizes are often erratic, and the assumption of constant production costs for all octavo sheets problematic, profit margins appear to be greatest for the middle price range of books of between *1s.* and *2s. 6d.*[91] This was also by far the most numerous category of total new publications by title.

Exact calculation of profits from aggregate production costs remains hugely frustrating. Philip Gaskell's much-cited figure of 0.5*d.* a sheet in production was for printing and paper, but the costings of many operators were often higher than this. They ranged from Ann Ward's 0.7*d.* a sheet for printing and paper, to John Trusler's usual 0.5*d.* a sheet for paper only, and some of Gavin Hamilton's calculations for his Edinburgh press of 1*d.* a sheet.[92] 'Extras' also figure largely, marked up in surviving accounts, rather like those given by Strahan in his printing ledgers. About a tenth of Trusler's 'profits' went on stock insurance and a further tenth on warehousing charges.[93] Although Gaskell's average *retail* costs per sheet are lower than the estimates given above, the higher estimates of production costs suggest that the late eighteenth-century retail price in England was far lower than five times the cost of production. In Trusler's case, it averages as just over three times production expenses as calculated retrospectively on the highly questionable assumption that all copies were sold. To underline how variable this was, however, calculations from the first John Murray's account ledgers suggest mark-ups of up to eight times the production cost.[94] Just as striking as the variation in price and cost differentials is the weak relation that retail prices bore to production costs, not only because of inflated prices where monopoly protection applied, but also because of the general and extremely variable calculation of risk according to the particular work in hand.

Other surviving ledgers suggest that for much of the century the greatest production expense resulted from composition and presswork, but in the Longman accounts of book publication from the late 1790s paper costs are almost always greater than printing costs. The proportion of both to total production costs varied greatly, however, and depended upon the additional contribution of advertising, copyright and incidental costs. The ledger entries for pre-1800 books in the surviving Longman accounts suggest that paper costs

91 The average advertised price differential between sewn and bound twelves remained at about *6d.* a volume.

92 NLS, Ledger of Adam Neill, 1767, in McDougall 1974; Monkman 1970, 22.

93 BL, Add MSS, 28, 121, f. 381, and further references in Raven 2007, chaps. 8 and 10. Cf. Maslen, chap. 9, below.

94 Raven 2000a, 95; Zachs 1998, 255–409.

ranged from just over a quarter to one-half of total production costs. Printing expenses, always less than those of paper in the Longman accounts, ranged between a fifth and a third of total costs. Bills for printing sent to Longman were calculated at rates per sheet, with additional labour charges for the corrections made to the presswork before the sheets left the printing house.[95] Changes to the unit costs of publication remain difficult to recover, however. A major consideration in the economics of publishing was the nature of the flow of income, primarily as the turnover of stock by retail or by exchange and sale among wholesaling booksellers. This turnover depended upon a number of circumstances, from the range of publications held to the availability of retailing networks and the ability, both financial and physical, to store stock. As discussed above, it is safe to assume that editions of more than 1,500 copies were contemplated only for the most fêted of authors or works. Patricia Hernlund shows that 90 per cent of the 514 books printed by Strahan between 1738 and 1785 were in editions of fewer than 2,000.[96]

What we can conclude is that in addition to start-up costs (workplace, press, type and other permanent necessities), the overall economics of publication included job-specific costs of paper, the labour involved in all stages of printing (including collating the sheets) and, much more rarely, whatever might have been paid to the author or begetter of the text. These factors alone, however, cannot explain the price structure adopted by particular publishers; to understand this fully we have to allow for several additional considerations.

Bookselling

In establishing a wholesale price structure, the London publishers had to consider the mark-up necessary to make the participation of retailers worthwhile. The trade discount offered to booksellers, some of whom, after the mid-eighteenth century, were also library managers, was especially important for provincial retailers developing local markets for new literature. A large proportion of trade offers in the final quarter of the century were advertised as bound; earlier discounts often specified sheets. The novel and belles-lettres specialist Thomas Hookham allowed his trade customers a free copy for every twenty-five bought.[97] From their earliest years, the even more populist Noble brothers, John and Francis, offered a trade discount of 14 per cent on twenty-five volumes of the same title. If country booksellers were able to sell their

95 RUL, Longman Archives (Chadwyck-Healey film, reel 37).
96 Hernlund 1967, 1969; and cf. Raven 2000a, 93–100.
97 Ledgers of Hookham and Carpenter, 1791–8; Raven 2000a, 93, 96.

volumes for, say, the metropolitan price of 3*s*., the potential for profit appears large. In practice, however, the largest profits were taken by the London wholesalers.[98]

The one outstanding complication remained the securing of payments. In sales from the bookshop, the vagaries of payment and credit arrangements to both individual and trade customers had to be taken into account. A credit allowance of six months seems to have been quite normal, and some overseas customers expected eighteen months' or even two years' grace between order and the payment of an invoice.[99] Reliance on credit and the uncertainty of many credit notes added to the overheads carried by all types of booksellers and to the niceties of calculations in pricing and sizing an edition. One radical solution, Lackington's discounting of remaindered and second-hand books for cash only, was condemned by rival booksellers as unfair practice, given that they could not, like Lackington with his large emporium, break free of the retailing and newspaper-led advertising structure that customers now expected.[100] Certain retail specialization in the book trade by the end of the century did allow booksellers like Alexander Hogg and John Bell to develop new services, but many booksellers remained tied to older practices and relatively inflexible trading relationships.

In the popular market, and particularly in the publication of novels where high risk was moderated by high retail pricing, other production decisions followed during the final third of the eighteenth century. The most conspicuous of these was the distribution of the text over more than one volume, attempting to ensure, at standard pricing per volume, greater returns from retail or from library lending receipts.[101] Duodecimo proved the favoured format for popular book production, certainly in the century after 1740, but octavo was also adopted when booksellers aimed to give publications a certain distinction.[102] In some cases it promoted more efficient as well as more elegant composition when, in difficult times, the amount of text per page was increased. Towards the end of the eighteenth century, more volumes seem to have been sold already bound (titles were often marketed as 'sold, bound, unless otherwise stated'), but by far the most common advertised price remained that of the volume sewn in paper or boards, allowing the purchaser to have the book bound according to his or her choice.[103]

98 Raven 1990, 313.
99 Barker 1994, 293; Raven 1997a, 153–6; 2002b, 116–32.
100 See Harris. chap. 20, Ferdinand, chap. 21, Turner, chap. 23 and Tierney, chap. 24, all below.
101 See Sutherland, chap. 35, below.
102 See Suarez, chap. 1, above.
103 See Potter 1997. Cf. Green, chap. 28 and Shaw, chap. 29 both below.

Production monopolies

As this account has already insisted, the final but crucial consideration in understanding the economics of the book trade is that much pricing fundamentally turned on production monopolies and protected reprinting rights. For at least the first eighty years of this period, increased output was not necessarily propelled by the pursuit of more efficient production, especially when publishing was driven by investment opportunity as well as by the possibility of immediate returns on work in hand. The publishing syndicates and partnerships organized from the late seventeenth century were driven by both long-term and speculative investment, and lessened the extent to which the rate of product sale determined price and the economic development of book and allied trades.[104] The ranks of booksellers were fundamentally divided between those who invested and dealt in the ownership of the copyright to publication, and those who either printed, sold or distributed books for the copyholders or who traded entirely outside the bounds of copyright materials.[105] This division remained in effect throughout this period, even after new freedoms to reprint out-of-copyright titles following the legal decisions concerning copyright in 1768 and 1774, which led in particular to a great outpouring of anthologies and abridgements (including the Bible).[106] New restrictions were imposed by further Copyright Acts in 1808 and 1814. After the passage of these Acts, the number of titles coming out of copyright fell sharply.

The victories of Donaldson and Carnan did challenge the proud cartels with their private trade auctions of literary properties, and Carnan did end the Stationers' Company almanac monopoly.[107] Adventurous publishing businesses, such as those of John Bew and John Bell, selected newly reprintable titles (from almost anything published before 1746 save for patented titles) and were hugely invigorated. In a certain sense, after 1774, Shakespeare and many older plays and prose (including Bell's *Poets of Great Britain* and his *British theatre*) did become newly accessible commodities.[108] Both before and after those landmark cases, however, the greatest profits in book publication in England (but far less so in Scotland) still derived from the ownership of enforceable copyrights to successful works. From the late 1770s onwards, the

104 Blagden 1951; Belanger 1970, 1975; G. Mandelbrote 1997.
105 See Bonnell, chap. 37, below, for a discussion of booksellers' reinterpretation of the 1710 statute to claim perpetual copyright. See Walters 1974; Belanger 1975; M. Rose 1993. Cf. Rose, chap. 4, below.
106 St Clair 2004, chap. 4.
107 See Myers, chap. 39, below.
108 See Bonnell, chap. 37, below.

leading booksellers established new associations to reassert their interpretation of copyright contracts and to share publication expenses. Although each collaboration generally involved fewer firms than in the conger heyday, each also shadowed earlier, exclusive practices.[109] Of approximately 1,000 books published by John Murray I between 1768 and his death in 1793, nearly 40 per cent were co-published, some on his own initiative when he invited others to join in the financing, some after similar invitations to join others, and some resulting from the purchase of copyright shares in the trade auctions.[110] What the late eighteenth-century window of opportunity did create was a raft of cheaper reprints that certainly contributed to the fourfold increase in publication in the three decades after 1770,[111] but most new in-copyright publications were more expensive than ever, and by the 1810s the reproduction of obsolescent literature for lower-income book buyers was renewed.[112]

From the congers of the early eighteenth century to the new associations and partnerships of the early nineteenth century, part-shares and outright literary property ownership continued to form the staple investments to be bought at the London trade auctions.[113] The greatest accumulator of the second half of the eighteenth century was probably George Robinson who, by the early 1770s, proved a keen rival to the established literary investors. Before 1780, Robinson claimed, according to John Nichols, 'the largest wholesale trade that was ever carried on by an individual'.[114] By 1800, the businesses of Cadell and of Longman and Rees surpassed all others in the extent of their holdings,[115] although already, considerations of high risk pointed towards the primacy of what John Murray I called the 'simple publisher',[116] that is the bookseller, risking all (and often failing), and acting on his own in negotiations with the author and the rest of the trade.[117] The further consequence was that many of the most successful operators had raised their start-up capital from assorted outside sources and entered the trade with practical and financial expertise learned from a previous profession. Many of the bookseller-publishers marking up prices well above production costs, and protecting their position by astute copyright accumulation, died with immense fortunes. The wealth of dozens of the entrants to the trade – notably Thomas Osborne, George Robinson, Robert

109 See Briggs, chap. 19, below.
110 Zachs 1998, 77–81.
111 See Suarez, chap. 1, above.
112 St Clair 2004, chap. 6.
113 See Briggs, chap. 19, below.
114 Nichols 1812–16, III, 445–6; literary assignments of Robinson in Raven 2007, 175, 242–3.
115 See Briggs, chap. 19, below.
116 Cited in Zachs 1998, 61.
117 Raven 2007, chap. 8.

Dodsley, Thomas Cadell and Charles Dilly – was sensational to contemporaries, and the more so given that so many of the new book-trade grandees were born to families outside the profession or were first trained in trades unrelated to bookselling.[118]

Marketing and advertising

Commodification was therefore very much dependent on ensuring that demand could be promoted to justify artificially high prices (themselves appealing to fashionable consumerism). Bookselling success derived far less from supply-led production than it did from the successful exploitation of cartels and techniques to create the appearance of new markets (however limited they might in fact have been). To encourage demand, booksellers had to persuade buyers that expensive books were in fact necessaries – affordable, of high quality and beneficial. Attractions intended to entice custom ranged from the illumination of winter evening sales and exotic retail environments of the Thames ice fairs in the 1690s to the summer spa resort sales flourishing by the 1750s. Sales promoted as events and entertainments in themselves gained new prominence, and outings to great bookstores such as that of Christopher Bateman, or later, to fashionable parlours of booksellers like Lowndes and the Dillys, became frequent subjects for diarists and travel writers.[119]

At the beginning of this period, the established method of informing the public of new works was by the issue of printed proposals and booksellers' lists, the successors to the Term Catalogues.[120] The pioneers among the 'Catalogists', as Nichols described them, included 'Honest' Thomas Payne and Daniel Brown in the 1740s.[121] Far from being abandoned, individual booksellers' catalogues remained pivotal to the courting of custom, particularly for those London booksellers seeking to tap the retail markets in the provinces.[122] Cadell, Dilly, Longman, Dodsley and other established names continued to compile and advertise catalogues. Further catalogues were issued by circulating library publishers, including the Nobles, Bell, Hookham and Lane, as well as by booksellers and auctioneers offering libraries and second-hand books. As might be expected, the design of such lists was given a more fashionable appearance towards the end of the century. Lane led the way with

118 Details of individual fortunes are given in Raven 2001b, 28–30; 2007, 215–20. Cf. Turner, chap. 14, below.
119 Examples are given in Raven 1992, 274–6.
120 Pollard and Ehrman 1965; *CHBB* IV 19, 76, 677, app. 1.4.
121 Nichols 1812–16, VI, 439–40.
122 See Suarez 1999a.

his decorated 'Prospectus' issued every season from the late 1780s. One of the most elaborate was Lane's 'General Prospectus' of 1798 – a four-page, highly ornamented production listing more than eighty publications and bearing little resemblance to the plain conservative book lists of former years.

Many booksellers also advertised in their own publications. End-page and prefatory advertisements became common features, and were printed from standing type set to be split according to available space.[123] Again, this was no new practice – 1551 has been cited as the first example,[124] and lists of books were stitched into publications from 1650 and advertised in journals from the 1680s.[125] A century later, however, advertising achieved new levels of audacity. The juxtaposition of advertisements for very different titles is striking testimony to booksellers' awareness of the diversity of readers' tastes. Ostentatious dedications and special subscriber lists were similarly used to puff publications, even though no dedicatee or subscribers were required for their financing. Francis Newbery included a list of prominent junior subscribers in his *Lilliputian Magazine* and dedicated more than one children's book to the king.[126]

Such advertising was often fiercely competitive. New Year publications were an excellent case in point. In November 1780, for example, Robinson, James Russel, Samuel Bladon and Newbery were all announcing the publication of their pocket-books for 1781 from neighbouring boxes on the front page of the *Daily Advertiser*. Robinson boasted that his book, neatly bound in red leather and with pockets for bills and notes, was 'embellished with elegant engravings of two ladies in the dress of 1780 and twelve of the most fashionable Head Dresses'. Russel offered an engraved view of the Camp in St James's Park as well as the smartest dresses of the year. Bladon and Newbery advertised similar illustrations of voguish attire, but with the added flourish of plates of the royal family and of the Duke of Cumberland 'with his Prize Cup'.[127]

This salesmanship did not always require subtlety; there was much reliance upon the puff direct. Handbills and strident notices in journals and newspapers broadcast unmissable bargains.[128] The finely printed prospectus for James Harrison's *Novelists Magazine* detailed forthcoming highlights of the series and assured the public that 'the Neatness of the Print, Paper and Engravings as well as the Quality of delightful Reading will be well worth more than three

123 Cameron 1975, 200; Raven 2007, 282–93.
124 Miller 1959, 212.
125 *CHBB* IV, 240, 497–8, 677–9.
126 Roscoe 1973. Cf. Immel, chap. 40, below.
127 *PA*, 7 Nov. 1780.
128 See Harris, chap. 20, Ferdinand, chap. 21, Tierney, chap. 24 and Maidment, chap. 25, all below.

Times the Purchase-Money'.[129] According to notices in the leading London newspapers, *Harrison's Protestant's family bible: a new family bible* was 'the cheapest, most elegant, and far the most convenient sized Bible ever printed'.[130] The Newberys, having experimented with advertising gimmicks for their patent medicines, indulged in ingenious book-trade advertising in London newspapers, in handbills in the streets, and in well-placed asides within the actual tales.[131] Occasionally, the Newberys' advertising audacity was too much even for the printers, who refused to execute certain commissions.[132]

Of obvious related importance is what has been called the 'open-access character' of the engraving trade, involving men and women from various crafts.[133] Picture sellers, printsellers, mapmakers, printers and booksellers worked closely together, and some notable booksellers, including the Knaptons at mid-century, claimed regular involvement with the prints and picture trade.[134] Of the technological changes in the eighteenth-century book trade, the most significant were those concerned with papermaking, but also with engraving and with the design and manufacture of type.[135] The value of new founts in attracting customers and satisfying clients was swiftly appreciated.[136] As well as commanding attention, finely printed decoration became a status symbol, much in the manner of modern letter-headings and printed logos. Exquisite London creations also contrasted with provincial jobbing work. As the elegance and ingenuity of London print novelties continued to amaze, printers setting up in the country and specializing in jobbing printing or the publication of weekly newspapers were often too poor to buy the most modern type or ornaments.[137]

The increasing influence of critical reviewing[138] could also be turned to advertising advantage. Many of the brasher booksellers 'puffed' works by citing from recent or imaginary notices. By the early 1780s, review quotes were sprinkled liberally across the verso of title pages of subsequent editions by the Nobles, Bell and many others. A decade later, this practice appears to have been abandoned in preference to puffs inserted in end-page advertisements. The source of these notices was almost never given and the authenticity of

129 *A pleasing publication* ... handbill for the *Novelists Magazine* (1779).
130 *PA*, 2 Oct. 1780, 30 Nov. 1780, and notices thereafter.
131 Welsh 1885, esp. 106–9; Jackson 2003. Cf. Immel, chap. 40, below.
132 BL, Add. MSS 28,275 fol. 98, Newbery to Tonson (n.d.).
133 Harris 1997, 97–100. Cf. Mosley, chap. 7, below.
134 Lippincott 1983. Cf. Clayton, chap. 10, below.
135 Ball 1973; Bruntjen 1985; Clayton 1997; cf. Mosley, chap. 7 and Bidwell, chap. 8, both below.
136 See Barker, chap. 11, below.
137 Clayton 1997.
138 See Forster, chap. 33, below.

many remains now, as then, unproven. Critics certainly claimed that booksellers were fabricating the tributes.[139] By the late 1780s Lane had so perfected the technique that end-page or prefatory advertisements to his works bear striking resemblance to the modern book jacket with its battery of short but glorious quotations from respected authorities.[140]

Other booksellers preferred to dazzle by depth. Robert Baldwin's newspaper puffs for his second edition of S. J. Pratt's *Emma Corbett* featured a three-paragraph extract from the *London Magazine*.[141] Other advertisements featured extravagant titles, a ploy ridiculed by Goldsmith when his imaginary bookseller Mr Fudge claimed to have 'ten new title pages now about me, which only want books to be added to make them the finest things in nature'.[142] As Timperley sneered, 'in announcing the embellishment of these publications, language failed; and the terms "beautiful", "elegant", "superb" and even "magnificent" became too poor to express their extreme merit'.[143] Certainly, no review puff was required where titles provided their own recommendation and description of contents. Booksellers expanded both title lines and the imprint and publication notes at the foot of the title page. Many booksellers provided their full addresses and those of shops or circulating libraries where their books or periodicals could be bought or perused. Some booksellers used the imprint line to insert references to other printing, publishing or editorial services they offered. William Lane followed the Newberys and included puffs within the actual plot of a work.[144] In one of their 1771 novels, the Nobles placed 'An Introductory Dialogue between the Publisher and one of his Subscribers' in which the publisher declares, 'It doesn't become me, Sir, to puff my own publications,' but proceeds all the same to assure the purchaser of the unmatchable quality of that which follows.[145]

Courting fashionable custom remained hazardous, however. Significantly, in terms of pricing practices, many of these energetic publishers were outside the comfortable shared wholesaling arrangements of booksellers' associations. Many Harrison, Cooke and Hogg advertisements flamboyantly urged customers to check with their local bookseller that they were ordering original publications. In an address 'To the Public' in a second issue of his *British theatre*, John Bell warned of the 'several interested Booksellers' who had 'even gone so

139 *MR*, Mar. 1789, 288, warning against spurious reviews.
140 Examples given in Raven 2007, chap. 9.
141 *PA*, 18 July and 23 Aug. 1780.
142 Goldsmith 1762, letter 51.
143 Timperley 1842, 838. Cf. Cumberland 1791, I, 267–84.
144 Blakey 1939, 70–1.
145 *The undutiful daughter*, 3 vols., London, 1771, I, v; other examples in Blakey 1939, 194–205.

far as to copy the original Advertisement for this Work, and nearly the Title Page, in order that they may obtrude their own futile productions with less suspicion, when the above may be wanted'.[146] For all booksellers, another early difficulty was that advertising expenses could amount to a large charge on total publication costs. In 1760 the publishers of Smollett's *History* spent £300 in advertising the first issue, and another £80 advertising the second.[147] Packets of advertisements for the 6*d.* weekly numbers of the *History* were also sent to parish clerks, together with half a crown and a request that the prospectuses be placed in all church pews.[148]

The newspaper offered the solution to the search for wider advertising.[149] Across the country the maintenance of newspaper circuits secured the solvency of the main book distributors for the London publishers. Newspapers became the mainstay of many printer-booksellers, most notably in the fastest growing of the towns outside the capital. Success was clear to government and the exchequer: after the initial 1711 excise tax on home-produced paper, followed by the infamous Stamp Act of 1712, twenty-six further Acts imposing duties on paper, newspapers and advertisements were passed in the next 150 years.[150] As the numerical and geographical circulation of London and provincial newspapers increased during the century, so also did the number of columns devoted to advertisements.[151] Total sales of all newspapers in England (excluding tens of thousands of unstamped weeklies) amounted to some 7.3 million in 1750, 9.4 million in 1760, 12.6 million in 1775, and more than 16 million in 1790. In 1781, some 76 newspapers and periodicals were published in England and Wales; by 1821, this total reached 267.[152] It was, of course, a great advantage if the publisher of books also published a newspaper. The front-page top column of Bell's *World* regularly announced his latest publications, and in his *Morning Post* Bell promoted his works whenever he pleased, notably inserting home-grown reviews and commentaries praising himself and his works.[153] William Lane was expert in using his *Star and Evening Advertiser*, acquired in 1788, to similar effect.[154] It has also been suggested that the *Star*

146 Bell's *British theatre*, 2nd issue (1786), I, 6.
147 BL, Add.MSS 38,730, fol. 135.
148 Saunders 1964, 153.
149 See Ferdinand, chap. 21 and Turner, chap. 23, both below.
150 Collet 1899. Cf. Bidwell, chap. 8, below.
151 Cranfield 1962, chap. 10; Wiles 1965; Harris 1987; Tierney 1995; Raven 2001a, 24–6.
152 Snyder 1968, 1976; Harris 1987.
153 Werkmeister 1963, 150.
154 Blakey 1939, 10.

had been founded by booksellers specifically looking for an advertising vehicle.[155]

It was here, in the newspaper columns, that the sensationalist puff vied with the 'cloud', the closely worded, usually lengthy list of books offered by the more respectable of the booksellers. Such notices remained unchanged in format for most of the second half of the eighteenth century, and they were particularly associated with the ventures of Cadell, Dodsley, Longman and the Rivingtons. Dodsley often listed more than thirty works at a time, while Cadell relied on a half-column advertisement unchanged throughout the season. Such booksellers were jealous of their reputation for the sale of serious and useful publications. Nevertheless, according to Daniel Stuart of the *Morning Post and Star*, newspaper proprietors were not enamoured of the booksellers' advertisements. Cadell and Longman and company were regarded as arrogant and demanding, and 'each was desirous of having his cloud of advertisements inserted at once in the front page', refusing to agree to 'a few and pressing advertisements at a time; . . . he would have the cloud'. Such booksellers were 'affronted, indignant' by the offer of a cloud on the last page, and so, recalled Stuart, 'when a very long advertisement of a column or two came, I charged enormously high'.[156]

Advertising was expensive; the more so when it attracted successively increased taxation (not reduced until 1834, nor finally abolished until 1853). Woodfall, publishing his *Public Advertiser* from his large shop at the corner of Ivy Lane and Paternoster Row, took in advertisements 'of moderate length' at 3*s*. each.[157] If 'moderate' was average and charging remained proportionate to size, then many of the full-column booksellers' advertisements must have cost more than a guinea each. Historians of the newspaper industry have argued that the direct profits accruing from advertisements were vital to newspapers unable to survive by sales alone.[158] Even so, the costs of advertising in newspapers, catalogues and separate notices proved a shock for many authors. In 1816 John Murray II charged Jane Austen £50 for advertising *Emma* in the first nine months of publication, some of which was a charge for advertising in Murray's own catalogue.[159]

As a further consequence of the expansion in advertising, styles greatly diversified. Much in evidence was the reliable but eye-catching line, 'This

155 Werkmeister 1963, 221.
156 Stuart 1838, 25–6.
157 *PA* footline.
158 Wiles 1957, 149–53; Munter 1967, 57, 61–6; Harris 1978a.
159 Fergus 1991.

Day is Published', an announcement in the continuous present usually repeated the next day, next week, or even in successive weeks thereafter.[160] Lane, Harrison, Bew and others also began to devote the bold-face first lines of advertisements to their own names rather than to the titles of works. Other booksellers preferred a more self-effacing presentation of advertisements, trying to avoid both the sensationalist puff and the longer cloud. Charles Dilly, for example, varied his experiments in cloud insertion with an investment in three or more separately boxed notices in a single newspaper, the whole repeated a few days later. Some booksellers used a combination of advertisements to puff a particular work. The Duchess of Devonshire's *Sylph* reached three editions possibly only because it was partnered with *Evelina* in advertisements. Certainly, Frances Burney thought that this was so. Advertising in the provincial newspapers was especially important to the expansion in wholesaling operations. More than half the books bought by customers of John Clay who were also subscribers to the critical reviews were bought before the books were publicly reviewed.[161] Advertising appears to have been the main avenue for such promotion.

As competition advanced, further customer services were invented. Bell, Cadell, Harrison and many others boasted that books and opening numbers of serials could be 'perused *gratis* and returned if not approved'. Money-back guarantees were volunteered in addition to promises that prices would not increase during a set-length subscription to a part-issue or journal. Advertisements did not (as they often do not today) mention the payment of return carriage, nor indeed of ordinary delivery charges to confirmed subscribers. Notices also failed to specify the time an unsatisfied reader might keep a book before return. By the 1820s, the paper wrappers on many serialized number publications proclaimed the full worth of the run. John Saunders's 25-part issue of the 1823 *Widow's choice* was enfolded by confident puffing even though its endurance seemed uncertain: 'This truly interesting Work will be printed from Stereotype Plates, embellished with beautiful Copperplate Engravings, and completed in about 25 Numbers.'[162]

The more adventurous booksellers resorted to fanciful promotions. Harrison offered a 'square pianoforte' to subscribers to the entire run of the *Musical Magazine*.[163] Newbery offered purchasers of children's books free games, pull-outs and models.[164] Give-away prints and gifts accompanied

160 For an example, see Turner, chap. 23, below.
161 Fergus and Portner 1987, 158.
162 Garside 2000, 96.
163 Rees and Britton 1896, 23.
164 Noblett 1972, 269.

certain adult series, while spin-off prints and plans were also sold.[165] Robinson and Hogg used the newspaper notices to list all the pull-outs, embroidery patterns, song-sheets, prints and other free gifts to be offered in their latest monthly or weekly numbers. Cooke's weekly *New and authentick history of England*, printed by Russel in eighty numbers, contained in its first issue a promissory note for the free 'overplus' (an additional number or volume) and for the inclusion in the final volume of a separate neatly printed list of full subscribers.[166] It must be added that booksellers did not guarantee to fulfil their post-completion promises should they themselves decide to cancel the series. The outcome of Thomas Becket's pledge (in advertisements printed by Strahan) to provide plaster casts of Nollekens's bust of Sterne once his 1773 edition of *Tristram Shandy* reached a hundred subscribers remains 'something of a mystery'.[167] Trusler's *Habitable world described* fell silent before a single circumnavigation. No delivery of a Harrison pianoforte is recorded.

Conclusion

The basis of any analysis of the book as a commodity in this period is therefore that copyright was cheap, protected and investable, and that both the cartels of booksellers and those outside the associations (but conveniently adopting derivative business strategies) were able to sustain and increase the relative price of books and serials. Although the output of nominally inexpensive literature was maintained and its volume increased, any commodification certainly did not depend upon price cutting. Bookseller-publishers benefited, indeed, from the presentation of modish publications as exclusive and as the very antithesis of popular and cheap.

The consequent cultivation of demand did rely increasingly, however, upon innovative marketing techniques, sustained by capable and adaptable distributive mechanisms. First-generation entrants to the London trades introduced new business and marketing strategies, while the more versatile deployment of new money brought into the book trade from outside interests and investments was also the more striking given how broader resource limitations continued to constrain business expansion and technological advance until well into the nineteenth century. Where bookseller-publishers took on the full financial risk, the production expenses of paper, labour and type were balanced against protected monopoly rights (at least until 1774 and, for many

165 Examples given in Raven 2007, chap. 9.
166 *PA*, 22 June 1780.
167 Barker 1994, 294.

publishing ventures, until the end of this period). In most cases during these 135 years, book prices fell and print runs increased only when a title was free of asserted copyright restriction. Both before and after the challenges to the syndicates in the 1770s, however, bookseller-publishers embraced design and market profiling that placed a premium on skilful sales promotion. Under the high-price regime, luxury and expense had to be justified; in the years of cheaper reprints, price could be made a selling point (although often with some creativity by certain booksellers given the continuing inflated prices of new in-copyright publications). Books published by profit-sharing arrangements or on commission (with whole or part financing by the author) have usually been seen as low-risk undertakings by booksellers, but given the relative loss limitation assured by copyright protection and the high potential returns of reprinting, some profit sharing might now seem to us to have been something of a charitable operation. Even so, authors remained vulnerable to booksellers' sharp practice, including the silent production of more copies than agreed, or, conversely, the failure to advertise or distribute.[168]

The introduction of steam-driven printing presses from 1814 shattered the principal technological constraint of three and a half centuries, and introduced the means to create more fundamental distance between literary commodity and luxury.[169] Before 1814, publishing, as had been the case since at least the late seventeenth century, was dominated by questions of monopoly price fixing, capitalization, centralized production and control, technological constraints (and breakthroughs), and the efficiency of distribution networks. Within this structure, popular publishing responded during the eighteenth century to fast-growing consumer demand, advanced by the continued expansion of part-issues, periodicals and newspapers, school-books and instructional manuals, private and circulating libraries, the fracturing of the high-price protectionist regime, and, increasingly, by a lively if problematic colonial market.[170] Cheaper and more popular literature and reprint series (and the relaunch of the one-volume novel) heralded the transformation of print in the railway age. In turn, larger print runs, exploiting the new economies of factory print production, required more accurately forecasted demand.[171] Additional distributive capacity remained critical, but its configuration, together with the continuing centrality of London as both production centre and radial distribution hub, offered a sharp contrast with many other developing industries.

168 Fergus 2007, chap. 1.
169 See Bidwell, chap. 8, below.
170 See Green, chap. 28 and Shaw, chap. 29, both below.
171 Weedon 2003, 60–2.

The relocation of manufacturing sites in pursuit of raw materials and new sources of power scarcely affected the production of books, magazines and newspapers until the very close of this period. The transformation in printing capacity, first in the 1820s, and then the astonishing distributive possibilities of the railways, proved the means to create not just new markets, but pricing regimes more closely allied to true production costs. Although we do not yet have the detailed studies to be sure about price movements in the first three decades of the nineteenth century, the pressure to lower prices in many categories of publication is abundantly clear – and new research does indicate that in the seventy years after 1846 book prices were halved (with a fourfold increase in production).[172] In theory at least, popular consumption no longer had to seem so conspicuous.

172 Weedon 2003, 159.

4
Copyright, authors and censorship

MARK ROSE

The Statute of Anne

In 1695 the Licensing Act expired.[1] This Act, which was the lineal descendant of various printing ordinances and decrees dating back to the early sixteenth century, provided a comprehensive system for the examination and approval of materials to be printed. In addition, it confirmed the Stationers' Company's near monopoly on the British book trade and its powers to enforce its dominance. The lapse of licensing threw the book trade into disorder – members of the Company no longer were able to restrain others from printing their 'copies' – and led directly to the enactment in 1710 of the world's first copyright statute, the Statute of Anne, and consequently to a fundamental change in the legal institutions within which the book trade operated.[2]

Under the old system of Stationers' Company regulation, a stationer who wished to publish would establish his right by entering the title as his 'copy' in the guild register. Once secured, a 'copy' continued forever and might be bequeathed, sold or split into shares, but only members of the guild – booksellers and printers, not authors – could own 'copies'. When disputes over rights arose, they were generally settled within the confines of the guild. Publishing rights under the guild system were thus not quite property in the modern sense, even though stationers were accustomed to speaking of their 'literary properties'. Rather, they were guild-conferred privileges that depended upon the company's crown-chartered monopoly.

The Statute of Anne provided a regulatory system modelled on Company practices, but the statute departed from the guild system in that it specified that copyright would be a limited privilege, not a perpetual right. For books

1 14 Charles II c. 33. Astbury 1978.

2 8 Anne c. 19. On the making of the statute, see Patterson 1968, 143–50; Feather 1980; M. Rose 1993, 31–48. On the SC generally, Blagden 1960a. For a general survey of the law in relation to the book trade in the eighteenth century, see Feather 1982.

already in print the Act established a twenty-one-year term; for new books it established a fourteen-year term with the possibility of a second fourteen-year term if the author were still living at the end of the first. The statute also departed from the guild system in that for the first time authors – non-guild members – were empowered to own copyrights. At this time polite authors rarely sought or received payment for their writings, and those who did generally sold their manuscripts outright to booksellers. Therefore, copyright was not usually considered to be an authors' matter. Nevertheless, the stationers had long argued that they owned literary properties by virtue of having bought them from authors. Moreover, some authors such as Daniel Defoe and Joseph Addison were beginning to talk about authors' rights, and their agitation may have had an effect on the explicit provision for authors.[3]

The title of the statute – 'An act for the encouragement of learning, by vesting the copies of printed books in the authors or purchasers of such copies, during the times therein mentioned' – emphasized both the legal constitution of authors as the first owners of their works and the establishment of term limits. These terms, modelled on those that the Jacobean Statute of Monopolies[4] had set for patents, reflected the anti-monopolistic sentiment of Parliament and were conceived as an instrument to break the system whereby a small number of booksellers were able to dominate the trade through their control of the most valuable copyrights. Probably the inclusion of the author in the Act was also intended at least in part as a strike against the booksellers' monopolies.

It is worth noting, too, that the title emphasized the statute's civic purposes – the encouragement of learning – rather than simply speaking of securing the booksellers' literary property claims. In this the statute reflected the late seventeenth-century emergence of what Jürgen Habermas has called the 'public sphere' and its manifestation in such newly founded institutions of public benefit as the Royal Society and the Bank of England and in the spread of newspapers, periodicals, coffee houses and public pleasure gardens.[5] The passage of the statute was in fact epochal because, at least in principle, it marked a shift from the kind of culture of regulation represented by licensing and by the guild system to a new regime based more on Enlightenment ideas of individualism, property, and civil society as a collectivity. Henceforth, matters related to literary property would be adjudicated not by royal decree or by

3 M. Rose 1993, 34–42.
4 21 Jac. I c. 3.
5 Habermas 1989.

private panels assembled within the confines of the Stationers' Company, but in the legislature and public law courts.

The battle of the booksellers

Terry Belanger estimates that at the beginning of the eighteenth century the book trade was effectively controlled by fewer than a hundred London booksellers.[6] The basis of their dominance was control of old copyrights, especially standard religious works or reference books such as dictionaries for which there was steady demand.[7] Most of these had been, over the years, split into shares in order to spread the financial risks of bookselling and to maximize the worth of the copyrights themselves. Thus the heart of the system consisted of copyrights on works already in print.

The Statute of Anne's specification of a twenty-one-year term for books already in print was a transitional provision designed to ease the shift from the Company system to the new statutory regime. When the old copyrights began to expire in the 1730s, however, the London booksellers, by no means willing to surrender their properties, attempted to secure an extension of the term. What they proposed was a single twenty-one-year term for all copyrights old and new. This change would reduce the protection for new copyrights but, more important from the booksellers' point of view, it would start a new twenty-one-year term running on old copyrights. But Parliament – and especially the House of Lords, which remained suspicious of the booksellers' monopolies – twice refused to grant the booksellers the extension.[8] As one pamphleteer remarked, to grant the booksellers' plea would open the door to further requests each time the term expired.[9] Such an action would be tantamount to piecemeal re-establishment of perpetual monopolies.

The major booksellers were not yet ready to acknowledge that their old literary properties were no longer protected, however. Barred from securing parliamentary relief, the booksellers turned at times to aggressive business practices. When the independent London bookseller Robert Walker challenged Jacob Tonson's control of the Shakespeare copyrights by bringing out a very cheap edition of Shakespeare in 1734, for example, Tonson responded by producing an equivalent edition at an even lower price and driving Walker's

6 Belanger 1982, 11.
7 Belanger 1982, 16–18.
8 M. Rose 1993, 52–6.
9 *A letter from an author* 1735.

Shakespeare off the market.[10] To certain other 'piratical' challenges in the 1730s, however, Tonson and other major booksellers responded by securing Chancery injunctions against the offenders.[11] These injunctions were merely temporary decrees – that is, they did not determine the legal merits of the booksellers' claims; nonetheless, at this point they were sufficient to allow the booksellers to maintain control of their old properties and to protect both their profits and their domination of the trade.

In the 1740s, however, the struggle took a new turn when a group of Scottish booksellers, frustrated by the London booksellers' domination of the trade, began actively reprinting popular works on which the statutory term had expired. Because of certain specifications in the statute, the London booksellers had to respond to this challenge in the Scottish Court of Session rather than the more sympathetic Court of Chancery. It was in the context of this litigation of the 1740s that the London booksellers, represented by the brilliant lawyer William Murray, began to elaborate their most powerful argument for perpetual copyright, the theory of the author's common-law right.[12]

The essence of this argument was that authors had a natural right of property in their works as a consequence of the labour of writing and that this property was in principle no different in kind from property in houses or fields. The Statute of Anne, the booksellers argued, merely provided a supplement to an underlying and perpetual common-law right. The common-law theory was powerful because it grounded the London booksellers' claims in a discourse of individualism and property, drawing upon such fundamental Enlightenment assumptions as that of the freedom of the individual to create and dispose of property as he saw fit. Moreover, because it framed the literary property debate in terms of authors' rights, not booksellers' rights, the common-law argument disguised the fact that what was truly at stake was the continuing dominance of a small number of powerful London booksellers. Ironically, the common-law argument, grounded in Enlightenment ideas, was marshalled to preserve a system of centralized commercial control that had evolved in the pre-Enlightenment regime characterized by crown-chartered regulation.

The Scottish case developed into a long, complex and inconclusive litigation that was eventually dropped by the London booksellers.[13] After William Murray, now Lord Mansfield, was elevated to the position of chief justice of the Court of King's Bench in 1756, however, the London booksellers sought to

10 Dawson 1946, 30–1.
11 Feather 1987, 6–7.
12 M. Rose 1993, 67–70.
13 McDougall 1988, 5–9.

test the common-law theory in the English courts. *Tonson* v. *Collins*,[14] the first of a series of important cases in which the common-law theory was argued, was aborted when it emerged that the plaintiff and the defendant, Benjamin Collins, a respected provincial bookseller from Salisbury, were acting in collusion to establish a precedent. Thirteen years later, in 1769, Lord Mansfield's court gave the London booksellers the judgment they had sought, the landmark case of *Millar* v. *Taylor*.[15] By a vote of three to one, Mansfield's court upheld the theory of the author's common-law right and determined that literary property was, as the London booksellers had claimed, perpetual.

As an English court, the jurisdiction of King's Bench did not extend to Scotland, where the reprint industry continued to thrive and where a scrappy Edinburgh bookseller, Alexander Donaldson, was determined to break the London booksellers' hold on the trade.[16] Donaldson specialized in inexpensive reprints of standard – and, he maintained, out of copyright – works by such authors as Shakespeare, Milton, Locke, Defoe, Pope, Swift, Fielding and Thomson. In 1773, the London bookseller John Hinton brought suit against Donaldson and several others in the Court of Session in an attempt to resolve the question of literary property in Scotland. The Scottish court reached the opposite decision from King's Bench, however. Whatever the law in England, the majority said, in Scotland there was no common-law right of literary property.[17]

For a brief period, then, copyright was perpetual in England but limited in term in Scotland. With the Court of Session decision in *Hinton* v. *Donaldson* in hand as a precedent to offset the King's Bench decision in *Millar* v. *Taylor*, however, Donaldson was determined to bring the matter to the House of Lords. Moving quickly, Donaldson appealed a Chancery writ that had been obtained against him by Thomas Becket and a group of other London booksellers for reprinting James Thomson's *Seasons*, first published more than forty years earlier and thus clearly unprotected by the statute. Perhaps by coincidence, the work in question was the same as that which had figured in *Millar* v. *Taylor* five years earlier. In any case, *Donaldson* v. *Becket*[18] in effect constituted an appeal of that earlier landmark decision.

In major cases the House of Lords summoned the judges of King's Bench, Common Pleas and the Exchequer and solicited their opinions on the legal

14 1 Black W 301, 96 *English Reports* 169 (1761).
15 4 Burr 2303, 98 *English Reports* 201 (1769).
16 See Bonnell, chap. 37, below.
17 Boswell 1774.
18 4 Burr 248, 98 *English Reports* (1774), 257; 2 Bro PC 129, 1 *English Reports* (1774), 837.

issues involved. The judges' opinions in *Donaldson* v. *Becket* were very divided – and the record of their speeches is in some respects defective – but it appears that a majority held that there was a common-law right of literary property, that the right survived the publication of a work, and probably also that the common-law right was not taken away by the Statute of Anne. In this period, however, even in technical legal questions the actual decision was made by a general vote of the House as a whole, laymen and lawyers alike. In 1710 Parliament had resisted the London booksellers' desire for confirmation of the old Stationers' Company system of perpetual copyright, and in the 1730s it had also resisted the booksellers' attempts to maintain control of their old copyrights by extending the statutory term. The vote of the peers was consistent with these earlier anti-monopoly actions: by a strong majority the House of Lords in 1774 overturned the injunction against Donaldson.[19] Thus, some sixty-four years after the passage of the Statute of Anne, the limited duration of copyright was finally established.

Consequences of *Donaldson* v. *Becket*

There was great public interest in the booksellers' battle and the decision of the House of Lords. In Edinburgh the ruling was celebrated as a Scottish national victory; in London, however, it was met with anger and concern. A paragraph appearing in the *Morning Chronicle* and in a number of other periodicals after the decision claimed that a vast amount of property had been annihilated:

> By the above decision of the important question respecting copy-right in books, near 200,000 l. worth of what was honestly purchased at public sale, and which was yesterday thought property is now reduced to nothing. The Booksellers of London and Westminster, many of whom sold estates and houses to purchase Copy-right, are in a manner ruined, and those who after many years industry thought they had acquired a competency to provide for their families now find themselves without a shilling to devise to their successors.[20]

The London booksellers' desperation was sincere enough: all the great properties of the book trade that they had been accustomed to treat as private landed estates were suddenly declared open commons. The consequences of *Donaldson* v. *Becket* extended well beyond the immediate losses of the

19 M. Rose 1993, 97–103.
20 *MChr*, 23 Feb. 1774, quoted in M. Rose 1993, 97.

major booksellers, however; the decision altered the landscape of the trade in fundamental ways.

Since the heart of the eighteenth-century book trade consisted of old copyrights split into shares, the typical publishing project of that time involved multiple booksellers acting in combination. The surest way to turn a profit in the book business was to acquire a share in a standard work; to be financially successful in a large way it was necessary to become part of the inner circle of the trade. Characterized by co-operation rather than competition, and by close ties that were cemented by long histories of personal and family relationships, the book trade even as late as 1774 was still in many ways a traditional guild system.[21]

This system did not survive *Donaldson*. The end of perpetual copyright meant the opening up of the trade to previously excluded groups such as the Scottish reprinters. Thus shortly after the Lords' decision, John Bell began to issue his monumental *Poets of Great Britain* (109 volumes, 1776–82) and his *Bell's British theatre* (21 volumes, 1776–80).[22] The possibility of inexpensive reprints such as these meant both a change in the trade and the creation of a much wider book-buying public, a development that had enormous social consequences.[23] Moreover, since copyrights now expired after at most two fourteen-year terms, the *Donaldson* decision meant that booksellers had a new interest in investing in current literary productions to replace a continuously expiring stock. In addition, because very large accumulations of capital were no longer tied up in old copyrights, the share system became less attractive.

The changing circumstances of the trade, including the decline of the share system, made possible an increase in specialization. The typical bookseller of the early eighteenth century was both a publisher – one who purchased copyrights and arranged for the printing of books – and a retailer who sold his own and others' books in his shop. In the late eighteenth and early nineteenth centuries, however, it became feasible to make a good living by publishing alone, and such firms as Rivingtons, Longmans and John Murray developed into true publishers as distinct from retailers. Thus the modern publishing industry – specialized into publishers, wholesalers and retailers – emerged in the aftermath of the *Donaldson* decision.[24]

21 See Belanger 1982.
22 See Bonnell, chap. 37, below.
23 See generally Altick 1998. Cf. Raven, chap. 3, above.
24 On changes in the trade, see generally Belanger 1978, 1982.

Professional authorship and the Copyright Act of 1814

By increasing publishers' interest in new copyrights and by contributing to the development of a broader reading public, the *Donaldson* decision also affected authors. A few major authors of the late seventeenth and early eighteenth centuries, notably John Dryden and Alexander Pope, made substantial profits from their publications, often through elaborate contractual schemes such as those which Pope negotiated for his translations of Homer. Pope was also unusual in the extent to which he made use of the standing granted to authors by the Statute of Anne to control his copyrights. Despite his active commercial and legal engagements, however, Pope always presented himself as an amateur rather than as a professional author.[25]

Pope's self-representation was a social necessity. Before the middle of the eighteenth century, professional authorship was associated with hacks rather than with gentlemen. Indeed, as late as 1774, Lord Camden, arguing the literary property question in the House of Lords, could speak with contempt of 'Scribblers for bread, who teize the Press with their wretched Productions'.[26] Yet, Camden's scorn was a relic of an earlier time. By the time of *Donaldson* v. *Becket*, in part through the model and influence of Samuel Johnson,[27] respectable professional authorship was an established social fact, and Camden's remarks provoked a heavily ironic response from the historian Catharine Macaulay, who pointed out that for an author to sell his literary work was no more degrading than for a rich landowner to sell his grain and cattle.[28]

The usual arrangement between author and publisher throughout the eighteenth century was outright sale of the copyright, and this continued to be the usual arrangement in the early nineteenth century as well.[29] Some publishers favoured schemes whereby author and publisher would contract for a division of profits after expenses, but these generally put the author at the mercy of the publisher's bookkeeping and therefore were regarded with scepticism by writers. An alternative was publication by commission, a scheme whereby the author paid the publisher's expenses plus a commission fee and received the balance of receipts based on a regular accounting of sales. The disadvantage

25 On Pope's involvement with the trade, see generally Foxon 1991.
26 Quoted in M. Rose 1993, 104.
27 Kernan 1987.
28 Macaulay 1774, 14–15.
29 See Griffin, chap. 5, below.

of commission publishing, however, was that it offered little incentive to the publisher to market the author's book aggressively. A few popular authors such as Scott and Byron were able to earn substantial sums from their writings, but the lot of the average writer was not enviable. As Victor Bonham-Carter reports, the publisher William Lane generally paid between £5 and £30 for copyrights around 1800, and there were plenty of novelists glad to accept.[30] The modern royalty system was introduced in the mid-nineteenth century, but it did not really become practicable until the end of the nineteenth century when the Net Book Agreement established a firm price on which to base the author's payment.[31]

Nonetheless, as professional authorship increased in respectability and, at least for some, in profitability, authors became more concerned with legal matters such as copyright. Authors' and publishers' issues together led to the passage of a new Copyright Act in 1814.[32] The immediate impetus behind this Act was the controversy over the publisher's deposit requirement – that is, the provision that each publisher transmit a free copy of every book published to each of the major libraries in Britain. First instituted by the Licensing Act of 1662, and thereafter incorporated into the Statute of Anne, the number of deposit libraries had expanded to eleven after the Act of Union with Ireland in 1801, but in practice the requirement was generally ignored by publishers and libraries alike. The situation changed in 1812 when the Cambridge University Library successfully sued to secure its deposit copies. Unable to ignore the deposit requirement any longer, the book trade sought relief from the legislature, pointing out that the requirement made it difficult for them to publish small editions of specialized interest and maintaining that the requirement in effect amounted to an unjust tax imposed upon them for the benefit of the libraries.[33]

The Copyright Act of 1814 did not resolve the deposit controversy even though it made a few minor changes in the requirement, but the new statute did include a provision that was symptomatic of the changed status of professional authorship. Instead of basing the term of copyright protection solely on publication – fourteen years with the possibility of a second fourteen years – the Act related it to the author's life by providing protection for twenty-eight years or the life of the author, whichever was longer. This marked a major

30 Bonham-Carter 1978, 32.

31 On authors' payments and publication schemes, see generally Plant 1974, 410; Bonham-Carter 1978, 25–32; Belanger 1982, 21–3.

32 54 Geo. III c. 56.

33 On the deposit controversy, see Feather 1988b.

conceptual evolution in copyright. Nonetheless, the new term did not satisfy such writers as Robert Southey and William Wordsworth, who insisted that an author's writings should be protected forever. Interestingly, whereas in the eighteenth century the proponents of perpetual copyright had been the London booksellers, in the nineteenth it was the authors who revived the natural rights arguments and who sought to reopen the issues decided in *Donaldson* v. *Becket* in 1774.

Writing about the status of copyright in the *Quarterly Review* in 1819, Southey called for a correction of the Lords' decision. The value of many of the best authors' works, Southey said, was not quickly discovered and therefore the authors and their heirs were deprived of their rights by the limited term.[34] Wordsworth concurred, and – together with his friend and admirer Thomas Noon Talfourd, an author as well as a member of Parliament – Wordsworth and Southey actively campaigned for a new Copyright Act. The authors' campaign proved controversial – it was in the context of this controversy that Thomas Babington Macaulay made his famous statement about copyright being 'a tax on readers for the purpose of giving a bounty to writers'[35] – but the matter was finally resolved in 1842 with a compromise that set the copyright term as the author's life plus seven years or a total of forty-two years, whichever was longer.[36]

Censorship after licensing

The lapse of the Licensing Act ended pre-publication censorship and radically changed the power of the state to regulate the press, but it did not totally end regulation. After 1695, works that the state found offensive or dangerous might still be restrained after publication through the application of various criminal laws. Indeed, in 1698 Parliament passed the Blasphemy Act, which specified the categories of blasphemy and profanity that would be considered criminal, and which probably was intended as a general warning to authors and booksellers not to take the end of licensing as a sign that anything might now be published.[37] Moreover, in the 1720s the foundations of the law of obscenity were established in the successful prosecution of the notorious Edmund Curll for the publication of several titles with sexual content, one being a new English edition of the French pornographic classic, *Venus in the cloister*; the

34 Southey 1819, 212–13.
35 Macaulay 1896–7, VIII, 201.
36 On the making of the 1842 Act, see Feather 1989; Seville 1999.
37 9 William III c. 25. For discussion, see Thomas 1969, 63–73.

principles established in the prosecution of Curll were later applied in other obscenity cases, among them the many cases which involved John Cleland's *Memoirs of a woman of pleasure*, alternatively known as *Fanny Hill*.[38]

The blasphemy and obscenity laws were significant, but the most important legal instrument for press control in the eighteenth and early nineteenth centuries was the law of seditious libel. This law, which had its roots in the concept that the monarch was to be protected from false rumour, was quickly turned into a potent device for the suppression of various kinds of materials that the authorities found objectionable.[39] Often these cases involved matters that were concerned as much with religion as with politics. Thus, in 1703 Daniel Defoe, as is well known, was fined and pilloried in connection with his satirical pamphlet, *The shortest way with the Dissenters*. A few years later, in what was probably the most famous libel case of the early part of the century, Dr Henry Sacheverell was tried and convicted of libel for his sermons against 'false brethren', which were seen as an attack on the settlement of 1688 and specifically on the Earl of Godolphin.[40]

Prosecutions for seditious libel continued to be used as an instrument of press control throughout the century – most notably in the trials of the notorious Thomas Woolston[41] – but a turning-point came in the 1760s in the John Wilkes affair and the subsequent 'Junius' controversy. In 1763, Wilkes, a Member of Parliament and the editor of a periodical hostile to the current Tory administration, published an essay, the *North Briton* no. 45, in which he attacked Lord Bute in the fiercest personal terms as a corrupt despot who had brought dishonour upon the crown. The House of Commons declared the publication a libel and expelled Wilkes, but he in turn roused public support in the name of 'liberty' and was re-elected to Parliament multiple times with the House of Commons repeatedly refusing to seat him throughout the 1760s. Then in 1769 a series of scathing attacks on prominent figures began to appear in the *Public Advertiser*, signed only with the name 'Junius'. The identity of 'Junius' was never determined and so there was an attempt to prosecute the newspaper's publisher, Henry Woodfall, in 1770. This was unsuccessful, however, because, even though the question of Woodfall's responsibility as the publisher was beyond the jury's purview – juries at this time were merely asked to determine whether an accused person had in fact published alleged libels – the jury refused to acknowledge that Woodfall could be held

38 Thomas 1969, 74–91.
39 For general discussion, see Siebert 1965, 269–75.
40 Thomas 1969, 65–6.
41 Suarez 2005.

criminally responsible merely for publishing the letters. The Wilkes affair in the 1760s had popularized the ideal of a press free from political restraint. The subsequent jury revolt in the 'Junius' case indicated the depth of popular dissatisfaction with the use of libel law for press control. Moreover, the rising sentiment against the use of the libel laws for political purposes led eventually to the 1792 Libel Act, championed by Charles James Fox, which placed a limit on the state's power to prosecute for seditious libel by giving to juries rather than judges the authority to determine whether a particular publication actually constituted a libel.[42]

The eighteenth century thus witnessed a gradual growth in government tolerance of the press; nonetheless, the story of the struggle for freedom of the press is not one of steady progress. The 1790s and early 1800s, the period of the French Revolution and the subsequent Napoleonic wars, were a time of anxiety characterized by fears of invasion or revolt in which political anxiety led to fierce battles over press freedom.[43] One index to the repressive temper of the period was the prosecution of Tom Paine and others in connection with Paine's enormously popular anti-monarchical tract, *The rights of man* (1792). Another was the passage of the Seditious Societies Act of 1799, which required that all printing presses, makers of presses and founders of type be registered with the authorities; that every item of printed matter include the printer's name and address; and that all printers keep copies of every item printed and be prepared to produce them on demand.[44]

Libel law was one eighteenth-century instrument for press regulation; the so-called 'taxes on knowledge' were another. These included excise duties on paper and stamp duties on newspapers, pamphlets, advertisements and almanacs. Taxes of various kinds had been imposed on paper from time to time in the seventeenth century, but the first duties on printed matter were introduced in 1711, shortly after the passage of the Statute of Anne, with the imposition of a tax on almanacs. This was followed by the Stamp Act of 1712, which introduced duties on newspapers, advertisements and pamphlets.[45] This statute provided for a duty of one penny a sheet on newspapers, together with a duty of one shilling per advertisement. It also mandated a two-shilling-per-sheet tax on pamphlets, which were defined as publications larger than one sheet but fewer than six sheets in octavo. Moreover, it introduced a complex

42 On the Wilkes and 'Junius' affairs, see Thomas 1969, 92–100; and on the Libel Act of 1792 (32 Geo. III c. 60), see Thomas 1969, 112.

43 See Wood, chap. 48, below.

44 30 Geo. III c. 79; Feather 1982, 58–9.

45 10 Anne c. 19. For a summary of the provisions of the Stamp Act and of subsequent changes in rates, etc., see Feather 1982, 52–6; and for fuller discussion of the duties on paper, see Dagnall 1998b.

schedule of duties on various kinds of papers distinguished by size and quality. This tax applied to domestic as well as imported papers, although the rates for domestic papers were lower than for those from abroad.

Whether the Stamp Act of 1712 was intended as an instrument of press regulation to replace the lapsed licensing laws is a matter of debate. The taxes were imposed in a climate of official complaint about licentiousness and many contemporary writers regarded them as an attack on the press. Nonetheless, recent scholars point out that the Act also established duties on a host of other manufactured goods from soap to textiles. They conclude that its primary purpose was to raise revenue to fund the war then being waged in Europe.[46] However true this might be, it is evident that in later times of crisis the taxes were used as a means of press control. In 1815, for example, in the context of post-war social conflict, newspaper duties were raised to a punitive four pence per sheet, a measure that meant, as John Feather notes, that a single copy of a newspaper cost as much as a working man's daily wage.[47]

Issues related to the stamp duties thus became entwined in the early nineteenth century with more general questions of social reform and with the movement for working-class education. Some of the pressures related to these duties and taxes, along with other social discontent, began to be relieved after the passage of the great Reform Bill of 1832. By the time of the Reform Bill there was also, as Donald Thomas reports, a significant decline in the number of political prosecutions for libel.[48] The stamp duties and the excise taxes on paper were not finally abolished until 1855 and 1861 respectively, but it appears that in the first three decades of the nineteenth century the principle of a freer press was gradually becoming accepted.[49]

Conclusion

The period from 1695 to 1830, from the lapse of the Licensing Act to the eve of the Reform Bill, thus saw major transformations in the legal culture within which the book trade operated. In the late seventeenth century, the highly centralized book trade still operated in a style characteristic of the hierarchical society of the Tudor–Stuart period. The key to this system in which a small number of London booksellers dominated the trade was the authority of the

46 Siebert 1965, 305–22, sees the Stamp Act of 1712 as essentially a device to muzzle the press. This view is challenged by, among others, Foxon 1978 and Downie 1979, 149–61.
47 Feather 1988a, 87.
48 Thomas 1969, 176.
49 Downie 1981 discusses the growth of press toleration in the period to 1790; see Thomas 1969, 129–78, on the period 1792–1832.

Stationers' Company over publishing rights. Even when the guild system was supplanted by the Statute of Anne, however, the great booksellers managed to maintain control of their valuable old copyrights for the better part of a century until in 1774 the House of Lords declared copyright to be limited in term. The consequences of this decision were great. The trade was opened up to new entrepreneurs; reprinting flourished; books became cheaper; and the audience for books grew.[50] Moreover, publishers became distinct from booksellers and the modern profile of the trade began to emerge.

Authorship, too, underwent major transformations. In the late seventeenth century, writing for money was regarded as undignified. By 1774, however, professional authorship was accepted. The House of Lords' decision in some ways enhanced the position of authors, but except for a few unusually successful writers, the lot of the professional author was still difficult. Propelled by a sense of injustice, some major authors such as Southey and Wordsworth took it upon themselves to lobby for greater authors' rights. Professional writers thus became actively involved in helping to define copyright law.

The lapse of licensing set in motion a process that led to the transformation of the book trade. But the end of licensing did not mean the end of attempts to regulate the content of published materials. After 1695, however, the state was limited to punishing criminal offenders after the fact and to the enactment of taxation measures, presumably for the purpose of raising revenue. The new modes of press regulation, then, like the liberalized structure of the book trade and the emergence of authors as respectable professionals, reflected the general transformation of Britain in the late seventeenth and eighteenth centuries from the patterns of Tudor–Stuart society to those of a new regime based on ideals of individualism, property and freedom. Gradually over the course of the period, the principle of a press free from overt political pressure and coercion also became accepted.

50 See Raven, chap. 3, above.

5
The rise of the professional author?

DUSTIN GRIFFIN

The standard model of authorship in the 'long eighteenth century' (*c.*1660–1830) is a narrative of transformation and modernization. In this model the eighteenth century witnesses the 'emergence' of 'modern authorship' (whether one dates the symbolic moment of 'birth' as the Copyright Act (8 Anne c. 21) of 1710 or Johnson's famous letter to Chesterfield in 1755, or even as early as Dryden's distinction in the preface to *All for love* (1678), between 'men of pleasant conversation' and 'true poets' who write for 'subsistence').[1] As late as 1675 the symbolic centre of literary culture is still the court, but by 1800 the centre is the 'literary marketplace' of the book trade. The writer at the beginning of the period is typically a financially independent gentleman amateur or else a dependant of the patronage system. By 1800, the writer, now a proud and respected 'professional' man or woman who deals directly with booksellers, has been freed from the shackles of patronage, and can aspire to make a living by the pen. What was once a 'scribal' culture, in which new writings typically circulated in manuscript within a relatively small set of elite readers, becomes 'print culture', in which writing is reduced to standardized type, reproduced in thousands of copies and distributed to a vastly increased readership. Not only does the number of readers increase dramatically; so too does the number of printers, writers, titles and books. As Johnson claimed, the eighteenth century could be called 'The Age of Authors'.[2] The changes in the material and legal conditions of authorship – from 'print technology' to improved systems of distribution and the century-long debate about copyright – help explain the larger change in the way in which authorship was conceived. From the hordes of authors a few familiar figures consistently emerge: Dryden, the 'professional' who resists the cultural authority of 'amateurs' such as the Earl of Rochester; Pope, the first writer to make a living by

1 Shadwell makes essentially the same distinction (between a 'Drammatick Writer' and 'Men of quality, that write for their pleasure') in his preface to *The sullen lovers* (1668).

2 *Adventurer*, 115 (1752–4).

his pen (unless that honour be accorded to Aphra Behn); or Johnson, who by applying his talents to a variety of humble writing tasks virtually 're-invented authorship'.[3]

This composite narrative emerges from most of the recent scholarly work on eighteenth-century authorship – books by Alvin Kernan, Mark Rose, Harold Love, Brean Hammond, Lawrence Lipking, Clifford Siskin and Linda Zionkowski.[4] But the story is as old as James Saunders's *The profession of English letters* (1964), A.S. Collins's *Authorship in the days of Johnson* (1928a) and Alexandre Beljame's *Men of letters and the English public in the eighteenth century* (first published in French in 1881), which established the main lines of the argument on the progressivist assumption that the social and economic conditions of authorship improve over time. Even if the received narrative is broadly accurate about the crucial importance of the eighteenth century as the period of most significant change, it is imprecise and misleading in many of its details. For example, while it is true that patronage was by and large replaced by the so-called 'literary marketplace', the change was very slow and gradual: the patronage system persisted at least until the end of the eighteenth century. Both Pope and Johnson were deeply enmeshed in it.[5] In other respects too authorship was slower to change than the standard model suggests. The 'professional writer', the centrepiece of most accounts of the change in authorship in the period, was by no means established as the dominant model by the end of the eighteenth century.

What is new?

Debunkers might insist that the 'professional author' did not 'emerge' or 'rise' in the eighteenth century: there have always been 'authors' who wrote primarily for money (the 'professional' men of the Elizabethan theatre), surveyed by Edwin Miller in *The professional writer in Elizabethan England* (1959). As for the claim that it is only in the eighteenth century, through the efforts of Johnson and others, that authorship acquires the kind of dignity, status and authority implied by the modern term 'professional', it is easy to show that seventeenth-century writers as diverse as Jonson, Milton and Dryden invoked and exemplified the idea that the 'true poet' (as opposed to the mere hack or drudge) has a high calling (to teach, to adorn the language, to record glorious deeds), and

3 Lipking 1998, 241.
4 Kernan 1987; M. Rose 1993; Love 1993; Hammond 1997; Lipking 1998; Siskin 1998; Zionkowski 2001.
5 Griffin 1996.

readily took on both lofty and humble tasks – from epic poems to histories, dictionaries and grammar books.

Some have argued that our very idea of 'author' itself does not emerge until the eighteenth century. Foucault has theorized that it is only in this period that authorship, formerly a legal category (the author is somebody to whom legal responsibility for a piece of writing can be assigned, somebody who can be punished by the state for writing), becomes an economic category (the author is somebody who owns what he has written).[6] But as any careful historian of copyright observes, eighteenth-century authors almost always immediately sold their owner's right to a bookseller, and, once it was sold, did not think of themselves as legal proprietors of their work: copyright in the eighteenth century is essentially a bookseller's exclusive right to copy (and sell) a work, and not a key to authorial self-images.

Likewise, it is misleading to claim that prior to the eighteenth century the 'author' was essentially regarded as an imitator – of Nature and (since Homer and Nature were the same) of earlier writers – and that by the latter part of the century the 'author' came to be regarded as an 'original genius' whose imagination was 'creative'. The prominence of discussions of 'original genius' in critical essays of the later eighteenth century points to a new term for an old idea: critics and theorists before 1750 assigned a high value to the 'invention' or 'creative imagination' of a true poet such as Homer or Milton (and deplored mere mechanical copying or plagiarism),[7] just as poets and critics after 1750 in fact continued to invoke ideas of mimesis and of the author as the inheritor of literary tradition. One powerful and intriguing idea about literary inheritance – that the poet has literary forefathers and descendants – seems to have dropped out of circulation shortly after 1700. Its most prominent advocate was Dryden, who in his critical prefaces developed the idea that poets belong to lineal 'families', and that poetic fathers transmit something to their sons, and in his poems (notably *MacFlecknoe* and the verses on Oldham and Congreve) speculated about his own poetic father and sons. For whatever reason, eighteenth-century poets and critics did not adopt Dryden's idea. When Harold Bloom picked it up he focused on only one part of the family relationship.[8]

Much about authorship in the long eighteenth century is fundamentally continuous with what came before. Certainly Johnson's *Lives of the poets*, which treats writers from about 1650 to 1750 and notices broad trends in the

6 Foucault 1977.

7 Engell 1981 shows that the idea that the imagination was a 'creative' faculty long pre-dates the late eighteenth-century critics.

8 Bloom 1973.

history of English poetry, records no revolution in the nature of authorship. Perhaps he was too close to the world of authorship he described, for it is clear to most literary historians looking back on the eighteenth century that something – and not just a quantitative increase in writers, books and readers – is new about authorship in the period.

One distinctive feature of the writing of the period is that for the first time authorship is widely thematized. The 'bad poet', a stock figure in Roman satire, takes centre stage in *The rehearsal*, Dryden's *MacFlecknoe* and the lampoons exchanged among the courtiers at the court of Charles II. Recast as the 'hack author', he populates the 'digressions' in such canonical works as Swift's *Tale of a tub*, Pope's *Dunciad* and Fielding's *The author's farce*, and such peripheral works as John Oldham's verse letters, Richard Savage's *Author to be let*, James Ralph's *The case of authors* and Isaac D'Israeli's *Calamities of authors*. Many of Goldsmith's 'Citizen of the World' essays comically treat the humble hack, and much of Johnson's writing focuses (with a mixture of comedy and sympathy) on the humble writer as Everyman, representative of human aspirations and failings.

As Johnson's *Lives* remind us, it is in the eighteenth century that for the first time the author is commonly conceived as a biographical subject. Brief biographical sketches of writers appeared before 1690, but it is only in the eighteenth century that the genre of the poet's 'life' is widely found, from the *Biographia Britannica* (1747–66) to the *Lives of the poets* (1753) attributed to Theophilus Cibber,[9] and the 'life' that was increasingly a standard part of an eighteenth-century edition of a poet's works.[10] As Johnson's tripartite biographies invite us to think, an 'author' is normally someone who produces not a single work but an intelligible sequence of writings; who possesses a consistent 'character'; and whose 'life' can be instructively juxtaposed to (if not found consistent with) his writings.

Within the larger biographical tradition, it became conventional in the eighteenth century to conceive of 'the author' in at least three distinct ways: as figure of fun, as victim and as hero. In its comic version, the author is a hungry fool, confined to his garret (whether for lack of decent clothes, or to escape the bailiff), where he racks his brains to squeeze out copy for the bookseller. In eighteenth-century biographical tradition the author is usually male, despite the fact that after 1700 women enter the ranks of authorship in

9 In fact written by Robert Shiels.
10 'Lives' of Milton by Edward Phillips, John Toland, Elijah Fenton, Jonathan Richardson and Thomas Newton appeared in editions published between 1694 and 1749. Three different lives of Swift appeared in the 1750s, lives of Pope in 1756 and 1769. Mason's edition of Gray (1775) contained a 'Life'.

sharply increasing numbers.[11] It is an image familiar from the pages of Pope, Fielding and Goldsmith, securely comic because, in Pope's terms, we assume the authors are 'not bunglers because they are poor but are poor because they are bunglers' ('A Letter to the Publisher', prefixed to the *Dunciad*). The hungry author in his garret has a seventeenth-century predecessor in Marvell's 'Flecknoe, An English Priest at Rome', but it is in eighteenth-century writing that the type is standardized and widely copied.

The hungry author turns easily into the second type, an unrewarded victim of heartless or careless patrons and booksellers, whose neglect is an indictment of a callous society that has failed to discharge its obligation to support literary merit. This figure is prominent in the mind of Richard Savage, who regarded himself as unjustly neglected, and commonly appears in laments about the decline of patronage in the period, and one writer after another – Spenser, Cowley, Butler, Dryden, Oldham – was fitted to the model by eighteenth-century literary historians. The 'mournful narrative' of authorship – Johnson's term for the 'volumes' of tales of the 'miseries of the learned' and of their 'unhappy lives and untimely deaths'[12] – was updated by Ralph and Goldsmith with later victims: Richard Savage, William Collins, the political writer Nicholas Amhurst, the dramatist Edward Moore. Again, the author-as-victim is not strictly speaking an eighteenth-century invention. Dryden had complained, in a letter asking for payment of his salary, that ''Tis enough for one Age to have neglected Mr Cowley, and sterv'd Mr Buttler.'[13] But the eighteenth century popularized the figure, still prominent at the end of the period in the martyred Chatterton and in D'Israeli's compilation of the *Calamities of authors*.

If the struggling writer overcomes all obstacles and manages to win his due reward, or at least to achieve his sturdy independence, he can turn into a third incarnation: the author as hero, a figure most familiar from the pages of Boswell's *Life of Johnson* and from Pope's satires in the 1730s. In many eighteenth-century versions, from Akenside's odes to Gray's 'Bard', the poet is a kind of legislator, or a patriotic servant of his country. The classical models are Pindar and the Greek lyric poets.[14] Milton is probably the major seventeenth-century model, and Johnson, ordinarily suspicious of authorial heroics and hero-worshipping biographers, does not hesitate to call Milton a 'hero'. But elsewhere Johnson richly recombines and ironizes the century's

11 See Grundy, chap. 6, below.
12 Johnson 2006, III, 120
13 Dryden 1942, 20.
14 Griffin 2002, 63–7.

images of author as fool, victim and hero; in the early 'Life of Savage' (where the self-pitying victim is at least half to blame for his plight); poetic portraits of the inevitably disappointed 'Young Author';[15] the many *Rambler* essays dealing with authorship; and the late *Lives of the poets*, where again and again a poet's aspirations are ill-matched with his accomplishments, and a streak of self-destructiveness dogs his end. Robert Burns thought of the *Lives* as 'martyrologies'.[16]

The author may inevitably fall short of his hopes, but that does not prevent Johnson from regarding authors as a kind of national treasure: 'the chief glory of every people', he wrote in the 'Preface' to the *Dictionary*, 'arises from its authours'. This is another common image of authorship in the period, albeit one designed to promote the interests of authors. It is found as early as John Dennis's claim in 1701 that advancing the arts and learning of a nation will enhance its 'Reputation' and 'Power',[17] and appears in James Ralph's *Case of authors* ('If Heroes and Patriots constitute the first Column of national Glory, Authors of Genius constitute the second') and in D'Israeli ('It is a glorious succession of AUTHORS . . . which has enabled our nation to arbitrate among the nations of Europe').[18] The European reputation of England's great writers – Shakespeare, Milton, Pope – depends in turn on other eighteenth-century developments: the invention of Shakespeare as a 'national' writer, the establishment of 'English Milton' as the modern equivalent of the Greek and Roman epic writers, and the construction of a native English canon of which they are the leading members.[19]

The 'author by profession'

Much, then, is new about the way authorship is conceived in the eighteenth century. But what is probably most important is the appearance of a new figure: the 'author by profession'. The term had no precise meaning: it could be used with derision or pride; and it has often been confused with the later idea of a 'professional writer' – a term that does not appear in the eighteenth century. The essential points to make are two: that 'author by profession'

15 'The Young Author' (1743), in Johnson 1964, 72–3, the portrait of the scholar ('the young enthusiast') in 'The Vanity of Human Wishes', II, 135–74, and the Latin verses written in 1772 after Johnson finished revising the *Dictionary* (Johnson 1964, 271–3).

16 Fussell 1971 on the 'vanity of literary wishes' and the 'irony of literary careers'.

17 Dedication to the Earl of Mulgrave of *The advancement and reformation of modern poetry* (1701), in Dennis 1939–43, I, 207.

18 Ralph 1966, 3; D'Israeli 1793, II 280.

19 Griffin 1986; Kramnick 1998; Terry 2001.

signifies an alternative to the traditional models (whether that of the learned man who writes for fame or the gentleman who writes for pleasure), and that this alternative took a very long time to attain widespread respectability.

'Professional' (as an adjective) is found in Johnson's *Dictionary*, where it means 'relating to a particular calling or profession'. So of course is 'author', which means (among other things) 'a writer in general', and 'profession', which is a 'calling; vocation; known employment', particularly of 'divinity, physick, and law'. 'Known employment' points towards another eighteenth-century term, the 'professed author', which should probably be distinguished from the 'author by profession'. When Johnson says that Swift 'became a professed author',[20] he seems to mean that by putting his name on a title page in 1708 Swift publicly professed himself an author – his previous works having been published anonymously. Likewise, Johnson regards Pope's life as an 'author' as having begun in 1704, when he wrote and circulated his 'Pastorals', but it was only with their appearance in print in 1709 that Pope 'declared himself a poet'.[21]

Johnson does not regard such professed authors as having a 'profession'. His dry remark that Savage, 'having no profession, became by necessity an author', seems to mock the idea that authorship might be a 'profession'. Savage wrote for what Johnson calls 'means of support' – for money. Opportunities to sell one's work – or one's time – had been increasing as booksellers began to look for copy to keep their printers and their presses busy. Since about 1700 writers who wrote – so it was said – simply to support themselves had been dismissed as 'hacks' (from 'hackney', a horse available for hire).[22] Of course, no writer referred to himself as a hack, except in jest.[23]

Over time the numbers of those who wrote 'for bread' increased, whether they took their pay from reputable booksellers who offered 'copy money' for copyrights or simply literary services (so-much-per-page for a translation, a compilation of previously printed material or a pamphlet), from editors like Edward Cave of the *Gentleman's Magazine*, from the ministry or the political Opposition, or from theatre managers like Colley Cibber. Anecdotal evidence suggests that the prospect of earning money from writing was beginning to attract ambitious provincials to London, where such work might more likely be found. When Johnson went up to London in 1737, he reportedly told a

20 Johnson 2006, III, 193.
21 Johnson 2006, IV, 5.
22 *OED*'s first citation for 'hackney' in this sense is 1700.
23 See Iscariot Hackney in Savage's *An author to be let* (1728), and Blotpage, who in Fielding's *The author's farce* (1730) sings of the miseries of the 'hackney for bread'.

bookseller that he intended to 'get his livelihood as an authour'.[24] Such livelihood as was to be found there was pretty much hand-to-mouth. Although stories of Johnson's poverty in his early London days are much exaggerated, it remains true that trying to make a living from writing was still a risky business. When Johnson calls Collins, newly come to London, a 'literary adventurer', he probably has in mind not Collins as bold explorer of the uncharted realms of fancy but, as 'one who puts himself in the hands of chance' ('adventurer', *Dictionary*) – like Shakespeare before him, who also 'came to London a needy adventurer' ('Preface').

Culturally conservative writers such as Pope continued to regard such authors as debasers of literature, but by the second quarter of the century the authors themselves began to declare openly that they wrote for money: they 'professed' themselves to be authors-for-pay. In 1748 Fielding grumbled, a bit defensively, that he did not think 'a Writer, whose only Livelihood is his Pen, to deserve a very flagitious Character, if, when one Set of Men deny him Encouragement, he seeks it from another, at their Expence'.[25] In 1759 Ralph's *The case of authors by profession* is explicitly written to dispute disparagement of contemporary writers for pay as 'profligate Scribblers',[26] and as a kind of quasi-legal defence of their dignity. One wonders if William Guthrie had Ralph in mind when he wrote to one of the new king's advisers in 1762, asking that his pension be continued. The basis for his appeal? 'I am an author by profession' – that is, a man prepared to provide any literary 'services' that the court might need.

Acceptance of such claims came slowly, and even the defenders display some hesitation in making the case for the 'author by profession'. Ralph regards it as inevitable that booksellers and theatre managers will be 'Masters of all the Avenues to every [literary] Market', and implicitly asks political paymasters to reward their hired writers with places. He longs not for the arrival of a new day in which writers will be well paid for their work, but for a return to the days when 'the Link of Patronage . . . held the Great and the Learned together'.[27] Goldsmith too shows considerable ambivalence about the author who writes for money. In one series of essays he adopts the voice of an 'indigent philosopher', a self-confessed hack who says he 'must write, or I cannot live'. Why, he asks, should I be 'ashamed of doing this?' In another

24 Boswell 1791, I, 102. A friend more delicately stated that Johnson planned 'to try his fate with a tragedy [i.e. to get his play performed], and to see to get himself employed in some translation'.

25 *The Jacobite's journal*, in Fielding 1974b, 215. Fielding was defending Ralph against charges of being a political turncoat.

26 Ralph 1966, 13.

27 Ralph 1966, 72.

series he declares, as 'Citizen of the World', that the 'man of letters' in England today can expect both reward and respect from the public who buys his books. In the *Enquiry into the present state of polite learning in Europe*, however, he speaks as a gentleman of leisure, opining that 'writing for bread' reduces the writer to little more than 'the fellow who works at the press' – that is, a printer's boy.[28]

Sir John Hawkins, Johnson's biographer, is a good index of conservative contemporary opinion. He allows 'necessities' as a proper motive for writing, but is uncomfortable if he cannot find that a writer's principles co-operated with his 'necessities', and prefers the 'more liberal motive' of the 'impulse of genius' or the desire for fame. He was 'astonished' to hear Johnson assert 'that he knew of no genuine motive for writing, other than necessity' and the 'assurance of pecuniary profit'.[29] Hawkins implies that 'authors by profession' were beginning to win respect, especially if they acted as independent contractors, 'and vended their compositions when completed' to the bookseller 'who would give most for them'.[30] Fielding is placed in this category. Next in rank come the 'pensioners of the booksellers',[31] who in effect take commissions for work. Here he would put Johnson. And last comes the 'mere literary drudge, equal to the task of compiling and translating, but little capable of original . . . composition'.[32] Here he puts Goldsmith. Lord Camden, who voted against perpetual copyright in *Donaldson* v. *Becket* (1774), shared Hawkins's conservative prejudice, separating 'Men of Genius' who write for 'Glory' and 'Scribblers for bread' who write for 'Gain'.[33] Camden's attitude towards a mere 'author by profession' is confirmed by Boswell's anecdote about Goldsmith complaining that his lordship 'took no more notice of me than if I had been an ordinary man'.

While traditionalists like Hawkins and Camden refer disapprovingly to the 'authors by profession' as 'scribbling' for 'bread', we nowadays are more likely to refer to their decision to enter the 'literary marketplace'. This term, now common in our critical vocabulary, conveys our admiring sense of writers as enterprising and independent producers, freed from the shackles of patronage, appealing directly to the 'reading public', and seeking to earn an honourable living by meeting the needs of those who would buy their books. But it probably also carries our nervous sense, as beleaguered academics in a world dominated by commerce, that writing – by the middle of the eighteenth century – is

28 Goldsmith 1966, III, 182–3; II, 344–5; I, 316.
29 Hawkins 1961, 15, 46.
30 Hawkins 1961, 94.
31 Hawkins 1961, 94.
32 Hawkins 1961, 182.
33 M. Rose 1993, 104. Cf. Rose, chap. 4, above.

becoming a commercial product, and is perhaps on its way to becoming a mere 'commodity', so many sheets of paper covered by printed marks.

'Literary marketplace', like 'professional author', is under-defined and undertheorized. It is now used loosely for three or four different transactions: (1) the author sells a copyright to a bookseller; (2) the booksellers sell shares in copyright to each other; (3) the bookseller hires a writer and pays him so much per page; (4) the bookseller, acting as retailer, sells printed books to the reader. If the term 'marketplace' is used with any precision, it should imply a means, if not an actual place, whereby demand is met by supply, whereby willing buyers meet willing sellers, and where competition among buyers and sellers leads to a price, set by the impersonal force of 'the market' itself, that recognizes merit.

There is little reason to think that the eighteenth-century literary marketplace worked in this way. Historians of the book trade show that very few authors would have had any bargaining power in selling copyrights. Pope may have prompted a 'bidding war' between Tonson and Lintot for his Homer, but he was an exception. Johnson never pressed hard on his own behalf, asking only 200 guineas for his *Lives* and receiving £300, and his refusal to accept less than £10 from Dodsley for 'London' – since Paul Whitehead had received that amount for a poem – is exceptional enough to serve as an amusing anecdote. Even Boswell was sceptical, as we should be, of Johnson's boast about 'the power of his pen in commanding money'. Instead of competing with each other for copyrights, eighteenth-century booksellers sometimes combined into a 'conger' to spread the cost of buying copyrights to proven bestsellers, or to spread the risk of taking on an unproven book, to which they claimed perpetual copyright. Booksellers apparently had little difficulty in hiring needy authors to write for them, and notoriously did not have to pay much. The only real competition within the bookselling system seems to have come from pirates. If this picture is accurate, Ralph was right to claim that all the avenues to the market were controlled by the booksellers. Before literary historians build more claims for the rise of an independent writer who earns his own way, they need to consult the work of historians of the book, and to use the term 'literary marketplace' with more care.

The same applies to the term 'professional writer'. Although Boswell, Goldsmith and Hawkins all refer to writing as a 'profession',[34] it is a mistake to assume that they regard it as similar to the traditional learned professions, or even to the newer emerging ones (estate agent, surveyor, architect). If the term 'professional' is used carefully, it should refer to the fundamental features of

34 Boswell 1970, 801; Goldsmith 1966, I, 308, 312, 314; Hawkins 1961, 97.

the established 'professions' – formal training procedures, entry qualifications, a deliberately limited membership, a career ladder, 'professional' associations that set standards (and thus ultimately maintain prices), and at least the pretence that the prime motivation is not gain but service or the practice of and advancement in an art.[35] Siskin proposes 'disciplinarity' – confining one's attention to a single discipline – as a sign of the 'professionalization' of writing in the period. But it is notable that the characteristic later eighteenth-century author – Johnson, Goldsmith, Hume, Gibbon, Burke, Boswell, Smith, Priestley, even Gray – was not a specialist but a polymath.

As for 'entry qualifications', it was commonly remarked in eighteenth-century England that anybody could be an author.[36] No training, no credentials, no special talents, except a confidence that one possessed them, were required. Pope self-consciously shaped what we would call a 'career' (although the word was not yet used in this sense), but Johnson – more typical of eighteenth-century authors – was still essentially an occasional writer, responsive to both events and invitations. Standards were set not by authors themselves but by the booksellers, though their authority was being challenged by the book 'reviewers' for the new *Critical Review* (1756–) and *Monthly Review* (1749–).[37] Prices for copy were set not by authors but by what booksellers were willing to pay. Such associations as existed were private 'literary clubs', charitable 'societies' (like the Society for the Encouragement of Learning, which provided support to indigent authors) or the airy 'republic of letters' – a French invention that was never really domesticated in England, and was commonly regarded by English writers as more like an 'anarchy', in which authors, far from combining for their common advantage, seemed intent on undoing each other.[38]

Even by the end of the eighteenth century, the 'author by profession' was simply someone who wrote for money in a steady and public way as (in Johnson's terms) an 'occupation' or 'known employment'. Johnson called learning a 'trade' and regarded the humbler authors of London as the useful 'manufacturers of literature'.[39] By the force of his talent, his record of publications and his personality, Johnson struck his contemporaries as a dignified champion of the life of letters. But he is the exception – no one else puts you in mind of Johnson – and we should not extrapolate from his example. In the minds of

35 Cf. Corfield 1995; Holmes 1982; Reader 1966.

36 Johnson, *Idler*, 2 (1758–60), *Adventurer*, 115 (1752–4); Goldsmith, 1762, 29. Cf. *The connoisseur*, 116, 133 (1754–6), on 'lawyers and physicians without practice' who become authors.

37 See Forster, chap. 33, below.

38 Goldsmith, 1762, 20; Johnson, *Rambler*, 145 (1750–2); Fielding, *Covent Garden journal*, 2, 14, 23 (1752), and *Jacobite's journal*, 6, 15, 26 (1747).

39 Johnson, *Rambler*, 145 (1750–2). Cf. Swift 1939–68, x, 81 on the 'Trade of a writer'.

many of Johnson's contemporaries it was not yet clear that (in Hawkins's terms) authorship was yet an 'eligible' profession.[40] Women authors, of course, laboured under a special burden, sneered at as 'prostitutes' since before 1700, merely because they dared to present themselves in print.[41] In 1792 Charlotte Smith, in the 'Preface' to her novel *Desmond*, still feels obliged to apologize for becoming an 'Author by profession', pleading that she is 'compelled by [financial] circumstances'.[42] But, quite apart from the powerful cultural prejudice that branded them, few such authors ever made their living wholly by their pens. In the early part of the period, those few who earned great sums – Dryden, Pope, Gay, Prior – derived much of their proceeds from subscription (a form of patronage). Even after 1750, only a few writers – Fielding, Sterne, Hawkesworth, Gibbon, Burney – received as much as £500 for a single title. Poetry paid less than prose. Not until after 1800 did a bookseller pay as much as £500 for a poem. Scott, who grew rich, was an exception among writers.[43] Wordsworth's total literary earnings – as late as 1835 – were less than £1,000.

Most authors in the first quarter of the nineteenth century retained traditional ambivalence about embracing the emerging 'profession' of letters. Coleridge received income from a variety of sources – lecture fees, copy money, the dramatic author's 'third night'. But he warned the aspiring author to take on some regular employment as the primary means of support – Coleridge himself received a salary for a minor civil service position. The writer who pursues 'the profession of literature, or (to speak more plainly) the trade of authorship' will be tempted to produce what the market requires and to engage in the mere 'manufacturing of poems', recombining the words of other writers into something that will satisfy most readers. And yet, in terms that recall Pope's conception of the 'true poet', Coleridge insisted that there is 'no profession on earth which requires attention so early, so long, or so unintermitting, as that of poetry'. Like Hawkins, Coleridge distinguished between mere talent for 'appropriating and applying the knowledge of others' and real 'genius'.

The gentleman-author

Given the generally discouraging reception that an 'author by profession' received from eighteenth-century contemporaries, it is not surprising to

40 Hawkins 1961, 97.
41 See Grundy, chap. 6, below.
42 Smith 2001, 46.
43 Scott received far more for his novels than his poems, receiving about £1,000 per year as a poet, £15,000 as a novelist.

discover that an alternate model of authorship – the gentleman who wrote for pleasure or fame – continued to shape the way authors thought of themselves right to the end of the long eighteenth century. The ageing Congreve still had before him the example of the gentleman-wits of the Restoration court when he told Voltaire in 1726 that he wished to be considered 'not as an author but [as] a gentleman'.[44] Pope too liked to present himself as a latter-day Restoration wit. In the 'Preface' to his *Works* (1717) he insisted that he 'writ because it amused me . . . and I publish'd because I was told I might please such as it was a credit to please'. Decades later, Gray also preferred to be thought 'a private independent gentleman, who read for his amusement'.[45] Whether or not these claims are credible – Johnson scoffed at them – the fact that they were made at all suggests the lingering power of the old model of the gentleman amateur. Cowper claimed in 1786 to use his pen only for his own amusement: 'I only take it up as a gentleman performer does his fiddle.'[46] Gibbon was pleased to be regarded on his first visit to Paris 'as a gentleman who wrote for his amusement', plainly distinguishable, by his dress and manner, from 'the tribe of authors'. At the end of his life he embraced the title of 'man of letters' – another French import – and even of 'author', but only because he distinguished between the 'Gentleman, possessed of leisure and competency' who is 'encouraged by the assurance of an honourable reward', and the 'wretched' writer whose 'daily diligence is stimulated by daily hunger'.[47]

Authors who could consider themselves gentlemen shared the prejudice against writing for 'necessity' or 'livelihood'.[48] But 'gentleman' (a very broad social category) clearly meant quite different things to Gibbon at the end of the eighteenth century and to the Earl of Rochester or the Earl of Dorset at the end of the seventeenth. We can distinguish at least three varieties of gentleman-writers in the period. First, are what Pope called the 'holiday writers' of the Restoration – 'gentlemen that diverted themselves now and then with poetry' – distinguishing them from 'true poets' – such as himself – who wrote day in and day out.[49] Second, what have recently been called the practitioners of 'social authorship',[50] are men – and women – who wrote not simply for their own pleasure but for a small circle of friends, to whom they circulated their

44 Johnson 2006, III, 70.
45 Johnson 2006, IV, 179.
46 Cowper 1979, III, 101. Cowper commonly claims he writes for 'amusement' or 'employment' – i.e. to keep busy.
47 Gibbon 1966, 126, 153–5, 188.
48 Johnson 2006, III, 76, notes that the physician Sir Richard Blackmore was made a poet 'not by necessity but inclination, and wrote not for livelihood but for fame'.
49 Spence 1966, I, 469.
50 Ezell 1999; Griffin 2005.

works in manuscript. Authorship for such writers – and the early Pope perhaps belongs in this group – was a 'social' activity, in which the consolidation of social bonds was a leading motive. Third, are the gentleman-writers who accepted and even negotiated for money from the booksellers and made writing the primary 'business' of their lives.[51] Typically, they had other sources of income, insisted proudly on their 'independence' from patron, bookseller and even from readers,[52] and claimed to write primarily for fame. Hume, Gibbon, Gray and Cowper belong in this group, as do Pope (who liked to pretend he cared nothing for fame) and Boswell (when not occupied as a full-time lawyer). It is notable that most of these writers belong to the latter part of the century, suggesting that the model continued to have validity in 1800. Byron carried on the mode: he wanted his poems to sell, but maintained his literary identity as a titled gentleman.[53]

Can we call such writers 'professional'? Not without misrepresenting their own views of themselves, and not without blurring important distinctions between them and the 'author by profession'. One of the ironies of literary history is that it was probably the combination of the hard-pressed humble eighteenth-century 'authors by profession' with the successful gentleman-authors – who made up a relatively small proportion of the authors of the day but kept alive the idea that the true author was animated by genius and the goal of literary fame – that set the stage for the appearance, by the mid-nineteenth century, of the talented 'man [or woman] of letters' who might lead a well-rewarded life, and might aspire to be regarded as the equivalent of the members of the honourable learned professions.

51 See Johnson on Pope: 'He considered poetry as the business of his life' (Johnson 2006, IV, 63); and Hume: 'Almost all my life has been spent in literary pursuits and occupations' ('My own life', in Hume 1879, I, x).

52 Here the gentleman and author by profession converge. Johnson proudly proclaimed the dignity of the 'independent' writer (*Rambler*, 208), and Goldsmith celebrated the writer's 'independence (Goldsmith 1966, II, 345; cf. 396–9).

53 Magnuson 1998 argues that Romantic authors carefully identified themselves as qualified to publish by their education, rank or office (e.g. '. . . of Jesus College, Cambridge').

6

Women and print: readers, writers and the market

ISOBEL GRUNDY

What difference did women make to the book trade during the long eighteenth century? Female authorship and female readership burgeoned during this period, and some women were also active in the trade itself. If this had not been the case, if women had been illiterate and if writers, publishing workers and readers had all been male, would the production and consumption of books, what Robert Darnton calls 'the social and cultural history of communication by print', have developed differently?[1]

Such hypothetical questions are clearly unanswerable, up there in the lunar sphere along with questions about the survival of Queen Anne's son and Wolfe's defeat on the Plains of Abraham. Nevertheless, just asking them may help to clarify the issue of what is being investigated in a study of women and eighteenth-century print culture. Any account of women's contributions to the eighteenth-century book trade and the practices of reading and writing, or of the difference between their experience and that of men, keeps one eye on the unanswerable questions.[2]

Women's participation was already considerable when this period began, and more so by the end. If their part in the actual production of books shows no signs of growth, the opposite is the case in every activity surrounding the book trade. Female literacy rates have been estimated as 25 per cent in 1714, as against male rates of 45 per cent, as 40 per cent by mid-century (with male rates at 60 per cent), and as increasing steeply thereafter. But this rise in literacy was far outstripped by the rise in proportionate numbers of women publishing or otherwise circulating their writings. In 1988 Judith Stanton estimated the long eighteenth century's published and identified women writers as 913; the count today would be higher, owing to identities newly established for some of those

1 Darnton 1990, 107.

2 Stanton 1988 gathered material for research, in a bibliography of work up to 1988, mostly in English, which runs to almost a thousand titles; Broomhall 2002 asked how women's experience differed from men's in sixteenth-century France.

publishing as 'a Lady', 'a Gentlewoman' and so on. The numbers per decade, having risen fairly steadily during the first half of the century, took off around 1760, and thereafter virtually doubled every decade, including the early decades of the nineteenth century.[3]

Stanton deals with women publishing across the whole generic range. James Raven, looking at just the novel from the 1770s to the end of the century (a period during which the genre became both more dominant and more frequently seen as feminized), finds women in the majority among the most prolific novelists, and equally numerous with men among the most successful novelists, whether success is measured in esteem or in numbers of reissues and reprints. His investigations take into account the absence of an author's name from any but a minority of novels by writers of either sex at this time. With this proviso, he notes that among novels claimed by name, only one year of the 1770s produced more with female than with male names. Over the 1780s the proportion of named female novelists was twice that of named male novelists, though it was a mere 10 per cent of the whole; during the last three years of the decade, as more novelists began revealing their identity, the proportion of named women novelists soared to 33 per cent of the total, or four times as many as named men. While the general trend away from reticence continued during the 1790s, the relative proportions shifted; the proportion of named women went down by a third, while that of named men doubled. The deliberate promotion of female authorship which Raven perceives was of short duration; nevertheless, when the identifications made by modern scholarship are applied, women novelists increased their share of new fictional titles from 14 per cent over the 1750s and 1760s, through something under a third in the 1770s, to almost 50 per cent for the last three decades of the century reckoned together.[4]

This remarkable rise in numbers of women readers and authors is reflected in the steady rise, both in amount and in shrillness, of commentary on them in these roles. Criticism of literary behaviour in women grew more strident even as some of their former public roles disappeared. For instance, the seventeenth-century habit of personal distribution of one's own works survived through the Restoration period among radical-sect writers, many of them women. If we can believe their own statements, such women as Margaret Fell and Joan Whitrowe often delivered printed exhortations into the hands of William III (either in person or by proxy), as they had into those of Charles II before him.

3 Brewer 1997, 167; Stanton 1988, 247, 248.
4 Raven 2000a, 39–40, 45, 48.

Elinor James, as a manager of a substantial publishing business and a supporter of the establishment in church and state, may never have accosted a monarch in this way, but the titles of her works reflect the custom.

While this practice did not survive the Stuarts, literary patronage retained its importance throughout the period, and ladies of the nobility and gentry, from Queen Caroline downwards, remained significant in the ranks of the patrons and dedicatees, particularly for women writers. They also figured in the less rarefied ranks of subscribers and supporters, and sometimes later on as reviewers. Though few of the leading book collectors were women, a surprising number of them did amass substantial personal collections, and country-house libraries carried the lasting impression of the reading choices of female as well as male family members.

In the Augustan period, as English print culture grew towards maturity, writing 'was first brought to market in something like the modern way ... By the end of the century there were words for sale in every village in the nation.'[5] Female workers clustered around the lowlier tasks of this emerging trade in London and the provinces. Dr John Campbell reputedly married a printer's devil (who is famous for Johnson's crediting her with 'a bottom of good sense'[6]). Women (and often children) hand-coloured illustrations, mostly for children's books. Women worked in the binding trades, though as the century wore on the better-paid areas like finishing began to exclude them. They served as bookshop employees, like the novelist Eliza Fenwick working as manager and sales clerk in the Juvenile Library, the children's bookshop owned by William and Mary Jane Godwin.

In the book trade itself, family involvement was not something that would be specifically noted at a time when most publisher-booksellers lived in the same building with their business operation. Women's contribution was nevertheless a factor at every level – from operators of established publishing houses and their staff, though the trade publishers, mercuries and owners of circulating libraries, to those who staffed bookshops and libraries, and to the hawkers who cried broadsides and pamphlets about the streets – amounting to what Paula McDowell calls 'a vast network of women printers and publishers'.[7] Feminist historians have recently expressed the hope of synthesizing two

5 McIntosh 1998, 5.

6 Boswell 1934–50, IV, 99. Neither the old *DNB* nor the new *ODNB* dignifies this anecdote with a mention.

7 Correspondence with M.L. Turner, 14 July 2003; McDowell 1999, 145, 135. Though a woman is credited with being the first bookseller to branch out into lending, only one woman (Ann Ireland of Leicester) is named among library proprietors in 1770, a year when lending libraries were flourishing all around the country – Blain, Clements and Grundy 1990, under Circulating Libraries; Raven 2000a, 84–5.

areas of enquiry: about women in the book trade and about writing by women.[8]

The hawkers' trade, like other forms of rock-bottom retailing, was much practised by urban labouring-class women.[9] Such women achieved potential visibility for historians chiefly when they fell afoul of the law, in which condition they showed remarkable nerve and resourcefulness. One of them petitioned a minister of state for release from prison; others, sentenced to the pillory, took up a collection from the sympathetic crowd; others advertised their wares by singing, or altered the printed title to something more inflammatory, or distorted or embroidered the text.[10]

Parallels may be drawn between women's print-trade experience and their writing experience. As labouring-class women hawked paper wares for a hand-to-mouth subsistence, so women of the middling sort who were desperate to earn money turned to authorship (which, apart from teaching, sewing, retail sales at the micro level or prostitution in one form or another, was their only option). If the higher reaches of the book trade were driven by pursuit of profit and the higher reaches of literature by the pursuit of fame, women in the lower reaches of each often had their sights on survival.

While the hawkers, the hand-colourers and Fenwick urgently needed the money, the book trade seems also on occasion to have found casual or amateur work for middling young women with pretensions to gentility. Robert Dodsley 'employed' Elizabeth Cartwright (later Coltman, mother of the anti-slavery writer Elizabeth Heyrick) in rather the same fashion that Edmund Cave employed Elizabeth Carter: in each case a genteel young woman worked, probably unwaged, at jobbing journalism (and in Heyrick's case at proof-reading) in the way that family members did in family businesses. Carter developed into a full-fledged author, Coltman into a letter-writer and the mother of a publishing woman activist.

The largely hidden contribution by women, minor but significant, tends to be mentioned by contemporaries only in the absence of a visible male hand. By custom the Stationers' Company, like other guilds, allowed masters' widows to trade. Widows make up the vast majority of the 3,000 women already in Michael Turner's database on members of the London book trades (in progress) from about 1557 to 1830, though only a minority actually traded. Almost all the women

8 McDowell 1999, 136 – quoting Bell, Parfitt and Shepherd 1990.

9 There is an echo of their calling in the street ballad-singer in Isabella Kelly's *Joscelina, or the rewards of benevolence* (1797), who doubles as a prostitute but whose friendship helps to save the heroine from prostitution. The ballads these two sing at St James's Coffee House are melancholy-romantic, not political.

10 McDowell 1998, 58, 84–5, 96–7; 1999, 143.

active in the trade were active as wives or daughters if not as widows, and about 10 per cent of London publishing houses were in fact run by women.[11] *The new Oxford dictionary of national biography* has kept its promise to improve coverage of women in the book trade, but without changing the overall picture. Meanwhile, the two volumes of the *Dictionary of literary biography* that deal with the eighteenth-century book trade (volumes CLIV and CLXX, edited by James K. Bracken and Joel Silver) number four female names (two each) among their entries: Tace Sowle, Abigail Baldwin,[12] Anne Dodd and Mary Jane Godwin. Of these it was leading Quaker printer Sowle who had the most distinguished career: a success story spanning the reigns of William III to George II. She took over the family firm from her elderly father and ran it herself during her marriage and her long widowhood, distributing books in England, Europe and the colonies.[13] Baldwin and Dodd each took over from her husband and became a name to be reckoned with in the trade. While these three women were, it seems, raised in the London commercial/industrial scene, Mary Jane Godwin came from further up the middling ranks. As second wife of William Godwin, she brings to mind other associations than that with the book trade; but because she had experience in children's bookshops and in translating, the couple addressed their financial problems by launching a children's publishing house and attached shop, the Juvenile Library, in 1805. In the new, juvenile market niche, writing (and commissioning books from friends) had come together with publishing and selling.

The Juvenile Library, stocking school supplies as well as books, resembled those small-scale shops, commonly run by women, in which books or pamphlets shared shelf space with a highly miscellaneous stock. Mary Chandler of Bath probably stocked her own extremely popular *Description of Bath* at her shop opposite the Pump Room, as a sideline among her millinery goods. Laetitia Pilkington combined running a pamphlet shop with writing letters to order. Elizabeth Boyd, raised by the subscribers to her novel *The happy-unfortunate, or the female page* (1732) 'from almost the lowest Condition of Fortune', used her capital to realize her dream of opening a pamphlet and stationery shop.[14] From it she later printed and sold works of her own.

11 Correspondence with M. L. Turner, 14 July 2003; Simonton 1998 (quoting Olwen Hufton), 49, 61. The Company's dealings with widows mostly concerned inheritance of shares in the English Stock or pensions (see Turner, chap. 14, below).

12 Abigail Baldwin is called 'Anne' in Bracken and Silver 1996 and in one of the *ESTC*'s expansions of the 'A.' in her colophons. Among many other potential inclusions are Elizabeth Nutt, Mary Cooper and Elinor James, who said she spent forty years in the print trade and thought of masters and journeymen as her brothers (James 1702). A discussion of late eighteenth-century printers who worked on novels mentions only one firm in which a woman was partner (Raven 2000a, 82).

13 Bracken and Silver 1996, 249–53; McDowell 1998, 42 n. 13.

14 Boyd 1732, prelims.

An equally porous line divided such shops from circulating libraries, which also dealt in fancy goods as well as books.[15] The novelist Mary Collyer worked with her husband, Joseph, in his bookselling and circulating-library business; while her tenuous place in history comes from her writing, the trade probably absorbed the larger part of her time. The circulating-library ownership of Ann Yearsley has entered the public mind as part of a good story: an untaught labouring-class poet who clashed with her genteel patrons and then proved a failure in business. This generally accepted version masks the more complicated ascertainable facts. As a milkwoman, owner of the cows whose milk she sold, Yearsley had belonged to the bottom rung of the capitalist ladder. Running a library, as the best possible way of drawing an income from her literary earnings, bore some similarity to running a small dairy herd. She opened her library in January 1793, in the Colonnade or Crescent at Bristol Hot Wells. While tradition says it was a business failure, evidence suggests the opposite. The family lived well in the building which also housed the library, and the sale of it a few years later probably launched the highly successful business career of Yearsley's one surviving son.[16]

To be a woman in business at this period, even as a widow, was to be an anomaly. R. Campbell's *The London tradesman* (1747) – designed, as its full title explains, to help parents choose careers for their offspring – goes into informative detail about trades like that of milliner (for girls) and 'bookseller' and printer (for boys); the latter description mentions an opening for girls, but only for colouring illustrations.[17] Of Bracken and Silver's publisher women, all but Baldwin filled positions that were in some way marginal. Sowle was the dominant publisher for a sect that was 'every where spoken against',[18] though its energy and influence were disproportionate to its numbers. Dodd, as a mercury, was something of a shadowy figure, an agent for the actual owners of copyrights.[19] The Godwins (at a date when huge fortunes had been made in publishing, and the great houses were major players on the cultural scene) published in a genre which, even if radicals had hopes invested in it for social engineering, was of low status and largely associated with women. By the time of the Juvenile Library, the mainstream book trade coexisted with the specialized sub-field of female-gendered children's publishing.

15 Benedict 2000, 162.
16 Waldron 1996, 209–11, 272.
17 Suarez 2000, 132.
18 The phrase is from the opening of Margaret Fell's hard-hitting pamphlet *A declaration and an information from us the people of God called Quakers* (1660).
19 Treadwell 1982a, 123–4.

Were the day-to-day business decisions of book-trade women influenced by their gender, and was women's presence in the trade useful to women writers? One would suppose not. The path to success would seem to have involved behaving like a man, not being deflected into inappropriately female behaviour. A few clues to specific incidents are insufficient to form a judgement. *The Female Tatler*, a pseudonymous periodical launched on 8 July 1709 in response to what were perceived as anti-woman opinions in Steele's original, split in two with the nineteenth number. *Female Tatler* 19 from the original publisher, Benjamin Bragg, squared off against *Female Tatler* 19 from Abigail Baldwin. Bragg having issued the first eighteen numbers, it appears that he and the unidentified author had a difference of opinion which produced the switch to Baldwin. If indeed the author was female, the grounds of complaint against Bragg *may* have been gendered; and the most likely author of the early numbers, Delarivier Manley, *may* already have been in a position to take an inside view on account of her common-law relationship with a publisher, John Barber.[20] Certainly Lady Mary Wortley Montagu was indignant when in 1737 the (male) printer of her political journal *The Nonsense of Common Sense* sought to spice up her argument by foisting in a bawdy joke (a joke, moreover, about a man forcing sex on a woman for her own good).[21] Deliberate choice of a female publisher was not, however, really an option for either Manley or Montagu – although Sarah Gardner's unpublished play *The advertisement* (1777) imagines its heroine selecting a hack writer on account of her female gender.[22]

If women were anomalies in business, they were to some extent anomalies in property-holding too. Books might fairly rank as personal effects, a category of possession which did not automatically pass from wife to husband on marriage. Women, however, no matter what their marital status, had generally 'smaller disposable income[s]' than men, and this restricted their book-ownership. Several (like Catharine Cockburn, née Trotter, and Isabella Kelly) later owned no copy of works they had written: it seems that publishers did not offer free copies except in lieu of cash payment.[23] Among the clientele of one provincial book business, women made up a higher proportion of borrowers than of buyers, even while they remained a minority of borrowers.[24] Borrowing,

20 Prescott and Spencer 2000, 44, 45 and n. 7, 48–9. An Everyman selection of the *Female Tatler* edited by Fidelis Morgan (1992) is not to be recommended.

21 Montagu 1993, 112 n. 3, 127.

22 Manuscript in private hands. See Grundy 1988.

23 Dorothea Primrose Campbell, for instance, received twenty copies from A. K. Newman as sole remuneration for her Shetland novel *Harley Radington: a tale* (1824) (Royal Literary Fund MSS, Royal Literary Fund, London).

24 Fergus 1984, 178.

meanwhile, carried some stigma among the moneyed or cultivated. Susanna Haswell Rowson shows herself unusually sympathetic towards the circulating library when she makes it a site of self-education for the lower-class heroine of her *Rebecca, or the fille de chambre* (1792).

Books owned by women usually passed on or back into undifferentiated stocks. When they appeared in the sale room, they often came decorously and anonymously as 'the property of a lady'. The first Duke of Kingston, father of Lady Mary Wortley Montagu, died during the printing of his private library catalogue (the first in England). This sumptuous folio lists some seventeenth-century titles which seem likely to have reached the library through former Pierrepont brides: early works either written by women, or about women in general, or about individual women, most of them saints or queens. It powerfully suggests the way the country house library, no matter how masculine its ambiance in furnishing and decoration, must have been amassed by individuals of both sexes.[25]

Women were, however, no strangers to the masculine world of book ownership. Elinor James, having got her hands on her late husband's library against his wishes, donated it in 1711 to Sion College, where it helped to found a major religious institutional collection. Elizabeth Elstob and Elizabeth Thomas each lost a considerable collection of books when poverty overtook her: Thomas sold hers for a third of their value; Elstob left hers with a friend and was never able to reclaim them. The sale catalogue of the great Shakespearean collector George Tollet explicitly combined his library with that left him by the poet Elizabeth Tollet, his aunt.[26] One of the greatest female collectors, Frances Mary Richardson Currer, of Eshton Hall, Craven, in Yorkshire, specialized in the higher-status, masculine-gendered classical and scientific texts. She had her library catalogue privately printed in successive forms: forty copies in 1820, a hundred copies of a longer version in 1833, which, like the Duke of Kingston's, contained engravings of the owner's house and its library rooms.[27]

While subscribers' or metropolitan libraries were mostly male in membership (Liverpool in 1760 had a single female member), they held plenty of female-authored work.[28] In Catherine Hutton's novel *Oakwood Hall* (1819), the library of the Hall's patriarch contains only one woman author (Elizabeth Inchbald), but his spinster sister is a mine of information about authors of her own sex, including Eliza Haywood, Frances Brooke, Elizabeth Griffith,

25 Grundy 1994, 3.
26 Grundy 1994, 4.
27 James Burmester bookseller's catalogue no. 49, part II, 27; catalogue of the Bodleian.
28 Brewer 1997, 180; Raven 1992, 128–9.

Wollstonecraft, 'Miss Owenson', Phebe Gibbes (not identified by name), and the moderns Burney and Edgeworth.

Hutton seems to suggest that women owned more female-authored books than men did. This hypothesis needs to be considered in the light of eighteenth-century women writers' gradual penetration of the market. The women customers of Samuel Clay of Warwick did not select books according to sex of author; but in an era of frequently anonymous authorship, this was hardly an obvious criterion. It seems highly likely that women of professional or upper-class families, who were better informed about the nature of authorship and of patronage, sometimes selected books on account of the author's gender. The library of the late Queen Charlotte, auctioned by Christie's on 9 June 1819, included Jane Austen's works, plus titles by Catherine Cuthbertson, Georgiana, Duchess of Devonshire, Christian Isobel Johnstone, Alethea Lewis, Anna Seward, Jane West and many more. The 560 works identified as in the possession of Lady Mary Wortley Montagu (either at the time when she went abroad in 1739 or after her return in 1762) include 87 titles by (or translated or adapted by) women.[29]

Montagu's library was a fluid, unstable entity. As a young woman she was equally energetic in exchanging books with female correspondents (novels in French and English, current poetry, Bath lampoons, as well as unpublished work) and in applying herself to the classics and to works of scholarship in the family library. She built up her collection over her entire adult life, even though she lived on a tight budget. In London she no doubt frequented booksellers' shops; in Venice in the late 1750s she methodically scanned the advertisements in English newspapers for titles (mostly novels and memoirs) to request from home.

The circulation of women's books is richly if unsystematically recorded in surviving inscriptions: books were given by parents, siblings, spouses, godparents, friends – and authors. Housed in closets rather than libraries, they were often disrespectfully treated. Margins or endpapers were used for sums or shopping lists; children wrote their names over and over again in books belonging to adults. More serious annotators included some eminent women. Mary Astell comprehensively defaced Montagu's copy of *Pensées diverses écrites à un Docteur de Sorbonne* by Pierre Bayle (4th edn, Rotterdam, 1704) because 'no lover of Truth can read it without a just Indignation'.[30]

29 Grundy 1994, 5, 7. The total excludes books for which details were not recorded.
30 Grundy 1994, 7.

Hester Lynch Piozzi too was a tireless annotator, both knowledgeable and opinionated.

Patronage through subscription or dedication was important to publishing women, the great majority of whom would have wished to extract an income from their work if this had been possible, and had no prospect of doing so through their publisher alone.[31] A sample of 230 dedications by women writers shows female dedicatees outnumbering males by 119 to 102.[32] Women receiving dedications fall into various groups: a high proportion of royalty; peeresses and others chosen for rank; personal friends or relations apparently chosen for affection or solidarity.

A few writers (Elizabeth Carter, Eliza Fenwick, Joanna Baillie, the didactic novelist Maria Susanna Cooper, Barbarina, Lady Dacre) garnered dedications by their literary achievements; others, like Mary Champion de Crespigny and Georgiana, Duchess of Devonshire, were no doubt chosen for their patronage record rather than for their published novels. Similarly, the 'Ladies of Llangollen', Eleanor Butler and Sarah Ponsonby, gleaned dedications because of their personal reputation. Some writers (like Ann Hatton or 'Anne of Swansea', who was born a Siddons) looked to the theatre for dedicatees: when Hatton dedicated to the Countess of Derby, the title was no doubt less important to her than the countess's stage career as the comedienne Elizabeth Farren.

Regular, professional dedicators – such as the Restoration playwrights Aphra Behn and Mary Pix, and the novelists Mary Davys, Eliza Haywood, Charlotte Lennox, Ann Hatton and Barbara Hofland – were obviously interested in building brand-name recognition for themselves as well as garnering the conventional ten-guinea fee. Multiple volumes or revised editions offered chances for extra dedications. A proto-feminist concept of networking is evident in writers who dedicated to women only, like Davys, Elizabeth Elstob and Isabella Kelly. Some writers (or the same writers on a different occasion) preferred to use the dedication for a *jeu d'esprit*, an assertion of personality or a gesture of affection. Davys, who began by addressing useful contacts such as a Dublin judge's daughter, Swift's friend Esther Johnson

31 See Fergus and Thaddeus 1987. Over the last three decades of the century the average publisher's payment to a woman for a novel was around £80, but this average is skewed by a few spectacular payments, for instance to Ann Radcliffe (Raven 2000b, 51).

32 These 230 dedications are those by women made between 1695 and 1800 and currently mentioned in Brown, Clements and Grundy 2006 (results of tag search on Dedication, October 2008). Group dedications (Margaret Cavendish, Duchess of Newcastle, to the universities of Oxford and Cambridge; Jane Sharp to midwives; Hannah Wolley to ladies skilled in housekeeping) have been counted where they imply uniform gender.

('Stella') and the future Queen Anne, inscribed later novels 'To the Ladies of Great Britain' and 'To the Beaus of Great-Britain'. Haywood, who regularly chose the powerful in various fields, may have intended irony in addressing *The fatal secret; or, constancy in distress* (1724) to Sir William Yonge (about to divorce his wife with immense profit to himself). In dedicating her tragedy *Lucius, the first Christian King of Britain* (1717) to Richard Steele, Delarivier Manley perhaps hoped to engineer a rapprochement after a quarrel. Late in the period wit gives way to whimsy or sentiment, in dedications to the public, or the author's subscribers, or young children, or even grandchildren.

A comparable sample of subscription publishing (a later tactic for women than dedication) yields more evidence of female networking. Subscription, already well established for specialized publications like Elizabeth Elstob's *An English-Saxon homily* (1709, translated from Ælfric), was first used for fiction in 1724 by Mary Davys (*The reform'd coquet*). Sarah Fielding followed with *Familiar letters between the principal characters in David Simple* (1747). The name most frequently seen on women authors' subscription lists is that of Elizabeth Montagu, closely and equally followed by Samuel Johnson, Frances Boscawen and Georgiana, Duchess of Devonshire. It may not be fanciful to discern here three interlocking spheres of influence: social, intellectual and bluestocking (the last paralleled later by the less cohesive group of the 1790s radicals). Writers themselves, even when very far from rich, subscribed occasionally for others' works: Elizabeth Carter appears as often as the aristocratic one-time novelist Lady Hawke; Joanna Baillie is prominent; even such obscure, provincial or non-affluent figures as Elizabeth Ryves, Ann Jebb, Elizabeth Helme, Mary Meeke, Elizabeth Bonhote, Charlotte Smith and the young Jane Austen subscribed on occasion.

Subscription publishing was no panacea. Charlotte Lennox never turned a satisfactory profit this way, and abandoned two subscription projects unrealized. Mary Barber (who seems to have made a number of business errors in organizing her subscription[33]) imagines in 'To a Lady, who commanded me to send her an Account in Verse, how I succeeded in my Subscription' her work being scorned on sexist grounds. Elizabeth Boyd wrote indignant 'Verses on Capt. D—s, who after subscribing to a certain Pamphlet, and keeping it upwards of Nine Months, both refused to pay for it, and returned it Unsalable'. But a number of women writers (including those remote from the metropolis) commanded impressive and surely profitable subscription lists: Jane Cave's swept the west country, Ann Gomersall's brought together Leeds and the

33 Budd 2002.

Portsmouth area, Henrietta Battier's involved many of the big literary and cultural names of Dublin and London (where she had visited, though she lived in her native Ireland). Mary Barber's poems mustered more subscribers than Pope's Homer (though to disappointing financial effect), and Frances Burney famously supported her family on the subscription proceeds of *Camilla*.

In Jean Marishall's account of her economic travails as a novelist, set out in *A series of letters* (1788), subscription saves the day. She became disillusioned with sale of copyright when Francis Noble's offer of a 'very genteel price' for a novel in progress proved to be not a hundred guineas but five. (She managed, at least, to negotiate an additional entitlement to unlimited copies at trade price.) She became likewise disillusioned with dedicating to the queen when her paltry ten-guinea donation had to be offset against the cost of a special, expensive binding. For her, subscription proved the best among unsatisfactory options.[34] Eliza Kirkham Mathews's posthumous *What has been* (1801) features another publisher who (like the fictionalized Noble) uses a veneer of jovial compliment to mask absolute disbelief in female talent. The publishing section of *What has been*, in which the heroine's husband struggles to negotiate from a position of weakness, is a forcefully realistic moment in this novel's thickets of Gothic horror: the modern business practices of publishing, it seems, are the equivalent of Dark Age oppression.

Though women produced cultural comment on publishing practices (notably the conservative opinions voiced by Elizabeth Montagu in her contributions to her friend Lord Lyttelton's *Dialogues of the dead* (1760) and in her two unpublished dialogues in the Huntington Library), their fictionalized treatments are generally more compelling than their arguments. Countess Brillante in Mary Herberts's eccentric romance *The adventures of Proteus* (1727) has a self-referential function (the book she is writing turns out to be *The adventures of Proteus*), and she is a commercial success, with a sixth edition of her works in press – yet she has some of the qualities for which women writers are satirized, being an irrepressible talker and a glutton for praise. Charlotte Smith too transmutes the pains of authorship into comedy in her portrait of Mrs Denzil in *The banished man* (1794), but satire and bitterness surface in Denzil's relations with her illiterate and politically time-serving publisher Joseph Clapper (a barely veiled allusion to Joseph Bell). Both Laetitia Matilda Hawkins in her first identified novel, *The countess and Gertrude, or modes of discipline* (1811), and Sydney, Lady Morgan, in *Florence McCarthy: an Irish tale* (1818),

34 Marishall 1789, II, 151–2, 156, 162ff., 169.

present fictional women writers who are part-idealized, part-mocked, part-autobiographical.

It is hard to generalize about women writers' remuneration, but easy to see that it was lower than that of men. No women approached the level of profit made by Dryden from his Virgil translation (£1,200) or by Pope from Homer, and while authors' earnings stayed ahead of inflation over the course of the century, the gender gap did not narrow.[35] While Frances Burney's £2,000 for *Camilla* (half for subscription, half for sale of copyright) looks munificent as a lump sum or even as a year's income, her lifetime earnings from authorship compare very badly with the proceeds of land-ownership or steady paid employment. Scholars have only recently addressed the professionalization process self-administered by eighteenth-century women writers, and the outcomes of choices about different modes of publication (sale of copyright as against bearing the risk in hopes of profit, for instance).[36] Charlotte Lennox's literary profits, Betty Schellenberg suggests, should be computed to include the fees she received for dedications, on one hand, and her husband's earnings in his job (which was bestowed in compliment to her works) on the other.[37] If Hannah More was 'almost ashamed' to look back on a lifetime's literary earnings of about £30,000,[38] that was because the computation, either of a lifetime's expenses or of a woman's literary work, was unfamiliar, and she had no scale for comparison.

High earnings enabled Dryden and Pope to say they cared for fame rather than profit; low earnings might render the very idea of seeking fame problematic. After printing her hope that her radical novel might prove 'IMMORTAL', Eliza Fenwick found herself running a 'school' for six children under five in order to earn £32 a year, or less than her husband could make in a month by translating with her as amanuensis. The school was, however, more reliable.[39] It does not appear that she ever finished her second novel, though the *Monthly Magazine* ran a puff in 1800 and Charlotte Smith was watching for it to appear. Fenwick did publish at least six children's books during the years 1804–6, besides others later. These offered a smaller, but quicker and surer return than writing for adults. Noble had told Marishall that genteel novelists like Maria Susanna Cooper (whose husband was a clergyman) were happy to write for

35 Suarez 2000, 132, 133.
36 Fergus and Thaddeus 1987.
37 Schellenberg 2002.
38 M. G. Jones 1952, 186.
39 Fenwick 1998, 37; Grundy 1998, 11.

two guineas a volume.[40] Here the non-professional proved the enemy of the professional.

Despite this rehearsal of woes and problems, the century ended with women active in some new book-trade trends: in new ways of illustrating and binding, and in content-related developments. Circulating libraries, which enjoyed their heyday between 1790 and 1820,[41] did cater effectively if not exclusively for female clients, and were a major outlet for women's works. Women practised in most of the new or newly dominant genres: the novel first and foremost, but also children's literature, the national tale, the album and gift book, colonialist travel writing, the major literary series or collection, reviewing,[42] popular science and many more. Less hearteningly, they were prominent among the clients of the Royal Literary Fund, founded in 1791 to offer charitable support to indigent authors. The question of what difference they made to the book trade might be answered cynically (they kept prices and authors' earnings low; they supplied foot-soldiers for literary combat and boosted the figures of the literary marketplace), but the question as to what difference they made to literature is only just being addressed by literary historians.

40 Marishall 1789, I, 159.
41 Benedict 2000, 164.
42 The apparently unproblematic practice of reviewing books for children gave Sarah Trimmer an entrée into all the most vexed controversies of the day (M. Myers 1990).

PART III THE TECHNOLOGIES AND AESTHETICS OF BOOK PRODUCTION

7

The technologies of printing

JAMES MOSLEY

Introduction

The technique of printing and its ancillary processes is more certainly known for the eighteenth century than for any previous period. This is due above all to the publication of a series of technical manuals, of which the outstanding example is Joseph Moxon's *Mechanick exercises* of 1683–4, but also because many of the processes of the 'hand-press period' survived in common use in the printing industry until the last quarter of the twentieth century and were familiar at first-hand to historians of the book, some of whom created their own 'laboratory' or 'bibliographical' presses in order to replicate the conditions in which early texts had been produced.[1] The correction of composed type and the assembly of lines into pages is one example, but a fundamental one, of this continuity. Although in Britain after 1900 books were increasingly set on the Monotype machine, its product consisted of justified lines of separate type, and although the first proofs were made on slips from type in long galleys (a practice that did not become common until after the period covered by this volume), type was still corrected, letter by letter, by a compositor using a bodkin, and was then made up into pages by hand, and imposed in the manner described by Moxon and his successors.

This long continuity was broken with the disuse of printing from relief type during the last quarter of the twentieth century, leaving the historian increasingly dependent upon other sources of information. This needs to be borne in mind because it can sometimes be discerned that technical literature gives a partial or even a misleading account of contemporary technology. Moxon's one-sided promotion of the 'new-fashioned' printing press is one example. Disagreements about the details of the introduction of mechanized printing given in British and German sources provide another. Where inventories of printing offices and detailed records of production have been located and

1 Gaskell 1965.

studied, they may give a more reliable picture of the nature of the materials that were available at a given period and the way in which they were used. McKenzie's incomparably detailed study[2] of the unpredictable realities of the working of specific printing offices needs to be supplemented with many more case studies, especially from the later period.

During the later eighteenth century a sense of 'improvement' entered printing. New techniques were introduced at an increasing pace, as they were into other manufacturing processes, and the appearance of books and other printed matter changed noticeably. While these innovations did not generally affect the essential principles by which texts were composed in type and impressions were made with ink on paper, the speed of production accelerated steadily and the economics of the trade changed with the reduction of the unit cost of printed matter. A trade that during the eighteenth century was craft based had by 1830 become to some extent an industrial one, making use of power-driven machines in the major centres of production. The new techniques of this post-hand-press period, which are far more varied than those described by Moxon, have been less thoroughly studied, and the documents and artefacts have been less systematically preserved. In some areas their history has yet to be written and sources are scanty.

The use of a steam-driven cylinder printing machine for printing *The Times* in 1814, and the contemporary development of papermaking machines, is commonly held to mark the decisive shift from craft to industry in the printing trade.[3] But type was set by hand during the whole of the period under review, and many books and even newspapers continued to be printed at the hand-press. More powerful versions of the traditional hand-presses were introduced during the first decades of the nineteenth century, but they did not materially alter the rate of production of the printed sheet. Nor were the new printing machines invariably driven by steam engines. During the first decades of their use many were equipped with handles to enable them to be turned by hand.

Some innovations that were developed during the early nineteenth century were to have a long-term effect on the economics of printing. A few of these techniques were in existence but did not become widely used until the period of industrialization. Some wholly new inventions, like lithography, a new planographic[4] process for making images based on a chemical principle, or

2 McKenzie 1969.

3 See Bidwell, chap. 8, below.

4 *Planographic* – printing from a flat surface that has been treated to make it attract or repel ink.

aquatint, a development of existing intaglio[5] printing, were capable of development into new industrial processes when they were aided by photography. Michael Twyman has shown that many texts, some of which were quite substantial, were produced by lithography during the early nineteenth century,[6] but these processes would not be widely exploited on a major commercial scale for book or periodical production until the early twentieth century.

Printing will therefore be examined first of all as a craft, and what is written here may be taken to describe a process that in its essence was probably already practised by the middle of the sixteenth century. A later note will be made of the innovations that were introduced with greater frequency towards 1800 and in succeeding decades.

The chief aim of this chapter is to survey the means by which text and images were reproduced during the period 1695 to 1830. It does not attempt, except incidentally, to evaluate the use that was made of these processes, an aim that underlies many standard texts.[7] It is necessarily dependent on manuals, but it should always be borne in mind that these are prescriptive works, which state what should ideally be done. There are very few texts that convey the full flavour of working life in a printing office. One or two prominent figures of the period had been printers, but Benjamin Franklin gives only a few paragraphs of his autobiography to his working experience in London during the 1720s, and Balzac's sketches of a provincial office in Angoulême in the 1820s in his *Illusions perdues* (1837) are memorable but brief. However, Nicolas Contat, known as Le Brun, painted a vivid picture of life in a Parisian printing office in about 1760.[8] And in *The working man's way in the world*, Charles Manby Smith, although some of his general historical details have been shown to be flawed, wrote many lively and probably essentially trustworthy scenes drawn from his experiences in printing offices in various locations, including London and Paris, between 1826 and about 1840.[9]

The printing house

The equipment of a *printing house* or *printing office* comprised a printing press or presses, frames bearing type in cases, storage racks for cases that were not in

5 *Intaglio* – printing from a surface in which the image or text is cut into a metal plate with an engraving tool, or etched with acid, or a combination of both methods. The whole surface is inked, wiped clean, and the ink remaining below the surface is transferred to the paper under pressure. The term *letterpress* is commonly used to distinguish printing with a relief surface from the planographic or intaglio processes.

6 Twyman 1990.

7 McKerrow 1928; McKenzie 1969; Gaskell 1974.

8 Contat 1980.

9 Smith 1967; Nowell-Smith 1971.

use, and a flat stone-topped table on which pages were made up for the press. A sink and a source of water were needed for damping the paper beforehand and for washing and rinsing the formes after printing. After the sheets were printed and still damp, a space was needed to hang them up to dry. Since it was possible to place all the equipment, including the press and the cases of type, in the rooms of a conventional 'dwelling house', few special buildings were designed for printing until the industrial period, unless the dignity of the printing office or the exceptionally large scale of its operation required one.

A 'New Print House' adjoining the Sheldonian Theatre was built in about 1670 for Fell's press at Oxford, with five presses (later eight) and thirteen frames for the compositors. Its successor, a building that still survives as the 'Clarendon Building', was the new printing house to which the university printers moved in October 1713, built to the designs of Nicholas Hawksmoor. Of this Harry Carter remarked that, 'of its two purposes, to ornament the University city and to accommodate printers, it served the former better ... The pressmen, relegated to the basement, can have been served little better by the light of day than by their tallow candles.' But the compositors were on the first floor, with their frames placed by the windows.[10] It was perhaps in emulation of this building that the printing office at Trinity College, Dublin, 'a singularly beautiful specimen of the true Doric', was built with the aid of a gift of cash from John Sterne, Bishop of Clogheer, in 1734.[11] In 1689 a visitor noted that the 'Printing Room' of the University Press at Cambridge measured 60 by 20 feet and contained six presses.[12] Samuel Palmer, giving up his premises, advertised to let his apartment and printing room, '65 Foot long and 27 wide, with glaz'd lights all round, and very strong and airy': this was the former Lady Chapel of the Church of St Bartholomew the Great in Smithfield.[13]

Moxon observes that the term 'printing house' may be applied to 'a House, or Room or Rooms' in which printing is carried on.[14] He gives the area required by a press and pressmen as 7 feet square, and for a frame with a pair of cases, an area 4 ft 6 in square. A compositor setting roman and italic would need a double frame to provide room for two pairs of cases. The double frames made for the University Press at Oxford in 1668 are 5 ft 4 in wide.[15] Moxon

10 Carter 1975, 66–7, 198–9. The exact placing of the compositors' frames is shown on one of Hawksmoor's drawings (Colvin, 1964, fig. 112).
11 Timperley 1842, 600.
12 McKenzie 1966, I, 16–35.
13 Winkler 1993, 109.
14 Moxon 1962, 16.
15 Shown in Moxon 1962, fig. 1.

recommended that compositors should ideally have light from their left, and that the pressmen should have 'a clear, free and pretty lofty Light, not impeded with the shadow of other Houses, or with Trees'. The press needed to receive light from the north, to keep the pressmen cool, to give them a constant light by which to judge their work, and to avoid sunlight that shone directly on the dampened paper and dried it. Paper windows were made as an expedient to keep out direct sunlight where it was unavoidable, but had the disadvantage of giving poor protection from freezing in winter.[16]

Early illustrations of printing show compositors and pressmen working in the same space. Of this arrangement Moxon remarks that 'in England it is not very customary',[17] and Momoro says that the two are separated, so that the pressmen can talk freely while the compositors are left in peace to concentrate on their work. Hansard, in his manual of 1825, concurred.[18] However, the *Encyclopédie*, showing the two areas separately, says that this was done in order to illustrate the two processes clearly, but that compositors and pressmen generally work in one space, and the type cases should be nearest to the windows.[19]

Small to medium-sized printing offices occupied conventional town houses, and the master printer, together with some of the apprentices, often lived over his shop. The compositors needed the good natural light that was found on an upper floor, where the weight of a substantial quantity of type sometimes caused structural problems. In 1755 Samuel Richardson was compelled to leave his printing office in Salisbury Square for this reason: 'The very great Printing Weights at the top of it, have made it too hazardous for me to renew an expiring lease ...' He rented a court of houses 'ready to fall', pulled them down, and 'built a most commodious Printing Office; and fitted up an adjoining House which I before used as a Warehouse for the Dwelling-House'.[20]

The inventory of the materials of Samuel Darker in 1700 shows little distinction between printing office and dwelling house. The parlour and kitchen were on the ground floor and the chamber or bedroom was on the first floor. The 'working rooms' were 'up two & three Paire of Staires' and contained '40 paire of printing Cases, about thirty Hundred [*sic*, for

16 Moxon 1962, 17.
17 Moxon 1962, 16–17.
18 Momoro 1793, 210; Hansard 1825, 746.
19 'Imprimerie en caractères', plates 1, 14, from D. Diderot and J. Le R. D'Alembert, *Encyclopédie ou dictionnaire raisonné des sciences, des arts et des métiers*, 17 vols., Paris.
20 Richardson to Lady Echlin, 22 Mar. 1756, National Art Library, Forster MS, XI, fols. 163, 173 (cited by Sale 1950, 12–13).

'hundredweight'?] of letters, twenty Cases, tenn Frames two Presses', and in the garret were a bed, twelve reams of paper and 'some books'.[21]

The damped sheets that were hung up to dry after printing, often in the attic or loft, were a recurrent source of danger from fire. Some major London printing houses burned down, notably those of William Bowyer in 1713 and John Baskett in 1738. Thomas Bensley's warehouse, containing manuscripts as well as stock, was destroyed by fire in 1807 and the whole of his printing office, as well as the warehouse and dwelling apartments, was destroyed again in 1819.

When Charles Eyre and William Strahan in London acquired the reversion of John Baskett's patent of King's Printer in 1766, they decided against taking over his printing office in Printing House Square and between 1767 and 1770 had one specially built in East Harding Street to the designs of Robert Mylne (1734–1811). The building, which survived until 1940 when it was destroyed by a fire bomb (there was paper stored in its roof space), was on three storeys above ground, with a frontage of 44 feet. There were 'ware rooms' and a gathering room on the ground floor, two press rooms and a wetting room on the first floor, and three composing rooms on the second floor, where the continuous fenestration on three sides of the building resembled the traditional windows of the houses of hand-loom weavers. On the same floor there was a correcting room lit by a skylight and without an external window, presumably in order to isolate it from external noise.[22]

Manuals

Although original copies of the technical manuals which supply much detailed knowledge of the processes of printing are often hard to locate, the significant titles have almost all been reprinted, and the editorial matter to these new editions often provides a commentary to the practice of the processes that they describe. Moxon's *Mechanick exercises* (1683–4) is the first extensive account of printing and typefounding to be published in any language. The edition by Herbert Davis and Harry Carter[23] reproduces Moxon's original text and supplements it with a critical commentary, making use of later manuals in English and in other languages, and adding observations drawn from Carter's personal knowledge of trade practice in type founding and printing since the late 1920s. John Smith's *Printer's grammar* (1755), which does not include work

21 Winkler 1993, 669–74.

22 Five drawings for 'The King's Printing House near Fleet Street', Sale of architectural drawings, Christie's, London, 29 Nov. 1983, lot 24. Bought for St Bride Library.

23 Moxon 1962.

at the press, is a valuable work because, although aware of Moxon's text, the author clearly had personal knowledge of compositor's work. Very little is known about the author, although his recollection of an event of 1704 gives a clue to his age, and the addition of 'Regiom.' to his name on the title page suggests that he came from Königsberg. His text shows that he was familiar with trade practice in Germany and France as well as England. The other English manuals that provide additional information – Luckombe (1770) and Smith (1787) – are largely drawn from the texts of Moxon and Smith, as are C. Stower, *The printer's grammar* (1808), John Johnson, *Typographia* (1824), T.C. Hansard, *Typographia* (1825) and W. Savage, *A dictionary of the art of printing* (1841). These all make use of Moxon's text for their accounts of press-work and of Moxon's and Smith's for composition, but they add independent remarks based on their personal experience of the trade and include notes on new developments: Stower describes the new Stanhope press, Johnson and Hansard both refer to the new printing machines, and Hansard has a section on stereotyping. There are remarks on composition and presswork in W. Savage, *Practical hints on decorative printing* (1822).

Manuals for printers that supplement the texts in English were published in other European countries. These have been listed by G. Barber, M. Boghardt, P. Gaskell and others,[24] and many of the major texts have been reprinted.[25] Although there were some minor variations from British practice in these countries and they must therefore be used with caution, these manuals supply details that are sometimes lacking from the British manuals. One of the most considerable collections of technical information and images regarding printing and related trades in the hand-press era is contained in the main and subsidiary articles in the *Encyclopédie* of Diderot and D'Alembert and in the separate volumes of plates.[26] However, there are also useful articles in contemporary British encyclopaedias that have been less systematically identified and evaluated. The articles 'Printing' and 'Letter founding' in Ephraim Chambers's *Cyclopaedia* (1728 and later editions), and Abraham Rees's revision of it in 1786, were independently written. In the nineteenth century the encyclopaedias and some other technical works give information about new processes and provide illustrations of new machines that are lacking from the manuals. These are referred to later in this chapter.

24 Gaskell, Barber and Warrilow, 1968–71; Barber 1969; Boghardt 1983.
25 A Dutch manual of 1844 and an Italian manual of 1789, in manuscript when the first of these lists was compiled, have subsequently been published with a commentary: Wardenaar 1982; Campanini 1998.
26 Barber 1973.

Type

Punch-cutting and matrix-making

The traditional processes for making type were described during the sixteenth century by two writers, Biringucci (also spelt Biringuccio) in 1540 and in a little book published and perhaps partly written by Christophe Plantin in 1564.[27] Later, two detailed and largely first-hand accounts of the processes were published, and no comparable description has been published since the second of these accounts appeared. The first is contained in the *Mechanick exercises* of Joseph Moxon (London, 1683–4), and the second is the first volume of the *Manuel typographique* of Pierre-Simon Fournier (1712–68) (Paris, 1764). (The account in the *Encyclopédie* of Diderot and D'Alembert, for which Fournier supplied the information, is allied to this text, although the images are wholly different.[28]) A third account of punch cutting and type founding was prepared in Paris in about 1700 for the project known as the 'Description des Arts et Métiers', and currently remains in manuscript. It tallies essentially with the other two, supplying some additional details.[29] The illustrations that were made for it have been published.[30] For supplementary information on this subject and for its later development, some technical works and encyclopaedias of the eighteenth and nineteenth centuries should be consulted.[31]

Making type in the sizes that were used for the text of books required the services of a punch-cutter, a matrix-maker and a caster. The punch was fashioned in steel, hardened, and stamped into a block of copper to make a matrix. A set of *matrices*,[32] one for each character, was prepared with great precision, and they were used in a specially designed mould to cast a quantity or *fount* of type.

The punch was *cut* with files and gravers on a squared rod of high-quality steel that had been softened or annealed. Because it was to be subjected to stress by striking, it was important that the metal should not conceal the slightest flaw. Early punch-cutters appear to have forged their own steel blanks, and the manner in which they finished their punches can often identify

27 Carter 1969, 5; Fahy 1986.

28 Barber 1973.

29 Some of these are summarized in Fownier 1995.

30 Mosley 1991.

31 For a summary, see Fournier 1995. The encyclopedias include Chambers, *Cyclopaedia* (2nd edn, London, 1738); Chambers, *Cyclopaedia*, ed. A. Rees (London, 1786); *Encyclopaedia Britannica* (Edinburgh, 1771); *Encyclopaedia Londinensis* (London, 1814); Rees, *Cyclopaedia* (London, 1819).

32 The plural of *matrix* was generally the Latin (which coincided with the French) *matrices*. The spelling *matrixes* is sometimes found, but manuscript forms like *matrisses* indicate how the term was generally pronounced.

their work. The end of the blank was filed flat and polished, and a design was sometimes scribed or scratched on the surface. If the character had a *counter*, or a space that was wholly or partly enclosed such as o, this was generally created by first filing a *counterpunch* to the shape that was needed, hardening it and driving it into the steel blank. The same counterpunch would sometimes serve for more than one letter with the same shaped counter, such as d and p. Some commentators reproached punchcutters for failing to use counterpunches and preferring to dig out the counters with the graver, claiming that the result was a shallow counter which filled readily with ink.[33]

After the counter was made, the rough external shape of the character was prepared with coarse files, for which finer ones were substituted as the outline approached the desired result. Progress was observed from time to time by holding the end of the punch in the sooty flame of a candle or a lamp and by pressing it on slightly damp paper to make a *smoke proof*. When the design was judged to be satisfactory, the steel of the punch was hardened by heating and plunging in cold water. Hard steel was too brittle to stand the shock of striking, however, and as Joseph Moxon explained in the first part of his treatise, to make a steel that would not break, 'you must let it down, (as Smiths say) that is, make it softer, by Tempering it'.[34] This was done by controlled reheating.

The finished punch was struck with a heavy hammer into an oblong block of copper. The striking distorted the copper and made it bulge. It was the job of the justifier, who was sometimes also the original punchcutter, to file it to shape in order to match the dimensions of all the other matrices in the set. The dominant strokes of black letter and roman type were vertical, and roman characters like m, n and x stood on horizontal *serifs* that could be visually aligned. But the uniform slope of italic characters, or in the case of certain characters the subtle variations of their slope, was determined by the angle at which the punch was struck in the copper, an angle that could be changed by the justifier but only within very fine limits.

Metal was removed from the surface that received the impression in order to give each matrix an identical *depth of strike*. It was also critically important that the dimension from the letter to the top or head of the matrix, which was the part that would enter the mould, should have the same measurement, since this determined the horizontal alignment of the cast type. The width of each matrix varied according to the width of the letter it bore, from wide characters like W and Œ to narrow ones like i and the *points* or signs for punctuation such as the

33 Fournier 1995, III, 398–400.
34 Moxon 1962, 99–100.

comma and full point. In many sets of matrices a uniform space was left in the copper on each side of the letter to accommodate overhanging or *kerned* characters such as the roman and italic f and long s and their ligatures.[35]

Casting and dressing

The descriptions by Moxon and Fournier and surviving old examples show that a common design for the type founder's mould had been reached by the seventeenth century, with a few regional variations. Modern reconstructions have been based on both sources.[36] It was a hand-held device that was employed to make all the type used to set text until the process was mechanized towards the middle of the nineteenth century.

The design of the mould is essentially simple, although its detail, being internal, is difficult to represent clearly in a diagram. It comprised two L-shaped parts that slid against each other, leaving a space for the cast type that was constant in one dimension (the *body* or type size), while the parts moved apart or together to accommodate the varying widths of the matrices for different characters. A wire in one half of the mould worked in a rounded groove in the other half, and made a *nick* in the type which indicated to the compositor which direction to set it. The width of the type could be varied by setting the *registers*, which held the side of the matrix and could be adjusted laterally. The matrix was secured in the mould by the *bow*, an iron spring that engaged in a groove on the back of the matrix and pressed it against the *stool*, a separate part of the mould that could sometimes be removed and replaced with another that gave a different alignment to the type. This principle was used for casting several different music types from a single matrix by using different stools.[37] The sides of the mould were clad with wood to insulate the caster's hands from the hot metal.

Typemetal was an alloy of which the two main constituents were lead and antimony.[38] Lead, plentiful and cheap, melted at a relatively low temperature. Antimony hardened the alloy, gave sharper casts than pure lead, and (expanding as it cooled) counteracted the contraction of the lead. Typecasting was in effect diecasting, carried out to a higher degree of precision than was required by any other contemporary craft. The melting point of typemetal, 486 °F (or 252 °C), is lower than that of its components. Analysis of old type shows that small quantities of tin, copper and iron were sometimes present.[39] Tin, which

35 Fournier 1995, III, 347–8.
36 Nelson 1985; May 1996.
37 Morison with Carter 1967, 195–9.
38 Moxon 1962, 379.
39 Pelgen 1996.

made up a large part of the typemetal described by Biringucci, assists the flow of the molten metal. It is not mentioned by the authorities of the seventeenth and eighteenth centuries, but during the nineteenth and twentieth centuries it again became a significant constituent of typemetal.

The caster held the mould in the left hand and gave it a sharp upwards *shake* as the molten metal was poured from a ladle, in order to drive it quickly down to the matrix before it cooled, and thus to make a good *face* on the type. The output of a single typecaster was something like 3,000 pieces of type in a working day, with variations according to the size of the body.[40] After casting, the type was *dressed*. The *jet* of surplus metal was broken off and put back in the pot. The type was rubbed on an abrasive stone to get rid of fins of metal that had crept between the surfaces of the mould. The rough projection left by breaking off the jet was ploughed away, making a groove that left the type on two *feet*. Finally the body of the type was scraped to give the whole *fount* exactly the same dimension: Fournier observed that by the time a big fount had been cast and the mould had opened and closed 300,000 times, it was noticeably worn, and the last types had a smaller body than the first ones.[41]

The *fount* (or single 'casting') of type was made according to a *bill*, which listed the quantities of each individual *sort* that would be required. For a fount of Pica roman and italic weighing 800 pounds, the bill printed by Smith[42] specifies 12,000 'e's, 7,000 't's and 'a's, 4,000 commas, 2,000 full points, 600 'q's and 400 'z's. Such lists were, as he allows, very rough approximations, and the need to set a different kind of copy could throw the calculation out: a Latin text would need more 'q's and 'u's than an English one, and this might make it necessary to order additional sorts for the fount, known as *imperfections*, from the type founder. In 1753 the London printing office of Daniel Browne had a fount of Pica weighing 1,433 pounds. According to figures given by Smith, this fount would have comprised about 308,000 individual pieces of type or *sorts*, including the spaces.[43] A fount of 500 pounds was, says Smith, a small fount, and one of 2,000 pounds or more a large one.

The body of the type, its dimension from top to bottom, was known by a series of traditional names. Nonpareil and Brevier were small bodies, Long Primer, Small Pica, Pica and English were used for setting normal text, Double Pica was often used for poetry in big quartos or folios, and French Canon was a

40 Fournier 1930, 104.
41 Fournier 1764–6, 104.
42 Smith 1755, 42–5.
43 Winkler 1993, 691–4; Smith 1755, 42–6.

big type used for title pages.[44] Small Pica was known as an 'irregular size' because it was an intermediate size between two traditional bodies: Long Primer and Pica. Although Pica was considered 'the ever-best size for Printing Letter', and the Pica em quad of about 4.2 mm was, and still remains, a standard unit of measurement in typesetting, the smaller body of Small Pica 'took in' so much more matter that there was a vogue for it after it was used for setting Chambers's *Cyclopaedia*.[45] None of the sizes had a dimension that could be exactly defined.[46] The relationships between them were uncertain, and the Pica of one founder was still likely to be a slightly different size from another's, well into the nineteenth century.[47] Similarly, the *height to paper* of type might vary from one office to another, and it was common practice to send a sample type for the founder to match before a fount was cast.[48] German printers were said sometimes to have found it convenient to have their founts cast to a height unique to their office in order to make them useless to fellow-printers who might wish to borrow them.[49]

Compositor's work

Type

Type for setting was kept in *pairs of cases*. Early illustrations of printing offices show type being set from a single case, and the single case continued to be used in Germany, Switzerland and Italy, but by 1700 in France, the Low Countries and Britain, type was normally held in two long cases which were placed one above the other on a *frame* which held the upper case at a steeper angle to make it easier to reach. They were known as the *upper case*, which held the capitals, the small capitals, figures and the characters that were less frequently used, and the *lower case*, which held the small letters (also known as *lower case* characters), punctuation and spaces. There were also 'half cases' but it is not

44 For a very approximate table of the traditional type bodies expressed in millimetres, see Gaskell 1974, 15.

45 Smith 1755, 21–2.

46 A system of standard measurements for type bodies, based on nationally defined units of measurement, originated at the Imprimerie Royale, Paris, in the 1690s. The history of the 'typographical point' is complex and has no bearing on British trade usage at this date. For a summary, see Fournier 1995, III, 400–8.

47 Savage 1841, 802.

48 All type is just under one inch (25.4 mm) high. A surviving fount of type (at St Bride Library, London) cast for the Chiswick Press in 1854 has a height of 23.3 mm, which is close to the standard height used in Britain and the USA during the twentieth century. Founts in the same collection that were cast by the Caslon foundry for the Oxford University Press during the eighteenth century have heights of 23.7 and 23.9 mm. These appear to correspond to the two distinct type heights employed at the press: one (23.65 mm) for the Bible Press, and another (23.86 mm) for the Learned Press. The standard French height prescribed by the *Code de la librairie* (1723), 10.5 *lignes*, was about 23.69 mm.

49 Gessner and Hager, 1740–5, 132.

clear what these were.[50] Normal cases were generally 32½ inches wide, a dimension that must have been determined, like the maximum width of the normal paper mould, by the span of a workman's arms. They were 14½ inches from front to back and 1½ inches deep. Each case could hold about 30 pounds of type. The upper case, which contained 98 boxes, was divided into a regular grid of two sections of seven by seven small boxes. The basis of the lower case was a grid of two sections based on eight boxes by eight, but the divisions were absent from many boxes in order to make bigger compartments. The rest of the fount was stored either in more compositors' cases kept in racks, or in baskets, or in bigger and deeper *fount* or *barge* cases, which were divided in more or less the same way as the compositors' type cases,[51] and were used to recharge them as they emptied.

The compartments into which the cases were subdivided were arranged according to a system, known as the *lay*, that was a compromise between alphabetical order, which was easy to remember, and the frequency of the character and its combinations in practical use, which made setting easier.[52] It also reflected a pattern that was set in the sixteenth century: capital J and U were not included in the alphabetical sequence of letters in the upper case but placed separately.

Lower case e is the most frequent character in English and French, and it had the biggest and most central compartment. This order of frequency was reflected in the *bill*,[53] the name for the list of the different quantities of single characters or *sorts* that made up the fount. Other common letters were placed nearby, so that words like 'the' were quick to set. The lay in most printing offices followed a pattern, with only slight variations among the smaller boxes at the top and sides of the lower case. The University Press at Oxford used two lays of its own for the 'learned' and 'bible' sides of the printing house which differed from those used in the trade generally, and it retained one of them in use until it abandoned the use of metal type in 1983.[54] Savage shows distinct lays that were used in Edinburgh and Dublin.[55] The authors of most printers'

50 The inventory of the materials of Thomas Ilive in 1725 lists '30 setts of cases' and 'twelve half cases'; Daniel Browne in 1753 had '92½ pairs of Whole Cases' and '14 pairs of Half cases', as well as '4 pairs of Font Cases' (Winkler 1993, 684, 691–4). An unpublished plate engraved in 1694 by L. Simonneau for the account of printing prepared for the 'Description des Arts et Métiers' shows the upper and lower cases each divided in half, to make a set of four square cases.

51 Stower 1808a, 152. They were called 'barge cases' at the University Press, Oxford. The inventories of Thomas Ilive and of Cassandra Meere, both of 1725, list 'bump cases', which may possibly be a term for the same thing (Winkler 1993, 684, 687).

52 Gaskell 1974, 34–7.

53 Bills for English and other languages are given in Legros and Grant 1916, 128–43.

54 Carter 1975, 206, 208.

55 Savage 1841, 209, 210.

manuals showed what they regarded as the normal lay of their period and offered proposals for a more logical arrangement. Details of the lay, like the bill of type, might also be decided by the kind of work to be printed: commercial work would make more use of numerals; Latin texts (until the nineteenth century) more of the æ and œ ligatures. A rearrangement of the case was brought about generally by the abandonment of the long s and its ligatures, together with the ct ligature, during the decade from about 1795, which freed about eleven boxes.

The composing frame was a unit that would accommodate two pairs of cases, side by side, as illustrations in manuals and surviving examples from the seventeenth century at Oxford show.[56] There would be room for two compositors to work side by side, but if the copy required much setting in italic, cases with italic type were probably placed by the side of the cases with roman, as shown in an engraving made in 1694 for the 'Description des arts et métiers' by Louis Simonneau.

Composing

The compositor stood before the frame. In his[57] left hand he held a *composing stick*. This was of iron or brass, with an adjustable width or *measure*, or of wood (sometimes lined with brass) with an invariable width that was suitable for the fixed-column measure of newspapers. Moxon showed a stick with a supplementary part for the setting of shoulder notes to a narrower measure.

According to Moxon some compositors placed the *copy* or text in a *visorum*, a device with a horizontal bar which held the sheets of the copy and marked the line being set. A spike at the foot was inserted in the bar of the case or the frame. This remained normal in continental Europe, but its use seems to have declined in British practice. The right-hand side of the more steeply inclined upper case, which held the less-used small capitals, was a convenient location for the copy, and a combined weight and line-marker could be contrived, as Hansard shows, with a piece of leaden spacing material pierced to take a cord acting as a counterweight.[58]

Having read so much of his copy as he could remember accurately, the compositor took types from their compartments with his right hand and

56 Hansard 1825, 408; Moxon 1962, 401. Moxon's own engraved illustration (p. 32) shows one pair of cases on a frame with room for two, but the image does not show the essential transverse support for the backs of the cases and is in this respect defective.

57 The gender-specific term reflects contemporary trade practice, which did not admit women to any of the skilled operations of the trade. With very few exceptions, this rule was applied in England until letterpess printing ceased in the twentieth century. It was less rigidly observed in Scotland.

58 Hansard 1825, 408–9.

assembled them in the stick without looking at them, having already seen the *nick* below the type body that would tell him which way up to place them, and trusting to touch to confirm its presence and to detect a wrong type by its thickness.[59] Each word was separated by a space, a piece of type lower than the rest, without a letter cast to it. There were five spaces. The *em quadrat* or *quad* was the square of the *body* of the type. The *en* quad was half its width. Then came the *thick*, *mid* and *thin* spaces, of which there were three, four and five to the em respectively. Even thinner *hair spaces*, sometimes made of copper, were used to space out the letters of words set in small capitals or to help out in a tight line, but they were fragile and it was not good practice to use them generally between words. This system, which was described by Smith in 1755[60] and prevailed into the twentieth century, seems not to have been generally settled in the time of Moxon.[61] There were thicker quads cast to multiples of the em of the body which were used to fill a short line or to make an empty or *white* line between paragraphs. The em and en quads had boxes of their own, but the spaces appear to have been mixed indiscriminately together; later they had boxes of their own. According to Smith, a middling or mid space between words was sufficient for lower-case matter, but an en quad was needed between words set in capitals and small capitals.[62] A convention for compositors was for spaces to be wider or narrower according to the characters they separated: a letter like f, the top of which was *kerned* or overhung its body, was followed by one of the wider spaces, and words ending with ascending characters like l and d were separated by a wider space if they were followed by similar tall characters like h or b. Conversely spaces could be narrower between round letters or v and w.

In practice, a compromise was almost always needed. The line was *justified*, or made to fit the measure snugly, by adjusting the spaces so that it would stand in the stick without falling over. This fit was achieved experimentally by trying spaces with different widths and if necessary breaking words and adding a hyphen. After setting the line and before justifying it, the compositor read it for obvious errors like wrong or *turned* (inverted) letters, or words left out or repeated, faults which if not spotted on this occasion would be more troublesome to set right later. The compositor held the stick away from him, so that the type, although in mirror image and upside down, was easy for a practised eye to read from left to right. Before the next line was started, a *setting rule* cut

59 Stower 1808, 159.
60 Smith 1755, 111.
61 Moxon 1962, 103, 207, 353.
62 Smith 1755, 112–17.

from the kind of brass rule used for borders was placed on the line already set, so that the types of the new line would slide along it easily when the spaces were adjusted. Moxon's stick, like other early examples, looks as if it had room for no more than two or three lines of type. Later sticks were nearly two inches deep, and would accept about twelve lines of Pica type.

When the stick was full enough, the justified lines were lifted out on the setting rule and placed in the open-ended wooden tray known as a *galley*. As Moxon remarks in passing, and as his image implies,[63] while the lines were loose, the galley was kept at an angle on a sloping type case in order to prevent the type from falling over. When enough lines had been set to make a page, a *direction-line* containing a *catch word* (the first word of the following page) was supplied at the foot as a guide to the correct imposition of the *forme* from which the sheet would be printed, and to the correct folding of the printed sheet. The compositor whipped the page firmly around with four or five turns of *page-cord*, a thick thread, tucking in its end to secure it. The galley had a *slice* or sliding bottom part on which the tied-up page was carried and from which it slid on to the imposing stone.

Imposition

Pages were made up on the imposing stone into *formes*, comprising two, four, eight or more pages, according to the format of the work, whether *folio*, *quarto*, *octavo* and so on. They were placed in a *chase*, a wrought-iron frame, generally with an internal transverse bar or a cross, with wooden sticks or *furniture* to separate them. Small wooden wedges or *quoins* were driven against wedge-shaped *side sticks* and *foot sticks* to lock all the elements of which it was composed tightly in place so that the forme could safely be lifted. Two matching formes were made for each sheet, with the pages arranged, according to schemes that were published in the printers' manuals, to make the correct sequence of pages when the sheet, having been printed on both sides, was folded.

Correction

The making of proofs and their formal reading against the author's copy did not take place until the pages and formes had been made up. Occasional instances are recorded of the use of long metal galleys to hold the type as it was set, but it was not until the later nineteenth century that it became normal to take long *slip proofs* of the type in the galley before it was made up into pages,

63 Moxon 1962, 34, 36.

thus avoiding the tedious, expensive and hazardous process of *over* or *under running* by moving whole lines from page to page, when corrections or second thoughts required text to be added to or removed from them.[64]

When the edition had been printed, and the forme cleaned of ink with the hot alkaline solution known as *lye*[65] and rinsed with clean water, the compositor *unlocked* the forme and *distributed* the type, picking up words or groups of words and dropping the type back in the right compartments of the case, letter by letter.

Presswork

The form of the press of earlier periods is known from the many engraved images that were made when it was depicted as an icon of the new art of printing, but the exact interpretation of the detail of these images is often difficult. For the eighteenth century, there are paradoxically (given the dominant cultural and industrial importance of printing) very few images indeed of what was known as the 'common press'; but there are enough surviving examples to make its construction and working reasonably certain.[66] Measured working drawings have been published of the parts of one of these presses.[67]

The construction of the English common press matches in most of its essential details the press shown in the French texts of Fertel (1723) and the *Encyclopédie* of Diderot and d'Alembert. It differs slightly from the German press, illustrated by Von Werdt (1676)[68] and in the German manuals of Ernesti (1721) and Gessner (1740), of which the upper part was solid.

The basis of the common press was a frame made of two upright *cheeks*, held together by a transverse member, the *winter*, below and the *cap* above (a part that is absent from the French images). The *head*, a solid beam, was suspended from the cap and had tenons that enabled it to slide up and down in slots in the cheeks. Most of the parts were of oak and some other native woods (elm, beech) specified by Moxon.[69] Mahogany came into use later.[70]

64 Gaskell 1974, 194.
65 Moxon 1962, 310–11.
66 Gaskell 1956a, 1970.
67 Harris and Sisson 1978, based on an English press of the eighteenth century at the National Museum of American History, Washington, DC (Gaskell 1970, USA4).
68 Moran 1973, fig. 11.
69 Moxon 1962, 49.
70 Stower 1808, 325.

A steel *spindle* or screw with a steep pitch worked in a brass *nut* let into the head. A square wooden box, the *hose*, was attached to a groove in the spindle, and from hooks at its four lower corners was suspended the *platen*, a block of beech wood, 14 by 9 inches and 2½ inches thick,[71] that made the impression. The hose worked in an aperture cut out of the *till*, a pair of stout planks held between the cheeks, which kept the twisting action of the turning spindle from being transmitted to the platen. An iron *bar* with a wooden handle passed through the spindle and served to turn it through about ninety degrees before being checked against the nearside cheek. The *toe* of the spindle worked in the *stud*, a pan mounted centrally on the iron *platen plate* which was let into the upper surface of the platen.

A separate part, the *carriage*,[72] was designed to slide to and fro under the platen on *wooden ribs* on which were mounted steel rails to reduce the friction. It was a stout elm plank 1½ inches thick on which was built a box, the *coffin*, containing a *stone* (of real marble or 'Purbeck marble', a hard limestone) about 3 inches thick,[73] which was bedded on a foundation of bran or sheets of paper. Iron *cramps* fixed below the plank made contact with the ribs and slid along them. The *tympan*, an open wooden frame covered with vellum or calico, was hinged to the end of the coffin. An *inner tympan* fitted into it, and a woollen blanket was held between the two to spread the pressure of the platen. A lighter wrought-iron frame, the *frisket*, was hinged to the top of the tympan and folded down over it. It was covered with paper from which windows were cut for the pages, and served both to hold the paper to the tympan and to keep its edges clean. A *rounce* or windlass with *girths* moved the carriage under the platen and back again.

These are the parts of the press described by Moxon, and called by him the 'old-fashioned' press. The hose of his 'new-fashioned press'[74] consisted of an open framework of iron bars instead of the traditional enclosed wooden box. Moxon attributed the design and introduction of this press to the printer Willem Janszoon Blaeu (1571–1638) of Amsterdam and praised its advantages. Most of the surviving presses at the Museum Plantin-Moretus, Antwerp, have hoses of this kind, but since they are found on only four of the fourteen common presses that survive in Britain, it is doubtful whether Moxon's advocacy of their adoption had been effective. It should be noted that, although he

71 Moxon 1962, 77.

72 Moxon (1962, 60), Stower (1808, 320) and later writers gave a different meaning of *carriage*, changing it from the parts that moved, bearing the coffin, to the 'frame ... on which the ribs are placed', a less logical usage.

73 Stower 1808, 328.

74 Moxon 1962, 47.

omits the rounce and spindle from his illustration of the old-fashioned press, it was certainly present (it is seen in illustrations of presses dating from the first decade of the sixteenth century). On the other hand, Moxon makes no mention of another of its features: a thin platen with mouldings at the edge which, judging from his illustration of the 'new-fashioned' press and a separate illustration of its platen, appears to have been made of brass rather than wood.[75] The printing press described in the general description of machines (1607) by the Italian engineer Vittorio Zonca had a platen of cast brass.[76] In sale catalogues of Dutch printing offices in the seventeenth century, a brass platen is often mentioned to recommend a press, and in the eighteenth century a brass platen was usual in Germany too. But when John Baskerville described his equipment to the Parisian printer Philippe-Denis Pierres in 1773, the 'stones' and platens of brass are mentioned in terms that imply that these were unusual refinements in England.[77]

The press was operated by two men who worked alternate stints:[78] the *puller*, who placed the paper in position, pulled the bar and removed the printed sheet, and the *beater*, who applied ink to the forme with two round *balls* of leather stuffed with wool, and spent the rest of his time in beating it out on the ink block so that the impressions would maintain a consistent *colour*. A boy might be employed to help to increase production slightly by removing the printed sheet from the press and placing it on the heap.

As the platen covered only one half of the surface to be printed – covering the area of a single folio, two quarto or four octavo pages – the carriage was run halfway in, a pull was made, and then it was run in all the way for a second pull. One disadvantage of this practice was that the two pages in the middle of a six-page forme of duodecimo received two overlapping half-impressions, with a consequent risk of slurring the impression if the paper shifted between pulls.

The making and maintenance of the ink balls was one of the more tiresome chores of the printing office. After work, surplus ink was scraped off, the nails holding the leather to the stocks were pulled out with the tool known as a sheep's-foot, the woollen stuffing was removed to preserve its elasticity, and the leather was steeped overnight in what Moxon calls *chamber lye* (urine) to keep it supple. The next morning the balls had to be reassembled.

Printing ink was made from a clear varnish to which a pigment was added. The chief constituent of the varnish was an oil that, having been boiled, would dry on

75 Moxon 1962, 75.
76 Zonca 1607.
77 Straus and Dent 1907, 104.
78 Moxon 1962, 292.

exposure to the air and not remain sticky: linseed or walnut oil were the most suitable. Materials could be added to assist the drying. The making of the varnish, which could easily catch fire, was a dangerous process that was generally carried out by professional inkmakers who supplied the ink to printers in barrels, ready-made. The pigment for black ink was lamp-black, specially made for the purpose from suitable materials. Ink in other colours was made by adding the traditional pigments used by painters: printing ink was, in effect, oil paint.[79]

Paper for printing needed to be damp in order to soften the gelatine sizing that was added by the papermaker. Although Moxon calls the process *wetting*, a slight but perceptible humidity was all that was needed. Quires of paper (conventionally twenty-four sheets) were drawn through the water trough and alternated with dry ones. The heap was then left under a heavy weight. In order for the damp to become consistent throughout the heap, it was done many hours before printing, generally last thing at night for use the next day.[80]

The pulp that seeped under the deckle of the mould gave handmade paper an uneven edge, so that – unlike machine-made paper of the nineteenth century which was cut cleanly from a continuous band – it had no consistent square edge. *Register* was obtained by pressing each new sheet on two *points* that projected from either side of the tympan frame. The points held the sheet securely under the frisket. When the *reiteration* (the second side of the sheet) was pulled, the sheet was turned over and placed back on the points, using the same holes. If the formes matched each other exactly, and if the tympan was steady, the second impression matched the first, and each page *backed up* another page. The nominal rate of production of the common press was a *token* of 250 sheets in an hour, or one every fifteen seconds.[81] Although the real rate might vary considerably for many reasons, from the flow of work and the state of repair of the press to the quality of work required by the master printer, as the records cited by McKenzie amply demonstrate,[82] a figure of 1,250 completed sheets or 2,500 impressions during a working day of about ten hours appears in many contemporary estimates of normal output.

Woodcuts

Images and decorative elements that were cut in wood were the same height as the type, and could be placed in the text and printed at the same time. Although

79 Bloy 1967.
80 Moxon 1962, 281.
81 Moxon 1962, 262, 484–6.
82 McKenzie 1969.

they were vulnerable to accidental damage and sensitive to both the alkaline lye with which the forme was washed and the water in which it was rinsed, woodcuts were more resistant to wear than typemetal. Yet the medium, which had achieved great refinement in continental Europe during the sixteenth century, was increasingly displaced by copperplate engravings, both for illustrations and for decoration. Woodcuts, known as *cuts*, were used for simple illustrations and diagrams in the text.

The term 'woodcut' is generally applied to a raised image engraved on a block cut from the 'plank' (side grain) of a hardwood, while 'wood engraving' is reserved for blocks cut on the end grain, a technique which became normal in the nineteenth century. However, the two techniques may have coexisted for longer than has normally been believed.

Two handbooks deal with the subject of engraving on wood, one French and one German. J.-M. Papillon's treatise of 1766, developed from information that he supplied for the *Encyclopédie* of Diderot and d'Alembert, is consciously a work that is designed to promote a skill of which the status had declined, and which the author, a virtuoso of the medium, was attempting to redeem. The little manual of various related trades published at Erfurt by J.M. Funcke in 1740, however, offers the woodcut as an expedient, a technique that can be learned by any printer, 'even one who cannot draw'. Both Papillon and Funcke give recipes for transferring printed images to the wood in order to make facsimiles of existing designs.

Papillon named box as the most suitable wood for engraving, and also pear, the wood of the service tree (*cormier*), cherry and varieties of apple.[83] Funcke wrote that pear was the most usual wood; apple and box were also recommended, but the latter was expensive and not easy to get.[84] The normal cutting tool was a knife with a short, robust blade and a handle made to fit the hand well. Both manuals give much attention to the judging of the quality of the steel and the technique for the sharpening of the edge, but Papillon also illustrates a great variety of other tools and equipment for the professional engraver. He mentions in passing the possibility of cutting on the end grain rather than the plank, and reports with disapproval on contemporary engravers who 'use the graver (*burin*) on wood as if they were engraving metal', a technique that was later generally used.[85]

There are engravings cut on the end grain of boxwood among seventeenth-century blocks that are preserved at the University Press, Oxford.[86] From this

83 Papillon 1985, II, 57.
84 Funcke 1998, 4.
85 Papillon 1985, II, 124.
86 Morison with Carter 1967, 188–94.

evidence, it appears that this technique, the introduction of which has often been attributed to the English engraver Thomas Bewick (1753–1828), may not have been uncommon at a far earlier date. Nonetheless, Bewick was one of the engravers who towards the end of the eighteenth century restored the reputation of wood engraving as a medium for illustration in books, taking advantage of changes in materials and tools – notably the introduction of wove paper and improved presses – along with developments in the marketing of books.

Decorative head-pieces and tail-pieces are common in English books during the first half of the eighteenth century, and sections within the text were commonly divided by woodcuts forming bands of ornament, called *slips* by Smith.[87] They had a practical function, since they served as *bearers* which filled blank spaces in the forme and thus helped to make an even overall impression. Yet, the fashion for their use declined sharply in the 1760s. Little printers' ornaments or *flowers*, often derived from arabesque ornaments introduced in the sixteenth century, combined into decorative patterns and were sometimes used as a substitute for engraved blocks. They are common in the 1750s.[88] Flowers had the advantage to the printer that they could be set to fill different measures. But the use of typographical ornament of any kind became rare in British books after about 1770.

Duplication of image and text

Wood-engraved initials and other ornaments were occasionally duplicated by casting replicas in typemetal. The practice has a long history: the use of cast duplicate initials in Italy in the 1490s has been documented, and metal initials, comprising a thin typemetal plate mounted on blocks of wood to the height of ordinary type, survive in the stock of Christophe Plantin in Antwerp. It appears to have been generally a temporary expedient, however, and no notice of the technique was taken in published manuals. During the eighteenth century accounts of the practice began to be published in Germany, and by the end of the century 'cast ornaments' replicating wood engravings were sold commercially in Britain.[89]

The mould was sometimes of sand. Plantin owned wooden pattern letters which were used for casting big types in this way. But the use of a mould of plaster, as described in a German manual of 1713, produced finer work. A third

87 Smith 1755, 202.

88 Dodsley's *Collection of poems by several hands* (1748 and later editions) is a familiar example. On the printing of this work, see Suarez 1997, esp. 41–7, 57–65, 69–71, 79–80, 87–8.

89 Funcke 1998, Introduction.

technique, first described in 1740, used a matrix made by stamping a wood block into typemetal just before it cooled. It was a difficult operation, but if it succeeded the matrix could be used in the same way to make multiple relief replicas of the original. This technique was known in German as *abklatschen*, in French as *clichage* (the product was a *cliché*), and in English as *dabbing*.[90] The quality of the image was often high, and if the work was well done, there is now no way of telling from the printed page whether an impression of a wood block is from the original or a replica.

Duplicate casts were also made of whole pages of type. The history of *stereotyping*, as it later became known, is still uncertain. It is now widely accepted that Johann Müller, who printed in Leiden, made stereotype plates between 1701 and 1718, when he produced a folio Dutch bible for which a cast plate survives in the British Library. It has also been suggested, but with less agreement, that J. Athias of Amsterdam printed stereotyped bibles in English with a false Cambridge imprint in the late seventeenth century. William Ged of Edinburgh made some experiments in stereotyping, printing a duodecimo Sallust in 1739, but was discouraged by hostility from printers and typefounders. The technique used for this early stereotyping of text was probably the one that was largely adopted in the nineteenth century, which was to take moulds of fine plaster from pages of type and to cast plates from these. However, there is a circumstantial and convincing set of instructions in German dated 1696 for making stereotyped pages from moulds of papier mâché, a technique that was not commercially exploited until the 1830s. The stereotyping practices of the nineteenth century are described below.

Copperplate printing

Copperplate engraving and printing was a technique that differed radically from that of letterpress printing, and the two trades were generally carried on separately.[91] Some major printing houses may have had several copperplate presses if an important part of their work included the printing of maps and charts.[92] The big Amsterdam printing house of W. J. Blaeu was one of these. Plate printing was also done at the university presses at Oxford and Cambridge, both of which were out of easy reach of the London trade printers. In 1785 Pendred's directory of the London printing trade, which gives the names of 124 letterpress printers, lists 25 copperplate printers, 14 of whom were both

90 *OED*, *dab*, n[1], 9.
91 Gaskell 2004.
92 See Hodson, chap. 42, below.

'printers and engravers'. The latter no doubt contracted with letterpress printers to supply printed illustrations to be used as frontispieces or in the text – there has been little detailed study of the relationship – but a significant part of their output was of prints to be retailed separately.

An image for engraving was transferred to or drawn on a thin coating of wax applied to the surface of a copperplate, then engraved or etched into its surface. The tool for engraving was the v-shaped graver or *burin*, which cut the lines forming the design into the surface of the plate. For etching, the plate was first coated with a ground of varnish through which the design was scratched, revealing the metal. Acid was then poured over the plate, and this etched the design into the metal. Finer detail was added with the engraver's burin. The plate was warmed to soften the printing ink with which it was then coated, which penetrated the engraved lines, and surplus ink was wiped from the surface. The technique was incapable of rendering a solid colour, which was simulated by creating a dense pattern of parallel or crossed lines.

The rolling press had two rollers set horizontally into two uprights. The gap between the two, which could be adjusted with packing above and below, admitted a wooden plank. The inked plate was placed on the plank, a sheet of damped paper was laid on it, and then a woollen blanket. These were drawn together through the press by turning four long arms attached to the upper roller. Great pressure was applied, which the blanket spread evenly, pressing the paper against the plate from which it received the ink in the etched and incised lines.

The standard handbook, which was reprinted and spread into many countries by translation and adaptation, was that of Abraham Bosse, *Traicté des manières de graver en taille douce sur l'airin* (Paris, 1645). Bosse himself developed a hard ground for etched plates.

Plate printing was a much slower process than letterpress printing, and the finer detail of plates wore out quickly. It was customary to retouch them as this happened. Although relatively expensive, this was the normal process for the illustration of books and the monthly magazines during the eighteenth century. A variant of copperplate engraving, the *mezzotint*, had been introduced in the seventeenth century. A grain was created evenly over the surface of the plate with a tool known as a *rocker*, and the image was made by smoothing away the grain, working from dark to light, and adding detail in line where it was needed. The technique was much used for reproducing the tonal range of oil paintings for sale as individual prints, but the density of the ink on the paper made it less suitable for use to illustrate books.

The industrial trade

The introduction of industrial techniques to printing seems at first halting and partial if one compares it with contemporary changes in other industries. The process has not been studied in great detail. A public sense that new developments were taking place was promoted during the later eighteenth century by alterations in the look of printing that were in reality more cosmetic than essential, and which have their roots in events in British publishing. The case of *Donaldson* v. *Becket* and the consequent collapse of the concept of perpetual copyright protection, 'one of the most momentous decisions in [British] book trade history',[93] opened opportunities for the production of editions of popular texts that based their appeal on the use of new styles of type and on the use of wove paper. The sheets were sometimes hot-pressed between metal plates to eliminate the impression of the type and add a surface gloss that resembled the smooth surface of a print from a copper plate. Well-documented examples of this treatment can be found in the productions of the entrepreneur John Bell, whose new titles include the *Poets of Great Britain* (109 vols., 1776–92), *British theatre* (21 vols., 1776–8) and *Shakspeare* (11 vols., 1788). Of one title published by him, a play by Arthur Murphy, Bell wrote that:

> J. Bell flatters himself that he will be able to render this the most perfect and in every respect the most beautiful book, that was ever printed in any country . . . He is at present casting a new type for the purpose upon improved principles.[94]

Bell drew attention to a change in the appearance of his printing in the Advertisement to the volume of *Prolegomena* to his *Shakspeare*. By abandoning the long s (something that had been done some years earlier in Paris by François-Ambroise Didot in books printed in his new types, as Bell, an importer of French books, must have been well aware), 'the regularity of the print is by that means very much promoted, the lines having the effect of being more open'.

During the 1780s machines were introduced in Manchester which printed decorative patterns in several colours from cylindrical rollers bearing engraved copper plates on a continuous 'web' of cotton, using principles that were only adapted to printing on paper much later.[95] There was a conspicuous gap between the powered technology of the northern industrial mills and the

93 Altick 1998. See Rose, chap. 4, above.
94 Morison 1930.
95 Turnbull 1951, 50–98. The reference is to the machine of Thomas Bell, patented in 1783 and set up in 1785. There had been patents for earlier machines on similar principles since the 1740s. See Bidwell, chap. 8, below.

slow, laborious handwork of the printing office. A patent was taken out by William Nicholson in 1790 for a printing machine using the principle of a cylindrical printing surface,[96] a machine that was designed for printing not only on paper but on 'linen, cotton and other articles'. This device, which appears never to have been constructed, was later claimed by patriots in Britain as the true forebear of the cylinder printing machine.

Some movement towards change in the technology of printing can be seen in the improvement of the hand-press and the strong growth of interest in the use of stereotyping towards the end of the eighteenth century in Britain and in France, but in both cases this was largely a matter of the refinement of existing tools and processes. Developments of greater significance were the introduction of lithography[97] to Britain during the first decade of the nineteenth century – the first wholly new principle of printing devised since the fifteenth century – the application of steam power to printing in 1811, and the development of paper-making machines. In none of these cases was the inventor British, but capital for the exploitation of steam-powered printing and paper-making machines was raised in London.[98]

These developments would change the environment of printing. A symbolic event was the action for nuisance brought by the Duke of Northumberland against the printer William Clowes, which was heard in June 1824 in the Court of Common Pleas. The objection was to the noise and smoke of the steam engine that drove the printing machines in his printing office in Northumberland Court, next to Northumberland House, Charing Cross, which was 'some times like thunder, at other times like a thrashing-machine, and then again like the rumbling of carts and waggons'. When the case against Clowes was dismissed, the Duke agreed to pay the cost of moving his printing office to the former premises of Augustus Applegath in Duke Street on the other side of the River Thames.[99]

James Moyes, a contemporary printer working on a less ambitious scale than Clowes, was convinced of the need to organize the printing office on a more rational basis, particularly with attention to the resistance of the building to fire, a hazard that had so often devastated printing houses, including his own in Greville Street in 1824. His Temple Printing Office in Bouverie Street, which was lost to him by his bankruptcy during the economic turbulence of the mid-1820s, was said to be the first erected in London specifically as a printing

96 British patent no. 1748, 29 Apr. 1790.
97 See Twyman, chap. 2, above.
98 See Bidwell, chap. 8, below.
99 Smiles 1884, chap. 8: 'William Clowes'.

office.[100] Although Mylne's building for Strahan, already discussed, has a prior claim, the Temple Printing Office by William Pilkington (1758–1848) is among the earliest British examples for which there is detailed evidence of planning for the operations of printing, making use of new techniques of construction to create an industrial building on four storeys. After the loss of his new building, Moyes moved his printing office to an eighteenth-century 'dwelling house' in Castle Street.

The buildings of the University Printing Office in Glasgow, 'established on a small scale in 1811', were developed in 1818 and succeeding years by the addition of several single-storey buildings in order to accommodate more press-rooms and a stereotype foundry producing 300 pages weekly.[101] Shortly afterwards the two English university presses were also provided with new buildings, a development that was driven partly by the rising sales of the Authorized Version of the Bible for which they shared the monopoly with the King's Printer in London. At Oxford the press was moved from the Clarendon Building in Broad Street to a new site in Walton Street to the west of the city, where two separate ranges of buildings were built for the bible and learned presses to the design of Edward Blore in 1829–30, with a grand classical entrance front by Daniel Robertson, 1826–30. At Cambridge, the existing buildings were expanded piecemeal during the first decades of the nineteenth century in order to accommodate more presses and a stereotype foundry. Blore designed a grand front building in Trumpington Street, paid for by public subscription, which was built in 1833 and known as the Pitt Press in commemoration of William Pitt (d. 1806), prime minister and Member of Parliament for Cambridge.[102] Unlike the printing offices of Clowes, none of these new buildings was built to house steam-powered printing machines.[103]

Improved hand-presses

During the 1780s descriptions of two new and improved printing presses were published in France, by E.A.J. Anisson-Duperon, director of the Imprimerie Royale (1783), and by the printer Philippe-Denis Pierres (1786).

100 Moyes 1826; Bigmore and Wyman 1880; Bain 1968. Architect's drawings for Moyes's printing office (Memoranda from the working-drawings prepared by Mr Pilkington for erecting a printing-office in Bouverie-Street, London for J. Moyes Esq., 1824) came to light and were acquired after the publication of Bain's study (St Bride Library, London, 34411).

101 *Specimens of types and inventory of printing materials belonging to the University Printing Office of Glasgow . . . offered for sale by private bargain* (Glasgow, 1826).

102 Crutchley 1938; McKitterick 1998, 310–12.

103 It was decided to introduce printing machines at Cambridge in 1838: Roberts 1921, 137.

François-Ambroise Didot, who introduced influential new types during this decade, also devised an improved press. Isaiah Thomas praised the ingenuity of the improved press of Benjamin Dearborn of Portsmouth, New Hampshire, made in about 1785.[104]

There is less evidence of comparable activity in Britain. Indeed, towards the end of the eighteenth century some improved presses were said to have been imported from France by London printers.[105] Little is known about the press of Joseph Ridley, to which a premium was awarded by the Society of Arts in 1795, nor that of Roworth, made at about the same date.[106] However, at some date after 1800 a press was made in cast iron to the design of Charles, 3rd Earl Stanhope (1753–1816).[107] Stanhope had studied in Geneva, and it seems probable that his ideas were influenced by the iron press invented in 1772 by the typefounder Wilhelm Haas of Basel.[108] The earliest dated document relating to the press is a leaflet of 1803.[109] The Stanhope press had a conventional screw, but its innovation, a principle that was incorporated in all later iron hand-presses, was compound leverage, by which power was progressively increased as the platen descended.

Lord Stanhope, who was dedicated to libertarian principles and the freedom of the press, declined to patent his press, and it appears in contemporary caricatures as a political symbol. Iron hand-presses were widely used in Britain throughout the nineteenth century, and were still commonly a part of the equipment of printing offices in the twentieth century, used either for printing small editions or for proofing. In addition to the Stanhope press, there were the Columbian press, patented in London in 1817 by George Clymer of Philadelphia, and the Albion, first made in the early 1820s by Cope and improved in about 1830 by his foreman, Hopkinson.[110] The iron hand-presses had platens that printed the full area of the forme at one pull. Since the pulling of the impression was only one of several actions of the pressmen, the effect of this innovation on the rate of their output appears to have been negligible. The importance of the new presses lies in their greater power and the precision of their manufacture, which improved the quality of impression in books and

104 Thomas 1810, II, 538–9.
105 Johnson 1824, II, 502; Hansard 1825, 420.
106 Hansard 1825, 421.
107 The earliest surviving Stanhope press, No. 4, is dated 1805 (Gunnersbury Museum).
108 Haas 1790.
109 *Specimens of typography, without the use of balls; executed at the printing press lately invented by Earl Stanhope. The printing press made by Mr Robert Walker, of Vine-street, Piccadilly. The inking roller made by Mr Charles Fairbone, of New Street, Fetter Lane.* Printed by William Bulmer and Co. at the Shakspeare Printing Office, Cleveland-row, 1803.
110 Moran 1973.

enabled the new bold poster types to be printed well.[111] For the first time 'fine printing' appears in trade manuals as a distinct category of work for a luxury market, a term that was applied to the careful printing on fine paper of books illustrated with the new style of wood engraving.[112]

The inking roller

The traditional pair of leather balls for inking the type was superseded during the early nineteenth century by a single hand-roller. Papillon had illustrated a leather-covered roller with which impressions could be taken from wood blocks without using a press.[113] The earliest reference to an inking roller appears in Bulmer's *Specimens of typography without the use of balls* (1803; see above). This may perhaps have been covered with leather, but such rollers must always have had a seam that would tend to accumulate a line of thicker ink and transfer it to the printing surface. A seamless cast *composition* was adopted, consisting of a mixture of glue and molasses, the latter of which, by absorbing humidity from the atmosphere, gave the substance elasticity. According to Hansard, who gave detailed instructions for making composition rollers and an account of their use, the recipe was derived from *dabbers* that were used in the Staffordshire potteries.[114] The use of composition inking rollers probably contributed to the quality of 'fine printing' by hand. Although the inking rollers of Koenig's first power-driven press of 1810 were described in the patent as being covered with felt and leather, there is no doubt that, as Hansard observed, machine-printing would never have succeeded without composition rollers.

Printing machines

The powered printing machine was developed in London. Friedrich Koenig (1774–1833), born at Eisleben near Halle, served an apprenticeship in the Breitkopf printing office in Leipzig. He found backers for some experimental work towards improvements to printing techniques, but having failed to arouse interest in his inventions in Germany, Austria or Russia, Koenig travelled to London in November 1806. There he was at first employed at a

111 See Twyman, chap. 2, above.

112 Stower 1808, 490–8; Savage 1822.

113 Papillon 1985, II, 352–4. Papillon's roller was intended for applying pressure to the paper, and not, as Hansard mistakenly believed, for inking.

114 Hansard 1825, 622–36; Bloy 1967, 55–65.

printing office, probably that of Richard Taylor, who remained his friend long after his other business partnerships ended in disagreement and bitterness.

Koenig's first agreement for the development of his printing press was with Thomas Bensley. Taylor and George Woodfall entered the partnership; John Walter of *The Times*, after showing some interest, declined. Koenig was joined by Friedrich Andreas Bauer (1783–1860) from Stuttgart, who had practical and theoretical knowledge of engineering. The result of their co-operation, patented in 1810, was a hand-press with a conventional flat platen that was driven by steam power. It was first used in April 1811 in Bensley's office to print 3,000 copies of sheet (H) of the *New annual register* for 1810, which Koenig claimed to be the first printing ever executed by machine.[115] Koenig's second machine used a cylinder for the impression, and pointed the way to the later development of the powered printing machine. The cylinder machine, completed at the engineers' own workshop in White Cross Street in December 1812, printed 800 sheets an hour. It was shown to some newspaper proprietors, and it reawakened the interest of Walter, who privately commissioned the 'double machine', with two cylinders, that was used to print *The Times* of 29 November 1814.

The partnership, in which Bensley remained the largest shareholder, broke up acrimoniously in 1817. Koenig and Bauer left England to establish a factory for making their machines in Wurzburg. The fairest summary of the problems that led to the rupture is probably that of Richard Taylor, written many years later.[116] Other British engineers took advantage of the opportunity provided by the withdrawal of Koenig and Bauer to make machines on similar principles, claiming to have introduced radical improvements. David Napier made a machine, the Nay-Peer, illustrated by Hansard,[117] a development of a design of Koenig's that was also exported to Paris.[118] The partnership of Augustus Applegath (1788–1871) and Edward Cowper (1790–1852) made alterations to the Koenig and Bauer machines in the Bensley office and at *The Times*,[119] and became major manufacturers of machines of their own at their factory in Stamford Street, Lambeth. The Applegath and Cowper partnership was bankrupted during the trade crisis of 1826. Edward Cowper continued to develop printing machinery in partnership with his brother Ebenezer, contracting out their manufacture. Obituaries record that they installed machines in England,

115 *The Times*, 8 Dec. 1814.
116 Taylor 1847.
117 Hansard 1825, 710–14. The name is a word play on 'Napier' and 'nonpareil' or 'without equal'.
118 Goebel 1906, 187–9.
119 Cowper 1828.

Scotland, Ireland and Italy, and that they supplied the twelve machines to the Imprimerie Royale, Paris, that were broken up in the Revolution of 1830. Applegath, who continued to design machines, saw one with four feeding-stations installed at *The Times* in 1828, which produced 4,000 completed sheets an hour, probably the greatest output that was achieved on a machine with a conventional flat bed.[120]

Taylor's personal papers show that he saw the printers of newspapers and periodicals as the main market for printing machines, at least during the second decade of the century. They were later joined by book printers who had long, predictable runs of work, like the participants in the bible monopoly, and entrepreneurs like William Clowes.

Images

The buoyant market for images during the first decades of the nineteenth century, whether as illustrations in books or as separate prints,[121] encouraged the enhancement of existing techniques and the introduction of new ones.[122] As a consequence of the introduction of smooth wove papers, more refined styles of wood engraving were developed. Wood blocks had the great practical advantage that they could be placed in the page with type and printed with the superior quality of the improved hand-presses or with the commercial advantage of printing machines. They could also be stereotyped.

Engraving with a metal engraver's tools on the end grain of boxwood was not an invention of Thomas Bewick, but his illustrations to the *History of quadrupeds* (Newcastle, 1790) demonstrated ingenuity in exploiting the potential of the technique. The result was seen and widely appreciated in the successive editions of the *Quadrupeds* and in his own *British birds*, first published in 1797. The celebrity of Bewick's work was a powerful influence in promoting appreciation of the medium, and it created opportunities for a new generation of British wood engravers, some of whom, like Charlton Nesbit, Luke Clennell and William Harvey, had been his pupils. Another gifted wood engraver, Robert Branston, the son of a copperplate printer, had taught himself the technique on his arrival in London in 1802, and his pupil, John Thompson, became one of the most versatile and skilled of the new English wood engravers, providing blocks for many of the works finely printed by Charles Whittingham

120 Taylor 1997.
121 See Clayton, chap. 10 below.
122 Harris 1968–70.

the Elder at the Chiswick Press during the 1820s, and becoming well known in France.[123]

The rate at which intaglio prints could be produced remained low, at a period when the speed of mechanized letterpress printing was increasing. But the construction of the rolling press was improved. Cast-iron frames and steel rollers were introduced. The use of reduction gearing made the operation of the press easier and smoother, and enabled larger plates to be printed.[124] A new technique of etching copper was also introduced: the *aquatint*. Particles of resin were deposited on the plate and the etching was restricted to certain areas, producing a series of graded flat tints that emulated water-colour washes, and which were well suited to the production of hand-coloured topographical illustrations.

The problem of the rapid deterioration of the plate that had inhibited the use of copper for large editions was largely overcome by the use of steel. Interest in the use of this metal was stimulated by the need of banks for a medium that would resist wear. To this end, during the 1790s Jacob Perkins of Newburyport, Massachusetts, developed the process known as *siderography* by which an identical impression of an engraved design could be transferred under pressure to other plates. Having failed in 1820 to secure a commission for the use of his process from the Bank of England, Perkins joined in partnership with the engraver Charles Heath and sought clients among the London engravers for the supply of plates and the printing of their work. Thirty thousand copies of the frontispiece to Mavor's spelling book were printed by Perkins in 1821.[125]

Lithography

A wholly new process, stone-printing or lithography,[126] was introduced during the first decade of the nineteenth century. It made use of the capacity of certain varieties of fine-grained limestone to absorb water. An image was drawn on the stone with a greasy crayon. When the stone was damped and then inked, the ink adhered to the marks made by the crayon and was rejected by the unmarked areas. Unlike letterpress printing, in which the printing surface was in relief, or intaglio, where only the recessed lines retained ink, lithographic printing was a *planographic* process, in which the image was printed from a flat surface. Although it initially lacked the precision of line of

123 Chatto and Jackson 1861, 446–549.
124 Bain 1966; Dyson 1983, 1984.
125 Hunnisett 1980b, 17.
126 See Twyman, chap. 2, above.

the etched or engraved plate, and was just as slow to print, it offered access to printmaking by skilled draughtsmen who had neither the professional training nor the specialist technical skills required in order to engrave on wood or copper; its use grew steadily as a medium for book illustration and for the occasional production of whole texts.

Alois Senefelder, its inventor, came to London in 1800 to obtain a patent that was granted on 20 June 1801; he left the administration of the patent in the hands of Johann André, whose brother Philipp appears on the first examples of the process published in Britain, *Specimens of polyautography*, published in April 1803, comprising works drawn on the stone by twelve artists, including Benjamin West, the president of the Royal Academy, Henry Fuseli, and Thomas Barker of Bath, who later published *Forty lithographic impressions of rustic figues* (1813) and initiated the use of the term *lithography*.[127] However, the growth of lithography in Britain was due to Rudolph Ackermann, already known as a publisher of works illustrated by aquatint, and to Charles Hullmandel, who did much to improve methods of printing. Ackermann was responsible for producing an English edition of Senefelder's treatise, *A complete course of lithography*, in 1819. This event, and the establishment of a press by Hullmandel, signalled the real birth of English lithography. 'From 1818 onwards other presses were set up in London and in the provinces as well, but Hullmandel's influence remained paramount in directing the course of lithography for another twenty years.'[128] The first edition of Hullmandel's own manual, *The art of drawing on stone*, was published in 1824.

The lithographic press used a similar principle to that of the rolling press, but applied gentler pressure to the fragile stone. Paper was laid on the inked stone, a tympan was folded over them, and they were drawn together under a horizontal scraper to which pressure was applied. A substitute for the stone, generally a zinc plate, was eventually found. The printing process was not mechanized until the second half of the nineteenth century.[129]

Type founding

The change that was seen in the style of British type during the 1790s was a reflection of a European movement that began in about 1780. The printing of François-Ambroise Didot and his son Firmin played a prominent part in this movement, which (as Firmin's brother Pierre freely acknowledged) owed

127 Twyman 1970, 27, 35.
128 Twyman 1970, 40. Cf. Twyman, chap. 2, above.
129 Twyman 1967. Cf. Twyman, chap. 2, above.

something to the example some decades before of the Birmingham printer John Baskerville. The new types, with their greater contrast of thick and thin strokes, reflected new styles of calligraphy and their brilliant effect when printed from copper plates. Baskerville's use of wove paper, and of hot pressing the sheets after printing between metal plates, can be seen as helping to initiate the new fashion. Type founders used the term 'modern cut' types for the new style, and the name 'modern' would continue in use colloquially for these types when 'old face' types made a partial return later in the nineteenth century.

The most conspicuous innovation among the products of the type foundries during the first three decades of the nineteenth century was the introduction of big types, which were used for the printing of the handbills and posters that promoted the sale of goods and services, a specialized branch of the trade that grew very fast between 1800 and 1830.[130] The biggest type normally made by type founders had been 6-line Pica, a size equivalent to about one inch. Bigger types for poster printing, as large as 3 inches high, were cast in sand by the Caslon foundry during the 1780s using brass patterns that still survive.[131] The style of the big types changed too, even more radically than the style of type for text setting. First of all, in about 1805, the contrast between thick and thin strokes was hugely inflated. These 'fat faces' were used for the handbills and posters printed for the agents for the state lotteries, and it is probable that one of these agents, Bish, may have had some influence in their introduction. Simultaneously a new style of so-called 'Egyptian' letters was introduced into the work of signwriters. It provoked scandalized public comment, but these new letters, which would later be known as 'sans serif', have a complex history that includes genuine antiquarian sources. Such styles, though they are sometimes seen on the wrappers of books that were issued in parts, rarely penetrate to the text pages. They were, however, to become a permanent part of the repertoire of types for the printers of posters.

During the 1820s an entrepreneur with no experience of type founding, Louis John Pouchée, attempted to break the monopoly of the major London founders by undercutting their prices. He imported and patented a device, the *machine polyamatype*, invented in Paris by Henri Didot, for casting up to 200 types simultaneously. It was also used for making big decorated types and reproductions of wood engravings by means of a technique similar to 'dabbing'. Pouchée was bought out by London type founders and his machine was destroyed.[132]

130 Twyman 1970. Cf. Twyman, chap. 2, above.
131 At the Type Museum, London.
132 Pouchée 1993, Introduction.

Two technical innovations were introduced into type founding. A trigger was added to the hand mould to lift the matrix and enable the type to be more quickly ejected.[133] It was claimed to accelerate the speed of hand-casting significantly. A new kind of matrix called *Sanspareil*, cut from brass sheet, was introduced in about 1810, and it enabled big new poster types to be cast with greater precision and speed than was possible with casting in sand.

A practical casting machine for making types in the sizes used for text setting, invented by the New York type founder David Bruce Junior in 1835, employed a pump to inject the type metal. This innovation, which made it possible to cast the more delicate and complex ornamented types that were introduced after 1830,[134] may already have been in use to cast type with the hand mould. The Bruce machine was widely adopted by British typefoundries.[135]

Stereotyping

Towards the end of the eighteenth century there was revived interest in France in the technique of casting plates that duplicated typeset matter and experiments were made with several different techniques. The process became generally known as *stereotyping*, after the name given by Firmin and Pierre Didot to the *formats stéréotypés*, the technique for which they obtained a patent on 6 *nivose*, *an* 6 (26 December 1797).[136]

Intermittent experimental stereotype printing had also taken place in Britain during the eighteenth century. Alexander Tilloch and Robert Foulis, printer to the University of Glasgow, began experiments and brought them to Lord Stanhope, who set up a stereotype foundry with the assistance of Foulis at the family house at Chevening, Kent. The commercial exploitation of the process began when Andrew Wilson, a printer by trade, set up a foundry with Stanhope's support in London at 12 Duke Street, Lincoln's Inn Fields in 1802, and began to offer to supply plates to the printing trade.[137] A pamphlet dated 1804 was claimed as the first work stereotyped by the process. Surviving examples of stereotype moulds made in Stanhope's own workshop at Chevening are of fine plaster.

133 It appears to have been more or less simultaneously introduced in Britain and the United States. In Britain there was a patent by John Peek, No. 3194, 23 Jan. 1809, 'A machine for the more expeditious casting of printing types'.

134 Gray 1976.

135 De Vinne 1900, 20–4.

136 Camus 1801, 113.

137 M.L. Turner 1974.

In 1804, Wilson began negotiations with the University of Cambridge for the use of his stereotype process at the University Press, and these led to its adoption, although there were protracted disputes about payment. Shortly afterwards he was also conducting negotiations with the University Press at Oxford, where a similar agreement was concluded, and a stereotyped prayer book was completed by October 1806.[138] Having fallen out with Stanhope, Wilson set up as an independent stereotype printer and publisher and acquired additional premises in Camden Town, which were put up for sale in 1816.[139]

T. C. Hansard, who gave some account of the cool reception of stereotyping by London printers and publishers during this initial period in his printer's manual of 1825, set out the perceived advantages and disadvantages of the technique.[140] Among the disadvantages were that it caused wear and damage to the type, and opened owners of texts to the danger of fraud by the copying of plates. The quality of the printing surface was not always good to start with, and it was easily damaged when plates were repeatedly re-mounted for reprinting. And, in a period when the style of type was evolving, the look of the plate soon became out of date. He reported that the University Press at Oxford, having spent large sums on the licence and on setting up a foundry, had partially abandoned its use, preferring to print many works from type. The economic advantages of stereotyping for certain classes of work were undeniable, however. It freed the type for further use and enabled a work to be reprinted many times without incurring the expense of resetting it. Moreover, there were special advantages to publishers of works that comprised complex, accurate setting, such as mathematical tables, of creating fixed plates that were immune to accidental alteration.

Conclusion

The technical innovations that had been introduced into printing by 1830 would be developed during subsequent decades. Printing in multiple colours, which was still seldom attempted on a significant scale before 1830,[141] would be exploited by the printers of magazines, such as the *Illustrated London News*, within little over a decade. By the 1860s, newspapers were beginning to print at a rate of tens of thousands of copies an hour from a cylindrical printing

138 Hart 1966.
139 Inventory of his stock in M.L. Turner 1974, 55–64. See McKitterick 1998, 275–6, 281.
140 Hansard 1825, 815–87.
141 The pioneering work is Savage 1822.

surface on a continuous web of paper, employing the principle already established in machines for the printing of cotton during the 1780s.

Changes in the technology of printing were driven by an increase in the scale of production, which was the fruit of the rapid increase in the population and its urbanization during the course of the nineteenth century, and of the improvement in networks for the distribution of products. The term 'printing house', which seems apposite for most of the centres of production from the time of Moxon until the start of the nineteenth century, soon becomes inadequate for the large-scale industrial premises of Clowes and other major printers. Increasingly, their premises were located outside London, the capital city to which printing had been largely restricted for centuries, for political as well as economic reasons. One consequence of these changes of scale in the printing industry was the development of trade unions that would participate in the control of its operation.[142]

Notwithstanding the alteration that took place in the appearance of printed matter between 1695 and 1830, many techniques remained essentially the same. Type was laboriously assembled, letter by letter, and after it had been used each letter was put back again in the case. The correct setting of text long remained the responsibility of the printing trade. The practice of the craft was passed from generation to generation of skilled compositors, to whom authors and publishers entrusted their manuscripts in the expectation, seldom disappointed, that careless and inconsistent spelling and punctuation would be silently corrected before the words were set in type. The printing office was a place of arcane traditions that were often concealed from the outside world, and its practices must be understood by the historian of the book who wishes to trace the many processes through which a text passed before it reached the reader.

142 Howe 1947.

8
The industrialization of the paper trade

JOHN BIDWELL

French imports dominated the British paper trade until the end of the seventeenth century. Protected by tariffs, nurtured by capital investment and sustained by a steady demand for their products, British papermakers learned to manufacture cheap printing grades, drove the French out of the lower end of the market, and competed successfully against higher-quality goods imported from Holland and Italy. During the eighteenth century, they established a completely independent, highly efficient, well-organized and generally prosperous paper trade, ripe for technological innovations.[1]

Scientific discoveries and engineering advances revolutionized their business, but not so thoroughly and not quite so quickly as they claimed. Legal disputes and financial obligations complicated the diffusion of machine technology, which did not consist of any one invention, but rather a series of inventions, each needing the others to achieve its full potential. As far as printers were concerned, this process did not reach its logical conclusion until the advent of rotary presses capable of printing paper in the form of rolls rather than sheets – but in this period web printing was not yet technically feasible (or even legally permissible).[2]

Nevertheless, printers and publishers extolled the economic and cultural benefits of industrialization in terms of one machine, the Fourdrinier, a name used even now to signify progress in the papermaking trade. In 1837, friends of Henry Fourdrinier testified that he deserved recognition and recompense for the sacrifices he had made to develop the machine – not just a labour-saving device but a mechanism for social change, increasing capacity and cutting costs so dramatically that its products could enhance and redirect the power of the

1 Bidwell 2002b. The fourth chapter of Coleman 1975 (1958), 'Growth and Consolidation in the Eighteenth Century', remains the best overview of the paper trade in this period. See Shorter 1957 for a geographical survey of trade as well as a comprehensive account of all the known paper mills in England up to 1800.

2 See Mosley, chap. 7 above. In 1835 proposals for web printing were denied by the Excise, which still insisted on taxing paper in sheets; see Dagnall 1998b, 64.

printed word. They promised that cheap paper would be a vehicle of learning, that it would bring knowledge, instruction and enlightenment within the reach of readers eager to improve themselves with books previously beyond their means. Charles Knight credited the machine with the phenomenal success of his *Penny Magazine*, just one of his publications 'which I think do in some degree advance the civilization of the country'. Additional panegyrics could be cited, all based on the premise that mechanization lowered the cost of production, that papermakers passed the cost benefits on to publishers, that publishers passed them on to consumers, and that the consumption of books and periodicals rose in response to these inducements.[3]

Indeed, the price of book paper did fall significantly, but not until many years after Fourdriniers were first adopted by enterprising members of the trade who had made other manufacturing improvements in the meantime. Paper remained one of the most expensive ingredients of book production during the period covered in this volume, which ends when they were just beginning to recoup their investment in industrialization and when their customers in the book trade were just beginning to notice its effects. To give credit where it is due, the paper manufacturers' accomplishments should be viewed not so much as triumphs of technology, but as daring speculations, requiring financial acumen and managerial skills as well as mechanical ingenuity. Like the friends of Henry Fourdrinier, I will trace the development of the papermaking machine, but I will portray him in a different light. Moreover, I will concentrate mostly on the business conditions that made this invention possible, especially the robust growth and rising profitability of the paper trade during the eighteenth century.

At the beginning of the century, printers and publishers still depended on imports from Italy and Holland. They could purchase papers as large as atlas or as small as pott, but for book work they usually opted for demy, measuring around 15¾ by 19¾ inches, but growing to around 17½ by 22 inches by the 1780s. Between 1720 and 1750 imported demy cost about 12*s.* or 13*s.* a ream, although premium grades used for fine paper copies might bring as much as 20*s.* a ream. The Ackers and Bowyer ledgers record occasional purchases of English demy, always at less than the going price since it was less desirable than the standard fare obtained from abroad.[4]

In the 1730s, however, English papermakers began to hold their own against foreign competition. By that time, they could claim that they had brought their techniques 'to great Perfection' and could display specimens of their work that

3 'Report from the select committee on Fourdrinier's patent', *Parl. Papers* (Commons), 1837 (351), xx, 59, 70.
4 Dagnall 1998b, 17, 27; McKenzie and Ross 1968; Maslen and Lancaster 1991.

'even excels the *Genoa* Paper'. The Ackers and Bowyer ledgers gradually ceased to specify foreign and domestic varieties, apparently because the clerks no longer needed to designate quality by place of origin. Imports of writings and printings, the two highest-quality grades of paper, fell from about a hundred and twenty thousand reams a year in 1711 to just over forty thousand reams in 1743, even though demand was climbing higher than ever, and the supply was not impeded by any new tariff barriers between 1714 and 1748. Conversely, the number of paper mills in England and Wales increased from approximately 200 in 1712 to 280 in 1738, 380 in 1785, 420 in 1800 and 450 in 1816. No more than 10 mills were operating in Scotland before 1764, but the Excise licensed 25 concerns in 1785, 33 in 1800 and around 60 in 1816. Although Ireland had only 3 mills in 1710, as many as 50 were at work in the 1780s, after local authorities had encouraged investment in the trade by offering premiums for superior workmanship and by subsidizing the construction of new facilities, which were exempt from excise taxes until 1798.[5]

Investors helped to build these mills by contributing capital, cautiously at first but more confidently after learning what profits could be made in this rural industry. So remote were its water-powered manufactories that many investors might not have noticed its potential had they not been able to see for themselves signs of prosperity both at the manufacturing end and at the point of sale. Financiers in London could easily observe the manufacturing career of James Whatman II, proprietor of the renowned Turkey Mill in Kent, 'the most curious and the most compleat in the Kingdom'. Few papermakers could afford to run more than one or two vats, but Turkey Mill contained five of them, each capable of making around two thousand reams a year. Between 1781 and 1787 Whatman manufactured fine writings, drawings and plate papers in such quantities that he paid about a tenth of the total excise taxes collected on those high-priced commodities. His profits sometimes amounted to more than five thousand pounds a year, more than enough to acquire a country estate, refurbish a manor house, and furnish it with an extensive library and a picture gallery featuring the work of Van Dyck, Tintoretto, Reynolds and Romney. After he retired, he was able to give each of his two daughters a dowry of more than ten thousand pounds. In many respects, he personified the achievements of the paper trade, having built his business and

5 Coleman 1975 (1958), 94, fig. 2; *The case of the paper-makers, humbly address'd to the honourable the House of Commons* (London, *c.*1737), printed on paper made by William Jubb; *The case of the paper-makers in the kingdom of England* (London, *c.*1737), printed on paper made by Samuel Gibbon and Company; Richard Parker, *Proposals humbly offer'd to the consideration of the honourable House of Commons* (London, 1711?); Shorter 1971, 75–6, 123, 227; Phillips 1998, 163–72; Thomson 1974, 72–5.

made his fortune by matching and even surpassing the quality of imported goods. Around 1757, he and his father collaborated with the printer John Baskerville on the invention of wove paper, a new fashion eagerly adopted by French papermakers who hotly disputed the honour of being the first to imitate this English innovation. Foreigners also admired his Antiquarian paper, the largest sheet made by hand, commissioned by the Society of Antiquaries in 1773 to print an enormous reproduction of a painting in Windsor Castle. Other notable commissions lent more lustre to the Whatman name, itself such a valuable commodity that it was licensed for use in the watermarks of two competing firms.[6]

Whatman sold his products through London wholesale stationers, who could also impress investors with their wealth, rank and prestige. A stationer might start as a proprietor of a paper mill and then move to London, where he could expedite the distribution of his wares and deal in rags on advantageous terms. Most stationers took a career path in the opposite direction, however, beginning in sales and amassing in the course of trade sufficient capital to buy mills that could keep them supplied with goods made to their specifications. After producing thirteen sons in two marriages, Christopher Magnay bequeathed his stationery firm and the mills he had acquired in Ireland, Surrey and Hertfordshire to the senior members of his brood, who bought and sold other mills after he died in 1826. A prominent and respectable member of the business community, he served as Master of the Stationers' Company in 1816 and Lord Mayor of London in 1821. Likewise, Sir Matthew Bloxam rose to high office on his profits in the stationery trades, serving as Sheriff of London and Member of Parliament. He invested his surplus capital in a bank and for a while made his living as a bill broker before spending his last years as a paper buyer for the Stationery Office. The bank failed; his bills were protested, and he went to prison for his debts, albeit with the privilege of living in the Rules of the King's Bench – but in his prime he was discounting notes to the value of two million pounds a year.[7]

Investors in the paper trade incurred formidable risks in hopes of opulent returns like those enjoyed by Whatman, Magnay and Bloxam. Political developments greatly increased the risks and rewards during the 1790s, when papermakers were just on the verge of adopting industrial methods and were

6 Balston, 1979 (1957); Balston, 1998. The output per vat during this period was determined by the 'day's work', the production quotas set by the trade for different sizes of paper. In Kent, a vatman would have to make seven reams of demy printing a day, six days a week. For the production quotas of this period, see Bidwell 1990, 30–6 and *Instructions to be observed by the officers employ'd in the duties on paper* (London, 1729), 14.

7 Ormes 1997; Dye 2001; Maxted 1977, 23; 'Report from the select committee on printing and stationery', *Parl. Papers* (Commons), 1822 (607), IV, 649, 674–6.

in desperate need of them to keep up with demand and to cope with market forces difficult to predict and impossible to control. The financial pressures of the French war drove up prices in the paper trade as well as other sectors of the economy. Manufacturing costs rose relentlessly along with the price of imported rags – an essential ingredient already scarce and dear, but even more so when European conflicts disrupted foreign trade. And to make matters worse, Parliament financed the war effort with an array of new taxes, including one on paper introduced in 1794. This tax was based on weight, not on value or quantity, a great improvement in some ways since it simplified the task of excise officers, who previously had to tally a bewildering profusion of specific and *ad valorem* duties. Yet, the Act of 1794 was fundamentally a regressive measure penalizing those least able to bear the burden of taxation, the manufacturers of printing grades. The higher-priced writing grades paid proportionally lower taxes, although they were charged the same rate of 2½*d.* per pound. Writing demy got off easily in comparison with printing demy, two reams in a bundle of 41 pounds assessed at 8*s.* 6½*d.*, more than twice as much as the previous specific duty of 3*s.* 10*d.* per bundle. In 1801, Parliament raised the rate again to 5*d.* per pound, but soon reduced it to 3*d.*, heeding the protests of the trade and hoping for an upturn in the economy after the Peace of Amiens. Taxation, inflation and the increasing cost of raw materials forced papermakers to raise their prices during the 1790s, good demy peaking near 30*s.* a ream, coarse demy around 18*s.* a ream. After Parliament doubled the tax rate in 1801, prices soared higher than many customers thought they could afford, but still lagged behind the rate of inflation.[8]

These were not the best times to be in the papermaking business, unless one could count on it to recover quickly. Investors watched closely the development of two new inventions that seemed ready to solve the problems of the 1790s: the steam engine and chlorine bleaching. Both had proved themselves in other trades. The steam engine could overcome the constraints of water power, which ran the beating engines in paper mills. The topography of the mill seat and the terms of the water privilege dictated the productivity of the mill, for in most cases the available head and fall of water could run no more than three engines, providing sufficient pulp to keep no more than two vats at work. In theory, a steam mill could contain any number of vats with the requisite beating engines as well as other types of machinery, not to mention drying lofts heated by the excess steam. Likewise, chlorine bleaching could eliminate

8 Johnson 1794; 'Report from the committee on the booksellers and printers petition', *Parl. Papers* (Commons), 1801–2 (34–2), II, 102, 113. Representative prices of demy can be found in this report and in the impression books of the Longman firm, RUL (Chadwyck-Healey film).

another bottleneck in production, the chronic shortage of rags fit for the manufacture of writings and printings. Papermakers with bleaching facilities could produce acceptably white printing grades from low-quality coloured rags or alternative sources of fibre such as straw or wood. By increasing output and cutting the cost of raw materials, an enterprising papermaker might hope to capture the market in printings, an easy target during this turbulent decade.

Matthias Koops promised credulous investors that he would exploit these inventions in an enormous manufacturing complex containing thirty-two vats, an eighty-horsepower steam engine, a steam-heated drying loft, a bleaching house, boilers, tanks, and other facilities for generating pulp from large quantities of cheap, non-rag fibre. He had no experience in the papermaking trade and no qualifications for running a business on this scale beyond a gift for promoting his schemes and convincing others to take part in them. In 1800 and 1801 he patented methods for de-inking recycled paper and for making paper 'fit for printing' from straw, hemp, flax and wood. Although the patents are in his name, they probably are based on techniques developed by his partner Elias Carpenter, who had been experimenting with bleaching at the Neckinger Mill in London in 1795. Koops proclaimed the commercial potential of his patents in his *Historical account of the substances which have been used to describe events, and to convey ideas from the earliest date, to the invention of paper* (two editions, 1800 and 1801), printed on straw, wood and recycled papers manufactured at the Neckinger Mill. Under a scholarly veneer, the *Historical account* was actually a prospectus designed to impress investors. In another bid to attract attention, Koops complained to Parliament that he could not profit from his discoveries as long as foreigners were free to read the patent specifications in the Court of Chancery or in *The repertory of arts and manufactures*. Parliament took him seriously enough to hear the testimony of his associates, who announced that he was building a manufactory that would employ five hundred people and would cost a hundred thousand pounds. His methods would succeed only if he could implement them on a mass-production basis – an expensive proposition, but worth the risk if he could eliminate the problems posed by imported rags.[9]

With these ambitions, Koops, Carpenter and twenty investors formed the Straw Paper Company in 1801. The machinist John Rennie built a pilot plant on the premises they rented for this grandiose venture, a sixteen-acre estate in Millbank conveniently close to London's business district. They laid the foundation for the steam engine, and, as an interim measure, installed a much smaller

9 Hills 2001; Crocker and Clarke 2001; 'Report on Mr Koops' petition', *Parl. Papers* (Commons), 1801 (55), III, 127–34.

one to run four vats manufacturing mostly wrappings. Designs for the mill and the steam engine survive in the papers of the engineers Boulton & Watt, who would have built the machinery if the company could have paid for it.

While these preparations were being made, Koops's publicity campaign attracted so much attention that people began to inquire into his past. They learned that he was an uncertified bankrupt with debts dating back to 1790, when he defaulted in a mercantile venture, and that he had also dabbled in an insurance business, which had collapsed within a year. The bankrupt was obliged to meet with his creditors, who agreed that he should repay them at 5*s.* to the pound, but he could not repay the second dividend. In 1802, they demanded the seizure of his household goods along with assets of the Straw Paper Company to satisfy debts amounting to nearly £9,000, far beyond the means of the company, which had goods and facilities valued at £3,500. The proprietors cut their losses, closed the mill and put it up for sale in 1804, eventually recovering enough cash to pay £1,000 to Koops's assignees. Certainly, they would have failed to make paper from straw in large enough quantities to turn a profit even if they had not been betrayed by the founder of the firm. Straw proved to be less practical and economical than the esparto grass grown in Spain and Algeria, successfully adopted as a substitute for rags in the 1860s. Although doomed from the start, their efforts are worth noting here because they were prompted by the same enterprising spirit (or speculative fervour) that inspired the Fourdriniers to finance the development of the papermaking machine.[10]

Henry and Sealy Fourdrinier agreed to sponsor the machine in 1801, at a critical moment in the trade when it was contending with soaring prices and other hardships that seemed to call for desperate measures. If they had started any sooner or later, they might have been less eager to assume the risks of underwriting such a radical innovation in papermaking technology. The convoluted history of this invention does not have to be repeated here except to explain how the Fourdriniers became involved with it and how their strategies for exploiting it influenced the industrialization of the paper trade. Like many other inventions, the papermaking machine evolved gradually from an original idea to a working model, which still needed improvements before it could prove its commercial potential and be adopted widely enough to have a significant economic impact. Its development conforms to the classic paradigm of technological diffusion formulated by Nathan Rosenberg, who suggested that inventions reach economic maturity in four stages, beginning with 'initial

10 Goulden 1989.

conceptualization' and proceeding through 'establishment of technical feasibility (invention) to commercial feasibility (innovation) to subsequent diffusion'. The Fourdriniers played an important part in this process, but did not participate in the beginning or the end.[11]

The Fourdrinier was a French invention, starting as a crude, hand-cranked apparatus devised by Nicolas-Louis Robert, a clerk in one of France's largest, busiest and most labour-intensive paper mills, owned by Leger Didot. Robert and Didot began to dispute the rights to the discovery soon after Robert applied for a patent in 1798, but neither had the means or skills to proceed beyond the initial conceptualization. At one point, Robert sold his rights to Didot, who commissioned his brother-in-law John Gamble to patent the device in England, where Didot and Gamble hoped to find the technical facilities and financial resources to build a commercially viable machine. Gamble made the acquaintance of the Fourdrinier brothers, who immediately perceived the potential of his project and agreed to advance all the necessary funds in return for part of the profits. Leger Didot later came to England and took a third share of the patent. John Gamble owned another third, and the remainder belonged to various members of the Fourdrinier firm.[12]

Gamble and Didot could not have chosen better partners – if they were looking for trade connections and financial expertise. Henry and Sealy Fourdrinier were junior members of the leading firm of wholesale stationers in London, founded in 1719 when their grandfather emigrated to England and went into business as a stationer and engraver. The Fourdriniers sold paper to Bowyer and bought paper from Whatman, who campaigned for the reform of the excise duties in association with a Henry Fourdrinier, probably their father. By 1800, their family was running two separate and highly lucrative concerns: a retail store in Charing Cross – which stocked blank books, office supplies and fancy writings – and a large wholesale establishment first on Lombard Street and then on Sherborne Lane, where papermakers could purchase rags and publishers could order bulk quantities of printings. The Fourdriniers on Lombard Street recorded profits of more than £14,000 in two years running, 1800 and 1801. Like many successful merchants, they provided informal banking services on the side, using their accumulated capital to discount or endorse bills of their colleagues in trade. This was such an important part of their business that some of their partners were assigned to manage their banking operations in a separate division known as the 'cash department'. During a

11 Rosenberg 1972–3.

12 'Minutes of proceedings of the committee, to whom was referred the bill [concerning the Fourdriniers' patent]', *Parl. Papers* (Lords), 1807 (36), XIV, 25–6 (internal numbering); Clapperton 1967, 15–25.

downturn in the economy, they would have to cope with losses in this department, but in periods of prosperity they could call on it when they needed money to spend on their schemes for industrial development.[13]

At great expense they acquired the services of the brilliant engineer Bryan Donkin and a team of English mechanics who set out to construct an efficient and reliable machine on the basis of the French patent and a working model, which Gamble brought over for their examination. Robert's ideas had to be thoroughly revised and significantly improved before satisfactory paper could be made. The basic principle of pouring pulp on a moving wire web was sound, but several years of hard work were required to solve all of the technical problems and to increase the output of the machine. In 1807, a Fourdrinier operating at peak efficiency could make as much paper in a day as handworkers could produce in seven vats. By that time, however, the Fourdriniers' investment in research, machinery and manufacturing facilities had consumed so much of their private funds and capital in trade that they petitioned Parliament for an extension of their patent. Donkin testified before a parliamentary committee about their various expenditures, amounting to more than £31,000. They paid for a specially equipped workshop in Bermondsey where Donkin's technicians devised the precision metalwork needed for the smooth operation of the machines. They erected or enlarged three paper mills, all expressly designed to provide sufficient power, raw materials and workspace for mass-production papermaking. In addition to their flagship enterprises, the Frogmore and Two Waters mills, they owned a majority interest in the St Neots Mill, where they intended to install not one but two paper machines to make it the largest mill in England. Obviously, they were trying to accomplish too much too soon. One paper mill would have been enough to display the potential of the Fourdrinier. Yet, they had other ideas for the management of the patent and the future of the firm. They planned not only to sell this new technology to papermakers, but also to exploit it themselves – to combine their vastly enhanced production facilities with their extensive distribution network to build the foremost, vertically integrated, wholesale stationery business in the nation.[14]

Not even their great wealth could support these ambitions, even though the House of Commons did consent to prolong their monopoly so they could

13 'Select committee', 1837, 42; Balston 1979 (1957), 90–6; Clapperton 1967, 288. The following account of the Fourdriniers' affairs is based on Bidwell 1992, which recounts in greater detail their attempts to increase and protect the capital resources of their firm.

14 'Minutes of proceedings', 1807, 11–15; 'Select committee', 1837, 86; Bodleian, Fourdrinier Papers, 'Bill in Chancery & Answer Bloxam & Hollingsworth ag^{t} Towgood & others', *c.*1816?, fol. 84; 'The joint and several answer of Wm Abbott, Francis Morse, Joseph Brooke Hunt and Charles Fourdrinier . . . to the bill of complaint of Henry Bloxam and Willm Hollingsworth', *c.* Dec. 1817, fol. 11; Cowell 1994, 3–4.

recoup some of their expenses. Gamble and Didot had to relinquish their rights to the invention when they could not pay their share of the investment. For a while the Fourdrinier brothers were the sole proprietors of the patent and related business ventures, but then, reluctantly, they admitted other partners in the firm to attract additional capital. As the toll of debt mounted, some partners withdrew and were replaced by others who prudently disavowed the obligations of their predecessors. The retiring partners were either paid off or induced to leave some money in the firm, for which they demanded sureties of various kinds.

Sealy retired abruptly after becoming entangled in the schemes of the rogue industrialist James Bartholomew O'Sullivan, who had ordered two or maybe three machines for his family's paper mills in Ireland. The Fourdriniers lent him large sums from their house in Sherborne Lane and almost made him a partner, even though he had gone bankrupt more than once, and his defalcations had been publicly announced in the *Dublin Gazette*. In addition, without telling Henry, Sealy allowed O'Sullivan to draw between £10,000 and £12,000 in bills on the retail outlet at Charing Cross, apparently intending to divert these funds for a papermaking venture in Ireland. When Henry learned of their intrigues, he forced Sealy to surrender his share in the patent, or, according to a more indulgent interpretation of the affair, Sealy left voluntarily to seek his fortune with O'Sullivan. Whatever his misdeeds, Sealy no longer figured in the business of the firm except as a charity case, or in his brother's claims for recognition and compensation except as a vestige of the patent. If he followed O'Sullivan, he did not get very far, for the creditors later learned that he was 'in extreme distress & totally destitute'. They gave him the right to run a machine free of charge, but even so he never regained his place in the paper trade.[15]

After Sealy left in November 1809, the house at Sherborne Lane was reconstituted as Fourdrinier, Towgood, Hunt & Company. The new firm included two silent partners, William Abbott and Francis Morse, who contributed £30,000 secured by an encumbrance on the patent rights and on the workshop at Bermondsey. If the other partners failed to pay their debts, Abbott and Morse could take over the patent concern, which was then producing about £3,500 a year in licensing fees – a handsome sum, but already jeopardised by the brothers' debts. Henry had mortgaged one of his customer's payments and had submitted bills for collateral, not knowing that Sealy had previously entrusted them to O'Sullivan, who was on the verge of bankruptcy. When the customer failed, the mortgagee tried to collect the collateral, which, however, had

15 'The joint and several answer of Wm Abbott' *et al.*, fols. 17–23, 54–5. Charles Benson, TCD, very kindly provided information about O'Sullivan's bankruptcy notices in the *Dublin Gazette*.

become worthless after O'Sullivan succumbed, again, in July 1810. Henry's creditors soon learned about his difficulties and harried him so vindictively that he had to hide from officers of the law and a solicitor who succeeded in having him arrested, if later testimony can be believed.[16]

More discreditable transactions emerged when bankruptcy proceedings began in November 1810. The assignees estimated the brothers' debts at nearly £40,000, but could not be sure of this figure after discovering that the bankrupts or their accountant had made unauthorized transfers between the firm's ledgers and their private ledgers. The assignees paid a dividend of sixpence on the pound by liquidating assets such as the workshop at Bermondsey, purchased by Bryan Donkin. Although Donkin could now make machines independently, the right to grant licences and collect royalties still belonged to the patentees. The Fourdriniers had relinquished the patent in such dubious circumstances, however, that no one knew to whom it rightfully belonged.[17]

The controversy over this most valuable part of the estate divided the creditors into three hostile factions: (1) Abbott and Morse staked their claim on the encumbrance of the patent they obtained when they joined the firm in November 1809; (2) a previous partner demanded a share of the royalties as an indemnity for the brothers' failure to pay an annuity secured by the St Neots Mill; (3) the assignees argued that the patent should devolve on the creditors along with the rest of the bankrupts' holdings. They disputed Abbott's and Morse's claims on the grounds that the brothers had ceded the patent to their partners in the full knowledge of their impending bankruptcy and in an attempt to preserve some of their property. If Abbott and Morse colluded with the bankrupts to evade their legal obligations, then the deeds of November 1809 could be overturned as a fraudulent conveyance of assets properly belonging to the creditors, a subterfuge iniquitous enough to constitute an act of bankruptcy then and there.

This confused state of affairs impeded the diffusion of the papermaking machine. Until the patent expired in 1822, papermakers who wished to invest in this promising new technology could not be sure where to begin, whom to contact and how much to pay. The feuding creditors sometimes tried to compromise by placing the licensing fees in an escrow account pending the outcome of litigation, but even that failed to clarify the situation. Henry was thought to be the agent for some of the creditors and to control the licensing of machines, but suspicions of misconduct diminished his authority. After he

16 'The joint and several answer of Wm Abbott' *et al.*, fols. 19–27, 37–8.
17 'The joint and several answer of Wm Abbott' *et al.*, fols. 32–4, 55–7.

defaulted on his debts and forfeited the patent, his customers suspended payment while waiting for the courts to designate the true proprietor of the machine. His assignees were not able to collect patent dues between 1810 and 1816, and were still trying to sue delinquent debtors as late as 1827.[18]

Thirty papermaking machines were operating in England by 1816. Quite possibly, many more would have been in use if papermakers had been allowed to invest in a cheaper alternative to the Fourdrinier, the cylinder machine invented by John Dickinson. Like the Fourdriniers, Dickinson borrowed money to finance his invention, which he repeatedly improved, and installed in facilities specially designed to meet the demands of mass production. He was running two cylinders side by side in the Nash Mill, Hemel Hempstead, Hertfordshire, as well as a Fourdrinier close by in the Apsley Mill, both establishments acquired and enlarged at great expense. He mortgaged both mills to the printer Andrew Strahan, a family friend, who helped him start his business and supplied the means to sustain it by buying machine paper for bibles, statutes, periodicals and other large printing jobs. Dickinson recruited another valuable customer by forming a partnership with George Longman, brother of the publisher Thomas Norton Longman. After George Longman died, he was succeeded by his nephew Charles Longman, who paid £20,000 as his price of admission to the firm, thus allowing the inventor to repay a debt of precisely that amount to Thomas Norton Longman.[19] Longman and Dickinson sold to the Longman publishing house substantial quantities of machine paper for major publishing ventures such as Rees's *Cyclopædia* (1819–20, issued in parts beginning in 1802), the Gifford edition of Jonson's *Works* (1816) and John Pinkerton's *General collection of the best and most interesting voyages and travels* (1808–14).[20]

The inventor of the cylinder machine incurred many of the same business risks that ruined the proprietors of the Fourdrinier. He adopted similar methods to finance his experiments, purchase paper mills and appease his creditors, who pressed him hard for repayment, but not so hard as to drive him out of business. They were more lenient than the Fourdriniers' creditors because they knew his business, understood his problems and bought his products. Nevertheless, he did not want to contract any additional debts to finance the marketing and manufacture of the cylinders. Similarly, the Fourdrinier

18 'Select committee', 1837, 38.

19 See Briggs, chap. 19 below.

20 Spicer 1907, 249; Hertfordshire Record Office, Records of John Dickinson and Company, ACC 2495, deeds of 1 July 1809 and 30 Oct. 1821, box 17; 'Articles of partnership between Mess[rs] John Dickinson & Charles Longman', 11 Apr. 1832 (updated to 1840), box 16; day books, boxes 10 and 11.

assignees had already spent enough on legal fees and did not want to spend any more on attempts to compete against the cylinder, which could easily undersell its larger rival on the open market. Compact and durable, the cylinder mechanism was not only simple to build, but also different in design, so it could not be considered an infringement of their patent. Therefore, the assignees protected their investment by negotiating a truce with Dickinson, who agreed to suppress the cylinder for the right to use their machines on advantageous terms. Possibly he obtained a rebate or an exemption from royalties, for he is never listed among the earliest licensees although he acquired his first Fourdrinier in 1812. In turn, the contract restricted the exploitation of his invention so stringently that he had to pay £100 a year for permission to move his cylinders from the Apsley Mill to the Nash Mill. The exact terms of the contract remained a tightly held secret, but the assignees admitted that they were colluding with Dickinson when they announced that he was using one of their machines and that he had 'relinquished all right of selling' his invention.[21]

Dickinson, the Fourdriniers and the Fourdriniers' assignees successfully concealed the legal problems they incurred and the financial expedients they devised to develop and exploit their papermaking machines. To this day, historians have been hard pressed to explain why the cylinder was not readily adopted in Britain and why Dickinson never challenged the assignees' monopoly on machine technology. One early commentator supposed that the cylinder was too complicated to achieve widespread acceptance, apparently unaware that it was comparatively easy to build and maintain. At a loss for a better reason, the economist D.C. Coleman suggested that papermakers preferred the Fourdrinier and that Dickinson himself turned against his invention to install Fourdriniers in his mills. Actually, British papermakers had no choice in the matter, and Dickinson did not consider one machine better than the other, but preferred to have both in his widely dispersed, fully diversified manufacturing concern. Likewise, Henry Fourdrinier's friends tactfully neglected to mention the circumstances of his bankruptcy when they were urging the parliamentary committee to endorse his claims for compensation. The whole gruelling story of his failure has yet to be told, although some of the key legal documents have been preserved and have been summarized by Coleman. A few depositions may have been tainted by guile and malice, though even the harshest accusations must have contained a grain of truth to be introduced in a court of law. One can trust the complaints of Henry

21 'Select committee', 1837, 89; 'Bill in Chancery & Answer Bloxam & Hollingsworth', fol. 96; 'The joint and several answer of Wm Abbott' *et al.*, fols. 51–2.

Fourdrinier's enemies more than the testimony of his friends, who conveniently forgot about his machinations while praising the achievements of the machine.[22]

No one could doubt the achievements of the Fourdrinier, capable of making paper larger, faster and cheaper than vat mills, even though they too had become more efficient. In a machine mill, the size of the sheet was limited only by the width of the web, measuring up to 54 inches by 1813. Book printers could employ sheets twice the usual size to produce twice as much text in one impression, a feat easily accomplished on cylinder presses designed to accommodate larger formats. For a while, newspaper publishers could take advantage of a legal loophole allowing them to pay the same duty on a mammoth sheet as they would pay for the standard double-demy size, the extra space more appealing to the subscribers and more lucrative for the proprietor, who could fill it with additional advertisements. The greater speed of the Fourdrinier changed the way publishers allocated capital – a major concern when they had to cover the costs of warehousing and stockpiling paper in case of shortages or delays – but now they could buy only as much as they needed and only when they needed it. A Fourdrinier fitted with steam-heated drying cylinders, introduced around 1820, could fulfil an order for newsprint in less than a week.[23]

Above all, the book trade appreciated the higher output of the machine and the lower cost of its products, as the price of paper was still a significant factor in setting the price of books. Paper prices had already fallen noticeably by 1837, when booksellers and printers came before the Fourdrinier committee to testify how much money they had saved, and how much of their savings they could pass on to the consumer. But that was thirty years after the Fourdrinier firm began to license the machines. The confusion over the licensing rights makes it difficult to measure the economic impact of this invention, adopted tentatively by papermakers apprehensive about the litigation it had provoked and the capital investment it required.

Even if the diffusion of machine technology had proceeded smoothly, it would still be hard to detect changes in the price of paper, which varied greatly in size, weight and quality in the early industrial period. Coleman dealt with this problem by tracking the price of demy purchased by the Longman firm between 1797 and 1860, thus eliminating most of the variables, since he chose the most common printing size and an excellent source of data, the remarkably

22 *London encyclopædia* (London, 1826–9), part 32, 558; Coleman 1975 (1958), 180–91.
23 'Select committee', 1837, 52–60, 87; Dagnall 1998a.

consistent accounts of a large and diversified publishing concern. Rendered as a graph, the price of demy drifts down in a gently sloping curve from around 30*s.* per ream in 1810 to about 22*s.* in 1836, a convincing image of mechanization at work in the economy, but perhaps only part of the picture.[24]

Although Coleman was headed in the right direction, he was still proceeding on the assumption that printing demy was a staple product employed indiscriminately in all kinds of book work. In fact, Messrs Longman shopped around for different types of demy, each suitable for a certain class of publications, coarse grades for school-books, middling varieties for novels, the better sorts for standard authors, and the finest qualities for prestige editions. In one year, 1815, they could pay 26*s.* 6*d.* for an ordinary demy used in an abridgement of Lindley Murray's *Grammar* and nearly twice as much for a thick superfine demy used in Wordsworth's *White doe of Rylstone*, an elegant quarto designed for an elite clientele. Faced with this predicament, Coleman plotted his graph on the basis of prices he chose toward the top of the scale, where the effects of mechanization were more immediately apparent.

If he had chosen coarse demy for his yardstick of value, his graph would have told a different story. The price would begin at 15*s.* in 1795, peak at 27*s.* in 1809, fall back to around 20*s.* in 1810, drift up to 22*s.* 6*d.* in 1814, and slip occasionally afterwards, but keep returning to that level until 1830, when it weakened slightly and then dropped sharply to 15*s.* in 1836. Adjusted for inflation, the cost of coarse demy actually increased by 10 per cent between 1810 and 1836. One usually expects cheaper products to be more amenable to mass production and more likely to show its influence in the marketplace. This does not seem to be the case here, although more research will be needed to ascertain when the Longmans began to buy machine-made coarse demy for spelling books and other publications they produced at minimal expense and in large editions.

Instead of sampling paper prices, one can take a more direct approach and compare the aggregate cost of paper with other expenses of book production such as typesetting, presswork, illustration, advertising, binding and payments to the author. Here too, however, a number of variables have to be considered, mainly the size of the edition. The rule of thumb has been that the cost of paper would represent just over half of the total production costs of a typical edition in the hand-press era, rarely amounting to more than two thousand copies. The proportion might rise as high as 75 per cent in larger editions on better paper or fall below 50 per cent in smaller editions on inferior grades. The cheap demy

24 Coleman 1975 (1958), 203.

Ackers used to print 500 copies of Stephen Duck's *Poems* in 1742 comprised 39 per cent of the production costs, whereas paper accounted for more than two-thirds of the total due Bowyer for printing the 1743 editions of Pope's *Dunciad* and *Essay on man*, each consisting of 1,500 copies on fine demy and 100 copies on royal. To take an extreme example, the Longmans' purchases of middling-quality papers between 1807 and 1810 constituted around 80 per cent of their expenditures on their 18mo abridgement of Lindley Murray's *Grammar*, kept in standing type and regularly reprinted in editions of 12,000 copies.[25]

The accounts of the Longman firm do not display any striking changes in the ratio of paper costs to total production costs after the Fourdrinier was introduced in 1806. Entries for the abridgement of Murray's *Grammar* show that its cost of paper compared with the outlay on presswork still hovered around 80 per cent in 1830, after it had appeared in more than a hundred editions. In 1813, Thomas Norton Longman looked back at his accounts to find figures he could submit to a parliamentary committee considering revisions in the copyright laws and inquiring about the effect of those laws on the economics of book production. The committee questioned him about the ratio of paper costs and asked him to estimate what it would be in an edition of 500 copies. 'Generally speaking', he replied, 'it may be two-thirds of the whole.' This was either a mistake in transcription or a slip of the tongue for one-third, the usual ratio for 500-copy editions. Longman then went on to contradict himself by tabulating how much the firm paid to produce multi-volume works in 1,000 or 1,500 copies, requiring an investment in paper averaging about 44 per cent of the total costs. Nevertheless, his testimony was accepted at face value in Marjorie Plant's *English book trade* and, on her authority, in Richard Altick's *English common reader*, as if paper was so expensive in 1813 that it would amount to twice as much as all the other production expenses combined. The Longmans usually spent less on paper than on printing unless they were buying premium grades or printing from stereotype plates or standing type.[26]

They kept scrupulous records of their share in Samuel Johnson's *Works*, frequently reprinted in the same format and on the same quality of paper, a superior but not quite fine demy. They paid more than usual for this grade of demy, but did not incur any significant savings by buying it from mills running Fourdrinier machines. Table 8.1 shows that the ratio of paper costs remained at around two-thirds despite declining prices in the period 1810–23. These falling prices must be viewed in the context of the English economy, which was

25 Bidwell 2002b, 587–8; McKenzie and Ross 1968, 140; Maslen and Lancaster 1991, 239.

26 'Committee on acts respecting copyrights of printed books', *Parl. Papers* (Commons), 1812–13 (292; 341), IV, 1015–16; Plant 1974, 327; Altick 1998 (1957), 262.

Table 8.1 *Production costs of Samuel Johnson's* Works *in twelve volumes, demy octavo*

Date of edition	Size of edition	Price per ream	Price in 1823 currency	Cost of paper	Total production costs	Percentage of paper costs
1806	1,500	30*s.*	22*s.* 8*d.*	£1,497. 15*s.*	£2,262. 10*s.*	66 (hand-made)
1810	1,500	35*s.*	23*s.*	£1,746. 10*s.*	£2,615. 8*s.*	67 (hand-made)
1816	1,500	33*s.* 6*d.*	27*s.* 5*d.*	£1,685. 1*s.*	£2,512. 10*s.*	67 (machine-made)
1823	1,250	28*s.* 6*d.*	28*s.* 6*d.*	£1,275. 7*s.* 6*d.*	£2,031. 5*s.*	63 (machine-made)

Note: Based on entries in the Longman impression books at RUL and the Strahan Papers, BL, Add. Mss. 48813, vol. xv. The total production costs for the 1810 edition do not include an additional 250 copies on royal, which would have increased the ratio of paper costs to 69 per cent. The prices in 1823 currency are derived from historical price indexes tabulated in McCusker 1991c.

recovering at that time from the inflationary pressures of the Napoleonic wars. How far did they fall in relation to the increasing value of the currency in this period? A commodity price index reveals that the price of paper in Johnson's *Works* was actually rising in real money terms, and was rising even faster when the publishers switched from hand-made to machine-made demy.

The great leap in output and the most noticeable decline in prices occurred just before 1837, a propitious moment for Henry Fourdrinier to press his claims for public compensation. During the early 1830s, prices of printing grades decreased to the point where the injustice of taxing them by weight became more apparent to government officials, who appointed 'commissioners of inquiry' to recommend changes in the excise regulations. The most influential commissioner, Sir Henry Parnell, was an ardent advocate of free trade and the author of a treatise on tax reform, which blamed the paper duties for the artificially high price of books. 'By this', he noted, 'a great obstacle is thrown in the way of the progress of knowledge, of useful and necessary arts, and of sober and industrious habits.' The commissioners obviously hoped that the duties would be repealed along with the newspaper duties and other 'taxes on knowledge', but suggested as a provisional measure simplifications in the tax code that would increase efficiency, prevent fraud and preserve most of the public revenue. Parliament followed their advice and reduced the duty on writings and printings to ½*d.* per pound in 1836, thus pushing prices down even lower, and giving Fourdrinier's friends even more impressive figures to report when they described the economic impact of the machine. Like the commissioners, they predicted that lower prices of paper would spur the production of cheap and wholesome literature, an easy thing to say when most people still believed in technological progress. The Victorians would later lose their faith in the Industrial Revolution, but in 1837 they were enthralled with inventions like the Fourdrinier, which was finally producing significant savings in the book trade, after consuming an enormous investment in the paper trade.[27]

27 Spicer 1907, 241–2; 'Fourteenth report of the commissioners of inquiry into the excise establishment: paper', *Parl. Papers* (Commons), 1835 (16), xxxi, 159–344; Parnell 1830, 37–8.

9
A year's work in the London printing house of the Bowyers

KEITH MASLEN

Facing the New Year

The London printers William Bowyer, father and son, entered the year 1731 with justifiable confidence.[1] The elder Bowyer had been in business since 1699, his skill and integrity securing valuable customers. Chief among these were the London booksellers, the wholesaling and retailing entrepreneurs who together virtually monopolized the British book trade. The younger Bowyer was growing into a considerable printer in his own right. After studying for two years at St John's College, Cambridge, for the purpose of mastering the learned languages, he joined his father in 1722 as corrector to the press, continuing in this role to the end of his life in 1777. The firm's heightened ability to deal with learned texts brought further commissions, notably from scholars publishing by subscription. The younger man was also branching out in new directions. In 1728 he had acquired the first of many copyrights, generally of shorter pieces, which he could print and sell without blatantly competing with the booksellers. More remarkably, in 1730 he obtained the valuable right to print the *Votes of the House of Commons*, then the only publicly available day-to-day record of doings of the House. Other parliamentary printing was expected. Perhaps best of all, young William's four-month-old son and heir was thriving.

The Bowyers' location in Temple Lane, White Friars, just off Fleet Street towards the more fashionable West End, was conveniently close to major bookseller customers such as the Lintots. Nearby in the Temple were members of the legal fraternity who brought profitable work. The commercial life of the city was all around them. As members of the Stationers' Company, the Bowyers were in regular touch with other book-trade members, binders, booksellers, stationers as well as other printers.

Their commodious dwelling-cum-printing house, which paid by far the highest property rates in Temple Lane, had room for family and apprentices,

1 For the sources of this article see Maslen and Lancaster 1991; Maslen 1993.

as well as for journeymen, a larger number of whom were employed at peak times, and for all the equipment, cases of type, composing frames, printing presses and so on. A total of seven presses were available for use, although two or three sufficed for much of the time. Supplies of type accumulated over the years were ample. Founts included large quantities of the latest romans and italics produced by William Caslon, plus an exceptional range of exotic types for printing in remoter languages, such as Coptic. (Trade specialization, and in particular the distinction between book and job houses, was still far off.) A warehouse was necessary for storing paper. Trade customers normally supplied their own, but private customers expected the printer to supply paper and print. Printed sheets had to be housed until required, and deliveries were often prolonged. The Bowyers' tenancy of a warehouse at Puddledock down by the river, although not attested before 1739, is very likely.

The firm had not only excellent capacity but sound management and the operational systems in place ready to cope with more than a score of workers, many customers, large and small, and a considerable workload characterized by seasonal and unexpected highs and lows.

At the heart of the business was a sophisticated accounting system. Necessary in all save the smallest printing house was a wages and production book, the keeping of which in this very year was passed by the father to the son. This book, covering most of the 1730s in almost unprecedented detail – the nearest comparison is with the provincial Cambridge University Press some thirty years before – reveals the work done in successive pay periods by named compositors and pressmen in terms of pages or sheets set and formes printed, and the wages claimed. The father retained control of two other records: customer accounts (such as survive for several other London printers of the time, including Charles Ackers and William Strahan) and a paper stock ledger. The customer accounts record details of works charged to individual customers, specifying price per sheet and the precise number of sheets (signatures) in the work. The paper stock ledger is a running account of paper received (in reams and quires) for each piece of work, balanced against the subsequent delivery of printed copies of that work.

The younger Bowyer's 'Rules & orders to be observed in this Printing House', though belonging to the mid-century, no doubt apply equally to 1731. The 'Rules' specifying sums to be paid to the Chapel (or team of workers as a whole), for instance on a journeyman's first or second 'coming', particularly benefited the workers, but the 'orders' concern the careful handling of materials so that these may be freed for further use as soon as possible. One 'Rule', against leaving a candle burning in the workplace, affected all.

The requisite operational flexibility was secured mainly through management of a skilled workforce, the art being to satisfy customers while using resources efficiently. The practices adopted by the Bowyers were typical of their time and place. The journeymen compositors and pressmen available to them, as to other London printers, had with very few exceptions served formal apprenticeships according to rules maintained by the Stationers' Company, and could be put to most tasks likely to be encountered.[2] Three internal work practices, all monitored by the wages book, were of prime importance to the good conduct of the business. The first consisted in the ability to adjust the number of production workers to the amount of work on hand. The second was the method of payment of each worker by piece-rates according to their output. The third had to do with work-flow, and in particular a system of concurrent printing whereby works in hand were allocated piecemeal to compositors and pressmen so that, whatever the length of work or the number of copies required, all could progress through the press, meeting their respective delivery dates and making optimum use of men and materials.

These practices were not unique to the Bowyers or to other printers. The booksellers too employed as many or as few printers as they required, mainly to hasten production or control costs. The booksellers thus effectively drew on the productive capacity of the trade as a whole. One way they did this was by sharing a work among two or more printers. As the Bowyer accounts show, of the 147 works they printed during 1731, 15 were shared with other printers.

Through the year

A closer sense of the resultant rhythms of work may be gained by surveying the year's work as a whole, with the aid of Table 9.1, and then by focusing on work done in one period of two weeks.

Table 9.1, showing pay periods, numbers of compositors and pressmen employed and their earnings during 1731, throws light on the first two of the three basic work practices.

There were twenty-five pay periods for the year, each ending on a Saturday. Seventeen covered the previous two weeks' work, the others either one or three weeks. Departures from the norm, observable in other years as well, seem to have been governed by the incidence of holy days, principally Christmas and the variable feast of Easter, and of quarter days, usual times for settling

2 The work of employees on a set wage, such as the paper warehouseman and domestic servants, is not here considered.

Table 9.1 *Earnings of Bowyers' compositors and pressmen during 1731*

Period ending:	Weeks	Compositors	Earnings £.s.d.	Pressmen	Earnings £.s.d.
16 January	3	7	£14 14*s.* 0*d.*	6	£8 7*s.* 9*d.*
30 January	2	9	£14 19*s.* 10*d.*	9	£16 16*s.* 6*d.*
6 February	1	7	£6 1*s.* 6*d.*	7	£4 19*s.* 11*d.*
20 February	2	10	£18 17*s.* 0*d.*	6	£10 2*s.* 2*d.*
6 March	2	11	£12 10*s.* 9*d.*	8	£12 10*s.* 5*d.*
20 March	2	12	£22 11*s.* 1*d.*	8	£12 11*s.* 5*d.*
3 April	2	10	£18 10*s.* 4*d.*	8	£13 10*s.* 2*d.*
17 April	2	11	£22 4*s.* 2*d.*	8	£14 0*s.* 2*d.*
1 May	2	10	£15 18*s.* 4*d.*	8	£13 4*s.* 2*d.*
15 May	2	12	£17 7*s.* 9*d.*	6	£6 19*s.* 6*d.*
29 May	2	12	£19 3*s.* 10*d.*	8	£11 17*s.* 2*d.*
5 June	1	12	£10 11*s.* 6*d.*	6	£4 5*s.* 1*d.*
26 June	3	11	£21 6*s.* 5*d.*	6	£9 15*s.* 1*d.*
17 July	3	10	£22 13*s.* 0*d.*	7	£14 12*s.* 1*d.*
31 July	2	10	£16 7*s.* 7*d.*	6	£10 17*s.* 2*d.*
14 August	2	9	£12 19*s.* 11*d.*	8	£9 7*s.* 7*d.*
21 August	1	9	£10 11*s.* 4*d.*	8	£8 8*s.* 0*d.*
4 September	2	8	£11 1*s.* 7*d.*	8	£8 14*s.* 7*d.*
25 September	3	10	£29 10*s.* 10*d.*	9	£25 7*s.* 1*d.*
9 October	2	8	£11 2*s.* 5*d.*	9	£12 10*s.* 1*d.*
30 October	3	9	£19 1*s.* 5*d.*	10	£20 17*s.* 4*d.*
13 November	2	9	£15 11*s.* 4*d.*	11	£15 06*s.* 7*d.*
27 November	2	10	£11 3*s.* 9*d.*	10	£11 01*s.* 0*d.*
11 December	2	10	£17 6*s.* 5*d.*	8	£8 16*s.* 7*d.*
24 December	2	11	£19 9*s.* 7*d.*	6	£13 14*s.* 2*d.*
	52		£411 17*s.* 0*d.*		£298 11*s.* 9*d.*

accounts.[3] The number of journeymen employed at any one time is seen to vary considerably: compositors ranged between seven and twelve and pressmen between six and eleven. Mean numbers of compositors and pressmen employed at any one time were ten and eight respectively; annual totals were seventeen and thirteen respectively. Counted among the pressmen is the apprentice John Mazemore, who, though in the seventh and last year of his time, is paid as a journeyman. Variations in the number employed are related, if rather loosely, to changed levels of earnings and output. Two markedly low periods were mid-winter and high summer, when Parliament and the law courts were in recess and the town empty.

3 In 1731 Easter Sunday fell on 18 April.

What Table 9.1 cannot show – the wages book with its record of individual journeymen and their work must be directly consulted for this – is that the basic workload was carried by a core of workers comprising compositors and pressmen in approximately equal numbers assisted by the two apprentices at case. Some of these men stayed for months or even years. In 1731 there were six long-term employees among the compositors and pressmen, who could be relied upon to observe established procedures and standards.

The wage totals for each period shown in Table 9.1 are interesting for several reasons.[4] Taken in conjunction with the number of weeks worked and the number of men employed, they give an approximate idea of average individual earnings. Between Christmas and 16 January, for instance, the seven compositors earned on average 14*s*. per week. The totals, based as they are on piecework, also indicate fluctuations in output. The correspondence is not exact. Some unusually large claims are explicable in terms of the higher rates paid for setting urgent parliamentary work, others for the printing of exceptionally large quantities of particular jobs, such as almanacs for the Stationers' Company. Occasionally an apparently excessive individual claim recorded in the wages book may be found to extend over two pay periods, the clue being the amount of copy money paid. This was a weekly payment of 1*d*. to journeymen-compositors and pressmen, but not apprentices, in lieu of a traditional claim to a copy of each book on which they had worked.

In some pay periods there is little correspondence between numbers employed and levels of earning. This is usually because the desired level of output has been achieved by giving more or less work to existing staff. Again, precise answers must be sought from the wages book itself. For instance, the remarkably high total of compositorial earnings for the three weeks ending 25 September, achieved without a noticeable increase in staff, results largely from urgent parliamentary work on *Lists of the officers and their deputies, belonging to the several courts*, 21 sheets, 2,000 copies, and *Additional lists of attornies and solicitors*, 65 sheets, 1,500 copies. The very high pressmen's totals for the periods ending 30 January and 30 October reflect the printing of fifty-nine reams five quires of malt books (ledgers ruled in red for the collection of malt tax), while the low total for 21 August would have been almost halved but for the printing of another twenty-three reams. Although the rate for printing such large quantities was reduced to 1*s*. per token, extra was paid for altering signatures, and the press crew were evidently able to work much faster than usual. They may have been able to keep up well over 300 impressions an hour,

4 Halfpence are not shown.

much beyond the norm of 250 impressions indicated by Joseph Moxon in 1683. The printing for the Stationers' Company of large quantities of single sheets of psalms (40,000 copies in all) and almanacs *Poor Robin*, *Culpeper* and *The ladies diary* (26,000 copies in all), claimed for the periods ending 17 April, 1 May, 25 September, 13 and 27 November, was also a boon to the pressmen.

Weekly averages per person over the whole year have to be calculated from the full record in the wages book. The highest earner, at 19*s*., was Thomas Hart who later became his own master. The lowest, at just over 12*s*., was paid to the much older Gater Grantham. The median was 16*s*. 6*d*. A levelling effect was exerted by the frequent practice of working together in a 'companionship'. On such occasions wages seem to have been split equally. During 1731 fourteen of the seventeen journeymen-compositors worked in companionships, usually in pairs and on a particular job, and hence for a limited time. This was especially so for the *Votes*, which were often set by a companionship of two experienced men. New hands at case sometimes began by working with an established staff member. Pressmen worked in pairs nearly all the time, presumably taking it in turns at pulling or beating (inking) the forme. Overall, despite the considerable but not wild variation in individual earnings, the impression is gained of trained and competent men who worked fairly steadily and sometimes very hard indeed.

The relation between earnings and output is complicated by the question of piece-rates. The rates paid by the Bowyers may well have differed little from those of their fellow London printers. Pressure from the booksellers would have seen to that. This is because the Bowyers, like their peers, were similarly paid. Their charge for bookwork was at so much a sheet (or signature), and was reached by adding 50 per cent to the combined costs of composition, correction (whether or not done by the master) and presswork. The master's share was meant to cover overheads and profit. But what the rates for composition and presswork were in any particular case is not easy to predict because of the number of variables involved. Samuel Richardson packed the whole subject into a nutshell when in 1756 he informed lawyer Blackstone that he generally fixed his prices by 'Practice, by Example, by Custom, and by Inspection' (taking due note of variables such as size of type and width of measure). The reference to example and inspection acknowledges room for negotiation between master and men over such matters as the ease or difficulty of setting. Presswork was in theory more straightforward. The Bowyers' usual rate for presswork hovered around 1*s*. 2*d*. per token of 250 perfected sheets, and this was perhaps a standard London rate for bookwork. A token was traditionally regarded as equivalent to two hours' work for a press crew of two. For a sixty-hour six-day week one pressman might thus in theory earn 17*s.* 6*d.*, somewhat less than the 21*s.* per week said by informed contemporaries to be attainable by an expert, hard-working compositor.

The third basic work practice, that of concurrent printing, may be explained with the aid of entries in the wages book for the fortnight ending 20 March 1731. The topic of earnings and piece-rates is also further illustrated. In the twelve working days in question no fewer than twenty-five texts were steered at differing speeds through the printing house.

Working at case, twelve compositors plus the two experienced apprentices set part or all of twenty different texts. Each work was advanced more or less in accordance with its urgency, available supplies of type, requirements of correcting and proofing by a perhaps dilatory author, and so on.

How individuals participated in the flow of work can be seen from the following examples. Daniel Redmayne, who had for some time been working alone on a 'Greek Grammar', set half-sheet 2C, and charged 10*s.*, also part of the Index to Rymer's 'Foedera', vol. XVIII. For all this he earned £1. 2*s.* 2*d.*, the 2*d.* representing two weeks' copy money ('2 WCM'). Redmayne was the senior compositor. John Harte set sheet Z in No. 37 of 'Rapin-Thoyras' (*The history of England*, issued in parts) for 9*s.* 6*d.*; also half-sheets B–G in Twell's 'Critical Examination', for £1. 4*s.* For 'overrunning' (of lines, incidental to correction) in Wesley's 'Prolegomena' he was paid 3*s.*, his total earnings for the fortnight amounting, with 2 WCM, to £1. 16*s.* 8*d.* Harte too was a long-time employee. Charles Micklewright, third in seniority, composed in Marshall's 'Sermons', vol. I: signature 2K 5 pages, vol. II: B 6 pages, C 7 pages, D 6 pages, E 13 pages, F 4 pages, G 14 pages, H 10 pages, making 4 sheets 1 page at 5*s.* per sheet. He was also paid for filling up the blanks and overrunning (to get in additional text) in the 'Lawton Gate Bill', for setting signature B half-sheet in Pilkington's 'Poems' (2*s.*), and for setting the title of Sir Thomas More's 'Life' (1*s.*). Altogether he claimed £1. 10*s.* 11¾*d.* Micklewright was the most important hand of the 1730s, and by 1738 was serving as the younger Bowyer's overseer.

Clement Knell, of a well-known printing family, comes low in the wages list as a newcomer who had worked for just one week. He set part of the 'Importance of the British plantations' by Fayrer Hall, namely signature H 3 pages, I 5, K 4, L 5, M 3, N 4, O 5, P 5, title 1 page and preface 3 pages, totalling 2 sheets 6 pages; and claimed 13*s.* 2½*d.*, which included 1 WCM. The complementary pages of these half-sheet signatures were set by another newcomer, James Morgan, though not claimed for until 17 April, without payment of copy money. The explanation for this irregularity is apparently that Morgan had not yet quite served out his time as apprentice. On the death in February 1731 of his master, Ichabod Dawks, brother-in-law to the elder Bowyer, the Bowyers came to the young lad's rescue. Knell and Morgan are shown as working independently, but in this same pay period four other men were working in two companionships.

During this fortnight twenty-three works were wrought at four presses (numbered 1, 2, 3 and 7), each operated by two men. At press 1 the leading hand, William Diggle, who had been apprenticed to Bowyer senior in 1720, was assisted by John Mazemore, in his last year of apprenticeship, but apparently earning a journeyman's wage. Output and pay show that the team at press 1 deserved their ranking. They claimed £4. 1*s*. 0*d*. for working 44 formes and producing 80 tokens (of 250 perfected sheets); the crew at press 2 claimed £3. 2*s*. 5*d*. for working 39 formes and 54½ tokens; press 3 claimed £2. 5*s*. 3*d*. for 26 formes and 45 tokens; and press 7 claimed £3. 2*s*. 9*d*. for 35 formes and 58 tokens. The pressmen together more than kept pace with the compositors by printing 144 formes and 80 tokens, relating to eighteen of the works set by the compositors in this same pay period and to another five mostly smaller items, set in the immediately preceding pay period.

How work was allotted to any or all presses may be exemplified by the first line of the press record for this same 7–20 March period which records the printing of John Hutchinson, *A new account of the confusion of tongues*.

Press 1 500 Hutchinson F1 G1 K1 N1 O1	5*s*. 10*d*.
Press 2 500 Hutchinson G1 H1 K1 L1 N1 O1 P1	8*s*. 2*d*.
Press 3 500 Hutchinson H1 I1 P1	3*s*. 6*d*.
Press 7 500 Hutchinson I1 L1 M1 Q1	4*s*. 8*d*.

Press 1 produced 500 sheets printed on one side of each of five formes (equivalent to five tokens at 1*s*. 2*d*. per token), while press 2 printed the other side of four of these formes (G H K N O) and two others. The record does not say which press printed the white paper and which perfected the sheets.

Not all press claims are so straightforward, because numbers printed were not always neat multiples of 250, while the rate paid per token varied between 1*s*. and 1*s*. 2*d*. according to the relative difficulty of the task, with a lower rate of 10*d*. for the *Votes*. In this same pay period successive drafts of private parliamentary bills were printed at 50 and 200 a time, while from formes of John Friend's 'Hippocrates' in Greek (in his *Opera omnia*, 1733) were printed 500 copies on ordinary crown paper, 53 on Genoa demy and 27 on Holland demy. In such exceptional instances a special rate was no doubt agreed after 'Inspection'.

Something more should be said of the twenty-five works themselves that were in production during the two weeks up to 20 March. Seventeen were books or rather parts of books (including titles for a reissue), one was a set of proposals for a work not completed until 1736, and one was a pamphlet. As regards format, there were twelve items in octavo, eleven in folio (including the six parliamentary and legal pieces), one in quarto and one in duodecimo. Edition quantities ranged between 12 and 2,000, with four works at 1,000, six at around 750 and seven at 500. Speed through the press varied greatly, between two or three weeks and twenty-two months, but no fewer than nine works took between five and seven months. Works being printed directly for the author tended to take the longest time to print, the printer alone having little power to hasten copy preparation and proofing. At the other extreme political pamphlets, small and topical, were quickly dispatched. Parliamentary work had its own rather different set of practices. The daily *Votes* were usually set from segregated cases of type and were given priority at press.

All save three of the twenty-five works were in English, but there were two in Greek and one in Latin. Sixteen works were being printed for London booksellers, four were scholarly subscription editions for authors or editors (one of these jointly with a bookseller), three were printed to the order of the House of Commons and three, including two private bills, for legal clients. These figures underline the printer's dependence on the London booksellers, especially when it is also noted that Bowyer had been given the printing of only part of seven works. Parliamentary work was thus all the more sought after, for it eventually yielded Bowyer (and his competitor Richardson) something like double the profit.

Year's end

Between Christmas and New Year was a time for English tradesmen to reckon profit or loss. For the younger Bowyer, who had begun the year so hopefully, there was deep personal loss, for his wife, Ann, had died on 17 October. But how did the two masters rate their success in business?

During the year 128 works had been completed, and another 19 were still in progress. The number of sheets composed during 1731 totalled approximately 1,350, predominantly in the octavo and folio formats. The known total of sheets set by Samuel Richardson's compositors for the same year has been reckoned as 661. However, his business was still young and growing rapidly, whereas the Bowyers continued during the 1730s, and indeed long after the elder Bowyer's death in 1737, to coast along comfortably. The number of sheets of paper plucked off the Bowyers' presses in 1731 was close to 1.25 million – about as many as printed by Charles Ackers at his most productive in 1745.

What was the financial result of all this production? The gross annual return, crudely estimated as half the £780 paid for composition, correction and presswork plus the value of work done by the two apprentices at case and the premium yielded by the relatively small quantity of government printing, would have amounted to perhaps £450. To find net profit by deducting the cost of overheads is more problematic. The son tried this ineffectually in 1738 shortly after his father's death. In 1731 he or his father must have kept details of rents, purchases of new type and other printing materials, consumables such as ink, coals and candles, and costs of maintaining buildings and equipment – the presses needed frequent attention from joiner and blacksmith. Information of this class is partially available for the late 1730s and 1740s from receipts and from the so-called Dawks–Bowyer–Nichols notebook containing an inventory of types and equipment.

The administration of business and personal finances was probably delegated to outside professionals. In later years, Bowyer junior is known to have relied upon an accountant. In 1731, as at other times, there is no sign of a shortage of working capital, despite the necessity of allowing trade customers something like six months' credit after completion of their order.

What kinds of works did the Bowyers print in this year? No newspapers or periodicals, nothing as yet for learned societies, but much else. Works of scholarship are much in evidence, including editions of classical texts, works of (mainly British) history and a Greek grammar. There are nine broadly scientific works: four medical, including Lobb on the smallpox, also George Smith on distilling and Switzer on gardening. The twenty-three works of theology, controversial and otherwise, include six sermons or collections of sermons. Political works number fifteen. Among these are lumped two short pieces by Swift, of which the younger Bowyer had secured the copyright, thanks to his friendship with the Dublin printer George Faulkner. Imaginative literature also features strongly, with eight of verse and two of prose fiction, also two single plays. Education and travel are little represented. There were no fewer than eleven orders for proposals or receipts to do with author's subscription editions, including Serenius's Swedish dictionary, printed in Hamburg in 1734. Such works tended to bring more reputation than profit. However, Bowyer senior and especially his son saw themselves as promoters of scholarship, and, as the century went by, with ever-increasing justification.

During 1731 the Bowyers printed much parliamentary work. There were seventy-six numbers of the *Votes* printed during the session. There were also six public bills and eight private bills, as well as the two lengthy *Lists* mentioned above. The *Votes* contract remained with the firm until 1940, but the younger Bowyer's hope for more than a minor share of the House of Commons work ended in 1733 when Richardson secured the right to print bills and other papers.

There were also thirty small jobs (loosely defined as anything which, when printed, does not exceed a sheet), for instance, three book lists for booksellers, and hymn sheets for use at the annual church services held for the children of charity schools. The one major item of commercial stationery consisted of repeat orders of malt books for the Excise Department, ledgers for entering payments of excise tax. However, the Bowyers' business lay chiefly in the printing of books.

Customers dealt with in 1731, as in other years, were many and various. Most important were the booksellers, the more than two score forming a cross-section of the trade. It is not always easy to say which of these especially favoured the Bowyers because shares in the large and popular works were usually owned by a considerable number of booksellers. The Old or Printing Conger and the New Conger, more permanent associations of booksellers, are also represented. The majority of works, however, had just one or two publishers. Long-established firms are well represented: Fletcher Gyles, William Innys (who had for many years favoured Bowyer senior), James and John Knapton, and Jacob Tonson. Among the new men were Charles Davis, who in the years to come gave much work to the younger Bowyer, and Andrew Millar. The Bowyers also printed many smaller pieces for John Peele and James Roberts, specialists in publishing on commission. The outsiders, Cornelius and John Crownfield and William Thurlbourn, belong to Cambridge.

The next most prominent group were authors, editors and translators, and a clergyman's widow. During 1731 the Bowyers printed works for ten such persons.

The seventeen customers for small jobs came in the main from lawyers, including Alexander Hamilton of Lincoln's Inn (for six House of Lords appeal cases), and functionaries of local bodies, such as the Registrar of the Bedford Level Corporation. There was also a sprinkling of commercial agents, including a Mrs Sarah Underwood, who twice ordered commercial bills.

Printing for the House of Commons had been secured through the patronage of Sir Arthur Onslow, Speaker of the House. The six private bills for consideration by the House were ordered by four individuals identifiable as solicitors acting as parliamentary agents.

The Bowyers were also their own customers. The father as a member of the Company of Stationers had acquired shares in the printing of several almanacs and the Psalms, and his son inherited these rights. However, the younger Bowyer was venturing to print on his own account. Five of the six pieces of this kind printed in 1731 came through the Bowyers' friendship with the Dublin printer and bookseller George Faulkner. Most of these are said in the imprint to have been printed 'For James Roberts', though he was only the publisher. The most considerable was a volume of poems for Jonathan Swift's young protégé, Matthew Pilkington. Despite the imprint 'for T. Woodward, Charles Davis, W. Bowyer', young Bowyer was the prime undertaker, as shown by the entry in the paper stock ledger ('WBowyer and Ch. Davis').

The Bowyers' dealings with the public were not limited to those who commissioned print. Especially in the case of works printed for the author, deliveries of printed sheets were made to a multitude of others. Copies of the Pilkington, for instance, were delivered not only to the booksellers named in the imprint, but to bookseller Caesar Ward, to Mr Faulkner in Ireland, to the subscribers generally, and to a number of private individuals, such as 'Mr ——, Irishm[an], the King's Corrector', and Mr Pope, surely Alexander.

All these are a reminder of how closely a major London printer was in touch with the rich and multifarious life of English society. It may fairly be claimed that what went on in the Bowyer Press during 1731 exemplifies the patterns of work in perhaps all but the smallest London printing houses during the lifetimes of both father and son, if not beyond.

10

Book illustration and the world of prints

TIM CLAYTON

The use of prints to illustrate books was one branch of a wide-ranging business in the production of printed pictures. Away from the context of books, prints are usually thought of as decorative objects, but in the eighteenth century many were made for practical use. There were playing cards and printed fans, children's games and watchpapers, but there were also prints used by craftsmen and by amateurs teaching themselves a skill. Such were the many cheap 'books of ornament' and 'drawing books' listed in printsellers' catalogues – usually a handful of small printed sheets stitched together with or without a blue wrapper. Prints were used and consumed (literally destroyed through use) as well as admired and studied.

However, the most valuable and prestigious prints, along with many cheaper ones, were sold as art objects. Presented as individual sheets or in small sets, they were usually destined for a decorative role – to be framed or otherwise displayed on a wall. Alternatively, individual prints or sets of prints might be pasted or bound in volumes. Such volumes might contain a collection of portraits, views of a country or city, the works of an artist, or a compilation of political or social satires. Print collections were usually kept in volumes. Large prints on copperplate paper (usually heavier and sturdier than that employed for letterpress) were sometimes bound into albums; other prints were glued to sheets of sugar paper, often coloured blue. Albums of prints were intended to serve as sources of information for study, or for leisurely perusal to amuse company on a rainy day in the library or closet.[1]

As a rule, the purchaser determined the arrangement of his or her albums of prints, although some were bought ready-made from printsellers or artists.[2]

1 On print collecting, see Griffiths 1991, 127–39; 1993, 19–36; 1994, 37–58; Clayton 1992, 123–48; 1997, 41–8, 25–31, 167–9, 232–4.

2 It was quite common for printsellers to compile the œuvres of artists and for engravers to sell their own complete works; see Clayton 1997, 169. Caricature printsellers made up albums for sale or hire; see, for instance, *Holland's catalogue of humorous prints, &c.* reproduced in Turner 1999, 127–36.

Such albums consisted of independent items and were arranged according to a plan invented by the collector or recommended by one of several guides to print collecting. The earliest example in English of such a guide was John Evelyn's *Sculptura* (1662), although the relevant sections in Florent le Comte's *Cabinet des singularitez* (1699) and in Roger de Piles's *Abrégé de la vie des peintres* (1696, translated 1706) were more up to date and probably more influential. At a later date, William Gilpin's *An essay on prints* (1768), which was translated into German and French that year, was matched by a plethora of French, German and Italian guides. The most important of these were François Basan's *Dictionnaire des graveurs anciens et modernes* (Paris, 1767), Carl Heinrich von Heinecken's *Idée générale d'une collection complette d'estampes* (Leipzig and Vienna, 1771), Michael Huber's *Notices générales des graveurs divisés par nations et des peintres rangés par écoles* (Dresden and Leipzig, 1787) and his nine-volume collaboration with Carl Christian Heinrich Rost, *Manuel des curieux et des amateurs de l'art* (1797–1808), although there were many others.[3]

In the library, albums compiled from prints bought as separate items complemented what printsellers advertised as 'books of prints', which normally consisted of bound sheets of copperplate paper. The plates were designed as a series, usually numbered to make the proper order clear. Explanatory text (of which there was often a great deal) was etched or engraved on the plate, usually by a writing engraver. Architectural prints, views of houses and gardens, collections of paintings or statues, books of natural history, anatomical studies, and military histories, together with drawing books and other technical manuals, were frequently produced as books of prints. Later in the period, it became more common for the text to be set as type and for prints to be issued together with sheets of letterpress. In a sense, these 'books' consist properly of prints explained by text, rather than text illustrated with prints.

A further distinction can be drawn between the long series of copperplates in 'books of prints' and books that were illustrated with prints. In illustrated books, copperplates were either superimposed in blank spaces on sheets of letterpress or inserted at locations determined by instructions to the binder within longer sequences of letterpress text. In antiquarian studies or works on botany, natural history or surgery, illustration was often essential to understanding. In other books, illustration was a luxury but, as time went by, an

3 Other interesting works include *Sculptura-Historico-Technica: or the history and art of ingraving . . . extracted from Baldinucci, Florent le Comte, Faithorne, the Abecedario pittorico, and other authors* (1747); Strutt, *A biographical dictionary* (1785–6); Caulfield, *Calcographiana: the printsellers chronicle and collector's guide to the knowledge and value of engraved British portraits* (1814). Watelet and Lévesque's *Dictionnaire des arts de peinture, sculpture et gravure* (1792) contains some remarkable appreciations of English paintings and engravings.

ever more desirable and affordable one. At the beginning of the century, literary works occasionally had engraved frontispieces, but after about 1760 frontispieces were commonplace and it was not unusual for several other plates to be inserted as illustrations. By the 1760s, history books were commonly illustrated with portraits, and plans and views of campaigns and engagements. An engraved illustration was much more expensive to produce than a page of text, so its inclusion pushed the price of a book up markedly. The more work in a plate (to be judged by extent or intricacy), the more expensive it was.

Until the second decade of the nineteenth century, it was rare for a book to be sold in a permanent binding.[4] Normally, the purchaser bought a book either in sheets, or in a paper or card binding, and had it bound to his own personal specification. Consequently the precise content and arrangement of bound volumes was inconsistent; one of the principal variables was the inclusion or exclusion of printed images. Prints for bibles and prayer books were made small enough and printed on large enough paper to suit different formats. In this manner Richard Ware advertised 'A curious Sett of Cuts for the Bible and New Testament, containing upwards of Two Hundred Histories, so contriv'd as to Bind up with equal Advantage, either with Quarto or Folio'.[5]

After investing time and money in a copperplate, its publisher hoped to exploit its commercial potential in every conceivable way. In 1733 the booksellers John and Paul Knapton agreed with the engraver George Vertue to publish a series of portraits suitable to illustrate Paul de Rapin-Thoyras's *History of England*. They were not, however, produced in direct conjunction with Knapton's translation of Rapin, which was complete by 1731, but were an optional addition to the text.[6] The prints were issued at 6*d*. each in groups of four and, by Vertue's account, 'all the prints from these plates to be published & sold for our joint interest, as well by me as them in every way or manner we coud [*sic*]'. Presumably they anticipated selling the prints as decoration and to collectors of portraits, as well as to those wishing to adorn their histories. In 1736 the portraits could be bought from Vertue as a series for binding with a dedication, four pages of text and the title, *The heads of the kings of England proper for Rapin's history*. In 1737, to Vertue's indignation, the Knaptons proposed a further set of *Heads of illustrious persons of Great Britain* to

4 See Pickwoad, chap. 12, below.
5 *DJ*, 1 Jan. 1723.
6 Lippincott provides a fascinating insight into the business life of Arthur Pond, but she is mistaken in supposing that in this case there was a production schedule tied to text; see Lippincott 1983, 149ff.; Clayton 1997, 117. The advertisements that appeared in the *LEP* were 21 May 1734, 23 July 1734, 12 Nov. 1734, 17 May 1735, 18 Oct. 1735, 10 Apr. 1736, 20 May 1736.

be engraved in Amsterdam by Jacob Houbraken at 1*s*. each.[7] By 1743, these were also presented as a book, *Heads and characters of illustrious persons of Great Britain*, with text by Thomas Birch. However, they were also designed to be suitable illustrations to Rapin's history and its continuation by Nicholas Tindal. In 1747 the Knaptons advertised that all their portraits could be bought on large imperial paper – chiefly suitable for albums – for 1*s*. 3*d*. each, or as a set. They also printed them on smaller sheets of cheaper paper for use as illustrations:

> For the Accommodation of the Purchasors of Mr Rapin's History of England, and Mr Tindal's Continuation, who may chuse to add them to, or have them go with their Books, a Number of the same Heads is printed on fine Paper of the same Size with the History, and may be had at the small Price of 6d. each, for the whole Collection, or for any Head singly.[8]

Other printsellers also proposed their products as suitable additions to books. Henry Overton issued a set of copies of his rival Thomas Bowles's prints of the life of Charles I and advertised them in the press as 'very proper to bind up in Rapin's History of England (being printed on a Paper of that size)'. Claude Du Bosc had already announced a set of portraits of kings and 'Personages mentioned in Mr Rapin's History' in direct rivalry with Vertue's set. It was only a short step, if any step at all, from the addition of such independent illustrations to a body of text to the 'Grangerizing' – the illustration of a book by later insertion of prints, especially those cut from other works – that became increasingly common in the wake of the publication of James Granger's *Biographical history of England* in 1769.[9]

Books of prints routinely expanded and changed as a publisher acquired more plates. Early in the century, Joseph Smith was the principal specialist in architecture and topography, a British counterpart to Jean Mariette in Paris. By 1709, he had a share in the collection of views of houses originally undertaken by Leonard Knyff and issued by the printsellers and booksellers who bought Knyff's plates as *Britannia illustrata*. To this body of views of houses, each publisher added his own publications. Smith introduced a set of *Views of all the cathedrals* in 1712 and sold the set in two volumes. He subsequently added many further plates that had initially been sold as individual items or short series and eventually packaged the whole in 1724 in four volumes as the *Nouveau théatre de la Grande Bretagne*, but the contents of these volumes vary.

7 Vertue 1736; *Craftsman*, 12 Feb. 1737; for Vertue's reaction, see Lippincott 1983, 150.
8 *GA*, 25 Feb. 1747.
9 *Craftsman*, 1 Feb. 1735 and 15 Aug. 1733; see Pointon 1993, 53–78.

The best-known architectural series, *Vitruvius Britannicus*, evolved similarly over time as Smith published more prints.[10]

The organization of the trade

Throughout the long eighteenth century, specialists in printed pictures controlled their trade. Booksellers never dominated the business of printed pictures, although their interests frequently overlapped with those of printsellers. Booksellers occasionally published prints and London booksellers frequently helped with the distribution of prints, especially with expensive sets where a wide sale was needed to recover costs. It is likely that their provincial correspondence was more extensive than that of most printsellers. They may well also have helped to finance such expensive enterprises, although there is as yet a dearth of evidence.[11]

In London, prints were usually bought from outlets known at the very beginning of the century as 'picture shops', and later as 'printshops'. At the beginning of the century there were fourteen major shops and many smaller ones selling prints. The number of London printshops increased dramatically as time went by; in the provinces, the situation was different. In the early part of the period, picture shops were rare outside the capital and prints were usually supplied from London through the agency of the local bookseller. In May 1718, John Browne, bookseller in the Market Place in Norwich, announced in the *Norwich Gazette* that he had procured a 'great Choice of Books, Maps, and Pictures' together with other small items such as patent medicines, tea, coffee and chocolate. He pointed out that 'Any Gentlemen or others who have a Fancy for any particular Books, Maps, Prints, or Pictures, if they please to give or send Orders, they shall have them in 8 Days from London, as Cheap as if I had them in my Shop.'[12] As Browne's advertisement demonstrates, prints were just one of a number of sophisticated cultural goods and luxuries that provincial booksellers obtained from the metropolis for local customers. Sometimes he held auction sales of prints sent from London. Booksellers in the principal towns supplied others in smaller market towns as well as 'travelling hawkers' who served rural areas.

Throughout the period, the market for political prints remained distinct. At first, political, satirical and topical prints were sold primarily by the same people who sold political and topical pamphlets, rather than by the vendors

10 Clayton 1998, 46–8; Harris and Jackson-Stops 1984, 5–8; Harris 1990, 140, 145.
11 On the development of the print trade, see Clayton 1997, 3–23, 105–28, 209–34; O'Connell 2003.
12 *Norwich Gazette*, 3 May 1718.

of fine prints. The pamphlet-sellers sold views and plans of battles as well as satires and children's books. In the 1750s, it became common to group a year's output of political prints – originally issued individually – as a volume giving a political and satirical history of the year. In the great age of caricature, a few shops – notably those of Hannah Humphrey, Samuel William Fores and William Holland – specialized purely in satirical prints.[13]

Just as there were expensive books, middling books and cheap books,[14] so there were expensive prints, middling prints and cheap prints. Print production was also subdivided by size and by genre. Fine prints were intended for collectors and for display. In the mid-eighteenth century the price of individual prints was about 5–10*s*., rising sharply with inflation after about 1780. Such prints were often published by subscription. Their circulation was generally limited to hundreds until about 1770 when demand was augmented by a substantial export market. 'Middling prints' often reproduced the same design in smaller size or cheaper format. Views of battles and other topical subjects, as well as comical and satirical prints, were also usually produced in the middle price range of roughly 6*d*. to 2*s*. Cheap prints for widest distribution came in standard sizes, either as crude copperplates or as woodcuts. The designs engraved or cut on the 'royal sheets' were usually also available in smaller size as 'pot-sheets' and 'quartos'. There were also 'lotteries' on half a sheet of foolscap 'chiefly intended for children to play with'.[15] The retail price might be 1*d*. or less.

In nearly all cases, the publishers of prints were either shop owners (who sometimes, as in the case of the Overton and Bowles dynasties, had wholesale distribution networks to back them up) or artists (usually engravers or painters) seeking to publicize their own work. When an artist published a print, he usually made use of a subscription. He placed advertisements in the press proposing a print and invited subscribers to leave their addresses and a deposit at his studio. Their advance payments covered the cost of production, reducing the financial exposure of an undercapitalized entrepreneur. The method was quite as important to the publication of prints as it was to the publication of books and, as with books, the increasing circulation of newspapers greatly facilitated the process of making contact with potential subscribers.[16] Subscriptions were particularly effective in supporting expensive

13 *Holland's catalogue* suggests he still sold pamphlets about fashionable scandals and songs, but he advertises no prints other than caricatures; see Turner 1999, 127. Humphrey also sold fine prints. On caricature, see Donald 1996.

14 On book prices, see Raven, chap. 3, above.

15 Sayer and Bennett 1970, 150.

16 See Harris, chap. 20 and Ferdinand, chap. 21, both below.

series of prints with special appeal to a particular section of the community. They were used successfully for books of natural history and botany where communities of gardeners, druggists and scientific enthusiasts, along with the sympathetic nobility, could muster support.

Publication in parts was another innovation that was crucially important in the eighteenth century.[17] It helped to make the long series that became 'books of prints' more affordable, both to produce and to purchase, by spreading cost and payment. In 1760 the engraver and naturalist John Miller (born Johann Sebastian Müller in Nuremberg) launched a collection of botanical prints that was to consist of a hundred prints in fifty numbers, with one number appearing each month. The purchaser received two prints of a plant, one showing it in flower, the other in fruit, 'with the proper insects feeding on such plants'. The two plates with a printed sheet of letterpress cost 5*s*. This particular project failed after ten numbers, thus ending as a set of decorative prints rather than as an influential book.[18] Many other such projects succeeded, however, and from the botanical books of the 1740s to the topographical series published by Rudolph Ackermann (*c.*1800–32), publication in parts was the preferred method of bringing out numerous and expensive sets of prints.

It has been explained elsewhere in this volume that copperplate prints – the expensive end of the market – required a different type of press from the one used for printing type.[19] The copperplate itself was the first cost for a print. The cost of engraving it depended upon the process (which determined the time involved), upon the reputation of the engraver and upon the date since the cost increased over time. Within the art business, costs remained fairly stable until the 1760s, and then rose sharply. In the 1720s, the famous George White was paid 15 or 20 guineas for a mezzotint plate. In 1748 the young James McArdell received 7 guineas from Arthur Pond for a mezzotint, while four years earlier Pond paid Charles Grignion 18 guineas for an engraved portrait of Admiral Anson. These were all prices for plates of around 14 by 10 inches.[20] By 1785, costs had risen so much that John Raphael Smith had to pay one of his young assistants £42 for a 16 by 14 inch stipple. Prices paid to top engravers for large line engravings, which had always been much higher, became astronomical. In 1761, John Boydell paid William Woollett what he considered to be an extravagant £150 for *Niobe*. A quarter of a century later, the reward for a top

17 See Harris, chap. 20, below.
18 *PA*, 30 June 1760.
19 See Mosley, chap. 7, above.
20 Vertue 1933–4, 54; Lippincott 1988, 296, 264. Pond's journal contains numerous other examples of costs and prices.

engraver had increased tenfold: Francesco Bartolozzi received £2,000 for the *Death of Chatham* and James Heath the same for the *Death of Major Peirson* (1796). These fees were much higher than those paid to painters, chiefly because the engraver was required to commit more of his time.[21]

It was very common for plates to be used more than once: indeed, they tended to be used and reused until they were quite worn out, their progress and deterioration traceable as one owner after another engraved his (or occasionally her) address on them. For simple plates intended for a very large circulation, several identical plates might be engraved, making it possible to print impressions at least twice as quickly. This was inconceivable with a large, artistically distinguished engraving, but it became common with the sort of illustrations that periodicals used to increase their appeal. In 1761 Richard Baldwin, proprietor of the *London Magazine*, announced that 'The fine Print of her Majesty Queen Charlotte, intended for this Month, is obliged to be postponed till next; for altho' two Plates were engraved, it was impossible to work off a sufficient Number Time enough for this Publication.'[22]

Developments in the market

At the beginning of the eighteenth century, most fine prints and books of prints were imported from abroad, chiefly from France and Italy. Large numbers of imported prints were advertised in the newspapers after the cessation of hostilities with France around 1711, and huge quantities of foreign prints continued to flood the British market for many years. These showed off the glories of French and Italian design and the richness of their cultural history. The earliest British initiatives tended to emulate the style, presentation and subject matter of seventeenth-century Parisian productions and the prints published by the de Rossi family in Rome. Yet, by 1760 the battle that William Hogarth and his associates fought in favour of contemporary native design against the foreign and antique was paying dividends. During the following decade, London production took a dominant share in satisfying domestic demand.

At first, despite the arrival of some talented Huguenot refugees, there was a shortage of sophisticated designers and engravers; hence, in the early eighteenth century, many commissions to engrave prints for the British market were placed abroad. In 1700, wanting the best, Jacob Tonson sent a drawing of

21 Figures from Clayton 1997, 227. Boydell paid Copley £800 for the painting of the 'Death of Major Peirson'.

22 *PA*, 1 Dec. 1761

John Dryden by Godfrey Kneller over to Paris to be engraved by the leading French portrait engraver, Gérard Edelinck. Other lesser commissions were placed in Holland. During the long peace secured by Robert Walpole, several important French artists were lured to England to undertake lucrative engraving projects. Nicolas Dorigny came from Paris to engrave the famous Raphael Cartoons, then at Hampton Court, and brought Charles Dupuis and Claude Du Bosc to help him. Du Bosc in turn invited Bernard Baron and Nicolas-Dauphin de Beauvais to assist with a second commission. Both Du Bosc and Baron remained permanently in England, establishing lasting businesses. After publishing translations of several illustrated books originally issued in Amsterdam, Du Bosc launched in 1733 a subscription in weekly parts for *The ceremonies and religious customs of the various nations of the known world*, translated and with new illustrations. To help with this huge project, in which Jacob Tonson was also involved, Du Bosc hired Gérard Scotin and Hubert Gravelot. During his stay in England, Gravelot effected a considerable improvement in the draughtsmanship of young English artists, chiefly through his own drawing school and his teaching at the St Martin's Lane Academy. About the same time, Antoine Benoist arrived to work on the plates to Du Bosc's *Military history of the late Prince Eugene of Savoy and of the late John Duke of Marlborough* (1736).

During the 1750s and 1760s, it became evident that the quality of British drawing and printmaking had improved considerably. The period saw some remarkably lucid scientific productions, such as George Stubbs's *Anatomy of the horse* (1765) and Robert Strange's engravings for William Hunter's *Anatomy of the pregnant uterus*. Similarly, Robert Wood's *Ruins of Palmyra* (1753) and *Ruins of Baalbek* (1757), with views engraved by Thomas Major and architectural details by Paul Fourdrinier, set new standards in recording antiquity. Not long afterwards James Basire and other engravers produced plates for *Antiquities of Athens* (1762) by James Stuart and Nicholas Revett.

For the next thirty years Britain enjoyed an unprecedented export trade in cultural products. British literature was widely translated and exported,[23] and British prints enjoyed a pan-European vogue. This vibrant export trade and the phenomenon known as 'Anglomania' even helped the printseller John Boydell rise to become Lord Mayor of London. Ultimately, this market stimulated the vastly ambitious gallery productions of the 1790s – Boydell's *Shakspeare*,[24] Macklin's *British poets* and *Bible*, and Robert Bowyer's edition of Hume's *History of England* (see below).

23 See Suarez, Introduction, above; also Fabian and Spieckermann, chap. 27, Green, chap. 28, and Shaw, chap. 29, all below.
24 See Sutherland, chap. 35, below.

The discovery of cost-effective ways of printing in colour stimulated demand both for individual decorative prints and for books of prints.[25] The invention of aquatint – a means to imitate wash drawings –and the invention of wove paper – a smooth paper lending itself to a wash of colour – stimulated a market for books of views.[26] Aquatint, either printed in sepia alone or with added hand-colouring, became the characteristic form of presentation. In the nineteenth century, skilful washes of colour were often laid by hand over blue-printed sky and brown-printed earth. Some colourists acquired sufficient renown for their names to be printed on the plate.

Oriental scenery (1795–1808) by Thomas and William Daniell, J.A. Atkinson's *Picturesque representations of the manners, customs, and amusements of the Russians* (1812) and Edward Orme's *Collection of British field sports* (1807) provide three examples of the use of aquatint in books of views, costume and sport. However, the publisher who most thoroughly exploited the new vogue for colour was Rudolph Ackermann, a Saxon trained as a carriage designer who settled as a printseller in London.[27] His *Microcosm of London*, published in parts from 1808, represented the capital through 104 aquatints. Ackermann's *Repository of arts*, a monthly magazine of fashion and social news, launched in 1809, continued for twenty years with 1,432 plates. Between 1821 and 1827, he published *The world in miniature*, forty-three duodecimo volumes, revealing places such as Persia, China and Hindustan to the virtual traveller.[28] In some cases, details of the publication process have survived. Johann Isaac von Gerning's *A picturesque tour along the River Rhine*, completed in 1820, consisted of twenty-four coloured aquatints originally issued in six monthly parts, each containing four prints in wrappers with letterpress at 14*s*. for each part.[29] Ackermann published letterpress in German to serve that market and also in Spanish for the Latin American market that he developed in the 1820s. He published more than a hundred books in Spanish for export to the newly independent republics.

Working with Charles Joseph Hullmandel, who set up a press in 1818/19, Ackermann was also instrumental in the introduction of lithography[30] to Britain. After he published Senefelder's *Treatise* in 1818, books of coloured lithographs began to rival, then supersede, aquatints during the following

25 See Mosley, chap. 7, above.
26 See Bidwell, chap. 8, above.
27 On Ackermann, see Ford 1983. Ford is currently compiling a full bibliography of Ackermann's publications. The catalogue of the library of J.R. Abbey contains a considerable listing of books of aquatints and lithographs: see Abbey 1952, 1953, 1956–7.
28 See Rogers, chap. 43, below.
29 Abbey 1956–7, 189 ff.
30 See Mosley, chap. 7 and Twyman, chap. 2, both above; Maidment, chap. 25 below.

decades. Lithography was employed for the same sort of subjects as aquatint – it imitated drawing in pen, pencil and chalk, as aquatint imitated watercolour wash. Travel books and books of views, flowers, poetry and humorous sketches were illustrated with lithographs.[31] By the mid-1820s, the Asiatic Lithographic Press at Calcutta provided a local source for subjects with subcontinental appeal such as J. Grierson's *Twelve select views of the seat of war* (1825).[32]

Another development with lasting results was the revival of white-line engraving on the end grain of boxwood by Thomas Bewick.[33] Using this method, he produced finely detailed and lucid wood engravings, his chief works being *A general history of quadrupeds* (1790), *The history of British birds* (1797, 1804) and *Aesop's fables* (1818). Wood engravings could be set with letterpress and would yield many thousands of impressions without wear, and Bewick's method was regularly employed thereafter for book illustrations. His own popularity rests on his accurate and charming observation of nature and on the lively vignettes that embellished his books.

Wood engraving did not lend itself to fine tonal gradation of the kind obtained through line engraving on copper, however. In order to satisfy the demand for larger editions to serve the ever-widening public, various innovators explored the possibility of engraving on steel.[34] One difficulty with steel was that it was too hard to work; another was rust. Purists felt (and continue to feel) that steel could never be made to yield the tonal range and subtlety of copper. Nevertheless, there is no denying that the low-cost, high-quality line engravings produced from steel plates were 'one of the biggest bargains associated with the movement to make art cheap'.[35] The boom for steel illustration between 1825 and 1845 yielded many more books about art than had ever been published previously, in much larger editions.

The discovery that mezzotints scraped on steel plates would yield ten times as many impressions before retouching as those scraped on copper injected new life into mezzotint. J.M.W. Turner used steel for at least six of the twelve celebrated mezzotints he scraped for the 'Little Liber' in the 1820s.[36] John Martin also produced steel plates for his illustrations to *Paradise lost* (1825–7). Various processes were developed to facilitate engraving on steel, some associated with the American Jacob Perkins. Steel certainly yielded large editions. Whereas a copperplate treated gently might yield a few thousand impressions,

31 For the early history of lithography, see Twyman 1970, 1990.
32 See Shaw, chap. 29, below.
33 See Mosley, chap. 7 and Twyman, chap. 2, both above; Maidment, chap. 25, below.
34 See Mosley, chap. 7 and Twyman, chap. 2 both above.
35 Hunnisett 1980b, 3.
36 Lyles and Perkins 1989.

William Holl's plates for the *Methodist Magazine*, produced using Charles Warren's process for engraving on softened steel, yielded 24,000 copies.

Literary illustration

At the beginning of the eighteenth century, portrait frontispieces – typically produced by specialist engravers – were widely available as optional additions to large or small volumes. In George Clarke's library, preserved at Worcester College, Oxford, several volumes are embellished with portraits that were given to him by their respective authors. Booksellers sometimes published portraits in conjunction with works that they were selling. In 1718 Edmund Curll advertised 'A very curious Print of Mr Addison', pointing out that he had just published 'Mr Addison's Poems ... in one Volume', but Curll also envisaged the use of such prints for display: his 'Effigies of the most celebrated poets' were advertised as 'proper Ornaments for Closets and Libraries'.[37]

Other illustrations of works of literature were uncommon and confined to expensive books. Jacob Tonson commissioned designs by John Baptist Medina for his folio *Paradise lost* of 1688 and by François Boitard for his 1709 Shakespeare. The illustrations for his Beaumont and Fletcher (1712) were among the earliest engraved by Elisha Kirkall, a technical innovator, who was the first to produce a design cut in relief in metal that could be set with ordinary type. This proved to be a popular invention and Kirkall cut a large number of head-pieces, tail-pieces and capitals. His engravings for books also include plates to illustrate Terence (1713), Ovid (1717), Dryden (1717), Lucan (1718) and Pope's *Iliad* (1715–20).[38] Booksellers commissioned plates to add interest to a new edition of a classic or an established modern work; it was unusual for first editions of new works to be embellished. Important exceptions include the first edition of *Robinson Crusoe* in 1719 with a frontispiece engraved by John Pine and the first edition of the *Beggar's opera*, which included music. Music also had to be engraved on copperplates, though it cost less to engrave than a complicated picture.[39]

The first modern British work to be heavily illustrated was Samuel Richardson's *Pamela*. Between the publication of the first volume in 1740 and the second in 1741, Samuel Richardson mooted the idea of getting William Hogarth to design two frontispieces. This scheme came to nothing, but *Pamela* proved so popular that it went through five editions within a year.

37 *EP*, 24–26 July 1718, 24–27 Jan. 1719.
38 Hodnet 1976, 195–209.
39 See Mosley, chap. 7 above; Hunter, chap. 41 below.

In 1741, Richardson commissioned no fewer than twenty-nine illustrations for the sixth edition of 1742. Francis Hayman designed twelve, while Hubert Gravelot undertook the remainder and all the engraving. The prints were attractive and elegant but, in order to defray their cost, the price of the book had to be doubled from 12*s*. to 24*s*. At that price it sold insufficiently well to tempt Richardson ever again to adorn his work with copperplate illustrations.[40]

In the immediate wake of *Pamela*'s phenomenal commercial success, the artist Joseph Highmore decided to paint and publish a series of twelve designs for it, as large, decorative engravings 'by the best French Engravers'. This series of large prints emulated such recent French publications as Charles-Antoine Coypel's cycle on *Don Quixote* (1723–4) and William Hogarth's similar series illustrating *Hudibras* (1726). Highmore launched a subscription in 1744, explaining that in these prints he 'endeavour'd to comprehend her whole Story, as well as to preserve a Connexion between the several Pictures, which follow each other as Parts successive and dependent, so as to Complete the Subject. This is more distinctly illustrated in a printed Account given to the Subscribers, wherein all the 12 pictures are describ'd, and their respective Connexion shewn.'[41]

It is worth noting just how many words sometimes accompanied separately published prints. Eighteenth-century libraries contained single-sheet prints with huge quantities of text engraved on them. An example from Hogarth's *Hudibras* set, *Hudibras encounters the Skimmington*, had thirty-six lines of verse selected from Part II, canto III, lines 753–832 engraved on it. Highmore's *Pamela* prints had explanatory pamphlets issued in association with them. Framed prints are sometimes found with such letterpress explanations glued to the canvas that, at this period, was normally used as backing. The relationship between printed word and printed image was unstable and multi-faceted.

An uncommon permutation is exemplified in *Designs by Mr R. Bentley, for six poems by Mr T. Gray*, published by Robert Dodsley in 1753 for 10*s*. 6*d*. In this volume the juxtaposition of word and image invited comparison and created interplay to an unusual degree. Each poem received a full-page illustration, as well as head- and tail-pieces designed by Richard Bentley and engraved by Johann Sebastian Müller or Charles Grignion. The poems had been published previously and so Gray, nervous of attracting spite, insisted that the book should be presented as a vehicle for Bentley's designs. Accordingly, an 'Explanation of

40 Allen 1987, 149–51; Eaves 1950–1, 349–69; Halsband 1985, 870–80.
41 *LEP*, 26–28 Feb. 1744.

the prints' by Horace Walpole accompanied the whole. This kind of product, though common in France by the 1760s, was as yet unusual in England.[42]

Like Richardson, Laurence Sterne looked to Hogarth to design illustrations for him. 'I would give both my Ears ... for no more than ten Strokes of *Howgarth's* witty Chissel to clap to the front of my next Edition of *Shandy*,' he wrote to Richard Berenger in March 1760 before publication of the first London edition of volumes I and II of *Tristram Shandy*. Unlike Richardson, he succeeded in persuading the great artist by suggesting a design of *Trim reading the sermon*, his pose describing the 'Line of Beauty', a scene that deftly flattered him. Hogarth produced this plate in time for publication on 2 April 1760 and a second was ready to be a frontispiece to volumes III and IV in January 1761. These were the only prints made for binding with *Tristram Shandy* until the first collected edition of Sterne's works in 1780.

However, *Tristram Shandy* and, more especially, *A sentimental journey* also inspired a much larger number of separately issued 'furniture prints'. The earliest were comic subjects designed by William Henry Bunbury, who was also responsible for several of the numerous sentimental scenes that followed.[43] The first few were mezzotints, but after about 1775 they were usually engraved in 'the dotted manner' and printed in reddish brown or in colours for display in a gilt frame. A title and a quotation with a page reference normally appeared beneath the design. Most were sold by purveyors of expensive prints, but there were some cheaper exceptions. Carington Bowles, one of the most important wholesale printsellers for the middle bracket of the market, published *Twelve prints, representing the most interesting, sentimental, and humorous scenes in Tristram Shandy* (1785), designed by Robert Dighton. In the same series, Bowles issued a set of the *Surprising events in the life and adventures of Robinson Crusoe* (1783), which, like the stories of George Barnwell and Moll Flanders, was also copied more crudely as cheap woodcuts of the kind that decorated cottages.

Nevertheless, the vast majority of literary prints ornamented much more affluent homes. People (especially women, perhaps) who read novels and poetry decorated their walls with scenes taken from them. Indeed, women played a considerable part in inventing, selling and engraving such prints – Angelica Kaufmann, a Swiss artist settled in London, was the most prolific designer of literary prints. Caroline Watson and Mary Ogborne figured amongst the engravers of subjects that seem often to have been chosen to appeal to a female audience.

42 Griffiths 2004.
43 Many of these have been discussed in a series of articles in *The Shandean*; see D'Oench 1999.

Among modern works, James Thomson's *Seasons*, Goethe's *Werther* and Marmontel's *Contes moraux* followed *A sentimental journey* in popularity as sources of incidents. While Goethe and Marmontel were certainly read in England, their use may also reflect the wide export market on the Continent for such prints. Pictures did not need translation to be appreciated internationally, and the quotations engraved beneath them were sometimes translated into French, the most widely understood international language. Prints illustrating scenes from literature became very common between 1775 and 1800 and a large proportion of them were exported.[44]

Shakespeare led the way. The print of William Hogarth's portrait of *Mr Garrick in the character of Richard the 3d* (1746) was the first of a large number of engravings and mezzotints showing the great actor and his colleagues in Shakespearean and other roles. The most notable reproduced paintings by Johann Zoffany.[45] The twelve *Shakespeare heads* (1775–6) designed and etched by John Hamilton Mortimer were outstanding early Romantic interpretations of Shakespearean characters. Garrick and Elizabeth Montagu actively collected subscriptions to fund the enterprise.[46] The series of mezzotints scraped by John Raphael Smith after Henry Fuseli's paintings (1784–5) were also engaging, if idiosyncratic, responses to Shakespeare. John Pine's efforts (1781–4) were another important, albeit prosaic, attempt to 'bring those images to the eye, which the writer has given to the mind; and which, in some instances, is not within the power of the Theatre'.[47]

Meanwhile, a growing body of smaller illustrations was available to embellish editions of Shakespeare's works.[48] Hayman and Gravelot, who had illustrated *Pamela*, were employed again by Sir Thomas Hanmer for his edition of Shakespeare, published at Oxford in 1743–4. In this case, a copy of the contract between Hanmer and Hayman survives, as well as the record of payments to Hayman and Gravelot in Hanmer's bank account. Hanmer paid Hayman 3 guineas for each design, which was to follow (according to the contract) the patron's written instructions. It appears that Hayman did not complete the drawings within the stipulated time and may not have been paid in full. The bank account shows that £217 7*s*. was paid in instalments to Gravelot for thirty-six engravings and five drawings, suggesting a fee of about five guineas for each plate.[49]

44 Alexander 1993; Clayton 1997, 246–56.
45 Lennox-Boyd 1994.
46 Sunderland 1988, 76–82.
47 Alexander 1993, 10.
48 See Suarez, chap. 34 and Sutherland, chap. 35, both below.
49 Allen 1987, 153. According to George Vertue, the plates for Thomas Newton's edition of Milton (1749) cost four guineas for each drawing by Hayman and eight guineas for each plate by Simon François Ravenet.

During the 1770s, the effective end of perpetual copyright opened the works of Shakespeare and other major authors to all publishers and made it possible to publish canonical anthologies of the works of many authors.[50] This stimulated fierce competition, with illustrations providing a prominent distinction between rival editions. The most daring entrepreneur in this field was John Bell, who took on the combined might of the rest of the trade.[51] For his edition of Shakespeare (1773–5), published weekly in sixpenny parts, Bell originally commissioned illustrations by Edward Edwards but soon substituted a series of thirty-six portraits of actors in character. As he announced, their use was not limited to being bound with his own edition:

> fine Proof Impressions of the whole are sold at 10s. 6d. per Set, in loose Prints for ornamental Furniture, or which may be bound up with any edition of Shakespeare's plays; others at 12s. per Set neatly done up in Marble Paper. A few Sets will be coloured from Nature and sold when done at 36s. per Set.[52]

In 1776 Bell followed Shakespeare with a *British theatre* also published in sixpenny parts, each containing a play and an illustration. With each fifth part, Bell gave out a frontispiece and a title page. Illustrations showed portraits of actors 'painted from the life, by Permission, on purpose for this work *only*'. Both text and prints could be had in proof form on larger sheets of fine paper. A rival consortium of publishers led by Thomas Lowndes published a *New English theatre* (1777–9) with similar illustrations. Between 1777 and 1782, Bell published his *British poets*, employing the best of the literary designers, John Hamilton Mortimer, until the artist's untimely death. Each volume was 'calculated for a lady's pocket' while the whole would 'form a truly elegant ornamental appearance, in the drawing room, dressing room, or study'.[53]

Similar collected illustrated editions, including compilations of afterpieces and songs, proliferated in the years around 1800. It became commonplace for successful novels to be republished with illustrations. Artists could now make a career as illustrators, a turn of events from which Thomas Stothard, Edward Burney and Thomas Rowlandson were among the first to benefit. Illustrations were almost always engraved, since this was the process best suited to large editions. Small stipples were rarely used as book illustrations, but there were exceptions such as *Angelica's ladies' library* (1794). The dotted manner was sometimes also used for such fine luxury products as Peltro

50 See Rose chap. 4, above; Bonnell, chap. 37, below.
51 On Bell, see especially Morison 1930; cf. Burnim and Highfill 1998.
52 *PA*, 7 May 1776.
53 Brewer 1997, 485. Cf. Bonnell, chap. 37, below.

William Tomkins's edition of Thomson's *Seasons*, with illustrations designed by William Hamilton and engraved by Tomkins himself and Francesco Bartolozzi.

These developments culminated in the vastly ambitious projects launched by Thomas Macklin and John Boydell. Ostensibly vehicles for British history painters, they exploited the voracious international appetite for prints and British literature. Thomas Macklin was the first to envisage a planned programme of commissioned pictures from which prints would be made. In 1788 he announced *A series of prints illustrative of the most celebrated British poets . . . with explanatory letter press*. The plan was to publish one hundred prints after paintings displayed in the 'Poets Gallery' in Fleet Street. In fact, only twenty-four paintings were issued before the deterioration of international economic conditions after 1793 forced the abandonment of the project.

John Boydell's celebrated Shakespeare Gallery opened in 1789 with prints beginning to appear in 1791.[54] In its final form, the end product consisted of one hundred large plates, available individually for framing or as two imperial folio volumes at £63, and a nine-volume folio edition of Shakespeare, illustrated with ninety-five smaller plates at £42. The attempt to engage all the leading painters in Britain in illustrating the works of the nation's most famous writer was an enterprise of extraordinary ambition. The result was unsatisfactory, partly because the collapse of the European market enforced economies and partly because some artists failed to rise to the occasion. Nevertheless – with George Steevens as editor and William Bulmer as typographer – Boydell's claim that it 'surpasses in Splendour all former Publications, as far as the Genius of Shakspeare surpasses that of all other Dramatic Poets' was not empty bluster. In its sheer magnificence, the project remains a monument to the skill and scale of late eighteenth-century art and book publishing in London.

William Blake's illuminated books present a marked contrast.[55] In most respects Blake is an anomaly, but his prints might be compared with those etched by George Stubbs, Thomas Gainsborough and other artists for appreciation rather than profit. These plates are often experimental and technically ill-suited to the production of large commercial editions. With the help of his wife, Blake did his own printing and issued his prints more or less on demand. This led to a degree of variation from one example to another that would have been unusual when a copperplate printer undertook an edition for a

54 See Sutherland, chap. 35 below.

55 Blake literature is vast and most conveniently consulted through the website www.blakearchive.org.

printseller. Blake's price structures were also eccentric, possibly in order to render his work as accessible as possible. Initially, he sold *Innocence* and *Experience* for 5*s*. each, a quite unrealistic price in commercial terms. As priced at 6 guineas in 1806, they more closely mirrored the going rate for a series of colour-printed copperplates. Blake employed innovative and idiosyncratic methods in printmaking and printing to produce things of extraordinary beauty and apparent simplicity. Despite much valuable, detailed investigation into Blake's methods, the exact nature of his procedures still attracts lively debate.[56]

However low Blake might set his prices, his prints, along with most of those described above, remained out of reach for the working class. Labourers might see relatively fine engravings decorating inns and public houses, but they could not afford to own things more sophisticated than the chapbooks and the penny royal sheets represented in the wholesale catalogues of the Sayer, Bowles and Dicey firms. Although the variety of such cheap imagery increased after 1800, it was not until after 1830 that the working class could possess the sort of imagery that middling people consumed in the eighteenth century. The weekly *Mechanic's Magazine*, published for 3*d*. from 1823 and read mostly by 'Mechanics and Artisans', reached a circulation of 16,000 by 1824, but the real breakthrough came in 1832 with the advent of the *Penny Magazine* published by Charles Knight. This had a circulation of 200,000 (Knight reckoned this made its audience a million) and provided common people with prolific wood-engraved images of a sophistication 'which they never could behold before . . . and literally at the price that they used to give for a song!'[57]

56 Viscomi 1993. For debate between Viscomi and Essick and Martin Butlin, see Essick and Viscomi 2001–2, 2002.
57 Anderson 1991, 47, 49ff.

11

The morphology of the page

NICOLAS BARKER

The shape of words on a page, like the shape of the letters of which they were composed, followed conventions adopted without alteration from those of manuscript books. These protocols, generally derived from earlier continental examples, had altered little in Britain throughout the sixteenth and seventeenth centuries. Change in the sixteenth century was due not so much to insular taste as to the new French orthography, introduced by Huguenot émigrés. The seeds of another change in the layout and components of the printed page can be seen at the end of the seventeenth century, which may again be due to French influence and the release of more Huguenot printers. French taste was as fashionable in this as in other aspects of the decorative arts, in Holland as well as France. These phenomena may have provided the impulse that led others besides printers to re-examine accepted conventions for the printed page. Many factors contributed to this – social, political and economic – from the introduction of a tariff on imported paper to the improvement of communications, all of which led to a more conscious approach to the novel demands made for the layout of texts. The study of the changes thus induced constitutes the 'morphology' of the book, a phrase used by Henri-Jean Martin at a conference in 1977 to describe this process.[1]

At first sight, there seems a world of difference between the last great masterpiece of the seventeenth-century press in England and the first of the eighteenth. The contrast between the form provided by Jacob Tonson for his edition of Dryden's translation of Virgil (1697) and that provided by the press that Bishop Fell had set up 'at the Theatre' in Oxford for Clarendon's *History of the rebellion* (1702–4) is great. Although both are large folios, both texts for which 'classic' status was indicated, and both as dependent on copperplate as letterpress printing, the arrangement was otherwise very different. Dryden's Virgil seems

1 For the proceedings of the conference, see Barber and Fabian 1981. The word was coined by Goethe in or before 1817; cf. Gray 1880, 5n.

retrospective: the text type, although generously leaded, seems rough and old-fashioned; the title page – its words, in red and black, given irrational emphases ('Works' larger than 'Virgil') – is enclosed in a double-rule border horizontally divided by single rules, echoed in the running headlines. The full-page plates are separately printed, each endorsed with the name of the subscriber who had paid £5 for it, a method of financing such books invented by William Dugdale and given greater currency by John Ogilby in his illustrated editions of Virgil, Homer and Aesop. The type used for Clarendon is cleaner and newer in appearance, though closer set; the open title page has the relative importance of the words better arranged, and the copperplate printing – with initials, head- and tail-pieces – is integrated with the text. But these seeming differences are illusory. Whereas Dryden's Virgil is set in relatively new types,[2] Clarendon is in the types that Peter Walpergen cut to match the far older ones that Fell had acquired. If the pages of Clarendon look more modern, they in fact imitate the style set sixty years earlier by Cardinal Richelieu for the Imprimerie Royale (Fell's exemplar), as do the engraved decorations. The Virgil plates are in fact the same as those originally engraved by Pierre Lombard and Wenzel Hollar for Ogilby in 1654. The contrast is not one of time, but between a national or British and an international or Franco-Dutch style.

The use of rules, as opposed to the characters of printing type, is perhaps the least considered aspect of the history of printing. They were already in use in the fifteenth century, some visibly cast in a type-mould, others already made differently, being drawn in strips, probably in brass, as they certainly were later. The first use of such rules was utilitarian, for tables. The decorative use of lines enclosing or accentuating the page was not new when printing was invented, however. Ruling the page (as well as lines) was an essential part of the manuscript book and could again be ornamental as well as utilitarian. At some point, about the middle of the sixteenth century, it became customary to set off the black printed page with a red-ruled outline extending into the margins. This was by no means universal, but rather a way of distinguishing copies, especially those on large or fine paper. Again, a decorative border, particularly on the first or title page, was a practice inherited from illuminated manuscripts and facilitated by the invention of fleurons. Some books, especially those with woodcut illustration, such as emblem books, had decorative borders on every page. All these methods of finishing the printed page were in

2 The types are those of Robert Andrews (*fl.* 1674–1735), some of his own, some acquired from Joseph Moxon, some from Peter Walpergen; the bold two-line English heading type is that of Nicolas Kis, and may have been acquired from Holland around 1690 and supplied by Andrews to the Oxford University Press.

use in England before the end of the sixteenth century. At some point in the second decade of the seventeenth century, it became the fashion, and subsequently the custom, to enclose the type page with a boxed-rule border, with the headline and margin similarly boxed off, especially if the latter contained notes in small type. Just why this practice came in when it did is not clear, but it may be in imitation of the manuscript book, which about this time achieved a wider commerce due, paradoxically, to the increasing efficiency of censorship and the Court of Star Chamber. That the practice was ornamental not functional – that is, the rules were not intended to hold the page together[3] – can be shown by the parallel development of the marginal fillet rule on contemporary British plain calf bindings.[4]

By the end of the seventeenth century, this distinctive practice had eroded, but the habit of keeping skeleton formes standing may have led to the preservation of rules above and below headlines. The Dutch predilection for footnotes had yet to reach Britain, and marginal source references or comment continued, without vertical rules to enclose them from the text. When page folios were included in the headline, as they generally were, they were set out into the margin, whether side notes came beneath or not. This atrophied form of the ruled margin was given a new function by the insertion of the numeration of chapter or section followed by a brace on its side, forming a support to the letters or figures above. This detail survived over half a century, from Berkeley's *Alciphron: or the minute philosopher* (1732) to Gibbon's *The decline and fall of the Roman Empire* (1776), during which many other aspects of the printed page altered considerably.

If increasingly obsolete details thus dominated the shape of the printed page familiar to the seventeenth- and eighteenth-century British reader, they seem no less easy to anyone who reads such pages today. A phenomenon equally familiar then is less so now, namely 'black letter', the French *lettre de forme* adopted by English printers for vernacular texts. Already rare by the seventeenth century, it persisted in four uses: the 'Authorized Version' of the Bible (as distinct from the roman type of the Geneva version); the Book of Common Prayer (last printed in black letter in 1706) and its occasional supplements; Acts of Parliament, other statutory instruments and a few other legal texts; and as a display type, to distinguish a key-word in title pages and drop-head titles. All these uses had diminished by 1700, except for Acts of Parliament, which did not change to roman type until 1794, and as a display type, where it lingered on

3 A page divided by rules holds together more poorly than one of solid type.

4 Red-ruling was not made obsolete by this practice, but gradually came to be restricted to bibles and liturgical books, where it was emphasized by multiple ruling of lines as well as the page.

in varying contexts throughout our period, but it is important to remember that it was once as common and as easily read as roman type, to which it presented an alternative no more different than italic type. Italic too had more complex purposes than its present limited use largely for emphasis. Originally used for Latin words (even in black letter), it came to serve a variety of needs – highlighting proper names, an important noun or reported speech – all in various rhetorical ways emphatic. The arrival of Huguenot compositors after the Revocation of the Edict of Nantes in 1685 altered this, as it did conventional English spelling. A degree of irregularity and licence was no longer tolerable to those on whom the nuances of English speech were lost. Francophone spelling, 'chace', 'risque' and the like, was matched by a more orderly use of italic, now mainly restricted to proper names. Like black letter, however, it maintained its use as an alternative to roman for the purposes of display, in headings, epigraphs and citations from Latin and other foreign languages.

All these habits and uses had implied certain restrictions, some based on mechanical necessity, others on immemorial habit. The structure of the hand-press did not change much, although minor improvements, attributed by Moxon to Willem Janszoon Blaeu, improved its efficiency, and perhaps its size.[5] There was also the long-standing uniformity in the matter of format effected by the traditional and invariable sheet sizes of paper. A slow but marked increase in the size of the average octavo, quarto and folio book, due to the adoption of larger sizes of paper, matched the improvements in the structure of the common press. The sizes themselves, canonized by the Act of 21 Geo. III in 1781, remained unaltered,[6] but the extra expense (paper was charged by weight, and a larger sheet meant higher cost) was matched by a decline in quality, offset by the increased use of writing paper for better quality work. Larger sheets created larger formats: the enlarged folio ultimately made the format, long the preserve of the 'serious' book, extinct as such, its place taken by the new large quarto. Accordingly, the new octavo succeeded to all the purposes of the old quarto, while duodecimo and smaller sizes filled the needs met by the old small octavo, as well as new ones, notably in the new and expanding field of children's books.[7] Duodecimo was never as popular as a format for new books as it was in Holland and France. Whereas paper of good quality had been imported from Genoa or Holland, the former always white, the latter cream, the paper mills of Kent – to which the 'hollander beater' and

5 Moxon 1962, 373–4; Gaskell 1974, 121–2.
6 The sizes are given in c. 24; Gaskell 1957, 41.
7 See Immel, chap. 40, below. On changes in the popularity of various formats, see Suarez, chap. 1, above.

other improvements were introduced, again by Huguenot refugees – could now produce a cleaner, more even sheet. The growth of local manufacture was protected by a duty on imported paper from 1712.[8]

It was this change in the availability and quantity of raw material that, perhaps more than anything else, provoked dissatisfaction with the restrictions implicit in the current formats of British books and brought about change. Its first vigorous expression came with Jacob Tonson. Although Dryden's Virgil had been successful enough commercially, there may have been objections to its old-fashioned appearance that led him a year later to call on Cornelius Crownfield, the newly established printer to Cambridge University. His *Proposals for printing Horace, Virgil, Terence, Catullus, Tibullus and Propertius, In the new press at Cambridge*, printed in the late summer of 1697, announce 'That the Authors above-mentioned shall be printed in the same Form; with the same Letter; and upon the same Paper, as the *Specimen* annex'd', 'That there shall be a new *Frontispiece* to each Book, with other Ornaments, Design'd and Engrav'd by the best Hands', and 'That every Subscriber, paying one Guinea in Hand, shall have a Receipt given him, wherein the Undertaker *Jacob Tonson* obliges himself, upon the payment of a Guinea more, to deliver to the Bearer one compleat Set of the said Books, in Quires, as soon as printed.'[9] There were 286 subscribers listed in the editions that followed between 1699 and 1702. The engravings were by the Huguenot artist Simon Gribelin, then at the mid-point of his long career.[10] Prompted, perhaps, by his experience with Crownfield, Tonson paid a visit to Holland in August 1700, in company with William Congreve and Charles Mein, returning again in May 1703 and in 1707. He brought back copperplates, paper and ideas, ideas for publications that would rival the international appeal of the Dutch trade, now (as he shrewdly saw) in decline. He was fortunate enough to find a printer in John Watts, nearer at hand than Crownfield, and as able to provide composition and presswork equal to his ambitions.

It was to match these aspirations that Thomas James also made a journey to Holland in 1710, with the object of buying the equipment for producing types that would equal Tonson's determination to do better than the Dutch. He was fortunate to find type founders – who had hitherto regarded their English counterparts and English printers as a captive market – willing to sell, and what he bought, if not new, included some of the best work of Christoffel van Dijck and his contemporaries. All these new initiatives in the first decade of the

8 See Bidwell, chap. 8, above.
9 McKenzie 1966, I, 178.
10 O'Connell 1985.

eighteenth century culminated in the grandest publication of all, Samuel Clarke's edition of Caesar (1712). Its title page, in black only and with no rule border, the lines of roman and italic capitals generously letter-spaced, emulates its Dutch exemplars and the classical inscriptions that lay behind them. Its appearance is in every way a contrast with Tonson's tour de force of fifteen years earlier, Dryden's Virgil. The specially engraved double-page title by R. van Audenaerde, the head-pieces and historiated initials by J. Baptist after T. Goeree (their subjects echoing the text), and the generously spaced Dutch types (the text in Christoffel van Dijck's 'ascendonica') maintain this imposing appearance, which was amplified by plates engraved by C. Huijberts, and also paid for by subscription. Although all this was revolutionary in terms of contemporary typographic form, it also referred back to Ogilby's sumptuous editions of a generation earlier, an allusion to the past not lost on contemporaries.

The imprint of Clarke's Caesar was 'Sumptis et typis Jacobi Tonson'. Next year Michael Maittaire's editions of the classics began to appear 'ex officina Jacobi Tonson & Johannis Watts', a partnership that lasted until Tonson retired in 1717 and Watts moved to what Benjamin Franklin, who worked there in 1725, called his 'still greater Printing House' in Wild Court, off Lincoln's Inn Fields. The Maittaire classics reflect the current enthusiasm for the Dutch style, due originally to James Talbot, editor of the Cambridge quarto Horace in 1699. In November 1700, he put out a duodecimo edition, and wrote to his friend Matthew Prior, *en poste* at The Hague: 'I wish you would order my friend and your humble servant, old Elzevir, to recommend this impression in his namesake's types to Leers of Rotterdam, so that he may take off a number of copies, which shall be afforded at a reasonable price ... I am my own bookseller, and without Jacob Tonson's assistance have already six hundred copies bespoken ...'[11] In 1709, the *Tatler* responded to Henry Hills's piracy of its first hundred numbers with 'a very neat Edition, fitted for the Pocket, on extraordinary good Paper, a new *Brevier* letter, like the *Elzevir* editions'. Tonson advertised his ninth edition of *Paradise lost* as 'with a very neat Elzever Letter, in 12mo. for the Pocket', and his rival Lintot followed suit. In *Miscellaneous poems and translations* (1712), in which 'The Rape of the Lock' first appeared, Gay underlined the point: 'neat old *Elzevir* is reckon'd better / Than *Pirate Hill*'s brown Sheets and scurvy Letter ...'[12]

11 H.M.C., *Calendar of the manuscripts of the Marquess of Bath*, III (1908), 428–9; cited in McKenzie 1966, I, 197.

12 John Gay, *On a miscellany of poems to Bernard Lintot* (ii. 91–2).

Gay was not the only poet to appreciate the new, clean style, applied to English as well as Latin classics. This revolution, for such it was, in the appearance of the printed page was not lost on one of its youngest admirers, Alexander Pope. Pope may have 'lisp'd in numbers',[13] but their visible form was no less innate than his aural sense of poetry. His earliest manuscripts show that his feeling for the appearance of his poetry was intimately connected with print: the shape of his verse was typographic, as finished to the eye as its sound to the ear. What is interesting is that the form in which he wrote it was not that in which it actually appeared in print, nor in some version of the 'classical' form envisaged by Tonson and Watts. Instead, it harked back to the form current when he was born, or to a still earlier exemplar. His capacity to imitate print was precise enough not merely to distinguish roman and italic, but even, in headings, to identify the exact type he had in mind. Yet, the page he emulated was the folio in which *Absalom and Achitophel* appeared before Pope was born, and the headings recall the same typographic style. He was the child of the revolution that had then made verse the *lingua franca* of self-expression, as well as of the political revolution in the year of his birth. When Locke's *Two treatises of government* appeared two years later in 1690, the word 'Government' on the title page was in black letter, a not unconscious echo of the type appropriate to parliamentary statutes. But when *The works of Mr Alexander Pope* (a far from unconscious assertion of 'classic' status) appeared in 1717, although the title page was also still enclosed in a double boxed-rule border, the main word was in spaced roman capitals with a vignette of a lyre and two trumpets, clear acknowledgement of the new classic style of typography.[14]

The other poetic bestseller of Pope's youth had been *Poems on affairs of state*, which had canonized the 'miscellany' as the form in which occasional verse was to circulate for the next century. Comparison of the pages of the *Miscellany* (1709) in which Tonson first printed Pope with the pages of his manuscript shows that here too Pope had anticipated print in the headings. Where he did not anticipate typographic form, or where the compositor (surely acting on instructions) did not follow his copy, was in the use of italic. The text in the manuscript is in Pope's fine imitation of italic, but where current convention required italic for emphasis, his script simulates roman type. Was this not another deliberate allusion? Italic had been first cut in 1500 for Aldus to print the editions of the classic verse of the ancient Roman poets and the equally classic Petrarch; it was also used in contemporary print for dedicatory

13 *Epistles and satires of Horace imitated* (1735), prologue, line 127.
14 Foxon 1991.

epistles. No doubt Pope could write it faster than his equally faithful imitation of roman type, but the other implications in its use should not be ignored. *An essay on criticism*, his first separate publication, was printed by Watts in quarto in 1711 with the title page in a rule border, the words of the title exactly following, in size and letter-space, Pope's manuscript; the 'A' in ESSAY has even had the peak gouged by hand to match it. The second edition shrank to octavo in 1712 (post-dated 1713); in the latter year, before the second was exhausted, another edition (interchangeably 'third' or 'fourth') appeared in duodecimo, without the title border and without the emphatic italics of the previous editions. Is he not, here again, asserting an early claim to classic status?

If there are uncertainties in Pope's earliest encounters with print, they disappear with his *magnum opus*, the translation of Homer. There were to be two editions, one for the trade in the familiar 'old' folio form with well-spaced lines, the other for subscribers in quarto. They paid 'for the Expence the Undertaker must be at in collecting the several Editions, Criticks and Commentators', but the elaborate and evocative 'head pieces and tail pieces and initiall letters' were to be 'engraven on Copper in such manner and by such Graver as the said Alexander Pope shall direct and appoint'. It was a manifesto for a new style of printed page, which was to dominate the printing of verse, and it was not lost in the many other applications required of prose. Pope's new dominance extended to the least details in the use of capitals and italics. He had, with reason, trusted Watts in such matters, and may have followed Watts's lead in reducing the heavy capitalization of substantives, as did Gay. The corrected proofs of the *Iliad*, the only surviving example of Pope adjusting his compositors' work,[15] show that they worked from rough, not fair copy, which he rarely disturbed in accidentals, though he corrected errors and sometimes himself rewrote, even leaving a gap to be filled in during the proof stage. He gave no such licence to Wright, who succeeded Watts with *The Dunciad*. From then on, he watched over all details, constantly moving towards a simpler, more classic, style.[16]

If he was the author, in many ways, of the revolution in the form of the printed book that took place during his lifetime, Pope was also a mirror of the conventions that he found. His precise layout for the title page of *The works of Mr Alexander Pope* (1717) shows very clearly which details he felt free to improvise and innovate, and which he accepted as essential to the structure of the page. The title page had slowly evolved from the simplest note on an

15 Le Gal 1952.
16 Foxon 1991, *passim*; for comment see 'The Author as Editor', *BC*, 41 (1992), 9–27.

otherwise blank leaf to an elaborate set of differently arranged words in groups that had independent purposes. Rules, often dividing what was enclosed in a border into compartments, had an important part in these arrangements, and probably influenced the continuation of the apparent straitjacket of the boxed-rule border. Rules commonly divided off the title, longer and more explanatory than is now customary, the volume number (essential to distinguish otherwise identical books), an epigraph or vignette, the name and style of the author, and the imprint. Apart from the last (itself a complex and not always self-evident body of information), any part of the foregoing words might be picked out for prominence, in ways that sometimes seem illogical. They were designed not to meet the present-day cataloguer's need for descriptive information, however, but to catch a more passing and wayward eye, that of a potential purchaser. 'Extra for (it may be) 250 titles' is a regular feature of early printers' accounts; they served as posters, pasted up in a bookseller's shop, and the eccentricities of their arrangement reflect a feeling for the 'impulse buy' that would be familiar to any modern advertising agent. In Locke's *Two treatises*, mentioned above, the next most prominent words after 'Government' are 'Treatises' and 'Essay', both descriptive and clearly attractive in roman capitals, the latter leading on to the last of the thirty-eight words of the title, 'Civil Government'. The fact that twelve words are devoted to identifying Filmer's *Patriarcha* as the target of the first treatise was of negligible interest, but the words that follow, 'Detected' and 'Overthrown', are picked out as sensational in black letter. The same scale of values can be seen in the arrangement of a still more familiar title, that of Bunyan's *The pilgrim's progress* (1678). The two most familiar words are decently large in roman capitals and lower case – they run on without any visual break into 'from this World, to That which is to come' – and the whole, again thirty-eight words, is dwarfed by the one word, in huge roman capitals, 'DREAM', a word infinitely more eye-catching in the great age of almanacs and fortune telling.

It is interesting to compare the approach to advertising Locke with the titles of three other famous philosophic works spread over the next sixty years. Berkeley's *A treatise concerning the principles of human knowledge* (1710) was printed and published in Dublin. Here the four principal words of the title are given due prominence, the shortest largest, probably for no better reason. Where the length of the two preceding titles atrophies the horizontal rule compartments, they are now given full use, one for 'Part I', another for the twenty-two-word sub-title, setting out its inquiry into the grounds of disbelief, a third for Berkeley's name (Bunyan's is in small type, Locke anonymous) and qualifications, 'MA Fellow of Trinity-College, Dublin', and the last to the imprint. It is hard to be sure whether the author's hand can be seen here, but his purpose, as well as the bookseller's, has been admitted. There can be no such doubt about *Alciphron: or, the minute philosopher* (1732), now 'Printed for J. Tonson in the Strand'. The title visually runs on to the next words, 'in seven dialogues', and that to a shorter explanatory sub-title, again aimed at 'Free-thinkers', with the first word 'APOLOGY' in eye-catching caps and small caps. The compartments serve their conventional purpose, but the central and far the largest is given to a vignette of what the epigraph below from Jeremiah proclaims to be 'the Fountain of living waters', with the distant figures of the Israelites hewing 'broken cisterns that can hold no water', rounded off with a neat pun from Cicero. The unfamiliar name *Alciphron* is picked out in italic capitals with exaggerated letter-space. Both this and the vignette show the influence of Tonson and Pope, but the conceit is entirely Berkeley's. The last example is Hume's *A treatise of human nature* (1739). Like Locke and Berkeley, the author's words attempt to sum up his purpose, but as set they do not so much exploit as break the Procrustean bed of the rule border. 'Treatise' dominates in the old way, the horizontal rules remain but serve little purpose save to double underline the subject of the first volume, 'Understanding'; the casual reader would be uncertain whether this, or 'Moral Subjects' or 'Human Nature' was the main topic.

The title pages of all these philosophic works serve two purposes, the author's and the trade's, even if they are somewhat at odds with each other. All of these writings are famous today, but all were less popular in their own time than another, Lord Shaftesbury's *Characteristicks*, a collection of essays, not a treatise, inculcating moderate deism. It was first published in 1710, already with a circular vignette on the title page and head-pieces by Simon Gribelin; these decorative and pedagogical elements were extended in the second edition (1713) and retained in its many subsequent printings. It may have been the subject, uncontroversial in an age of controversy, that ensured its popularity, but the more likely source of appeal is its decoration. Like Tonson's classics and Pope's Homer, it appealed to an age interested more in visual than in verbal stimulus, to which a monument meant more than a direct statement. *Characteristicks* achieved the unusual distinction, unique for a text still relatively modern, of being reprinted both by Robert and Andrew Foulis and by John Baskerville, proof of the extent to which it appealed to the new classicism. The Foulis brothers printed it without the plates in 1743–5; Baskerville in 1773 retained them. The plates made it, perhaps, a special case, but other decoration, vignettes on title pages, head- and tail-pieces, initials and factotums, all cut on wood, proliferated, filling the vacuum left by the absent rules. By now the sense of the page as enclosed space had markedly diminished. One of the great bestsellers of the age, in Europe as well as England, was Young's *The complaint: or, night thoughts on life, death, and immortality* (1742–5), which shows a new spaciousness, not only in the arrangement of the title page (black letter for the two key-words perhaps a consciously sepulchral use), but also in the interlinear space in the text. The other great success of the age of sentiment, *Tristram Shandy* (1759–67), subverted the page with blank, black and marbled pages, skipped pagination, and other surreal devices.

Besides the new taste for classicism – a monumentality that requires the eye not just to be caught but also to engage with what is there to be read – there was another factor that changed the appearance of English books, less conspicuously but no less dramatically. By 1720, Thomas James was effectively the sole type founder in London; the others were small businesses, all in decline, whose stock and business he was mainly to absorb: he must have thought his commercial position impregnable. His reckoning did not anticipate the emergence of a genius, the more unexpected since no such talent had yet appeared in the British Isles. William Caslon was one of the rare breed of punch-cutters capable of informing the alphabet with an individual yet familiar style. His early training as an engraver of musket barrels for the Board of Ordnance gave him a grounding in the 'English vernacular'; the letters inscribed on tombstones and brass plates by generations of stone masons and other letter-carvers. If his immediate model was the types that James had brought back from Holland in 1710, he improved upon them. Updike, pondering his success, saw that 'he introduced into his fonts a quality of interest, a variety of design, and a delicacy of modelling, which few Dutch types possessed'.[17] Besides these gifts, Caslon added facility and business sense. Where James was limited to the stock of matrices that he held, Caslon could add anything required of him, from new Arabic types for the SPCK to fleurons.[18] It was exotic types, first the Arabic and then a Coptic for David Wilkins's *Pentateuch*, that first made his reputation. It was not until 1725 that his first romans and italics appear in Bowyer's *Anacreon*, but from then on, his success was assured. The quality of his metal was good and his delivery was punctual – virtues that William Bowyer may well have expected as much as his letter-cutting ability, when he, Bettenham and Watts advanced the £500 that established Caslon's foundry in 1720.[19]

The rapidity with which Caslon's new types spread throughout the English printing trade, reaching both Scotland and Ireland, and America before the end

17 Updike 1962, II, 105.
18 See Mandlebrote, chap. 32, below.
19 Nichols 1812–16, II, 720.

of the century,[20] was remarkable. They had already superseded the Fell types at Oxford for Sir Thomas Hanmer's elaborate six-volume illustrated Shakespeare in 1743–4, and the new Caslon fleurons were used as dividers between acts. The excellence of the types also had a retarding effect, however. Their ability to make the commonplace or familiar seem better than it was inhibited further experiment. It excluded England from exploring the new rococo typography, or, with rare exceptions, from experimenting further with the interaction of type and copperplate engraving. This limitation is the more surprising since the links between France and England had in other respects never been closer. Voltaire had found much to admire during his stay in England in the 1720s, and had promoted it in *Lettres philosophiques* (1733–4). Like others on the periphery of France – from Brussels and Amsterdam to Strasbourg, Bouillon and Neufchatel – English printers readily took to producing works that increased censorship made difficult to print in France, from Voltaire's *La Henriade* (1728) to Diderot's *Jacques le fataliste* (1796). Little attempt seems to have been made to disguise this trade: *La Henriade* 'Chez Woodman & Lyon' in 1728, if not overtly English, is certainly not French, as is the 'nouvelle edition' of 1734, nominally 'A Londres, Chez Jacob Tonson'. The first edition of Marivaux's *La vie de Marianne* (1742) may have been genuinely for sale 'A Paris, Chez Prault, Fils, Quay de Conty, vis-a-vis la descente du Pont-Neuf, à la Charité', but its origin is betrayed by that exclusively English phenomenon, press-figures. How many more French books were first printed in England (to say nothing of English piracies of books first printed in France) remains to be discovered. Yet, the fact is that French taste – whether exemplified in the engravings after Moreau or Eisen or in the elegant and equally decorative types of Pierre-Simon Fournier – failed to catch on in England. French engravers such as Gravelot found a ready market in England, and so too did English printers for books smuggled into France, but in other respects taste failed to travel. It is no coincidence that the only use of French type in England so far discovered is in the Sallust of William Ged, whose innovatory stereotype shut the doors of all English typefounders against him.

By the mid-century the format of books had stabilized. If Pope had now canonized quarto as the invariable form for new poetry, as folio had been earlier, books in general were smaller. William Shenstone, a sensitive observer, wrote: 'I am always in Hopes that whenever an Author is either a tall or even middle-size Man, he will never print a Book but in Folio, octavo, or duodecimo; & on the other Hand, when he is short & squat, I collect that his

20 Silver 1965, 123.

partiality to a Figure of that kind, will induce him, to my great discomfort, to publish in Quarto.'[21] That satisfaction with the status quo was not universal is demonstrated by *Designs by Mr R. Bentley for six poems by Mr T. Gray* (1753). To his friend Horace Walpole, Gray was a poet of revolutionary talent, whose work deserved a novel frame, and he spared no effort to provide it. Faced with the choice between an amateur artist who understood what he wanted to achieve and a professional who might not, Gray may have made the wrong decision, but it was the poet's embarrassment (and subsequent withdrawal) at being transformed into a manifesto for a new style of book production that left the volume imperfect, a sketch for a book rather than the finished article. One person who saw its revolutionary potential was John Baskerville of Birmingham, who was a writing master and japanner before he took to printing. As we now know, Baskerville recognized *Designs* as the ideal showcase for his new types, and was frustrated by his own inability to get them ready in time.[22] His early career, and independent and active mind, both qualified him and disqualified him as an innovative force. He refused to be satisfied with anything less than the best, and measured his success by a calligrapher's standard. The punches cut for him by John Handy copied his own style of roman and italic, as written and engraved on stone, echoing the same progress of script and engraving visible in Caslon's work a generation earlier. He made his own ink, and his correspondence with James Whatman exhibits the same desire for perfecting the surface on which his types were to be printed, accentuated by the 'hot-press' finish that so struck contemporary admirers. The publication of his quarto Virgil in 1757 was rightly seen as a landmark in European, as well as English, book printing.[23]

Baskerville's limitation, as an influence on the shape of printing in Britain, was his inability to compromise. So long as the object of his work was in itself simple, as in the quarto and duodecimo Latin classics, or already fully worked out, as in the Books of Common Prayer of 1761 and 1762 and the 1763 Bible, his application of his typography to it was successful; it was less so in more ordinary contexts. His career – first as a printer on his own account, then as employee or lessee of the University Presses at Oxford and Cambridge – exemplifies the same tendency, but as he himself wrote in the preface to his second work:

21 Letter to Lady Luxborough, 1 June 1748; cited in Bronson 1968, 333.
22 Bidwell 2002a.
23 Gaskell 1959, 19–22.

> It is not my desire to print many books; but such only, as are books of Consequence, of intrinsic merit, or established Reputation, and which the public may be pleased to see in an elegant dress, and to purchase at such a price, as will repay the extraordinary care and expence that must necessarily be bestowed upon them. Hence I was desirous of making an experiment upon some of our best English Authors, among those Milton appeared the most eligible.[24]

Within those limitations, and to those who shared his tastes, Baskerville's typographic experiments had a lasting value, and it is appropriate that his punches, *aere perennius*, should have come to be preserved at Cambridge two centuries later.

If Baskerville left little mark on the way that ordinary books were printed, his influence was felt indirectly through the imitations made of his types, especially by Joseph Fry at Bristol. Fry could undercut Caslon's London prices, an important factor as the spread of printing to the provinces, rapidly increasing in the second half of the century, caused a corresponding rise in the market for type. The intense rivalry between the two firms was expressed in further imitations of each other's work, both of which were proclaimed to be superior to the other. More influential than either were the types of Alexander Wilson, in the hands of Robert and Andrew Foulis. Their work as printers to the University of Glasgow, spread over a much longer time (thirty years) than Baskerville's, was aimed at a competitive and commercial market. Beginning in 1743, two years before the last Stuart attempt to regain the throne, they profited thereafter from the rapid commercial and intellectual growth of Scotland. They were fortunate enough to find in Alexander Wilson an equally able punch-cutter and type founder, who followed them to Glasgow from St Andrews, becoming professor of astronomy in the university. From this combination came a wholly distinctive typographic style: clear, uncluttered with rules or ornament of any kind, and monumental in appearance, whether in large or small format. The deployment of letter-space, the use of the squarer shape of small capitals in multiple lines and the well-judged balance of interlinear space were influential, not only through the diffusion of their own books – found all over Europe to a degree not achieved by any earlier British press – but also in their imitation by almost all other British printers. Such restrained and self-conscious elegance was a new phenomenon in printing outside France. It was not entirely self-generated, since the Foulis brothers benefited from the prizes offered by the Select Society of Edinburgh for

24 Preface to *The works of John Milton* (Birmingham, 1758), A3v.

well-printed editions of the classics. At the same time, the Royal Dublin Society also awarded premiums for well-made local paper. Both these initiatives show that there was, for the first time, an interest outside the trade in making a conscious effort to improve the quality of the printed page by extending control to its smallest details.[25]

If the example of the Foulis editions can be seen in the later monumental editions of the Didot brothers in Paris and Bodoni in Parma, it was not lost at home, where it vied with various other influences. The use of Whatman's wove paper came of age in 1760 in Edward Capell's *Prolusions*, a revolutionary work in multiple ways: no catchwords and the use of type-facsimile to reprint old texts are other signs of a new typographic awareness. Capell's printer was Dryden Leach, the printer of Charles Lloyd's *Poems* (1761), Francis Fawkes's translation of Theocritus (1767) and many other books between 1758 and 1769. He printed both William Caslon and Son's *Specimen of types* – the first English specimen published in book form – and *The north Briton* for John Wilkes, himself a connoisseur of printing, and was arrested for it, barely escaping prosecution.

The traditional form of the page had now withstood impulses to change from several quarters: from the classicism of Tonson and Pope, from the new types inspired by Baskerville, and from the monumental typography of the Foulis press. Change had indeed taken place, but much had remained unaltered: not just the atrophied remnants of earlier compositorial practice, but also the means of production and the way the trade worked. The next impulse had more serious consequences, since it threatened the essentially London-based structure, described so vividly by Johnson in his famous letter to the Vice-Chancellor of Oxford.[26] The arena of change was complex and various: improved communication by water and then by road, the growth of manufacturing industries in the midlands and north of England, challenges from Methodism and renascent Catholicism to a latitudinarian Church of England, improved and increased school education, and the growth of the periodical press and its extension outside London.[27] All these tendencies spread literacy and the market for print faster than the metropolitan system could support. Unacknowledged provincial reprinting of books successful in London, a practice more common and earlier than is obvious, became overt. Both in Dublin and Glasgow, reprinting became complicit; a single misprinted letter in the imprint signalled Berwick reprints, in not inconsiderable numbers.[28] But this

25 Gaskell 1986, 209.
26 12 Mar. 1776; Boswell 1934–50, II, 424–6
27 See Ferdinand, chap. 21, below.
28 See Benson, chap. 17 and Beavan and McDougall, chap. 16, all below.

guerrilla warfare led to open conflict; the challenge came from the Edinburgh bookseller Alexander Donaldson. In 1774, the House of Lords overturned the principle of perpetual copyright, and with it the dominance of the London trade.[29] Those who had pioneered modernity just lived to see it triumph; the next year, both Baskerville and Andrew Foulis died, and Robert Foulis the year following, and it was left to John Bell to exploit the vacuum in trade as well as typographic terms.

Donaldson himself had printed several English 'classics' in small format, but it is impossible to underestimate the impact of Bell's series: the acting edition of Shakespeare (1774); *The British theatre* (1776) issued in sixpenny weekly parts in octavo; *The poets of Great Britain complete, from Chaucer to Churchill*, beginning in 1779; and a second Shakespeare, beginning (again in weekly parts) in 1785, in duodecimo. His first printer was C. Etherington of York, but the major part of the series went to Gilbert Martin in Edinburgh, where the 109 volumes of the *British poets*, completed in 1792, were printed in large quantities.[30] Both printers employed the same types, cast, like those of the Foulis press, by Alexander Wilson. The uniform layout of the text pages had numbered lines and headings separated from the text by double rules. The same rules appeared on the title page under the title and came before the imprint, in black letter, featuring the name, 'Apollo Press', that the Martins gave their business. In front of this appeared an engraved title page, with an engraved frontispiece facing it, both within a monumental border, in the French manner. All the main artists and engravers of the day were employed on these, and the use of black letter for the imprint and the rules, which Bell later converted to thick and thin rules, became a trade mark, not only of Bell and his series, but later of the revolution in British typography that they inspired. The parallel volumes of the Shakespeare 'were printed for Mr Bell by Messrs Frys & Couchman in a brand new Burgeois letter cast and hand-drest on purpose by Messrs Fry, the eminent typefounder', further evidence of Bell's interest in appearance. The London trade, under no illusion as to the threat that Bell's series represented, responded with heavy artillery: the sixty-eight volumes of *The English poets*, for which Johnson wrote his famous prefaces.[31] His bookseller friend, Edward Dilly, explained this to Boswell in 1777 in dismissive terms that fail to conceal his alarm:

29 See Rose, chap. 4, above.
30 See Bonnell, chap. 37, below.
31 Bonnell 1995.

> The first cause that gave rise to this undertaking, I believe, was owing to the little trifling edition of *The Poets*, printing by the Martins, at Edinburgh, and to be sold by Bell, in London. Upon examining the volumes which were printed, the type was found so extremely small, that many persons could not read them; not only this inconvenience attended it, but the inaccuracy of the press was very conspicuous. These reasons, as well as the idea of an invasion of what we call our Literary Property, induced the London Booksellers to print an elegant and accurate edition of all the English Poets of reputation, from Chaucer to the present time.[32]

If Johnson's *Poets* was a success, it was as nothing to Bell's, which was not limited to the sales of his little volumes. The Bell style, lightweight types with rules to punctuate rather than enclose, took universal hold, and Thomas Bewick's discovery (or rediscovery) of the extra subtlety of wood engraving on the end grain instead of the plank made it possible to combine it with finer and more graceful vignettes.[33] In addition, each of the little books had a specially commissioned engraved frontispiece and title page before the letter-press; this revived the art of book illustration, dormant (other than for technical purposes) since Hanmer's Shakespeare and Bentley's *Designs for six poems by Mr T. Gray*.

Bell's francophile taste now took a new direction. For almost a century, the *romain du roi* had offered an alternative letter form to the traditional 'old face', which the trade had been slow to follow, since the Imprimerie Royale discouraged imitation. François-Ambroise and Pierre-François Didot, however, introduced the first 'modern face' types in 1784, which Bell, visiting Paris in 1785, was quick to admire. On his return, he issued the prospectus of a 'New Printing Letter Foundry' in 1788, which advertised the types cut for him by Richard Austin. His new 'transitional' design had an immediate effect. The two printers who were to pioneer the typographic revival at the turn of the century, William Bulmer (a Northumbrian like Bewick) and Thomas Bensley, previously had very ordinary equipment, as their early work shows: for example, Bulmer's *Guide to the Shakspeare gallery* (1787), or Bensley's *The six princesses of Babylon* (1785) by Lucy Peacock. Austin's design for Bell's embryo foundry was quickly copied, and William Martin, who had learned under Baskerville, was employed by the 'Shakspeare Printing Office' of Bulmer and George Nicol, the royal bookseller, with John and Josiah Boydell, 'to cut sets of types after approved models in imitation of the sharp and fine letter used by the French and Italian printers'. Bensley, supported by their rivals, Thomas Macklin and

32 Boswell 1934–50, III, 110.
33 See Clayton, chap. 10, above.

Robert Bowyer, went first to Caslon's former apprentice, Joseph Jackson, and after his death in 1792 to Vincent Figgins, for equally monumental and rather more versatile types. The Boydell Shakespeare (nine volumes, 1792–1802) and Macklin Bible (seven volumes, 1800), printed on huge sheets of wove paper, achieved a splendour that could be confidently compared with the finest books of Bodoni and the Didot brothers. Boydell's large investment in engraved plates, both for the Shakespeare Gallery and for books like Farington's *River Thames*, set a new fashion. The smaller productions of both Bulmer and Bensley had the same grace and greater variety of typographic design. To an American observer, reviewing the course of British typography in 1802, it seemed a *ne plus ultra*:

> The person whom I above mentioned as superceding all these, and bringing the British press up to the highest perfection was Bulmer. The luxury of the age, and other circumstances, such as the printing for the Shakespeare Gallery in England, introduced a rage for fine printing upon vellum and hot pressing. To render typography equally worthy of regard, Bulmer adopted many improvements from the engravers, and taking the bold stroke of Baskerville, adopting the swelling shape of Fry, he added thereto the delicate and brief curves of the Italians and their fine hair stroke. The types of Bulmer are now to be seen in every work of elegance or taste printed in England, and are sought after in various parts of Europe. But what is a remarkable circumstance it is necessary to wait a year before an order is executed, so great is the demand – and spare sorts are not to be had at all.[34]

The last decade of the eighteenth century and first of the nineteenth, a period of prosperity in time of war, were thus a high point in the appearance of books in Britain. If contemporary connoisseurs were chiefly impressed by the two Bs, there were many other printers whose compositors had as sure a touch. Miller Ritchie, Thomas Rickaby, Thomas Davison, D.S. Maurice and the young Charles Whittingham all produced fine work in London. Eyres in Warrington, McCreery at Liverpool, Joseph Aston of Manchester, Cruttwell at Bath, and Bewick's printers Beilby and Davison in Newcastle showed that equally good work could be produced outside London, while James Ballantyne maintained the Scottish tradition of careful and elegant composition. It was also a period of great technological change, with the introduction of machine-made paper by the Fourdriniers, Lord Stanhope's iron press and first stereotype office, and finally the steam-powered press of Koenig and Bauer, of which Bensley and Richard Taylor were joint patentees. The

34 William Duane, in the Philadelphia *Aurora*, 2 Mar. 1802; cited in Silver 1965, 123.

elaboration of aquatint, the perfection of the stipple technique by Francesco Bartolozzi and the invention of lithography offered new potential for the illustrated book.[35] All these improvements left their mark; at the same time, collecting famous and beautiful books of the past vied with patronage of the contemporary press.[36] The 'Bibliotheca Parisina' sale in 1791 attracted fierce competition for books released after the French Revolution, whence too came the émigré labour that made possible the great colour-plate books of Rudolph Ackermann and others.

Both the types used by Bulmer and Bensley and their contemporaries and the pages they produced have a grace that is appreciable even now, which makes it hard to understand why this style of typography was of relatively short duration. The explanation lies in another change: if books had hitherto been the main staple of the press, they were no longer so. The increase in the number of newspaper and periodical titles in the last half of the century had been dramatic, and with it the demand for posters, playbills, forms and other jobbing work.[37] Large letters, first cast and then engraved on wood, were a new necessity; smaller letters had to become more legible to convey more information more economically in an increasingly competitive market. Anthony Bessemer devised a revolutionary solution to this problem in 1795, when he cut the first types with markedly thicker strokes, 'fat face' as they came to be called.[38] John Bell was quick as ever to grasp the economic advantage, inserting this notice in his newspaper:

> *Bell's Weekly Messenger* is now printed in a New Type cast by Mr Thorne – the graceful formation and present Arrangement of which enables us to introduce Intelligence equal to One-Eighth more than we have formally done, and with a distinct and more agreeable effect to the eye of the Reader than is observed in any other Newspaper.[39]

Robert Thorne's genius in this respect was acknowledged when he was summoned to Paris to cut types of the new design for the Imprimerie Nationale. This reversal of the trend of imitation speaks for itself, but by the time it came, the economic prosperity of the first decade of the century had waned. The great colour-plate books were fewer, although Ackermann's smaller landscape series prospered, and the *Repository of arts, literature, fashion and manufactures* (a telling conjunction) continued till 1828. Steel engraving, with finer detail,

35 See Clayton, chap. 10 above.
36 See Landon, chap. 38 below.
37 See Harris, chap. 20 and Tierney, chap. 24 below; also, Twyman, chap. 2 above.
38 Bessemer 1930 (1830).
39 Morison 1930, 123.

provided the new medium for the frontispiece and engraved title of the 'Magnum' edition of the Waverley novels, with which Scott sought to rebuild the fortunes of Ballantyne and the Constables, his printer and publisher, as well as his own.[40] They were set in new types from the Wilson foundry, in the new 'modern face' style, and inaugurated a new taste for what came to be called 'Scotch' types.

By 1820, almost any combination of type, ornament and illustration seemed possible, no format, large or small, beyond the capacity of the press. Old constraints were forgotten, and in a market wide enough to absorb all competition there was no entrenched cartel to enforce uniformity. When Pickering launched his 'Diamond Classics' in 1822, there was no Dilly to criticize types still smaller than Bell's or texts immaculately set by Charles Whittingham; their little pages appealed to connoisseurs now more historically conscious than they had been in Pope's day, when Elzevirs were their equivalent. Those connoisseurs had founded the Roxburghe Club in 1812 to canonize their taste, and its laureate, Thomas Dibdin, was as enthusiastic in praise of the new achievements of the press, as of the 'black letter tracts' that his heroes contested in the sale room. Yet, enthusiast though he was, he had a not uncritical eye for the present, a feeling for the merits of the past as well as the infinite possibilities of modern progress:

> In regard to *Modern Printing*, you ask me whether we are not arrived at the topmost pitch of excellence in the art? I answer, not quite at the topmost pitch: for our types are, in general, too square, or sharp; and the finer parts of the letters are so *very fine*, that they soon break, and, excepting in the very first impressions, you will rarely find the types in a completely perfect state. There is more roundness, or evenness, or, if you will allow the word, more *comfortableness* of appearance, in the publications of Tonson and Knapton, than in those of modern times.[41]

This perceptive criticism, anticipating the revival of 'old face' types, in which Pickering was to have so large a part, is doubly interesting, since it shows an aesthetic appreciation of type as well as of typography, of the merits of the old as well as of the new. A sense of the evolution of the printed page is not new, and, consciously or unconsciously, has always informed reactions to what is read.

40 See Beavan and McDougall, chap. 16, below.
41 Dibdin 1817, II, 378.

12

Bookbinding in the eighteenth century

NICHOLAS PICKWOAD

Likewise with books bound after what manner you please.[1]

It is as well to remember this statement when looking at the work of the hundreds of binders active throughout the United Kingdom over the period covered by this volume, who would have laboured for much of the time on individual commissions from retail booksellers (if they did not serve this function themselves), institutional libraries or private individuals, seeking to have books bought in sheets, paper wrappers or other temporary bindings put into permanent ones. For most of the eighteenth century, only the very cheapest end of the trade, such as school-books, popular romances and devotional works, typically sold books bound and delivered direct to the end-user, though the sale of bound bibles and liturgical works was something of an exception to that. It is in the second decade of the nineteenth century that significant numbers of editions were for the first time issued bound in what were intended to be permanent bindings. It is also important to remember that the bindings we know best from the literature – generally the more extensively decorated bindings – formed only a very small part of the trade. This chapter will therefore take as its main focus the more standard types of binding and the more ephemeral protection offered to text blocks within the book trade; the reader is directed to the existing literature for a more detailed account of the more extensively decorated books.[2]

In terms of the tools used to make books, however, the period sees remarkably little innovation: a binder from 1830 could have walked into the shop of his late seventeenth-century counterpart and recognized virtually every piece of equipment (Plate 12.1). The first piece of 'industrial' equipment to find its

1 From the ticket of Richard Randall, Newcastle, late seventeenth century (Hunt 1975, 75).

2 For a general account of the development of English decorated bindings, see Nixon and Foot 1992 and Nixon 1978. A comprehensive account of English bookbinding technique will be found in Middleton 1978.

way into bookbinding workshops – the rolling machine designed to replace the manual beating of text blocks in preparation for binding – was not invented until 1827, but in London soon resulted in the dismissal of fifty men whose sole job was the beating of books.[3] What did change, and quite dramatically, was the appearance and levels of finish applied to bindings of almost all qualities, together with the introduction of a small number of highly significant new structures and materials which paved the way for the industrial development of the trade later in the nineteenth century.

The bookbinder occupies the territory between the bookseller/printer and the client, taking the product of the former and turning it into the readable book required by the latter. As such, it was essential that the bookbinder be accessible to the client, which meant that, outside the major book-producing centres where many bookbinders had always found work, there was a need for bookbinders to provide bindings for local needs. The growth in the provincial book trade through the eighteenth century was substantial and widespread,[4] and had a considerable impact not only on the numbers of provincial bookbinders, which greatly increased towards the end of the eighteenth century, but also on the levels of skill required of them. The period 1780 to 1830 saw a remarkable flowering of bookbinding in provincial centres, where work of high quality and originality was produced for the local market.[5] In the smaller regional centres, however, a local bookseller might have to wait for the arrival of a 'tramp', usually a journeyman binder from London looking for work.[6]

Workshops remained small, and in the provinces, bookbinders often had to take on other trades to make ends meet. The most common of these was bookseller, though printer and stationer followed close behind, and other trades associated with the distribution networks established by the book trade, such as druggist and patent medicine vendor, were also popular. Bagford observed early in the eighteenth century that many binders, who were generally speaking not well paid, moved into bookselling to improve their lot;[7] and in the provinces especially a bookseller might well find it convenient to add bookbinding to the services he could offer his local clientele. In the early eighteenth century the London bookseller Rhodes used several binders almost as his servants, fetching and carrying and acting as

3 Middleton 1978, 228–30. A hydraulic press was patented in 1795, but is not recorded as being in widespread use until 1837, and was not mentioned by Hüttner in his description of binding in 1802 – Middleton 1978, 225.

4 See the British Book Trade Index (http://www.bbti.bham.ac.uk) for further information.

5 Hobson 1940, 195.

6 Howe and Child 1952, 23.

7 Davenport 1904, 140–1.

agents for the sale of books.[8] Towards the end of the century, the publisher John Bell established his own bindery to cope with the demand for his books and to give him control over, as well as the profit from, binding them.[9]

The bookbinding trade in London at the beginning of the eighteenth century was concentrated in the City, close to the printers, but as the West End of London became more fashionable, the bookbinders who catered to the wealthier clients began to move westwards, and by the end of the century most of the best-known names had workshops west of Temple Bar.[10] The growing size of the trade also encouraged the journeymen and masters to form trade associations, and from the 1780s a number of trade disputes broke out.[11] In London the highest paid craftsmen, always the finishers who carried out the tooling of the bindings, could earn a good living, but generally it was not thought a highly paid craft.[12] In spite of the growth of the trade, few workshops, even by 1830, employed more than a dozen people,[13] and an individual journeyman could set up a workshop at modest cost.[14] Bagford at the beginning of the eighteenth century and Baxter a hundred years later both record that women were mostly employed to fold, sew and headband books.[15]

Below the top end of the trade, the work of bookbinders often remains anonymous, and it is frequently difficult to relate bindings to the names that we have from other sources. A handful of earlier binders tooled their names on their bindings,[16] but bookbinders' tickets, which first appear in the 1720s,[17] remain scarce until the last quarter of the eighteenth century. Even then, they are mostly found in decorated bindings, often on books of fashionable prose and verse, indicating not only a growing class of readers with time and money to spare for such books, but also a market for them to be sold already bound. Not all those advertising bookbinding on their tickets actually bound books; many acted as agents responsible for getting the work done.

Before the appearance of large-scale edition binding in the 1820s, it is difficult to assess the extent to which books were sold bound. (Bennett 2004 argues powerfully that many more books were sold bound than previously thought, but the evidence is difficult to interpret.) Booksellers certainly sold

8 Blagden 1954, 107–8.
9 Morison 1930, 38–40.
10 Howe 1950a, xxix; Ramsden 1956, *passim*; Potter 1991, 34.
11 Howe and Child 1952, 9–50.
12 Howe 1950a, xvi.
13 Potter 1993, 259.
14 Nixon 1970, 33–52.
15 Davenport 1904, 137; Baxter 1809, 95.
16 Munby 1953, 179.
17 Maggs Bros., *Catalogue* 1075, pt 1, no. 130, 202 Brotherton. Munby 1953, 183.

bound copies of books in their shops, and certain books for which there was a reliable market, such as bibles, were regularly sold bound, though such bindings, commissioned a few at a time by retail booksellers according to sales, are not edition bindings and cannot necessarily be distinguished from bindings commissioned individually from the same bookbinders. From the fact that law books were often bound in a standard style, with white, unsprinkled edges and no sprinkling on the calf, it would appear that many law books were also sold bound. This characteristic appearance, noticed by Bagford in around 1700[18] and again by Cowie in 1828,[19] was clearly well established as a style.

Booksellers' advertisements from the beginning of the eighteenth century offered some books for sale 'bound', but the rationale behind the selection is often obscure. A small percentage of the books listed in the *Term catalogues* are similarly described, and the most likely titles came under reprints and divinity, for which, presumably, a reliable market was already established.[20] In the second half of the eighteenth century, such references to bound books become increasingly common, though the terminology is limited and not always easy to understand.[21] The word *bound* is the most frequently found, and would usually have meant a plain calf leather binding in boards, unless qualified as *in sheep*, *in red*, *in vellum*, etc. *Calf* (or *sheep*) *lettered* would have been much the same with the addition of a lettering piece, and *calf gilt* would have had a gold-tooled spine. *Neat*, *handsome* and *elegant* are regularly found, but what exactly was meant by such distinctions is harder to assess, though a distinction is clearly implied in one advertisement which offered books in either '*neat or Elegant Bindings*'.[22] *Stitched* is straightforward, but *sewn* is somewhat ambiguous, though when qualified, as in *sewn in blue*, the meaning is clear: a sewn text block in a blue paper wrapper. From the mid-century, the terms *boards* and *in boards* are more and more frequently encountered, describing paper-covered bindings in boards with uncut edges. In the early nineteenth century the term *extra boards* appears, possibly referring to books with boards cut larger than the text block,[23] and from 1825 books covered in bookcloth could be described as *cloth*, *cloth boards* or *extra cloth boards*.[24] Options were sometimes given, such as *sticht 4d. bound 6d.*, and from the last quarter of the eighteenth century the term *half-bound* makes its appearance.

18 Davenport 1904, 140.
19 Cowie 1828, 32.
20 Arber 1906, entries for the years 1695–1709.
21 Peddie 1943, 20–1.
22 Stewart-Murphy 1992, pl. 25.
23 Hill 1999, 259.
24 Carter 1932, 20.

The highly detailed list of prices issued by the bookbinders of Newcastle in August 1813 conveniently defined what was then meant by some of the commonly used terms:

Calf, Gilt.– Forwarded [i.e. sewn, put in boards and covered] as calf lettered, with the addition of silk headbands.

Calf, Half-extra.– Forwarded carefully, marble papers, two-coloured silk head bands, narrow registers [i.e. silk bookmarks], narrow rolled round the sides [i.e. a narrow gold-tooled border to the boards].

Calf, Extra.– Well beat and forwarded, better marbled paper, three-coloured silk head bands, registers, narrow rolled round the sides and inside.

Calf, Super extra.– Beat and forwarded in the best manner, extra marbled paper, three coloured ribbon, or fancy head bands, broader registers, rolled inside, and double rolled outside, with narrow rolls or one broad roll.[25]

In London, ordinary bindings would appear to have been charged at standard prices which would have followed those recommended in the bookbinders' price lists published at intervals in the eighteenth and nineteenth centuries.[26] These lists generally give prices for standard bindings in calf and sheep according to different sizes of book, with and without some extra decoration, in an attempt by the binders to establish minimum prices for such work.

Although many bookbinders must have bound books at all levels of cost, there was, by the mid-eighteenth century, at least in London, a distinct division, based on the cost of the bindings produced, between the 'calves leather binder' and 'the binder in sheep'.[27] A third category was 'vellum binder', the binder of blank books for the stationery trade, which was accounted the most profitable of the three branches,[28] and a distinct part of the trade by 1695.[29] Government offices, the military and, of course, the business community would all have needed such books, and the vellum binders were said to have benefited greatly from work commissioned by the Admiralty during the Napoleonic wars.[30] By 1806, this part of the trade was large enough to form its own Vellum Binders' Trade Society.[31] The years 1780–1830 also saw a rapid growth in 'bible binding', a profitable business based on the output

25 Isaac 1997, 22.
26 Foot 1984; Pollard 1956.
27 Collyer 1761, 68–9.
28 Collyer 1761, 68.
29 Howe 1950a, 60.
30 Howe 1950b, 113.
31 Howe 1950b, 116.

of organizations such as the Society for Promoting Christian Knowledge (founded 1699) and British and Foreign Bible Society (founded 1804).[32]

Until the 1760s, the construction of books at all levels of the trade remained essentially static, whatever the developments in decoration. For high- and medium-quality work there were leather-bound books in boards with raised supports. At the lower levels, stitched books, with or without boards, were produced in larger numbers than surviving examples might suggest, and other cheap books continued to be sewn in the seventeenth-century manner on recessed alum-tawed supports to the end of the eighteenth century. The 1743 Dublin bookbinders' price list gave prices for testaments and grammars 'saw'd per 100' (i.e. with recessed supports) and covered in 'grains',[33] presumably the tanned grain-split of sheep leather, which the Dublin Guild of St Luke the Evangelist had forbidden twenty-two years previously.[34]

Within the decade of the 1760s, however, a number of significant changes took place that took the trade in two different directions. At the lower level, the introduction of both case binding and the use of linen canvas as a covering material set precedents not fully realized until the end of the period. At the upper level, there was a distinct movement towards greater precision of work in both forwarding and finishing, a development that was recognized by the master binder James Fraser in 1781.[35] This decade saw also the reintroduction at the upper levels of the trade of sewing on recessed supports (always cord and never skin at this level), which contributed to the increasingly slick appearance of the more elegantly bound books and, when combined at the end of the century with the new artificial hollow back, set the structure and appearance of hand-bound books for the whole of the next century.

This new standard of appearance gradually worked its way down through the trade; by the end of the eighteenth and in the opening decades of the nineteenth century, there were huge numbers of neat-looking, inexpensive calf or sheepskin bindings on small format books available on the market, sewn on only two or three thin, recessed cords, with some gold-tooled fillets, if not lettering. James Fraser claimed that duodecimos and octavos 'occup[ied] four days out of six in the Week' and that profits from quartos and folios did not make up the profit lost through the smaller formats.[36] J.C. Hüttner, a German resident in England, had, however, harsh words about the work at this level of

32 For a brief account, see Potter 1993, 264–8. For a more comprehensive history, see Howsam 1991.
33 Foot 1984, 310.
34 Pollard 2000, xvi–xvii.
35 Quoted in Howe 1950a, xxvi.
36 Howe 1950b, 161.

the trade, claiming in 1802 that 'There is also very bad work in London. In the City it is all botched work because it is poorly paid. The booksellers, especially in Paternoster Row, are not worried about quality; they pay very late, and get bad work.'[37] Hüttner was comparing their work with that of London's West End trade, and it could only suffer by comparison, but if the comparison is made to similar work of the early part of the previous century, it is clear that the materials are more accurately cut, the leather is thinner and the finish neater – though no more and probably less durable in many cases.

The great majority of printed books intended for domestic and institutional libraries were bound in boards and covered in leather. Limp parchment bindings had virtually disappeared from printed books,[38] to be found almost exclusively in the blank book trade, though the laced-case parchment binding over stiff boards (commonly known in England as Dutch vellum; Plate 12.3) was still current, but much more commonly found as a stationery binding (Plate 12.4). It was only in the hands of high-class binders, such as Edwards of Halifax[39] and their imitators in the second half of the century, that Dutch vellum binding achieved prominence in Britain. Tight-back bindings with parchment on the spines and foredges, and often also along the head and tail edges to create a frame filled in with marbled or coloured paper, seem to have been a speciality of Oxford, a unique example of a distinct regional binding type (Plate 12.5).

Variations between bindings were largely controlled by cost, which showed itself both in the amount of decoration applied to a binding and also in the quality of the materials used. The prominent use of printed waste as endleaves had almost entirely disappeared by the end of the seventeenth century, though marbling on printed waste is found well into the nineteenth century on less expensive books. More typically, endleaves were made from good quality writing paper, suited to manuscript inscriptions, and marbled papers were used only on the more expensive bindings, often associated with an increase in the amount of gold tooling. On the most expensive bindings, the more costly decorated papers – such as British-made or more usually imported metallic varnish and embossed papers, woodblock printed papers and pastepapers – would be commonly found, with Scottish bindings favouring in particular the German embossed papers.

The sewing structures of books bound in boards used either raised or recessed supports. The latter, although very much in decline by the 1690s,

37 Middleton 1978, 256.
38 Middleton 1978, 142.
39 Marks 1998, 186–9.

were still occasionally found on standard texts at the very beginning of the eighteenth century, surviving only among the cheapest books until revived for all types of work in the third quarter of the century. By the end of the seventeenth century, the practice of sewing leather-bound octavos and quartos on five single cords appears almost universal, with four for smaller books and three only for the smallest formats. Folios, except for the very largest and grandest, were usually sewn on six cords.

The reintroduction of recessed support sewing, resulting in smooth spines (unless false bands were added), was probably imported from France, but was quickly taken up across Britain. Matthewman, the binder working for Thomas Hollis, was regularly sewing books this way in the 1760s,[40] and it would appear that the initial interest in the structure was aesthetic, as evidenced by its appearance on relatively expensive bindings in which the binders often took full advantage of the decorative possibilities of the smooth spine. However, the trade soon realized the economies offered by sewing on recessed supports and their use spread rapidly for the rest of the century,[41] to the extent that when binders in the 1790s wanted to use raised bands for the decoration of the spines of their books, they mostly used false bands.[42] Roger Payne, the most inventive and talented of English binders of the late eighteenth century, was swimming against the tide when he insisted that one of his bindings was 'sew'd in the very best Manner on six Bands on the outside (the Bands are not saw'd in and their is not any false Bands)'.[43] He was fighting a lost battle, however, and in the decade after his death in 1797, false bands became almost universal and sometimes took on enormous, if not grotesque, proportions, having lost all pretence of looking like real supports. Combined in the same decade with hollow backs, false bands became standard practice.

By the end of the seventeenth century, the use of millboards made from rope fibre was well established and within the first quarter of the eighteenth century it became almost the only board used. In 1711, its manufacture was presented to the House of Commons as a means of reducing dependence on imported boards from Holland, and some of the wealthier London binders set up a mill near Windsor to make it.[44] At the beginning of the eighteenth century some binders, especially at the cheaper end of the trade, continued to use boards made from paper pulp, which binders were able to make for themselves, largely

40 Nixon 1978, 168–9; Bond 1990, 39.

41 Smith 1810, 284. 'Bookbinders now generally use a saw to make places for the bands.'

42 Parry 1818, 9 claims that folios and quartos were generally 'sewd to bands, that is stand up bands', but actual examples are rarely encountered by then.

43 Rothschild 1947, text to pl. II.

44 Middleton 1978, 66.

from the trimmings of the cut edges of the books they bound (it was estimated that a sixth part of the paper was cut off and recycled).[45] Occasional pulp boards are found as late as the early nineteenth century, but generally of very poor quality and most probably provincial work.

Spine shapes change during the period, with the even round of the spine found at the beginning of the century giving way to a half elliptical spine in the 1770s and then to almost flat spines around 1800.[46] Spine linings are seldom found until the reintroduction of recessed supports, except on the larger books where binders clearly felt that extra support was required. With the reintroduction of recessed supports, the use of spine linings, cut to the height and width of the spine, in both paper and textile, became increasingly common, to compensate for the flexibility of the spines of books thus sewn.[47] Linings in soft sheep leather were often used in combination with the early hollow backs (known at first as 'open backs'[48]), which arrived in England at some point towards the end of the eighteenth century. They were designed to allow books printed on thick paper to open more easily without damaging the tooling on the spine, giving the books the two qualities so greatly admired at the time: solidity and elasticity.[49]

Headbands had long since lost any structural function, and served only to decorate and establish the status of a binding. According to cost, they might be worked in linen thread, worsted or silk, with the number of colours used increasing in line with the elaboration of the rest of the binding. Cheaper bindings would reveal their status by the absence of headbands, and vast numbers of the most inexpensive books were produced without them. The cheapest headbands might use only an uncoloured thread, but most have two colours, blue and white being popular at the beginning of the period and red and white thread for the rest, always with a front bead and very few tiedowns. More elaborate endbands were given crowning cores (thin cores running along the top of the main core), and double-core headbands are found by the end of the century. Curiously, the German binders working in Britain from the 1760s rarely used the stuck-on headbands which were to be found on almost all German bindings of the period.[50] The use of stuck-on headbands did, however, become established in the United Kingdom in the early years of the nineteenth

45 Middleton 1978, 66.
46 Middleton 1978, 59–61.
47 Arnett 1837, 150.
48 Parry 1818, 23–4.
49 Arnett 1837, 154.
50 A copy of Torquato Tasso, *La Jérusalem d'livré*, 2 vols., Paris: P. Didot, 1796, in the Pierpont Morgan Library (PML 75002–3) bound, with a ticket, by Staggemeier and Welcher, has stuck-on endbands.

century, though Cowie pointed out that they should not be used 'for extra binding'.[51]

The choice of covering material was essentially dictated by cost, but for leather bindings the skins of only three animals – sheep, calf and goat in ascending order of cost – were in regular use, decorated and tooled in a wide variety of ways, again depending on cost and, on occasion, subject matter. Tanned sheep, which makes a comparatively weak skin, will only be found on the cheapest bindings, and was particularly associated with school-books (Plate 12.7). It was mostly used plain, but is also found sprinkled and, at the end of the period, even marbled, but is rarely tooled with anything more than a few gilt fillets and perhaps a title. Basil, much used as a cheap substitute for goatskin in the early nineteenth century, and roan, a tanned sheep leather of rather higher quality, were used extensively for small stationery bindings as well as cheap printed books.

Tanned calf was by far the most popular skin, a reflection both of its comparative strength and of the British diet. It was produced in a variety of shades of brown, depending on the tanning process, but the very dark brown skins popular in the seventeenth century are not found in the eighteenth. Coloured calfskins are not commonly found until the beginning of the nineteenth century. The bookbinders' price lists, as well as occasional advertisements, constantly refer to the escalating rise in the price of leather. The increased cost would appear to have been due to a shortage of supply,[52] and was sufficient in 1768 for the booksellers of London to try to persuade their customers to buy books in paper wrappers and boards instead of leather.[53]

It was perhaps the rather featureless appearance of calf, especially when taken from very young animals, that encouraged the used of stain decoration, from the simplest sprinkling with black ink to the most elaborate marbling using many different colours. Spines, board edges and turn-ins were often stained black to give a better contrast to gold tooling (Plate 12.8). The first tree-marbling is usually associated with the German binder Baumgarten,[54] but once introduced, the decoration of leather took on a new life and a great deal of the content of early nineteenth-century bookbinders' manuals is devoted to recipes for different colours and patterns. The same freedom was extended to the decoration of the cut edges of the text blocks as well, and some of the most striking work in this line was carried out by the provincial binders.

51 Cowie 1828, 48.
52 Vallancey 1780, iv.
53 *LC*, 21–24 May, 1768 quoted in Roscoe 1973, 394.
54 Nixon 1978, 180.

Bagford noted the use of russia calf on books in around 1700,[55] and Harley, Sunderland and Coke used it on their books in the 1710s and 1720s.[56] More widely used in the second half of the century, russia calf became very fashionable towards the end of the eighteenth and at the beginning of the nineteenth. Typically made from the skins of relatively mature animals, most probably reindeer,[57] it made a thick leather that is usually found on larger format books. An imitation was made in France in the mid-eighteenth century,[58] but there is a noticeable loss of quality and permanence in imitation skins from the 1790s. The characteristic graining was rolled into the skins during manufacture, and it was usually rather irregular; as a result it was often done again on the book by the binders (Plate 12.9).

The use of goatskin presents a slightly complicated story in the eighteenth century, but it was always the most expensive of the conventional binding leathers. At the beginning of the period, high quality skin was imported into England under the name of Turkey leather, named after its country of origin (Plate 12.10). This would appear to have come from the same ultimate source as the *maroquin* used in France, and was an immensely durable skin with a rich grain, mostly used in various shades of red, but also in dark blue and black and less frequently green and yellow (citron). It is quite distinct as a skin from what the English called morocco, which was used by both Lord Harley and the Earl of Sunderland[59] for their books in the 1720s. Although thought to have first been used in 1721 to make up for a shortage of suitable skins for Harley's growing library,[60] there is evidence to suggest that it was used by the Earl of Sunderland some ten years earlier.[61] Morocco has a much finer grain than Turkey leather, is nowhere near as durable and is probably the skin of the hair sheep rather than true goat (Plate 12.11).[62] Until the mid-century, a clear distinction was usually made between Turkey and morocco, but thereafter the distinction became blurred until the word morocco was used for both. Both types of skin remained in use, however, the hair-sheep skins often revealing themselves by their inferior durability. Straight-grain morocco, introduced in the 1760s and immediately fashionable, was made by folding the skins hairside to hairside and rolling the dampened leather backwards and forwards in one direction only (Plate 12.12).

55 Davenport 1904, 138.
56 Swift 1985, 28.
57 Garbett and Skelton 1987, 18, 42.
58 Vallancey 1780, 195, etc.
59 Swift 1985, 23–4.
60 Nixon 1975, 164–5.
61 Swift 1985, 25.
62 Swift 1985, 23–4.

The use of parchment with tight backs over books bound in boards with raised bands is less common, but through the century had its enthusiasts, who used sheep parchment for the cheaper variety and calf vellum for the more expensive bindings (Plate 12.6). Horace Walpole asked specifically for a vellum binding from Dublin, which was said to produce the best examples.[63] White alum-tawed skins in general were seldom used, except when there was need to obtain brighter colours for special bindings, though white alum-tawed sheep or hair sheep was more often used for almanac bindings in the last quarter of the eighteenth century. The prepared skin of the shark or the ray, either polished or unpolished, and known in England as shagreen, was used as a covering material for a wide range of small domestic articles and occasionally for a limited range of books that included pocket-books, almanacs and small-format bibles, prayer books and psalters. Thomas Edlin advertised binding in shagreen as well as 'vellum extraordinary' in the 1720s, but the skin was not commonly used.[64]

Silk and velvet, materials used for the most expensive bindings from the Middle Ages onwards, were still occasionally used in the eighteenth century for special books, particularly for presentation copies, and the binder Thomas Elliott is known to have bound in velvet in the 1720s,[65] but by 1800, the situation had changed and silk and velvet bindings, whilst never common, formed part of the repertoire of most of the better quality binders.

The prevalence of paper as a full, permanent covering material is harder to assess, as a low rate of survival has probably skewed our perception of its use; only a handful of scattered examples survive from the early part of the eighteenth century. Starting in the mid-century, 'Dutch gilt' papers were often used to make bright colourful bindings for John Newbery's children's books,[66] and the same papers were used for Osborne's book sale catalogues. In the 1820s, the arrival of the annuals saw the introduction of printed, glazed, coloured paper covers on case bindings. The most widespread use of paper on books bound in boards is found on the temporary bindings known as boarded books, which mostly used white and/or blue paper up to the early nineteenth century, after which both drab and brightly coloured Cobb papers[67] are also found. On up-market versions, marbled paper was used,[68] suggesting that different retailers may have adjusted even these simple bindings to their particular clientele.

63 Craig 1954, 18–19.
64 Howe 1950a, 33.
65 Nixon 1975, 167.
66 Roscoe 1973, 396.
67 Middleton 1978, 38; Krill 1987, 95–6.
68 Wakeman and Pollard 1993, pl. 15.

There is some evidence that inexpensive quarter bindings with uncut edges made their appearance within the trade before the end of the seventeenth century, and it is in this guise that quarter and half bindings are commonly found before the last quarter of the eighteenth century. Pepys's use of quarter bindings in his library was unusual for his time.[69] By the end of the century and throughout the next, their use on books with cut edges was widespread, presumably encouraged by the economical use of leather that they offered; examples in goatskin, calf and sheep were augmented occasionally in the early nineteenth century by books which had either their foredges covered with a continuous strip of leather or the whole board framed with leather, filled in with plain coloured or marbled paper.

The varieties of tooled decoration used on books within this period cannot be covered within this chapter, and it is difficult to divide them up into neatly defined categories, as the tooled decoration of bindings is best seen as a continuum – at one end books with little or even no tooled decoration at all, and at the other books with every surface covered with gold tooling, and perhaps also with onlays of coloured leather or paper. The more expensive end of the trade has been thoroughly researched for many years and there is an extensive literature already available.[70] The general trade made use of a series of widely accepted standard tooling patterns on the boards, the board edges and the spines, and these have also recently been discussed in some detail.[71] It is as well to remember, however, that all the tooling patterns were subject to variations and embellishment according to the taste and pocket of the customer and the skills of the binder, and whilst normally executed on the boards in blind (that is, without gold foil in the impressions), they can all be found from time to time tooled in gold.

The spines of many of the simpler bindings in calf and sheep leather were left either without tooling, or with nothing more than horizontal blind- or gold-tooled fillets on each side of the bands and at head and tail, with no other tooling beyond perhaps a volume number in Arabic numerals to identify sets.[72] The choice of title was frequently left to the owner of the book, and may be found executed many years after the book was bound. The same is also true of at least some of the decorative spine tooling, as purchasers of books sold bound in plain calf or sheep might choose to have the spines tooled in gold. This could have been done by a binder of their own choice, and thus not necessarily the

69 Nixon 1984, xxi, pl. 21. See also Kiessling 2002, xxv–xxvii.
70 For a general introduction, see Nixon and Foot 1992.
71 D. Pearson 2004, 41–114, 178–83.
72 Pollard 1956, 77.

binder responsible for forwarding and covering the book. Such secondary tooling also resulted from books being decorated after being turned spine outwards on the shelves, and this may have happened at any time in the eighteenth century.[73] James Fraser, master bookbinder in London at the end of the eighteenth century, advertised on his trade card: 'Gentlemen's libraries . . . beautified', by which he would have meant tooling the spines of the books.[74]

Many, if not most, binders would have taken in work from the very simplest to the most complex and demanding that their skills allowed. The so-called Geometrical Compartment Binder[75] certainly carried out work at the end of the seventeenth and beginning of the eighteenth century which ranged from the simplest sprinkled calf to the most elaborately gold-tooled Turkey leather; Christian Kalthoeber, in his work for the Whitbread family, bound in all styles from half calf and marbled paper to finely tooled straight-grain morocco.[76]

Both Ireland and Scotland developed their own highly recognizable decorative fashions in design independently both of each other and of England, though forwarding and covering techniques in all three countries appear to show few significant differences. The use of plain and marbled paper onlays on coloured goatskin bindings is highly characteristic of Irish binding (though not unknown elsewhere) and the richness and inventiveness of tooling found on the best work[77] was quite unlike anything found in London. In Scotland designs based around both a wheel and herringbone (or ladder) design were extensively used,[78] though not by the most inventive Scottish binder, James Scott of Edinburgh, whose unusual kit of tools included large classical columns and figures.[79] He, like John Brindley and the Geometrical Compartment Binder before him, also used methods of edge decoration that set him apart from other British binders. Welsh binding offers nothing to compare with the best decorative work in Ireland and Scotland, but otherwise follows the general pattern of the rest of the British Isles.[80]

Perhaps the most creative English binder of the period was Roger Payne (d. 1797) who set himself apart from other binders of the period by his attention to structure and high quality, rather soberly coloured materials (such as drab purple paper endleaves and dark green silk headbands), tooling

73 Pollard 1956, 74.
74 Howe 1950a, 38.
75 Nixon 1978, 128.
76 Several hundred bindings by Kalthoeber remain in the library of the Whitbread family, Southill Park, Hertfordshire.
77 Craig 1954, *passim*.
78 Sommerlad 1967, *passim*.
79 Loudon 1980, *passim*.
80 Rees 1983–4.

patterns built up with finely cut small tools, and the mass of small gold-tooled dots he called studded work, to say nothing of his highly detailed bills. He worked for many of the most active and discriminating collectors during a period marked by its extravagant expenditure on book collecting, and his designs influenced binders on both sides of the English Channel for a decade or more after his death. The most decisive influence on English fine binding, however, came in the form of a succession of German immigrant binders – starting with Andreas Linde in the 1750s and continuing with binders such as Kalthoeber, Staggemeier, Welcher, Hering and Charles Lewis, amongst others[81] – who dominated the London's West End book trade until well into the nineteenth century. Their work is marked by a richness of design and materials, often using coloured onlays, leather joints, watered silk doublures and decorative false bands arranged in pairs or even in threes, which was quite in keeping with the tastes of the Prince Regent and his court.

Thomas Gosden[82] was one of the first British binders to use large blocks to decorate the boards of books, an ancient technique revived in and taken over from France.[83] By the end of the second decade of the nineteenth century, the use of embossed plates to decorate mass-produced bindings was widespread, though the technique used was different from the more traditional one; the leather, most commonly black and maroon goatskin or hair sheep, was usually embossed before the books were covered, allowing for a measure of mass production that leant itself to more durable bindings for the Christmas annuals than the paper and silk first used for them.[84]

At all periods, however, elaborately decorated bindings constituted only a tiny proportion of total output, and it is the medium-range books of the book trade which constitute the vast bulk of what has come down to us in what can be described with any confidence as permanent bindings. Much less visible today are the cheaper and less permanent bindings that once formed a large proportion of the trade. It is difficult to assess not only what was typical when so much has been lost, but also the degree of permanence they had in the minds of their original owners. In the end, permanence is a matter of choice or necessity, and what is permanent to one, possibly impecunious, owner, may be thought temporary to a wealthier one. There is only one sure sign of temporary status within the period 1695–1830: the presence of uncut deckle edges on the leaves of a book. Up to the introduction of machine-made paper,

81 Marks 1984; Ramsden 1956, 9–13; Howe 1950a, xxvii–xxviii; Nixon 1984, 152–3, 182–7, 191–2.
82 Nixon 1978, 198–9.
83 Arnett 1837, 156.
84 Jamieson 1972, *passim*.

most owners of books bought to be read would have had the deckle edges cut off as a necessary precursor to permanent retention and regular use.

From at least the beginning of the seventeenth century, stitched books, held together by thread stabbed through the inner margin of the text block, were mostly issued with uncut edges (Plate 12.13). Controlled to some extent by the Stationers' Company (to protect the work of the binders),[85] stitching offered a simple and efficient means for booksellers at all levels of the trade to move ephemeral material or part issues out on to the streets as quickly and cheaply as possible. By the end of the seventeenth century, most stitching conformed to a fairly standard pattern using three holes, though by the end of the eighteenth century only two holes might be used. Simple though the structure may have been, there was room for considerable variety in the ways in which they were assembled. Many had no covers at all, but if there was a cover, it could be added either before or after the book was stitched, the latter being a little more sophisticated. The quality of paper used for the cover ranged from plain blue through marbled to gilt and embossed.[86] The edges could also be cut, and left plain, sprinkled or even gilded.

Many of the blue paper wrappers were left plain, but from at least 1731, Edward Cave used the wrapper on the stitched issues of his *Gentleman's Magazine* for its advertising potential,[87] and from then on magazine issues regularly made use of printed wrappers. Printed labels were used on at least one occasion as early as 1736 (Plate 12.14),[88] though the rate of loss of this material means that we are unlikely ever to know if this was a common practice at that date, but we do know that by 1742, publishers' advertisements began to appear on the wrappers of part issues of books.[89] In the second half of the century, and particularly from the 1770s, paper wrappers on both sewn and stitched books became more and more frequently used for advertising. The early nineteenth century saw a great increase of decoration involving the use of type ornaments and illustrations on paper covers.

Sewing books immediately made them more expensive, and there is evidence that some books were sold as sewn text blocks without boards or cover at all. These certainly included books imported from abroad[90] as well, it would appear, as books printed in the United Kingdom; the advantage for imported

85 Foxon 1975b, 111–12.
86 Foxon 1975b, 113–14.
87 Pollard 1956, 76. See also Bennett 2004, 87 n. 87.
88 Simon Smith, *The golden fleece: or the trade, interest, and well-being of Great Britain considered. With remarks on the rise, progress, and present decay of our woollen manufactures* [London, 1736] (NT, Blickling Hall).
89 Foxon 1975b, 114.
90 Pickwoad 1994, 64–70.

books, at least until the repeal in 1739 of the 1533 Act forbidding the importation of bound books, was that sewn text blocks would not have been considered as bound. That this Act was still enforced is evidenced from Thomas Bennet's request in 1700 that bound books ordered from Holland should have their covers removed 'as the duty on bound books is very high'.[91] Sewn text blocks would have kept the text leaves together, have added very little weight and thus little extra cost in shipping, and have left decisions on the cover to the eventual owner. The London bookbinders' price list for 1744 lists prices for 'sowing & folding' books only.[92]

When booksellers' advertisements refer to books being 'sewn', it probably refers to sewn text blocks in paper wrappers. There is, however, an important difference between the sewn text block and the book 'sewn in blue': the former was given a substantial sewing structure to which could be added boards and leather, whereas the structure of the latter was quite flimsy and would have had to have been taken to pieces and rebound to achieve the same end. They are usually found with uncut edges and, although it is difficult to establish exactly when they first appear, they survive well into the nineteenth century. The early reference to an edition of 1732 issued at 'price two shillings and sixpence done up in blue covers' is antedated by an example of 1726.[93] Typical examples were economically sewn, very lightly beaten and pressed, and would have been very cheap to make. As such, they would not have represented a significant investment on the part of the bookseller who commissioned them – though whether that was always the bookseller responsible for printing them, or a wholesaler or even a retail bookseller preparing them for sale in their shop remains an open question.[94]

Books were also sold bound in boards with uncut edges without covering or, from at least the second quarter of the eighteenth century, with quarter leather spines and paper-covered boards, though there is evidence that such bindings were made at the end of the previous century.[95] Mid-eighteenth-century examples are often found in quarter sheep with Dutch marbled paper on the sides and uncut edges; this combination of materials is the one most commonly encountered, occasionally with vellum tips or leather corners, but calf leather (and parchment) and plain coloured papers (almost always either blue or grey) are also found. A reference to these bindings in 1810 shows that the practice

91 Hodgson and Blagden 1956, 24.
92 Foot 1984, 312–14.
93 See *The Statutes at Large* (London: R. Gosling, 1726). See also Sadleir 1930, 96.
94 Pollard 1956, 93.
95 Kiessling 2002, xxv–xxvii.

survived well into the nineteenth century,[96] and although many examples have survived, the majority would have been stripped of their covering materials and finished off in whatever style their owners desired.

By the 1740s it would appear that the trade was looking for a rather less substantial binding in boards. The first recorded use of the term 'boards' to describe books bound in boards and covered in plain paper appears in an advertisement in the *British Magazine* of August 1749.[97] A London edition of 1737[98] and another of 1749[99] in such bindings, covered in single pieces of blue- and cream-coloured paper respectively, have survived and would appear to be very early examples of the 'boarded books' which would become the mainstay of the retail book trade from the 1770s through to the 1830s.[100] Lightly beaten and bound by apprentices, these bindings, though simple and bound at great speed, were carefully thought out by the binders, who often used a sewing structure described as 'wide in the middle'[101] that allowed for efficient three-on or even five-on sewing whilst retaining the maximum strength for the book (Plate 12.15). For many readers this temporary binding proved permanent and numerous examples have survived. A variant with a hollow back is known from the 1760s, but does not become common until the early nineteenth century.[102] Boarded books occasionally found their way into circulating libraries where they offered the advantage, with their uncut edges, of preserving the full width of the margins to allow for rebinding when sold off by the libraries. This phenomenon explains the only examples of the retention of uncut edges in otherwise apparently permanent bindings, in the half and quarter leather bindings commissioned by the more up-market circulating libraries.[103]

A structure known as 'binding in the common manner' was used for school-books and other cheap, popular works, and Bagford observed (*c.*1700) that the binders 'use[d] neither sewing nor binding to these sort of books'.[104] Such books were in fact stitched, being held together by two thongs stabbed through the inner margin and laced into boards, and were mostly covered in sheep leather with a blind roll run up the back edge of each board (Plate 12.16),

96 Smith 1810, 283.
97 Cloonan 1991, 34, n. 41.
98 Wakeman and Pollard 1993, pl. 14.
99 Richard Rolt, *An impartial representation of the conduct of the several powers of Europe engaged in the late general war*, London: Printed for S. Birt, T. Longman, P. Vaillant, J. Waugh and W. Owen, 1749, 4 vols., vol. II (NT, Nostell Priory).
100 Hill 1999, 250–3.
101 Cowie 1828, 12.
102 Hill 1999, 261.
103 Pollard 1956, 77.
104 Davenport 1904, 142.

though quarter tanned sheep and marbled paper and plain paper covers are also found. Given the huge numbers in which primers, spelling books, grammars, etc., were produced in the trade, they must in terms of sheer quantity have outstripped the rest of the work of the binding trade by a fair margin. In London, this sort of work was done in the City by the firms that specialized in 'sheep binding', but comparatively little of it from the first half of the century has been preserved. How much of the output was bound and shipped direct to customers, and how much went to wholesalers, is not known, but the presence of sawcuts across the spines of many of these books suggests some form of preparation for sale before binding. Such sawcuts, perhaps made to twenty or thirty copies at a time, are redundant within a stitched binding; it is possible, if not likely, that they were used to allow glue on the spine to hold the books together as they moved through the trade, at some point in which process they would have been stitched, boarded and covered. By 1800 it would appear that the stitched and boarded school-book was becoming less common, though they were still to be found in the second quarter of the nineteenth century.[105]

The first commercial use of inexpensive cloth as a covering material and case binding both date from the 1760s, though neither translates by an easily recognizable path into the trade practices of the following century that they appear to foreshadow. The earliest datable examples of canvas used as a cheap substitute for leather have been found on five copies of Bunyan's *The doctrine of the law and grace unfolded ... sixth edition corrected and amended* (W. Johnston, London, 1760).[106] These were sewn two-on on two recessed alum-tawed supports, but other examples, up to at least 1800,[107] are also found bound in the common manner (Plate 12.17). The canvas is usually brown, and the latest recorded English example dates from 1830,[108] thus overlapping the introduction of bookcloth, which may have encouraged the pioneers of bookcloth, who did not wish to have their bindings associated with school-books, to find a method of disguising the weave of the cloth they used. Irish examples can be found from as late as the 1850s.[109]

In 1769, Newbery and Carnan advertised the fifth edition of Cordier's *Colloquia* as 'bound in Linen and sewed in bands [i.e. raised bands]', having

105 Davenport 1904, 186. Unfortunately, the type of stitching used is not described.

106 A copy belonging to Howard Nixon and now in the Book Arts Press collection in the University of Virginia at Charlottesville contains a note stating that he had found five copies of this edition, all bound in the same manner in canvas.

107 Foxon 1975b, 120.

108 Foxon 1975b, 120.

109 *Reading book for the use of female schools*, Dublin: by Alex. Thom and Sons for Her Majesty's Stationery Office, 1853.

undertaken to bind all copies of the edition in this manner to prevent other booksellers binding (i.e. stitching) them 'as School Books are usually done'.[110] In 1776, the bookseller Sylvanus Chirm also made an attempt to replace 'the deceitful Practice of stabbed Bindings' with books sewn on bands, but in his case covered in tanned sheepskin, a project taken over by his partner and successor, George Herdsfield.[111] Timperley claimed that after the reintroduction of recessed supports 'Bands or raised cords were ... only used for school books, which species of binding is now universally known as sheep bands.'[112]

The introduction of canvas was largely in response to the high cost of leather, and Newbery used the same reason to justify his bindings 'in the vellum manner'[113] which were the first commercial case bindings used in the British book trade. Only one British example, on an edition of 1750, has been found of a case made from a single piece of cover paper,[114] though the type was well known in German-speaking countries, where case binding had been in common use since at least the end of the previous century. The more typical German three-piece case binding of the eighteenth century (the *gebrochener Rück*) was, however, virtually unknown in Britain in the 1760s; the earliest examples I know of are on some books privately printed for Sir Richard Colt Hoare in 1817,[115] and it is not, I think, unreasonable to connect them to his patronage of Charles Lewis, son of one German immigrant binder, Johann Ludwig, and apprentice to another, Henry Walther.

Newbery's case binding, announced in 1761,[116] was more probably derived from Dutch vellum bindings, which, if the sewing supports are not laced through the joints, effectively become case bindings. For Newbery they had the selling points of low cost and replaceability; if 'stained or rubbed' new bindings could be produced for a penny, clearly a benefit for children's books, and one that shows that Newbery was from the outset aware of the structural advantage of providing a binding that can be made in two separate units (the sewn text block and the cover). From the circular dated 22 September 1774, it would appear that they were highly successful ('... Fourteen Thousand Volumes have been sold bound in this manner, and not One Hundred of them have been returned to be new covered'). To date, more attention has

110 Potter 1993, 261.
111 Munby 1950, 180–6.
112 Timperley 1842, 681. Also Arnett 1837, 150.
113 Roscoe 1973, 394–5.
114 *Mr Cooke's edition and translation of the comedys of Plautus*, vol. I, London: Printed by and for J. Purser, 1750 (NT, Calke Abbey).
115 Sir Richard Colt Hoare, *Recollections abroad*, Bath, 1817 (NT, Stourhead).
116 The text of Newbery's circular is given in Sadleir 1930, 11.

been given to the early printed labels used on their spines than to the pioneering structure, but Sadleir's astonishment at the failure of the rest of the British book trade to make use of the printed label for a further thirty years (*vide* 1930, 11–12) is more than matched by the trade's failure to adopt case binding for another sixty years (Plate 12.18).

It would appear that the reintroduction of case binding in the 1820s came from two different directions: one British, one German. The earlier would appear to be of the German *gebrochener Rück* type, probably imported with the original idea of the *Taschenbuch* for Ackermann's *Forget me not; a Christmas and New Year's present for 1823* (Plate 12.19).[117] The printed, glazed paper covers of these early British gift books, protected when first issued by paper-covered slip cases, continued to use the German-style three-piece case into the 1830s, and it was also used for the annuals bound in watered silk. *The keepsake* and *The amulet* both used silk, with titles hand-blocked in gold, usually with the ticket of R. Westley, Binder, who specialized in this sort of work. Heath is recorded as having sold (and therefore having had bound) 15,000 copies of *The keepsake* and to have ordered in advance 4,000 yards of silk for a single edition.[118] It is, however, something of a structural dead end in the English trade, though it no doubt helped to establish the idea of case binding as a viable proposition for the edition binding of large numbers of books.

The case binding that appeared in the pink, glazed calico on William Pickering's edition of Johnson printed in Oxford in 1825[119] shows some similarities to the German model, but also looks forward to the cloth case bindings that dominated the trade from the 1830s (Plate 12.20). However, not all binders followed the lead offered by this (and possibly earlier) case bindings: many bookcloth-covered books in either full or half bindings of the later 1820s and 1830s, and even the 1840s, were still bound in boards – that is with laced-on boards – before the books were covered, just like the paper-covered, boarded books of the same period. It was exclusively the combination of case binding and bookcloth that prepared the way for the industrialization of the trade later in the century. It is significant that these important developments, from the 1760s onwards, all grew out of that part of the trade which first began to sell books directly to the public in standard – or edition – bindings, and for which economies of scale, rapid production, and innovative thinking and design became all important.

117 Renier 1964, [5].
118 Potter 1993, 267.
119 The subject is dealt with at length by Sadleir 1930, 41–3; Carter 1932, 23–30; 1935, 24–7; Potter 1993, 268–9. The arguments are usefully rehearsed in Ball 1985, 11–15.

Books of maps produced with flexible, drawn-on leather covers without boards, making them, as one title page put it, 'portable either for cloak-bag, portmanteau, or pocket',[120] seem to have created a precedent which was taken up later in the century in other areas of book-making. Before the end of the century, volumes of Cooke's *Pocket edition of English poets* could be bought in flexible, drawn-on green goatskin with an artificial plated straight-grain finish, an overlap at head, tail and foredge, and titled and filletted in gold on the spine.[121] The word 'pocket' on the title page suggests that such bindings were offered as an option for these books from the start. Similar bindings also appear at the same time on small format liturgica, as well as on certain small format legal manuals on which the covers were sometimes stiffened by the insertion of pieces of thin card under the leather.

Another printed book which was almost always designed to be carried around was the almanac, frequently bound as a pocket or memorandum book; by the end of the eighteenth century, in London at least, there were binders who clearly specialized in this type of binding and described themselves as 'pocket-book maker' or even 'fancy pocket-book maker'.[122] Almanacs are distinguished from other binding types by a variety of optional features, such as the inclusion of pockets inside the boards, foredge flaps with adjustable clasps (Plate 12.2), metal furniture, and sometimes fastenings which use a silver stylus to hold them together. The silver styluses were used to write on specially prepared leaves which could be wiped clean and reused.[123] In the early nineteenth century, the almanac or memorandum book trade came to be dominated by pocket-books bound in plated straight-grain goat or sheep with a foredge flap from the front board shaped with a tongue that slipped under a leather strap on the other board (often with a fold of leather to take a pencil on the inside of the flap). Throughout the period, of course, almanacs were also available in plain stitched wrappers, bound in the 'common manner' in sheepskin or sewn in paper wrappers or in boards in plain sheep and calf bindings. As with all other books, the trade provided for all tastes and pockets.

By 1830, the bookbinding trade in Great Britain had in place most of the elements which would shape the books of the following half-century and beyond. The increasing mechanization that followed would serve more to consolidate and refine structures already developed than create new ones,

120 *The English gentleman's guide: or, a new and compleat book of maps of all England and Wales*, London: Philip Overton and Thomas Bowles, 1717 (NT, Felbrigg Hall).

121 *The poetical works of Alexander Pope*, London: C. Cooke, 3 vols., 1795.

122 Howe 1950a, 60, 77.

123 Smith, 1810, 289–90, describes how to make these 'white Tables for Memorandum Books, to write upon with a silver Bodkin or wire'.

with the sole exception perhaps of adhesive bindings. Although traditional hand skills still dominated the trade, the move increasingly was towards larger workshops (and more often incorporated into larger printing or publishing businesses), a more organized and unionized workforce, more specialization and something more closely resembling production-line work.[124] In 1830 customers could still expect a high degree of personal service and a variety of bindings designed to meet their individual tastes and pockets, but within two decades a larger and larger proportion of books was to be sold already bound, and the element of choice was steadily eroded, until left in the hands of the wealthier customers only. In the first half of the eighteenth century, by contrast, the bookbinding trade and craft had changed little in its essentials since the mid-sixteenth century. It is the sixty years following the 1760s that saw the greatest change, though it may not have seemed so at the time as their full impact only came later. The fact that this period also witnessed the growth of an increasingly industrialized and mechanized society is no coincidence, and the work of individual entrepreneurs in developing the means both of production and of marketing of their products played no small part in this. The book trade was no exception, and bookbinders, as the servants of the trade, had no choice but to follow suit.

124 See Mosley, chap. 7, above.

PART IV THE BOOK TRADE AND ITS MARKETS

I
LONDON AND THE 'COUNTRY'

13
London and the central sites of the English book trade

JAMES RAVEN

New building schemes, new commercial agendas and new trading practices reshaped the topography of the London book trade between 1695 and 1830. Fixed sites of sale increasingly replaced (but by no means completely supplanted) itinerant traders supplied by cheap book depots. Greater book-trade concentrations in particular streets and precincts supported new trade specializations. Bookshops, printing houses and subscription and commercial libraries followed developers and builders as fashionable London devoured the fields to the west and north of the City. As is often the case, change, especially rapid change, also highlighted continuities and encouraged the exploitation of tradition.

Mapping the location of printers, booksellers and allied businesses deepens our understanding of the commercial and cultural orientation of the book trade between the late seventeenth and the mid-nineteenth centuries. As the following seeks to demonstrate, the business of publishing and bookselling, characterized by increasing diversity and a steady expansion of production, was closely allied to the transformation of London during this period. From a relatively modest European capital city, London became an imperial metropolis. The compact clusters of streets and public spaces within the medieval walls turned into the nucleus of a sprawling conglomerate of different neighbourhoods. The practical (if not administrative) fusion of London, Westminster and Southwark during the eighteenth century stretched from the elegance of western and northern squares to the wharves and squalor of the East End, to the workshops and market gardens south of the Thames. By means of its products – and notably by books and periodicals – London was highly visible to the country at large. Commentators acclaimed the flow of goods in and out of the city as a marvel of the age. As John Macky noted in the

1720s, London boasted open gates rather than being encircled by continental-style bastions.[1]

With some important exceptions, seventeenth-century London printers continued to congregate in two broad areas of activity, one outside the City focused on Smithfield, and the other stretching broadly southwards from the cathedral to Paul's Wharf and London Bridge.[2] For booksellers, street location had proved of particular importance, whether in proximity to a major thoroughfare or to the custom of a monastery, cathedral, Inn of Court or place of business. As Macky claimed, bookshops were scattered all over London, but certain locations mattered more than others. In addition to ancient and isolated sites in Westminster, Fleet Street, Chancery Lane, Charing Cross, the Exchange, Blackfriars and the eastern fringes of the City, the established axis for the stationery, scribal and publishing trades of London ran from St Paul's to London Bridge, the sole road crossing the Thames in London until 1755. Famous Bridge addresses continued to flourish, such as the Looking Glass occupied by Thomas Norris, bookseller and bookbinder between 1695 and 1732, while the wealthy Bridge House remained an important landlord within the increasingly powerful book-trade district of St Paul's and Paternoster Row.[3] The Marshall family, among others, ensured that Aldermary Churchyard stayed synonymous with chapbook production. For very different markets, Thomas Cadell rejuvenated bookselling in the Strand (made famous by the Shakespeare's Head of the Tonsons and then by Andrew Millar), while the 'Tully's Head' of Robert and then James Dodsley cut a dash in Pall Mall, close to St James's, Whitehall and the fashionable coffee houses and pleasure gardens.[4]

Both old and new London venues sustained the advance of the eighteenth-century book trade. Several ancient sites had supported book-traders, some under the same distinctive trade sign, for generations stretching back before the Civil War, but recent research also reveals the recurrent reuse of many print and book shops by different trades.[5] Rapid turnover in occupancy resulted as much from the fragility of bookselling careers as from the condition of the sites (although fires and building collapse were frequent), and tenements were required to be extremely adaptable. In the second half of the eighteenth century, however, the impermanence of so many tenancies was matched by the unprecedented size and fitments of the grandest of the printing houses and

1 Macky 1714–22, I, 205.
2 Hetet 1987, 39.
3 A simple guide to early addresses is given in McKerrow 1910, 323–35. It was not repeated in later volumes. See also Blayney 1990; Raven 2004.
4 Solomon 1996, 50–1.
5 Hall and Raven 2000.

shops, founded on the fortunes of the most successful booksellers. In the way that those fresh to business often do, many embarking upon bookselling took brazen advantage of particular traditions of place.[6]

Across Georgian London certain districts reaffirmed or developed bookselling interests. Macky's guide book, begun in 1714, identified 'divinity and classicks' on the north side of St Paul's Churchyard, 'law, history and plays' near to Temple Bar, 'French-booksellers' in the Strand, and 'booksellers of antient books in all languages' sited in Little Britain and Paternoster Row.[7] These were very general associations and to them we might add law books, newspapers and political tracts in and around Westminster Hall;[8] financial news and guide books in the Exchange and Cornhill; and novels, magazines and fashionable titles in Covent Garden, Fleet Street, the Exchange and the Row. The booksellers and printers who flourished in Cornhill and the Royal Exchange by the late seventeenth century were proud of a bookselling tradition that dated from before the mid-sixteenth century. In 1750 at least nine booksellers, printsellers and stationers operated from Cornhill proper (with others in Pope's Head Alley and Exchange Alley), and a further eight traded from the booths of the Royal Exchange itself. By 1790, the Cornhill book trades were even more populous, with a marked continuity in the use of long-established shops as they passed from one bookseller to another (even despite a disastrous fire that destroyed many properties and stocks in 1748). Many booksellers like William Meadows opposite the Exchange at the Angel published a broad range of books and pamphlets, but many also like Meadows's neighbour, John Brotherton at the Bible, and Elizabeth Nutt on the south side of the Exchange, produced a large number of publications relating to trade and commerce. From at least 1697, when John Castaing commenced his *Course of the Exchange*, providing currency exchange rates and stock prices, a succession of brokers and merchants also maintained important publishing activities in Cornhill.[9]

The stalls of Westminster Hall (some forty-eight, hosting various trades by 1666 and each about eight feet in width) offered freedom from Licensing Law provisions to those booksellers established in or within twenty yards of the hall before the end of November 1661. Business prospered, and the Westminster bookstalls, in close proximity to the courts,[10] continued to flourish even after the lapse of the Laws in 1695. Several booksellers, including Henry Mortlock

6 Raven 2003, 91–3, 95, 109.
7 Macky 1714–22, I, 205, cited in Mumby 1930, 173.
8 Mandelbrote 1995, 50, extending Macky.
9 Worms 1997.
10 In addition to the Exchequer, the Courts of Chancery, Common Pleas and King's Bench; Common Pleas moved to a new adjoining room in about 1732; King's Bench remained until 1820.

and his successor, with main shops elsewhere, used the hall as a lucrative outlet. Exactly when the stalls were removed remains obscure. Although the question was posed by Henry Plomer a century ago,[11] the best answer to date is that after temporary removals for coronations, most booksellers seem to have left the hall by 1780, although a term catalogue of 1797 still cites the hall as a selling place. The coffee shops built alongside the entrance were removed in 1807, and a print of 1808 shows no stalls in the hall. The remaining law courts were permanently moved out in preparation for George IV's coronation in 1820.[12]

The other famed haven of booksellers, at least for a period of brief brilliance from the Restoration to the early eighteenth century, was the area between Smithfield and Aldersgate Street known as Little Britain. This 'plentiful and perpetual emporium of learned authors', in the words of Roger North, attracted 'a mighty Trade; the rather because the Shops were spacious, and the learned gladly resorted to them where they seldom failed to meet with agreeable Conversation'.[13] North, dejectedly recalling Little Britain in 1744 when 'this emporium is vanished', exaggerated the commodiousness of its shops. The area around the Mourning Bush tavern and the crowded tenements of Duck Lane, so beloved of Swift, hosted mixed trades with small shops of booksellers and printers, all on very intimate scale and much disadvantaged as the volume of trade advanced. In the 1710s a dozen or more booksellers traded in this area, but by 1720 Macky charted the decline: 'it seems, then, that the bookselling business has been gradually resuming its original Situation near this [St Paul's] Cathedral ever since the beginning of George I, while the neighbourhood of Duck Lane and Little Britain has been proportionately falling into disuse.'[14] By 1750 only Samuel Ballard, bookseller at the Rising Sun, and Richard Reilly, printer of Pelican Court (with another premises at the nearby Town Ditch), continued the once populous Little Britain book trade lauded by Pepys and Swift.[15]

The decline of these bookselling resorts contrasted with the steady commercial enhancement of St Paul's Churchyard and Paternoster Row. At the hub of the book trade for four centuries or more, St Paul's Churchyard housed Stationers' Hall within and then just beyond its precinct.[16] Great coaching inns, like those at Ludgate and the Poultry, stood at either end of the

11 Plomer 1905, 390.
12 Gerhold 1999, 47 (1808 print), 51; Cooke 1987, 61; Saunders 1951, 211.
13 Roger North cited in Mandelbrote 1995, 59.
14 Macky 1714–22, 1724 edn, cited in Mumby 1930, 173.
15 Raven 2007, 167–8.
16 In 1606 the Stationers moved from St Peter's College to Milk Street, and then in 1611 to Abergavenny House, sited off Ave Maria Lane; Blayney 1990, 95.

Churchyard and served discrete carrier routes to country merchants and retailers. To the immediate north of the Churchyard, Paternoster Row was as well known at the Restoration for its mercers, silkmen and lace makers as it was for its historic association with binders and bookshops. From the early eighteenth century, however, the Row attracted dozens of new bookselling tenants. Just to the south of Grub Street and Little Britain, the Row became by the 1770s the premier publishing district of the country and home to the majority of leading English booksellers of the second half of the century. About sixty or so bookmen and women (and some two dozen at any one time) established the Row as the centre of the wholesaling of books and magazine and periodical publishing.[17] Until the close of the eighteenth century almost all booksellers lived over (and sometimes also behind) the shop or printing house (with some printing presses, we now know, sited on an upper floor). By 1800 the Churchyard and the Row comprised one of the greatest publishing centres in Europe. From here, throughout the nineteenth century, booksellers despatched books, magazines and other printed works not only to the country towns of England, but also to the colonies in North America, the Caribbean, India, Africa, Australasia and the Far East.[18]

The diversity of sites is telling. Some of the foremost producers of fashionable titles worked within the established network of the trade and as prominent members of the Stationers' Company; others relished the out-of-City challenge in their battle for public and commercial success. After mid-century, many of the major novel and magazine publishers like John Bew and the firm of George Robinson operated from the Row. Other novel specialists, such as John and Francis Noble and Thomas Hookham with his partner James Carpenter, set up shop in the newly built squares and lanes of the West End.[19] Still others, like William Lane and his Minerva Press in Leadenhall Street or, later, James Lackington at the Temple of the Muses in Finsbury Square, made an address famous despite an unusual site.[20] For more than forty years, until his retirement in 1844, John Hatchard's shop in Piccadilly offered another celebrated literary meeting place, especially after he was able to lure evangelical customers from the most popular bible shop in London, the Rivingtons' 'Bible and Crown' in the Churchyard (founded in 1711).[21] John Murray II's move from Fleet Street to Albemarle Street in 1812 inaugurated one of the most famous of

17 Maxted 1977; Raven 1997c, 2003.
18 Raven 1997b.
19 Raven 1990, 2000b, 71–86.
20 Blakey 1939; Raven 1994.
21 Howsam 1991, 152.

all bookshop-rendezvous, while at the very end of this period Henry Colburn and Richard Bentley further exemplified the enterprise of the West End and Mayfair, with their fashionable premises in New Burlington Street.[22]

Imprints and newspaper advertisements carried this recognizable topography to every town in England – and beyond. The expansion of sites of printing across the country after the 1695 repeal of the Licensing Laws, and with it the establishment of newspapers outside London, created a network of booksellers serving all the leading London publishers.[23] Before the early nineteenth century, regional publication of more than the newspaper or local sermon was rare. The most reliable estimates to date suggest that even by 1830 London imprints comprised about three-quarters of all book titles published in Britain and Ireland.[24] Those living in remote parts of the country ordered books either through the offices of their nearest provincial bookseller or directly from the London publisher (whose address was usually cited both in the local and in the widely circulated London newspapers). Readers of every type of book and magazine were made familiar with addresses and trade signs from Paternoster Row, St Paul's Churchyard, Fleet Street, Amen Corner, Ave Maria Lane, Ivy Lane, the Poultry, the Exchange, and distinctive western offerings such as St Martin's Lane, Covent Garden, Charing Cross and Pall Mall.

The mosaic of London stationery, print and book shops was first clearly revealed by Ian Maxted's plotting of the book trade after 1775 and then by Peter Blayney's mapping of the sixteenth- and early seventeenth-century Churchyard.[25] During the past ten years more precise mapping for eighteenth-century London has allowed investigation of the nature and turnover in occupancy and the relationship of tenants and subtenants to their commercial and built environment. New research, beginning with St Paul's Churchyard and Paternoster Row, Ludgate, Fleet Street and its extensive hinterland of courts and alleys, Little Britain and Cornhill, incorporates post-Fire surveys and maps, annual land tax evaluations, surviving shop leases, fire insurance records, fragmentary ward and site maps, and sketches of elevations.[26]

For those seeking books and prints, following perhaps in the footsteps of Pepys, the physical changes to favourite resorts often appeared stark. As rebuilt

22 Smiles 1891; Mumby 1930, 323–4; Garside 2000, 88.

23 See Ferdinand, chap. 21 below.

24 Weedon 2003, table 2.2, where totals given suggest 74 per cent of all British and Irish titles in 1800–29 were published in London (and 71 per cent in 1820–9), although these are *title* counts only, and necessarily heedless of often unknowable total editions sizes and of continuing research on provincial printing.

25 Maxted 1977; Blayney 1990.

26 Raven 1997c, 2001c; Hall and Raven 2000; see also Raven 2001a.

after the Great Fire, the area around St Paul's was distinguished by its narrowness and height, although clearances near to Wren's cathedral created new space in the Churchyard proper.[27] Bookstalls reappearing against the new cathedral walls were removed as well as some late seventeenth-century bookshops on the northern side.[28] Paul's Alley, leading to the cathedral, was described by John Strype in his reworking of Stow in 1720 as 'a Place of small Trade, and very narrow', but close by was Petty Canons Alley (or Canon Alley) 'a good open Place, with a Free-stone Pavement leading into Paternoster Row'.[29] After the Fire the large shops in the triangular block bounded by Anchor Alley, New Jewry proper and Paul's Alley north were reconstructed before 1669, but all were demolished by parliamentary Act by the end of 1702 because they were too close to the new cathedral.[30] Strype's comments confirm that demolition had tended to enhance the situation of the Row and the shops lining the northern side of the churchyard. Buildings boasting four or five storeys, often with split working levels, contributed to what John Summerson described as an idiomatic and insistent verticality.[31] In 1720 Strype declared that 'of all the Streets in the whole City, there is none to compare to [Paternoster Row] for handsome Signs, and uniformly hung'.[32] By mid-century, however, the clutter was increasingly denounced as obstructing traffic and trade, and an Act of 1762 ordered all trade signs to be fixed flat against the walls. Further action followed to restrict the dozens of 'rubric' or advertising posts lining both sides of the street and pasted with title pages and other printed sheets.[33] A century after the rebuilding, the streetscape changed again, with the removal of the trade signs and rubric posts outside the bookshops.

Changes to buildings affected modes of production, how business was conducted and how customers treated the bookshop as the destination for orders and commissions, for browsing and conversation, and for the exchange of news and information. Paternoster Row, reconstructed after the Fire to twenty feet in width, served a succession of confined alleys and courts, especially on the northern side towards Newgate Street. Some of the yards and passages, like Lovell's Court with its concentration of binders' shops, were packed with ramshackle warehouses and small tenements. Strype described the

27 Jones and Reddaway 1962–7.
28 Blayney 1990, 81–9; Raven 2003, 104–5.
29 Strype 1720, I, 195b.
30 Blayney 1990, 82–3.
31 Summerson 1978, 67.
32 Strype 1720, I, 195b.
33 Malcolm 1810–11, II, 392.

Row premises of 'Stationers, and large Warehouses for Booksellers; well situated for learned and studious Mens access thither; being more retired and private'.[34] Two generations later, admiration was mixed with complaints about having to fight off bad air on the way to the best bookshops. In 1785 William West 'could only just perceive St Paul's with its dome towering amid the smoke and fog that surrounded it', and in his approach to London-House Yard, linking the Row and Churchyard, his 'mind was pervaded with a kind of awe at the gloomy appearance of the stores of literature before me'.[35]

However toxic the smells of the printing house troughs, of the stables (and nearby cattle slaughter houses) and of the fires burning during periods of long labour, the progression of booksellers' premises in the long strips of the Row and the north side of the Churchyard made good commercial sense. The warehouses against Stationers' Hall stood close by, and other storage buildings were often shared. All booksellers benefited from adjacent tradesmen, including oilmen, tallow chandlers and silver smiths. The narrow alleyways fronted by many of the bookshops proved helpfully congested passages, necessitating the relatively slow movement and foot traffic; accordingly, especially after the decline of the rubric posts, window displays seem to have become fuller and more elaborate. The ancient crossroads of Paternoster Row, Paul's Alley and Ivy Lane developed as a particular business focus, its corners sentinelled for much of the eighteenth century by booksellers James Bayley and John Beecroft at the north-west corner; printer Henry Woodfall at the north-east; booksellers Benjamin Bragg, Sarah Popping, Thomas Field and the binder, Christopher Norris, at the south-east; and the Chapter Coffee House at the south-west. The Chapter Coffee House hosted meetings of bookseller associations, the proprietors of newspapers, and literary clubs, as well as the regular sales of copyright shares carefully controlled by the leading booksellers.[36]

Eighteenth- and early nineteenth-century commentators gave much attention to the antiquity of such sites, although none offered great precision. Many early book-trade venues had adjoined the doors of the old cathedral whose nave and transepts served as public thoroughfares.[37] While some traders – notably George Robinson – converted shops formerly associated with other crafts, many others setting up as booksellers – Thomas Longman, Samuel Bladon, Thomas and Mary Cooper, and above all John Coote, John Cooke and James Harrison – succeeded to premises with long-standing literary associations.

34 Strype 1720, I, 195.
35 West 1837, 44.
36 Further detailed in Raven 1997c, 2003, 103–4, 126.
37 Raven 2004, 430–1.

Stationers and book artisans had traded in the cathedral churchyard at the beginning of the fourteenth century, and binders worked in the Row from at least 1312. The first of the Bridge House shops in the Row date from the early 1280s, built between Paul's Alley (running right through old St Paul's) and what was to become known as Pissing Alley. Paul Christianson has charted much of this history,[38] although his allocation of the tenements to four main sites has been challenged by new research. The south-west of the Row did not comprise Bridge House holdings; the greatest block of twenty-nine or thirty Bridge House tenements (still under the same ownership by 1830) stretched on the south side of the Row from Paul's Gate to the eastern side of Paul's Alley postern or North Gate.[39] Located on the northern side of the Row on the corner of what was to become Queen's Head Alley, the site (if not the exact buildings) of the Peter et Poule house of Peter Bylton – given to the Bridge House at his death in 1454 – supported a series of different bookshops for more than five centuries until destroyed by the incendiary bombs of January 1941. It was a site that particularly flourished in the eighteenth and early nineteenth centuries: what were to be known as nos. 16, 17 and 18 the Row were occupied by the various partnerships of the literary entrepreneurs James Harrison and son, John Coote, John Cooke, Jonathan Kendall and Alexander Hogg. The combined shops presented a formidable Row façade of more than sixty feet in width with a further frontage of thirty-three feet on Queen's Head Alley and more back shops besides.[40]

For both customers and traders, neighbourhood reputations developed increasing commercial importance. In particular, Paternoster Row came to boast many of the most noted bookshops and imprints of the eighteenth century. Among the earliest, Christopher Bateman, of Holborn and then Little Britain, extended his business in 1698 to the prime corner site, later styled no. 36, where the Row joined Warwick Lane. From here Bateman specialized in second-hand books and book auctions.[41] As Henry Plomer wrote, 'probably no bookseller's shop in London was better known in the days of Swift and his contemporaries'.[42] The German traveller Conrad von Uffenbach thought Bateman's shop 'the best in England . . . the floors piled up with books'.[43] Opposite Bateman's shop, most of the land on the south-western sector of the Row was owned by the Bishop of London, and situated

38 Christianson 1987, 1989.
39 Raven 2003, 91–3, 106–7.
40 See Raven 2003, 94–6, 119–20; 2004, 436.
41 See Landon, chap. 38, below.
42 Plomer 1922, 24.
43 J.E.B. Mayor cited in Plomer 1922, 25.

either just north of or within the site of the Bishop's Palace. A few large residential houses remained in 1700, but by 1800 all were commercial premises, including the long-standing bookshop (at no. 39) occupied by Awnsham Churchill between 1681 and 1711. Until 1723 the Churchill shop was taken over by William Taylor (the 1719 publisher of *Robinson Crusoe*), by John Osborn in 1723/4, and then from 1724 by Osborn's brother-in-law, Thomas Longman, and his equally celebrated successors.[44]

As London bookseller-publishers combined to share production costs but also to protect investments in literary properties and maintain prices,[45] the physical proximity of partners became of increased relevance. Many cartels included prominent booksellers relatively widely scattered, from the Strand and Fleet Street to the Exchange, but increasingly more associations featured many neighbouring or nearby firms. The ability of booksellers to remain within particular neighbourhoods, irrespective of changing needs for space, proved a valuable feature of the changing city. The continued availability of differently sized tenanted properties enabled booksellers to expand, contract or relocate easily within the same street or adjacent to it. The recent historical mapping of the Row, Fleet Street and other key book-trade areas suggests that the plasticity of occupied space offered traders an important flexibility during years of high-risk expansion and commercial unpredictability.[46]

Especially as reconstructed after the Great Fire, the permanent and notably productive and retail shops of the Row and Churchyard appeared entirely unlike the stalls and lock-ups near or against the cathedral walls. Whatever might be argued about the processes of production and whether the book was finished in one shop or in several adjoining, separate shops, those in the Row were all now fixed sites – although the permanence of the occupant was quite another matter. Before the mid-twentieth century, leaseholding was not only the most commonly practised form of property tenure in Britain but carried with it a more varied approach to tenancy, repair and rebuilding, according to the conditions of the lease or tenancy agreement. Almost every stationer and bookseller, like almost every other trader in London, possessed his or her shop and tenement not as a freeholder but as a leaseholder or as the tenant or subtenant of leaseholders. Most early modern leaseholders were able to sublet and all leaseholds and most tenancies were readily assignable to heirs and others within the original term of years, with no changes to rentals or rights until the lease – of variable duration – expired. Many booksellers repaired, extended or even completely

44 See Briggs, chap. 19, below.
45 See Bonnell, chap. 37, below; Raven, chap. 3, above.
46 Raven 2007, 162–7.

rebuilt their shops and houses, and let all or part of them to others when they wished, without recourse to the actual owner of the property. The freeholder took an interest only at the time of lease expiry and renewal (in the case of the booksellers of this period – averaging about fifty years).

Much of the Row, Churchyard and Fleet Street in the eighteenth century was marked by rapid turnover of occupancy and by migration among nearby properties. A preliminary survey suggests that during the century more than a thousand separate property units stood in the lanes and courts off Fleet Street between the Fleet ditch in the east, Temple Bar in the west, the Thames in the south and New Street in the north. The density and quick-changing tenancies of this compact area attracted law booksellers serving the Inns of Court that bordered this maze of lanes and alleys. Also trading from these streets, early newspaper and periodical proprietors and general printers, booksellers and circulating librarians included William Strahan, Samuel Richardson, Thomas Lowndes, George Kearsley and John Murray I.[47] Bernard Lintot and Abel Roper (proprietor of the *Post Boy*) had presided at well-situated shops on Fleet Street, near to Temple Gate and the main Inns of Court, but the courts and alleys off Fleet Street also continued to offer particular versatility in the choice of premises. Richardson and Strahan were able first to move to larger buildings when required, and then to exploit variations in building leases to demolish groups of small properties and construct new printing shops.[48]

Of much slighter acreage than the Fleet Street area, Paternoster Row was no less dense or adaptable, housing a total of about six hundred different tax-recorded occupancies (not counting, of course, further subtenanting). About 40 per cent of the primary tenancies were taken by booksellers, stationers, printers or bookbinders.[49] Relocation was frequent. Seven years and five weeks represents the average length of tenancy in the seventy-three different Row property units. Much-moved booksellers included Joseph Johnson and John Payne who swapped various properties up and down the street between 1749 and 1794, taking their distinctive trade signs with them.[50] Other traders, such as Bladon and Stanley Crowder, were easily able to find temporary premises close by after fires or a building collapse.[51]

Certain book-trade sites seem to have specialized in quick-change occupancy. No. 3 the Row accommodated fifteen different tenants over fifty

47 Hall and Raven 2000.
48 Raven 2007, 163–6.
49 Hall and Raven 2000; Raven 2003, 109–10.
50 Johnson began business *c.*1761; Payne died in 1787.
51 These and further examples below are detailed in Raven 2003, esp. 115–26.

years. A partitioned shop next to what became known as no. 14 housed eleven tenants between 1725 and 1797, giving an average occupancy of six-and-a-half years. These included the booksellers James Buckland (before he moved to no. 57), accounting for five years, J. Wilson and Isaac Fell, six years, and Alexander Hogg, more than thirteen years. To the east of the Longman and Bloss shops on the south side of the Row stood (after two large residential properties) a line of five very small properties, all subject to a swift turnover of booksellers (among others). The tiny Bridge House properties in the south-east end of the Row sustained many short-lived tenancies by booksellers. Neighbouring these premises, no. 47 achieved greater stability. For long an apothecary's shop, from 1760 it was taken by Richard Baldwin II who resided there for the rest of the century. The ground floor of Baldwin's 'Rose' measured no more than 14 ft (frontage) by 18 ft 10 in. Like other extended book-trade families, however – including the Rivingtons, Harrisons, Bowleses and Newburys – the Baldwins traded (with significant overlaps) from other locations, first in Creed Lane, then in St Paul's Churchyard, and from 1761, Henry Baldwin and family in Whitefriars, Fleet Street and later New Bridge Street.

Some modest properties in the Row, Churchyard and courts off Fleet Street appear to have served either as early-career stepping stones to larger nearby shops or as convenient additional storage buildings. The eighteenth-century history of several Row shops further demonstrates the ease with which they were converted and reconverted in and out of bookselling. No. 33, home to the booksellers Crowder, John Osborne, Henry Woodgate and Thomas Moore, intermittently housed grocers and wax chandlers. Just as versatile was no. 24 (18 ft Row frontage with a depth of 26 ft 8 in),[52] occupied by bookseller Richard Baldwin between 1747 and 1758, but a butcher's shop from 1759 until 1765 and then a linen draper's until reverting to a bookshop under John Wheble's tenancy after 1771. By contrast, premises such as no. 16 the Row, in continuous occupation by booksellers during the eighteenth century, was tenanted by six booksellers between 1709 and 1797 with an average tenure of a little over fourteen-and-a-half years. The eighteenth-century tenancies of no. 16 (the prime part of the Peter et Poule site, adjacent to Queen's Head Alley) were dominated by those of just two: the booksellers Jonathan Kendall, residing here for forty-five years, and Hogg (also tenant of the partitioned no. 14 after 1784) for twenty years.[53]

52 Jones and Reddaway 1962–7.
53 Raven 2003, 109, 119–23.

In the buoyant market of eighteenth- and early nineteenth-century London, movement between shops usually resulted from commercial expedience (sometimes caused by rent increases when leases were renewed), but fires also occurred with a frequency that made insurance policies no small consideration for leaseholders.[54] No less dramatic than the 1748 Cornhill calamity, an early 1770 fire in the Row destroyed the bookshops of Johnson and Payne and Crowder, and the houses of the printer Charles Cock and the auctioneer Edward Upton. Upton's back room had contained the entire stock of bibles and common prayerbooks from the Oxford Press. The Aldine Chambers were built on the site of the gutted shop in the Row. The Oxford stock was re-established nearby, with William Dawson, bookseller to the university, later trading from no. 7 from 1793 until 1810. Payne either gave up completely after the fire, or – according to one account – moved to Marsham Street, Westminster, and after 1792 to Paddington, where he worked under different names. Johnson moved to the large but oddly shaped no. 72 St Paul's Churchyard where he continued business – when not imprisoned for seditious publication – until his death in 1809.

Early nineteenth-century commentators add a further perspective to changes in the trade: wonderment at the increased size and grandeur of the shops of leading London booksellers. The interior of Lackington's Finsbury Square 'Temple of the Muses' appeared in an Ackermann print, and was also vividly recalled by Charles Knight when, as a ten-year-old, he was taken in 1801 by his bookseller father to this great mecca of literature:

> We enter the vast area, whose dimensions are to be measured by the assertion that a coach and six might be driven round it. In the centre is an enormous circular counter, within which stand the dispensers of knowledge, ready to wait upon the country clergyman in his wig and shovel-hat; upon the fine ladies in feathers and trains; or upon the bookseller's collector, with his dirty bag . . . We ascend a broad staircase, which leads to 'The Lounging Rooms,' and to the first of a series of circular galleries, lighted from the lantern of the dome, which also lights the ground floor. Hundreds, even thousands, of volumes are displayed on the shelves running round their walls. As we mount higher and higher, we find commoner books in shabbier bindings; but there is still the same order preserved, each book being numbered according to a printed catalogue. This is larger than that of any other bookseller's, and it comes out yearly.[55]

54 J. Cardwell 2004.
55 Knight 1865, 283.

For many established booksellers, notably the Longmans and the Rivingtons, improvement of shops did not necessitate moving site, and we should be careful not to regard all ancient bookshops as small and confined, however crowded the immediate neighbourhood. Although many bookshops and printing houses were crowded together and often featured complex arrangements of shared sheds and zig-zagging boundary walls crossed over by rooms on upper floors, not all premises were small and unimposing. The line of six shops (all some-time bookshops) between Paul's Alley and Pissing (or Canon's) Alley on the south side of the Row boasted large frontages. We know from the post-Fire property surveys that these shop fronts averaged 28 ft 10 in, with the depth of the ground floor varying between 18 and 28 feet.[56] Together, the shops comprised one part (but definitely not the whole) of the site of the Bridge House rents, some originating from the 1280s. Also in the Row, large shops included those of John Bew, with a 33 ft frontage and a depth of 44 ft. The four storeys of Bew's shop and house must have offered a relatively spacious living area. The Longman shop boasted an 18 ft 3 in frontage, while next door, the stationery shop of John Bloss represented, at 25 ft, the median size of all frontages in the street. These were not small façades and, although overshadowed by the fame of Longman, Bloss's firm (opening in 1713 and his successor continuing into the early nineteenth century) became another celebrated fixture of the Row. The Bateman shop similarly boasted a 26 ft 4 in façade on the Row and a further 22 ft on Warwick Lane. The average frontage of a book-trade premises in Paternoster Row can be calculated as 25 ft 4 in, and many, as already noted, were much larger.

The grandeur of the few, nevertheless, disguises huge differences in sizes between bookshops in close proximity to one another. Ludgate, Fleet Street and the courts off it, High Holborn, Cornhill and Westminster all maintained an often rickety jumble of the imposing and the squalid. The miniature shop of Zachariah Stuart in the Row (13 ft 4 in frontage and a depth of only 11 ft) stood within sight of the enormous property of John Beecroft on the corner of Row and Ivy Lane (a shop that also reaffirmed the strategic commercial importance of the corner and passageway site). Some very distinguished and successful bookselling and publishing firms were reconciled to very confined quarters (in which neighbourliness could also break down, as in the case of the Robinson–Wheble magazine war of the 1770s). The very small sites also remained an unchanging feature of the book trade. The corner shop to a small Row passage into Newgate Market offered a frontage of only 11 feet, and yet supported the

56 Jones and Reddaway 1962–7.

firms of William Innys (1744–56), and of Robinson and John Roberts (1766–71), possibly because of substantial back storage sheds (such sheds are usually neglected by ward maps and civic taxation records). Still smaller properties stood in the south-eastern sector where the Dean's wall limited the depth of some shops to 10 feet. Although few familiar names traded in this part of the Row, the shops here were more notable for the successions to properties between women (many of whom were probably ribbon sellers).

A further constant was that, in both the new and the traditional London bookselling sites, the positions of buildings remained more important than their fitting up (and sometimes even than their size). Among booksellers' premises, middle-sized shops continued to be readily convertible between different trades. These changes and frequent refurbishments tell us much about the risks of leaseholding and the various ways in which leaseholder and tenants might exploit their possession of a property, usually without any interference by the freeholder. In the case of many Churchyard and Paternoster Row properties, the owners were the Bishop of London, the canons of the cathedral, the Bridge House or a livery company, but the identity of many landowners often seems irrelevant to questions of occupancy and succession.

Despite such continuities, the relocation of booksellers and of their shops became the most obvious feature of the topography of the early nineteenth-century London book trade. The Row remained at the heart of publishing and bookselling, but Lackington's establishment in Finsbury Square and John Murray II's move to Albemarle Street more obviously typified the expansion of the trade and new metonymies of place. The Piccadilly triumphs of John Stockdale (rival, from 1781, to Debrett, successor to the political and strong-willed bookseller, John Almon) and of John Hatchard (from 1797) exemplified the lively and often controversialist bookselling trade of the West End. The book-trade profile of the Strand, Covent Garden, Pall Mall and Charing Cross was extended by the stately succession of the Tonson–Millar–Cadell establishment, the importer and royal bookseller John Nourse, and the more publicity-prone Dodsley, Thomas Davies and the Noble brothers (heading a cast of other colourful entrepreneurs including Rudolph Ackermann and John and Josiah Boydell). Now a further generation of dealers such as the Hookhams, James Ridgway, James Carpenter, Samuel Fores, the much-moved John Bell and James Lackington's heir, George, and his partner, Allen, stretched the bookselling map to include notable sites in Piccadilly and St James and other western and northern extremities.

These new (if sometimes transient) fashionable resorts for book and print buyers contrasted with the diverse and faintly old-fashioned heartlands of the

London trade. The changing neighbours and shared courtyards and walls of Harrison, Cooke, Woodfall, Johnson, Crowder and the others typified the variegated and versatile community of the Row – of populists and scholars, radicals and loyalists, pious Anglicans and sober nonconformists, astute entrepreneurs and humble aspirants, gentlemen and rogues, and many who, in one way or another, moved between such associations. But the reputation of the Row suffered. When Byron accused Murray of mistreatment of his manuscript he wrote that 'it was a book-selling, back-shop, Paternoster Row, paltry proceeding'.[57] These were the ancient and crowded lairs of bookselling despised by Charles Lamb, writing on behalf of authors in 1833: 'You know not what a rapacious, dishonest set these booksellers are . . . those fellows hate us.'[58]

By the early nineteenth century, printers had also found premises in the book-trade heartlands of the Row and Churchyard increasingly unattractive (especially as compared with the expansion of bookselling in the area). Even by the 1750s and 1760s many printers had moved to new districts well beyond the city walls. Other, rather different, migration followed. By the close of the eighteenth century, most of the grander booksellers no longer lived over the shop and many purchased country estates (the confident badges of success and status). The Robinsons retreated to Streatham, the Longmans to Hampstead, William Strahan acquired a large acreage in Norfolk and Francis Newbery bought Heathfield Park in Sussex. Bookselling avenues such as Paternoster Row were soon featured in the nostalgic memoirs of mid-nineteenth-century bookmen, but their favoured haunts were in fact far from abandoned by popular London publishers. From familiar street addresses (trade signs had now all but disappeared), a new generation of booksellers, mostly with off-site and often far-flung and contracted-out printers, confronted new challenges in the provincial market.[59] The dominance of the London trade was never threatened, even if, by the 1820s, booksellers were forced to reconfigure both the organization of printing and their distributive networks. That this was most famously led by Simpkin, Marshall and Co., successor to Benjamin Crosby of Stationers Court and to the Robinson firm of Paternoster Row, only demonstrated the endurance and versatility of long-standing associations.

57 Byron to Mr Dallas, 23 Sep. 1811, cited in Smiles 1891, I, 209.
58 Charles Lamb to Bernard Barton, cited in Mumby 1930, 276–7.
59 See Bell and Hinks, chap. 15 below.

14

Personnel within the London book trades: evidence from the Stationers' Company

MICHAEL L. TURNER

Introduction

Many years ago[1] I suggested that Fernand Braudel's view of society as *l'ensemble des ensembles*, or a *set of sets*, was a particularly helpful way of approaching the book trade, of describing it and mapping it. In choosing this expression Braudel wished to remind us 'that any given social reality we may observe in isolation is itself contained in some greater set; that as a collection of variables, it requires and implies the existence of other collections of variables outside itself'. He recommended the idea of sets 'to provide an approach to a problem, to lay down some guidelines for preliminary observation. If it makes that observation easier, both at the beginning and in later stages, if it helps to produce an acceptable classification of the material and to develop the logic of the argument, then the definition is useful and has justified itself.'[2]

Book-trade historians have long been involved in defining such sets of one sort or another. Biographical listings by trade and/or locality have been an important element in the way the subject has been approached and have played a major part in the publishing activities of the Bibliographical Societies. In the period covered by this volume there are many relevant works including Plomer's two 'Dictionaries'; Maxted on the 'London Trade'; Pollard on the 'Dublin Trade'; McKenzie's 'Apprentices'; Humphries and Smith's 'Music Publishers'; both Ramsden's and Howe's 'Bookbinders'; Todd's 'London Printers'; Twyman's 'Lithographic Printers'; Tyacke's 'London map-sellers'; Hodgson and Blagden's identification of the membership of the various congers; Belanger's tracing of publishing partnerships through the trade-sale catalogues; and Treadwell's listing of the London trade publishers in the early

1 In the second Pollard Lecture before The Bibliographical Society, 15 Apr. 1986.

2 For Braudel's discussion of this topic see chap. 5 'Society: a set of sets' in Braudel 1982.

eighteenth century.[3] Though many of these are predominantly concerned with the London trade, there is also a great deal available relating to the provinces. In particular, the work of the late Peter Isaac's team is now manifest in the *British book trade index* and the contributions listed by John Feather.[4] All may be said to be defining subsets within the principal set that is our concern – the book trade.

When Samuel Negus compiled his list of the various printing houses in London in 1724 and classified them by their political and religious alliances, such as 'Known to be well affected to King George', 'Nonjurors', 'Highflyers' and so on, he was describing sets which take us outside the limits of our principal set, immediately and dramatically tying us into those of mainstream history.[5] Similarly, at the end of our period, when Wiener and Hollis in their individual works identify the printers and publishers of the radical unstamped newspapers of the early nineteenth century we enter the same area.[6] It is perhaps from such examples that we can best demonstrate the importance of book history to *l'histoire totale*.

We must never forget that the individuals who make up our sets will undoubtedly all belong to other sets outside the limits of our principal set, involving allegiances which may or may not carry levels of loyalty and motivation greater than those involved in membership of the set in which we are interested. Just as in analytical bibliography we would be suspicious of theories based on arguments which treated a book as having been produced in isolation, and have thus – for example – learnt to take on board the problems of concurrent printing; so in studying the personnel of the trade we must be aware of other relevant sets and all that they imply.

The exercise will be judged on a true understanding of the quality of the raw data on which we base our work; the care with which we delineate our sets; and our ingenuity in discovering the questions that this will allow us to ask. Moreover, we must recognize that over a period of time neither the size of our sets nor their overlap with other sets, through which still further sets will be identified, will remain constant – thereby illustrating historical trends. However, just as the Hinman Collator merely draws our attention to the existence of variants between two printed texts, but offers no explanation for

3 Plomer 1922; Plomer, Bushnell and Dix 1932; Maxted 1977 together with many other of his useful listings at www.devon.gov.uk/localstudies/100158/5.htmlands=NIrqBe8FW9D; Pollard 2000; McKenzie 1974b, 1978; Humphries and Smith 1970; Ramsden 1956; Howe 1950a, 1950b; Todd 1972; Twyman 1976; Tyacke 1978; Hodgson and Blagden 1956; Belanger 1970, 1975; Treadwell 1982a.

4 For *BBTI* see www.bbti.bham.ac.uk; Feather 1981.

5 Negus 1724.

6 Wiener 1970; Hollis 1970.

those variants, so too will our models only point out to us the existence of sets and their changing relationship to other sets; the task of explication remains with us.

A great deal has been done within the context of the *London book trades* database in gathering information and in recording it in ways which will allow for its interrogation.[7] That task is by no means complete; it never will be. For the Stationers' Company, where most effort has so far been concentrated, it is possible to start assessing the quality of some of the information available throughout this period. This chapter will attempt to do just that.

The shape and size of the Company

Irrespective of any discussion of the role of the Stationers' Company within the business of the book trade during the period under consideration, there is no doubt that the archives of the Company provide our richest source of biographical material for members of the London book trades. Almost anything that one looks at in it will provide a name, an event or other pertinent fact that can be recorded. The eighteenth century and the first decades of the nineteenth saw a growth in the membership of the Company, an improvement in the record keeping and a wider range of information being recorded. Moreover, during this period the Company remained predominantly tied to the members of the book trade when other City companies were relaxing their guild connections. As with earlier periods, McKenzie made impressive inroads into the eighteenth-century records by listing the apprentices; that work has been invaluable to what follows.[8] Apart from Blagden's general history of the Company, we have his article 'The Stationer's Company in the Eighteenth Century', which is unsurpassed in understanding and information.[9] Nor can the work of Myers, in laying out the archive for us in such a detailed fashion and making it more generally available, be underestimated.[10]

Briefly,[11] apprentices – they could be male or female – were presented at the Hall usually around their fourteenth or fifteenth year, though there could be a

7 The *London book trades – a biographical resource* is a database, currently containing more than thirty thousand individuals active in London from the introduction of printing up to 1830. It is hoped to convert it into a website in the near future.

8 McKenzie 1978.

9 Blagden 1960a, 1959.

10 Myers 1990 and Chadwyck-Healey's film of the archive. For earlier descriptions of the archive in relation to this project, see Turner 1985a, 1985b.

11 In what follows it should be remembered that at all stages of progression through the Company a fee or 'fine' was imposed by the Company. The present context will not allow for much detailed discussion or the citing of many examples. Blagden 1959 is fuller on both counts. His statistical tables should be read

deal of variation in this. They were bound to a master who must be free of the City and in good standing in regard to his quarterage fees. Sometimes a fee, a 'premium', was paid to the master, sometimes not. These premiums might be paid by one or other of the child's parents, a relative, a well-wisher or a charity. By 1700, the usual length of service was seven years, and this remained standard throughout our period. The apprentice ought to 'live in', but as time went on this was not always the case, and there is evidence that the Company connived at the practice of 'living out' as early as 1737. This remained a matter of contention with the journeymen into the nineteenth century.[12] In theory, at the end of the period of service the master would return to the Hall with the apprentice and present him to be made free of the Company 'by servitude'. In this way he qualified to enter into the lowest ranks of the Company, the 'Yeomanry'. During the course of his apprenticeship various reasons might lead to an apprentice being turned over to a new master – apprentices of members of the book trade in other Companies who wished to become members of the Stationers' Company might be turned over to a Stationer; or the opposite situation might apply, that the apprentice of a non-book-trade Stationer might have wished to become free of a more appropriate Company and be turned over to make that possible. The original master may have died, be leaving off trade or simply moving out of London to another location. The apprentice himself might wish to widen his experience by moving to a master in a related trade. Some apprentices were turned over on more than one occasion. It was not uncommon when an apprentice became free and was setting up in trade on his own account, for his old master to turn over another apprentice to him, usually someone he had worked alongside during his own training. Throughout the period there was a certain relaxation of the theoretical rules – it is often pointed out that some apprentices were, in effect, working as journeymen before their full time was served.

Serving an apprenticeship and entering the Company by servitude was not the only way to obtain the freedom of the Company. Providing the child's father had been free of the Company at the time of the child's birth, that person, whether male or female, could be freed 'by patrimony' from the age of

alongside those that follow. Note that Blagden follows the guild year, i.e. July to June, whereas our tables follow the calendar year. Minor variations do not alter the general trends. Actual figures often need adjusting as further information comes to light. An earlier discussion of these matters will be found in the introduction to Howe 1947. For other illustrations of how the information in the database may be used, see Ferdinand 1992.

12 In 1818 Francis Place was told by an unknown informant that, of 600 printing trade apprentices then in London, not more than 90 were 'in-door'; see Howe 1947, 132.

twenty-one.[13] Some of those freed in this way may already have served an apprenticeship. Others could, in effect, buy their way into the freedom of the Company, if the Court of Assistants agreed, 'by redemption'. Often such entry was forced on to the Company by decisions made in the Lord Mayor's Court; the candidate might be possessed of 'foreign indentures', meaning he had served an apprenticeship outside London. More rarely, and not always clearly distinguished from redemption, is the 'translation' of a tradesman from another City company into the Stationers' Company. Very unusually, freedom of the Company might be presented in an honorary fashion or 'by gift'.

Technically, in order to trade within the City of London it was necessary to gain the freedom of the City – and to do that one had to be a Freeman of one of the City livery companies.[14] On presenting documentation from one's Company to the City and paying the necessary fine, freedom of the City followed more or less automatically. A Freeman could bind his own apprentices. During this period, restrictions on the number of apprentices which had historically been placed on masters within the Stationers' Company no longer applied.

From time to time the Company made 'calls on the Livery' and members of the Yeomanry would be summoned to attend the Court to be 'cloathed' and thereby enter the Livery of the Company. Not all Yeoman were called, nor did all those called wish to be cloathed, or were able to pay the necessary fine. On becoming a Liveryman, one's status very definitely changed and one was on the ladder to advancement within the Company. Liverymen literally entered the strict hierarchical lists of the Company and, as the more elderly died and younger ones were cloathed, they gradually and slowly progressed up that list. Women, at that time, were never called on the Livery.

Within a few years, there was another hurdle. Each March the Court summoned a number of Liverymen to show why they should not serve either as the Senior or Junior Renter Warden for the following year. These two officers assisted the Upper and Under Wardens of the Company in the day-to-day running of the Company. Becoming a Renter Warden was a good way to gain first-hand knowledge of the workings of the Company and to get oneself noticed. Three options lay open – to serve in the office; to pay a fine in lieu

13 The Company's archive is sometimes uninformative as to the identity of the father of those being made free by patrimony. In order to resolve such questions patrimony papers in the bundles relating to City freedoms in the CLRO need to be consulted. References to them are being added to the database. Very occasionally a City freedom will be identified for a person where no record of freedom has been picked up in the Company's archive.

14 By the late eighteenth century this exclusivity was being ignored more and more. It came to an official end in London in 1856.

of serving; or to refuse to serve or pay the fine. The first two options ensured that one would retain one's position in the hierarchy of the Company; the third committed one into a limbo in the lower levels of the Company, listed below those who were currently serving as Renter Warden. Each year those serving or paying the fine would leapfrog over this group and continue to climb the ladder.

If a Liveryman impressed, could afford to pay and, perhaps most importantly, survived in the trade, then many years later he might be called to the Court of Assistants, the governing body of the Company. The Court was self-appointing and chose whom it wished to include from those near the top of the Livery list. As a Court member it was then a matter of further survival before one served or fined for the offices of Under Warden, Upper Warden, and finally, Master of the Company. The only way in which it was possible to ensure that one was called to the Court, or to drastically shorten this life-long process, was to become an Alderman, the Sheriff or Lord Mayor of the City, upon which event one was immediately invited on to the Court and accelerated into the highest office.[15]

Against this background it is clear that the simplest and most obvious subsets that can be defined within the set that is the Stationers' Company are the apprentices bound through the Company, the Yeomanry, the Livery and the Court. By examining these categories we should be able to gain some idea of the size of the Company at various times, and to demonstrate its hierarchical nature.

Table 14.1 simply counts the numbers of those identified as having been bound, freed, cloathed and elected to the Court in each decade from the 1700s to the 1820s, based on calendar years, while Table 14.2 looks more closely at the numbers freed by different means in the same decades. Unless otherwise stated, all the figures have been derived from the *LBT* database (March 2003), which allows for the identification of all the individuals counted in any set.

The overall figures show a fairly even level of activity during the first sixty years of the century followed by a steady growth over the rest of our period. The largest jump in bindings, which takes place in the first decade of the nineteenth century, is partly accounted for by the industrial problems of 1805–7 when the printers were recruiting large numbers of so-called apprentices in order to break

15 It was earlier the custom for those elected Lord Mayor to be a member of one of the 'Twelve Great Companies'. In 1732 when John Barber was about to be elected Lord Mayor he translated from the SC into the Goldsmiths' Company. However, in 1742 Sir Robert Willimott, a Cooper, refused to follow the custom. The first Stationer to serve as Lord Mayor, as a Stationer, was Sir Stephen Theodore Janssen in 1754.

Table 14.1 *Bindings, turnovers, freedoms, cloathings and elections to the Court within the Stationers' Company, 1700–1829, each decade*

	Bindings	Turnovers			Freedoms	Cloathings	Assistants
		First	Second	Third			
1700–9	661 (2)[a] [7][b]	71	10	3	364 [6][b]	64	21
1710–19	590 (4) [4]	91	10	2	332 [2]	72	17
1720–9	588 (7) [4]	113	13	1	313 [4]	83	18
1730–9	581 (5) [8]	85	5	1	343 [6]	65	8
1740–9	543 (5) [12]	104	6	0	379 [12]	72	16
1750–9	629 (2) [22]	98	5	0	353 [11]	101	23
1760–9	837 (1) [22]	142	12	1	378 [9]	103	18
1770–9	704 (0) [6]	155	15	0	482 [3]	126	21
1780–9	801 (1) [6]	70	6	0	353 [4]	123	16
1790–9	1,039 (4) [1]	127	4	0	417 [5]	183	11
1800–9	1,487 (1) [0]	97	2	0	474 [2]	150	25
1810–19	1,437 (0) [0]	113	5	0	498 [1]	110	14
1820–9	1,523 (0) [1]	98	7	0	516 [0]	110	25
Total	11,420 (32) [93]	1,364	100	8	5,202 [65]	1,362	233

Notes: [a] The figures in parentheses in the first column after the number of bindings represent additional rebindings.
[b] The figures in square brackets in the bindings and freedoms columns represent the number of women included in that decade's figure.

the strikes of their compositors and pressmen. A similar influence probably slightly inflated the figures for the 1820s. The years 1805, 1807 and 1825 each saw more than two hundred bindings in the year, with 1806 at 199. However, the second decade of the nineteenth century shows that the higher growth rate was more or less sustained. A small decrease in the 1830s followed by a steady decline in the binding of apprentices at Stationers' Hall made the first three decades of the century the busiest in the history of the Company.

Table 14.3 takes a closer look at those bound in each decade and follows them through their careers, showing how many and what percentage of them made the successive steps into the Yeomanry, through the Livery and into the Court.

The rate of fall-out and the pyramidal structure of the Company are well illustrated by this table. The most noticeable trend is the decline in the second half of the period in the percentage of apprentices taking their freedom. Though arrived at in a different way, the figures suggest that Blagden's

Table 14.2 *Freedoms within the Stationers' Company, 1700–1829*

	Freed	by servitude		by patrimony		by redemption		No record of binding	
		No.	%	No.	%	No.	%	No.	%
1700–9	364 [6][a]	291 [2]	79.95	56 [4]	15.38	3 [0]	0.82	14 [1]	3.85
1710–19	332 [2]	259 [0]	78.01	62 [2]	18.67	2 [0]	0.60	9 [0]	2.71
1720–9	313 [4]	241 [0]	77.00	60 [4]	19.17	8 (1)[b] [0]	2.56	4 [0]	1.28
1730–9	343 [6]	261 [0]	76.09	61 [6]	17.78	21 [0]	6.12	0 [0]	0.00
1740–9	379 [12]	279 [1]	73.61	69 [11]	18.21	30 [0]	7.92	1 [0]	0.26
1750–9	353 [11]	285 [5]	80.74	44 [6]	12.46	23 (2) [0]	6.52	1 [0]	0.28
1760–9	378 [9]	327 [2]	86.51	45 [7]	11.90	5 [0]	1.32	1 [0]	0.26
1770–9	482 [3]	421 [1]	87.34	45 [2]	9.34	15 [0]	3.11	1 [0]	0.21
1780–9	353 [4]	271 [0]	76.77	56 [4]	15.86	26 [0]	7.37	0 [0]	0.00
1790–9	417 [5]	316 [0]	75.78	54 [4]	12.95	47 [1]	11.27	0 [0]	0.00
1800–9[c]	474 [2]	345 [0]	72.78	74 [2]	15.61	50 [0]	10.55	4 [0]	0.84
1810–19	498 [1]	384 [0]	77.11	72 [1]	14.46	39 [0]	7.83	3 [0]	0.60
1820–9	516 [0]	382 [0]	74.03	105 [0]	20.35	29 (1) [0]	5.62	0 [0]	0.00
Total	5,202 [65]	4,062 [11]	78.09	803 [53]	15.44	298 [1]	5.73	38 [1]	0.73

These two tables may be compared with Table I in Blagden 1959, remembering that his figures are based on Guild years.

Notes: [a] The figures in square brackets represent the number of women included in that decade's figure.

[b] The figures in parentheses in the redemption column indicate the inclusion of the four translations.

[c] The decade 1800–9 included the one freedom by gift, ignored in this table.

estimate of around 60 per cent of those bound in the eighteenth century failed to make it into the Company is perhaps a little high, and that the addition of the first three decades of the nineteenth century makes it a little low for the period as a whole (1700–1830). It is very clear, if not surprising, that as the numbers of apprentices rose dramatically in the later decades, the incidence of making it into the Company fell to below half of what it had been in the mid-century. Although some would die, some would run away, and some would leave the book trade, this is not to say that such large numbers were lost to the trade; presumably, most continued working as journeymen in London or moved out into the provinces. The increasing number of apprentices no doubt also reflects the growth of larger establishments employing ever-larger numbers of workers during the second half of our period.

Table 14.3 *Progress of those bound in each decade to freedom, Livery and the Court of the Stationers' Company, 1700–1829*

	Bindings	Bound to freedom		Bound to Livery		Bound to Court	
		No.	%[a]	No.	%	No.	%
1700–9	661 [7][b]	293 [0]	44.33	62	9.38	14	2.12
1710–19	590 [4]	241 [0]	40.85	45	7.63	22	3.73
1720–9	588 [4]	266 [0]	45.24	37	6.29	14	2.38
1730–9	581 [8]	285 [1]	49.05	46	7.92	17	2.93
1740–9	543 [12]	291 [4]	53.59	79	14.55	17	3.13
1750–9	629 [22]	319 [3]	50.72	85	13.51	20	3.18
1760–9	837 [22]	411 [1]	49.10	109	13.02	24	2.87
1770–9	704 [6]	313 [0]	44.46	89	12.64	7	0.99
1780–9	801 [6]	318 [0]	39.70	115	14.36	24	3.00
1790–9	1,039 [1]	372 [0]	35.80	119	11.45	22	2.12
1800–9	1,487 [0]	421 [0]	28.31	94	6.32	13	0.87
1810–19	1,437 [0]	391 [0]	27.21	73	5.08	17	1.18
1820–9	1,523 [1]	314 [0]	20.62	61	4.01	11	0.72
Total	11,420 [92]	4,235 [9]	37.08	1,014	8.88	222	1.94

Notes: [a] Percentages are always of those bound.
[b] Figures in square brackets represent the number of women included in that decade's figures.

We must remember that an apprenticeship was not the only way to achieve the freedom of the Company, however, and that the Livery and the Court contained people who had followed other routes. Tables 14.4 (a)–(c) compare the advancement rates of those who had entered the Yeomanry by servitude, with those who had entered by patrimony and redemption.

It is not surprising that the progress of those who had joined the Company by redemption should be better than those who had come in by servitude as they already had demonstrated that they were well established and respected in order to qualify. It is perhaps surprising that the figures for those who came in by patrimony are as low as they are for moving on into the Livery. Of course, this method brought sons into the Company who were not in the book trade and who saw no point in pursuing the matter because of the added financial commitment. The figures of those freed by patrimony also included a number of daughters who could not progress into the Livery. Also, it is noticeable that a significant number of those receiving pensions from the Company had been freed by patrimony, and that some had been so freed only shortly before

Table 14.4a *Progress of those freed by servitude into the Livery and the Court of the Stationers' Company, 1700–1829*

	Freed by servitude	to Livery		to Court	
		No.	%[a]	No.	%
1700–9	291	59	20.27	13	4.47
1710–19	259	56	21.62	18	6.95
1720–9	241	47	19.50	15	6.22
1730–9	261	37	14.18	15	5.75
1740–9	279	43	15.41	15	5.38
1750–9	285	75	26.32	19	6.67
1760–9	327	91	27.83	18	5.50
1770–9	421	108	25.65	16	3.80
1780–9	271	74	27.31	8	2.95
1790–9	316	120	37.97	23	7.39
1800–9	345	87	25.22	14	4.06
1810–19	384	83	21.61	13	3.39
1820–9	382	61	15.97	16	4.19
Total	4,062	941	21.49	203	4.64

Note: [a] Percentages are always of those freed by servitude.

Table 14.4b *Progress of those freed by patrimony into the Livery and the Court of the Stationers' Company, 1700–1829*

	Freed by patrimony	to Livery		to Court	
		No.	%[a]	No.	%
1700–9	56	4	7.14	1	1.79
1710–19	62	10	16.13	1	1.61
1720–9	60	16	26.67	6	10.00
1730–9	61	13	21.31	8	13.11
1740–9	69	12	17.39	3	4.35
1750–9	44	7	15.91	2	4.55
1760–9	45	15	33.33	3	6.67
1770–9	45	15	33.33	3	6.67
1780–9	56	30	53.57	4	7.14
1790–9	54	16	29.63	4	7.41
1800–9	74	23	31.08	3	4.05
1810–19	72	24	33.33	2	2.78
1820–9	105	27	25.71	9	8.57
Total	803	212	26.40	49	6.10

Note: [a] Percentages are always of those freed by patrimony.

Table 14.4c *Progress of those freed by redemption into the Livery and the Court of the Stationers' Company, 1700–1879*

	Freed by redemption	to livery		to court	
		No.	%[a]	No.	%
1700–9	3	1	33.33	0	0.00
1710–19	2	1	50.00	0	0.00
1720–9	8	6	75.00	1	12.50
1730–9	21	12	57.14	6	28.57
1740–9	30	7	23.33	1	3.33
1750–9	23	15	65.22	4	17.39
1760–9	5	3	60.00	0	0.00
1770–9	15	10	66.67	1	6.67
1780–9	26	11	42.31	1	3.85
1790–9	47	31	65.96	1	2.13
1800–9	50	26	52.00	4	8.00
1810–19	39	9	23.68	4	10.26
1820–9	29	8	27.59	2	6.90
Total	298	140	46.98	25	8.39

This table has included the four translations in the redemptions.

Note: [a] Percentages are always of those freed by redemption.

receiving the pension. It would appear that in these cases the prime reason for taking the freedom was in order to become eligible for a pension. It also seems clear that many less well-to-do families would, as it were, retain only one member of the family in the Livery and that only when the father died would an eligible son pick up his freedom by patrimony. On the other hand, the high figures for entry into the Court from those obtaining their freedom by patrimony in the years between 1720 and 1740 is probably the knock-on effect of the use of privilege by the more well-to-do families earlier in the century to advance sons into a position where they were eligible for the higher shares in the English Stock.

Having identified those who joined the Yeomanry, and being enabled to identify those who would go on to join the Livery, we still have a problem in defining the Yeomanry at any particular time. This is due to the loss of the 'Quarterage Books' during the Second World War. A member of the Company had to pay his dues to the Company every quarter, and these books were the records of those payments. Their loss makes it impossible to keep track of those who did not make it into the Livery. Some work which has been done on the records relating to the eleemosynary activities of the Company reveals part of the history and dates of death for some of the Yeomanry and their widows who fell on hard times, but a great deal still remains to be done in this area, and for the bulk we will never know how long they remained or the reasons why they left.

The Livery is a different matter in that there are many listings. The Calls on the Livery themselves originally covered protracted periods and are consequently not as useful in defining the numbers of Liverymen on any given date, though the more dates of death that we discover improve our attempts to do that. Lists attributed to given dates clearly are more helpful. Bearing in mind all the cautions that one should make about any such printed list, it is worth pointing to the sequence of broadside listings that survive for 1721 and then annually from 1733 throughout our period. Table 14.5 shows the numbers revealed by these lists.

Although the size of the Livery was just over two hundred in the earlier part of the eighteenth century, we discover that in the late 1730s it fell below that level and did not regain it until the early 1750s. This lapse requires some investigation. From the mid-1750s, the rise is steady until the all-time peak of just over five hundred is reached in the late 1820s.

The members of the Court unsurprisingly are the group best documented within the Company; the size and membership of the Court in theory and in practice can be stated for almost any day during our period. There are relatively few individuals whose death or burial dates remain to be ascertained, and attendance lists for meetings of the Court have been compiled throughout the period. It must be emphasized that the column giving the size of the Court on the day of an election in Table 14.6 need not give a true impression of the active Court at that time: some members may not have attended for a while due to age, infirmity or merely retirement to the country. Most did manage to appear for the annual elections, but not all, and some may not have been seen for years.

Trades within the Company

Users of McKenzie's *Apprentices* will be familiar with the information that the record made at the time of binding might provide – the date; the forename and surname of the apprentice; the father's forename; the father's trade or occupation; the father's address;[16] the master's forename and surname; the master's trade or occupation; the master's address; the amount of any premium paid;

16 From around the 1720s it is not unusual to be given an indication of whether the father was already dead at the time of binding, and it would usually be noted if the intended master was the apprentice's father.

Table 14.5 *The size of the Livery of the Stationers' Company, 1721 and 1733–1829*

1721	218	*1756*	225	*1781*	306	*1806*	493
		1757	223	*1782*	308	*1807*	495
1733	212	*1758*	233	*1783*	314	*1808*	514
1734	211	*1759*	242	*1784*	309	*1809*	521
1735	204	*1760*	240	*1785*	309	*1810*	517
1736	201	*1761*	241	*1786*	309	*1811*	509
1737	198	*1762*	246	*1787*	312	*1812*	509
1738	187	*1763*	244	*1788*	323	*1813*	500
1739	189	*1764*	247	*1789*	339	*1814*	502
1740	187	*1765*	252	*1790*	357	*1815*	502
1741	191	*1766*	245	*1791*	382	*1816*	501
1742	191	*1767*	248	*1792*	390	*1817*	507
1743	188	*1768*	257	*1793*	398	*1818*	505
1744	191	*1769*	266	*1794*	411	*1819*	498
1745	183	*1770*	263	*1795*	413	*1820*	500
1746	196	*1771*	271	*1796*	418	*1821*	498
1747	–	*1772*	–	*1797*	428	*1822*	492
1748	191	*1773*	272	*1798*	433	*1823*	492
1749	187	*1774*	273	*1799*	431	*1824*	497
1750	195	*1775*	275	*1800*	453	*1825*	500
1751	193	*1776*	284	*1801*	472	*1826*	505
1752	199	*1777*	288	*1802*	468	*1827*	502
1753	206	*1778*	294	*1803*	481	*1828*	494
1754	216	*1779*	294	*1804*	482	*1829*	482
1755	226	*1780*	303	*1805*	488		

Source: Stationers' Company Archive, 'Beadle's Book', p. 93.
Notes: The figures appear to have been compiled by the Beadle from the Sheet Lists surviving from 1733 onwards; 1721 has been counted. The numbers never reached 500 again after 1827. See Treadwell 1992 for an annual count of the Livery and for a more detailed discussion of the problems involved.

who paid the premium; and the length of service. Such would be an ideal entry, but throughout the period not all of this information appears in every entry. From 1705 to 1717 the information given is particularly sparse. Nevertheless, the opportunities for much more sophisticated set-making open up. Blagden's 1959 article provides us with some snapshots. His Table II looked at some of the fathers – whether they were dead at the time of the binding; did they work in London or outside? In Table III he counted apprentices from the home counties. Table IV looked at the occupations of the fathers. Table V examined some of the aspects surrounding the payment of

Table 14.6 *The size of the Court of the Stationers' Company, 1700–1829*

Date of election	Before	Elected	After	Date of election	Before	Elected	After
8 Apr. 1700	25	4	29	16 Mar. 1773	30	1	31
4 June 1705	20	4	24	7 Apr. 1778	19	8	27
7 Oct. 1706	21	1	22	1 Oct. 1782	21	1	22
2 Dec. 1706	22	1	23	4 Nov. 1783	21	5	26
25 Mar. 1708	20	8	28	6 Dec. 1785	22	5	27
3 May 1708	28	3	31	1 July 1788	25	5	30
2 May 1715	20	6	26	3 Apr. 1792	24	5	29
6 May 1717	24	1	25	6 Oct. 1795	23	6	29
6 Apr. 1719	20	1	21	6 May 1800	21	5	26
1 June 1719	21	8	29	1 Mar. 1803	21	5	26
6 July 1719	29	1	30	21 Aug. 1804	25	8	33
4 Mar. 1723	24	7	31	5 Feb. 1805	32	1	33
1 Apr. 1723	31	1	32	14 Mar. 1809	25	6	31
7 Nov. 1727	25	4	29	6 Mar. 1810	28	1	29
6 Feb. 1728	27	6	33	7 Apr. 1812	24	6	30
2 Mar. 1736	25	8	33	5 Dec. 1817	21	7	28
1 Dec. 1741	17	15	32	3 July 1821	27	1	28
5 Mar. 1754	23	10	33	11 June 1822	27	6	33
6 Apr. 1756	26	1	27	6 May 1823	29	1	30
4 May 1756	27	11	38	1 Dec. 1823	28	1	29
6 Nov. 1759	32	1	33	20 Oct. 1824	28	4	32
1 Nov. 1763	24	18	42	5 July 1828	25	5	30
2 Mar. 1773	18	12	30	13 Oct. 1829	25	6	31

Notes: The table is based on the dates of elections to the Court, showing how many members were entitled to attend on the day of the election, how many were elected on that day and the number to which the Court had risen as a result of the election.

premiums. In the context of this chapter it is not possible to follow all the possibilities through, but we ought to say something about the trades to which people were bound, and how those trades measured up in the general scheme. The naming of the master's trade was not a systematic practice until the 1720s and again became a little lax with the larger numbers of apprentices in the nineteenth century (see Table 14.7).

A little needs to be said about the designation of trades. In the first place, it is not very common for a master to have more than one trade mentioned in a record, and we all know that many, if not the vast majority, worked or offered services in several branches of the book trade. Nor was it uncommon for many

Table 14.7 *Trades to which Stationers' Company apprentices were bound or turned over, 1700 1829*

1700–9	1710–19	1720–9
Printer 129	Printer 175	Printer 204
Bookseller 56	Bookseller 54	Bookseller 117
Bookbinder 55	Bookbinder 71	Bookbinder 97
Stationer 35	Stationer 63	Stationer 63
{Mathematical instrument maker} 13	{Mathematical instrument maker} 18	{Mathematical instrument maker} 20
Letter founder 9	Letter founder 9	Letter founder 11
Writing master 6	Writing master 5	Writing master 8
Copperplate printer 2	Copperplate printer 3	Engraver 6
Scrivener 2	Engraver 2	Copperplate printer 5
		Scrivener 2
No trade mentioned 321	No trade mentioned 115	No trade mentioned 3
1730–9	**1740–9**	**1750–9**
Printer 237	Printer 237	Printer 257
Bookseller 91	Bookbinder 86	Bookbinder 121
Bookbinder 72	Stationer 71	Stationer 85
Stationer 71	Bookseller 67	Bookseller 67
{Mathematical instrument maker} 21	{Mathematical instrument maker} 24	{Mathematical instrument maker} 22
Copperplate printer 8	Copperplate printer 9	Copperplate printer 16
Engraver 8	Engraver 7	Engraver 12
Writing master 7	Letter founder 1	Letter founder 2
Letter founder 3		Publisher 2
Map colourer 1		
No trade mentioned 1	No trade mentioned 2	No trade mentioned 0
1760–9	**1770–9**	**1780–9**
Printer 371	Printer 328	Printer 362
Bookbinder 150	Stationer 132	Stationer 149
Stationer 126	Bookbinder 117	Bookbinder 105
Bookseller 67	Bookseller 51	Bookseller 62
Engraver 23	{Mathematical instrument maker} 21	Engraver 35
Copperplate printer 21	Copperplate printer 13	Copperplate engraver 24
{Mathematical instrument maker} 20	Pocket-book maker 4	{Mathematical instrument maker} 17
Publisher 5	Bookbinder – vellum 2	Pocket-book maker 6
Letter founder 2	Limner 1	Bookbinder – vellum 3
	Papermaker 1	Limner 1
No trade mentioned 0	No trade mentioned 1	No trade mentioned 2

Table 14.7 (*cont.*)

1790–9	1800–9	1810–19
Printer 476	Printer 820	Printer 653
Stationer 177	Stationer 193	Stationer 160
Bookbinder 115	Bookbinder 142	Bookbinder 160
Bookseller 89	Bookseller 88	Bookseller 150
Engraver 48	Copperplate printer 44	Stationer – law 44
Copperplate printer 31	Engraver 37	Engraver 43
{Mathematical instrument maker} 15	Stationer – law 20	Copperplate printer 40
Pocket-book maker 6	{Mathematical instrument maker} 10	Bookbinder – vellum 11
Bookbinder – vellum 5	Letter founder 4	{Mathematical instrument maker} 6
Letter founder 4	Bookbinder – vellum 2	Engraver – map 3
Stationer – law 3	Chart seller 1	Letter founder 3
Book-clasp maker 1	Engraver copperplate 1	Pocket-book maker 3
Box maker 1	Engraver map 1	Engraver – chart 1
Engraver – copperplate 1	Map colourer 1	Papermaker 1
Stationer – writing 1	Papermaker 1	Stationer – wholesale 1
	Pocket-book maker 1	
	Printer's press-maker 1	
No trade mentioned 6	No trade mentioned 11	No trade mentioned 2

1820–9	1820–9 cont.	1820–9 cont.
Printer 700		
Stationer 219	Letter founder 4	Account-book maker 1
Bookbinder 145	Pocket-book maker 4	Engraver – historical 1
Bookseller 124	Papermaker 3	Engraver – portrait 1
Stationer – law 76	Chart seller 2	Map mounter 1
Copperplate printer 37	Map seller 2	Page gilder 1
Engraver 36	Music seller 2	Paper gilder 1
Bookbinder – vellum 7	Publisher 2	Scrivener 1
Bookseller – law 5	Stationer – manufacturing 2	Stationer – ornamental 1
{Mathematical instrument maker} 5	Stationer – wholesale 2	No trade mentioned 22

Note: The evidence for this table is based on the trade assigned to the master in the record of the binding. This information was not systematically given in the early years of the eighteenth century. Only those whose trades are connected with the book trade have been included, apart from 'Mathematical instrument makers' who are included for comparative purposes, being by far the largest group throughout the period of non-book-trade members of the Company.

in the book trade to be active in other 'non-book-trade' activities. Some masters do have various trades allotted to them within their set of apprentices, but whether this is indicative or not of the emphasis on an individual's training is unknown. On the other hand, some masters whom we know followed more than one trade are consistently referred to as though they only had the one. Second, the trade or trades, which the records imply were the object of the apprenticeship, are by no means always the one we know the individual followed later in life.

Of course, not all members of the Stationers' Company were members of the book trades, in spite of the Company's reputation for remaining one of the most closely tied to its original guild connections. Throughout the period, something like two hundred and fifty individual trade descriptions have been recorded. For the purposes of our exercise slight variations have been edited to gain greater cohesion – for example, booksellers and book dealers have been treated as the same; makers and manufacturers have been treated as identical; type founders and letter founders have been amalgamated, as have copper plate printers and rolling-press printers. Some might have gone further: should paper gilders and page gilders be treated as identical, or was one more to do with the stationery trade and the other with bookbinding?

Two groups of non-book-trade masters deserve special mention in view of the numbers of apprentices involved – mathematical instrument makers and the associated optical instrument makers, who during the eighteenth century clearly had a special connection with the Stationers' Company. The mathematical instrument makers, the largest of the non-book-trade groups, have been included in the lists of Table 14.7 for comparative purposes. Haberdashers and milliners should perhaps also be noted as trades providing opportunities for female apprentices, though many of them – together with freemen's widows – were active in the book trade, particularly in bookbinding.

Out of this number of around two hundred and fifty trades, some thirty-nine have been regarded as book trades – a small proportion, but dominant in numbers of apprentices. Here again there is room for discussion – does a box maker (included) have any book-trade connections; machine rulers (not included) were presumably connected with stationers; were gold beaters and shagreen case makers (neither included) linked to the bookbinders? How far along the line of wholesale stationers and papermakers, into paper stainers, paper hangers and wallpaper makers does one go? It seems clear that the last two mentioned should not be included, but (although paper stainers have been left out), there may be occasional doubt: sometimes such appellations are given to individuals who at other times are merely described as stationers and have thus been included. Engravers have been listed, though the general term may apply to individuals who never had any connection with printing (the only exclusion was in the specific case of 'engraver on glass').

Table 14.7 provides 'league tables' for the book trades to which apprentices were apparently bound or turned over for each decade of our period. It is my impression that the practice of applying trade designations to the masters in this context was somewhat conservative and that the common words 'printer', 'bookseller', 'bookbinder' and 'stationer' were the simplest and most convenient to enter. Certainly, so far as printers, booksellers and bookbinders are concerned, little specialization is indicated, which is a pity for the closing decades of the eighteenth century and the early ones of the nineteenth, when more specialization was emerging. No stereotypers appear, even though Hodgson informs us that there were 'at least twelve establishments for the casting of stereotype plates' in London by 1820.[17] Nor are any lithographers mentioned.[18] The five instances of the word 'publisher' occur surprisingly between 1759 and 1769 and relate to the one 'master', Mary Lewis, presumably the widow of John Lewis and a trade publisher in what Treadwell referred to as 'the Augustan' sense.[19] The Longmans, Rivingtons and their colleagues are listed as booksellers throughout the entire period. A number of vellum bookbinders make themselves known from the 1770s.[20] The growth of the copper plate-printing trade is clearly demonstrated through its printers and the engravers.[21] Some specialization in the engraving trade is indicated by the occasional master's designation.

It is the stationers, the rising force in the Company throughout our period, who begin to fragment – some denoting their wholesaling role, others a specific field of activity such as 'writing' or 'fancy'. Perhaps most significantly, we may observe the 'law' stationers who entered the lists as late as the 1790s, but may be said to have had a meteoric rise over the next three decades.[22] Similarly it is 'law' bookselling that begins to distinguish itself in the 1820s.[23]

It must be repeated that it is the master's trade designation that is being used to define this particular group of sets. We can therefore pursue it in possibly another useful way by trying to determine the relative number of printers, booksellers, etc. within the Company who were actively taking on apprentices

17 Hodgson 1820, 121.
18 Cf. Twyman 1976.
19 See Treadwell 1982a.
20 See Pickwoad, chap. 12, above.
21 See Twyman, chap. 2, above.
22 See Twyman, chap. 2, above.
23 See Prest, chap. 44, below.

Table 14.8 *Numbers of bookbinders, booksellers, printers and stationers binding apprentices each decade, 1700–1829*

	Bookbinders	Booksellers	Printers	Stationers
1700–9	38	55	88	27
1710–19	55	59	108	49
1720–9	86	92	109	51
1730–9	61	77	128	62
1740–9	61	56	122	67
1750–9	79	58	119	79
1760–9	83	62	186	101
1770–9	71	48	143	114
1780–9	60	46	147	109
1790–9	66	62	183	112
1800–9	86	56	193	134
1810–19	84	72	185	169
1820–9	87	75	214	168

Notes: These numbers represent the masters and their widows identified as binding apprentices within the given decade and those involved in any subsequent turnovers of those apprentices whenever they took place. All types of stationers listed in Table 14.7 are included in this table.

at a given time or through a given period. One must be careful, however, not to convert this into the number of shops or houses in operation at any given time, as partners in and managers of such businesses may also have been serving as master alongside, or in place of, the nominal owner.[24] Many small operations may never have taken on apprentices. Also we must constantly remind ourselves that – as the trades spread beyond the City limits and traditional restrictions weakened – membership of the Company was a matter of choice not a requirement. In Table 14.8, the four principal groups of printers, booksellers, bookbinders and stationers have been analysed to show how many masters in each group have been identified in each decade.

As we have seen in Table 14.7, so far as numbers are concerned, the printers are dominant throughout the entire period, but the stationers' numbers grow in the most dramatic fashion. In spite of the reservations about the nomenclature already expressed, the emerging picture is suggestive. There are engaging questions arising from these figures relating to differences in labour intensity between trades; to the differences in the cost of capitalization and profitability;

24 Cf. Howe 1947, 40.

to the loyalty of certain trades to the Company – which, in turn, may be a reflection in changes in the concentrations of location;[25] and so on. The implications of these figures might be considered in connection with the changing balance of trades illustrated in the membership of the Court.[26] The swing in the balance of power within the Company over our period from the booksellers to the stationers revealed by Blagden can be clearly observed.

The English Stock

Another very important factor within the Stationers' Company and in the possibilities it creates for defining further sets, or divisions within the membership, is the English Stock. This is not the place for an extended discussion of the business of the Stock,[27] but a short description of the mechanics of becoming a share-holding member and progressing through the different values of shares will reveal further possibilities for defining sets relating to the more successful (affluent) members of the Company.

The English Stock was a joint trading company operated from within the Stationers' Company itself. It emerged from a grant made by James I in 1603 and related to the production of almanacs, psalters and certain school-books, giving the Company a monopoly in these areas. Once again, Blagden is the authority to whom one should turn for a detailed discussion of its origins and progress in the earlier period.[28] The capital on which the dividends were distributed at the beginning of the eighteenth century was £14,400 divided into three equal portions of £4,800 each. The first portion was in the name of the members of the Court of Assistants and their widows in fifteen shares, each worth £320; the second for the Liverymen and their widows in thirty shares, each worth £160; and the third for the Yeomanry and their widows in sixty shares, each worth £80. In 1695, the annual dividend was already yielding a sum of £40 (11.11 per cent) on an Assistants' share, £20 (12.5 per cent) on a Livery share and £10 (12.5 per cent) on a Yeomanry share. The only exceptions to this in our period occurred in 1697, 1699–1702, 1711, 1713–16, and 1779

25 See Raven, chap. 13, above.

26 There is a listing of masters of the Company to 1872 with trades in Arber 1875–94, v, lxi–lxxv. However, the trades of members of the Court are somewhat problematic in that the more successful some of them became the more they diversified their interests. For instance, in this period several moved into banking, most notably the Gosling family.

27 See Myers, chap. 39, below.

28 Blagden 1955, 1957; see also Stationers' Company 1893.

(midsummer and Christmas)–1780 (midsummer only). In some of the earlier years the payment included books. The dividends were paid annually at Christmas until in May 1723 it was decided that the amount should be divided into two payments – midsummer and Christmas. The by-laws regulating the Stock also provided that at least £200 per annum from the profits of the Stock should be distributed at the quarterly Pension Courts to the poor of the Company.

The by-laws also stipulated that the numbers of shares in each category should not exceed those mentioned above, but that if there were members of that degree exceeding the number of shares, then they should have a share from the level below. This provision, together with a growth of the Company, meant that by the end of the seventeenth century the Yeomanry were, in effect, excluded from their shares, which were all owned by members of the Livery. At the top end of the table, as early as 1700, William Phillips served most of his first term as Master not having achieved an Assistants' share, a situation that soon became a common occurrence. In fact, the situation had progressed even to the point where, at the beginning of our period, many of the Yeomanry shares were divided and the halves – 'half-Yeomanry shares' – held by separate Liverymen. This was partially rationalized in 1729 when the Court ordered that the Yeomanry shares be re-divided into forty Yeomanry (£80) and forty half-Yeomanry (£40) shares. The pressure continued however, and it was not long before no one could obtain a share until he had first served or fined for the office of Renter Warden. From time to time, further shares were created, as laid out in Table 14.9 – the biggest change taking place in 1805 when for each category an 'Additional' group, pitched somewhat above the historic levels, was created. Nevertheless, no one below the level of Renter Warden was ever again able to own a share.

The Stock year remained tied to the old-style calendar. On 1 March, or the next day if it fell on a Sunday, the Court and the Partners met to hear the by-laws read out and to choose the officers of the English Stock for the following twelve months – two Stock-keepers for the Court of Assistants, two for the Livery and two for the Yeomanry. The Treasurer of the English Stock and the porter were also elected on that day. The business of the Stock was managed by the Master, Wardens and the six Stock-keepers, and was in the day-to-day control of the Treasurer (Warehouseman). When a share became vacant, an election was held at a meeting of the Court, and although at least two names were reported as going into the box, the choice seemed regularly to go with precedence. In the early part of the century, there was some evidence that members of the Court worked the system in favour of their sons. On 7 October

Table 14.9 *Changes in the number and value of shares in the English Stock, to 1805*

Before 1729	£320 share 15	£160 share 30	£80 share 60	£40 half-share
6 May 1729	15	30	40	40
3 Feb. 1736	16	32	42	44
7 July 1747	18	36	46	52
5 Feb. 1754	19	38	48	56
6 Apr. 1756	20	40	50	60
1 May 1759	22	44	54	68
1 Feb. 1763	24	48	58	76
12 Apr. 1768	25	50	60	80
3 Apr. 1770	27	54	68	80
6 Dec. 1796	29	58	68	96
5 Mar. 1799	33	66	72	120
21 Aug. 1804	36	72	78	132
2 Oct. 1804	38	76	82	140

	£400	£360	£200	£160	£100	£80	£50	£40
6 Aug. 1805	20	18	40	36	40	42	80	60

1717 Daniel Brown successfully persuaded the Court that his son Jonas, who dwelt 'out of the Freedom' of the City but followed the trade of bookseller, should be allowed to take up his freedom, be accepted into the Livery and pay the fines for Renter Warden 'forthwith', 'provided that' he was then elected to the next available £40 share and on the Christmas following to an £80 share. This done, Richard Mount immediately obtained a similar deal for his son Richard. Those who entered the Court as Aldermen were also usually accelerated into an Assistants' share, though in the second half of our period this became regarded as not correct and most of them chose to wait until their proper turn. An election, at any level other than in the half-Yeomanry group, caused a knock-on effect as one person being elected to a share in the group above caused a vacancy in his own group. If an Assistant or his widow died, the effect went all down the line.

On being elected, the stationer had to find the capital to pay for the higher share; at times this clearly led to individuals declaring they did not want to accept the share. The practice, if not the rules, changed from time to time. The Company became much firmer on the principle that only Liverymen who were practising book-trade members could own shares, non-book-trade members having to renounce their eligibility. One could mortgage one's share, but one was only meant to do so within the Company and preferably through the Treasurer, although this did not always happen. One could bequeath one share to one's widow and she would hold the benefits until her death or remarriage. There is evidence that, in the earlier part of the period, the Court was reasonably lenient with widows whose spouses had died without actually having made the bequest, but later in the period it adopted what can only be described as a draconian view in such situations. If one was declared bankrupt, one's share was immediately forfeited, but it became the policy that once the Commissioners were satisfied, then the individual concerned would be allowed back into the chain again and accelerated to his original position at the earliest opportunity. On relinquishing a share, the party (or his executor) was 'paid out' – theoretically in four instalments, but this could vary.

Clearly, a great deal of record keeping went along with all this activity. For our period the picture is now fairly clear. All the dividend payments have been recorded for the *LBT* database and most of the share transfers found and entered. It was quite clearly essential that the Company keep in contact with shareholders; therefore, the associated records are particularly informative – addresses, dates of death; later, notes on wills give dates for the wills and the probate, information as to whom the share had been bequeathed (only the widow could retain it and draw the dividends), and the names of executors.

There is little doubt that the possibility of owning a share in the English Stock was one of the major attractions in membership of the Stationers' Company; to say the least, it was a very good pension plan. The fact that one's widow could continue to hold the share until death or remarriage could only have added to the attraction, though it could cause problems for the Company. There were occasions in the eighteenth century when the majority of the Assistants' shares were in the hands of surviving widows rather than active Assistants. Some Assistants' widows were able to retire to Bath or Brighton with the help of their £40 a year, and some widows survived a long time –William Fielder's widow drew her £5 per annum from 1764 until her death in 1820, whilst John Davidson's widow, Anne, enjoyed £20 per annum from 1799 until 1843.

Pensions and charity

There is another large area of the records where the information will lead to a fuller understanding of the sociology of the Company and the London trade. These relate to the paying of pensions and giving of charity to the less financially successful members of the Company. It has already been noted that some small proportion of the profits of the English Stock was annually set aside for this work, and as the period progressed more and more of the wealthy members of the Company gave or bequeathed monies for one-off distributions or for the establishment of regular pensions.[29] Just as with the activities of the English Stock, this resulted in a great deal of record keeping. Several hundred more widows of members of the Company have been revealed, and approximate death dates for most of those receiving regular pensions or benefits should be ascertainable. This work has only just started, however. Although it is revealing possibilities for further analysis, it is still too early to report on any results. Such work is invaluable for obtaining a greater understanding of the family relationships existing within the trade.

Beyond the 'Company'

There was within the book trade what might be described as a penumbra around the immediate membership of the Company. Legally, the City treated the widows of Freemen as they had their husbands unless they remarried – they were, for example, allowed to bind apprentices. Daughters were allowed into the freedom by servitude and by patrimony. We have seen that in the Stationers' Company widows could inherit and continue to benefit from all levels of shares within the English Stock, until their death or, again, until they remarried. Modern scholarship has recognized that women were active within the trade much more than is made clear by the bibliographical evidence.[30] A similar situation should be recognized for other members of the family, particularly while it was common 'to live above the shop' or close to it. Sons and daughters, together with parents and siblings of the master and mistress, could all be active within the family business. It is obvious and true today in such a situation, and it was no doubt always so. The connection was perhaps somewhat weakened when the family's residence separated from the place of business. Such moves came with growing affluence and allowed for the development of a kind of gentility, especially for the female members of the household, though it does not necessarily even then prohibit their involvement. In the last decades of the eighteenth century it can be seen from the addresses of the Livery that such a shift was taking place. Islington, in particular, was extremely popular with the book trade, as with many other City-located

29 In the later period the Company regularly produced updated versions of a booklet entitled *Abstract of the charitable donations in the disposal of the Court of Assistants of the Worshipful Company of Stationers*.
30 See Bell 1988, 1989, 1992.

trades.[31] The more affluent naturally were attracted by the West End, while a few early commuters were moving to Clapham or similar locales.

If one thinks of the business in terms of the 'extended' family throughout the first half of our period, it is easy see the possibilities for ever-increasing connections and complications: a husband and wife, with several children, and perhaps one or more of their parents and siblings all living under the same roof, together with one or more living-in apprentices. The costs of becoming a member of a City company were not negligible, and we have seen that restricting participation to one individual per household was often a common strategy. If the husband was a member of the Company, then his apprentices should have been bound through the Company. Some of the apprentices would have served their full time and might have stayed on to work as journeymen, with or without having taken their freedom. It is important to recognize that many apprentices were regarded as part of the extended family – as a number in fact were – quite often receiving legacies and occasionally taking on a family business on the death of the master. Fellow apprentices often retained connections throughout their careers, going into business with each other either openly or silently.[32] Siblings were often apprenticed to the same master. These young men provided a convenient pool of possible husbands, not only for the widow of a deceased master – the traditional scenario – but also for daughters and their spinster aunts. Examples abound. Wills often reveal the involvement of brothers, or other members of families, in partnerships, when they are not members of the Company or even generally recognized as having been in the trade. We are considering a relatively small number of people within a particularly restricted geographical area, though it should be noted that as the century progressed there were more and more trade connections with the provinces, as sons came in from the provinces to serve London masters and London-trained journeymen moved out into the provinces. Several prominent provincial members of the trade were members of the Stationers' Company and even bound their apprentices through the Company.

The same arguments would apply to those members of the book trades in other City companies. Our period saw some translations into the Stationers' Company, but there was little effort to bring them about, as there had been in earlier times. Just as we have seen that one or two apprenticing families of scientific instrument makers could make an impact in the Stationers'

31 From 1773 to 1824 the incumbent of St Mary's Islington was even a member of the Stationers' Company: Revd George Strahan, William's son, who had served an apprenticeship with his father before going up to Oxford.

32 The value of focusing on apprentices is well exemplified in Stoker 2004.

Company, so could one or two book-trade members in other companies. The expansion of the trade westwards, and elsewhere,[33] away from the confines of the City proper, together with the decline in strict City restrictions on trading, reduced the need to be a member of a City company. Stationers' Company apprentices and journeymen, and those traditionally described as having 'foreign indentures', were free to trade within the ever-growing metropolis at their will, with or without being formally 'free of the City'.

Finally, it must be recognized that listings of members of the book trades during the second half of the eighteenth century, published or unpublished, show that the relative number of Stationers' Company members was in a sharp decline. There are more and more lists, many associated with other newly formed groupings, which emerged amongst the masters and, from the 1780s, among the workforce at large. The 'combinations' and 'self-help' associations of printers, compositors and bookbinders became particularly active and evidence of their membership abounds.[34] Esther Potter's work on the bookbinders' groups documented in the Jaffray papers in the British Library[35] has revealed around three and half thousand entries for individuals, of whom only a handful can be identified as members of the Stationers' Company – usually people who had become masters in their own right. Only when work has been undertaken for groups other than the Stationers' Company will we have a real chance of understanding the demography of the London book trade throughout our period.

33 See Raven, chap. 13, above.

34 In particular see Howe 1947 and Graham Pollard's appendices in Pendred 1955. Many of the documents referred to contain lists of signatures, sometimes in the hundreds, omitted in these sources. The task of identifying these people is often very difficult.

35 Potter 1993, 1997.

15

The English provincial book trade: evidence from the *British book trade index*

MAUREEN BELL AND JOHN HINKS

During the past twenty years, an increasing amount of scholarly attention has been focused on the spread of the book trade in the English provinces and the character of that trade as it developed from the late seventeenth to the early nineteenth centuries. Local historians and historians of the book alike have focused on the specific details of the book trade and its personnel in particular towns and cities; the first monograph on the provincial trade in England was published by John Feather in 1985.[1] The series of annual British Book Trade Seminars initiated by the late Peter Isaac has encouraged a particular research focus on the provincial trade,[2] and his accumulation of data from willing contributors to the *British book trade index* began, in the 1980s, a process which continues with the recent incarnation of an augmented *BBTI on the Web*.[3]

BBTI's evidence for the systematic study of the provincial book trade is now beginning to be explored,[4] though the collection and entry of data is still in progress and the database will continue to grow, at a slower rate, after the funded project ends; in a sense, it can never be complete. Nonetheless, the growth of *BBTI* to its current size of approximately 120,000 records, representing those who worked in the book trade and its allied trades in England and Wales from the earliest times to 1851,[5] provides a data set which, while in some respects inconsistent and incomplete, is at least large enough to enable some

1 Feather 1985. For an overview of the state of current research, see Feather 2004.

2 Much of this work has appeared in the *Print Networks* series of papers, edited by Peter Isaac and Barry McKay.

3 *The British book trade index on the Web*, funded under the Resource Enhancement Programme of the Arts and Humanities Research Board, is freely accessible at www.bbti.bham.ac.uk. The continued input of data renders the database a moving target, and the search results reported here offer a snapshot of the database records as they stood in spring 2004.

4 'Evidence for the personnel of the English provincial book trade ... is inconsistent and incomplete' was the judgement of Barnard and Bell 2002a, 671, though they made use of *BBTI* CD-ROM data.

5 *BBTI* does not encompass Scotland. The *Scottish book trade index*, edited by John Morris, is hosted by the National Library of Scotland at www.nls.uk/catalogues/resources/sbti/index.html.

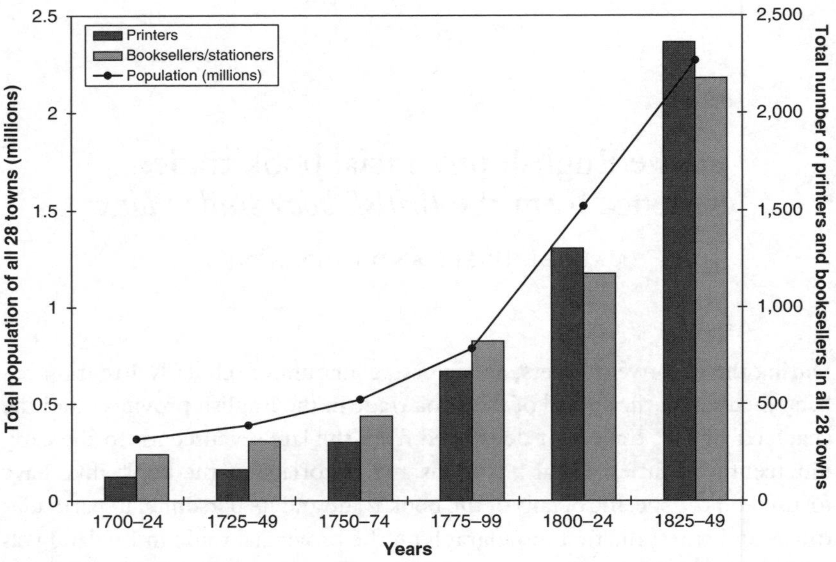

Figure 15.1 Total printers and booksellers/stationers in the twenty-eight towns studied, 1700–1849

useful statistical analysis.[6] While necessarily hedged with caveats, findings from searches of the database are reliable enough both to suggest broad historical trends in the development of the provincial trade and to indicate areas deserving further investigation at a more detailed level.

In attempting to identify the scale of book-trade activity in the provinces between 1700 and 1850, *BBTI* records have been used to create a series of comparative 'snapshots' at twenty-five-year intervals for twenty-eight selected English provincial towns.[7] The results, plotted against population trends, enable some comparisons of the scale and nature of the trade to be made between towns of different types and sizes.[8] As well as establishing similarities, some significant differences between towns emerge. Figure 15.1 presents the overall picture of the development of the book trade, as represented by *BBTI*-recorded individuals engaged in printing, bookselling and stationery businesses, from 1700 to 1850. The same data divided into trade groups are shown in Figures 15.2 (printers) and 15.3 (booksellers/stationers). These raw

6 For a fuller rehearsal of the caveats to be applied when searching *BBTI*, see Hinks and Bell 2005.

7 Bath, Birmingham, Bristol, Cambridge, Canterbury, Carlisle, Chester, Colchester, Coventry, Exeter, Gloucester, Hull, King's Lynn, Leeds, Leicester, Liverpool, Manchester, Newcastle, Norwich, Nottingham, Oxford, Plymouth, Portsmouth, Salisbury, Sheffield, Shrewsbury, Worcester and York.

8 For a detailed description of methodology, see Hinks and Bell 2005.

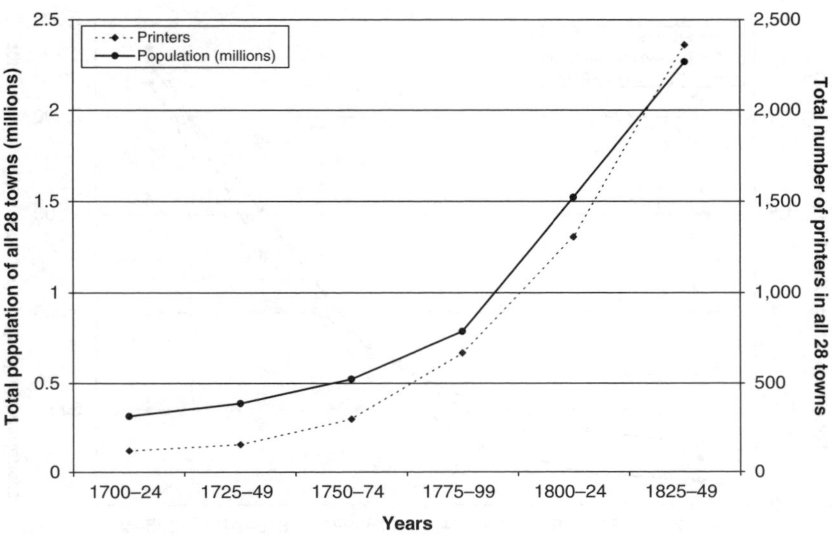

Figure 15.2 Total (from urban sample) of printers, 1700–1849

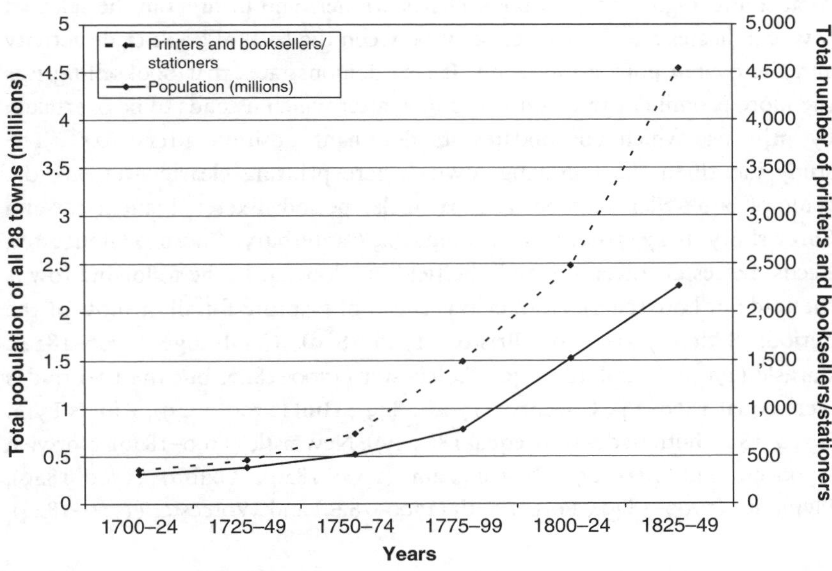

Figure 15.3 Total from urban sample (printers plus booksellers/stationers), 1700–1849

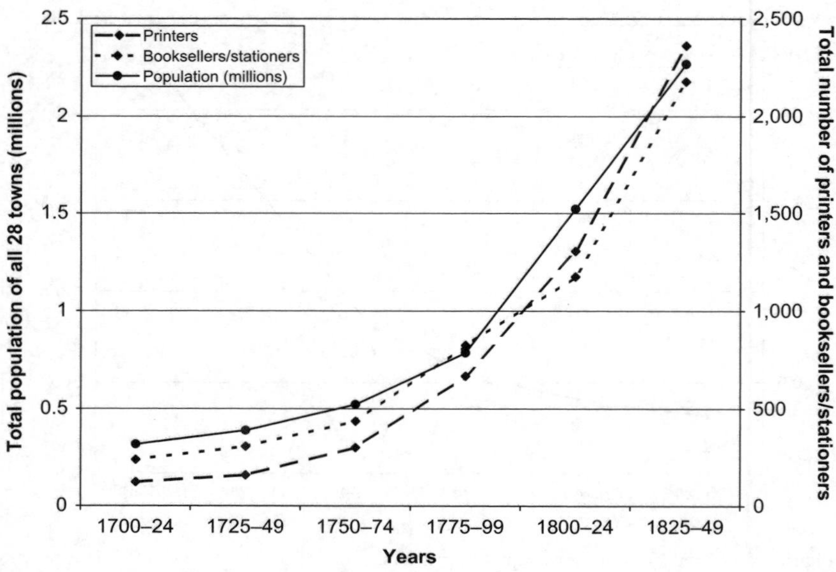

Figure 15.4 Total (from urban sample) of printers and booksellers/stationers, 1700–1849

totals suggest a growth in trade broadly in line with population trends. The total count (Figure 15.4) of bookseller/stationers and printers in the selected towns indicates a reasonably close fit between the level of book-trade activity and the overall population trend. It also demonstrates that bookselling was the more prominent trade until 1800/24, after which it tends to be overtaken by printing, which consolidates its dominant position after 1825.[9] The study identified the following towns where printing clearly overtook the trade of bookseller/stationer at a particular period: Exeter, Manchester and Shrewsbury in 1775–99, and Birmingham, Canterbury, Chester, Gloucester, Leeds, Leicester, Liverpool and Sheffield in 1800–24. In the following towns the trade of bookseller/stationer was ahead of printing for all or most of the period: Bath (1700–1849), Bristol (1700–1849), Cambridge (1700–1824), Carlisle (1700–74 and 1800–49), Colchester (1700–1849, but the two trades were equal 1800–24), Coventry (1700–1849), Hull (1700–1849), King's Lynn (1700–1825; both trades were equal 1825–49), Newcastle (1700–1849), Norwich (1700–99 and 1825–49), Nottingham (1700–1824), Oxford (1700–1849), Plymouth (1700–1849), Portsmouth (1700–1849) and Worcester (1700–1824).

9 More detailed graphs relating to individual towns will be made available on the *BBTI* website.

In only one town, York, was printing ahead of the trade of bookseller/stationer for most of the period (1725–1849).

Raw totals can, of course, easily mask important differences, both geographical and chronological, and more detailed analysis is needed to identify any significant patterns and disparities in the scale and development of book-trade activity in towns of comparable size and character during this period. One way of approaching this problem is to classify towns according to type, based on various mixes of social, economic and cultural factors (for example, industrial/non-industrial, market towns, cathedral cities, ports). Examples of the results of such comparisons are offered here, briefly, as case studies.

Industrial and non-industrial towns

The most significant differences between types of town proved to be between industrial and non-industrial towns.[10] Figures 15.5 and 15.6 depicting printing and bookselling in these two groups show that there were fewer printers than

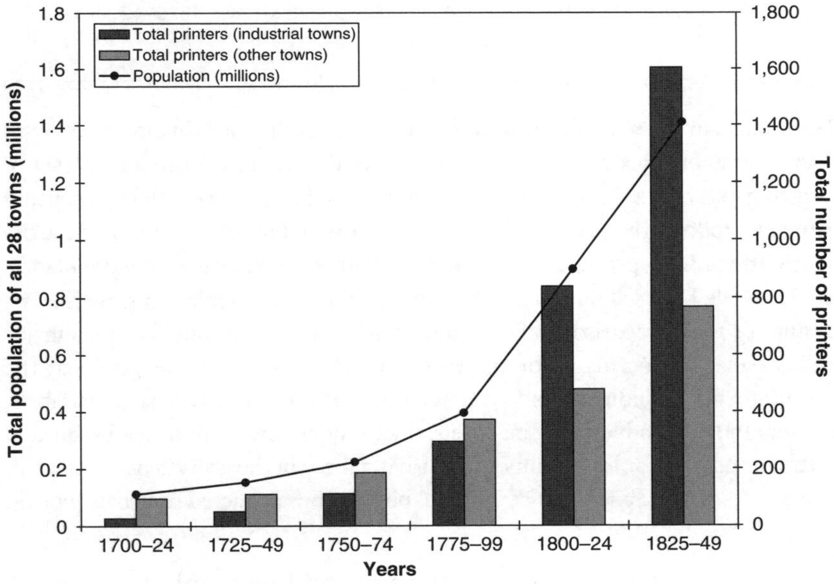

Figure 15.5 Total number of printers in industrial and other towns, 1700–1849

10 Towns classified as 'industrial' were: Birmingham, Bristol, Leeds, Liverpool, Manchester, Newcastle and Sheffield; 'non-industrial': Bath, Cambridge, Canterbury, Carlisle, Chester, Colchester, Coventry, Exeter, Gloucester, Hull, King's Lynn, Leicester, Norwich, Nottingham, Oxford, Plymouth, Portsmouth, Salisbury, Shrewsbury, Worcester and York.

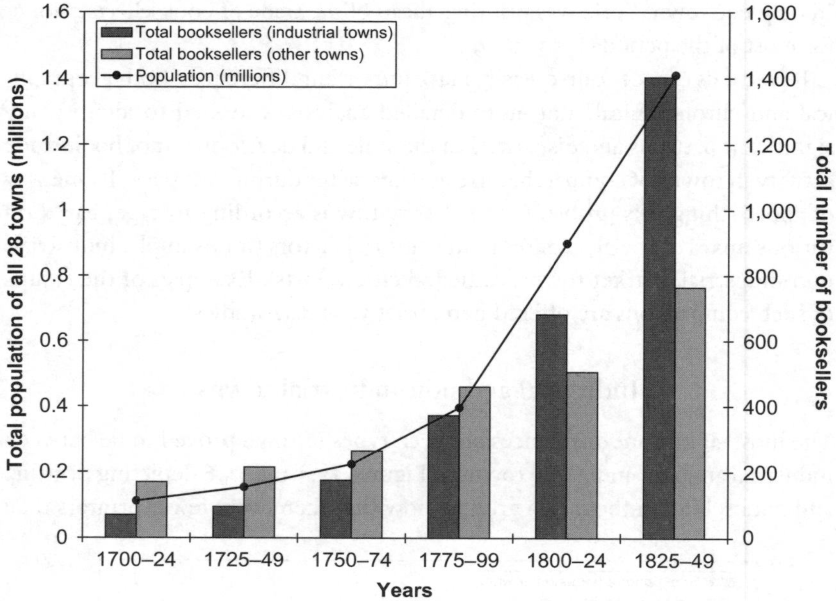

Figure 15.6 Total number of booksellers/stationers in industrial and other towns, 1700–1849

booksellers in the industrial towns before 1800, but that printing in these towns increased enormously in the first half of the nineteenth century. The level of printing and bookselling activity in both groups during the eighteenth century generally follows the pattern of population growth, but after 1800 – and particularly after 1825 – printing in the industrial towns leaps ahead of the population trend, while bookselling remains broadly in step with population growth. The results of the comparison reflect quite strikingly the obvious fact that major industrialization occurred for the most part after 1800, and suggest that the requirements of industry and commerce for printed material (such as labels, posters and other advertising materials, ruled ledgers and account books, bill and letter heads) were at least as much of a driving force in the growth of the trade as the increasing (and increasingly literate) populations attracted to urban centres.

Two major ports: Bristol and Liverpool

Bristol was, for a time, the second largest town in England, and was larger than Liverpool until around 1775. After that year, however, it was overtaken by the massive growth of that northern port, which by 1850 had acquired a population more than two-and-a-half times that of Bristol. This pattern is reflected in the

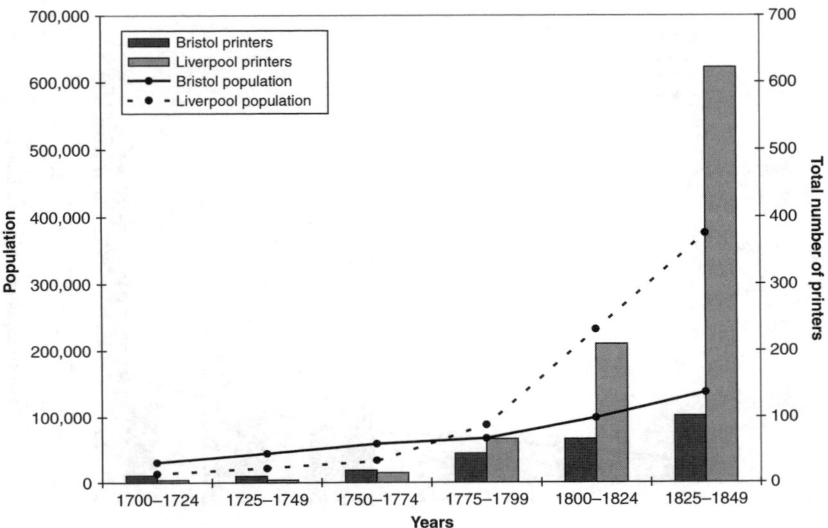

Figure 15.7 Number of printers in Bristol and Liverpool, 1700–1849

position of printing in both towns (see Figure 15.7): Bristol leads until 1775, and then Liverpool leaps ahead suddenly, with three times the number of Bristol printers by 1800–24. This rapid expansion continues at least until 1850, by which time the printing trade in Liverpool is six times larger than in Bristol.[11] Bookselling in the two ports (see Figure 15.8) follows a broadly similar pattern to printing, except that Bristol remains well ahead of Liverpool in 1775–9; after 1800 a pattern similar to that observed for printing is resumed.

Printing and bookselling in both towns more or less follow the rise in population, with the exception that in Liverpool both trades apparently grew much more rapidly than population after 1825. This is strikingly clear in Figure 15.9, which shows the ratio of printers per thousand population in the two towns: Liverpool rises steeply from a ratio of 0.9 in 1800–24 to 1.65 in 1825–49. Bristol's printing in the same period rises only very gently from a ratio of 0.68 to 0.74. Figure 15.10, showing the ratio of booksellers per thousand population, reveals a quite surprising leap up to 1.42 in Bristol in 1800–25 (when Liverpool has 0.78), compared with 0.72 in the previous twenty-five-year period and 0.85 in the following period (declining further to 0.76 by 1850). Ratios, however, can be misleading: rises and declines revealed by ratio-counting often do not indicate an actual rise or decline in trade, merely that trade development has not kept

11 Dr Jonathan Barry's data for Bristol, not yet incorporated into *BBTI*, could alter the scale of the apparent difference between Liverpool and Bristol.

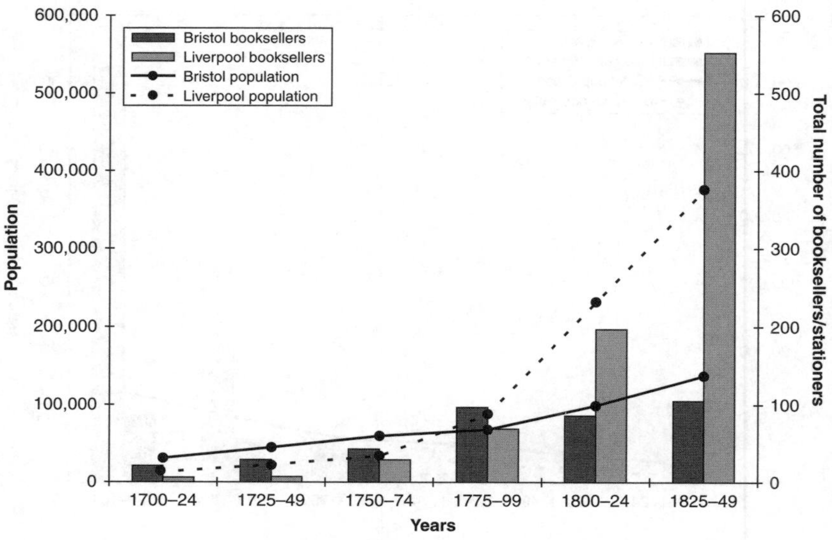

Figure 15.8 Number of booksellers/stationers in Bristol and Liverpool, 1700–1849

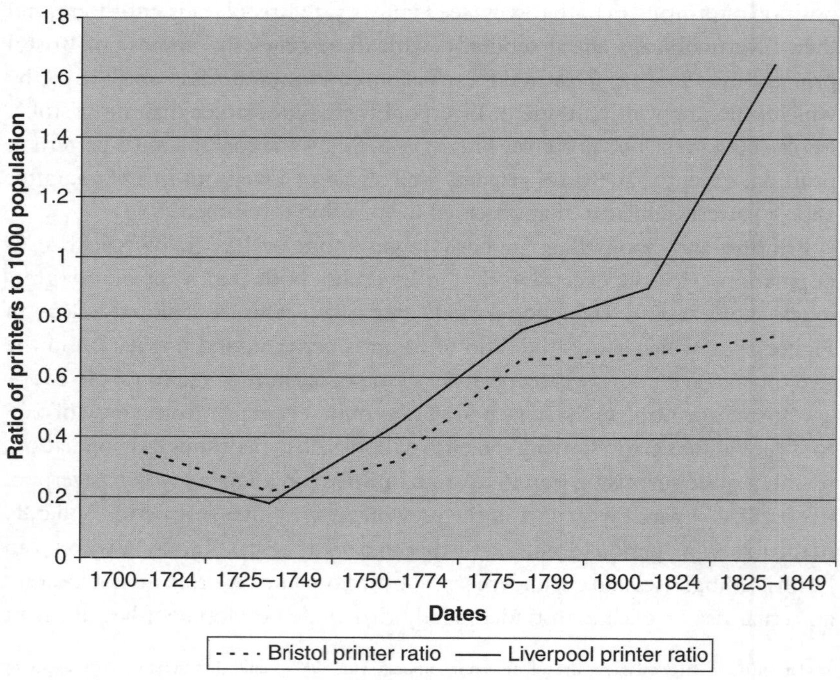

Figure 15.9 Printer ratios, Bristol and Liverpool, 1700–1849

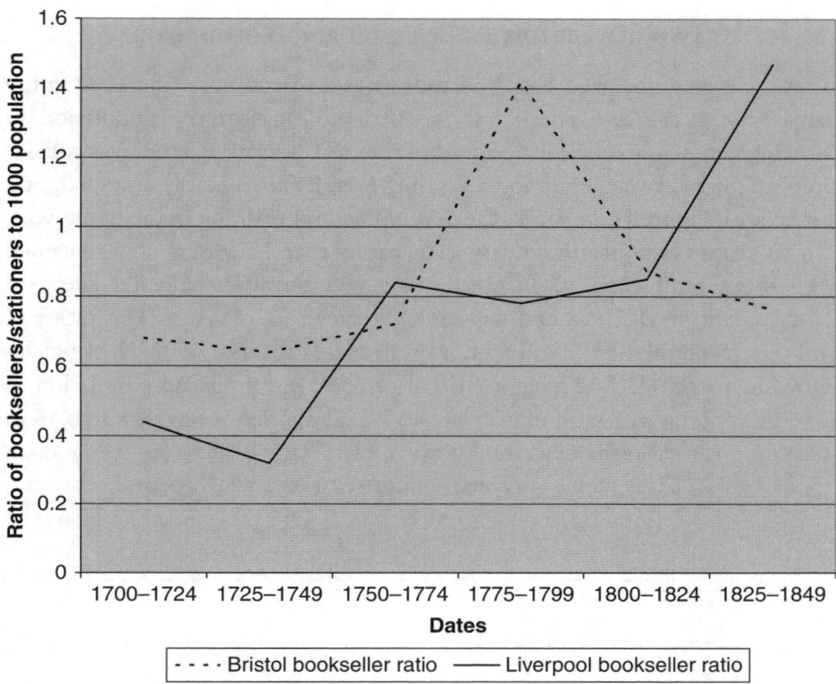

Figure 15.10 Bookseller ratios, Bristol and Liverpool, 1700–1849

pace with a (perhaps rapid) growth in population. Moreover, trade growth does not *need* slavishly to follow population growth because a thriving book trade of a certain scale may well have had sufficient capacity to service a growing population for some time before needing to expand to meet significantly increased demand. It is of course possible that the generally high values for Liverpool, compared with those for Bristol, reflect not only a real, historical difference in trading levels, but also a different level of activity by book-trade historians. Liverpool's book trade has been quite thoroughly studied;[12] Bristol seems not to have benefited from the same degree of diligent research. This discrepancy would of course be reflected in the level of *BBTI* records for the two towns and therefore in the results of this research.[13]

12 See, for example, the publications of the Liverpool Bibliographical Society's Book Trade in the North West Project: Perkin 1981, 1987a.

13 The figures comparing Bristol and Liverpool are a good example of one of the problems inherent in expressing research data graphically: the very high count for Liverpool (both printing and bookselling) in 1825–49 means that the values shown for earlier periods are rather compressed. The gently sloping line therefore masks a considerable growth in both trades that would be shown as a much steeper line if the very high value of the final column did not have to be accommodated.

Two market towns: Leicester and Nottingham

These two medium-sized East Midlands market towns were compared in the same way as the two ports.[14] It is worth noting that the population of Nottingham, while only a little ahead of that of Leicester in 1700, was considerably higher between 1725 and 1825; however, by 1850 Leicester was slightly in the lead. Figure 15.11 shows the development of printing in the two towns. Nottingham began printing thirty years earlier than Leicester[15] and remained well ahead until 1800, when there was a reversal, with Leicester ahead of Nottingham in 1800–24 and substantially ahead in 1825–49. The ratios of printers to population (Figure 15.12) reflect this reversal, with Nottingham showing a steep decline from a ratio of printers per thousand population of 0.76 in 1775–99 to a ratio of 0.25 in 1800–24, although it recovers to 0.36 in 1825–49. The ratio for Leicester shows a less drastic decline (1775–99: 0.59; 1800–24: 0.41), but then a very sharp increase to 0.82 in 1825–49.

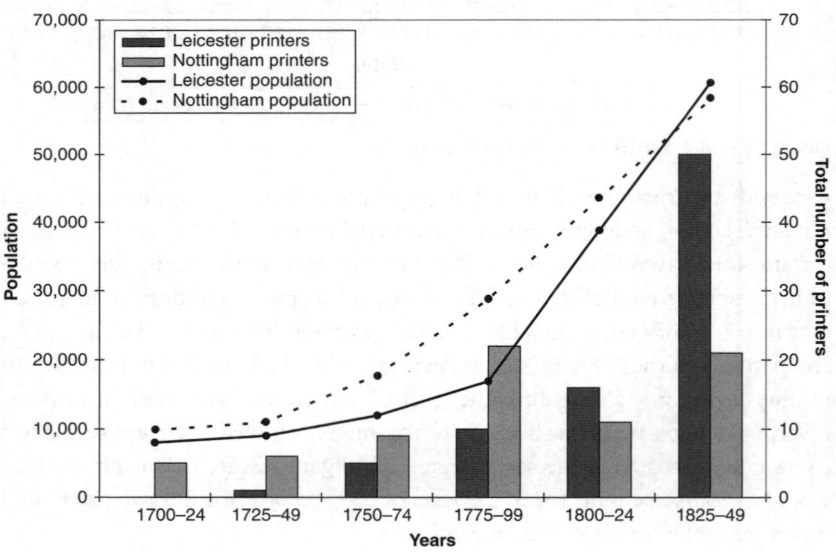

Figure 15.11 Number of printers in Leicester and Nottingham, 1700–1849

14 For the book-trade history of Nottingham, see Clarke and Potter 1953; Creswell 1863; Cropper 1892; Walton 1968; and Fraser 1963. For Leicester: Hinks 2000, 2001, 2002.

15 Printing began in Nottingham in 1710. *BBTI* shows five printers active in the town in the period 1700–24. Leicester had to wait for its first printer until 1740/1: Hinks 2002, 301.

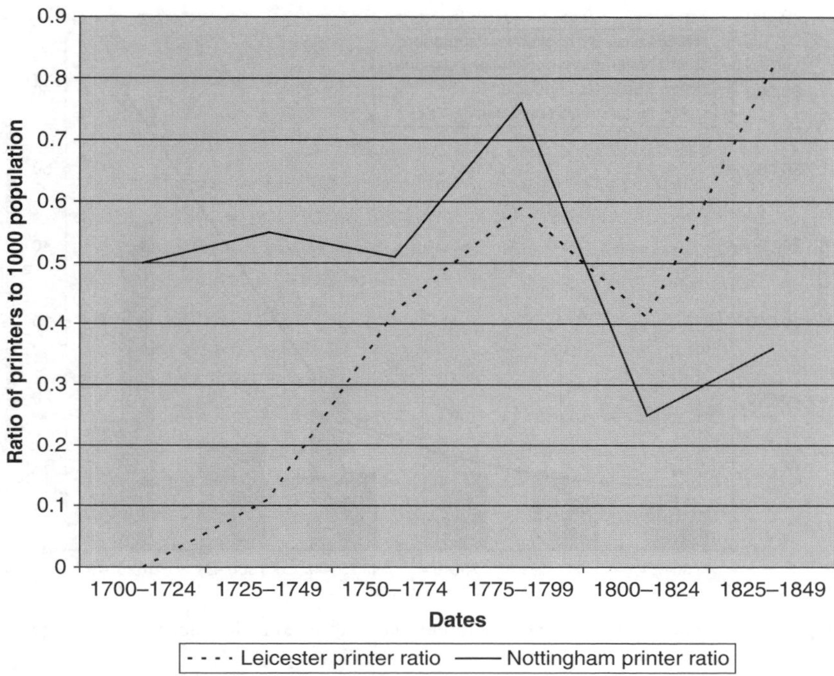

Figure 15.12 Printer ratios, Leicester and Nottingham, 1700–1849

The level of bookselling activity in the two towns is shown in Figure 15.13. Nottingham is a little ahead of Leicester up to 1775, but is almost two and a half times higher in 1775–99. By 1800–24, however, the two towns are equal, both having fourteen booksellers/stationers. Although the population size of the two market towns converges around 1825 (after which Leicester edges ahead until mid-century), the number of booksellers/stationers in Leicester (forty-three) in 1825–49 is very much higher than in Nottingham (seventeen). Figure 15.14, representing ratios of booksellers per thousand population, indicates the divergence between the two towns after 1750, with Nottingham's ratio of booksellers to population increasing a little between 1750–74 (0.68) and 1775–99 (0.83), but then declining very steeply (down to 0.29 by mid-century). Leicester's ratio of booksellers declines more steadily between 1750–74 (0.83) and 1800–24 (0.36), but then – while Nottingham's is still in slow decline – increases to 0.71 by mid-century.

The differences between Leicester and Nottingham – rival regional capitals of the East Midlands – are intriguing. Leicester was known, rather later in its history, as a major printing town, and the beginnings of this printing boom

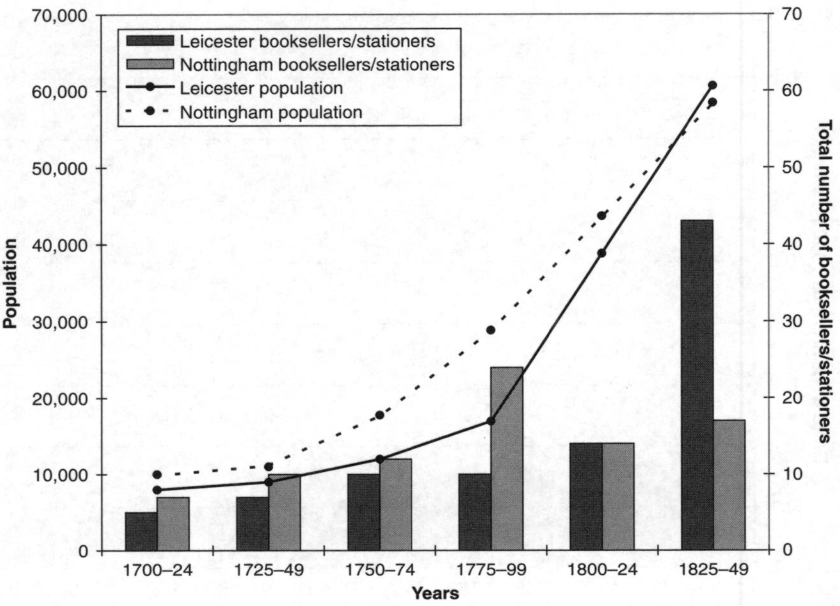

Figure 15.13 Number of booksellers/stationers in Leicester and Nottingham, 1700–1849

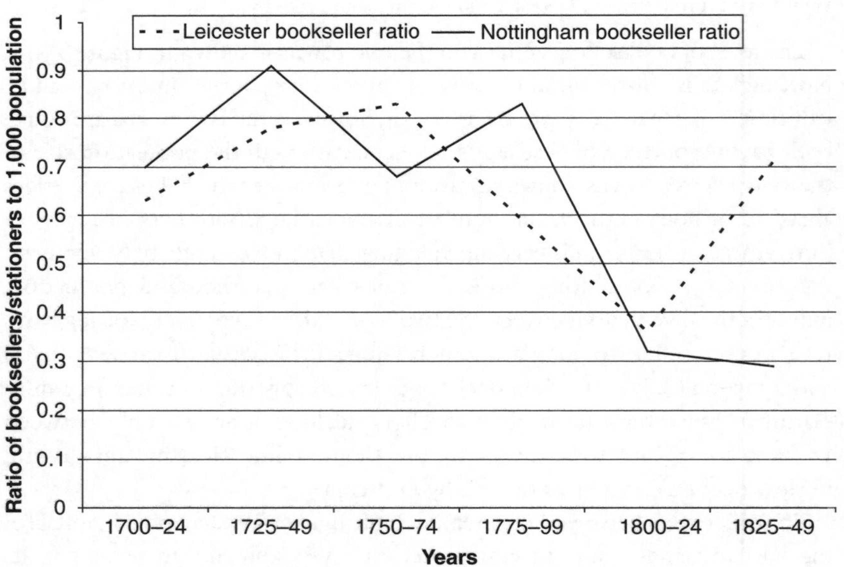

Figure 15.14 Bookseller ratios, Leicester and Nottingham, 1700–1849

may be reflected in the sudden increase, in sharp contrast to Nottingham, of printing activity in the second quarter of the nineteenth century. Less expected, however, is the sharp rise in bookselling activity in Leicester in the same period. This increase is supported by an earlier comparative study of Leicester, Nottingham and Worcester, which indicated that, although the overall level of eighteenth-century book-trade activity in the three towns was closely comparable – with fifty-two individuals in Leicester, sixty-one in Nottingham and fifty-nine in Worcester – Nottingham was exceptional in having twenty-six printers in addition to twenty-eight bookseller/stationers (only two of whom also printed), whereas in Leicester and Worcester virtually all printing (and binding) was carried out by bookseller/stationers.[16] These simple counts may not be conclusive, but they at least indicate that the book trade in Nottingham became specialized much earlier than in Leicester or Worcester.

Printing

The case studies undertaken so far using *BBTI* data broadly confirm the established view that, in the eighteenth century, the mainstream provincial book trades developed steadily, with printing in particular becoming increasingly important as the century progressed.[17] The trade of printer, especially in the industrial towns studied, became considerably stronger than that of bookseller/stationer, particularly after 1775 in the industrial towns, and in non-industrial towns after 1800. This noticeable 'surge in printing' most probably resulted from printers meeting the growing needs of new and developing industries for printed matter (packaging, publicity, commercial stationery), rather than from a significant increase in book printing, though this rather broad assertion merits further research. It does not explain why, in several of the towns studied – Bristol, Cambridge, Carlisle, York – printing was apparently ahead of bookselling for all or most of the period 1700–1850; further investigation might reveal why this is so.

Clearly, in order to understand the apparent surge in printing activity in the last quarter of the eighteenth century, we need to delve beneath the broad term 'printer' to discover what exactly the traders so described were doing. Valuable evidence for the day-to-day work of the 'jobbing' printer has been presented by John Feather who cites, for example, the specialist box printer John Varden and the printer Cheney in Banbury in 1790.[18] Three of Cheney's customers – Hawtyn,

16 Hinks 2002, 302–3. Leicester had just one specialist printer (and no specialist binder) and Worcester two.
17 Feather 1985.
18 Feather 1985, 104–5.

Table 15.1 *Printers and booksellers in selected towns, 1750–1850*

Town	Printers	Booksellers	Printers who were also booksellers No. (%)	Printers who were also newspaper proprietors No. (%)
Birmingham	790	457	193 (24)	13 (2)
Bristol	319	303	61 (19)	14 (4)
Hull	99	120	40 (40)	7 (7)
Leeds	246	180	43 (18)	10 (4)
Leicester	255	171	90 (35)	21 (8)
Liverpool	1,182	694	161 (14)	41 (3)
Manchester	551	285	58 (11)	16 (3)
Newcastle	233	271	79 (33)	7 (3)
Plymouth	167	163	76 (46)	11 (7)
Sheffield	306	205	92 (30)	11 (4)

an auctioneer and wholesale brazier; Young, a papermaker; and Bignall, a lawyer, banker and auctioneer – provided more than half of all Cheney's printing orders: auctioneers' bills and catalogues, posters, labels, bills of sale, legal documents and blank forms. Cheney also produced tickets for carriers, stationery for a Fire Office agent, toll tickets, medicine labels, bank stationery, playbills and notices for local societies. While *BBTI*, itself merely an *index* to sources, does not contain information at this level of detail, it is possible to use the records to refine the term 'printer' so far used in this study. A smaller and more detailed sample of printers in selected towns has therefore been undertaken with the aim of exploring the term.

Table 15.1 clearly reveals the extent to which bookselling and printing were often practised by the same people. Whereas in Manchester 11 per cent of printers between 1750 and 1850 also sold books, in Hull the proportion was as high as 40 per cent. Printers who were concerned with newspaper publishing were a much smaller proportion: between 2 and 8 per cent. It is immediately clear that the terms used for our initial statistical survey in the case studies presented above – printer, bookseller and stationer – frequently overlap and that the results are therefore distorted to some degree by an element of double counting. *BBTI*'s records, which often provide multiple trade descriptors and information about an individual's ancillary trades, can allow us to go a little further in adding discrimination to the term 'printer', taking Bristol as an example.[19]

19 Statistics retrieved from *BBTI* in June 2004.

About 60 per cent (194) of the 319 records retrieved for 'printer' in Bristol for the period have no further trade description in *BBTI*: for these individuals and businesses, 'printer' remains a broad and impenetrable term. But a sizeable proportion, the remaining 40 per cent, are recorded as having practised a variety of other trades; in some cases an individual printer practised several.[20] It is immediately apparent that the meaning of the term 'printer' – as far as *BBTI* is concerned – is in fact very broad, covering many kinds of printing and including, for example, type founding and copper engraving.[21] Table 15.2 groups this activity into broad categories.

The majority of the printers for whom ancillary printing trades are known were involved with letterpress trades, including a significant group concerned with newspaper production. The separation of copperplate printers is a useful refinement of the broader term 'printer', and the small group of 'other trades' acts as a reminder of the extent to which traders diversified their activities, often through economic necessity. Yet, while some printing specializations (music printing, account-book printing, pocket-book printing) are evident here, there is no possibility of retrieving from *BBTI* information about the kinds of general and jobbing work that presumably formed the bulk of most printers' daily activity. Nor is there any way of knowing how many of the 60 per cent of Bristol traders excluded from this table – recorded in *BBTI* only as 'printers' – were in fact (but unknown to us) also engaged in some of the various and specialized activities noted for the 40 per cent represented by Table 15.2. Further research could identify the extent to which the results of this study of Bristol printing could meaningfully be extrapolated, although the differences already noted between the book trades of Leicester and Nottingham suggest that application of the Bristol data to other towns would be unsound and that every town would need to be studied individually – a huge research task.

Further research

BBTI data can provide the preliminary data for numerous further and more detailed studies of particular types of towns, classified according to a range of

20 The fact that one printer may be described as also a bookseller, stationer and bookbinder, for example, means that the figures given in Table 15.2 should not be aggregated. It should be noted, of course, that here we are reliant on the detail of the various sources for *BBTI* data (i.e. the ancillary trades recorded may well be incomplete for certain individuals). Thus, as noted above, the data no doubt under-represent multiple trading activities.

21 Trade denominations entered in *BBTI* rely on the many sources as recorded by *BBTI*'s many contributors. The variety of sources used (printed secondary sources, primary sources such as trade directories and newspapers, manuscript archives, parish records and other more serendipitous finds) leads to inevitable inconsistencies. A full list of sources is available on the *BBTI* website.

Table 15.2 *Bristol printers, 1750–1850: other trades recorded*

Book trades	
bookseller	61
stationer	41
bookbinder	27
publisher	16
library proprietor	8
Printing trades specified	
newspaper printer	5
music printer	3
lithographic printer	3
type founder	3
pocket-book printer	2
account-book printer	1
Newspaper trades	
newspaper proprietor	14
newsagent	6
newspaper printer	5
Engraving	
copperplate printer	23
engraver	15
printseller	2
Other trades	
auctioneer	2
wood cutter	1
rag dealer	1

factors, and will enable additional comparisons of the kind described above.[22] Using the data for preliminary mapping and then following up with more detailed research in other sources will inevitably be required, because of *BBTI*'s gaps in coverage and because it is the product of many hands over many years. In particular, the fairly low trader counts in some of these towns at certain periods might well distort historical realities. The picture of the provincial trade emerging from this study should be at least broadly accurate in outline, however, and will tend towards understating the scale of book-trade activity in any of the towns in any 25-year period. While not in itself sufficient to the task of answering all our questions about the development of the book trade in the

22 A brief study of Bath as a spa town, based on *BBTI* data, was included in Hinks 2004.

provinces, it can support and indeed prompt further study of aspects of the provincial trade, such as the family and business networks that developed in particular towns and within regions. Such investigations might usefully inform our understanding not only of the provincial trade itself but also of the relationship between the London and provincial trades.[23]

23 See Stoker 2004 for an excellent study of the relations between the Norwich and London trades between 1695 and 1725.

16

The Scottish book trade

IAIN BEAVAN AND WARREN McDOUGALL

I

Scotland had not been subject to the same form of official control of its printing as England, yet in 1700 its book trade was small – a press at Aberdeen, another at Glasgow, a half-dozen printing establishments in Edinburgh, and some booksellers in the major centres and a few country places – comprising perhaps fewer than ninety workers for a population of a million.[1] There were probably six paper mills.[2] By the early nineteenth century, booksellers and printers had set up business in many of the smaller towns, and Scotland had printing, publishing and paper industries operating on a British scale. This enlarged trade can be viewed against a broader social and economic context. Scotland manifested many of the features of a 'traditional underdeveloped economy' at the end of the seventeenth century, but the following eighty years or so witnessed, particularly after mid-century, a more stabilized political and economic climate and significant commercial and trading developments, such as the tobacco trade and the banking system. Employment opportunities became more varied; personal incomes increased, contributing to a heightened demand for commodities, and many Scots had more comfortable lifestyles.[3] In consequence, readers, including tradesmen and artisans, acquired books printed domestically and imported from London and elsewhere. The Union of 1707 gave Scotland access to English markets at home and in the colonies without payment of customs duties, and classed Scottish vessels as British, bringing privileges and protection.[4] In 1710 came the Copyright Act of 8 Anne; by mid-century, these opportunities

1 Mann 2001, 198 and 2000, 219–23, estimates twenty-nine printing workers, and fifty-four booksellers, stationers and bookbinders; Aldis 1970, 105–24 for trade names and places; Smout 1987, 240 for population.
2 Thomson 1974, 9.
3 Smout 1987, 265–71; Colley 1994, 120; Whatley 1997.
4 Devine 1999, 54.

enabled the Scots to have a sizeable book export trade and a growing reprint industry.[5]

In Edinburgh, rivalries at the beginning of the century were carried on by characters of a type recognizable in later years: the entrepreneur, Agnes Campbell, who successfully exploited her printing monopolies and privileges between 1676 and 1716,[6] and the printing improver, James Watson the younger, operating 1695 to 1722.[7] Two great thrice-weekly Edinburgh newspapers were started, the *Edinburgh Evening Courant* (1718–1886), by the booksellers James McEuen and William Brown and the printer John Mosman, and the *Caledonian Mercury* (1720–1867), which came to be owned by the scholar Thomas Ruddiman and his family for forty-three years.[8] The Jacobite printer and bookseller Robert Freebairn published a series of scholarly books, several bearing the editorial hand of Ruddiman, who with his brother Walter printed from 1721 to 1734 the works of Allan Ramsay, poet, bookseller, founder of a circulating library, and a leader of the early Edinburgh literati.[9] Scottish medical books (written in English, rather than Latin) began to receive international recognition. When the Edinburgh Philosophical Society's *Medical essays and observations* (edited by William Monro and printed by Ruddiman) first appeared in 1733, Charles Mackie, professor of civil history at Edinburgh, sent a parcel containing the edition to Thomas Johnson, the scholarly printer and book pirate at Amsterdam, with copies to be given to Boerhaave and Albinus at Leyden. Johnson gave a reply that looked down the century: 'I am glad that you begin to publish som[e]thing in Scotland that may make your ingenious men known to the rest of the world, I wish that Spirit may continue & find encouragement, & may extend to other arts and Sciences as well as medecine [*sic*].'[10] The *Scots Magazine*, started in 1739, was printed by Sands, Brymer, Murray and Cochran, and became a record of Scottish politics and culture.[11] David Hume appeared in an Edinburgh imprint with the publication by Alexander Kincaid of *Essays, moral and political* (1741). Printing innovation included the use of William Ged's stereotype plates for Edinburgh editions of Sallust in 1739 and 1744 – although the trade's acceptance of this technique lay in the future. In 1743 Hamilton and Balfour initiated Scottish fine printing of the classics with an edition of Virgil, the title page setting a style with its

5 See Bonnell, chap. 37 below.
6 Mann 1998.
7 Evans 1982.
8 Couper 1908, II, 19–62.
9 Duncan 1965; Phillipson 1974, 407–8.
10 Thomas Johnson, letter to Charles Mackie, 22 Dec. 1733, EUL, La.II.91.
11 Brown, Holmes and McDougall 2002.

sparing use of type on white space.[12] This development, with the fine printing by the Foulis Press from this period and the design of type by Alexander Wilson and John Baine, were deliberate efforts to improve 'the art of printing' in Scotland at a time when societies of gentlemen were seeking to improve the linen industry, fisheries, agriculture and manufactures.[13]

II

Cheaper versions of London originals were imported illegally into Scotland by various means: Thomas Johnson of Holland supplied Edinburgh with reprints of Pope and other poets between 1719 and 1733; Irish reprints were brought in through Irvine on the west coast, while clandestine reprinting in Edinburgh included Robert Fleming's editions of James Thomson between 1730 and 1737.[14] By 1743 the Scots were reprinting openly books they considered not protected by the Copyright Act or whose term had expired; these were sold at home and in England while contributing to a significant Scottish export trade from the Clyde ports to America.[15] The piracy prosecution Millar and sixteen other London booksellers brought that year against twenty-four principal booksellers of Edinburgh and Glasgow[16] changed the face of the Scottish book trade. The defence was nationalistic – Scotland would benefit economically, socially and culturally if the monopoly on literary property were limited and Scots gained the right to reprint – and this vision of improvement began to materialize when the Court of Session ruled that copyright prosecutions brought under the 1710 Act were subject to certain limitations.[17] Apart from a brief price war with London,[18] and the unsuccessful London prosecution over Stackhouse's *History of the Bible* in 1773, the trade was left free to reprint and distribute within Scotland; up to the settling of the literary property question in 1774, litigation took place in England.[19] Consequently, a Scottish reprint industry grew rapidly from mid-century. Scottish readers had access to an increasing volume of literary, historical, philosophical, scientific, religious, social and economic publications, as well

12 Gaskell 1952.
13 Phillipson 1974, 436–48.
14 For Edinburgh piracies, see Foxon 1975a, Y138–48, T210, T234, T326; McDougall 1988, 3.
15 McDougall 1988, 2–5, 14–20; McDougall 1990b.
16 McDougall 1988, 2–9; Feather 1994, 81–3.
17 Prosecutions were to be valid under the 1710 Act only if begun within three months of an offence and if the book were registered at Stationers' Hall. Pursuers were entitled only to the small penalties of the Act, not to damages.
18 Over the *Spectator* (Glasgow, 1745); Burnet's *Exposition of the thirty-nine articles of the Church of England* (Edinburgh, 1745); Tillotson's *Works* (Edinburgh and Glasgow, 1748).
19 See Rose, chap. 4 above.

as translations of foreign work.[20] Reprints (including many works of English literature) were also distributed in England.[21] Alexander Donaldson set up a printing shop in Edinburgh to supply the new market and, with his brother John, opened a shop in the Strand in 1763, where he would sell popular titles at nearly 50 per cent below regular London prices.[22]

By 1774, Edinburgh's reprinting was said to give employment to many hundreds of paper-mill workers and a still greater number of booksellers, bookbinders and printers.[23] William Creech, a shareholder with Londoners who supported the idea of monopoly, gave a picture of Scotland in this year, thinking it was lamentable:

> in every little town there is now a printing press. Cobblers have thrown away their awl, weavers have dismissed their shuttle, to commence printers. The country is overrun with a kind of literary packmen, who ramble from town to town selling books. In the little inconsiderable town of Falkirk there is now set up a printing press, and there are several editions of the same book carrying on in Berwick upon Tweed, in Edinburgh, in Glasgow, in Dumfries, and in Aberdeen.[24]

The resolution of the copyright question attracted London interest in Scottish printing projects, such as the Glasgow and Edinburgh editions of the British poets. London booksellers also increasingly employed Edinburgh printers for their own ends, while exercising care at times. In 1802, Creech told Thomas Cadell that 'There are a set of pirates in London' watching for the expiry of every book at Stationers' Hall: 'they give information to the pirates here, and the moment a Book expires they have an edition ready for the Market. To take the odium off themselves they say – some Copies sent us from Scotland – while they are the employers.'[25]

In 1804, the 106 Edinburgh journeymen compositors who took court action for higher wages said their houses were printing more books, mainly reprints, than almost all the other cities of Britain put together, London excepted, and 'even London booksellers have come of late years to employ Scotch printers to print for their market'.[26] The regularity of cheap sea transport, with smacks setting out daily for a three- or four-day journey to London, and the lower

20 *ESTC* for Scottish reprints; McLean 1914 for Urie's; Gaskell 1986 for Foulis's; McDougall 1990a for Hamilton, Balfour and Neill's; and McDougall 1988, 9–14, for the book trade's output.

21 Walters 1974, 292.

22 Zachs 1998, 56–8. *Donaldson* v. *Reid* papers 1769, National Library of Scotland, R.234.b.2., describe eighty-eight titles printed for Donaldson by John Reid 1760–5.

23 Walters 1974, 305.

24 Walters 1974, 308.

25 Creech to Thomas Cadell, 15 Apr. 1802, National Archives of Scotland, R.234.b.2.

26 Compositors against master printers of Edinburgh, 1804–5, no. 2, 2, Signet Library, Session Papers 225/19 – for which see Howe 1947, 248–50.

printing costs and wages in Edinburgh made such transactions practical. The city was said to be traditionally a penny below London for the cost of setting 1,000 letters, but by the beginning of the nineteenth century the compositors were paid 3½*d.* per 1,000 for ordinary work, compared with the London scale of 5¼*d.* The Court of Session increased this to 41/2*d.* in 1805 (a scale that lasted until 1862), but the gap with London widened again in 1810. The 1805 increase raised the weekly wages of the Edinburgh compositors by 5*s.*, to an average of around £1 3*s.* 5*d.*[27]

Cheaper reprints of books currently in copyright were in demand in the second half of the eighteenth century. Irish reprints of such titles, illegal if imported, at first came through the western Scottish ports if the duty were paid, although from the 1760s a number of stoppages by Customs hindered this traffic. Reprints were smuggled instead: either bluffed through Customs, unloaded to a lighter before landfall, or taken straight to a quiet spot and put into a carrier's wagon for distribution to booksellers around the country. These books had false London titles or were without title pages, which were printed in Scotland bearing the names of the London or, occasionally, the Edinburgh literary proprietor. It was an extensive trade.[28] Readers in Scotland and England were also served with illegal Edinburgh reprints in the latter end of the century, which caused the London proprietors to mount a series of prosecutions at the Court of Session, not on principle this time, but for particular cases, such as the edition of Lord Chesterfield's *Letters* (1775), published by the printer Colin Macfarquhar, the bookseller Charles Elliot and the papermaker George Douglas. This four-volume duodecimo sold for 10*s.* in boards, 12*s.* bound in calf, as opposed to James Dodsley's legitimate four-volume octavo at £1 1*s.* in boards or £1 4*s.* in calf; 1,500 copies were printed, most of which were sent to England.[29]

III

The publication of Scottish authors from the 1750s saw the advent of copy money and a tension between the nationalistic imprint and the more pragmatic London one. Below the title of David Hume's *The history of Great Britain*, vol. I (1754), was simply *Edinburgh: printed for Hamilton, Balfour, and Neill.* Alexander

27 Howe 1947, 248–50; Compositors against master printers of Edinburgh, no. 4; Gillespie 1953, 21–4. The average wage was around 14*s.* 6*d.* in 1773–9, 19*s.* 8*d.* in 1791 and 18*s.* 5*d.* in 1802.

28 McDougall 1997, 151–72.

29 Gillick 1979, 9–11; Elliot ledgers, John Murray Archives, NLS, for sales of Chesterfield – e.g. L1/201 for piracy, L1/204 for legitimate; McDougall 1997, 172–9 for this and other piracy prosecutions.

Kincaid with his partners Alexander Donaldson (1751–8) and John Bell (1758–71) also published authors of the Scottish Enlightenment – David Hume, Lord Kames, Adam Smith, Alexander Gerard, Thomas Reid and Adam Ferguson – but did so in collaboration with the London Scots Andrew Millar and William Strahan, generally above London/Edinburgh imprints carrying all their names, although at times Edinburgh was put first as the place of printing. This style of imprint prevailed in the decades after Hamilton, who had not shared profits with a Londoner and was unable to penetrate the London market with Hume's *History*; yet, his startling offer to Hume of £1,200 for the proposed three volumes (in actuality he paid £400 for the one) introduced the notion that Scottish authors could obtain huge rewards from the booksellers. After Millar died, several Edinburgh booksellers took shares with Londoners in large ventures. In 1769, John Balfour, Strahan and Cadell paid William Robertson £4,000 for the copyright of *Charles V*.[30] Creech participated with Strahan and Cadell and their successors in publishing James Beattie, Kames, Ferguson, Robert Burns and Hugh Blair, and Balfour joined this consortium in publishing John Gregory and Sir John Dalrymple. There was rivalry in the business: John Bell of Edinburgh and George Robinson of London combined to pay £300 to Thomas Reid for *Essays on the intellectual powers of man* (1785), beating a Cadell offer by £100.[31] In the 1780s, Charles Elliot took payments by an indigenous Edinburgh bookseller to a new level when he defeated London bidders and paid Dr William Cullen £1,200 for the copyright of the fourth edition of *First lines of the practice of physic*, the most copy money yet paid in Britain for an octavo. He was in the pro-Scottish mould of Gavin Hamilton; but while he retained his copyrights for each publication, he had an agent or collaborator in London – primarily Cadell, Robinson or John Murray – who bought copies at a special rate and was given due prominence in the Edinburgh imprint. The greatest payment to a Scottish author for an edition in the eighteenth century appears to have been made to James Bruce of Kinnaird. He negotiated a fee of £6,666 from George Robinson for *Travels to discover the source of the Nile* (1790), paying James Sibbald and James Ruthven of Edinburgh to print 2,000 copies in five volumes quarto and buying the paper from the Auchendinny mill near Edinburgh.[32] The book was published in London with the imprint *Edinburgh: printed by J. Ruthven, for G.G.J. and J. Robinson, London*; materially it is a British book.

30 Cochrane 1964, 84–5.
31 Robinson to John Bell, 6 Sep. 1784, NLS, Acc. 10662/9.
32 'James Sibbald', see *ODNB*.

Charles Elliot's business in Edinburgh illustrates the extent of the book trade's distribution networks by the 1770s and 1780s. Elliot corresponded in Scotland with ninety booksellers at twenty-seven locations; in the English provinces, with fifty-nine booksellers and two printers in twenty-nine places;[33] and no fewer than eighty in London, including all the major firms established at the time in the metropolis. In Ireland, he had three booksellers in Belfast, ten in Dublin and one in Newry. Abroad, Elliot had a bookselling agent at Gothenburg, Sweden; booksellers in Holland at Rotterdam, The Hague and Leyden; in Germany at Göttingen, Berlin and Leipzig; in France at Lyons, Versailles and Paris; in the West Indies book-buying correspondents in Grenada and Jamaica; and in America agents or booksellers in New York, Philadelphia, Charleston, SC, Boston, and in Virginia at Petersburg and Fredericksburg.[34] Elliot employed these networks, as well as his correspondence with individuals, for one of the monuments of the Enlightenment: the *Encyclopaedia Britannica*. In 1785, Elliot paid £3,000 to buy up the remaining copies of the ten-volume second edition from the Edinburgh publishers (the printer Colin Macfarquhar, the engraver Andrew Bell and the papermaker John Hutton) and sold the edition in collaboration with George Robinson of London, who advised on the trade and retail prices. Elliot's enthusiasm about selling the book – 'take care of my Child' he told Robinson – helped to ensure the edition was an international success, and when the third edition began to appear in parts in 1788, he was a major buyer, this time selling it in London through his partnership with Thomas Kay.[35]

The middle decades of the eighteenth century witnessed the steady growth of the trade beyond Edinburgh. The monopoly of printing in Aberdeen – hitherto held by a series of 'printers to the town and university' – came to an end in 1752 when Francis Douglas (initially with William Murray) set up business. Their output and, a little later, that of John Boyle stand in contrast to that of the Chalmers family, who were very much civic printers and owners of the highly lucrative *Aberdeen Journal*. While the Chalmers dynasty continued its cautious way, Douglas (and Murray) appealed to the educated groups of the north-east with editions that included Addison's *Cato* (1754, 1757) and

33 Alnwick, Berwick, Burlington (Bridlington), Cambridge, Carlisle, Birmingham, Chester, Durham, Eton, Gainsborough, Halifax, Hull, Lancaster, Leeds, Liverpool, Manchester, Newcastle, North Shields, Nottingham, Oxford, Ripon, Sheffield, Southampton, Stockton, Sunderland, Warrington, Whitby, Whitehaven, York.

34 McDougall, index to entries in Elliot papers (in preparation); McDougall 2002 for Elliot's European and American trade; McDougall 2004 for the Philadelphian.

35 Elliot papers, John Murray Archives, NLS, letters to Robinson 1785–6; purchase price, letter of 7 Jan. 1786; quotation, letter of 5 Mar. 1785.

Alexander Gordon's *History of Peter the Great* (1755). John Boyle, printer, bookseller and paper manufacturer, undertook *A collection of the English poets* in twenty volumes in 1776, though not without first seeking subscriptions.[36]

In Perth, the Morison family, already well established as booksellers, increased their options, and financial risk, by becoming printers in 1774. James Morison was sufficiently ambitious to have gained for himself the role of printer to the University of St Andrews where, under the editorship of John Hunter, professor of humanity, a number of works by the Latin authors emanated from his press. Yet, the testament to the printing skills of Robert Morison (brother to James), the *Encyclopaedia Perthensis* (1796–1806), stands also as partial witness to the firm's lapse of commercial judgement in assessing its likely success in the face of competition, in spite of having London agents including Vernor and Hood. The production of the *Encyclopaedia*, combined with other demanding publication ventures, led the Morisons towards severe financial difficulties.[37]

The appointment in 1743 of Robert (and Andrew) Foulis as printers to Glasgow University enabled the professoriate to go some way towards their wishes to support the changing curriculum with a wider range of texts and more reliable editions. The careers of the Foulis brothers as university printers demonstrate a driving concern to provide accurate and legible texts, supported by well-cast and designed founts (from the Glasgow foundry of Alexander Wilson, himself later appointed a professor of astronomy) and a preoccupation with *mise en page*. The brothers' folio two-volume editions of Homer's *Iliad* (1756) and *Odyssey* (1757) – the Greek fount by Wilson – were recognized at the time as unsurpassed, and won Silver Medals from the Edinburgh Society, as did their Callimachus (1755), Horace (1756), Virgil (1758) and Homer, *Minor poems* (1758). Their only rival for a medal was Hamilton, Balfour and Neill of Edinburgh, who won in 1757 with an edition of Terence produced by the young printer William Smellie.[38] Robert Foulis's aspirations to establish an Academy of the Fine Arts came to fruition in 1754 after the university granted permission for its establishment on its premises. Yet, the Academy appears to have been a drain on resources, and on the founder's time, to the extent that one commentator (with some exaggeration) commented that 'During the rage of this fancy, they forgot their former business, and neglected an art which, from their editions of Homer and Milton, might have made them immortal.'[39]

36 Beavan 1987; also see Bonnell, chap. 37, below.
37 Carnie 1960, 20–1.
38 Hillyard 1984, 295–319; Carnie 1987, 301–2.
39 Topham 1776, 180–1.

Nearest to the Foulis brothers in quality of printing at Glasgow was Robert Urie, whose finest works were a Greek New Testament and an edition of Buchanan's *Psalms* (both 1750), and who also printed many translations from the French and reprinted literary works.[40]

In the latter part of the century, a number of prominent bookselling partnerships were operating in Glasgow, including Dunlop and Wilson, while at Greenock the agents handling American, Irish and English book shipments were Gordon and Millar.[41] In 1792 James Duncan of Glasgow brought his son Andrew into a bookselling partnership that appears to have dealt extensively in America, supplying their own books or their shares of others' editions, as well as a considerable number of bibles, testaments and other King's Printer productions. The Duncans were Glasgow University Printers in 1815, when grandsons John M. and James joined the business; they gave up the export trade through lack of profit in 1819, and bookselling in 1820 to carry on a printing concern that employed sixty hands.[42]

IV

Following the establishment of the *Scots Magazine*, other periodicals appeared in Edinburgh which reflected or encouraged a specific Scottish viewpoint.[43] Hamilton and Balfour's *Edinburgh Review* of 1755–6 (contributors to which included William Robertson, Hugh Blair and Adam Smith) had in its outlook towards literature and in its frankness the seeds of an Edinburgh style of reviewing that was carried further by the aggressively critical *Edinburgh Magazine and Review* (1773–6, edited by Gilbert Stuart and William Smellie, co-owners with the booksellers William Creech and Charles Elliot) and that looked towards the *Edinburgh Review* of 1802.[44] James Sibbald's monthly *Edinburgh Magazine, or Literary Miscellany* (1785–1804) gave in 1786 the first and highly favourable review of the poetry of Robert Burns.[45]

The magazines of the nineteenth century devoted much space to politically informed discussions.[46] The principles and opinions of the Whig *Edinburgh Review* – first published, quarterly, in 1802 by Archibald Constable, and edited

40 Gillespie 1990, 59–60.
41 Elliot papers, John Murray Archives, for letters to these firms and others in the west of Scotland.
42 Duncan and Co. Correspondence with Mathew Carey, Philadelphia, 1792–1820, Historical Society of Pennsylvania, and American Antiquarian Society.
43 See Maidment, chap. 25 below.
44 Brown, Holmes and McDougall 2002; Zachs 1998, 203–5.
45 'James Sibbald', see *ODNB*.
46 See Maidment, chap. 25 below.

soon after its inception by Francis Jeffrey – diverged from those of John Murray's rather stolid Tory *Quarterly Review*, copies of which came north of the border through Blackwood's agency. In May 1817, William Blackwood, driven by a variety of motives, not least the wish to provide a more effective vehicle for younger Tory views, began his *Blackwood's Edinburgh Magazine* and, with editorial input and contributions from John Gibson Lockhart, James Hogg and John Wilson, supplied the contemporary literary and political scene with an unprecedentedly lively, satirical and biting publication. Murray at first was happy to back it, and bought a share in the title for £1,000, but subsequently became uncomfortable with the level of personalized attacks, and backed out.[47] The *Scotsman* newspaper, no ally of *Blackwood's*, appeared for the first time in January 1817, rapidly establishing for itself a reputation for 'independence with intelligence, and moderation with zeal' and becoming 'immeasurably the best newspaper that exists . . . in Scotland', with the avowed aim of sweeping away the (often self-imposed) restrictions on what was reported. Cockburn commented, 'the newspaper press of Edinburgh, though not as much fettered as in St Petersburgh (as it has been said to have been) was at least in as fettered a condition as any press that is legally free could be'.[48]

By the 1830s, issues relating to 'taxes on knowledge', set against increasing demands for a reformed Parliament and for greater democratization, contributed to the defiant production of a large number of unstamped periodicals throughout Britain, including Scotland. In Aberdeen, for example, the *Aberdeen Pirate* took to the often adopted course of frequently changing its title and publication date to avoid the attentions of the Stamp Office, evolving finally into the *Aberdeen Shaver*. Other, more explicitly radical titles also appeared, and survived into the 1840s: in Glasgow, the unstamped *Loyal Reformers' Gazette* 'started as the organ of Glasgow radicalism' in 1831, witnessed the Reform Act and continued to 1841.[49]

V

Chapbooks continued to be sold in parts of Scotland through much of the nineteenth century. Hawkers and chapmen travelled the country areas, regularly calling in at farm towns, fairs and markets. Street sellers took up station at the most populous or appropriate points, to maximize their sales of chapbooks, song sheets, and crime, execution or confession broadsides. Tolerance towards

47 Smiles 1891, I, 476–80.
48 Cockburn 1856, 308.
49 Wiener 1969, 190–1; Harrison, Woolven and Duncan 1977, 298.

speech criers diminished as the nineteenth century progressed, and their categorization with beggars and vagrants became codified as they became subject to social control. Thus the day patrol of the Edinburgh Police Establishment were instructed, in 1837, to 'apprehend all Vagrants and common Beggars . . . and all Ballad-singers or others, causing a crowd of idle people to collect on the streets'.[50]

The production of such material was concentrated through the central belt – Glasgow, Edinburgh from mid-century onwards, and, a little later, Airdrie, Paisley, Falkirk and Stirling – which offered (relatively) good communications to other parts of the country, thus facilitating widespread distribution.[51] Chapbook consumption north of the border included titles printed in England. The Angus family of Newcastle upon Tyne was responsible for a large number of chapbooks, many of which had Scottish references (for example, *A collection of new songs. 1 Kitty o' the Clyde. 2 Donald of Dundee . . .*), and were widely available in that country. Conversely, Scottish chapbooks sold in northern England. 'Hawkie' (William Cameron) records his moving through the Scottish borders and on into Northumberland (Morpeth, Blyth, North Shields), but not without first calling at Wooler Fair, where standards (to Hawkie) were questionable. He commented damningly, 'Little to the credit of the clergy and magistrates of that place, the most infamous and abominable songs that can be picked from the works of the lowest poets that ever wrote, are the articles which sell in Wooler.'[52]

VI

In his description of Paternoster Row at the end of eighteenth and beginning of the nineteenth centuries, Dr Thomas Rees (brother of Owen Rees) identified the Rivingtons, Robert Baldwin and the Robinsons as 'book-merchants, who were chiefly wholesale dealers and carried on an extensive and important trade with country booksellers: they were also publishers upon a large scale'.[53] The function of wholesaler also grew in importance in Edinburgh, as London publishers' attempts to maximize their sales in Scotland aided the consolidation of such a role.[54]

50 Edinburgh Police Department 1839, 3.
51 McNaughton 1990, 165; Morris 1997, 108–9; Harvey 1903.
52 Cameron 1888, 41.
53 Britton 1849–50, pt 1, 253–4, 258–64.
54 Beavan 2000, 70.

Bell and Bradfute, formed in November 1788 (though John Bell himself had worked in the Edinburgh trade since 1754), became the largest wholesale house in the late eighteenth century, though throughout they retained a role as publishers, and supplied the London trade with their own titles.[55] They also bought much stock – at the request of Scottish provincial booksellers, but presumably also on occasion for their own resources – from the regularly held trade sales arranged by Scottish and English publishers. Their knowledge of the Scottish market, and London publishers' dependence on them, is ably demonstrated by George Kearsley's letter to the firm, enclosing copies of the prospectus for the *British Magazine*, and asking for them to be circulated to best advantage. The letter also included wording for a number of advertisements to be inserted by Bell and Bradfute in the 'four best Edinburgh papers', and asked the Edinburgh firm to recommend a correspondent who could provide commercial and agricultural reports on Edinburgh and its surrounding area.[56]

Copyrights were routinely purchased outright, though frequently publishers agreed to forms of profit-sharing arrangements with their authors. However, essentially new departures included having to adjust to publication and marketing strategies effectively built around the lease of a copyright for a particular edition or impression, and the participation of the author, whose interests were advanced through his own agent. Any publisher who put into print the writings of Sir Walter Scott knew that he was dealing with an exceptional individual – and a publishing phenomenon – and had to accept that the author appreciated the commercial value and potential of his copyrights in ways that others at that time did not.[57] The influence of the author was henceforth established in unprecedented ways.[58] Yet, the consequences of financial incautiousness by the agents of Scott's primary publishers were to send them into insolvency and bankruptcy. In 1826, Archibald Constable tried (ultimately in vain) to stave off the financial ruin of himself, the printers, James Ballantyne and Co., and Walter Scott himself, who, as partner in the firm, was also legally involved. This was not through any waning popularity on the part of Scott, but as a direct result of a complex series of ultimately unsustainable mutual credit arrangements between Constable, the printers, and the publisher's London agent, Hurst Robinson, whose

55 For example, fifty copies of *Collectanea graeca majora*, which was one of the editions of Andrew Dalzel's often republished school-book, and twenty copies of an edition of one of Thomas Reid's *Essays* (probably *Essays on the powers of the human mind*, 1808) to Rivingtons in autumn 1809. Bell and Bradfute papers, Edinburgh City Archives, SL138/4/6.

56 George Kearsley letter, 10 Jan. 1800. Bell and Bradfute papers, NLS, Acc. 10662/17.

57 Garside 1983. See also Hewitt 1995, 357–64. The authors are also grateful for many discussions with Prof. David Hewitt.

58 See Griffin, chap. 5, above.

speculations led to their downfall, followed by the collapse of the supposedly mutually supportive financial arrangements they had established.[59]

Constable's own ex-partner, and son-in-law, Robert Cadell, extricated himself from the financial morass, and exploited the situation by buying up Scott's copyrights and initiating his own forty-eight-volume collected edition of Scott's work (with the author's active editorial participation).[60] Nevertheless, along with his reputation and the Scott copyrights, Constable lost ownership of the *Edinburgh Review* to Longmans (who had always retained a financial interest in the title) and the *Encyclopaedia Britannica* to the relative newcomer, Adam Black.[61]

Publishing, though centred in Edinburgh, was not confined to that city. The firms of Collins and Blackie and Son, both based in Glasgow, published a considerable quantity of religious and expository material. William Collins, teacher and evangelist, developed a close friendship with Dr Thomas Chalmers (a founder of the Free Church of Scotland in 1843), and became for many years the theologian's publishers. From the 1820s, the firm's output expanded to include religious series, and drew in the Edinburgh wholesalers, Oliver and Boyd. In some contrast, though no less successfully, John Blackie remained, with his various partners, heavily committed to publishing in numbers, particularly popular religious titles, for at least a half-century after the foundation of his business.[62] Both firms continued into the twentieth century.[63]

In late 1819, John Murray transferred the agency for his publications in Scotland to Oliver and Boyd. Founded in the first years of the nineteenth century, Oliver and Boyd had, during the 1820s, flirted with the notion of becoming literary publishers (firms like Blackwood were more prepared to take on such risks), but preferred to rely on more secure investments in educational texts, along with many chapbooks kept constantly in print, the promotion of which was partially effected by commercial travellers, at least from 1811. By the late 1820s, other Scottish publishers were pursuing the same strategy.[64] By the 1830s, the firm had become the largest wholesale house in Scotland, its agency having included the publications of the Society for the Propagation of Christian Knowledge, and Charles Knight and the Society for the Diffusion of Useful Knowledge.[65] Oliver and Boyd's role as agent for the SDUK placed them as competitors with W. and R. Chambers, within a very

59 J. A. Sutherland 1987; Millgate 1987; Bell 1998, 123.
60 Millgate 1987.
61 Newth 1957, 2.
62 See Harris, chap. 20 below.
63 Blackie 1959; Keir 1952.
64 Bell 1998, 121–2.
65 See Mandlebrote, chap. 32 below.

similar market; when the Society's *Penny Magazine* and *Chambers's Edinburgh Journal* appeared in 1832, both publications were apparently resisted as 'cheap trash' by the 'regular booksellers' who, to their cost, found that the demand for such material was quickly met by 'a shoal of new rivals'.[66]

VII

Publishers in both London and Edinburgh were frequently competing in a single British market, and Oliver and Boyd's roles as wholesalers and publishers in their own right exemplify some features of the interdependence and the rivalries of the trade in Scotland and England. A tension is evident in the fact that Oliver and Boyd had to contact Murray over the appearance, in Edinburgh, of copies of Thomas Hope's *Anastasius*, before they (as Scottish agents) had received any.[67] On occasion, the two firms were in competition. Oliver and Boyd's own newly commissioned series, the Edinburgh Cabinet Library, was extensively advertised throughout Britain, and the publishers used their own wholesale agents in London (Simpkin, Marshall) to maximize distribution. However, John Murray (probably justifiably) became concerned that Oliver and Boyd were less than assiduous in promoting his series, the Family Library, because it was a close market competitor.[68]

Other commercial developments tested the relationship between the English and Scottish book trades. By the mid-1830s, the Scottish trade was complaining about the intense competition that had led to the frequent undercutting of the full retail prices. Yet the controversy was not remotely new. The Edinburgh Booksellers' Society had confronted the problem in 1796 and found one of their number, George Mudie, guilty of a practice 'highly detrimental to the interest of the fair trader'.[69] Mudie gave in, but the problem nevertheless slowly grew. The Edinburgh trade recognized that a unified approach was necessary, and that the active support of London publishers and wholesalers was needed to control underselling (largely by refusing stock to transgressors). Yet, the booksellers could not even find agreement amongst their own number. By the 1850s, the debate was no longer primarily conducted amongst members of the trade, but had widened to include the views and interests of authors and readers. The principles of free trade were about to envelop the British book trade.[70]

66 'Johnstone's *Edinburgh Magazine*: the cheap and dear periodicals', *Tait's Edinburgh Magazine*, 4 (1834), 491.
67 Isaac 2005, 133–4.
68 Beavan 2000, 72.
69 Edinburgh Booksellers' Society, minutes of meeting, 19 Dec. 1796, NLS Dep.303/23; Sher 1998, 68–79.
70 Beavan 2001; Barnes 1964.

17
The Irish trade

CHARLES BENSON

The late start of printing in Ireland, in 1551, is an indication of the relative isolation and backwardness of its economy. Printing was introduced to the country as an instrument of government policy to promote its secular aim of securing power and religious objective of promoting the reformed religion. The complete dominance of English rule did not occur until the early seventeenth century, however, and the reformed religion of the state church never received acceptance from the majority of the population. The development of printing was slow. With the exception of a few items printed in Kilkenny and Waterford during the 1640s and 1650s[1] and a modest trickle of works printed in Cork from 1644[2] on, printing was confined to Dublin. Moreover, before 1680 there was never more than one printer in business in Dublin at any one time.[3]

The potential growth of the book trade was hampered by the highly exclusive nature of the powers granted in the patents of the successive King's Printers. The terms of the last of the patents granted to John Frankton in 1609 were extremely wide-ranging, giving him complete authority over the printing, binding and bookselling of everything and forbidding others to engage in any aspect of the trade without his licence.[4] Significant penalties were laid down for any infringement. The successive patents issued in the seventeenth century followed the same terms. The last of these, granted on 26 June 1693, was in force until 1727. It was not until the second of George Grierson's patents was enrolled on 18 June 1730 that printers in Ireland became at last entitled to print everything except the Bible, service books and state publications. Enforcement was another matter, however, and in

1 Dix 1916.
2 Dix 1912.
3 Pollard 1989, 2; Welch 2002.
4 Pollard 1980.

practical terms the trade in Dublin had liberated itself from the oppressive terms of the patents by the early 1680s.

A real sign of the development of the trade came with the establishment of the Guild of St Luke in Dublin in 1670. This was a tripartite association with separate faculties of cutlers, painter-stainers and stationers. The charter of the guild gave a monopoly of the book trade in Dublin to the stationer-citizens, which created an immediate conflict of powers with those held under the King's Printer's patent.[5] Bookselling increased as an activity, to judge by the growth in membership of the stationers' faculty from four in November 1670 to twenty-seven in 1680. Of the twenty-seven members of the guild in 1680, at least eight were British immigrants.[6]

The market in Ireland had singular features. The government of the country was English-speaking and Anglican in religion; the majority of the inhabitants were Irish-speaking and Roman Catholic in religion – and there was a sizeable minority of Presbyterians of Scottish origin in Ulster. The Treaty of Limerick (1691), which ended the Jacobite war in Ireland, finally assured English rule with Anglicanism as the state's official religion. It was followed within a few years by a series of laws intended to restrict severely the civil liberties of Roman Catholics. For the book trade, the most material legislation was *An Act to Restrain Foreign Education* (7 William III c. 4 IR) which forbade Catholics to send their children to be educated 'into any parts beyond the seas, out of this Majesty's obedience' and denying Catholics the right to 'publickly teach school, or instruct youth in learning'. On the other hand, the Act enjoined strict observance of an Act of Henry VIII called *An Act for the English Order, Habit and Language* (28 Henry VIII c. 15 IR), which required every incumbent of each parish to keep a school for pupils to learn English. Roman Catholic education was largely driven underground for most of the succeeding century.

As the language of administration, and, increasingly, of commerce, English made considerable gains as the daily language during the eighteenth century. Towards the end of the eighteenth century and in the beginning of the nineteenth century, Whitley Stokes, a Fellow of Trinity College, Dublin, and an enthusiastic promoter of evangelization through Irish, made estimates of the state of that language. Writing in 1799, he was of the view that 'for the diffusion of religious knowledge it is necessary, that it should be conveyed in the language the people understand. I have reason to believe, from various inquiries, that at least eight hundred thousand of our countrymen speak Irish only, and that there

5 Pollard 1980.
6 Pollard 2000, *passim*.

are at least twice as many more who speak it in preference.'[7] This amounted to about half of the population. Returning to the topic in 1806, he found that the Irish language was dominant in four counties in Leinster, in only two in Ulster, in most of Munster outside the large towns, and generally in Connaught, where 'even the gentlemen often find it convenient to acquire the language, in order to be able to deal with the peasantry without an interpreter'.[8] One of his correspondents, Mr Graham, curate of Kilrush, county Clare, noted that young people 'are universally learning to read English'.[9] As late as the census of 1851 almost 1.5 million people spoke Irish (315,482 of them monoglots) – almost one-quarter of the population.[10] However, a contemporary writer noticed that a mistrust of the government's motives of inquiry in the census led many bilingual speakers to deny their knowledge of Irish.[11]

Despite the continuing importance of Irish, the number of items printed in the language before the nineteenth century is negligible, and the majority of these were printed in continental Europe.[12] In the book trade in Ireland, it was the book in English that dominated. At the start of the 1680s, after twenty years of peace, trade was expanding. Figures from the overseas port book of Chester reveal that exports of books to Ireland amount to about five and a half tons in 1681.[13] The bulk of these were being shipped to Dublin with only three hundredweight being put on a boat to Carrickfergus. The majority of the importers on a larger scale can be readily identified in the Dublin book trade, among them Patrick Campbell, Eliphal Dobson and John Worth, each of whom imported more than half a ton of stock. Operating on a smaller scale was Samuel Helsham, who is the only figure of whose business any detail remains. M. Pollard has analysed the fragments of his shop day book for the period 2 March to mid-May 1685[14] and suggests that nearly '75 percent of the books he sold would be printed in England, 20 percent only in Ireland and 5 percent on the continent'.[15] His main stock-in-trade at the time was sermons and devotional works, school and university textbooks and pamphlets of ephemeral interest. In the fifteen days of recorded business, he dealt in sixty-one different titles.

7 Stokes 1799, 45.
8 Stokes 1806, 2.
9 Stokes 1806, 8.
10 *The Census of Ireland for the year 1851* (UK *Parl. Papers*, 1856, xxxi, 633), 777.
11 MacAdam 1858, 172.
12 This is not to deny the continued existence of an active scribal tradition, and a vigorous composition of poetry; see, for example, Tuama 1981; Welch 2002.
13 Hunter 1988.
14 Pollard 1989, 42–61.
15 Pollard 1989, 55.

Figures for imports to Ireland in the late 1690s show that Dublin was the dominant destination, receiving more books than the rest of the country in the proportion of more than three to one – the imports to Dublin for the three years 1698–1700 being 194.5, 284 and 216 hundredweight against 56.5, 69 and 63 hundredweight for the rest of the country.[16] There is a snapshot of the trade in Dublin in 1698 in the splenetic memoir *The Dublin scuffle*, by John Dunton. Dunton came to Dublin in April 1698 with a stock of books of 'near ten tun' weight to dispose of at auction. Four auctions and a remainder sale were held.[17] Auctions appear to have been a comparatively recent feature in the Irish book trade, the earliest recorded being in 1693.[18]

By the turn of the eighteenth century, the Irish use of English books had begun to change with a shift towards reprinting more than retailing imported works. Nonetheless, the proportion of British exports to Ireland was high. Giles Barber has shown that in the period 1701–80 Ireland was second only to continental North America in terms of books exported from London.[19] M. Pollard has demonstrated that the level of imports of unbound books oscillated between 150 and 300 hundredweight per annum prior to 1775, and then – despite sudden troughs – moved gradually upwards in the 1780s. With the exception of the disastrous year of 1798, imports were above 400 hundredweight for the rest of the century and then enjoyed accelerated growth in the nineteenth century.[20]

The British Copyright Act of 1710 (8 Anne c. 21), which came into force on 10 April 1710, never had any counterpart in Irish legislation. All through the eighteenth century it remained entirely legitimate for an Irish bookseller to have a British work reprinted in Ireland.[21] A legal offence was committed only by someone importing a reprint into Great Britain. Between 1710 and 1739, the prohibition on importation was implicit in the terms of the protection of literary property granted under the Copyright Act, and was made explicit in the Importation Act of 1739 (12 George II c. 36).

During the course of the century, there were several attacks by the British trade on the Irish reprint trade. These ostensibly attacked the illegal importation into Britain but were, in fact, criticizing the lack of equivalent legislation in Ireland. Evidence was given to a committee of the House of Commons in

16 Pollard 1989, 41.
17 Dunton 1699, 5 and *passim*.
18 *A catalogue of books in several faculties . . . to be sold by way of auction on 23 November 1693, by William Norman* (Dublin, 1693).
19 Barber 1976.
20 Pollard 1989, 154–5.
21 See Rose, chap. 4 above.

1735 of the availability of Dublin reprints in London and in York which were underselling the authorized editions, and of the arrival in Preston of a bale of books from Dublin.[22] The number of Irish books legitimately sent to London was small; figures for the period 1701 to 1780 show that bound books to a value of £6,587 and unbound books to a value of £2,940 were shipped to the British capital.[23] There is evidence of some smuggling – generally from Dublin, but also from Belfast – into places ranging from Beaumaris in Wales to Irvine in Ayrshire, but in an examination of official records for fourteen selected years M. Pollard found only six definite instances of seizure of smuggled books, and most of those of insignificant quantity.[24]

The absence of any legislative framework or rules from the Guild of St Luke led to the development in Dublin of a customary right in literary property. The practices are elaborated in a newspaper and pamphlet dispute between George Faulkner and George and Alexander Ewing in 1758 over the publication of Jonathan Swift's *The history of the last session of Parliament*. In a riposte to an attack from Faulkner, the Ewings refer to 'a known rule among booksellers here, that, whoever is first in possession of the manuscript of any work, or the London edition; and actually puts it to press or publishes his intention of so doing, has the undoubted right of publication'.[25] Later on in the quarrel, they refer to the rules as being well established when the first Dublin edition of *Gulliver's travels* was produced in 1727.[26] While there were some cases of breach of custom, these were sufficiently infrequent for it to be clear that the system worked well enough for London and Dublin booksellers to be able to collaborate on a regular basis for the exchange of copy.[27] Samuel Richardson was able to sell the Dublin reprint rights of *Clarissa Harlowe* to George Faulkner in 1747 for seventy guineas.[28] Robert Dodsley wrote to Faulkner in October 1757, 'I transmitted to you an Ode on terror & pity [*Melpomene*] which I hope you recd. I have not put my name to it here, but if you think it is worth reprinting, you may prefix or omit it as you please.'[29]

Some of the commercial links between Irish and British booksellers are obvious from imprints. A. and J. Churchill appear variously as London outlets for three books printed in Dublin between 1682 and 1712. J. Churchill's

22 *Journal of the House of Commons* [of England], xxii, 411–12.
23 Barber 1976.
24 Pollard 1989, 77–81.
25 *Dublin Gazette*, 28 Mar. 1758.
26 Ewing 1758, 2.
27 Phillips 1998, 127–47.
28 Richardson 1762, VII, 429.
29 Dodsley 1988, 300.

enthusiasm for the productions of the Irish trade was limited, however. He was agent for Jeremy Pepyat, who published George Berkeley's *A treatise concerning the principles of human knowledge* in 1710, and failed to promote it in London. Writing on 20 October 1710, Berkeley remarked that Pepyat suspected the lack of enthusiasm in Churchill 'to be his apprehending that the encouragement of a printing trade in this kingdom would interfere with his intent; since there are yearly exported great sums of money to him and other booksellers in London for books, which if that trade were encouraged might be printed much cheaper in Dublin because there is not here so great an impost on paper'.[30] Later in the century, John Murray established trading connections with a dozen booksellers in Dublin and a couple in Belfast. He enjoyed convivial occasions on his visits to Dublin in the 1770s.[31] Despite the well-known outburst of Samuel Richardson against the Irish over the publication of *Sir Charles Grandison*, the true pattern of English attitudes to the Dublin trade is that of attention paid to an important export market.

A selection of advertisements from George Faulkner's *Dublin Journal* for the years 1758 to 1760 gives a sense of the variety of connection between the Irish and British trades. A joint advertisement on 8 April 1758 by G. Faulkner, Abraham Bradley and William Watson announced the importation of T. Leland, *The history of the life and reign of Philip King of Macedon*. Irish subscribers to the edition could obtain their copies by sending their receipts and second payments to A. Bradley. On 29 April 1758, James Rudd advertised a variety of architectural books published by R. Sayer in London, while G. Faulkner advertised the importation of Baskerville's edition of Virgil on 12 September. There were stock lists of publications of George Keith and J. Richardson on 27 May and 4 July 1758, both from London. T. Wilkes, *A general view of the stage*, advertised on 14 April 1759, was a joint publication between J. Coote of London and W. Whitestone in Dublin. Subscriptions for a quarto volume of original pieces by Samuel Derrick, to be printed in London by R. Dodsley, were touted for on 21 June 1760 by G. Faulkner and T. Wilkinson.

There was also some traffic in newspapers and periodicals. The Corporation of Youghal ordered on 16 January 1695 that the mayor should arrange for the 'public news' to be sent to the town by every post.[32] Charles Delafaye, employed in the Secretary of State's office and involved in the distribution of newspapers under franks at the start of the eighteenth century, had about thirty-two Irish customers mainly living around Dublin and Cork, but

30 BL Add. MSS 47026, fols. 44–5; Berkeley 1948–57, VIII, 42.
31 Zachs 1998, 109–16; 120.
32 Caulfield 1878, 393.

including places like Tullow, county Carlow and Portarlington. His agent, John Tyrrell, was apparently receiving about 120 papers a week when Parliament was sitting.[33] Delafaye had a long connection with Cork where the Corporation ordered on 4 January 1714 that he be paid £36 for six years' newspapers and ending his contract. Rising costs, rather than indifference to news, appears to have been the problem; later that year, on 6 August, the Corporation ordered the mayor-elect to make arrangements in London for the supply of the *Postman*, *Flying Post*, *Evening Post* and the *Votes* of Parliament, when sitting, and 'to send an account before agreement'.[34] By 1721, this was costing £7 3*s*. a year.[35] Youghal clearly continued to take papers, resolving on 11 December 1786 that the Corporation should not in the future be supplied with more than one two-day English and one two-day Irish paper.[36] Monthly periodicals were frequently advertised in Ireland. Such London delights as the *Grand Magazine*, the *Royal Female Magazine; or, The ladies' general repository of pleasure and improvement*, the *Public Magazine*, the *Imperial Magazine*, the *British Magazine*, the *Musical Magazine* and the *Universal Review* were advertised in Faulkner's *Dublin Journal* in the first four months of 1760.

For a few literary genres, the main function of the British book was to serve as a copy text for an Irish reprint. This is particularly the case with plays, which were very widely reprinted, most obviously in Dublin, but also in Cork, Belfast and Newry. Irish reprints tended to coincide with stage productions, being sold at the theatre as well as in bookshops. There is evidence of amateur acting in the eighteenth and early nineteenth centuries[37] and of plays being read in domestic surroundings.[38] Fiction was proportionately less frequently reprinted. Of the 1,421 novels first printed in England between 1779 and 1799, almost a third, 459, received a Dublin reprint and a handful were printed elsewhere in the country.[39] According to James Raven, original publication in Ireland was uncommon; during the 1780s, eleven novels were first printed in Dublin, but none in the 1790s when three were published in Cork.[40] During the first half of the century, poetry was comparatively infrequently reprinted. A survey of Foxon's *Catalogue of English verse, 1701–1750* for the years 1703, 1723 and 1743 showed that, exclusive of collected editions, reprints in Ireland

33 Harris 1975, 141, 146.
34 Caulfield 1876, 363, 368.
35 Caulfield 1876, 416.
36 Caulfield 1878, 513.
37 Moore 1825, 1–10.
38 Fitzgerald 1949, I, 84.
39 Garside, Raven and Schöwerling 2000, I, 36–7.
40 Garside, Raven and Schöwering 2000, I, 71.

ranged between 1 and 5 per cent of British originals.[41] This meagre total of original work reflects the weakness at the heart of the Irish book trade. The lack of any copyright protection led those with copy to sell to take it to England, principally to London.[42] William Preston, in an essay presented to the Royal Irish Academy in 1796, identified the evils of having no copyright law in force: 'it exposes to a certain loss, from piracy, the author of any original work, who shall publish it, at his own expence . . . it precludes all improvement in the typography of this country, with respect to correctness, or beauty of type. Should any printer, of taste and enterprise in his art, prepare an elegant and costly edition of any work, he is liable to have the sale of it ruined by a spurious and disgraceful republication.'[43]

The Act of Union (39 & 40 George III c. 67), which came into force on 1 January 1801, was followed in July the same year by a Copyright Act (41 George III c. 107), which extended the legal regulations current in Great Britain to Ireland. The immediate result was to undermine the basis on which the Irish trade of unauthorized reprints had developed and to increase greatly the opportunities for British publishers. Within two decades, informed sources were dismissive in their comments on the state of Irish publishing. Writing around 1816, R. Walsh described the Dublin printing business as 'confined to devotional and moral tracts, which are paid for by charitable societies for gratuitous distribution – to printing handbills and playbills – to some half-dozen newspapers, which are by no means remarkable, and to one or two middling magazines, which can scarcely maintain an ephemeral existence'.[44] William Wakeman was asked his opinion on the state of printing by the Commissioners of Inquiry into the collection and management of the revenue arising in Ireland. He replied, 'it is comparatively nothing in Ireland, except a description of Catholic books of a very cheap sort, which are sold at a lower rate, that they could not be printed in England for the same money, and also a few schoolbooks used exclusively in Ireland', adding that the book-printing trade had been almost annihilated since the Act of Union.[45]

Book imports, already increasing in the 1790s, rose rapidly. Despite the establishment of the United Kingdom, the two exchequers were separately maintained until 1824, and it is possible to draw annual figures from the Customs ledgers for the first eighteen years of the century. As had been the

41 Foxon 1975a.
42 See Green, chap. 28, below.
43 Preston 1803, 404.
44 Warburton, Whitelaw and Walsh 1818, II, 1158.
45 *Third Report of the Commissioners of Inquiry into the collection and management of the revenue arising in Ireland* (UK *Parl. Papers*, 1822, xiii, 1219), 15.

Table 17.1 *Imports of unbound books in hundredweight from Great Britain to Ireland, 1802–18*

Year ending	Dublin	Belfast	Cork	Other ports	Total
5 Jan. 1802	560	59	51.75	19.00	689.75
5 Jan. 1809	1,192	165	203.00	91.25	1,651.25
5 Jan. 1814	2,021	198	271.00	114.63	2,604.63
5 Jan. 1818	1,354	240	174.50	57.375	1,825.875

Source: Irish Customs Ledgers, PRO Customs 15/105–128.

Table 17.2 *Imports of unbound books in hundredweight from England and Scotland to Ireland, 1802–18*

Year ending	England	Scotland	Total
5 Jan. 1802	622.50	67.25	689.75
5 Jan. 1809	1,447.25	204.00	1,651.25
5 Jan. 1814	2,036.63	568.01	2,604.63
5 Jan. 1818	1,593.375	232.5	1,825.875

Source: as Table 17.1.

case before the Union, a value is given only for bound books; the weight is given for unbound books, which since 1730 had been valued at £10 a hundredweight. Imports were principally of unbound books. (See Tables 17.1 and 17.2.)

The continued dominance of the trade by Dublin is clear, but there is a rapid rise in the importance of Belfast, which eclipsed Cork as a centre for distribution by 1817. Scotland became a major supply centre and this may reflect partly the literary success of Sir Walter Scott.[46] Figures for importation to individual ports show that Scotland was a relatively more important source of supply for Belfast than for Dublin or Cork. The importation of bound books was comparatively small and irregular (see Table 17.3). With the advent of prefabricated publishers' bindings in the 1820s and 1830s, however, the balance between bound and unbound books was to change rapidly.

So long as the separate exchequers were maintained, there were serious administrative handicaps to the development of trade. A system of countervailing duties and drawbacks was in place and operated slowly and at

46 See Beavan and McDougall, chap. 16, above.

Table 17.3 *Imports of bound books from Great Britain to Ireland, 1802–18 (value in Irish pounds)*

Year ending	Dublin	Belfast	Cork
5 Jan. 1802	£337 11*s*. 4*d*.	£48 18*s*. 3*d*.	£319 0*s*. 1*d*.
5 Jan. 1809	£1 18*s*. 7*d*.	£374 4*s*. 10*d*.	£348 0*s*. 0*d*.
5 Jan. 1814	£711 0*s*. 0*d*.	£469 10*s*. 0*d*.	£122 5*s*. 0*d*.
5 Jan. 1818	£377 8*s*. 2*d*.	£43 10*s*. 0*d*.	£123 0*s*. 0*d*.

Source: as Table 17.1.

significant cost. In 1800, the duty on unbound books had been set at 3*d*. per pound weight.[47] The working of the system was explained by William Wakeman – resident agent in Ireland of the London publishers Baldwin, Cradock and Joy – to the Commissioners of Inquiry into the collection and management of the revenue arising in Ireland in 1821:

> when importing large parcels entered for a drawback by Liverpool, or by long sea, that is, from London direct, we have to enter into bonds, the expense of which is £1 2*s*. 6*d*. British; the cost of entry at the Custom House here 5*s*. 6*d*.; and the expenses after we have got a certificate of landing, in getting the drawback from the broker on the other side, that is double postage both ways. The expense of forwarding the certificate to the broker, and receiving money from him, that is 4*s*. 6*d*.[48]

Such was the scale of the administrative costs that it was not worthwhile entering any quantity of books weighing less than 160 pounds for drawback.[49] Charles Palmer Archer, giving evidence to the same body, found every importation attended by a 'certain degree of inconvenience, expense, annoyance and unpleasantness; for instance, if I pay £50 duty here on importation, perhaps it is six or twelve months before I get that back again'.[50]

Potential sales were lost because publishers found it uneconomic to send over copies of new books on approval, even though this was their custom for the English trade. If the books were not taken, there was the double loss of duty paid on importation into Ireland and on returning them to Britain.[51] The system also made Irish booksellers behave with great caution. As Archer

47 40 George III c. 4 Ireland. Schedule A.
48 *Third Report*, 1822, xiii, 1217, 13.
49 *Third Report*, 1822, xiii, 1218, 14.
50 *Third Report*, 1822, xiii, 1221, 17.
51 *Third Report*, 1822, xiii, 1218, 14.

testified, 'if I have orders for twenty-five copies of a work, perhaps I would not get thirty, I would not like to risk the chance of the sale, there is no profit, there is nothing to induce us to import them'.[52] Nor would London publishers 'send a book latterly on sale or return, except in very few circumstances; they do not wish to do it; if they send a hundred copies of a work to Dublin on the chance of sale and they do not sell, the expenses on getting them back are so very great, that it deters them from attempting it, except in very few cases'.[53] Longman and Co. had apparently given up the practice by 1815, finding it a ruinous way of doing business.[54] Archer continued his saga of woe when discussing the importation of periodicals. This, he maintained, was almost profitless – for the sake of speed, the booksellers were obliged to transport them from London by coach and across the Irish Sea by mail packet.[55] Wakeman concurred, giving evidence that many booksellers refused to import monthly publications such as reviews except for the convenience of particular customers.[56]

The expense of postage was a hindrance in both islands until the advent of the penny post. Evidence given to the Select Committee on Postage in 1838 suggested that many booksellers would have sent out more circulars had postage been cheaper. The cost of letters was such that orders were often delayed and sent off in batches. L. Fenwick de Porquet received one letter from Ireland which contained orders for three other publishers in London and which cost him 1*s.* 3½*d.* He was expected to cut it into four and to distribute the other parts to the relevant booksellers.[57]

Despite these handicaps, the Irish market was a growing one. Stock selection was made in a variety of ways: through commercial travellers, visits of Irish booksellers to other centres or from trade catalogues. There seems to have been considerable growth in the number of commercial travellers in the early nineteenth century. T.F. Dibdin, writing in 1824, believed they had doubled over the previous few years with the result that 'three orders are now received where one formerly was scarcely given'.[58] Owen Rees, partner of T.N. Longman, was a regular traveller to Ireland, taking in both Dublin and Cork. This enabled him to check on the creditworthiness of his customers as well as promoting the firm's products. In 1811, he heard unpleasant rumours in Dublin about W. Figgis and on his return to London the company wrote to Figgis saying

52 *Third Report*, 1822, xiii, 1220, 16.
53 *Third Report*, 1822, xiii, 1220–1, 16–17.
54 Longman Archive I, University of Reading, 102 no. 159 [draft].
55 *Third Report*, 1822, xiii, 1220, 16.
56 *Third Report*, 1822, xiii, 1218, 14.
57 *First Report from the Select Committee on Postage* (UK *Parl. Papers*, 1837–8, xx, 278–83), 274–9.
58 Dibdin 1824, xxii.

that Rees was sorry 'to observe that he did not find you so regularly in your shop as he had formerly the pleasure of seeing you' and that the company declined to fill Figgis's order.[59] The surviving correspondence in the Longman Archive indicates that Rees expected to be in Dublin in July and August 1817 and again in 1821 and 1827.

In 1838, G.B. Whittaker of London employed two travellers who visited the leading towns of England and Wales and the great towns in Ireland (presumably Belfast, Cork and Dublin) twice a year;[60] Oliver and Boyd of Edinburgh had a traveller who visited Dublin regularly between 1825 and 1827.[61] Adam Black toured Ireland in 1830 finding few shops outside Dublin and Cork worth visiting and relating that, in some towns, few books other than Roman Catholic prayer books were sold. He took exception to the style in which his Dublin wholesaler, John Cumming, lived, recording that he had two carriages, a town and a country house, and that he frequently gave sumptuous dinners 'for which his creditors had to suffer in due time'.[62]

There was some immigration, particularly to Dublin. John Cook, brother-in-law of the law publisher Joseph Butterworth, set up business in Dublin in April 1802 - arriving with a cargo of law books - and continued until 1826. Baldwin, Cradock and Joy employed William Wakeman as their resident agent and he also traded on his own account. Alexander Thom, who established his printing business in 1825, came over as the barely teenage son of Walter Thom from Scotland. The father was a journalist and newspaper proprietor much favoured by the government and, from the 1830s on, Alexander Thom was able to engage in much official printing. Cyrus Westley of the London bookbinding family established a short-lived partnership with Gerrard Tyrrell in Dublin in the bookselling and circulating library business in 1825, and a branch of the Tegg business was established there in 1834.

There is evidence too of visits to London by Dublin booksellers. John Archer was in London in July 1799 and intended going on to the Continent to build up his stock.[63] He advertised in 1802 that he planned to visit France and Germany, presumably via London, and sought commissions.[64] Archer was in London again in 1807.[65] Richard Milliken travelled regularly to England, being there

59 Longman Archive I, 97 no. 154.
60 *First Report from the Select Committee on postage*, 1837–8, xx, 265, 261.
61 *Oliver and Boyd Travellers' Logbook*, National Library of Scotland, Acc. 5000.1109.
62 Black 1885, 74–5.
63 Bellew Papers, NLI MSS 27, 923 (3).
64 *Saunders's Newsletter*, 25 Apr. 1802.
65 Bellew Papers, NLI MSS 27, 293 (6).

early in 1821[66] and again in 1831.[67] Matthew Neary Mahon was in London in September 1811, using Longman and Co. as his postal address.[68]

Publishers' lists inserted in books and periodicals at the time of boarding up were clearly influential in attracting the attention of the private collector, particularly those who lived outside the cities. The most successful instance of this advertising occurred in 1831. It was then, at the height of the success of Sir Walter Scott's Waverley novels, when a volume of his works was being published each month, that the Dublin bookseller John Cumming wrote to John Murray in London thanking him for being given the management of a new edition of Lord Byron's *Works* for the Irish market. He wrote that 'it would be of great advantage, if I could have 2,500 Prospectuses without covers sent off by return of coach as I may have them in time to paste into the December volume of the Waverley novels and standard novels where they will be sure to meet the view of the very persons who will be the most likely to subscribe', and promised to delay the issue of the Waverley novels for a day or two, regarding it as more important to have the prospectuses inserted.[69] Two years later, he wrote again to Murray enclosing a statement of the expenses of publishing Byron's *Works*; these were £95 for advertising and £88 for carriage, set against a sales return to Murray of £5,000.[70]

Although the figures for imports to Ireland give the impression of a healthy trade, it is evident that in the early years of the nineteenth century the Dublin booksellers were frequently under financial pressure. The change from the pre-copyright era – when Dublin booksellers would publish fiction and plays in congers – to a post-copyright dependence on individual contracts with British publishers clearly involved a need for more capital. Such evidence as we have about this period originates in a remarkable series of letters from Dublin booksellers to one of the most important Irish collectors, Christopher Dillon Bellew, of Mountbellew, county Galway, written between 1799 and 1824. Hardly a year passed without one or more of the major booksellers expressing anguish. On 4 December 1807, John Archer wrote to Bellew thanking him for sending £280, 'this money is a very timely supply. The London booksellers had drained me of the last shilling . . . to be candid, I never had more occasion for your assistance'.[71] Charles Palmer Archer wrote to him on 22 January 1816 when enclosing his account, 'I never in all my life

66 Longman Archive I, 101 no. 19.
67 Longman Archive I, 102 no. 175A.
68 Bellew Papers, NLI MSS 27, 298 (1).
69 Murray Archives, NLS, Miscellaneous correspondence 1820–40.
70 Murray Archives, NLS, Miscellaneous correspondence 1820–40.
71 Bellew Papers, NLI MSS 27, 293 (6).

knew business so bad, nor have I ever known such difficulty in getting monies – although there are five or six thousand pounds due to me I can scarcely get in a guinea'.[72] Four years later in January 1820, he was writing in the same vein: 'never have I known money so scarce, or difficult to be got . . . as to my engagements in London I cannot possibly meet them next week, unless my kind friends will assist me'.[73]

Although the major booksellers in Dublin continued to maintain close links with London, the figure of the wholesaler clearly emerges in the second decade of the century. While subscription-list entries for booksellers for large numbers of copies of a hundred or more imply the function of wholesaling, the first use of the designation in Ireland seems to be by W. Pickering and Co. in the subscription list for N. Caussin, *The Holy Court*, published in Dublin in 1815. The man who became the chief wholesaler in Ireland was John Cumming, who started in the bookselling business in Dublin in 1809. Over the next three decades, he combined publishing, wholesale and retail bookselling, and property development. At the start of the 1830s, Cumming was taking fairly small quantities of general books from Richard Bentley. He is listed in March 1830 as taking 25 copies of L. Lloyd, *Field sports of the north of Europe*; 40 of L. A. F. Bourrienne's *Private memoirs of Napoleon Bonaparte*; 25 of P. Dobell, *Travels in Kamtchatka*, and in April 25 of each of J. Howison, *Tales of the colonies*, C. MacKenzie, *Notes on Haiti* and J. Smith, *English army in France*. In the following year, he ordered 250 copies of J. F. Cooper, *The pilot*, the first novel issued in Bentley's Standard Library.[74] At its peak in 1846, the profits of Cumming's business were reckoned at £2,500 a year, though in the following year he was one of the many casualties of the fall of the business consequent on the Great Famine.[75]

The Irish market was viewed as less sophisticated and less wealthy than the English one. Robert Walsh, writing around 1816, was scathing about the effect of the Copyright Act, declaring that 'great numbers who formerly were in the habit of reading are by this Act interdicted from doing so, as the books which once, by their comparative cheapness, were within their means of purchasing, cannot be procured'.[76] Yet, he also blamed the trade itself: 'it is true, there is no encouragement for literary exertion in the Irish metropolis, because the cautious Dublin bookseller will run no risk in publishing an original work,

72 Bellew Papers, NLI MSS 27, 301 (7).
73 Bellew Papers, NLI MSS 27, 301 (15); postmarked 22 Jan. 1820.
74 Bentley Papers, BL Add. MSS.
75 *Saunders's Newsletter*, 27 July 1848.
76 Warburton, Whitelaw and Walsh 1818, II, 1158.

however great its merit. It must appear in London, or not at all.'[77] We may infer something of the perceived unsophisticated nature of the Irish market from the reply of Messrs Darton and Harvey on 5 January 1809 to Mary Leadbeater about a proposed publication which she contemplated having printed in Dublin, saying that they would take twenty-five copies of it unseen, 'but in general the form and manner of printing books in Ireland are not calculated for the meridian of London' and suggesting that she sell them the rights to print for the English market.[78] A few years later, Longman and Co. expressed a similar view when offering Richard Milliken an option in Henry Grattan's *Speeches* which were being edited by his son: 'Mr G. wishes to have the work printed in Dublin, stating that it will not be in his power to arrange so as to have the printing carried on in London. We need not tell you that it is almost impossible to have a handsome book printed in Dublin either as to paper or type: at least we have never seen such.'[79]

The perceived poverty of the market is illustrated by the Dublin subscription edition of James Gordon, *A new history of Ireland* in 1804. While this was being printed in London in quarto for the English market, a prospectus was issued for the publication in octavo for the Irish market because the author, an Irish clergyman, wished to accommodate his fellow countrymen with a less expensive edition available 'on a very fine paper at £1 2*s.* 9*d.* and on a less fine paper at 17*s.* 4*d*'.[80]

A significant measure of the extent to which Dublin publication was unfashionable, and Irish authors flocked to London publishers, can be seen in the figures produced for the publication of fiction between 1800 and 1829 by P. Garside and R. Schöwerling.[81] For this period they record a total of 2,265 novels being published for the first time in the British Isles. Of these, 2,030 were published in London, 133 in Scotland, 71 in the English provinces and a mere 27 in Ireland. Yet, novelists such as Maria Edgeworth, Lady Morgan and Charles Maturin were living in Ireland, and even writing fiction with Irish settings. The meagre total may reflect the reluctance of Irish authors to offer their manuscripts locally as much as the unadventurousness of publishers.

There is no doubt that there was plenty of appetite for fiction in Ireland. As in Great Britain, there was continued growth in reading clubs and circulating libraries. Artisan reading clubs were numerous in counties Down and

77 Warburton, Whitelaw and Walsh 1818, II, 1162–3.
78 NLI MSS 19082.
79 Longman Archive I, 101 no. 44.
80 *Hibernian Journal*, 18 June 1804.
81 Garside, Raven and Shöwerling 2000, II 76.

Antrim.[82] Eight such societies, for example, subscribed to the publication of W. Anderson, *Collection of moral, instructive and religious poems* (Belfast, 1830).[83] An analysis of the content of four northern Irish subscription libraries showed that imaginative literature comprised 21 per cent of the *Catalogue of the books in the library of the Down Literary Society* (Downpatrick, 1801); 5 per cent of the books in the *Rules of the Belfast Society for promoting literature, with a catalogue* (Belfast, 1808); 32 per cent of the *Catalogue of the Newtownlimavady Library* (Belfast, 1815); and 22 per cent of the *Catalogue of books belonging to the Comber Society for acquiring knowledge* (Belfast, *c.*1828).[84]

The commercial libraries were strong purchasers of fiction. A list of novels was the feature of an advertisement of new publications just arrived from London at Jackson's Circulating Library at 3 New Sackville Street, Dublin in 1801.[85] These were to be lent to read at 8*d.* per week or £1 2*s.* 9*d.* per year. John Kempston of Dublin had about 2,000 volumes of fiction in his circulating library in July 1816,[86] while J. Hodgson of Belfast had 1,144 such volumes among the 'upwards of 6,000' contained in his *Catalogue of Hodgson's new circulating library* (Belfast, 1821). By 1824 he had added a further 256.[87] Such libraries as these offered a service to country subscribers as well as to their town's middle classes.

Fiction was one part of the market in which the British product had a near monopoly. Drama was another. The eighteenth-century pattern of little original production or publication continued into the nineteenth century. The theatre's existence in Dublin had ranged from the affluent to the precarious and in the early part of the century only one theatre was in regular use in Dublin. Other centres – Belfast, Londonderry, Limerick, Cork, Waterford and Wexford – were very dependent on touring companies. The repertoire reflected that of the English, indeed mostly the London, stage. Interest in play reading continued to be lively; John Wiseheart advertised the opening of the theatrical circulating library in Dublin in 1825.[88] This comprised a 'very rare collection of new and scarce tragedies, comedies, operas, melodramas and farces', and weekly membership cost 6½*d.* Plays were lent singly for the night.

The extent of the domination of the British book in Ireland was enormous in all areas, except for pamphlets of immediate local, political and religious

82 Adams 1987, 124.
83 Adams 1987, 124.
84 Adams 1987, 125–6.
85 *Hibernian Journal*, 4 Aug. 1801.
86 *Saunders's Newsletter*, 30 July 1816.
87 Supplementary catalogue bound with TCD copy of Hodgson's *Catalogue* (Belfast, 1821).
88 *Saunders's Newsletter*, 23 June 1825.

controversy and educational books.[89] An anguished notice by the journeymen printers in Dublin in 1825, intended to deter potential apprentices, stated that the art of printing in Ireland had been rapidly decaying under the withering influence of English monopoly, and that since the Copyright Act 'no work of sterling merit has ever issued from the Press of Ireland – the brilliant productions of the prolific genius of her sons have been executed by English capital and English workmen'.[90] However true this was, change was at hand. The 1830s and 1840s were to see the stirrings of independent Irish publishing feeding a growing appetite for nationalist literature.

89 See Green, chap. 28, below.
90 *Saunders's Newsletter*, 2 Apr. 1825.

II
TWO CASE STUDIES

18

Richard Francklin: a controversial publisher, bookseller and printer, 1718–1765

JAMES J. CAUDLE

The career of Richard Francklin (*c.*1696–1765) – bookseller, publisher and printer – spanned a crucial period in the history of the eighteenth-century book. Born soon after the lapse of the Licensing Act (1695), he died soon after the furore over the *North Briton* (1764). Examining Francklin's mix of business activities, this study considers Francklin's career as a representative example of early to mid-Georgian stationers.

The shop

The Stationers' Company Registers do not show Francklin's name among the listed apprentices and, indeed, only record one apprentice of Curll's, a 'Thomas Dyer' or 'Dryer' turned over to Curll in 1711 and freed in 1713; nonetheless Ralph Straus claimed Francklin was Edmund Curll's 'own apprentice'. From 1750, Francklin was a London 'Citizen and Cordwainer', freed of that company.[1] Certainly he was working for Curll by September 1717, when he produced a 'true Copy' for Curll and authenticated it with the words, 'Witness my Hand'.[2] His name first appeared on a title page in 1718. Francklin's original shop in 1718 was 'at the *Sun* against St *Dunstan's* Church in *Fleetstreet*', near Curll's shop at the Dial and Bible; the title page of *The art of beauty* (1719 [1718]) claimed he was also at the '*Court* of *requests*'.[3] From about 1726 to 1758, he was located 'under Tom's Coffee-house in Covent Garden', later no. 17 Russell Street.[4] His move was paradigmatic of the book-trading

1 Straus 1927, 86; cf. McKenzie 1978, entries 3021, 2260.

2 *Evening Post*, 3 Sep. 1717; Sherburn 1928, 415.

3 Plomer 1922, 121.

4 Plomer, Bushnell and Dix 1932, 96; Lillywhite 1963, item 1366.

world's shift from the traditional St Paul's and City environs into the newly emergent West End, and the continuing influence of coffee houses as centres for political and cultural discussion.

There are several sources for the daily conduct of his business. One is Nicholas Amhurst, who expressed his hope to escape his 'servile Garret' in 'An epistle' (1720). Francklin's shop followed the common pattern of a cramped set of residences for apprentices and authors located above the shop floor and the master's residence ('my Lodgings up Three Pair of Stairs, at Mr Francklin's'). In 'A Familiar epistle' (1720), Amhurst noted that Francklin was often importunate for copy, and 'Sends in warm Terms for Copy by next Post'. In 1738, Amhurst joked about the overflow of unsold publications in 'poor *F__nkl__n's* lean Abodes'.[5]

The second major source is the cache of papers seized from Francklin's shop during a government raid of 3 September 1730. These papers, preserved in the Cholmondeley MSS, give details of elements of his business in December 1726–March 1730.[6] The only portions relevant to book production (rather than periodicals) are the accounts dealing with 'the [*Craftsman*] published in pamphlet form'. Francklin kept his accounts in double-entry form with columns of 'Dr' (debtor) and 'Cr' (creditor), although Harris observes that Francklin's 'arithmetic was sometimes inexact'.[7] The accounts record charges common to all printed matter (paper, printing fees, delivery charges, money paid for advertising publications in news or magazines). They reveal a standard set of costs for paper – from 8*s*. 6*d*. for a ream of newspaper paper upwards to 16*s*.–17*s*. for a ream of pamphlet paper. They suggest commercial printing-house charges – about 19*s*. per issue for a one-page periodical, or 17*s*.–18*s*. per sheet of a pamphlet 'Collection'. They show the prices charged for 'Publishing' (in the case of periodicals, 2*s*. per 1,000 copies) and the fee levied by middlemen to serve as a point of transfer from printer to vendor. They record the sums paid for a title to be entered into the Stationers' Company Registers, at 10*s*.–12*s*. per pamphlet. They even uncover petty daily costs (6*d*. 'paid for a letter'; 4*s*. in 'Incidental Expenses'). They sketch, in part, the types of people who frequented Francklin's shop and others like it: the 'Printers Men' of the outsourced printing house (paid 1*s*.–2*s*. 6*d*. for each number of the paper), the 'Men' or 'Man' sent by retail vendors, the three or four 'Porter[s]' who undertook deliveries (paid about 3*d*.–8*d*. for each delivery of the periodical, or 3*s*. for

5 Fielding 1989, xviii.

6 *Craftsman* accounts December 1726 to May 1727, *Craftsman* profits May 1727 to March 1730, and *Craftsman* pamphlet collection accounts January 1727.

7 Harris 1970.

a large single job of delivering a book), and the 'Carman' (paid *2s. 6d.*). In addition to these, as the *Craftsman* itself pointed out,[8] the shop was 'where advertisements and letters to the author are taken in', so various contributors and correspondents would have visited during the day. The accounts also expose Francklin's politically polymorphous links to advertisers: Whigs, accused High-Flyers and a Roman Catholic. Although he himself was a Whig, either the cross-party appeal of the *Craftsman*'s Country Party rhetoric or exigencies of business motivated him to advertise across party lines. These records suggest the profits to be gained by even one successful title in a world in which bestselling books under the imprint of any given publisher were fairly rare. Publication of the *Craftsman*, the leading Opposition journal of the day, from May 1727 to March 1730 brought in just over £1,990 in profits.[9]

To this might be added a third source, accounts relating to the Westminster election of November–December 1749. These accounts involve Francklin's work as a printer (in this case, of ephemera) rather than publisher.[10] In a surviving bill, Francklin noted that on 29 November 1749 he printed 3,000 copies of *Reasons for voting for Lord Trentham.* He also billed for 13,000 copies of the ½mo one-issue political squib *The Covent-garden Journal* printed 5–6 December. The 5 December charge was '6000 Covent Garden Journal', for which he charged £7 10*s.*; a second series of print runs on 6 December added 7,000 more copies (in clusters of 5,000 and 2,000), for which he billed £8 15*s.* in printer's fees. The cost was 'in folio at 25*s.* a thousand' (just over a farthing a copy). Distribution costs were 8*s.* for the deliverymen of the 5 December run, and 9*s.* 6*d.* for delivery of the 6 December order.

A fourth source for Francklin's business practices is the record of testimonies given at his trial for 'False, Scandalous And Seditious' libel in December 1731. Witnesses revealed that the master vended materials in the section of his 'own house' known as 'his shop', and that 'Mr Francklin himself' sold current and back issues of the *Craftsman* in small amounts (two to six copies) or larger orders ('threescore quires a week', or 'about 7*l.* a week, or upwards' for 'between 40 and 50 quires weekly') from a place 'standing by the counter'. Granted, 'his man' (or 'his servant') often 'look[ed] out' the copies needed, and also delivered them to retailers, and sometimes accepted the reseller's money. Alternately, a retailer sent a 'man' to 'fetch' copies, which were sometimes even paid for by another servant. However, Francklin was, not surprisingly, a daily presence in 'Mr Francklin's house', resident as well as businessman. On a

8 No. 45, 13 May 1727.
9 Harris 1970.
10 Battestin and Battestin 1977–8, 164–8.

typical Saturday, he accepted payments (for example, 10–12 guineas) and counted out money; the money in retail sales was paid 'Sometimes to Mr Francklin, and sometimes to his servants'. When he did not send 'his servants', Francklin himself paid the advertising duties at the Stamp Office. The papers relative to the business, including copy-text manuscripts and accounts, were kept in 'house and shop', either 'wrapped up in a bundle' or locked in a 'scrutoire'. Francklin's wife was a presence in the shop, and attempted to save his papers during the 1731 seizure. All these petty encounters testify to the face-to-face nature of the London book world. Despite the expansion in numbers of printed materials after 1695, the scale of commerce was still such that retail booksellers frequently went in person on behalf of individual clients, and dealt for much of the process with masters rather than men. However, the selective use of shopmen as go-betweens allowed masters and mistresses to preserve a pretence of not knowing what precisely was in their stock.[11]

A fifth source is Henry Haines's pamphlet of 1740, *Treachery, baseness, and cruelty, display'd to the full* . . ., an attack on Francklin's alleged abandonment of Haines, who had been 'retain'd in the Capacity of a Journeyman to Mr *Francklin*' in December 1726, and whose 'Conduct in managing the Business' had been praised by his master. Haines noted that 'he was capable to get a Guinea a Week by his own Hands, as a Journeyman Printer', which, presuming a week of six days, amounted to 3*s.* 6*d.* per day. He explained that in 1731 'all the Printing Materials ... of his [Francklin's] House' were 'looked upon [by Francklin] to be worth 500£.'; these 'Printing Materials' were 'torn from him by Force of Arms' when he was gaoled. Yet Haines, while acting as a front for Francklin, found the *Craftsman* less lucrative in 1735–7 than Francklin had in 1727–30; he complained that 'as to the Profits of the Paper, he got but a bare Living by it'. Haines 'printed 4500' per issue, but after 'the *Mercuries* returned some' unsold copies, his 'nearest Computation' was that 'the Paper clear'd Ten Guineas a Week, all Charges paid'.[12]

In contrast with larger shops like Tonson's, which employed fifty men in 1730, Francklin's verifiable employees were few.[13] Our knowledge of the numbers and names of personnel employed by any given master is patchy given the small number of printing and publishing houses whose detailed ledgers survived. Anecdotes about the printer Henry Haines provide evidence of at least one journeyman associated with Francklin's business around 1726–38. Francklin's only documented apprentice was a late addition: William Bunce

11 Howell 1816–26, XVII, 641–61.
12 Haines 1740, 8–11, 15–16, 20–1.
13 Feather 1984, 207.

served Francklin for twelve years (1750–62), was probably a journeyman before 1765 when he became a partner and co-printer, and ultimately became Francklin's 'successor'. Although Francklin is known to have printed books in his own right, the *Craftsman* accounts that survive mostly document outsourced printing by Samuel Aris. Haines's printing house in (Great) Hart Street was furnished with Francklin's printing equipment, and used to produce works 'printed by H. Haines' in 1734–7 until Francklin repossessed the equipment in 1737–8.[14]

Unlike those printers and offices renowned for the beauty and accuracy of their texts, Francklin was a commercially driven stationer; he was more eager to get the text to market than to make it correct or visually appealing. Like other eighteenth-century publishers, he thought the first state should only be mended if the market called for new impressions of the work. Accuracy in eighteenth-century books was undermined by print-shop beer breakfasts, by slapdash or rushed typesetters, by farming out segments of the same work to different printers, and by the rarity of professional proofreaders' 'correctors' in smaller printing offices before the 1750s. The fines traditionally levied on typos do not seem to have prevented the slovenliness of compositors directly or indirectly employed by Francklin. The blunders were present even in 'revis'd and corrected' works. In the composition of at least seven books, the number of errors spotted required an errata list, and some tardily spotted mistakes only received an 'errata slip'. Anomalies of pagination suggest continuous composition by different printers, or at least different presses in the same house. There is no evidence that Francklin himself or his journeyman Haines were great sticklers for perfection. Of those men known to have been associated with Francklin's shop, only Bunce, who during his brief post-apprenticeship career worked mainly in a luxury and art book printing market, seemed less prone to errors.

Francklin's life as a London 'Citizen and Cordwainer' ran contrary to the stereotype of publishers as confirmed urbanites who aspired to be founders or upholders of book-trade dynasties. The bourgeois grasping of such traditional businessmen was derided by the literati of the period who called them 'cits', a derogatory word used to describe – in the words of Johnson's *Dictionary* – 'An inhabitant of a city, in an ill sense. A pert low townsman; a pragmatical trader'; the implication, of course, is that cits could never, try as they may, be true gentlemen. Francklin aspired to attain the symbols of gentility pursued by so many other would-be gentlemen in the Georgian period: a country villa (he

14 Plomer, Bushnell and Dix 1932, 113–14.

leased a modest cottage), and his son in the clergy, not a city trade. After Francklin's retirement in 1765, the shop descended not to his son, as one would have ordinarily expected in dynasties such as the Mottes, Bowyers or Rivingtons, but to his former apprentice, who was not related to him by blood or marriage.

Relationships with authors

The alliance of the author to his or her stationer was one of the more important associations in the eighteenth-century literary world. The almost feudal or patronal attachment that an author like Swift demonstrated towards someone like Benjamin Tooke or George Faulkner, and the personal betrayal Swift felt from Benjamin Motte II, suggest the intensity of feelings which author–publisher relations inspired.

Francklin's first major alliance with an author was speculative, and fateful. In his first year of credited publication, Francklin was already associated with the oppositionist Whig Oxford wit Nicholas Amhurst. Amhurst would prove a major influence on Francklin's publishing career for nearly a quarter-century, from 1718 to 1742. He appears to have met Amhurst through Curll, who had published Amhurst between 1717 and 1719. Francklin, especially in the early period, can be described as 'Amhurst's publisher', and Amhurst even inhabited a garret in Francklin's Fleet Street shop. In slow business years, Amhurst's poems seemed to have made up the bulk of Francklin's credited business in new titles. Amhurst was presumably the reason that the fairly obscure Francklin later obtained the commission from aristocratic sponsors to publish the highly controversial *Craftsman*.

Francklin's work for the *Craftsman* connected him with other major contributors such as Lord Bolingbroke and William Pulteney (later (1742) Earl of Bath), who became authors and patrons for his publishing house. Their patronage was more than a symbolic genteelism: 'Without sponsorship from a wealthy patron ... or a distributor of subsidies ..., a paper's existence depended ... on its marketability.'[15] Pulteney was the man who most directly adopted the role of Francklin's patron. He was one of only three backers who paid the promised £50 to recompense Francklin for his gaol time on their behalf. Pulteney was also the initial academic sponsor of Francklin's son Thomas, and was supposed to help him into a place in the church, though he later ceased to be the son's patron.

15 Varey 1993, 61, 75 n. 12.

Bolingbroke seems to have personally chosen Francklin as a publisher by the early 1730s, although it is difficult to determine how many of the *Craftsman*-related squibs were owned by Francklin by virtue of appearing in 'his' paper. Of twenty-three 'Separate Prose Works' from 1710 to 1754, about 30 per cent of Bolingbroke's works were published by Francklin.[16] Bolingbroke elected to continue with Francklin to publish his still-anonymous works: the fifth and subsequent editions of *A dissertation upon parties*, *Remarks on the history of England* and *A collection of political tracts* were all printed for Francklin. Bolingbroke's new association with Andrew Millar in 1749 seems to have set his compass away from Francklin towards the Millar alliance.

It is uncertain whether this continuing connection from 1727 to 1735, and perhaps even until 1748, was a matter of Bolingbroke's patronage of Francklin or Francklin's pre-existing copyrights. It is clear, however, that Bolingbroke never offered Francklin exclusive rights over all his works. When Bolingbroke died in 1751, Francklin's presumption that he had been tacitly given copyright was the only basis for his posthumous Bolingbroke editions in the ensuing years. By 1749, however, Bolingbroke's publisher of choice was Millar, who owned most of the subsequent new Bolingbroke texts that were first published from manuscripts in 1749–66. Bolingbroke confused matters horribly by appointing David Mallet as his literary executor with an eye to a posthumous edition of his complete *Works*. This appointment led to the Francklin–Mallet dispute of 1754–63 over ownership of the reprint rights.

Even after the split between Bath and his quondam oppositionist allies in 1742, Francklin maintained his connections with most of them. It was rumoured that Francklin had paid for the tomb when Amhurst, by then a poor man, was buried in 1742. Francklin was alleged to be author of the anonymous *A new year's gift for The R[igh]t H[onourabl]e, the E[arl] of B[ath]* (1744).

The role of personal 'connection' in the book trade is revealed most strongly in Francklin's patronage of his own son's works. Somewhat unusually, rather than planning to create a dynasty of stationers in his family as Jacob Tonson I, Benjamin Motte I, Charles Rivington I and others had done, Richard chose instead to help his son Thomas Francklin to a career within the Church of England's clergy. As clerical preferment was often connected to publication, and booksellers were reluctant to take on works by unknown parsons, having a father in the book trade was a great help to the son. Richard published more than ten of Thomas's early works and translations in the years 1741–63. This

16 Barber 1965, 531–7.

relationship between young Francklin and his father's shop continued under Bunce's supervision even after the elder Francklin's retirement.

In the 1740s and 1750s, Francklin increasingly turned to safer authors – light poetry and serious and comic stage plays – to augment his chiefly political and scientific stock. These included the works of the fabulist and dramatist Edward Moore, the translator and dramatist Thomas 'Hesiod' Cooke, and the actor-playwright Samuel Foote. Francklin presumably knew Cooke because he took over the editing of the *Craftsman* around 1741 after Amhurst's departure from its helm. However, this focus on individual authors and Francklin's relation to them should not obscure the fact that many of the authors whom Francklin published were anonymous. The persistence of literary anonymity among so many of Francklin's authors lends credence to questions about the 'birth' or 'construction' of authorship often claimed for the period.

Publications

Like most stationers, printers were far less frequently credited than publishers; the words 'printed for' were far more common than 'printed by'. It is particularly challenging to discover the full range of books that Francklin printed. His documented work as a printer began in 1720. He was infrequently credited as a printer during his career in the trade, and more commonly appeared in the imprint as 'printed for'. A careful study of the ornaments in these known printing jobs would probably reveal more uncredited imprints by Francklin's print shop. His printing was farmed out to others in the trade: Bettenham, Aris, and perhaps Woodfall.

Until the *Craftsman* and its allied titles skyrocketed Francklin's sale of copyrighted materials, his publishing was modest and depended heavily on alliances with other booksellers. The year 1726 might be taken as a 'border' year for Francklin, since it was the last before the *Craftsman* began in earnest, and indicates the typical level of publication he might have achieved had he never dared to take on the *Craftsman*. The *Craftsman* provided a huge boost for Francklin's output in 1727–31, but in the wake of the 1731 conviction, he went underground. Furthermore, all of the books from 1732 to 1736 were apolitical works, and mainly reworkings of old titles. From 1732 until 1739, the polemical publisher Francklin *seemed* to have almost ceased to exist. The truth about his vanishing act was quite different. Books in these years credited to Henry Haines or his wife were actually false imprints of a sort, published on Francklin's behalf, with the Haines name acting as a screen or a front to protect Francklin from further litigation. From 1732 to 1736, imprints 'printed by

H. Haines' at 'R. Franklin's' or 'at Mr Francklin's' appeared and the *Craftsman* was credited only to 'H. Haines' in this period. Once Haines himself was imprisoned, his wife took over, publishing until Francklin repossessed the equipment. The final three decades of Francklin's career were less fraught than either the period of founding his business in 1718–25, or the 'peak *Craftsman* decade' from 1726 to 1735. At the end of his final decade, in 1765, Francklin began to hand the reins over to his successor, William Bunce (active 1765–9), who moved the house towards production of art books.

In Table 18.1, each column contains three numbers in sequence, divided by virgules. The first is the number of separate titles recognized by the *ESTC*, whether they be spurious 'new editions' repackaged to sell old stock, multi-volume works or broadsheets. The second is the number of separate volumes, a crucial statistic given the number of multi-volume works under Francklin's name. The third is a sheet count of the paper expended in publishing the book. These numbers are suggestive rather than definitive: given the amount of joint publication and investment, the numbers in column two are less reliable as indicia of Francklin's investment and resources than are those in columns one and three. The many ways in which Francklin employed false and misleading imprints means that the fifth column is probably an undercount. Including periodical ephemera not usually classified as 'books' (such as the uncompiled 2° *Terræ-Filius* of 1721 and the individual *Craftsman* papers) would add roughly fifty-two sheets per annum for the relevant periods when Francklin and Haines published the *Craftsman* weekly.

The numbers presented in Table 18.1 reveal much about the rhythm and flow of operations for a smaller publisher or printer (aside from the sale of existing books printed or published by him or others). Much of Francklin's work, especially on books from the first years of his business, 1718–26, was collaborative, with risks and profits shared among several stationers; multi-volume large works (Defoe's *Tour*, Pluche's *Spectacle*, Voltaire's *Dramatic works*) were almost always undertaken in such coalitions. Most of the titles which Francklin owned outright were minor pamphlets printed in only one or two editions; the *Craftsman* essays were an exception. Had he not been asked to publish the *Craftsman*, Francklin would have been spared persecution by Walpole's agents. Yet his profits would have been far more modest, and his name even less well known. Capital flow problems in Francklin's business, though they cannot be proved by ledgers, are inferred by the number of years in which the shop produced a handful of titles or none; to stay in business he presumably relied on the sale of books and pamphlets, production of new ephemera (printed items below the level of pamphlet or periodical) or the

Table 18.1 *Richard Francklin's publishing activity, 1718–65*

	Published by Francklin alone	Published by Francklin and other(s)	Printed by Francklin	Imprint states 'sold by' Francklin	False imprint ('A. Moore', H. Haines)	'Pirated' editions
1718	3 / 3 / 10	6 / 6 / 20				
1719	3 / 3 / 32	7 / 7 / 60		1 / 1 / 4		
1720	8 / 8 / 53	1 / 1 / 5	1 / 1 / 12	1 / 1 / 12		
1721		2 / 2 / 56				
1722	1 / 1 / 3					
1723	2 / 2 / 11				1 / 1 / 6	
1724	6 / 6 / 85		1 / 1 / 27[a]	1 / 1 / 27		
1725	2 / 2 / 5		1 / 1 / 28[a]	1 / 1 / 28[a]		
1726	3 / 5 / 36		4 / 4 / 77	2 / 2 / 13		
1727	5 / 5 / 97	1 / 1 / 10			2 / 2 / 7	
1728	4 / 4 / 86			2 / 2 / 8		
1729	8 / 8 / 22	2 / 2 / 30	1 / 1 / 1		4 / 4 / 6	
1730	7 / 7 / 10	2 / 3 / 54	1 / 1 / 2		1 / 1 / 1	1 / 1 / 2
1731	29 / 35 / 160		3 / 3 / 5			
1732	1 / 1 / 3				3 / 3 / 6	1 / 1
1733		1 / 1 / 39			10 / 10 / 36	1 / 1 / 2
1734		2 / 2 / 15			7 / 7 / 26	1 / 1 / 5
1735		1 / 1 / 27		1 / 1 / 39	5 / 5 / 52	
1736		3 / 6 / 111			2 / 2 / 5	
1737	1 / 7 / ?97	2 / 2 / 55			2 / 2 / 4	
1738					1 / 1 / 4	
1739	4 / 4 / 88	5 / 5 / 89				
1740		4 / 10 / 187			1 / 1 / 2	
1741	1 / 1 / 19					
1742						
1743	2 / 2 / 40	1 / 3 / 45				
1744	3 / 3 / 19	1 / 1 / 15				
1745						
1746	1 / 1 / 12	2 / 2 / 11				
1747	1 / 1 / 22	2 / 3 / 81				
1748	5 / 5 / 62	1 / 3 / ?84				
1749	3 / 3 / 51	2 / 4 / 58	1 / 1 / 1			
1750	1 / 1 / 3	2 / 4 / 60				
1751	1 / 1 / 7	1 / 2 / 38				
1752	2 / 2 / 7					
1753	5 / 5 / 23 [4 / 4 / 20 'sold by R. Dodsley']	1 / 3 / 43				

Table 18.1 (*cont.*)

	Published by Francklin alone	Published by Francklin and other(s)	Printed by Francklin	Imprint states 'sold by' Francklin	False imprint ('A. Moore', H. Haines)	'Pirated' editions
1754	5 / 5 / 73 [1 / 1 / 3 'sold by R. Dodsley']	1 / 1 / 16			2 / 2 / 2	
1755	4 / 4 / 26 [1 / 1 / 6 'sold by R. Dodsley']					
1756	1 / 1 / 3					
1757	3 / 3 / 8 [1 / 1 / 4 'sold by P. Vaillant']	4 / 4 / 60				
1758	4 / 4 / 55					
1759	1 / 1 / 38					
1760	1 / 1 / 3					
1761	2 / 2 / 30	1 / 1 / 13	2 / 2 / 132			
1762		2 / 4 / 44				
1763	2 / 2 / 4	4 / 5 / 67				
1764		1 / 2 / 25				
1765			2 / 2 / 107			

Note: [a] Printed by Francklin with others.

sale of old stock-on-hand.[17] The importance of fronts and false imprints in an age of sporadically vengeful post-publication censorship is amply shown by the role which numerous imprints by 'A. Moore' and 'Haines' play in the table of Francklin's publications. Finally, the appearance of demonstrable piracies (surely an undercount) suggests the publishers' constant risks of copyright theft or of the legal, but nonetheless undercutting, imprints produced in Edinburgh and Dublin.

Imposters, pirates and copyright disputes

Because imprint information is not always reliable, eighteenth-century contemporaries and later scholars have sometimes faced great difficulties in discerning who actually printed and published particular works. The number of

17 Battestin and Battestin 1977–8.

piracies and 'false and misleading imprints' meant that every element in a book's imprint – 'printed by', 'printed for' and 'sold by' – could be faked. Even when a publisher did wish to claim credit for a work, typographical errors abounded; Francklin often saw his name in print as 'Franklin', 'Francklyn', 'Franckling', 'Francklain', 'Franklaine', or even the jocular 'Franck-Lynn'. This thicket of variant spellings, though a bane to bibliographers, was a godsend to printers, publishers and retailers. Under interrogation, Francklin was honestly able to claim that unscrupulous publishers frequently expropriated his name; therefore, the crown could not prove that the 'R. Francklin' on a libellous imprint was indeed the bookseller himself.[18]

Francklin, like others in the trade, resorted to spurious imprints when printing controversial material. Indeed, he became so well known for the practice of deceptive imprints that when John Mottley mentioned Francklin in Scene I of his *The Craftsman, or weekly journalist, a farce* (1729) his character was named 'Sham-Title the Bookseller'. Superficially, *The report of the committee* (1723) was 'printed for A. Moore'. However, 'A. Moore' was well known in the London book world as a fictitious imprint of choice.[19] Presumably, Francklin's publications include those titles that are first printed by 'A. Moore' and later credited to Francklin. There is also reason provisionally to place in a Francklin bibliography those 'A. Moore' imprints related to the *Craftsman* or to Bolingbroke, Pulteney or Amhurst.

Not all subterfuges involved fabricated names. Henry Haines, an employee since 1726, worked from 1732 to 1738 as a screen for Francklin. Francklin, while imprisoned, persuaded Haines to use his name as a false imprint; although Haines became nervous about this arrangement, Francklin continued the ruse. The Haines-at-Francklin's publications were essays by Pulteney or *Craftsman* reprints; all were strongly critical of the policies of Walpole's administration. Francklin was still allowed to publish under his own name after his conviction, and he did not shift the *entirety* of his titles to Haines. He simply made certain that *Craftsman*-related materials appeared as credited to Henry Haines. The apolitical matter he kept for himself. The success of the deception inspired a new printing house using printing materials owned by Francklin, of which Haines was seemingly the proprietor. The house of Haines was not a genuinely fictitious imprint such as 'A. Moore'. Yet, it was assuredly a front designed to screen Francklin from further prosecution.[20] The ruse employed by Francklin, though clever and effective, was transparent enough to be known to a New Yorker unfamiliar with London life

18 Varey 2001, 57.
19 Treadwell 1989, 41–6.
20 Plomer, Bushnell and Dix 1932, 113–14.

who was visiting in February–March 1735.[21] Furthermore, Francklin's name was still popularly connected with the journal in the press.

One of the few good things that could be said about a failed publication was that it was the only sure protection of copyright. Any title which succeeded was open to three forms of expropriation. The first was the publication, under a Scottish or Irish publisher's own imprint, of works first copyrighted in England. There is debate over whether these ought to be described as 'piracies', as Scottish and Irish property law provided some exemption from English copyright. Those Scottish and Irish stationers who proudly placed their names on copies of volumes originally issued in England did not likely see themselves as pirates or reivers. More pernicious were reprintings of the second sort: those which not only reproduced Francklin's copy without authorization, but bore a faked imprint purporting to be from Francklin's own shop. Those based in Edinburgh or Dublin who faked a known London imprint would less easily escape the posthumous charge of fraud, even though, because of the loopholes of literary property law, the courts did not judicially recognize their guilt. The third kind of publishing fraud was even odder: the creation of new titles which do not appear in Francklin's catalogue, but which claimed to be from Francklin's house: counterfeits. In this case and others, a typographical error in the publisher's name helps to flag a possibly unauthorized copy. Vexingly, not all twenty-three instances of 'Francklin' printed as 'Franklin' are unauthorized, but the botching of one's own name on the title page is the sort of printing error one would expect a publisher to catch. Besides the piracies flagged as definite or probable by *ESTC*, there are other suspicious imprints.

The defence of violated or disputed rights of literary property often provoked publishers to seek remedies in courts of law or in arbitrations by fellow members of the trade, and Francklin's career included one such great battle over copyright. Near the end of his life, when Mallet threatened Francklin's old literary property in Bolingbroke's essays, he was called to defend his stock in trade. Francklin supposed that 'Many of the political pieces' written by Bolingbroke had been 'given to Fran[c]klin ... in perpetuity'.[22] Bolingbroke's transferring his authority for the edition from Francklin to Mallet meant that no individual (or group) clearly owned the full rights to all of Bolingbroke's *Works*. Whether this right to reprint 'in perpetuity' was a specific arrangement, or simply a supposition based on the common-law customs of the trade, is unclear. However, Bolingbroke was (wrongly) believed to have willed the rights to

21 Katz 1971.
22 Johnson 1905, III, 407–8.

Mallet, who included *Craftsman* materials in his 1754 edition. This misunderstanding of Bolingbroke's wishes created a legal conundrum: who owned the texts? The matter was said to be 'so complicated by the anonymity necessitated by the political situation of the 1730s that it was settled out of court'.[23] It was not in fact so great a mess as that: Francklin had at risk of name and safety placed his true name on most of the debated Bolingbrokeana. Francklin and Mallet both agreed to turn the question over to binding arbitration by two 'judges' whom they chose. On 28 March 1754 the literary arbitrators instructed Mallet to pay Francklin 200 guineas,[24] but as Johnson noted, Mallet 'refused to yield to the award'. Thomas Davies, a stationer himself, noted that 'Mr Mallet did by no means approve the decision; and Francklin, by trusting to his honour, in not having insisted upon bonds of arbitration, was deprived of the benefit of the award.'[25] Francklin's weapon of choice for revenge against Mallet was itself a pamphlet, which he issued twice: in 1754 as a *Short state of the case* and *c.*1763 as *An act before the first act.*

Conclusion

In concluding this brief account of Francklin, one is reminded of McKenzie's dictum that 'all printing houses were alike in being different'.[26] One could say the same for publishers and mere retailers, and indeed Georgian stationers in general. Francklin's extraordinary and roguish life, seemingly from the pages of Defoe or Fielding, offers a glance into a still underexplored world of printing, publishing and selling. That world – similar to Darnton's 'Literary Underground' of 'Forgotten Middlemen' in Ancien Régime France – existed beneath the more refined stratum which included the famous houses of the Tonsons, Strahan, Richardson and the Foulis brothers.[27] Those great houses have previously received (well-deserved) scholarly attention in the form of careful checklists and reconstructions of the lives and shops of those famous men, remembered either for their cordial links with celebrated authors, or for the beauty or accuracy of their productions. By means of further microhistorical 'local studies' of the individual lives and output of previously ignored printers, booksellers and retailers such as Francklin, book historians investigating this period will better be able to reconfigure and re-evaluate generalizations about the world of books, producers, dealers and consumers in this era.

23 Barber 1965, 528–37, esp. 530.
24 Riely 1974.
25 Davies 1780, II, 45.
26 McKenzie 1969, 60.
27 Darnton 1982.

19

The Longmans and the book trade, *c.*1730–1830

ASA BRIGGS

The House of Longman, founded in 1724, which survived for 270 years, through seven generations, might well have come to an early end in 1755 with the death of its founder, Thomas Longman (1699–1755). The first member of his family to become a bookseller, Thomas had arrived in London from Bristol in 1716, the orphaned son of a prosperous soapmaker, to be apprenticed to John Osborn(e) 'At the Sign of the Oxford Arms'. In 1724, having just secured his freedom and having conveniently inherited family property, he purchased the premises of William Taylor 'At the Sign of the Ship' in Paternoster Row, later to be numbered 39. A year afterwards, Osborn, who briefly had an earlier business partner, Thomas Varnam, became Thomas's partner, and in 1731 Osborn's sister, Mary, became his wife. They had no children, however, and his partner, John Osborn, died in 1734, leaving Thomas eventually to take on his own nephew. He too was called Thomas (1730–97) (hereafter Thomas II), and had served his apprenticeship with Thomas I, starting it at the age of fifteen and becoming sole head of the House even before Mary's death in 1762.[1] He remained in full control until a few years before his death, having taken into partnership in 1793 his oldest surviving son, Thomas Norton Longman (1771–1842) (Thomas III).

From the start, Thomas I added shrewdly and unobtrusively to the list of books and copyrights that he obtained from Taylor in 1724. It was a list, however, that did not include Taylor's greatest success, Daniel Defoe's *Life and strange surprizing adventures of Robinson Crusoe* (1719).[2] Many of Thomas's later titles, including a share in the tenth edition of *Robinson Crusoe* in 1753,

1 The wills of two John Osborn(e)s make the relationships clear. John, 'of London, Stationer', died on 12 Mar. 1734 and his will (PROB 11/664/68) was proved on 21 Mar. 1734. His father, John 'of Coney Hatch ... Middlesex, Gentleman', made his will a day or so after his son's death on 15 Mar. 1734 (PROB 11/665/118) and it was proved on 21 May 1734. The father was described as of 'Ashborne in the Peake, Derby, Yeoman' at the time of the son's binding in 1703. See also Cameron 1954.

2 Rogers 1979.

were acquired at exclusive booksellers' sales to which, with his Taylor and Osborn connections, Thomas was admitted from the start.[3] Thus, as early as 1725 at a sale in the Queen's Head Tavern, he acquired for £5 a sixth share in John Dunton's *Athenian Mercury*.[4]

Such auction sales were occasions which combined food, drink and business, exclusiveness and conviviality. Necessary capital was raised at a time when liquid capital was short, and financial risks were spread through business associations. Shares in a title might be 'wholes' or 'parts', as small as 1/128th. Thomas acquired both. There was an obvious element of competition in this process as well as of co-operation, but the fact that sales – like the holdings in the deliberately circumscribed Stationers' Company's 'English Stock' – were open only by catalogue, and almost always only to certain members of the metropolitan trade, kept the system closed.[5] The word 'conger', describing the group participating in the sale, was familiar to both Thomas I and Thomas II, although its meaning changed over the course of the eighteenth century, as did the words 'publisher' and 'publishing'.[6]

The so-called Printing Conger, formed a few years before Thomas I started business, was followed in 1736 by a so-called New Conger, which in turn gave way to a bigger organization, based on the Chapter Coffee House in Paternoster Row. Sales there might be held in quite different circumstances – the death, retirement or bankruptcy of an owner; the settlement of a family account; the breaking up of a partnership; or simply the need to raise more money. When, for whatever reason, a book went out of print, shareholders would meet to settle on a new price for a reprint or, if they chose to do so, to keep the book out of print. As the reading public increased, new titles, including part publications, gained in importance; in order to keep pace with the developing market, Thomas II belonged to a 'Literary Club' of booksellers who met – first in the Devil's Tavern, Temple Bar, and later at a monthly dinner at the Shakespeare Tavern – to discuss together 'the germ of many a valuable production'.[7]

3 For 'trade sales', see Belanger 1970, 1975.

4 For Dunton, see McEwen 1972 and Parks 1976.

5 The best description of eighteenth-century structures of economic organization and their dynamics is still Ashton 1955. Ashton 1948, 187: 'the characteristic instrument of economic and social purpose was not the individual nor the State but the club'.

6 Pollard 1978; McKenzie 1976; Curwen 1873, 29, suggested that the word 'conger' derived from eels. The conger as an association would collectively 'swallow all the smaller fry'. Another possible source of the word was said to be *congerie*.

7 *The Aldine magazine of biography, bibliography, criticism and the arts*, Letters to my son at Rome, Letter V, 22 Dec. 1838.

Thomas II took an active part too in the protective politics of copyright. The passing of the so-called 'Copyright Act' of 1710, which stands out in retrospect as a landmark date,[8] had ushered in a new phase in the history of the book trade. Yet, when the law stipulated that a right in an author's work should be secure for only fourteen years, or for a further fourteen if the author were still alive, it did not dispose of the entrenched view of many London booksellers that the common law upheld 'perpetual copyright' in books. Because the Act did not apply to Ireland or Scotland, it opened the way to complaints of Irish or Scottish 'piracy', adding aggressive colour to a debate which seldom transcended protective 'interest'.[9] An Act of 1739, to be renewed every seven years, forbade the import into England and Wales of foreign reprints, and in 1759 Thomas II contributed £100 to a common fund to help enforce it; this was the same size of contribution as his slightly older near-neighbours, the Rivingtons.[10]

Thomas I, within a decade of starting his business, acquired rights in new and old titles. Through the Taylor succession, he acquired as early as 1725 a share in the three-volume *Philosophical works* of the chemist Robert Boyle (1725), edited by Peter Shaw (1694–1763), who became his doctor and friend. This acquisition was followed by a steady flow of publications on science and medicine. It proved useful to Thomas I, as it did to his successors, that some of these publications involved institutional collaboration, in particular with the Royal College of Physicians of London, whose *Dispensatory* was 'printed for T. Longman and J. Nourse' in 1751. In 1733–4, Thomas I and Osborn acted as the London booksellers for the second edition of the Philosophical Society of Edinburgh's *Medical essays and observations*. John Quincy's *Pharmacopoeia officinalis et extemporamen* – 'printed [solely] for Thomas Longman' in 1742 – is a representative example of a Longman reference work, a genre that was already becoming a House speciality. Thomas I also became the biggest shareholder in Ephraim Chambers's *Cyclopaedia of arts and sciences* (1728), and a major shareholder in *An universal history from the earliest account of time to the present* (first instalment, 1730, first five folio volumes, 1744). This ambitious work was immediately translated into foreign languages – the first of them, French, published in Holland in 1731. Volumes on the 'modern' period appeared in 1758 in octavo for half the price of a folio volume.[11]

8 The much investigated Act, described at the time as an Act for the 'encouragement of learning', referred to 'the sole liberty of printing and reprinting' not to copyright as such. It recognized for the first time the prime interest of the author. See M. Rose 1993 and chap. 4, above; Kaplan 1967; and Feather 1994.

9 See Beavan and McDougall, chap. 16 and Benson, chap. 17, both above.

10 Walters 1974.

11 Abbattista 1985.

The most-celebrated consortium to which Thomas I belonged was that which published Samuel Johnson's *Dictionary* in 1755. Johnson was not the first editor of an eighteenth-century English dictionary, however: Thomas I had a share in Nathan Bailey's *An universal etymological English dictionary* (1725). Thomas's was one of the names attached to Johnson's *Prospectus* in 1746; others included Andrew Millar, John and Paul Knapton, and Robert Dodsley, footman turned bookseller, who had set up a bookshop in Pall Mall in 1735; he had published all Johnson's major works between 1738 and 1755. Thomas I died only two months after the *Dictionary* appeared and we know nothing of his reaction to Johnson's great work.[12] Unlike the *Prospectus*, the *Dictionary* bore two Longman names: Thomas I and Thomas II, who had become Thomas I's partner in 1753. The two long-awaited folio volumes of the first edition of the *Dictionary*, priced at £4 10*s*. a set and weighing 25 pounds, were followed by new editions in 1755 (published in 165 sixpenny weekly numbers), 1765, 1773 (revised by Johnson himself and now carrying the imprint of twenty-five booksellers), 1784 and 1786. A 1790 edition to which was prefixed 'a grammar of the English language' was described as 'printed for J.F. and C. Rivington', with fifteen other names to follow. Thomas II's name came third. In his *Dictionary*, Johnson chose to place first in his definitions of publishing the religious use of the word 'publish' – 'proclaiming the good news of the gospel to all mankind' – before giving as his second definition the more humble task of 'putting out a book into the world'. Although the proportion of sermons in the Longman list diminished during the course of the eighteenth century, religion still remained a staple, though not the main staple, in 1830.[13]

Thomas I and Thomas II acquired a major share in the hymns of Isaac Watts which included some of the most famous hymns in the English language. Shares in Watts, like shares in Johnson, were also held by the Rivingtons. In 1711, they acquired the bookselling business of Richard Chiswell, described by Dunton as 'the Metropolitan of Booksellers', who operated on Paternoster Row under 'The Sign of The Bible and Crown'. Charles Rivington (1688–1742) and, later, his sons were committed Church of England booksellers, particularly after John Rivington (1720–75) was appointed publisher to the Society for Promoting Christian Knowledge (SPCK) in 1760.[14] Yet, like the Longmans, the Rivingtons were not exclusively concerned with one line of

12 Sledd and Kolb 1955; Reddick 1990.

13 *Gentleman's Magazine*, May 1734, 259: 'As to *Religion*', a bookseller reported, 'if we take a view of our *Stock* and *Copies*, or our *Accounts*, we find ourselves indebted to it for so great a proportion of our *Income* as three parts in Four.'

14 See Mandelbrote, chap. 32, below; for the Rivingtons, see Rivington 1919 and Fitzpatrick 1995.

publishing and added greatly to their income when they brought out Samuel Richardson's novel *Pamela* in 1740.

The fortunes of the Rivingtons, prominent in the affairs of the Stationers' Company, and those of the Longmans often converged, and in 1890 the Longmans were to take over the House of Rivington in the most dramatic – and surprising – of Victorian publishing takeovers.[15] Nevertheless, between 1724 and 1842 there was never the same kind of intimate relationship between the two Houses as there was, both through rivalry and through co-operation, between the Longmans and the Murrays. The relationship was summarized in a fascinating letter written years later in 1879 by Thomas IV's son after his father's death. 'My dear father', he told Murray, 'was so closely connected with yourself in so many things and in a manner more closely than any one else.'[16]

We have no information as to why Thomas I was apprenticed to Osborn, nor why he or his family decided that he should become a bookseller. There are no personal records of his experiences as a bookseller, nor indeed of those of Thomas II. Institutional records were lost in fires in 1861 and, devastatingly, in the Blitz of 1940.[17] For contemporary impressions of the eighteenth-century book trade – a trade that changed significantly before the advent of major alterations in production technology – and for contemporary impressions of the Longmans' significance within the trade, we have to turn to other booksellers. One valuable source is John Murray I (1737–93), who in different circumstances from Thomas Longman I – and in parallel to Thomas Longman II – also founded what came to be thought of as a publishing dynasty. Fresh from Scotland, he moved into bookselling at 32 Fleet Street in London not through apprenticeship, as Thomas I had done, but through the navy. He died four years before Thomas II, who was already established when he began. Murray knew nothing then about the book trade that he was entering. His most substantial asset was confidence. 'Many blockheads in the trade are making fortunes', he told the friend he hoped would become his partner, 'and did we not succeed as well as these, I think must be imputed only to ourselves.'[18] Of course, access to capital in an age without an organized capital market mattered almost as much as brains. Unlike Thomas I and II, Murray was short of capital when he first undertook the trade in 1768, relying on a loan to acquire 32 Fleet Street from the bookseller William Sandby for £1,000. In

15 See, for example, the *Daily Telegraph*, 31 May 1890.
16 Letter of 6 Sep. 1879 in the Murray archives, NLS.
17 Accounting for the title of Blagden 1949 – *Fire more than water*.
18 Zachs 1998, 24.

contrast, Thomas I had been able to pay the large sum of £2,282 9*s*. 6*d*. from his inheritance in 1724 for Taylor's premises and its contents in Paternoster Row. Location mattered too, and the situations of the Longman and Murray premises figure differently and in contrast to each other in publishing history. Many memories and myths gathered round Paternoster Row,[19] but Fleet Street, where Murray first operated – by coincidence also at the 'Sign of the Ship' – subsequently became associated not with bookselling but with the production of newspapers. The history of such serial publications, particularly in the eighteenth century, could never be completely separated from the history of books.[20]

With two interesting, if qualified, exceptions, the Longmans never printed their books themselves. The first exception arose from the fact that John Osborn II bequeathed to his brother-in-law his moiety of a share as 'King's Printer in the Latin, Greek and Hebrew tongues'. (Buckley, who had launched the *Daily Courant* in 1702 and who had been the first joint-publisher of the *Spectator* in 1711, held the other moiety.) The second exception was that, in the second decade of the nineteenth century, a number of imprints bear the words 'from the private press of Longman & Co'. These were all associated, however, with one man, Sir Egerton Brydges (1762–1837), a committed bibliophile, who also bought rare books from the Longmans and sold some to them for their Old Book Department. Characteristic private press books were Brydge's *Censura literaria* (1815), 'containing titles, abstracts and opinions of old books', and John Brady's *Clavis calendaria or a compendious analysis of the calendar* (1812). Thomas Davison was the printer. In 1824, Brydges claimed that 'the publication of the *Censura* did far more in promoting a taste for old English Bibliography than all other works that were ever published, but unfortunately the number of collectors is considerably reduced'.[21] Eleven years earlier, a four-page folio catalogue for Longman's had given details, with prices, of first or rare editions, 'fifty great works', including Lysons's *Environs of London* and Walton's *Compleat angler*, and whether or not the number of collectors had subsequently declined, the Longman Old Book Department had augmented its stock by acquiring a large collection of scarce and curious books from the great collection of Thomas Hill.[22]

19 Raven 1997c; Harvey 1863.
20 See Harris, chap. 20, below and 1978b; Asquith 1978; Ferdinand, chap. 21, below; Cranfield 1962.
21 Longman Archive, University of Reading, MS 1393/29/1.
22 The Hill Catalogue, *Bibliotheca Anglo-poetic*, was prepared by a Longman clerk. For Hill, the original of Poole's 'Paul Pry', and other collectors, see Roberts 1895, 79–80. Cf. Landon, chap. 38, below.

Murray and his son after him had no interest in dealing in old books or in appealing to book collectors. They were like the Longmans, however, in having close relations with the printer William Strahan (1715–85), who built up a fortune from shares in books as well as from printing. Later, there were Longman links through marriage with the Spottiswoodes – Andrew Spottiswoode was Strahan's great-nephew – and with the papermakers John Dickinson and Sons. Such dynastic connections did not stop the Longmans from turning to other printers or other papermakers, however. Like Strahan, they treasured their independence.

Both Thomas I and, even more, Murray I were interested in extending the scope and range of their own business. Thomas I and his nephew preferred building up a substantial home trade – wholesaling books as well as retailing them – and developing a foreign trade (Murray did this too) to making bold innovations and diversifying their business, as some other booksellers, notably the Newberys, chose to do.[23] The Longman domestic business was less influenced by fashion than was that of the Newberys, but novels figured prominently in their late eighteenth-century lists. In foreign trade, Murray looked to India – Warren Hastings was a customer – where later the Longmans were to build up a publishing empire of their own.[24] Thomas Longman II looked to America.

The expanding Longman home trade rested on a network of contacts, some of them expressed in imprints that were not always consistently framed and not always straightforward to understand. (Shrewsbury, for example, figures particularly frequently in imprints that included the Longman name.) Strahan too kept his name off many books in which he had a substantial financial interest. The provincial booksellers named in many imprints were even less of a homogeneous group than the metropolitan 'publishers'. Although some of the books they handled were by local authors and were sold mainly within a local and regional network, the geography of the trade changed considerably with the eighteenth-century development of physical infrastructures and of commercial and cultural networks. Crucial to provincial publishing was advertising in local newspapers, which increased in numbers and in circulation throughout the century.[25]

Longman's foreign trade was mainly transatlantic, and Thomas II's interest in the American market, real but not unique, is reflected in his transatlantic correspondence with Henry Knox, a bookseller in Boston with whom he

23 Welsh 1885.
24 Zachs 1998, 37.
25 Cranfield 1962; Briggs and Burke 2002. Cf. Ferdinand, chap. 21 and Turner, chap. 23, both below.

provided catalogues and to whom he sent books and periodicals, warning him not to 'undersell' the former.[26] The two men became personal friends, and their friendship survived the American War of Independence. Enterprising though this trade was, Thomas I's most important business strategy was to move into educational publishing, which was to become a lucrative Longman speciality. In 1725, he was among the publishers of John Locke's *Some thoughts concerning education*, and in 1736 – three years after the death of his partner – he combined with another bookseller, Samuel Buckley, to purchase 'the Royal Grant and Privilege' of printing William Lily's sixteenth-century Latin grammar; their 'revised and improved' edition was printed in the hope that it would 'win the Approbation and Encouragement of those Gentlemen who have the Care and Instruction of Youth'.[27] The purchase was deemed so important by Thomas that the name Norton, that of the family from whom he acquired it, passed into the Longman family with Thomas Norton Longman (hereafter, Thomas III), the first of the Longmans to be called (mainly in retrospect) a publisher and not simply a bookseller.

It was Thomas III who in 1799 purchased a major share in the copyright of Lindley Murray's *English grammar*, a valuable property, written by a man born in America in 1745, who had moved to Britain in 1784. This and other works by Murray added to a sizeable backlist of widely used Longman educational books – soon to appear regularly in separate catalogues – most of them regarded as textbooks. Murray, who wrote French as well as English grammars, was sometimes called 'The Father of Grammar', and his *English grammar* remained in Longman catalogues for more than a century. Murray also wrote an *English reader*, used on both sides of the Atlantic, along with many related books, including 'exercises and keys'.

A Longman interest not extended far beyond 1815 was publishing for the theatre. It has sometimes been suggested that this line of business was the result of the marriage of Thomas II in 1760 to the sister of Thomas Harris, who for many years was the proprietor and manager of Covent Garden, one of the three licensed theatres in London at that time. In fact, Longman had previously published several plays performed outside London. The Longman interest in the theatrical market is also reflected in translations of plays, among them August von Kotzbue's *The East Indian* (1799). Some British dramatists had the majority of their books published by Longman; others were 'printed under the authority of and by permission of the managers from the prompt books'.

26 The correspondence has fortunately survived and is in the possession of the Massachusetts Historical Society. There are copies in the Bodleian Library.

27 Cox and Chandler 1925, 9.

Longman playwrights included John O'Keeffe (1747–1833), William Pearce (1738–95), Thomas Morton (1764–1838) and Frederick Reynolds (1764–1841).

Neither John Murray I nor the Rivingtons were greatly involved with the theatre, but Murray was very quickly interested in extending his business by bringing out newspapers and periodicals as well as books. As early as the summer of 1769, a close adviser of Murray, Gilbert Stuart, told him (less than a year after he moved to Fleet Street) to 'connect' himself with 'some review or periodical work'. 'The advantage of such things to a bookseller is inconceivable,' he explained.[28] A newspaper came first: a twentieth share in the *Morning Chronicle and London Advertiser*. Murray soon disposed of it, however, planning instead, with Strahan, a different newspaper, which never took off. In 1770 he founded a review, the *Repository or Treasury of Politics and Literature*, which he quickly discontinued, the first of a number of ventures in reviewing, including the *English Review* (1783). Ten years later, the Rivingtons brought out the *British Critic* just as Britain was going to war with revolutionary France.

Thomas II was more cautious – and prudent – than Murray, although in 1788 he canvassed support for 'a periodical paper called *The Times*'.[29] Two years before his death, he published along with John Debrett an eight-page periodical, the *Sylph*, which lasted for less than a year.[30] It may have been Thomas III who was responsible for the *Sylph*; certainly, he preceded John Murray II in introducing a new phase in the history of the periodical when – with the pioneering Scottish publisher, Archibald Constable (1774–1827) – he co-launched the *Edinburgh Review* in 1802. Murray's Tory *Quarterly Review* followed in 1809. Both reviews survived into the twentieth century, the former remaining Whig in outlook until its end in 1929.

John Murray II was as determined as his father had been to enter directly into the newspaper business, planning in 1825 to establish another new Tory newspaper to rival *The Times* in much the same way that the *Quarterly* rivalled the *Edinburgh*. In 1826, he started the *Representative*, providing half the financial backing. A young and ambitious Benjamin Disraeli, son of a long-standing friend of the Murrays, had promised the rest.[31] In a critical year in the history of publishing and, indeed, for the economy,[32] the venture failed, placing Murray

28 Zachs 1998, 200 and chap. 11, *passim*.
29 C.W. Dilke, *Diary*, 4 Jan. 1788: 'Mr Longman wrote to me desiring my support to a periodical paper called *The Times*.'
30 Marr 1924, 238–40; Sullivan 1983b, 399.
31 Blake 1966, 27–43 for an account of the relationship of Disraeli and Murray and for the disastrous history of the *Representative*.
32 Gayer, Rostow and Schwartz 1953, I, 180–210; J.A. Sutherland 1987.

in a difficult financial position. He never again attempted to publish another newspaper.

Thomas I and Thomas II, like Murray I, always called themselves 'booksellers', not publishers, although they all produced books on their own account. In contrast, Thomas III and his partners and John Murray II – still calling themselves (and being called) booksellers – have passed into history as 'publishers', a term whose meaning had changed during the course of the eighteenth century. The shift was not sudden; there was a gradual development in both the function and the status of 'publisher'. Dunton had dreamed of dispensing with a bookshop; James Dodsley (1724–97) did so. By 1818, another new-style 'publisher', (Sir) Richard Phillips (1767–1840), described in his *Book of English trades* the 'Bookseller of the present day' as 'a person of considerable importance in the republic of letters, more especially if he combines those particular branches of the trade denominated *Proprietor* and *Publisher*: for it is to such men that our men of genius take their publications for sale'. Nonetheless, Phillips, who had sold only his own publications since 1806,[33] did not include a separate entry on 'publishers'.[34] He himself concentrated on school-books, dealing extensively with Thomas III who acquired some of his property in 1818 and the remainder ten years later.

In the supplement to the third edition of the *Encyclopaedia Britannica* (1818), a contributor stated that the firm of Cadell and Davies provided 'the example of an establishment avoiding all business, even wholesale, except what relates to books printed for their own account. These sub-divisions tend exceedingly to facilitate business: they cause it to be done both better and to a greater extent.'[35] Nevertheless, Thomas III continued, whatever the scale of his own new publishing business, to run a retail shop and to promote an active 'country market'. (It was not until 1886 that the Longmans' shop in Paternoster Row, producing regular catalogues of books it could 'supply from stock', was closed.) Thus, in a characteristic letter of 1813, 'Messrs Longman and Co' told a would-be customer in Londonderry how to open an account with them, adding that there was a nine-month credit period from the receipt of an invoice or a 7½ per cent discount. They sent him a catalogue and asked him to refer to 'some house in Belfast, where we correspond pretty extensively'.[36]

33 Pollard 1978, 35, where he quotes an anonymous author of a *Memoir of Sir Richard Phillips* (1808) who stated that 'he is now the first publisher in London: he sells only his own publications'.
34 *The book of English trades* (1818), 36 – 'to be had of all booksellers'.
35 Pollard 1978, 36.
36 22 Feb. 1818.

While the reputation of Longman remained high – and its output of new books substantial, more than that of any other publisher – it was their friendly rival John Murray II who did most to establish the role of the 'publisher' as it subsequently came to be pursued during the Victorian years. He was clearer than his father or Thomas I and II had been about the scope and direction of his publishing enterprise. Inheriting his father's business as a minor in 1793, Murray II got rid – in 1804 – of Samuel Highley, the partner he inherited, and took full charge of the business as quickly as he possibly could. Two much-quoted statements of his demonstrate his lack of interest not only in retailing but also in wholesaling his own as well as other people's books. 'Country orders', he told Constable in 1805, 'are a brand of business which I have ever totally declined as incompatible with my more serious plans as a publisher.'[37] 'The business of a publishing bookseller', he told Sir Walter Scott, 'is not in his shop or even in his connections but in his brains.'[38] Nevertheless, Murray continued sometimes to describe himself as a bookseller.

Constable, a pioneering publisher who figures explicitly in the first of these quotations and whose haunting presence lies behind the second, was just as articulate as Murray when describing the scope of his own enterprise, and it is significant that for Scott it was not Murray but Constable who was 'the prince of publishers', the man 'who knew more of the business of a bookseller [Scott reverted to the still-most-common term] than any man of his time'.[39] Constable, who had dealings with both Murray and Longman, must always be considered when the shift from bookselling to publishing is under review. Yet, as he was located in Scotland, Constable depended on connections in London, just as all English provincial booksellers did.[40] When he opened business on his own account at the age of twenty-one in 1795 – ironically dealing at first in old books – it was to Thomas III that he first turned.

When Thomas III acquired a half-share in the *Edinburgh Review* and a major stake in Scott's *Minstrelsy of the border* from Constable in 1802, he told Constable that he recognized him as 'a real man of business, of honourable mind, and of universally acknowledged talents in [his] profession'. A year later, he expressed his hope that 'by a liberal exchange of copyright, and thus promoting our interests, we shall infallibly raise our fortunes and our names infinitely higher and to a more important station than has yet been known in

37 Smiles 1891, II, 511.
38 Smiles 1891, II, 512.
39 Scott 1890, II, 11.
40 For Scotland, see Millgate 1996; for the English provinces, see Feather 1985.

the annals of our profession'.[41] Yet, it was not to be (nor was a mutual arrangement made in 1806 between Murray and Constable to work either). In 1807 Longman sold his share of the *Edinburgh Review* back to Constable, only to re-secure it in 1814. Meanwhile, in 1809 Murray had launched the *Quarterly Review* which, from 1827 to 1853, was to be edited by Scott's son-in-law, John Gibson Lockhart.

The triangular relationship between Longman, Murray and Constable is at the core of early nineteenth-century publishing as it came to define itself and of the literary history of Scott, Wordsworth and Byron, among others. Yet, as is well known, Constable's fall into financial crisis was even more rapid than his ascent into prosperity, and in 1826 Scott fell with him. Ballantyne and Company, publishers as well as printers, a company in which Scott had been a secret partner with no limited liability, went down too, forcing Scott, who refused to declare himself bankrupt, into a period of strenuous and ultimately wearing literary activity.[42] Of course, the relationship of Murray to Byron raised many other issues beyond the financial sphere – including the critical role of the *Edinburgh Review*, also an important factor in the case of Thomas III and Wordsworth.[43] Byron's vitriolic diatribe, *English bards and Scotch reviewers*, was refused by Longman because of its onslaught on Wordsworth and Scott's poetry; the 'Lake poets' themselves, including Wordsworth, were sharply criticized in the *Edinburgh*. Byron moved over to Murray, and there was never such a dramatic event in the history of the House of Longman as the burning of his memoirs in Murray's own drawing room on 17 May 1824, a month after the poet's death.

Murray II and Thomas III were alike in giving parties for their authors and other invited guests; Murray even kept portraits of 'his' authors – Coleridge, Scott, Byron, Southey and Tom Moore – in his drawing room. Moore, however, was above all a 'Longman author', a term beginning to become common, and in 1814 Thomas III agreed to pay him the unprecedented sum of £3,000 for a romantic poem, to be called *Lalla Rookh*, which Moore had not yet started. It was not published until 1817 and, unlike Wordsworth's collected *Poems* (1815), was an immediate financial success, running into six printings in its first year. In making deals with authors and in entertaining them before and after he had signed them on, Thomas III had an invaluable partner from 1799

41 Constable 1873, III, 47: letter of 31 Dec. 1803.

42 For the unsigned Waverley novels, see Millgate 1984. Longman published Scott's *Guy Mannering or the astrologer* (1815), the first novel to appear under the name of 'the author of Waverley'. See Beavan and McDougall, chap. 16, above.

43 Francis Jeffrey's 'campaign' against Wordsworth and the 'Lake poets' went on until 1822 when he pronounced the Lake School of Poetry 'pretty nearly extinct' (*Edinburgh Review*, 23 (1822), p. 449).

to 1837, Owen Rees (1770–1837). Describing a dinner party at Thomas's house in Hampstead, the American writer Washington Irving (1783–1859) recorded that the two ends of the dining table were occupied by the two partners of the House: 'the grave gentleman' and 'carving partner [Longman], who attend[ed] to the joints' and 'the laughing partner [Rees] who attend[ed] to the jokes'.[44]

The partnership between Thomas III and Rees, the initial date of which has often been misrepresented,[45] has rightly been identified as a landmark event in the history of the publishing house. Inadequate attention has been paid, however, to the significant introduction of two other new partners in 1804: Thomas Hurst (1775–1847) and Cosmo Orme (1780–1859).[46] It is noteworthy that Hurst's name was placed second, before that of Rees, in Longman imprints between 1804 and 1825, by which time two other partners had been added: Thomas Brown (1784–1829), who had entered the House at the age of fourteen and became a partner in 1811, and Bevis E. Green (1794–1869), who had been apprenticed to Hurst when he came to the Row in 1807 and who became a partner in 1824. Brown, the son of a bookseller, lived at 39 Paternoster Row longer than any of his fellow-partners until the fire there in 1861; he was known then as 'the Nestor of the Row'. Green was in charge of both the country trade and the foreign trade and was succeeded by his son.

'Messrs Longman' was now 'the Long Firm', as Sir Walter Scott called it, with as many as six partners on its imprint in 1832. Another more colourful description of Thomas III and his fellow partners was 'the Divan'. Murray II was nicknamed 'Emperor of the West' and Constable, while he lasted, 'the Czar of Muscovy'. Nicknames were not required, however, to direct attention to the increasingly specialized tasks the various Longman partners carried out, still with a small staff, and their increasing need to confer on their decisions. They developed the habit, to be continued deep into the twentieth century, of transacting business late in the morning, meeting informally and (until 1957) not keeping notes or putting matters to the vote.[47] They were financially successful too: Thomas III left a private estate of more than £200,000 when

44 Wallis 1974, 18–19.

45 The date of the Thomas Norton/Rees partnership is not given on a nineteenth-century list of Longman partners (probably recorded by the head of the Binding Department). It has often been stated that Rees became a partner before Thomas II died and Wallis 1974, who used the House list, not only described Rees as 'active from 1797' but included in his list of Longman imprints Messrs Longman and Rees 1797–9. There is no such imprint.

46 Hurst and Orme had been joint partners at a neighbouring bookselling business at 32 Paternoster Row, and they took with them to no. 39 capital derived from a substantial wholesale business with strong provincial connections. Orme, in particular, had many literary and social contacts.

47 Wallis 1974, 52.

he died in 1842; Brown left more than £100,000, and Green almost as large a sum as Thomas III.

Rees, the first of the strangers to the Longman family firm – and the most important of them – was active until his retirement to Wales just before his death in 1837. He had been still in his twenties in 1799, when he arrived in London from Bristol, as Thomas I had done, but having been apprenticed to a Bristol bookseller and afterwards having set up a shop of his own, he had already had valuable experience of authors and printers as well as of booksellers. As soon as he arrived in Paternoster Row, he established an effective working relationship with Thomas III; it is evidence of their energy and drive that they brought out no fewer than ninety titles in 1800, including the second edition of Wordsworth and Coleridge's *Lyrical ballads* in two volumes.

This was not the first edition of the *Ballads*, of course. That – in one volume, with an 'advertisement' and not a preface, and with no authors' names attached to it – had appeared in Bristol in 1798 under the auspices of a local bookseller, Joseph Cottle (1770–1853), whose shop was near to that of Rees. In 1798, Cottle was in serious financial difficulties and as a consequence he disposed of 108 of his copyrights to Longman and Rees.[48] *Lyrical ballads* was not among them. Cottle had paid Wordsworth 30 guineas for the copyright but subsequently returned it to the poet; Longman and Rees acquired it from Wordsworth – and from 1800 to 1836 they continued to be Wordsworth's publishers, not always to his satisfaction.[49] Indeed, he moved over in 1836 to Edward Moxon, who had been a much trusted employee of Longman and Rees, but who subsequently set up business on his own. The Longman/Rees relationship with Coleridge was to be even more complex. Brilliant though he was, Coleridge proved unreliable in meeting his authorial obligations.

Wordsworth was concerned not only for his own finances, but also for the financial future of his children; supported by Southey, he accordingly took an almost obsessive interest in problems of copyright.[50] Thomas III's concern, going back much further in time, was less emotional but equally real. He gave informative evidence to the select committee on copyright in 1813, one year before the new 'Copyright Act' of 1814, which extended the term of fourteen years laid down in the 1710 Act to twenty-eight years, or – if the author was alive at the end of that time – for the rest of his or her life. It was soon after that

48 For Cottle, see Bracken and Silver 1995, 66–74.
49 For a meticulous study of the finances as seen by the publisher, see Owen 1954.
50 Gill 1955. Cf. Rose, chap. 4, above.

Southey argued the case for perpetual copyright in the interest of authors: 'With what justice, or under what pretext of public good, are men of letters deprived of a perpetual copyright in the produce of their own ideas?'[51]

The views of Thomas III and Rees on copyright were set out in evidence they gave to select committees of the House of Commons, and which covered many other matters, including pricing, the effect on turnover of fluctuations in trade, the impact of the paper duties, and advertising. Southey joined Longman and Rees and John Murray II in complaining too about the statutory obligation to supply copies of books to academic libraries, the number of which had been increased in 1800 to eleven, an obligation said to have cost Messrs Longman £3,000 in four years and Murray £1,875. At times, they were advised by Sir Egerton Brydges who was a specialist not only in old books but in copyright. Brydges extravagantly described the 'Copyright Act' as it was being enforced as 'the most perfect instrument of collecting and disseminating all the mischiefs flowing out of an abuse of the Liberty of the Press, which human ingenuity has yet contrived'.[52]

Neither Thomas III, who died in 1842 (the year that the Literary Copyright Act became law), nor Murray II, who died a year later, was a believer in 'free trade in books', which became a rallying cry later in the century. Murray, like Constable before him, however, believed, at least for a time, in supplying cheaper books that would be accessible to a larger public. Constable had talked of tapping 'millions' of readers for his *Miscellany* (begun 1827): inspired by him, Murray launched a 'Family Library' (begun 1829) on the same day that Charles Knight, most eloquent advocate of and publisher of 'cheap books', issued his first volume in a 'Library of Entertaining Knowledge'. For different reasons, both ventures failed, and Murray had to dispose of his forty-seven volumes to Thomas Tegg, who was already flourishing by dealing in what came to be called 'remainders' and in cheap reprints.[53] In 1828, both Thomas III and Murray II refused to provide books for W. Pickering, a London bookseller who was prepared to 'undersell' to the public – that is, to charge lower prices than the rules of the metropolitan booksellers dictated. Longman and Co., as they described themselves, stated succinctly, as did Rivingtons, that 'they could not let Mr Pickering have books, his name not being on the list of recognized Booksellers' (that is, a list drawn up by a self-constituted committee of booksellers conforming to standard procedures), while Murray

51 *Quarterly Review*, 21, 61 (1819), 211–13; Letter of Wordsworth to J. Forbes Mitchell, 21 Apr. 1819 in De Selincourt 1937, II, 844.

52 Parsons 1974, 46.

53 See Bonnell, chap. 37, below.

went further and declared that he 'would not sell any body a book that sold Mr Pickering one'.[54]

In the evidence they gave to Parliament, Thomas III and Rees maintained that prices were high during the Revolutionary and Napoleonic wars, higher than they had been before the wars began, 'simply because costs were high', although the 'monopoly' of the publishers surely had its effect too. Different publishers responded to the price rise in different ways, but when the financial downturn came in 1826, two of the most important publishers who were not forced back by it were Longmans, whose reputation was scarcely shaken, and Henry Colburn,[55] a new kind of publisher who established a 'three-decker' mode of publication with three post-octavo volumes costing 31*s*. 6*d*.[56] Thomas III and Rees pursued a steady course, producing educational books at all levels alongside novels and Thomas Bowdler's painstakingly abridged and adapted bestselling *Family Shakespeare* (1818).

One Longman/Rees strength that remained was the preparation of substantial works of reference that in previous generations might well have demanded a consortium to finance them. These included two innovative encyclopaedias: Abraham Rees's *New cyclopaedia* (1802–19), which competed in quality with the *Encyclopaedia Britannica* and ran to forty-five quarto volumes, and *The cabinet encyclopaedia* (1826–46), a part-work which ran to 133 numbers, each with its own author and its own title, and costing only 6*s*. There could be intellectual pleasure even in such 'steadiness' and there was genuine excitement at 39 Paternoster Row on 'Magazine Days (and Nights)', when periodicals of all kinds, some associated with Longman, like the *Athenaeum* founded in 1828 and taken over in 1830 (with Longman support) by Charles Wentworth Dilke, were disposed of for ready money and there was 'constant bustle kept up from morning till night'.[57] Thus, there was both great continuity and genuine innovation in 'the Long Firm' in the first several decades of the nineteenth century. Still greater changes were soon to come, however. With the development of a cheaper and more regular postal system, pressed for by Thomas III, and a railway system on which it depended, all publishers great and small would soon enter a new period in the history of the book.

54 The replies are quoted in Pollard 1978, 46.

55 Crabb Robinson reported in June 1826 that an informed visitor had told him that 'booksellers' were 'in a deplorable condition . . . with the possible exception of Colburn and Longman', he doubted 'whether any of them are solvent'. Robinson 1938, II, 337. Cf. J.A. Sutherland 1987.

56 Sutherland 1986. Colburn extended himself, however, and in 1829 was forced into an 'ill-fated' partnership with Richard Bentley.

57 Pollard 1978, 39, quoting James Grant, 'Magazine night' (1838); Francis 1888.

III
SERIAL PUBLICATION AND THE TRADE

20
London newspapers

MICHAEL HARRIS

Introduction

Serial publication was the engine that drove the generalized expansion of print through London and the nation during the long eighteenth century. This period saw the transition of the London print business from a small-scale workshop activity, supported by modest lines of distribution and catering to a coherent and identifiable audience, towards an industrialized system geared to a highly diversified and expanding market. Underlying the pattern of change in this as in most other forms of commercial activity was the general process of population increase. In London the population of just over half a million in 1695 remained fairly static until the middle of the next century. By 1801, the momentum of increase had pushed the population over one million, a number that more than doubled by 1841. The pattern of population increase in the nation at large followed a similar trajectory. Through the eighteenth century changes within the print business were organizational rather than technological and it was the serial that came to provide the main framework for the internal structure of the London trade. When the new commercial possibilities of the expanding market began to open up in the early nineteenth century, the impulse to mechanization and specialization was again focused in serial publication. The London print trade synchronized its response to changes in the market through this commercial device. That is not to say that the serial simply represented a response to economic circumstances, a means of adapting and responding to market forces; the serial also provided a medium through which many of the internal tensions in play in the London trade itself, as well as in the wider worlds of politics and commerce, could be expressed.

Serialization as a publishing strategy offered benefits to a range of producers, readers and users. For the producers, printers, booksellers and to a lesser extent authors, the serial became a means by which output could be organized – presses kept in motion, stock replenished and work time-tabled.

At the same time, serial publication itself became the primary medium for promoting all other forms of print. Systematic advertising by members of the London trade, whether with a direct commercial interest in serial publication or not, created and sustained audiences predisposed to participation by consumption of the serials themselves. Serials offered members of the trade a means of spreading commercial risk. Producers were able to reduce the level of start-up costs and minimize working capital on projects which, by staged publication, could be monitored for symptoms of public interest or lack of it. Built into the serials in general and the newspapers in particular was a form of continuous market research. For the consumer, serialization offered parallel benefits. Cheapness, the outlay of a few pence at a time, the value and interest of continuously updated material, the means of direct access to the communities implicit in the form (primarily, though not only, by advertising), combined to hold the readers of newspapers and other serials in place.

The conditions that supported the flow of serial print both within London and across the nation were taking shape by the 1690s but were developed and extended across the next century. In the metropolis itself the network of public houses, particularly the coffee houses, rapidly became associated with the production, distribution and consumption of serial news. The number of coffee houses in London in 1700 is, to some extent, unknowable since the use of premises for public leisure could ebb and flow unpredictably and contemporary estimates were based on uncertain definitions and were widely variable. A figure in the region of 400 or 500 might make sense for the early eighteenth century. In the crammed spaces of metropolitan London sociability, particularly at a middling level, was centred in the public houses with their inescapable components of news and gossip whether in spoken or written form. Under the Licensing Act, coffee houses became the primary focus for the construction and distribution of manuscript news and consequently for attack by government. The relationship with news began to shift from the mid-1690s when the move away from manuscript to print created an alternative centre of gravity in the printing office. While the coffee house continued to provide a base for manuscript news publication, it also became a crucial centre for access to printed newspapers. This relationship was not uncontested but the existence of an infrastructure of public spaces in London was crucial to the development of the newspaper as a form.

At the same time, the road network, as the basis of physical communication, played an equally important part in fostering the production and distribution of printed news. The roads linking London to all parts of the United Kingdom were progressively subject to the interventions of private enterprise through the turnpike trusts. As surfaces were improved and journey times were cut, the flow of information was also speeded up. For newspaper proprietors and readers it was the use made of the road system by the Post Office that had a primary and growing importance. The Penny Post, set up by Robert Docwra in 1680, had created a rapid and effective means of local communication within London, which extended beyond the Bills of Mortality and provided services based partly on the public house network. This entrepreneurial venture was rapidly absorbed into the state monopoly, becoming part of the well-established general post. From the 1630s London was plugged into a national and international communication system through the Post Office, whose services were extended to Ireland, the Continent and America by way of packet boats scheduled out of the leading ports. By 1700 the posts were leaving London for the English provinces three times a week on Tuesdays, Thursdays and Saturdays, returning on the intermediate days. Posts going further afield arrived and left every day of the week. News moved through the posts, arriving in multiple forms – in manuscript and in varieties of print. In London this material was collected, translated if necessary, repackaged and supplemented to be redistributed through the posts to a new set of consumers. The Post Office was at the heart of this system. The six Clerks of the main roads, which lead into and out of London like the spokes of a wheel, were from an early date complicit in the collection of news and the distribution of the reconstituted product. Their right of franking materials through the post free of charge, a right extended to other official groups during the eighteenth century, had been applied under the licence to the distribution of the *London Gazette*. From 1695 the emergence of commercial news publications geared to the postal services created an immediate circuit linking producers, clerks and readers. By the mid-eighteenth century the arrangements had been centralized within the Post Office and the Clerks, who individually held shares in the London tri-weeklies, purchased copies on a growing scale to send on to their customers at a reduced postal rate. Provincial readers of London newspapers rapidly became dependent for their supply, whether by way of a local bookseller or public house, on the six Clerks at St Martin's-Le-Grand.

Among the conditions usually cited as necessary for the development of the London press was the level of literacy in the capital, which was unusually high. Estimates put the extent of male literacy at around 80 per cent of the total population at the beginning of the eighteenth century and female literacy at about 40 per cent.[1] Both were rising. The circumstances of urban, and in

1 For a comparative analysis of male and female literacy in London and elsewhere based on signatures, see Cressy 1980. See also Suarez, Introduction, above.

particular metropolitan, life made reading a key skill. It was promoted by the prevalence of print at street level where posters and notices, a torrent of handbills, and the general paraphernalia of commercial activity pushed the ability to read well down the social scale. Access by purchase also became widely available. Through the seventeenth century and until the tax of 1712, newspapers cost 1*d*. The familiar images of street-corner readings and group purchase, endlessly repeated, have served to emphasize the element of democratic engagement.[2] It is clear that some kinds of trickle-down access to newspapers and other forms of serial print were becoming increasingly widespread. However, the construction and growth of the London newspaper press during the eighteenth century was not dependent on a widening of the target audience. The papers remained inherently part of the culture of the dynamic and entrepreneurial group characterized as the middling ranks of society or even, subsequently, as the 'middle class'.[3] Taking in the upper levels of the business community, as well as the shopkeepers and artisans earning £50 a year or more, they formed just over 20 per cent of the metropolitan population and constituted the core element of the readership. The expansion of output that took place across this period can be directly related to the increase in the numbers of this sector and of equivalent groups in other urban centres across the United Kingdom.

It was the 'Glorious Revolution' that laid the platform for the development of the London newspapers by creating the conditions for a general commercial expansion as well as for some political regrouping. What has been called the 'Financial Revolution', with its complex elements of joint-stock finance and improved systems of credit, created a new level of demand for information and publicity.[4] The longest running serials in London had been based on the supply of updated commercial information and the earliest newspapers had been produced and published in the immediate vicinity of the Royal Exchange. This line of interest was reinforced in 1688 and again in 1695 with the lapse of the censorship arrangements. As the business serials increased in number and variety, so the new generation of commercial newspapers were saturated with materials of value and interest to the widely dispersed trading community; ship news, the prices of stocks and commodities, as well as the more generalized coverage of national and international news, locked in widening circles of individuals to the readership of the London serials.[5]

2 The most frequently quoted account of group purchase by shoeblacks and others was given by de Saussure 1995, 101.

3 For example, in Earle 1989.

4 Dickson 1993.

5 For newspaper coverage of trade and shipping, see Harris 1999b. Cf. McCusker, chap. 22, below.

The impact of the Revolution on the structure of politics also had considerable importance for the development of the news and news-related serial. The emergence of a formally constituted two-party system, whereby distinct sets of ideology were identified within an acknowledged framework of authority, created an environment in which public debate became an integral part of the political process. The post-1695 London papers were engulfed by the publications generated by party conflict which, during Queen Anne's reign, centred on series of dedicated essay sheets linked in various ways to the leading Whig and Tory politicians. The deployment of money in support of propaganda to complement the use of legal action against the London papers was initiated early in the eighteenth century. This dual policy of benefit and threat continued fitfully, taking on a particular force under the administrations of Robert Harley, Robert Walpole and the elder and younger Pitt when substantial amounts of time and public money were applied to sections of the London press.[6] Commercial newspapers adopted political positions for financial as well as ideological reasons, and into the next century the character of content and readership continued to be influenced by party considerations.

Business and politics became, and remained, key elements in the development of the London newspapers, although the cultural interests of the English middle class – behaviour and manners, sport, the theatre, and other respectable and increasingly commercialized activities – figured prominently within the nexus of news, information, comment and advertising. All these elements were brought together in the commercial newspapers, which were legitimized in the key event of the 1690s, the lapse of the Printing Acts. From 1662 onwards, the Acts had required that all material should be submitted to a licenser before being printed, but its application by the state had ebbed and flowed through the seventeenth century as executive authority broke down and was reconstituted. The system of pre-publication censorship had centred on the Stationers' Company. The mutual interests of the leading members of the book trade and of the political authorities coincided in the control of printing which in turn was centred on the restraint of serial news. Under the Printing Acts, only the *London Gazette* offered a printed narrative of events. The lapse of the Acts in 1695, for a variety of political, cultural and commercial reasons, opened up the market to the commercial publication of serial news and, after a brief flourish of competition, the London-based output stabilized in a few titles aimed at a national market. The models adopted for the first generation of commercial

6 Among the studies which provide an account of the links between political interest and London newspapers across the period are Downie 1979; M. Harris 1987; R. Harris 1993; Peters 1980; Aspinall 1948.

papers were the manuscript newsletters for timing and domestic content, and the *London Gazette* for style and layout. The use of tri-weekly publication to synchronize with the postal services out of London was emphasized in their titles. The *Post Boy*, the *Post Man* and the *Flying Post* were only the leaders in this respect. The second immediate outcome of the lapse in the Acts was the diaspora of printers who moved out of London to a widening circle of urban centres where competition was less severe and a new set of commercial opportunities was offered. In almost every case a new printing business in the provinces was marked by the publication of a weekly newspaper.

During the 1690s modified and reconfigured elements of the commercial, political and cultural life of the nation began to form new patterns, which were most clearly visible in London and within which print played an increasingly important role. The newspapers were woven into the fabric of life at a middling social level and, as the long eighteenth century unfolded, it was through the lines of serial print that some of the circuits that have come to form such a pervasive part of recent analysis were constructed and maintained.[7] The models of how print worked in general, linking producer and consumer and bringing a range of external interests into play, apply with particular force to the serial forms. Whatever one's reservations about parts of the Habermas thesis, his identification of the newspaper as a crucial component in the construction of a bourgeois public sphere has a particular resonance in the context of coffee-house society in eighteenth-century London.[8] The newspaper was a highly interactive form in which the reader could gain access to the text in a variety of different ways: through correspondence, through news paragraphs and through advertisements. Until a layer of professional staff began to be introduced to the newspaper establishment, the form had some of the characteristics of the internet and, by its association with public space, engaged directly in social and cultural formation. Across this period the London newspapers formed coherent groupings identified by periodicity and by the location of readers; dailies, tri-weeklies and weeklies were each geared to compatible but distinct lines of distribution. It was not a highly differentiated system. The titles that made up the post-1695 London newspaper press shared a range of characteristics, which were reinforced over the next century. Owners and readers, form and content were all held in place by a combination of vested interest, competition, political pressure and market acceptability. At any given point, the London press formed a dense cloud of material in which each text

7 Darnton 1990, 107–35, 'What is the history of books?'; Adams and Barker 1993.
8 Habermas 1989.

formed part of a massive but coherent whole. Between 1695 and 1830, the London press formed an inescapable element of the output of the book trade and the structure of middling society. There is a long way to go before the detailed history of this period can be written and the newspaper can be realistically identified in the context of the history of print.[9]

This chapter in a volume dedicated to 'the history of the book' can only attempt to identify some of the established features of a generalized and necessarily incomplete view. The method used here is to offer a short sequence of temporal snapshots within which some of the variables in the history of the newspaper during this long period can be indicated. The years chosen, 1720, 1775 and 1830, are not key years; nor are they closed off here for detailed investigation. They simply offer an evenly spaced sequence from which it is possible to take stock of the changes that crystallized around them. This will be a supply-side view with the emphasis placed on the newspaper as a part of the output of the general trade in print. This chapter will not contain a systematic statistical analysis but when numbers can provide perspective they will form part of the picture. The aim here is to offer an outline of the development of the newspaper during this period and to suggest how its relationship to the market developed over time.

1720

By 1720 a structure of serial publication had been established in London composed of a variety of interlocking elements. Some of the output published in this year had been established under the Printing Acts and continued to roll forward under the more competitive circumstances that developed after 1695. The *London Gazette* (1665) still provided a core element of news coverage authenticated by its state sponsors. It was constructed through the Secretaries of State's offices in Whitehall, and in 1720 was organized by the London printer and bookseller Samuel Buckley. Buckley had been involved in the production of the first London daily paper, the *Daily Courant* (1702), and it may have been through this connection that he was drawn into the orbit of the Hanoverian Whigs. In 1715 he had replaced Jacob Tonson on the imprint of the *Gazette* and in 1719 he was appointed gazetteer for life. Whatever his personal skills, the commercial circulation of the *Gazette* had plummeted. Its position in the market had already been undermined by the more dynamic,

9 While there has been a slow accumulation of detailed studies of the history of the newspaper, Morison 1930 remains the most useful (though flawed) survey of the form.

post-1695 papers and, when it reverted from tri- to bi-weekly publication in response to the stamp tax of 1712, the game was up. In 1720 the Tuesday and Saturday issues sold only a few hundred copies each.[10] Even so, along with the official newsletter, it remained a highly regarded source of news and, particularly in time of international crisis, its content was ruthlessly recycled in the commercial papers. At the same time, a raft of news-related information serials with a very long pedigree were still in publication, although elements of their content had been absorbed into the commercial newspapers. The *Bills of Mortality* in their weekly printed form, the *Proceedings* at the Sessions House in the Old Bailey, and the proliferating business papers all remained on the market. So did the latest generation of periodicals, which succeeded the monthly translations of continental news serials that had been syndicated in London, Edinburgh and Dublin from the 1680s. Abel Boyer's monthly *Present State of Great Britain* (1711) and the quarterly *Historical Register* (1715), the last in a sequence of serials published by the Sun Fire Insurance Office, offered serious compendia of national and international news.

The initial skirmishing that followed the lapse of the Printing Acts had rapidly given way to the market dominance of the three main tri-weekly *Posts*, which were still in publication in 1720. By this time, in the more hectic commercial environment, they had been joined by several new tri-weekly titles whose proprietors had identified a commercial advantage in adopting a later publication time to synchronize more closely with the postal services out of London. The *Evening Post* (1709), the *St James's Evening Post* (1716) and the *Whitehall Evening Post* (1718) established a line of output which was later to be exploited by the most successful tri-weeklies of the century: the *London Evening Post* (1727) and the *General Evening Post* (1733). The *Daily Courant*, with its tacit government connections, was published through most of the first two decades of the century without any direct competition. However, in 1720 it was faced by two rival dailies offering readers a modified formula in which a brisker news cover was combined with a more active advertising policy. The *Daily Post* (1719) and the *Daily Journal* (1720) successfully challenged the *Courant* and outlasted its separate existence.

The tri-weeklies and dailies published in London in 1720 provided the main framework of the metropolitan news service. None the less the structure of output had been both extended and polarized by government intervention in the Stamp Tax of 1712. Whether intended as a form of policing or simply as a means of raising revenue, it created a split in output that emphasized a division

10 Alsop 1986–7.

already present in the London printing trade. Dominating the business were the respectable booksellers whose interests had already coalesced outside the Stationers' Company in the shareholding of literary property. After 1695 this form of group ownership was gradually extended to the property of commercial newspapers. As early as 1708 the *Daily Courant* was said to be in the hands of 'a club' of twenty booksellers and the new dailies in publication in 1720 were both set up under this form of ownership.[11] The process of annexation was far from complete and alternative control by individuals or small groups probably continued in the tri-weeklies. In a trade increasingly dominated by the booksellers, the printers held a subordinate position. Their control of the means of production made them essential to the cartels but, as in the Stationers' Company itself, their access to the hierarchy was limited. Printers had set up and run newspapers since the lapse of the Printing Acts in 1695, but with the identification of a loophole in the tax law this line of independent publication was reactivated. Existing single sheets published daily or tri-weekly either increased their price to 1½*d.* or were substantially modified. The loophole arose from a failure to envisage a newspaper consisting of more than one sheet of paper folded into four pages. Any serial of more than four pages could therefore be registered as a pamphlet and pay the tax of only 2*s.* for an entire edition. Even the *London Gazette* appeared briefly in a six-page format to avoid the stamp, but it was the commercial possibilities of weekly publication in this form that attracted investment by individual printers. Filling up the available space with an essay or serial, providing a digest of news together with an easily assembled mix of information and advertisements, the miscellany could be sold at the same price as a single-leaf paper. By 1720 a number of highly successful journals were published each Saturday from printing offices clustered in the south-east corner of the City or south of Fleet Street. James Read, John Applebee and Nathaniel Mist owned and ran six-page news journals, which were associated with their personal interest through their titles and were very widely distributed.[12]

The impact of the tax also registered lower down the economic scale among printers who scratched a precarious living from the production of pamphlets, ballads and various kinds of jobbing work. The value of the serial was universal and at this level a number of six-page, unstamped tri-weeklies appeared on the market at ½*d.* Published between the post days, they were printed on bad paper with a page size roughly half that of the printer-owned journals. Their

11 Defoe 1955, 263–4.

12 For a view of the print trade in this geographical setting, see Harris 2003.

content was borrowed wholesale from any available source but was made up of the same elements as the other news serials. The papers of Francis Clifton, William Heathcote and George Parker circulated through the streets of London, catering to a readership that probably overlapped with and extended beyond that of the main publications. By 1720 the serial publication of books in fascicules or parts, initiated in London in the 1670s, had begun to coalesce with the cheaper forms of London newspaper. Books on history, geography and similar subjects, as well as works of fiction, began to appear in long sequences in the content of the six-page weekly and tri-weekly papers. The first two parts of *Robinson Crusoe* ran through Heathcote's halfpenny *Original London Post* between October 1719 and October 1720.[13] However, it was not until the next decade that the publication of cut-price newspapers in conjunction with issues of distinct part-works, a device pioneered by William Rayner and Robert Walker, gave a substantial boost to the output of cheap, news-based serials.[14]

The newspaper output of London in 1720 consisted of three dailies and about five tri-weeklies, all stamped, together with about six weekly journals and possibly half a dozen tri-weeklies whose proprietors evaded the tax. Circulation information is sketchy and limited. A few tax figures in 1712–13, a limited number of government accounts and a few claims in the papers themselves provide the roughest of guides.[15] In 1720 it might be possible to suggest that the dailies had an average sale of about 800 copies each, the tri-weeklies around 2,500 copies and the weeklies perhaps 3,500. The cheap tri-weeklies may have sold 250 copies per issue. Individual titles reached far higher levels. Mist's weekly journal was said to have sold 10,000 copies per issue in the early 1720s, although this was clearly an outer limit for a weekly paper. The grand total for the sale of the London newspapers based on these estimates would have amounted to about 50,000 copies a week.

The distribution of this volume of material was a complex process involving a variety of access points for purchasers and non-purchasers. In London itself copies were supplied directly to subscribers by the printers who sometimes organized the general publication. By 1720 specialist trade publishers were handling the primary distribution of some papers, including the delivery from the printer to the 'mercuries' or pamphlet sellers and to the Post Office.[16] The mercuries, whose shops were strung out along London's east–west axis marked off by the Royal Exchange and Westminster Hall, supplied the hawkers who

13 Wiles 1957, 27.
14 For Rayner and Walker, see Harris 1989.
15 See, for example, Price 1958; Snyder 1968.
16 Treadwell 1982a.

ran the papers through the streets for casual sale or operated a delivery service. The cheap papers were probably entirely dependent on street sales. A significant proportion of the retail distribution in London was made to the coffee houses, which supplied their customers with a cross-section of newspapers under the inclusive charge for entry. Newspaper reading in 1720 was a public activity and the material they contained was a primary resource for sociability and conversation. Similarly, a proportion of the provincial readership was organized through public houses and access to copies was probably even more eagerly sought than in the capital. Copies seeped out into the communities where they were available for second-hand reading as well as for use in lining pie dishes or as lavatory paper. The social uses of news pushed up the de facto readership to high if largely unknowable levels. Addison's famous estimate of 1711, which suggested twenty readers to a copy, has a specific and local reference, although some contemporaries put the figure much higher.[17] At all events, the readers and users of the dense, useful, inescapable London newspapers may have numbered a quarter of a million a week.

As a postscript it should be added that in 1725 the loophole in the tax law was finally closed partly at least through the lobbying of the bookseller proprietors of the taxed papers. The move was aimed at the two categories of unstamped serials: the weekly journals and the halfpenny tri-weeklies. Both survived by raising their prices by a halfpenny and cutting their size from six pages to four. They were printed on what was accepted to be a half-sheet of paper. All the main titles survived, suggesting some elasticity in the market, and the pattern of split-level publication identified in 1720 continued in place, becoming even more pronounced in the 1730s through widespread tax evasion.

1775

By the year in which the American war broke out, the newspaper and related serials had settled into a position of practical importance in the economic, political and cultural life of middling society across Europe.[18] In London the newspapers had stabilized within the framework that had begun to take shape early in the century; however, by 1775, they had been consolidated across the output of serial print which had been purged of many of the elements of tension and conflict. The long-established publications, including the *London Gazette*, the business serials, the *Bills of Mortality* and the sessions *Proceedings*,

17 The *Spectator*, see Bond 1965, I, 44.
18 For the European dimension of serial publication, see Goldgar 1995. Also Blanning 2002, 103–82.

continued to move along their well-defined tracks, although in each case the formulaic character of their contents had been emphasized and their relationship to the newspaper press had become more distant. Their notice-board function in the supply of updated information of a reliable and useful sort was both a benefit and a limitation in the market. In the case of the *Proceedings*, the more sensational and interesting elements had moved over into book form and were already appearing in the multi-volume sets later known under the generic title of the *Newgate calendar*.

The number of commercial newspapers had not increased dramatically but the status and durability of individual titles was more clearly established. In 1775 there were about seven of each of the main categories of daily, tri-weekly and weekly newspapers in publication with a scattering of essay sheets moving through the market on a short-term trajectory. In terms of circulation, the morning dailies had started to edge ahead of the tri-weeklies, with the weekly papers taking on a subordinate position. Only one of the titles in print in 1720, the *Whitehall Evening Post*, was still in publication in 1775, although others had merged or been reconstituted over time, making this sort of chronological assessment uncertain. All the morning tri-weeklies had been squeezed out and the long-running evening papers, notably the *London Evening Post* and the *General Evening Post*, continued to dominate this sector. Two dailies from the 1730s, the *Daily Advertiser* and the *Gazetteer*, were jostling for position at the top of the market while the rest of the London titles in print in 1775 were newer foundations strung out across the previous decades. Among the weekly papers, only the *Craftsman* (1726), in title at least, had some sort of continuity from the 1720s.

The primary difference between the two dates in terms of the structure of the London press, as well as the main reason for the heightened stability, was the extension and consolidation of bookseller ownership of the London newspapers. By mid-century the cartels had established an iron grip on the newspaper press in London. In 1775 all the London papers fitted into an interlocking pattern of carefully controlled shareholdings secured by closely applied agreements and contracts. Shares were not released into the open market and the groups of partners, usually between twelve and fifteen in number, engaged in a common system of management and oversight. Although some individuals from outside the print trades were admitted – auctioneers, brokers, even the occasional 'gentleman' – the great majority of the newspaper proprietors were leading members of the London book trade.[19]

19 For a view of the membership and initial correspondence of a shareholding group in mid-century, see Fitzpatrick 1994.

The booksellers' interest in the newspaper press had arisen through its capacity to promote their own products, exclude those of competitors and produce a serial income. In each case advertisements provided the central component and by 1775 the prevalence of advertising in the content of the leading London papers was clearly signalled. From the 1730s almost every London daily incorporated the word 'advertiser' in its title or sub-title, following the trend set by the *Daily Advertiser*. In 1746 the *London Daily Post and General Advertiser* had carried 12,254 advertisements bringing in a post-tax profit of £753 10*s*., and thirty years later the emphasis on advertising content, probably producing similar yields, was evident across both the dailies and the tri-weeklies. As newspapers spread through the nation the government income from the advertising tax rose steeply; the national figure for 1720 was £1,456 1*s*., and by 1775 it had reached £33,381.[20]

The identity of the shareholders and the character of their involvement can usually be deduced only from internal evidence in the newspapers themselves, particularly through the recurrent book-trade advertisements. However, in the case of two of the leading newspapers in publication in 1775, the survival of business records through legal proceedings provides a clearer view. The papers were the *Gazetteer*, the subject of the only full-scale account of an eighteenth-century London daily paper, and the *General Evening Post*. Both had been established in the 1730s, although the *Gazetteer* could claim a longer pedigree as it was formed in part from the *Daily Courant* in 1735 when Robert Walpole's newspaper interests were rationalized.[21] By 1775 it had been involved in mergers and changes in title but, even so, of its approximately seventeen partners, about eight had held shares in the paper for more than twenty years. The *General Evening Post* had a less changeable history and the property in 1775 was in the hands of about a dozen members of the London book trade.

The papers had close links. Some of the partners held shares in each: the daily and tri-weekly papers, together with the weekly *Craftsman*, the sole property of the printer, formed one of the standard combinations of forms permitted under most agreements. This pattern of ownership may help to explain the equivalence in the number of daily, tri-weekly and weekly papers in print in 1775. All three papers of the *Gazetteer* group were printed by Charles Green Say, although there had been a series of rows over his involvement with the rival *London Evening Post*, as well as the quality of the printing. He died in July 1775 and was succeeded as printer by his wife, Mary. Charles Say had held

20 Table in Aspinall 1948, 208.
21 Harris 1987, 85–6.

shares in the properties, which were passed on to his widow. The partners in the *Gazetteer* and *Evening Post* followed the usual practice of appointing a publisher and treasurer, usually a shareholder, and selecting an executive committee of about half a dozen of their number to handle the routine management decisions and to monitor the paper's organization, content and finances. They met with varying degrees of frequency in the coffee houses and taverns around Fleet Street and the Strand. The minutes of the committee of the *General Evening Post* indicate that only four meetings were held in 1775, although this number had risen dramatically by 1781 when, after a management shake-up, they met twenty-one times. In 1775 a share in the paper was valued at £120 and meetings were mainly concerned with assessing the partners' dividends, which ranged from £11 to £23 a share.[22] The main decisions about the conduct of these papers and probably most others were ratified at the general meetings held semi-annually or quarterly in the same locations.

Conflict within this tightly organized system was not uncommon and the most frequent outbreaks of hostility seem to have been between the bookseller partners and the printers. The cartels, consisting largely of respectable London booksellers associating with each other in the Stationers' Company, were inclined as much to co-operation as to competition. At the same time, even when conflict in the market was inescapable, it was manifested in the papers themselves partly through a process of imitation. Every change in size, typeface and organization of content tended to be followed in a cascade effect through the press. A good deal of sniping went on in the papers and claims for precedence in terms of accuracy or circulation were part of the currency of the exchanges between direct rivals; occasionally the undertow of conflict could erupt into open war. Even so, the protection of the status quo usually seemed as important as gaining an advantage. Shared content, which had always been a feature of the London papers, continued to emphasize a general uniformity and the political prosecutions of the late 1760s and early 1770s swept up handfuls of printers from across the newspaper system for publishing the same materials.

If a shared organizational structure underpinned the control of the press by the London booksellers, the absence of any external challenge by individuals or groups outside the charmed circles of commercial self-interest reinforced the sense of regimentation. The unstamped and pseudo-newspapers, which had been prefigured in 1720 and which multiplied during the 1730s, had been

22 *General Evening Post*, Minute book of partners, 31 May 1754–9 August 1786, British Library [ms. facs.* 761].

crushed by the legislation of 1743.[23] This had effectively closed down the street-based distribution networks of the illegal news serials by blanket prosecution of hawkers. The stamped 1*d.* papers staggered on through the 1740s but do not appear to have survived beyond mid-century. Commercial pressure was aggravated by a tax increase in 1757, while a further rise was implemented in 1776. Legitimate cheapness could not be sustained in this environment. In the event, the challenge to the London booksellers had been transferred from London to the English provinces, and particularly to Ireland and Scotland where the struggle against the claims of perpetual copyright led to a final victory in 1774.[24] The production of cheap print, outside the long-established forms of ballads and chapbooks, came to be centred on magazines, part-works, small books of practical information, and collections of texts released from copyright. All these figured in the output of such large-scale London publishers of the 1770s and 1780s as John Cooke and Alexander Hogg. To some extent they skirted the main interests of the respectable London booksellers; none of the active outsiders were involved in or had access to newspaper publication.

While the number of titles stabilized, circulation levels had continued to rise at a rate that may have reflected population increase as much as the formation of a wider readership. The constraints of hand-press technology, the rising stamp tax and the tight focus of interest, which united producers and their target audience, limited the possible expansion. By 1775 the half-sheet papers had increased in size and most papers had adopted a four-column page layout. Real numbers for circulation levels in 1775 are in short supply but it seems that the *Gazetteer* had overtaken the *Daily Advertiser* as the most successful London daily, with a print run of about 5,000 copies per issue. The first figures itemizing the sale of the *General Evening Post* appeared in the partners' minutes for March 1780, when it averaged just over 4,500 per issue. In both cases it seems likely that the sale per daily and tri-weekly issue hovered between 4,000 and 4,500 copies. The records of Henry Woodfall's *Public Advertiser*, which had generated huge public interest through the Junius letters, fell back to a daily sale rather below this.[25]

For the *General Evening Post*, Post Office distribution remained crucial; much of the discussion at the partners' meetings came to be concerned with the arrangements for getting copies from the printer to the Clerks to synchronize with the outward postal services. At the same time, the Clerks were

23 Harris 1987, 27–30.

24 The end of perpetual copyright was signalled by the case of *Millar* v. *Donaldson*. Feather 1994. Cf. Rose, chap. 4, above.

25 Haig 1960, 79.

increasingly finding themselves bypassed by supply organized through Members of Parliament, who had been added to the list of those with franking privileges in 1764. The total scale of movement through the post was considerable and by 1775 may have involved the national distribution of some of the leading dailies as well as the tri-weeklies. During 1764 just over 1 million newspapers left London by post; by 1782 this had risen to just over 3 million, and by 1796 the outward flow had jumped to over 8.5 million copies. Distribution within the metropolitan area could also involve the postal services; in 1782 it was estimated that 60,000 papers were sent out by this means.[26] Clearly the London papers were very widely available and, if the readership was socially limited, the extent of penetration in this sector of the market was extremely high.

The range of market penetration by serial print was greatly extended by the burgeoning output in London, and occasionally in the provinces, of the periodical.[27] Usually published monthly and offering a digest of news alongside a heterogeneous collection of letters, essays, commentary and engravings, the magazines were directed at different sections of the audience identified in their titles. Though far from the first, the most influential of the monthlies was the *Gentleman's Magazine* (1731). It was initially published by Edward Cave, previously a Clerk in the Post Office, as a vehicle for extracts from the essays published in the weekly newspapers. It was soon converted to a miscellany and was joined by a mushroom growth of competitors, some of which had considerable staying power. In 1775 the *London Magazine* (1732), the *Scots Magazine* (1739) and the *Universal Magazine* (1747) were running alongside more recent and up-to-date monthlies, like the *Town and Country Magazine* (1769) and the *Lady's Magazine* (1770), as well as some hard-core political titles. In 1768 a contributor to one of the London magazines estimated that, besides the London newspapers, there were seventeen magazines in publication as well as the two monthlies devoted to reviews of current literature.[28] The continued expansion in the serial publication of works in parts, which formed an important element in the output of printing offices in both London and the provinces, had moved away from the sphere of interest of the newspapers. Books repackaged as serials were big business by 1775 and they added to the rising tide of print. However, it was the magazines rather than the news serials that provided a medium for the secondary circulation of their content. The two forms of material came into a particularly close conjunction in the serial

26 Harris 1978b, 90.
27 See Tierney, chap. 24 below and Maidment, chap. 25, below.
28 *The Court Miscellany; or, Gentleman and Lady's Magazine*, 4 (1768), 3.

anthology entitled, perhaps rather misleadingly, the *Novelist's Magazine* (1780). Each week a section of text from a work of prose fiction, such as Samuel Richardson's *Pamela*, was published without any additional material until the entire book could be made up as a separate volume.[29] In combination, the total volume of serial output was beginning to rise steeply and this was having a knock-on effect in some obscure areas of the print trade. In 1768 an obituary of Anne Price included an aside that by the time of her death she had assembled a fortune of £5,000 from the modest business of supplying rags for the manufacture of paper.[30]

The year 1775 fell within the period in which the newspaper remained an adjunct to the business of the London booksellers, although political interests had developed around the perimeter of the trade, which sometimes impinged on the finances of production. The Wilkes affair had heightened public demand for political information and his intervention had served to open up the debates of Parliament to the press. The reports were of prime interest and had become a conventional, even a dominant, element in the news cover of the dailies and tri-weeklies by 1775. This in itself helped to push forward the development of the newspaper as a distinct business. The need for parliamentary reporters, employed on a regular basis, added to the number of individuals hired to carry out various specialist tasks. In 1775 full-time editors had not generally begun to replace printers and take responsibility for a general oversight of content. However, during the next decade, individuals such as James Perry, who was employed in 1783 to edit the *Gazetteer*, began to assert a distinct authority within the organization of the London newspapers and to modify some of the side effects of bookseller control.

1830

The number of news and news-related serials in publication had risen considerably by 1830. *Robson's London directory* for that year listed fifty-three titles under 'London newspapers', mostly printed in the traditional printing neighbourhoods of Fleet Street, the Strand and Blackfriars. They included thirteen dailies (seven published in the morning and the rest in the evening) and four tri-weeklies (divided between Monday, Wednesday and Friday, and the established pattern of Tuesday, Thursday and Saturday). Except for the bi-weekly

29 The *Novelist's Magazine* ran for nine years, the weekly issues making up twenty-three volumes of British and foreign fiction. At the height of its popularity it was said to be selling 12,000 copies of each number; Mayo 1962, 363–7.

30 *Court Miscellany*, 4 (1768), 55.

London Gazette, the remaining titles were published weekly, thirteen on Saturday and ten on Sunday. The old forms of information serials, the lists of financial information, the *Bills of Mortality* and the Old Bailey sessions *Proceedings*, were still in print, although by 1830 they had taken on an entirely formal character. On the other hand, the generalized interest in commerce pushed the business listings towards a new lease of life through the later emergence of specialist financial journalism.[31] The presence of the *London Gazette* in the directory and its continuing survival resulted from its statutory role in the publication of official and legal actions. The notices concerned with bankruptcy, which had figured in the paper since the seventeenth century, had long been a required part of the process; by 1830 most lines of public administration were represented in government notices in the *Gazette*.

Robson's list indicated a growing diversity in the frequency and timing of publication as well as some specialization of content, although this was centred on the weekly papers. The two forms that most clearly separated the output of 1830 from the equivalent in 1775 were the evening dailies and, more importantly, the Sundays, which had first appeared in the late 1770s and were to become a focal point for the growth of newspaper output in the mid-nineteenth century. By 1830 the distinction between metropolitan and provincial distribution was becoming blurred as the postal services speeded up, increased in number and became more accessible. Under the Act of 1825 the long-established system of franking privileges was ended and all newspapers were permitted to pass through the post free of charge. Sixty thousand a week were sent out of London by the middle of the next decade, many still by way of the Clerks who were able to exploit their late access to the services for commercial gain.[32] The most successful of the various forms were the morning dailies led by *The Times*, already known in 1830 as 'the Thunderer'. The direct challenge of the *Morning Chronicle* had faded with the death of James Perry in 1821. In 1830 *The Times* sold about 3.5 million copies, a figure that was rising steeply; it amounted to sales of just over 10,000 per issue.[33]

If the general shape of the London newspaper press had been modified since 1775, changes to the internal organization of individual titles had also taken place. This amounted not to a radical alteration but to a series of readjustments that ebbed and flowed within the London papers. The cartels of bookseller shareholders had, by the end of the eighteenth century, proved too unwieldy to cope with the expanding newspaper business. By 1830 the benefits of control

31 See McCusker, chap. 22, below.
32 Hemmeon 1912, 48.
33 *The Times* 1935, 245.

by a single individual or a tight-knit group of partners had been generally established across the main publications. The *Gazetteer* had collapsed in 1797 under the weight of its long-established and self-perpetuating management structure.[34] On the other hand, the *Morning Post* and the *St James's Chronicle* had been rescued from an apparently terminal decline under the old system of management by the personal interventions of Daniel Stuart and Charles Baldwin in 1795 and 1808 respectively.[35] The property of *The Times*, established in 1785, was still divided into sixteen shares in 1830. However, the various strategic sub-divisions made in 1816 and 1827, which left the Walter family as substantial stockholders, also served to reinforce the business structure. In 1830 control of the content and organization of *The Times* was in the hands of the professional editor Thomas Barnes, while the printing business remained the property of John Walter II. Barnes received a salary of £1,000 a year but he was also a shareholder; this combination ensured his personal engagement to the success of the paper.[36] During the 1820s there was a revival of syndicated ownership as a means of spreading the burden of rising costs but, for the most part, editorial control and financial management remained distinct.

The second and related shift in the internal organization of the London newspapers involved a move away from the relationship with the book trade. The printing office had remained a primary focus for the organization and construction of the newspaper through the eighteenth century, although the printers had always been subordinated to the direction of the bookseller shareholders. As the staffing of the newspaper became more complex and the role of the editor took on a greater importance, so the technology of production began to experience the first spasms of modernization. The mechanization of printing, which was essential to get past the bottleneck in output created by the hand-press, again shifted the industry's centre of gravity. In this area, as in most others, *The Times* was in the vanguard of change. The introduction of the Koenig steam-powered, flat-bed press in 1814 multiplied the potential output to 1,100 sheets an hour, a capacity that was increased with the introduction of multi-feeder presses in 1828. In 1830 the paper was worked off on two Applegath and Cowper machines, which could print 4,200 sheets an hour on both sides. A third machine was kept in reserve for emergencies. As the paper increased in size and length, the workforce on the printing side increased. In 1832, of the total of nearly a hundred *Times* employees, fifty were compositors.

34 Haig 1960, 266.
35 Asquith 1978, 102.
36 *The Times* 1935, 174–6.

Technology centred the newspaper on the printing office and the expanding numbers of editorial staff were inevitably drawn to this location. *The Times* may have been the first London newspaper to be produced entirely on its own premises at Printing House Square in Blackfriars. The layout, which reflected the specialist division of labour involved in producing the paper, was probably in place by 1830. The printing machines were located in the basement while rooms for the reporters and the editor, as well as separate rooms for setting news and advertisements, were deployed through the two upper floors of the building.[37]

The paper itself and its business organization created a strong impression on contemporaries, making it increasingly expensive to attempt to enter the market to compete with the established morning dailies. It has been estimated that setting up or buying into a newspaper before 1820 usually cost between £2,000 and £5,000 while by the 1830s this had risen to between £30,000 and £50,000.[38] An important additional cost was imposed by the stamp tax, which had risen by progressive stages to 4*d*. per copy printed. In 1830 *The Times* sold for 7*d*. but although this price limited sales, it also represented a financial challenge to potential interlopers. The tax was, as it always had been, a buttress for the commercial elite against competition.

If costs were high, profits were also buoyant, primarily through income from advertising. These had been of primary interest to the proprietors of the London newspapers in 1720 and 1775 but, by 1830, income from advertisements had become even more critical. *The Times* advertising supplement, issued (to general amazement) free of charge, was an indicator of both demand and commercial value. According to Ivon Asquith, the *Public Advertiser*, selling just over 3,000 copies per issue in 1771, contained 24,613 advertisements, which produced an annual profit of about £2,300. Fifty years later, the *Morning Chronicle*, with a roughly equivalent sale, contained just over 40,000 advertisements producing a profit of £12,400.[39] These levels of income enabled the newspaper owners to loosen the grip of political interests on the press though it made them increasingly vulnerable to commercial dependence on advertisers. Not surprisingly, this alternative form of influence was generally manifested in the publication of non-contentious and miscellaneous forms of content, though the scope for political intervention remained.

In 1830 the leading London papers, supported by advertising income and the application of the stamp tax, faced a challenge from outside the charmed

37 *The Times* 1935, 414.
38 Asquith 1978, 109.
39 Asquith 1975.

circles of established interest. The tax itself was re-designated as a 'tax on knowledge' and became the target of a systematic attack which combined middle-class ideology, working-class radicalism and forms of commercial self-interest. An initial charge by the publishers of radical, unstamped newspapers published in London and the English provinces from 1816 had been beaten back by the legislation passed at the end of the decade, the notorious 'Black Acts' of 1819.[40] In 1830 a new assault was initiated through the publication of unstamped serials, in which working-class newspapers were joined by what have become known as 'useful knowledge' papers in a direct challenge to the validity of the stamp duty. In 1836, after a decrease in the advertising duty, the stamp tax itself was strategically reduced to 1*d*. Joel Wiener listed 559 separate periodicals published in London and elsewhere between 1830 and 1836 and the split-level output of this period contained echoes of the tax-related divisions of the 1730s.[41]

The year 1830 was pivotal in the history of the London newspapers. Change had begun, but the elements that linked the publications of 1720, 1775 and 1830 were probably stronger than the differences. In organisation, scale of production and character of content and readership, the main London newspapers stood in a recognizable evolutionary relationship to each other. After 1830 a series of seismic shifts, centred on Fleet Street and involving a quickening flow of serials, part-works and print generally, led inexorably towards the emergence of the mass market.

40 See Wood, chap. 48 below.
41 Wiener 1970.

21

Newspapers and the sale of books in the provinces

C.Y. FERDINAND

Introduction

The provincial newspaper trade was an entirely new development in the eighteenth century, enabled by the lapse of the Printing Acts in 1695. The London printing trade had made a good recovery after the Great Fire and plague in the 1660s and the capital was overcrowded with printers by the end of the century; the regulations that had attempted to control their numbers and restricted book production to London, Oxbridge and York were no longer in force, and some printers began to think of making a fresh start in the country.[1] Often they returned to towns where they already had family or trade connections. The migration of printers from London was evidently anticipated by an increase in the numbers of booksellers and stationers who serviced the provincial reading and writing market.[2] But the economic reality of London's traditional dominance in book production, supported by networks to distribute books throughout the country, meant that the new provincial printers could not easily compete on that front. Instead they turned at first to jobbing printing or publishing the occasional local sermon or verse, often combining that with the retail sale of London imprints. The more imaginative, looking for a firmer financial base and steadier employment for their presses, perceived a potential market for locally produced newspapers, and the first provincial papers, the *Norwich Post* and the *Bristol Post-boy*, were begun soon after the turn of the century.[3]

Communities in the provinces were long accustomed to reading and hearing newspapers read, for London and continental serials, like books, had always been available to subscribers and their families, friends and customers through the post, along the book-trade networks that radiated from the capital and by

1 McKenzie 1976; Treadwell 1982a.
2 *CHBB* IV, appendix 1, table 9, 793.
3 Wiles 1965, 14–16; Cranfield 1962, 13–15.

means of personal agents. Nevertheless, there was a gap to be filled in the provincial market, for the London papers and newsletters were expensive and scarcely addressed local issues, in either their news or advertising. Country newspaper proprietors were able to capitalize on both the ready availability and the expense of the London papers: they subscribed to several at once to mine them for the latest news – a sort of proto-wire service – at the same time as they drew attention to the fact that in a single relatively inexpensive and locally produced paper the country reader could find the best of the London and continental press. A small section of local news, usually presented in a formulaic fashion, might be included, but more important, the advertisement columns in provincial newspapers developed into a medium for local notices as well as for nationwide campaigns.

Just as the first London serials had followed earlier continental models in format and presentation, so the first provincial newspaper proprietors – many of them London-trained printers – naturally looked to the capital for guidance. Early provincial newspapers looked much like their London counterparts, with familiar mastheads, the same broadsheet formats and arrangement in columns. The London papers carried news, of course, and an ever-growing number of advertisements, including a significant proportion of book-trade advertisements. While the earliest English newspapers had carried few advertisements of any description, the booksellers soon learned the marketing potential of the periodical press. The first print-related advertisements appeared in the periodical press in the 1640s. These were simple notices with only a minimal amount of information. The periodical *Perfect Occurrences of Every Daies Iournall* carried this advertisement typical of the 1640s: readers were invited to a London bookseller's address to purchase something vaguely described as 'a new book, of the beauty of Providence', that, thanks to the *ESTC*, can be identified as John Wilkins's *A discourse concerning the beauty of providence in all the rugged passages of it: very seasonable to quiet and support the heart in these times of publick confusion*, a duodecimo book of 142 pages printed for Samuel Gellibrand.[4] By the end of the century, the most widely distributed seventeenth-century paper, the *London Gazette*, was running nearly seven hundred advertisements a year, about a quarter of them book-related and addressed to a more sophisticated readership who knew something about typefaces, formats, bindings and paper, and expected information on price and methods of payment and delivery before they made up their minds.

4 *ESTC* R1664.

The practice of advertising books in periodicals was driven by a number of factors. First, proprietors learned that advertising had the potential to generate more income than periodical subscriptions could, and so encouraged advertisements of all kinds. As early as 1706 one acquaintance could write that 'the Norwich Newspapers are the principal support of our poor printer here [Francis Burges], by which, with the Advertisements, he clears near 10*s.* every week, selling vast numbers to the country people'.[5] Another factor was the increasing physical separation between book production and retail sale, so that traditional methods such as posting title-pages outside printing offices and booksellers' shops – although still regularly employed – were less effective at reaching the wider reading public. The newspaper advertisement not only went out and met the market, but it was taken up precisely by those who were already equipped to buy books, the literate who could afford the time and money to read. (This is not to discount the illiterate who never actually read, but had the papers read to them – and may have learned to read at one of the educational establishments routinely advertised in the papers.) A third factor promoting book advertisements in periodicals was the fact that the newspaper and book trades shared much the same infrastructure and personnel throughout the eighteenth century, in London but especially in the provinces, where newspaper printer-proprietors regularly provided a multi-faceted local service including jobbing printing, selling stationery supplies, binding, and ordering London and perhaps continental imprints for their customers. A successful periodical provided regular employment for equipment and workers. It could also offer a medium for advertising the proprietor's and his colleagues' own print productions, usually at preferential, duty-only rates, and was a means of underwriting book-trade contacts and networks.[6]

Many early provincial proprietors were careful not to take overtly political positions on most issues, particularly if theirs was the only newspaper in town, for politics could alienate readers and decrease revenue. Owners made a point of describing their paper's impartiality, but it is sometimes possible to detect political leanings in the choice, presentation and editing of reports. Occasionally some incident was controversial enough to force country editors out of neutrality. For example, the political uncertainty after Queen Anne's death provoked the *Newcastle Courant*, the *Worcester Post Man* and the *Stamford Mercury* to fly their Tory colours, while some of their rivals seized the opportunity to increase their Whig readership. Local editors could draw upon the

5 Thomas Tanner to Browne Willis, 1 Aug. 1706; cited Allnut 1878.
6 Bodleian Library, MS Pollard 280, fols. 163–4.

periodical essays of great political writers such as Swift, Bolingbroke, Fielding and Defoe. Despite those resources, a general impartiality – with exceptions to prove the rule – was to characterize the reportage of the provincial periodical press for much of the eighteenth century.

1720

Thirty-seven provincial newspapers were started in the first twenty years of the eighteenth century. It was not easy to get it right, and about half had failed by 1720 under the pressures of government duties, poor marketing, bad management, underdeveloped networks and/or competition. Nevertheless the provincial newspaper trade was gathering momentum, and at least nineteen were still circulating in major towns throughout the country from Newcastle and Leeds to Bristol, Norwich and Exeter.[7] It was no coincidence, as R.M. Wiles has noticed, that the early eighteenth-century towns that hosted the most successful newspapers were populous and at some distance from London.[8] While the earliest provincials had followed the format of the London papers – some of them imitating the *Gazette*'s two-column layout on a single half-sheet, a few reflecting in type the more intimate setting of the handwritten newsletter – the 1712 Stamp Act had pushed many newspapers, suddenly subject by government definition to an inconvenient duty on every single copy, into the shape of more economical twelve-page pamphlets, which attracted only a single tax on the whole edition. It was a Londoner who first discovered this loophole, but within a month or two it was exploited in the provinces, beginning with John White in Newcastle. Newspapers settled back into a familiar folio format after the government closed that loophole in 1725.

Ownership of eighteenth-century newspapers is often difficult to determine, and is complicated throughout this period by a dearth of hard evidence. Unless account books or other documents happen to survive, there is little to go on, for the imprints of newspapers sometimes conceal more than they reveal. Nevertheless, it is likely that many of the first provincial papers were owned and managed by small partnerships or by individuals, such as William Bonny, who established the *Bristol Post-boy* – 'printed and sold by' him – around 1704. The imprint of the *Norwich Post* (est. 1701?) suggests that Francis Burges might merely have printed it, but a long letter from a rival, Samuel Hasbart, written after Burges's death, is more informative. Hasbart, recognizing that Norwich

7 Wiles 1965, appendix B: Chronological Chart.
8 Wiles 1965, 16.

was not big enough for two newspapers, proposed partnership with Burges's widow, Elizabeth. His letter makes it clear that Francis Burges had himself 'first set up the Trade here', but that Hasbart, a distiller, was indeed the real owner of Norwich's other newspaper, the *Norwich Gazette*, printed by Henry Crossgrove.[9] Their titles suggest that the newspapers established around the south-west by the amazing Farley family were probably owned by them. These include *Sam. Farley's Exeter Post-man* (1704), *Sam. Farley's Bristol Post-man; or, Weekly Intelligencer* (1713), the *Salisbury Post-man* (1715), printed by Samuel Farley, *F. Farley's Bristol Journal* (1725, probably continued as *Farley's Bristol Advertiser* from 1743), and *Farley's Bath Journal* (1756). It would be difficult to prove the Farleys were sole owners, however. On some occasions imprints do seem to tell the whole ownership story. There is evidence that the founders of Stamford's first newspapers, the *Stamford Post* (1710) and the succeeding *Stamford Mercury* (from 1712), were the partners Thomas Baily and William Thompson, whose names both appear in the imprint of the earliest extant copy of the *Stamford Mercury*.[10] At the beginning of the eighteenth century, this local newspaper circulating in the low hundreds, along with the usual retail sales and jobbing, suggests a diversified family business that could have been managed without outside backers.[11]

Whether capital came from a few shareholders or a single owner, no country newspaper could survive long without a reliable distribution network. The commercial success of a serial depended on this multi-layered structure that was ultimately shaped, financed and controlled by the proprietors. They might well hire a manager to look after the printing office and oversee distribution. The relationship between the managers and their customers was mediated by newsagents, distributors, newsboys and hawkers, and to some extent the postal and carrier services. At the top of the distribution hierarchy were the newsagents scattered in towns and villages around the hub of the printing office. They were usually tradesmen, often book tradesmen: for example, more than half (97 of 172) the *Salisbury Journal* agents between 1736 and 1785 were booksellers, printers, stationers or bookbinders. Mapping the newsagents listed in a country newspaper's colophon can produce a fairly reliable outline of its 'sphere of influence'.[12] When it came to distribution and sales, there was every incentive for transparency – local customers needed to know exactly

9 *Norwich Gazette*, 20 Dec. 1707; Wiles 1965, 29–30.
10 For 13 Aug. 1713, in the Cambridge University Library. Two 1712 numbers of the *Post* are extant, both in the Codrington Library, All Souls College, Oxford.
11 Ferdinand 1997, 18–19.
12 Ferdinand 1997, 95–134; 1990.

where to find the paper. London agents, frequently coffee-house proprietors, supplied the reading needs of a population that was often on the move, from those who left home to find work in London to the gentry who took up residence in London as the season dictated. A striking instance of the universal availability of the provincial press is found in an account of a dinner at Sion House, 'where, after two courses, the [Newcastle] Courant of the 3rd inst. was served up among the dried sweetmeats in the desert'.[13] Besides providing a local focus for newspaper sales, agents also organized the teams of distributors, newsboys and hawkers who actually delivered the paper and sundry other goods to outlying subscribers. The benefits of an effective distribution network went beyond simply making sure readers received their newspapers; commercial contacts between the proprietor and other tradesmen were promoted, and reliable carriage for other goods, such as books, could be ensured. The system remained little altered into the nineteenth century, although there were improvements in transportation, adjustments to catchment areas and the emergence of specialized London agents.[14]

Newspapers were a natural source of information for the book-buying public, but they were always part of a larger book-marketing strategy and it is useful to remember that the booksellers continued to attract their country readers' attention in other ways. Promotional title-pages were still posted around town, but now they could be delivered to subscribers along with, or even inserted in, the newspaper. In 1740 Charles Rivington advised the Society for the Encouragement of Learning to 'order 2 or 300 single titles of every Book they publish, to be printed in order to disperse thro' the Town and in the Country; It will be of advantage to the sale, and is what I always do in my own Books'.[15] Charles Ackers's account books show that he regularly printed extra title pages for a provincial market that included Salisbury and Gloucester.[16]

Selling books serially, in affordable parts that had to be collected and bound by the purchaser, was another marketing technique that suited the periodical trade. The first part-book, Moxon's *Mechanick exercises*, was published 1677–84. In the eighteenth century bookseller-newspaper proprietors saw the advantages of books that could so readily be incorporated into their serial business: part-books allowed the trade to engage with readers who might not be able to afford the full purchase price, but felt easier about regularly parting with small amounts for small portions of the book and probably did not think too hard

13 John Brand to Ralph Beilby, 5 Apr. 1784, cited in Gardner 2003, 36.
14 See Turner, chap. 23, below.
15 Rivington to the Society for the Encouragement of Learning, 5 Feb. 1740: BL Add. MSS 6190, fo. 106.
16 McKenzie and Ross 1968.

about the cumulative price. This was a particularly attractive proposition for local newspaper owners who worked with a clientele that had become accustomed to weekly deliveries of other reading material and goods. Part-books are known to have been published in huge editions and many parts, evidently sustained by thousands of patient customers who were willing to buy a book in (occasionally) hundreds of unbound pieces.[17]

After some experimentation, most of the provincial papers settled into weekly publication timed according to the thrice-weekly postal deliveries from London that brought fresh stocks of news, as well as some regular local event such as the weekly market. Publication the morning after a post day could produce the very 'freshest advices' so valued by newspaper readers, a strategy that actually got some of the news to some of the provincial readers a few hours before it was published in the London evening papers. The flow of news at this time was generally from London to the country via the London serial press, although unusual local concerns such as the Melksham weavers' riots in 1738, first reported in the *Salisbury Journal* and the *Gloucester Journal*, might temporarily reverse the trend. There are only a few clues to the anonymous news-gatherers and the way they worked: editors publicly thanked occasional contributors to their serials, but usually without naming them, and made it clear that more such reports would be welcome. It is clear that many amateur reporters were book-trade colleagues. The postscript to a letter from a London bookseller to a colleague asked for any news, 'w$^{ch.}$ tho' trivial at Oxford may still have the Advantages of being *new* here. And if any Peice of wit, humour, Poetry, usefull Science or any way Literary or entertaining is to be had from any ingenious Friend of yours, pray communicate it.'[18]

The brief local news sections, the way other news was edited, and especially the advertising in provincial newspapers, were adjusted to local developments and interests. For example, in some of the port towns, serials supplied the shipping trade with such detailed reports that they had become virtual trade journals by the early 1750s, and were censored in times of war.[19] Recent studies have quantified regional differences, such as the larger proportion of book-trade advertisements in Wessex papers, compared with those of Newcastle and Leeds.[20] The successful weekly local paper became a distinctive part of the rhythm of country life, in a cycle of publication, delivery and

17 For a case study, see Ferdinand 1999, 170–2.
18 J. Whiston, S. Baker and L. Davies to J. Fletcher: Bodleian Library, MS Top. Oxon. c. 787, fol. 4v.
19 Cranfield 1978, 181.
20 Newcastle: Gardner 2003; Wessex: Ferdinand 1997; Yorkshire: Looney 1983.

reading that was repeated on a more intimate scale with informally shared subscriptions.

1775

One hundred and fifty provincial English papers had been started by 1760. Many of them were short lived, but the fact that there were thirty-nine titles still published in 1760 alone suggests a moderately healthy country trade. The number of provincial papers increased to fifty in 1782, and over one hundred in 1808.[21] By 1775 the usual pattern of serial ownership outside London seemed still to be family-oriented. Ivon Asquith suggests that in 1840 thirty-three provincial papers were owned by inheritance of two or three generations.[22] He also places the beginning of newspaper 'chains' (one man or consortium owning a number of serials) in London after 1820, but this trend was anticipated much earlier in unusually successful serial publishers like Benjamin Collins, who, based firmly in Wiltshire, founded the *Salisbury Journal*, the *London Chronicle* and the *Public Ledger*, took over the *Hampshire Chronicle* and owned shares in the *Monthly Review* during the mid-eighteenth century. Many local serials were run by partnerships – generally smaller than their London counterparts – that shared the risks and profits. Wiles thought that as many as forty provincial newspaper partnerships had been started by 1760. The issue of ownership remains blurred, however. One publisher admitted during the course of a lawsuit that it had become 'customary amongst printers to make use of the Names of Persons as Publishers who have no concern therein'.[23] There were obvious legal advantages when government restrictions on what the press could report were in force, but the deception could be useful in other ways. When Collins and Company bought out a nearby competitor in the 1770s, long-time readers of the *Hampshire Chronicle* could not know from its imprint that the new owners were the very group that had probably engineered the bankruptcy of the old.[24]

That the country periodical was regarded as an effective source of information for book buyers is clear from the increasing numbers of advertisements that appeared in them. Bookseller-proprietors continued to enjoy the usual advantages of advertising their own printed wares, and self-advertising could have added commercial value in a new publication. When the Oxford

21 Wiles 1965; Read 1961, 59.
22 Asquith 1978, 104–5.
23 Thomas Brewman's Answers, *Collins* v. *Faden*: PRO CH. 12/1254/11.
24 Ferdinand 1997, 63–4.

bookseller James Fletcher was invited to become a partner in a new London paper, he learned that each partner had to buy twenty-four advertisements each month. Fletcher argued that, as a provincial bookseller with fewer publications, he would be disadvantaged. His colleague John Whiston convinced him that 'it wou'd be both impracticable and absurd to publish a News paper without a proper shew of Advertisements, wch are the means of bringing others to advertise in it'.[25] Anecdotal evidence suggests that ordinary readers benefited too. Wiles describes how the naturalist William Borlase read the *Western Flying Post* in the 1770s and found it convenient to order books and pamphlets he had seen advertised there to be delivered by the paper's distributors.[26]

Certainly a growing population of readers living in Britain's towns and villages continued to hear of new books through newspaper advertisements, but from the middle of the eighteenth century, review journals and miscellanies began to promote reading material in a new language and medium.[27] The editor of the *Monthly Review* suggested that a book's title page, on its own or reproduced in an advertisement, was no longer to be trusted – if it ever had been – and that 'few readers care to take in a book, any more than a servant, without a recommendation' (1749). There were many reviewing titles, including the *British Magazine* (est. 1760), which not only reviewed books, but was the first to serialize a major piece of fiction written in the first instance for the periodical press, Smollett's *Sir Lancelot Greaves*.[28] The new serials were popular throughout the country: it is estimated that in 1797 Ralph Griffith's *Monthly Review* (est. 1749), the first regular literary review, was selling about 5,000 copies a month; the *Critical Review* (est. 1756) and the *British Critic* (est. 1793) were each selling about 3,500; the *Monthly Magazine* (est. 1796), which published essays as well as a biannual 'Retrospect of literature', was selling 5,000.[29] One study suggests, however, 'that less than half of the books bought by subscribers to the reviews [sold by John Clay, bookseller of Daventry] in 1758–59 and 1764–66 were actually reviewed at all during the twelve months before they were purchased'.[30] The rise of book clubs and circulating libraries played a part too.[31] Ordinary bookshops, which were more numerous by this time, were another option for the provincial reader. Their current stock might

25 J. Whiston and D. Browne to Fletcher, 26 Feb. 1750/1: Bodleian Library, MS Top. Oxon. c. 787, fol. 6.
26 Wiles 1968, 56; Borlase's account books, according to Wiles, are in the Royal Institute of Cornwall.
27 See Forster, chap. 33, below.
28 Mayo 1962, 276–7.
29 Sullivan 1983a, xvii. Cf. Forster, chap. 33, below.
30 Fergus and Portner 1987, 158.
31 Kaufman 1964, 24.

have been of questionable quality – James Lackington thought there were 'a few (and but a very few) good books' in the Leeds and York shops, and 'in all the other towns between London and Edinburgh nothing but trash was to be found' – but of course orders could be placed there for better-quality imprints.[32] Both the suppliers and their markets responded to these developments, sometimes with fluctuations in the proportion of book advertisements in the local newspaper press.[33]

The overall pattern for the periodical outside the capital was never a simple one that reflected or lagged behind London. There were real differences in character and rhythm that came to distinguish the country from the London serials, and country proprietors were aware of them. When four northern proprietors – Walker of the *Newcastle Courant*, Hodgson of the *Newcastle Chronicle*, Brown of the *Newcastle Advertiser* and Ware of the *Cumberland Pacquet* – combined to protest against Pitt's proposed extra duty on newspapers and advertisements in 1797, they spoke in terms of those differences. The Londoners, 'by living on the Spot', might benefit from an ameliorating discount, 'but the Country Printers are obliged to have their Stamps from a Stationer or Agent in London, whereby they lost this Discount'. They had to pay for a 'wide and extended Circulation' too, which would become even more expensive if an anticipated turnpike duty came into force. Country printers, they said, charged for advertisements according to their length, while 'in London a distinction is made according to the part of the Paper the Ads are placed in'.[34] By this time too, London could support a concentrated daily and Sunday press, while the local papers continued in their more stately weekly pace. Indeed the first successful daily outside London, Glasgow's *North British Mail*, was not to be established until 1847.[35]

Around the time of the American Revolution and the beginning of the reform movement, country papers generally began to find greater political voice.[36] International and national news from the London papers was still edited into the local press, and could be selected to support one position or another, but more and more material that reflected popular debates was published. Readers turned to their country papers to find out about local elections, what their MPs were up to, when reform meetings were to be held, as well as developments at the national level. This new freedom of the

32 Lackington 1792, letter 36.
33 Looney 1983; Ferdinand 1997; Gardner 2003.
34 A printed notice, signed in manuscript; BL Add. MSS 50240, fol. 36.
35 Koss 1981, 56.
36 Barker 1998, 135–78.

press was not entirely welcome and a nervous government looked for ways to control it, especially in the unsettling aftermath of the French Revolution.[37]

1830

By 1830 there were approximately 150 local newspapers. Provincial readers still had access to all the London papers – more than fifty by then – as well as to numerous specialized periodicals. By the beginning of the nineteenth century the local newspaper had developed into an important and sociable part of country life, read for its news as well as for its local and national advertisements. Its diffusion through all social levels is illustrated in a letter from a descendant of a late eighteenth-century reader of the *Stamford Mercury*, who recounts the travels of a shared subscription paper from its arrival at the home of a Gainsborough lawyer on the Friday and its transfer the following Tuesday (market day) to the other paying subscriber, whose entire family read it. After they had finished with it, it was passed on to a neighbour, who handed it to the curate, and then it made the rounds of the rest of the village. Since most of the villagers were illiterate, they had the paper read to them, and finally it was returned to the Hall. The whole circuit evidently took a fortnight.[38] Thomas Flindell observed the same phenomenon when he was describing his difficulties in compiling a list of subscribers in 1811 ('In some cases a single copy serves a whole village or little country parish').[39] More evidence is found in the particular history of a Blyth public house – where regularly 'Old Ebenezer Kell, a custom house officer read the paper aloud, while the company sipped their grog and smoked their pipes' – but was no doubt repeated in countless coffee houses, inns, and meeting places throughout the country.[40]

Newspapers still carried book advertising, although not in the same proportions. On the one hand, proprietors relied more than ever upon the income brought in by advertising of all kinds. Thomas Flindell justified his travel expenses for the *Cornwall Gazette* with the argument that 'these journies had the additional object of extending our advertising connexions, obtaining orders, etc. it being frequently necessary to *court* connexions by civilities and expense, and advertising connexions were actually obtained in many instances by these means'.[41] On the other hand, many readers still relied on their local

37 See Wood, chap. 48 below.

38 Letter to the *Manchester Guardian*, reprinted in the *Stamford Mercury*, 9 Mar. 1914; cited in Newton and Smith 1999, 75.

39 Maxted 1996, 8.

40 Wallace 1869, 59, cited in Gardner 2003, 33.

41 Exeter, Devon CRO, 48/26/13 DC. 6327; cited in Black 2001, 110.

papers for information about new publications. G.B. Whittaker, testifying in 1836 before the Commissioners of Inquiry into the Management of the Post Office, acknowledged that newspaper advertising had been a necessary marketing tactic, 'and the reason is, there are many persons who would like to buy the books whom we know nothing of, and consequently could not send our lists to, who would see them in the newspapers'.[42]

Journalism did not develop into a serious profession until later in the nineteenth century, but meanwhile the news networks exploited by the country newspapers had become more varied and sophisticated.[43] The London papers still supplied news, but provincial and continental papers appeared with increasing frequency in the credit lines. During 1830 one country paper, *Jackson's Oxford Journal*, credited stories from *The Times*, the *Monthly Magazine*, *Whittaker's Monthly Magazine*, the *Morning Herald*, the *Weekly Dispatch* and the *Gazette*, but also used such diverse periodicals as *Le messager des chambres*, the *Wolverhampton Chronicle*, the *Coventry Observer*, the *Taunton Courier*, the *Bucks Gazette*, *Limerick Evening Post*, *Journal de la Belgique*, *Constitutionnell*, the *Moniteur*, *New York Mercantile Advertiser*, *Belfast Newsletter*, *Cork Constitution*, the Russian *Gazette of Health* and the *United States Service Journal*.[44]

On the whole, distribution of provincial serials continued to follow traditional lines, radiating out from different points of production and supply, from the printing office to newsagents and on to the subscribers through various routes. Flindell's prospectus outlines the plan for his *Western Luminary* (1813):

> Such of the inhabitants of Exeter as are disposed to receive it, are requested to give their orders to the person appointed to wait on them for that purpose; or leave their address at the printing-office as soon as convenient. Other persons within the four counties (if not personally waited on by the Traveller for the Luminary) will have the goodness to give their orders through some reputable bookseller or news-agent in their nearest post town. All persons wishing to have it sent to them beyond the boundaries of Devon, Cornwall, Dorset and Somerset, must send their orders through some respectable inhabitant of Exeter who will at the same time undertake for the payment, quarterly.[45]

There were some developments, such as the advent of London agents who specialized in country newspapers. The most prominent of these was William Tayler, who matched advertisers and local papers in the 1790s, and organized

42 Commissioners of Inquiry into the Management of the Post Office, *Fifth report* (1836), 33; cited Bodleian Library, MS Pollard 280, fol. 195.

43 Chalaby 1998; Lee 1976, 104–17.

44 Unpublished study of *Jackson's Oxford Journal*, by N. Aubertin-Potter, All Souls College, Oxford, 2003.

45 Cited Maxted 1996, 2.

the efficient supply of London and country papers in both directions.[46] He is described as 'Printers Agent' in the will of his friend, the Hampshire newspaper proprietor James Linden.[47] The introduction of mail coaches in 1784 led to improvements in delivery time.[48] The railway was just beginning to make an impact in the 1820s and early 1830s with the inauguration of the Stockton–Darlington line in 1825 and the Manchester–Liverpool line in 1830.[49]

Developments in printing technology were not felt in the provinces until the end of this period.[50] Iron presses were introduced at the beginning of the nineteenth century and offered some improvements: they were sturdier and could take a slightly bigger sheet, but were built to much the same design as the old wooden presses and were not much faster. The *Manchester Guardian* did not begin printing on iron presses until 1821, following London's lead. The Stanhope and improved Columbian hand-presses proved inadequate to the growing production demands of the better circulating papers, and *The Times* was the first to purchase the radically faster steam-driven machines, installed 29 November 1814 – at night to avoid hostilities with the printers. The *Manchester Guardian* became steam-driven fourteen years later, with little disruption to employment relations. After making 'a trial of the machine for a week or two', the Manchester Typographical Society evidently decided steam was all right. A more violent story would be told when the composition room became mechanized at the end of the nineteenth century.[51] The local printing trade followed London in the acquisition of new machinery, but when it did, the periodical press was always the motivating force.

Literacy was rising in the nineteenth century and overall there were more readers,[52] but there were ever more competing newspaper titles inside London and out, so the steady rise in readership individually enjoyed by the major provincial papers in the eighteenth century – from one or two hundred subscribers at the beginning to a few thousand – generally levelled off in the early 1800s. Provincial circulation and advertisement-duty figures for this period were published in the *Stamford Mercury* in 1833. The leading provincials enjoyed weekly circulation rates that year ranging from about 2,000 (*Cambridge Independent Press*, *Gloucester Journal*, *Ipswich Journal* and *Norfolk Chronicle*), to around 3,000 (*Salisbury Journal*, *Newcastle Courant* and *Manchester*

46 See Turner, chap. 23 below.
47 Hampshire Record Office: 1806/A/56.
48 Ellis 1958.
49 Musson 1958, 411–12.
50 See Mosley, chap. 7 above.
51 Musson 1958, 425.
52 Altick 1998.

and Salford Advertiser), to exceptional figures of more than 5,000 (*Leeds Mercury* and *Stamford Mercury*).[53] Others seemed to manage with much lower sales, particularly when they had to divide the market with competitors. The *Nottingham Journal*, *Nottingham Mercury* and *Nottingham Review* had weekly circulation averages of 865, 846 and 1,361 respectively in 1833; likewise, the *Northampton Free press*, *Northampton Herald* and *Northampton Mercury* had 490, 692 and 1,615.

The law-abiding press laboured under an increasing burden, the so-called taxes on knowledge, which were introduced at ½*d.* in 1712, but had risen to 2*d.* by 1789, and to 4*d.* in 1814. Raising revenue on a popular commodity was one government motive, but another was to put the periodical press out of the financial reach of the working classes. This proved futile. Scores of unstamped, affordable (and mostly ephemeral) periodicals appeared, promoting the reform movement and other causes, which were also picked up by the 'legitimate' press. The provincial press played a part in the narrative of growing press freedom, for many of the new radical papers originated outside London. The unpopular taxes on periodicals were later reduced (which saw off most of the unstamped), and finally withdrawn in 1855.

In the 130 or so years since its foundation, the local periodical press as a whole had become more popular, more political, and above all more commercial. In 1830, the provincial newspaper was still in the ascendant. One commentator, looking back on the history of the provincial press in the nineteenth century, was in no doubt:

> The provincial press has made wonderful advances in ability and energy during the last twenty years. How almost invariably has the pen displaced the scissors – the ink supplanted the paste! Some of the best reporters in the kingdom are engaged on the country press; whilst the leading articles of the first country newspapers are quite upon a par with most of the daily London press. The country editors, therefore, may be set down as an able body of men, and in general ... they are upright and honourable men. From the peculiar position and local influence of a country paper, its editor has often the interests of a local party greatly in his power; ... How many a member of Parliament has owed his seat to the exertions of the local journal, which, for concentrating its efforts to one particular spot, and to one great party purpose, has achieved a triumph of which the metropolitan press itself might be proud![54]

53 Newton and Smith 1999, 'Appendix 1: Comparative circulation figures, 1833/1839', 277–9.
54 *Eclectic Review*, cited in *Reynolds's Miscellany*, 2 Jan. 1847, 143.

22

British commercial and financial journalism before 1800

JOHN McCUSKER

Beginning in the late 1530s, Europe experienced an explosion of business newspapers, but time has muffled the report. Before the end of the sixteenth century – and, therefore, well before the beginnings of what may be called the 'political newspaper' – commercial and financial newspapers were being published in more than half a dozen cities. Amsterdam, Hamburg, Frankfurt, Rotterdam, Middelburg and Venice had their commodity price currents; Antwerp, its exchange current; London, its bills of entry. This is an understatement since it is quite likely that additional research will add both to the number of cities and to the variety of newspapers published in each.[1]

Additional research is called for because very few copies of these newspapers survive and there is little contemporary mention of them. So few survive because they were instantly ephemeral; the news in one of them was superseded by the news published in the next number. Thus, there was no reason to keep them; they were quickly discarded. Some of their characteristics – such as the lack of a title – have made it difficult for librarians successfully to incorporate the few copies that have survived into their collections, sometimes treating them instead as curiosities. Contemporaries made little mention of them because they were so common within the circle of those who used them as to be hardly worthy of comment. Everyone who mattered in the financial world knew what a commodity price current was. The lack of surviving copies renders almost unintelligible what little contemporaries did write about them.

Additional research is justified by the significance of these early business newspapers. They were important as a source of economic information for contemporaries and they continue to have importance as a source of economic information for historians of the economy of the early modern Atlantic world. Indeed, given the published and therefore public nature of the information

1 This chapter has its antecedents: McCusker 1985, 1986, 1991a, 1997; McCusker and Gravesteijn 1991. Also see Harris 1987; Winkler 1993; and Nelson and Seccombe 2002.

they broadcast, these early business newspapers are a uniquely valuable source. This chapter has as its purpose to sum up what we know about the origins of the English business press so as to provide a starting point for all who would pursue the subject further.

It is appropriate to begin this exposition by defining terms. Table 22.1 distinguishes between two broad types of early commercial and financial newspaper. The first type – the 'current', to adapt a word in use at the time – published information produced by the local market. This information was essentially price data: the price of commodities; the price of foreign bills of exchange; the price of money; and the price of securities. Thus publishers produced 'commodity price currents', 'exchange rate currents', 'money currents' and 'stock exchange currents'. The second type of newspaper published information about shipping and trade. The 'bills of entry' recorded the shipment of commodities into and out of ports; the 'marine list' published information about the arrival and departure of cargo vessels. These two types are called 'A' and 'B', not only to group them and to designate the groups simply, but also because doing so permits us to establish a category 'C' to allow for the eventual incorporation into a single newspaper of more than one of the originally separate kinds of publication.

By defining what these newspapers were, we are better able to describe them and to distinguish them from what they were not.[2] These were all newspapers in the classic, even modern meaning of that word. They were printed and published on a frequent, regular basis, as a commercial venture, for sale to a paying public. An editor or publisher employed individuals who gathered the desired information. The editor assembled the information into a consistent format and sent the copy to a printer who set and printed the newspaper. It was then sold about town both to regular subscribers and to occasional purchasers. The newspaper appeared as a serial; that is, it was printed and distributed regularly, usually weekly, on the same day of the week, at the same time of the day. The publisher expected to make a profit over his costs, which many times included not only the sums owed to the people he employed, but also charges involved in obtaining and maintaining the licence under which he operated.

Consequently, there are several things that these newspapers were not. Most emphatically they were not the same as the lists of rates or prices that one merchant sent privately to another merchant, frequently as an addition to or insert in a letter. It is necessary to distinguish between a 'price current' and a list of 'prices current', the former public and published, the latter personal and

2 See Harris, chap. 20, above, and Harris 1987.

Table 22.1 *Catalogue and description of the types of early commercial and financial newspapers published in Europe prior to the end of the eighteenth century*[a]

Catalogue

A Publications that reported on the local economy ('currents')
- 1 Commodity price currents
  - (a) General price currents
  - (b) Specialized price currents
- 2 Foreign exchange rate currents
- 3 Money currents
- 4 Stock exchange currents

B Publications that reported on overseas trade and shipping
- 1 Bills of entry
  - (a) General bills
  - (b) Specialized ('small') bills
- 2 Marine lists

C Publications that combined two or more of the elements from categories A and B
- 1 Exchange rate current/stock exchange current
- 2 Exchange rate current/marine list
- 3 Exchange rate current/stock exchange current/marine list

Description

A Local market publications or 'currents'

1 Commodity price currents

Published the local currency prices of goods offered for sale in a specific market. The general commodity price currents included the prices of a broad range of goods; the specialized price currents were limited to particular kinds of commodities, e.g. cloth, grain, sugar, imported colonial goods, etc. The general commodity price current also usually listed a few exchange rates and sometimes insurance rates and money rates.

2 Foreign exchange rate currents

Published the going rates on the local exchange or bourse for bills of exchange against a list of cities in other countries. Bills of exchange are negotiable instruments for the transfer of funds, usually to another country. They were similar to modern bank cheques but were drawn on funds held by individuals or businesses rather than on funds held by banks.

3 Money currents

Published the value in the local money of account of a variety of foreign and domestic coins and, sometimes, gold and silver bullion. As this implies, even domestically minted coins sometimes fluctuated in value against the local money of account.

4 Stock exchange currents

Published the prices at which shares of stock, bonds and government securities were traded on the local market.

B Overseas trade and shipping publications

1 Bills of entry

Published lists of commodities that had been entered into the local custom house books as being offloaded and imported or as being loaded on board for export.

Table 22.1 (*cont.*)

2. Marine lists Published lists of ships entering into or clearing from various ports, particularly the port at which the list was published, but sometimes other domestic and foreign ports also.
C Combined publications As economies grew more complex and business publishing became more sophisticated and competitive, some publishers produced newspapers that incorporated more than one of the elements in categories A and B. Modern business newspapers and the business sections of modern political newspapers combine everything distinguished above.

Note:
[a] Compare McCusker 2005, 320–1.

private. Published information reported the doings on the exchange and in the market; private correspondence was one step removed from the market, no matter how dependent upon it the information may have been. By the eighteenth century, many merchants had begun to use printed or partly printed forms to distribute to their correspondents lists of their own buying and selling prices. At the same time, brokers had begun to use similar forms to tell their correspondents about exchange rates and stock prices. This is a key point because some of the very earliest published commodity price currents and exchange rate currents of the sixteenth and seventeenth centuries *looked like* the printed forms of the eighteenth century: they were only partly printed with the data filled in by hand. Whatever the similarity in appearance, however, the distinction is essential. Lists prepared by individuals for occasional distribution to their own customers recording their own offering prices are fundamentally different from published newspapers. This chapter deals only with the published newspapers.

None of the developments discussed herein was peculiarly English. The earliest traceable commodity price current was published at Antwerp before 1540, although it may have been modelled upon an even earlier Italian commodity price current, possibly Venetian. Antwerp was also the place of publication of the first known exchange rate current, dating from as early as the 1580s, although it, too, may have started concurrently with the Antwerp commodity price current in the 1540s.[3] Although the dating of these earliest newspapers to within a century of the invention of movable type printing may at first seem surprisingly early, upon reflection it is quite understandable. Business people across the ages have pushed at the frontiers of information technology.

3 McCusker 1996.

Although printing came to England fairly quickly, the first indication of the publication there of a business newspaper is the suggestion somewhat after the fact that the London bills of entry had their origins in the 1580s. The earliest extant copies of an English commodity price current are from London, dating to the first and second decades of the seventeenth century. Both the London bills of entry and the London commodity price currents were appearing regularly by the 1620s and 1630s, the former daily, the latter weekly. Over the next several decades, other business newspapers began to be produced. Merchants not only subscribed to them for their own enlightenment, but also sent them to overseas correspondents on a regular basis. Provision had been made for such newspapers in government and in law. The postal service and the taxing authorities had taken note of them and decisions had been made to limit charges levied against them in order to encourage them as part of government's general promotional efforts for the English economy. Well before 1700, business newspapers had become an essential part of English commerce and finance.

At the turn of the eighteenth century, there were four basic types of commercial and financial newspaper published at London during the business week: the bills of entry; the commodity price current; the marine list; and the exchange rate current. It is now possible to sketch the history of each of them.

Bills of entry

The 'bills of entry' were newspapers that published lists of commodities imported and exported at a given port of entry. In 1678, John Vernon, writing in his book *The compleat comptinghouse: or, the young lad . . . instructed . . . in all the mysteries of a merchant*, described the newspaper in the following words: 'By a Custom-house Bill is meant a sheet of paper that comes out every day, (except Holy days); in which Paper there is set down all the Goods by themselves that are Imported; and all them that are Exported by themselves; and there is put the Place they are Imported from, the Merchant's Name that Imports them, and the quantity of Goods; and so for the Exportation of Goods.'

Vernon's description underscores two important characteristics of the bills of entry: the source of the information published in them and the market for them. The information in the newspaper came directly from the records of the custom house, where the importer or exporter of any commodity had to enter the details of the shipment. The handwritten documents recording these details were called the 'bills of entry'. It was on the basis of this document that the Customs assessed duties. Custom house clerks made several copies of the entries inwards and outwards for the internal administration of the Customs. Two of those copies are of special interest to historians of the Customs. One copy was sent on to the Exchequer and became the basis of the port books; after the mid-1690s another was sent to the office of the Inspector-General of Imports and Exports where his clerks compiled the data into the large, annual ledgers of imports and exports. The custom house bills of entry were the primary fiscal and statistical documents of the Customs.

The bills of entry were also of great importance to businessmen. Importers and exporters were interested in the information that the bills contained as a means to keep track of what their competition was doing. Shopkeepers were interested in the information in order to find out where to buy wholesale the things they sold retail. By long-standing tradition, all could apply to the custom house clerks for handwritten copies of summaries of the bills of entry. Someone thought to print and publish these summaries, apparently as early as the reign of Elizabeth I. The venture was such a success that in 1619 James I found ready buyers for the office of Clerk of the Bills in two of his courtiers, Alexander Foster and Richard Grimes.

Although the monopoly granted by letters patent in 1619 extended to all the ports of England and Wales, the newspaper was published at first only at London; the London bills of entry published lists of imports and exports only for that port. It appeared, as Vernon said, every day the custom house was open, six days a week excepting only public holidays. It was a single-sheet publication, dictated in its dimensions and shape by the amount of information generated by a day's business (see Plate 22.1). Thus it grew in size as the trade of the port of London grew. By the 1770s, the newspaper was considerably larger than those from a century earlier. As it grew, it acquired other characteristics that we associate with the more modern newspaper, but it originally lacked any title or any printer's information or publisher's imprint.

In addition to its growth in size, there were other changes. Sometime in the seventeenth century, the publisher of the London bills of entry started issuing several shorter compilations – called 'small bills' – besides the complete or 'general bills'. Of these 'small bills', the import bills listed only goods imported; the grocers' bills, only groceries; the linen bills, only linens; and the wine bills, only wines. Later, in the 1730s or 1740s, provincial publishers, operating under licence from the holder of the monopoly, began to publish bills of entry at Liverpool and Bristol. The same thing happened at Dublin as early as the 1690s; at Hull beginning as early as 1753; and at many other British ports beginning in the early nineteenth century. Almost all of these newspapers continued to be published until the start of the Second World War.

Although business newspapers were widely sold and well known to contemporaries, relatively few copies have survived from before the end of the eighteenth century. Yet, several hundred copies of the London bills of entry were printed and published every day in the seventeenth and eighteenth centuries; they were subscribed to not only by individual merchants, but also by such institutions as London coffee houses and government agencies; and contemporaries turned them to good use both inside and outside of government. The records of the publishers show print orders for the general bills of 260 in 1672, 350 in 1676 and 500 in 1798. In 1696 there were eleven bound volumes of the London bills of entry in the library of the Commissioners for Trade and Plantations. John Houghton extracted information from the newspaper and published it in his own periodical, *A collection for improvement of husbandry and trade*, in the 1680s and 1690s; Charles Whitworth used it for his *Register of the trade of the port of London; specifying the articles imported and exported*, begun in 1777; and several compilations appear to have been based upon it, beginning as early as one prepared under the direction of Sir Lionel Cranfield during his term of service as Surveyor General of Customs, 1613–18. Nevertheless, for the period before 1775 there are no known extant copies of any of the 'small bills' and only approximately two hundred of the general London bills of entry.

In lieu of surviving copies, the best sources of information about the newspaper are the records concerning the monopoly on its publication, especially the papers of two of the patent holders. Charles II granted the monopoly to Andrew King in 1660 and he and his heirs held it until 1722. In that year, it passed to the Lewis family, who published the newspaper for the next century. King was a London merchant originally engaged in the Spanish trade; he was knighted and given the patent for services rendered to the Royalist cause during the Civil War. The Lewises of Harpton Court were an important Welsh landed family. Members of the family held local and national governmental offices throughout the period and included Thomas Lewis, Member of Parliament for New Radnor Boroughs, and Henry Lewis, Collector of Customs in the port of London. After the 1620s, the patent never strayed far from the hands of men involved in trade.

Government support of the monopoly greatly enhanced the value of the patent, which guaranteed the active, if sometimes reluctant assistance of the Customs authorities both in providing access to the requisite information and in denying it to others. It protected the patent holder from any competition from either inside or outside the Customs establishment. In the seventeenth century, the custom house clerks, who had previously obtained some of their income from the production of handwritten copies of the bills of entry, mounted repeated but consistently unsuccessful campaigns to keep – and, later, to regain – the right to produce at least some copies of the bills. In the eighteenth century the publishers of some provincial political newspapers tried to improve their competitiveness by obtaining and printing information about cargoes entered in at the custom house for import or export. The battle was particularly fierce at Liverpool in the 1780s and early 1790s. Victory always went to the monopolist.

Government support involved more than defence of the monopoly, however. The bills of entry – and, indeed, all of the newspapers discussed herein – were afforded special status in the mails.[4] Instead of paying the usual postage rates, which were very high, newspapers paid nothing. They went free – free of postage, that is, but not quite free of any transportation costs. The carriage of newspapers at fees to be arranged between publishers and themselves was a perquisite of the Clerks of the Roads who administered the transport of the mails between the cities of England. Newspapers were, as a result, distributed with the mails, but at much less than the usual postage costs. As William, Lord Lowther, president of the Board of Trade, observed in 1835: 'The principle of the Post-office at its establishment . . . was to afford advantage to trade and commerce. The direct revenue to be derived from the Post-office was not the primary consideration.'[5]

While all newspapers eventually came to share such treatment with regard to the post, government promotion of commercial newspapers went even further. When all other newspapers were brought within the scope of the stamp duty in 1712, business newspapers were exempted. The exemption extended to all of those discussed in this chapter, although the bills of entry were mentioned explicitly in the statute. The distinction made between business newspapers and other newspaper publications was based on the omission from business newspapers of any advertisements. One anomalous result of this exemption is that studies of eighteenth-century English newspapers based on records created in the collection of the stamp duty omit mention of almost all of these business newspapers.

The special status afforded the bills of entry – and, perhaps, the commodity price currents – included one other element that serves additionally to camouflage them in the historical record. Until the very end of the seventeenth century, the English government kept strict control of printing through a

4 See Tierney, chap. 24 below.

5 Great Britain, Parliament, House of Commons, 1836, *The fifth report of the Commissioners appointed to inquire into the management of the Post-office Department*, London, 6.

licensing procedure. It is not clear how and why it happened, but the printer of the bills of entry was excused from this control, apparently by custom up to 1662, when the new 'Act for preventing the frequent abuses in printing' was brought in, and afterwards directly by proviso in that statute. This exclusion would explain why these men are not picked up in the contemporary lists of licensed printers. However inconvenient for historians, this exception from licensing requirements served to cut printers' costs and, thereby, to promote the publication of bills of entry still more.

The protection and promotion of the publication of the bills of entry emphasizes the significance of these newspapers both for the contemporary consumer and for the modern user. Government sanction served to enforce a certain care and caution in the gathering and presentation of the published data that permitted merchants at the time – and economic historians in later years – to rely on their accuracy and consistency. At the very least, the grant of a monopoly, by implying the possibility that it could be withdrawn, worked to prevent obvious misuse of the rights conferred. Only twice were the letters patent for the bills of entry withdrawn and the patent granted to others. This was done once in the time of the Commonwealth when the motives were purely political. On the other occasion, the patent was withdrawn after complaints about the quality of the service rendered. One expects that the lesson was not lost.

Commodity price currents

The second of these four business newspapers, the commodity price current, published lists of commodities and the wholesale prices at which they sold on the local market. Writing roughly a century after it had first appeared in England, Edward Hatton described it thus: 'Price Current. A weekly account published in London, of the currant [*sic*] value of most commodities.'[6] The earliest extant copies of the London commodity price current – four of them dated between 1601 and 1614 – are not especially impressive. They were only partly printed on two sides of a long, narrow sheet of paper (25 by 6cm); the date and the prices were filled in by hand in pen and ink. Under a full title, *Pris des marchandises en Londres*, some ninety commodities were listed in alphabetical order. They bore no imprint. In these same years the *prijs-courantiers* of Amsterdam were producing a larger, completely printed, two-page list with title and imprint that gave the prices on the Amsterdam Exchange of

6 Hatton 1697.

many more commodities than did the considerably humbler London publication. Indeed, if it were not that we possessed copies of more than one number published in the same format several years apart, legitimate doubt could be registered about whether these early examples were actually of commodity price currents. Nevertheless, by the 1630s London's commodity price current had come to rival that of Amsterdam and, by the end of the century, to better it (see Plate 22.2). Viewed in this light, the history of the publication of the two cities' commodity price currents paralleled the changes in their comparative commercial and financial positions across the seventeenth century.

An added reason to think that the earliest examples of the London commodity price current were a true published newspaper is the close control exercised at that period over all printing and publishing. Mention has already been made of this matter in connection with the history of the bills of entry. Printers were licensed; publishers of newspapers such as the bills of entry and commodity price currents sought grants of monopoly rights from the crown and the City. Where extant copies of these publications fail us, it is to the records of both the national and the local government that we can turn in order to learn what was happening. Thus, as at Amsterdam, all of the publishers of the London commodity price current who have been identified were licensed brokers. At Amsterdam, they operated under cover of a city ordinance that not only granted them a monopoly to publish a commodity price current, but also exercised strict control over it. Similar rights and obligations seem to have operated in London, although – given the traditional tensions between crown and City – in a somewhat different way. In the seventeenth century, the publishers sought and received grants of letters patent from the king to establish their monopoly. They complied with City regulations about the price they charged – and were empowered to display the City's arms in the masthead of their newspaper as a result. Presumably, too, the printers they employed fell within the Acts regulating printing. At least until the end of the century, ancient rights and privileges circumscribed what was possible. It would have been impossible, therefore, to have sustained publication of an extra-legal *Pris des marchandises en Londres*.[7]

Much of this changed during the two decades after 1680 when controls of the press were ended.[8] Nothing testifies better to this change than the sudden proliferation of published business newspapers including several different commodity price currents. Yet, the publishers continued to be licensed brokers,

7 Nelson and Seccombe 2002, 535: 'Unauthorized publication was severely punished and rarely attempted.'

8 See Rose, chap 4 above.

and so were not without some constraints upon their actions. Indeed, there may have been even greater constraints than before, exercised this time by the need to satisfy their customers. Should one commodity price current prove to be unreliable, London merchants had others from which to chose, others to which to give their custom. There is even a suggestion that one group of brokers subsequently threatened to start a new commodity price current to compete with an existing one because they were dissatisfied with the publication available to them. The visible hand of government was replaced by the invisible agency of the market to ensure due care in the publication of the London commodity price current.

By the middle years of the 1690s, there were four different commodity price currents being published in London. They resembled each other in many ways. All were completely printed in two or three columns on both sides of a single sheet of paper. Almost all had proper titles and imprints. They were all weekly newspapers and, in so far as we know, cost the same per copy to buy both individually and on a subscription basis. French, which seems to have been the language of the London commodity price current in its first decades, continued to be important throughout the period. In the 1690s, one of the four was published exclusively in that language and the others had parallel French translations. Contemporary comments tend to confirm the impression that there was not much to distinguish between them, while contemporary records also reveal that merchants and others bought more than one of these newspapers, if only because they appeared on different days of the week. In 1696, the Commissioners for Trade and Plantations had on their library shelves several bound volumes of some of these newspapers, including two of Samuel Proctor's and three of James Whiston's, having subscribed to them regularly over the years.

The competition between the several publishers seems to have continued down at least into the 1720s, but something happened at that point which is very difficult to explain. For some fifty years, between roughly 1725 and 1775, there are almost no known extant numbers of any London commodity price current. If it were not for the very occasional mention of the commodity price current in contemporary sources and the existence of a short run of the *London Price Current on the Royal Exchange*, for 1754, one could easily have been convinced that there was no such newspaper published in London during those five decades. Why the number of commodity price currents published there fell off so fast and so far after about 1720 and why one can find almost no copies from this period are questions for which there is as yet no satisfactory answer.

The London Price Current published by William Prince began production in April 1776 and continued to be issued until nearly the end of the nineteenth century. Many copies of it and its competitors survive in various archives and libraries. Prince proclaimed in his masthead that the information he published was 'regulated by near fifty eminent brokers, factors, and others'. His statement reinforces the point made above about how important, in the name of accuracy and reliability, the exercise of some control over the newspaper was thought to be. Prince's invocation of nearly fifty prominent people as having some interest in and oversight of his enterprise is reminiscent of a similar pronouncement in the Amsterdam commodity price current almost two centuries earlier. The brokers who oversaw its publication (the *prijscourantiers*) repeated in each number that it was 'checked over by the five of us' – 'Ghecorrigeert by ons vyven'. It also suggests the broad base of support for the newspaper and hints at a possible reason for the decline over the years in the number of London commodity price currents that were published. Perhaps the London brokers, in uniting behind one such publication, had thereby forced any others into an untenable position: they had no backers and they had no customers. Despite the paucity of known copies, there appears to have been a London commodity price current printed and sold in the City from 1601 or before until 1800 and beyond.

Apparently, there were no commodity price currents published in the provinces. The publication nearest to a provincial commodity price current of which mention has been found was a newspaper that combined a marine list and a list of commodity prices, printed at Liverpool for a short while in the mid-1760s. It disappeared quickly, however, because, as one contemporary commentator put it, the commodity prices in it 'proved often very incorrect'. The situation in England was analogous to that in the Low Countries. The Amsterdam commodity price current had no competition within the city because of monopoly licensing, and no competition from elsewhere in the country because the Amsterdam market dominated the region. In a parallel fashion, London wholesale prices – and, therefore, the London commodity price current – constituted the point of reference for all in England and beyond.[9]

The sudden burgeoning of newspaper publishing consequent upon the effective lifting of censorship controls in the 1680s and 1690s brought with it the establishment of two other English business newspapers. Intriguingly, both of these newspapers continue to be published today. They are *Lloyd's List*,

9 McCusker 2005.

a marine list, founded sometime before January 1692, and the *Course of the Exchange*, an exchange rate and stock exchange current, initially published in March 1697, the modern descendant of which is called the *Daily Official List*. After the *London Gazette* (1665), they are the second and third oldest continually published newspapers in the world.

Marine lists

A marine list published information about the arrival and departure of vessels at various ports at home and abroad. *Lloyd's List*, the first known marine list, was the work of one man, Edward Lloyd, the proprietor of a London coffee house. While it is one of the better known of England's business newspapers – if only because its continued publication has interested people in its early history – much about its origins has only recently been clarified by the discovery of a handful of very early numbers.[10] Lloyd's marine list was pretty much what he described it as being in his early running title: a listing of *Ships arrived at, and departed from several ports of England . . . [and] an account of what English shipping and foreign ships for England, I hear of in foreign ports*. It is no wonder then that someone, perhaps Lloyd or perhaps one of his successors as editor and publisher, shortened the title sometime between 1704 and 1741. (See Plate 22.3.)

The earliest numbers of *Lloyd's List* – if we may be permitted the anachronistic use of the shorter title – were printed on one side of a single sheet of paper. Like the London commodity price currents, it appeared weekly, for sale by subscription or to individual purchasers. Like them, too, and as distinct from the bills of entry, *Lloyd's List* had both a title and an imprint that spelled out who published it and from whom it could be purchased. In 1735, major changes were effected in the composition and issuance of the newspaper when it began to be published twice a week and when, with the marine list proper relegated to the second side of the sheet, the front page was given over to publishing other business news. That 'other business news' was, in fact, a wholesale copying of the *Course of the Exchange*, about which more information can be found below (see Plate 22.3; compare Plate 22.4). Obviously, the editor of *Lloyd's List* sought to strengthen his competitive position by combining his marine list with an exchange rate and stock exchange current and by changing the frequency of appearance to compete

10 McCusker 1991a.

directly with the very successful *Course of the Exchange*. *Lloyd's List* continued to be published in much the same manner down through the next century – as it continues to be into our own.

Richard Baker, the editor of *Lloyd's List* in 1735 who instituted the changes just mentioned, was also Master of Lloyd's, as had been his predecessors. Under Edward Lloyd's leadership – solidified by his publication of the *List* – the London marine insurance industry had coalesced around his coffee house. While the extent of that development was extraordinary, its nature was not. Many of the coffee houses of London were recognized gathering places for businessmen with specialized interests and Lloyd's coffee house was a place where those concerned in shipping sought each other out. It was certainly these men who provided the facilities upon which Lloyd initially depended for the information he published, although he quickly set up a more elaborate and more formal network of accredited agents throughout the country to collect and pass on news about shipping. Since such news was of particular importance to those interested in marine insurance, they naturally gravitated to the source. Lloyd's coffee house quickly became the centre for marine insurance brokers and underwriters who then organized an association headed by a Master. Under Edward Lloyd the ownership of the coffee house and the publishing of the newspaper had been united in the same person. The association of marine insurers eventually took control of both coffee house and newspaper, probably sooner rather than later. The Master of the association quite naturally assumed the editorship of *Lloyd's List*. The parallel between the history of *Lloyd's List* and the London commodity price current, the publication of each eventually taken over, one way or another, by the association of professionals who dominated the businesses that the newspapers served, will be seen below to have been matched by the history of the newspaper that published the news from the Stock Exchange.

To guarantee the rapid, reliable flow of information from his network of correspondents, the editor of *Lloyd's List* relied on a unique relationship with the Post Office. Letters from the newspaper's agents addressed to Lloyd's received favoured treatment in the post: they travelled free of postage; they were sorted specially and conveyed with dispatch; and they were held out for collection by a Lloyd's clerk once they arrived at London. For all of this the newspaper paid a set fee; it amounted to £200 a year by the 1780s. No other newspaper could avail itself of these services, at any price, however. Given what was said above about government's attitudes towards business newspapers, this privilege can be simply viewed as another promotional device. We do not know when it first started, but we do know that Lloyd moved his establishment from Tower Street to new premises in Lombard Street, near the General Post Office, just after Christmas in 1691, suggesting a new development in the relationship between Lloyd's and the Post Office. The initial number of *Lloyd's List* in the series from which we have the two earliest copies started immediately thereafter, in January 1692. It seems reasonable to presume that the newspaper had had its origins in the old coffee house in Tower Street sometime before that date.

Lloyd's List repaid these promotional efforts handsomely, both to the London business community and to government. As early as 1693, the Hudson's Bay Company had come to rely so greatly on 'Mr Loyd the Coffee Man for his Intelligence of the Comp[an]ies Shipps' that the governor and the committee of the company awarded him a subvention of £3. The master of Lloyd's also made it his business to see that government was speedily apprised of news that was of particular importance. Indeed, one historian has concluded that, because of its maritime intelligence capability, during wartime *Lloyd's List* became in effect an arm of the Admiralty.

These factors assume some significance for our understanding of the development and the importance of this newspaper. As with the other business newspapers, both institutional and commercial constraints operated to insure the completeness and the accuracy of what the editor inserted into his columns. Edward Lloyd's new newspaper could not have survived long had he not exercised due care. The organization of accredited correspondents in all the major ports and the elaborate preferential arrangements with the Post Office that sped the flow of reports to Lloyd's office helped establish and maintain the reputation of the newspaper. Subsequent editors not only had Lloyd's example as their guide, they also had to answer to the association of marine insurers gathered under the name of Lloyd's. Later in the century, for several years after 1769, as a result of disputes between two groups of marine insurers, a second, rival *Lloyd's List* appeared. It was published alongside the older one until the dispute was settled and a single publication once again sufficed. One element in the continuing competition was the question of the quality of the paper's news coverage. So important to the marine insurance industry had *Lloyd's List* become that neither contending faction felt comfortable without its own newspaper.

Exchange rate and Stock Exchange currents

The fourth and last type of early English business newspapers that concerns us here is a variation on an exchange current. Exchange rate currents published the rates at which foreign bills of exchange sold locally. As Gerald de Malynes wrote in 1622, 'exchange is the rudder of the ship of trafficke'. Without knowledge of the set of the rudder, merchants could not navigate well in the world of commerce. As was noted above, the earliest known exchange current was published at Antwerp probably as early as the 1540s. Many others followed later. While John Castaing did not invent the exchange rate current, he did tailor it to his own time and place. Castaing, a Huguenot émigré who became a citizen in 1688, had his origins in a continental tradition where such newspapers were well known. A rising broker on the Royal Exchange, Castaing found himself caught up in the London of the 1690s amid a rapidly developing market for all kinds of business and government securities. He took advantage of this booming business to establish a newspaper. In his *Course of the Exchange*, he published not only the rates of foreign exchange, but also the prices of stocks and bonds. Castaing's was the first exchange rate and stock exchange current.

The first part of Castaing's twice-weekly newspaper resembled all other exchange rate currents (see Plate 22.4). There he printed a list of European cities in one column and the price at which bills of exchange in those cities sold on the Royal Exchange. The rest of the page was taken up with information about the prices and conditions of sale of numerous forms of investment: company shares, company bonds, lottery tickets, annuities and government securities. The *Course of the Exchange*, started by Castaing in March 1697, continued to be published down into the nineteenth century, in much the same form, always fully printed, always on one side of the sheet, headed by the title, footed by an imprint giving the names of the successive publishers. Now published by the London Stock Exchange and called the *Daily Official List*, it still plays an important commercial role today in a considerably expanded format – and, of course, online.[11]

In January 1707, John Castaing, Jr., succeeded his father as publisher. Four years before his death in 1729, the younger Castaing started publishing the newspaper in partnership with Edward Jackson, his sister Arabella's husband. Sometime after Jackson's death in 1735, she remarried and, as Mrs Arabella Wharton, continued to be involved in the publication of the newspaper for at least forty-five years, always in partnership with a man who was a broker on the Exchange, but apparently taking a leading publishing role in the business herself (see Plate 22.4). In 1786, what had been the arrangement in fact for

11 In October 2003, the London Stock Exchange launched an electronic version of the *Daily Official List* (DOL); in December of that same year, the electronic publication superceded the printed publication.

some time, was made explicit in the imprint for the first time when the newspaper was said to be 'published... by Edward Wetenhall, Stock-broker, appointed by the unanimous vote of the gentlemen of the Stock-Exchange, October 30, 1786'. In ways very similar to what had happened with *Lloyd's List*, Castaing's *Course of the Exchange* – long a de facto ward of the Royal Exchange if only because its publishers and many of its readers were licensed brokers – was taken formally into its custody.

Castaing's *Course of the Exchange* always had an excellent reputation and deservedly so. He and his successors organized the collection of information carefully and published the compilation with due caution. Business was concluded on the walks of the Royal Exchange by mid-afternoon and Castaing's clerks then circulated among the various brokers noting down the latest prices for bills of exchange and shares of stock. The newspaper was set – presumably from standing type – printed, and ready for distribution within a matter of hours. Copies could be collected at the editor's office or, by arrangement, they were delivered to subscribers. When an error was made, Castaing took pains to correct it in the next number. Much about all this is available in a deposition in an Exchequer Court case of the 1740s during which the then-current editor of the newspaper, Richard Shergold, was called upon to testify about the price of the South Sea Company's stock over the fateful year of 1720.[12] He brought along to court with him the bound office copy of the newspaper for that year, which was then admitted as evidence. In reply to a direct question, Shergold testified that the *Course of the Exchange* was 'of good credit and esteem among the persons who usually bought and sold stocks'. Something similar could have been said about the other early business newspapers discussed in this chapter.

Perhaps the best evidence of how successful and how valuable these newspapers were is the eager competitors they attracted. The *Course of the Exchange* seems to have been a particularly popular target. We have already seen how Richard Baker altered *Lloyd's List* in 1735 to the point that it became a near clone of Castaing's newspaper. Others did the same thing. For at least eight years from 1714 to 1722, John Freke published his *Prices of Stocks* at London. In the mid-1730s, a newspaper appeared called *The London Course of the Exchange* that so mirrored Castaing's paper as to be virtually indistinguishable from it, except for the added word in the title and the different names in the imprint.

12 PRO/TNA – deposition by Robert Shergold, 16 Nov. 1743, *Percival Lewis* v. *Jacob Sawbridge*, depositions taken under commission, E 134, 17 Geo. II, Michaelmas, no. 7.

Imitation sprung from more than mere flattery. There was money to be made in publishing business newspapers.

These newspapers served a growing clientele that was anxious for the latest news, the 'freshest advices', about every aspect of the business world. They found paying customers for the news they printed both at home and abroad. They flourished and developed. Their success highlights how very important they were to the economy of seventeenth- and eighteenth-century Great Britain.[13]

13 For an example of their distribution in the late eighteenth century, see Turner, chap. 23 below.

23

Distribution – the case of William Tayler

MICHAEL L. TURNER

> I am from Grantham where the great North Road passes through 8 miles, and from Melton 7 miles and from Leicester where the other North Road goes 22 miles. Melton and Grantham are our Markets, but the Peterborough waggon with other Assistance comes to Waltham which is within 3 miles of me tho' Waltham is neither a Post Town nor a Market Town but there is a Carrier meets the Peterborough Waggon at Stamford every Wednesday and brings all the Parcels into our part of Leicestershire ...
>
> Thomas Wright, the compiler of the *Seasons almanac*, writing to the Clerk of the Stationers' Company, June 1775[1]

This passage illustrates the problems of communication that still had to be dealt with entering the final quarter of the eighteenth century. As Christine Ferdinand and Michael Harris have both discussed,[2] networks were required – networks for the communication of information,[3] for the passage of goods and for the payment of monies. Of course, some networks had been established for many years – those of the chapmen, the carriers, the letter-writers and the Post Office were all of great importance to the book trades – yet, during the eighteenth century a number of more specific enterprises emerged aimed at dealing with these concerns.[4] This case study takes a preliminary look at one such business – that of William Tayler. Beginning with the imprint of Pendred's *Vade mecum* of 1785, it attempts to identify Tayler; to look at possible antecedents; describe the scope of his activities; and, finally, to explain the succession of the enterprise, placing it in a historical context.

1 Stationers' Company (SC) Archive, Supplementary documents. Box C: Almanack accounts and advertisements.

2 See Ferdinand, chap. 21 and Harris, chap. 20, both above.

3 For advertising in newspapers, see Raven, chap. 3, above.

4 See Saurez, 'Introduction', above.

John Pendred

On 7 June 1784 John Pendred announced that 'This Day is published' his *List of the master printers in London, Westminster, and Southwark with the number of each house, and their situation*.[5] More importantly for our present concern the publication also included 'A List of those residing in the several Towns of England, Scotland, and Ireland, With the Number of Miles each Town is distant from London'. It emphasized that 'Those who print Newspapers are particularly distinguished' and pointed out how the publication was 'Very necessary for all Printers, Booksellers, Stationers, &c. Likewise for all Lottery-Office-Keepers, Shopkeepers, and others, who have Occasion to advertise in any of the Newspapers in England, Scotland, or Ireland.'[6] It was said to cost 4*d*.

Nothing published in 1784 has been identified with this handbill but, from the following year, a copy has come down to us of *The London and country printers, booksellers and stationers vade mecum* printed and sold by Pendred from no. 1 Featherstone Street, Bunhill Row, Moorfields.[7] It is perhaps unlikely that there was a previous publication to this, for at the end of it Pendred says, 'The Compiler, since the Publication of his Handbills, thought proper to change the Title of his book ...' The *Vade mecum* does appear to be a more ambitious publication than the one envisaged by the handbill, for it includes a 'correct List of Newspapers published in Great Britain, their Agents, and Days of Publication; and an useful Table of Stamps and Duties as are now in Use. Also a List of the Master Printers in Ireland.' It cost 1*s*., promised 'To be continued annually', and help was solicited in improving the lists. No later issue of the *Vade mecum* is known to survive.

In his edition of the *Vade mecum* Graham Pollard proposed two aims for the publication. First, bearing the handbill in mind, Pendred 'sought his market among the advertising agents – not a numerous trade at that date, except for lottery offices – and among wholesale booksellers'.[8] Second, he made the reasonable inference, considering Pendred's occupation as a compositor, that it was intended 'to be used by journeymen printers like himself, when in search of work'.[9] Pollard also drew attention to a few members of the country trade

5 The fullest account of Pendred is given by Pollard in Pendred 1955, xi–xiv. It may be added that he became free of the City in Nov. 1763: CLRO/ELJL/0901.

6 Pendred 1955, frontispiece: 'original is bound up in the front of Wyman's Copy of *Rhynd's printer's guide* now in London University Library'.

7 Pendred 1955; the introduction and appendices to Graham Pollard's edition of the *Vade mecum* provide essential background to this article. The original publication is in the Bodleian Library, Vet. A.5 g.5.

8 Pendred 1955, xxii.

9 Pendred 1955, xxii. For other publications of this type see Pollard's appendix B.

who Pendred appeared to have missed. John Feather, in rightly emphasizing the importance of Pendred's publication to matters of distribution, makes the point that these were unimportant people who did not publish newspapers, were therefore of no use to the distribution network, and that Pendred had been 'deliberately specific'.[10] If the list were to be regarded solely as a guide to advertisers and not perhaps also as a guide to compositors this is a reasonable argument, but the fact is that there is a long list of provincial members of the trade given, of which Pendred himself says, 'We have omitted distinguishing the News-paper Printers, they being affixed to the Titles of their Papers' which are listed elsewhere in the volume. It would seem that the intention was to be inclusive.

The 1784 announcement only mentions the involvement of Pendred; the title page of 1785, however, adds, 'And to be had of Mr Tayler, No.5, Warwick-Court, Warwick-Lane; and of Mr. Rich, No.55, Fleet-Street'.[11] Tayler was to be a key player in the information networks of the late eighteenth and early nineteenth centuries. When Pollard did his work he knew more about Pendred than he did about Tayler. Pendred was more accessible, being an author and a member of the Stationers' Company. Tayler was a much more shadowy figure: he is listed in the *Vade mecum* itself and described as an 'Agent to the Country Printers, Booksellers, &c. 5 Warwick Court, Warwick Lane',[12] exactly the kind of person that Pendred was targeting; or, maybe, a source for much of Pendred's information.

The Taylors of Bolt and Tun Court

On 9 December 1777 the *Manchester Mercury* had carried the following rather lengthy advertisement:

> The London News Papers, Continue to be sent by Post to all Parts of England, Scotland, and Ireland, free of Postage by TAYLOR and Co. next the Inn, in *Bolt and Tun Court*, *Fleet-street*, London, three Times a Week at Threepence Halfpenny the Paper, or *2l.* *5s.* *6d.* the Year, to be paid Quarterly or Half-yearly in London. Daily Papers, London Gazette, Votes in Parliament, &c. in Proportion.

10 Feather 1985, 67.

11 Pollard knew nothing of Rich beyond the information given by Pendred – that he was a bookseller and printseller – nor do I. The only relevant 'member' of the Stationers' Company within the time-frame is a John Rich, bound to the printer Edward Say on 2 Mar. 1762. There is no record of him ever having been freed.

12 Pendred 1955, 6. At this date Pendred only mentions Tayler's name as an agent for three country newspapers – Routh's *Sarah Farley's Bristol Journal*, Harward's *Gloucester Gazette*, and Smart and Co.'s *Reading Mercury, and Oxford Gazette*.

> Gentlemen who pay for the Year in advance when they begin, thereby save us the Trouble of collecting small Sums are supplied at Three-pence the Paper, or 1*l*. 19*s*. for the Year; and should any Gentleman be necessitated to discontinue the Paper before the Expiration of the Year, we return the prime Cost or Two-pence Half-penny each for all the Papers countermanded.
>
> Orders (Post paid) specifying the Mode of Payment, and where in London the Money is to be received, will be executed (if desired) by return of the Post (but we shall be obliged to Gentlemen for more early Notice when it can be given). It is usual for Gentlemen who have no Acquaintance in London, to get their Payments made by one of their Country Tradesmen, or by the Book-keeper of their nearest Stage Coach or Carrier.
>
> We could have fixed our Prices something lower, did we (as is frequently done) send Papers that have been first read in the London Coffee-Houses; but we flatter ourselves, that the Neatness and strict Regularity which have distinguished us for above 20 Years, will be a stronger Recommendation to the public Favour than the specious Abatement of a few Pence per Quarter in the Price. All Letters must be Post paid.[13]

A similar advertisement in the same newspaper a year later, on 15 December 1778, expands a little more:

> Threepence the Paper being the Ready Money Price in *London* (and on a small Profit) we humbly submit to the judicious Public, if, considering the additional Postage, – Expence of Paper, writing 156 Covers for an Evening Paper in a Year; paying Part of the Time; laying down Ready Money for the Papers in *London* (all which, all Dealers in News-Papers must do) and losing Five per Cent. by bad Debts, any Person who honestly sends a Gentleman all his Papers, cannot send them into the Country on Credit, under Threepence Halfpenny. Indeed the Customers continually coming to us, from those who have misled and abused them with fallacious Prices, sufficiently prove the contrary . . .

The first obvious point in respect of these advertisements, which no doubt appeared in many other provincial newspapers around the same dates, is that the style of the name and the address are different from those of Mr (William) Tayler of 5 Warwick Court associated with Pendred in 1785.[14] It is tempting to assume a connection, but I have found no evidence of a positive link between the two businesses. Moreover, the land tax assessment records for Farringdon Without at the Guildhall show no connection of anyone called Taylor or Tayler

13 I am grateful to the late Elizabeth Swain who provided me with copies of the advertisements from the *Manchester Mercury* mentioned in this chapter.

14 William Tayler signed himself with an 'e' rather than an 'o', and that is how it is usually spelt, though there are exceptions: in the advertisement found in the *Manchester Mercury* for 12 Dec. 1786; Trusler 1790, see below; and the obituary notice in *The Times* on 3 May 1817.

with Bolt and Tun Court between 1776 and 1785.[15] Second, Taylor and Co. speak of 'having distinguished' themselves 'for above 20 years', which puts their establishment back into the 1750s. William Tayler died in 1817, aged seventy-seven, which gives a birth date around 1740.[16] Also, later evidence speaks of William Tayler's firm having been established in 1786, though we have already met him at Warwick Court in 1785 through Pendred, and we shall see other evidence of him being active just one year after the second advertisement quoted above, in December 1779. Third, Taylor and Co. did not confine themselves to sending out just newspapers to the country gentry, but were also willing to supply the 'London Gazette, Votes of Parliament, &c.' This fits with what we shall shortly learn of William Tayler's activities a year or so later, but was probably common for those involved in this type of business, and I believe links us into the long-established line of the suppliers of written newsletters.[17] Fourth, it is clear that they did not have the field to themselves but that they were in competition with others.

Two such must have been J. Hamilton, bookseller and stationer, at no. 73, Shoe Lane, Fleet Street, who offered to send newspapers and periodical publications into the country in an advertisement in the *Salisbury Journal* on 26 November 1770, and A. Norman, at Mr Leece's, no. 1, Sweeting's Alley, Cornhill, London, to whom one could apply for almost identical services as those provided by Taylor and Co., according to an advertisement placed in the *Hampshire Chronicle* for 6 October 1777.[18]

In respect of Taylor and Co., it is interesting to see the attention paid to the arrangements that people in the country must make in order to pay their debts in London. The suggestion that customers can contact 'the Book-keeper of their nearest Stage Coach or Carrier' in order to arrange payments with London tradesmen is all part of the pattern which Chartres has described in his work on the inns in London and their provincial connections.[19] The

15 Guildhall, MS 11316, Land Tax Assessments, Farringdon Without.

16 It is probable that Tayler was born in Lincoln. In his will (PROB 11/1592) there are one or two bequests with Lincoln connections, including one 'to the poor of the Parish of St Paul in the Bail of Lincoln where I was baptized'.

17 Ben Jonson was parodying 'factors' of news in *Newes from the new world discover'd in the moone* in 1620. Though such letters have been studied for their content, a thorough study of their production and distribution is a major desideratum. For the circulation of information on prices and commodities, see McCusker, chap. 22, above.

18 I am grateful to Christine Ferdinand for this information. Probably somewhat later in the century another person in the field was one William Turner of no. 12, Cloak Lane, Dowgate Hill. A circular letter of his is illustrated in Turberville 1957, 351. This is said to be 'of the 'nineties'; interestingly it includes a list of London newspapers, giving the name, when published, the politics and the charge. Unfortunately the left-hand edge of the document appears to be missing. Elizabeth Swain once mentioned to me an Ann London as also advertising similar services.

19 Chartres 1977.

evidence from the country newspapers themselves is also informative on this score. Their imprints commonly list their agents in surrounding towns, mapping out what Cranfield described as the newspapers' 'sphere of influence';[20] but they themselves needed a London connection where 'files of the newspaper can be seen' and where 'advertisements can be placed'. Coffee houses tend to predominate – the London, the Chapter or Peele's are common ones; there will be the occasional inn; sometimes a well-known member of the London book trade; and sometimes, simply a name and address.[21] During the last thirty years or so of the century, one name and address that occurs with more and more frequency is that of Mr W. Tayler of no. 5 Warwick Square (or Court), Warwick Lane (or Newgate Street), London.

William Tayler of Warwick Square

If Taylor and Co. felt the necessity to spell out in their advertisement how the country customer could get round the problem of paying his London creditors, the evidence makes it clear that William Tayler was providing this service from at least 1779.

In that year James Linden of Southampton, the publisher of the *Hampshire Chronicle*, sent an invoice on 22 November to the Treasurer of the Stationers' Company for payment for advertising their annual almanacs in his paper. At the foot of the invoice is written:

> Sir, Be pleased to pay the above to Mr Wm. Tayler, or his order, whose Receipt shall be a full discharge from Sir, Your very hble. Servt. [Jas. Lindon]

Underneath this is written – 'Rec. Dec. 17 1779 the Content for Mr. Lindon, Wm.Tayler'.[22]

20 Cranfield 1962; see also Ferdinand, chap. 21, above.

21 See Pendred 1955, 22–37 for how important the coffee houses were in this respect. Examples of late eighteenth-century provincial newspapers naming members of the London book trade as their agents include: Bulgin and Rosser of the *Bristol Mercury and Universal Advertiser*, using Fourdrinier, Bloxam and Co. in 1796; Woolmer of the *Exeter Gazette*, using Richardson of the Royal Exchange in 1792; and Simmons and Kirkby of the *Kentish Gazette*, using Richard Baldwin and Joseph Johnson at various times. Other well-known members of the London book trade acting as agents included Thomas Astley, Stanley Crowder, Bedwell Law, John Newbery and John Souter.

22 SC Archives. Christine Ferdinand has pointed out to me two entries in the cashbook of the *Hampshire Chronicle* that nicely bracket this date: one on 20 Sep. 1779, 'By Mr Taylor on acct. of Gazette' and the other on 20 Mar. 1780, 'by Wm.Taylor Gazette's Papers on acct'; PRO, E.140/90. It may be significant that James Linden, who is the earliest member of the provincial trade with whom we have established a connection for Tayler, mentions Tayler in his will; also in Tayler's will there is a substantial bequest 'to my dear ffriend Elizabeth Lindon now or lately of Southampton Spinster'.

Unfortunately, there is no address for Tayler on this invoice. In fact this type of evidence rarely gives him an address; the mere mention of his name, or the phrase 'handed by Mr Tayler', seems to be sufficient, and to have indicated to everyone who was meant. From this time onwards his name is probably the one most often found on the invoices of country newspaper publishers – that I have seen – as being the London agent through whom the bill should be settled. Some members of the country trade included a printed statement on their invoices indicating to whom payment should be made; most of these usually left a blank for the name to be filled in, but James Blowing of Leeds was one who actually printed Tayler's name in the statement.[23] In 1791 John Monk of Chester printed 'Having resigned the Business in Favor of my Son, and wishing to settle my Affairs, I have taken the Liberty of sending your Account; your payment thereof to Mr W. Tayler, (whose Receipt shall be your Discharge) . . . ' on his final invoices.[24]

The earliest evidence so far found connecting Tayler with the Warwick Court address is in the land tax assessments where his name first appears in 1784 and continues there until his retirement in 1813.[25] We have seen it given in the imprint and content of Pendred's book in 1785, but several later documents imply, or actually state, that 1786 was the year in which the Warwick Court business was established.

The *Manchester Mercury* once again contains an advertisement on 12 December 1786, which this time is without any doubt for William Tayler. It provides apparent evidence that 1786 was the year in which the Warwick Court office was opened, and also gives us a useful resumé of some of Tayler's activities at that time:

> NEWS PAPERS.
> Warwick-Square, Warwick-Lane, near St Paul's
> *LONDON*
> AN OFFICE is opened at No. 5, in this Square, by *W. TAYLOR*, for the purpose of sending into the Country all the LONDON NEWS PAPERS, viz. *Morning Papers – Evening Papers – Weekly Journals – Gazettes – Votes of the House of Commons* – {*Minutes of both Houses* (sent in *Manuscript* every Night the House sits) – *Addresses – King's Speeches – Proclamations – Lloyd's List of Shipping – Weekly Prices of Merchandize*, and all the Foreign Gazettes of *Paris*, *Amsterdam*, the *Hague*, *Philadelphia*, &c. all which will be regularly sent, *free of the Duty of Postage*, under Privilege of Parliament, to any Part of *England*, *Scotland*, or

23 Bodleian, John Johnson Collection.
24 SC Archives, ses. 1, box c.
25 Guildhall, MS 11316, Land Tax Assessments, Farringdon Within.

> *Ireland*}, on the most moderate Terms. Clerks attend daily at the Office to receive Orders, who are employed in sorting the Papers after they are made up into Packets previous to their being carried to the General Post-Office, by which Method Disappointments are prevented, and every News-paper, Gazette, or Vote of Parliament, is punctually forwarded to Order.
>
> Gentlemen are respectfully recommended when they send their Orders, to direct to *W. Taylor*, as above, and to appoint Payment Half-yearly, in *London*, if convenient, as it will save the Duty on Bills and Receipts, as well as Postage of Letters.
>
> Orders taken in by the Printer of this Paper.

The words that I have placed within brackets are quoted by Pollard in his introduction to Pendred as appearing in the *Maidstone Journal* for 25 January 1786;[26] further research reveals that they are taken from a fuller advertisement that is essentially word for word the same as that published in the *Manchester Mercury* at the end of that year.[27] So, the Warwick Court office probably was open in 1785 after all.

Pollard gave us a further account of Tayler's activities, quoting from the second edition of Dr W. Trusler's *The London adviser and guide* published in 1790:

> To those who wish to advertise in the Country Newspaper, the following is a list, –
>
> Files of these papers are kept at W. Taylors, No. 5, Warwick-court, Newgate-street, where persons sending their advertisements through him, may refer to them. Mr Taylor charges sixpence or one shilling for sending an advertisement, besides the postage of the letter... [28]

This activity was illustrated by Pollard from the publisher's own file copy of the *Maidstone Journal* where across each advertisement is written the name of the person through whom the advertisement had been received. The practice seems to have been common to other publishers of country newspapers and no doubt had something to do with the bureaucracy surrounding the administration of the advertisement duty. These annotations show Tayler submitting advertisements to the *Journal*.[29]

26 Pendred 1955, xxi.

27 It is strange that Pollard did not quote the whole advertisement. In 1955, he located the publisher's file copy of the *Maidstone Journal* in the Maidstone Museum. It is now held by the Maidstone Library, and I am grateful to Joanna Pateman for providing me with a copy of the full text. In this instance 'Tayler' is spelt in the more regular way, and the final paragraph quoted above is omitted in favour of the more specific 'Orders taken in by Mr Blake at the King's Arms Printing Office, Maidstone', placed as a penultimate paragraph. Otherwise the wording, if not the typography, is identical.

28 Trusler 1790, 137–8, quoted by Pollard in Pendred 1955, xxii.

29 Pendred 1955, xxi. They show him to have placed advertisements for T. Hodge's State Lottery Office and for Elliot's silver tea service. This type of evidence may help us to identify some of Tayler's competitors in the field; for example, Pollard, at this point, mentions that Champante and Whitrow, the publishers of *The universal British directory*, have their names written across several advertisements.

Further evidence of Tayler's activities in 1790 is provided by a broadside list of English newspapers. It confirms Trusler's account and perhaps implies the existence of what may well have been the first regular 'directory' of the British newspaper press. It is headed:

> (No. 14 corrected, with Additions) No. 5. Warwick-Square, Warwick Lane, London, May 20, 1790.
>
> ADVERTISEMENTS for all the COUNTRY NEWS-PAPERS in England, Scotland, and Ireland, are taken in by W. TAYLER, at his Office . . ., to whom ALL the *English* and *Scotch* Country Papers are sent up every Week, by the respective Printers, as they are published, for the Inspection of those who bring Advertisements. – Gentlemen are requested to send their Advertisements written or printed upon Half a Sheet of Paper, as there is a Convenience in it with respect to Postage.
>
> At this Office Files of ALL the Country Papers are kept COMPLETE.[30]

Then follows the list of papers.

One other similar broadside issued by Tayler is known. It carries no number and is undated.[31] It is simply headed 'A complete List of all the COUNTRY NEWS-PAPERS throughout England'. At the foot, giving the Warwick Court address, it assures its readers that 'Particular Care will be taken . . . that the Advertisements are inserted as paid for, an Account of which, taken from the Papers, shall, if requested, be sent to the Advertiser. – A Convenience, the Want of which, has heretofore with-held many Gentlemen from advertising in the Country-Papers.'

Returning to the evidence given by the names of advertisers written across their submissions in the official files of country newspapers, another such copy is a short run of *Jackson's Oxford Journal* in the Bodleian.[32] In the calendar year 1799, more than a hundred and sixty advertisements are attributed to Tayler, though something between a quarter and a third of these are repeated insertions. Book-trade advertisements are present but not dominant – Bunney and Gold of Crane Court, Fleet Street advertise a pamphlet on income tax; Sampson Low advertises a novel by Elizabeth Helme and an instruction manual for sword exercises; Joseph Johnson and

30 This broadside, which was in the private collection at Four Oaks Farm, was brought to my attention by the late David Fleeman many years ago and first kindled my interest in Tayler. The collection is now at the Houghton Library, Harvard University.

31 I am again grateful to Christine Ferdinand for bringing this to my attention. There is a date of 1786 written on the piece, but Christine Ferdinand thought it might be earlier on the evidence of the Goadby name against the *Sherborne Mercury*. Robert Goadby died on 12 Aug. 1778. However, his widow was not buried until 13 Apr. 1790, and the inclusion of the Warwick Lane address must, I think, argue in favour of accepting the date of the annotation.

32 Bodleian, G.A. Newsp.a.4*.

others a book on ruptures; J. and A. Arch announce that 'this day was published' Edmund Fry's *Pantographia* on six separate occasions over as many weeks; James Wallis of Paternoster Row advertises a book on agriculture; W. Clarke and Son of Portugal Street a pamphlet on equity; and the Stationers' Company announce their forthcoming almanacs for 1800. Lottery advertisements figure largely, but Tayler also seems to have had good connections in the legal, insurance and business worlds, and also amongst the public schools: he took in notices for the anniversary meetings of Harrow, Winchester and Cheam schools. There are a few properties for sale and the odd job vacancy. There are other trade advertisements, perhaps the most interesting – in view of one of the books mentioned – for Fry's chocolate. Fry's also provide another instructive detail. In the issue for 2 November 1799 there is what appears to be a short article rather than an advertisement, reporting medical advice against drinking tea, and going on to recommend Fry's chocolate. This 'article' has been marked down to Tayler.

Other evidence too shows that Tayler particularly targeted the legal profession as a source for their legal notices. Entries in the legal sections of the several editions of the *Universal British directory of trade, commerce, manufactures* during the 1790s not only include informative entries about his activities, but also provide very full listings of the nation's newspapers and journals.[33]

Tayler's subsequent partner: Thomas Newton

It is clear that Tayler's business must have been quite an organization, the hub of a national network. The 1790 broadside list of newspapers and other sources, which states that 'At this Office Files of ALL the Country papers are kept Complete', indicates a miniature Colindale! There must have been quite a few employees. There are a number of names of those who signed the receipts on Tayler's behalf – particularly in the early 1790s. One of the earliest, appearing in the 1780s, is one Elizabeth Gisbey.[34] Another is John Rieder.[35]

33 For example, *The Universal British directory*, 1791, 427–9: 'PUBLIC Office for NEWSPAPERS and ADVERTISEMENTS ... At this Office all the Newspapers are filed, and Advertisements for Decrees in Chancery, Sales under Statutes of Bankruptcy, Notice to Debtors and Creditors, and all other Concerns, either in Law, Equity, or common Business, which Masters in Chancery, Attorneys, or others, may from time to time have occasion to make public in any particular Precinct or County, are taken in, and forwarded immediately to the Newspaper-Printers in any Part of England, Scotland, or Ireland ... *File-Clerk* J. Poyntell.'

34 Bodleian, John Johnson Collection, 5 July 1787 on an invoice of Hooper and Keenes, Bath. In his will Tayler left a bequest for 'my Old Servant Elizabeth Gisbey'.

35 E.g. 4 Sep. 1788 on an invoice of Richard Cruttwell, Bath. Tayler leaves a bequest to a William Rieder now or late of the city of York, and to his two sisters, Elizabeth and Ann.

There is a name I read as J. Poyntell by 1789,[36] and this is confirmed by one of the *Universal directory* entries where his name appears as the 'File Clerk'. This position, according to other editions of the same source, was held by a James Taylor who regularly signs in the early 1790s,[37] though the name is spelt with an 'o' as opposed to William's 'e'. On one occasion there is a clear 'Joseph Taylor',[38] as opposed to the more frequent James. Then there is a Thomas Newton,[39] who signs more and more in the late 1790s.

Newton proves to be a significant addition. His progress in the firm seems to have been rapid and by July 1803 the imprint of the *Leicester Journal* is referring to 'W. Tayler & T. Newton, Printers Agent, No. 5 Warwick Square, Newgate Street'. This style was to continue for the next ten years. That the firm had become a genuine partnership is further confirmed by a bill dated 1 June 1806 with an engraved head beginning: 'To W. Tayler & T. Newton Printers Agents', followed by the usual address and a version of the now familiar form of wording describing their activities.[40] A further broadside listing of newspapers is also to be found in the Bodleian,[41] headed 'Tayler & Newton, General Advertising Office (Established 1786)', the blurb of which confirms that their activities in all spheres remain the same and draws them to the attention of 'Auctioneers, Surveyors, Land Agents, Brokers, Solicitors, Attornies, Booksellers, and every Class of Advertisers'.

Tayler's retirement and death

At the end of June 1813, it seems that the eighteenth century finally yielded to the nineteenth. The *London Gazette* carried a notice of the dissolution of the partnership:

> Notice is hereby given, that the Co-partnership lately carried on by the undersigned William Tayler and Thomas Newton, in Warwick-Square, in the City of London, as Agents to the Proprietors of Provincial Newspapers, was resolved and determined on the 30th June last, when the said William Tayler retired

36 Bodleian, John Johnson Collection, 23 Mar. 1789 on an invoice of Williamson and Billinge, Liverpool. Tayler leaves a generous bequest to a John Elmhurst Poyntell, and a smaller one to Mrs Jane Brown of Newark upon Trent, 'formerly the Wife of Thomas Poyntell'. There are reasons, as yet unverified, to believe that there may have been family relationships between the Tayler, Rieder and Poyntell families.

37 Bodleian, John Johnson Collection, 11 May 1792 on an invoice of Hall and Elliot, Newcastle upon Tyne.

38 Bodleian, John Johnson Collection, 28 Aug. 1794 on an invoice of Crouse and Stevenson, Norwich.

39 Bodleian, John Johnson Collection, 11 May 1795 on an invoice of Richard Cruttwell, Bath.

40 Bodleian, John Johnson Collection.

41 Bodleian, 258 h.90 (11).

> from the concern; and from which time the business has been and will be continued under the firm Newton and Company ... [42]

Gradually, in the succeeding months, the imprints of the country newspapers began to reflect the change, and Tayler's name gave way to the new style along the lines of 'Messrs Newton & Co., Printers' Agent'.

William Tayler was around seventy-three years old when he retired, after a long and seemingly significant career. He lived for almost another four years. Simply, but with some precision fortunately in view of his name, *The Times* announced his death on 3 May 1817: 'In his 78th year, after a few hours indisposition, William Taylor [*sic*] Esq. (formerly of the firm Tayler [*sic*] and Newton, printers' agents, Warwick-square)'.[43] The *Gentleman's Magazine*, under 30 April, records his death 'In Boston Lane, near Brentford, in his 78th year, Mr Wm. Tayler, late of Warwick-square, Newgate-street; a truly benevolent Christian', a description which his will seems to justify.[44] Significantly, in spite of his retirement and death in the Brentford/Ealing area, he returned to the City to be buried in the Old Church at Christchurch, Newgate, within a stone's throw of his old business, on 6 May 1817.[45]

Aftermath

One wonders if Tayler felt himself to be a member of the book trade. He was undoubtedly connected with it and his activities facilitated its workings. He was not a member of the Stationers' Company nor was his partner and successor, Thomas Newton, but Newton had two sons who were. Nelson Norman, or Norman Nelson – the records give both forms – was apprenticed to John Harris, the bookseller of juvenile publications in St Paul's Churchyard. He received his freedom on 3 February 1824 and was cloathed on 3 August of the same year. On 5 July 1825 his name duly appears in the Livery List, giving his address as Warwick Court. The Beadle's Book records him there until 1840. The second son, Raymond D'Arcy, was apprenticed to James Scatcherd, the bookseller, of Ave Maria Lane on 1 December 1818; he did not become free until 3 May 1853. Thomas Newton's will makes it clear that the 'agency business' was bequeathed to these two sons, though there were

42 *London Gazette*, 29 June 1813, 1281.

43 *The Times*, 3 May 1817, 3e.

44 *Gentleman's Magazine*, 1817, 475. Cf. PROB 11/1592.

45 Guildhall, Christchurch Newgate Street (also known as Christchurch Greyfriars), tr. of extracts [by William McMurray] from burial registers 1667–1853, MS 3713/1. In his will Tayler says he was baptized at St Paul in the Bail, Lincoln to which parish he left a bequest. He also left another bequest to the County Hospital in Lincoln, but so far his family and background have largely evaded me.

other younger children. Under the Newtons the business flourished and took its place alongside the other great nineteenth-century newspaper and advertising agencies, such as Algar and Street, Clarke and Lewis, and the Mitchells. Perhaps it would be more correct to say that these agencies took their place alongside the firm of Newton and Co., in view of its antecedents.[46] More and more broadside lists of newspapers survive from these various agencies as the nineteenth century proceeds, until they finally give way in the second half of the century to the great annual newspaper directories of Mitchell and Sell.

46 Thomas Newton did not long outlive his old partner, dying on 3 August 1825. *The Times* reported, on 5 August 1825, 3f.: 'On Wednesday morning, after a procrastinated illness, at his residence, north-side Clapham-common, Thoms Newton, of Warwick-square. He was many years agent to the provincial press, and a man highly respected by a numerous circle of friends, by whom his loss will long be severely felt and deeply lamented.' A somewhat longer obituary appears in *Gentleman's Magazine*, 1825, 186, which reveals that he was a native of Hereford. For his will, see PROB 11/1703. Another broadside list of newspapers by the firm is reported by *NCBEL*, col. 1787 dated *c*.1840.

24

Periodicals and the trade, 1695–1780

JAMES TIERNEY

Introduction

Distinguishing between eighteenth-century 'newspapers' and 'periodicals' has been a thorny problem for modern scholars. Unlike modern newspapers, magazines and journals, whose physical appearance easily distinguishes them, many eighteenth-century newspapers and periodicals were published on the same size sheets and the same cheap paper. A further complication arises from the tendency of eighteenth-century publishers to experiment with format and subject matter, hoping to hit upon the happy formula to sustain a regular readership. Ultimately, the only reliable rule of thumb for differentiating them derives from the nature of their predominant content (though, of course, there was some overlap). Newspapers primarily comprised ephemeral material, today's news being superseded by tomorrow's news; periodicals, on the other hand, were principally composed of more enduring content – essays, poetry, biographies, literary criticism, book and drama reviews, etc.[1] The clearest evidence that eighteenth-century readers made similar assumptions derives from the practice of contemporary publishers, who collected, bound and offered for sale copies of past periodical issues on an annual or semi-annual basis; the fate of newspapers, however, depended upon the industry of private collectors like Charles Burney.[2]

Late seventeenth-century periodicals

Periodicals of the latter half of the seventeenth century were usually characterized by two traits: first, their authors were generally not professional writers but amateurs who took up their pens for a cause; and, second, when the cause

1 See Harris, chap. 20, above.

2 Upon his death, the collection of newspapers and periodicals compiled by the classical scholar Charles Burney (1757–1817) was purchased by Parliament for the British Library and today represents the Library's principal holdings of the era's newspapers.

no longer proved of political, religious or social consequence, the periodical was discontinued. Most periodicals, then, were serious and short lived. Some undertakings collapsed after only an issue or two from lack of reader interest. Other projectors, enthusiastic but lacking the proper journalistic or business experience, probably underestimated the demands of maintaining a regular publication schedule and distribution network. It is possible that some publishers had no intention of carrying on a periodical for longer than a few issues; many may simply have had something to say, and thought the periodical, which implicitly promised readers continued coverage, offered a more effective public medium than a single pamphlet.

The vast majority of periodicals lasted less than a year. Some, like *Mercurius Reformatus; or, the True Observator* (1691), *Merlin* (1692), the *Weekly Memorial* (1692), *Miscellanies over Claret* (1697) and the *English Martial* (1699), lasted only an issue or two; others, like *The Test-paper* (1688), the *Dilucidator* (1689), the *Moderator* (1692), the *Jovial Mercury* (1693) and the *Ladies Mercury* (1693), fell far short of ten issues. Even some of the better-known titles enjoyed a life of only two or three years. Motteux's the *Gentleman's Journal*, for instance – an unprecedented miscellany that published the full range of literary genres – ran only from January 1692 to November 1694. Likewise, Ned Ward's unique first-person sketches of London social life, the *London Spy*, appeared only from November 1698 to April 1700.

Politics and religion generated the most late seventeenth-century periodicals; scholarly and scientific interests prompted the next largest category. The earliest and most common among these scholarly publications were the review journals, which covered a wide swath of both domestic and foreign books on philosophy, theology, the classics, medicine, science, history, foreign travel, etc., and often included essays on learned subjects. Identical wording in the titles of many periodicals – 'memoirs', 'works of the learned', 'ingenious' – makes it difficult to keep them distinct. The two *Weekly Memorials for the Ingenious* (1682, 1682–3) – one published for the author by Chiswell and the other published by Faithorne and Kersey – represent the first book-reviewing journals that showed some endurance. These were followed by review journals edited by the Huguenot Jean Cornand de la Crose, including the *Universal Historical Bibliotheque* (1687), *History of Learning* (1691) and *Works of the Learned* (1691–2).[3] Randal Taylor's *Mercurius Eruditorum* (1691), a counterblast to de la Crose's dissenting position, elaborated the dialogue format that would evolve into the popular 'club' gimmick employed by later essay sheets and journals,

3 See Forster, chap. 33, below.

including Addison and Steele's *Spectator*. Largely consisting of summaries, extracts and little or no critical comment, the review tradition continued in later publications: John Dunton's monthly (later quarterly) *Compleat Library* (1692–4); de la Crose's *History of the Works of the Learned* (1699–1712), which was the longest running; and Michel de la Roche's *Memoirs of Literature* (weekly, fortnightly and then monthly, 1710–14, 1717), which followed the publication of European theological, political, scientific and literary writings.

Intellectually curious Englishmen were also interested in serious discussions of learned subjects, as well as historical accounts of foreign countries and events. Once again, the energetic, sober-sided de la Crose led the way in 1693 with *Memoirs for the Ingenious: containing several curious observations in philosophy, mathematicks, physick, philology, and other arts and sciences*, a 32-page quarto intended to 'make men more learned and good'. The *Memoirs*, cast in the format of letters written to eminent scholars of the day, was followed the next year by *Miscellaneous Letters, giving an account of the works of the learned* (weekly, then monthly, 1694–6). John Phillips addressed historical interests with such periodicals as *Modern History; or, a monethly* [*sic*] *account of all considerable occurrences, civil, ecclesiastical, and military with all natural and philosophical productions and transactions* (1687–90?) and the long-running *The Present State of Europe; or, the historical and political monthly mercury, giving an account of all the publick and private occurrences, civil, ecclesiastical and military* (1690–1738).

This period also saw the beginning of a popular periodical format that exercised considerable influence well into the eighteenth century: the 'question-and-answer' publication introduced by Sir Roger L'Estrange, a loyal Tory and, as licensor of the press, a rigorous censor. His uncompromising royalist position permeated his single-sheet folio the *Observator: In question and answer* (1681–3; *Observator in dialogue*, 1684–7), but the long-running success of this rhetorical device prompted several imitators in the coming years. Probably the most significant periodical patterned on the technique was the twice-weekly, half-sheet folio the *Athenian Mercury* (1691–7), published by Whig bookseller John Dunton, who answered questions submitted by readers. Dunton's success attracted further imitators: Thomas Brown's *London Mercury* (1692, later *Lacedemonian Mercury*), the short-lived *Jovial Mercury* (1693) and *Ladies Mercury* (1693). The question-and-answer format carried into the eighteenth century, the best implementation being the *British Apollo* (1708–11), a four-page folio appearing twice weekly, later thrice weekly. It should be noted that late seventeen-century periodicals with 'mercury' in their titles, unlike most serious mid-century mercuries, usually carried little or no news. There was no news, for example, in the post-Revolution *Mercurius*

Reformatus: or the New Observator (1689–93?), a government-sponsored reflection on the times based on L'Estrange's defunct *Observator*. The same is true of *Mercurius Infernus; or, news from the other world discovering the cheats and abuses of this* (1680), *Mercurius Librarius; or, a Catalogue of Books* (1668–1711), *Mercurius Eruditorum; or, News from the Learned World* (1691), and *Mercurius Musicus* (1699–1702).

A unique publication and an extraordinary achievement, Daniel Defoe's *A Weekly Review of the Affairs of France* (variously entitled thereafter, 1704–13), entered the market as a twice weekly on 19 February 1704. Defoe alleged political neutrality while writing on behalf of the moderate Tory agenda of Secretary of State Robert Harley. In the lead essays, Defoe aimed at middle-class merchants and coffee-house patrons, whom he instructed on politics, trade and related subjects. One feature of the *Review*'s secondary material during 1704–5 – the question-and-answer *Mercure Scandale*, 'Advice from the Scandalous Club' – became so popular and took up such space that it led Defoe, first, to issue many supplements and then to create a separate four-page twice-weekly periodical, the *Little Review* (1705). This question-and-answer format links Defoe's *Review* with Dunton's Athenian Society of the previous decade (above), while his advice on the 'nonsense, impertinence, vice, and debauchery' of the times anticipates the moral perspective of the *Spectator*. Defoe's most extraordinary accomplishment, however, was churning out the *Review* three times a week over nine years for a total of 5,610 pages.

Factors influencing the growth of the periodical in the eighteenth century

The 1690s proved a harbinger of major developments for the British periodical trade; the decade introduced a number of substantial periodicals and major trade names that carried well into the eighteenth century. These developments owe their origins to a number of domestic and foreign phenomena. Across western Europe, the Enlightenment had already bred new intellectual interests and increased exchange of ideas through printed media. As early as 1663, Dryden's enumeration of scientific discoveries by his fellow Englishmen in his 'Epistle to Dr Charleton' had signalled the new spirit of inquiry and debate that would foster the growth of periodicals. Likewise, an influential and ever-expanding merchant class grew keenly interested in commentary on foreign affairs, particularly wars that might have an impact on trade routes and the safety of shipping. Also of pressing concern were reports of natural disasters, new foreign products and markets, and successful enterprises like the East

India Company. In the political arena, the ever-weakening authority of the monarchy and the church gave way to the increased power of the House of Commons, the formation of parties, and a new public awareness of the potential for political influence. Perhaps, as Joad Raymond contends,[4] the evidence falls short of Habermas's criteria for the establishment of a 'public sphere' in 1694–5, but certainly there was a pervading sense of enfranchisement felt among all ranks in the second half of the seventeenth century; clearly a forum was required for the discussion of gradually emerging democratic thought, practices and legislation.

Especially instrumental in promoting the reading and circulation of newspapers and periodicals was the seventeenth-century phenomenon of the coffee house, whose owners subscribed to various serial publications to entertain their customers. While inns, taverns, barbers and even brandy shops also provided reading material, it was the coffee house that served as the major forum for the discussion of politics, drama and news. From the introduction of coffee to London through to Queen Anne's reign, it is estimated that some 2,000 coffee houses had served the capital;[5] in 1739 alone, London is estimated to have had 559 coffee houses.[6] In their short history, coffee houses developed close relations with the periodical trade. Their proprietors contributed to the growth of periodical circulation through subscriptions, of course, but announcements and advertisements in newspapers and periodicals reveal many other services provided by coffee houses for publishers:[7] the collection of book subscriptions, of advertisements, of charitable donations, and of lost and found items. These favourite resorts of gentlemen also served as the settings for monthly or quarterly business meetings of newspaper and periodical owners. By the late 1720s, newspapers and periodicals had become such an integral part of the coffee-house trade that owners had begun to complain of the expense they endured to satisfy customer demand for an increasing supply of titles. Their resentment, aimed at the proprietors of the publications, resulted in a protracted debate between the two interests, as reflected in such pamphlets as *The case between the proprietors of news-papers and the subscribing coffee-men* (1729). Frustrated in their case, coffee-house owners even proposed publishing their own newspaper.

Increasing literacy rates likewise contributed to the growth of periodicals. The charity school movement alone had trained 5,225 students of the lower

4 Raymond 1999b, 112–17; Habermas 1989.
5 Clark 2000a, 162.
6 Lillywhite 1963, 23.
7 See Turner, chap. 23, above.

class within thirty years of its founding in 1699.[8] The growth of the reading public, and the attendant profits, induced printers and booksellers to invest in both the newspaper and periodical markets. Michael Treadwell indicates that, by 1680, booksellers had begun to consolidate their control of the trade, and Michael Harris charts their growing influence after 1710 through the large-scale bookseller investment in London newspapers in response to the formalization of the system of shares in papers.[9] As Harris demonstrates, the same system pertained to periodicals as well. Moreover, by the third quarter of the eighteenth century, clearly discernible growth in middle-class consumerism meant that proprietors of newspapers and periodicals could make more money by taking in advertisements. The drive to capitalize on this new consumer phenomenon is perhaps best illustrated in the *Daily Advertiser* of the 1770s: into its daily four pages, the *Advertiser* squeezed an average of 180 advertisements in almost illegible, reduced type.

Not surprisingly, the new robust periodical market in the early eighteenth century attracted a new breed of writer. Whereas the seventeenth-century periodical had primarily been produced by amateurs, the eighteenth-century periodical was largely written and conducted by what would later be called the 'professional' writer.[10] In fact, a listing of authors who wrote for, edited or conducted their own periodicals reads much like a roll call of major figures of the age. Daniel Defoe wrote for at least a dozen newspapers and carried on his own *Review of the Affairs of France* single-handedly for nine years. Jonathan Swift wrote for various periodicals including the *Spectator*, the *Examiner* and the *Intelligencer*. Addison and Steele produced the *Tatler*, the *Spectator* and the *Guardian*. Alexander Pope contributed to the *Spectator* and to the most popular weekly of the early 1730s, the *Grub-street Journal*. Samuel Johnson produced biographies and parliamentary reports for the *Gentleman's Magazine* in the late 1730s, later turning out the twice-weekly essay sheet the *Rambler* and contributing regular essays to the *Adventurer* and the *Universal Chronicle*. Samuel Richardson contributed to Johnson's *Rambler*[11] and likely authored several pieces that appeared in the *True Briton* and half a dozen other serials. Oliver Goldsmith wrote his 'Citizen of the world' essays for the *Public Ledger*, edited the *Bee*, and contributed to the *British Magazine* and the *Westminster Magazine*. Henry Fielding conducted at least four periodicals, including the *Champion*, the

8 Newman 1997, 113.
9 Treadwell 1982a, 128, 131; M. Harris 1987, 66. Cf. Harris, chap. 20 and Raven, chap. 3, both above.
10 See Griffin, chap. 5, above.
11 Dussinger 2000.

True patriot, the *Jacobite's Journal* and the *Covent Garden Journal*;[12] and Tobias Smollett founded the powerful *Critical Review* and conducted the *British Magazine*. The ranks of the newspaper and periodical world were further swelled by writers of the second and third order who were pushed to make a living in journalism as a result of the decline in royal and noble patronage during Robert Walpole's administration.[13] Walpole himself paid the journalists James Pitt and William Arnall for defending the ministerial position in the *London Journal* and in the *Free Briton*, respectively; and John 'Orator' Henley was employed in 1730 to attack the writers of the anti-Walpole weekly the *Craftsman* in his *Hyp-doctor* (1730–41). In literary talent alone, the eighteenth-century periodical clearly distinguished itself from its predecessors.

Innovations in eighteenth-century periodicals

If we judge by the host of imitators they generated, then the most important developments in periodical literature in the eighteenth century were Addison and Steele's single-essay half-sheets, the *Tatler* (1709–11) and the *Spectator* (1711–14); Edward Cave's *Gentleman's Magazine* (1731–1907); and Ralph Griffiths's *Monthly Review* (1749–1844) and Tobias Smollett's *Critical Review* (1756–1817). In the *Tatler* and *Spectator*, Addison and Steele introduced a new kind of single-essay sheet that entertained and instructed readers on a variety of subjects, distinguishing itself from all predecessors by its informal, witty and urbane prose. Cave's monthly *Gentleman's Magazine* initiated a new miscellany tradition by borrowing the best from the weekly newspapers and periodicals, and then, eventually, turning to original material, primarily submitted by his readers. The *Monthly Review* and the *Critical Review* were distinguished by their comprehensive reviewing of recent English publications (not just works for learned readers) and by their inclusion of critical commentary with the standard summary/extract.[14]

The Tatler *and the* Spectator

Addison and Steele arrived in the wake of the moral reform that had swept England in the last decade of the seventeenth century, but the legacy of the *Tatler* and the *Spectator* lies outside their role as reformers of the age. Their

12 On the basis of internal and stylometric evidence, Martin Battestin also attributes to Fielding forty-one essays in the *Craftsman* during the period 1734–9; in addition, he calls attention to nine other pieces attributed to Fielding elsewhere; see Fielding 1989.

13 See Griffin, chap. 5, above.

14 See Forster, chap. 33, below.

enduring success lay in their projectors' commercial and literary genius: to perceive that a new polite audience would support such publications, to employ cleverly the organizational strategies of earlier periodicals, and to lift the prose of their predecessors to new heights. Imitating a gimmick used by such predecessors as the *English Lucian* (1698) and the *Merry Mercury* (1700), the *Tatler* essays achieved an air of realism and local appeal by dating the papers as originating from various London locales. To capture the coffee-house atmosphere of discussion and camaraderie, the *Spectator* employed the artifice of the 'club', as had its predecessors the *Mercurius Eruditorum* (1691) and the *British Apollo* (1708–11). To appeal to a broad market of interests, the *Spectator* took a cue from Ned Ward's *Weekly Comedy* (1699) and *Humours of a Coffee-house* (1707) by creating a circle of humorous characters to people its pages.

These deft strategies notwithstanding, it was an informal but urbane prose style that remains their major contribution to developing periodical literature. In its own century, the *Spectator* became *the* recommended model of prose style. In his biographical account of Addison (*Lives of the English poets*, 1781), Samuel Johnson would write: 'Whoever wishes to attain an English style, familiar but not coarse, and elegant not ostentatious, must give his days and nights to the volumes of Addison.'[15] The most conspicuous testimony to the *Tatler*'s and the *Spectator*'s influence surfaces in the many imitators that immediately appeared on their heels. Three months after Steele began his thrice-weekly *Tatler*, Thomas Baker made clear his intent when he began to publish his own thrice-weekly *Female Tatler* (1709), with essays familiarly dated 'From My Own Apartment'. Shortly after the discontinuation of both the *Tatler* and the *Spectator*, a number of essayists, employing the same titles, cheekily pretended to publish continuations of the famous originals.

Within the next two decades, close to a hundred new periodicals exploited the essay-sheet model established by Addison and Steele, including the *Whisperer* (1709), the *Moderator* (1710), the *Tory Tatler* (1710), the *Free-thinker* (1711), the *Plain Dealer* (1712), the *Mirrour* (1719), the *Visiter* (1723–4), *Titt for Tatt* (1710), the *Grouler: or Diogenes robb'd of his tub* (1711), the *Grumbler* (1715), *Terrae Filius* (1721) and the *What-d'ye-call-it* (1733–4). None of these equalled the originals, and many were short-lived. Among the more notable were Sir Richard Blackmore's *Lay Monk* (1713–14), which employed the 'club' motif under the guise of a monastery; Lewis Theobald's single-sheet folio the *Censor* (1715, 1717), which offered extensive literary criticism on diverse authors; Ambrose Philips's twice-weekly half-sheet the *Freethinker* (1718–21), a consistently well-written and timely publication; Thomas Sheridan's Dublin weekly essay sheet the *Intelligencer* (1728),

15 Boswell 1934–50, I, 225.

which spoke in defence of Ireland against British exploitation and included contributions from Jonathan Swift; and Aaron Hill's twice-weekly, half-sheet folio the *Prompter* (1734–6), one of the earliest theatrical periodicals. Eliza Haywood's *Female Spectator* (1744–6) was the first periodical written by a woman for women and was penned in the original *Spectator* tradition, but it differed significantly by reason of its monthly publication and its extremely long essays.

Addison and Steele themselves attempted to replicate their early success with later essay sheets like the daily *Guardian* (nos. 1–175, 1713) and Steele's own the *Englishman* (nos. 1–57, 1713–14; nos. 1–38, 1715), but these attempts were disappointing. Although the *Guardian* blended moral, social and literary criticism like the *Spectator*, the publication could not recover from the long absences of both authors as they campaigned for or sat in the House of Commons. In Steele's solo management of the thrice-weekly *Englishman*, the author/editor abandoned the organizing strategies employed in the *Spectator* to speak more directly as a Whig patriot on the critical political issues of the day.

By the 1730s, however, the essay sheet had begun to lose its readership to newspapers and ultimately to magazines, which often included essays, letters and poetry to attract additional readers. Nonetheless, the essay sheet would endure through to the end of the century, enjoying a resurgence in the 1750s with such works as Samuel Johnson's the *Rambler* (1750–2), John Hawkesworth's the *Adventurer* (1752–4), Edward Moore's the *World* (1753–6) and, of course, Samuel Johnson's the *Idler* and Oliver Goldsmith's 'The Citizen of the world' (1760–1), which appeared as single essays in the *Universal Chronicle* (1758–60) and the *Public Ledger* (1760–1), respectively.

Origins of the magazine: the *Gentleman's Magazine*

The modern magazine had its origin in periodicals comprising materials so various that the early eighteenth century referred to them as 'miscellanies'. The *Gentleman's Journal* (1692–4), edited by Peter Motteux and published by Richard Baldwin, is generally regarded as the first magazine. Carrying the subtitle 'Monthly Miscellany', Motteux printed fiction, translations, dialogues, allegories, scientific accounts, reviews, music and news. Running to thirty-four pages in quarto, the *Journal* was more comprehensive than any preceding periodical. Other monthly miscellanies followed, but there was no rush to imitate the form. Notable miscellanies from this period include John Dunton's *Post Angel* (1701–2), which comprised incidents illustrative of God's judgment, biographies of eminent persons, questions and answers from the *Athenian Mercury*, foreign and domestic news, and accounts of recently published books; John Oldmixon's *Muses Mercury* (1707–8), which addressed the literary coterie with a wide selection of poetry and accounts of books, plays and operas; and James Petiver's longer-surviving *Monthly Miscellany* (1707–10), which initially featured articles on the arts, biography, sciences, mathematics, husbandry, travel and trade, before moving to specialist scientific interests.

A major landmark in the development of English journalism occurred when Edward Cave published the first issue of the *Gentleman's Magazine; or, Monthly Intelligencer* on 8 January 1731. None of the foregoing miscellanies would have the impact on the periodical trade enjoyed by the *Gentleman's*, the first periodical to feature the term 'magazine' in its title. Affecting the ubiquitous editor with the nom de plume 'Sylvanus Urban, Gent.' on the title page of the *Gentleman's*, Cave claimed that his new monthly carried 'more in Quantity, and greater Variety, than any Book of the Kind and Price' (6*d*.). This new periodical, which consisted primarily of extracts of the best essays that had appeared in the past month's London newspapers and periodicals, offered London readers a welcome alternative to keeping up with the plethora of weekly, twice-weekly and thrice-weekly newspapers and periodicals that existed in the early 1730s. In one monthly, readers could enjoy abridged accounts of the 'best' that had appeared during the past month, at least as determined by Cave. According to Titia Ram's calculation,[16] over the first twenty-five years of the *Gentleman's* existence, Cave extracted essays from eighty-seven different London newspapers and periodicals, including the Opposition papers *Common Sense*, the *Craftsman* and *Fog's Weekly Journal*; the government newspapers the *Daily Courant* and the *Daily Gazetteer*; and the non-partisan papers the *Grub-street Journal*, *Old England; or, the Constitutional Journal*, the *Universal Spectator* and the *Weekly Miscellany*.

With slight variation, the organization of the *Gentleman's* monthly numbers remained essentially the same for its first quarter-century. Following the opening extracts, accounts of parliamentary debates appeared, sometimes followed by more essays (in later years by 'Letters to the Author') and a section of poetry borrowed from other publications. Next came the last substantial prose section, the 'Historical Chronicle', containing domestic and foreign news, activities of the royal family, accounts of crime and unusual happenings, and miscellaneous matters for the curious. Series of lists ensued, accounting for births, deaths and marriages in notable families; government promotions and ecclesiastical preferments; shipping news; and prices of stocks and grain.[17]

16 Ram 1999, 36–7.
17 See McCusker, chap. 22, above.

Usually a section on foreign politics followed, and the issue concluded with a list of recently published books and advertisements for works printed and sold by Cave. By its third year, the *Gentleman's* had begun to mature into something more than a digest by including original material. As Ram notes, extracts were replaced by original essays and letters submitted by readers. By 1735, according to Ram's calculation,[18] the number of original essays had risen to 11 per cent; by 1737, almost half of the articles were original, and by Cave's death in 1754, 94 per cent. In another significant evolution, the *Gentleman's* occasionally included fold-out maps and woodcuts, illustrating recent inventions, architecture and mathematical puzzles.

Much of the *Gentleman's* success can also be attributed to Cave's perception of the emerging need to have the *vox populi* represented in the press. Heretofore, newspapers and periodicals generally comprised material wholly reflective of the cultural perspectives of their proprietors and editors; the content of a periodical was produced either by its editor and his stable of authors or directly solicited by the editor from friends and associates. As the *Gentleman's* developed, however, Cave encouraged the more democratic submission of original material from readers in all segments of society.

Cave enjoyed one special advantage that explains much about the periodical's incredible success, however. As early as 1721, besides operating as a printer and reporter, Cave worked in the General Post Office; in 1723, he succeeded to the position of Inspector of Franks, a job he held until his retirement from the GPO in 1745. Through this post, he enjoyed the privilege of franking newspapers and periodicals (sending materials free of postage), which meant that Cave, like his fellow Post Office associates, could carry on his own commercial enterprise by supplying copies of newspapers and periodicals to both private citizens and distributors along the post roads, a practice informally condoned by the government as a salary supplement. As Michael Harris observes, 'By the mid-1720s the clerks had established [such] a substantial newspaper interest' that the *Craftsman* complained of them as '*licensed Hawkers* over the whole Kingdom'. 'By the 1740s, a number of postmasters were acting independently on behalf of local printers [of newspapers]', some of them, by the mid-1750s, holding shares in the ownership of both the *General Evening Post* and the *Whitehall Evening Post*. In 1764, a Post Office committee report 'estimated that between them the clerks were earning £3,000 or £4,000 per annum from newspapers'.[19]

18 Ram 1999, 38.
19 Harris 1987, 42–6.

In this sideline enterprise, Cave and his fellow postal clerks could obviously restrict or 'push' the circulation of periodicals as their personal financial interests dictated, generating bitter complaints from slighted newspaper and periodical publishers, as well as from country customers disappointed in their orders. This influence of Post Office officials on the periodical trade is markedly evident in the attempt by Robert Dodsley, the mid-century's major bookseller, to succeed with the publication of his *Public Register; or, the Weekly Magazine* (1741). Although the periodical got off to a good start, Dodsley would later blame its premature demise on the 'ungenerous usage' of Cave, 'who has prevail'd with most of the common newspapers not to advertise it'.[20]

Clearly, Cave feared competition from the lesser-sized weekly and fortnightly journals that nibbled at his market share. Like the miscellany, weekly journals had antedated the *Gentleman's* existence, but, unlike the miscellany, they did not all collapse into the 'magazine' market after the *GM* appeared. Indeed, the weeklies proved rather successful. In 1727, Nicholas Amhurst ('Caleb D'Anvers') changed the format of his anti-Walpole journal from the twice-weekly, single-sheet essay the *Craftsman* (1726–50) to the four-page weekly the *Country Journal; or, the Craftsman*. Henry Baker's the *Universal Spectator and Weekly Journal* (1728–46) ran for 907 numbers and carried the typical fare of the emerging magazine, including announcements of births and deaths, but on a weekly basis. Lyttelton and Chesterfield advanced their 'young Patriots' cause with a weekly anti-Walpole periodical, the witty *Common Sense* (1737–43). Fielding also switched to a weekly schedule with the fifty-fourth number of the *Covent Garden Journal* (1752), in which he played moral censor of current social ills. Social satire was also the principal fare of the *Connoisseur* (1754–6), another weekly set up by the young Bonnell Thornton and George Colman, with contributions from their Nonsense Club friends, Robert Lloyd and William Cowper. Undeniably, the weekly journal held its own against the onslaught of the *Gentleman's* and its many imitators through the mid-century, as did the many weeklies that opted for the title 'magazine'.

Nonetheless, the *Gentleman's* impact on the periodical trade was sudden, pervasive and enduring. The term 'magazine' quickly replaced 'miscellany' as the title of choice for this kind of publication: by 1780, well over a hundred periodicals had carried the term 'magazine' in their titles, whereas 'miscellany' appeared in only half a dozen titles, such as the *Student, or the Oxford [and Cambridge] Monthly Miscellany* (1750–1). Most of the 'magazines' that emerged immediately upon the heels of the *Gentleman's* were magazines only in the

20 *The Public Register*, no. 24, 13 June 1741.

nominal sense, however, and not true imitators of Cave's publication. Many were weeklies and therefore considerably smaller, meaning they fell far short of the *Gentleman's* in content and generic coverage. A number of titles were addressed to women, but few survived for long. The *Lady's Magazine; or, Universal Repository* (1733) lasted but five numbers. A few more successful weeklies – like the *Weekly Amusement; or, Universal Magazine* (1734–6) and the *Queen Anne's Weekly Journal; or, the Ladies Magazine* (1735–9) – ran for several years. Ephraim Chambers's monthly *Literary Magazine* (1735–6), subtitled as *The History of the Works of the Learned*, ran for two years and offered book reviews, biographical accounts of authors and extracts from the *Philosophical Transactions of the Royal Society*. Less enduring were the *Lady's Magazine; or, the Compleat Library* (1739) at eighteen numbers and the *Universal Spy; or, London Weekly Magazine* (1739) by 'Timothy Truepenny' at twenty-six numbers. The *Universal Spy* began as a four-page weekly, and then expanded to a twelve-page miscellany, but with its slight size and high price (double the *Gentleman's*), it simply could not compete. The *Country Magazine; or, Weekly Pacquet* (1739) lasted but two numbers, and the *Lady's Weekly Magazine* by 'Penelope Pry' (1747) saw only a single issue. On the unpopular fortnightly schedule, the *Ladies Magazine; or, the Universal Entertainer* (1749–53) by 'Jasper Goodwill of Oxford, Esq.' flourished through four volumes, providing readers with such fare as extracts of books, serialized fiction and the 'History of England in Question and Answer'.

Most of the *Gentleman's* true competitors would not appear for several decades, but Cave's chief rival, the *London Magazine; or, the Gentleman's Monthly Intelligencer* (1732–85), was published within fifteen months, imitating the *Gentleman's* in every respect. Cave quickly complained about the newcomer's exact replication of the *Gentleman's* organization and typical contents, as well as its appropriating most of his periodical's name and many features of his title page, including Cave's motto: 'More in Quantity and Greater Variety than in any Book of the Kind and Price'. In response, the *London*'s proprietors charged Cave with piracy for having abstracted material from their monthly *Chronicle* (1728–32) and thereby undermining its sales, a complaint echoed by the publishers of many weeklies whose circulation was curtailed by the emerging magazine.[21] The *London Magazine*, like the *Gentleman's*, initially extracted much of its content from the dailies and weeklies, but by the 1740s, it also

21 To Cave's charge of piracy on the part of the proprietors of the *London Magazine*, the latter responded by printing the following in the *St James's Evening Post* of 6–9 May 1732: 'Your Assurance we think is very extraordinary, in reflecting upon us for compiling a Book of this Kind from the Publick Papers, in several of which we have a Property; when you have not the least Share in any of them: which makes

began to publish original material. Among its most notable pieces were essays on acting and 'The Hypochondriack' columns by James Boswell, who, by the 1770s, would become one of the *London Magazine*'s owner-managers.

The next significant competitor, the *Scots Magazine* (1739–1817), proudly announced itself as the advocate of the 'Caledonian Muses' and the repository of the best from the Edinburgh papers. Although it did print extracts from the latter, it relied heavily upon London periodicals and, contrary to expectations, did not attract the works of native poets. Later, the Scottish trade would be represented by three other magazines: Walter Ruddiman, Jr.'s *Edinburgh Magazine* (1757–62) and its resurrection in his *Weekly Magazine; or, Edinburgh Amusement* (variously entitled, 1768–84); and the ambitious, liberal and controversial *Edinburgh Magazine and Review* (1773–6), a monthly edited by Gilbert Stuart.

In March 1746, the protean and prolific Sir John Hill entered the competition with a 48-page monthly *British Magazine* (1746–50), which he seems to have compiled and written mostly by himself. Some material was extracted from other sources, but Hill departed from the competition by introducing the familiar essay technique: the 'Occasional Spectator' (with club members) and later 'The Visiter' columns on current fashionable life. The *Literary Magazine; or, Universal Review* (1756–8) is notable primarily because Samuel Johnson was the first editor of this monthly and contributed numerous reviews and political essays until the fifteenth number, after which it began to decline. One of the *Gentleman's* most successful imitators was the long-lived monthly *Universal Magazine of Knowledge and Pleasure* (1747–1814), 'intended for Gentry, Merchants, Farmers and Tradesmen'. Like the *GM*, the *Universal* enjoyed correspondence from its country subscribers, and many of its articles were aimed at educating its readership, especially youth.

Beating Cave at his own game was the intent of a number of imitators, one boldly appropriating Cave's title. The *Gentleman's Magazine and Monthly Oracle* (1736) by 'Merlin the Second' – carrying a woodcut of Merlin's *cave* on the cover, together with Cave's motto – imitated the original *Gentleman's* content, but lasted only seven numbers. The *Magazine of Magazines, Compiled from Original Pieces* (1750–1) logically extended Cave's method by abstracting the monthly magazines, supposedly to provide a 'compleat literary and historical account of the period'. The predatory practice was carried on by a nominal successor, which, by its seventeenth number, was entitled the *Grand Magazine of Magazines; or, Universal Register* (1758–9).

your Work little less than a downright *Pyracy*. As to supplanting you, in your Design, Pray Sir, Who gave you (a Proprietor in no one Paper) a Right, exclusive of all others, even of Proprietors themselves, to a Design of this Nature?'

While the *Gentleman's Magazine* was primarily an informative periodical, many monthly magazines, especially after the 1760s, turned to entertainment as well. In some cases, these periodicals were more in the tradition of the literary miscellany, but now newly branded as 'magazine'. Christopher Smart's fifty-page monthly *The Midwife; or, Old Woman's Magazine* (1750–3, intermittent after 1751) by 'Mary Midnight' did not follow Cave's model, but rather offered commentary on the theatre, essays, letters, verses and parodies. A similar focus on entertainment marked Tobias Smollett's *British Magazine; or Monthly Repository for Gentlemen and Ladies* (1760–7), which carried book reviews, poetry and essays on aesthetics, history, philosophy, biography and more fiction than any of its predecessors, including the first serialized novel (Smollett's own *The life and adventures of Sir Launcelot Greaves*).[22] Similarly, Hugh Kelly's *Court Magazine* (1761–5) published a considerable amount of poetry, fiction, translations, epigrams, book reviews, essays on theatre and literature, historical pieces, travelogues – as well as domestic and foreign news and a range of informative essays on religion, science, social issues, trade and politics. Kelly's next undertaking, the *Court Miscellany; or Lady's New Magazine* (1765–71), included poetry, fiction, essays on drama, and a chatty section on domestic and foreign events, and was initially addressed to women, though its focus alternated between science, literature and politics. The *St James Magazine* (1762–4), founded by Robert Lloyd, also sought to publish original material; its first three volumes were composed almost exclusively of poetry and criticism, much of it contributed by fellow members of the Nonsense Club: William Cowper, Charles Churchill, Bonnel Thornton and George Colman.

Numerous magazines directed to women were set up immediately upon the heels of the *Gentleman's* or within the next four decades. In addition to those mentioned above are Oliver Goldsmith's *Lady's Magazine; or, Polite Companion for the Fair Sex* (1759–63), Robert Lloyd's *Royal Female Magazine* (1760), Hugh Kelly's *Court Miscellany; or, Ladies New Magazine* (1765, mentioned above, continued the next year with 'Gentleman' in the title) and the *Lady's Magazine; or, Entertaining Companion for the Fair Sex* (1770). Other magazines place women beside men: the *Country Magazine; or, the Gentleman and Lady's Pocket Companion* (1736–7), the *Traveller's Magazine; or, Gentleman and Lady's Agreeable Companion* (1749–50), the *New Universal Magazine; or, Gentleman and Lady's Polite Instructor* (1751–9), the *Weekly Magazine; or, Gentleman and Lady's Polite Companion* (1759–60), the *British Magazine; or, Monthly Repository for Gentlemen and Ladies* (1760–7), the *Universal Museum; or, Gentlemen's and Ladies' Polite Magazine* (1762–72) and the *Monthly Miscellany; or, Gentleman and Lady's Compleat Magazine* (1774–6?).

22 See Suarez, chap. 34, below.

One of the longest-running literary magazines of the second half of the century – twenty-seven years – was Archibald Hamilton's *Town and Country Magazine; or, Universal Repository of Knowledge, Instruction, and Entertainment* (1769–95), which published 14,000 copies in 1772. The magazine printed the usual run of literary types, but distinguished itself from others by its essay serials, notably its 'History of the Tête-à-têtes', disguised exposés of the lives of the rich and famous. Also durable and of an especially literary character was the *Westminster Magazine; or, the Pantheon of Taste* (1773–85), which printed a frequently biting review section, essays on major authors of the century, satires on customs, manners and fashions, regular accounts of Parliament's proceedings, summaries of foreign and domestic news, and the usual lists of prices, births, preferments, etc. Keeping with fashion, but with 'Chastity of Sentiment', the *Sentimental Magazine; or, General Assemblage of Science, Taste, and Entertainment* (1773–7) printed the standard fare of essays, essay serials, letters from readers, pieces of fiction and poetry, superficial commentary on the theatre, and the expected lists.

In the latter half of the century, publications catering to special interests moved further from Cave's original conception of the magazine. In these periodicals, where the term 'magazine' constricted to designate a miscellaneous collection of material directed to a specific audience, we see movement towards the modern magazine. This adjustment can be detected in titles such as the *Poetical Magazine; or, the Muses' Monthly Companion* (1764), the *Musical Companion; or, Songster's Magazine* (1768), the *Biographical Magazine* (1773–6), the *Musical Companion; or, Songster's Magazine* (1777) and the *Vocal Magazine; or, British Songster's Miscellany* (1778). Professional and occupational interests are reflected in such publications as the *Country Magazine Calculated for the Gentleman, the Farmer and his Wife* (1763), the *Lawyer's Magazine* (1773), the *Medical Magazine* (1773), the *Builder's Magazine; or, Monthly Companion for Architects, Carpenters, Masons, Bricklayers, etc.* (1774), the *Trader's Magazine and Monthly Treasury of Trade, Commerce, Arts, Manufactures and Mechanics* (1775) and the *Farmer's Magazine* (1776–80). Magazines catering strictly to the concerns of formal religion also make an appearance in the *Christian's Magazine; or, a Treasury of Divine Knowledge* (1760–7), the *Spiritual Magazine; or, the Christian's Grand Treasure* (1760, merged with the *Gospel Magazine* in 1784), the *Gospel Magazine; or, Spiritual Library* (1766–73), the *Gospel Magazine; or, Treasury of Divine Knowledge* (1774–84), and John Wesley's *Arminian Magazine* (1778–98, continued as the *Methodist Magazine*).[23]

23 See Rivers, chap. 30, below.

Contrary to modern assumptions, then, although Edward Cave introduced a new kind of periodical with the *Gentleman's Magazine*, and although clever tradesmen were quick to capitalize on the term 'magazine', a large percentage of periodicals employing 'magazine' in their titles did not truly imitate Cave's invention; rather they appropriated a fashionable term for their own economic interests.[24]

Review journals

The book review had been part of the stock-in-trade of periodicals reaching back into the second half of the seventeenth century and had comprised departments of most miscellanies and magazines ever since, but the founding of Ralph Griffiths's *Monthly Review* (1749–1844) and Tobias Smollett's *Critical Review* (1756–1817) ushered in a new phase in book reviewing.[25] Earlier review periodicals were almost exclusively concerned with books of interest only to the learned, as demonstrated by their titles: *Weekly Memorials for the Ingenious*, *Bibliotheca Literaria*, *History of the Works of the Learned*. Andrew Reid addressed the same audience but departed from the standard in his eighty-page monthly, the *Present State of the Republick of Letters* (1728–36), which included essays on varied intellectual subjects among reviews of a surprisingly vast range of scholarly interests. Other review journals focused almost exclusively on foreign authors, as in the two quarterlies with the same name, *A Literary Journal*, and conducted by two Huguenots, Michel de la Roche and Jean Pierre Droz. De la Roche's *Journal* (1730–1), published in London, differed little from contemporary standard reviews, offering a summary of the book and extended extracts. In contrast, Droz's 200-page *Journal*, published in Dublin from 1744 to 1749, has been called by Walter Graham a 'bridge' between the earlier reviews and Griffiths's *Monthly Review* because of its many original articles and emphasis on critical analysis in later reviews. Nonetheless, Droz did not address the growing need for more comprehensive and discriminating review journals – driven by an ever-increasing literate British reading public and its ever-expanding book supply.

24 Probably much of the impression that all periodicals with the term 'magazine' in their titles were imitators of the *Gentleman's* derives from the well-known 'Address to the Reader' prefacing the 1738 annual volume of the *GM*, which Cave extracted from his new, 27-year-old editor, Samuel Johnson: 'The Success of *The gentleman's magazine* has given rise to almost twenty imitations of it, which are either all dead, or very little regarded by the World. Before we had published sixteen Months, we met with such a general Approbation, that a Knot of enterprising Geniuses, and sagacious Inventors, assembled from all Parts of the Town, agreed with Unanimity natural to Understandings of the same Size to seize upon our whole Plan, without even changing the Title.'

25 See Forster, chap. 33, below.

Although Griffiths's eighty-page *Monthly Review* made modest claims when it first appeared, it soon attempted to account for every book recently published in England, which meant that the general reader was now apprised of popular and imaginative works – poetry, drama, fiction – not merely of learned books. Moreover, while Griffiths's announced policy was to provide reviews consisting of the standard summary and extracts, he and other reviewers occasionally included opinions of a work's quality. Initially, most of the opinion was expressed as short comments in the extensive list of recently published books, which followed the major reviews (usually ten) that opened the *Monthly*. Griffiths's review journal was more comprehensive (except for foreign publications) and more critically informed than anything that had preceded it. That Griffiths read his market correctly is evident in the *Monthly*'s longevity. Nonetheless, having abandoned his main bookselling business to dedicate himself solely to the *Monthly Review*, Griffiths occasionally struggled. In 1761, he sold a share to Benjamin Collins, a provincial bookseller and publisher of the *Salisbury Journal*; two years later, Becket and De Hondt are listed on the title page as publishers; and in 1767, to satisfy his creditors, Griffiths sold the whole interest to Collins, who retained Griffiths as editor until 1803.

The *Monthly*'s prime competitor until 1817 was Tobias Smollett's 120-page *Critical Review*. Like most of his peers, Smollett justified the need for his new review journal by pointing to the shortcomings of his predecessors; thus he attacked the *Monthly*'s 'obscure Hackney writers'. Yet, despite its intention to restore 'the true Spirit of Criticism' and defend the 'cause of Literature', the *Critical* generally followed the successful format of its predecessor, the summary and extract formula. The *Critical* differed, however, by courting readers for reviews and by censuring works considered unfit for its readers' attention. Readers could entertain themselves by comparing the two journals' reviews of the same works or by perusing the *Critical*'s caustic dismissal of some books; the fun was kept up by the *London Magazine*'s savage attacks on the *Monthly*'s reviewers. Smollett's own protracted controversies with offended authors were usually carried on outside the pages of the *Critical*. However, ill health and overwork caused him to resign his connection with the periodical in 1763.

Succeeding review journals often imitated the *Monthly Review* and the *Critical Review*, but none really compare. Both the *Monthly and Critical Review* (1756) and the *Repository; or, General Review* (1756) lasted only five numbers, and the *Universal Review; or, a Critical Commentary on the Literary Productions of these Kingdoms* (1760) saw but a single number. The *Edinburgh Magazine and Review* (1773–6), while studded with literary talent, had a reputation for abuse. William Kenrick's eighty-page *The London Review of English and Foreign*

Literature (1775–80), reflecting the editor's personality, anticipated the stinging commentary of some nineteenth-century review journals.

While it is difficult to estimate the effect of review journals on book sales, booksellers clearly thought they had a significant impact. From the late 1750s on, newspaper and periodical advertisements for new publications often carried references to favourable reviews in the *Monthly Review* and the *Critical Review*, sometimes even quoting from them. Also, London booksellers' earlier practice of advertising all new publications fell off markedly by 1765, perhaps suggesting their reliance upon the reviewing journals to acquaint the public with their new productions.[26] In the end, probably the greatest impact the *Monthly Review* and the *Critical Review* exercised was forcing authors, publishers and the reading public to realize the need for the comprehensive and discriminating review of literature. Taking over the role of the coffee house, the influence of these two journals was so pervasive that less specialized magazines expanded their review sections, and it was rare for a new periodical to come on the scene without a review department. The trade never looked back.

26 Tierney 2001.

25

Periodicals and serial publications, 1780–1830

BRIAN MAIDMENT

Although the period between 1780 and 1830 provides the moment when the idea of seriality begins to become identifiable (and indeed popular) as a mode of textual production, the borderlines between periodical and book, 'issue' and volume, or serial and series remained through these years both blurred and increasingly contested. The whole period might be characterized by an often unselfconscious and unresolved – even haphazard – dialogue between seriality, periodicity and the volume format, a dialogue that can, historically, be given shape through the wider growth and democratization of print culture in the period. Literature directed towards children, for example, shows relatively few titles that can be clearly identified as 'magazines', but many projects dependent on seriality or part-issue, such as miscellanies or series. Frequently, part-issues were later turned into volumes, a transition that clearly shows how far periodicity was conceived as an accumulative rather than an occasional form of publication.[1] The *Youth's Monthly Visitor*, for instance, published in 1822 and 1823 in serial form, became the *Youth's Miscellany of Knowledge and Entertainment* on volume republication. The emergence of something clearly identifiable as a magazine from what John Brewer calls the 'labyrinth' of late eighteenth-century publishing forms a recurrent narrative of the period.[2]

Uncertainty over generic boundaries at this time did not solely concern the clarity of the distinction between 'book' and 'magazine', but rather involved broader issues concerning the transformation of the cultural commodities marketplace, the changing nature of readerships, and the increasingly complex recognition of the social prestige and political importance of 'literary' culture. To take the obvious example of fiction, Mayo has calculated that 1,375 novels or novelettes were published in British magazines between 1740 and 1815, and his list is by no means complete.[3] For Victorian readers, periodicity was often

1 See Tierney, chap. 24, above.
2 Brewer 1997, 140.
3 Mayo 1962, 382–620.

associated with topicality and ephemerality and represented a version of commodity culture marked by the repeated consumption of a reduplicated commodity; if you missed one issue of a magazine, another similar one would appear the following month. For late eighteenth-century readers, however, seriality was seen not necessarily as a mode of publication driven by commercial imperatives, but rather as a valuable mechanism for mediating texts into the more permanent formats offered by bookbinders and volume republication. As one historian of print has put it, 'some literary papers existed as periodicals only until sufficient issues had appeared for a reprint in book size'.[4]

However subordinate periodicals may have remained for literary historians, for contemporary readers they were largely regarded as equivalents to, or even embryonic versions of, volumes. Indeed, one of the fundamental purposes of periodical literature in this period was to sustain and develop book culture through the medium of the review, a shift of interests immediately apparent not just by the founding of such influential review-led journals as *Blackwood's Magazine*, *Fraser's Magazine*, *New Monthly Magazine*, the *Quarterly Review* and the *London Magazine* between 1814 and 1832, but, more particularly, by the close identification of these magazines with individual publishers and their 'stable' of authors and reviewers.[5] The development of periodicals in the first few decades of the nineteenth century was driven as much by the agenda of the book trade and its entrepreneurs as by the needs and demands of an ever-increasing reading public. Accordingly, it is entirely appropriate, and indeed necessary, to consider periodicals in any history of the book in the late eighteenth and early nineteenth century.

Even allowing for these fundamental uncertainties over the relationship between periodicity, seriality and textuality, a number of clear themes can be identified that define magazine and serial culture in this period. These narratives are usefully figured and summarized in an etching by the satirical artist Robert Seymour called 'The March of Intellect', which humorously depicts, like many comparable images produced in the 1820s and 1830s, the ways in which print culture exemplified wider social change (see Frontispiece).

This image was drawn and etched by Seymour in 1829, three years before the launch of the *Penny Magazine*, that icon of the new mass-circulation journalism, which redefined the reproductive technology, distribution networks and potential audience for mass-circulation periodicals. It is a characteristically crowded and complex caricature, drawn in response to the many technological

4 Handover 1960, 142.
5 See Forster, chap. 33, below.

and cultural changes that made up the 'March of Intellect'. The confusions and energies implicit in such major social upheaval are recognized in the frenzied assemblage of caricature tropes through which the image is constructed. The mocking of the cultural aspirations and ambitions of the mass of the populace forms a familiar topic for caricatures of this period, which used laughter and the grotesque both to publicize and to manage the threats and uncertainties of a 'world turned upside down'. This etching draws on the contemporary repertoire of caricature motifs to delineate 'progress'; several of these commonplaces can be immediately recognized. A burly coachman, for instance, neglecting the immediate and the practical for the distant and the theoretical, is so absorbed in his route book that he fails to notice a baby lying in his path. Elsewhere, in a parody of genteel manners, two hod carriers exchange cards, the one seated with a volume from the St Giles Reading Society on his lap.

Equally characteristic for this date is a recognition of the centrality of periodicals and serial publication to this humorous overview of disturbing yet exciting social change. Indeed, the 'March of Intellect', which proceeds uncertainly down the obstacle-strewn street, is framed by images of part-issue or serial reading matter. To the left of the image, a bookseller's window and advertisement hoardings offer a list of wares that brings together major Romantic authors (Byron, Crabbe, Rogers, Scott and Hogg among them) and serious literary journalism (represented here by the weighty *Edinburgh*, *Quarterly* and *Monthly* magazines). Yet, even such an obvious statement of the dependence of establishment literary culture on the relatively recently founded, but already well-respected, metropolitan journals is subverted here. A poorly dressed tailor, his eyesight ruined by years of close stitching, takes off his eyeglasses and squints at the advertisements in the hope of making something out. The books, and therefore the cultural aspirations traditionally associated exclusively with the rich and cultured, have become accessible to the poor and artisan classes, however distorted their vision might be.

Such developments of, and tensions within, the literary market are equally obvious from the row of hoardings and posters that form the backdrop of the right half of the image. Among the competing claims of various literary commodities for the reader's interest – and, indeed, his or her cash – are included such representatives of the new print culture as practical advice on abortion (*Every woman's book*), Gothic romances, volumes of 'useful knowledge', and posters offering rewards for the apprehension of criminals or information about forthcoming spectacles such as the 'Great Eliphant'. Such a mélange of proclamations – reduced in two instances to the single word imperative: 'read' – serves to reinforce a recognition of the interdependence of serial and volume publication in the late eighteenth and early nineteenth century. Equally, this image suggests the indistinctness of the dividing line between the ephemeral and the permanent, a fraught issue for historians, given the consumption of periodicals in both part-issue and volume form.

Prominently located among this mass of serial publication is an advertisement for the *Mechanicks Magazine* (*sic*). Founded in 1823, the *Mechanic's Magazine* is one of the significant new journals of the 1820s, described by one commentator as 'an important vector of knowledge for the middle class'.[6] Like the influential and widely distributed miscellany, the *Mirror of Literature*, founded in 1821, the *Mechanic's Magazine* employed a small, double-columned octavo format profusely illustrated with wood-engraved vignettes (often of considerable intricacy and detail), that shifted periodical literature away from an elite readership towards a more democratic and technocratic circulation among the self-educating middle classes and ambitious artisans. The emblematic title page of the first issue made full use of an iconographical vocabulary that aligned the classical with the technocratic, traditional forms of knowledge and understanding with images of paddle steamers and beam engines.

Coming at the end of the period discussed in this volume, Seymour's print suggests, if only retrospectively, several of the central narratives concerning periodicals and magazines emerging from these years. Most obviously, it is an image that registers, entirely unequivocally, the centrality of print culture to both the actuality and the perception of social change. Such a centrality was the product both of the exemplary nature of the book as an increasingly successful and widely desired commodity, and of the printed word as a mechanism through which social change was managed and understood. The melodramatic equation drawn here between selfish self-improvement and its human costs – in studying the printed version of his route, a coachman steps on a helpless baby – suggests the considerable anxiety felt about print culture and its effects on the social fabric. Equally, it constitutes an image of the dangers of the book-learned against the experiential, of theory against practice, of concept against event. Every bit as unequivocal in Seymour's image is his depiction of periodicals as the most obvious representatives of, or even the driving force behind, the complex of social change given the shorthand title of 'The March of Intellect'. Much of the literature on display comprises periodicals, serials or part-issues, drawn from across a broad spectrum of readers' interests. Within a commercial marketplace, of course, seriality was primarily a mechanism for creating an often illusory cheapness; Seymour's magazines, aimed at artisans,

6 Rauch 2001, 59.

were depicted with a certain disdain as the recourse of the irredeemably vulgar seeking forms of knowledge dangerously beyond their immediate needs. Yet, there is no mistaking Seymour's main theme: periodicals both led to, and were most characteristic of, the profound cultural changes occurring in the late eighteenth and early nineteenth century.

It has become a commonplace for cultural historians to reinforce Seymour's perception of the central role of magazines in both constructing and reflecting social change, albeit for a variety of reasons. John Brewer, in his magisterial overview of the development of eighteenth-century cultural forms within both genteel and vernacular discourses, sees the central role of periodicals as facilitating access to print: 'The world of eighteenth-century publishing is best understood as an expanding maze or labyrinth, and it offered the potential author many entrances and numerous routes to eventual publication, each full of hazards, pitfalls and dead ends. How did such a heterogeneous body of authors find their way into print? The crucial vehicle was the periodical press.'[7] In his study of the relationship between developments in the publishing industry and the writing of literature in the first half of the nineteenth century, Lee Erickson not only acknowledges the importance of periodicals for their role in developing new literary forms, such as the familiar essay, but also argues that a concentration on the book has seriously distorted literary history: 'Today's critical view of early nineteenth-century literature has been obscured by ... privileging the book form in the production of literature, when, in fact, to this day intellectual discourse on all levels usually appears first within and is always mediated by a periodical context.'[8]

Both Jon Klancher and Marilyn Butler, two of the most important cultural historians to have considered late eighteenth- and early nineteenth-century periodicals, have developed sophisticated models for their history that suggest a complex dialogue between the construction of a precise implied readership for (and by) each magazine and a broader address to the 'general' or 'national' reader. These models will be briefly considered later in this chapter, but the point to emphasize is the central role both scholars give periodicals as agents of cultural change at this time. 'The periodical, long the least prestigious and most nearly invisible element in this cultural effort [that is the shift from a court-centred elite culture to one dominated by a broader leisured class], is in fact its matrix,' Butler remarks.[9] Similarly, Klancher, in describing the 'whole cultural machinery [that] had to be formed to channel books to their readers', builds his

7 Brewer 1997, 140–1.
8 Erickson 1996, 12.
9 Butler 1993, 121.

entire study on periodicals, citing Leo Lowenthal's judgement that they formed 'the newest and most characteristic medium of the age'.[10]

Underlying these various models of the transformative presence of periodicals in late eighteenth- and early nineteenth-century society, and central to Seymour's satirical vision, is the role magazines played in extending readership and offering this extended readership a sense of shared identity – essentially a process of making a middle-class audience 'self conscious of its own cultural power' to use Klancher's phrase.[11] 'To us,' Marilyn Butler observes, 'it looks as though the eighteenth-century journals accomplished remarkable feats of homogenization, creating a market for the booksellers and a single English-speaking culture, straddling the Atlantic, of which readers themselves could have had no apprehension before.'[12] Brewer underlines the ways in which the construction of such homogeneity might be read as a form of democratization: 'Periodical editors were conscious of their importance in creating a republic of authors, a world of temporary equality, in what was otherwise a highly stratified society' and goes on to cite the editor of the *Bee*, writing in the last decade of the eighteenth century, who saw magazines as offering 'full liberty ... for every individual to become a writer'.[13] But of course it was readers as much as authors who sought access to a shared world view, and strove, however unconsciously, to become a 'reading community' that transcended simple economic definitions of communality and common interest.

Though an apparent paradox, it was the miscellaneous nature of the magazines of the late eighteenth century that made homogeneity possible. 'Within the covers of a single unbound periodical,' Butler observes, 'readers encountered a lively, eclectic mix of fables, dreams, letters, poems, travels, natural science, history and biography; of book reviews in any of these fields; of obituaries and tables listing the price of commodities.'[14] In attempting to describe the vast field of late eighteenth- and early nineteenth-century periodical literature, Klancher develops the central argument that the combination of regular serial appearance and apparent openness to readers' contributions (through letters to the editor or other forms of submitted comment) sought to construct a community of interests which, through the emergence of a shared language, defined itself against ideas of the national or of precise class interests. Klancher sees this project of both democratizing and defining

10 Klancher 1987, 19.
11 Klancher 1987, 15.
12 Butler 1993, 122.
13 Brewer 1997, 142.
14 Butler 1993, 122.

readership through periodicals as ultimately a fractured or illusory ideological undertaking, largely because the miscellaneous information, knowledge and opinion that periodicals presented to readers finally frustrated rather than enabled comprehensive understanding.

The model for such miscellanies had been set by Edward Cave, a printer by trade, who had launched the *Gentleman's Magazine* in 1731; each separate issue cost 6*d*. and was clearly intended to be bound up in volume format to create an accumulative record of topical matters.[15] Not only opinion but information, much of it gathered unapologetically from other serial resources like almanacs, was at the centre of the *Gentleman's Magazine* in its early years. As the century wore on, however, it increasingly introduced an admixture of interpretative and factual knowledge in the form of letters from readers and, in an embryonic and sketchy form, reviews of new books. The reading community posited by the *Gentleman's Magazine* was essentially anti-clerical and anti-scholastic, formulating itself in opposition to the traditional interests of a wealthy elite. 'Without having a radical editorial stance, the *Gents Mag* managed by its very representativeness to reflect middle-class attitudes that could become egalitarian and oppositional,' Butler notes.[16] Certainly the idea of enlightened (or even Enlightenment) progress, managed by the entry that periodicals gave their readers to the public sphere, was something the new miscellanies self-consciously offered to their readers.

Central to this process was a new concentration on print culture as a defining characteristic of a progressive society. Such a concentration manifested itself in the form of the 'Review'.[17] Anonymous notices of new and recent publications encouraged ideas of equality and the capacity of the ordinary man of intelligence to contribute to public life as either reviewer or reader. Two key periodicals – the *Monthly Review* (founded in 1749) and the *Critical Review* (founded in 1756 and edited initially by Smollett) – spanned the later half of the century and offered their readers reviews of travel books, literature, biography, science and, to a limited extent, popular theology. These reviews were egalitarian in their assumptions about the reader's knowledge and intelligence and deliberately eschewed narrow scholarly, antiquarian and sectarian themes. The review rapidly became the most successful form of periodical literature, essential to the stock of reading rooms and circulating libraries, and offering the topicality and urgency of the metropolitan to the provinces. Derek Roper's extremely useful study of the reviews between 1788 and 1802 gives, despite a lack of

15 See Tierney, chap. 24, above.
16 Butler 1993, 124.
17 See Tierney, chap. 24, above.

available detailed evidence in many cases, a clear sense of the publications' wide variety of known readers, including luminaries such as Walpole, Beckford and Gibbon, as well as landowners, scholars, clergy, professionals and commercial men. Yet, if 'these upper- and middle-class readers gave the Reviews their solid core of support', a 'still wider and very influential audience was reached through educational institutions and learned societies', and 'the reviews reached an even wider public through the subscription libraries, literary societies and book clubs'.[18] Roper concludes that the combined sales of reviews in the 1790s represented one-sixth of the contemporary reading public, and gives yearly figures for the key periodicals: the *Monthly Review* (3,500 in 1776), the *Critical Review* (also 3,500), the *British Critic* (3,500) and the *Analytical Review* (1,500).

The reviews of the last three decades of the eighteenth century represented a key moment in the bringing together of a reading community that shared Enlightenment ideas of the egalitarian potential of information, the necessary relationship of knowledge to understanding, and the progressive and accumulative nature of knowledge. As Roper argues, 'numbers of the *Monthly* and *Critical* were not meant to be read for entertainment and thrown away. They were conceived as instalments of a continuous encyclopaedia.'[19] Nevertheless, maintaining such an ambitious overview of knowledge and making it available as democratically as possible became unsupportable; ultimately, the early years of the nineteenth century gave way to a new wave of journals that set themselves a more disciplined and limited agenda and signalled the end of the attempt to create what Butler describes as 'the bourgeois republic of letters'.[20] The first two decades of the nineteenth century saw the successive founding of magazines that sought deliberately to influence and shape public opinion rather than to represent an inclusive, if indiscriminate, overview of available knowledge. The most famous of these was the *Edinburgh Review*, which first appeared in October 1802; this was followed by magazines that, however different they sought to be, nonetheless existed in the shadow cast by the *Edinburgh*.

The *Quarterly Review*, founded in 1809, was largely written by ex-*Edinburgh* alumni, and proved every bit as sententious and opinionated in maintaining the high cultural conservatism of the earlier journal. Both sought a new purpose for magazines, one that was less concerned with expanding readerships and seeking intellectual common ground and more focused on constructing a core

18 Roper 1978, 24–5.
19 Roper 1978, 36–7.
20 Butler 1993, 130.

of knowledge and opinion based on philosophy and science rather than the practical 'arts' and literary orientation of the earlier journals. The *Edinburgh* and the *Quarterly* were joined in 1817 by *Blackwood's*, another Edinburgh-based monthly journal, followed by two London-based competitors, the *London Magazine* (1820) and the *Westminster Review* (1824), as well as some less ambitious review-based magazines like the *New Monthly Magazine* (1814). These magazines expressed differing political viewpoints – the *Edinburgh* was as staunchly and famously Whig as the *Quarterly* was Tory – but they came to represent a new professionalization of journalism both in their aggressive and confident tone and in the more literal sense of representing professions like the law, the social sciences and medicine as the arbiters of public opinion. More approachable than the *Edinburgh* and willing to devote more space to literary topics, the *Quarterly* was nonetheless equally hostile to the political views of the younger poets.

By 1820, these two innovative and yet deeply conservative periodicals had enjoyed their most influential moment, both having won circulations of around 12,000 in the years between 1812 and 1814.[21] The journals that took their place in popularity and influence were more avowedly middle class and literary in their orientation, and were especially dependent on the discursive prose of late Romantic authors like Hogg, Hazlitt, Lamb, De Quincey and Leigh Hunt. *Blackwood's* came to represent the Scottish literary scene, while the *London* was regarded as the most 'literary' of the London-based monthlies. In these journals and magazines, for the first time the professional writer took centre-stage within periodicals;[22] the anonymous snippetry that had characterized late eighteenth-century journals and the ideological mission that had informed the *Edinburgh* and the *Quarterly* quietly receded. There is not space here to explore the complex and animating relationship between Romantic authors and the periodical press, a relationship that has been studied in detail by Erickson, Klancher and Parker among others, but it is still worth noting Butler's conclusion that, in bringing together these literary responses from professional authors, the magazines of the 1820s represented 'the all-important gatheredness which early journals supplied only in ideas'.[23] It was a sense of place, and the community it implied – the idea of the 'town' – as well as a sense of the egalitarian and civilizing potential of the professional writer's trade that characterized the new 'literariness' these periodicals brought into the Victorian period and which resonated so fully there within middle-class culture.

21 Butler 1993, 140.
22 See Griffin, chap. 5, above.
23 Butler 1993, 146.

The above narrative describes the rise and fall of an egalitarian and inclusive Enlightenment vision of progressive bourgeois periodical culture in the last three decades of the eighteenth century and its replacement by a conservative, high cultural vision of ambitious journalism, expressed in review-based monthlies in the first two decades of the nineteenth century. In the subsequent twenty years leading to the Victorian period, magazines began to represent the values of a middle-class social vision represented by meritocratic professional writers. There are several ways in which such a coherent narrative needs to be modified and sophisticated, however.

One necessary narrative concerns the dependence of the development of magazines and their readerships on technological change. Caricature provides a particularly interesting example of the intersection between the drive towards the wider readerships and sustained modes of consumption represented by periodicity and the constraints of technical processes, especially the reproduction of images. The generic constituents of eighteenth-century caricature – a costly reprographic method for the production of topical satirical images on individual and fragile engraved plates – would seem to have precluded the idea of periodicity. Aimed at wealthy consumers who assembled their miscellaneous and discrete images into portfolios for use at genteel sociable occasions, caricatures seemed – by their ephemerality, topicality, political partiality and general contempt for the ruling elite – to be beyond both the reproductive technology and the usual social discourses found in periodicals.

Yet, the periodical idea clearly excited and exercised the ingenuity of the producers of caricatures in the early nineteenth century. One solution was to organize reprints of outstanding stocks of much earlier images into a miscellany with a newly engraved emblematic title page and tail-piece. The multi-volume *Caricature Magazine* produced by Thomas Tegg in the second decade of the new century characterized this approach. Another was to include caricatures within the format of a more conventional political journal, an idea successfully carried out by the *Attic Miscellany* in the 1790s using fold-out etched plates drawn by Samuel Collings. Yet, as caricature shifted its central topic from politics to social conduct, artists began to decrease the size of their images and to organize them into thematic groupings, sometimes introducing a narrative element that prefigured the comic strip.[24] By the second decade of the nineteenth century, the emerging technology of lithography made it clear that caricature, partly because of its miscellaneity of interest, could be adapted

24 Kunzle 1990, 18–25.

to meet the needs and interests of a much wider audience, even if sold at a high but not entirely prohibitive price. The *Glasgow Looking Glass* from 1825, a fortnightly publication drawn by Henry Heath, was the first full-fledged periodical to use caricature as its sole focus, thus demonstrating that lithography could reproduce letterpress far more effectively and cheaply than the limited resources of metal engraving or etching.[25] At about the same time, the potential of wood engraving, reinvented by Thomas Bewick and his London-based pupils as a decorative and illustrative medium at the turn of the century, was also being adapted for satirical purposes. Exploited by William Hone in the pamphlet wars of the Regency, the fluency, rapidity and expressive clumsiness of wood engraving made its use in satirical and comic periodicals inevitable, and by the early 1830s such periodicals as *Figaro in London* (founded in 1831) were looking forward to the launch of *Punch* in 1841 and the many subsequent wood-engraved comic journals of the first years of Victoria's reign.

But, while technological change offers an important gloss on the periodicals' sustained quest (*c*.1780 to 1830) to find a broad-based and coherent middle-class readership, the drive towards what Butler calls 'homogenization' was a far more fractured and contested project than so far suggested. A contributor to *Blackwood's Edinburgh Magazine* in 1824 described the countervailing tendency towards fragmentation, specialization and diversity evident in the dominant miscellany and review format: 'Instead of a Magazine being a repository of papers on a great variety of topics ... almost every one department was sufficient to support and fill its own peculiar Magazine. Thus we now see such a variety of these periodical publications: the mechanic, the chemist, the man who dabbles in physic, &c. &c. has his own magazine.'[26] Erickson notes that 'reviews and magazines in stiff competition with one another effectively segmented the reading public along existing political, religious and class lines'.[27] Similarly, Butler, writing of late eighteenth-century periodicals, contrasts apparent 'remarkable feats of homogenization' with the journals' organization, which 'underline[d] the compartmentalization of knowledge and its increasing specialization' with the result that they did not 'attempt to group, still less to hierarchize, knowledge'.[28] Klancher's persuasive model for describing the period and its magazines originates in ideas of fracture and conflict consequent upon responses to the French Revolution, and he structures his book around three emergent notions of readership that characterize the early

25 Twyman 1990, 190–1.
26 Stevens 1824, 524.
27 Erickson 1996, 72.
28 Butler 1993, 122.

decades of the nineteenth century: 'a newly-self-conscious middle class, a nascent mass audience, and an insurgent radical readership'.[29]

Certainly, increasing specialism was characteristic of the periodicals market. Some of this specialization was the outcome of the Enlightenment quest for knowledge – a knowledge newly liberated from the pages of impenetrable learned journals – and lay largely outside the intense ideological contests described by Klancher, despite magazine culture's sustained critique of courtly and establishment culture. Numerous popularizing magazines on natural history, for example, were rapidly developed to cash in on the market opened up by the Bewick illustrated volumes on British birds and animals, another interesting example of how technological change (in this case sophisticated white-line wood engraving) drove changes in the marketplace. Previously 'unknown as a popular science but only to a few profound individuals', the interest in natural history nonetheless supported the launch of at least eight journals between 1828 and 1834.[30]

The struggle to establish the social purposes and readerships of other segments of the market for periodicals was much more fraught, however. Magazines aimed specifically at children, for example, were slow to build on the example of Newbery's the *Lilliputian Magazine* (1751); only eleven juvenile titles were published between 1752 and 1800.[31] Most of these were projected by John Marshall and comprised both visual material and text likely to be chosen by adults as suitable to support the home education of their children. In appearance and content these magazines remained very close to the more established literature for children published in volume format, and sought to maintain a balance between 'instruction and delight'.[32]

Magazines for children only really took off when sectarian interests became actively involved in the first quarter of the nineteenth century. With the organizational potential and funds of large organizations behind them, religious groups formed the central agency for developing this important sector of the periodical market. Moreover, because of their extensive experience producing and distributing tract literature for the weekly devotional activities and practices of individual congregations, religious groups were alert to the potential of mass-circulation literature. The *Youth's Magazine*, for example – from 1805 the first widely successful and much-imitated children's magazine – was the product of a young enthusiast called William Lloyd and the

29 Klancher 1987, 15. Cf. Wood, chap. 48, below.
30 Ritvo 1987, 10.
31 Drotner 1988, 17. Cf. Immel, chap. 40, below.
32 Drotner 1988, 17–27; Jackson 1989, chaps. 5 and 6.

interdenominational vision of the Sunday School Union. Such magazines either cost very little or had their costs absorbed by church or chapel members who distributed free copies as part of their daily devotional routine. By 1839 the first halfpenny paper, the *Children's Missionary Record*, was being published on behalf of the Scottish Presbyterian Free Church. By 1824, the Religious Tract Society, founded twenty-five years previously,[33] had begun to publish the *Child's Companion*; *or*, *Sunday Scholar's Reward*, a miscellany of anecdotes, fables and narratives illustrated with vignette wood engravings. The title suggests both the attempt to befriend children – Drotner perceptively points out that such periodicals 'gave no reason for the pervasive influence of religion in their lives'[34] – and the close relationship between periodical literature and the public practices of religious observance.

If such sectarian hijacking of the periodical format in pursuit of proselytizing impulses seems nakedly ideological in its trajectory, nonetheless there were contradictions even within the content of such ostentatiously purposive kinds of literature. As Drotner helpfully comments, 'The religious magazines ... were neither a monolithic medium of indoctrination, nor did they offer juveniles universal, spiritual consolation. They operated on several psychological levels ... The pious fictional surface that adults perceived and commended as morally beneficial hid a narrative structure that ... gripped their [children's] imaginations with a forceful hold, which the readers had different means of rehearsing and reformulating for their own ends.'[35] Additionally, such journals evolved the distribution systems, the low-cost mass-publication technology and the social occasions that made 'entertaining' periodical literature for children a commercial possibility when the increasing secularization of education and the growth of middle-class leisure became features of early Victorian culture.

Even where a less overtly ideological project informed the development of specialist periodicals in the first three decades of the nineteenth century, the shift to wide circulation and popular formats often involved the kind of weakening of the Enlightenment ideas of knowledge, social participation and egalitarianism described by Klancher in his chapter on mass-circulation journals. Consider, for example, the *Mirror of Literature*, a relatively down-market journal that translated the traditional interests of the middle-class miscellany into a newly industrialized world. Founded in 1822, but continuing successfully into the mid-nineteenth century, the *Mirror* provided the key personnel,

33 See Mandelbrote, chap. 32, below.
34 Drotner 1988, 60.
35 Drotner 1988, 60.

expertise and technology from which Victorian middle-class illustrated journalism grew – many of the staff of the *Mirror* were involved, for example, in the creation of the *Illustrated London News* in 1842.[36] For Klancher, the creation of a mass audience 'displaces all discourses of political argument, philosophical speculation, and cultural discrimination one finds in *Blackwood's Magazine* or *Edinburgh Review*. Excluded from the dialogues of cultural power, the mass reader discovers an allegorical world overcrowded with signs.'[37] In this way, Klancher reads the 'contentless' mélange of information and images which characterized the *Penny Magazine* (1832) and the *Saturday Magazine* (1832) as politically and intellectually debilitating, offering their readers not so much a reflection of their own world as 'a longing, a utopian desire' that could never be fulfilled.[38]

It might also be argued that women's magazines undergo a similar transformation in this period from Enlightenment aspiration to something more cosily bourgeois; the ambitions of magazines like the *Lady's Monthly Miscellany* (founded in 1798) set up a paradigm of instruction and entertainment that was slowly eroded by the loss of news and political commentary from women's journals, the emergence of women as professional journalists, and the development of question and correspondence pages, pioneered by *La Belle Assemblée* in 1806.[39] The apparent broadening of the agenda of women's magazines in fact concealed a potential narrowing of focus in the early Victorian period. Beetham characterizes this dialogue as a 'flux between an older aristocratic definition [of femininity] and a new set of values associated with the bourgeois family'.[40] She also notes the shift from eighteenth-century 'magazines ... which positioned readers as members of a reading/writing community rather than simply as consumers' to early Victorian journals which 'openly articulated ... the argument that intellectual activity was incompatible with women's moral role'.[41] In short, women's magazines, like many other periodicals, abandoned the late eighteenth-century attempt to construct an egalitarian community of writers and readers and instead began to construct a role devoted to the ideological project of a newly proselytizing middle class.

Klancher's third 'division' of periodicals and their readers in the early nineteenth century comprised 'radicals', represented by an extraordinary group of magazines founded between 1816 (when William Cobbett's *Political Register*

36 Maidment 1992, 5–9.
37 Klancher 1987, 81.
38 Klancher 1987, 81.
39 White 1970, 38–9. Cf. Grundy, chap. 6, above.
40 Beetham 1996, 18.
41 Beetham 1996, 20, 29.

first appeared in a cheap serialized form familiarly known as 'Twopenny Trash') and the mid-1820s.[42] Such notorious journals as Thomas Wooler's the *Black Dwarf* (founded in 1817) and William Hone's *Reformist's Register* (also from 1817) sought to articulate an oppositional social position distinct from the philosophical radicalism of the 1790s, which concentrated on abstract debate, but perhaps equally distant from Chartist agitation around the franchise and the economic relationships between employer and employed, which constructed the next generation of radical journalism in the 1830s and 1840s. Whereas preceding and succeeding journals sought to build a more inclusive reading community of politically active radicals, the journals of the 1820s sought to speak on behalf of the oppressed and the marginal rather than to speak with them. Indeed, their defining characteristic was an extraordinary verbal energy. As Klancher puts it, 'In stark contrast to the mass journals, where no one speaks, but everyone is spoken for, the radical text is all talk, a stormy representation of one social discourse by another.'[43]

The periodicals produced between 1780 and 1830 undoubtedly performed a number of major transformative roles within society and helped to thrust print culture to the centre of national consciousness. Markets for periodicals both expanded and diversified, and at one level the magazine represented a triumphant new mass-produced commodity. Periodicity became a commonplace and respected mode of producing a huge variety of texts and a popular form of consumption. Yet, the central project of periodicals in the 1780s – the uniting of readers within a well-informed, egalitarian middle-class reading community – was never realized. Any enlightened vision of the socially unifying potential of magazines and journals was increasingly lost among the fractured or competing readerships and ideological conflicts of a periodical press substantially and increasingly committed to the representation of middle-class value systems and beliefs. By 1832, magazine culture was both technologically and ideologically prepared for the culture wars of 'useful knowledge', the unstamped press, and the emergence of a mass-circulation illustrated journalism that sought to address, if not include, every member of society.

42 See Wood, chap. 48, below.
43 Klancher 1987, 100.

IV
THE INTERNATIONAL MARKET

26
Continental imports to Britain, 1695–1740

P.G. HOFTIJZER AND O.S. LANKHORST

In 1733, the London printer and publisher Samuel Buckley presented a petition to Parliament, asking for protection for his impressive, seven-volume folio edition of Jacques-Auguste de Thou's *Historia sui temporis*. Fearing that the work might be pirated on the Continent, he requested a ban against the importation of any foreign edition for a period of fourteen years. Although Buckley was well aware that the Copyright Act of 1710 had declared free the importation of all books in foreign languages, he argued that the Dutch government in particular had given its publishers an unfair market advantage by conferring numerous privileges while simultaneously conniving at the reprinting of what he described as 'the most useful and vendible books published in the neighbouring nations, in the learned languages, or in French, the common language almost of Europe'. He concluded: 'Great estates have been gained in Holland by reprinting books written in France, with which, as well as with the classics, and other books of literature, the Dutch have for many years largely supplied England, Scotland, and Ireland, as well as Germany and the Northern parts of Europe.'[1]

Samuel Buckley knew perfectly well what he was talking about. During the early years of his career in the 1690s, before he went into the newspaper and publishing business, he had been a prominent Latin trade bookseller, importing large quantities of old and new books from the Continent through his contacts in the United Provinces.[2] In the following decades, there were quite a few other London booksellers engaged in this trade. The stationer Samuel Smith, to whom Buckley had originally been apprenticed, was active until his death in 1708, after which the business was continued by his partner and

1 Buckley 1733; van Eeghen 1960–78, I, 102, 126–7.
2 Roberts 2002, 169, 171–2; on Buckley, see Plomer 1907; for his catalogues, Munby and Coral 1977, 6, 18, 19.

brother-in-law, Benjamin Walford. As booksellers to the Royal Society, Smith and Walford held a key position in the Latin trade, and – as the surviving part of their foreign trade correspondence over the years 1683–92 demonstrates – they dealt with a large number of (mainly Dutch) colleagues, who supplied them with scholarly books and text editions of the classical authors.[3] Other London players in this field were – to name only a few – Thomas Bennet and Henry Clements, who were active up to 1719;[4] William and John Innys, who continued Benjamin Walford's shop until 1732; the booksellers-auctioneers Thomas and Edward Ballard; and, from 1730 onwards, John Nourse. In addition, there were numerous French and some Dutch immigrant booksellers active in the import trade. Outside the metropolis, several bookdealers in Oxford and Cambridge had links with Holland,[5] while in Scotland leading members of the trade – such as Robert and Andrew Foulis in Glasgow and John Paton and Gavin Hamilton in Edinburgh – dealt extensively with the Dutch.[6]

Although the preponderance of Dutch book imports on the English market had a long history, it was much strengthened by the long sequence of wars between Britain and the Dutch Republic on the one hand, and Britain and France on the other. During the War of the League of Augsburg (1689–97) and again during the wars of the Spanish (1702–13) and Austrian Succession (1740–8), book imports from France came to a complete standstill due to the prohibition of trade between England and France. The Dutch, on the contrary, maintained book trade relations with France – both directly through their contacts in Paris and other cities, and indirectly via the Frankfurt and Leipzig book fairs. They were thus able to act as intermediaries in the Anglo-continental book trade, continuously supplying their British colleagues with books from all over Europe. Even during periods of peace, however, no imports from France – or for that matter from any other European country – could match the constant flow of books from the United Provinces. This state of affairs is clearly demonstrated by the British Customs records that have been preserved for the years 1696 to 1780, listing the value of a great variety of imported and exported goods

3 On the Smith correspondence, see Hodgson and Blagden 1956; Lankhorst 1983; Hoftijzer 1987, 1991a; Roberts 2002. On 27 June 1709, the Leiden bookseller Pieter van der Aa settled a claim on Smith and Walford to the value of 1,000 guilders (Leiden Municipal Archives, Notarial Archives 1531, deed no. 61).

4 For their memorandum book, containing, among other items, part of their foreign correspondence, accounts and book lists, see Hodgson and Blagden 1956.

5 On the books-for-books exchange between Cornelius Crownfield, printer of the newly founded Cambridge University Press, who himself was of Dutch origin, and booksellers in the Netherlands, see McKitterick 1998, chap. 4. In Oxford, John Owen was active in the Latin trade around 1700.

6 Robert and Andrew Foulis and John Paton are among a small group of British booksellers present in the ledgers of the firm of Luchtmans in Leiden; see Luchtmans Archive, Boekverkopersboeken, vol. 7 (1747), 425 and vol. 8 (1751–2), 371 (Library of the Royal Dutch Booksellers Association, Amsterdam University Library); for Hamilton, see McDougall 1974, 45.

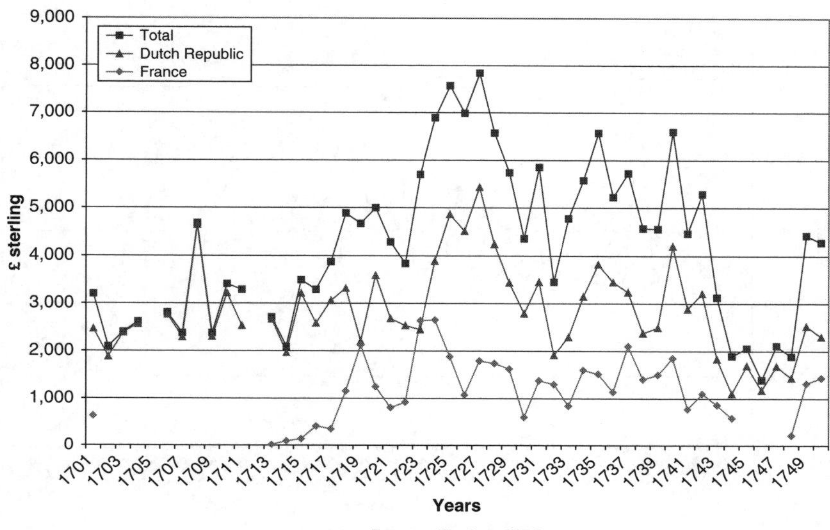

Figure 26.1 Dutch and French book exports to Britain, 1701–51, estimated value in pounds sterling

and merchandise, including books. These records, which provide the first statistical information on the Latin trade, have been analysed by Giles Barber.[7] Figure 26.1, based on his data, shows the total value of book imports, bound and unbound, from 1701 to 1751, and the Dutch and French shares in it.

The average annual value of Dutch imports fluctuates around £3,000 sterling, with a high peak of £5,432 in 1727. French imports, which were virtually non-existent between 1702 and 1716, rarely exceed the £2,000 mark. After 1740, however, a steep overall decline set in due to the outbreak of the War of the Austrian Succession, affecting both Dutch and French imports.

Because of the difference between import duties on bound (antiquarian) and unbound (new) books,[8] the Customs records make it possible to compare these two categories. As Figure 26.2 shows, the value of bound books imported from Holland remained fairly modest until the mid-1720s, when there was a sudden increase, which is paralleled by a significant rise in the value of unbound imports. On average, however, the value of the imports of bound books does not exceed £500.

7 Barber 1976, 1977, 1982.

8 These figures may be somewhat distorted. As a letter from Thomas Bennet to his Leiden correspondent Pieter van der Aa shows, the bindings of bound books were sometimes removed in order to avoid the higher tax duty on bound books. Hodgson and Blagden 1956, 56.

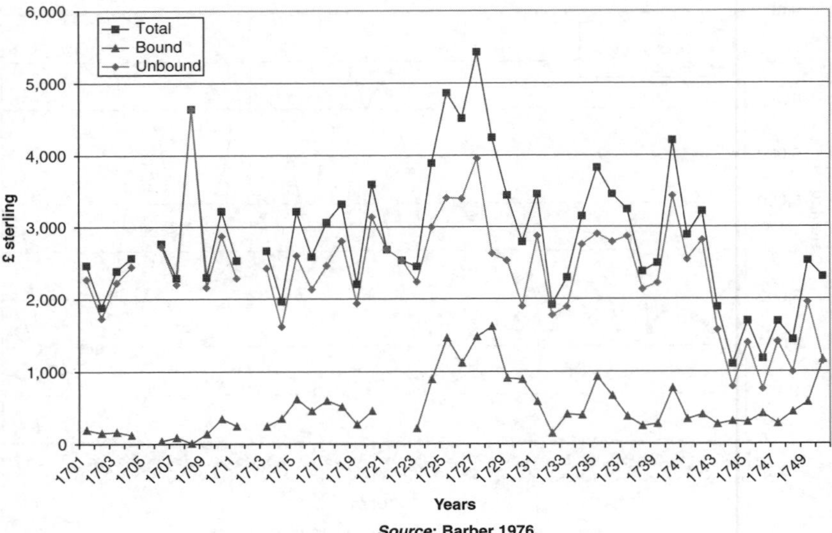

Figure 26.2 Dutch book exports – bound and unbound – to Britain, 1701–51, estimated value in pounds sterling

Yet, with regard to the physical volume of book imports, one has to keep in mind that these figures are somewhat misleading. The duty on bound books was £1 sterling per hundredweight, against an average of £8 per hundredweight for new books. As the value of bound books imported from the Dutch Republic in, for example, 1727 was £1,477, this amounts to an impressive 75,000kg of second-hand books (one hundredweight=50.8kg). Although the value of unbound books for the same year comes to the much larger sum of £3,955, this figure stands for 'only' 25,000kg of new books.

A category of imported books about which the Customs records do not provide separate information are the pirated editions of both continental and English works produced in the United Provinces. Piracy was one of the mainstays of the Dutch publishing industry and many printers and publishers in cities such as Amsterdam, Leiden and The Hague were involved in this truly international enterprise. While the once-profitable production of English bibles and prayer books at Amsterdam appears to have lost most of its lustre during the first half of the eighteenth century,[9] other branches were still flourishing. The greatest of all book pirates in Amsterdam around 1700 was

9 van Eeghen 1960–78, IV, 107–16; 1966. Cf. McMullin, chap. 31, below.

the firm of the Huguenot brothers Marc, Jean Henry and Pierre Huguetan, about whom one contemporary remarked that they had twelve or thirteen presses at their disposal, which they kept in constant operation, 'without making any distinction whom they damage or where'.[10] Little is known about the reprints of English titles by the Huguetans and whether or not these were sold on the British market, but the firm clearly had several agents in England, including David Delgas in London and John Crosley in Oxford, who in 1694 had books in commission worth 10,000 guilders, or approximately £1,000.[11]

A figure who obviously caused serious financial damage was the Scotsman Thomas Johnson. He had begun his career in the Dutch book trade in 1705 when he entered a short-lived partnership with the Huguenot bookseller Jonas l'Honoré in The Hague. Johnson's bookshop catered for a varied clientele including British diplomats, students and travellers and is said to have been a meeting place for the sympathizers of the deist and freethinker John Collins, who at the time was living in exile in the Dutch Republic.[12] In 1728, Johnson moved to Rotterdam, 'the centre of all English affairs and business in these provinces', as he described it in his *Guide for English travellers, through Holland* (Rotterdam, 1731).

Until his death in 1735, Johnson produced an extensive list of English books, which – apart from sale in his own shop – were intended mainly for distribution on the British market. Among his publications, we find not only treatises by English philosophers such as John Toland, Anthony Collins and Anthony Ashley Cooper, 3rd Earl of Shaftesbury, but also numerous pirated editions of literary publications. In 1710, he began a series of small format (duodecimo) reprints of English plays, among them the works of Shakespeare as well as those of more recent authors.[13] By the end of 1711, some forty titles were available, issued separately and as a ten-volume set entitled *A collection of the best English plays*. In total, Johnson envisaged a series of nearly one hundred texts, but of the 'other plays now printing, or proposed to be printed, to make the collection complete' as advertised in 1711, more than half remained unpublished. He also reprinted the works of contemporary writers, such as Pope, Dryden, Swift, Burnet, Addison and Prior, again in small (octavo or

10 Letter of the Amsterdam paper merchant IJsbrand Vincent to Balthasar Moretus at Antwerp, dated 24 Jan. 1695; cf. van Eeghen 1960–78, III, 175. See also van Eeghen 1982.

11 van Eeghen 1960–78, III, 168–79; Hodgson and Blagden 1956, 35–40. One pound was approximately 10 guilders.

12 Kossmann 1937, 205–10.

13 It has been said that Johnson was responsible for 'the passing of the 4° and advent of the 12°' in the publication of Shakespeare's plays; Ford 1935, 47.

duodecimo) formats, 'pocket editions, small volumes fit for the pocket' as he called them. In 1718, for example, he published *The Works of Mr Alexander Pope* and the first three books of Pope's translation of Homer's *Iliad* in octavo. According to the advertisements in his own periodical, the *Journal Litéraire*, his Pope editions were printed 'proprement & correctement', and with a price of only 24 'sols' (= one guilder and four stuivers, i.e. just over 2*s*.) per volume, they cost a fraction of the original English folio edition.

Johnson used various imprints for his piracies. Whereas the early title pages of his plays have 'Printed for T. Johnson, Bookseller at the Hague', later (re-)editions give London as the place of publication, mostly without mentioning him as the publisher.[14] His edition of Pope's *Works* has the imprint 'printed by T.J. for B.L.', the latter initials standing for the London publisher Bernard Lintot who owned the copyright, but surely had not consented to Johnson's using his name. The 1726 edition of the *Works* of John Sheffield, 1st Duke of Buckingham, equally has a spurious imprint – 'Printed for John Barber, Alderman of London' – together with Johnson's monogram 'T J' on the title page. Still, Johnson may well have co-operated with others in these piracies. In their resistance against the new English copyright legislation, some London publishers must have welcomed any attempt to break the monopoly of their more powerful colleagues in the trade.[15]

Not much is known about the distribution of Johnson's books in England. With regard to the transport and sale of books in Scotland, however, information is provided by his correspondence with Charles Mackie, professor of universal history at the University of Edinburgh. Mackie had studied in Groesningen and Leiden, and was tutor of Alexander Leslie, Earl of Leven, to whom Johnson was related through his wife. He apparently acted as an intermediary between Johnson and various Scottish booksellers by passing on illicit consignments of books, handling orders and addressing other matters. In August 1719, Johnson wrote to Mackie concerning a despatch of books from Holland: 'the English books are put between the leaves of the latin & french ones in such a way as they'l not be easily seen at the Custom house'. Following the shipment of a number of copies of his edition of Swift's *Miscellaneous works* in January 1721, he informed his correspondent: 'Your bound books are most at the bottom of the box & the unbound above, the English books are in the middle.' And in July 1733 Johnson asked Mackie to propose to the Edinburgh bookseller Thomas Heriot a three-month monopoly for the exclusive distribution of Johnson's

14 For example, 'London, Printed in the year . . .', 'London, Printed for the Company' and 'London, printed for T. Johnson'.

15 Feather 1992, esp. 153.

edition of Shaftesbury's *Characteristics*, published anonymously that same year.[16]

While Thomas Johnson worked from The Hague and later Rotterdam, other foreign booksellers set up their business in London. The majority of them were Huguenot refugees, who had come to England either directly from France or via the Dutch Republic following the Revocation of the Edict of Nantes in 1685.[17] As the strict naturalization laws made it almost impossible for them to enter publishing or become members of the Stationers' Company, they clustered outside the City boundaries, particularly in the Strand, in the vicinity of the French church in the Savoy, where they specialized in retail bookselling to the expanding Huguenot population as well as to English customers. Many of the 'French booksellers' in London – the Vaillants, Cailloués, Riboteaus, de Varennes, Marrets and others – came from old bookselling families in France and maintained close relations with members of the Huguenot diaspora elsewhere in Europe. This international network enabled them to offer a wide variety of new and antiquarian books, in many cases imported directly from or via Holland.[18] The Huguenot booksellers had their heyday in London around 1700, but their prominence was short lived. By the 1730s, most of them had disappeared again, mainly because the Huguenot community, which constituted a substantial part of their clientele, was gradually dissolving into the metropolitan population.

The aim of the native Dutch booksellers who came to London was first and foremost to promote the bookselling interests of their family businesses and partnerships at home. David Mortier, who had arrived in England in 1696 at the age of twenty-two, represented the big Amsterdam firm of his elder brother Pieter. He was quite successful, dealing from his shop 'at the sign of Erasmus's head' in the Strand in all sorts of old and new imported books – some of them issued with London imprints – as well as maps and prints, and eventually was able to obtain denization in 1706. Three years later, he sold his shop to Pierre Dunoyer.[19] Similarly, Jacob (or James) Moetjens, a nephew of The Hague bookseller Adriaan Moetjens, arrived in London in 1711 and ran a bookshop in the Strand together with his partner Michel Charles le Cène.[20]

After the death of James Moetjens in 1721, his business was jointly continued by his former overseer, Abraham van der Hoeck, who had come to London in 1716, and Johannes Groenewegen from The Hague. The man behind their

16 The correspondence between Johnson and Mackie is preserved in the Edinburgh University Library, La.11.91. Cf. McDougall 1974 and Mijers 2002.

17 The following is based chiefly on Swift 1986, chap. 3, Swift 1990 and 1992.

18 See Landon, chap. 38, below.

19 Swift 1992, 268–70.

20 Swift 1992, 270–7.

partnership, however, was Pierre Gosse the elder, one of the most important international booksellers in The Hague, who had grasped the opportunity to fill the gap left by Mortier and Moetjens. In an agreement with his factotum Groenewegen, Gosse stipulated that he would be their exclusive supplier of old and new books. When Van der Hoeck left the partnership in 1726 – he later would found the still-existing firm of Van der Hoeck in Göttingen – a new company was founded by Groenewegen and Nicolas Prevost in London, and Pierre Gosse and Jean Neaulme in The Hague. For several years, they flooded the English market with old and new foreign books of mixed quality, a cause of considerable concern among the established booksellers in the City. But trouble was looming. In 1728, Groenewegen suddenly departed for Paris and – although Prevost desperately tried to continue the enterprise, while at the same time involving himself in various hazardous publishing projects – business began to fail. In December 1733 Prevost finally disappeared from the London stage after a fraudulent bankruptcy.[21]

Operating on the fringes of the established book trade, these foreign booksellers used all the means available to them to dispose of their books. In order to promote direct sales in their bookshops, they printed traditional stock catalogues to inform the public about the books 'lately imported from abroad'. They also placed advertisements in popular periodicals like the *Post Man*, the *Monthly Catalogue* and the *Gentleman's Magazine*. In 1730, Nicolas Prevost even began a monthly journal of his own, entitled *Historia Litteraria, or, an exact and early account of the most valuable books published in the several parts of Europe*. Seemingly modelled on the successful scholarly review journals published in Holland, it was really intended as an outlet for his vast assortment of unsold books.[22]

A major distribution channel for imported books was the book sale.[23] Many of the book auctions held in London during the first half of the eighteenth century contained imports, in some cases even entire foreign libraries.[24] In December 1701, Samuel Buckley organized a major auction, which (according to the title page of the catalogue) consisted of books 'collected chiefly' from three major collections sold previously in Holland.[25] At the numerous auctions held by French booksellers at Exeter Exchange in the Strand, old and new books of diverse continental origin were sold, as can be gauged from the titles

21 For the relationship with Gosse, see Kossmann 1935–6 and Swift 1992, esp. 273–8.
22 Swift 1992, 277.
23 See Landon, chap. 38, below.
24 Mandelbrote 2001.
25 Buckley 1701. A similar auction was held by an anonymous auctioneer in Exeter Exchange in 1702; see Munby and Coral 1977, 19.

of their catalogues, such as *Catalogue des livres françois anciens et modernes* or *A catalogue of Greek, Latin, Italian, Spanish, French and English books, collected chiefly from several libraries beyond sea*. The less risky fixed-price sale – held at a specific place and date on the basis of a printed catalogue with set prices – was also routinely employed, particularly by Van der Hoeck and Groenewegen from 1721 onwards. Often, the fixed-price sale was used to sell quality books, while auctions were an outlet for books that were more difficult to dispose of.[26]

Notwithstanding the considerable success of the import trade, it should be realized that foreign books did not arrive in Britain only through the services of commercial booksellers. Because of the increasing contacts between Britain and other European countries, there was a lively traffic across the North Sea and the English Channel of merchants, diplomats, scholars, students, soldiers, tourists and others. Many of them returned home with books, especially since books as a rule were much cheaper on the Continent than at home. Many public and private collections in Britain to this day bear witness to the intensive book buying by private individuals travelling in continental Europe. The most impressive buyers were the English bibliophiles. Some stayed abroad for years, hunting for manuscripts, rare books and works of art. Richard Rawlinson, who travelled in the Low Countries, France and Italy between 1719 and 1726, bought so extensively that a manuscript catalogue lists well over 2,000 titles.[27] When in Naples, he praised the government for not charging him for an export licence for books, commenting: 'No country but England knows a tax on learning.'[28] Others commissioned agents (such as John Bagford) to search for books and manuscripts and to buy whatever they could lay their hands on at auctions in The Hague and Paris.[29]

Rare information on the much more modest book buying by British students abroad is provided by the correspondence of John Clerk, a Scottish student at Leiden, with his father, Sir John Clerk of Penicuik. When young Clerk arrived in Leiden in November 1694 to study Roman law, he had only two books in his luggage: a copy of Emperor Justinian's *Institutiones* and the accompanying *Compendium*. His father, who also had been to Leiden and apparently spoke from experience, had urged him not to buy too many books, as four or five books would suffice for his studies. In October 1695 John wrote to his father:

26 Swift 1992, 265–7; cf. Suarez 1999a.
27 See Landon, chap. 38, below.
28 Enright 1955, 1990, 33.
29 De Ricci 1930, 41–2.

> As for books, I have bought only about ten or twelve good ones, which I have made use of since I came here. It would be my best to begin and pick up these books I yet must have, in different auctions. For I can get them cheaper at several times than to buy them all in one auction . . .[30]

By the 'books I yet must have', he meant modern Dutch editions of classical Roman authors such as Tacitus, Cicero, Suetonius and Seneca, which were lacking in his father's library. Although a few months later he promised not to buy books that he did not want, considering it 'foolishness in any man' to read many books, he somewhat anxiously informed his father in October 1696 that he had acquired a library worth 400 guilders: 'all choice books and few or none to be had in Scotland'.[31]

During the first half of the eighteenth century, the Continent, and the Dutch Republic in particular, continued to send vast numbers of books, old and new, to the British Isles. This phenomenon can be partly explained by the long-lasting isolation of the British publishing industry with regard to mainland Europe, partly by the unique position of the United Provinces as the 'intellectual entrepôt of Europe'.[32] This situation changed slowly: the most important development during the second half of the century was the slow decline of the Dutch dominance of the British market for imported books to the benefit of French and German, and to a lesser degree Flemish and Italian, booksellers. By 1740, the first signs of a shift were becoming visible. As readers on the Continent were becoming increasingly interested in English-language British books – particularly in the fields of science, theology, philosophy and literature – opportunities were finally created for a redress, however modest at first, of the long-standing imbalance in the Anglo-continental book trade.

30 Van Strien and Ahsmann 1992/3, 27–8.
31 Van Strien and Ahsmann 1992/3, 57.
32 Gibbs 1971.

27

The English book on the Continent

BERNHARD FABIAN AND MARIE-LUISE SPIECKERMANN

1

In the history of intellectual exchanges between England and the Continent, the eighteenth century stands out as a period of special significance. In all of the major and many of the minor European countries, the literature of England was absorbed to an extent and with an intensity which only a new word, current in the second half of the century, could describe accurately – Anglomania.[1] The flow of ideas from England to continental Europe began in the last decades of the seventeenth century and continued uninterrupted into the nineteenth. It was not confined to the belles-lettres and *humaniora*, but included many other, if not all, fields of contemporary knowledge.

There were, of course, political reasons for this interest in English life and letters. The accession of William of Orange to the English throne in 1688 strengthened relations between Holland and England, and the Hanoverian succession in 1714 brought Germany and England closer together, though the English disliked George as much as he did them. Nevertheless, the spell which England cast on the Continent was not primarily due to dynastic affiliations. It originated in a political and cultural pre-eminence, which was widely praised and held up, often in the wake of Voltaire's *Lettres philosophiques*,[2] as an idealized model for other European countries.

The major obstacle to the discovery of English culture was the linguistic barrier which had existed earlier and continued to be an important factor, in many parts of the Continent well into the nineteenth century. In 1700, English was, in nearly every respect, a foreign language of which only merchants doing business with England and, perhaps, some polymathic scholars or men of letters had a more than rudimentary knowledge. English became the new, and fashionable, foreign language of the century which many tried to learn but

1 Maurer 1987; Graf 1911.
2 Voltaire Foundation 1979.

few really mastered. By 1800, a heterogeneous cultural elite had acquired not only an uncommon command of the language, but also an impressive familiarity with English culture.[3]

The reception of British authors on the Continent occurred in a multilingual context in which English was not the dominant language. Original-language books were of course imported, but they were – in number and in importance – plainly outweighed by translations. There were primary and secondary translations into Latin (as the traditional language in the world of scholarship), into French (as the habitual language in the world of the elegant and educated) and into German (as the new lingua franca in many parts of central, northern and eastern Europe). There were – smaller in number but not inferior in significance – translations into Italian, Spanish and Portuguese, Polish and Russian, Swedish and Danish, and other languages as well. The 'English book' was no longer exclusively a book written in English. It was also a book originally written in English which was felt to be worth translating into another language and, if need be, adapting to a different cultural context from that in which it had originated.[4]

2

In the early eighteenth century, book-trade relations between England and the Continent were primarily determined by the needs of scholars. For centuries the scholarly market had been an international market dominated by the Latin book. This tradition continued because Latin remained – on the Continent longer than in England – the major medium of communication in fields such as theology or history, and frequently in medicine and the sciences. English editions of classical authors figured prominently in this market, chiefly on account of their reputation for textual accuracy and attractive printing.[5]

The high production costs of many scholarly works made it important to achieve the widest possible distribution. Holland came to act as the chief intermediary between England and the Continent – an obvious choice for English publishers when many Dutch printers were employed by English presses. Via Holland, other publishers and booksellers appear to have become business partners, especially in Germany (several Leipzig firms) and in France. Payment was often in books, so that publishers on both sides of the Channel

3 Schröder 1975, 1989; Fabian 1985; Klippel 1994. See also Loonen 1991.
4 For Germany, see Fabian 1992a.
5 Brüggemann 1797, ix–xi.

gradually acquired a sizeable stock of foreign publications in Latin.[6] Sharing an imprint as a measure for cutting costs and enlarging the market was not unusual. Occasionally, co-operation resulted in complicated arrangements – as, for instance, in the case of *Hortus indicus malabaricus*, revised by John Hill (1774), an illustrated work jointly produced by Dutch and English scholars and engravers, printed for the author, and distributed by twenty booksellers in twelve cities between Edinburgh and Rome (north–south), and London and Vienna (west–east).

At times, Latin books originating in England appear to have been committed to Dutch printers, presumably to reduce the cost of production. Partly they were sold in England, partly they appear to have been intended for sale on the Continent through Dutch agents.[7] John Ray's *Methodus plantarum emendata et aucta* was printed at Leiden for Janssohn and Waasberg bearing the imprint 'Londini: impensis Samuelis Smith & Benjamin Walford. Et veneunt Amstelaedami apud Janssonio-Waasbergios, 1703.' There were also trade arrangements between English and continental publishers, negotiated by French Huguenots in England who still had contacts with France and other countries – for example, Tacitus' *Opera* with the imprint 'Parisiis: ex typographia Ludovici-Francisci Delatour; Londini, apud Paulum Vaillaint 1771'. Between 1740 and 1742 Vaillant had a magnificent quarto edition of Cicero produced in Paris, where he supervised the printing himself.

Most frequently, however, the works of English scholars reached their European readers in continental reprint editions either of the original Latin edition or of a Latin translation first published in England or Scotland. Publishers residing in various parts of the Continent were involved in this business. Many, but not all, were based in university towns (e.g. Leiden) or in commercial centres (e.g. Leipzig). Other centres were Basel and Geneva.[8] In general, these reprints were less expensive than the original editions, as they were reduced in format, with ornaments or illustrations omitted, and were frequently printed on paper of inferior quality. Of course, there were exceptions. The publishing house of the brothers De Tournes in Geneva (originally established by French Huguenots in Lyons in 1555[9]) produced high-quality reprints which were widely appreciated for their correct texts and their handsome printing. Among the important reprint editions of major English scientists are single and collected works by Robert Boyle (1680–96). The De

6 McKitterick 2001, 247–50.
7 Barber 1977. See Hoftijzer and Lankhorst, chap. 26, above.
8 Welti 1964; Bonnant 1999, 240–85.
9 Cartier 1970; Kleinschmidt 1948, 98–104.

Tournes also published Thomas Sydenham's *Opera medica* (1696, with later editions until 1769), and – together with other Geneva publishers (Chouet, Cramer, Partachon and Ritter) – William Cave's *Scriptorum ecclesiasticorum historia litteraria* (1705). The firm played a significant role in the dissemination of English scholarship until about 1775. They and other publishers from Geneva attended the Frankfurt and Leipzig book fairs and had trade relations in the Mediterranean countries as well as in France and in the Netherlands.

3

Remarkably, the early continental trade in English books appears to have bypassed the traditional distribution centres of the eighteenth century, the Frankfurt and Leipzig book fairs. During the first two or three decades of the century practically no English imprints were listed in their semi-annual catalogues.[10] Customs records show, however, that there were exports from England to a number of countries: in the first place to Holland but also to France, Flanders and, on a smaller scale, to Germany. Marginally small exports are reported to Scandinavia and to the southern European countries before the middle of the century.[11] Thus, as is to be expected, the Dutch book trade provided the major channel through which English books were distributed on the Continent in the early eighteenth century. At the turn of the century, the Leiden bookseller Pieter van der Aa had 'considerable dealings with London booksellers', notably with Samuel Smith, who appears to have had a number of continental contacts.[12] Two Amsterdam booksellers, Bruyning and Swart, specialized in English books (primarily religious) and were active from the late seventeenth century through the first decades of the eighteenth.[13]

The international relations of the Dutch trade cannot easily be traced in detail. There were apparently continuous transactions with some of the major Leipzig booksellers, who in turn operated internationally in central and northern Europe.[14] The House of Weidmann, *primus inter pares*, was among the first to offer English books in the early 1730s and from then on remained a leading, perhaps the leading, German stockist of English authors in their original language. Moritz Georg Weidmann the younger appears to have been the first German bookseller who, as early as the 1720s, went to England as part

10 Fabian 1982.
11 Barber 1976.
12 Hoftijzer 1992. Cf. Hoftijzer and Lankhorst, chap. 26, above.
13 Hoftijzer 1987.
14 On the business relations of Dutch booksellers to the Frankfurt and Leipzig fairs (still to be explored in detail), see Laeven 1992.

of his training. Serving an international learned clientele, Weidmann first offered new and second-hand scholarly works, mainly on historical topics, and later a medley of titles of learned and popular interest. A striking feature of his stock was nearly seventy plays, which represented the repertory of the London stage in the 1720s. These texts were apparently not imported from England, but came from the press of Thomas Johnson, an émigré reprinter in The Hague and, later, in Rotterdam.[15]

Although the Leipzig booksellers relied heavily on imported books from Holland, they were also strongly opposed to the intrusion of the Dutch into their own territory. Moritz Georg Weidmann made repeated attempts to prevent Dutch booksellers from opening branches in Leipzig. He failed, finally, when Arkstée en Merkus were granted a charter and, in 1737, established a business which continued for several decades. One of their specialities was French translations of English authors, which they supplied - obviously to a widening range of customers - as original publications or reprints of Paris editions with an 'Amsterdam & Leipsic' imprint.

In the second half of the century, the Dutch trade retained its leading position, but it appears to have gradually lost its key function as distributor of English books to the Continent. The business transactions, on exchange account, between John Nourse and the Luchtmans in Leiden - which can be traced in the Luchtman archives from about 1740 to 1780 - were largely confined to scholarly, scientific and medical books, though belletristic works, primarily novels, were not altogether excluded.[16] Johannes Luchtmans himself went on a buying tour to London.[17] In general, the number of imported English books increased - in Holland, France and most notably in Germany - and their range expanded. In 1755, for instance, the Leipzig bookseller Johann Wendler announced, in an unusual block entry in the autumn fair catalogue, the availability *inter alia* of the works of Pope, Thomson and Bolingbroke, together with the *Spectator* and Johnson's *Rambler*, in addition to various novels from Richardson to Smollett. This and similar attempts to introduce contemporary or quasi-contemporary literature appear to have been successful. Wendler issued catalogues with hundreds of titles (which were probably not all in stock), and soon published the first number of *Brittische Bibliothek* (1756), a review journal devoted exclusively to English books.[18] It was the first in Germany, but as a source of information about books from

15 Fabian and Spieckermann 1995. On Johnson, see Hoftijzer and Lankhorst, chap. 26, above.

16 Barber 1977.

17 Hoftijzer 1991a.

18 Fabian 1976a, 141–2.

beyond the Channel it had been preceded by the *Bibliothèque angloise, ou histoire littéraire de la Grande Bretagne* (Amsterdam, 1717) and the *Bibliothèque Britannique, ou histoire des ouvrages des savans de la Grande-Bretagne* (The Hague, 1733).

In the 1780s, when Dutch booksellers stopped attending the fair, several Leipzig booksellers offered imported books of various kinds in the semi-annual catalogues, usually on a commission basis, sometimes as joint publications. Evidently, direct contacts of some sort existed with London publishers, but no archival records appear to survive to document the business arrangements. In the early 1770s, Karl Heydinger, a Swiss bookseller and publisher in London, was also present at the Leipzig fairs.[19]

An exclusively English bookshop, purportedly the first on the Continent, was opened in Hamburg in 1788 by William Remnant, a former language teacher, whose brother James was later active in London as a German bookseller.[20] Remnant, who served private customers but also offered 'good allowance to booksellers', was from the beginning unusually successful (Dorothy Wordsworth and Coleridge visited the shop on their German tour, presumably at the suggestion of Joseph Johnson). Remnant's business extended to Switzerland, Denmark, Sweden, Poland and even Russia. His catalogues, all preserved, contain, in addition to established authors, much of the ephemeral literature of the period.[21]

The 'Circulating Library' which in 1803 Remnant added to his shop – 'at the repeated request of many Friends to English Literature' – was, by contrast, not an original undertaking. Half a century earlier (in 1750), Hendrik Scheurleer, publisher in The Hague, attempting 'to fulfill the wishes of scholars and cultivated amateurs of the arts and sciences', had made available his large collection of English (and French) books to the general public as a lending library. Though a commercial project, the *Bibliotheca Scheurleeriana* was intended to promote cultural knowledge and serious learning rather than to provide light reading (despite a section of new *romans)*, and accordingly contained an impressive range of scholarly and scientific works.[22] In conjunction with his library, Scheurleer published (from 1750) the *Journal Britannique*, edited by Matthew Maty, which gave an account of the productions of the English press.[23] It circulated not only in the Low Countries but also in Paris, Geneva, Venice and Rome.

19 Van Vliet 2002; Kirchoff 1894; Fabian 1982; Jefcoate 2004.
20 Fabian 1978b, 1992b.
21 The catalogues were issued, from 1788 to 1790, with the *British Mercury*, a journal edited by Johann Wilhelm von Archenholtz.
22 Janssens-Knorsch 1993, 290.
23 Janssens 1975.

Remnant's library, though planned to 'vie with the best similar Institutions in London', appears to have been less scholarly and directed at an audience primarily interested in belles-lettres. It was obviously intended to rival the 'Brittische Lesebibliothek' which an otherwise unknown Thomas Harbridge had opened in Hamburg in 1802. No catalogues of either institution appear to survive, but the existence of these two commercial libraries indicates the contemporary interest in English reading matter. On a smaller scale, Rudolph Sammer (originally also a language teacher) was active as an international bookseller in Vienna in the last decades of the eighteenth century and the early decades of the nineteenth. Although he offered books in many languages, English books were his speciality, and he must be supposed to have served a market that extended beyond Austria into the corners of the Habsburg empire. Among almost four hundred 'English' titles in a catalogue of 1814 are some continental reprints and many dictionaries and language learning aids, testifying to the intense interest in the 'new' foreign language.[24] Sammer also reprinted literary works in neat paperback editions.

Numerous collections of English books – large and small, private and institutional – were formed in our period.[25] Not a few are impressive and suggest an intimate familiarity with the contemporary culture of England. Two in German libraries are outstanding by any standard. The first is in the University Library at Göttingen (founded in 1737). It was built up as an integral part of a research library and is generally regarded as one of the largest and perhaps the most significant collections of pre-1801 English imprints outside the English-speaking world.[26] Its nucleus consisted of the private library of Joachim Heinrich von Bülow, a rich general collection (not only of English books) bought primarily in Holland. The Dutch trade continued to be a major, though not the exclusive, source for early institutional purchases of antiquarian books from England. From the 1760s onwards, 'new' books were bought directly from London booksellers (mostly from John Ridley) through the Hanoverian Legation and brought to Göttingen by diplomatic couriers.[27]

The second notable collection forms part of the private library of the Prinz von Ratibor und Corvey at Corvey Castle in Westphalia. It consists of late eighteenth- and early nineteenth-century books of general appeal and includes among its 67,000 volumes what is 'probably the most extensive single

24 *Catalogue général des livres français, anglais, italiens, espagnols et portugais, hollandais et flamands, bohémiens et polonais, danois et suédois, hongrais, russes, illyriens etc* ... 1814.

25 Some are described in Fabian 1976a, 154–65.

26 See Fabian 1979a; Jefcoate and Kloth 1987 (catalogue).

27 Jefcoate 1996.

collection of novels belonging to the British Romantic period', with near-complete coverage of the production of the 1820s. The library was assembled by a bibliomaniac ancestor of the present owner through contemporary purchases which involved both the local and the international book trade.[28]

4

The dissemination of British authors in vernacular translations on the Continent was a gradual, sometimes even slow, process influenced by many accidental factors.[29] Broadly speaking, it moved from west to east and from north to south. The central areas from which it radiated were France and, somewhat later, Germany. Translations into the minor languages of the Continent were strictly vernacular books distributed through the channels of the domestic trade. Those into Italian had a slightly wider currency and were occasionally read outside Italy.

Translations into French and German were disseminated both nationally and internationally and were read, sometimes in reprints, by linguistically proficient social or cultural elites in a variety of countries. As a special category, Latin translations of scholarly or scientific books – still produced in the latter decades of the eighteenth century – continued to circulate among learned readers as a matter of course.

There is as yet no reliable information about either the total number of translations (certainly amounting to many thousands) or their linguistic distribution. Bibliographical evidence suggests that the largest number of translations was published in the German-speaking area, followed by translations into French, chiefly issuing from France and the Netherlands.[30] The prevalence of German translations is to be attributed to the massive attempt, especially in the second half of the eighteenth century, to assimilate a foreign culture in all its manifestations and to use it as a stimulus in efforts to modernize the country.

28 Huber 2004; Garside, Raven and Schöwerling 2000. Catalogue: *Historische Bestände der Fürstlichen Bibliothek Corvey*: Herausgegeben von der Universitätsbibliothek der Universität-Gesamthochschule Paderborn, Paderborn, 1999, 8 vols. Quotation from Peter Garside, 'The significance of Corvey', www.shu.ac.uk/schools/cs/corvey/articles/Significance.html, accessed October 2005.

29 The reception of British authors on the Continent is currently being documented in a multi-volume series. See Shaffer 2002.

30 For French translations see Rochedieu 1948 and Streeter 1970; for German translations Price and Price 1934, 1955. A bibliographical catalogue documenting the publication of British authors in the German-speaking countries (1680–1810) is in preparation. On English translations of German and French novels, see Garside, Raven and Schöwerling 2000.

The vast number and extensive range of attractive titles that seemed to call for translation in the wake of the 'discovery' of English culture opened up a new field for continental publishers. English books had of course been translated before, but not until the middle decades of the eighteenth century did the publication of translations appear to be so culturally prestigious and financially promising. As a result, the first tentative moves were made towards international publishing – albeit cautiously and sometimes awkwardly in the absence of a legal framework to regulate business transactions and intellectual commerce across national boundaries. At least two of the leading continental publishers went to London, evidently to gain a first-hand impression of the English publishing scene: Charles-Joseph Panckoucke, the richest and most enterprising Paris publisher,[31] and Philipp Erasmus Reich, head of the House of Weidmann and doyen of the Leipzig book scene. Panckoucke appears to have been interested in possible translations. Reich went to see Samuel Richardson in order to elicit from him a volume of genuine letters as a counterpart, as it were, to the fictional letters of the novels.[32]

The number of publishers trying to bring British authors to the notice of continental readers is surprisingly large. French translations originated not only in Paris and Amsterdam, but also in the French provinces as well as in Belgium and in Switzerland. In Germany, traditionally regionalized, more than a hundred publishers produced at least some translations of British works, though the bulk came from a few publishers in Leipzig. Weidmann surpassed all others by producing several hundred translations. As a rule, translations of major works (in every field) were marketed by major publishers, though there were significant exceptions in the case of provincial booksellers.[33] Much depended on how titles suitable for translation came, or were brought, to the notice of the individual publisher.

Little is known as yet about the information networks of particular publishing firms. No doubt, many scholars and scientists who went to England from the late seventeenth century onwards[34] must have made suggestions to booksellers and may even have supplied copies of the works they recommended. Philipp Erasmus Reich certainly solicited academic advice. More formally, he placed paid agents or correspondents in Paris and London to find out about recent titles and to secure early copies of new books. One of these agents was

31 On Panckoucke's extensive business relations, see Tucoo-Chala 1977. His visit (or one of his visits?) to London is attested by Georg Forster in a letter of 22 Oct. 1776.

32 Fabian, *English authors and German publishers in the eighteenth century*, Lyell lectures 1993 (publication forthcoming).

33 Fabian 1976a, 126–37.

34 Selling 1990.

Johann Friedrich Schiller, a relative of the poet, who also seems to have negotiated translation agreements for Reich.[35] On the whole, however, direct contacts between English and continental publishers appear to have been few and far between. Occasionally, translators approached the authors they translated. Johannes Stinstra, the Dutch translator of Richardson, carried on a prolonged correspondence with him, which is a significant literary document in its own right.[36] Johann Arnold Ebert, the German translator and editor of Edward Young, reported to Young about his work and – a rare piece of information – about the sale of 5,000 copies of the *Night thoughts*.[37]

Perhaps the most noteworthy aspect of this publishing scene developing in the middle and later decades of the eighteenth century is the emergence of cultural intermediaries. Previously unknown as a link in the eighteenth-century 'communication circuit', they rapidly and firmly established themselves among men of letters on account of their expertise and their linguistic competence. Their intense efforts to familiarize their respective countries with the culture of England often gave the reception process a special impetus or a decisive turn. They were active in a variety of countries, but – coming from different walks of life – they did not form a homogeneous group. One of the early intermediaries was Justus van Effen in Holland, a member of the Royal Society (1715) and equally important both as a translator of key works and as a journalist spreading knowledge of English literature.[38] Later, Johann Joachim Eschenburg was perhaps the most informed and – as the owner of a large personal library – best-equipped intermediary in Germany.[39] He translated and interpreted major aesthetic treatises as well as the works of Shakespeare (1775–82), and instituted novel channels for disseminating information about new English books. The outstanding figure in this regard, however, is Giuseppe Baretti – the author, among other works, of a *Dictionary of the English and Italian languages* (1760) – who promulgated, widely and with sustained success, English culture in Italy and Italian culture in England.[40]

The corpus of vernacular translations varied from country to country, and the differences in size and content were considerable. Yet, each body of translations comprised, as a core element, English literature in the narrow sense of the word and, within limits, was composed of essentially the same authors and the same works. For the eighteenth-century continental reader 'English

35 Buchner 1874, 117–18.
36 Slattery 1969.
37 Fabian 1978a.
38 Pienaar 1929; Schorr 1982.
39 Meyen 1957; Paulin 1986.
40 Lubbers-Van der Brugge 1951.

literature' basically meant the contemporary literature of England with the inclusion of Shakespeare and Milton. The continental canon, if it can be so called, was, by and large, the familiar canon, albeit with certain modifications.

Early on, it included the obvious: the *Spectator*, soon imitated from Paris to Warsaw and from Stockholm via Hamburg and The Hague to Venice and Madrid;[41] *Robinson Crusoe*, adapted in many tales of shipwreck and survival, called *Robinsonaden*;[42] *Gulliver's travels*, admired alike by enchanted readers and imitative satirists;[43] and the *Essay on man*, appreciated as a poem, discussed as a philosophical treatise and finally celebrated in 1801 by Bodoni in a polyglot edition (English, Latin, Italian, French and German).[44] The canon also comprised Edward Young, whose *Night thoughts* took the entire Continent by storm,[45] James Thomson, whose *Seasons* was no less highly acclaimed (and adapted by van Swieten for Haydn's oratorio), and, of course, *Ossian*.[46] Many of the early translations were secondary translations, usually from French. The Abbé Desfontaines' rendering of *Gulliver's travels* (Paris, 1727), for instance, was reprinted in France until the beginning of the twentieth century and served as the basis of the first translations into Italian, Russian, Portuguese, Spanish and other languages.[47]

Milton, a favourite of literary critics and a model for aspiring epic poets, was available in translation from the middle of the century. Shakespeare, linguistically difficult, followed later. After crude translations of single Shakespearean dramas in the 1740s, collected works followed in later decades – the translations by Wieland and Eschenburg into German (1762 and 1775), and by Le Tourneur into French (1776) were the earliest. The classic German rendering by Schlegel and Tieck (from 1797 onwards) heralded the nineteenth-century translations of selected or complete works – repeatedly into German, but also into Danish (1807), Swedish (1820), Italian (Leoni, 1819) and other languages in the 1830s and later.[48]

The mid-eighteenth-century novelists were almost immediately (and in many cases repeatedly) translated into various languages – French and German as a matter of course, but also Italian, Spanish, Dutch, Danish, Swedish, Norwegian, Polish, Russian and others. These translations were

41 Rau 1980.
42 Ullrich 1898 (1977).
43 Real 2005. For German translations, see Fabian and Spieckermann 1997.
44 For German translations, see Fabian and Spieckermann 2000.
45 Forster 1970.
46 Gaskill 2004.
47 Real 2005.
48 For translations into German, see Blinn and Schmidt 2003.

marketed for a growing public of enthusiastic readers in editions which included both the precursor of today's paperback and the 'Anglophile' book with an engraved title page[49] or specially commissioned illustrations. Richardson's novels were perhaps even more highly esteemed on the Continent than in England, and Goldsmith's *Vicar of Wakefield* was universally liked and admired. *Tristram Shandy* produced peculiar continental manifestations of Shandyism as well as a number of respectable imitations.[50] There is a classic German translation by Johann Joachim Bode (1774) with a subscription list which uniquely documents the international readership of Sterne, and a classic Italian translation of the *Sentimental journey* by Ugo Foscolo (1813).

The mid-century novelists paved the way not only for the reception of the popular novel of the late eighteenth and early nineteenth century, but also for the popular drama of the period.[51] The growing number of fiction writers in England provided for an ever larger reading public on the Continent a kind of literary entertainment which was not obtainable from elsewhere. And theatregoers, even in distant Budapest, developed a taste for plays – sentimental or humorous – by George Colman the elder, Richard Cumberland and others. A note on the title page of a German novel, 'As good as translated from the English',[52] testifies to the high reputation which serious and trivial novels and plays of English origin then enjoyed – and have increasingly enjoyed ever since. Publishers old and new in both France and Germany were meanwhile sufficiently equipped to 'manufacture' translations, and by the end of the century enough ill-paid hack writers with a working knowledge of English were available as translators.

Apart from the continued presence of eighteenth-century writers, the early decades of the nineteenth century were dominated by Scott and Byron. Wordsworth, Coleridge and Keats did not receive immediate attention and were 'discovered' only much later. Shelley was not entirely ignored but, with the possible exception of *The Cenci*, not widely received either. Surprisingly, Thomas Moore's *Lalla Rooke* (1817) was soon translated into French, German, Polish and Swedish, to be followed somewhat later by extensive selections in French. Hardly any translations of the non-fiction prose writers appeared in our period apart from the adaptation of De Quincey's *Confessions* by Alfred de Musset (1828). Jane Austen's major novels came out in French (1811–24), but

49 An example is the German translation of *Joseph Andrews* (Berlin, Stettin, Leipzig, 1761).

50 De Voogd and Neubauer 2004.

51 Garside, Raven and Schöwerling 2000. The bibliography includes translations from continental languages into English. For France, see Streeter 1970; for Sweden, Ostman 1983.

52 Johann Timotheus Hermes, *Miss Fanny Wilkes* (1766).

considerably later in other languages, while those of Maria Edgeworth found early translators both in France and in Germany.

The major cause of the singular popularity of Scott was apparently the familiarity of the continental reader with the 'English' novel as a genre (including, as a favourite sub-genre, the Gothic novel). Scott's own proximity to French, German and Italian Romanticism was no doubt an additional factor. In 1822, Heinrich Heine reported from Berlin that everybody was reading Scott – 'from the Countess to the sempstress, and from the Count to the messenger'.[53] He could have been reporting from anywhere in Europe: the enthusiasm for Scott was ubiquitous. Translations of single novels into various languages (French, but also Polish and Russian, Spanish and Portuguese) abounded. Upon publication of *The pirate*, no fewer than four translations into German were immediately announced in Berlin. In due course, diverse collections of his novels, ballads and other works were compiled by a variety of publishers. Together with Shakespeare, Thomson and Byron – as well as Calderón, Tasso and Washington Irving – Scott was included in a mammoth *Taschenbibliothek der ausländischen Klassiker*, put together by the then-new and fast-rising publishing house of the brothers Schumann in Zwickau (Saxony), which specialized in the publication of foreign authors.[54] The bibliography of Scott in translation is hardly less intricate than that of Scott in English – and still awaits its compiler(s).

The vogue for Byron on the Continent is well known, and the contemporary publishing record of his works was unprecedented. No other English author was at once translated into so many languages and so extensively disseminated in translations and reprints. Single works – *Childe Harold's pilgrimage*, *The giaour*, *The bride of Abydos*, *The corsair* – as well as selections and collections of his works were made available in many languages, eventually including Armenian and Icelandic. Byron himself noted that his works sold better in Germany (where he was exorbitantly praised by Goethe), in France and in America than in England. Long after his death, the Byronic myth still hovered over most of the national literatures of Europe.[55]

In the total corpus of continental translations, literary works constituted the central element. They were read, or at least noted, everywhere, though not always at the same time, or with the same intent and purpose. In many cases – chiefly the countries of southern and eastern Europe – they were the dominant component in a vernacular corpus which included relatively few

53 *Briefe aus Berlin*, 13 Mar. 1822.
54 Schmidt 1902, 876–8.
55 R. Cardwell 2004.

non-belletristic works. In other countries – primarily France and Germany – literary translations, regardless of their number and significance, constituted only one category among many others. As a group, they were balanced, perhaps even outweighed, by translations of works that can only be called literary in a wider sense or that must be assigned to other fields altogether. The number of translations of British medical works, for instance, published in Germany during the eighteenth century amounts to nearly one thousand.[56]

Philosophers were translated – Locke, Berkeley, Shaftesbury, Hume and Adam Smith – together with lesser writers such as Thomas Burnet, William Derham or Adam Ferguson, at least into French and German, and often also into other languages.[57] Historians and major political writers were widely received, in particular those of the middle and late eighteenth century – Bolingbroke's *Letters on the study and use of history*, Edmund Burke's *Reflections on the revolution in France* and other works, William Robertson's *History of America* and, above all, Edward Gibbon.[58] The literature of travel and geographical exploration was of great interest on the Continent – not only were the reports of James Cook and other individual works translated, but large new collections of travel accounts were also compiled (alongside collections of popular novels). Technical literature was much in demand, especially in Germany. And the literature of science from Newton to Priestley was decidedly of interest to both experts and laymen.[59] In many cases, a lengthy introduction was added, annotation was supplied or a critical discourse was attached, so that the translation became an 'enriched' work, substantially different from the original.

The reception of this vast body of literature is in some respects more properly part of the history of individual scholarly and scientific disciplines than part of the history of the book. In some fields such as classical and oriental studies, the intellectual exchanges between England and scholarly centres on the Continent were particularly intense. Many details of this traffic in ideas across the Channel are also of interest to the book historian. Thus, for instance, the German translation of Robert Wood's *Essay on Homer* was published before the first English edition;[60] the 1714 Amsterdam edition of Newton's *Principia* was issued as the 'ultimate edition'; the earliest collection of Francis Bacon's works called *Opera omnia* appeared in 1665 in Frankfurt (later continental

56 Fabian and Spieckermann 1980.
57 See Price, chap. 45, below.
58 Norton 1940.
59 See Walters, chap. 46 and Topham, chap. 47, both below.
60 Fabian 1976b.

editions 1684–1730);[61] and after two Oxford editions of John Wallis's *Grammatica linguæ anglicanæ*, the 'third' (so numbered) was published in Hamburg, later to be followed by an edition with 'Londini & Lipsiæ' in the imprint.[62] Collectively, these and many other bibliographical items suggest that the English national printed archive was being opened up internationally, and that with the ascent of English to the lingua franca of the modern world the intellectual heritage of Britain was gradually appropriated as a common heritage – in Europe and, later on, in the world at large.

5

English-language printing and publishing on the Continent began in the sixteenth century and was, for a long time, largely confined to religious works. Many religious books originating in France and in the Netherlands were intended for British expatriates or for the British market. Colleges founded in Catholic countries on the Continent produced religious pamphlets as well as devotional and educational books. In France, these books came from Paris and two colleges near Calais, Douai (founded in 1568) and St Omer. In Belgium, Catholic material came from Brussels, Antwerp and Bruges. In Holland, Protestant exiles from England and Scotland established presses which produced bibles and other religious literature for (illegal) export to England. This trade, which often also included political tracts, flourished until the 1720s.[63]

Early in the eighteenth century, some émigré printers in Holland began to reprint English books for an emerging continental market. The most significant of these, Thomas Johnson – a Scot, active in The Hague (1705–28) and in Rotterdam (until his death in 1735) – reprinted, among other books, from 1710 onwards a series of contemporary London plays as 'A Collection of the Best English Plays' intended for sale on both the English and the continental market.[64] These reprints, traceable in Leipzig, appear to have been used, *inter alia*, by avant-garde learners of English, who had but few language-learning aids at their disposal. After the death of Johnson, Dutch reprinting – in contrast to Dutch bookselling – appears to have been confined for the rest of the eighteenth century almost exclusively to religious and commercial works.[65]

61 Gibson 1950, nos. 235–6, 239–43b.
62 Alston 1974, I, 7–8.
63 Mann 2000; Hoftijzer 2002.
64 Feather 1992.
65 Cf. Hoftijzer and Lankhorst, chap. 26, above.

In France, reprinting in the first half of the eighteenth century was largely determined by the activities of expatriate communities which had been founded earlier. Religious books, political tracts, grammars and dictionaries made up the bulk of their production. The number of reprints, small anyway, did not increase appreciably in the second half of the century. During the revolutionary period, political works were naturally of interest, and reprints of the writings of Tom Paine and Joel Barlow figured prominently. Of the approximately two hundred titles reprinted in the second half of the century, nearly half are literary or belletristic works. Reprints of *Paradise lost* (1754) mark the beginning of this phase, which reached an initial peak in the 1780s.

With few exceptions, the reprint publishers were based in Paris. The most prominent, the House of Barrois, published – occasionally in partnership with Pissot – some twenty classical or popular works, many in several editions, from Milton, Addison, Swift, Defoe, Gay, Fielding and Young to such favourites as Lady Mary Wortley Montagu and writers of popular minor fiction including Elizabeth Helme.[66] The neat duodecimo volumes were first printed by J. G. G. Stoupe, and later by the distinguished firm of Didot. At the turn of the century, Didot launched a reprint project of its own, the *éditions stéréotypes*, a series of French, Italian and English classics in small formats. The venture was a flop, and had to be discontinued in 1802 after the publication of only four English titles, although two, Lady Mary's *Letters* and *The vicar of Wakefield*, went into second editions. Apparently Didot had overestimated the market, which – for the time being – was saturated with small format reprints of Anglophile favourites. Perhaps the Didot partners had been ahead of their time: the era of stereotype editions was still to come.[67]

Reprinting in the German-speaking area presents a different picture, at least initially. An abridgement of John Strype's *Life of... Thomas Cranmer* (1725), a scholarly work, appears to have been the first substantial reprint. Above all, in the early eighteenth century, language-learning aids were required. Among these were familiar texts, such as Fénelon's *Télémaque*, in English translation (Jena, 1729; also reprinted in France). The earliest anthology came out in 1712, with a Latin title (*Selecta anglicana*) and a Latin preface. The most successful was *English miscellanies* (1734), compiled by John Tompson, who taught at the University of Göttingen and was given, *ad eundem*, the title of professor – the first professor of English. Throughout the century, anthologies

66 Cooper-Richet 2001.
67 Piton 1856.

proliferated – not only in Germany – and played a key role in familiarizing educated language learners with a large variety of predominantly literary texts.[68]

When, around the middle of the century, imports from England increased, reprinting also began on a larger scale. Major incentives for German (and other continental) publishers were the high price of imported books, which made them unaffordable for impecunious members of the intellectual elite, and the frequent unavailability of original editions even in the centres of the book trade. The leading Leipzig publishers abstained from reprinting to underline their protest against the unauthorized reprinting of their own books in southern Germany and Austria. As a result, most of the reprinters were smaller publishers, often operating in provincial places.

The first continental attempt to launch a comprehensive collection of English authors was made by Friedrich Nicolai, the Enlightenment publisher in Berlin, who created the German equivalent of the *Monthly Review* and published the first bibliography of late eighteenth-century British and American writers.[69] In 1762, Nicolai reprinted Warburton's edition of Pope as part of a series which was to include 'the Works of Milton, Addison, Thompson, Shakespeare, Young, Prior, Akenside, and other classical English Writers'.[70] Nicolai's grandiose plan to establish for the German reader a classical canon in reprint editions came to nothing. The market simply did not support the vision of the first German *Kulturverleger*. Another mammoth project devised in 1783 by the Göttingen publisher Johann Christian Dieterich – a reprint of Johnson's *English poets* at half the price of the original – likewise collapsed after the initial reprint of *Paradise lost*.

Consequently, the 1770s and 1780s were, with rare exceptions, a period of single-volume publishing, concentrating on works which could be linguistically managed even by those who had not yet fully mastered the new language. Some publishers tried to build up smaller series. Among them, the Richtersche Buchhandlung in Altenburg (Saxony) – which had already produced a deluxe quarto edition of the *Essay on man* (1755) as a showpiece for the Anglophile book lover – stands out for its number of reprints and for its pragmatic choice of titles. The Richters produced twenty-four octavo volumes (1770–88) of works well known to German readers, such as *The vicar of Wakefield*.[71] In Dresden the *Hofbuchdrucker* Georg Conrad Walther published, in addition to translations in a variety of languages, reprints of standard authors in

68 Fabian 1983a, 1985; Schröder 1989.
69 Fabian 1979b, 1983c.
70 See Bonnell, chap. 37, below.
71 Spieckermann 1979.

fashionably Frenchified typography (1789–1806),[72] and in Gotha Steudel and Keil assembled a multi-volume *English library* of 'authors in prose' and 'authors in verse' (1805–7). The international bookseller Rudolph Sammer in Vienna issued, as duodecimo paperbacks, a uniform *Collection of the best English authors in an exact – and corrected – edition* (1787–1801) which comprised the works of the most popular authors, from Pope to Henry Mackenzie, some with parallel German translation.

Dictionaries, grammars and other learning aids were produced in a number of countries which otherwise must be supposed to have depended on imported books or reprints produced elsewhere.[73] This would apply to Denmark and Sweden, where very few reprints were published. Production in Italy was slightly larger (about forty titles by various publishers), and included some literary and political works. The sumptuously produced Bodoni reprints of *The castle of Otranto* ('printed with Bodoni's characters for Edwards booksellr. of London'), of Gray's *Poems* and of Thomson's *Seasons* (1790–4) constituted a unique contribution from Italy.[74]

The most ambitious and successful series of eighteenth-century reprints was produced in Switzerland by the Basel printer and publisher Johann Jacob Thurneysen, who had previously reprinted the Kehl edition of Voltaire. It was announced as 'a collection of the principal English historians, philosophers and poets' and comprised more than 180 volumes published between 1787 and 1803.[75] The series was launched with a reprint of Gibbon's *Decline and fall of the Roman empire*, and ended abruptly, on account of Thurneysen's sudden death, with a reprint of Warton's edition of Pope. It included Bolingbroke and Hume, Ferguson and Robertson, as well as popular works of current interest such as Keate's *Account of the Pelew Islands* (1788). Sold at about a quarter of the price of the original editions, Thurneysen's reprints were nevertheless produced with exceptional care. He appears to have had expert advice on the selection of titles and on the choice of editions to be reprinted. His reprints were in a uniform octavo format, so as to give the impression of a 'library'. They were obviously proofread by native speakers, and followed the style and conventions of contemporary English typography. Gibbon, who was in Switzerland when Thurneysen's reprint of his work appeared, was impressed by its elegance and accuracy, but he also warned Cadell, his publisher, of the 'unexpected invasion of *foreign* pirates'.[76]

72 Vinz 1969.
73 For titles, see Alston 1974, II.
74 Brooks 1927.
75 Barber 1960; Germann 1973; Fabian 1983a.
76 Norton 1940, 96–7.

Thurneysen commanded an efficient distribution network. His agent for Germany was Karl Wilhelm Ettinger in Gotha (Thuringia), who marketed the reprints at the Leipzig fairs, so that they would ultimately reach central, northern and eastern Europe. In France, his associates were Pissot and Barrois in Paris and Levrault in Strasburg, who covered not only France but presumably also the Netherlands and perhaps Italy. Some reprints list Pissot and Levrault on their imprints as joint publishers. Finally, William Remnant, the English bookseller in Hamburg, included the reprints in his catalogues. All new titles were widely publicized and reviewed, and *in toto* the collection was praised as a 'sanctuary of good taste'.[77]

In the early nineteenth century, mass production of English reprints – impossible in the eighteenth century – became financially viable. There were more continental readers who could read English books, and more English readers (among them the new travellers) who appreciated inexpensive continental books. Thus, at the same time that the import of books from England increased, continental reprinting also entered a new phase. The European centre of activities shifted to Paris.[78] Established publishers (such as Théophile Barrois, Martin Bossange, Treuttel and Würz, Parsons and Galignani) and relative newcomers (Louis Claude Baudry and J.B.M. Baillière) shared the expanding market for English books. Most of them had contacts with London booksellers and branches in London, New York and elsewhere, while their Paris bookshops and reading rooms served as meeting places for English travellers. Bossange, who founded Bossange and Masson in London around 1815 (later Bossange, Barthès and Lowell), could boast the most extensive trade, with offices in New York, St Domingo, Montreal, Mexico, Rio de Janeiro, Madrid, Naples, Leipzig and Odessa.

English-language books from Paris were usually duodecimo editions of contemporary poets, novelists and playwrights – especially Byron, Thomas Moore, Scott[79] and James Fenimore Cooper – which were mostly marketed, sometimes under shared imprints, as series or collections. Baudry frequently shared imprints with Truchy and Barrois in his substantial *Collection of ancient and modern British authors*, while Didot and Galignani jointly published a *Collection of modern English authors*. Parsons and Galignani (who came from London to Paris in 1800) started, in 1804, *Parsons and Galignani's British library in verse and prose*, with more than sixty numbered volumes, mostly of classics.[80]

77 *Göttingische Gelehrte Anzeigen*, II, 1793 (26 Aug.), 1368.
78 The following account is largely based on Barber 1961 and Cooper-Richet 2001.
79 For reprints of Scott's works, see Todd and Bowden 1998.
80 On Galignani in particular, see Barber 1961; Barnes 1970.

Somewhat later, this was followed by a more prestigious series advertised as 'Standard modern novels and romances, beautifully printed in 12mo., in a bold and clear type, on vellum paper and illustrated by engravings from designs of eminent artists.' Set in Didot characters and issued in paper-covered boards, they cost, Galignani claimed, one-third to one-fifth of the London editions. From 1831 onwards, Galignani associated himself with Baudry, who henceforth issued his *Collection of ancient and modern British authors* under his own and under Galignani's imprint. The reprints were marketed not only throughout the Continent but also, in large numbers, in England and in the colonies, where they seriously impaired the sale of the original editions.[81]

In Germany, Scott was a special favourite with reprint publishers[82] – among them established firms such as Friedrich Vieweg in Brunswick or H.K.R. Brönner in Frankfurt who obviously wanted to cash in on the frenzy of the reading public. There were a number of multi-volume collections, in particular the huge *Pocket edition of English classics* (1819–31) published by Friedrich August Gottlob and Friedrich Schumann in Zwickau, who supplied their texts also in translation (partly undertaken in-house by Friedrich Schumann himself). Of the 232 volumes of mainly nineteenth-century authors (Byron, Thomas Moore), 156 contained the works of Scott, which in part appear to have been secondary reprints of Galignani reprints.[83] The companion series, *Pocket edition of the most eminent English authors of the preceding century* (1830–2), comprised the preferred eighteenth-century authors, among them Swift, Sterne, Goldsmith, Sheridan and 'Ossian'. While the Schumanns appear to have catered primarily or exclusively for the domestic market, Friedrich Campe in Nuremberg may have reached the American market with his cheap and flimsy *Pocket editions of classics* (more than fifty volumes, now difficult to trace)[84] – provided his imprint 'Nurnberg and New-York printed and published by Frederick Campe and Co.' is not a fake, as many other prestigious imprints were.[85]

When, in 1787, Gibbon warned of 'foreign pirates', hardly anybody would have suspected that within decades unauthorized foreign reprinting of English authors might become a serious problem. The conquest of the Continent by early eighteenth-century authors – Addison, Pope, Swift – did not cause any disturbances. The reading public was small, and knowledge of English

81 On the importation of French reprints into England, see St Clair 2004, 293–306.

82 For reprints, see Todd and Bowden 1998.

83 Todd and Bowden 1998, 853.

84 A list is to be found in the reprint of Thomas Campbell, *The pleasures of hope and other poems* (n.d.).

85 A reprint of *The Black Dwarf* carries the imprint 'Pest, Leipzig and London: printed for Otto Wigand, 1831'. Wigand was first active in Budapest, later in Leipzig, and does not appear to have had any connections with London.

minimal. In contrast, the enthusiastic reception of British writers on the Continent towards the end of the eighteenth century was potentially dangerous. The number of authors had rapidly increased, and the circle of readers had greatly expanded. The triumph of Byron and Scott in Europe occurred at a time when a new mass reading public, much smaller than today's but considerably larger than the educated public of the later eighteenth century, asked for 'English' reading matter that was inexpensive and readily available. Accordingly, the publishing system and its legal basis urgently needed readjustment. In 1837, a German publisher – Christian Bernhard Tauchnitz – ushered in a new era of international publishing by founding in Leipzig, at the age of twenty, a publishing house which secured for itself, by individual contracts with authors or publishers, the right to publish English books for sale on the Continent. The modern phase in the ubiquitous and continuous European presence of English literature had begun.

28

The British book in North America

JAMES N. GREEN

The colonial period

Throughout the colonial period, most books read in America were British, as was to be expected in a mercantilist colonial system; however, in the first half of the eighteenth century, the London book trade paid little attention to the colonies.[1] In the second half of the century the book trade awoke to the potential of the American market, just as it was slipping away.

In his *Autobiography* Benjamin Franklin recalled that

> At the time I establish'd myself in Pennsylvania [i.e. in the 1720s], there was not a good Bookseller's Shop in any of the Colonies to the Southward of Boston. In New York and Philadelphia the Printers were indeed Stationers, they sold only Paper, etc., Almanacs, Ballads, and a few common School Books. Those who lov'd Reading were oblig'd to send for their Books from England.[2]

This passage highlights all the important features of American book culture at the beginning of the eighteenth century. First, nearly all the books in the colonies were British, and apart from the staples – Franklin could have added Bibles, Testaments, and psalters to the list – most books were either brought in by immigrants or ordered from London by their readers. Very few gentlemen dealt directly with London booksellers, however; instead they used agents with whom they had personal acquaintance and credit, and who often had to act through other agents to locate, pay for and ship the desired books. Colonials without an agent in London had to find someone better connected at home who was willing to vouch for them.[3]

Another feature highlighted by Franklin was the uniformity of the staple reading material available in all the colonies in the early eighteenth century. In

1 See *HBA* I.
2 Franklin 1986, 63.
3 For the use of agents, see Wolf 1974 and Raven 2002b. For books immigrants brought with them, see Wolf 1988.

most places, the book trade was indeed a subsidiary of the stationery business. If books were not an absolute necessity for a civil society, paper, ink and quills were. For many people the most important British book was a blank account book. Every town and even most villages had a store that stocked stationery along with a wide variety of other imported merchandise, and where stores were absent, pedlars plied the roads. Books, if they were to be found at all, were part of this stock and they came from the same source: psalters, school-books and almanacs from the Stationers' Company English Stock, and Bibles and Testaments from the King's Printer. Throughout the eighteenth century these accounted for the bulk of all book imports.[4]

For the most part these staple books were imported by merchants who exchanged American produce – furs, tobacco or sugar, depending on the colony – for a long list of manufactured goods, with books and stationery always at the bottom. These merchants were used to giving the kind of long credit required by planters, because of the seasonal nature of their livelihood and because of the length and circuitous nature of ocean voyages; whereas most stationers and booksellers offered only six months to wholesale customers. That was barely enough time for the American merchant to receive the goods, much less sell them and collect money, assuming he gave credit to his customers in turn. The only proper bookshops outside Boston in Franklin's youth were those kept by printers William Bradford in New York and his son Andrew in Philadelphia, who, as Franklin observed, knew little more than ordinary merchants about importing books.

What, then, were the 'good Booksellers' of Boston like? From the anecdotes of John Dunton we know that the trade in imported books was so lively in the 1680s that it was worth his while to make a journey across the ocean to cultivate his bookseller customers.[5] The Boston booksellers sold a wide assortment of imported books by wholesale and retail, but more and more often – from the 1680s on – they also published books at their own risk or in partnership with others of their trade. When they published books, they put up all the capital and employed printers and binders as mere manufacturers. With a populace as literate as any on earth, and several clergymen who wrote more voluminously than all but a handful of English divines, the Boston booksellers had plenty of books to publish and plenty of readers to sell them to. What made the Boston stores 'good' from Franklin's point of view, then, must have been their similarity to those of London, with a mix of imported books with books

4 *HBA* 1, 26–45.
5 Dunton 1818, 90–137.

written and published locally.[6] That the booksellers of Boston attempted to emulate their colleagues in London is perhaps not remarkable, but in no other colony was the book culture so deep that bookselling on such a scale could even be contemplated.

The early Boston booksellers who were active publishers were not deeply involved in importing books, or so the scanty evidence suggests. Where we have information about their stock, their own publications outnumber imported books. This is due partly to the simple fact that the books they published remained on their hands for years, whereas the books they imported were mostly single copies – or at the most a dozen of a popular title – that sold quickly, even immediately if they were specially ordered. The earliest surviving Boston bookstore stock list is the 1700 estate inventory of Michael Perry, who like most of the booksellers occupied a shop or stall measuring less than forty square feet under the Town House. His inventory consisted of some 191 titles, of which 28 are Boston imprints. If we count copies, however, local imprints outnumber imports seven to one, because he had hundreds of copies in sheets of titles in which he had a share.[7] When Franklin left Boston in 1723 there were, judging from imprints in books they published, about ten booksellers in Boston. The most eminent of these was Daniel Henchman. His business papers survive, and they show that his printing and bookselling business was indeed very large, but he imported very little. When he wanted English books he bought them from his son-in-law, Thomas Hancock, a bookseller soon to become one of Boston's richest merchants.[8]

Hancock imported some of his books from the prominent bookseller Thomas Longman, that is, until 1737, when another London bookseller, Thomas Cox, sent an agent to Boston with a consignment consisting of 'eight trunks and a Box or too of Books'. This modest cargo was enough (if Hancock's complaints to Longman are to be believed) to glut the largest book market in the colonies. But Hancock obtained only some of his books from Longman. He imported staple books along with stationery from a London paper merchant named Rowe. In 1736 he ordered from Rowe a thousand Bibles at 2*s*. 4*d*. a copy, 'well bound in Calves Leather Claspt and with New England Psalms'. In London as well as in the colonies, much of the transatlantic book trade was in the hands of merchants.[9]

6 For Boston bookshops generally, see Ford 1917; Littlefield 1900.
7 Amory 1993b.
8 *HBA* I, 319–25.
9 Baxter 1945, 41–2.

The records of book exports from England suggest that despite Boston's lively book publishing trade, the overwhelming majority of books owned by early eighteenth-century New Englanders were imported. In the period 1701 to 1711, an annual average of about 7,500 pounds by weight of books was exported from London to New England.[10] In that same decade on average seven extant books of a hundred pages or more[11] were published annually in Boston. If we assume editions of 750 copies and an average weight per book bound of half a pound (both surely on the high side), the annual average weight of locally produced books was about 2,600 pounds, about a third of imports. In the 1720s the average annual weight of imports more than doubled, but the number of books of a hundred pages or more produced annually in Boston rose only by half. The proportion of imported books seems to have been increasing.[12]

In other colonies the preponderance of imported books was still greater. Boston publications were seldom transported beyond Massachusetts Bay, and in Philadelphia and New York the Bradfords published a book only every year or two. Yet the middle and southern colonies accounted for 44 per cent of all North American book imports in the first quarter of the eighteenth century.[13] Outside Boston, as Franklin observed, virtually all books were British.

Benjamin Franklin's move from Boston to Philadelphia in the 1720s was the first in a chain of events that led to a new organization of the book trades in all the colonies. He not only transformed Philadelphia from a scene of monopoly to one of intense competition, he also exported his entrepreneurial ideas to other colonies. Precisely because he understood too much competition was worse than too little, he encouraged his journeymen to move to other towns when it came time for them to set up business on their own. To prevent his protégés from becoming his competitors, he made them his partners, setting them up in business in half a dozen towns from New Haven to Antigua, wherever there was an opportunity to establish a similar jack-of-all-the-book-trades business. Thus, by 1750 most of the printers in the middle and southern

10 Barber 1976, 219.

11 Defining a book as containing a hundred or more pages is arbitrary, but is simply meant to exclude the pamphlets, broadsides, job printing and newspapers that made up a large proportion of the output of the colonial press, but surely a very small part of the book exports noted in Customs records. The count of imprints is based on the North American Imprints (NAIP) database, not counting imprint variants.

12 Raven 1997b, 33 and 2000a, 183–7 demonstrate how problematic these figures are, but if anything they understate the total quantity of books exported. Amory in *HBA* 1, 197–8 argues that because editions printed in the colonies were sold over many years and may not have sold at all, their numbers cannot be directly compared with book imports. While this may be true, his complex calculations do not seem to change the general order of magnitude, which is what I am comparing here.

13 Barber 1976, 219–20.

colonies were either protégés of Franklin's or emulators of his way of doing business.[14] Meanwhile the generation of Boston booksellers that flourished during the Puritan ascendancy was dying off, along with many of the prolific divines who had kept them so well employed. By 1750 almost all the book publishing and importing was in the hands of printers, and the London-style bookseller who employed printers as mere manufacturers was a thing of the past.[15]

The early Boston booksellers very seldom expended their capital in printing their own editions of books they could get at less risk, in smaller quantities and in greater variety from London. The new generation of printer-booksellers was somewhat less reluctant to attempt to compete with imports. This trend may have been accelerated by the lapse of licensing in England and the passage of the Copyright Act of 1710 (8 Anne c. 21), which established the author's right to literary property but also set limits to it. The Copyright Act was never enforced abroad, but nevertheless most American printers appear to have observed its spirit if not its letter. The reprinting of English properties at first happened only sporadically and often in circumstances where copyright status was in doubt. For example, the first American edition of the Brady and Tate Psalms was printed in New York by William Bradford in 1706 as part of a Book of Common Prayer commissioned by Trinity Church, with Queen Anne's licence facing the title page. He reissued it in 1710, just after the Copyright Act was passed, and thereafter the metrical psalms were reprinted freely in America.[16] However, the English Bible and its parts were not reprinted openly, most probably because the patent that reserved it to the King's Printer was more respected than the statutory law of copyright. Simple economics must also have played a role, however; if Bibles could be imported from London for 2*s.* 4*d.* per copy well bound with clasps, it is difficult to see how an American printer could beat that price. It is also doubtful that colonial buyers would have chosen an American edition of unproven accuracy over an authorized printing supposedly free of errors and unorthodox interpolations. Despite all these inhibitions to printing the Bible in the colonies, several editions appear to have been printed, though no copies have been located. They presumably had false London imprints that headed off the threat of prosecution and any suspicion of textual unreliability.[17]

14 J. N. Green 2000, 270–79.

15 Thomas 1970, 213.

16 McAnear 1949.

17 For Franklin's *c.*1745 New Testament, see Miller 1974, no. 368. Thomas 1970, 103 claimed a Bible and a New Testament were printed in Boston in about 1750.

It is sometimes difficult to know why some British properties were reprinted in the colonies and others were not. Some seventeenth-century staples, such as Baxter's *Call to the unconverted*[18] may have been presumed to be in the public domain. Books first published shortly before the copyright law was enacted seem to have been considered fair game as well, such as Jabez Earle's *Sacramental exercises*,[19] and Robert Russel's *Seven sermons*.[20] American publishers may have felt that copyright died with an author. Popular devotional works by Matthew Henry and Elizabeth Rowe began to be reprinted a year or two after their deaths in 1714 and 1737 respectively. Pope's *Essay on man* was first printed in America in 1747, three years after his death. In other cases the publisher's disregard for the law was flagrant, as with Franklin's edition of Samuel Richardson's *Pamela* (2 vols., 1742–3).

The first printers in Canada came from Philadelphia and Boston, and they brought the bookselling business as it was practised in those towns with them.[21] The first recorded book exports from England to Canada were to Nova Scotia in 1750, five years after Louisburg fell to New England troops. In 1751 Bartholomew Green, son and grandson of Boston printers, set up a short-lived press in Halifax, and this first shipment of books may have been an order placed in advance of his arrival. Green died without printing anything that survives and was replaced by his Boston partner John Bushell, who began the *Halifax Gazette* and possibly ran a bookstore as well, since more book exports are recorded for 1752–4.[22] In 1764, the year after France ceded New France to England, a printing office was established in Quebec by two young printers from Franklin's orbit, William Brown and Thomas Gilmore.[23] Again, a small importation of books from England is recorded the year before, but in 1764 quite sizeable imports began. Gilmore died young, but Brown's Scottish nephews Samuel and John Neilson continued the business into the next century. The first printer in Montreal (and the first French printer in Canada) was Fleury Mesplet, who was working in London when he was recruited to come to Philadelphia in 1774. In 1776, he proceeded to Montreal with a commission from the Continental Congress to print a newspaper representing their interests. He was far more active as a book publisher than his colleagues in Halifax

18 First published London, 1658, reprinted Boston, 1717 and 1731.
19 First published London, 1708, reprinted in Boston, 1715, 1725 and 1729.
20 Reprinted in Boston with edition statement reading 'Licens'd & enter'd according to order' in 1701, 1705 (twice) and 1709; thenceforth reprinted in Boston without license in 1715, 1718, 1727, etc.
21 On the business of printing and bookselling in Canada in the eighteenth and early nineteenth centuries, see Fleming, Gallichan and Lamonde 2004.
22 Barber 1976, 222.
23 Thomas 1970, 597.

and Quebec, and much less of a book importer.[24] As in the older British North American colonies, the trade in imported books to Canada was not confined to printers. General merchants soon were adding Bibles, prayer books and primers to their orders for imported dry goods and hardware. In Halifax most of those books came from London but in Quebec about half the books were imported from France for Catholic readers.[25]

At the mid-point of the eighteenth century, most colonial printers were native to America, and had no direct knowledge of, or family ties to, the book trade in London. Because they were often preoccupied with newspaper and jobbing printing, bookselling was only a sideline for them, but an expanding one, and their lack of personal contacts in the London trade was an increasing handicap. By the same token the London booksellers paid little attention to the colonial trade, much of which was in the hands of merchants anyway. They offered the same discounts and credit terms as they gave their provincial customers, and those terms made the business unattractive to colonial printers. Without knowing the printers, or even the men who endorsed their bills of exchange, the London booksellers saw no reason to take an extra risk. The difficulty of dealing with London booksellers affected the calculus of risk and reward that led some printers to reprint their own editions of popular English books. This state of affairs began to change after 1750, and once again Franklin played an important role.

The first sustained and profitable relationship between a London bookseller and an American printer-bookseller was William Strahan's with Franklin. Part of the reason it worked was that they were both printers – Strahan was the only London printer who was also a major bookseller and copyright owner – and both held lofty views of their profession and its power to make a better world. Even though they did not meet for years, they developed a warm epistolary friendship. The human link between the two men was David Hall, a journeyman of Strahan's whom he loved as a brother. Hall went to America in 1744 to be Franklin's foreman, and the two men got on so well that when Franklin retired in 1748 he made Hall his partner. According to the terms of their partnership agreement, Hall was to share the profits on printing, but whatever he made by bookselling was his alone. When Hall took over Franklin's book stock, it was valued at only £681, but from then until his death in 1772, he imported more than £30,000 worth of books and stationery from Strahan, plus some 20,000 Bibles and three tons of books from Strahan's Edinburgh friends, Hamilton and Balfour.[26] Whereas Franklin had occasionally reprinted English

24 Fleming 2002, 232, 243.
25 Black 2004, 121.
26 See Beavan and McDougall, chap. 16, above.

properties, including *Pamela* and a number of psalters, Hall never did. He was lukewarm in his opposition to the Stamp Act, which all the other printers strongly opposed, and when the non-importation movement began in the late 1760s, he was the only Philadelphia printer who was not a supporter. Though he carried on Franklin's printing office, his talent and his financial interest kept him focused on bookselling. Until the 1760s, he was by far the largest book importer in the colonies.[27]

Not long after David Hall took over his bookshop, Franklin wrote to Strahan that Thomas Osborne was 'endeavoring to open a Correspondence in the Plantations for the Sale of his Books'. Osborne had sent parcels to Franklin's protégés in Philadelphia, New York and Williamsburg, and having seen two of the invoices, Franklin thought the books 'very high charg'd'.[28] This marks the beginning of an ever-increasing interest on the part of the London trade in the American market. At issue was not only the invoiced prices of the books, but also the discount and the time allowed for payment. Some exporters invoiced the books at the full London retail price; others allowed a small discount, perhaps 6 per cent, which barely covered the cost of transport and insurance. In the middle colonies it was normal for the importer to set his retail price in local currency at twice the sterling invoice price. Since local currency was worth about two-thirds sterling, this rule of thumb allowed for a small profit to the importer, and left room for a discount on copies sold wholesale.[29] Thus, the Americans were eager to do business with anyone who offered lower invoice prices.

In 1755 David Hall learned that the Williamsburg bookseller William Hunter was buying books from the London bookseller James Rivington at a discount of 16 per cent off the London retail prices, plus a year's credit and the privilege of returning unsold books. The discount alone brought the price below what Strahan himself paid at wholesale. Strahan explained to Hall how Rivington was able to offer these unheard-of terms. First, he hired low-paid printers in the provinces and in Scotland to pirate all the most popular literary properties, using inferior paper in smaller formats. Second, he marked down a few of the most popular books as loss leaders; on less popular books his prices were actually higher than usual. Third, he sent without order many old, unsaleable books, which Strahan called 'books of no price' or 'waste paper books', which he got for little or nothing. Strahan believed Rivington was exporting more than all the other London booksellers together. He reported

27 J. N. Green 2000, 276–9; Harlan 1966, 1–14; 1976.
28 Franklin 1961, Franklin to William Strahan, 19 Oct. 1748.
29 J. N. Green 2000, 265, 282, 575–6 n. 37.

that 'the Booksellers are about contriving some Plan, by which they will make a difference in the Price of those Books that are sold to go abroad, and those for Home Consumption, in order to save the Trade to America from falling into the Hands of a Man who will stick at nothing to accomplish his Designs'. By his unorthodox methods, Rivington drove the London trade for the first time to adjust its export terms to make the business worthwhile to American booksellers.[30]

Then in 1760 Rivington emigrated to America, opening shops in New York, Philadelphia and Boston. He proclaimed in advertisements that he was 'the only London book-seller in America', and indeed publishers were sending him books as soon as they were published, without waiting for specific orders. While David Hall never listed more than a dozen novels in his catalogues, Rivington's 1762 catalogue listed 782 'Books of Entertainment, &c.', and the entry for Rousseau's *Nouvelle Heloise* included an eleven-page extract from the preface that was in effect a primer on how to read a novel. Best of all, his prices were low, almost as low as in London. He announced that he was better acquainted with the prices and characters of books than any American bookseller, that the booksellers of America did not know how to deal with the London trade, and that their customers were being robbed as a result. The high point of his American career was his 1768 edition of the poems of Charles Churchill, sold by subscription. He secured 2,200 subscribers from all over the colonies, though primarily from Virginia, Maryland and the West Indies. He had intended to reprint the book in America, and had he done so it would have been the most valuable property ever to be pirated there. (Churchill's copyrights were rumoured to be worth £3,000.) In the end, he imported an entire authorized edition (the third) in sheets and bound them in blue boards, with a list of the American subscribers and a title page with the imprint 'Printed in the Year 1768'.[31] This was yet another example of Rivington doing business in America as if he were in London. At least since Michael Perry's time, the general practice of American booksellers was to import their books already bound, usually in plain trade bindings of calf or sheep.[32] At about the same time, Robert Bell, a Scot recently arrived in Philadelphia, began pirating valuable London properties in earnest. By

30 Cochrane 1964, 80–7; Stiverson and Stiverson 1983, 154–8.

31 Hewlett 1966; Botein 1983, 73–81.

32 Many American booksellers imported books ready bound, including Michael Perry (Amory 1993b), William Hunter (Stiverson and Stiverson 1983, 145) and David Hall (Harlan 1966, 6). Reilly 1983, 88, 105, claimed Jeremy Condy imported books in sheets, but all the binding accounts in his account book at the American Antiquarian Society are for his own publications. Bennett 2004 argues that in the eighteenth century most books were retailed already bound in England.

means of a continental subscription campaign he published Robertson's *History of the reign of Charles V* in three volumes octavo (1770) and Blackstone's *Commentaries on the laws of England* in four volumes octavo (1771–2). American and English literary culture had never been so close.[33]

Historians have argued that the closer the colonies came to breaking with England, the closer they came culturally; and the expansion of the book trade with America in the second half of the century bears this out.[34] Until 1748 (the year Hall took over Franklin's bookshop) the growth in book imports roughly kept pace with the increase in population of the colonies. Over the next twenty years, however, annual imports rose fourfold, from about 35,000 pounds in 1748 to almost 140,000 pounds in 1768, while the population increased by only 80 per cent. In the final seven years of trade before the Revolution, imports averaged 165,000 pounds with a high of more than 230,000 pounds in each of the years 1771 and 1772.[35] By then more books were exported from England to the American colonies than to Europe and all the rest of the world combined, with exports to America accounting for 5 per cent of the total English annual book production.[36] In 1772, thirty-nine books of a hundred or more pages were published in the colonies. Allowing an average of a pound weight per volume (these include several folio law books) and estimating the average edition at 750, the total would have weighed 29,250 pounds, an eighth of the weight of imports that year. Though rough, these figures suggest that even as American book production increased over the course of the colonial period, the quantity of books imported grew faster and was never at any point exceeded by native production.[37] Books in colonial America were overwhelmingly British.

Early national period

In the years following the Revolutionary War, a vigorous American book publishing enterprise emerged; paradoxically, Great Britain supplied both the initial capital that got the trade off the ground and the texts that Americans printed. The war had not changed the basic fact that London was the centre of English-language book culture and America was on the periphery. The primary goal of the American book trade was to replace British imports

33 J. N. Green 2000, 282–91.
34 Greene 1988, chap. 8 sums up this argument.
35 Imports from Scotland added at least another 10,000 pounds a year from 1743 to 1757. See McDougall 1988, 16–17; 1990b.
36 Barber 1976, 223–4; Raven 2000b, 183–4.
37 Imprint statistics from the North American Imprints (NAIP) database.

with its own editions of the same texts. This turned out to be a difficult goal to achieve, and progress towards it was fitful.

During the war, hardly any large books were printed – with the notable exception of the Bible printed in 1782 by Robert Aitken in Philadelphia. This was the first full Bible with an American imprint. Aitken claimed he was nearly ruined by the venture, both because he was paid in worthless paper money and because the advent of peace precipitated an avalanche of cheap imported Bibles. British merchants continued to dump books in America for the rest of the 1780s as the American economy slumped. Several booksellers sent agents with large stocks of books. Some of them returned home as soon as they sold their books for whatever they could get, but others stayed on.

In 1784 Thomas Dobson arrived in Philadelphia from Scotland with a large stock of books, which immediately made him one of the more substantial booksellers in town. Within a few years, however, he embarked on publishing reprints of the very books he had been importing. His first major venture was an American edition of Adam Smith's *Wealth of nations* in 1788. To undersell imports – both the original London quarto and the pirated Dublin octavo – he reprinted in duodecimo. In 1789 he began reprinting the new edition of the *Encyclopaedia Britannica* (with American material added) as it arrived part by part from Edinburgh. When completed in 1798 it totalled eighteen volumes with more than 400 engraved plates, and was by far the largest book yet published in America. This very risky venture required large reserves of capital to sustain it through the ups and downs of a turbulent and immature economy. The source of Dobson's capital was a mystery until recently when Warren McDougall discovered that his original stock of British books was provided by his erstwhile employer, the Edinburgh bookseller Charles Elliot. Elliot wanted his lavish backing to remain a secret so his protégé would be more easily accepted in America. Dobson sold the stock and put the returns into publishing, but he refused to pay Elliot back despite increasingly desperate appeals. His debt rose to tens of thousands of pounds. Elliot died in 1790 in considerable financial difficulty, in part due to Dobson's default. Thus Elliot unwillingly supplied the capital for the largest American publishing venture of the Federal era.[38]

Another emigrant of 1784 was Mathew Carey of Dublin, a radical Catholic printer forced to flee because of his newspaper's opposition to British rule. With support from the likes of Franklin and Lafayette he began a newspaper in

38 McDougall 2004. Dobson finally settled his debt with Elliot's estate in 1805.

Philadelphia and then in 1786 launched *The American Museum*, the leading Federalist magazine during the first Washington administration. In 1792 he began using his extensive political connections to obtain the credit necessary to import books from several London booksellers, as well as from his Dublin associates.[39] Much like Dobson, he used imported books as capital for publishing reprints, more than $50,000 worth in 1794 and 1795. When they did not sell as quickly as he had hoped, he simply suspended payments to his British creditors. This cut off much of his supply of imported books, but he had determined henceforth to be the publisher of the books he sold. His motivation was political as well as economic. Like Dobson and the other reprinters of the Federal era, he advertised his reprints of popular British books in patriotic 'buy American' terms. At the same time the Federalist party was splitting over Jay's Treaty of 1795, which was meant to repair trade relations with Britain. Carey sided with the anti-British faction, which made it easier for him to defy the London booksellers. To sell off his vast stock of reprints, he exchanged his books with those published by other like-minded booksellers, and he hired the famous travelling book salesman Mason Locke Weems to gather subscriptions and open bookshops in the towns of Virginia and Maryland. Thus he succeeded in diverting much of the region's book trade from Britain to Philadelphia, and he fostered an American publishing trade based on reprints.[40]

Isaiah Thomas took another path to publishing, not through bookselling but through printing. During the war he had moved inland from Boston to Worcester, Massachusetts, where his business was much like a colonial printer's. After the war, he imported $9,000 worth of type from Caslon and others on credit extended to him by Worcester merchants. He intended to use the type to print original books by American authors, but commissions did not materialize.[41] Since he had little capital besides his type, he chose the smallest books there were, the children's books published in London by John Newbery. These were fantastically profitable sheet for sheet; he sold 119 editions in the 1780s, easily paying for the type.[42] By 1789, he felt firm ground under his feet, and he switched from these trifles to the largest and most serious book of all, the Bible, no edition of which had appeared in America since Aitken's.

39 Carey's business correspondence is in the Lea and Febiger Papers, Historical Society of Pennsylvania; for imports from Dublin, see Kinane 1994, 321.
40 J. N. Green 1987; Remer 1996; Green forthcoming.
41 Shipton 1948, 45–6; Updike 1962, II, 157.
42 Nichols 1912, 132–3.

Many American printers felt that some protection analogous to the British Bible patent was needed. On 10 January 1789, Hugh Gaine and four other New York printers sent a circular letter to all the trade calling for a joint petition to Congress for protection or financial support for an American Bible printing company that would share the risk and reward of supplying the nation.[43] This was the first proposal for national co-operation in the book trade, but it had precisely the opposite effect. The letter touched off a chain reaction of Bible proposals. Within days, William Young and Mathew Carey, both of Philadelphia, and Isaac Collins of Trenton, New Jersey all announced their intention to print Bibles, a group of New Yorkers announced a folio and a quarto, and Gaine himself ordered type for a duodecimo already composed from England, which he proposed to keep standing. Shortly thereafter, Thomas announced Bibles in all three formats. Where there had been none, now there were nine Bibles announced as in press.

In 1790, Congress passed a Copyright Act that protected only books written by American citizens and residents, a step that neatly evaded the Bible problem and set the stage for a non-monopolistic reprint trade characterized by a constant tension between co-operation and competition. Carey and Thomas became the principal Bible publishers – with Carey even keeping the quarto in standing type – and they more or less divided the country between them. With this capital base, they became the leading reprinters as well. In 1802, Carey convened the first national 'literary fair' in New York to which fifty publishers came.[44] Even at this early stage, most of the publishers had given up printing and were hiring others to manufacture books for them, a development that marked the end of the domination of the American book trade by printers. Out of these fairs grew a system of self-regulation modelled on Dublin's, called 'courtesy of the trade', whereby the first to advertise the reprint of a title had the right to it;[45] others could have a share in the edition in exchange for their own publications. In 1804, the booksellers of Boston published a *Catalogue of all the books printed in the United States*, listing 1,339 American editions in print, most of which were reprints, though some disguised the fact by 'Americanizing' text in order to obtain a copyright.

In 1810, some Philadelphia printers summed up the state of the book trade:

> For many years after the peace of 1783, books could be imported into the United States and sold cheaper than they could be printed here and indeed

43 The unique copy of the circular letter is at the Library Company of Philadelphia.
44 Nichols 1924.
45 See Benson, chap. 17 above.

> until 1793 nothing like a competition with English Printers and Booksellers could be maintained. The war then raging in Europe and added duty on paper made some difference but it was not until the union of Ireland and England (in 1801) that a decided advantage was ascertained to exist.[46]

In the absence of Customs data, it is difficult to confirm how decided this advantage was. For example, members of the book trade ceased importing Bibles, but general merchants continued to do so. The Union of Ireland and England may have stopped the Irish reprint trade, but Patrick Byrne of Dublin emigrated in 1802 with a stock of books in sheets as large as any in America.[47] Certain types of books continued to be imported because the demand was too small to justify reprinting: novels by unknown writers; books in foreign languages; professional literature in law, medicine, theology and the sciences; luxury books such as fine illustrated books, books in fine bindings, fancy pocket-books, and albums. Most large libraries and many private gentlemen continued to order books from London, but almost every book that had a good sale or even a good review in England was reprinted in America.

During the Revolution, book imports to Canada (and to Florida as well) had risen steeply, suggesting that books were being shipped from there to the rebellious colonies. After the war, Canada was of course still subject to British copyright law, and so a reprint industry did not take root there, though just after the war a couple of Canadian printers launched trial balloons to see whether reprinting would be allowable.[48] These took the form of proposals for publication by subscription of Buchan's *Domestic medicine* at Quebec in 1786 and Burns's *Poems* at Charlottetown in 1789, but neither edition was ever printed.[49] At least until the 1820s, the press in English Canada confined itself to newspapers, government printing, almanacs, sermons and other local fare. All other books were imported either from England, or – increasingly – from the United States, where they were considerably cheaper. Some American publishers offered Canadian booksellers discounts of 30–40 per cent, which alleviated the burden of a 30 per cent duty. This made American reprints of British books competitive with British imports, at least in some regions, and it encouraged Canadians to buy American editions of American authors as well, notwithstanding frequent warnings from civil and religious authorities about their pernicious effects.[50] The legal and economic barriers to book production

46 *The Evening Star*, Philadelphia, 30 Oct. 1810, quoted in Nichols 1924, 84.

47 Byrne 1802.

48 For Canada, see Fleming, Gallichan and Lamonde 2004.

49 Tremaine 1952, nos. 476, 584. Black 2004, 124 notes that in 1789 Buchan's *Domestic medicine* was on sale in Halifax at less than it sold for in Scotland; this must have been the 1784 Philadelphia edition.

50 Parker 1985, chaps. 2 and 3.

in Canada before the 1820s were much stronger than they had been in the lower thirteen colonies before 1776. Even reprints of French books were uncommon, despite the fact that they were legal to reprint and more difficult to import. Up to 1810 reprints of French books were almost entirely limited to primers, elementary school-books, catechisms and prayer books that were tailored to the use of local schools and religious orders. French translations of English books were actually more common than reprints of books originally published in France.[51] In the late 1820s and 1830s, a few editions of the Bible and reprints of some standard English school-books proved the viability of domestic book production, although some of these books were printed from imported stereotype plates, and some were printed in the United States with the names of Canadian publishers in the imprint.[52]

After the war of 1812, the poems of Scott and Byron and, later, the Waverley novels were so popular in America that each new title was reprinted almost simultaneously in Boston, New York and Philadelphia, often within days of receipt of the first copy or even purloined advance sheets. At this hectic pace, no one could afford to wait and see if someone else had advertised the title, and courtesy of the trade went by the board. The Philadelphia firm of Mathew Carey, now run by his son Henry Charles, urged a revision of the rule, whereby the first to publish any work by a given author had the right to all subsequent works.[53] Carey's chief antagonist was the Harper firm in New York. The brothers Harper started as book printers after the war of 1812, but they were so entrepreneurial that they began to propose books to the trade instead of waiting for the booksellers to start the ball rolling. They would write to all the booksellers in and sometimes out of New York, saying, 'we propose to reprint such-and-such; how many copies will you take at the cost of paper and print?' It was a short step from this to publishing. Most other publishers had long ago given up doing their own printing, but the Harper brothers reunited printing and publishing, which gave them an advantage in the race to reprint new books.[54]

Traditionally, the Philadelphia trade had supplied the hinterland to the south and west, Boston had supplied New England, and New York took what was in between. The Harpers destabilized this system every time they filled a bookseller's order from Worcester or Richmond. After the Erie Canal

51 See Tremaine 1952, nos. 583, 919.

52 For a proposed reprint of a British spelling book (1828), see Fleming 1988, 323. For an 1830 New Testament printed from imported stereotype plates, see Fleming 1988, 464. For a Bible and a school-book with Canadian imprints but actually printed in the United States, see Fleming 1988, 760, 823.

53 Todd 1999; Accardo 1998; Kaser 1957, chap. 6.

54 Exman 1965, chap. 1.

reached Buffalo in 1825, they began to capture business from the Susquehanna and Ohio valleys that previously had come to Philadelphia. Cut off from the interior, Boston stagnated as a publishing centre, but at least until 1840 Philadelphia and New York battled it out, more or less evenly sharing the honours until the 1830s.

In 1825, US Customs began recording book imports separately; the value of book imports from Great Britain for 1827, a typical year, was just under $80,000.[55] That same year, the Carey firm alone published fifty book titles in a total of more than 80,000 copies, costing almost $100,000 to produce, with a potential retail value of at least $200,000.[56] This certainly suggests that by 1830 domestic book production had long outstripped importation, but imports were still an important part of the book trade. It is also worth noting that of those fifty books published by Carey in 1827, twenty-nine were by American authors. Since at least the 1790s when an American publisher spoke of an American book, he meant a book of American manufacture, but by 1830 an American book increasingly meant a book written by an American. The British book in America was becoming foreign for the first time.

55 US Government Documents 167: 174, pp. 8, 104, including imports from Scotland and Ireland and books imported free of duty, 1 Oct. 1826 to 30 Sep. 1827.
56 Kaser 1963, 52–106, 730–47, excluding pamphlets.

29
The British book in India

GRAHAM SHAW

Three stages may be distinguished in the book-trade relationship between Britain and India during this period. Up to and including the third quarter of the eighteenth century, the British in India were entirely dependent for reading matter upon books published in Britain, only the few Christian works and almanacs printed by missionary presses such as Tranquebar and Vepery (Madras) being available locally. During the last quarter of the eighteenth century, commercial book and newspaper publishing sprang up in India on a limited scale, so that some information and recreational reading needs could be satisfied locally, but the overwhelming majority were still met through imports. Finally, during the early nineteenth century, a recognizably two-way traffic in books between Britain and India began to develop, as interest in Indian affairs increased in the former, driven by career opportunities as much as by intellectual curiosity.

This chapter describes the various purposes for which books were exported from Britain, the scale of that export trade, and the emergence of an embryonic infrastructure for book selling and distribution within India. Publication in India of English-language works remained in its infancy, however, and book imports from Britain still vastly outweighed exports from India to Britain at the end of our period. The attention of London booksellers was confined principally to contemporary works on Indian affairs and history, and pioneering investigations into the languages, literatures and culture of the subcontinent. By 1800 only thirty-six works of creative literature in English had been published in India.[1] By 1830 that figure had increased, but not dramatically. India remained on the periphery of an English-language book culture centred on London, even if books were no longer imported only from Britain.

1 For details see Shaw 1987, 15. This work contains (pp. 5–12) summaries of the scope and output of all presses in India up to 1800.

The earliest importation of books by individuals

By 1695 British books had been percolating into India, albeit on a small scale, for more than three-quarters of a century. This stemmed from the activities of the East India Company which from 1600 until 1833 enjoyed a monopoly on trade between Britain and Asia. By 1695 it had already established a number of settlements or 'factories' in India. From the earliest decades of the seventeenth century, the Company's employees frequently took books out with them for their personal use, carried freight-free in the Company's ships, or had them sent through the agency of family or friends.

The titles of the books are never given – only rare glimpses of subject matter or language, as in 'three trunks mathematical books and instruments' belonging to Captain Lewis D'Illens, a passenger on the *Montford* in 1752, or Armenian books worth £13 6*s.* 8*d.* taken by Stephen Cogigian on the *East Court* in 1755. These were usually one-off consignments, but occasionally certain individuals made regular shipments, such as David Salomons sending to his brothers Abraham and Henry at Madras, one box of books and newspapers and another of just newspapers (the earliest such known to have been exported to India) by two ships of the 1736 fleet; one case of books in 1740, and two more in 1742 and 1743.[2] Whether these consignments were solely for private reading or for some commercial purpose it is impossible to say. Later, there is some evidence for the kinds of books individuals bought specifically to equip themselves for service in India. Just before embarking in June 1796, for instance, Arthur Wellesley, the future Duke of Wellington, bought forty-one titles from the London bookseller Faulder. Of these, twenty-four related specifically to Indian affairs; among the remainder were Caesar's *Commentaries*, Plutarch's *Lives*, the works of Locke and Paley, and a twenty-four volume set of Swift.[3]

The four-month voyage provided ample opportunity for reading. Some, such as Thomas Twining in 1792, turned this to educational advantage: 'During the heat of the day, I went very little upon deck, but occupied myself below with Sir William Jones's excellent Persian Grammar,' Persian being used for revenue and justice administration over most of India.[4] Others, such as Bishop Heber in 1823, combined language learning with leisure reading, in his case Persian and Hindustani with Scott's *Quentin Durward* and Scoresby's *Journal of a voyage to the northern whale-fishery*.[5]

2 Madras Record Office 1911–70, XXXIX–XLI, 146, 148; XLV–XLVII, 20; XLVIII, 89; LVIII, 99.
3 Guedalla 1931, 54–7.
4 Twining 1893, 17.
5 Heber 1829, I, xvii–xx.

Once in India, books needed care if they were not to fall prey to climate or insects. In the hot weather, as Emma Roberts observed in Bengal around 1830, the bindings would warp, and the monsoon encouraged rust and mildew.[6] Anne Elwood arriving at Bombay in 1825 recorded that 'several trunks which had left England, properly packed and full of valuable books, maps, and dresses, now presented a melancholy spectacle of shreds and rags', destroyed by the chewing of white ants.[7]

Books changed hands quite regularly owing to the short life-expectancy of Europeans in India. For instance, in September 1701, a 'chest of books' at the auction of Ambrose Thompson's effects was bought in Bombay by Vincent Broom, and on his death just nine months later, the same chest was sold on to Mark Warring. More often than not, collections of books were split up after death. When Captain D'Illens died at Fort St David (Cuddalore) in 1757, his eighty-eight books were bought by five fellow soldiers and eleven civilians. In the early nineteenth century such auctions also allowed Indians to acquire British books, either for their own use or for re-sale to Europeans. Aderjee Framjee and five other Parsees, for example, bought twenty-eight books at the sale of the effects of Lieutenant-Colonel John Bond at Surat in 1821.[8]

The importation of books by the East India Company

The Company itself also regularly exported batches of Christian literature – bibles, prayer books, catechisms and sermons – to its settlements in India, out of concern for the spiritual well-being of its employees, isolated in distant places amid alien cultures. For instance, in 1737 Madras received a consignment of bibles with size matched to status: 'The largest Bibles and Prayer Books are for the Chaplain's Desk and the Clerks, the others in Folio for the Deputy Governor and Council, the Octavos for the rest of our Covenant Servants, and for the use of the Military.' Books that were necessary for administrative or military purposes were also shipped out. In 1742, for example, *The new method of fortification*, *The art of gunnery* and other works by the French military engineer Sébastien de Vauban were sent to Madras. The Company was always keen to promote the learning of Asian languages by its

6 Roberts 1835, III, 9.
7 Elwood 1830, I, 402–3.
8 India Office Records: East Indies Wills 1618–1725 (G/40/23), Madras Wills 1753–7 (P/328/60), Bombay Inventories 1818–22 (L/AG/34/27/390).

servants, and in 1756 shipped to Madras again a copy of Mesgnien Meninski's *Thesaurus linguarum orientalium*.[9]

These initially small shipments of books formed the nucleus of the factory libraries, placed in the care of the local Company chaplain. For instance, in 1697 the Company sent the Madras chaplain, Revd Mr George Lewis, seventy-two copies of the Portuguese common prayer book to be distributed to Portuguese-speaking servants and slaves. These were to be kept in the church library and borrowers were 'to subscribe their names . . . under a title obliging them to return the books when demanded under the penalty of paying one Pagoda each'.[10] Thus as early as the 1690s these factory libraries were being run as lending libraries with fines imposed against defaulters. Books were valuable assets that were difficult to replace. In 1711, for example, the books of divinity in the Madras library were valued at £438 6*s*.[11]

The surviving 1729 catalogue of the Madras library illustrates the size and composition of these factory libraries. It lists 1,235 works, and alongside it are also catalogued 640 books belonging to the Madras chaplain, the Revd Thomas Consett. Together the two collections offered the Company's servants in Madras an impressive total of 1,875 titles.[12] Of these, 1,016, or just over half the total, were in English, with Greek and Latin (728 titles) making up another third, the remaining one-sixth (131 titles) being in various European and Asian languages (French, German, Dutch, Hebrew, Arabic, Persian, Tamil and Telugu). The Company's library contained Christian works primarily, being particularly rich in English sermons, and there were many editions of classical authors. There were also utilitarian works on medicine, surveying, accounting, elocution and other practical subjects, as well as some leisure-time reading, including travels, history and antiquities, trade with Asia, the works of Shakespeare, Vanbrugh, Cowley, Denham, Norris and Waller. Consett's collection naturally included titles such as Johnson's *The clergyman's vade mecum*, but also showed a wide range of interests, including medicine, mathematics, history and politics, languages, and English literature including Milton, Herbert, Oldham and Prior.

These libraries were often augmented by bequests or purchases of books from Company servants. For instance, Richard Eliot in 1696 bequeathed his books to the Fort St George library, and when John Landon transferred from Madras to become chaplain at Batavia in 1709, £45 was paid for his collection.[13]

9 Madras Record Office 1911–70, XLII–XLIV, 23; XLV–XLVII, 63; LX, 23.
10 Lockyer 1977, 28–9.
11 Lockyer 1711, 20.
12 India Office Records: Home Miscellaneous Series CCLX, 1–84.
13 Love 1913, III, 150; Madras Record Office 1911–70, XIV–XV, 96.

Inevitably, the factory libraries were vulnerable to the unstable political situation in India at the time, particularly as a result of Anglo-French rivalry in the subcontinent. During the Austrian War of Succession, for instance, the French occupied Fort St George from 1746 to 1749, and the library had to be replenished with fresh stock from London in 1753. Similarly, the Fort William library was destroyed when the Nawab of Bengal, Shuja-ud-Daula, occupied Calcutta in 1756.[14]

From the middle of the eighteenth century, the factory libraries became less important, for several reasons. The number of Company employees with their own collections grew steadily; books began to be imported as just another commodity for sale; learned societies in India formed their own libraries; and, not least, commercial circulating libraries opened in the principal settlements. In short, the Company no longer felt a primary obligation to supply reading matter to its employees in India.

Military and missionary imports

That concern did, however, partially resurface in the 1820s when military libraries were established among 'measures for the better preservation of the health of the European soldiery' serving in the Company's three presidency armies. Libraries would contribute to the soldiers' 'mental exercise', especially during the hot and rainy seasons when they were 'generally prohibited from leaving their barracks from breakfast until 5 o'clock p.m.' By stocking 'histories of our Commanders and their exploits, and the heroic traits of national character from the time of the Black Prince to Wellington', libraries would also improve the men's fighting spirit and esprit de corps. In 1821 the Company sent out sets of books to Bengal to equip seven libraries, but by 1823 only two had opened, at Kanpur and Meerut. In Bombay presidency seven military libraries were also planned, initially stocked with purchases from the local book depositories of the Society for Promoting Christian Knowledge (SPCK). In Madras in 1829 steps were taken to establish twelve libraries, again starting with SPCK stock and on a small scale, those at Bangalore and Vizagapatam containing just fifty-four and sixty-two titles respectively. Apart from religious and historical works, some novels were provided, together with instructional titles, including some aimed specifically at the education of young soldiers.[15]

14 Lockyer 1977, 36–7, 53; for the development of the Company's Bengal library, see Kabir 1987.
15 Baxter 1993, 26–8.

Next to the Company and its employees, the most prominent early exporters of books from Britain were missionary societies, principally the SPCK. Its secretary, Henry Newman, sent regular consignments of books, at least once every two years, to the Danish missionaries – first at Tranquebar and then in Madras. Between 1712 and 1739 he exported ten chests and sixteen boxes or cases of books to Madras.[16] This pattern was continued by his successor, William Watts, from the 1740s onwards. The missionaries were also responsible for the introduction of western-style education, through their charity schools at Madras and Cuddalore, and books were supplied for teaching purposes for the first time in 1717: 'Several Primers, Spelling Books, Psalters, Catechisms and other Religious Books, and Small Treatises as also Testaments for the use of the children and some for the Schoolmaster', sent freight-free as were all SPCK consignments.[17] This import of educational literature from Britain continued throughout the period. When Bishop's College opened in 1820, the Incorporated Society for the Propagation of the Gospel in Foreign Parts sent out books as the foundation of its library. Oxford University then gifted all the works printed at the Clarendon Press, and in 1826 Cambridge likewise presented copies of all works printed at its University Press.[18]

Manpower and materials for presses in India

Apart from the end products of the printing trade, Britain was also the essential source of manpower and materials for the fledgling book trade in India. Trained personnel began to reach India in the late eighteenth century specifically to man the presses of the expanding expatriate printing market in Calcutta, Madras and Bombay. For instance, James Augustus Hicky, a former apprentice of William Faden, arrived at Calcutta in 1772, and George Gordon, who had worked for his uncle, William Strahan, the King's Printer, in 1783.[19] Some, however, chose India as an escape from the book trade in Britain by enlisting as soldiers in the East India Company's army. To take just one sample, between 1718 and 1755 eighteen men from the British book trade are listed embarking as soldiers for Fort St George: six printers, five bookbinders, four papermakers, one hot-presser (of paper), one copperplate printer, and even one bookseller. They came from London, Kent, Suffolk, Lincolnshire, York,

16 Madras Record Office 1911–70, XVI–XVII, 12, 105, 110; XVIII–XIX, 109; XX–XXI, 137; XXII–XXIII, 82–3; XXIV–XXVI, 61, 143; XXX–XXXI, 28; XXXIX–XLI, 99, 155; XLII–XLIV, 65, 130.

17 Madras Record Office 1911–70, XX–XXI, 82.

18 Long 1848, 452–3.

19 Shaw 1981, 48–52.

Lancashire, Durham, Scotland and Dublin. Their ages ranged from seventeen to thirty-four, presumably a mix of young men escaping apprenticeships and those more experienced but unsuccessful.[20] It is unlikely that they resumed their book-trade careers once in India. Only one such instance is known, that of Thomas Jones in 1779, released from military service to assist Hicky in printing Bengal Army regulations and then a successful printer-publisher in Calcutta until at least 1792.[21]

All printing materials had to be imported from Britain, especially paper as locally made varieties were found unsuitable for the process. The SPCK was among the earliest exporters of printing equipment to India. In 1712 Henry Newman sent out to Madras by the *Frederick* '2 cases of paper, books & types, 2 cases of Mallabarick [i.e. Tamil] types, 1 case of iron, lead and steel, &ca., 1 case of tulls [i.e. tools] for printing press, 2 barrils lamp black, 3 barrils oyl & antimony'. In 1723 he shipped twenty-nine reams of paper, and in 1724 two cases of printing paper and a printing press.[22] The principal commercial exporter of paper into India was James Whatman II, who secured the contract for supplying paper to the East India Company. His success was no doubt assisted by his marriage in 1776 to Susanna Bosanquet, sister of Jacob Bosanquet, a director of the Company for some forty years and thrice elected chairman. Whatman's stated primary object was 'to supply such papers as would stand the Indian climates in exclusion of the Dutch papers which til then the Company had exclusively used'.[23]

Private libraries of Europeans in India

By the end of the eighteenth century, the professional elite of British society in India possessed private libraries of considerable size. For instance, when John Hyde, justice of the Supreme Court of Judicature in Bengal, died in 1797, he had 1,321 titles in his personal library.[24]

Taking a sample of inventories from Bombay, Calcutta and Madras across this whole period, excluding technical or profession-related works, we can reconstruct the typical personal library of the late eighteenth- or early nineteenth-century British officer, Company administrator or professional in India. Poetry is by far the largest category represented, with Byron's *Childe*

20 Madras Record Office 1911–70, XXII–XXIII, 79; XLII–XLIV, 123; XLV–XLVII, 29; XLIX–L, 56; LIV, 64–5; LV, 88; LVI, 95; LVII, 134, 137, 140; LVIII, 114, 117, 122, 125; LIX, 106, 109.

21 Shaw 1981, 55–6.

22 Madras Record Office 1911–70, XVI–XVII, 110; XXIV–XXVI, 61, 142.

23 Balston 1997, 48, 113–14.

24 India Office Records: Bengal Inventories 1797 (L/AG/34/27/19).

Harold perhaps the most popular work of all, followed by Thomson's *The seasons*, Milton's *Paradise lost* and Butler's *Hudibras*. The works of Addison, Burns, Cowper, Crabbe, Dodsley, Dryden, Gay, Goldsmith, Gray, Ossian, Pope, Shenstone, Southey, Spenser and Wordsworth are also frequently listed, as are the songs of Dibdin. Apart from the works of Shakespeare, the only play found at all often is Sheridan's *School for scandal*. Among novels, the works of Scott are most frequently mentioned – *Ivanhoe*, *Redgauntlet*, *Rob Roy* and so on, followed by Smollet's *Humphrey Clinker*, *Peregrine Pickle* and *Roderick Random*, Sterne's *Tristram Shandy* and *Sentimental journey*, Goldsmith's *The vicar of Wakefield*, Fielding's *Amelia*, Swift's *Gulliver's travels* and Defoe's *Robinson Crusoe*. Cervantes's *Don Quixote* is the only foreign novel commonly found, but *Gil Blas*, *The Arabian nights*, Goethe's *Sorrows of Werther* and *Letters writ by a Turkish spy* also recur. The essays of Bacon and Hume were popular, as well as Locke's *Essay concerning human understanding* and Chesterfield's *Letters to his son*, the works of Franklin and Voltaire, Smith's *Wealth of nations*, Pitt's speeches and the controversial *Letters of Junius*. History and travel were also popular, the leading titles being Mill's *The history of British India*, Lyttleton's *The history of England*, Rollin's *Ancient history*, Gibbon's *Decline and fall of the Roman Empire*, Robertson's *The history of America* and Anson's *A voyage round the world*. Among reference works, Johnson's *A dictionary of the English language* is almost ubiquitous, with Boyer's *Royal dictionary: English and French*, Guthrie's *A new geographical, historical and commercial grammar*, the *London pharmacopoeia*, Blackstone's *Commentaries on the laws of England* and Chambers's *Cyclopaedia; or an universal dictionary of arts and sciences* also often listed. Classical authors were well represented, Ovid's *Metamorphoses* above all, along with Virgil, Horace, Terence and Cicero. Finally, the two most popular periodicals were the *Spectator* and *Tatler*.

The commercial importation of books and newspapers

The commercial importation of British books into India began with the captains and officers of East Indiamen who were allowed to ship out freight-free a certain weight of speculative cargo according to rank. For instance, Captain Henry Kent of the *Dragon* bound for Madras in 1750 took one case of books among his cargo.[25] In 1772 John Shore indicated that such trade was already extensive and geared to popular taste: 'The libraries brought out by the

25 Madras Record Office 1911–70, LIV, 34.

captains and mates of Indiamen into this country for sale, though very voluminous, consist mostly of novels, and such books as are termed, by the London shopkeepers, "light summer reading".' Shore boasted that 'I had the good luck, last year, to furnish myself, at a very cheap rate, with some Latin and Greek Classics; which one of the captains, ill judging for the mart to which he brought them, imagined to have sold at a high premium.'[26]

By the 1780s when the first newspapers appeared in India, there were frequent advertisements for British books, journals and newspapers imported as speculative cargoes and bought up by local 'houses of agency', i.e. general merchants. For instance, in 1784, Messrs Baxter and Ord at Calcutta purchased the investment of Captain Johnson of the *Berrington* including 'an assortment of new music' (always a popular category) and 'debates in the House of Lords and Commons'. The same year, Roach and Johnston bought the cargo of the *Monte de Carmo* together with Captain Asquith's investment from the *Surprise*, including 'all the late pamphlets, trials, &c., and complete sets of the most esteemed morning and evening newspapers, and magazines to the latest periods' and 'a large collection of books for children and youth learning to write or draw; Westminster, London Town and Country, Universal, Political, and Rambler Magazines for 1783'.[27]

Newspapers from Britain were especially eagerly awaited. The information available locally to the eighteenth-century British expatriate in India was extremely limited: 'In this part of the world . . . the channels of intelligence are few, the novelty of character trifling, the follies and vices of the people, from a confined sphere of action, not strikingly conspicuous. The subjects of merriment and laughter but thinly scattered. The vicissitudes of fortune, tho' oftentimes extraordinary, seldom worth relation.'[28] By the 1780s, London newspapers were a common feature of Calcutta social life: 'At the coffee-houses your single dish of coffee costs you a rupee (half-a-crown); which half-crown, however, franks you to the perusal of the English newspapers, which are regularly arranged on a file, as in London.'[29]

English newspapers and magazines were also cannibalized to provide column inches for the local press. Just how dependent for copy on imported titles newspapers and magazines published in India were can be gauged from the *Bengal Weekly Messenger* for 1825. Its stated aim was to emulate the *London Literary Gazette* (by far its principal source of news), but twenty-seven other

26 Shore 1843, I, 45–6.
27 Seton-Karr 1864–5, I, 27, 53, 60.
28 Shaw 1981, 6.
29 Barwick, Macfarlane and Cotton 1908, 59.

British serials are also cited in that year's issues: national and provincial newspapers, the journals of learned societies in Scotland as well as England, literary magazines, and more popular titles such as the *Helter-skelter Magazine* and the *Ladies' Monthly Museum*.

When launching the *Bombay Gazette* in 1790, the proprietors sought to capitalize upon Bombay's geographical superiority over Madras or Calcutta as the first port-of-call for ships from Europe: 'Bombay, from its peculiar situation, is much better adapted for being a channel of general and early information than any other of the British settlements in India.'[30] Diaries often express frustration at not being up to date with news at home. For instance, Sir James Mackintosh at Bombay in April 1811 complained of 'seven months from the date of the last London news – a pause of unexampled length'. The British in India were victims of distance and entirely dependent for information upon the safe arrival of the fleet. When a new batch of print did arrive, it was greedily devoured. Mackintosh in 1810 read through numbers 28–31 of the *Edinburgh Review* between 9 June and 4 July.[31]

Circulating libraries and bookshops in India

One of the biggest markets for imported British books was that of the circulating libraries which opened in the three British presidency capitals. These were mostly operated by local printers who had perforce to diversify their business to survive. The British communities in India – at least before 1800 – do not seem to have been large enough to support more than one circulating library at a time. When two opened in competition, one inevitably failed or they were combined. Calcutta boasted the largest number of these libraries and the earliest, that of John Andrews established by at least 1774. In 1786 John Hay, a Calcutta printer, provided competition with the New Circulating Library, but a year later they were amalgamated under new owners, Messrs Cock, Maxwell and Company, to form the General Library. This lasted until 1792 when another printer, Joseph Cooper, opened his own circulating library; in 1797 a New Calcutta Library began under P. Mathison but closed under R. Grant in 1800.[32] By 1815 Greenway's Library had been established; and by 1830 J.J. Fleury's Library. Some circulating libraries also offered reading room facilities such as the Hurkaru Circulating Library and Reading Rooms (allied to the *Bengal Hurkaru* newspaper) and the 'Bengal Subscription, Reading and

30 Seton-Karr 1864–5, II, 514.
31 Mackintosh 1836, II, 23, 32–3, 97.
32 Shaw 1981, 22.

Billiard Rooms'.[33] The first subscription library at Madras opened in 1792. A second library operated by Brown and Ashtons started in 1794 containing 4,000 volumes, and seems to have been more successful as it was still in business in 1799.[34] The Bombay Library opened *c.*1790, but the original owner is not identifiable. In 1795 ownership changed first to J. D. Richardson and partners, then to Messrs Maclean and Greenway, and finally to Leonard Jaques who continued to operate it beyond 1800 when he added some 2,000 new titles to stock. By 1797 a Bombay Medical and Literary Library was also in business.[35] Learned societies and educational institutions also had sizeable collections of English books, such as the Asiatic Society of Bengal, the Bombay Literary Society, the College of Fort William, the Hindoo College and the Calcutta Library Society.

The circulating libraries were also the first local booksellers, as printers diversified still further by selling books directly to the public. In 1785 John Hay opened a bookseller's and stationer's shop in Calcutta, continued by his successor at the India Gazette Press, James Shakell. In 1787 Shakell at the New Library was advertising for sale books and magazines just landed from the *Minerva*, including natural history, works for children, novels by Smollett, Burney and Gwynn, plays and farces by Sheridan, Moore and Inchbald, and comic operas.[36]

Thacker, Spink and Company, later to become one of the leading booksellers under the Raj, was founded in 1819 by William Thacker. He was connected with the East India Company's London booksellers as he settled in Calcutta 'to dispose of Messrs Black, Parbury and Co.'s consignment' and opened St Andrews Library.[37] Already by the 1830s his bookshop had achieved pre-eminence, as Emma Roberts records that 'next to the jewellers' shops, the most magnificent establishment in the city is that of . . . Thacker and Co. . . . the splendid scale of this literary emporium, and the elegance of its arrangement, place it far above all its competitors'. Thacker was clearly aiming at the elite of Bengal society. 'The most expensive standard works are always procurable at this establishment; and though it may be cheaper to literary clubs and book societies to import their own supplies from London, so much must be left to the discretion of the agent employed, and, in the trade, there is such great temptation to get rid of unsaleable volumes, that, in the end, little saving is effected.'[38]

33 Das Gupta 1959, vi, 173, 608–9.
34 See notices in the *Madras Courier*, 26 Apr. 1792, 3 Oct. 1794, 23 Oct. 1799.
35 See notices in the *Bombay Courier*, 21 Feb. and 20 June 1795, 18 Mar. 1797, 17 May 1800.
36 Seton-Karr 1864–5, I, 219–20.
37 Cotton 1931, 157.
38 Roberts 1835, III, 8–10.

By 1830 the importation of books into India had become quite sophisticated, with shipments targeted at different market segments, such as schools, book clubs and libraries, as well as private individuals. Compressed editions were particularly sought after, such as the London series of classical texts in eighteenmo, 'Regent's Classics'. These reduced the costs of shipping and were more portable once in India for the Company's peripatetic employees. The trade had also become international, involving English-language books from France and the United States of America as well as Britain. The Paris editions of A. and W. Galignani, such as all Scott's novels in six octavo volumes, were frequently advertised in Calcutta at one-third to one-sixth of the price of London editions. From New York came the stereotype editions of J. and J. Harper such as 'The Family Library' series.[39] As Emma Roberts ironically noted: 'American editions of works of eminence also find their way into the market at a very cheap rate; and those who are content with bad paper, worse printing, and innumerable typographical errors, may furnish a library of the best authors at a small expense.'[40] But there was also a steady 'luxury' trade in fine editions beautifully bound, such as Tulloh and Company of Calcutta advertising in 1807 'an excellent collection of new books, [in] elegant bindings . . . [including] a splendid edition of Shakespeare's plays, printed on royal octavo wove paper and bound in yellow Russia leather'.[41]

Book distribution outside Calcutta, Bombay and Madras, however, was not at all developed. As Anne Elwood observed in the late 1820s, there were as yet very few circulating or other libraries up-country and 'unless care is taken to have a regular private supply from England, you stand a chance of never meeting with a new publication'.[42] This was echoed by Emma Roberts at Kanpur: 'The supply of books is seldom equal to the demand; for though there are numerous clubs established in the various [army] corps, and a few private collections belonging to the residents, the works which are to be found in all are chiefly of a light and desultory nature.' The problem was the kinds of books available as well as the lack of quantity: 'Books of instruction and reference are rarely to be purchased or borrowed, and however anxious young men may be to make themselves acquainted with the natural productions of India, or to study its political history, they must remain destitute of the means, unless they can afford to send to Calcutta or to England for the necessary materials.'[43]

39 See advertisements in the *Calcutta Courier*, Apr.–Oct. 1832; cf. Green, chap. 28, above.
40 Roberts 1835, III, 10.
41 Sandeman 1868–9, iv, 426.
42 Elwood 1830, II, 99.
43 Roberts 1835, I, 68.

It is clear that novels quickly became the most popular category of British books in India, much to the chagrin of one newspaper correspondent at Calcutta in 1816:

> A list of Books was put into my hands the other day ... Almost all the best English works were unsold: there appeared to be no demand for the histories of Greece, Rome, Melmoth's Cicero, or, in fact, for any of a serious or national nature. Under the head 'sold', I found on the file 'The sorrows of Werther, Spirit of English Wit, Spirit of Irish Wit, Life of Rochester, Ladies' Museum, Ackermann's Repository', &c., &c. Is it not a disgrace, Mr Editor, that such trash ... should be sought after with so much avidity in India?

Emma Roberts concurred when describing how popular British titles were offered for sale to Europeans in Calcutta: 'Books are thrust into the palanquin-doors, or the windows of a carriage, ... by natives who make a point of presenting the title-pages and the engravings upside down. Some of these books seem to be worthy of the Minerva Press [the leading publisher of popular fiction in Britain] in its worse days; and it is rather curious that novels, which are never heard of in England, ... are hawked about in the highways and bye-ways of Calcutta.' In 1830 one Calcutta editor even regarded the continuing vogue for cheap novels and magazines from Britain as detrimental to the emergence of a truly 'Anglo-Indian' literary culture: 'The predilection that exists for them is natural enough, but their popularity is an additional obstacle to the growth of an indigenous literature, the early shoots of which are choked and overshadowed by the more favoured vegetation of a foreign soil.'[44]

The scale of book imports into India

For the last four decades of our period, there are annual statistics (see Table 29.1) for the export of books from Britain to the 'East Indies', that is, principally India but including also the very small amount exported to China and south-east Asia (for example, in 1828 just £305 worth went to China). During the 1790s the value of books exported was over £150,000, more than doubling in the 1800s to over £340,000, and staying at that level more or less for the next two decades. By the end of 1830, therefore, books worth well in excess of £1 million had already been exported from Britain to India.

From 1814 onwards more detailed statistics (see Table 29.2) show that the export of books from Britain to India was overwhelmingly conducted as private trade; only a minute proportion was due to the Company's own

44 Sandeman 1869, v, 144; Roberts 1835, III, 11–12; *Bengal Annual* 1830, 5–6.

Table 29.1 *Book imports into India, 1791–1830, in pounds sterling*

Year	Value £	Year	Value £	Year	Value £	Year	Value £
1791	8,725	1801	25,530	1811	26,120	1821	45,459
1792	8,063	1802	22,151	1812	no figures[a]	1822	40,419
1793	7,450	1803	36,922	1813	no figures[a]	1823	47,219
1794	17,442	1804	18,630	1814	21,052	1824	41,082
1795	15,388	1805	19,860	1815	38,678	1825	41,814
1796	20,163	1806	25,403	1816	47,897	1826	32,424
1797	18,287	1807	25,040	1817	46,656	1827	30,973
1798	18,714	1808	56,140	1818	47,265	1828	22,587
1799	14,435	1809	48,500	1819	40,843	1829	34,296
1800	25,118	1810	66,180	1820	39,730	1830	27,426
Totals cumulative	153,785		344,356		348,241		363,699
			498,141		846,382		1,210,081

Note: [a] The total for the decade 1811–20 can only be approximate as no figures are available for 1812–13, the records for those years having been destroyed in the 1814 London Custom House fire. For the purposes of this table, a conservative value of £20,000 has been assumed for each of these two years.

Table 29.2 *Book imports into India: private trade and East India Company imports contrasted, 1814–30*

Year	Private trade £ sterling	EIC imports	Private trade tons	EIC imports
1814	21,022	30	58.95	0.05
1815	38,430	248	102.95	0.85
1816	47,851	46	124.75	0.15
1817	46,357	299	85.50	0.70
1818	47,265	0	126.75	0.00
1819	40,814	29	107.00	0.05
1820	39,156	574	136.95	0.20
1821	45,385	74	151.75	3.35
1822	39,429	990	135.55	3.35
1823	47,219	0	163.15	0.00
1824	40,549	533	131.50	1.65
1825	37,865	3,949	105.80	6.15
1826	31,751	673	54.40	0.80
1827	29,418	1,555	41.30	3.90
1828	21,785	802	36.20	1.45
1829	30,481	3,815	54.95	3.10
1830	27,189	237	35.15	2.00
Total	631,966	13,584	1652.60	26.15

requirements. In terms of sterling value, private traders imported forty-six times more books than the Company itself. During the two years 1825 and 1829 the Company's exports (no doubt connected with the new military libraries) peaked at just under £4,000. This compares with an average annual private trade export value of over £37,000. According to weight, the difference is even more stark, as private tonnage was sixty-three times greater than the Company's.

From being the prime exporter of British books to India up to the middle of the eighteenth century, the Company had been reduced by the second decade of the nineteenth to playing a very minor role in this trade.[45]

The two-way trade in books and its economics

During the first three decades of the nineteenth century we can trace the gradually increasing export of books published in India back to Britain, from advertisements placed in the *East-India register and directory*. These imports were mostly on Indian languages, religion and history, the fruits of the researches of the first great generation of British Indologists centred around Sir William Jones. In 1812, 52 works on Asia were advertised, in 1815, 96, and in 1820, 182. At the same time, books were also being published in London catering specifically for the man about to embark. A broadsheet, *Necessaries for a writer to India* printed around 1800, included 'Moorish [i.e. Hindustani] grammar, Persian ditto, ditto dictionary, ditto Interpreter, Ousley's Persian Miscellanies, and Carlisle's Arabian Poetry'.

The economics of publishing in India compared unfavourably with those in Britain. First, the potential market remained comparatively small. Unlike the United States, Canada or Australia, in India the European population was not a gradually expanding one of permanent settlers. People came, worked, and then returned to Britain, to be replaced by new fortune-seekers. During our period the total European population in India probably never exceeded 30,000 at any one time. Additionally, books exported from Britain were in effect 'subsidized' because of the lower unit costs of production:

> It may seem unreasonable that sixteen rupees should be charged for *The Bengal annual*, when some of the London ones are sold for twelve rupees in India, and twelve shillings in England. But a price affixed to an Indian Annual that would not cover the cost of publication in this country, would produce a handsome

45 Moreau 1825, *passim*; Parliamentary Papers Session 1828 xxiii, paper 178; 1829 xxiii, paper 344; 1830 xxviii, paper 22; 1830–1 ix, papers 168, 217; 1833 xxv, paper 229.

> profit to the London publisher of a work of the same nature . . . Not only is the sale of works in India most miserably limited in comparison with those of London, but the expenses of printing and paper are nearly doubled.[46]

It was these same high production costs that led many would-be authors among British expatriates in India to send their works to London to be printed and published, particularly if any kind of illustrations were required, rather than have them produced locally.[47]

Conclusion

The extent to which these small communities were able to transplant their intellectual world from Britain to India is impressive. Within the constraints of contemporary forms of transport and communications, this was a periphery determined to stay connected with the centre. Reading was essential in maintaining the 'spiritual' link with home. As Maria Graham put it: 'Every new book that reaches us, every poem, especially if it recall the legends of our native land, is an object of discussion and interest beyond what I could have thought possible, till I felt in a foreign country how dear every thing becomes that awakens those powerful associations.'[48]

46 *Prospectus*, [1–2]. *The Bengal Annual and Literary Keepsake for 1830*.
47 See Green, chap. 28, above.
48 Graham 1813, 139–40.

PART V BOOKS AND THEIR READERS

I
RELIGIOUS BOOKS

30
Religious publishing

ISABEL RIVERS

Introduction: denominations and publishers

Religious books and pamphlets of all kinds indisputably constituted the largest part of the publishing market in the period 1695 to 1830, just as they had since the invention of printing.[1] They fell into three main categories, doctrinal, controversial and practical (the last meaning didactic and devotional in the widest sense), though with inevitable overlap between them. This chapter will concentrate on aspects of the third and largest category, which contained a huge range of books of different size, length and price aimed at different audiences. It included aids to religious worship, such as hymns and guides to communion; didactic aids, ranging from manuals for divinity students to catechisms for children; and devotional aids, teaching the reader how to live a devout Christian life both private and public. The writers of such books were mostly clergy or ministers of different denominations, though there were some lay authors; their readers, depending on the kind of book and how it was distributed, were the clergy and large numbers of the laity. Religious books were written and produced for clearly defined markets: the most expensive folio or quarto volumes – usually collected works or commentaries – for scholarly or ministerial or gentry libraries, medium-priced octavo handbooks or duodecimo pocket-books for clergy and prosperous laity, and cheap duodecimo or smaller pamphlets or tracts for the middling sort or for the prosperous to distribute to the poor. Denominational factors as well as economic and social ones determined the size and kind of publications: thus specific books were published for the differing liturgical and doctrinal needs of different denominations, though it is clear that some of the most popular works crossed denominational boundaries.[2]

1 I. Green 2000; Collinson, Hunt and Walsham 2002; Green and Peters 2002.
2 For a sketch of the religious spectrum, see Rivers 2005.

By far the largest number of books were published by and for members of the established Church of England. A minority of Anglican works – though they often made a great deal of noise – addressed the controversial or doctrinal concerns of its opposing high church and latitudinarian wings. The Trinitarian dissenters – Presbyterians, Congregationalists, Baptists and Quakers, who were free to worship under the Toleration Act of 1689 – produced a disproportionately large number of books in relation to the small percentage of the population they represented. The evangelical revival beginning in the late 1720s and gathering strength throughout the later eighteenth and early nineteenth centuries was stimulated by and also generated an increasing number of publications written and distributed by Methodists and evangelicals both within and outside the Church of England. Two important but smaller denominations, Roman Catholics and Unitarians, suffered from legal constraints, which in the earlier part of the period restricted their ability to publish and distribute their works freely. The statute of James I prohibiting the printing and selling of Catholic books remained in force, and in the first half of the eighteenth century Catholic booksellers were still being harassed.[3] Unitarians, who were not covered by the Toleration Act until 1813, were fairly cautious in the earlier part of the period, but in the later eighteenth century there was a marked increase in the number of Unitarian publications, though they sold in small numbers in comparison with evangelical works. For all these denominations, the widespread dissemination of printed works was essential, supporting and extending different communities of believers, and serving the purposes of worship, instruction and evangelism.

This survey begins with a brief account of the main booksellers involved in the publication of religious books. Though some large booksellers might have eclectic lists which mixed religious books with history, literature and natural philosophy, and some Anglican booksellers might own shares in dissenting books and vice versa, a number specialized in publishing works of a particular denomination. The long-lived firm of Rivington was perhaps the one that became most closely associated with the established church. It was begun by Charles Rivington in 1711, when he acquired the business of Richard Chiswell, publisher of works by prominent late seventeenth-century churchmen such as Gilbert Burnet, Simon Patrick and John Tillotson, and was continued by his sons John and James and John's sons Francis and Charles and their heirs through the nineteenth century.[4] Rivingtons published both high church

3 Williams 1968, 9–11.
4 Rivington 1919.

authors such as William Cave and Robert Nelson, and low church evangelicals such as James Stonhouse and the extremely popular James Hervey. Despite bringing out a few early works by John Wesley and George Whitefield, they steered clear of Methodists.[5] They were official publishers to the Society for Promoting Christian Knowledge (SPCK) from 1760 to 1835 (Joseph Downing was the publisher closely associated with SPCK at the beginning of the century), and published the high church magazine the *British Critic* from 1793 to 1843. Yet it should be noted that in the later eighteenth century they also had shares in posthumous editions of the moderate dissenter Philip Doddridge. The Knapton family (James, John and Paul) were part of the London book trade from 1687 to 1770.[6] Important churchmen they published included Samuel Clarke (notably his much reprinted Boyle lectures of 1705–6), Benjamin Hoadly, Joseph Butler and William Warburton. William and John Innys, who specialized in natural philosophy and medicine as well as theology,[7] published not only William Derham's very popular Boyle lectures on physico-theology and astro-theology, but also the influential devotional and mystical writings of the nonjuror William Law. The university presses, whose function was printing rather than publishing, produced fewer religious books than one might expect apart from the all-important Bible and Book of Common Prayer. At Oxford the University Press at the Theatre (later the Clarendon Press) frequently reprinted in the earlier part of the period Thomas Marshall's *Catechism* and the collection of devotional and didactic works attributed to the author of *The whole duty of man*; the most important religious writer printed at the Clarendon Press in the later eighteenth century was the high churchman George Horne.[8] At Cambridge the liberal theologians Edmund Law, Richard Watson and John Hey had their works produced by successive University Printers, Joseph Bentham, John Archdeacon and John Burges. Bentham also printed Christopher Smart's Seatonian prize poems on the divine attributes.[9]

Religious publishing for dissenters was carried on by a much smaller number of booksellers in London, who worked for certain denominations of which they were themselves members. The most important were Richard Hett and his son, also Richard, who were in business successively from 1724 to 1785.[10] Hett,

5 On the breach between Rivington and Wesley, see Baker 1941, 82.
6 Plomer 1922, 181; Plomer, Bushnell and Dix 1932, 148.
7 McKitterick 1998, 124; Rousseau 1982, 231; Plomer 1922, 167.
8 Carter 1975, appendix.
9 On these printers and Bentham's predecessor, Cornelius Crownfield, see McKitterick 1998, chaps. 4–12.
10 Plomer, Bushnell and Dix 1932, 123. The dates are of the earliest and latest recorded titles in *ESTC*; Plomer gives the dates 1726–76.

together with John and Barham Clark, Richard Ford and James Waugh,[11] published seventeenth- and eighteenth-century moderate Presbyterian and Congregational authors such as John Howe, Isaac Watts, Elizabeth Rowe and Philip Doddridge.[12] George Keith, who was in business from 1749 to *c.*1782, specialized in Particular (i.e. Calvinist) Baptist authors such as John Gill (his father-in-law) and Calvinists of other denominations such as the Anglican and Methodist George Whitefield.[13] Quaker books from 1692 to 1775 were largely in the hands of two families, Sowle and Hinde. In the period up to 1749 books published by the Sowles appeared successively under the imprint T[ace]. Sowle, J[ane]. Sowle, the assigns of J. Sowle, and T. Sowle Raylton [Tace's married name] and Luke Hinde;[14] Hinde began publishing in 1735 and was succeeded in 1769 by his wife, Mary. These families published the principal seventeenth- and eighteenth-century Quaker authors, George Fox, William Penn, Thomas Ellwood, Robert Barclay and Joseph Besse.[15] The Hindes' business was carried on from 1775 to 1800 by James Phillips,[16] who published the Anglican abolitionist Thomas Clarkson. The leading publisher of Unitarian books was Joseph Johnson, in business from 1761 to his death in 1809.[17] By upbringing a Baptist and apprenticed to George Keith, in the 1760s Johnson published the evangelical John Newton and the American Calvinist Jonathan Edwards. Gradually abandoning his Trinitarian views, he was involved in the establishment of the Unitarian Essex Street Chapel and published liturgical works on behalf of the Unitarian Society. His prominent Unitarian authors included Joseph Priestley and Theophilus Lindsey, yet he continued to publish evangelicals such as Newton, William Cowper and Thomas Scott. Commercial considerations must have played their part, but at the same time his list illustrates the open attitude to other denominations on which Unitarians prided themselves.[18] It is worth noting the work of some provincial dissenting printers who produced books for London dissenting booksellers. The best known is William Eyres of Warrington, who was in business from 1756 to 1803 and printed works by tutors at the Warrington academy, including William Enfield and Gilbert Wakefield.[19]

11 For John (but not Barham) Clark, see Plomer 1922, 72; for Ford and Waugh, see Plomer, Bushnell and Dix 1932, 95–6, 258.

12 For letters from and to Doddridge discussing negotiations with Hett, see Nuttall 1979, letters 492, 963.

13 Plomer, Bushnell and Dix 1932, 144; Tyson 1979, 6–7. See also Whitley 1916–22.

14 Plomer 1922, 277–8 and Plomer, Bushnell and Dix 1932, 125–6, with corrections.

15 Smith 1867.

16 Maxted 1977, 176.

17 Plomer, Bushnell and Dix 1932, 141; Tyson 1979; Braithwaite 2003.

18 E.g. J. Johnson, *A catalogue of books composed for children and young persons, and generally used in the principal schools and academies in England* (London, 1790) has a clear Unitarian bias but includes the evangelical Mrs Trimmer.

19 Perkin 1987b; O'Brien 1993.

Eyres produced at least sixty-five items for Joseph Johnson, a significant proportion of them religious works. On a much smaller scale, from 1796 to 1800 the Yorkshire Baptist pastor and tutor John Fawcett had his own press and employed a printer in his successive homes, Brearley Hall and Ewood Hall near Halifax, where he produced a number of his own works and some seventeenth-century classics for booksellers in London (ten of twenty-one surviving items were sold by Johnson).[20]

Roman Catholic booksellers, like the dissenters, formed a closely connected group in London. Thomas Meighan took over Thomas Metcalfe's business in about 1710, and on his death in 1753 was succeeded by his wife, Martha, followed by his son Thomas. James Marmaduke was in business from around 1741 to his death in 1788; from about 1760 he was in competition with James Peter Coghlan, who bought the stock of Thomas Meighan the younger on his death in 1774. On Coghlan's death in 1800 his partner and nephew Richard Brown joined forces with Patrick and George Keating as Keating, Brown and Keating.[21] These publishers specialized in liturgical, historical, didactic and devotional works for the Catholic community, such as *The laity's directory* (Marmaduke and Coghlan published competing versions) and the voluminous output of Bishop Richard Challoner.[22] Though Meighan senior was several times under investigation, Catholic books were freely advertised and sold; their numbers suggest that some must have been bought by Protestants.[23]

For the booksellers named so far, religious publishing was essentially a business. However, an important development in the eighteenth century was the systematic publishing and distributing of religious literature on a large scale not for monetary profit but to further the saving of souls. John Wesley kept the burgeoning Methodist Societies under his control supplied with books (the majority cheap duodecimo pamphlets either written or edited by him) from a variety of sources. Before 1778 most of these were printed by the Farleys and later William Pine in Bristol, William Strahan, Henry Cock and Robert Hawes in London, John Gooding in Newcastle, and Samuel Powell in Dublin; they were distributed by Book Stewards (first appointed in 1753) at the Book Room at his London headquarters, the Foundery, and his preaching houses around the country. In 1778 Wesley moved the Book Room to the new City Road Chapel in London and established a printing press in the Foundery,

20 Fawcett 1818, 282–90. Several items mentioned by Fawcett Jr. are not listed in *ESTC*.

21 Gillow 1885–1902, I (1885), 322–5 (Brown), 526–7 (Coghlan); III (1888), 675–6 (Keating); IV (1895), 462–4 (Marmaduke), 558–9 (Meighan); Plomer, Bushnell and Dix 1932, 167–8 (Meighan, but information limited); Blom *et al.* 1996, xi–xiii; Blom *et al.* 2007.

22 Williams 1981; Luckett 1981, 77–81.

23 Blom *et al.* 1996, xi, xiii.

where he employed his own printer, John Paramore. After Wesley's death the Book Room and printing office moved in 1808 to premises in the City Road, and then in 1818 to Paternoster Row.[24] Though Wesley kept tight control of what was published, his choice of authors was extremely eclectic, including Roman Catholics, Anglican churchmen, and seventeenth-century puritans and nonconformists.[25] Surviving catalogues of books published at City Road after his death show that the majority of his publications were kept in print, with the addition of works by later Methodist leaders such as Joseph Benson and by eighteenth-century dissenters excluded by Wesley, such as Philip Doddridge.[26] In 1782 Wesley and Thomas Coke began a Society for the Distribution of Religious Tracts among the Poor,[27] but (contrary to what has been claimed by Methodist historians) this was not the first such society: it was preceded by the long-lived but now almost unknown dissenting and evangelical Society for Promoting Religious Knowledge among the Poor, usually called the Book Society, founded in 1750 by Thomas Gibbons and others, and still going strong until the early twentieth century,[28] and followed by Hannah More's Cheap Repository Tracts (1795–8) and the Religious Tract Society, founded in 1799.[29] The Unitarian Society for Promoting Christian Knowledge and the Practice of Virtue by the Distribution of Books, founded in 1791, had difficulty raising enough subscriptions, whereas the Methodist Tract Society, instituted in 1809 and reformed in 1828, was responsible for giving away millions of its own publications.[30]

Guides for the clergy and biblical commentaries

Divinity students, clergy and ministers of different denominations were in urgent need of guides to the mass of religious publications that poured from the presses and of commentaries to help them interpret the Bible. Several such guides, most of them written for members of the Church of England, became standard works and were revised and reprinted for the benefit of generations of students; they are also invaluable to the modern reader who wants to find out exactly which religious books were most often recommended at the time.

24 Green 1906; Baker 1939–40, 1947, 1966; Cumbers 1956.
25 Rivers 1982b, 152–8.
26 Six Methodist catalogues dating from 1807 to 1820? are in a collection of ephemera in the Bodleian Library (G.Pamph.2920).
27 Green 1906, no. 363n; Baker 1947, 171.
28 Rippon 1804?; Bullock 1963; Rivers 2007.
29 Spinney 1939; Quinlan 1941, 83–9, 122–6; Jones 1850; Altick 1998, 100–3. Cf. Mandelbrote, chap. 32 below.
30 Mineka 1944, 18, 102; leaflet entitled 'The Methodist Tract Society; Instituted, October 25, 1809' Bodleian Library (G.Pamph.2920 (31)); Cumbers 1956, 50.

John Wilkins's *Ecclesiastes: or, a discourse concerning the gift of preaching, as it falls under the rules of art*, first published in 1646 and revised and expanded in 1669 by the author, now Bishop of Chester, was posthumously revised and expanded further in 1693 by John Williams and again in 1704, and was last reprinted in a ninth edition in 1718.[31] The expansions, especially the later ones, were largely to the book lists in Section 4, 'Concerning a regular scheme of the chief heads in divinity', and they provided the erudite clergyman with a full and up-to-date catalogue of Reformation and seventeenth-century religious writing in all its aspects, with a noticeable latitudinarian slant in the post-Restoration authors. *A discourse of the pastoral care* by the Bishop of Salisbury, Gilbert Burnet, first published in 1692 and enlarged with a new preface for the third edition of 1713, was written at the suggestion of Archbishop Tillotson and Queen Mary with the object of improving the clergy's education, and it became one of five books for students and young clergy adopted by the SPCK.[32] Chapter 7, 'Of the due preparation of such as may and ought to be put in orders', contains a relatively compact account of the most suitable books for a clergyman who does not intend to be a divine (i.e. a theologian – unlike the putative reader of *Ecclesiastes*). The last London edition, described as the fifth, was published in 1766. *Directions for young students in divinity, with regard to those attainments, which are necessary to qualify them for holy orders* (1766), another work adopted by the SPCK, was specifically addressed by the clergyman and biblical scholar Henry Owen to candidates for orders who were not university educated. It reached its fifth edition in 1809. Owen's list was avowedly extracted from other divines (borrowings from Burnet's *Pastoral care* are evident, with mid-eighteenth-century additions). To the objection that he had recommended too many books, he answered that '*some* of these books they can certainly buy: and the *rest*, I presume, they will be able to borrow' (p. viii).

Some guides were written by tutors at Oxford and Cambridge, initially for their own students. Daniel Waterland, Fellow and later Master of Magdalene College, Cambridge, after discovering that his 25-year-old guide had been unofficially and inaccurately published in 1729,[33] brought out his own version as *Advice to a young student. With a method of study for the four first years*, printed in London and sold in Cambridge by Cornelius Crownfield, the University Printer. A second enlarged edition was published in Oxford in 1755. An introductory chapter recommends personal devotional books, a table gives

31 Rivers 1991, 38–9.

32 Clarke 1944, 22. For books actually owned by a contemporary clergyman, see Salter 1978.

33 In *The present state of the republick of letters*, IV, 412–43.

instructions for philosophical, classical and religious reading, and an appendix lists books relevant to the making of a preacher after the four years of study have been completed.[34] Edward Bentham, Fellow of Oriel College, Oxford, and later Regius Professor of Divinity, similarly put in print works originally designed for Oxford students, including *An introduction to moral philosophy* (printed at the Theatre, 1745, with a second edition in 1746) and *Reflexions upon the study of divinity. To which are subjoined heads of a course of lectures* (printed at the Clarendon Press, 1771, with a second edition in 1774).[35] The *Introduction* was not explicitly designed for divinity students, but it contains 'A table of reference to English discourses and sermons upon moral subjects', listing a wide range of late seventeenth- and early eighteenth-century authors, mostly but not exclusively Anglican clergy. At the end of the table Bentham draws attention to Wilkins's catalogue, to which his own was presumably intended as a supplement. *Reflexions* gives a much shorter list of 'plain and easy' books of divinity through which he took his Oriel students for many years (pp. v–viii).

Far more comprehensive than these university guides in pamphlet form were the lectures Philip Doddridge gave his ministerial students at the dissenting academy at Northampton, which were published posthumously in quarto as *A course of lectures on the principal subjects in pneumatology, ethics, and divinity*, edited by his former student Samuel Clark (1763). Each lecture in Doddridge's course of 230 lectures in ten parts was dependent on a series of precise references to texts which often expressed opposing points of view; his students were required to follow these up in the library and discuss them at the next lecture. The course was used in other dissenting academies as a textbook, and later editors (Andrew Kippis, 1794; Edward Williams and Edward Parsons, 1803–4) added further references, as had Clark. Williams and Parsons described it as 'the most complete syllabus of controversial theology, in the largest sense of the term, ever published in the English language'.[36]

The guides so far mentioned assumed that the reader would somehow find access to books, in college or academy libraries or through the kindness of clergy or ministers. Two very interesting attempts were made to surmount this difficulty by publishing collections of essential religious books. John Wesley regarded his itinerant lay preachers as university students nominally under his supervision, and he required them to spend seven hours a day in addition to their pastoral activities reading books chosen only by him. In 1746 Doddridge

34 Rivers 2000, 195–6.
35 McKitterick 1998, 131; Carter 1975, 526, 529, 591, 598; Greaves 1986, 403–4, 407–10.
36 Doddridge 1802–5, IV, 282. Also see Rivers 2003. For other collections of lectures by dissenters, see McLachlan 1931.

sent him a lengthy letter of advice on the subject, published by Wesley in the *Arminian Magazine* for September 1778 under the title 'A scheme of study for a clergyman'. From 1749 to 1755 Wesley issued for the preachers' benefit fifty duodecimo volumes of *A Christian library*, which contained his editions and abridgements of a very wide range of authors of different denominations, the majority from the seventeenth century. The larger Methodist Societies were urged to acquire the *Library* for the preachers' use. With a print run of one hundred for each volume, the *Library* had a much narrower circulation than Wesley's other publications in his lifetime, and was probably more influential in Thomas Jackson's revised second edition (30 vols., 1819–27, with some additions).[37]

Richard Watson, Regius Professor of Divinity at Cambridge, edited his six-volume *Collection of theological tracts* (printed by John Archdeacon, the University Printer, in 1785, with a second edition in 1791) for the benefit of university students and younger clergy, including those ordained from country schools. Unlike Wesley's collection, it contained a large number of eighteenth-century works, several of them by dissenters, and was very successful, with a sale of nearly a thousand copies in less than three months. For those who wanted to progress beyond the tracts, Watson appended to volume VI a lengthy annotated (but unpaginated) 'Catalogue of books in divinity', which provides an exceptionally useful guide to Anglican and moderate dissenting religious writing from the mid-seventeenth to the late eighteenth century.[38] The titles are arranged by size – folio, quarto and octavo, but not duodecimo (thus excluding the cheap pocket-books in which Wesley specialized and which formed such an important part of the lay religious market).

The Bible was of course at the heart of clerical education, and it was assumed by most Anglicans and dissenters in this period that it could not be properly understood without the help of commentaries.[39] Most of the guides described above, including Doddridge's letter to Wesley, gave advice about suitable commentaries and other kinds of aid to interpretation, though Henry Owen warned that it was much more important to read the Bible than its expositors: 'no person, who is possessed of a BIBLE with good *marginal references*, and has not at least a competent knowledge of the Holy scriptures, can fairly charge his want of knowledge on the want of books'.[40] Such books ranged from

37 Green 1906; Monk 1966, appendix 1; Rivers 1982b, 149–52.
38 Rivers 2000, 340–5.
39 Relevant studies include McLachlan 1934, chap. 1; Preston 1982; Reedy 1985; I. Green 2000, chap. 3; Mandelbrote 2001.
40 Owen 1766, 35.

multi-volume and sometimes multi-author commentaries, containing detailed verse by verse analysis, comparisons of different authorities in Latin and the vernacular, and explanations of different readings of the Old Testament Hebrew and the New Testament Greek, to shorter and more elementary introductions to the interpretation of Scripture. Some commentaries included a translation or paraphrase. There was a marked shift in the mid-eighteenth century in the audience for whom commentaries were designed, from clergy or ministers to the laity, especially the family, but both kinds had a very long life.

The most important of the longer works in the earlier part of the period by both churchmen and dissenters were Henry Hammond's *A paraphrase and annotations upon all the books of the New Testament* (folio, 1653), Matthew Poole's *Annotations upon the holy Bible* (2 vols. folio, 1683–5, the second volume by eleven others), William Burkitt's *Expository notes, with practical observations, on the four evangelists* (folio in two parts, 1700), Samuel Clarke's *A paraphrase on the four evangelists* (2 vols. octavo, 1703), George Stanhope's *A paraphrase and comment upon the epistle and gospels appointed to be used in the Church of England* (4 vols. octavo, 1705–9), Matthew Henry's *An exposition of all the books of the Old and New Testaments* (5 vols., 1708–10; the Epistles and Revelation were by others), and a multi-volume amalgamation (1727–60) of separate commentaries and paraphrases of the Old and New Testaments by Simon Patrick, William Lowth, Daniel Whitby and Richard Arnald. More introductory works included William Lowth's *Directions for the profitable reading of the holy Scriptures* (1708) and David Collyer's *The sacred interpreter* (2 vols., 1726; the date of 1732 usually given is that of the second edition).[41]

The longer, more scholarly works, though frequently reprinted, could be very expensive, as can be seen from advertisements in the *Monthly Catalogue* from 1724 to 1729: thus a new edition of Henry's *Exposition* published in June 1725 cost £6 10*s*. for six folio volumes; Collyer's *Sacred interpreter* published in October 1726 cost 10*s*. for two octavo volumes; the fifth edition of Whitby's *Paraphrase and commentary on the New Testament* published in March 1727 cost £2. 2*s*. for two folio volumes; the third edition of Patrick's *Commentary upon the historical books of the Old Testament* published in August 1727 in two folio volumes cost £2. 2*s*. in sheets (the subscription proposals in April 1727 stated that the previous edition of nine quarto volumes was so scarce that it sold for £6 or £7); the ninth edition of Burkitt's *Expository notes* published in December 1728 in folio cost £1. 2*s*. 6*d*.; the fifth edition of Clarke's *Paraphrase* published

41 This list is largely derived from Preston 1982, 103–6, and I. Green 2000, 118–24, 149–51 (some of their information has been corrected). For a useful guide from a dissenting perspective, see Orme 1824.

in March 1729 in two octavo volumes cost 12*s*.[42] One way for booksellers and buyers to spread the cost was through the sale of commentaries in parts.[43] Thus *Bibliotheca biblica*, a digest of early interpretations up to the year 451, was printed at Oxford in monthly parts from 1720 to 1735, though the project ground to a halt at the end of the Pentateuch;[44] the parts were regularly advertised in the *Monthly Catalogue* at 6*d*. At the other intellectual extreme *Biblia; or a practical summary of the Old and New Testaments*, advertised in the *Monthly Catalogue* for December 1727 as suitable for New Year's gifts for the young, cost 9*s*. a dozen bound in calf or 15*d*. each with gilt leaves.

From the mid-eighteenth century there was a concerted move on the part of clergy and ministers, particularly those who promoted the evangelical revival, to provide serious commentaries for a lay readership without knowledge of Hebrew or Greek. Three were particularly influential and were regularly republished through the nineteenth century: Doddridge's *The family expositor: or, a paraphrase and version of the New Testament* (6 vols. quarto, 1739–56); John Wesley's *Explanatory notes upon the New Testament* (quarto, 1755); and Thomas Scott's *The Holy Bible, with notes* (4 vols. quarto, 1788–92). Doddridge explained in the preface to the first volume of the *Family expositor* that his aim was 'chiefly to promote *family religion*' and that he wrote for those without a learned education who did not have access to commentators.[45] But the book, dedicated to the Princess of Wales, was designed to appeal to the great and the good. The subscription lists prefacing volumes I, IV and V, with approximately 2,800 names in all, include members of the aristocracy (many of them women), the Archbishop of Canterbury, bishops and clergy, Fellows of Oxford and Cambridge colleges, Scottish professors, and dissenting ministers in addition to the large number of provincial commoners.[46] Doddridge was paid 400 guineas for the work by his publisher Hett, who issued 1,750 copies of the first volume.[47] The *Family expositor* rapidly established its popularity among Anglican as well as dissenting readers, clerical as well as lay: Henry Owen thought it 'better calculated for the improvement of a young divine' than earlier paraphrases such as Clarke's (recommended by Bentham), and it figures in Watson's list.[48] Wesley's quarto of 759 pages, costing £1 bound, was much

42 Wilford 1964.
43 For the commercial motivation and some mid-eighteenth-century examples, see McKitterick 1998, 223. Cf. Harris, chap. 20 above.
44 Carter 1975, 309.
45 Doddridge 1802–5, VI, 9.
46 For an analysis of the subscription lists, see Everitt 1985, 229–33.
47 Nuttall 1979, letters 492, 663.
48 Owen 1766, 33; Bentham 1771, vii.

longer and more expensive than his other individual publications (the third revised edition of 1760–2 in three volumes duodecimo cost 7*s*. 6*d*. or 9*s*. bound),[49] but his characteristically terse annotations were much shorter than Doddridge's (to which he acknowledged a debt). His *Explanatory notes* achieved authoritative status and hence steady sales among Methodists through its adoption in 1763 as the standard for doctrines to be taught in his chapels, along with forty-four of his sermons,[50] but in this period it seems to have been largely ignored outside his own societies – Watson's catalogue contains no Methodist publications. Thomas Scott's heroic experiences illustrate the real risks of serial publication. He was commissioned to write a commentary on the whole Bible in a hundred weekly numbers for a guinea a number, but was soon asked to finance the project himself. On its completion in 174 numbers the publisher went bankrupt and Scott found himself in debt, and he became embroiled in further difficulties and lawsuits over later revised editions.[51] Despite this unhappy start, it became a standard work, and William Orme thought it unlikely to be soon superseded.[52]

Continuities and innovations in religious publishing: sermons, devotional works, hymns and magazines

Over the period 1695 to 1830 there were significant continuities as well as innovations in religious publishing. For the period from the Reformation up to about 1720 Protestant books which were regularly reprinted have been studied very fully by Ian Green, who has divided them into the broad categories of catechisms, sermons, treatises, devotional works, handbooks on preparation for communion and miscellaneous works combining entertainment with instruction.[53] Certain forms remained standard, and several popular works first published in the seventeenth century continued their steady sales right through the eighteenth and into the nineteenth century; at the same time this period witnessed the development of new forms which were to become increasingly influential. The following account, necessarily highly selective, is concerned first with examples of older forms, sermons and devotional or

49 Prices taken from 'Catalogue of books published by the Rev. Mr Wesley', 1790? (Bodleian shelfmark G.A.Glouc.b.4a (f.175)).
50 Rack 1989, 343.
51 Scott 1823, chap. 10.
52 Preston 1982, 122; Orme 1824, 393.
53 I. Green 2000, 188–9. There is as yet no comparable study for the eighteenth century, but see Rivers 1982b and 2012. On catechisms up to 1740, see Green 1996.

didactic works, and then with the two principal new ones, the collection of hymns for congregational worship and the religious magazine for family reading.

Sermons almost certainly constituted the largest category of religious publishing.[54] Two lengthy indexes, Sampson Letsome's *The preacher's assistant* (1753) and John Cooke's revision and expansion of Letsome under the same title (2 vols., Clarendon Press, 1783), provide a very full guide to what was published. Cooke's subtitle explains the method and time-span: *Containing a series of the* [biblical] *texts of sermons and discourses published either singly, or in volumes, by divines of the Church of England, and by the dissenting clergy, since the Restoration to the present time, specifying also the several authors alphabetically arranged under each text – with the size, date, occasion, or subject matter of each sermon or discourse.* His first volume, 'A series of the texts of sermons, &c.', is arranged under seven headings: chapter, verse, authors, edition (including size and date), volume, title, and occasion or subject; his second, 'An historical register of authors, &c. in the series', gives the same information arranged alphabetically by author, together with the authors' degrees and livings or appointments and the libraries where the sermons are held – public and private libraries in both universities, the British Museum and Dr Williams's Library (Cooke regretted not being able to include cathedral and parochial libraries). Dissenters are indicated by italics, and Cooke's large number of additions to Letsome by asterisks. Cooke lists more than 24,000 items, 81 per cent by clergy of the established church and 19 per cent by dissenters (a disproportionately large representation). The largest annual number of Anglican sermons (nearly 2,500) was published in 1710, the largest number of dissenting sermons (nearly 1,000) in 1770. The largest category by topic was practical (27 per cent of Anglican sermons as against 35 per cent of dissenting), the second largest doctrinal (19 per cent as against 23 per cent). Far more Anglican sermons were on political topics (13 per cent as against 7 per cent); Anglicans published far fewer funeral sermons proportionately than did dissenters (3 per cent as against 9 per cent).[55]

New single sermons in octavo were frequently advertised in groups of different authors, usually but not invariably priced at 6*d.* each;[56] thus the *Monthly Catalogue* for June 1724 lists four by dissenters printed for J. Clark

54 Feather 1986, 38, tables 1–2; Lessenich 1972.

55 These figures are taken from the useful analysis by Deconinck-Brossard 1993, 106–11. She warns (p. 111) that published sermons represent the tip of the iceberg and the impression that the churches wanted to convey rather than the reality of regular preaching.

56 For interesting comments on the cost and size of single sermons, see Carter 1975, 284.

and R. Hett, priced respectively at 1*s*. 6*d*., 4*d*., 1*s*. and 6*d*. Advertisements in the catalogues give a clear indication of the range of public places and occasions at which Anglican sermons were preached: before the House of Commons, at assizes, consecrations of bishops, episcopal visitations, Act-Sunday at Oxford and Commencement at Cambridge, on 30 January for the anniversary of Charles I's execution, royal birthdays and accession days, thanksgiving days (for example, for the suppression of the '45 rebellion) and fast-days. Many sermons were addressed to societies and published on their behalf: for example, the Society for the Reformation of Manners, the Sons of the Clergy, charity schools, the Three Choirs and the Society of Ancient Britons. Single sermons of this kind were far more typical than the well-known series of Boyle lectures to which Richard Bentley, Samuel Clarke and William Derham contributed, or the Rolls Chapel sermons, of which Joseph Butler is the most famous exponent. It is difficult to discover who bought these huge numbers of single sermons, whatever their topics. Did the laity buy them, or were they brought out at the expense of organizations or individuals for free distribution? It appears from the experience of Rivingtons that booksellers did not put up the capital costs.[57]

Collected sermons, whether of an individual or a series by several hands, were usually published in several volumes in folio or quarto; their cost suggests that only the prosperous would have bought them. Two multi-author collections published in the 1730s illustrate the different possible purposes of sermon publishing of this kind. *A defence of natural and revealed religion: being a collection of the sermons preached at the lecture founded by the honourable Robert Boyle, esq.*, was edited by Sampson Letsome and John Nicholl and published in three volumes folio (1739) by Daniel Midwinter. Advertised at three guineas in sheets in the *Monthly Catalogue* for February 1739, *A defence of natural and revealed religion* represents a commercial publication of material of considerable importance for the philosophical definition of eighteenth-century Christianity, which would presumably have been bought for college and gentry libraries. Richard Watson recommended it strongly: 'If all other Defences of Religion were lost, there is solid Reasoning enough (if properly weighed) in these three volumes to remove the Scruples of most Unbelievers.'[58] Another multi-volume set, *Faith and practice represented in fifty-four sermons on the principal heads of the Christian religion; preached at Berry-Street 1733 . . . published for the use of families, especially on the Lord's Day evenings*, was published in two volumes

57 Rivington 1919, 30; Carter 1975, 283.
58 Watson 1791, VI, 'Catalogue of books in divinity'.

octavo (1735) by R. Hett and J. Oswald, advertised at 11*s.* in the *Monthly Catalogue* for February 1735. This collection of lectures by Isaac Watts and five other dissenting ministers known as the Bury Street sermons, supported by the Congregational philanthropist William Coward, represents a charitable publication to teach the principles and practice of Christianity to dissenting families in their own homes. 'This book, does, indeed, constitute a pretty little system of practical divinity', Doddridge told Wesley, 'and I advise my young people [i.e. at his academy], when entering upon their studies, not only to read but to abridge it.'[59]

The much reprinted sermons of Archbishop Tillotson clearly illustrate the different status and cost of single items and collections. Tillotson published a large number of single sermons and discourses in his lifetime, as well as six collections of sermons. By his death in 1694, 54 sermons and the anti-Catholic treatise *The rule of faith* had appeared, but Tillotson left 200 unpublished in manuscript; these were edited by his chaplain, Ralph Barker, and brought out in fourteen volumes from 1695 to 1704. Tillotson's widow, Elizabeth, sold the copy for £2,500.[60] Up to 1735 there were ten collected editions of the 54 sermons and *The rule of faith*; between 1712 and 1735 there were five editions of Barker's posthumous collection of the 200 sermons; in 1728 the two collections were brought together, totalling 254 sermons and *The rule of faith*. In 1752 Thomas Birch in his new three-volume folio edition containing his important scholarly life of Tillotson increased the number to 255 by including Tillotson's first published sermon from a collection edited by Samuel Annesley in 1661. Over the same period single sermons were repeatedly reissued. In July 1729 the *Monthly Catalogue* under the heading 'Books reprinted' advertised four different collections and single works by Tillotson: *Six sermons* at 2*s.* bound or 18*s.* a dozen to those intending to give them away; *Works* in three volumes folio (containing 254 sermons and *The rule of faith*) at £2. 10*s.*; *A persuasive to frequent communion* at 3*d.* or 20*s.* per 100; *A discourse against transubstantiation* at 3*d.* or 20*s.* per 100. This advertisement illustrates very clearly the high and low ends of the sermon market and the importance attached by the clergy to the free distribution of sermons and other kinds of exhortation to their flocks.

A very large number of popular devotional and didactic books of different kinds were published by clergy and ministers for the benefit of the laity, and clerics of all denominations urged their people to read. In his much reprinted devotional handbook *The garden of the soul* (1740), the Roman Catholic bishop

59 Doddridge 1829–31, IV, 489, 18 June 1746 (first published in the *Arminian Magazine*, Sep. 1778).
60 *Tatler*, 101 (1 Dec. 1709); see Bond 1987, II, 122.

Richard Challoner gave precise instructions 'Of reading good books, or hearing the word of God':

> Let not a day pass without employing at least one quarter of an hour in reading the Scripture, or some spiritual book; and a more considerable time on *Sundays* and holidays: advise with your director what books may be most proper, and endeavour to procure them for yourself and family.
>
> Begin your reading by an humble invocation of the Holy Ghost, that you may profit by it: read leisurely and attentively, so as to let the lessons you read have time to make proper impressions upon you, and to sink deep into your heart. Pause awhile upon such places as touch you most: and from time to time excite affections and resolutions in your soul, suitable to the subject you are reading of ...
>
> If you are the master or mistress of a family, see that those under your charge want not the advantage of frequent reading or hearing what is good. It is a care your great master expects from you.[61]

Similar instructions, stressing the method and function of devotional reading and its influence downwards through different social strata, can be found in comparable Protestant works, such as William Law's *A serious call to a devout and holy life* (1729) and Doddridge's *The rise and progress of religion in the soul* (1745). These three works represent significant and (judging by the number of editions) very successful attempts to reinterpret older devotional traditions in eighteenth-century terms for Catholic, Anglican and dissenting readers.

What is striking, however, is the large number of earlier works that continued to be recommended and reissued, not always in their original form. Such works were sometimes altered to make them acceptable to different denominations, and shortened to make them cheaper to distribute and easier to read. Commercial, religious and educational motives all played their part in this process. Works that were officially adopted by societies – for example, the high church SPCK, John Wesley's Methodist Societies, or the dissenting and evangelical Society for Promoting Religious Knowledge among the Poor – thereby gained a much wider and longer lasting circulation.[62] The SPCK was partly responsible for the extraordinary longevity of the two most important and substantial Anglican handbooks, *The whole duty of man* (1658), usually attributed to Richard Allestree, and Robert Nelson's *A companion for the festivals and fasts of the Church of England* (1704).[63] *The whole duty*, though usually

61 Challoner 1755, 172–3. At the end there is a catalogue of books sold by James Marmaduke; *The garden of the soul* is listed at 1*s*. 6*d*.

62 See Mandelbrote, chap. 32, below.

63 Stranks 1961, chaps. 5–6; I. Green 2000, 353–5.

published in full, sometimes appeared in abridged or epitomized versions in 24mo size, or in Latin or Welsh translations, or even in verse. Both these works were republished regularly until the 1840s. The Society for Promoting Religious Knowledge among the Poor gave away long-established works by seventeenth-century nonconformists, such as Richard Baxter's *Call to the unconverted* (first published 1658 and later abridged) and Joseph Alleine's *An alarme to unconverted sinners* (1672), in addition to works by eighteenth-century dissenters such as Watts and Doddridge.[64] John Wesley also printed Baxter's *Call* and Alleine's *Alarme* in abridged versions to be given away.[65]

There was an established tradition after the Reformation of Protestants adapting Catholic handbooks for their own purposes,[66] and eighteenth-century editors and distributors similarly felt free to make earlier works fit the requirements of their own different denominations. Three interesting examples are the *Imitatio Christi* by the fifteenth-century German monk Thomas à Kempis, *The life of God in the soul of man* by the Scottish Episcopalian Henry Scougal, and *The pilgrim's progress* by the English nonconformist John Bunyan. The *Imitatio Christi* was available in several different versions under different titles for Roman Catholics, Anglicans and Methodists, the most regularly reprinted in a range of sizes and prices being the Anglican George Stanhope's wordy paraphrase *The Christian's pattern* (1696), John Wesley's *The Christian's pattern* (1735), based on John Worthington's revision (1654) of an earlier version, Wesley's abridgement *An extract of the Christian's pattern* (1741), and Richard Challoner's *The following of Christ* (1737).[67] *The life of God in the soul of man* (1677) first appeared posthumously with a preface by Gilbert Burnet, and was subsequently edited by other Protestants of varying sympathies: John Wesley (1744), the moderate Scottish Presbyterian William Wishart (1756), and the Unitarian Joshua Toulmin (1782).[68] Though Toulmin's version (sold by Joseph Johnson) was little known, Wesley's was published in the main Methodist centres, London, Bristol and Newcastle, and Wishart's in Edinburgh, Glasgow, Berwick and Belfast. The Society for Promoting Religious Knowledge among the Poor added *The life of God in the soul of man* to its list in 1765. The edition published by W. Phorson of Berwick

64 *An account of the Society for Promoting Religious Knowledge among the Poor. Began anno 1750*, (1769, London), 'The names and number of books given away by the Society' (pull-out table); I. Green 2000, 337–9; Rivers 2007.

65 Green 1906, nos. 362, 363, both in 1782.

66 I. Green 2000, 305–9, on à Kempis and Parsons; Collinson, Hunt and Walsham 2002, 44–55, on 'Catholic books'.

67 Copinger 1900, nos. 9, 11, 16, 17; Baker 1941; Rivers 1982b, 153–5.

68 Butler 1899; Henderson 1937, chaps. 6, 10.

in 1791 with the prefaces of Burnet and Wishart contains a revealing list of Phorson's other publications at the end, including seventeenth-century Puritan and nonconformist authors such as Lewis Bayly, John Owen and John Flavel, together with early eighteenth-century authors such as the Scottish Calvinist Thomas Boston and the English dissenters Watts and Defoe. *The pilgrim's progress* (1678, part 2 1684), already a bestseller in Bunyan's lifetime, was increasingly available in a multiplicity of versions for different social and religious groups, abridged, edited, annotated or illustrated.[69] A large number of eighteenth-century editions included the spurious third part, first published in 1692. In 1728 J. Clark and J. Brotherton published a subscription edition in octavo with twenty-two copperplates by John Sturt, advertised in the *Monthly Catalogue* for March 1728 at 6*s*., quite unlike all previous cheap editions; this suggests a deliberate attempt to boost the work's standing at a time when Bunyan's literary reputation was still low. In contrast Wesley's much reprinted abridgement of the first part (Newcastle, 1743), with careful doctrinal excisions,[70] sold at 4*d*. for forty-nine pages duodecimo. In the later eighteenth century the Congregationalist George Burder and the Anglican evangelicals John Newton, Thomas Scott and William Mason produced separate annotated editions, sometimes with illustrations, which were repeatedly reissued in the nineteenth century. Burder was also at least the third person to turn *Pilgrim's progress* into verse.

Many English devotional works found a ready market overseas, though only a few examples can be given here.[71] Several seventeenth-century classics were translated into German, and increased in popularity in the eighteenth century: thus there were ten German-language editions of *The whole duty of man* published by German and Swiss booksellers (including one in Copenhagen) in the period 1700–50, with only four in the later seventeenth century; there were twenty-four German-language editions of the first part of *Pilgrim's progress* published by German and Swiss booksellers (including one in Amsterdam) in the period 1685–1750, seven of these published in the 1730s.[72] Among eighteenth-century works, Doddridge's enormously influential *The rise and progress of religion* was translated into German (Hanover, 1750), Dutch (Amsterdam, 1747, 1749, 1767, 1775, 1776) and French (The Hague, 1751).[73] The SPCK regularly sent out large numbers of *The whole duty of man* among

69 Harrison 1936, 1942; Greaves 2002, 610–19.
70 Rivers 1991, 219.
71 See Fabian and Spieckermann, chap. 27 above.
72 McKenzie 1997, nos. 108–21, 485–508.
73 Nuttall 1979, xxix–xxx, letters 1557, 1668; Van den Berg and Nuttall 1987, 35–7, appendix 1.

other books to parochial libraries in the American colonies.[74] *The pilgrim's progress* was already being printed in New England in 1681, and *The rise and progress* represented the largest order for imported books by the Boston bookseller and minister James Condy in the period 1754–68.[75]

Alongside these traditional forms of religious publication, major new forms emerged as a consequence of important developments in religious culture among the dissenters and evangelicals. The spread of congregational hymn singing among the dissenters in the early eighteenth century, taken up by Methodists and evangelicals in the mid-eighteenth century and by Anglicans in general in the early nineteenth, produced an explosion in the publication of hymn books.[76] Some of these books were wholly or largely the work of individuals, notably the Congregationalist Isaac Watts, the Methodist Charles Wesley, the evangelical John Newton and the Anglican John Keble; others were editions and compilations. The most influential early eighteenth-century collections were those of Isaac Watts, *Hymns and spiritual songs* (1707, enlarged 1709) and *The Psalms of David imitated in the language of the New Testament* (1719), which were often printed together: there were 163 editions of the *Hymns* by 1791, and very many more in the nineteenth century, a large number of them American.[77] John Wesley issued several hymn books under various titles from 1737, the most important being *A collection of hymns for the use of the people called Methodists* (1780), the majority of which were by his brother Charles; this became the standard book for the Methodist Societies.[78] Newton's *Olney hymns* (1779), written in collaboration with the layman and poet William Cowper, were originally intended for use in prayer meetings in Olney, Buckinghamshire, not as part of the church service. It was not until the nineteenth century that hymns became tied to the Anglican liturgy. The key text in bringing about this development was Keble's *The Christian year, thoughts in verse for the Sundays and holydays throughout the year* (1827), though this was designed for private reading, not congregational singing. In addition a number of popular compilations established themselves, for example, George Burder's *A collection of hymns from various authors. Intended as a supplement to Dr Watts's hymns, and imitation of the psalms* (1774), John Rippon's *A selection of hymns from the best authors, intended to be an appendix to Dr Watts's psalms and hymns* (1787)

74 Allen and McClure 1898, 22, 23–5; Laugher 1973, 44, 53, 96, 100; Beales and Green 2000, 400; cf. Mandelbrote, chap. 32 below.

75 Amory 2000b, 100; Reilly and Hall 2000, 389.

76 Watson 1997, chaps. 7–12. On metrical psalms, which for reasons of space cannot be considered here, see I. Green 2000, chap. 9.

77 Bishop 1974.

78 Wesley 1983.

and James Montgomery's *The Christian psalmist; or, hymns selected and original* (1825). Hymns by writers from different denominations, and by members of the laity as well as ministers, women as well as men, appeared together in such books. *A collection of hymns adapted to public worship* (1769), edited by John Ash and Caleb Evans, included hymns by Elizabeth Rowe, Elizabeth Scott and Anne Steele not originally designed for congregational singing. Several of these works had provincial imprints – Burder's were published in Coventry – and some were sold by the ministers themselves: Rippon's *Selection* (1787), printed in London, was 'sold on week days, at the Vestry of Mr Rippon's Meeting-House', and successive editions of Joseph Hart's *Hymns, &c. composed on various subjects* (1759) were sold at the house of the author, his widow and his daughter. Hymn books would repay further study both as a means whereby the doctrines and practices of different denominations were disseminated or countered (for example, Calvinist hymns were modified in Unitarian hymn books), and as an illustration of the variety of routes through which popular religious literature reached its audience.

The other crucial new form to develop was the religious magazine. The hymn book as Wesley saw it gave lay people 'a little body of experimental and practical divinity',[79] and involved them directly in the lives of their societies and churches; the magazine in addition gave them a sense of the history and current development of the denomination or movement to which they belonged.[80] The first important magazines, John Lewis's London-based *Weekly History* and *Christian History*, were the product of the Calvinist revivals from 1741 to 1746 associated with George Whitefield in England, Wales, Scotland and North America; there were parallel magazines in Scotland and New England in the same period, the *Glasgow Weekly History* and the *Christian Monthly History*, and the Boston-based *Christian History*. These magazines emphasized religious news at home and abroad and included large numbers of letters describing the various revivals, which were also read aloud at society meetings; converts could thus share publicly or privately in the experiences of others, most of them members of the laity, in an international movement. At one point Lewis printed an advertisement in the *Weekly History* inviting the poor who could not afford the magazine (the usual price of such publications was from 1*d.* to 3½*d.*) to read it for nothing at his printing house.[81] Later monthly

79 Wesley 1983, 74.

80 For an excellent history, see Mineka 1944, chap. 2; also Altholz 1989 and the listings in *NCBEL*, II cols. 1291–312, III cols. 1839–44.

81 Durden 1976; this is an exceptionally useful and informative article. See also O'Brien 1986, 1994; Lambert 1994.

magazines tended to be clearly identified by doctrinal or denominational affiliation, and sometimes took a combative stance towards their rivals. Calvinist evangelicals were catered for from the 1760s to the 1780s by the *Spiritual Magazine* and successive series of the *Gospel Magazine*, to which John Newton contributed his *Omicron Letters* in 1771–4. The *Gospel Magazine* was edited from 1774 to 1776 first by William Mason and then by Augustus Montagu Toplady (also the compiler of a hymn book).[82] John Wesley's *Arminian Magazine* was explicitly started in 1778 in opposition to Toplady's editorial stance; it was renamed the *Methodist Magazine* in 1798 and the *Wesleyan Methodist Magazine* in 1822, with *Wesleyan* dropped from the title in 1914, and was to prove the longest running of the religious magazines founded in the eighteenth century.[83] Thomas Jackson, its editor from 1824 to 1842, also edited Wesley's *Works*, his *Christian library* and *The lives of early Methodist preachers*, autobiographies commissioned by Wesley and first published by him in the *Arminian*. Both Calvinist and Wesleyan magazines published a wide range of material, divinity, biography, autobiography, letters, essays, reviews, hymns and poetry; Wesley's statements of editorial policy in the prefaces to volumes 1, 4 and 7 show how he regarded his magazine as an educational medium and as a transmitter of a new kind of religious literature.

From the 1790s there was a large increase in the number of religious magazines, with clearly defined audiences and intellectual levels. The *British Critic* (1793–1826) was high church in its sympathies; the *Christian Observer* (1802–74), one of whose editors was Zachary Macaulay, catered for the increasingly influential body of Anglican evangelicals; the long-lived and very popular *Evangelical Magazine* (founded 1793) addressed both dissenting and church evangelicals, as had the earlier *Gospel Magazine*, and included George Burder among its editors.[84] Other dissenting magazines aimed at a more cultured and liberally minded readership: the *Eclectic Review* (1805–68) took an interest in non-religious literature; the *Monthly Repository of Theology and General Literature* (1806–26), edited by the Unitarian minister Robert Aspland, published a great deal of material on the history of dissent and its political status.[85] Religious magazines thus filled a wide range of functions: in some ways they overlapped with traditional devotional and didactic literature, or reinforced the identities

82 Mineka 1944, 37–9; Hindmarsh 1996, 247–9.
83 Cumbers 1956, 115–17, appendix 2.
84 For the cultural role of magazines for evangelicals, see Rosman 1984.
85 Mineka 1944, chap. 3. On the earliest Unitarian periodical, Priestley's *Theological Repository*, see McLachlan 1923, chap. 3.

of particular religious communities; in others they encouraged the critical examination of doctrine and the historical and political basis of the often conflicting relations between the denominations; they further provided some of the pleasures of secular literature, especially poetry and history. They provided the laity with a new kind of religious material which was separate from devotion, yet their success demonstrated that the appetite for religious publications in the early nineteenth century was insatiable.

31

The Bible trade

B.J. McMULLIN

In the overall history of the book in Britain, the lapse of the Licensing Act signals a fundamental change in the circumstances of printing and publishing, but for the Bible trade the year 1695 was essentially uneventful.[1] The production of the Authorized (or King James) Version (AV) of the Bible, along with the Book of Common Prayer (the liturgy of the established Church of England), continued to be the subject of a privilege enjoyed in England by the King's Printer in London and the Universities of Oxford and Cambridge, in Scotland by the King's Printer for Scotland, and in Ireland by the Printer-General. Similarly, the metrical psalms – in the version of Thomas Sternhold and John Hopkins – continued to form part of the English Stock of the Stationers' Company, to be printed by members on behalf of the shareholders, and often bound up with Bibles and prayer books from the privileged printers.

The privileged printers

The history of the office of the King's Printer in England is a complex one,[2] reflected in the imprints of London Bibles: there were competing claims to the office and overlapping patents; moreover, the nominal incumbents frequently assigned their rights to others, either exclusively or in fractions, such arrangements being indicated by imprints reading 'By the assigns of ...'. In January 1710, the office passed to the heirs of Thomas Newcombe and Henry Hills for a period of thirty years. John Baskett, who was subsequently to secure a virtual monopoly of Bible printing in Britain, bought a one-sixth share of this privilege in May 1710, and by 1732 – when his name first appears alone in the imprint of a London Bible – he had bought out the other interests. At his death

1 This chapter is a continuation of the chapter with the same title in *CHBB* IV; like that chapter, it is based essentially on published sources; only the principal ones, which provide further references, are identified in the footnotes.

2 Carter 1975; McKitterick 1998.

in 1742, Baskett was succeeded by his sons Thomas and Robert, and by dint of purchasing the competing rights of Benjamin Tooke and John Barber – due to take effect in 1740 – members of the Baskett family remained as King's Printers until 1769, when Charles Eyre purchased the remaining thirty years of their privilege. Thus began the reign as King's Printer of what was to become the firm Eyre and Spottiswoode, King's/Queen's Printer until 1990.

The first London Bible to bear the names of Eyre and William Strahan did not appear until 1772. In addition to Bible printing, the privileges and duties of the King's Printer included Acts of Parliament, proclamations and the like, and the attraction of the office for Eyre and Strahan was the profit to be made from this government printing. In practice, they licensed other London printers to undertake the printing of Bibles. Not that buyers were deprived by the inactivity of the King's Printers: for much of the previous fifty years the market for Bibles in England had been satisfied by Oxford University.

Although Oxford University was to be the dominant printer of Bibles and prayer books in the eighteenth century, by agreements extending from 1693 to 1713 it had been the university's practice to forgo the right in return for an annual payment of £200 from the Stationers' Company, an arrangement superseding that previously made with the London booksellers Peter Parker, Thomas Guy, Moses Pitt and William and Ann Leake. Thus, beginning with the New Testament of 1694 and ending with the Bible of 1713, Oxford Bibles were issued over the imprint of 'The University-Printers'. In 1713, John Baskett supplanted the Company when the university granted him a lease of twenty-one years, again at £200 a year. Beginning in 1715, therefore, Oxford Bibles bear the imprint of John Baskett, 'Printer to the King's most excellent majesty, and the University'.

At Oxford, the Baskett interest came to an end in 1765, on the expiry of the lease granted in 1744 to Thomas (d. 1761), who had been succeeded by his son Mark. The lease now passed to the London stationers Thomas Wright and William Gill, at £850 a year. In 1780, however, when the lease fell vacant again, the university could find no bidders and at this point entered into a partnership – covering the whole of the university's publishing – with a succession of master printers, designated 'Printer to the Univerity', the first being William Jackson (in Oxford) and Archibald Hamilton (in London). The partnership arrangement was to survive until 1884.

The third privileged printer, Cambridge University, was effectively silent as far as Bible printing is concerned for sixty years following the publication of the quarto Bible of 1683. After that date, there were editions of the Book of Common Prayer in 1694, 1696 and 1701; a Sternhold and Hopkins in 1696;

and editions of the new Tate and Brady metrical psalms in 1698, 1699 and 1702. Otherwise – apart from a brief interlude in the 1730s – the Cambridge Syndics abandoned the field to London and Oxford, apparently feeling financially disadvantaged by the lack of access by river to London. The decision to re-engage with the other privileged printers was taken in December 1740, when Joseph Bentham was elected to succeed Cornelius Crownfield as University Printer. The first fruit was the duodecimo Bible of 1743. Thereafter, there was an uninterrupted flow of Bibles and prayer books from Cambridge, which – unlike Oxford – incorporated Bible production into the general work of the printing house. Bentham was succeeded in turn by John Archdeacon (1766), John Burges (1793), Richard Watts (1802) and John Smith (1809).

In 1695, the holder of the office of King's Printer for Scotland was Agnes Campbell, widow of Andrew Anderson (d. 1676), whose forty-one-year privilege expired in 1711. The patent was then granted to Robert Freebairn, but temporarily forfeited by him because of his participation in the 1715 Rebellion, whereupon a new patent was granted to John Baskett and Agnes Campbell (d. 1716). James Watson had already acquired a share of Freebairn's grant, so that until 1752 the office was shared by Baskett, Watson and Freebairn or their assigns or heirs. Until 1725, however, when he set up a printing house in Edinburgh, Baskett was content simply to import Bibles that he had printed in Oxford or London. Alexander Kincaid joined the patentees in 1747, and in 1785 the privilege passed to Sir James Hunter Blair and John Bruce.

The office of Printer-General in Ireland had been held since 1660 by members of the Crooke family, culminating in Andrew, whose patent was renewed in 1693 for the term of his natural life. Holders of the office preferred to do government work, however, and left Bible printing to others. On Andrew's death in 1732, the office passed to George Grierson, and remained with members of the Grierson family well into the nineteenth century. The earliest surviving Bible printed in Ireland is a folio AV of 1714,[3] printed by Aaron Rhames, but there had clearly been earlier editions of which no copies survive. In predominantly Roman Catholic Ireland, the demand for the AV was limited and was satisfied largely from England or Scotland; nonetheless, prior to 1830 twenty-odd editions of the whole Bible or the New Testament (NT) in the AV were printed in Ireland.[4]

3 Darlow and Moule 1968, no. 928.
4 Pollard 2000.

Competition in Bible-printing

The privileges granted to the King's Printers, dating from Christopher Barker's patent of 1577, were rehearsed in 1799, when John Reeves joined Eyre and Strahan in a thirty-year arrangement. This new patent records that in 1716 George I had granted to John Baskett the right to print 'all ... Bibles and New Testaments whatsoever, in the English tongue or in any other tongue whatsoever of any translation, with notes or without notes; and also of all Books of Common-Prayer and Administration of the Sacraments and other Rites and Ceremonies of the Church of England, in any volumes [i.e. formats] whatsoever'.[5] Despite the broad terms of their patents relating to Bibles, the privileged printers sought to protect only their monopoly on printing the AV without notes. Most would-be competitors no doubt lacked the capital necessary to produce a work of biblical length in a variety of formats;[6] but – given the problems of producing frequent long runs of bulky texts in the hand-press period – the privileged printers themselves probably lacked the capacity to produce anything more than an unadorned text of the one version in several formats. Yet, competition did exist.

From 1743, when Cambridge resumed Bible printing, and more particularly from the late 1760s, when the Baskett interest at Oxford had come to an end and Eyre had become King's Printer, there was competition within England among the three privileged printers. Further competition was afforded by the King's Printer for Scotland, particularly after 1757 (when the Basketts ceased to be involved) – until the end of the eighteenth century, there appears to have been no objection by the various patentees to the circulation of Scottish-printed Bibles in England or, for that matter, of English-printed Bibles in Scotland.

In January 1802, however, the two universities sought an injunction forbidding the London booksellers Messrs Richardson from selling Scottish-printed Bibles without their consent or that of Eyre and Strahan. As the universities did not proceed against any other English bookseller, Hunter and Blair continued to supply Bibles to England – until, that is, the King's Printers began to take a renewed interest in the Bible branch of their patent. By 1820, through pursuing individual booksellers, they had managed to exclude Scottish-printed Bibles from England, whereas English-printed Bibles continued to be sold in Scotland, a situation which led Sir David Hunter Blair and John Bruce to seek

5 Reprinted in Hansard 1825, 183.

6 For example, in 1772 Oxford-printed Bibles extended to 262 sheets in folio, 164 in quarto, 83 in octavo and 35 (no Apocrypha) in duodecimo.

an injunction – granted in March 1823 – forbidding the sale of English-printed Bibles in Scotland.[7]

At no stage do the British patentees seem to have considered Irish Bibles a threat to their interests. In the second half of the seventeenth century, however, Holland had been a significant source of Bibles and editions of Sternhold and Hopkins (but not prayer books) for the English-speaking market.[8] Contemporaries attributed the attraction of Dutch-printed Bibles principally to their being cheaper than editions produced by the King's Printers. The situation changed, however, in the 1680s, when the sub-lessees of the Oxford privilege engaged in competition with the King's Printers, driving down domestic prices and thus depriving the Dutch editions of their prime advantage. Dutch editions with Geneva notes presumably continued to find buyers, but after 1700 there appear to be few Dutch-printed English Bibles, the last probably being the quarto dated 1730.

As the privileged printers countenanced the production of the AV with notes, the only constraints on printing such editions were financial ones. Annotated editions of the complete Bible came to be commonplace from the late 1750s. Often incorporating in their titles the word 'family', many of them were folios, often with illustrations, but they were obviously not intended for lecterns: their ostensible market implies a growing level of literacy (however limited) and the increasing emphasis on 'self-study' in the home.

On the one hand, the proliferation of folio family Bibles may reflect the more substantial resources of mid-century printers. On the other, their popularity coincided with the rise of publishing in numbers, whereby the cost of a book could be spread over a period of time by purchasing a gathering or two each week or month, so that it could be said that the family Bible was actually made possible by this form of publication.[9] The earliest of the eighteenth-century annotated editions, Samuel Parker's five-volume *Bibliotheca biblica*, was published in this form: a monthly, its publication extended, extraordinarily, from 1720 to 1735.

One device adopted specifically to circumvent the privilege was to print annotated Bibles with the notes placed so far below the text that in binding they could be ploughed off – indeed, that must have been the intention, for the notes are at best perfunctory, at worst vacuous or nonsensical. Moreover, with

7 The decision fell heavily on the Scottish Bible Societies, whose needs were not being met from Edinburgh – hence Lee's *Memorial*, which constitutes an exhaustive account of Bible-printing in Britain, especially as it bears on the question of importation.

8 See Hoftijzer and Lankhorst, chap. 26, above.

9 See Harris, chap. 20, above.

the notes in place, duodecimos, for example, are abnormally tall in relation to their width, but, with the notes removed, assume more usual proportions. The earliest Bible of this kind is Pasham's (1776).[10] Bound copies of all such editions have survived with and without the notes.

Bible printing at Cambridge

As already noted, from 1743 there was an uninterrupted flow of Bibles and prayer books from Cambridge. This section is devoted to three episodes in the history of Bible printing at Cambridge in the eighteenth century, the first actually anticipating the resumption by the university itself.

The 'brief interlude' in the 1730s mentioned above is the attempt by William Ged to apply his invention of stereotyping to the Bible and the Book of Common Prayer.[11] The Bible (and, less obviously, the prayer book, with its unstable text) was the very work for which printing from stereotype plates was especially suited: the text was – at least in principle – fixed, and editions in large numbers were called for frequently. Because printing the AV in England was the preserve of the three privileged printers, Ged's partners – who supplied the necessary technical and financial support – successfully approached Cambridge to have him appointed Printer to the University in 1731 so that the experiment could go ahead. Disagreement among the partners and resistance from type founders, compositors and pressmen led to the project being abandoned in 1733, however.

Possibly the only surviving result of Ged's Cambridge venture is a single copy of an octavo prayer book dated 1733, the imprint bearing the name of William Fenner (one of the partners, a bookseller); the initial gatherings seem to have been printed from plates, the remainder – beginning with gathering H – from type. There is considerable uncertainty as to whether any further prayer books or Bibles printed from plates were produced at Cambridge, though Ged himself claimed that, after his departure, the Press printed three prayer books (including the 1733 octavo) and a Bible using his process.[12] The successful application of stereotyping to British printing had to await the foundation of the British and Foreign Bible Society in 1804, by which time Ged's process had been forgotten.[13]

10 Darlow and Moule 1968, no. 1249.
11 Carter 1960. Cf. Mosley, chap. 7, above.
12 Ged 1781.
13 See Mosley, chap. 7 above and Mandelbrote, chap. 32, below.

A similar interlude began in December 1758 when, in order to satisfy his ambition to print the Bible and the Book of Common Prayer, John Baskerville had himself elected Printer to the University for a period of ten years.[14] Baskerville's folio Bible, printed in his own type, finally appeared in July 1763.[15] It bears comparison with Oxford's Vinegar Bible (see below) in terms of execution; moreover, both were 'remaindered' and both have survived in large numbers, no doubt because of their visual attributes. In addition to the Bible, between 1760 and 1762 Baskerville printed at Cambridge four editions of the Book of Common Prayer,[16] a Sternhold and Hopkins[17] and a Tate and Brady.[18]

Despite his election as printer, Baskerville faced direct competition from the university itself when in July 1759 the Syndics decided to print a new edition of the Bible, its preparation entrusted to F.S. Parris, of Sidney Sussex College, who had been involved with the revival of Bible-printing in the early 1740s. Parris's edition was imposed first for printing in quarto and then 'lengthened' by being reimposed for printing in folio. Herbert[19] observes that:

> In this Bible a serious attempt was made to correct the text of King James' version by amending the spelling and punctuation, unifying and extending the use of italics, and removing printers' errors. Marginal annotations, which had been growing in some Bibles since 1660, although excluded from others, were finally received into the place they have occupied ever since, sundry new ones being added. Lloyd's dates and chronological notes[20] ... were also adopted and increased, and the marginal references were much enlarged.

As a result of this care, Parris's edition became recognized as the 'Cambridge standard Bible', for some time the ultimate source for editions produced by the university.

Bible printing at Oxford

The Oxford Bible press was the most active of the three privileged printers in England in the eighteenth century, though when members of the Baskett family were concurrently printers to the university and King's Printers there

14 Gaskell 1959.
15 Gaskell 1959, no. 26.
16 Gaskell 1959, nos. 12, 13, 19, 20.
17 Gaskell 1959, no. 21.
18 Gaskell 1959, no. 22.
19 Darlow and Moule 1968, no. 1142.
20 William Lloyd, Bishop of Worcester, was apparently responsible for assigning the dates BC and AD, which first appeared in the London folio of 1701 (Darlow and Moule 1968, no. 868).

is the possibility that imprints do not reflect the true place of printing. This section is devoted to three notable editions bearing Oxford imprints.

The first folio printed by John Baskett at Oxford, in 1717 (NT 1716), is one of the finest products of the hand-press in Britain.[21] Among Bibles, its only rival is probably the Baskerville folio (see above). Textually, the 1717 folio is not so well regarded: it is known variously as 'A Baskett-ful of errors' and 'The Vinegar Bible' (from an erroneous running title in Luke xx, reading 'The Parable of the Vinegar' instead of 'Vineyard'). Presumably, Baskett's greater concern was with producing a sumptuous edition: typographically it is undeniably impressive. In addition to the three issues on paper, at least three copies were printed on vellum: one for the king, one for Oxford University and a third probably for the Treasurer, Lord Harley.

The 1743 Oxford quarto, the first Bible printed entirely by Thomas and Robert Baskett, is unremarkable in appearance, but certainly remarkable as evidence of the efforts made to produce an accurate text.[22] Whatever their motive, they went to great lengths: in its 'corrected' form at least 132 of its 622 leaves (21.2 per cent) are cancellantia. Since copies of the 'uncorrected' form have survived, the changes are identifiable: some genuine errors are corrected, but most of the changes are 'indifferent', and, despite the concern for accuracy (extending to the marginal notes), the reset leaves introduce errors of their own. From a bibliographical standpoint the most interesting feature of the cancellantia is their signatures. The volume is gathered in eights, signed $1–4, and the cancellantia in $5–8 are signed 'by the page' – that is, according to a system whereby a cancellans $5 is signed $9, $5r being the ninth page in the gathering. No satisfactory explanation for this practice has yet been advanced.

As at Cambridge in 1762, a determined effort was made at Oxford in the 1760s to produce an accurate text of the Bible when Benjamin Blayney, of Hertford College, was engaged to produce a new edition. It appeared in 1769, and, like Parris's edition, it was issued in both quarto and folio. Blayney's text became the Oxford standard, though it has not met with universal approval – Herbert[23] observes that 'Blayney quietly incorporated most of Paris's [*sic*] improvements, increased his marginalia, and repeated not a few of his errors.' Copies of Blayney's edition were destroyed on 8 January 1770 in the fire at the London auction house of Mr Upton, where Oxford Bibles and prayer books were being stored. This fire is the source of the mistaken belief that Parris's

21 McMullin 1984.
22 McMullin 1998.
23 Darlow and Moule 1968, no. 1194.

edition was substantially lost in a fire at the warehouse of Benjamin Dod, Cambridge's London agent: there is no evidence that such a fire occurred.[24]

Physical aspects

Apart from folios in general and Baskerville's and the Vinegar in particular, Bibles of the eighteenth century are not, in physical appearance, especially distinguished. Those printed by the University Printers at Oxford in the years around 1700 – from worn small type in small formats on poor paper – could be particularly bad. When shoddy materials and slovenly workmanship were combined with corrupt texts, the resulting editions duly earned the wrath of critical readers. The poor reputation of Bibles printed in Britain can probably be attributed to the monopoly conditions under which they were produced, particularly before 1743, whereby carelessness in textual matters might be accepted and poor paper employed in an attempt to increase profits.

Within the ordinary printing house, the main procedures remained constant until the very end of the hand-press period in the early decades of the nineteenth century. The Bible trade, however, requiring large numbers in frequent editions in various formats, was necessarily innovative. Two notable aspects of production are described in this section, the second – applied initially on a large scale to the printing of Bibles – heralding the introduction of a new technology to printing in general.

As in the seventeenth century, particular markets for Bibles and prayer books were satisfied not only by various formats but often also by various qualities of paper. Editions might be produced on two (occasionally three) separate papers, though the differences are not always obvious. At times, two issues of the one edition can be distinguished only on the basis of their discrete watermarks. Paper-quality marks continued in use at Oxford until 1718, albeit sporadically. Such marks were intended to guide members of the trade, however, rather than to assist purchasers, whose only protection against misrepresentation was that the royal order of 24 April 1724 (issued in response to complaints about paper, type and text) required, among other things, that the retail price be printed on the title page. The importance of being able to distinguish issues on different papers may be illustrated by the 1770 Cambridge folio Book of Common Prayer, available on demy paper (2,000 copies) at 8*s*. and medium paper (1,000 copies) at 15*s*.

24 McMullin 1996.

After the aborted Ged experiment at Cambridge, the process of stereotyping was not applied in British printing until the conjunction of two events provided a new impetus: the reinvention of the process and the foundation of the British and Foreign Bible Society (BFBS).

Stereotyping was newly invented in Glasgow by Alexander Tilloch and Andrew Foulis, who in 1784 secured a patent for fourteen years. Several works are said to have been printed by Foulis from plates, but for some reason the process was abandoned until, in the late 1790s, Earl Stanhope took an interest in it and had Tilloch and Foulis transfer to him the technical details. In order to implement the stereotyping process, Stanhope enlisted the London printer Andrew Wilson, who was able to print substantial books from plates by 1804.[25]

The BFBS was established in 1804 with the aim of distributing copies of the AV without notes worldwide, in English and in other languages. Since the society is discussed elsewhere in this volume,[26] it is sufficient here to note its impact on the workings of the printing trade. The need for large numbers (almost entirely in octavo and smaller formats), produced as cheaply as possible, suggested that the new process, as with Ged's earlier invention, was ideally suited to the printing of Bibles, even if standing type eventually was preferred. Constrained by the privilege in England, the society had to enlist the services of the patentees, and, since Wilson had already arranged with Cambridge to print Bibles from plates, it was from Cambridge University Press that the first BFBS stereotyped New Testament appeared, in 1805.[27] Soon the society was having stereotyped Bibles printed by Oxford, in 1808,[28] and the King's Printers, in 1812.[29] No one printer had the capacity to meet all the society's needs, and spreading orders introduced a degree of competition that served to keep down printing costs, which were further restrained by using cheap paper.

The textual condition of the Authorized Version

As with any frequently reprinted work, the text of the AV was subject to progressive 'corruption', much of it, however, resulting from changing conventions in the printing house. Yet, the supposed divine origins of the Bible extended to the AV and ensured that the state of the text was a concern as early

25 M.L. Turner 1974.
26 See Mandelbrote, chap. 32, below.
27 Darlow and Moule 1968, no. 1485.
28 Darlow and Moule 1968, no. 1512.
29 Darlow and Moule 1968, no. 1562.

as the middle of the seventeenth century. At one extreme was an insistence – sometimes qualified by excluding printer's errors[30] – on a literal fidelity to the first printing (1611), even in typographical conventions. The 1611 itself was not free from error, however, even in translation. The accuracy of setting and the accidentals (including spellings) were, of course, no more than reflections of early seventeenth-century usage or compositors' preferences, while those of later editions are generally no more than indifferent modernizations.

Equally of concern by the early nineteenth century was the authority for the various intentional changes that had been introduced over the course of two centuries, particularly in Blayney's edition – indeed, the extent of the various 'improvements' and additions became part of the argument for abolishing the Bible privilege. Lee was particularly critical of the marginal notes, which, without any ecclesiastical authority, had increased from about 9,000 in the first edition to 64,983 in Blayney.[31] In response to Curtis's enquiries, Oxford claimed that it accepted Blayney as its standard; Cambridge did not know what the appropriate standard was; and the King's Printers were happy to let the universities sort things out and then to follow their example. In truth, it was easy to conclude that the privileged printers were not particularly concerned about the textual condition of their Bibles – especially the King's Printers, who took no responsibility for the printers to whom they sublet the privilege. So seriously corrupted was the text of the Bible in 1833 that it was estimated that in current editions there were more than 11,000 'intentional departures' from 1611 in wording alone, quite apart from variations in spelling and punctuation.[32]

The order of April 1724 had required that new settings be scrutinized by correctors appointed by the Archbishop of Canterbury or the Bishop of London, though if the requirement was ever implemented it had no noticeable effect. Reference has already been made to the attempts at Cambridge and Oxford to 'correct' the text, but by the 1760s the AV – as exemplified by 1611 – was couched in a form of English which was already seriously dated. That is, there was a clear conflict between fidelity and intelligibility; yet, it was to be another century before this inherent difficulty was resolved by the making of a new translation of the Bible.

30 For example, the frequent 'As the heart [*vere* hart] panteth after the water brooks' (Psalms 42, 1) or the perversion of the sense by the addition of 'not' in 'Make me to go in the way of thy commandments' (Psalms 119, 33) in the 1791 Edinburgh quarto printed by Mark and Charles Kerr (Darlow and Moule 1968, no. 1355).

31 Lee 1824, 231–2.

32 Curtis 1833, ii.

Other translations and languages

In effect, during the period covered by this volume, the AV was the sole translation read by Protestant readers in Britain whose working language was English. Also available, however, were Roman Catholic versions and translations of the AV into British languages other than English, as well as new translations of various parts of the Bible.

Despite new translations of the New Testament (NT) in current English by Cornelius Nary (1719)[33] and Robert Witham (1730),[34] the Roman Catholic community continued to use editions derived from the Douai-Rheims translations of 1582 (NT)[35] and 1609/10 Old Testament (OT),[36] finally in the revision made by Richard Challoner, 1749/50,[37] several times reprinted.

Translations were made into four other British languages: Welsh, Erse, Gaelic and Manx. The whole Bible had been available in an independent Welsh translation (Morgan's Bible) since 1588, and it had been reprinted several times during the seventeenth century. Further Welsh Bibles appeared during the eighteenth century, including one from the SPCK (1718), and several from the privileged printers in England; the first BFBS editions appeared in 1806/7. No Irish translations of the whole Bible for Roman Catholic use had been published by 1830, though one for Protestant use was published in 1681–5, in Irish characters, and then reset in roman in 1690 for use in the Scottish Highlands. Thereafter the NT was published in Gaelic in 1767, the OT in four volumes, 1783–1801. The earliest Manx Bible appeared progressively in 1763–5; the BFBS published a Manx NT in 1810, the whole Bible in 1819.

Several new translations were made of portions of the Bible, ranging from single books, such as Lowth's *Isaiah* (1778),[38] to the NT, as in William Whiston's *Primitive New Testament* (1745),[39] or the occasional whole Bible, as in Anthony Purver's *New and literal translation of all the books of the Old and New Testament* (1764).[40] In addition, paraphrases were sometimes published in family Bibles. Nonetheless, the AV had no competitor in general use until the publication of the Revised Version in 1881–5.[41]

33 Darlow and Moule 1968, no. 951.
34 Darlow and Moule 1968, no. 1009.
35 Darlow and Moule 1968, no. 177.
36 Darlow and Moule 1968, no. 300.
37 Darlow and Moule 1968, nos. 1086, 1089.
38 Darlow and Moule 1968, no. 1269.
39 Darlow and Moule 1968, no. 1071.
40 Darlow and Moule 1968, no. 1154.
41 Darlow and Moule 1968, nos. 2017, 2037.

32

The publishing and distribution of religious books by voluntary associations: from the Society for Promoting Christian Knowledge to the British and Foreign Bible Society

SCOTT MANDELBROTE

> I could say much concerning the good effects of this most excellent charity upon thirty years' experience: that whereas at first there came many young men and women in hopes of the Bibles, that, at sixteen or seventeen years of age, could not say (though perhaps the Lord's Prayer) the Commandments, and much less the Creed, there are now numbers that can, both these and the entire Catechism, at six or seven years of age, ... and many other people's children have been taught to read in hopes of getting Bibles.[1]

Writing of the charity that Philip, Lord Wharton (1613–96), established formally in July 1692, the Yorkshire antiquary Ralph Thoresby (1658–1725) expressed several of the most important characteristics of the voluntary distribution of religious literature during the long eighteenth century. Charity was a gradual and incremental process. Its purpose was not simply to increase the circulation of Bibles and devotional literature, but rather to promote a particular vision of Christian behaviour, in which reading and the practice of piety helped to construct an image of virtuous poverty. The recipients of charity earned the spiritual benefits that were eventually bestowed upon them, in the form of religious books and tracts, through their labour in learning to read and, especially, in the missionary work of converting their unlettered family and neighbours. The individual's small reward of a Bible, prayer book, catechism or devotional tract might thus become an investment towards the moral transformation of an entire society. Private generosity, however, carried with it something of the stigma of Popery and ran the risk of encouraging

I am grateful to Isabel Rivers, John Walsh and Tabitta van Nouhuys for advice and assistance with this essay.

1 Thoresby 1830, I, 195–6; cf. Findlay 2002.

idleness or rewarding cunning. The careful rules with which voluntary organizations circumscribed the freedom of their collaborators and subscribers helped to guarantee the seriousness of their purpose. The enthusiasm for the giving of time and money that was displayed by the burgeoning membership of charitable societies helped to maintain the independence as well as the virtue of the respectable members of a state whose interference in the daily lives of its citizens remained for the most part local and consensual.[2] Although involvement in religious charity appeared at first to smack of excessive zeal, by the middle years of the eighteenth century it had become the polite pursuit of gentlemen and ladies. There were moral and social benefits to giving, as well as to receiving.[3]

Thoresby was one of a small number of laymen who assisted Lord Wharton, most of whose collaborators were nonconformist ministers, in the distribution of godly books, as well as Bibles and catechisms, to poor children and their parents in selected locations in the counties of Westmorland, Cumberland, Yorkshire and Buckinghamshire from 1690.[4] From London, Wharton sent out by carrier boxes of Bibles, copies of the Westminster Assembly's shorter catechism, and godly books by Joseph Alleine and Thomas Lye.[5] After 1693, the terms of Wharton's trust specified that Bibles were to be in large duodecimo, bound in calf together with a copy of the metrical psalms, and fastened with a strong brass clasp. They should be given to children on condition that they learn to recite particular psalms. Financial inducements, in the form of a shilling for coals, were also offered to the children's parents. By the 1780s, Wharton's trust was entirely under the control of the Harley family, two of whose members had been among the original trustees. Later generations of Harleys, however, were less sympathetic to dissent, and, with the exception of twenty Bibles intended each year for Swaledale, north Yorkshire, the trust's distribution by the early nineteenth century had come into the hands of local priests of the Church of England. The trust adopted the distribution of the church catechism and of the Book of Common Prayer, which were preferred by conformist clergymen, in 1786.[6] In 1830, Wharton's trust distributed

2 Innes 1996, 1999; Roberts 1998.

3 Heyd 1995; Langford 1991, 558–81.

4 Heywood 1881–5, IV, 195, 235, 242, 244, 246, 254, 277–81.

5 Lancaster 1912, 25–6; Samuel Clark to Wharton, 20 June 1691, 'Correspondence of Philip, Lord Wharton', MS Rawlinson Letters 53, fol. 384, Bodleian. For catechisms and godly books, see I. Green 1996, esp. 82, 680; 2000, 193, 338, 594. Joseph Alleine's *An alarme to unconverted sinners* (London, 1672) was frequently reprinted in whole or in part throughout the eighteenth century; Wharton preferred the version entitled *A sure guide to heaven* (1688) and its reprints, together with Thomas Lye *The principles of Christian religion* (1677).

6 Dale 1906, 109–73; Wadsworth 1987–92; Thoresby 1830, I, 215, 344, 464; Hunter 1832, I, 106–8.

its standard annual total of 1,050 Bibles, many of which still found their way to Leeds and other northern towns.[7]

The bindings of Bibles given out by Wharton's trust were stamped with their provenance and each carried a bookplate setting out their donor's intentions. The trust established on the death of the banker Henry Hoare (1677–1725) employed a similar device. It used the profits from an initial capital of £2,000 'to the purchasing, dispersing and giving away Yearly, Bibles, Common-Prayer Books, and such other Books as are entirely agreeable to the Principles and Doctrine of the Church of England'.[8] The distribution of the books was in the hands of up to seven trustees, who were either members of the Hoare family or close associates with an interest in Hoare's Bank. Between 1725 and 1759, Hoare's trust distributed 3,952 Bibles, 447 copies of the New Testament, 4,870 copies of the Book of Common Prayer, 3,431 copies of *The whole duty of man*, as well as smaller numbers of several other tracts.[9] The trustees used a number of London booksellers to supply and distribute the books according to their shares, initially buying from Joseph Hazard, then from John Worrall (beginning in 1739), who had already acted as binder for the Hoare trust when he was resident in Fleet Street, then, for one year (1751–2), from William Watts, and finally from Benjamin Dodd.[10] The books appear to have been purchased in sheets and bound relatively cheaply. There seems to have been little consistency in the editions chosen by the trustees. For example, 210 Bibles were supplied in 1742 at 3*s*. each. These were presumably in duodecimo, yet in 1745, when only 77 Bibles were purchased, the choice was for octavos costing 6*s*. each in sheets.[11] Once the trustees began to purchase books from Benjamin Dodd, and later from John Rivington (starting in 1767), it may have been

7 Thoresby 1830, I, 196.

8 The quotation comes from one of the bookplates of Hoare's trust, on this occasion in a copy of [Richard Allestree], *The whole duty of man* (London, 1744), *ESTC* N25737; the full terms of the trust are set out in Henry Hoare's will, proved on 19 July 1725, a copy of which may be viewed at C. Hoare & Co., 37 Fleet Street, London. I am grateful to the archivist at Hoare's Bank, Ms Barbra Sands, for her assistance.

9 These figures are taken from the annual expenses given in the minute book of the Bible Fund, C. Hoare & Co. In 1729, fifty copies of *The whole duty of man* were purchased as a special donation for distribution on discharge to patients in St Bartholomew's Hospital. Other works purchased from time to time by the trustees included William Beveridge, *The great necessity and advantage of publick prayer and frequent communion* (London, 1724), *ESTC* T126793 (of which 125 copies were ordered in Dec. 1730 and 162 in Apr. 1739, in both cases apparently to be bound with the Book of Common Prayer); Robert Nelson, *A companion for the festivals and fasts of the Church of England*, 17th edn (London, 1739 1st edn, 1704), *ESTC* T164852 (of which 133 copies were ordered in Oct. 1740); *A new manual of devotions*, 8th edn (London, 1742) *ESTC* T227948 (of which 105 copies were ordered in Mar. 1742 and a further 72 in Aug. 1752).

10 For these individuals (other than Watts), see respectively Plomer 1922, 151; Plomer *et al.* 1932, 121, 272, 76.

11 These details come from two surviving booksellers' bills, from 1742 and 19 Sep. 1745 respectively, both in File Box 1, envelope 1, C. Hoare & Co.

possible for them to benefit from the special rates offered by these booksellers to members of the Society for Promoting Christian Knowledge.[12] Between 1787 and 1812, the trustees paid bills for books of approximately £150 roughly every other year, which would have purchased rapidly decreasing numbers of copies given the steep rise in costs and prices at this time. This pattern appears to have continued after 1812.[13]

Henry Hoare's personal activities crossed the boundary between private and public charity. He was one of the four founders of the Westminster Hospital in 1715, a leading figure from about 1703 in the Society for Promoting Christian Knowledge and a supporter of Thomas Bray's plans for establishing parochial libraries.[14] Bookplates, whose design Hoare helped to supervise, were also placed in volumes that the SPCK sent out to parochial libraries in England and Wales.[15] These benefactions included copies of the life and works of the Cambridge Platonist, Henry More (1614–87), which had recently been reprinted by Joseph Downing (who acted as the society's bookseller until his death in 1734),[16] as well as an edition of Eusebius's church history.[17]

The Society for Promoting Christian Knowledge represents the best exemplar of a voluntary organization engaged in the distribution of religious literature for most of the eighteenth century. The SPCK was founded in London in 1698 and quickly established a wide correspondence with Anglican clergymen and lay people throughout the country. It was interested in building contacts abroad, notably with the Lutheran and Reformed churches in Denmark, Germany and Switzerland which had been influenced by the teachings of August Hermann Francke. Although it did not establish its own press, as Francke had at Halle, the SPCK was soon involved in the commissioning and distribution of printed works. Catechetical works and small books of practical piety, especially those that had been generated by the contemporary campaign for the reformation of manners, were prominent in early lists of books that

12 The prices charged to Henry Hugh Hoare in the late 1780s seem, however, to have been slightly higher than the current rates for members of the SPCK. This may, however, reflect a decision to bind the books to a higher standard. For this and other details, see the ledgers of C. Hoare and Co., especially new series 26, fols. 433v–434r. Cf. Rivers, chap. 30, above.

13 The minute books of the trustees and entries in the ledger books at C. Hoare and Co.

14 Woodbridge 1970, 15–17; Clay 1994; Hoare 1955, 33–5.

15 Minutes of the Library Committee, 1705–30, 50–2, SPCK Archive.

16 The relevant titles are Henry More, *Theological works* (London, 1708), *ESTC* N98975; Richard Ward, *The life of the learned and pious Dr Henry More* (London, 1710), *ESTC* T145602; More, *Enchiridion ethicum*, 4th edn (London, 1711), *ESTC* N7326; More, *A collection of several philosophical writings*, 4th edn (London, 1712–13), *ESTC* T98967; More, *Divine dialogues*, 2nd edn (London, 1713), *ESTC* T97823; for Downing, see Plomer 1922, 106; Plomer *et al.* 1932, 79; Minutes of the Library Committee, 1705–30, 141, SPCK Archive; Jefcoate 1995.

17 Eusebius of Caesarea, *The history of the church* (London, 1709), *ESTC* T142058; Minutes of the Library Committee, 1705–30, 47, 71, SPCK Archive.

were made available to the society's correspondents.[18] Various works by Josiah Woodward (1660–1712) remained staples of the SPCK's lists until the nineteenth century, as did translations of the writings of the Neuchâtel divine, Jean Frédéric Ostervald (1663–1747).[19] The society's initial interest in moral reform was also apparent in its sponsorship of works attacking the stage.[20] Despite such links with the aims and membership of the Societies for the Reformation of Manners, the SPCK was generally suspicious of religious dissenters. During its early years, the society supported the campaigns of George Keith (1639?-1716), a missionary convert from the Quakers.[21] Its hostility to nonconformity later manifested itself in attacks on Methodism and suspicion of the motives of the urban Sunday school movement, to which it was reluctant to donate books. Such suspicion derived in part from a wish to protect the interests of the charity schools. Usually associated with local clergymen, and often promoted by sympathetic members of the gentry, charity schools were the principal beneficiaries of the SPCK's generosity.[22] The society issued accounts of the progress of the schools, to accompany the annual sermons that it sponsored for their gatherings in London from 1704.[23] The charity children, and to a certain extent their teachers, were also the targets for many of the society's publications, which were often distributed as rewards for suitable attainment and religious conformity.[24] The success of the charity school movement certainly played a part in the continuing vitality of the Church of England, especially in rural areas. Nevertheless, its political biases, in particular suspicion that charity schools might become breeding grounds for Jacobitism and sedition, generated uncertainties about the motives of the SPCK that lasted well into the 1720s.[25]

18 McClure 1888, 121; C. Rose 1993.

19 Works by Woodward included *The seaman's monitor*, 2nd edn (London, 1701), *ESTC* N21417, which was in its fourteenth edition by 1799; *The soldier's monitor* (London, 1701), *ESTC* T221494, in its eighth edition by 1796; *A disswasive from the sin of drunkenness* (London, 1701), *ESTC* T188022, for which there are fourteen entries published by the SPCK's booksellers in *ESTC*; *A kind caution to profane swearers* (London, 1701), *ESTC* T195820 or *ESTC* N33369, for which there are sixteen entries published by the SPCK's booksellers in ESTC. Those by Ostervald included a catechism, *The grounds and principles of the Christian religion* (London, 1704), *ESTC* T87841, translated by one of the SPCK's secretaries, Humfrey Wanley, which had reached its seventh edition in 1765, and *An abridgment of the history of the Bible* (London, 1715), *ESTC* T150442, which was reprinted throughout the eighteenth century and reissued in 1800 as one of the SPCK's religious tracts.

20 Barry 2001; Shoemaker 1992.

21 Allen and McClure 1898, 166–8.

22 For example, Minute book 30 (1787–91), 53–4, SPCK Archive; the usefulness of rural Sunday schools to the established church is, however, made clear by Snell and Ell 2000, 274–320.

23 Allen and McClure 1898, 146–50; Clarke 1944, 69–70.

24 Unwin 1984; James Talbot, *The Christian school-master* (London, 1707), *ESTC* T96612, which was still being reprinted in 1811.

25 Jones 1938; Rose 1991.

The work of the Society for Promoting Christian Knowledge depended on the activities of its members and correspondents. Outside London, it was heavily reliant on the support of rural clergymen.[26] The society was strict in confining the benefits of membership, particularly the right to order its publications and selected other books at reduced rates through its bookseller, to those who had paid its subscription. Members were supposed to distribute their purchases free of charge.[27] From the middle years of the eighteenth century, the nature of the SPCK's subscribers underwent considerable change, with a large expansion in its membership and a growth in the number and significance of female members. In 1745, there had been 167 subscribers and 3 female annual contributors. In 1765, by contrast, there were 425 subscribers and 42 female annual contributors. The rate of increase in the society's membership was sustained. By 1785, there were 939 subscribers, 7 foreign members and 162 female annual contributors.[28] The expansion of the society's membership, however, did not protect it from financial concerns. In 1787, for example, it was forced to limit the distribution of its books to members applying for their own use or on behalf of charity schools with which they had a personal connection.[29]

To an even greater extent than the activities of private charities, the philanthropic efforts of the SPCK depended on successful collaboration with individuals in the book trade. A succession of London booksellers acted for the society, initially taking advantage of the captive market that it provided to support pious publishing ventures of their own. Increasingly, the SPCK's bookseller acted as a publisher as well as a supplier for the society, which used its own name on publications that it sponsored from the middle of the eighteenth century.[30] For particular projects that it promoted, the SPCK made use of specialist skills, for example those of William Caslon, who cut some of the types with which editions of the New Testament and Psalter in Arabic were printed by Samuel Palmer in the 1720s, or those of the Whitehaven firm John Ware and Son, who printed the Bible in Manx in the 1770s.[31] Decisions to

26 Spaeth 2003, esp. 135–6.

27 Allen and McClure 1898, 185–7.

28 Annual Reports for 1745 (the first year in which such statistics were printed), 1765 and 1785, SPCK Archive. The three female annual contributors listed in 1745 had all been admitted to the Society in 1732.

29 Annual Report, 1787, 120, SPCK Archive.

30 After Joseph Downing's death in 1734, his widow acted as the SPCK's bookseller. Following a competition held in Mar. 1745, she was succeeded by Benjamin Dodd, and, from Oct. 1765, John Rivington and his heirs. Others, including John Oliver from the late 1740s, printed books for the society and helped to maintain its warehouse. See Allen and McClure 1898, 188, and the relevant minute books in the SPCK Archive. The details given in Plomer *et al.* 1932, 76, 79, 214, should be revised accordingly.

31 Ball 1973, 331–3, 339–43; Minute books 26–8 (1769–81), SPCK Archive; Darlow and Moule 1903–11, II, 67, 1068–70; 'Collections relating to the Isle of Man', MS Gough Islands 1, Bodleian.

promote ventures like these were the consequence of the enthusiasm of individual members, who succeeded in persuading the society to support their schemes, and who were often involved themselves in supervising or distributing the resulting publications.

The SPCK's interest in the publication of the Welsh translation of the Bible derived from an older concern with evangelism. The activities of the Welsh Trust, which had distributed Bibles mainly in north Wales in the 1670s and 1680s, provided both an example of how to go about such proselytizing and a warning that dissenters might in future act alone and steal the thunder of the established church.[32] A group of gentlemen from south Wales, of whom the most important was Sir John Philipps of Picton Castle, Pembrokeshire, encouraged the society to take on an edition of the Welsh Bible in 1713. With Moses Williams, vicar of Devynnock, Philipps was prominent in raising funds for the project. In 1717, Williams undertook a tour of north Wales to collect subscriptions. Williams also acted as the corrector for the press, helping to ensure that the Bible would be accurate enough to be useful. Two issues were printed in 1717 and 1718, the second including a translation of the Book of Common Prayer. Although there were concerns that the distribution of the Bible in Welsh would hamper the work of charity schools that depended largely on English texts, the educational activities of Griffith Jones, the founder of the circulating schools, and other loyal churchmen soon dispelled any doubts. Jones and others pressed the SPCK to maintain the supply of Welsh Bibles for their schools and parishes, and helped to ensure that new editions were prepared in 1727, 1746, 1752, 1769, 1799 and 1809.[33]

Concern for the spiritual care of Wales and the Isle of Man was in part a reflection of the changing nature of the SPCK's charitable imperatives. The relatively unsuccessful Arabic Psalter (1725) and New Testament (1727) and some early work in distributing books in North America and the Caribbean aside, the society was limited in its engagement with overseas Christians by the activities of its sister, the Society for the Propagation of the Gospel. Although it maintained links with the Danish mission at Tranquebar and was involved in a number of schemes to assist European Protestants, the main focus for its evangelism, at least until the early nineteenth century, was at home. However, its activities in this sphere were initially hampered in several ways. The SPCK was a centralized and hierarchical charity that believed in monitoring the social and religious effects of its giving. The system of distribution that

32 Jones 1939.
33 Clement 1952, 1954; Shankland 1904–5; Allen and McClure 1898, 203–4.

it adopted was ad hoc and concerned principally with ensuring that books and pamphlets went to deserving individuals or institutions. It was wary of the costs that might be generated by large-scale charity, yet it was easily diverted into ventures in translation that were time-consuming and often highly expensive. By volume, far and away the most important aspect of the SPCK's activities lay in the distribution of cheap pamphlets and tracts, often purchased by subscribers in bulk. The SPCK was, however, interested in other parts of the book trade, in particular the functioning of the monopoly on the publication of the Bible.

For its early editions of the Welsh Bible, the Society had had to co-operate with John Baskett and his heirs, who had established an effective monopoly over the printing of English Bibles in Britain. During the late 1710s and early 1720s, however, the society's correspondents were increasingly critical of the quality of production of English Bibles. Comments were particularly addressed at the legibility, paper quality and binding, as well as the price of Bibles in smaller formats that were made available through the SPCK's lists.[34] The society explored the possibility of breaking Baskett's monopoly by purchasing Bibles printed by rivals in Edinburgh or in Dublin.[35] Eventually, the episcopal supporters of the SPCK and the city contacts of Henry Hoare managed to obtain an order from George I, dated 24 April 1724, which attempted to regulate the quality and price of Bibles printed by the King's Printer.[36]

The society's relationship to the trade in Bibles was altered by the receipt in 1735 of a donation of land in Romney Marsh from Edwin Belke, a gentleman from Kent. This allowed the creation of a separate fund, Mr Belke's charity, from which the SPCK could distribute Bibles, New Testaments and other religious literature to its correspondents free of charge. During the 1720s and early 1730s, the society seems to have distributed slightly fewer than 1,000 Bibles, together with a couple of hundred New Testaments, each year. The immediate effect of Belke's bequest can be gauged in the period from 1736 to 1745, during which the SPCK increased the number of Bibles it gave away through its subscribers to an average of 1,188 per year, but began to distribute more than double the previous number of cheaper New Testaments. The

34 For example, Abstract Letter Book 9 (1718–19), nos. 6151, 6171; Abstract Letter Book 10 (1719–21), nos. 6298, 6421, 6615; Abstract Letter Book 11 (1721–3), no. 7262; Society Letters, CS2/12, 72–5, SPCK Archive. Cf. McMullin, chap. 31, above.

35 Minute Book 10 (1722–4), 19, 22, 46–7, SPCK Archive.

36 *London Gazette*, 21–25 Apr. 1724; for Hoare's involvement, see Abstract Letter Book 12 (1723–5), nos. 7341, 7371, 7646, 7829, SPCK Archive; for the role of Edmund Gibson, Bishop of London, see Lewis 1739, 350–1; Edward Gee to Gibson, 6 May 1724, 'Gibson Papers', MS 1741, fols. 28–9, Lambeth Palace Library. Complaints continued despite this measure; see Abstract Letter Book 13 (1725–7), nos. 8939–40, 8993, 9005; Society Letters, CS2/17, 22–5, 33–4, 37–8, SPCK Archive.

increasing size of the society in the middle years of the eighteenth century was reflected by distributions of more than 3,000 Bibles and between 1,500 and 2,000 New Testaments each year during the 1750s and 1760s. At this time, members were also purchasing and giving away up to 46,000 of the society's briefer, moral pamphlets each year. These figures continued to rise throughout the 1770s and 1780s, despite the changes in regulations introduced in 1787. During the moral panic of the 1790s, the SPCK distributed around 5,000 Bibles, 9,000 New Testaments and 9,750 Books of Common Prayer each year, as well as an average of 68,348 cheaper pamphlets.[37] At the same time, the society's relations with the printers of English Bibles was altered by the role played by its bookseller, John Rivington, as a distributor for the publications of Cambridge University Press, which had resumed the printing of Bibles in 1743. Into the nineteenth century, it was normal for the SPCK's bookseller to offer to members a full range of Bibles and prayer books, itemized according to printer, format, type and binding. Although the volume of purchases by subscribers rose exponentially, due to the continuing expansion of the society at this time, the number of books given away completely free of charge by the society remained small. The success of the society thus depended almost entirely on the enthusiasm of those who chose to join it.

This situation was transformed in the early nineteenth century. In these years, the society became a formidably large and relatively active charity, chiefly in response to pressure from rival bodies that seemed likely to promote different ecclesiastical values from those of the SPCK. In 1821, the society could boast more than 14,500 members and claimed to have distributed 3,540 packets of books, containing 31,983 Bibles, 45,455 New Testaments and psalters, 84,975 Books of Common Prayer, 74,904 other bound books, and 821,044 small tracts. In 1830, the society issued 1,715,560 books and tracts, many of which were sent to India. This huge expansion of activity was achieved through fundamental changes in the structure and purposes of the SPCK. The most important of these were the creation, after 1810, of separate diocesan societies and district committees, and the improvement of links with the colonies. These developments altered the relationship between the society and its subscribers and generated new opportunities for organized charity at a local level, although the SPCK even so continued to depend heavily on networks of local clergymen. The costs that they generated, however, did not prove to be sustainable in the long run. In addition to these organizational

37 These figure all derive from the relevant annual reports in the SPCK Archive. On the responses of voluntary societies to the moral climate of the 1790s, see Innes 1990.

changes, the society altered the design of its booklists to draw attention to the stitched tracts that were available singly or in hundreds. In 1811, a complete library of these could be purchased, bound in calf in twelve volumes, for £1 10*s*. The level of direct charitable giving by the SPCK, however, was limited in 1830 to 216 Bibles, 227 New Testaments, 326 Books of Common Prayer, 646 other bound books and 6,000 tracts.[38]

The changing nature of the SPCK was a feature of broader developments in voluntary religious activity within the British Isles.[39] The most important of these was the growth of evangelical piety and its stress on lay involvement in philanthropy and the improvement of the lives of the poor. Dissenting laymen were prominent, for example, among the founders of the Society for Promoting Religious Knowledge among the Poor, which was established in London in 1750. This was a voluntary society that aimed to distribute Bibles, New Testaments and other religious books free to the poor by supplying them at low cost to interested ministers and gentlemen. Later known as the Book Society, it survived until the early twentieth century. Books were ordered through its bookseller and publisher, Thomas Field, and were supposed to carry its bookplate. Titles that the society sponsored included reprints of some of the most successful puritan and nonconformist works of practical piety written during the seventeenth century, notably Richard Baxter's *A call to the unconverted* (1658) and Joseph Alleine's *An alarme to unconverted sinners* (1672).[40] Although subscribers often gave away Bibles and testaments, it seems that other books were lent out and that the society in this way promoted the formation of local libraries and reading groups. The similarity of these methods to those of the SPCK is apparent, but the Society for Promoting Religious Knowledge among the Poor was both more openly democratic and more interested in interdenominational co-operation than was the SPCK. Nevertheless, the majority of its members seem to have had Calvinistic leanings. Although subscribers were widely distributed through the country and even in North America, the most influential seem to have been London dissenters. A subsidiary society, which published similar works, existed in Edinburgh as early as 1757. Several works by Isaac Watts were also sold by the society in Welsh.

38 Annual Reports for 1811, 1820–1 and 1830, SPCK Archive.

39 See Rivers, chap. 30, above.

40 *ESTC* R2096 and *ESTC* R8216, and cf. note 3 above. For this and other information about the society, I have relied on Rivers 2007. All figures are taken from two editions of the society's *Account*, published in 1769 and 1779, *ESTC* T186045 and *ESTC* T196779. On Field, see Plomer *et al.* 1932, 93.

By 1769, the society had 695 members, many of whom were women, each subscribing one guinea annually. This comparatively impressive number does not seem to have increased as quickly as subscription to the SPCK, nor were members as likely to be peers or bishops. The society distributed 48,246 volumes (of which 6,470 were Bibles and 6,381 New Testaments) between 1750 and 1759, and a further 119,987 volumes (of which 16,037 were Bibles and 10,287 were New Testaments) between 1760 and 1769. From 1770 to 1779, it gave away 130,871 volumes (of which 22,110 were Bibles and 10,741 New Testaments). For larger books, these figures compare reasonably well with those for the SPCK during this period. The prices charged to its members by the Society for Promoting Religious Knowledge among the Poor were, however, rather higher than those of the SPCK. These differences may indicate divergent views about the quality of production required in books for the use of the poor. Nevertheless, the Society for Promoting Religious Knowledge among the Poor seems only to have published two pamphlets for circulation in bulk, which could be purchased by the dozen.[41] The Society's most successful title, of which 29,797 copies were distributed between 1750 and 1779, was John Reynolds's *A compassionate address to the Christian world* (1730 or earlier), which was priced at 4*d*.[42] The Society for Promoting Religious Knowledge among the Poor was clearly a much more serious rival to the SPCK than Lord Wharton's charity, which was in any case no longer so clearly favourable to Old Dissent by the late eighteenth century. Yet, despite their propagation of a godly version of practical piety, neither of these institutions figured among the complaints of the SPCK's committees. Instead, anxiety was expressed about competition from New Dissent and about the unnecessary duplication of charitable endeavour. As early as the 1740s, the SPCK had been worried about Methodist interest in the circulation of literature in bulk to the poor, and concerned to prevent the abuse of its own publications by the followers of John Wesley (1703–91).[43]

For much of his long career, Wesley published cheap pamphlets himself, using a variety of London and provincial printers. He also produced editions, abridgements and translations of other works of practical piety. Many of these he offered to purchasers in bulk at reduced prices for giving away to the poor.

41 These were 'Toms against Intemperance' and 'Toms against Impurity'. They can be identified as *The heavy guilt of the sin of drunkenness*, of which five editions are recorded between 1763, *ESTC* N46547 and *ESTC* N51554, and 1788, *ESTC* T104356, and *The heinous guilt and destructive consequences of impurity displayed* of which one edition is recorded in *ESTC*, printed for the Society in 1794, *ESTC* N70278. The author may be Isaac Toms (1710–1801).

42 *ESTC* W11899; an edition of this work was published by T. Field in 1791, *ESTC* T118970.

43 See Evans n.d.

In 1782, he formalized this charity by founding the Society for Distributing Religious Tracts among the Poor, with his assistant Thomas Coke (1747–1814). Subscribers to the society were to pay a guinea or half a guinea, in return for which they could make bulk orders from its list of tracts. The society did not distribute Bibles, which Wesley believed to be unsuitable for those whose piety had not yet been awakened. Instead, it concentrated on a list of thirty works of practical piety, mostly written by seventeenth-century non-conformists or by Wesley himself. These tracts were printed for the society by John Paramore and advertised in Wesley's *Arminian Magazine*. For the most part, they were extremely cheap and, in some cases, they undercut similar publications sold by the Society for Promoting Religious Knowledge among the Poor.[44]

The publications sponsored by the Society for Promoting the Knowledge of the Scriptures were rather different, both from Wesley's and from those of the other societies discussed so far. Sold to subscribers in parts through the society's bookseller, Joseph Johnson,[45] these were relatively erudite works that were designed to combat an injudicious or enthusiastic approach to religion, such as that found in so many popular tracts. Instead, they encouraged the application of reason in religion and recommended the writings of leading moderate churchmen, such as the great commentator on Hebrew poetry and Bishop of London, Robert Lowth. More worryingly for bodies like the SPCK, however, they also stressed the right to make private judgements on matters of religion. Many of the publications that the society sponsored were openly sympathetic to Unitarianism.[46]

The most obvious example of the SPCK's concern with the duplication of charity came in its decision in November 1780 to curtail donations of Bibles and other books to the army and the militia. Although the justification given at the time was the cost and relative ineffectiveness of this activity, and the society resumed donations on an increased scale to the Royal Navy during the Revolutionary and Napoleonic wars, at least part of the explanation for the change of policy in 1780 must have been the foundation of the Bible Society for the Use of the Navy and Army of Great Britain. This society was supported through voluntary subscriptions, usually of a guinea annually, and by collections taken in churches. By 1794, it had around 400 members, of whom 156

44 This account of Wesley's activities depends on Rivers 2007 and on Rivers 1982b.

45 See Rivers, chap. 30, above.

46 See *Commentaries and essays published by the Society for Promoting the Knowledge of the Scriptures*, 2 vols. (London, [1784–96]), *ESTC* P3240, which contains 'A sketch of the plan of the Society'; Plomer *et al.* 1932, 141.

were annual subscribers. It had distributed 21,951 Bibles to 120 ships and 100 regiments. Its members, many of whom also subscribed to the SPCK, included a number of moderate divines, as well as some Methodists. It was, however, dominated by evangelical churchmen, including Granville Sharp (1735–1813) and William Wilberforce (1759–1833).[47]

Evangelical ideas for national regeneration through the moral reform of the poor lay behind a number of other new publication societies, several of which distributed cheap tracts on the basis of charity. These included the Religious Tract Society, founded in 1799 with an equal representation of churchmen and dissenters on its committee, whose products paralleled the *Cheap Repository Tracts* that Hannah More (1745–1833) and her friends had distributed on a monthly basis between 1795 and 1798. Eventually underwritten by subscription, the *Cheap Repository Tracts* were moral pamphlets, ballads and stories that were sold directly to the poor at a penny each or less through the existing network of chapmen, as well as being sold in bulk for charitable distribution.[48]

A narrow group of evangelicals was similarly prominent in the Church Missionary Society, which was founded in 1799 by John Venn (1759–1813), rector of Clapham, and his clerical associates. Initially dedicated to sending out catechists to India and Africa, in particular to the new colony of Sierra Leone, the CMS rapidly began to promote schemes for translations into native languages. With this purpose in mind, it collaborated extensively with German and Swiss missionary organizations and with the East India Company's College at Calcutta. Although there was a distinctly millenarian tinge to the early programme of the CMS, its publishing activities took some time to get off the ground. In its early years, it thus depended on grants from the British and Foreign Bible Society. By the 1820s, however, it offered its subscribers a large number of publications, including histories of mission, works of practical piety, grammars and partial translations of the Bible in various African and Indian languages (as well as in Arabic, Italian and Maori). It helped to support missionary presses in Malta and Ceylon, as well as in Calcutta and Madras.[49] By concentrating on overseas missions, especially in areas of recent colonial

47 Only one of the reports of this society seems to have survived (in a single copy); see *Bible society, London, instituted 1780, for the use of the navy and army of Great Britain* (London, 1794), *ESTC* N46898. This is bound with an unrecorded flysheet about the society, printed by C. Boult at Egham. I am grateful to Dr Ian Patterson, Librarian of Queens' College, Cambridge, for allowing me to consult this item. Accounts for the society from 1807 survive in the ledgers of C. Hoare & Co., especially new series 98, third series 7, 17, 29.

48 Howse 1953, 101–5; Stott 2003, 169–90; More 2002.

49 This account is based on the Annual Reports and Proceedings of the Church Missionary Society, published from 1801. See also Stock 1899–1916, I. On the relationship between evangelical piety and missionary work in the 1790s, see Elbourne 2002, 25–70.

expansion, the CMS avoided the issue of competition with older societies such as the SPCK. Many of the sponsors of the CMS, however, were soon involved in another venture, the British and Foreign Bible Society, which did initially seem to threaten the SPCK. Its rapid success, moreover, helped to change the organization and structure of other voluntary societies during the early nineteenth century.

The British and Foreign Bible Society held its first meeting at the London Tavern on 7 March 1804, with Granville Sharp in the chair. The idea for such a society had developed at committee meetings of the Religious Tract Society during the previous two years. It intended to supplement the work of the CMS and other missionary charities through supplying copies of the Bible for use overseas, and meet the demand for Bibles in Welsh that the editions published by the SPCK had failed to satisfy. Members could subscribe annually for a guinea, in return for which they would be able to buy Bibles and New Testaments at reduced prices. It was not the intention of the BFBS itself to give away English Bibles within Britain. The BFBS rapidly attracted prominent patrons, especially the evangelical and former Governor General of India, Lord Teignmouth (1751–1834), and built a wide correspondence network that enabled it to sponsor many scriptural publishing ventures in continental Europe and further abroad.[50] Within England, it quickly attracted the attention of both critics and supporters of the SPCK, although many of its original members also belonged to that society. Its correspondents noted the persistence of poor typography and design in the cheap Bibles distributed by the SPCK, but also issued warnings about the superior nature of the new edition of the Welsh Bible on which the rival society was working. Links were rapidly established with the Naval and Army Bible Society and with the newly founded Hibernian Bible Society in Dublin.[51]

From the outset, the BFBS differed in a number of fundamental ways from the SPCK. The first of these was in terms of membership. The BFBS was open to members of all Christian denominations. Its committees were made up largely of merchants and professionals and were less responsive to clerical pressure. The BFBS distributed Bibles without notes, thus avoiding sectarian complaint, but encountered controversy in the early 1820s because of the hostility of members of the reformed churches, in particular Scottish Presbyterians, to its support for the circulation in Lutheran and Catholic Europe of Bibles that included the Apocrypha. The BFBS took a far more

50 See Fabian and Spieckermann, chap. 28, above.

51 See Bible Society Archive, Minutes of General Meetings, A1/1–2; Home Correspondence, D1/1/1–2; Canton 1904–10, I.

active interest in the workings of the Bible trade than did the relatively passive SPCK. From the beginning, it was responsive to the claims of stereotype printers that Bibles might be produced more accurately and perhaps more cheaply using this method. Although the early experiments in printing the English Bible in stereotype that it encouraged at the Cambridge University Press were marred by inaccuracies, the BFBS was soon publishing stereotyped editions of the Bible in most western European languages, using the labour of a variety of provincial printers. In 1809, the society began to supplement its orders from the Cambridge University Press with stereotyped English Bibles printed at Oxford, and, in 1812, it placed its first order with the King's Printers, Eyre and Strahan. The BFBS also encouraged the use of a number of technological developments, including the Stanhope press, machine printing and steam drying techniques. It sought to reduce the effects of the increase in paper prices, produced by the long period of war with France, by experimenting with bleaches for paper. In all these cases, the aim of the BFBS was to reduce the high prices to which Bibles had risen and thus to make them more readily available to the poor. From 1812, the BFBS also issued specific requirements for the sewing of its Bibles, designed to enable them to withstand repeated use.[52]

These innovations did not prevent criticism of the quality of production of Bibles sold by the BFBS. They did, however, succeed in multiplying the variety of Bibles offered to the poor and in maintaining or even reducing prices. Subscribers were initially promised Bibles and New Testaments at two-thirds of the normal retail price. In 1820, at the BFBS's depository in Blackfriars, a Bible in duodecimo would have sold for 4*s.* 2*d.* to a member of the society who might have bought an octavo Bible in brevier type for 4*s.* 8*d.* The comparable prices in 1830 were 3*s.* and 5*s.* In the case of New Testaments, the cheapest duodecimo was sold to subscribers at 1*s.* in 1820 and 1*s.* 1*d.* in 1830. These were not historically low prices, but they were effectively stable or falling.[53]

The real innovation of the BFBS, however, was not in lowering prices but in finding a way to increase the ability of people to afford to buy Bibles. This was largely achieved by the activities of auxiliary societies, the first of which was founded in Reading in 1809. Auxiliary societies were groups of local people who banded together to take out a subscription to the BFBS with one-half of their funds, using the other half to purchase Bibles and New Testaments at the

52 See Canton 1904–10, I and Howsam 1991.

53 These figures are based on information in the relevant Annual Reports, Bible Society Archive.

society's rates for local distribution. They were often interdenominational in character. Some auxiliary societies allowed Sunday school children to subscribe weekly sums of as little as 1*d*. towards the eventual purchase of a Bible from the BFBS depository. Gentleman visitors also took collections from poor families for subscriptions, usually to the cheapest Bibles that the society offered. In this way, the BFBS overcame the gap between donor and recipient that had dogged the charitable distribution of books by the SPCK and other societies. It allowed poor people to purchase the Bibles and New Testaments that they wanted for themselves, admittedly through an intermediary, but nevertheless at very low prices. The resulting relationship between the books that were purchased in this way and their owners was clearly different from that between those donated by the SPCK and their recipients.[54] By 1830, there were more than five hundred auxiliary and branch societies, and consideration was being given to the question of whether a Bible should be provided for every poor child. This was a significant change from the aim of providing Bibles for family use only, which had always been the policy of the SPCK as well as of the early BFBS. It perhaps suggests that the domestic market for Bibles, as understood according to earlier charitable imperatives, was becoming saturated through the efforts of a society that claimed that it had distributed 2,550,000 Bibles and New Testaments worldwide between 1805 and 1820.[55]

Despite the collaborative nature of many of the auxiliary Bible Societies, the success of the BFBS attracted adverse comment from many churchmen. The concentration on individual access to the Bible that marked the activities of the BFBS was in marked contrast to the interest in Christian education and practical piety that characterized the SPCK and a number of other organizations. Moreover, the work of the SPCK, in promoting the Welsh and Manx Bibles, seemed less heroic in the light of the efforts of the Bible Societies. A similar pall was cast over the activities of the Society in Scotland for Promoting Christian Knowledge (SSPCK), which had been incorporated in 1709. Its initial concern was mainly with the establishment of English-language charity schools in the Highlands, but, in the second half of the eighteenth century, it sponsored the publication of a Gaelic New Testament. The Gaelic Bible that it completed in 1801 sold out within the year, but from 1807, the editions that it sponsored had to compete with those published by the BFBS and distributed by the Edinburgh Bible Society.[56] There were also limits to the extent to which

54 See Canton 1904–10, I and Howsam 1991; *The report at the first anniversary of the Dudley Auxiliary Bible Society* (Dudley, 1813); see also Smith 1994, 227–42.

55 Annual Reports for 1820 and 1830, Bible Society Archive.

56 On the SSPCK, see Durkacz 1983, 45–95; Withers 1984, 120–40; Darlow and Moule 1903–11, II, 462–5.

the BFBS was willing to co-operate with other Christians. The Edinburgh Bible Society broke with the BFBS over the issue of the Apocrypha in 1826. In 1813, the BFBS discovered that the English Catholic Board had set up a Roman Catholic Bible Society to reprint the English translation of the Vulgate, with explanatory notes. This led to a heated dispute, which the BFBS turned into anti-Catholic propaganda by attacking the reluctance of Irish Catholic priests to support charity schools.[57]

The evangelical success of the BFBS was not entirely replicated by that of the Prayer Book and Homily Society. This society was founded in 1812 to supplement the work of the SPCK in distributing 'the daughter of the Bible', the Book of Common Prayer, and to promote editions of the edifying moral discourses of the early English Reformation as contemporary guides to practical piety.[58] Like the BFBS, it adopted an ambitious programme of publication that included translations into Welsh, Manx and many western European languages, as well as Arabic and Chinese. The Prayer Book and Homily Society experienced continual financial difficulties, however, which made it difficult for it to give books away free. Moreover, its faith in the usefulness of the Elizabethan homilies did not match the commercial realities of reprinting the entire volume of these texts. The society lost 2*s*. for each copy supplied at the subscription price for the edition that it published in 1814. Nevertheless, by 1828, it claimed to have distributed nearly 155,000 copies of the Book of Common Prayer, as well as 1.25 million tracts consisting of single homilies.

The rise of party within the church in the second quarter of the nineteenth century damaged both evangelical movements like the BFBS and the older voluntary societies.[59] It raised questions about the success of evangelical piety in tackling the religious and moral problems of the nation, and cast charitable work in less polite and universal contexts. In the process, it undermined the confidence with which charity might appear to be the answer to the religious needs of the poor and a solution to the related problems of how to encourage reading and, at the same time, control behaviour. Although this change in intellectual and religious fashion engendered doubt over the moral success of the societies, it did not obscure the very real impact that they had had on the practice of literacy within the British Isles, and, indeed, across the globe. The sheer bulk of the distribution of religious literature that the societies undertook represented a spur to innovation in the book trade. The publications of

57 See Blair 1813.
58 This account is based on reports printed with the annual sermons of the society. A run of these from 1813 is available in the British Library. See also Griffiths 2002, 230.
59 See Knight 1995, 175–6.

the societies supplied opportunities for reading that might otherwise have been lacking for many beneficiaries of charity. Both the content and the form of those publications generated debate about the nature and purposes of book production and about the relationship between religion and literacy that had broad social consequences. The publishing and distribution of religious books undertaken by voluntary associations must therefore be accounted a major element in the culture of print during the long eighteenth century.

II
LITERATURE AND THE CULTURE OF LETTERS

33
Book reviewing

ANTONIA FORSTER

In February 1749 the narrator of *Tom Jones* blames love of fame for the fact that 'some Books like Quacks impose on the World by promising Wonders; while others turn Beaus, and trust all their Merits to a gilded Outside'.[1] Four months later, Ralph Griffiths advertised the first number of his *Monthly Review* as 'Giving an Account, with proper Abstracts, of the new Books, Pamphlets, &c. as they come out.'[2] Griffiths's description of the purpose and content of the new journal was initially modest, although it was to become more complex and comprehensive, claiming for reviewing a central place in the literary world that it has never entirely lost. Although a great deal of attention has been given to the nineteenth-century development of the review journal – often as if the earlier period did not exist, or as if, at least, it was only in the nineteenth century that reviewing learned to walk upright – it was in the eighteenth century that the business of criticism and its place in the history of the book was established.

The *Monthly Review*'s decisions brought the critical enterprise from the fringes into the commercial centre of bookselling and thus established the grounds for later imitators – and, eventually, the jumping-off point for nineteenth-century reviewers and editors to change direction again. The rapid and practical processes by which the early reviews defined their role and moved into the book marketplace are the subject of this chapter. What were the reviews doing? Why were they there? How were they to sell their function and their judgements to the public? Even at the beginning it soon became clear that the goal of the review journal might be at variance with the booksellers' aim of selling books with as little interference as possible. The

1 Fielding 1974a, Bk.13, chap. 1, 685.
2 *London Evening Post*, 17–20 June 1749.

Reviews certainly liked to claim their independence – often ignoring their bookseller connections and emphasizing the reviewers' supposed disinterested role in serving the public by detecting the literary quacks and sorting out the good books from the bad – but the point was challenged early and justifiably in practice, even if the theory of the reviewers' purpose was almost instantaneously accepted.

Demonstrating this acceptance, James Elphinston comments in 1783 on the sad failure of the 'two volunteer-Associations: which patriotically erected themselves, one 34, the other 27 years ago [respectively, the *Monthly Review* and *Critical Review*], into Courts of Criticism: where the public was to be taught how to judge of every new Work, great or small ...'[3] Elphinston's picture of the ideal state of periodical criticism stands, as such pictures usually do, in contrast to the actual state he saw around him. A sound judgement of books requires 'refined science': few are capable of undertaking 'the Herculean task of candidly perusing all publications' and giving 'a clear, however concise, sketch of each respective plan' together with a dispassionate demonstration of 'the excellences or defects, intellectual, moral, and literary, alike of the plan and of its execution ...' Those capable of achieving such an ideal 'must be honored, admired, and followed, in the career of letters; as holding the torch, at once, of Science and of Virtue', but the model was unrealized – and has remained so ever since.[4]

Two hundred years later, explaining the shortcomings of the eighteenth-century reviewing periodicals in comparison with the revolutionary quarterlies, the *Edinburgh Review* (1802) and *Quarterly Review* (1809), John O. Hayden wrote that 'little attempt was made to go beyond providing readers with an idea of the content and relative worth of recent publications – the merest practical function of reviewing'.[5] While this assessment is intended to convey a sense of the intellectual superiority of the selective nineteenth-century journals and a sense of the vast gulf between them and their predecessors, Hayden's remarks sound like a definition of what most general readers are looking for in book reviews and reminds us that this lowly function is the principal reason for reviewing's success and survival. In 1749 Griffiths had explained the role of the reviewer in simple, practical terms to a reading public unused to the phenomenon of purchasing literary judgements or descriptions of books that might pre-empt any necessity of reading the books themselves:

3 Elphinston 1783, 4.
4 Elphinston 1783, 3–4.
5 Hayden 1969, 7.

> When the abuse of title-pages is obviously come to such a pass, that few readers care to take in a book, any more than a servant, without a recommendation; to acquaint the public that a summary review of the productions of the press, as they occur to notice, was perhaps never more necessary than now, would be superfluous and vain.
>
> The cure then for this general complaint is evidently, and only, to be found in a periodical work, whose sole object should be to give a compendious account of those productions of the press, as they come out, that are worth notice; an account, in short, which should, in virtue of its candour, and justness of distinction, obtain authority enough for its representations to be serviceable to such as would choose to have some idea of a book before they lay out their money or time on it.[6]

The notion that books, like servants, need recommendations to ensure against intellectual fraud and theft was a new and interesting one, placing the new Review in a mediating position between the booksellers and the reading public.

The *Monthly Review*'s English predecessors – such specialist, highly selective journals as *Memoirs of Literature* (1710–14, 1717), *History of the Works of the Learned* (1699–1712), all following to a greater or lesser extent the *Journal des sçavans* (established in 1665 and published in Paris and Amsterdam until 1753)[7]– had not presented their views and aims in this light. Their stated purpose was supplying information, and their coverage, as some of their titles suggested, was restricted. Michel de la Roche's *Memoirs of Literature*, whose stated purpose was 'to give the Readers an *Universal* Account of the State of Learning, especially beyond Sea', did not widen its reach even when 'the Performances of the Learned did not afford [him] sufficient Matter to fill up so many Sheets in a Year', forcing de la Roche to pad the publication with original pieces of his own and extracts from 'curious old Books'.[8] The *History of the Works of the Learned* was meant to assist 'those who are less conversant with Books', so that they could gain information about 'the state of Learning in the World' and 'maintain Conversation with the Learned upon any subject, at a small Expence of Money and Time'. Yet, the magazine was also intended to be not 'wholly useless to the Learned, who may hence have a brief View of the Progress of Arts and Sciences in all Parts of *Europe*, and be thereby timely informed of such Books as may be proper for their Libraries', and made a point of its selectiveness: 'We think fit likewise to assure the *Reader*, That we shall be

6 This 'Advertisement' is bound following the table of contents at the beginning of volume 1 of the *Monthly Review* in the Bodleian Library's copy (Griffiths's own annotated set) but is bound at the end of the first number, i.e. between pages 80 and 81, in the British Library's copy.

7 See Tierney, chap. 24 above.

8 *Memoirs of Literature* (1722), 'Preface', I, sigs. A4r–A4v.

so far from giving an Account of Books that are Trifling, or contrary to good Manners, that we will not so much as mention their Titles.'[9] A little more than a century later the revolutionary *Edinburgh Review* circled back to this position, with the editors making a point of proclaiming that they wished 'their Journal to be distinguished, rather for the selection, than for the number, of its articles' and reminding readers that 'Of the books that are daily presented to the world, a very large proportion is evidently destined to obscurity, by the insignificance of their subjects, or the defects of their execution . . .'[10] The *Edinburgh Review* 'opened a new chapter in the history of literary criticism', as Massimiliano Demata and Duncan Wu argue.[11] None of its predecessors 'had been so influential as to shape the taste of the reading public or to determine the agenda followed by writers themselves', yet it did not spring out of nowhere. The revolutionary change reviewing wrought in the relationship between authors, publishers and the reading public took place in the eighteenth century.

Griffiths's initial description of his journal's coverage of 'those productions of the press . . . that are worth notice' was in keeping with the principle of selectiveness. From the third number onwards Griffiths began the attempt to 'register all the new Things in general, without exception to any, on account of their lowness of rank or price' (*MR* 1, 1749: 238).[12] Thus, there began a two-tier approach to reviewing followed by the *Monthly* and its various imitators as they struggled to cover everything published, apart from chapbooks and some other items such as single sermons; this latter voluminous category was covered to some extent by the *Monthly*, but not much by the other journals. In the first tier were a number of main articles, averaging ten in the early decades and increasing as the century went on (the *Monthly Review* had an average of 15.3 main articles in the twelve numbers for 1800), and in the second tier a much longer list of briefer catalogue items, each item sometimes only a few words long, but sometimes more than a page of small type.

Placement in the catalogue was a value judgement by the editors. The 'lowness of rank' attached to the items in the monthly catalogues is confirmed in correspondence between the *Monthly*'s editor, Ralph Griffiths (and later his son George Edward Griffiths), and some of the reviewers, with various references to an item's being 'consigned to a little, obscure Nook in the Monthly Catalogue'.[13]

9 *The History of the Works of the Learned: for the Month of January* (1699), 'Preface', sigs.[A]1r–[A]1v.
10 *The Edinburgh Review, or Critical Journal* (1802), 1, 'Advertisement'.
11 Demata and Wu 2002, 4.
12 All references to the principal reviews – the *Monthly Review* (*MR*), the *Critical Review* (*CR*), the *London Review* (*LR*), the *English Review* (*ER*), the *Analytical Review* (*AR*) and the *British Critic* (*BC*) – will be thus abbreviated and given parenthetically in the text.
13 Samuel Badcock to Ralph Griffiths, 31 Oct. 1779, Bodleian – MSS Add. c 90, fol. 20r.

'A Corner – a *Catalogue*-Corner will do very well for such Company,'[14] writes Samuel Badcock in 1780. William Enfield, who reviewed a great deal of fiction along with many other things, maintains in 1796: 'I have no objection to catalogue articles, but you will of course always mix with them something more interesting than the general run of pamphlets, as you have opportunity.'[15] Sometimes the suggestion or instruction came from the journal's editor, as when Ralph Griffiths writes to William Taylor in 1796, 'you will probably consign it to the catalogue for November'[16] or George Edward Griffiths writes to Charles Burney the younger, 'They will require from us only Catalogue articles.'[17] Authors were aware of the distinction too, and we see Charles Lloyd writing in 1813 to offer thanks for his work not being placed 'in your *catalogue*, which I might have expected for so thin a volume'.[18] A list of the attributes of catalogue items is offered in 1799 in the *New London Review*'s Prospectus:

> Such, however, as have cost less pains, are on an inferior scale, more in the style of mediocrity, or betray a structure less lofty, ornamental and finished, and occupy none of the higher walks of genius and taste, must be ranked with the common-place of the Month, and be content, as in other Reviews, with such brief notice as the Catalogue admits.[19]

Fifteen years earlier the *Monthly* had replied to a correspondent asking about the frequent consigning of 'works of MERIT to the Catalogue part', explaining that the answer may be seen in

> the unequal proportion of our limits, to the increasing multiplicity of the publications which our plan obliges us to notice: a circumstance which renders it absolutely necessary for us to embrace every opportunity, not only of abridging our growing labours, but of making room for *some* mention, though ever so brief, of those productions of the press which have too long waited for a place in our journal. (*MR* 70, 1784: 327–8)

That the difference in review status between the main articles and the monthly catalogues was not merely a matter of length is made clear on many occasions by the inclusion of catalogue items that are significantly longer than main articles in the same monthly numbers. Many examples could be given, but see,

14 Samuel Badcock to Ralph Griffiths, 18 Jan. 1780, Bodleian – Add. MSS C 90, fol. 32v.
15 William Enfield to Ralph Griffiths, 3 Mar. 1796, Bodleian – Add. MSS C 89, fol. 97r.
16 Ralph Griffiths to William Taylor, 20 Sep. 179[6] in Robberds 1843, I, 135.
17 George Edward Griffiths to Charles Burney the younger, 4 July 180[6]. Osborn Collection, Beinecke Library, Yale University.
18 Charles Lloyd to Christopher Lake Moody, 4 Dec. 1813, Bodleian Add. MSS C 89, fol. 212.
19 *The New London Review; or, Monthly Report of Authors and Books* 1799, Prospectus, 2, British Library 898, f.1 (3).

for instance, the *Critical*'s number for July 1777 where the catalogue review of *Epistle to Dr Shebbeare* is four pages of small print, much longer than the three pages of normal type given to Frances Brooke's *The excursion* and one page to Henry Man's *The trifler*, both main articles. Similarly the *Critical*'s main-article review of *An answer to Mr De Lolme's Observations on the late national embarrassment. By Neptune* in March 1789, is only nine and a half lines long, shorter than many of the items in the monthly catalogue.

In the 1770s the *Critical*'s monthly numbers had an average of 11.8 full or main-article reviews of English works and the *Monthly Review* had 11.3; these constituted just over 30 per cent of the *Critical*'s total number of items and 23 per cent of the *Monthly*'s (the *Monthly*'s higher totals overall are substantially explained by the journal's much greater coverage, almost always in the catalogues, of individually published sermons). The number of main articles increased as the century went on and the journals struggled to keep up with the increasing number of publications[20] – a phenomenon that brought about a 50 per cent increase in both journals' pages when first the *Monthly* in 1790 and then the *Critical* in 1791 began new series in which three, rather than two, volumes were published each year. The proportion of main articles to catalogue items remained essentially constant, however: the *Critical*'s average of 13.35 main articles in the 1780s and 17.71 in the 1790s still represented 30 per cent in the 1780s and a very slight increase to 30.5 per cent in the 1790s. Similarly, the *Monthly*'s 12.7 average in the 1780s and 16.5 in the 1790s also represented only a slight increase to 23.6 per cent. In short, throughout this period the *Critical* reviewed a little less than a third of its items in the main-article sections and the *Monthly* a little less than a quarter.

Even in its early years, with little fanfare surrounding the new undertaking, the *Monthly Review* found favour with the public and book reviewing was soon an accepted part of the literary marketplace, with six major additional review journals starting up in the next few decades – the *Critical Review* in 1756, the *London Review* in 1775, the *English Review* in 1783, the *Analytical Review* in 1788, the *British Critic* in 1793 and the *Anti-Jacobin Review* in 1798 – and a number of short-lived minor ones, together with review sections in the general magazines. The principal new entries into the field after the *Edinburgh Review*'s October 1802 debut were the *Quarterly Review* in 1809, *Blackwood's Edinburgh Magazine* in 1817 and the *Westminster Review* in 1824.

Timperley gives 1797 circulation figures for the Reviews of between 1,500 (*Analytical Review*) and 5,000 (*Monthly Review*), with the *British Critic* and the

20 Forster 1997, xxxv–xxxvi.

Critical Review at 3,500.[21] In 1799, with the completion of its first volume, the *Anti-Jacobin Review* claimed a circulation of 3,250.[22] These numbers may be compared with the *Edinburgh Review*'s 2,000 in 1803, a figure considered a 'dazzling success' as Derek Roper has pointed out,[23] and the *Monthly*'s early circulation figures of between 500 and 1,000 copies in 1751, rising to 2,500 in 1758 and 3,500 in 1776.[24] Massimiliano Demata and Duncan Wu give figures for the *Edinburgh* of 9,000 by 1809 and 13,000 by 1815,[25] and Joanne Shattock reports that Murray's print run of the *Quarterly* for the 1830s was between 9,000 and 10,000.[26]

The *Monthly Review* itself lasted almost a hundred years (a figure later dwarfed by the *Quarterly* and *Westminster* Reviews), and the apparently penniless Griffiths became a rich, influential man of whom it was said at his death that he

> must have become acquainted with more characters, anecdotes, and circumstances ... than, perhaps, any other Critic from Dionysus of Halicarnassus, who, we gather from Polybius and others, was the first reviewer, downward, or indeed any other person of the bibliopolical or literary professions.[27]

The *Monthly*'s original utilitarian descriptions of its role soon expanded to more elaborate definitions of its literary/cultural functions, and great claims were soon made by its imitators, particularly the *Critical Review*. It is a long step from Griffiths's modest claims in 1749 to Smollett's outraged rhetorical flourishes six years later in December 1755 advertising the still-forthcoming *Critical Review*, then called *The Progress or Annals of Literature and the Liberal Arts*:

> This Work [will be] ... executed by a Set of Gentlemen whose Characters and Capacities have been universally approved and acknowledged by the Public: Gentlemen who have long observed with Indignation the Productions of Genius and Dullness; Wit and Impertinence; Learning and Ignorance, confounded in the Chaos of Publication; applauded without Taste, and condemned without Distinction; and who have seen the noble Art of Criticism reduced to a contemptible Manufacture subservient to the most sordid Views of Avarice and Interest, and carried on by wretched Hirelings, without Talent, Candour, Spirit, or Circumspection.[28]

21 Timperley 1842, 795.
22 *Anti-Jacobin Review* 1799, 'Prefatory Address to the Reader', 1, 1.
23 Roper 1978, 24.
24 Knapp 1958; Knapp's source is British Library – Add. MSS 48, 800.
25 Demata and Wu 2002, 3.
26 Shattock 1989, 12. See also p. 21 n. 20 where she gives some of the conflicting circulation figures for the two quarterlies.
27 *European Magazine* 45, 1804, 3–4, 'Memoir of Ralph Griffiths, LLD.'
28 *Public Advertiser*, Friday, 9 Dec. 1755.

Smollett's task in advertising and starting his new journal was, of course, different from that of Griffiths. With the early success of the *Monthly* it was no longer necessary to justify the existence of a review journal or show why it might have a place in the literary world; Smollett needed to show why his particular review journal was needed to meet the now-established market for reliable critical judgements. These judgements had practical consequences, of course, however much a higher purpose might be claimed for them: literary reputations could be increased and lessened, if not quite made and broken.

Griffiths had argued in an early advertisement for the *Monthly Review* that a review journal was something 'which no one, conversant in the Literary World, ought, in justice to themselves, to be without'.[29] Smollett and the *Critical Review* took this further, taking the need for granted and attempting to carve out a place for the sale of a journal, sublimely claiming its non-commercial purposes while essentially copying the *Monthly Review* – that 'contemptible Manufacture' – in almost all aspects, including its price.

Smollett's 'Set of Gentlemen' may have had their 'Characters and Capacities' 'universally approved and acknowledged by the Public' but they remained anonymous like the *Monthly*'s reviewers.[30] Much emphasis was laid on the unnamed predecessor and rival's 'most sordid Views of Avarice and Interest' and the new journal's supposed impartiality and lack of commercial prejudices or trade connections – 'They have no Connexions to warp their Integrity; they have no Prejudices to influence their Judgment' and 'they scorn to act as the Ministers of Interest, Faction, Envy or Malevolence' – but in practice the differences are difficult to see and the operation of prejudice, interest, faction, envy and malevolence is rather more striking in the *Critical Review* than the *Monthly Review*. The *Critical* might express sublime outrage that one anonymous author (Goldsmith) should confound 'a work undertaken from public spirit, with one supported for the sordid purposes of a bookseller' (*CR* 7, 1759: 372), but the similarities are more striking than the differences. Much later, the

29 *General Advertiser*, Thursday, 2 Nov. 1749.

30 Thanks to Griffiths's annotated set of the *Monthly Review* in the Bodleian Library and Benjamin Christie Nangle's long work on identifying the reviewers indicated by varying initials and partial names, most of the reviewers in the *Monthly Review* have been identified. See Nangle 1934, 1955. Lonsdale 1961 demonstrates that Nangle's decoding of Griffiths's annotations cannot always be relied on but it is generally useful. No such index exists for the *Critical* or any of the other Reviews, although identification, firm or tentative, of individual reviewers such as Tobias Smollett or Samuel Johnson has been done with varying degrees of authority. Roper 1955 clearly identifies the four additional contributors to the first volume of the *Critical Review* and Basker 1988 identifies many early contributions by Smollett, but only occasional identification is possible for the rest of the run. The initials used in the *London* and *Analytical* Reviews encourage identification of some reviews, such as many of Wollstonecraft's reviews in the *Analytical*, but the shifting and deceptive use of initials must often make this identification somewhat tentative.

Quarterly was similarly started in reaction against the *Edinburgh Review*, but 'lifted its format and technique from the *Edinburgh*'.[31]

The attempt by Smollett to portray the *Critical*'s reviewers as gentlemanly critics untainted by commerce caused some mirth among the new journal's rapidly acquired enemies. John Shebbeare, for example, in his ferocious 168-page pamphlet *The occasional critic; or, the decrees of the Scotch tribunal in the Critical review rejudged*, made much mock of the pretence: 'I suppose you mean, that the Authors of the *Monthly* Review are yet *more* sordid and avaritious, *greater* Hirelings and more miserable Critics than you, *Gentlemen Annalists*.'[32]

Each successive review journal was in a similar position to that of the *Critical*, however, each confirming the important role played by book reviewing in the literary marketplace, and each attempting to establish the need for its own particular approach. Each new review needed to appeal both to 'those Gentlemen and Ladies who ... are desirous of changing the Magazine they have usually taken for a better' and to those 'who have been accustomed to regard all Publications of this Nature with Contempt or Indifference, from the slovenly Manner in which they are in general executed ...'[33] Anonymity and decorum tended to prevent the public exhibition of the complicated web of connections between the reviewers and proprietors of reviews, and Smollett certainly did not point out his earlier reviewing for the *Monthly* any more than William Kenrick pointed out the same fact about his own career when he was busy establishing his *London Review* in 1775, or Gilbert Stuart with the *English Review* in 1783. In addition, many other reviewers wrote for two or more of the reviews. The process continued even after the *Edinburgh Review* changed the world of reviewing; Francis Jeffrey wrote reviews for the *Monthly Review* at almost the same time as he was engaged in the beginnings of the *Edinburgh Review*,[34] for example, and William Gifford, who had featured prominently in the *Anti-Jacobin Review*, went on to edit the *Quarterly Review*. After 1802, we see plenty of movement from one journal to another, as when Sir Walter Scott moved from the *Edinburgh* to help found the *Quarterly*, or J.G. Lockhart went on from large-scale reviewing for *Blackwood's Edinburgh Magazine* (established in 1817) to editing the *Quarterly*. Moreover, the journals' self-definitions are sometimes cyclical. Just as we see the *Edinburgh Review* proudly proclaiming in 1802 a revolutionary change which is in fact a return to the practice of a much

31 Demata and Wu 2002, 5.
32 Shebbeare 1757, 6.
33 Advertisement for no. 7 of the *British Magazine and Review; or, universal miscellany, of arts, sciences, literature, history, poetry, politics, manners, amusements, and intelligence foreign and domestic, public advertiser*, 1 Feb. 1783.
34 Nangle 1955, 33–4.

earlier period, so too do we observe the *Analytical Review* in 1788 staking its ground by attempting to return to the abstract-and-extract approach characteristic of the pre-*Monthly Review* journals and some of the early reviewing of the *Monthly* as well.

The *London Review*'s preliminary advertisements in 1775 are vague about the aspects of the new journal distinguishing it from its rivals. The only specific point stressed is the hitherto universal anonymity of reviewers, with the *London Review* pointing out with considerable justification that such protected reviewers are 'apt to indulge both their petulance and indolence, from the reflection that they are neither responsible to the Writer whom they insult, nor the Reader on whom they impose'. Kenrick knew this well, having taken full advantage of its possibilities when he reviewed for the *Monthly Review*, and in fact his promises of changing this situation were completely fraudulent; writers of individual reviews were never identified, except by shifting initials, and any public attempts by readers to raise the question were rudely or disingenuously dismissed.[35] Like the *Critical* in its early years, the *London* kept up its insulting attitude; as the journal survived Kenrick by only a year and ceased in 1780, it is not possible to know whether time might have mellowed its attitude.

The *Analytical Review* too, with its principal opening claim that the proper purpose of a literary journal was 'to give such an account of new publications, as may enable the reader to judge of them for himself' and its doubt whether 'the Writers ought to add to this their own judgment' (*AR* 1, 1788: i), promised what it did not perform and in fact offered critical opinions from the beginning. It too could lament the abuse of anonymous reviewing – 'men without a name, from the shade of obscurity in which they were concealed, have ventured to abuse at random the first literary characters' (*AR* 1, 1788: ii) – and fail to identify its own reviewers.[36] Surprisingly, five years earlier the *English Review* had not proclaimed any revolutionary changes or attacked aggressively, but had taken a mild approach sometimes reminiscent of Griffiths's first description of the public's need for the service the *Monthly* would provide. In the same year in which James Elphinston had commented on what he saw as the failure of the existing review journals to meet the needs of the reading public, the *English Review* was establishing itself by once again pointing out the 'endless multiplicity of performances' and the surprising fact that 'two publications only of the critical kind should have been able to establish themselves in England' (*ER* 1, 1783: 3). Perhaps this virtuous moderation seemed the most

35 Forster 1997, xvii–xx.
36 See note 28 above.

logical approach to take; following the *Critical*'s and the *London*'s start-up approach, it might have seemed hardly possible to step up the level of aggression. That raising of the stakes awaited the politics of the *Anti-Jacobin Review* in 1798.

Politics were of varying degrees of importance in the reviews, although there was also little consistency even within the early examples. Walter Graham's description of the *Critical* as 'established under Tory and Church patronage to maintain principles in opposition to those of the *Monthly*'[37] greatly oversimplifies the differences, although there is truth in it.[38] Certainly the *Monthly* and *Critical* often disagreed – a correspondent to the *London Chronicle* in 1760 said that he took the two reviews 'for the same reason, and with the same success too, that Mr Alworthy put his nephew under the tuition of *Thwackum* and *Square*'[39] – but politics were only a small part of this. In contrast, a much more obviously political line was taken by the *British Critic*, established in 1793 and arguing from the beginning that, while the existing journals might be doing a satisfactory job of simply reviewing, there was something else more important: the 'principal Reviews have long been animated by a spirit very hostile, not only to the whole establishment in Church and State, but to all that Englishmen in general hold most sacred, in the principles by which it is supported ... ' (*BC* 1, 1793: 1). By this time in the ferment of the 1790s the level of political engagement was much increased by periodical publications of many kinds.

The political differences between the *Monthly* and *Critical* Reviews can be greatly overemphasized, but the explicitly political purpose of the *Anti-Jacobin Review*, established in 1798, hardly can. Its Prospectus beats the drum ferociously against the 'Jacobin faction, in the bosom of our country' with its 'numerous presses' incessantly pouring forth a 'torrent of licentiousness'[40] and presents the pressing need to counter this flood:

> That the channels of criticism have long been corrupted; that many of the Reviews have been rendered the mere instruments of faction; that the Reviewers, sinking the critic in the partisan, have insidiously contributed to favour the designs of those writers who labour to undermine our civil and religious establishments, and, by a shameful dereliction of duty, to cast an odium on their opponents, is a fact which may easily be established by an attentive perusal of their works since the year 1788.[41]

37 Graham 1930, 213.
38 Roper 1961; Spector 1966.
39 *London Chronicle* (1760) 8, 85; letter dated 10 July 1760 and signed 'Tim Buck'.
40 See Wood, chap. 48 below.
41 *Anti-Jacobin Review*, Prospectus, 1799, 1, 1–2 (republished as pp. 1–6 of vol. 1).

By subjecting the other Reviews to criticism, exposure and analysis – especially the radical *Analytical*, whose 'death-blow' and 'dissolution' the *Anti-Jacobin Review* was proudly claiming to have hastened before the end of its first volume – and by providing in its own reviews and other miscellany items an opposing view, the *Anti-Jacobin*'s aim was to vanquish 'the spirit of Jacobinism'.[42] In this atmosphere it is not surprising to see the *New London Review* arguing in the following year that the 'learned labours of this enlightened age merit a record as independent as possible of [the] prepossessions' characteristic of the existing journals: 'Party politics, with all the feuds and asperities incident to the passions of venality and ambition, maintain an undue ascendancy in all.'[43] Such political rhetoric did not soon die down; ten years later the *Quarterly* was established as a Tory opposition to Jeffrey and its 'primary function was to counter the Whig principles of the *Edinburgh*'.[44]

Politics aside, the innumerable complaints, pleadings and attacks directed at reviewers in prose and verse and in newspapers, magazines, pamphlets and books soon made it clear that whether or not reviewers' opinions really influenced readers, there was widespread fear that they did. Yet the principal interest of those making such complaints was in neither the radical opinions of the *Analytical* nor the rabidly conservative ones of the *Anti-Jacobin*; it was in the supposed ignorance, malevolence and, above all, corruption of the reviewers. In 1760, a pamphlet entitled *The battle of the reviews* argued that 'Criticism is a Matter of too great Importance to be made a Trade of, or to serve Views purely lucrative, in either Author or Bookseller,'[45] but reviewing, of course, was a trade or commercial transaction. There is little evidence to support the view, popular among authors, that reviewers, who, 'like hangmen, are obliged to execute for bread'[46] actually would 'write for Booksellers and their own fraternity, and, as is commonly said, will insert any Character of any Publication for a Guinea'[47] or 'save or damn just as the authors pay'.[48] Nonetheless, many authors clung to their belief:

> they are all *the property* of three, four, or more booksellers; and as no hawker will cry stinking fish, it is their invariable practice to praise in the most extravagant terms *every publication* those booksellers originally vend, whether meritorious or otherwise; this forms the first and most important part of the

42 *Anti-Jacobin Review*, 'Prefatory Address', 1799, 1, iv.
43 *New London Review*, Prospectus, 1–2.
44 Demata and Wu 2002, 5.
45 *The battle of the reviews* 1760, vi.
46 Griffiths 1770, I, 10.
47 Sayer 1765, v.
48 A Lady, *Retaliation* 1791, 1.

> review: the second part of the performance is prostituted to the interests of *Bribery* – as thus, those authors who are resolved to acquire a fugitive fame independent of talents, send a copy of their works to the *Editor of the Review* with a *guinea*, and then they may either write the criticism themselves (which is done in nine instances out of ten) or receive more praise from the honest editor for their doggrel nonsense, than Virgil would think even just if describing his incomparable Aeneid.[49]

Until Griffiths retired from general bookselling in the early 1760s, his obvious conflict of interest was sometimes the subject of jokes in the *Monthly Review*. Similar observations might have been made about the other journals, with, for example, Joseph Johnson and the *Analytical Review*, John Murray and the *English Review*, and the Rivingtons and the *British Critic*. The network of connections between the booksellers was inextricably complicated and often hidden. The *St James's Chronicle*, for example, which began in 1761 and continued well into the nineteenth century and carried large numbers of book advertisements and other literary coverage, carried only the name of the printer Henry Baldwin, but its founding shareholders also included a number of booksellers: Griffiths, Thomas Becket, Thomas Davies, Robert and Lockyer Davis, Christopher Henderson, William Jackson of Oxford, and Thomas Lowndes.[50] Much of the reading public appears to have taken the pragmatic view expressed by William Boscawen in his Preface to his *The progress of satire* in 1798:

> Literary journals, it is true, are become of great use in the present state of literature, and, if conducted with but a moderate degree of liberality, afford an amusement unmixed with indignation or disgust. Although their criticisms, separately taken, be anonymous (for which they may plead a kind of prescription), the editors or conductors of the *publication* are generally known, and considered as responsible for its contents. No outrage on private feelings, no barefaced violation of candour, is likely to be committed; their connections and their prejudices are known, and intelligent readers will make due allowance for them.[51]

Yet the chief problem for the Reviews was sometimes not the unsavoury closeness of bookseller relationships but something like the opposite: difficulty in obtaining books for review.[52] As booksellers usually did not send out review copies – although there were some exceptions – it appears that the Reviews' collectors had to borrow or buy the copies; reviewers, who were paid by the

49 Williams 1791, iv, 'Declaratory dedication'.

50 The minute books of the *St James's Chronicle* are in the Manuscripts Department of the library of the University of North Carolina at Chapel Hill.

51 Boscawen 1798, iv.

52 Forster 1990, 1997, Introduction, especially xxxviii-xxxix.

sheet, were not normally able to keep the books unless they paid for them.[53] This procedure we know to be true in the case of the *Monthly Review*, both from its answers to correspondents, much more extensive than those in the other journals, and from many references in Griffiths's correspondence, now in the Bodleian Library. The occasional comments in and around the other journals suggest that they went about their business in much the same way. There are many testy responses to questions about why certain books have not been reviewed, as when the *Monthly Review* writes: 'Authors who print their works in Scotland, or at any country presses, and neglect to advertise them, must not be surprized if they pass unnoticed by the Reviewers – who, though they ought to be Critics, most certainly are not *Conjurors*' (*MR* 68, 1783: 288). We do know from the surviving agreement setting up the *British Critic* in 1793 that the Rivingtons were bound by it to supply all necessary books on temporary loan to the editor, Robert Nares.[54] The *London Review* encouraged authors to send in copies of their books and it is clear that some authors did send books to some of the Reviews, but this was a small part of the solution to the problem.

The early reviewers described their role in various terms including 'tasters to the public' (*MR* 13, 1755: 399), 'beadles of Parnassus' (*MR* 38, 1768: 248) and 'officers of the literary police' (*CR* 21, 1766: 60–1). These terms pointed to the dual nature of the reviewers' role: they were there to tell the public what to read, as they still do, and to keep order, as they saw it, in the literary world: exposing booksellers' tricks, repressing and encouraging authors, and giving advice as well. These two functions were often hostile to each other.

Walter Graham has said that the evolution of the Review has been 'most regular and dependable' among literary periodicals, and that from 1665 to 1790 'a very gradual change transformed the abstract of a book into an abstract-with-comment, then into a review, of a sort, with copious excerpts from the work reviewed'.[55] It is not as simple as that, however. Certainly it is true that Griffiths took for granted when he began that the well-established 'agreeable and useful method' of quoting extracts (*MR* 1, 1749: 67) and summarizing a book's contents was the accepted approach. Readers of the preceding *Works of the Learned* and similar journals were familiar with this method, but Griffiths, while aiming to meet the needs of these readers, was also focused on a far larger, more general reading public who might not be thoroughly familiar with the idea that the reviewers' 'business is to enter no farther into the province of criticism, than just so far as may be indispensably necessary to give some idea of

53 Forster 1990, 10, 16–17, n. 32.
54 Indenture 19 Aug. 1793, London Metropolitan Archives Library MS F/RIV/4. See also Forster 2001, 176–7.
55 Graham 1930, 196.

such books as come under [their] consideration' (*MR* 2, 1749–50: 260). The pretence that the early reviewers were not offering opinions and were leaving judgement to readers was a thin one, however, and there are few reviews which do not judge; at the same time the reviewers pointed out – as they did, for example, forty-one pages earlier than the above statement about the province of criticism – that they were 'expected . . . to have a voice' (*MR* 2, 1749–50: 219). Similarly, the *Critical Review* could in its first volume point out that 'appealing to an author's works, and supporting our judgment by quotations from them [is] the fairest method of determining their intrinsic merit that could possibly be made use of' (*CR* 1, 1756: 484), but also pronounce aggressively that 'Every author who writes without talents is a grievance, if not an impostor, who defrauds the public; and every critic has a right to detect the imposition' (*CR* 1, 1756: 287).

Reviewers' comments on the defrauding of the public usually referred to booksellers' tricks, however, with occasional mentions of authors. In 1730, Fielding's Mr Dash in *The author's farce* had said that 'A title page is to a book what a fine neck is to a woman, and therefore ought to be the most regarded as it is the part which is viewed before the purchase.'[56] The early decades of general reviewing were particularly likely to produce references to deceitful title pages while the reviewers were busy making quite sure that the reading public was persuaded of the utility and indeed necessity of the reviewers' efforts. 'Books like men, generally present the fairest side outwards,' the *Monthly Review* reminds its readers in 1763, 'and very few instances can be given in this pretending and superficial age, wherein the title page of a book hath not been by far the most promising part of it' (*MR* 29, 1763: 46). No matter how many the reminders that 'Authors and Booksellers, persuaded of the vast importance of a title page, have left unattempted no device which in the advertisement might serve to prejudice the world in favour of their productions' (*MR* 34, 1766: 273), reviewers continue to note that 'Some people are prepossessed in favour of a book by the speciousness of its first page' (*CR* 31, 1771: 58) and 'A specious title-page, it must be owned, frequently imposes upon readers' (*CR* 32, 1771: 229). 'It is a fundamental article in the creed of a Reviewer, that no trust is to be put in title pages,' writes Bentley in the *Monthly Review* (*MR* 46, 1772: 443), and it remains an often-mentioned, pivotal point of the reviewers' role to 'detect literary impositions' (*MR* 46, 1772: 627) and 'prevent those who know no better, from believing implicitly every assertion of [an] author' (*CR* 33, 1772: 120).

56 Fielding 1966, 28.

If the reviewers were reigning as 'absolute monarchs over literary merit'[57] and infuriating and terrifying authors on one hand and acting as literary policemen detecting the cheats of booksellers on the other, then they were also from an early stage functioning as sources of advertising material to aid booksellers in selling more books. Nearly forty years passed between Griffiths's very early advertisement for the forthcoming translation of *The revolutions of Genoa* – with a fifteen-line review quotation accompanied by the simple addition '*Vide*. The Character of the *Original*, in the *Monthly Review*, for *March* 1750'[58] – and the point where the *Monthly* complained of 'the practice of some unblushing Publishers, who, in their puffing advertisements, scruple not to insert *pretended* commendatory extracts from the Reviews' (*MR* 80, 1789: 288). By the late 1780s there was so much review-supported advertising in newspapers that hundreds of examples could be given. The most common way of using the reviews in advertisements throughout the half-century was the quotation of a brief passage preceded or followed by an identifying note: 'Monthly, Nov. 1778',[59] 'Critical Review, June 1767'[60] or 'The Appendix to the Monthly Review, published last Month says of this ... '[61] Some advertisements, in at least a pretended assumption that readers have regular access to reviews, do not quote but merely refer readers: 'For a Character of which Piece see the Monthly and Critical Reviews',[62] 'For a Character of this long-expected Work, see the last Appendix to the Monthly Review'[63] or 'For an account of this spirited and well-written Novel, see the British Critick, January, 1799; the Anti-Jacobin Review, December, 1798, and January 1799; and the Monthly Review, November, 1798.'[64] Many more elaborate phrases are also used, both with and without quotations. For example, Cadell, advertising Lennox's *Euphemia*, quotes fourteen lines from the *English Review*'s recent 'just and very forcible character of this most respectable production' and comments that if Lennox's reputation so required or if there were enough room in an advertisement, there 'might be added the very high character already given ... both by the Monthly and Critical Reviewers'.[65]

57 *Flights of inflatus* 1791, I, v.
58 *General Advertiser*, 14 Dec. 1750.
59 Advertisement for *A diary kept in an excursion to Little-Hampton*, *Public Advertiser*, 8 Mar. 1780.
60 Advertisement for *A letter to a Member of Parliament concerning the growth of popery*, *Public Advertiser*, 14 July 1767.
61 Advertisement for *An impartial account of the invasion under William Duke of Normandy* by Charles Parkin, AM, *Public Advertiser*, 6 Aug. 1756.
62 Advertisement for *The romance of a day*, in footnote to advertisement for Samuel Foote's *The Methodist*, *London Evening-Post*, 3–5 Nov. 1761.
63 Advertisement for *Les souvenirs; or recollections of Madame De Cailus*, *Public Advertiser*, 1 Dec. 1770.
64 Advertisement for second edition of *Arthur Fitz-Albini, a novel*, *St James's Chronicle*, 14–16 May 1799.
65 *London Chronicle* 69, 10–12 Mar. 1791, 245.

Advertisements appended to books very often included review material and, with little of the space restrictions of newspaper advertisements, sometimes at considerable length. William Lane, among others, made great use of these advertisements with extensive review quotations; at the end of volume II of George Walker's novel *The house of Tynian* (1795), for example, appear advertisements on facing pages for *Count Roderic's castle* and *The voluntary exile*, the first supported with an eighteen-line quotation from the *Monthly Review* for April 1795 and the second with a twenty-one-line quotation from the *Analytical Review* for March 1795.[66] John Bell and Thomas Longman were also frequent users of this advertising strategy. Longman's publication of August La Fontaine's *Clara Duplessis and Clairant*, for example, contains seven pages of advertisements in volume I, one even facing the title page with fourteen lines from the *Monthly Review*'s review of the French original, and six more pages advertising twelve of Longman's publications with quotations of between two and thirty-one lines from the *Monthly* and *Analytical* reviews, the *British Critic* and the *Gentleman's Magazine*.[67]

Some advertisements even took the opportunity to argue with the reviewers or point out the differences of opinion between them. Baldwin's and Dodsley's advertisement for *Newmarket; or, an essay on the turf* (1771) quotes very briefly the conflicting opinions of the *Monthly* and *Critical* reviews and ends with the note 'NB REVIEWERS, as well as DOCTORS differ.'[68] Wilkie's advertisement for *Sentimental tales* (1771) goes much further and comes out fighting: 'The Author of the Sentimental Tales takes this Opportunity of telling Malignitas the Critical Reviewer, that he scorns his impotent Malice, while favoured with the Approbation of the Public, and supported by the honourable Testimony of every other literary Journal.'[69]

There were many of these literary journals in existence and to come. The establishment and rapid spread of general book reviewing in the second half of the eighteenth century clearly altered the balance of book publishing, introducing a new factor into the marketing and reading of books.[70] In the *Critical Review*'s striking phrase, reviewing 'inclosed what was once a common field' (*CR* 30, 1770: 467) and – whether they liked or loathed it, fought it or exploited it – booksellers, authors and readers came to expect this further factor in the

66 Walker 1795, II.
67 La Fontaine 1797, I.
68 *St James's Chronicle*, 24–28 Sep. 1771.
69 *St James's Chronicle*, 16–18 Apr. 1771.
70 For a detailed study of the effect on literary careers, see Donoghue 1996.

publishing relationship. Advertising and the sight of the physical volumes themselves were no longer necessarily the primary means of initial acquaintance with books. Before ever reading booksellers' advertisements in newspapers or books, before encountering title pages, prefaces and other physical aspects of books in shops or libraries, consumers might well already have seen – and sometimes paid for – the opinions of reviewers. Bookselling has never been the same.

34

Publishing contemporary English literature, 1695–1774

MICHAEL F. SUAREZ, S.J.

Drama

Dramatic texts were steady sellers. Evidently, Samuel Johnson was not alone in believing that 'A play read, affects the mind like a play acted.'[1] There was a demand for copies of less popular works as well as standard parts of the repertory because readers commonly collected the works of important dramatic authors. Until *c.*1715, dramatic texts almost invariably were first published as quartos, following a tradition dating back to the Renaissance.[2] By the 1720s, however, most first editions were octavos, a change accounted for in part by the significantly increased size of the sheet.[3] Octavo continued to be the preferred format while a play was still enjoying publishing success, but many subsequently came on to the market as more economical duodecimos. According to B.J. McMullin, it was the Hague bookseller Thomas Johnson who established the small octavo and duodecimo formats for the reprinting of canonical English plays.[4] One advantage of printing plays in smaller formats was that they could be carried in the pockets of theatre audiences. Typically plays cost between 1*s.* and 2*s.*, depending on format, popularity and pressure from pirated editions; 1*s.* 6*d.* and 1*s.* were most common.

New productions of old plays, if they did reasonably well, often occasioned new editions. In the comic repertoire, for example, Congreve, Vanbrugh, Cibber, Farquhar and Steele were repeatedly staged and frequently reprinted.[5] Sales of the dead – and successful living – authors subsidized the publication of new works: plays as well as poems and, later, prose fiction.[6] Until John Bell's

1 S. Johnson 1968, 79.
2 For the important exception of Moseley's serial publication of octavo plays, see Kewes 1995.
3 Pollard 1941.
4 McMullin 1993, 100.
5 Kenny 1976.
6 See Bonnell, chap. 37, below. The bookselling business of the Tonsons is a particularly noteworthy example of this phenomenon. Foxon 1975a and Raven 1987 give some indication of the era's myriad minor authors, now largely ignored.

Shakespeare's plays (9 vols., 1773–4) and his *British theatre* (21 vols., 1776–81), printed plays seldom reflected alterations for performance made by the acting companies. Because the 1737 Licensing Act (10 George II, c. 38) imposed censorship only on the performance of plays, and did not govern the contents of printed texts, expurgated passages could be included without legal constraint. Naturally, publishers of plays that had been modified for the stage by the Licenser often made the printing of censored passages a primary selling point.

During the Restoration and eighteenth century, play texts were most commonly reprints of whatever edition was close to hand. Few playwrights showed much concern for the texts of their published plays – most attended neither to the first edition, nor to the correction or revision of subsequent editions, Congreve being the most obvious and important exception.[7] The surviving evidence suggests that very few playwrights even bothered to read proof.[8] Old cast lists and out-of-date prologues and epilogues are common evidence that the same texts were simply reprinted over and over again. A significant exception, however, is the bowdlerization of many Restoration plays from the mid-1730s onward to accommodate an increased female readership and to forestall moral censure that could damage sales.

Drury Lane (1674–1791) consistently performed about sixty mainpieces each season.[9] A survey of *The London Stage* suggests that the numbers for Covent Garden (1732–1808) were comparable. In addition, performances were taking place at Lincoln's Inn Fields (1714–44), at The New Theatre (or Little Theatre) in the Haymarket (1720–1820) and at Oldell's Theatre (1729–32) and The New Theatre (1732–42) – both in Ayliffe Street, Goodman's Fields – and elsewhere.[10] There were invariably several London booksellers who made it their business to keep on hand a large inventory of plays, both of titles they owned – either outright or, more commonly as the century progressed, through the purchase of shares in a copy – and of those available from other booksellers. Inventories were routinely expanded by exchanging stock with other members of the trade, or by purchasing books at the usual trade discount. Among the booksellers with substantial stocks of plays were William Lewis, Richard Wellington, Bernard Lintot, John Watts, Andrew Millar, Paul Vaillant, William Griffin (from 1749 onwards) and, of course, the Tonsons. David Garrick's 1768 purchase of 186 different play titles – both mainpieces

7 Congreve 2009.
8 Kenny 1980, 318, 319, 320.
9 Milhous and Hume 1994, 131.
10 See Van Lennep *et al.* 1961–5.

and afterpieces, mostly in multiple copies – from the London bookseller William Griffin highlights the considerable number of plays in print.[11]

Early in the period 1695–1774, the interval between production and publication followed no consistent pattern, although two to four weeks was about average. As the century progressed, however, plays were frequently published during the first run and were commonly sold near or even at the theatre itself, the orangewomen taking the role of hawkers.[12] From 1704, the bookseller Richard Wellington made certain that his newspaper advertisements for the texts of plays then being performed were juxtaposed with the theatres' advertisements, and this sensible practice was certainly carried on by his successors, as a survey of the *Daily Courant* clearly shows.[13] Publishing plays during the initial run or very soon thereafter meant that it became increasingly common practice for booksellers to purchase the copyrights to plays in advance of the first night. One advantage of later publication was that the length of the stage run helped the bookseller gauge the length of the press run.

If an author wanted to make a good living from his or her pen, playwriting was arguably the best bet. In addition to the money to be made from the stage, there was the prospect of significant income to be had from the page: from the lapse of the Printing Act up to the death of Queen Anne, a playwright could expect to be paid an average of about £22 copy money for the publication of a mainpiece, with prices ranging from the meagre £3 10*s*. given to Elkanah Settle for *The city ramble* (1711) to an astonishing £107 10*s*. to Joseph Addison for *Cato* (1713). Standard prices increased between 1714 and 1737: the average paid for mainpieces was £52, with afterpieces typically fetching between £5 and £10. Although the extant data from 1737 to 1774 – the advent of Stage Licensing to the Lords' decision in *Donaldson* v. *Becket* – are not as complete as one would wish, the average fee for the copyright of a mainpiece was approximately £95, for afterpieces around £40.[14] Milhous and Hume have determined that, throughout the century, the remuneration given to writers for their work appearing in print was consistently about 50 per cent of the income they typically earned from their work being performed on stage. In other words, publication generally accounted for about one-third of the total income a playwright could expect to make from a reasonably successful mainpiece. An exceptional run in the theatre would alter these proportions, however. It is

11 Griffin charged Garrick 6*d*. per duodecimo copy and 2*s*. 6*d*. per octavo; afterpieces were generally 1*s*. each; see Milhous and Hume 1994, 123.

12 Kenny 1980, 313–15.

13 Milhous and Hume 1994, 126.

14 Figures calculated from data given in Milhous and Hume 1999, appendix VII; they use the period 1737 to 1790 and arrive at a figure of £100 for a mainpiece and £40 to £50 for an afterpiece (p. 39).

generally believed that John Gay made £693 13*s.* 6*d.* from the production of *The beggar's opera.*[15] Yet, in February 1728 Tonson and Watts paid him just £94 10*s.* (90 guineas) for both *The beggar's opera* and *Fifty fables.*[16]

Perhaps the most lucrative of all eighteenth-century plays earned no income from performance. The considerable sums Gay made from *The Beggar's Opera* were relatively small when compared with the fortune he garnered from the *succès de scandale* of *Polly*. Suppressed by Walpole's government in December 1728 before it was staged,[17] Gay's sequel to his 'Newgate pastoral' became a publishing phenomenon. Taking a lesson from his friend Pope, Gay vigorously solicited subscriptions at a guinea (21*s.*) per copy and had the play printed for himself: 10,500 copies in quarto.[18] Gay's ordinary retail price was originally 6*s.* – four to six times the standard price for a mainpiece in those days – but the presence in the market of many pirated copies forced Gay to adjust the cost of his play about pirates to 2*s.* 6*d.* All totalled, Gay earned some £3,000 from the publication of *Polly*: the subscription alone netted more than £1,200.[19]

When Henry Brooke's *Gustavus Vasa* (1739) was denied a licence by the Lord Chamberlain, Brooke too decided to publish by subscription, and on 17 March 1739 he advertised in *The Daily Post* his intention to print the tragedy 'on a superfine Royal Paper' at 5*s.* per copy. All the leading Opposition figures subscribed; Robert Dodsley, himself associated with the anti-Walpole Patriot group, saw the work through the press. Among the subscribers, whose names occupy a dozen pages, are Lord Chesterfield (10 guineas), the Earl of Marchmont (four books), Jonathan Swift (ten books) and Samuel Johnson, who subsequently observed that the playwright was 'recompensed by a very liberal subscription'.[20] Brooke did not sell his play at 5*s.* to the general public, however, but reduced the price to 1*s.* 6*d.* 'to secure my property', having been 'appris'd that a pyrated Edition of my Play is intended to be publish'd this Day'.[21]

When James Thomson's *Edward and Eleonora* was also banned from the stage just ten days after the censorship of Brooke's play was made public, Thomson,

15 Winton 1993, 174 argues that the figure should be £200 less because it does not reflect the deduction of standard house charges by the theatre.

16 Ransom 1938, 59.

17 On stage censorship during the period, see Winton 1980. On print censorship, more generally, see Thomas 1969, 1977.

18 Maslen and Lancaster 1991, nos. 1427, 1432. See also Nichols 1812–16, I, 404.

19 Winton 1993, 133–5; Milhous and Hume 1999, 42. See also Sutherland 1942.

20 Boswell 1934–50, I, 141 n. 1. Provoked by the censorship of Brooke's tragedy, Johnson wrote the satirical pamphlet *A compleat vindication of the licensers of the stage* (1739).

21 Chapman 1925–6. At least two copies of the piracy survive: N17825 and Bodleian Vet.A4 e 1967, which is not recorded in *ESTC*.

similarly a prominent supporter of the Opposition, followed Brooke's example and offered his work to the public on the same terms. In all, 4,500 copies of the play were printed, 1,000 of them on fine paper.[22] Thomson's income from this venture, said to be £1,000, must have been considerable as he used the profits to move into a spacious new house next to Richmond Gardens.[23] In January 1740, another play, *Arminius*, by Thomson's friend William Paterson, was subject to a third ban from the Stage Licenser. Once again, the work was sold by subscription and sales were fuelled by political partisanship: although Paterson was an author of only moderate gifts, Henry Woodfall, Jr. printed 400 copies on fine paper and 2,000 ordinary copies for the first edition.[24]

In literature, as in other areas of publishing, print tended to breed print – a commercial and cultural phenomenon that occasioned considerable anxiety (most famously expressed in the *Dunciad*). When, for example, Tonson issued Rowe's edition of *The [dramatic] works of Mr William Shakespear* (6 vols., 1709), both Lintot and Curll promptly published volumes of the *Poems* in the same format to complete the set.[25] The 'Advertisement' to Lintot's edition merely refers to Tonson's publication (a2r), whereas Curll's book is entitled *The works of Mr William Shakespear, volume the seventh* and further maintains the illusion of an authorized supplement by including a commentary keyed to Rowe's text.

Although London was very much the theatrical centre of the kingdom, surprisingly few multi-volume collections of English drama published in the eighteenth century originated in the capital.[26] The first such dramatic assembly, *A collection of the best English plays* (1711–12, 1714, 1718, 1721, 1722, 1726) – with various imprint dates, places of publication (some false) and booksellers listed, as well as shifting contents – was issued by Thomas Johnson in The Hague and, like many subsequent drama collections, consisted of a combination of reprints and remainders.[27] By the early 1720s, the *Collection* consisted of sixty-four plays in sixteen octavo volumes, a hodgepodge of reissues and re-set texts. In 1750, another Hague bookseller, 'H. Scheurleer, Junior', reissued Thomas Johnson's remaining octavos (now 10 vols.) as *A select collection of the*

22 P., P.T. [unidentified], 1855a, 218. It appears that no subscription list was printed.

23 Sambrook 1991, 199;

24 P., P.T. [unidentified], 1855a, 218. Other censored plays in the period include John Kelly, *The Levee* (1741), William [not Jas.] Shirley, *Electra* (1763), and Miles Peter Andrews, *The Election* (1774). See Conolly 1976.

25 See *ESTC* T138085 and T138298.

26 Tonson was publishing multi-volume, small format editions of canonical authors, including dramatists, during the 1710s, but there is no evidence that he was marketing them as dramatic 'collections'.

27 On the several as yet unsolved bibliographical problems associated with Johnson's plays, see McMullin 1993, 100–3.

best modern English play's [*sic*]. By 1752, the stock, now down to six volumes, was sold as *The British stage* and bore a London imprint 'for J. Brindley'.

The English theatre (1731) was similarly compiled by the London bookseller William Feales from remaindered editions that he bought and then reprinted as his inventory was depleted. There is an 'edition' in eight volumes duodecimo – four volumes each of comedy and tragedy – and another collection published in the same year in four sixteenmo volumes.[28] Robert Dodsley's *Select collection of old plays* (10 vols., 1745, 2 additional vols., 1746 – all dated 1744) was an altogether different enterprise: it newly printed what was then the most complete collection of early English dramatic texts (dating back to 1547). Its success enlivened others to the market for more contemporary undertakings. *A select collection of English plays* (6 vols., 1755) was a Scottish venture by the Edinburgh booksellers G. Hamilton and J. Balfour, reprinting works whose copyright had expired. Predictably, Alexander Donaldson brought on to the market a three-volume supplement under the same title in 1760. G. Martin's and J. Wotherspoon's *The theatre: or select works of the British dramatic poets* (1768) in a dozen duodecimos also originated in Edinburgh, while parts of *Bell's British theatre* (1776–81, 1791–1802) were printed in Edinburgh and York,[29] and [*William*] *Jones's British theatre* (10 vols., 1795) was a Dublin publication. Two London anthologies were probably reactions to Scottish efforts. Donaldson's publication may have prompted the London bookseller T. Lowndes to cobble together *The English theatre ... containing the most valuable plays which have been acted on the London stage* (8 vols., 1762–3, with imprint dates on individual title pages between 1735 and 1763); his second collection, *The new English theatre* (12 duodecimo vols., 1776–77), was definitely a response to Bell.[30]

Poetry

David Foxon's *English verse 1701 to 1750* records 9,748 separately published poems and collections of verse by individual authors who were alive after 1701. The *ESTC* has helped scholars discover still more poetry publications outside the traditional canon, both in the Foxon period and beyond, demonstrating the degree to which poetry was a vital part of the eighteenth-century publishing scene. The variety and range of such publications is probably best indicated by Roger Lonsdale's two landmark anthologies, *The new Oxford book of*

28 See *ESTC* N66368 and T222315, respectively.
29 See Bonnell, chap. 37, below.
30 See Bonnell 1983; see also Bonnell, chap. 37, below.

eighteenth-century verse (1984) and *Eighteenth century women poets* (1989). The Tonson family,[31] Bernard Lintot (1675–36),[32] and Robert (1704–64) and James Dodsley (1724–97) were arguably the three most important publishers of poetry in the period. Yet, we should bear in mind that – even for these highly successful publishing booksellers remembered today chiefly as purveyors of poetry (and, in the Tonsons' case, of Shakespeare's plays) – poetic texts were by no means their only stock-in-trade. An analysis of Robert Dodsley's imprints, for example, indicates that he also had considerable investments in books on religion, theology and ethics; on government affairs and politics; and on science and medicine.[33]

We must remember too that poetry publication was hardly restricted to the medium of print and that poetry was the genre in which manuscript and print continued to interact most extensively during the century.[34] Sub-genres as diverse as classical imitation, contemporary satire, the verse epistle and biblical paraphrase all had vibrant lives in manuscript circulation and criss-crossed the putative barrier between manuscript and print with remarkable fluidity. Alive to the realities of the book trade in the seventeenth century and knowledgeable about the importance of patronage, the persistence of chirographic systems and cultures, the acute anxieties precipitated by print culture, the perdurance of orality and the world of the ear, and the complex and problematic circumstances of commercial authorship in the eighteenth century, book historians no longer imagine that 'an older system of polite or courtly letters – primarily oral, aristocratic, authoritarian, court-centered – was swept away at this time and gradually replaced by a new print-based, market-centred, democratic literary system'.[35]

A close survey of poetry publishing produces a number of surprises not revealed in conventional accounts. Daniel Defoe's greatest triumph as a writer, for example, is to be found neither in his journalism nor in his novels, but rather in the verse satire *The true-born Englishman* (1700 [1701]), a publication that conferred on him almost instant celebrity, became one of the bestselling poems of the century, and won its author an audience with the monarch himself. A rejoinder to John Tutchin's anti-Williamite satire *The Foreigners* (1700), Defoe's poem wittily argues that it is ethical excellence, rather than birth, that makes one a true-born Englishman. How well did the satire sell?

31 Jacob the elder (1655/6–1736), his nephew Jacob the younger (1682–1735), and the younger's son, Jacob (1714–67); see *ODNB*.
32 Lintot's business was carried on by his son, Henry (1703–58); see *ODNB*.
33 Dodsley 1988, 25–8.
34 See Fairer 2003, 1–20.
35 Kernan 1987, 4.

Defoe's own claim in *A second volume of the writings of the author of the True-Born Englishman* (1705) that 'besides Nine Editions of the Author' sold at a shilling each, the poem 'has been Twelve Times printed by other Hands; some of which have sold for 1d. others 2d. and others 6d.' may be true, though his assertion that '80000 of the Small Ones have been sold in the Streets for 2d. or at a Penny' beggars belief (A3r).[36] Defoe's modern bibliographers suggest a more modest but nevertheless impressive publication record: 'some twenty-two editions or impressions have been identified as appearing in Defoe's lifetime [he died in 1731], of which at least five seem to have been piracies [two in quarto and three in octavo]'.[37]

The most intriguing of these piracies was described by the *Post Boy* (no. 907, 28–30 January 1701) as printed 'in three [octavo] half-sheets only' by 'the White-Friars Sham-Printer ... having left out more than half of the Original'.[38] Quite possibly, this is the 'Small' version for which Defoe claimed such an extraordinary sale, though there is an even smaller publication, printed on two half-sheets octavo (some pages in double columns), which advertised itself as 'printed word for word from the shilling book'.[39] Defoe's satire also survives in multiple contemporary printed and manuscript miscellanies. The poem's impact need not be measured solely in numbers of editions, piracies and speculation about sales figures, however. More than a dozen published responses to *The true-born Englishman* attest both to its cultural currency and to the vitality of print culture at the beginning of the eighteenth century.

From a publishing perspective, perhaps the most audacious single volume of poetry to appear between the lapse of the Printing Act and the 1774 Lords' decision in *Donaldson* v. *Becket* was Pope's *Works* of 1717.[40] Issued at the same time as the third volume of Pope's *Iliad* translation, the publication was calculated – from its oversize author portrait frontispiece to its typography, illustration and ornament – to accord the 29-year-old poet the status, if not the *auctoritas*, of a classic author. Perhaps more than any other collection of its time, this volume exploits the resources of the book, not only to win a lucrative market for the author's wares, but also to construct a *monumentum aere perennius*. Employing William Bowyer, Lintot produced 750 illustrated quartos (a third of them on fine paper) to match the expensive subscription quartos of the *Iliad*, which at this juncture in the progress of the subscription had a print run

36 Defoe's *Second volume* is the companion of *A true collection of the writings of the author of the True-Born English-man* (London, 1703). See Furbank and Owens 1998, 3–6.

37 Furbank and Owens 1998, 20.

38 *ESTC* N306; see Foxon 1975a, I, D159 and Ellis 1970, 763.

39 *ESTC* T70653; see Foxon 1975a, I, D161.

40 See the exemplary treatment of this work in McLaverty 2001, 46–81.

of 660 copies (including 200 on fine paper). These copies of the *Works* were priced at a guinea (21*s*.) each. At the same time, Lintot also had ready for sale 250 illustrated folios for customers in the middle of the market and 1,000 unillustrated, pot-paper folios for sale at the bargain price of 12*s*.[41] If the *Iliad* was announcing that classical poetry could be modern, then no less did the *Works* proclaim that modern poetry could achieve the status of the classical.

The tastes of eighteenth-century reading publics are sometimes inscrutable to us, but even contemporary booksellers often found the market unpredictable. Publishing William Somerville's blank-verse poem on hunting, *The chace*, in May 1735, George Hawkins prudently called for a print run of 750 copies, having earlier circulated 500 quarter-sheet proposals in February, March and April. In June, another 1,000 copies went on sale, and in August 1,500 more, making a total of 3,250 copies of this substantial (fourteen-sheet) quarto – not counting an Edinburgh piracy and an unauthorized Dublin reprint – on sale in just four months. A fourth edition was required in 1743.[42] Yet, such a publishing history hardly constitutes a reception history: did the poem's success rest primarily on the fashion for blank verse established by Milton, Philips and Thomson? On Somerville's lively descriptions? Or on the work's political affinities and association with the Prince of Wales? At their most useful, literary history, bibliography and book history are often mutually informing – and all need to be marshalled in concert to develop an adequate answer.

The publication history of Thomas Gray's *Elegy written in a country churchyard*, arguably the best-loved poem of the century, is likewise instructive on several counts.[43] The author sent a copy of the manuscript to his friend Horace Walpole in June 1750. Gray's 'Stanza's wrote in a country church-yard', as it is called in the Eton MS, circulated in various manuscript copies for more than seven months – one of many indications that manuscript transmission continued to be an important vehicle for the dissemination of poetry in our period – when in February 1751 Gray learned that the *Elegy* was soon to appear without his permission in *The Magazine of Magazines*. Accordingly, he asked Walpole to obtain for the poem a more secure and dignified debut from Robert Dodsley's shop at Tully's Head, thus pre-empting the unauthorized publication. Gray's wishes were speedily executed and – although his poem was soon printed not only in the *Magazine of Magazines*, but also in the *London Magazine*, the *Scots Magazine*, the *Grand Magazine of Magazines*, the *True Briton* and a Glasgow

41 The author himself received 120 copies of the quarto, which would have brought him a minimum of 120 guineas (£126) and possibly as much as 200 guineas (£210) including benefactions.

42 See Foxon 1975a, S562–67; cf. Fleeman 1964.

43 See Lonsdale 1969, 110–13.

poetic miscellany – sales of the *Elegy* were exceptional: a fifth edition of Dodsley's quarto was called for within nine months, and twelve editions were published in as many years.

Newspapers and magazines were increasingly significant venues for poetry publication. Two of Swift's best-known poems, 'A description of the morning' and 'A description of a city shower', for example, first appeared in *The Tatler* (nos. 9 and 238). The London periodical press could help make a name for a writer, especially in publishing works by provincial and female authors, but many were no respecters of literary property and tended to regard almost all available writings as in the public domain. Gray's difficulties notwithstanding, periodical publication often played a significant role in writers' careers. When Thomas Chatterton came to the capital in late April 1770 to vanquish the Republic of Letters with his pen, he had already published thirty-one poems and essays in seven different journals, five of which were London publications. By the time of his death four months later, he had seen twenty-two more of his writings appear in six journals (only one of which was a provincial publication), and was earning a decent living by his pen.[44] Chatterton's purchase on the London publishing world is evident in his satirical poem 'The art of puffing by a bookseller's journeyman' (comp. July 1770), in which the persona purports to be an insider in the book trade revealing to the public how books are fraudulently promoted for sale.[45]

The importance of printed miscellanies is evidenced by the fact that there are some 1,136 surviving verse miscellanies and anthologies (including reprints and separate issues, but excluding songbooks) for the seventy-five years from 1700 to 1774 – more than fifteen per annum.[46] Chief among these was Robert Dodsley's *Collection of poems by several hands* (6 vols., 1748–58), which went through twelve editions in thirty-four years; gave rise to multiple piracies, imitations and unauthorized 'continuations'; and was consistently well reviewed in the public press.[47] The proliferation of poetic miscellanies – typically compiled by booksellers or their agents intent on pleasing and, at times, directing the aesthetic sensibilities of the reading public – suggests that this relatively neglected species of poetic text may have much to teach us about eighteenth-century reading habits, the formation of the poetic canon and the predilections of the public.

44 Suarez 1999b.
45 Chatterton 1971, 650–1.
46 Suarez forthcoming.
47 See Dodsley 1997, I, 1–119, and Suarez 2001.

The publishing history of Pope's *Essay on criticism* (1711) illustrates the importance of cultural capital supplied by patrons in directing both taste and consumption.[48] The bookseller had 1,000 copies printed, but the poem by a then relatively unknown author scarcely attracted any notice at all until Pope 'packed up and directed twenty copies to several great men' whose endorsements generated brisk sales.[49] The fifth edition was published in 1715, just four years after the poem was entered in the *Stationers' Register*.[50] Sometimes, however, a patron's influence was less efficacious. Lawton Gilliver related that he published David Mallet's *Of verbal criticism: an epistle to Mr Pope* (1733) – paying the author 20 guineas – because Pope had insisted he do so, but the poem sold only about a hundred copies.[51]

One of the most important forms of patronage was subscription.[52] Although Tonson's elaborate subscription edition of *Paradise lost* (1688), which enriched its publisher and substantially enhanced Milton's reputation,[53] was by no means the first work so financed and promoted in England, it nevertheless added substantial momentum to a publishing trend that was to have a considerable impact on publishing and authorship.[54] Another Tonson-sponsored subscription, Dryden's *Works of Virgil* (1697), earned its translator nearly £1,400.[55] Pope clearly had these precedents – as well as the remarkably successful subscription edition of the *Tatler* (4 vols., 1710) – in mind when in 1713 he undertook to market his own Homer translations in this way.[56] Pope seems to have made about £5,000 each for his *Iliad* (6 vols., 1715–20) and *Odyssey* (5 vols., 1725–6).[57] Although Pope's undertaking was atypical in several respects,[58] its fame added to the considerable vogue for subscription publication, a practice that was particularly popular around 1710–45. *The seasons* (1730), one of the most popular poems of the century, was also published by subscription.[59] Christopher Smart published both his *Poems on several occasions* (1752) and, less successfully, his *Translation of the psalms of David* (1765) by

48 On patronage, see Griffin, chap. 5, above.

49 Pope 1956, I, 128; Pope 1797, I, xviii; both cited in Johnson 2006, IV, 250–1.

50 The 'fourth edition' appears to be a reissue of the third, though we do not know if sales were sluggish or, more probably, if a long press run had been called for to save resetting; see Foxon 1975a, P806–13.

51 *Gentleman's Magazine*, 1791, 1181, cited in Johnson 2006, IV, 458 n. 7.

52 On subscription as a form of patronage, see Korshin 1973–4; Amory 1995; Griffin 1996; Brewer 1997.

53 Johnson 2006, I, 399.

54 Robinson and Wallis 1975, 1–2; see also Wallis 1996; cf. Cannon and Robinson 1995.

55 Barnard 2000.

56 Johnson 2006, IV, 257.

57 Foxon 1991, 63, 101. See also Nichols, 1812–16, I, 77–8 n., 109–10 n. and VIII, 169; Hodgart 1978; Mack 1985, 417; and McLaverty 1993.

58 See Foxon 1991, 51–101.

59 On the complex publication history of Thomson's poem, see Thomson 1981, xxiv–lxxix. See also Foxon 1975a, T211–46.

subscription. In *Jubilate Agno* (comp. 1758–63), he remembered those who had supported him: 'I pray God bless all my Subscribers.'[60] Hugh Amory rightly cautions that a subscription list is often taken as a precise indication of a work's readership, when in fact, 'Nothing in the list proves that [subscribers] ever paid the second half of their subscription, much less that they ever read their copies if they did.' He also points out that 'Subscribers ... were [often] greatly outnumbered by subsequent purchasers, and their weight in any account of the work's reception and readership must be gauged accordingly.'[61]

Fiction

Most literary historians regard the eighteenth century as the era, if not when the modern novel was invented, then at least when it came of age.[62] Certainly, the reading public showed great appetite for extended prose fiction. *Robinson Crusoe* (1719) was published in six editions (not counting piracies and serialization) of 1,000 copies each in just four months.[63] The turning point in novel publishing, however, was Richardson's *Pamela* (1740; Part 2, 1741). By the end of December 1741, nearly fourteen months after it first appeared, *Pamela* had been published in six authorized editions (including one in French) comprising an estimated 20,000 copies.[64] In addition, there were London piracies, a Dublin reprint from the press of George Faulkner, and ongoing serial publication.[65] According to Keymer and Sabor, Richardson and his allies had variously marketed the novel as piety, pornography and pedagogy, and would soon package it as an elaborate octavo to adorn the polite library.[66] *Pamela* gave rise to a flood of responses to the novel – including Richardson's own sequel.[67] Illustrated editions with engravings by Hayman and Gravelot (1742) and Joseph Highmore (1744) further augmented sales.[68] In Philadelphia, Benjamin Franklin reprinted *Pamela* (2 vols., 1742–3), attempting to undercut British imports; his experiment failed, and it was more than thirty years before another unabridged novel was published in the American colonies.[69]

60 Smart 1980, 128 (frag. D, line 221).
61 Amory 1995, 102, 104.
62 Watt 1957; Richetti 1969; McKeon 1987; J.P. Hunter 1990.
63 Maslen 1969.
64 Keymer and Sabor 2005, 17; they call the French edition a 'masterstroke of market maximization' (37).
65 Keymer and Sabor 2005, 2, 39.
66 Keymer and Sabor 2005, 37, 38. McKillop 1936, 155 notes that sheets from this lavish octavo (the 1742 'sixth edition') 'were remaindered as late as 1772'.
67 Keymer and Sabor 2005, 2–3; see also Keymer and Sabor 2001.
68 On the illustrations for *Pamela* and for other novels of the period, see Clayton, chap. 10, above.
69 See J.N. Green 2000, 267–8; see also Giles 2001, 70–91; Raven 2002b, 70.

The most enduring rejoinder to *Pamela*, Henry Fielding's *Joseph Andrews* (1742), was remunerative far beyond its author's expectations: Millar bought the copy for £183 11*s*. when Fielding had imagined selling it for as little as £25. The novel proved profitable for its publisher as well: the first edition of 1,500 copies sold out in some four months, leading to a second edition of 2,000 copies. The appearance of the third edition nine months later, in March 1743, indicates that trade remained brisk. Although Millar's print run of 3,000 was not exhausted for another five years, the sale of 6,500 sets in less than seven years made *Joseph Andrews* a very sound investment.[70]

Readers increasingly continued to consume novels as luxury products and emblems of their status and leisure.[71] Like other books, fiction was expensive: novels in trade bindings[72] typically cost 3*s*. per volume; unbound fiction ordinarily sold for 2*s*. or 2*s*. 6*d*. per volume. Richardson – himself a printer, and, hence, able to control the physical form of his novels more than most authors – at least tried to make *Clarissa* (1747–8) affordable by asking for a smaller type to fit material that should have taken eight duodecimo volumes into seven.[73] Yet, although it sold well, this tragic and morally complex tale did not enjoy anything like the popular success of *Pamela*.[74] In Dublin, Faulkner's authorized *Clarissa* (1748) reached only a single edition, as did an unauthorized two-volume abridgement (1756) selling for 6*s*. 6*d*.

A very different and far more accessible novel, Tobias Smollett's *Roderick Random* (1748), was such a hit that between January 1748 and November 1749 Strahan printed 6,500 copies.[75] From a publishing perspective, the early history of *Roderick Random*'s market rival, *Tom Jones* (1749), might best be considered an exercise in favourable prolepsis. Millar paid Fielding £600 in advance for the copy; the contemporary observer Joseph Spence noted that the whole press run was sold 'before it was publisht' as 'the way here generally is to send in their number of Books to each of the Booksellers they deal with, four or five days before the Publication; that they may oblige people, who are eager for a new thing' – 'all the books were disposed of' before its publication

70 Fielding 1967, xxix–xxxiv; see also Battestin and Battestin 1989, 325–6. On the Fielding–Millar author-publisher relationship, see Dobson 1916.

71 Raven 1992; 2000a. In all genres, the book trade kept the price of new literature artificially high, a well-documented practice that has far-reaching implications for the nature and scale of its readership. See also Raven 2007, 301–3; cf. St Clair 2004, 186–209, for a discussion of prices in the early nineteenth century.

72 On the prevalence of trade bindings in the period, see Bennett 2004. Pickwoad 2005 expresses some reservations about Bennett's treatment of the available evidence.

73 Eaves and Kimpel 1971, 219–20.

74 Eaves and Kimpel 1971, 306, 317.

75 Knapp 1932, 284.

date.[76] The first two editions totaling 3,500 six-volume duodecimo sets (18*s.* bound, 16*s.* 'sew'd in Blue Paper and Boards') – 21,000 volumes in all – were followed by a more economical four-volume duodecimo reset in small pica (12*s.* bound, 10*s.* 6*d.* sewed) in 3,000 copies. Even a vigorous market could be glutted, however. The fourth edition of 3,500 – bringing the overall number of copies printed to 10,000 in just nine months – was not exhausted for a dozen years, and the fifth edition did not come on to the market until 1763.[77] In Ireland, John Smith's unauthorized 1749 Dublin reprint – in three economical volumes costing just 8*s.* 8*d.* – saw two editions in as many years.[78]

Given the triumph of *Tom Jones*, it is no wonder that Millar probably paid £800 for the copy in *Amelia* (1752 [1751], 4 duodecimo vols.; 12*s.* or 10*s.* 6*d.* sewed). Contrary to legend, however, Fielding's novel did not meet the high commercial expectations of Millar, who rashly ordered an initial print run of 5,000.[79] First sales were sufficiently promising for the publisher to commission a new edition of 3,000 copies within a month of publication, but this was quickly terminated and a new London edition did not appear until Millar printed Fielding's *Works* (1762).[80] Notably, two unauthorized Dublin reprints – both available for as little as 4*s.* 4*d.* – were published just nineteen days after *Amelia* went on sale in London.

The first four volumes of *Sir Charles Grandison* (3,000 copies duodecimo and 1,000 octavo) were published in November 1753, but in that same month – despite Richardson's elaborate security measures in London and foresighted business arrangements with Faulkner in Dublin[81] – a bootleg edition of the first six volumes appeared in Ireland's capital, forcing Richardson to publish volumes V and VI in December. By the time volume VII was ready in March 1754, the original 4,000 copies of volumes I–VI had been disposed of for some months. A third edition of 2,500 (7 vols., duodecimo) entered the market in March as well.[82] During the eighteenth century, there were two periodical serializations and four known unauthorized editions.[83]

76 Wright 1950, 232 n. 29, quoted in Battestin and Battestin 1989, 451–2. See also Fielding 1974a, xlvii–xlviii.

77 Fielding 1974a, xlvii–li.

78 In all genres, the high price of literature repeatedly attracted piracies, many of which may remain unknown to us because the cheap paper, smaller formats, abridged texts and casual presswork such productions routinely employed would potentially have contributed to their low survival rates; see Suarez, Introduction, above.

79 Fielding 1983, xlv–xlvi.

80 Fielding 1983, xlvi–l.

81 *Pamela II* had been 'pirated' in Dublin, much to Richardson's ire.

82 See McKillop 1936, 214–15, 215 n. 132.

83 Richardson 1972, xiii.

Evidence from the Strahan Ledgers shows that, once *Tristram Shandy* captured the popular imagination, its two-volume instalments had initial press runs of 4,000.[84] Knowing that the popularity of his novel would attract unauthorized imitations and, quite possibly, piracies, Sterne took the unusual (but not unprecedented) precaution of signing his name in every copy of volume v of *Tristram Shandy* before it and its companion volume vi appeared in December 1761 (dated 1762).[85] Advertisements in the *London Chronicle* alerted would-be purchasers to look for the signature, a feature that Sterne's audience would come to regard as an emblem of the author's celebrity and éclat.[86] Sterne was by no means being overly cautious: when Smollett's *Adventures of Ferdinand Count Fathom* (1753) was pirated almost immediately after its initial publication, the pirates had very little time to determine whether the novel would be a popular success (it was not); rather, they were gambling on the commercial strength of *Roderick Random* (1748) and *Peregrine Pickle* (1751).

Despite these and other remarkable successes, most novels were published anonymously, most never reached a second edition, the average edition size was 500 or fewer, and most authors made little or even nothing from their labours.[87] Although counting titles is fraught with methodological and practical difficulties, there were approximately 45 works of fiction published in the first decade of the century, 135 titles in the second, a downturn of 95 in the third, and a healthy 210 in the 1740s. This more than doubling is partially an artefact of the low output in the 1730s, and partially a sign of the genuine reinvigoration of the fiction market in the 1740s, propelled in the first instance by the *Pamela* phenomenon.[88] Fiction publishing then rises significantly, with 238 recorded titles in the 1750s and 292 in the 1760s; this surge may be accounted for, in part, by a significant rise in reprinting.[89] Some 315 novels were first published in the 1770s, 405 in the 1780s and 701 in the 1790s.[90] Another 10 per cent of the known output of fiction has probably vanished without a trace. Of the 2,500 or so fiction titles published during the century, fewer than twenty-five are read for pleasure by non-specialists today.

84 Monkman 1970.
85 For the printing of a spurious continuation, see Maslen and Lancaster 1991, no. 4273.
86 Cash 1986, 113.
87 Garside, Raven and Schöwerling 2000, i, 35, *et infra*; see also Raven 1987.
88 See Suarez, chap. 1 above; Keymer and Sabor 2005, 2001.
89 Raven 1987, 9, 10.
90 Garside, Raven and Schöwerling 2000, i, 26, table 1.

If we measure the popularity of novelists 1750–69 by numbers of editions published – irrespective of the size of print runs[91] – then there are few surprises at the top of the list: Sterne (35), Henry Fielding (33), Eliza Haywood (31), Smollett (28), Defoe (28) and Richardson (23) occupy the first six places with more than 20 editions each. There are some unexpected names, however, among those having between 15 and 19 editions in this period: Madame Riccoboni (17), Edward Kimber (17), Sarah Fielding (16), Charles Johnston (16), John Langhorne (15), Jean François Marmontel (15) and Voltaire (15) – an indication of both the popularity of translations and the fugitive nature of literary reputation. Other highly popular fiction authors included Cervantes (13) and Rousseau (11), Charlotte Lennox (14) and Frances Brooke (11), John Cleland (14) and Goldsmith (14), whose *Vicar of Wakefield* was published in 1766.[92] If we consider the century as a whole, then the two most popular novelists (by numbers of editions printed) are Defoe and, remarkably, Goldsmith.[93]

The presence of Haywood, Riccoboni, Sarah Fielding, Lennox and Brooke – Burney, Radcliffe, Robinson and Yearsley would come later – testifies that the novel was a highly congenial genre for female authors. Of new novels that can be positively identified as having been written by women, there were 33 in the 1750s, 43 in the 1760s, 45 in the 1770s, 118 in the 1780s and 260 in the 1790s.[94] Yet, in her study of provincial readers in eighteenth-century England, Jan Fergus has shown that women did not comprise the largest reading audience for fiction.[95] Accordingly, she urges us to 'see [the] reading of fiction in the last half of the eighteenth century as more complicated, more fluid, [and] less gender-bound' than is usually assumed.[96]

The connections among female writers, female readers and the proprietors of circulating libraries who were both promoting and publishing novels have been well established – especially during the years 1770–4 and, on a far larger scale, 1785–9 – but we should not overestimate the importance of fiction as a staple of such libraries before the final three decades of the century.[97] The catalogue (*c.*1766) of the London circulating library owned by the bookseller Thomas Lowndes lists 6,290 works, of which 1,132 (or 18 per cent) are plays;

91 Although the size of many print runs is unknown, 500–750 copies should be considered as typical: see Hernlund 1967, 104; Garside, Raven and Schöwerling 2000, II, 39; cf. Chard 1977, 144; Altick 1998 (1957), 18–19; and Besterman 1938, xxxi.

92 Data from Raven 1987, 14.

93 Raven 1987, 16.

94 Data from Raven 1987, 19 and Garside, Raven and Schöwerling 2000, I, 46–7, table 6.

95 Fergus 2006a, 41–74.

96 Fergus 2006a, 8–9.

97 Jacobs 2003, 4–14. Cf. Hamlyn 1947; Kaufman 1967; Varma 1972; Fergus 1984.

only about 10 per cent of the available titles are fiction. Yet, Jacobs notes that 'both in size and percentage of fiction, Lowndes's catalog is typical of the surviving catalogs of [the London proprietors] Samuel Fancourt (1748), William Bathoe (1757), and John and Francis Noble (1767)'.[98]

Among the most important fiction publishers in the 1750s were Millar, the Dodsleys, the Nobles, Lane and Hogg, and Robert Baldwin. Sterne's defection from James Dodsley to Becket and De Hondt was partially a cause and partially a symptom of that firm's rise to prominence as fiction publishers in the 1760s. In the 1770s John Bew, Thomas Cadell (Millar's former apprentice), John Bell and Thomas Lowndes were all conducting a healthy business in fiction. William Lane, who would come to be the doyen of novel publishing and purveying, entered the market in 1775. Meanwhile, in the 1750s–1770s, several Dublin publishers – the Hoeys (James and Peter), George Faulkner, Robert Main, Richard Moncrieff, Dillon Chamberlaine, Caleb Jenkin, Samuel Price and the Sleaters (William I and II) – were conducting a brisk trade in reprints of London novels.[99]

Another form of reprinting, serial publication – still insufficiently taken into account by many literary historians of the eighteenth century – was an important means of dissemination.[100] Defoe's *Robinson Crusoe*, first published in April 1719, was not only conventionally pirated soon thereafter, but also reprinted (both Part 1 and Part 2) serially in the *Original London Post* between October 1719 and October 1720.[101] *Captain Singleton*, published in June 1720, was serialized in a provincial newspaper, the *Post-Master*, in Exeter, between November 1720 and November 1721.[102] *Moll Flanders* (1722) too was serialized both in the *London Post* and in the *Kentish Post*, published in Canterbury.[103] For popular works, such piecemeal piracies were common. *Pamela* too was quickly pirated, and then serialized without sanction in *Robinson Crusoe's London Daily Evening Post*.[104] Yet, it was not until Tobias Smollett's *Sir Lancelot Greaves* – published serially (in twenty-five parts) in the *British Magazine* between January 1760 and December 1761 – that a major writer produced a work of fiction intended for initial publication in serial form; many others would follow.[105]

98 Jacobs 2003, 2.

99 Raven 1987, 34–7; Garside, Raven and Schöwerling 2000, I, 73, table 12; Plomer, Bushnell and Dix 1932; Maxted 1977; Pollard 2000.

100 See Harris, chap. 20 above; Wiles 1957, 1965; Mayo 1962.

101 Hutchins 1925, 157–8; cf. Wiles 1957, 27.

102 Furbank and Owens 1998, 196.

103 Shaw 2007.

104 Keymer and Sabor 2005, 39.

105 See Mayo 1962; see also Smollett 2002. The weekly sixpenny *Novelist's Magazine* (1779–89) serially reprinted more than sixty novels: see Mayo 1962, 363–7; Bentley 1977, 597–602.

Conclusion

The three score and ten years from the lapse of the Printing Acts to the Lords' decision in *Donaldson* v. *Becket* (1695–1774) witnessed many developments that materially affected the production, distribution and reception of English literature in Britain.[106] Among the more salient changes were the advent of new ideas about authorship, patronage and the market;[107] the efflorescence of the newspaper and periodical press;[108] the genesis and burgeoning of the literary reviews;[109] the rise of children's literature;[110] the growth of the reprint trade;[111] the arrival and proliferation of commercial circulating and subscription libraries;[112] the substantial enlargement of the provincial book trade;[113] and the emergence of an expanded reading public.[114] Concomitant with these and other events, the literary market was – for authors, booksellers and publishers alike – highly competitive. To a hitherto unprecedented extent, these are years that witnessed the thoroughgoing commercialization of literature in Britain.

106 On the impact of the Lords' decision, see St Clair 2004. Sher 2006, Fergus 2006a and Bonnell 2004–5 (2008) all contest St Clair's view, marshalling new information in support of their arguments. On the publishing of British literary works in the years after 1774, see Sutherland, chap. 35, below.
107 See Griffin, chap. 5, above.
108 See Harris, chap. 20, Ferdinand, chap. 21, and Tierney, chap. 24, all above.
109 See Forster, chap. 33, above.
110 See Immell, chap. 40, below.
111 See Bonnell, chap. 37, below.
112 See Sutherland, chap. 35, below.
113 See Bell and Hinks, chap. 15, and Ferdinand, chap. 21, both above.
114 See Suarez, Introduction, above.

35

British literature, 1774–1830

KATHRYN SUTHERLAND

Literary history is inseparable from the formation of nations and nationalities. It contributes powerfully to the recognition and celebration of collective practices distinguishing 'us' from 'them'. We write our history – the history of our particular moment in cultural and personal time – across the body of the works we read. The period that saw Britain's decisive stand in Europe against Revolutionary and Napoleonic France also saw the first systematic attempt to calibrate a British national character according to literature's agency. Reading became at this time a significant social and individual indicator and people participated in public culture by virtue of what and how they read. At the same time, the foundations were laid for the professionalization of the activities of the writer and the critic. In thinking about how and why certain works of literature gain status as cultural capital (as 'Literature'), war as the real test of value has always been important, and Britain was at war for twenty-eight of these fifty-six years.

In the years 1774–1830 literature became increasingly subject to modes of marketing and consumption that helped consolidate its functions, whether for entertainment or instruction, within a domestic space. One material sign of this was the rise in production of smaller format books – more octavos and duodecimos, and fewer quartos – signalling portability and accessibility. Domestication of print was the norm despite (and arguably because of) the threats posed by a renewed radical faith in the press and its power to rally public protest. Prosecutions under libel or blasphemy laws, the imposition of gagging orders, and taxes on paper and print were employed from time to time during the pamphlet wars of the revolutionary 1790s and again in the late 1810s and culminated in the arrests of prominent radical journal editors, booksellers and printers. Such restrictions were aimed as much at defining the acceptable sphere of mass reading and its agency in forming the social character as at precise individual targets. Repressive political measures paid tribute to the strength of the perceived link between reading and social action and the consequent need to establish readerships along exclusive lines.

Only a few decades earlier, the cultural revolution signalled by the House of Lords' 1774 decision in *Donaldson* v. *Becket* was apparently a decision against exclusive privilege. By breaking the English booksellers' right of perpetual copyright in texts, the decision altered the publishing industry for ever, dissolving old-established internal alliances, opening the way for brisker competition between London firms and from upcoming regional enterprises (William Creech and later Archibald Constable in Edinburgh, for example), and creating a climate in which profits must be turned quickly. In the short term, the price of books fell and, in the longer term, the boost given to a competitive reprint trade in out-of-copyright works inaugurated a canon of English 'classics' which accrued mounting national and literary significance throughout the period. What began as a trade dispute served to define a concept of literature as a set of significant works from the past which would gain cultural value (and extend booksellers' profits) by their freer circulation. Reprint series consolidated readerly interest in distinct literary forms and encouraged in their textual associations a concentration on their native generic evolution – the British drama, the English poets, the British novelists – demonstrating the capacity of literature at this time to absorb, enact and even anticipate nationalist agendas at work in society at large. The reader was confronted in these collections not just with drama, poetry or novels, but with an implied genealogy and classifying features of the forms. Leading the way were the major series from the resourceful John Bell, among them *The Poets of Great Britain complete from Chaucer to Churchill* (1777–83), a joint venture with the Martins at the Apollo Press in Edinburgh, in 109 volumes, at 1*s.* 6*d.* a volume, and later reissued on coarse paper at 6*d.* a volume. In the 1780s, John Harrison had enormous success with his *Novelists' Magazine*, issued in octavo with double columns, in 6*d.* weekly numbers, and in the 1790s John Cooke's editions of British poets, prose writers and dramatists appeared, also in 6*d.* weekly numbers. Books on the instalment plan, paperbound abridgements, and publications like Harrison's *British Classicks* (1785–7), reprinting extracts from the *Spectator*, *Tatler*, *Guardian*, *Connoisseur* and other quality eighteenth-century periodicals credited with establishing by mid-century a digest of polite taste, for the first time brought something like a standard English literature within the purchasing power of the many.

A stimulus to the production of Shakespeare editions had been given by the Jubilee celebrations of 1769, and the steady reprinting of the complete works, in cheap and more expensive form, over the next decades witnesses to their popularity among various kinds of readers. There were at least ten distinct reprintings in the 1770s; six in the 1780s; as many as twenty-three in the 1790s;

thirty between 1800 and 1809; and in 1811 alone, nine in London. The demand for cheap texts was met by Charles Jennens's issues of individual plays between 1770 and 1774, and by John Bell's performance-based texts of 1773–4, *Shakespeare's Plays, as they are now performed at the Theatres Royal in London* (9 vols.). Bell followed these up with his *British Theatre* (21 vols., 1776–81) in 6*d.* weekly parts; and beginning in 1791, he reissued both series at 1*s.* 6*d.* a volume, or 6*d.* on coarse paper. If Edmond Malone's ten-volume edition of the plays and poems (1790) appealed to a growing scholarly market for a historical and textually 'authentic' Shakespeare, there was experimentation with other forms of presentation, like Boydell's Shakespeare Gallery. John Boydell, printseller and entrepreneur, had opened his Gallery at 59 Pall Mall to great fanfare in May 1789 and produced an accompanying catalogue of engravings. The year 1807 alone saw several distinct attempts to package Shakespeare for a variety of markets: the six-volume, illustrated Stockdale edition, with copperplates by J. Heath after designs by the fashionable artists Thomas Stothard and Henry Fuseli; Francis Douce's *Illustrations of Shakespeare*, introducing him as a dramatist in touch with the culture of the people; Charles and Mary Lamb's children's adaptation, *Tales from Shakespeare*; and Henrietta Bowdler's four volumes of expurgated *Family Shakespeare*.

That was the situation with reprint literature, or more specifically with works whose copyright (a maximum of twenty-eight years from first publication) had expired. Other institutional practices proposed further ways to consolidate, diversify and cheapen new literature. The proliferation of varied methods of access, through circulating libraries, subscription libraries and reading clubs, and in the pages of magazines as well as in books, contributed to blur distinctions between the public-political and private-unpoliticized space of reading, between kinds of literature, and specifically between 'high' and 'low' genres and the tastes and capacities of socio-economically diverse audiences. Like the periodical press, which exploded into activity in the early nineteenth century, the circulating library branded readers as group-identified, sociable consumers and made literature accessible when the cost of new works remained prohibitively high and purchasing power beyond all but the very wealthy.

At the same time, the space which now appeared to open for the delineation of a common literature became in many ways more uncertain and more contested, reflecting the variety, complexity and sheer imprecision in the concept as formulated by the different interest groups of publishers, writers, readers and critics. Wordsworth's famous questions, 'What is a Poet? To whom does he address himself?', and Hazlitt's apparent rejoinder, 'What is the People?', confront from their different perspectives the dangerous fluidity of definition which is one consequence of a proliferation of print.[1] Efforts to align literature with the practices from which it was becoming increasingly distinct (specifically the authority of speech and intimate conversation among the like-minded) witness to the high Romantic anxiety about print's capacity to communicate in the right way and inscribe a paradoxical bibliographic unease into many publications. The implied situatedness of much Romantic literature – as table talk, autobiography and anecdote – attempts to reinstate within the passive encounter with the printed text the aura of exchange as the living dialectic of speech and the power of personality to stimulate response. Though chiefly a trade war, the copyright dispute also served to bring into focus a distinction that sharpened at this time between literature as creation and as consumption. For Wordsworth, who throughout his long career regularly lobbied Parliament in support of perpetual authorial copyright, originality and genius define authorship. It follows that they impress the work indelibly and constitute an inalienable right in it. Against this stands the idea of literature founded in reading rather than creation, promoted by a widely circulating canon of out-of-copyright works and a cheap reprint trade. If the former case rests on the uniqueness of the linguistic and experiential defamiliarization that attends the literary encounter, the latter emphasizes familiarity, public ownership and the reader's choice. The two definitions, as writing and as reading, come into headlong collision in the period, where for Wordsworth and other Romantic writers reading is a function of books and writing of the freedom before books – of drafts and revisions, of private manuscript circulation and a more dynamic exchange. Most famously, Wordsworth and Coleridge, both notorious in their deferring of print publication, consider the problem of how to discover the true reader among an amorphous mass readership – how to circumvent the levelling properties of print and address the 'clerisy' of readers through the 'living' text. For William Godwin the question of print's capacity to reproduce authentic relations is equally applicable to authorship:

> A book is an abstraction. It is but imperfectly that we feel, that a real man addresses us in it, and that what he delivers is the entire and deep-wrought sentiment of a being of flesh and blood like ourselves, a being who claims our attention, and is entitled to our deference. The living human voice, with countenance and manner corresponding, constrains us to weight what is said, shoots through us like a stroke of electricity, will not away from our memory, and haunts our very dreams.[2]

1 Wordsworth (1802) in Wordsworth 1963, 255; Hazlitt, 'What is the people?' (1817) in Hazlitt 1930–4, VII, 259.

2 Godwin 1831, 251–2.

The distinction between writing and reading, with its attendant implications of authentic and inauthentic communication, can also surface as one of genre, with poetry occupying the high ground and the novel relegated to a lesser space shaped by the low expectations of its mass readership and the commodifying strictures of the print industry. Dressed as an attack against mere bookmaking, it is heard in Coleridge's famous dismissal of the contents of circulating libraries – 'manufactured at the printing office, which *pro tempore* fixes, reflects and transmits the moving phantasms of one man's delirium, so as to people the barrenness of an hundred other brains'.[3] Earlier, in his *Morality of fiction* (1805), Hugh Murray argued for a similar correlation between printing, the downward spread of literacy and the proliferation of lowbrow fiction: 'The origin of this mode of writing is easily accounted for. The invention of printing, and consequent diffusion of books, has given birth to a multitude of readers, who seek only amusement, and wish to find it without trouble or thought.'[4] In his pamphlet *The use of circulating libraries considered; with instructions for opening and conducting a library, either upon a large or small plan* (1797), Thomas Wilson, bookseller and stationer of Bromley, Kent, provides advice on account-keeping, terms of subscription, uniform binding of books, and the kinds of businesses most suited to combine with a lending library. He also makes recommendations for proportionate purchasing of stock across the various literary categories. Imprecise though such divisions were, they point to the ascendancy of the novel within popular culture at the end of the eighteenth century. A modest library in a small provincial town should consist of 'fifteen hundred volumes, which should be well chosen from different subjects, in the following proportion: 60 volumes of History; 60 – of Divinity; 30 – of Lives; 20 – of Voyages; 20 – of Travels; 30 – of Poetry; 20 – of Plays; 1050 – of Novels; 130 – of Romances; 10 – of Anecdotes; 40 – of Tales; 30 – of Arts and Sciences.' And mindful of the contemporary political moment, he urges the appropriateness of a nationalist agenda for the library: 'There can be no reason to search foreign countries for authors to instruct, inform, or amuse: our own has produced the greatest men in the study of letters . . . and even the common people are better informed, than in most other nations.'[5] Almost twenty years later, A. K. Newman's *Catalogue* (1814, with supplements to 1819) of the Minerva Library in Leadenhall Street, London, lists about 40 per cent of its holdings under the unwieldy heading 'Novels, Romances, Imaginary Histories, Lives, and Adventures'. Catalogues from comparable commercial

3 Coleridge 1817, I, 49–50.
4 Murray 1805, 40.
5 Wilson 1797, 26–7, 50–1.

circulating libraries in other towns suggest similar high proportions (usually between 40 and 70 per cent) of fiction in their stock.[6]

The debate over the status of the novel in the period has only recently moved beyond the anecdotal and the single-author study, methods which perpetuated the familiar high Romantic dismissal of the form and of hack women writers as among its chief exponents. Thanks to new research, some revisions to these older views are now matters of fact. There was a statistical rise in the number of new novels from the 1780s which ensured that, despite occasional troughs in output (most interestingly in the middle years of the 1810s, when Jane Austen and Walter Scott began publishing), by the end of the 1820s it was the dominant literary form; and it remained so for the rest of the nineteenth century.[7] Two of the main factors in this expansion were an influx of women readers and the aggressive marketing of fiction by entrepreneurs like William Lane, who specialized in Gothic romances and sentimental novels. There is also evidence throughout the period for a talking up of a form which could be as mobile in its categorization as the fortunes of the heroes and heroines charted in its pages. Godwin again, in his essay 'Of history and romance' (1798), appears to argue that works of fiction alone release for the examination and profit of writer and reader the complexities of social and psychological behaviour as exhibited by the individual. Coming hard on the Treason Trials and attempts at censorship of the mid-1790s, his faith in the recording powers of fiction over history carries political conviction. It follows that if the novel at this time acquired new significance as the record of 'the very web and texture of society, as it really exists',[8] so too did the critical debate over its significance. The period saw not just a statistical rise in the output of novels, but also serious attempts to account for its contemporary value and to place the form in historical context, most notably in John Dunlop's *The history of fiction* (1814).

Lane's success was based on three interrelated enterprises which together allowed him to control the market for three decades: the Minerva Library, the Minerva Press and his activities as a commissioning publisher. From 1800 to 1829, Minerva held a dominant market share (estimated at 23 per cent) in new titles, far outstripping other primary fiction publishers: the consistently prosperous middle-market firm of Longmans, which had approximately 8.7 per cent of titles over the three decades; J.F. Hughes, the publisher of the best-selling Gothicist M.G. ('Monk') Lewis, who had brief spectacular success in the 1800s; and Henry Colburn and Co., the steadily rising star, responsible for as

6 Newman 1814–19; Garside, Raven and Schöwerling 2000, II, 18–19.

7 Garside, Raven and Schöwerling 2000, I, 26–8; II, 38–40.

8 'Standard novels and romances', *Edinburgh Review* (1815) in Hazlitt 1930–4, XVI, 5.

much as 12.6 per cent of new fiction imprints by the 1820s.[9] Lane was an acute businessman, switching early in life (in about 1770) from poultry to books; and in his case at least the charge of commodification is not unjust. Controlling both production and distribution from his base in London's Leadenhall Street, he made a huge fortune. He had grasped that in an undercapitalized industry fiction was a lucrative product for which the fashion-conscious and the pleasure-seeking would pay highly; but that being an essentially ephemeral commodity, profit lay in circulation figures rather than in sales alone. He offered for sale from his 'General Warehouse and Universal Repository of Literature' complete libraries, ranging from a hundred to ten thousand volumes, to jewellers, perfumers, tobacconists, purveyors of patent medicines and haberdashers eager to extend their leisure-directed trades into book-lending; and he provided advice on how to set up the business. In his own flagship operation, the Minerva Library, the annual subscription fee was high, between one and three guineas in 1798, depending on the type of subscription, and in 1814 one and a half to five guineas; by then the Library was open from nine in the morning to nine at night, Sundays included.[10] If such charges placed major circulating libraries beyond the reach of those below the middle classes, it was thanks to Lane's entrepreneurial drive that commercial libraries, in existence in some urban centres since the early eighteenth century, penetrated to lesser provincial towns. By 1801 there were thought to be a thousand circulating libraries in England.[11]

Where Lane's symbiotic formula succeeded, its long-term effect on the market for and reputation of fiction is more debatable. The wholesale trade in complete fiction libraries highlights the particular relationship to the material form of its manufacture that dogged the critical fortunes of the novel throughout the nineteenth century. After Lane, Charles Edward Mudie, who dominated the circulating library trade through the Victorian period, continued to influence by sheer economic clout the way the novel developed. The Minerva novel quickly assumed a corporate style with recognizable bibliographic codes or paratextual features which served both as self-advertisement and to anticipate how it would be read – to pre-engage the reader sensationally. Branding by layout and typographic design was not new – Bell and others engaged in the classic reprint trade were doing much the same to make recognizable (and in Bell's case, elegant) commodities. But in Lane's productions, such devices as well-rehearsed formulaic titles and lurid frontispiece

9 Garside, Raven and Schöwerling 2000, II, 83–4.
10 Newman 1814–19, 3–4.
11 *Monthly Magazine*, 11 (1801), 238.

engravings displaying frenzied villains and swooning, scantily clad heroines – at a time when illustration was still a rarity in fiction – slipped over into self-parody even as they fuelled demand. The typographic inaccuracies that reviewers remarked in the novel generally at this time were singled out for comment in notices of Lane's publications and contributed to their low esteem. His marketing strategies openly encouraged the identification of the formula-novel with women as authors and readers (a prospectus of 1798 lists ten 'particular and favourite Authors', all women) – the 'prolific ladies of the Minerva Press', as the *Critical Review* dubbed them in April 1808 – and with a consumer-oriented practice. His methods included elaborate newspaper promotions of forthcoming titles, fly-leaf advertisements of future novels in published books, and even the puffing of the Minerva Press and its works in the text proper, earning the charge of cynical trading and contributing to the culturally stagnant state in which the novel appeared to many contemporary commentators.[12]

But in the same years various projects, the joint conceptions of publishers, editors and authors, attempted to reverse critical perceptions and provide a respectable genealogy and textual authority for the form. Anna Laetitia Barbauld's *British novelists* (1810) was issued in fifty volumes by an association of booksellers, who banded together to spread the costs and the risk. The collection went farther than any other in the period in its comprehensive attention to the generic integrity of modern fiction, in its presentation of the novel in nationalist, wartime terms, cleansed of the European excesses levelled against Gothic, and in its positive critical observations on women as writers and consumers. The seriousness of the project was signalled by the thirty-seven booksellers (thirty-five from London, one from Edinburgh and one from York) who underwrote its initial print run of 1,000 copies and whose names alone form a conspectus of the trade in the early nineteenth century. This is no upstart enterprise: many of the names brought considerable cultural weight, like the old-established firms of Rivington and Strahan, and respected newer houses like Longman, Cadell and Creech (in Edinburgh), while others included the influential liberal publisher Joseph Johnson and successful commercial entrepreneurs like George Robinson and James Lackington. Barbauld, too, was by 1810 a highly regarded editor and cultural commentator, with editions to her credit of the poetry of Collins (1794) and Akenside (1797) as well as Richardson's *Correspondence* (1804) and *Selections from the Spectator, Tatler, Guardian, and Freeholder* (1805). As a sign of her stature and the confidence

12 Blakey 1939, 67, 91–3, 96–105.

felt in this new enterprise she was paid the considerable sum of £300 for her editorship of *The British novelists*. The chosen works of each novelist are prefaced by a biographical and critical introduction and the whole collection is fronted by an essay 'On the origin and progress of novel-writing'.

Barbauld's essay followed a characteristic Enlightenment trajectory, previously employed by Thomas Warton, James Beattie, Richard Hurd and Clara Reeve in their eighteenth-century literary histories of vernacular poetry and romance, where 'progress' is discernible as a shedding of non-native (typically oriental and European) superstition and improbability, in a steady march towards a superior native manufacture. According to Barbauld, the novel emerges from eastern origins, through medieval European romance, to its highest evolution as a British work of moral instruction, in which 'the interest, even of the generality of readers, is most strongly excited when some serious end is kept in view'.[13] Even her unapologetic insistence on the epithets 'novel' and 'novelist' constituted a bold defence at a time when respected writers like Fanny Burney and Maria Edgeworth approached the term nervously. 'The following work is offered to the Public as a Moral Tale – the author not wishing to acknowledge a Novel,' wrote Edgeworth in her 'Author's Advertisement' to *Belinda* (1801), a title Barbauld chose to include in her collection. On the contrary, in establishing the novel as a substantial ethical vehicle, the modern female novelist, she maintains, has been unsurpassed. Of the twenty-one British novelists represented in her collection, eight are women. Importantly, too, several (Burney, Edgeworth, Inchbald, Radcliffe) were still alive in 1810. If the convention to date in reprint collections had been to exclude contemporary writers, Barbauld and her bookseller collaborators actively promoted the concept of a living tradition for a form whose moral and literary significance they shrewdly conflated with its popularity.

Comparison might be drawn here with attempts to engage critically the substantial readership for printed plays. Elizabeth Inchbald's biographical and critical prefaces to her *British theatre* (25 vols., 1808), for example, argue the vitality of the relationship between printed text and performance, against a sense that modern theatre was in a state of decline if not degeneracy. Aesthetically and morally compromised for some by an emphasis on spectacle, the drama appeared, like the novel, to require special pleading to compensate for its sensational and popular appeal as a genre. Joanna Baillie's innovative *Series of plays, in which it is attempted to delineate the stronger passions of the mind* (1798, 1812), with important theoretical prefaces, take a different

13 Barbauld 1820, I, 57.

approach: emphasizing lyric intensity and complex psychological development, almost independent of the causality of plot, they demand to be discovered reflectively, through reading. It was in these years, too, that Shakespeare came to be represented as a dramatic *poet*, more profitably encountered on the page, as did other Jacobean playwrights – Ford, Webster, Massinger – in, for example, Charles Lamb's *Specimens of English dramatic poets, who lived about the time of Shakespeare* (1808).

Barbauld's *British novelists* was reissued in 1820, at which time, and spurred by her example, Ballantyne's *Novelist's library* (1821–4) combatively weighed in with its collection. Edinburgh-based and with prefaces by Walter Scott, the most famous novelist of the day, Ballantyne's enterprise diverted critical attention back towards an older male tradition, more in tune with Scott's own style. The shift signalled the success of a new northern challenge in the contemporary fiction market.[14] When Scott published his first novel, *Waverley*, in 1814 the form was dominated by women authors and London publishers, but only ten years later these trends were significantly modified. Stimulated by the energetic partnership of Archibald Constable and Scott, Edinburgh became in the 1820s an alternative centre of production associated with a marked masculinization of the genre. Constable published in the 1820s only two novels by women, both of these directed to him by Scott. The rival Edinburgh house of William Blackwood also had a strong male contingent – John Galt, J.G. Lockhart and John Wilson – and of its thirty-five original imprints in the 1820s, only five were by women.[15]

The Waverley novels (1814–32), Scott's monumental one-man fiction enterprise, took the novel to new heights of public seriousness, simultaneously inscribing in their historical narratives a middle-class agenda of reconciliation for British society and proposing, on more respectable terms than Lane's industrial model had done, the connection between literary and market value. Scott had turned to fiction after a hugely successful career as a poet, when for the space of about a decade (1805–15) he helped to fuel and in turn profited from an unprecedented boom in sales of verse. The boom was linked to manufacturing constraints on more diffuse literary forms (during war, paper, always the most expensive item in book production, is scarce) as well as to the greater respect enjoyed by a genre not yet tainted with associations of trade and an undiscriminating democracy of readers.[16] It is no coincidence that Scott, the aspiring aristocrat, and Byron, the born aristocrat, established in these years the

14 See Beavan and McDougall, chap. 16 above.
15 Garside, Raven and Schöwerling 2000, II, 88–90.
16 Erickson 1996, 19–48.

definition of poetry as a judicious blend of (financially) expensive and (socially) exclusive adventure. If there was a boom, it was, paradoxically, conditional upon exclusivity, linked to the exceptional poet who, like Byron and Scott, could command outrageous prices, well beyond general market values. Their medievalized and orientalized tales, in some respects verse Gothic, and produced on the same commercial scale, yet managed to align themselves bibliographically with the prestige and luxurious inutility of the antiquarian text at a time when the trade in early printed books was burgeoning.[17]

Scott's first long poem, a modern medieval romance, *The lay of the last minstrel* (1805), was issued as a large-format luxury quarto, priced at a guinea (21*s*.) a copy, when London skilled artisans, the highest paid workmen in the country, were earning between 20*s*. and (very exceptionally) 40*s*. for an average 72-hour week, and country workers 9*s*. or less. A tale about the recovery of a long-buried magic book, the *Lay* plays self-consciously with its internalized model in its address to an aristocratic patron and its simulation of the sumptuous appearance and format of an incunable. If Scott was the star of Constable's Edinburgh publishing house, Byron held the same high place with John Murray in his London firm in fashionable Albemarle Street. Between them Byron and Scott forced up the market value for new poetry – Scott's £4,000 for *The lady of the lake* (1810), selling more than 20,000 copies in the first year, is matched by 4,500 copies of Cantos I and II of *Childe Harold* (1812) within six months, a reputed 10,000 copies of *The corsair* (1814) on the day of publication alone, and Murray's offer of 1,000 guineas for *The siege of Corinth* (1816). It was a market in which Wordsworth's provincial moral poetry, issued without panache but with plenty of admonishment on the dangers of 'wrong' reading, could not compete – the 500 copies printed of *The excursion* (1814) were not sold out for six years, with a second edition in 1820, again 500 copies, lasting another seven.

When Scott turned to the novel in 1814, various magazines, reviews and journals were beginning to diversify and cheapen print for a growing readership, while the end of the war with France would soon cheapen paper itself. If between them Scott and Constable made poetry commercially successful before 1820, together they exploited the market for novels after 1820, as Scott acknowledged in this letter of 1822: 'They talk of a farmer making two blades of grass grow where one grew before but you my good friend have made a dozen of volumes where probably not one would have existed.'[18] Where

17 Dibdin 1811; Connell 2000.
18 Scott 1932–7, VII, 104.

Scott's medievalized poems make imaginative and paratextual play with many of the features of rare old books, his novels drive an industrializing model of manufacture deep into their structures (all share a narrative of the birth of commercial society from the warring factions of the past), collapsing together those issues of creation and production (of writing and reading) which Wordsworth found so incompatibly associated in true authorship. In elaborate pseudonymous prologues Scott engages metaphorically with the pressures of literature's commodification in an age of mass reading. In the preface to the late novel *The betrothed* (1825), for example, characters from the extended Waverley enterprise hold a meeting to discuss a proposal for the formation of a joint-stock company to turn out future fiction by machinery; overtaken by the sheer scale and mechanics of his bookmaking venture the author, as creative instigator, now appears redundant. Scott's joke at his own expense was not far from the truth: by 1825 he had made the novel the most potent literary form. Over the years, he had formed printing and publishing partnerships, with boyhood Edinburgh friends James and John Ballantyne, profiting from the manufacture of his novels several times over. By way of self-explanation or simply to keep the motor running, he developed a fictional formula which presented writing as a series of collaborations and business transactions between pseudonymous storytellers, savvy editors and survivors from a pre-print tradition of folklore and oral poetry; and at the height of his popularity, in 1816–19, he issued rival novels, under different pseudonyms and from different houses, and to stimulate curiosity reviewed his own work. It is not unreasonable to suggest that during this period the space opened up for literature as a set of cultural and critical practices lay between the extreme models provided by Lane and Wordsworth, and that by 1833 Scott had done more than any other single figure to weld their differences into a synthesis which would place literature and literary criticism, the property and identifying mark of a professional and sensitized middle class, centre-stage for the rest of the nineteenth century.[19]

Scott's runaway success was checked by the economic difficulties of the book trade in 1825–6, precipitated by the crash of Constable's London associates, Hurst, Robinson and Co. Constable and James Ballantyne both incurred massive financial losses in which Scott was also implicated; they all had over-extended their credit on the strength of unrealistic or distorted sales figures and the promise of future successes. Back in 1808, with Scott's verse romance *Marmion*, Constable had pioneered the advance system of authorial payment,

19 K. Sutherland 1987.

and thereafter he and Scott both built on the advance to capitalize their various ambitious ventures. While the reverberations of the crash through the wider publishing world have been exaggerated, Constable and Ballantyne went under and Scott, Constable's principal author, who had signed a complex series of accommodation bills, was left liable for a huge £120,000. Scott refused bankruptcy, in what was portrayed by his son-in-law and early biographer, John Gibson Lockhart, as a heroic gesture of personal responsibility; but in fact the alternative route – repaying his creditors under the terms of a trust deed – left him in relative comfort. Constable, on the other hand, was stripped of all his assets and died in misery in 1827. Scott and his creditors banked correctly on his continued huge earning potential; he died in 1832, exhausted by a punishing writing regime.[20]

Scott altered forever the landscape of literary publishing. *Kenilworth* in 1821 is credited with setting the mould for a standard nineteenth-century novel, in terms of format (the three-decker) and cost (sold at 31*s.* 6*d.*, or 10*s.* 6*d.* per volume). Within a few years, a third of new novels in three volumes commanded the same high price – the effect of Scott's example, but also of the aggressive marketing of the publisher Henry Colburn who, seizing this as well as every other opportunity, successfully standardized the primary form of fiction as three volumes, post-octavo, 31*s.* 6*d.* Subsequently Scott inaugurated between 1829 and 1833 an ambitious innovative reprint programme combining narrow profit margins with huge sales. Issued by Robert Cadell in forty-eight volumes over as many months, sales of the collected edition of the Waverley novels were estimated at a staggering 35,000 copies a month as early as the end of 1829. Extensively annotated in a uniform format, the edition for the first time raised to mass institutional status a living author and signalled a new departure for the modern novel; but at a cost of 5*s.* a volume it still would not have percolated much below the middle ranks of purchasers, despite the promise of its advertisement in the *Literary Gazette* for 18 April 1829, to be within reach of 'readers of all classes'.[21] After all, the three-decker at 10*s.* 6*d.* per volume for new fiction and the commercial lending library would hold sway until the end of the nineteenth century.

Influential on the careers of Dickens, Thackeray and Trollope, Scott's example undoubtedly skews our sense of the fortunes to be made from novel writing in the early part of the century. Peter Garside provides details for 2,256 fiction titles first published in Britain between 1800 and 1829, showing peaks in

20 J.A. Sutherland, 1987; 1995, 281–98.
21 Millgate 1987, *passim*.

output in the first years of the new century, a clear trough coinciding with the economic depression of the 1810s, and a steady rise in the 1820s. Annual production of new titles averaged between sixty and eighty (still only a small percentage of book production overall), and, contrary to some critical claims, there appears to be no uninterrupted upward trend, 1808 and 1824 standing out as high points (more than a hundred new titles in 1808, ninety-nine in 1824).[22] Throughout, impression numbers for first and subsequent editions were modest, with a run of 500–750 copies remaining a norm, only increasing to 1,500–2,000 for established authors by the 1820s. Scott was the exception – 6,000 copies of his third novel *The antiquary* (1816) disposed of in a few weeks, and first impressions of 12,000 copies of subsequent novels by the early 1820s. Against this, *Emma* (1816), Jane Austen's first novel to be published under the prestigious imprint of John Murray, ran to a healthy first impression of 2,000 copies, some 750 copies more than the first run of her previous novel, *Mansfield Park*, printed in 1814 for the less distinguished firm of Thomas Egerton.[23]

Where Scott's annual novel profits were estimated in 1818 at a colossal £10,000, Fanny Burney's excellent deal (up to £3,000) with the firm of Longman, Hurst, Rees, Orme and Brown for the manuscript of *The wanderer* (1814) gambled on the novel going through several editions. Burney, who in 1776 sold her first novel for only £20, to which her publisher Lowndes subsequently added £10 more, was now a big name and this much-delayed novel was eagerly awaited. Longman's plan to market an initial print run of 6,000 as a first edition of 3,000, dividing the remainder into three subsequent editions (a common enough ploy), collapsed when in the event, the novel was a critical failure, and copies were later pulped.[24] From a very respectable £300 given for *Belinda* (1801), Maria Edgeworth could command an impressive £1,050 for the second series of *Tales of fashionable life* (1812), followed by £2,100 for *Patronage* (1814).[25] Without the same fame, Austen failed to make more than small profits, though she managed with some skill the game of 'on commission' publishing, and there is no evidence that any publisher egregiously cheated her. With Cassandra Austen's sale of the five remaining copyrights to Richard Bentley in 1832 for £210 (only the copyright of *Pride and prejudice* was sold during the author's lifetime), the overall earnings from her novels can be estimated at around £1,625, most of which was received after her death.[26] It

22 Garside, Raven and Schöwerling 2000, II, 38–40.
23 Gilson 1997, 49, 69.
24 Garside, Raven and Schöwerling 2000, II, 45.
25 Butler 1972, 490–3.
26 Fergus 1991, 171.

is worth comparing these modest profits with the situation at the end of the eighteenth century, when the price for the average novel manuscript ranged from £5 to £20.[27] When we take into account the significant but by no means proportionate hike in the retail price for a three-volume work, which tripled from 10*s.* 6*d.* in 1800 to 31*s.* 6*d.* in the later 1820s, we discover a clear signal of the greater economic respect in which the profession was held post-1800. In general terms, though, and from the perspective of literary publication in book form, the period is best viewed as one of moderate financial rewards for a small proportion of writers and of consolidation and cautious expansion in the trade rather than innovation and risk-taking. An indication of the fragility of authorship as a professional career, as well as a clear recognition of its claims, was the establishment in 1790 of a Literary Fund (granted a Royal Charter in 1818 and still in existence) to assist distressed writers or their dependants.

An exemption from this caution must be allowed to developments in the periodical press. Partly owing to the slowness of the book trade to exploit expansions in technology and literacy, the early nineteenth century witnessed an unprecedented explosion in all kinds of magazine, review and journal publication.[28] With large print runs, lower prices, and high standards for manufacture and contribution, many of these periodicals achieved wide circulation and influence (readerships of 5,000–50,000 and more), and in some cases became the mainstay of publishing firms. Constable and Blackwood in Edinburgh and Murray in London established their formidable publishing networks around the critical periodicals they each launched: the *Edinburgh Review* (1802–1929), *Blackwood's Edinburgh Magazine* (1817–1980) and the *Quarterly Review* (1809–1967) respectively. These big periodicals attached to themselves schools of reviewers, selectively accommodated new authors and set the intellectual horizons of their readers. Among the evolving institutional relations of the modern literary market, the periodical represented the chance to control both the fortunes of particular books, by arranging for favourable reviews, and the opinions of readers, to whom they served up a digest of views on a variety of issues and across a range of genres. In 1817 Colburn set up the *Literary Gazette*, an innovatory weekly review which enjoyed a rapid success, providing prompt and influential comment on new works. Colburn in particular gained a reputation for manipulating his journals to his own ends; his caricature as Mr Puffall in Thomas Love Peacock's *Crotchet Castle* (1831) witnesses to his reputation among authors and rival publishers. Eventually, too, by

27 Blakey 1939, 73.
28 See Maidment, chap. 25 above.

the end of the period monthly journals combining essays, reviews, short fiction and poetry, like *Blackwood's*, the *London Magazine* (1820–9), and Colburn's *New Monthly Magazine* (1814–84), were challenging the high prices of volume publication and redirecting the tastes of readers towards the miscellany as a forum for new literature.

The identification of literary criticism at this time as a political activity and the coincident recognition of contemporary literature as socially influential (part of the shift in the definition of culture to include the current as well as the classic) were crucially made through the textual heterogeneity and diverse editorial policies of the periodicals. In their pages, reviews of the latest literary publications were contextualized alongside articles on the economy, the state of the wars against France and political concerns at home. The graphic alignments of the periodical's mixed texts fostered connections between the act of reading within the journal's space and the interpretation of society's juxtaposed 'texts' beyond it, making the case for an engaged literary practice far removed from the transcendent idealism which we still commonly associate with high aesthetic activity in the period. As editor and chief literary reviewer for the *Edinburgh Review* from 1802 to 1829, the Whiggish Francis Jeffrey was among the most powerful arbiters of national taste. His sense of the critic's public responsibilities as cultural leader and literary censor in a country at war exposes the political expediency of his campaign against much contemporary poetry and his ridicule in the 1800s of Wordsworth's experimental verse in particular. Later, the Tory reviewers J.G. Lockhart in *Blackwood's* and John Wilson Croker in the *Quarterly* based their dismissal of Keats's newly published *Endymion* (1818) on his poetic association (and presumed political sympathies) with the reformist Leigh Hunt, leader of the scornfully named 'Cockney School of Poetry'. In both reviews it is clear that Hunt and his politics as much as Keats and his poetry are the target.[29]

When we think about literature bibliographically, in its book-bound existence, we are thinking about several kinds of object – the book shaped by market and production forces as a particular publication 'event', the book the reader engages privately, the book located on a shelf or in a collection and from which it derives further significances, and so on. In this period, the material appearance of books took on newly recognized symbolic value in the context of markets that included, at one end, a fashion for antiquarian collecting[30] (and for deluxe and 'antiqued' publishing of certain new works) and, at the other,

29 K. Sutherland 1994.
30 See Landon, chap. 38, below.

ephemeral and occasionally 'dangerous' chapbooks or 'little books', as they were known, for mass circulation.[31] Literary writers expressed a new consciousness about forms and formats and how they contribute to reception and even meaning, as when George Crabbe apostrophized the physical appearances of books in his poem *The library* (1781), or Jane Austen joked 'I detest a Quarto',[32] or Scott's *Ivanhoe* (1820) signalled its importance by a departure from the usual novel format: issued in first edition as a post octavo rather than duodecimo, the slightly larger dimensions linked it with the superior style of the history and travel book. The lending library came to dominate the scene, whether as commercial businesses, large or small, or non-profit proprietary ventures attached to literary and philosophical societies, mechanics' institutes, or run as modest book clubs in which members clubbed together to buy and share publications.[33] The consequent importance of the library as spatial repository and, through its purchasing choices, as arbiter of value, to local or group-interest definitions of what Literature is (and is not) and to how it is read and categorized cannot be overemphasized. Like the periodical, the library was a means to widen access to new literature during a period of high purchasing costs. By its rules of membership the library could and did simultaneously democratize and affirm the exclusivity of its collections and therefore of its definition of good reading. Many subscription libraries made a point of distinguishing their stock from that held by the commercial libraries, their catalogues listing proportionately few contemporary novels, which would in any case occupy a separate category from 'Polite Literature' (usually defined as the classics in original languages and translation, older and contemporary poetry, critical, moral and aesthetic studies). By extension, the period saw the mounting importance of a distinction between renting and reading and owning and rereading books, with the emergence of an oppositional culture of rereading by the few as the means of transforming literary value into selective salvation. In immediate terms, this had consequences for the fortunes of both poetry and the novel, with the novel achieving only slowly and by the end of the period the status of a vendible and, in some circumstances, rereadable object.

31 See Wood, chap. 48 below.
32 Austen 1995, 206.
33 Altick 1998, *passim*; St Clair 2004, 235–67.

36

Scholarly editing: patristics, classical literature and Shakespeare

MARCUS WALSH

Editing, I have argued in another place, is not merely a function determined by social or political or economic conditions, but should be seen also as a discipline possessed of its own principles, procedures and purposes.[1] The editorial discipline nevertheless is not ideal but historical. Its methods, however characterizable and coherent, and yet more tellingly its objects, are and have been shaped in relation to changing circumstances, political, national, religious, cultural, social, institutional. Aldus Manutius set up his press in Venice, was joined by such scholars as Erasmus, and financed by Pico della Mirandola, not because of an abstracted and disinterested desire to restore the past to light, but out of an ideological, cultural and nationalist understanding of the value of classical writing. History does not repeat itself, but editing in the long eighteenth century – my task here is to survey the editing in Britain of patristic texts, classical texts and the writings of Shakespeare – similarly pursued its ideological purposes, was connected with the creation of its own mechanisms of production, and sponsored its own communities of scholarship.

The editing of patristic texts

The implication of editing in its ideological and material contexts is most broadly and consequentially manifest in this period, no doubt, in the case of the Bible, and particularly in the development in continental Europe and in Britain of a rational textual criticism, hermeneutic methodology and historical scholarship. The leading figures of this Enlightenment project – as it was commonly understood at the time and may be seen in retrospect – included Richard Simon in France; Richard Bentley, Henry Hammond, Matthew Poole, John Locke, Robert Lowth and Benjamin Kennicott in England; Alexander Geddes in Scotland; and Johann David Michaelis, Johann Gottfried Herder and

1 Walsh 1997b; see especially Introduction, 1–3.

Johann Gottfried Eichhorn in Germany.[2] The editing of patristic texts in England at the beginning of our period is a more restricted though methodologically and ideologically parallel case, displaying evident relations between editing and political, religious and social contexts. Patristic scholarship had of course been pursued and patristic texts had been edited long before the eighteenth century, both in England and, more extensively, in continental Europe. Cyprian, for instance, had been edited by Andreas (Rome, 1471), Erasmus (Basel, 1521), Pamelius (Antwerp, 1568), Paulus Manutius (Venice, 1563), and Rigault (Paris, 1648). Sir Henry Savile's edition of the Greek works of Chrysostom (Eton, 1611–12) was a founding monument of English textual scholarship. The issues of the religious debates of the decades following the Restoration, however, led Anglican apologists, embattled between papacy and dissent, to pursue with renewed urgency the Laudian appeal to the primitive truths of the Church Fathers. Patristic scholarship in England flowered, in the work of, for example, John Pearson, Bishop of Chester and Lady Margaret Professor of Divinity at Cambridge. Amongst a number of patristic editors, Johannes Ernst Grabe came from his native Germany to England in 1697, in search of a genuinely apostolic church, and published editions of Irenaeus (1702) and Justin (1706). The tide of patristic editing was at the full from the 1670s to the third decade of the eighteenth century; Edward Harwood, in his *View of the various editions of the Greek and Roman classics*, first published in 1775, cites many English as well as continental patristic texts but none later than 1728, by which date one of the last phases of the turn-of-the-century controversies, the war against deism, was coming to an end.

The pressure of ideological and more specifically religious imperatives, and the creation of mechanisms, communities and institutions of textual production, may be seen in spectacularly close association with the forms of patristic editing in the career and publications of Dr John Fell, Dean of Christ Church, Bishop of Oxford and Vice-Chancellor of the University. Fell was a follower of Laud almost by birth. His father, Samuel Fell, Lady Margaret Professor of Divinity, received a series of advancements from Laud, the most significant of which was to Dean of Christ Church in 1638. In post-Restoration Oxford John Fell played a leading role in the governance of the university, in the founding of the University Press, and in scriptural and patristic scholarship. No doubt his major public achievement was his implementation of Laud's plan of a learned institutional (rather than private) University Press. The Laudian statutes of 1636 provided for the

2 For an extended account of this project, see Walsh 1997a.

creation of a 'Universitatis Typographia', but until the Restoration that had taken no more ambitious physical form than a store room; Fell persuaded Archbishop Sheldon to make his intended gift to the university a theatre, begun in 1664 and completed in 1669, which would host not only the university 'acts', but also a new 'learned Imprimerie'. Fell was a member of the Delegates of the Press from 1662, and, during his Vice-Chancellorship (1666–9), chairman. Fell's major, certainly his most celebrated, contribution to the Press was his location and purchase (through his agent Thomas Marshall) of an extensive stock of the types, matrices and punches in the learned languages upon which the publication of scholarly texts depended; the 'Fell types' passed to the Press at his death.[3]

Like Aldus Manutius, however, Fell was interested in more than type. The new Press had an avowedly apologetical function, enabling not only the publication of learned books with the university's official stamp, but also the advancement of a particular Church of England programme, closely associated with Fell himself. For Fell as for Laud and the Laudians, the defence of the church rested upon Scripture and the Fathers. In the Preface to his translation of Cyprian's *Of the unity of the church* ('Printed at the Theater in Oxford', 1681), Fell insisted on the parallel between the primitive church, persecuted as it was by the emperor Decius and weakened by the schism of Novatian, and the late seventeenth-century English church, 'assaulted by the plots and machinations of idolatrous Rome ... molested by domestic dissentions from within'. As Cyprian's book was salutary in its own time, 'bringing back into communion, several of the most eminent partners in Schism', so, Fell hopes, his translation might now have a similar effect: 'Would to God ... men ... would diligently read the holy Fathers and Writers of the first ages of the Church, particularly S. Cyprian; which if they did, it would be impossible for them to continue their opinions, and be either Papists or Separatists' (pp. 39–40).

Fell sponsored and participated in patristic scholarship throughout his career. He encouraged Henry Dodwell to write his *Dissertations upon St Cyprian* (1682) and arranged for the collation of the Bodleian manuscripts of St Augustine on behalf of the Maurist community, who were preparing a new edition. His own editions, including Clemens Alexandrinus (1669), Athenagoras (1682) and Theophilus of Antioch (1684), were printed for the most part as small-format 'New-Year Books' prepared as gifts for the Fellows of his college, all with some annotation textual and explanatory, and proudly bearing on their title page the imprint, and an illustration, of the Sheldonian

3 The Fell types were used in the printing of the authoritative modern study, Morison 1967.

Theatre. The greatest product of his patristic scholarship, and at the same time his major contribution to the defence of a Laudian church, however, was the folio *Sancti Caecilii Cypriani opera* (1682). Fell's Cyprian includes extensive apparatuses – textual, explanatory and variorum – incorporating not only his own work, but also the fruits of helpers including John Mill and John Pearson (who wrote the 'Vita S. Caecilii Cypriani' that follows the Preface). It is beautifully printed, using the new types. More than that, it is a resonantly symbolic book. It was the first formal production of the new Press, announced in the 1681 *Proposal tending to the advancement of learning*. Its choice of subject had a particular contemporary ideological force: not only a Church Father, but that Father most appreciated by Anglicans, and particularly followers of Laud, for his stand against Rome and for his episcopal theory, which insisted both that bishops were answerable to God, and that their unanimous consent must be the standard of orthodox belief. (Laud had indeed been described by Heylin as 'Cyprianus Anglicus'.) The title page insists on the book's location and significance. Here Fell himself, in both his scholarly and episcopal capacity, is identified as the editor: 'recognita & illustrata per Joannem Oxoniensem Episcopum'; here too an allegorical figure, Minerva surrounded by the emblems of various learning, set against a background of the Divinity School, Old Schools and of course the Sheldonian, graphically represents Oxford and scholarship, theology and the book.

Classical editing

The broader field of the editing of Greek and Latin classical texts similarly reflected cultural, academic and social issues, though in more complicated ways. Classical editing of course addressed itself to that audience which had access to knowledge of the learned languages, public- and grammar-school and university educated, primarily male (though in a century when the processes of education were less formally prescribed, there were exceptions: Elizabeth Elstob, who learnt eight languages with her brother at Oxford; Elizabeth Carter, who acquired classical learning from her clergyman father; Lady Mary Wortley Montagu, who spoke of 'stealing the Latin language' in the family library). That audience in itself was not, however, homogeneous, and the procedures and concerns of classical editing, and indeed the physical forms of its books, relate to and reflect intellectual, and social, divisions. An early, involved and notorious such division, itself associated with the ongoing war between ancients and moderns, was that between the humanism of the aristocrat or gentleman, and that of the scholarly philologist.[4] Dryden's 1697 verse translation of Virgil is in every way an icon of the former: a superb folio printed in the handsomest style, with multiple dedications to senior peers of the realm, and 101 fine 'cuts', each sponsored by an armigerous subscriber. Dryden's translations of his ancient poet appear without annotation, in a large and elegantly readable type; neither the original text nor the translation of a classic poet requires explication to the educated gentleman reader, who values the poem as an aesthetic and moral whole, and understands at once (as Pope would insist in the programmatic note to the first line of his translation of the *Iliad* of Homer) 'all that an Author can reasonably mean'. Sir William Temple displayed and commended a similar gentlemanly *facilitas*, a dependence on intuitive rightness of judgement, claiming in his 'Essay upon ancient and modern learning' (1692) that the epistles of Phalaris – which he assumed, mistakenly, to be both genuine and classical – 'have more Race, more Spirit, more Force of Wit and Genius than any others I have ever seen, either ancient or modern'. Henry Felton, Principal of St Edmund Hall, defends the easiness of 'the politest Parts of Learning', and rejects 'sour, verbal Study'. His *Dissertation upon reading the classics* (1713) is addressed to the young aristocrat Lord Roos, and discards the gravity of the gown in favour of the more deferential voice of the private tutor. Felton assures his young charge, with a proper sense of community, that 'we have natural notions' of idiom, purity and plainness of speech. Understanding, according to this ethos, requires neither verbal exactitude ('we need not be too solicitous about the Words of an Author, to have a right Taste of him'), nor the dull empiricism of supporting example (Felton sets out his 'general Rules' without 'the Pomp of Quotations').[5]

The claim to so easy and so familiar an intimacy with the ancients came under withering attack in both the polemic and the rhetoric of Richard Bentley, King's Librarian and Master of Trinity College – though his origins were in the rural Yorkshire yeomanry, and he learnt his Latin rudiments from his mother, before grammar school and Cambridge. Bentley had an extensive and scholarly knowledge of the literature of the ancient world, prefiguring the *Altertumswissenschaft* of the late eighteenth-century German critics. That vast contextual learning, already displayed in his *Epistola ad Joannem Millium* (1691), he now turned against Temple in his *Dissertation upon the epistles of Phalaris*,[6]

4 The authoritative recent account is Levine 1991.

5 Felton 1713, 4th edn, 1730, vi, vii, xi, xix, 36.

6 The *Epistola ad Millium* was published as an appendix to John Mill's edition of the *Historia chronica* of John Malalas of Antioch. The *Dissertation upon the epistles of Phalaris* first appeared as a ninety-eight page appendix to William Wotton's *Reflections upon ancient and modern learning* (1697), and was republished in expanded form, as a 600-page book, in 1699.

where he established beyond question, by extensive reference to Greek chronology, language and literature, that the letters of Phalaris were spurious. Bentley was also, however, to the yet greater fury of his more gentlemanly opponents, a verbal critic. In his series of editions of Greek and Latin authors he challenged the idea of a *textus receptus*, making particular editorial decisions at every line. His standard method was the critical analysis of the readings of the existing text, with reference to previous emendations and the manuscripts; the diagnosis of possible error; and the proposal of his own emendation, frequently conjectural. The emendations are supported by careful and deliberated reasoning, an overwhelming and detailed knowledge of ancient metrics, grammar and history, and, most characteristically and influentially, by the adduction of parallel passages drawn from his own vast familiarity with ancient literature. Bentley's great edition of Horace, published in 1711 in Cambridge, provides only a few records of variant readings on the text page, but the 310 pages of text are followed by 460 pages of notes and other apparatus, printed in two columns in a smaller type, exploring issues of variance to the last detail, and treating his predecessors with an often ungentlemanly asperity. The 1713 Amsterdam *editio altera*, in a highly significant formal move, shifts the notes to the text page, where typically a few lines of Horace's verse sit over two tall columns of Bentley's distinctively voiced notes. The Amsterdam edition is a book of great beauty, but the reader's experience is inevitably different, the gentlemanly process of continuous reading with understanding remorselessly attended and diverted by the voice of the professional textualist.

To Alexander Pope, Bentley's divining eye, and the notes which expressed that eye's perceptions, was no more than 'the microscope of wit', laying bare the minutiae of the text, but failing to see 'the body's harmony, the beaming soul' of the poem in its entirety.[7] The Bentleian manner became a regular target, for example in an opportunistic *Translation*, published by Bernard Lintot in 1712, in which Bentley's Latin notes are not only made available to the less scholarly reader, but also parodied through an exaggerated brusqueness and a more bluffly colloquial lexis, and satirized by newly coined 'Notes upon Notes; Done in the Bentleian Stile and Manner'. Negative responses to learned classical editing continued through the century. Even as late as 1762, John Langhorne, in his review of Benjamin Heath's *Notae sive lectiones ad...Aeschyli, Sophocles, Euripidis quae supersunt dramata* (Oxford, 1762), complained of Heath's obsession with 'verbal observations', 'measuring lines, and weighing syllables', and 'collating manuscripts and editions', wishing rather

7 Pope 1743, Bk IV, line 236.

that Heath had offered 'sentimental' observations, pointing out the beauties of the poetry, which would be useful in 'forming the taste of the young reader'.[8]

Yet as the century progressed gentlemanly reading became increasingly hospitable to, and continuous with, a more scholarly humanism, in parallel with a significant increase in Britain of classical scholarship and publication. Editions of the classics became more widely available, produced by a broadening spectrum of scholars and available to a wider range of readers. Through the sixteenth and seventeenth centuries, scholarly editing of the classics had been predominantly continental. As Harwood's *View of the various editions of the Greek and Roman classics* clearly shows, editions bearing such imprints as Stephanus, Elzevir and Plantin remained available throughout the eighteenth century. The 'Delphin' classics in particular, with their notes and indexes, survived as school texts, in college libraries and in the hands of the general classical reader. During the eighteenth century, however, English and Scottish publishers assumed both a more dominant and a more prestigious place in the market, producing classical texts for a wide and various public. Within his extensive account of the modern editions of the Greek and Roman classics Edward Harwood lists at length the work of British publishers and editors in his own century, and celebrates especially the scholarly accuracy and beauty of the books issued by the two university presses, boasting that the University of Oxford 'has produced more splendid and accurate Editions of the Greek Classics, than all the other Universities in Europe. WEST'S PINDAR, HUDSON'S DIONYSIUS, DR MILL'S GREEK TESTAMENT, JEBB'S ARISTIDES, WARTON'S THEOCRITUS... are superior to any Editions other countries have produced, in correctness of text, splendour of execution, and sagacity of criticism' (p. xiv). School and university readers required textbooks, notable amongst which were the extensive series of Latin and Greek authors, in small as well as larger formats, produced by Robert and Andrew Foulis, and by the younger Andrew Foulis, in Glasgow from 1742 until 1800.[9] Numerous cheap and portable books appeared from other publishers, Elzevir and, more commonly, 'Delphin' reprints, or such uniform series as the 'Brindley' classics, duodecimos issued in the mid-eighteenth century by James Brindley in London. A more affluent and gentlemanly readership was served by fine large-format editions. An early and successful example is John Pine's remarkable 1733 Horace, printed from engraved brass plates. A later and particularly well-known example is John Baskerville's 1757 Virgil, a superb quarto printed by

8 *Monthly Review*, 26 (1762), 321–5.
9 For full details, see Gaskell 1986.

subscription in Birmingham, notable not only for the quality of its printing, but also for the new and expensive wove paper, produced by James Whatman, which made up most of its sheets, and Baskerville's own innovation of a coated finish.The subscribers' list for Baskerville's Virgil reveals the likely audience, to the extent that such lists do.[10] By far the largest class are Oxford and Cambridge figures, including professors and masters of colleges. Less numerous are the fifty or so non-university-based clergy. There are thirty-five titled subscribers, all male. Doctors and surgeons, lawyers, school-masters and merchants are numerous. About eighty names are local, some thirty of those from Birmingham itself (or what are now its modern inner suburbs, such as Edgbaston). Mark Akenside, Matthew Boulton, Benjamin Franklin, Thomas Gray and Samuel Johnson are amongst the most familiar names, and represent something of the variety, and distinction, of Baskerville's clientele. Just two women are named: Miss Charlotte Condill and Miss Harriet Hedge.

Editions both small and large in format – the more portable products of the Foulis house as well as Baskerville's Virgil – showed a marked tendency towards elegance and 'correctness', a clean and (particularly in the later years of the eighteenth century) stylish text page appropriate to gentlemanly reading, unencumbered with textual or explicatory machinery. The model for this development is the Horace published by Aldus in 1501, and its formal followers, rather than Bentley's 1713 Amsterdam edition of the poet. 'Beautiful' and 'correct' are a harmonized refrain of Harwood's 1775 *View*: the 1758 Foulis duodecimo Virgil, for example, is 'a very correct and beautiful edition' (p. 171). As the general prevalence of the clean page suggests, the emphasis for many editions was on the text and textual correctness. The sheets of the 1756 Foulis Virgil, famously, were displayed in the University at Glasgow, and a reward of £50 offered to anyone who could find a fault (though what might count or have counted as a fault begs a large editorial question). Yet if, as Harwood acknowledged, 'a correct text, and judicious punctuation indeed, are instead of ten thousand notes', he and others insisted on the value not only of textual criticism and 'sagacity', but also of contextualizing and explicatory commentary:

> critical annotations . . . elucidate the modes of diction, and illustrate the customs and usages which in those ancient ages prevailed . . . The Commentaries and Observations . . . of many illustrious Critics who have indefatigably expended the industry of a long life in collating manuscripts, or in restoring

10 The presence of the name of an individual in a subscription list does not of course prove that individual received his copy, or read his copy, or received as many copies as he subscribed for. Subscription lists can be evidence of patronage, as well as of purchase. See Amory 1995; Suarez 2002.

> the text, scrutinizing contemporary authors, and writing their remarks, are of the last utility, as their singular erudition and sagacity have shed light and beauty upon innumerable passages in these ancient Authors, which would otherwise have been obscure, and totally inexplicable.[11]

Bentley's two great and overlapping methodological legacies to English classicism, the contextualizing scholarship of the Phalaris and the textual scholarship of the Horace, were developed in the work of professional, university-linked, editors. Jeremiah Markland (1693–1776), Fellow of Peterhouse, Cambridge, and an associate of Bentley's later years, edited the *Sylvae* of Statius (1728), authored *Remarks on the epistles of Cicero* (1745) and provided notes on Euripides' *Hippolytus* for Samuel Musgrave's edition (1756). The work of Richard Dawes on Greek metre and grammar was collected in his *Miscellanea critica* (Cambridge, 1745). John Taylor (1704–66), Fellow of St John's, Cambridge, and a friend of Markland's, edited Lysias and Demosthenes. The greatest English classical scholar of the latter part of our period, Richard Porson (1759–1808), was born into an artisan's family in Norfolk. With the help of wealthy patrons he was educated at Eton, and at Trinity College, Cambridge, where he was appointed to a Fellowship in 1782. Having moved to London on surrendering his Fellowship, he was in 1792 appointed Regius Professor of Greek at Cambridge, but declined to lecture. Continuing to live in the capital, he was appointed Principal Librarian of the London Institution in 1806. His editions, notably of Euripides' *Hecuba* (1797), *Orestes* (1798), *Phoenissae* (1799) and *Medea* (1801), display a particular focus on issues of text, idiom and metrics, indebted to Bentley but amounting to a characteristic method, and giving rise to his own school: James Henry Monk (1784–1856), Porson's successor in the Regius Chair, editor of Euripides and biographer of Bentley; Peter Paul Dobree (1782–1825), who succeeded Monk to the Regius Chair in 1823, editor of Aristophanes; Charles James Blomfield (1786–1857), fellow of Trinity Cambridge and editor of five plays of Aeschylus, as well as works by Callimachus, Sappho and others. After Porson's death Monk, Blomfield and Dobree were together commissioned to edit his scholarly remains.

Yet if Bentley's example had pointed the way to a new academic professionalism, centred on Cambridge, it was also true that classical scholarship rapidly became a far more widely disseminated activity, by no means confined to the universities. By the middle of the eighteenth century Henry Felton's unwillingness to 'descend into the Provinces of the Grammarian and Rhetorician'

11 Harwood 1775, v–vi.

was no longer a universal, or indeed a typical, pose either within or without academe. Major editorial work was carried on by gentleman scholars and by professional men. Thomas Tyrwhitt (1730–86), though a Fellow of Merton College, Oxford, lived mostly in London attending to his duties as Deputy Secretary of War (from 1756) and Clerk of the House of Commons (from 1762), yet found time (amongst other literary interests and publications) to produce *Conjecturae* on Strabo (1783) and the Attic dramatists (1822). The classical publications of the London and West Country physician Samuel Musgrave (1732–80) included an edition of *Euripidis quae extant* (4 vols., Oxford, 1778). Many other readers pursued scholarship in more fragmented ways; as Joseph Priestley put it, 'criticism, which was formerly the great business of a scholar's life, is now become the amusement of a leisure hour'.[12] The pages of the *Gentleman's Magazine* and other periodicals of the time bear, in occasional textual notes contributed by their correspondents, repeated witness to the willingness of a wider readership to get its hands dirty with the ink of classical learning and textual enquiry.

Vernacular literary editing: Shakespeare

The editing of vernacular literary classics in the long eighteenth century shows a still more extensive and dramatic dissemination of reading, and development of professional institutions and practices and communities of scholarship. Shakespeare is the exemplary case: a native text, even by the beginning of the eighteenth century the great representative of a characteristically British literary genius, played with increasing frequency in the theatre, and the central ground of the exercises and battles of an emerging English literary scholarship. Through the seventeenth century the Shakespearean Folio of 1623 had been reprinted three times. In 1707 the great bookseller Jacob Tonson the elder bought the rights of the Shakespearean text from the publishers of the Fourth Folio, and throughout the eighteenth century Tonson and his successors (his nephew, Jacob II, and great-nephew, Jacob III) would energetically reassert, by repeated publication under the names of a series of editors, their property in the complete text of the plays.[13] The first two Tonson Shakespeares were edited by Nicholas Rowe and Alexander Pope, both well known as poets and hence the more saleable as editors. Rowe's edition of Shakespeare, published in 1709, in many ways set a new pattern: a modern-spelling text, with act and

12 Priestley 1765, 23.
13 See Suarez, chap. 34 above.

scene divisions and scene locations, in an octavo format, small enough to carry and read easily, with a 'Life' of Shakespeare which would be reprinted in successive editions. Nevertheless, though Rowe was conscious of textual problems and undertook 'to compare the several editions', his was not a scholarly edition to modern or indeed to later eighteenth-century eyes. Nor was Alexander Pope's, published by Tonson in the more imposing and less portable form of six quarto volumes in 1725. Pope was as conscious as Rowe had been that the inherited Folio text was faulty in many ways, and made extensive (though not consistent or comprehensive) use of the original Quarto editions of virtually all the plays, assembling 'parties of my acquaintance ev'ry night, to collate the several Editions of Shakespear's single Plays'. Nevertheless, his textual decisions are often arbitrary, and, more notoriously, he 'degraded to the bottom of the page' passages which were in his judgement 'excessively bad'.[14] Explanatory notes are extremely few, though eighteenth-century readers were already becoming very much conscious of the difficulties of comprehension posed by Shakespeare's language.

The first recognizably 'modern' scholarly edition of Shakespeare was that published by the Tonson house in 1733, and edited by Pope's celebrated adversary, Lewis Theobald.[15] A practising dramatist, Theobald was extensively read not only in Shakespeare but also in the drama of Shakespeare's time, and in earlier English literature, and was able to adduce copious supporting textual and cultural evidence. Trained as a lawyer, he knew secretary hand, and could appeal to the 'traces of the letters' to underpin his textual readings. The revolutionary nature of Theobald's Shakespearean work is explosively demonstrated in *Shakespeare restored* (1726), in which he provided, as the title announced, 'a specimen of the many errors, as well committed, as unamended, by Mr Pope in his late edition of this poet'. Both in *Shakespeare restored* and in his edition, Theobald deliberately applies the methods of Bentley the editor of classical texts, and in particular the copious and reasoned adduction of parallel passages, drawn in this case from the writings of Shakespeare and his contemporaries, and a wide range of earlier writing. The first edition of Theobald's Shakespeare appeared in seven workmanlike octavo volumes. At the foot of most text pages are to be found, in marked contrast to Pope's edition, a considerable body of notes, in which Theobald applies his knowledge of the literature of Shakespeare's period to the choice and explanation of readings. Bound to use the Tonsonian *textus receptus*, Theobald nevertheless claimed that

14 Pope 1956, II, 118: Pope to Jacob Tonson, Jr., 16 or 23 May 1722; *Works of Shakespear* (1725), Preface, i, xxii.

15 On Theobald, see Jones 1919; Seary 1990; Walsh 1997b.

his text was 'collated with the oldest copies', and indeed he made more extensive use of the Quartos as well as of the Folio texts than Pope had done. But like Bentley's, his emendations were based on reason as well as the textual witnesses, and he was prepared to make purely conjectural decisions on the basis of sense and evidence, as in his famous and brilliant proposal of 'a' babled of green fields' at *Henry V*, 2. 3. 16. Despite Pope's devastating revenge in the *Dunciad*, Theobald's Shakespeare remained popular with readers throughout the century; by 1773 there had been no fewer than seven London editions, in octavo and duodecimo formats, for a total (according to George Steevens) of 11,360 copies.

The name of Theobald was ritually abused after his warfare with Pope by many writers, and particularly by William Warburton, whose 1747 revision of Pope's edition is characterized by extensive unacknowledged borrowings from Theobald's letters and edition, and its free use of speculative, and occasionally fantastic, conjecture. Nevertheless, Theobald's work had effectively decided the battle, so far as Shakespearean scholarship was concerned, between gentleman and philological humanism. The 'pond'rous volume[s]' of Sir Thomas Hanmer's 1744 quarto edition, published by the Oxford University Press, presented a rare example of a gentleman amateur editing Shakespeare's plays, and a unique example of any editor or press challenging at this date the Tonson monopoly. Shakespearean editing was becoming recognizable by its economic, and its methodological, professionalism. The same was true for the editing of Spenser and Milton. The 1715 six-volume Spenser and 1719 *Paradise lost* edited by the poet and scholar John Hughes, and published by Tonson, were early landmarks of responsible textual collation. John Upton's 1758 two-volume *Faerie queene* remains deeply impressive for its textual basis in the 1590 and 1596 editions, and the hermeneutic precision, and breadth of scholarship, of its annotations. If Richard Bentley's 1732 *Paradise lost* notoriously exposed the dangers of textual conjecture inadequately fettered by contextual knowledge, Zachary Pearce's answering *Review of the text of Milton's Paradise lost* (3 parts, 1732, 1733) demonstrated the explanatory and textual value of relevant scholarship, in classical, biblical, Miltonic and modern vernacular sources. Thomas Warton's 1785 edition of Milton's *Poems on several occasions* is an exemplary case of late eighteenth-century scholarly editing, its text based on collation of 'the authentic copies', its commentary informed by a newly comprehensive grasp of the English as well as the classical poets, its hermeneutic method self-consciously theorized especially in regard to the use of parallel places – a practice whose source in English secular editing may be traced back to Theobald, and before him to Bentley the editor of the classics.

In the process of the professionalization of editing Samuel Johnson is pivotal and representative. For the Tonson house and the other publishers who joined together in undertaking the edition eventually published in eight volumes in 1765, Johnson, the celebrated author of the *Rambler* (1750–2) and the *Dictionary* (1755), was the obvious choice as editor, from a commercial as well as from a literary point of view. For Johnson himself, the 'revisal' of Shakespeare was an exercise perfectly adapted to his professional literary and linguistic skills and knowledge. The years of his lexicographical labours had added a sharper focus and a greater range to his reading in English literature of the sixteenth and seventeenth centuries, qualifying him for the editing of the playwright who was now, after half a century of rising prestige, clearly the jewel in the crown of British literary culture. As a professional editor must, Johnson took seriously the issue of the Shakespearean text, still using the *textus receptus* but aware at every point of the readings of the early editions, and conducting in his Preface a discussion of issues of editorial responsibility and textual authority that remains significant to these continuing debates. Physically, Johnson's edition is (like Theobald's) a utilitarian octavo, designed for reading with understanding, the text accompanied by copious notes, in which Johnson engages both with the text itself and with previous commentators. Johnson's may be regarded as a formal forerunner of the variorum Shakespeares of the later eighteenth century; if Warburton cited earlier editors for the most part to disagree with them, Johnson enters into a more genuine dialectic, understanding that the explication of a rich and allusive text from a distant cultural and linguistic past 'is not to be expected from any single scholiast', but requires the labour and discoveries 'of many men, in devious walks of literature'.[16]

This implied community and continuity of scholarship took a real form in the process and product of the major editions of Shakespeare of the late eighteenth century.[17] Johnson's edition was substantially expanded by George Steevens for the 1773 variorum edition published by a consortium of some thirty-three booksellers (Jacob Tonson III had died in 1767, and the Tonson rights had been sold in 1772). A second edition of the Johnson/Steevens Shakespeare, published in 1778, benefited from many suggestions and corrections by Edmond Malone; a further edition was published in 1785, with Isaac Reed's revisions. In 1790 Edmond Malone published his own great and innovative ten-volume edition of *The plays and poems of William Shakspeare*.[18] Malone rejects the

16 Johnson 1968, VII, 103; 1992, 162: letter to Thomas Warton, 14 Apr. 1758.

17 For a fuller discussion, see Walsh 2001, 206–9. For a key consideration of the profession of scholarship in the eighteenth century, see Jarvis 1995.

18 On Malone, see Martin 1995.

textus receptus in favour of a recognizably modern approach to textual authority, base text and textual collation. His explanatory notes continue the movement, already evident in Johnson and Steevens, towards a more tightly selective and argued hermeneutic logic. His prolegomena include his definitive 'Attempt to ascertain the order in which the plays of Shakspeare were written' (first published in Johnson and Steevens 1778), groundbreaking 'Historical account of the rise and progress of the English stage', and massively extended revision and correction of Rowe's much-reprinted *Life*. However distinctive and extraordinary, Malone's edition is nevertheless recognizably a continuation of conventions, contents and methods already prefigured in Johnson and taken forward in the editions of Steevens and Reed: a usable octavo format and a text based on an explicit and credible methodology, presented with a known and to some extent a communal paratextual scholarship, accompanied on the page with explanatory notes. Malone's volumes, like those of his predecessors, were products of expert, professionalized scholarship aimed at those who wished not only to read but to comprehend Shakespeare, and who expected the textual reliability, contextualizing information and rational exegesis that made such understanding possible. The sequence of learned multi-volume editions of Shakespeare, with expanding apparatus, continued after Malone with Steevens's 15-volume edition of 1793, and the 21-volume 'first variorum' of 1803, which was the work of Johnson and Steevens thoroughly revised by Isaac Reed. The achievement of eighteenth-century scholarly editing of Shakespeare reached its fullest expression in the great 21-volume 'third variorum' of 1821, a completion by James Boswell the Younger of Edmond Malone's work of expansion and revision of his own 1790 edition.

The scholarly grouping, and succession, of Johnson, Steevens, Reed and Malone was notoriously not simple, continuous, or always amicable. Nor did they exercise a monopoly. There were other scholars at work in the field of Shakespearean editing, outside this metropolitan group of professional or quasi-professional editors. Some had the resources to secure the publication of their work, most notably perhaps the independently wealthy gentleman amateur Charles Jennens, who produced punctiliously collated editions of a number of individual plays in the late 1760s and early 1770s.[19] Others confined themselves to more private scholarly activities, amongst them John Howe, Baron Chedworth, who wrote extensive marginalia in copies of the 1785 (Reed), 1790 (Malone) and 1793 (Steevens) variorums.[20] Nor was the variorum

19 *Lear* (1770), *Hamlet*, *Macbeth* and *Othello* (1773), and *Julius Caesar* (1774).
20 See Nelsen 1998.

the only possible intellectual mode or physical format even for recognizably scholarly editing. Edward Capell, notably, pursued a distinct approach, printing the plays themselves in ten small octavo volumes (1768) as a separate 'clean text', suitable for uninterrupted reading. Capell's edition presented itself as a humanist book, deliberately purged of the pedant's 'garniture of notes'. The ancestry of its form lies not in Bentley's Amsterdam Horace, but – no doubt via the classical texts of the Foulis brothers especially – in the clean pages of the Aldine Horace, stripped of the accretions of scholiastic commentary. Yet for all the purity of its first published form Capell's Shakespeare was a learned book. The 1768 text was based directly on the early printed editions, and was the product of exceptionally thorough, and critical, collation. The bare text was followed (after an extended interval) by the impressively scholarly glossary, textual and explanatory annotation, and contextualizing passages of his *Notes and various readings* (Part 1, 1774; 3 vols., 1779–83).[21]

If there was diversity in the social groupings, book forms and modes of production of scholarly editing of Shakespeare in eighteenth-century Britain it is nevertheless possible to detect directions and processes parallel to those evident in classical editing: a growing insistence on textual accuracy and the formulation of text-editorial methodologies; the development of contextualizing scholarship, historical, cultural, literary and biographical; an increasing sense of a national literature and a national scholarship; a productive self-consciousness amongst editors, printers and booksellers of the physical forms of the scholarly edition and the disposition of its contents; and the growth of readerships who demanded reliable texts and adequate explanatory annotation, capable of personal involvement not only in reading but also in textual criticism and exegesis. With whatever necessary qualifications, this is a recognizably Enlightenment project: the establishment by scholars, booksellers and their readers of a rational and knowledge-based community of understanding.

21 For a fuller discussion of Capell see Walsh 1997b, 175–98.

37
The reprint trade

THOMAS F. BONNELL

'Printing-presses, every where, are chiefly employed in reprinting.' In one succinct remark Robert Foulis of Glasgow defined what he perceived to be the heart of the book trade.[1] If the goal of business is to maximize profits while minimizing risk, a publisher can hardly do better than to reprint books for which there is a proven demand. Risk can never be erased – reprinters must guard against flooding the market with more books than can be absorbed, watch for signs of changing taste, choose their points of sale wisely, manage their distribution networks efficiently and so forth – but at least the goods at the centre of the equation are known to attract buyers. Midway through the long eighteenth century Foulis saw with unusual clarity where the trade stood and what lay ahead. He anticipated the historical verdict of John Feather, who observed that back lists of proven titles, coupled with the reprint series and its progeny (like Everyman's Library and the Penguin Classics), were 'destined to become the economic pillars of the British publishing industry'.[2]

To understand the dynamics of the reprint trade, an important subject generally neglected by book historians, it is necessary first to revisit the issue of copyright and to review how booksellers in Ireland and Scotland took advantage of their distance from London – in legal as well as geographical terms – to reprint the titles they wanted. Next to discuss is the cogent economic analysis put forward by members of the trade desperate for clarification of the often murky distinction between piracy and legitimate reprinting. Finally, an overview of the literary series that proliferated at the end of the century, once the statutory limits on copyright had been firmly settled, shows how vast and vital the reprint trade would become.

The evolution of a reprint trade in this period was interwoven with developing notions of copyright. After the lapse of the Printing Acts in 1695, the

1 Foulis 1774, 15.
2 Feather 1988a, 117–18.

principal asset in the book trade, intellectual property, remained without significant legal safeguards until passage of the Copyright Act of 1710 (8 Anne c. 19). This bill protected any title already in print for twenty-one years; new titles were protected for fourteen years, at the end of which, if the author were still alive, a fourteen-year extension was granted. Books as commodities tend either to thrive or to languish; as Andrew Millar quipped, 'a book, that did not sell quickly at first' amounted to 'a blank in the lottery of bookselling'.[3] To compensate for the losses stemming from such poorly selling titles, so greatly did they outnumber 'lottery winners', it was once reckoned that successful books would need to be protected for sixty years if a bookseller was to prosper in business. So argued Samuel Johnson to justify the peculiar custom of the London trade, whereby – never mind the statute – booksellers purchased copyrights as though they were obtaining the property in perpetuity.[4] When a book out of copyright kept up steady sales, the supposed copyright holder often allowed others to buy shares in the title – that is, in lieu of publishing their own editions, to procure shares of a monopoly in current and future reprints.

A case in point for the way such monopolies warded off a full-fledged reprint trade is offered by the remarkable career of Jacob Tonson, whose list of publications by the 1720s boasted 'something like the whole of English literature in duodecimo'.[5] In this list Milton was joined by Dryden, Waller, Addison, Congreve and numerous others, all held in copyright by Tonson. It is possible, surmised David Foxon, that the publisher 'saw himself as taking over the Elzevier tradition', given that he also reprinted a series of Greek and Roman classics in duodecimo from 1713 to 1719.[6] Only eleven years old when *Paradise lost* (1667) was published, Tonson acquired half the copyright to the poem in 1683. By virtue of the Copyright Act of 1710 (8 Anne c. 19), his exclusive claim on the poem was extended through to 1730, at which point the firm was managed by his nephew Jacob. By the time Jacob Tonson III inherited the business in 1735, much of his great-uncle's intellectual property was no longer covered by statute. Still, he lived handsomely off reprints of the old titles.[7] For booksellers owning no copyrights, nor the sort of 'honorary copyright' recognized by most of the London trade, it was risky to try to reprint valuable titles no longer under statutory protection.

3 Foulis 1774, 8.
4 Boswell 1934–50, I, 438.
5 See Suarez, chap. 34, above.
6 Foxon 1991, 26, 29.
7 Geduld 1969, 116; Feather 1988a, 101. See also Lynch 1971.

The challenge presented by this stranglehold on literary property was epitomized by the predicament of John Baskerville in the late 1750s. Wealthy from other ventures, the middle-aged Birmingham entrepreneur turned his mind to type design and printing. After lavishing his skill on Virgil – 'The best printed book the typographical art ever produced', judged Harwood[8] – he wished to show how exquisitely he could produce a Bible, a Book of Common Prayer and Milton's works. A bitter discovery awaited the newcomer to the trade: 'The Booksellers claim an absolute right in Copys of old books, as old as even Milton & Shakespeare; the former of which I did design to have printed, but am deterred by Mr Tonson & Co threatening me with a bill in Chancery if I attempt it.' To have free access only to ancient authors, he rued, 'I cannot forbear thinking a grievous hardship after the infinite pains & great expense I have been at'.[9] However absurd the situation, he finally negotiated the 'privilege' of printing Milton's works by adding the phrase 'for J. and R. Tonson in London' to his Birmingham imprint and by fulsomely acknowledging the 'singular politeness' and generosity of Tonson. (As for the sacred texts, guarded by royal patents, he finagled an appointment as Printer to Cambridge University that permitted him, under the strict eye of the Syndics, to print a single folio edition of the Bible and two octavo prayer books.) Ambitious to reprint '*books of Consequence*, of *intrinsic merit*, or *established Reputation*' – titles worthy of purchase at a price that repaid 'the extraordinary care and expense' laid out upon their 'elegant dress' – Baskerville was hemmed in by restrictions on all sides.[10]

While Baskerville's exasperation was common to all reprinters who felt that a system guarding 'Copys of old books' in this manner was anomalous and indefensible, his deluxe imprints were a far cry from the cheaper editions that typified the reprint trade. The bulk of the books that threatened the interests of London publishers came from places further afield than Birmingham.

In the absence of international copyright agreements (not to appear until the 1840s), nothing could be done to squelch the reprinting of English titles abroad. Irish and Dutch reprints, even when published immediately after a first edition in England, were legitimate products for domestic consumption and sale throughout the Continent. Given that literary property was not recognized in Ireland, the British statute 'virtually forced the Irish printers into the reprint trade' because it lured to England all writers seeking to sell their work.[11] Supplied by their London agents with copies of recently

8 Harwood 1775, 170.

9 Straus and Dent 1907, 97–8.

10 Milton 1758, sig. A3b. See also Gaskell 1959; and Pardoe 1975. Cf. Benson, chap. 17, above.

11 Pollard 1989, 70.

published works – or even the printed sheets as they were worked off, as with Richardson's *Pamela* and, more notoriously, *Sir Charles Grandison* – Irish booksellers were free to reprint whatever they pleased.[12] Only when such books were sold in Britain did they become piracies. (Every unwelcome reprint was decried as a 'piracy' in London, a habit that has muddied the definition of the term.) Of course numerous copies made their way into Britain, many bearing a false London imprint; one portion of a print run might be given a true Dublin imprint, and the rest a press-variant London title page. English booksellers who colluded in this traffic exposed themselves to prosecution under the Importation Act of 1739 (12 George II c. 36), and were liable to be fined for every contraband copy on their premises.[13]

London booksellers, reluctant to lose the Irish market outright, occasionally were able to negotiate payment in advance for the reprint rights to a particular title. But if a book could be reprinted in Ireland for the cost of paper and printing, why should anyone pay extra money, especially with the commercial value of the title as yet unknown?[14] Such arrangements were infrequent, but they could help a Dublin bookseller to deter competition, since an unwritten rule – though often breached – awarded the Irish market to the first reprinter.[15] Thomas Ewing paid John Murray fifteen guineas for a pre-publication copy of John Millar's *Observations concerning the distinction of ranks in society*, counting on his instant reprint to forestall other editions in Dublin. Ewing stocked some of Murray's imprints for customers who preferred the more prestigious London edition, and promised not to distribute his own reprint in Britain, thus alleviating worries over illegal imports.[16] The fraught relationship between London and Irish booksellers was simplified, much to the disadvantage of the latter, following the Act of Union in 1800, by a new Act in 1801 (41 George III c. 107) which brought Ireland under British copyright law and essentially reduced it to a market for imported books.

Scotland was another bastion of reprinting constantly reviled by the London trade, but unlike Ireland was subject to British statute after the Union of 1707. Its relative remoteness, however, along with a degree of juridical independence (disputes over piracy were heard by its own Courts of Session), mitigated somewhat the interference of London booksellers.[17] Lower production costs also contributed to make Scotland an ideal place for reprinting: wages were

12 Cole 1986, 11, 13.
13 Pollard 1989, 71–2, 82–3.
14 Pollard 1989, 97–101.
15 Cole 1986, 11–12, 64–7.
16 Zachs 1998, 112–13.
17 See Beavan and McDougall, chap. 16, above.

lower, profit margins were narrower, and there were no shares to be bought in titles out of copyright protection. The 1740s marked a period of aggressive growth in the Scottish reprint trade, as measured by the activity of the presses north of the Tweed and the alarm it caused in London. Inevitably legal confrontations arose, most notably a round of suits initiated by Andrew Millar. In the first, concerning the poems of James Thomson, an astonishing twenty-nine booksellers of 'differing temperaments and interests, and relative states of innocence and guilt' were summoned before the bar. Ultimately Millar dropped the case, possibly calculating that for the time being he had intimidated the Scots.[18]

They were, however, undeterred. Their reprint trade grew, with the partnership of Gavin Hamilton and John Balfour in the vanguard, provoking Millar in 1743 to set in motion a second legal process that lasted until 1749. Joined by sixteen other plaintiffs in London, he filed charges against two dozen booksellers – twenty in Edinburgh and four in Glasgow – lending to the case 'an air of national confrontation' that only galvanized the Scottish trade. Hamilton and Balfour, the most prominent defendants, were named in the memorial for the case, along with Andrew Stalker of Glasgow. Arguing on their behalf, Henry Home (later Lord Kames) insisted that a flourishing print culture in Scotland, grounded in reprinting, strengthened the British book trade by multiplying commerce in all directions. True, an established reprint trade might lead to London booksellers receiving payment in kind – that is, 'Returns in Books instead of Bills or Money' from their Scottish correspondents for the latest English titles – yet Scottish reprints would 'fetch them the Money, with additional Profits from other Quarters'. In other words, London booksellers would earn higher profits by selling reprint editions than they could get by straightforward monetary payment. In turn, the more prosperous Scots could 'furnish themselves vastly more extensively with London Books', but so long as they were confined to 'remain only Retailers of Books printed at London, they must remain generally poor'.[19]

Similar economic arguments were offered by Robert Foulis in opposition to the Bookseller's Relief Bill of 1774, drafted by the London trade in hopes of reinstating the status quo that governed their dealings prior to *Donaldson* v. *Becket* (1774). The price of books, Foulis stated, obeyed the law of supply and demand: 'Take away competition between buyers, and goods become cheap. Take away competition among sellers, and goods become dear.' As long as

18 McDougall 1974, 83–94, 121–2; 1988, 3–4.
19 McDougall 1988, 5–7.

monopolists held sway, consumers were unable to reap the benefits of 'free competition', that is, 'a contention for cheapness, for correctness, for elegance, for legibility'. If, on the other hand, books were 'more universally' printed, they would be more universally purchased and read. The taste for books in Scotland had spread on account of its reprint trade, and from Dublin itself, Foulis wagered, London booksellers gained as much as they lost by the Irish reprint trade, because 'wherever printing takes place, it diffuses the taste for books wider'. A market that attracted more book buyers would generate more customers able to afford prestigious London editions. To prop up the monopoly, perversely, would depress 'honest industry among the whole body of London booksellers themselves', not to mention its 'restraint on the industry of every printer and bookseller' outside London. In sum, Foulis scoffed at the idea that reprinting elsewhere in Britain in 'any way sensibly hurts the London trade'. The damage to their interests was self-inflicted; they 'diminish[ed] their own trade by endeavouring to bind the hands of their brethren all over the kingdom, who, if free and independent, would be able to trade with them more extensively, and on more equitable terms'.[20]

Internationally as well Foulis called for Britain to examine anew the whole balance-of-trade issue. Throughout the republic of letters, he pointed out, 'the learned and ingenious authors of one nation are reprinted by another' without legal interference or 'complaint of national injury'. No injury? A country that hobbled its reprint trade lost out on two fronts, surrendering 'the profit it brings as a manufacture' and becoming dependent on foreign presses for 'a great national benefit', namely affordable copies of its finest books. Self-defeating restrictions in France had led to Holland's becoming its rival 'in reprinting almost all their saleable books'. Until recently the British had relied on foreign-made paper, thereby subsidizing wages abroad, but now, fed by the demands of the reprint trade, a growing domestic paper industry contributed to 'the increase of the revenue and the national wealth'. To the extent that its monopolies drove up prices and crippled exports, Britain stunted its global economic reach. An opportunity was opening up: 'As the English language becomes more universal', Foulis prophesied, 'English books will be more frequently reprinted on the Continent.'[21] The might of Britain would be enhanced if printers were freely able to produce goods for the reprint market abroad as well as at home. The gist of these points would coincide with the arguments laid out by Adam Smith two years later in *The wealth of nations*.

20 Foulis 1774, 10–11, 13–14, 16, 21.
21 Foulis 1774, 6, 9, 15, 20.

Foulis practised what he preached. He and his brother Andrew were appointed Printers to the University of Glasgow, a post in which they published dozens of Greek and Latin texts for students and other educated readers.[22] While struggling to produce a sumptuous edition of Plato for serious scholars and elite consumers in the vein of the great Parisian printer Robert Estienne, the Foulis firm ironically paved the way for a mass market in reprints by applying to English poetry the paradigm of the multi-volume set of pocket-sized ancient classics. Begun in 1765 as an expedient to raise cash, *The English poets* reached fifty volumes by 1774. Their idea was copied in Edinburgh by William Creech and John Balfour (erstwhile partner of Hamilton), who brought out *The British poets* in forty-four volumes from 1773 to 1776. What distinguished these undertakings from previous reprints was their scope and uniformity, amounting to a difference in kind as well as degree: a whole field of writers – vernacular, not ancient – served as the object of reprinting, not merely this or that popular title. Ambitious, unprecedented and enormously expensive undertakings for the booksellers, such series figured crucially in the growth of the reprint trade.

The Foulis and Creech series reveal that a programmatic approach to reprinting classic English poetry antedated the landmark decision in *Donaldson* v. *Becket*. Owing to that decision, it has been claimed, on 22 February 1774 'literature in its modern sense began'.[23] Yet cause and effect were reciprocal; if the copyright ruling gave birth to the reprint industry in its modern guise, the very pressure of its impending birth had forced the legal issue in the first place. If fresh advances in criticism and aesthetic theory made room for this new concept of literature, so did the heightened material visibility of books: proliferating editions of this author or that work went hand in hand with the developing sense of a national canon.[24]

The expectation of dramatic increases in reprinting created tensions and challenged allegiances. William Strahan, the most influential printer in London and a mentor to Creech, was courted to take a financial interest in *The British poets*. Had he agreed, the series would have enjoyed a London distribution point, but he vehemently refused, fuming that the book trade 'must soon be destroyed if every body is permitted to print every Thing'. The Scots were naive to ignore the harm that threatened them too, not just the London trade: 'I find there are about ten Printers with you, that print every Thing,' Strahan

22 Gaskell 1986.
23 Ross 1992, 16.
24 See Bonnell 1989, 1997, 2008. Cf. Sutherland, chap. 35, above.

warned, 'and who are now beginning to print upon one another.'[25] Shaken by such harsh disapproval, Creech shied away from promoting his series in London, going so far as to ask John Murray to destroy the printed wrappers on a shipment of the *Edinburgh Magazine, and Review* lest an advertisement for the *British poets* cause offence. Murray chided him: 'If it appears to you (as it has done to the house of Peers [in *Donaldson* v. *Becket*]) that the perpetual property claimed by the London booksellers has been nothing but a villainous & unlawful usurpation, you ought boldly to join in a vigorous opposition to them.' Calling the legal decision 'a *magna charta* in fact to the Scotch booksellers', he taunted Creech for trying 'to reinstate [the London monopolists] in their usurpation' when his reprint series made him, in their eyes, 'as great a pirate as the worst'. Murray assured Creech, 'you have reason to be afraid of no trade, & your fears are dastardly & pusillanimous'.[26]

Despite Murray's outrage, Creech let himself be recruited into the rearguard battle to defend honorary copyrights. However effective it might be, the London booksellers' strategy 'to underprint every Person instantly that invades our Books', which Creech aided by turning informant, was bothersome to execute; the better way, Strahan hinted, would be for the Edinburgh trade to 'do their own Business, nothing being at present so dangerous as promiscuous printing of Copies out of the Protection of the Statute'.[27] In a word, he wanted them to police themselves, a wish that came true on 7 February 1776 when the Edinburgh Booksellers Society was organized. Strahan helped the group to shape its bylaws, and was heartened by their progress. By 'discouraging your little dirty pitiful Pyrates', he cheered Creech on, 'you may restore the Trade with you to some Reputation'.[28] It was the season for organizing. January 1776 saw the formation of a Society of Dublin Booksellers to regulate the influx of London publications and safeguard the commercial interests of its members.[29]

Temporarily Strahan had fended off the largest reprint enterprise to date, yet others would flood the London shops in the wake of *Donaldson* v. *Becket* as booksellers approached the business of reprinting ever more systematically. The benchmark for these ventures was set by John Bell, whose edition of Shakespeare (9 vols., 1774) was followed by *Bell's British theatre* (21 vols., 1776–80), a large project begun shortly in advance of an even more significant undertaking, *The poets of Great Britain complete from Chaucer to Churchill*

25 The Creech Letter books, Blair Oliphant of Ardblair Muniments, NRAS 1915; microfilm copy, National Archives of Scotland, RH4/26, Strahan to Creech, 1 Jan. 1773.
26 Murray to Creech, 8 Apr. 1774, Murray Archives, NLS.
27 The Creech Letter Books, Strahan to Creech, 27 Dec. 1774, 12 July 1774.
28 The Creech Letter Books, Strahan to Creech, 20 May 1776. See also Sher 1998.
29 Zachs 1998, 116–17.

(109 vols., 1776–82). By incorporating portraits, vignette illustrations and prefatory lives into his pocket volumes, in addition to formalizing his textual presentation (adding line numbers, classifying the contents by poetic genre and so forth), Bell set a standard of uniformity to be emulated by subsequent reprint series.[30] Whether or not he was 'indisputably the most versatile member of the London printing trade ever', the range of his activities – from type founding to running a large circulating library – was captured in the name Bell chose for his shop and imprint: the 'British Library'.[31] Less iconic than, say, the sign of Shakespeare's Head under which Tonson conducted business, Bell's epithet made a different play for authority; it offered the idea of access to the whole of British print culture.

Strahan and other London shareholders responded with an edition of their own, *The works of the English poets* (68 vols., 1779–81), which included Samuel Johnson's *Prefaces, biographical and critical.* Over a period of thirty-five years both editions found their market. Bell sold volumes collectively or separately, reprinting them as needed so that full sets were always available. In 1784 he reprinted nearly a third of his volumes with 'Bell's second edition' on the title page, and dozens more over the next ten years. Given the higher price of *The works of the English poets* – sold only in complete sets – a second edition was not called for until 1790, when Isaac Reed expanded the collection to seventy-five volumes. Continued sales of Bell's edition led to a reprint of the entire collection, with additions, by Samuel Bagster and a host of other publishers (124 vols., 1807). Three years later many of these same publishers became financial backers of a much expanded edition of *The works of the English poets*, printed in double columns in a hefty octavo format, edited by Alexander Chalmers (21 vols., 1810). It says much about the stability of the reprint trade by the early nineteenth century that the two collections, born of a bitter rivalry and once having represented fiercely antagonistic interests within the book trade, performed so reliably in their respective markets that publishers readily invested in and profited from both at once.

By now the field was full of poetry collections. Chalmers's large octavo format had been anticipated by a series called *A complete edition of the poets of Great Britain* when begun in Edinburgh but renamed *The works of the British poets* after a London firm joined in (14 vols., 1792–1807). In order to make the collection 'which goes under the name of Dr Johnson' much cheaper, the publishers set out to reprint it 'in *six volumes* large octavo' with double

30 See Bonnell 1987, 2008.
31 Handover 1960, 148. See also Morison 1930.

columns. Under the editorship of Robert Anderson, however, the project grew enormously. To unite 'ancient and modern poets in one comprehensive view', Anderson planned to include every poet from Chaucer onward who had 'obtained a classical distinction', a criterion satisfied by any writer who, 'though not generally read, is familiar to us in conversation, and constantly appealed to in controverted points of poetical taste'. The publishers ultimately drew the line at 115 poets, 26 fewer than the editor proposed.[32] Although Anderson found the adjective *complete* (adopted from Bell's title) to be a misnomer, under the banner of 'comprehensive' inclusion he came closer to realizing his predecessor's claim to having reprinted 'every English Classic published within a series of Four Hundred Years'.[33]

Objecting to the ponderous size of Anderson's tomes, Charles Cooke applied Bell's pocket formula to several genres in a co-ordinated fashion. He became the first full-service purveyor of English classics by marketing – in uniform pocket editions, all 'Superbly Embellished' – parallel series of novelists, poets, essayists, historians and devotional authors. Drama too was a favourite target of reprinting, from the late 1770s skirmish between *The new English theatre* (12 vols., 1776–7) and *Bell's British theatre* (along with its later expansions) to *Inchbald's theatre* (25 vols., 1808) and other series up through *Cumberland's theatre* (48 vols., 1826–61). Collections of every sort flourished in the early decades of the nineteenth century, including a series edited by Chalmers before he tackled the poets, *The British essayists* (45 vols., 1803), and *Walker's British classics* (ever-expanding from 1808), but they were outnumbered by the poetry collections that kept cropping up, from John Sharpe's *The British poets* (85 vols., 1805–12) to Charles Whittingham's *The British poets* (100 vols., 1822) and others.

The scale of these undertakings was unprecedented. By 1783 – with untold reprints yet to come – Bell reckoned he had produced 378,000 books for the initial run of *The poets of Great Britain*, his capital outlay of £10,000 supplying 'daily bread, upon an average, to not less that an *hundred manufacturers for many years*'.[34] *Cooke's pocket edition of select British poets* (56 vols., 1794–1805) entailed the production of more than two hundred engravings. Added to this tally, the commissions for his various series lend credibility to the claim that Cooke's reprints provided 'the first steady market for the work of English engravers and artists' in the realm of book illustration.[35] The image conjured by Bell's

32 Anderson 1795, 4; *Edinburgh Evening Courant*, 21 Nov. 1793.
33 Bell 1783.
34 *Morning Post*, 3 June 1783.
35 Amory 1993a, 140.

boast – printers, artists, engravers, binders and shippers at work, along with the makers of paper, type, ink, leather, etc. – differed from the busy labour of Mandeville's beehive by virtue of a new understanding of what drove such economic activity. Mandeville had turned the moral debate over 'luxury' on its head, explaining how necessary it was (not merely beneficial) for the hive to be kept abuzz by the demand for superfluous goods. Vestiges of the guild mentality in the book trade consistent with this economic model gradually receded once publishers like Bell began to see themselves as shaping vast new consumer markets and creating new wealth.

The economic arguments of Home and Foulis thus were borne out by events in the second half of the long eighteenth century. An earlier mode of bookselling faded away as the accelerating commodification of print gave rise to modern publishing. This change coincided with the conceptual shift described by Trevor Ross: property, once viewed as an 'object of ownership and right', came to be regarded as the 'subject of production and exchange', its worth acquired through 'circulation within a dynamic market economy'. If literature contributed to the formation of a national culture through the 'commerce' shared by ordinary readers, it did so as a function of 'the multiplicity of books and ... their wide diffusion'.[36] Reprinting was key to this burgeoning supply of books.

What Strahan had dreaded – 'The opening up of our old property' – led to a profusion of reprints of popular authors. Editions of individual favourites like James Thomson sprouted anew each year as predictably as the revolutions of nature described in *The seasons*, the title fought over in *Donaldson* v. *Becket*.[37] Multi-volume collections meanwhile provided the impetus for assessing the nation's cultural achievement as never before – for a Johnson to take under magisterial survey a vast sweep of poetry, or an Elizabeth Inchbald to render 'the first truly critical history, in essence, of the English drama'.[38] As prefacer and editor, Chalmers partook in defining 'a complete Library of standard English Literature' and 'a Body of the Standard English Poets', confirming the tangible measure of canonicity that Keats understood in predicting, 'I think I shall be among the English Poets after my death.'[39] That the process of measuring up – expressed in the dreams of personal ambition, the drive to embody a collective national culture or the grandiosity of publishing ventures – should have been altered so profoundly by changes within the reprint trade during this era shows how far-reaching were their ramifications.

36 Ross 1992, 8–9, 11.
37 Cohen 1964, 479–95.
38 Castle 2002, 10–11.
39 Chalmers 1809, IV, sig. Y6a; Chalmers 1810, I, v; Stillinger 1999, 115–20.

III
SPECIALIST BOOKS AND MARKETS

38
Collecting and the antiquarian book trade

RICHARD LANDON

The British public was introduced to formal book auctions with printed catalogues in 1676, when William Cooper sold the collection of Dr Lazarus Seaman.[1] By 1695 the practice of selling books by auction was firmly established: twenty-nine catalogues are recorded for that year,[2] all but two of them (Edinburgh and Dublin) issued in London. The considerable number of catalogues published before 1700 demonstrates not only the significant collections to be put on the market – eighteen of the catalogues for 1695 are for named sales – but also the presence of receptive consumers and a well-organized antiquarian trade. The sale of Sir Charles Scarburgh's library serves as a representative case in point. A prominent physician, Scarburgh had personally acted for Charles II, James II, Queen Mary and Prince George of Denmark before his death on 26 February 1694. In 1695, two sales were required to disperse his library, which was divided between his large assortment of the classics, history, theology and literature, and his more specialized assemblage on the history of mathematics and medicine. He was a typical collector of his time: well educated, prosperous and with an interest in the history of his profession. Less typical, but more historically significant, were the libraries of the fellow diarists Samuel Pepys and John Evelyn. Pepys secured a further sort of immortality by bequeathing his books and manuscripts to Magdalene College, Cambridge, where they can still be seen in their original furniture.[3] Evelyn's collection, much of it elegantly bound, fared less well. From 1706 until well into the twentieth century, individual volumes were alienated from

1 Mandelbrote 2001.
2 Munby and Coral 1977.
3 Smith *et al.* 1978.

the collection, the great bulk of which was finally sold by his descendants in 1977–8.[4]

Between the end of the seventeenth century and the beginning of the eighteenth, a brisk antiquarian book trade developed to cater to the needs of this newly flourishing group of collectors. Early in the eighteenth century, there appeared a new kind of collector – nobly born, very rich and fascinated by early printed books, especially those of the incunable period.[5] Leading this group were the 2nd Duke of Devonshire, the 3rd Earl of Sunderland, the 8th Earl of Pembroke, the 1st Duke of Roxburghe, and the 1st and 2nd Earls of Oxford, better known as Robert and Edward Harley. Two of these five collections remained intact until 1881 (Sunderland) and 1914 (Pembroke), but the only one remaining in the family seat, and far from intact, is Devonshire. The Harley manuscripts remain together in the British Library, but the printed books were scattered by Thomas Osborne immediately after the death of the 2nd Earl in 1741. The Roxburghe collection, considerably augmented, came under the hammer to much acclaim in 1812, after the death of the 3rd Duke.[6]

Ironically, such dispersal can provide scholars with a wealth of information. Much more is known about the collections sold at auction or through the trade than those that have remained wholly, or in part, *in situ*. For instance, one of the many spectacular books and manuscripts purchased by Thomas Coke, Earl of Leicester, during his extensive travels in Europe (between 1712 and 1718), is the prized 'Codex Leicester' by Leonardo da Vinci.[7] Apart from a brief appearance at the Royal Academy in 1952, it was kept at Coke's library in Holkham until 1980; up to that point, the codex had only been imperfectly described and transcribed. It remains in private hands.[8]

A significant feature of eighteenth-century collecting is the rise of the scholar-collector, a phenomenon that coincides, not surprisingly, with the increasing interest in English genealogy and topography, antiquarianism, and the editing of earlier English literature, especially Shakespeare's works.[9] The Rawlinson brothers, Thomas (1681–1725) and Richard (1690–1755) – the first appearing as 'Tom Folio' in Addison's *Tatler* no. 158 – were omnivorous.

4 Christie, Manson and Woods Ltd, *The Evelyn library*, four parts: 22–23 June 1977; 30 Nov.–1 Dec. 1977; 15–16 Mar. 1978; 12–13 July 1978; Barker 1995; Harris and Hunter 2003.

5 De Ricci 1930; Myers and Harris 1991, 1996; Myers, Harris and Mandelbrote 2001; Fletcher 1902; Quaritch 1892–1921.

6 See Connell 2000.

7 Hassall 1959.

8 It was sold at auction to Armand Hammer in 1980 for £2.2 million and again in 1994 to Bill Gates, Jr. for $31 million.

9 See Walsh, chap. 36, above.

Thomas's estimated 200,000 volumes required sixteen sales from 1721 to 1734 to disperse, while Richard left 5,700 manuscripts and books to the Bodleian Library. The remainder of his collection was sold in 1756 and 1757.[10]

Physicians, too, figured prominently as collectors. William Hunter (1718–83), the eminent surgeon and lecturer, left his great collection to the University of Glasgow. Composed of books, manuscripts, coins and natural history specimens, the collection included the Hunterian Psalter, one of the most beautiful examples of twelfth-century Romanesque art produced in England.[11] Physician Richard Mead (1672–1754), who 'lived more in the broad sunshine of life than almost any man' according to Johnson, also formed a major collection. When it was posthumously sold in 1754 and 1755, his colleague Anthony Askew (1722–74) not only participated in the sale but also privately bought all of Mead's Greek manuscripts. Askew enjoyed a similarly high reputation as both a doctor and a classical scholar; his own auction in 1775 attracted the attention of French collectors, returning some of his books and manuscripts to the Continent.[12] Among the libraries of the great eighteenth-century doctor-collectors, the only one that survives, albeit not intact, is that of Sir Hans Sloane (1660–1753);[13] his vast collections of books and manuscripts, natural history specimens, antiquities, coins and medals, and prints and drawings constitute part of the foundations of the British Museum and therefore the British Library. These prominent collectors were an integral and recognizable part of British society – so much so that in 1731 Alexander Pope could write, 'Rare Monkish Manuscripts for Hearne[14] alone:/And Books for Mead and Butterflies for Sloane' and confidently expect that the references would be recognizable to his audience.[15]

The reign of George III initiated a new phase of British book collecting, led by the king himself.[16] Although 'Farmer George' is typically remembered for his thick German accent, his 'loss' of the American colonies and the madness which clouded periods of his reign, we must not forget that he was also a sophisticated patron of the arts. His greatest cultural accomplishment was the formation of a library, beginning with the purchase in 1763 of a collection formed by Joseph 'Consul' Smith (1682–1770), the long-time British representative in Venice. Smith's 1755 catalogue lists a collection particularly rich in

10 Tashjian, Tashjian and Enright 1990.
11 Ker 1983.
12 McKitterick 1986, 326–36.
13 MacGregor 1994.
14 Harmsen 2000.
15 *Epistles to several persons: epistle IV to Richard Boyle, Earl of Burlington* (1731), lines 9–10.
16 Roberts 2004.

early editions of classical texts, with an emphasis on those printed in Italy. This glorious foundation initiated almost sixty years of concentrated collecting; by the time George IV presented the collection to the nation in 1823, there were 65,000 books and 19,000 pamphlets.

Frederick Augusta Barnard (who was not the king's natural half-brother, as was often rumoured) was employed as the king's librarian in 1768, after which he was sent on a three-year European tour to collect on behalf of his sovereign. He left with the written advice of Samuel Johnson that a royal library should contain 'at least the most curious edition, the most splendid, and the most useful'.[17] Domestically, the king's presence was apparent at many of the prominent book sales of the late eighteenth century. At the sale of James West's library in 1773, Pall Mall bookseller George Nicol, the sovereign's usual agent, bought on the king's behalf the 1460 *Catholicon* for £35 3*s*. 6*d*., along with thirty-six books printed by William Caxton. Another buyer at the West sale was Nicol's old rival, John Ratcliffe, a chandler from Southwark who reportedly became interested in early printing after looking at the printed leaves he used to wrap his goods. Ultimately, Ratcliffe accumulated more than fifty Caxtons, a dozen of which were purchased by the king at Ratcliffe's sale in 1776.[18]

The sale of West's library, however, is also significant for reasons other than the presence of the king's agent. The catalogue for the sale was compiled by Samuel Paterson (1728–1802), an auctioneer renowned for his knowledge of old books and a pioneer in his trade. Paterson was among the first to issue classified catalogues describing each book as a single lot and his *Bibliotheca universalis selecta* (1786), a listing of primarily European books imported by him for his 1786 sale, includes what is possibly the first index in an English auction catalogue. Lot 2112 in the West sale, catalogued by Paterson as 'A curious Collection of old Ballads, in Number above 1200, b.l. [black letter], with humorous Frontispieces, 3 vol.', contained most of the famous works that would come to be known as the 'Roxburghe Ballads'. The three volumes had originally been obtained, like much of the rest of West's collection, from the Harleian holdings. At the West sale, the ballads were purchased by Major Thomas Pearson (*c*.1740–81), who continued to add new materials, and when Pearson's library was sold at auction, Roxburghe paid £36 4*s*. 6*d*. for the lot. At the Roxburghe sale in 1812, the collection – now containing 1,594 ballads – was sold by the bookseller J. Harding for £477 15*s*. to Benjamin Heywood

17 Barnard 1820–9.
18 De Ricci 1909, 181–2.

Bright (d. 1843).[19] The Roxburghe Ballads were ultimately purchased for the British Museum by Thomas Rodd for £535 in 1844–5 and remain in the British Library, the greatest collection of their kind.

By the fourth quarter of the eighteenth century, antiquarian book collecting and bookselling had developed into stable, flourishing and mutually supportive interests. Indeed, the bookseller's business was largely supported by collectors, most of whom were clergymen, antiquaries and scholars, often with a particular fondness for Shakespeare. George Nicol acted for the Duke of Roxburghe as well as the king, for whom he secured Charles I's annotated copy of the Second Folio of Shakespeare, held to this day in the Royal Collection at Windsor. Shakespearean scholar Isaac Reed also developed a fine library, which was sold by King and Lochée in 1807. Edward Capell (1713–81) gave his collection, with its wonderful series of Shakespeare's plays, to Trinity College, Cambridge in 1779.[20] George Steeven's great Shakespearean library, sold by Edward King in 1800,[21] set record prices for his quarto editions of the plays, almost fifty in number. Steeven's most serious rival as a collector, Edmond Malone, died in 1812 and bequeathed his collection to his brother, Lord Sunderlin, who in 1822 presented it to the Bodleian. These scholar-collectors, typical of the late eighteenth century, presaged the golden age of British book collecting, best represented perhaps by the Duke of Roxburghe.

John Ker, 3rd Duke of Roxburghe (1740–1804) is remembered entirely as a collector of books and the progenitor of the most famous book sale ever held in Britain. In 1755, he inherited his title, along with the considerable estates in England and Scotland that went with it. In 1761, he won the heart of Christiana, the eldest daughter of the Duke of Mecklenburg-Strelitz. However, their marriage prospects were destroyed by George III's engagement to Christiana's younger sister; it was considered politically unwise for an elder sister to be the subject of a younger. Thus, as the *DNB* rather charmingly states, 'both parties evinced the strength of their attachment by devoting their after lives to celibacy'. The duke – whose close friendship with the king helped him become both a Knight of the Thistle and a member of the Order of the Garter – thereafter devoted his energies to amassing one of the finest libraries in England. Of course, he did not produce an heir and, following his death, a sale of the library was planned for 1807, as attested by an 1807 Preface by

19 Cf. Connell 2000.
20 Greg 1903.
21 Edward King commenced business in 1790, joined forces with Mr Lochée in 1805, and stayed in business until 1816.

George and William Nicol. When the sale actually took place in 1812, with a revised Preface, the catalogue was 'arranged' by the Nicols, but Robert H. Evans conducted the sale, the first of his illustrious career.[22] The catalogue contained 9,353 lots, followed by 752 in an 1812 Supplement and 1,383 more at an 1813 sale from his country seat near Kelso. The London sales, conducted in the dining-room of Roxburghe's house in St James's Square, lasted for forty-two days, Sundays excepted, from 18 May until early July.[23] The event became a landmark for several reasons: the quality and condition of the books was very high; several very rich aristocrats, and a few equally rich commoners, were eager to seize the opportunity to enrich their collections; and the Revd Thomas Frognall Dibdin was at hand to record and rhapsodize about the event.[24] The most famous book in the sale was lot 6,292, an edition of Boccaccio's *Decameron* printed at Venice by Valdarfer in 1471, and said to be the only known complete copy. It was bought by the Marquis of Blandford,[25] bidding against Earl Spencer,[26] for £2,260. As Dibdin writes, 'when the hammer fell ... upon the Valdarfer Boccaccio of 1471 the spectators stood aghast! – and the sound of Mr Evans's prostrate sceptre of dominion reached, and resounded from, the utmost shores of Italy'.[27] The price stood as a record for a printed book until 1873. Several other books in the sale, however, fetched considerable prices: Roxburghe's copy of Caxton's *Recuyell of the hystoryes of Troye* (1474) made £1,060 10*s*.; the three volumes of ballads brought £477 15*s*.; his 1470 Cicero £189; his Shakespeare First Folio £100; and a manuscript of Chaucer's *Canterbury tales* fetched £557. The total received from the sale amounted to £23,321, an astonishing amount, given that Roxburghe had paid approximately £5,000 for the whole collection.[28] For those collectors who possessed valuable books but few liquid assets, the success of the Roxburghe sale served as an even greater incentive to put their books on the market. In the British Museum list of book auction catalogues, thirty-three sales are recorded for 1812;[29] by 1815 the number had risen to fifty-two. Perhaps the most enduring effect of the sale, however, was the founding on 17 June 1812 (the day of the sale of the Boccaccio) of the Roxburghe Club, which continues to flourish as one of the most prestigious bibliophilic societies in the world.[30]

22 For Robert Harding Evans, see *ODNB*.
23 See Connell 2000.
24 Jackson 1965; Windle and Pippin 1999; Ferriar 2001.
25 For George Spencer, 5th Duke of Marlborough, see *ODNB*.
26 For George John Spencer, 2nd Earl Spencer, see *ODNB*.
27 Dibdin 1817, 62–4.
28 Cf. Connell 2000.
29 Pollard 1915.
30 Mersey 1928; Barker 1964.

Besides Blandford, two other collectors figured prominently at the Roxburghe sale: Earl Spencer and the Duke of Devonshire.[31] Spencer began collecting books as a young man, but it was not until 1807, when he retired from politics, that he began to devote his full attention to the development of his library. In 1790 he met Count Reviczky and persuaded the Hungarian to sell him his substantial library for an annuity, a transaction that proved to be quite a bargain as the count only lived for a further three years. With Reviczky's books serving as the foundation of the great library at Althorp, Spencer became the most enthusiastic of collectors. Sometimes he even bought whole collections, as he did in 1813 with Stanesby Alchorne's holdings,[32] but most of Spencer's acquisitions were made through purchases of single books. In this endeavour he was assisted by Dibdin, who became his unofficial librarian around 1805 and often represented the earl at sales. Dibdin also recorded Spencer's acquisitions, producing a sumptuous catalogue of his collection of books, the grandly named *Bibliotheca Spenceriana* (1814–23). The first four volumes were printed by William Bulmer and lavishly illustrated with woodcuts and engravings in an edition of 500 ordinary copies and a smaller edition of 50 large paper copies. The supplementary *Aedes Althorpianae* (1822) and *A descriptive catalogue of the books printed in the fifteenth century lately forming part of the library of the Duke di Cassano Serra* (1823) were printed by William Nicol, his successor. When the collection was sold to Mrs John Rylands in 1892, it contained 41,500 volumes, including fourteen block-books, many Bibles (including Gutenberg's), both Mainz Psalters, fifty-six Caxtons, and a huge trove of early editions of classical authors, including seventy editions of Cicero. It allegedly cost Mrs Rylands £250,000.

The Duke of Devonshire, like his uncle Earl Spencer, was also a major purchaser at the Roxburghe sale. Despite his young age (he was only twenty-two years old at the time), he carried off the Caxton *Recuyell*, which had belonged to Elizabeth Grey, the wife of Edward IV, and added a 1603 *Hamlet* to the collection of plays he had acquired from John Philip Kemble.[33] He later bought the library of the Bishop of Ely, Thomas Dampier.[34] Collectors like Spencer, Devonshire and Sir Mark Masterman Sykes[35] naturally accumulated considerable numbers of duplicates which were either used to perfect copies of books they already owned or put back on to the market. Copies used to

31 For William Cavendish, 6th Duke of Devonshire, see *ODNB*.
32 For Stanesby Alchorne, see De Ricci 1930, 74.
33 For John Philip Kemble, see *ODNB*.
34 For Thomas Dampier, Bishop of Ely, see *ODNB*.
35 For Sir Mark Masterman Sykes, see *ODNB*.

improve other books would likewise be put up for sale if they were in decent condition. In 1815, for instance, there were two sales of Devonshire duplicates and one for Spencer, and anonymous regular sales were also held for dispersals.

By the late eighteenth century, the antiquarian book trade had grown in size and sophistication, a development that is vividly seen in the careers of two of that period's most successful booksellers: James Edwards (1757–1816)[36] and James Lackington (1746–1815).[37] Despite their humble origins, both men evinced a striking talent for making money. Lackington, who had been apprenticed as a shoemaker, moved to London in 1773 to practise that trade, and in 1774 set up a combined cobbler/bookshop with £5 borrowed from one of John Wesley's special funds. In 1779 he issued a catalogue of 12,000 volumes and introduced the first of his innovations: the simple but revolutionary expedient of lowering his prices and selling only for cash. By the mid-1780s he had invented remainders, issued a catalogue of 30,000 volumes, and boasted a standing inventory that included 10,000 copies of Watts's *Hymns*. He wrote his *Memoirs* in 1791 and two years later opened the Temple of the Muses in Finsbury Square, the ground floor of which could accommodate a six-horse coach. He issued trade tokens and had the door of his carriage lettered with his motto 'Small Profits Do Great Things'. In 1798 he retired to the country and subsequently died at Budleigh Salterton, having built the parish a chapel.

Lackington does not seem to have been a collector, but Edwards certainly was. The second son of William Edwards of Halifax, scion of the famous firm of bookbinders, Edwards established himself in 1784 on Pall Mall, where he quickly created a carriage-trade business and began to issue catalogues and import large quantities of rare books from the Continent. By 1786, he had firmly established his reputation as a collector by outbidding the king for the Bedford Book of Hours (215 guineas) at the sale of the Duchess of Portland's holdings. In 1789 and 1790 he sold the famous Pinelli collection from Venice at auction, and in 1791 the small, but choice, *Bibliotheca Parisiana*. Around 1800 he began to turn over his business to R.H. Evans, and travelled to France on government business at the behest of his friend Earl Spencer. In 1805 he married and moved to a manor house near Harrow. His collection was described in glowing terms by Dibdin – Edwards is 'Rinaldo' in the *Bibliographical decameron* – but deteriorating health compelled him to sell it in 1815. Accordingly he prepared a catalogue, printed by Bulmer in both small and large paper copies. On 11 April the Dibdinians turned out in force and,

36 For James Edwards, see *ODNB*.
37 For James Lackington, see *ODNB*.

although five lots of Greek vases remained unsold, the sale was quite successful, netting £8,432 for 820 lots. The 'Bedford Hours' went to Blandford for £687 15*s*., Thomas Grenville acquired a 1470 Livy for £22 1*s*., and Longman bought an imperfect Caxton *Troye* for John Bellingham Inglis.[38] The highest price of the sale was the £903 paid by J. and A. Arch on behalf of Sykes for the 1469 Sweynheim and Pannartz Livy printed on vellum. Several lots were purchased by John North, a mysterious collector whose books were sold in 1819. He paid £315 for Piranesi's *Opere* in twenty-three volumes. Edwards's 1479 Jenson Bible printed on vellum brought £115 10*s*. (Triphook for Hibbert).[39]

The timing of Edwards's sale was prescient: he died on 2 January 1816 and was buried at Harrow in a coffin constructed from his library shelves. Annotated copies of his catalogue reveal something of the growth of the antiquarian book trade, with the names of booksellers like Triphook, Payne,[40] Arch,[41] Longman,[42] Clarke[43] and Rodd[44] appearing often. Many collectors' names are given as well because some bid for themselves while also employing booksellers as agents, even for the same sale. Dibdin's name, for instance, frequently appears as a buyer, but he was usually acting on behalf of other collectors. He often reports in his *Decameron* that he had purchased a particular item and then turned it over to a collector at no profit.

There were two collectors of the period who largely ignored the methodology espoused by Dibdin: Thomas Grenville (1755–1846)[45] and William Beckford (1760–1844).[46] Grenville was born into a powerful political family – they would eventually receive the dukedom at Buckingham and Chandos – and he initially pursued a political career, briefly serving as the First Lord of the Admiralty. In 1807 he withdrew from the political scene and spent the rest of his long life concentrating on his library. Remarkably, through the influence of his family, he procured the sinecure office of Chief Justice in Eyre South of Trent, which paid a comfortable £2,000 per year. Grenville's library contained many of the books beloved by the Dibdinians; he owned a Gutenberg Bible printed on vellum, the 1457 and 1459 Psalters, and both Caxton editions of Chaucer, along with a copy of the First Folio of Shakespeare that was said to be

38 For John Bellingham Inglis, see De Ricci 1930, 97–8.
39 Robert Triphook *fl.* 1820–30; for George Hibbert, see *ODNB*.
40 For both Thomas Payne the elder and the younger, see *ODNB*.
41 John and Arthur Arch *fl.* 1820s.
42 The publishing house of Longman sold antiquarian books from 1810 to *c*.1840. See Briggs, chap. 19, above.
43 William and George Clarke *fl.* 1810–35.
44 For both Thomas Rodd the elder and the younger, see *ODNB*.
45 For Thomas Grenville, see *ODNB*.
46 For William Beckford, see *ODNB*.

the finest in existence despite being rebound. He is chiefly remembered as an imaginative pioneer in several hitherto neglected areas of bibliophily, however. Voyages and travels relating to the British empire claimed a particular hold on his attention; his several editions of the Columbus *Letter* and magnificent sets of De Bry and Hulsius mark him as a pioneer of Americana.[47] Grenville was also conversant with Italian and Spanish literature and his run of the early editions of Ariosto was unequalled anywhere. He had intended to leave his collection to his great-nephew, the 2nd Duke of Buckingham and Chandos, but he had become very friendly with the charismatic Anthony Panizzi,[48] then Keeper of Printed Books at the British Museum. In the autumn of 1845 Grenville changed his will and donated to the nation the fruits of his sinecure. The 20,240 volumes – said to have cost more than £50,000 – thus went to Bloomsbury instead of Stowe, where they almost certainly would have been scattered in the sale of 1849.

William Beckford, 'England's wealthiest son', who in 1770 inherited property worth about £100,000 a year, bought his first collectors' books in Paris around 1785 and was still ordering books from his death-bed in 1844. He openly scorned collections built along the lines of the *Bibliotheca Spenceriana*, and cared neither for *editio princeps* of classical authors, nor for early black letter texts printed by Caxton, de Worde and Pynson. His taste was much closer to what was recognized as a French aesthetic: fine printing on special paper, lavish illustrations (preferably in variant states) and fine bindings (especially those with interesting provenances). In the course of his collecting, he acquired bindings from the libraries of Grolier, Maioli and De Thou, as well as many books with French and Italian royal and noble coats of arms. Beckford was also a reader and annotator of books, with a habit of pencilling notes on the fly-leaves of his books, providing critical commentary and pointing out passages of pomposity and ignorance, all of which make volumes from his library easily recognizable. He had a particular fondness for rare voyages and travels and the history and literature of Britain, France, Italy and Spain.[49] His most noteworthy acquisition was the library of Edward Gibbon, which he found in Lausanne in 1787 and attempted to read in a marathon session lasting several days.

In 1822, Beckford's extravagance and a decline in the income from his Jamaica estates forced him to sell Fonthill, his fantastic villa in Wiltshire. An auction was held in 1823 and most of Fonthill's contents and books were sold,

47 See Rogers, chap. 43, below.
48 For Sir Anthony Panizzi, see *ODNB* and Miller 1967.
49 See Rogers, chap. 43, below.

but the most valuable books were removed to his house in Bath. Throughout his later years, Beckford continued to add to his collection, as evidenced by his letters to the bookseller George Clarke for the years 1830 to 1834, which provide a charming glimpse of his book pursuits.[50] As one would perhaps expect, he is imperious and demanding, but also very amusing – he refers to the Revd T.F. as 'P.' Dibdin, the 'P' standing for 'Puppy'. At his death, the collection was inherited by his daughter and her husband, the 10th Duke of Hamilton.[51] Thus, the real Beckford 'sale' was not held until 1882–3, when four sales reached a total of £73,551 18*s*.[52]

With the first part of the Heber sale, held by Sotheby's on 10 April 1834, the golden age of book collecting came to an end. Whereas the Duke of Roxburghe had turned a £5,000 investment into a £20,000 windfall for his heirs, Heber's expenditure of more than £100,000 was only half recouped. Richard Heber (1773–1833),[53] who once declared that 'no gentleman can be without three copies of a book, one for show, one for use, and one for borrowers', had accumulated more than 200,000 books over a lifetime of collecting. Stored in eight houses in London, Oxford, Ghent and Paris, the collection covered virtually every field in a great variety of languages. Astonishingly, Heber seems to have perused a great many of the books he purchased, as testified by his handwritten notes on many of the fly-leaves. According to Dibdin, he began collecting at the age of eight and was represented, if not personally present, at almost every sale until the time of his death. His reputation as a scholar and generous lender of books drew friends such as Richard Porson, C.M. Cracherode, Robert Southey, Charles Burney the younger and Sir Walter Scott, all notable collectors in their own right. In *Marmion* (1805), Scott pays tribute to Heber's collection: 'Thy volumes, open as the heart, / Delight, amusement, science, art.' Dibdin published the first edition of his poem *The bibliomania; or, book madness* in 1809 and addressed it to 'Richard Heber, Esq.' In 1832 he again took up his pen, under the pseudonym 'Mercurius Rusticus', to publish *Bibliophobia: remarks on the present languid and depressed state of literature and the book trade*, addressed to 'the Author of the *Bibliomania*'. The low mood Dibdin reveals in *Bibliophobia* stemmed primarily from an Evans sale in August 1831, in which manuscripts of Scott's novels fetched rather low prices – individual sales ranged from £12 10*s*. to £50 6*s*., while the total for

50 Beckford 2000.
51 For Alexander Hamilton Douglas, 10th Duke of Hamilton, see *ODNB*.
52 Sotheby, Wilkinson and Hodge, *The Hamilton Palace libraries. Catalogue of… the Beckford library*, four parts: 20 June 1882; 11 Dec. 1882; 2 July 1883; 27 Nov. 1883.
53 For Richard Heber, see *ODNB* and Hunt 2001.

thirteen works was only £321 11*s*. Dibdin's gloomy prognostication about the state of the trade would be fully realized by Heber's executors from 1834 to 1837: with many Dibdinians either dead or retired, there were just too many books for the market to absorb.

Between 1695 and 1835, the collecting of antiquarian books and manuscripts moved from the country estate to the scholar's study – then returned from the study to the country estate or elegant town house. In the earlier period, many of the collections ended up in institutions; in the middle and later periods, many, but not all, went back to the auction rooms or booksellers' shops. The customs and fashions surrounding the antiquarian book trade ebbed and flowed, as they would for decades to follow.

39
The Stationers' Company and the almanack trade

ROBIN MYERS

'An Almanack-Maker', wrote Richard Brathwaite, 'is an annual author, no lesse constant in his method than matter.'[1] Designed as items to be replaced yearly, almanacks sold in huge numbers. Indeed, they had a nearly universal appeal, for while some almanacks had partisan political or religious affiliations, the vast majority did not. Moreover, since they were cheap to produce, it was possible to price them to suit almost everyone's purse. The better almanacks, in effect yearbooks, provided useful information for professional men, merchants and the gentry, while the poorer classes and semi-literate could enjoy the crude woodcuts and learn the jingles.

The English Stock and its government

The original letters patent setting up the English Stock in 1603 granted the Stationers' Company perpetual copyright in 'all manner of Almanacks and Prognostications in the English tongue' which it 'shall and may at all times and from time to time *for ever* print or cause to be printed' (my italics).[2] This, the Company believed, established its exclusive right to print and publish almanacks in perpetuity.

The English Stock was funded by shareholding members of the Stationers' Company and run by a stock board. Appointed by the Stationers' Court, the stock board met fortnightly or monthly[3] and consisted of the Master and Wardens, a paid Treasurer or Warehouse Keeper, the Clerk in attendance, and six Stock Keepers (two for each class of share: Court assistant, Livery and

I am grateful to Matthew Groom for much help in gathering material for this chapter. Items cited from the Stationers' Company Archive are indicated by the prefix 'St.Co.'

1 Briathwaite 1631.

2 The English Stock was set up as an independent publishing company 'for the benefit of the poore' as well as the profit of its shareholders. The Letters Patent of 29 Oct. 1603 were read out to the Company in the hall in Dec. 1603 and recorded in St.Co. Court Book B 485b. See also Blagden 1955, 1957.

3 Only one minute book, for 1755–66, survives before the long sequence from 1869 to 1972.

Yeomanry). While the Stock held a monopoly on a number of works, it was almanack sales that ensured its continuing prosperity. As Blagden notes, sales of almanacks allowed the Stock to earn the equivalent of its capital in just eight years, helping to maintain the numbers of those joining the Livery in the eighteenth century when the Liveries of other Companies were in decline.[4]

Circulation figures, numbers of titles

Even during the disastrous 1690s, which saw the debasement of the coinage and a record number of book-trade bankruptcies, almanack sales remained brisk.[5] Individual titles might come and go, but the number of titles published by the Company stayed constant: twenty-six in 1692, twenty-one in 1693 and twenty-five in 1695. As late as 1830, the Company was still publishing about twenty-five almanacks a year.[6]

Almanack print runs also remained remarkably steady. Blagden estimates annual printing numbers of 350,000 to 400,000 throughout the seventeenth century,[7] and by the time the 1830 Statement for Almanacks went to press, that number had only risen to 452,450 almanacks.[8] Run lengths, however, varied greatly from one title to another. In 1830, *Old Moore* was the front runner at 270,000 while the once popular *Partridge* had fallen to a mere 2,000, although it was not discontinued until 1871. Only two of the county sheets sold substantially fewer: Shrewsbury with 500 and the calendars with 250. The facetious *Poor Robin* saw a similar change in fortunes; in 1759 it sold 11,000 copies, comparing well with *Rider*'s 16,000 copies, but by 1829 it was discontinued altogether.

Printing, binding and paper

These mass-produced almanacks were, generally, badly printed on poor paper, making many of them practically unreadable. This was particularly so with the book almanacks or 'sorts', although the sheet almanacks – most of which were printed at Cambridge for many years – usually demonstrate better printing quality on higher-grade paper in keeping with their being displayed on walls. Quality, or even legibility, does not seem ordinarily to have concerned the

4 Blagden 1960a. Cf. Turner, chap. 14, above.

5 Treadwell 2003.

6 The number of titles appears in broadside advertisements for the years 1692 and 1794, reproduced in Blagden 1960a, figs. vi, xi.

7 Blagden 1957.

8 An annual Statement of Almanacks was kept from 1789. It is almost impossible to work out details of number of almanacks issued and print runs before that, the sole extant account book being the St.Co. Journal Book for Moneys Disbursed (1650–98).

Stock Keepers until 1711, when a price rise needed to be justified to prevent a drop in sales. In that year, their decision to increase the selling price in anticipation of a new stamp duty occasioned a Court order mandating that almanacks be printed with unworn type on higher-grade paper.[9] We do not know what prompted a 1752 report on various stock books and almanacks in which the Stock Keepers recommended improving the print quality of the Wing and Cambridge sheets and some of the 'sorts'.[10] However, a comparison of the 1752 almanacks with those of following years does show that the order was put into effect; there is an immediate and striking improvement in the presswork as well as the weight and colour of paper used.

Almanacks were generally sold unbound to be carried in pockets and constantly consulted; thus used, they rarely survive. Survival rates are much higher for the small number of almanacks interleaved to serve as pocket diaries and for the almanacks that were put aside to be bound up in sets and sold for gentlemen's libraries, often bound like royal bindings using tooled crowns, or else in plain calf. Greater care was also taken with gift almanacks, particularly the miniature Raven's sheets, frequently stitched and bound in either gold-tooled calf or painted silk in matching slip cases, making neat gifts in bespoke binding.

Shared printing

Book almanacks were by convention limited to three or, on occasion, five sheets, a practice that allowed even working and was convenient for shared printing. While one printer set section *A*, printed in red and black ink, sections *B* and *C*, printed in black only, could be set and printed by one or two other presses.[11] Shared printing accorded with the terms of the original patent of 1603, which stipulated that work should be distributed among many printers in order to help those in want of work. By 1671 the Court had ordered 'the Stock-Worke to be equally distributed among the Legal printers'.[12] Shared printing not only provided a fairer division of labour; it also increased production speed and reduced piracy. Almanack work was often a fierce race to get the Company's wares on to the market before the numerous pirates, waiting in the wings to reprint and undercut, arrived there first. Exacerbating this was the

9 St.Co. Court Book G, 191b, 4 June 1711.

10 St.Co. Court Book L, 27, 2 June 1752.

11 Printer A might be named on the title page, and C might sometimes appear in the colophon, while B might not be identified at all.

12 St.Co. Court Book D, 187a, 3 Aug. 1671.

fact that a single section was not saleable by itself, even in the rare event that it ended at a natural break in the text. To check infringement, the Company kept strict control over the amount of paper given out to their printers and maintained a watchful eye on the numbers of copies printed. They insisted that all waste sheets be returned to the Stock Keepers and that printers be compensated for the loss of over-runs, which were their traditional perquisites.

With time, the Company's ideal of equitably shared printing was diluted as more and more almanack work went to printers on the Court or those with influence in the Company. Smaller printers could not compete with the larger printing houses, which expanded greatly in the second half of the eighteenth century. Whereas more modest printers often faced constraints on the amount of work they could accept, printers such as the Strahans, Nichols and Son, and the Hansards welcomed work that filled down time when their presses would otherwise be idle. With a larger workforce, greater expertise and better equipment, the larger printing houses were simply more efficient. Moreover, they were considered more trustworthy and, thus, unlikely to pirate the company's almanacks.

The almanack-makers

In the political turmoil of the seventeenth century, almanack-makers often used astrology as a political or religious weapon, in the process achieving a cult of personality. John Booker (1602–67), Henry Coley (1633–1707), Nicholas Culpepper (1616–54) and William Lilly (1602–81) were among the best known; however, John Gadbury (1624–1704) and his chief rival, John Partridge (1644–1715), were household names and, thus, able to command much higher fees than their less colourful fellow almanack-makers. In 1695, the Company, never willingly overpaying its authors, was persuaded to pay Partridge £38 5*s.* for his *Merlinus liberatus* and Gadbury £31 10*s.* for his *Ephemerides of the coelestial motions*. In contrast, the author of the *Protestant almanack* earned a mere £2 and Dr Salmon received only £3 6*s.* 6*d.* for his steadily selling almanack. Partridge achieved unwanted publicity, however, when he and his audacious astrological readings became the butt of jokes in Swift's witty *Predictions for the year 1708* and *An elegy on Mr Partridge, the almanack-maker who died on the 29th of this instant, March 1708*. Partridge, who lived until 1715, was rather unappreciative of Swift's humour and grew still more distressed when Swift continued the cruel joke with *A vindication of Isaac Bickerstaff Esq. against what is objected to him by Mr Partridge* (1709) and *A famous prediction of Merlin, the British wizard* (1709).

Perhaps the most famous almanack-maker of the time was Dr Francis Moore (1657–1714), who outlasted the competition with his *Vox stellarum* (later *Old Moore*), an almanack renowned, or perhaps notorious, for its horoscopes and prophecies. The notoriety of the work continued even following Moore's death. As Richard Brathwaite wrote about the almanack-makers, 'If famous, he seldom dies for some inferior artist will assume to himself his name. But if he die, another phoenix-like, will be forthwith raked out of his ashes.'[13] As in the case of Dr Moore, the Company at times employed various professional mathematicians, surveyors, physicians and astronomers to update the old favourites after their original authors' deaths. However, this was ill-paid hack work, for which the compilers frequently recycled material – whether or not it was still appropriate. Similarly, the unvarying typography of the title page, assumed as a trade mark, was all too often a slipshod attempt to avoid the extra expense of re-setting. The results of such shortcuts could be absurd. Capp instances the sub-title of later editions of *Partridge*, which continued to celebrate, in 1828, the Glorious Revolution of 1688 and the 'deliverance of King William from Popery and Arbitrary Government ... from the Horrid, Popish, Jacobite Plot'.[14]

Many of these compilers promoted their own interests through the almanacks. For instance, Charles Leadbetter (*fl.* 1715–44), mathematician and gauger to the Royal Excise, used his editions of *Partridge* to advertise his professional expertise. His successor, Thomas Wright (1716–97), announced at the end of his 1768 *Partridge* that he surveyed, valued and sold timber, delineated maps, and surveyed lands. Both men also compiled almanacks for the Company in their own names.[15] In contrast, Henry Andrews (1743–1820), a mathematician and Royston schoolmaster, was no run-of-the-mill hack. A compiler of the *Nautical almanack* for the Board of Longitude for forty years and a long-term Company reader, Andrews brought astronomical expertise to the almanacks he compiled.

Over the course of the eighteenth century, astrology's prominence diminished as publishers gave more room to educational features and practical information. When astrology made a comeback in the turbulent and revolutionary 1780s and 1790s, it was not the Company but rather the radical press that published inflammatory predictions. As Michael Harris notes, having lost the monopoly on almanack printing, the Company no longer had 'the power to control' the content of such works. In an earlier age, he reminds us, the

13 Brathwaite 1631.
14 Capp 1979.
15 Capp 1979, 239.

Company would have denounced such printers within the pages of its own almanacks; now the Company responded to the revolutionary threat by offering loyal support to the government and the monarchy in a 1793 roll of association that included the signatures of the 250 members of the Livery.[16]

The effect of legislation on the Company's almanack trade

Surprisingly, the lapse of the Printing Acts in 1695 barely caused a ripple in the printing of almanacks. Theoretically, the Act had afforded the Company protection against piracy of its patents. Yet, as Michael Treadwell has shown: 'When the Act finally lapsed on 3 May 1695 leading members of the trade were not particularly disturbed. Forewarned as they had been by the earlier lapses of 1679–85, they had already made those adjustments they considered prudent to protect their businesses in the changed conditions which seemed to be coming ... and when it lapsed they seem, for the most part, to have gone about their business.'[17] Similarly, the Act for the Encouragement of Learning (1710), the first Copyright Act, had little immediate impact; it did, however, pave the way for the ultimately successful attack on the Company's 1603 grant.

The Stamp Act of 1711/12 was another matter.[18] It issued a levy 'upon all Books and Papers commonly called Pamphlets, and for and upon all News Papers ... printed in Great Britain', along with a disparate assortment of commodities and services, including soap, hackney carriages, fabrics and marriage licences. Partly a revenue-producing levy, partly a censorship measure, the Stamp Act would ultimately be dubbed a tax on knowledge; however, it was the resulting increase in costs that most immediately concerned the book trade, leading to feverish activity in the months leading up to the bill's passage. The Company had advance warning of 'the Resolution ... for laying a penny upon every sheet Almanack and two pence on every other Almanack' and, on 14 May 1711, the Master called a special Court 'to consider what it was most proper to do to prevent the said Duties being laid'.[19] On 14 June it reconvened to 'consider the manner and number of Almanacks to be printed this year'. On the advice of the Stock Keepers, the Company decided to halve the print run and ordered that: 'all the Red Letters shall be left out in the printing of all

16 Harris 1980. The Roll of Association is in the Company's muniment room.
17 Treadwell 2003.
18 Its actual title was *An act for laying several duties upon all sope and paper* ... It was introduced in Parliament in 1711 and became law on 1 Aug. 1712.
19 St.Co. Court Book G, 191a, 14 May 1711.

Almanacks both Sheet and Stitcht for the future and only Black Letters to be printed in their stead'.[20] In July and August of the same year, just before the bill became law, the Master and Wardens tried to negotiate a deal with the Commissioner of the Stamp Office, who initially rebuffed them: 'what was desired did not lye before them but before the Lord Treasurer'.[21] By September, however, the Master was able to report that he had 'with some difficulty prevailed upon the Commissioners ... to take a bond' of £3,000 for three months' worth of stamps.[22] The deal would be signed under the common seal of the Company in open Court in December. The Company had no choice but to accept what it could not prevent. In August 1712, the measure regarding coloured ink was rescinded, and black and red printing was restored. To accommodate the new tax, the Company raised the selling price of its almanacks, passing the burden to consumers, who paid 'a penny upon sheet almanacks ... added to the usual price besides the stamps'.[23]

The war against counterfeit and 'sham' almanacks

Infringing on the Company's almanack monopoly was a well-established practice. As Blagden notes, 'When 20,000 copies of a book are being distributed within a few weeks, it cannot have been difficult for a pirate, with the connivance of a wholesaler, to feed another 5,000 to the market.'[24] To combat this, publishers altered their printing schedule and worked to produce almanacks as early as feasibly possible. After all, if a counterfeit reached the market before the Company's almanack was out, the Company would be left with thousands of pounds of dead stock. Much of the information in almanacks was not time-sensitive material that would be affected by an earlier print date. Calendars, advertisements for false teeth and patent medicines, tables of kings and queens, and meteorological charts based on solar and lunar motion could all be prepared ahead of time with little risk. However, the physicians, mariners and farmers who routinely used these features in their daily lives also relied on forecasting. When forced to speculate too far into the future, the almanack-maker could be badly mistaken, with ludicrous results. Bernard Capp cites Gadbury's almanack for 1689: 'Written in the middle of the previous year, he informed the reader that 1688 had brought none of the expected

20 St.Co. Court Book G, 191b, 15 June 1711.
21 St.Co. Court Book G, 192b, 10 July 1711.
22 St.Co. Court Book G, 193b, 10 Sep. 1711.
23 St.Co. Court Book G, 193b, 13 Aug. 1711.
24 Blagden 1958, 111.

upheavals, and that the birth of the Prince of Wales was a guarantee of future security. By the time it appeared, the regime ... had been swept away, and Gadbury conceded in his edition for 1690 that "my muse hath of late been planet-struck, and I must waive prediction for a season".'[25]

Taking action against infringers

By the 1650s, the Company was attempting to stem the tide of piracy by buying counterfeit almanacks, and taking legal action against offending printers.[26] Transgressors who belonged to the Company, many of whom printed for the English Stock, were summoned to appear before the Court. Their Stock shares were confiscated and, in the worst cases, their presses were broken up and their type melted down; yet, they seem never to have been expelled from the Company. Non-members were prosecuted through the law courts.

Robert Stephens, the Company's dreaded messenger of the press, hunted for pirates. In October 1696 he obtained a search warrant,

> having had information that there was a private press in the house of one Roger Bradley, a frame-maker in Distaff Lane ... [He went] with a Constable and some Assistants and found it at work on a Sheet Almanack for the year 1697... They had printed 20 Reams of the red, and were beginning to draw for the black as he came ... [The Court ordered] that all the persons who shall be so found to be concerned in that printing presse be made Parties to the Bill in Chancery and the Sollicitor is ordered to take care in it and to take out sub poenas and serve them accordingly.[27]

For this, Stephens was paid 6*d*.[28]

With the spread of provincial printing after 1695, it became even easier for pirates to reprint and sell a small impression of the more popular almanacks before effective action could be taken against them.[29] On 22 June 1697 a complaint was made to the Court

> that a printer dwelling in Chester ... had printed severall of the Company's Almanacks of this yeare without Lycence of the Company and severall of them being produced in Court ordered that the said [printer] be forthwith proceeded against at Law for his soo doing and that the Master and Wardens

25 Capp 1979, 41.
26 St.Co. Journal Book for moneys disbursed 1650–98, the first detailed record of Stock expenditure.
27 St.Co. Court Book F, 251a–b, 17 Oct. 1696.
28 St.Co. Journal Book 183a.
29 Blagden 1960a, 235.

> and such other members of this Court as they shall think fitt do advise with and see Counsel in order to seek such Prosecution.[30]

Cheaply printed almanacks were also frequently imported from overseas. In 1708 the Company brought a bill in Chancery against the Chester carrier for importing 'severall quantityes of Almanacks from Ireland'.[31]

The Stationers' Company was particularly fierce in its prosecution of pirates during the 1770s. Remarkably, the printers of Welsh almanacks were spared such treatment since they were not seen as competition for the Company's trade; Wales itself was almost inaccessible and the readers of Welsh almanacks were generally non-English-speakers. Printing a foreign-language almanack within their jurisdiction was another matter entirely, however. In 1771, the Court 'received undoubted information' that the maverick William Gilbert II had printed a Hebrew almanack 'and on the opposite side of the page the same translated into English'.[32] The Master and Wardens drafted a letter, to be delivered to Mrs Gilbert, accusing Gilbert of 'a high infringement of the Company's right of publishing Almanacks only as an invasion of the Company of Stationers' property which you must answer at your peril'.[33] In the draft, 'Greek' is crossed out and replaced by 'Hebrew', suggesting perhaps that the Master or the Stock Keepers were not even able to identify the language of a text that surely posed little threat to the monopoly.

In another attempt to protect their assets from the infringement of pirates, the Stationers' Company marked their territory. The Company advertised its almanacks in some thirty-five provincial papers from Edinburgh to Exeter, and a handful of London papers. These advertisements, like the printed handbills distributed for display in bookshops, frequently carried a warning against counterfeits inserted by the Warehouse Keeper, George Hawkins:

> All the Almanacks printed for the Company of STATIONERS are to be known by the following Words being printed on the Title-Page, or at the Bottom of the Five Sheets of an almanack: Printed for the COMPANY OF STATIONERS, and sold by George Hawkins, at their Hall, in Ludgate Street.[34]

30 St.Co. Court Book F, 263a , 22 June 1697.

31 St.Co. Court Book G, 186b, 5 Feb. 1710.

32 Gilbert, freed by patrimony in 1771, printed in the name of his wife Ann in Creechurch Lane, Leadenhall Street, from 1767.

33 This letter, 10 Apr. 1771, from the Master, Paul Vaillant, and the Wardens, Thomas Gammuth and Joshua Jenour, 'Delivered to the above of which is the copy to Mrs Gilbert' is a rough draft in unidentified hand, Series I, Box B 2, vii.

34 St.Co. Series I, Box C 2.

The Stamp Act: an offensive weapon

The Company could afford to invest several thousand pounds in the bulk purchase of stamped paper, but most of its competitors could not; they would either be forced out of business altogether or driven into a risky illegal trade in unstamped almanacks. Although the Company was concerned to keep its prices down, it found that readers who bought such quality titles as *The ladies' almanack*, *Rider*, *White*, *Goldsmith* and the various county sheet almanacks would not balk at an extra 2*d*., 4*d*. or even 1*s*. 3*d*. The ever-popular *Old Moore* and *Poor Robin* continued to sell to all and sundry.

The duty had been doubled in 1742, 1757 and 1781, by which time the Company had seen its potential as a weapon against the pirates and had begun urging the government for additional increases.[35] The Act of 1757 empowered the arrest of hawkers of unstamped almanacks and, at a Court of 5 July 1757, the Master announced his hope that 'this law would effectually put a stop to the piracy of almanacks ... he [further] informed the Court [in tones of triumph] ... that the Clerk had been instrumental in procuring the clause to be inserted in the Bill'. The Clerk was rewarded with 'a gratuity of 20 guineas for his pains and trouble on this occasion'.[36] The new Act was made effective by the offer of 20*s*. (£1) for information leading to a conviction, to which the Company added a further assurance of 20*s*.

Between 1757 and 1775, one woman and seventeen men were recruited by the promise of a 40*s*. payment to act as informers. Collectively, these eighteen informers caught thirty-nine widows or labourers as they peddled their wares about the streets; convictions were subsequently secured in all cases but one.[37] Whereas earlier press managers like Robert Stephens had concentrated on identifying printers at work on illicit almanacks, these later informers generally focused on those operating at the point of sale. Isaac Brown was typical: he bought an almanack for a ha'penny (the Stationers' price being 6*d*. or more) from James Clarke of Berwick-on-Tweed and carried him before the magistrate, John Burn, on 8 February 1766. In 1757 and 1758, a number of individuals were caught hawking unstamped almanacks: ten mercury women in London and Middlesex, three women in Kent, and eight women and twelve men in Derby, Manchester, Preston, Penrith, Newcastle, Stockport and

35 The Act specified that 'For every Almanack or Calendar for One Particular Year, or for any Time less than one Year. Printed on One Side only of any One Sheet or Piece of Paper, over and above the Duty charged thereon by an Act made in the Ninth Year of the Reign of Her Majesty Queen Anne, an additional Duty of One Penny.'

36 St.Co. Court Book L, 278, 5 July 1757.

37 St.Co. Series I, Box B 5.

Chester. The depositions in the Stationers' archive give little more than the culprit's name and status. The women, such as Mary Gray of Preston, are generally identified as widows, while the men are vaguely designated by their occupation or nationality: Robert Lingard of Preston is listed as 'labourer', John Gordon of Penrith as 'Scotchman' and Andrew McCoullogh of Penrith as 'Irishman'. Only one of the thirty-nine pirates was caught reoffending: George Abercrombie (or Abercromby), convicted in 1763 and 1768, belonged to a notorious family of illegal book dealers which included Margaret Abercrombie, convicted in 1759, and Anne Abercrombie, convicted in 1767.

Thomas Carnan and the end of perpetual copyright

The Company continued to pounce on the sellers of unstamped almanacks, but, even by 1750, several formidable individuals had begun to infringe upon and challenge the principle of perpetual copyright.[38] Initially, however, the Company failed to perceive the challenge posed by respectable and established booksellers. In 1748 Robert Dodsley published *The new memorandum book*, and in 1749 *The ladies complete pocket book*. The same year, Richard Baldwin, a Liveryman, entered *The gentleman's and tradesman's daily journal for 1750* in the Stationers' Register.[39] In their attempt to evade the Company's monopoly, both men produced the memorandum books interleaved with blank pages to serve as diaries.

Dodsley and Baldwin revealed the direction of things to come. Nonetheless, the Company ignored such infringement until 1770 when Thomas Carnan and Francis Newberry entered *The ladies complete pocket book* in the Stationers' Register.[40] A rogue bookseller who had been refused entry to the Company in 1755, Carnan subsequently took out an injunction against the Company on the grounds that James I had no power to grant a perpetual monopoly in almanacks. The Company took notice immediately, and on the advice of Dr A.C. Ducarel of Doctors' Commons, it issued a warning in the press against 'publications which were almanacks in all but name'. The Court also pressed Carnan to accept an agreement like the 'covenant of forbearance' that the Company had established with the universities. In exchange for an annual payment of £200, Oxford and Cambridge had long ago agreed to refrain from infringing the Company's almanack patent; the Court hoped Carnon

38 This section is derived almost wholly from Blagden 1960b, and on evidence in the Stationers' Company Archive.

39 Blagden 1960b, 26.

40 St.Co. Entries of copies 1746–73, 341, 16 Nov. 1770.

would withdraw his injunction and agree to a similar arrangement. However, times had changed and, in the climate of the 1770s, the Court's strategy failed decisively. In large part, the Court's failure stemmed from its inept handling of an opponent whose motives had more to do with revenge than monetary gain. Playing directly into Carnan's hands, the Company sent the Master's son, William Strahan Jr., to make an offer. Subsequently, it was alleged that Strahan 'offered Mr Carnan £10,000 if he would relinquish his suit with the Stationers' Company and that he rose in his offers from smaller sums to £10,000 and concluded with an offer of £10,000 per annum for [the rest of] Mr Carnan's life'[41] – all with the blessing of the Court. Not a man to keep quiet, Carnan took delight in advertising the interview in all the newspapers. While the Court pretended that the offer was made in jest, its minutes reveal a conscious awareness that Carnan had made fools of them by his revelation of 'Proposals made by the Worshipful Company for an ignominious Compromise'. Their only recourse was to 'declare that this Assertion is totally Groundless'.[42]

The dispute remained unresolved in 1773 and, on 13 November of that year, Carnan published Reuben Burrows's *Diary for the year of Our Lord 1774*. Ultimately, the legal delays proved advantageous to Carnan, for, while he waited for his counsel to act, the High Court gave its decision in the long-standing case of Thomas Becket versus Alexander Donaldson.[43] Becket had claimed that Donaldson's Scottish edition of Thomson's *The seasons* infringed his copyright in the work, first published 1726–30, but the Lord Chancellor found for Donaldson. Therefore, the judges in the Company's case were unable to support similar claims against Carnan. On 29 May 1775 they gave their opinion that the Company's right to almanack publication could not be exclusive. Carnan had won.

The Company sought additional means to regain exclusive copyright, but their efforts were ineffectual; the Court minutes for 17 and 25 November 1775 make it clear that they had no further defence. Although they salvaged what they could, entering seventeen almanack titles in the register, Carnan had effectively ruined their trade. Over the next seven years, the Company's almanack sales dropped precipitously, even as they made a determined effort to improve the standard of both content and appearance. Cambridge and Oxford felt the loss too, as their annual payments from the Company ceased. Carnan's triumph, however, was short-lived. He died suddenly, and three

41 St.Co. Waste Book, 7 Apr. 1772 to 22 Dec. 1780, 108b, 7 Nov. 1775.
42 St.Co. Court Book M, 488–9, 7 Nov. 1775.
43 See Rose, chap. 4 above.

weeks later, on 29 July 1788, the Company acquired his copyrights from his heirs for £1,500. The upturn was immediate, as total almanack sales rose by 150,000 the following year, resulting in a profit of £10,000. In Blagden's words, 'Carnan was defeated ... by his own mortality – a weakness to which his opponent was not susceptible.'[44]

Conclusion

By the early years of the nineteenth century, the almanack trade had opened up to an even greater flood of small printers who cashed in on the lucrative market that had long been the monopoly of the Stationers' Company. Cheap imitations of *Moore* selling at 1*d.* seriously undercut the Company's original *Vox stellarum* by Dr Francis Moore, priced at 6*d.* In 1834, when the Stationers pressed for a further increase in stamp duty, Parliament 'decided that the privilege was outmoded and had been ill-requited and abolished the tax altogether'.[45] At the same time the Company was attacked for failing in its moral duty by pandering to the superstitious and sensation-loving lower orders rather than publishing educational and improving works. Subsequent attempts to recuperate the Company's image through a takeover of the respectable *British almanack* would end in failure.[46] In 1927 the Company sold most of what remained of the patent to Charles Letts, and in 1961 the English Stock disbanded.[47] *Old Moore* is still published, but is now owned by the Foulsham Press.

44 Blagden 1960a, 241.
45 Capp 1979, 268.
46 The original publishers were the Society for the Diffusion of Useful Knowledge.
47 Bowden 2001.

40

Children's books and school-books

ANDREA IMMEL

Of all the new markets for print that emerged between 1695 and 1833, the one for young readers was arguably among the most important to Great Britain's polite, commercial society. Recent scholarship on such topics as the constructs of the family, motherhood and childhood, the rise of consumerism, the expansion of educational provision, theories of the mind, cognition, developmental psychology and the emergence of child-centred pedagogies during the early modern era suggests that the expanding market for children's books was shaped by a complex nexus of familial aspirations, commercial interests, social programmes and intellectual rationales. Although an ambitious synthesis is beyond its scope, this chapter will show that during this period the proliferation of printed materials for children cannot be understood without analysing their production and reception.

In order to map the growing market's contours, the term 'children's book' is used here to mean all genres in the vernacular produced for youngsters. This sense contrasts with F.J. Harvey Darton's use of the term as a synonym for children's literature in his standard history.[1] His thesis, which viewed the genre's rise as a battle between instruction and amusement in which the latter ultimately triumphed, maintained a sharp distinction between literary and educational texts that seems less helpful here. Instead, an acknowledgement that the line between fiction and non-fiction was relatively fluid between 1695 and 1833 makes it possible to describe the growing market as a reflection of contemporary concerns rather than of our own. It is important to keep in mind that few people then envisioned such a radical change as the evolution of a separate literature for children, nor would they have thought it necessary or desirable.

1695–1739

Would boys have learned more Latin if they had not associated construing classical texts with the schoolmaster's rod? When Locke addressed this

1 Darton 1999, 1.

problem in *Some thoughts concerning education*, he argued for replacing traditional methods of teaching Latin with more enlightened ones evolved through trial and error. In doing so, he offered a rationale equally applicable to instruction in the vernacular. Learning to spell could be as agreeable as acquiring the physical skills to play a game, he suggested. He had observed parents who customized materials on the market such as dice, playing cards or lottery sheets for spelling lessons so that their children would not learn by rote memorization, reinforced by the fear of corporal punishment. Similarly, fluency in classical languages might be achieved in significantly less time, if they were taught like modern languages through conversation instead of grammatical rules. Locke himself edited an illustrated interlinear Aesop (A. and J. Churchill, 1703) based on Charles Hoole's bilingual version,[2] which may represent that 'easy pleasant Book' envisioned in *Some thoughts*, 'wherein the entertainment, that he finds might draw him on, and reward his Pains in Reading, and yet not such as should fill his Head with useless trumpery, or lay the principles of Vice and Folly'.[3] Locke's Aesop was also consistent with his larger purpose to devote more attention to subjects such as arithmetic, geometry, geography and history by reducing the time spent drilling Latin accidence. Even though most of the books Locke recommended were in Latin, his desire to reform the curriculum so that boys would be better prepared to assume adult responsibilities in the public sphere must have spoken eloquently to middle-class parents, whose sons were more likely to be educated in English.

Locke's legacy to this little-understood stage in the market's expansion was probably this pragmatic approach to developing better pedagogy and instructional materials. His greatest popularizer, Isaac Watts, subscribed to a similarly utilitarian view. Watts's rigorous self-imposed criteria when composing devotional verse for children reflected a serious desire that what he produced should be useful to a wide audience. In his *Divine songs* (1715), Watts restricted himself to metres that could be sung to the best-known psalm tunes to facilitate memorization, making the poems more versatile from the standpoint of a teacher or parent, who could assign them in class or incorporate them into family worship. (His preface implies that he went so far as to have a teacher he knew try out the songs on pupils.) Watts also scrupulously avoided anything that smacked of party, so that all children could participate in their recitation or singing, regardless of class or denomination. Presumably he succeeded, because the *Divine songs* remained a cornerstone of the children's literature canon well into the nineteenth century.

2 Horwitz and Finn 1975.
3 Locke 1968, 259.

Because so many critics have presumed that Locke articulated an embryonic concept of modern children's literature, few have questioned the assumption that the market did not respond to his ideas until the 1740s when John Newbery began publishing original literary works for young readers. It has also been taken for granted that there was little fiction available for children throughout the period except for chapbooks, based on allusions to them in Steele's *Tatler* no. 95 (15–17 November 1709), vol. vi, chapter 32 in Sterne's *Tristram Shandy*, and the poetry of John Clare.[4] In fact, the market for children's books was more diverse than that, but determining its extent is complicated by several factors. First, the formats and cheap bindings in sheep or calf make a children's book indistinguishable from a book for adults. The exceptions are school-books, which can often be recognized by a blind-tooled scalloped line parallel to the spine or later by canvas-covered boards.[5] Second, if long-winded title pages are not transcribed completely, the phrase describing the work as intended for young people may be omitted – information also frequently dropped in advertisements. Third, because there were no children's booksellers per se at this time, the presence of a particular name in the imprint is not necessarily a clue as to the text's intended audience. Many well-known members of the trade – among them James Hodges, Daniel Midwinter, Richard Hett, Charles Hitch, Thomas Norris, Arthur Bettesworth, J. Pemberton, Richard Francklin, J. Hawkins and Richard Ware – formed congers that collectively owned and marketed publications for children including school-books and the old chivalric romances. Fourth, when children's books began to be listed in the monthly catalogues of new publications in periodicals like the *London Magazine* during the 1730s, they were scattered throughout by subject, not grouped in a separate section.

Also easy to overlook are those eighteenth-century genres for youngsters that have no modern counterparts. Many of these works, including two of the century's mostly highly regarded children's books, were either translated from French or originally written for the education of the nobility. For three generations, Fénelon's epic *Télémaque* (1699), a continuation of the *Odyssey*'s fourth book written for Louis XIV's grandson the duc de Bourbon, was widely recommended in the original and in translation. Similarly Gay's first book of fables (1727), invented for George II's son, William, Duke of Cumberland, was reprinted countless times, and its contents constantly plundered without acknowledgement for inclusion in juvenile poetical miscellanies. Other

4 Blamires 1996–7.
5 Bennett 2004, 91–2.

important works were generic hybrids, such as the first children's encyclopedia, the abbé Pluche's *Spectacle de la nature* (1732–50). Instead of an alphabetical sequence of essays, male and female characters of different ages and ranks reviewed the state of knowledge in the natural sciences, arts and manufactures in a series of lively dialogues. Such books were expensive because they were lavishly illustrated with excellent copperplate engravings. In the mid-1730s, the first two volumes of the Humphreys translation of the *Spectacle* cost 14*s*., the second set of Gay's *Fables*, 6 *s*., and the two different two-volume translations of *Telemachus*, 6 *s*. and 10 *s*., respectively.

By far the most important category of books produced for children between 1695 and 1740 were non-fiction works of information or secular improvement for middle-class readers. Nathaniel Crouch's late seventeenth-century abridgements introduced many young readers to important works of history, travel and divinity,[6] circulating along with the equivalent for youngsters of what Lawrence E. Klein calls 'very useful manuals', books intended to teach the information necessary to master a particular subject or skill.[7] But they were also intended to help readers acquire the gentility that was an asset in a society whose robust commercial economy brought the middle and upper classes into more frequent contact, offering increased prospects for social advancement. Klein's concept of instructional books that also instilled ethical values, formed social identity, and promoted the level of cultural literacy appropriate to the reader's station (or the station aspired to) offers a more dynamic approach to analysing the heterogeneous mass of grammars, spellers, easy readers, writing books and miscellanies.

The way in which literary and educational materials were balanced in the 'very useful manuals' depended upon the social class of the child reader.[8] A speller for charity schools like Henry Dixon's *English instructor* (1725) would devote far less space to polite literature than to the articulation of religious principles because lower-class pupils needed to be reconciled to their lot, not tempted to aspire above their stations. Robert Wharton's elementary reader *Historiae pueriles* (1738), on the other hand, consisted of retellings from Plutarch's *Lives*, biographies of great English kings and Addison's fiction from the *Spectator*. This text was supposed to give a seven- or eight-year-old middle-class boy 'a notion of the strength and purity of his own language' to lay the foundation for correct English usage, a sign of full literacy.[9] The elegant

6 Mayer 1993–4.
7 Klein 1995.
8 Mitchell 2001, 153–62.
9 Wharton 1738, A2r.

Young clerks assistant; or penmanship made easy, instructive and entertaining (*c*.1740) was intended for middle-class boys and girls, with sets of exercises carefully adapted for each sex. Peter Motteux's 'Encomium on the pen' fed boys' hopes for power and wealth by promising that they would eventually 'deal the fate of Empires in a line', while the dedication to young ladies recommended that they cultivate penmanship as assiduously as needlework, because a prospective suitor might be put off by a scribbled letter.[10] Boys practised different hands by copying out the kinds of aphorisms the *Spectator*'s Sir Andrew Freeport freely quoted, while young ladies were to perfect their round hand by writing out poems by Gay, Roscommon and Atterbury that celebrated the feminine virtues of modesty and piety and deprecated the lures of high life.

There was also a demand for books that did not exhort children to embrace this world so enthusiastically. Many late seventeenth-century sectarian religious works for children remained in print until the early nineteenth century. Among the reissues, now suitably illustrated with relief cuts, were James Janeway's *A token for children, being an exact account of the conversion, holy, and exemplary lives and joyful deaths of several young children*, John Bunyan's *Divine emblems*, and Benjamin Keach's *War with the devil; or the young mans conflict with the powers of darkness*. Little William Godwin's desire to surpass Janeway's holy children suggests the power such texts could have for those brought up in strict dissenting families. The long publishing histories of these books, as well as those of Crouch, remind us that no survey of the children's books market or history of children's reading can focus exclusively on new titles if it is to be comprehensive.

1740–1775

This survey of the children's books market in the early eighteenth century, though not definitive, does deflate the romantic notion that the appearance of John Newbery's *Pretty little pocket-book* in the early 1740s forever changed the history of children's reading. His books, with their zeal to reform manners and morals, their hearty endorsement of British commerce and their delight in contemporary popular urban culture are as characteristic of the times as Hogarth's progresses. Newbery was also the first publisher to create, and his successors to sustain, something analogous to a quality brand of children's books, to which reviewers were still referring in the late

10 *Young clerks assistant; or penmanship made easy, instructive and entertaining* (London, *c*.1740), leaf 7.

nineteenth century.[11] Whether credit for the Newbery juveniles ought to be shared with the writers in his employ – among them Giles Jones, who probably wrote *Goody Two-Shoes*, and Christopher Smart, who may have edited the *Lilliputian Magazine* – is difficult to know, because few Newbery juveniles have been definitively attributed to particular authors.[12]

Fifty years of private and institutional collecting of Georgian juveniles has confirmed the Newbery firm's pre-eminence, but the effort has established the existence of several other equally innovative competitors. Thomas Boreman now receives credit for having devised the appealing package Newbery perfected: a small volume generously illustrated, distinctively bound, and priced competitively with sermons and pamphlets at 6*d.* or less. Trading adjacent to one of London's great tourist attractions probably inspired Boreman to publish by subscription the *Gigantick histories* (1740–3), a ten-volume series of miniature guidebooks for St Paul's, Westminster Abbey, the Tower of London and the Monument. Just as the book's exterior was carefully designed to distinguish it from a volume for adults, so were its contents. His tours (if indeed the texts were Boreman's) were more informative than the guides pilloried by Ned Ward's *London spy*. Boreman also tried to ingratiate himself with readers by telling ghost stories associated with the buildings, sprinkling imaginary purchasers' names in the subscription lists, and appending a lilliputian commendatory verse supposedly penned by a young subscriber.[13] Lists of Boreman's other juvenile publications and information about discounts extended to toymen and haberdashers appeared at the end.

Engravers were also quick to perceive that children constituted a new market for prints, picture books and fully illustrated volumes more stylish than anything Newbery attempted. In the 1740s James Coles offered delightful writing sheets such as *Youth's instructions* whose borders consisted of scenes from Aesop's fables and the school room. Around the same time, George Bickham junior, better known for libellous political prints, issued some handsome books. Their contents and illustrations were usually borrowed without acknowledgement from the works of others: *The first principles of geometry explained* (*c.*1745), for example, was adapted partly from Sebastian Le Clerc's *Practique de la géometrie* (1669). Henry Roberts, who specialized in theatrical portraits, also produced little square engraved picture books, including a Ten Commandments, a rhyming alphabet of moral precepts, and retellings of pantomimes appearing on the London stage during the 1770s. Sayers and

11 Roscoe 1973.
12 Mahony and Rizzo 1984.
13 Hounslow 1998.

Bennett's catalogue for 1775 offered lottery sheets, harlequinades and board games reasonably priced between 1*d*. and 6*d*. Drawing, writing and copy books were rather more costly, starting at 1*s*. 6*d*., but comparably priced with a set of any twelve small prints, and still a bargain compared with a volume of Wenceslaus Hollar's engravings of animals at 10*s*. 6*d*. bound. Of all the engravers who entered the children's market, Edward Ryland was perhaps the most ambitious. His output during the 1760s included abridgements of the Old and New Testaments dedicated to the infant Bishop of Osnabrug (George III's brother, Frederick, Duke of York) with 'bookplates' engraved on the front pastedown endpapers; a two-volume set of London cries moralized for the use of schools or families with illustrations after Marcellus Laroon; and *The conjurer*, a verse retelling of the popular farce *The devil to pay*, with a frontispiece after Hogarth's illustration of the skimmington in Butler's *Hudibras*. All of them cost 1*s*. plain and 2*s*. coloured, except for the Bible abridgements, which were 2*s*. 6*d*. each.

It can easily be shown that between 1740 and 1775 more members of the book and picture trades than ever before began producing a wider variety of materials for children. It is harder, however, to establish the relative importance of the two branches. A good example is the engraver Homan Turpin, who ran a well-diversified business between the 1760s and 1790s that included a charming line of children's books. Turpin's output of juveniles was comparable in number to that of John Newbery, judging by the advertisement at the end of *The seven ages of man* (*c*.1775), which lists fifty-six titles mostly of the entertaining sort. How many copies would Turpin have printed? A sample of subscribers' lists from Boreman's *Gigantick histories*, John Marchant's *Puerilia* (1751), the *Lilliputian Magazine* (1751), Fenning's *New and easy guide to the use of the globes* (1760) and Daniel Bellamy's *Ethic amusements* (1768) allows us to infer a figure between 200 and 500 copies. Only fourteen titles survive, according to *ESTC*, and each in just one or two copies. The low survival rate per title is by no means unusual: an edition of a Newbery juvenile that can be located at more than three institutions is the exception, not the rule. The difference is that almost three-quarters of Turpin's children's books have perished, whereas virtually all of Newbery's exist in some form. Because of the unusually high attrition rate of Turpin's books (probably exacerbated by their smallness), his contribution to the history of children's book publishing remains unaccessed.

These new books, which were intended to make leisure reading delightful yet useful, have always overshadowed contemporary school-books, the sector where the real money was to be made. On their trade cards, the booksellers Robert Withy and John Wilkie, for example, proudly advertised their stock of school-books along with the works of Addison, Boyle, Dryden, Locke, Milton, Pope, Shakespeare, Tillotson and Watts. The bestselling author for young readers at this time may have been Daniel Fenning, a schoolmaster in Bure, Suffolk, who produced several of the eighteenth-century's most important steady-selling school-books, including *The universal spelling book* (*c*.1755) which went through nearly a hundred editions by 1800. Sarah Fielding's *The governess* (1749), the first school story and a contemporary classic, was unusual for having reached a seventh edition by 1789. Members of the trade were much more likely to pick up shares in a school-book than an entertaining non-fiction work like *The travels of Tom Thumb over England and Wales* (1746). The innovative speller, *The child's new play-thing*, first issued in 1742 by the trade publisher Thomas Cooper, was by its fourth heavily revised edition of 1748 the property of a conger consisting of Richard Ware, Charles Hitch, Charles Corbet, Robert Dodsley and Mary Cooper, Thomas Cooper's widow. The *Play-thing* reached an eighth edition – again substantially revised – in 1763, and the conger now included Clark, Benjamin Collins, Hinxman and Charles Rivington. The foundation of Newbery's juvenile back list was its school-books such as *The museum for young gentlemen and ladies* (1750) and *The circle of the sciences* (1745–8), a multi-volume introduction to arithmetic, chronology, geography, grammar, logic, poetry and rhetoric. The *Museum* and *Circle* went into edition after edition during Newbery's lifetime, then those of his successors, who eventually sold the copyrights in the 1790s to William Darton senior when he was setting up his business in children's books. It is nevertheless ironic how little we know about the books teachers assigned or how they were used in classes, even in a school as famous as the Palgrave Academy.[14]

1776–1833

The children's book market's expansion between 1740 and 1775 facilitated further specialization within the book and picture trades. At the same time, the overall standards for contents, design and production rose even higher. Mrs Barbauld's *Lessons for children* (1778) for children of two to four years of age is an example of the era's enlightened book-making at its best, where text and mise-en-page were co-ordinated with exceptional intelligence. The square pamphlet, small enough for little hands, opened flat. The type was large and the leading and margins likewise generous, taking into account the way the human eye developed. The graded reading selections, in the form of

14 McCarthy 1997.

conversations between Charles and his mother, revolved around small incidents in their daily routine, which allowed her to introduce him to the symbol-systems and conceptual structures embedded in the world around him. Few elementary readers of any century could be considered literature, but *Lessons for children* transcended its genre: the adult who read it to a child could admire the art of Barbauld's deceptively simple language, as well as her apparently effortless presentation of the complex relationships between words and things.[15]

Sophistication of concept and skilful presentation are features that distinguished late Georgian juveniles from their predecessors. And for the first time, the larger world of letters recognized that writing for children was 'one of the most important, though not the most brilliant, among the literary improvements of the present age',[16] thanks to the works of Barbauld, Lady Ellenor Fenn, Maria Edgeworth and Sarah Trimmer. Volumes of occasional essays often included critical analyses of children's books, such as Vicesimus Knox's *Winter lucubrations* 45, which discussed picture bibles, or James Pettit Andrews's 'Books', the first survey of eighteenth-century juveniles, in *Anecdotes antient & modern* (1790).[17] Although children's books had been reviewed sporadically (and usually superficially) since the 1760s, a higher percentage of new works began to receive thoughtful notices in major review journals. Many of these anonymous pieces can be attributed to distinguished men of letters like Jabez Hirons or the dissenting divine and educator William Enfield.[18] By the 1790s, however, conscientious parents needed more assistance than the reviews or lists of recommended books for children in works like Erasmus Darwin's *A plan for the conduct of female education* (1797). In order to identify the mischievous books in the flood of new juvenile publications, Mrs Trimmer launched the *Guardian of Education* (1802–5), the first review journal of its kind. After the *Guardian*'s suspension, at least one person, the anonymous compiler of the *Juvenile Review* (1817), tried to provide parents and teachers with a one-volume guide to the best current publications for children.

Now that parents and reviewers had higher expectations, the savvy booksellers likewise needed to achieve higher production values for the printing, illustrations and bindings of their children's books. By the Regency, the Dutch embossed gilded paper ubiquitous since the 1740s had begun to look old-fashioned. Small volumes were now bound in red, green or black roan with marbled paper boards, or, less frequently, in sheep or calf. John Marshall was an

15 McCarthy 1999.
16 Unsigned review, *Critical Review* 62 (1786), 152.
17 Immel 2000.
18 See Nangle 1934, 227–55.

especially adroit packager of his titles, decking out pamphlets in brightly coloured glazed or mottled paper wrappers with oval engraved titling labels. Miniature libraries of tiny volumes bound in pastel paper boards were issued in wooden boxes with sliding lids designed to resemble book cases.[19] The Harris, Darton, Tabart and Godwin firms issued pamphlets in printed wrappers on buff, blue, pink, green or yellow papers, the titles within borders of typographical ornaments, and book lists on the rear. Illustrations reproduced from copperplate engravings continued to be of relatively high quality: William Darton senior frequently employed various members of the celebrated Taylor family of author/engravers in Ongar, while William Godwin hired the young William Mulready.[20]

The artistic quality of images reproduced from relief blocks improved markedly during this period. Contrary to modern assertions that he recycled blocks from existing stock, John Newbery illustrated his juveniles with relief cuts in wood or metal depicting actual scenes in the texts. But they could not compare with the Bewicks' wood engravings. John Bewick was one of the only children's book illustrators to receive title page credit for some sets of blocks he cut for John Stockdale, Dr Trusler, Elizabeth Newbery, and George Riley of the Sliding Black Lead and Coloured Pencil Warehouse.[21] Several other anonymous craftsmen also had styles of cutting so distinctive as to be instantly recognizable, such as the wood engraver who executed the blocks for Marshall's editions of the Kilners' stories, or the one who illustrated Harris's reformatted *Cabinet of amusement and instruction* of the 1820s (possibly Robert Branston). Maintaining similar standards for design was also possible in Scotland and provincial English towns. In his toy book manufactory in Glasgow, James Lumsden produced primly attractive pamphlets (many engraved throughout) pirated from other children's booksellers' wares, while James Kendrew in York turned out dozens of neat little two-penny and penny books of nursery rhymes and fairy tales.[22]

In addition to making their books' packaging increasingly enticing, children's booksellers continued to diversify by expanding into the market for children's educational toys, adapting formats such as playing cards and maps for instructional purposes. This development represented the culmination of a trend seen earlier in the century, which may have been initiated by engraver John Lenthall, who issued a hybrid deck of playing cards that could be used for

19 Alderson 1983.
20 Pointon 1986, 130.
21 Tattersfield 2001.
22 For Lumsden, see Roscoe and Brimmel 1981; for Kendrew, see Davis 1988.

playing games to learn the alphabet or games of chance. In the 1740s, Benjamin Collins sold battledores and the alphabet cards *A set of squares*, both claimed as his inventions, in addition to children's books. The engraver, map-maker and seller John Spilsbury marketed geographical jigsaw puzzles (then called dissected maps) in the 1760s. In the case of the Wallis firms, beautifully hand-coloured engraved race games and puzzles (the one mounted on linen, the other on wood) that introduced children to the manufactures of Great Britain, the succession of Roman emperors or the pleasures of astronomy may have been as important sources of revenues as the picture books. Other firms in the picture trade offered dainty novelties as much toy as book. Samuel and Joseph Fuller, proprietors of the Temple of Fancy, sold doll books, in which a moral tale could be acted out with a paper doll with a detachable head and several changes of costume. Rudolph Ackerman sold *Fables in action, by means of moveable pictures*, an early example of the slot book. Occasionally a member of the trade like E.S. Harding or Tabart issued comprehensive catalogues of all the books and games they published or sold, systematically arranged by price, subject, or the age for which materials were best suited.

By the 1790s, it was possible in London to make a living primarily from selling children's books, and shops catering to the needs of children, their parents and schools dotted the city by the early 1800s. The corner of St Paul's Churchyard, for example, was occupied by three generations of Newberys from the 1740s until 1801, then by the firm's successor, John Harris, and finally by Harris's son until 1843. John Marshall, also the publisher of the *Cheap repository tracts*, traded at Aldermary Churchyard, Queen and Fleet streets between 1780 and 1830. William Darton senior (Darton & Harvey subsequently) operated out of Gracechurch Street, while his son William junior had an establishment on Holborn Hill, known during its heyday in the 1820s as the Repertory of Genius. Benjamin Tabart, whose business was entangled with that of Sir Richard Phillips, had premises on New Bond Street, and Lucy Peacock, the only known female children's author and bookseller, offered translations and books in foreign languages on Oxford Street near Piccadilly. The political philosopher William Godwin traded under his second wife's name on Skinner Street, near the tanneries.[23] In addition to selling books in their juvenile repositories, the better capitalized booksellers like the Dartons and Harris offered their publications at a discount to schools and booksellers outside London. The separate section of children's booksellers

23 For the Darton firms, see Darton 2004; for Harris, see Moon 1992; for Tabart, see Moon 1990; for Godwin, see St Clair 1989 and Kinnell 1988.

in the 1823 edition of *Leigh's new picture of London* suggests that these shops had become destinations for many visitors. Indeed, the Darton firm was so well known that Thackeray mentions it in *Vanity Fair* as the place where Amelia buys Georgy copies of Edgeworth's *Parent's assistant* and Thomas Day's *Sandford and Merton* for his birthday.

Conclusion: readers respond

Booksellers continue to be treated in histories of children's books as if they were the *auteurs* of their backlists.[24] Focusing on the authors during this period remains problematic, as the majority of children's books were issued anonymously. Even successful authors like Dorothy and Mary Ann Kilner preferred to keep their identities secret. Little progress has been made in the attribution of anonymous works because few documents have surfaced like the day book of Richard Johnson, the hack employed by Elizabeth Newbery's business manager to write children's stories.[25] Nor is much known about author–publisher relations because so little correspondence has survived, even in the case of major figures like Joseph Johnson, and Barbauld, Edgeworth and Wollstonecraft, the great writers he published. New information about the career of Mme Le Prince de Beaumont, on the other hand, suggests that there are still discoveries to be made in the archives.[26]

Because publishers have received more credit than may be their due, the texts they produced have been regarded more frequently as disposable commodities than cultural artefacts. The Romantic writers' condemnation of contemporary children's books as soul-killing instruments inflicted by adults upon young readers – most notably Book V of Wordsworth's *Prelude* – supports this view, and has been cited in lieu of other evidence that could lead to a more balanced analysis of the genre's reception.[27] A systematic study of marks of ownership in children's books, for example, would yield up much new information about their owners and shed light on the status of texts over time. Just as Fielding's Tom Jones wrote his name throughout his bible when a boy, so did real children, including some like Thomas Carlyle or Florence Nightingale who grew up to be famous public figures, as well as the pioneering collectors of children's books – Joseph Ritson, Thomas Gaisford, Richard Monckton-Milnes and Robert Curzon. Portions of family libraries have survived, including Jane

24 Alderson and Oyens 2006.
25 Weedon 1949.
26 Shefrin 2003.
27 Myers 1992.

Johnson's charming instructional aids, the so-called Ludford box or the collection begun in girlhood by Lydia Heaton Haskoll.[28]

Signatures and bookplates cannot tell us if the book was chosen by a child or by an adult for a child, why it was selected or if its owners ever read it. But other sources can help to contextualize the raw data from the books, however. Booksellers' records, such as the ledgers of the provincial stationer John Clay, show that the boys at Rugby and Daventry schools did indeed spend their pocket money on Newbery juveniles.[29] Attitudes towards particular children's books can be gleaned from documents such as Mrs Thrale's *Children's book*, the diary of Marjorie Fleming and Lord Chesterfield's earliest letters to his son. Nor should literary works be overlooked: eighteenth-century occasional poems, for example, are surprisingly rich in references to child readers and texts they enjoyed. Allusions to Georgian children's books in Victorian novels suggest that their authors assumed their audience would instantly recognize them, undermining the prevailing notion that these books had little impact. In chapter 22 of Dickens's *David Copperfield*, Steerforth's old nursery tale proves to be the cautionary progress of two brothers from Fenning's *Universal speller*; and an ironic allusion to Fénelon turns up in chapter 28 of *Great expectations* when the local journalist describes Pumblechook as Mentor to Pip's Telemachus.

Studying the reception of children's books during this period will be a project for the future, but it is reasonable to conclude even now that while the increased availability of the books may have laid the foundation for a separate children's literature, it did not spark a revolution in reading habits. The Longman ledgers for the end of this period show that school-books such as those by Fenning and Lindley Murray continued to dominate children's book production, with the steady-selling titles reprinted as often as every few years in relatively large editions. Only a handful of literary texts – Aikin and Barbauld's *Evenings at home*, Gay's *Fables*, Watts's *Divine songs*, Berquin's *Children's friend* or Fénelon's *Telemachus* – were in such demand.[30] Likewise, certain habits of reading probably persisted well into the period. It is indisputable that eighteenth-century children read literary works for adults such as *Robinson Crusoe*, *Gulliver's travels*, the *Spectator*, *Tom Jones* and Madame d'Aulnoy's fairy tales, just as they read the unabridged and unexpurgated Bible. This kind of crossing over may also describe children's reading habits

28 For Johnson, see Styles and Arizpe 2006; for the Ludford box, see Alderson 1989; for Haskoll, see Hounslow 2004.

29 Fergus 2006.

30 Fyfe 1999.

in general before a largely autonomous market for juvenile books existed or circulating libraries began routinely stocking titles for younger patrons.[31] Many autobiographical writings suggest that young readers consumed whatever was available in the family library that struck their fancy or seemed useful: they did not necessarily gravitate towards those books intended primarily for them. Thus, Benjamin Franklin's description of what he read before being apprenticed at twelve - Bunyan, Nathaniel Crouch's chapbooks, Plutarch, Defoe's *Essay on projects* and Mather's *Essays to do good* - does not seem so extraordinary when compared with similar lists extracted from the memoirs of Edward Gibbon or Samuel Romilly. The rise of the children's book between 1695 and 1833 seems to have been a gradual rather than meteoric ascent: most of the necessary components for an organized market may have been present early in the period, but it was not until late in George III's reign that these new books were regarded as essential to a child's reading experience.

31 Grenby 2001.

41

Music

DAVID HUNTER

The dissemination history of music is shaped by a fundamental difference in comparison with the regular book trade, its authors and readers. Music on the page lacks the immediacy of apprehension that linguistic and even numeric text affords its readers. Unlike drama, written music requires performance in order for the signs to become meaningful to all but the most adept proficients. Music requires two special skills in order to be performed – musical literacy and performance ability – both of which necessitate training and practice. Two or more persons are usually required to make the text sound and the text may exist only as separate parts until performed. Performance is often restricted to specific instruments. Unlike the three Rs, music-making is not regarded as a skill necessary to worldly advancement, and thus must be specifically encouraged. The expense of the training and equipment, coupled with the need for active promotion, mean that music's diffusion through the purchase of texts and their transformation through performance is restricted. Music written in score or for keyboard instruments such as harpsichord or organ requires both horizontal and considerable vertical page space in which to unfold, and thus entails a different approach to printing. Like the trading of books in Latin during earlier times, music is distributable anywhere western notation is understood. These differences of use, market, technology, education and social utility will be highlighted in what follows, but they should not completely obscure the similarities – such as concerns with intellectual property protection, textual accuracy, technological advances, taxation, methods of distribution and profitability – between music and the other systems in the universe of textual reproduction.

For music historians, 1695 signifies the untimely death of England's leading composer, Henry Purcell, and the issuance of the first publications by John Walsh, whose firm quickly came to dominate music printing and publishing in London, and retained its supremacy until the death of John Walsh the younger in 1766. The year 1830 is close enough to several events to mark the end of one era and the beginning of the next. Between 1825 and 1829 these musicians, collectors or publishers who worked chiefly in Britain died: Domenico Corri, Michael Kelly, James Hook and William Shield. In 1830 Muzio Clementi retired from publishing. That same year the Novello publishing house, dedicated to the diffusion of music texts among the widest possible audience, was formally established by Vincent, Mary and their son J. Alfred Novello (and continues to this day as part of Music Sales Group). The previous year two men – Felix Mendelssohn and Michael Costa – who now symbolize a significant portion of the imminent Victorian musical world, arrived in England. That year, 1829, also saw the establishment of Keith, Prowse and Co. as a music selling and publishing firm in Cheapside, London, which has survived to the present as a leading international ticket agency. Of the notable musicians who worked primarily on the Continent, the years 1825–9 witnessed the deaths of Antonio Salieri, Carl Maria von Weber (who died and was buried in London), Ludwig van Beethoven, Franz Schubert and Mauro Giuliani, and of the publisher C.F. Peters (the firm is still in business).[1]

Accurate quantification of the output of printed music during our period is impossible at present owing to inadequate bibliographical control, but we can be sure that whatever the level of supply, copies could be purchased only by persons with sufficient funds.[2] The latest analysis of macro-economic data indicates that not only did inegalitarian trends of wealth distribution increase between 1795 and 1815 as many had thought, they also increased during most of the second half of the eighteenth century, as a result of rising population growth that drove down wages but increased demand for staples.[3] Much of this inequality derived from falling prices of luxury goods (such as printed matter, musical instruments and servants) relative to staples (such as grain, fuels and housing). In crude terms, not only did the rich get richer through raised rentals, the luxury goods they purchased fell in price both relatively (ticket prices for Italian or grand opera remained almost constant over the eighteenth century) and absolutely (as a result of pioneering entrepreneurs, scientific discoveries and mechanical inventions).

1 Krummel and Sadie 1990 has details on these and many more printers and publishers.

2 Most music is excluded from the eighteenth-century portion of *ESTC*, while music coverage of the *National Union Catalogue* (NUC) pre-1956 is inconsistent; the music catalogues – the *British union catalogue of early music* and Répertoire International des Sources Musicales: United Kingdom and Ireland (RISM), series A/I and B2 – terminate in or around 1800. In addition, there are problems of definition as publishers issued texts such as arias or choruses from operas and oratorios both collectively and as single sheets. Many of the latter have not survived; those that have are rarely catalogued individually.

3 Hoffman *et al.* 2000, 2002.

The most potent trope used as both cause and effect to explain the supposed expansion of the market for music over the long eighteenth century is the rise of the middle class. For example, the assertion of greater availability of printed music during the early nineteenth century is claimed to be dependent upon the adoption of the piano by the putative middle class.[4] Given an economic reality of little surplus income, no health or retirement insurance, and increasing costs of staples, purchase of a piano and continuing expenditures on lessons and music cannot have been priorities for the families that occupied the social space between rich and poor.[5] A far more likely explanation for any expansion of music's market over the long eighteenth century is a combination of greater market penetration among the elite and an absolute increase in the elite's numbers.[6] This is not a claim for an exclusively elite market (there were devotees from less wealthy families, as the country psalmodists found), but it is a claim that the market was far more restricted than has been stated heretofore. For most of our period at least 97 per cent of families were unlikely ever to buy music, given their more pressing economic needs.[7] The realization that so few of those families that had sufficient funds used them to buy music is even more startling and underlines music's highly restricted market. A few population and income figures for England and Wales will help make the point (see Table 41.1).

If music's potential marketplace expanded faster than the increase in population (1803b in Table 41.1 offers one scenario), that growth was still largely restricted to the wealthiest 3.4 per cent of the population. Real changes in income distribution did not begin until the last third of the nineteenth century. Any use of teleological terms such as 'spread', 'development', 'popular' and their amplifying adjectives to characterize change should be exceedingly cautious.

Without wishing to adjudicate the chicken–egg, priority-of-origin debate as it relates to publishers and the customers of their wares (let alone the place of

4 Ehrlich 1990, 16–17. As there is no unequivocal evidence over the fifteen years following the end of the Napoleonic wars in 1815 for a substantial increase in piano sales beyond the level necessary to substitute for the decline in output of the harpsichord and clavichord (the keyboard instruments previously preferred), let alone proof of a direct relationship between sales of pianos and of printed music, or who it was that purchased pianos, any such claim must be treated as propaganda.

5 Rather than consider competing definitions and quantifications of class, income, standards and costs of living, quality of life, aesthetic values, musical literacy and so forth, I provide a single viewpoint.

6 The rigidity of British social class conceptualization – any well-off family not part of the nobility or gentry is middle class – inhibits analysis, particularly as it subordinates economics to other aspects of distinction.

7 These figures for income distribution may shock, not least in terms of the poor constituting 85–90 per cent of the population. That music historians have been unwilling to assent to such exclusivity is unsurprising.

Table 41.1 *Families and incomes in England and Wales, 1698–1803*

	1698		1759		1803a		1803b	
Total number of families	1,390,586		1,536,140		2,227,629		2,227,629	
Type	elite	middling sort	elite	middling sort	elite	middling sort	elite	middling sort
Income range	>£200	£50–200	>£200	£50–200	>£700	£139–700	>£350	£139–350
No. of families in that range	29,890	98,322	34,000	104,256	49,703	250,204	76,543	223,364
Percentage of total families	2.1	7.0	2.2	6.7	2.2	11.2	3.4	10.0

Source: Statistics of families and income derived from the summary tables in Hay and Rogers 1997, though the table divisions there are unreliable.

the creators of texts in that avian conception), I begin consideration of those symbiotic elements of the book trade with customers, if only because less has been written about them. During the long eighteenth century, customer choice was constrained not only by wealth but also by geography, technology, distribution, aesthetics, religion, musical genre, fashion and developments in compositional practice that demanded increasingly complex technique or resources in performance. Thus an interest in old music, evangelical revival, domestic or local sociability, the sacralization of the performance of selected oratorios, and fashions for particular instruments or the works of particular composers, all played a part in determining preference. With few exceptions, books of psalmody – those volumes of basic musical instruction, hymns and anthems suitable for use in country churches – were not of interest to urban sophisticates, nor were collections of opera songs or selections from oratorios likely to be purchased by the church choirs.[8] Similarly, collectors of music were unlikely to be active in both areas, although in a few cases the wealthy did support the issuance of psalmody books by the itinerant music masters in their localities.[9] Publication of the repertory of collegiate and cathedral choirs provided the wealthy with patronage opportunities in sacred music. Publishers of vocal music typically issued selections from operas and oratorios adapted for single voice and accompaniment (flute and harpsichord, and later

8 For Charles Burney's disgust at the musical ignorance of the parishioners at King's Lynn where he went to be organist in 1751, see Burney 1991, 2.

9 D. Hunter 1990.

pianoforte) or instruments alone. Only two works of Handel's for multiple voices were issued complete during his lifetime, *Alexander's feast* in 1738 and *Acis and Galatea* in 1743, the former by subscription to raise funds for the composer. For professional musicians (including cathedral singers), serious amateurs and collectors wishing to own complete texts of works more complex than solo cantatas or songs, manuscript remained an important means of transmission.

The evidence for the music collections of individuals must be discerned from subscription lists, auction or sale catalogues, account books, correspondence and diaries, wills and inventories, surviving copies, and the catalogues prepared by or for collectors themselves. Subscription publishing is the obvious means of tying individuals to particular publications, but, whether used by an established publisher or as a method of self-publishing, it is not representative of the music market as a whole, so great care must be taken in terms of characterizing subscribers as regular purchasers of music (or of using the number of copies subscribed as a valid indicator of the size of print run for other publications).[10] Few among the collective 539 individuals and societies who subscribed to one or more of the ten Handel publications issued during his lifetime for which lists survive can be regarded as serious collectors if that is defined as subscribing to more than nine books of music.[11] During their lifetimes, such notable music lovers as Thomas Twining (a grandson of the eponymous tea merchant), Thomas Gray (the poet and Cambridge don) and John Marsh (the quondam lawyer, composer and diarist) respectively subscribed to three, none and two musical publications. A comparison of the subscribers to the art music of opera songs and instrumental works and those who supported the books issued by or for the country psalmodists shows little overlap and thus is a clear indicator of the differentiation of genres. In both cases, the motives of the subscribers may be a mixture of support for the composer and the desire to perform the works in their distinct contexts.[12] The contrast in price – art music costing a guinea or more, books of psalmody only a few shillings or less – signals the purchasing ability of the intended customers.

The pioneering studies of private collections focused on the printed catalogues of auction sales and those collections that survive in institutions.[13]

10 During the decades from 1721 to 1830, music comprised between 9 and 14 per cent of the subscription market (except from 1781 to 1790 when it peaked at 17 per cent), a proportion that is probably larger than the one between all music and all ordinary books.

11 Hunter and Mason 1999.

12 The extent to which music subscriptions conformed to general practice – about half the copies subscribed never entered the purchasers' libraries – has yet to be determined. Amory 1995.

13 King 1963; Coral 1974; Coover 2001.

Numerous manuscript catalogues, inventories and library borrowing registers now in county record offices, libraries and private hands also deserve close attention but are only beginning to receive it.[14] One such catalogue lists the collection of Queen Caroline, consort of George II, and, surprisingly, it reveals few works by Handel, but printed music of other composers with court connections such as William Croft and Maurice Greene, published volumes dedicated to the queen such as William Thomson's *Orpheus Caledonius* (1726), and manuscript scores of the operas produced in Hanover, complemented by a substantial collection of printed opera libretti.[15] Admittedly, a royal collection is unlikely to be representative, but that is just as true for any individual. The libraries of John Cousser and Philip Percival, in Dublin during the 1710s and 1720s, are quite distinct in scope, though Percival directed the Irish State Music and Cousser was its leader.[16] As an example of library borrowing we may note that Laurence Sterne took music by Albicastro, Marino and Vivaldi from the York Minster Library in 1752, though whether this was to oblige a musical friend or to satisfy his own interests remains unknown. Charles Burney borrowed from the extensive music library at Christ Church, Oxford while he was writing his *General history of music*. These cathedral and college libraries may be unusual; only further research will reveal whether the libraries in other cathedrals and colleges were similarly well provided or generous. Similarly underexplored are the catalogues of musical societies in London and elsewhere.[17] Almost nothing is known of the operation of the commercial lending libraries of music run by music publishers and sellers and by existing library proprietors, the earliest of which dates from about 1770.

The interactions of customers and shopkeepers are unlikely to be well documented, but initial evidence suggests that customers in London had favourite shops. Philip Percival wrote to his brother John (later Earl of Egmont) in July 1716 that 'when you see Ribeauteau I wish you would put him in mind that the figured bass of the six last concertis of Valentinis, which Cosin Usher bought of him is wanting and he ought to gett it or they will be of no use to me'.[18] Henry Riboteau was the London agent of Amsterdam publisher Estienne Roger, the leading north European music publisher of the day. In December 1737 Thomas Harris wrote to his brother James (the philosopher, MP for Christchurch from 1761, and trustee of the British Museum from 1765)

14 Ledsham 1999; Gifford 2002.

15 Daub 1994.

16 Cousser's commonplace book is now in the Beinecke Library, Yale University.

17 For the exceptions of Oxford and Edinburgh, see Burchell 1996.

18 BL Add. MSS. 47027, f. 95.

saying that he will take back to John Walsh junior his brother's copies of 'the favourite songs in those opera's which I am to buy' and exchange them for the new, more complete editions that Walsh was then putting out.[19] Apparently such exchanges were expected. According to her account book, on 8 May 1742, Gertrude Savile returned (probably to Walsh) four music books that she had purchased nine days earlier, and took away three others, paying only 1*s.* 6*d.*[20] Edward Weld, the wealthy Catholic of Lulworth Castle, bought opera aria collections and instrumental music from Walsh during the 1740s and 1750s.[21] Thomas Twining wrote to his college friend John Hey in July 1761 about a visit to Walsh's shop during which Walsh 'was revenged upon me for the many laughs I have had at him. He found out my taste, & flung a whole bundle of MS music before me . . . He got the money out of my pocket as easily as if I had been a lady of quality & had come in a coach.'[22]

Twining was an active member of a music club in Colchester.[23] These societies, initiated (and disbanded in some cases) by local music lovers in more than thirty capital, cathedral, university and port cities before 1760, were usually private and quite small. The oldest one still in existence is the Hibernian Catch Club founded by the singing men of the Dublin cathedrals around 1680. In the absence of commercial music libraries or a generous benefactor, the societies built up their own, often substantial holdings, such as at Aberdeen.[24] By 1830, catch and glee clubs or concert societies were established in numerous towns though not all were long lasting. John Marsh recorded in his journal that the Chichester Catch Club he founded in 1787 disbanded in 1792.[25]

As with other kinds of publication, customers of music could read newspaper advertisements to learn of new publications. For the first half of our period, if not longer, there was a marked contrast between the London papers, which catered to the elite and in which appeared advertisements for secular vocal and instrumental music, and the provincial papers, which carried advertisements primarily for sacred music suitable for parish churches.[26] The first firm known to have advertised art music in a provincial newspaper was that of Cluer and Creake.[27] John Cluer's brother-in-law William Dicey owned the

19 Burrows and Dunhill 2002.
20 Nottingham, Nottinghamshire Archives, DD.SR A4/45. See also Savile 1997.
21 Dorchester, Dorset Record Office, D/WLC/AE8–AE11, AF1.
22 Twining 1991.
23 Holman 2000.
24 Johnson 1971.
25 Marsh 1998, 416, 526.
26 D. Hunter 1990.
27 Hunter 1991.

Northampton Mercury and that paper announced, on 1 June 1724, the second edition of *A pocket companion for gentlemen and ladies: being a collection of the finest opera songs & airs, in English and Italian*, which included songs by Handel, Bononcini and English composers.[28] The second volume of *A pocket companion* was also advertised in the *Suffolk Mercury* of 13 December 1725. The other London publishers seem not to have followed the example, considering, perhaps, that the London newspapers sent into the country by MPs and to the nobility and gentry would suffice. Indeed, *A pocket companion* is anomalous for other reasons. The first edition of volume one lists 992 copies subscribed, and the second edition issued in the same year adds 259. Volume II, issued in December 1725, was subscribed for 945 copies. No other subscription music book sold as many copies until 1812.[29] With sellers from Plymouth to Edinburgh, the *Pocket companion* was the first trade publication of Italian music to reach across Britain and its distribution was not matched for decades.

Imprints, newspaper advertisements and publishers' catalogues were used by Humphries and Smith to augment the work of previous scholars and produce the standard list of music printers, publishers and engravers.[30] Subsequent work has resulted in much revision though it is as yet unsynthesized.[31] Furthermore, numerous provincial newspapers and local directories remain to be analysed for their music-related advertisements and businesses, and the scrutiny of other documentary evidence has hardly begun.[32] Account books of provincial booksellers can be especially helpful in revealing the extent of the distribution of music outside the major centres and specialist businesses, though they have yet to be investigated on a systematic basis.[33] Unlike the impression obtainable from Humphries and Smith, present evidence indicates that the majority of towns in Britain had seen the sale of music from fixed premises by 1760, and most of the rest did so over the next seventy years.

Music shops in cities carried not only British and imported printed and manuscript music, but also a wide variety of music-related material, including instruments, replacement strings and reeds, cases, stands, books and periodicals about music, music paper in sheets and bound, pens and ink, tickets to performances, and probably offered music lessons or contacts with local

28 Hunter 1997.

29 D. Weyman, *Melodia sacra* (Dublin, 1812), 1,335 copies.

30 Humphries and Smith 1970.

31 D. Hunter 1990; *Biography database* (first issued on three CD-ROMs but since 1999 available by subscription at www.ancestry.com); Pollard 2000; *BBTI*; Bodleian – John Johnson Collection; Temperley 1998.

32 For the exceptions of Aberdeen, Bath, Cambridge, Leeds, Norwich and Sheffield, see references in Pickering 1990; also Griffiths 1998; and Wollenberg 2001.

33 See Fergus and Portner 1987.

teachers. In London and major cities, the shops of the dominant publishers were also the leading music stores. A very few of London's publishers were equally if not more renowned as instrument dealers or makers, notably Longman and Broderip (bankrupted 1795) and the various Clementi partnerships. On the other hand, famous instrument-makers such as Broadwood and Erard never were active as publishers. In smaller towns, printed music and other music material was sold by general booksellers and by other traders. An advertisement in the *Derby Mercury* of 22 March–5 April 1754 placed by Samuel Fox, bookseller in Derby, indicates the availability of books of psalmody by East, Arnold, Knapp, Green and Clark, Greene, Barber, Tans'ur, Chetham and Playford. We should not imagine that any seller had the universal availability of publications as a goal. Even in the leading London shops, the full range of continental publications was not stocked, owing to the unacceptability of some languages for vocal music, differing traditions of dance or the lack of interest in a particular musical genre.[34] For example, none of Mozart's dance music or his songs of 1789 published by Artaria in Vienna were imported by Longman and Broderip, which sold other Mozart publications.[35] Competitor John Bland, who imported Hoffmeister editions, was similarly selective.[36] Too great an emphasis has been placed on the obvious growth of publishers' catalogues, from the forty-eight items listed by Walsh senior in 1703 to Clementi, Collard and Collard's 189-page list of 1823.[37] Length in itself tells us nothing about market depth or saturation, let alone the ability to buy; rather, it is a testimony to the efficiency of engraving as a technology and the preservation of plates. Back lists were never so extensive, nor publication-on-demand so easily undertaken, as during the early nineteenth century. No wonder, then, that plate sales became a significant part of the auction trade.[38]

Not until 1777 and the case of *J.C. Bach* v. *Longman and Lukey* were music publications held to be protected by copyright.[39] Prior to that composers and publishers had resorted to various means, notably royal licences and the Engraving Copyright Act (8 George II c. 13) of 1735, to prevent unauthorized issuance of their works.[40] Following the landmark ruling by Lord Mansfield, registration with the Stationers' Company quickly came to be seen as a benefit

34 See Krummel 1992, supplemented by studies of individual publishers such as Constapel 1998 and Rheinfurth 1999.
35 Wyn Jones 1996.
36 Woodfield 2000.
37 Washington, Library of Congress; BL Mic.A.2054.
38 Coover 1987, 1988.
39 Hunter 1986.
40 Almost fifty royal licences were awarded to composers or publishers between 1720 and 1770. Hunter 1987.

and registrations of music rose dramatically, briefly comprising some 25 per cent of all titles annually.[41] Music was now considered to be subject to legal deposit and thus library receipts became a regular, if not consistent, practice.[42] The Bach case was also significant in that it established that a foreigner resident in Britain was entitled to copyright protection for works published in Britain.[43] From 1789 to 1830, seven precedent-setting cases are to be found in the law reports.[44] Other aspects of copyright continued to be litigated, for which we can now be grateful as the depositions provide one of the few means of learning how much publishers paid composers, the length of print runs and other vital data. Given the philo-composer stance of music historians and biographers, the common characterization of composer–publisher relations has been one in which the publishers are villains.[45] Perhaps some publishers were cheats, but until 1777 none was under a legal obligation to pay composers for copy not received directly from them. From 1777, fashionable composers, including those from abroad, could expect to make lengthy agreements with publishers, as Haydn did with Frederick Augustus Hyde, Beethoven with Clementi and Storace with Dale.[46]

Intaglio engraving on metal plates run through a rolling press was the chief means of music printing, though typeset letterpress and relief engraving on wood blocks continued in use. The major innovations in engraving were implemented by Walsh senior between 1695 and 1700. These involved the use of pewter plates, which, in contrast with the harder copperplates, did not need to be etched with acid or warmed prior to inking; punches for certain signs (such as clefs and note heads, but eventually including almost all signs and letters); and passe-partout title-pages, both illustrated and not.[47] It was probably Walsh senior who introduced the practice of not dating music publications. As Oliver Goldsmith had Miss Hardcastle wittily remark in *She stoops to conquer* (1773), 'Women and music should never be dated.' Customers, dealers, bibliographers and cataloguers have wailed ever since, mollified in part by the innovation of Walsh junior, implemented about 1730, to number his firm's publications.

41 Kassler 2004.
42 Turbet 1997.
43 For discussion of additional music copyright suits 1750–89, see van Allen-Russell 2002; Mace 1996, 1999; Rabin and Zohn 1995; Price 1989, 1991.
44 For *Skillern and Goulding* v. *Longman and Broderip* (1792–4), see Milhous, Dideriksen and Hume 2001.
45 Cooper 2002; Hunter 2002. Evidence to the contrary has been ignored, e.g. following John Simpson's funeral, the *General Advertiser*, 11 Feb. 1749, noted that the London publisher was 'a Man of strict Honour, remarkable Industry, and universally beloved by all his Acquaintance'.
46 Rosenthal 1996; Tyson 1963; Cooper 2002; Girdham 1997.
47 Hunter 1989.

Unlike the music printers and publishers of continental Europe, British ones were slow to adopt lithography as the preferred means of reproduction despite the establishment by Philipp André, brother of Johann the music publisher in Offenbach, of the Polyautographic Printing Office in London in 1801. Although Twyman has attributed the late acceptance of the process to the reluctance of music engravers to work with stones, we should bear in mind that engraving retained an economic advantage, in large part due to the vast plate libraries that publishers created.[48] The development of the transfer process from 1809 meant that engraving could maintain its dominance as a form of reproduction even if printing gradually moved away from the rolling press. Engraving even came to dominate the printing of hymn books with music, traditionally considered to have been a bastion of letterpress. In England during the first decade of the eighteenth century only 6 per cent of newly issued hymn books (measured by titles) were printed by engraving, but by 1780 the proportion had risen to an overwhelming 90 per cent.[49] From 1781 to 1820, letterpress was used to print less than 3 per cent of new hymn books with music.

Despite the continuing importance of manuscripts, printed sources have significance in terms of documenting various repertories. The first books of music for bagpipes were published for the union pipes around 1745, and the Scots Highland pipes around 1784.[50] Welsh tunes were first published alone in *Antient British music* in 1742. Military music was issued as books of tunes and sets of parts for bands and combat musicians, and in a gentrified version for parlour performance. One form of publication, the periodical, even gave its name to a musical sub-genre, the periodical overture or symphony.[51] Attempts to market a serial comprised wholly of music usually foundered after a few issues or years.[52] Periodicals about music were similarly ill-starred.[53] Our period did see several important firsts in the music book trade: two comprehensive histories of music by Burney and Hawkins (issued almost simultaneously in 1776); autobiographies, memoirs and biographies of musicians; biographical dictionaries and books of musical travels. Likewise with scores: the first scholarly editions of old music, edited by William Boyce, Thomas Warren and John Stafford Smith, were issued between 1760 and 1779;

48 Twyman 1996.
49 These figures apply to books of hymns with English words, printed in England. Temperley 1998 did not tabulate comparable figures for Scotland and Ireland. No hymn books with music and English words were printed in Wales 1700–1820. The first printing of music in Wales was undertaken by Ishmael Dafydd of Trefriw in 1816; Griffiths 1998.
50 Cannon 1980.
51 See Teirney, chap. 24 and Harris, chap. 20, both above.
52 Krummel 1990.
53 Langley 1990.

complete or collected works of composers were attempted, for Handel by Samuel Arnold (1787–97) and for Purcell by Benjamin Goodison (*c.*1787–90), though both lacked subscribers sufficient to bring the projects to completion.

The unique contribution of dissemination history lies in explaining what happens at the intersection of individuals, the copies of texts and the environments in which those copies are made and used. Understanding the complexities of these intersections requires gathering data not only on texts and those who issued them (the focus of valiant individual and collective efforts over the past fifty years), but also on the individual buyers and users of those texts. Until we know the full extent of publishing and selling, of purchasers and collectors, of clubs and libraries, of costs and incomes, of print runs and imports, and can make meaningful diachronic and synchronic comparisons, the triumphant story commonly encountered in music histories – of rapidly multiplying demand for and supply of the products of the music trade over the long eighteenth century – will remain an empty boast.

42

Maps, charts and atlases in Britain, 1690–1830

YOLANDE HODSON

Introduction

The period between 1690 and 1830 was marked by five major wars, the loss of the colonies in North America, the development of the British empire in India and the exploration of the South Pacific. Maritime commerce was plied around the world. At home, the progress of agriculture, industry and communications altered the domestic landscape. All of these events were given cartographic expression in a variety of forms which, as the eighteenth century wore on, were capable of being ever more precisely rendered as a result of advances in scientific instrumentation and survey. The trade in the thousands of maps, atlases, charts and maritime atlases published in Britain during this time was in the hands of relatively few men: successive generations of the same family carried on the family business, often in ever-shifting partnerships with other map firms.

Such temporary trading partnerships were essential in spreading the high financial risk which was endemic in map publishing for most of this period.[1] The complexities of multiple ownership in any atlas could be of byzantine proportions, involving intricate transactions in the transfer of copyright. The fourth edition of *Britannia, or, a chorographical description of Great Britain and Ireland* (1772), for example, carried the names of thirty partners on the title page.[2] Sometimes income would be solicited in advance from subscribers, because the capital required to underwrite a successful original survey, followed by its publication, was too high to be borne by the publisher's purse alone. The cartographic community, on land or at sea, was characterized, until about 1760, by indigence. Thomas Jefferys (*c.*1719–71)

The author is most grateful to Laurence Worms for his generosity in making available his unpublished research material.

1 Most map-sellers also sold a wide range of prints, as exemplified in *Sayer & Bennett's catalogue of prints for 1775* (facsimile by Holland Press, 1970).

2 Hodson 1984, 109–10.

became bankrupt,[3] while Richard Chandler 'beset by debt', committed suicide.[4] The statutory provisions of the three copyright Acts of 1735, 1767 and 1777[5] appeared to have little impact on the practice of plagiarism which was, for many a map and chart publisher, an economic necessity. While much new material of good quality came to be published in the second half of the eighteenth century, old plates – refurbished with or without corrections, and published with new imprints – were generally the stock-in-trade of most.

The essential roll call of those involved in map and chart publishing for this period is not long: Robert Morden (d. 1703, *fl.* 1668–1703), the Mount and Page families (*fl.* 1677–*c.*1792),[6] John Senex (1678–1740, *fl.* 1702–40), the Overtons (*fl.* 1666–1744), the Bowles family (*fl.* 1683–1832),[7] Herman Moll (*fl. c.*1678–1732),[8] Emanuel Bowen (*c.*1693–1767, *fl.* 1714–67), George Willdey (*fl.* 1707–37),[9] Thomas Kitchin (1719–84, *fl.* 1739–84),[10] Thomas Jefferys (*fl.* 1732–71),[11] John Ainslie (1745–1828, *fl.* 1765–1828), Robert Sayer (*fl.* 1775–83),[12] John Cary and sons (*fl.* 1779–1850),[13] William Faden (1749–1836, *fl.* 1773–1836),[14] Aaron Arrowsmith (1750–1823, *fl.* 1777–1823; John Arrowsmith, 1790–1873, continued the business until 1873), Laurie and Whittle (1794–1818; R.H. Laurie 1818–54),[15] and Christopher Greenwood (*fl.* 1815–55).[16] Of these premier publishers, the Bowles family played an important part in the London map trade for more than a century; the founder of the firm, Thomas Bowles I (*fl.* 1683?–1714?) had been born some time before 1695, and his great-nephew, Henry Carington Bowles, who carried on the business with Samuel Carver, died in 1830. To these firms must be added the names of numerous surveyors, engravers and publishers, such as John Rocque (*c.*1704–62), and smaller enterprises such as the county surveying of Peter Burdett (d. 1793),[17] William Yates (*c.*1738–1802) and sons,[18] Andrew

3 Harley 1966.
4 Hodson 1984, 29.
5 Maps were mentioned for the first time in the Copyright Act of 1767: Harley and O'Donoghue 1977, xxix, xxxii.
6 Adams 1993.
7 Hodson 1984, 186–91.
8 Hodson 1984, 172–82; Reinhartz 1988, 1997; Tyacke 1978, 122–3.
9 Hodson 1984, 141–6; Tyacke 1978, 146–8.
10 Worms 1993.
11 Harley 1966; Pedley 1996, 2000.
12 Hodson 1984, 60–70; Tyacke 1978, 130–6.
13 Fordham 1925; Smith 1988.
14 Pedley 1996, 2000; Worms 2004.
15 Robinson 1962, 123–4.
16 Harley 1962.
17 Harley and Laxton 1974.
18 Harley 1968.

Dury (*fl.* 1755–76/80) and John Andrews (*fl.* 1766–*c.*1800), and A. Bryant (*fl.* 1820–35), all of whose work produced published maps of high quality.

The material output of maps was surprisingly diverse. Maps were printed on handkerchieves for the relief of a snuff-induced sneeze.[19] Playing cards (1717) by William Redmayne and John Lenthall were adorned with county maps.[20] John Spilsbury, who had been apprenticed to Thomas Jefferys, took printed maps, mounted them on thin mahogany and then cut them into jigsaw puzzles (1760s–1770s).[21] Jefferys himself produced map games of his own. Many books were printed in which maps supplied an illustration, and many periodicals were published in which maps of all parts of the world featured.[22] Even maps of fantasy places, or with a moral message, found a ready clientele.[23] Educational geography texts also carried maps, of course.[24]

Exploration, trade and conflict were together a prime impetus for map production. Thus Henry Popple's *A map of the British empire in America with the French and Spanish settlements adjacent thereto*, first published in twenty sheets in 1733,[25] was followed in 1755 by John Mitchell's *A map of the British and French dominions in North America*, engraved by Kitchin, and first published by A. Millar. Mitchell's map was reissued by Jefferys, and then by Faden to be used in the peace-making process at the end of the American War of Independence (1775–83).[26] It was not superseded until Arrowsmith's *Map exhibiting all the new discoveries in the interior parts of North America* was first published in 1795. Revised to incorporate the further discoveries of the explorers Lewis and Clark, it was to become, on its publication in 1814, 'a cartographic masterpiece'.[27] Thomas Jefferys's son, also Thomas, and Faden in partnership, engraved and published a plan of the battle of Bunker Hill (fought 17 June 1775) – *A sketch of the action between the British forces and the American provincials* – on 1 August, demonstrating a speed of information transmission and publication which was not to be surpassed until the Peninsular War, when the use of lithography made it possible for a sketch to be sent from the battlefield to be printed at the Horseguards in London within ten days.[28]

19 Christian 1986.
20 Kingsley and Mann 1972.
21 Shefrin 1999.
22 Jolly 1990, 1991.
23 Hill 1978, 27–38; Reitinger 1999.
24 McCorkle 1994.
25 Babinski 1998/2000.
26 Dunbabin 1998.
27 Heckrotte 1987.
28 Clark and Jones 1974.

Wherever possible, the more notable publishers would try to take account of new surveys. In 1759, for example, Jefferys obtained access to the surveys of the St Lawrence River and the battle of Quebec by Samuel Holland, Hugh Debbeig and J.F.W. Des Barres.[29] These were used to produce an attractive engraved map: *An authentic plan of the river St Laurence ... with the operations of the siege of Quebec* (1760). In India, some of the surveys by James Rennel in 1776 for the East India Company in Bengal[30] gave rise to *A Bengal atlas: containing maps of the theatre of war and commerce on that side of Hindoostan* (1781). Captain James Cook's charts for *The North American pilot for Newfoundland* were mainly engraved and published separately by Jefferys and later published in 1775 by Sayer and Bennett.

In the age before the advent of the national topographic and hydrographic surveys in the 1790s, government requirements and patronage played an important, if understated, role in the commissioning of new maps. Thus the Admiralty, for example, had contracted J.F.W. Des Barres to produce a set of coastal charts of Britain's newly acquired territories in French Canada.[31] Des Barres's *Atlantic Neptune, published for the use of the Royal Navy of Great Britain* was a sumptuous three-volume work published by the Admiralty between 1775 and 1781. The role of the East India Company in the surveying of India and the publication of its mapping in this period has been recently explored.[32] Similarly, the Office of Trade and Plantations had commissioned Mitchell's map of America, and the military made use of any available commercial mapping.

Scientific discoveries that changed the perception of the environment also found a place for cartographic depiction. In 1700, Edmund Halley, although not the first to map terrestrial magnetism, produced the data for his *New and correct chart, shewing the variations of the compass in the western and southern oceans*, first published around 1701. Closer to home, geological surveys had begun in Ireland in the middle of the eighteenth century.[33] In 1815, the field surveys of William Smith were engraved and published by John Cary under the title *A delineation of the strata of England and Wales with part of Scotland*, twenty years before the formation in 1835 of a national geological survey.[34]

The bulk of the map-seller's trade in Britain in the eighteenth and early nineteenth centuries was concerned with the production of atlases, maps and

29 Hodson 1988, 10.
30 See also Cook 1978.
31 Terrell 1995.
32 Edney 1997.
33 Davies 1983.
34 Winchester 2001; Boud 1975.

charts of other countries and seas. On the home front,[35] aside from urban mapping,[36] estate surveys,[37] and thematic mapping such as Milne's land-use map of the capital, *A plan of the cities of London and Westminster* (1800),[38] it is arguable that the four most important genres of domestic map-publishing at this time were county maps, county atlases, road books and maps, and hydrographic charting.

County maps

Original surveys for roads and county maps were rarely undertaken in the late seventeenth century. The years following the Restoration were marked by unsuccessful projects to produce new maps of the English counties. Maps were still based on Saxton (1579) and Speed (1612); a few – such as Ogilby's maps of Middlesex and Kent (1675–6) and Essex (1678), Seller and partners' Buckinghamshire, Hertfordshire, Oxfordshire and Surrey – had been published in the 1670s and 1680s.[39]

Nevertheless, the last five years of the seventeenth century saw, in the publication of Joel Gascoyne's map of Cornwall in 1699, the first new county survey to be published to a scale of one inch to a mile (1:63,360).[40] In this, the Cornwall map, which took six years to survey, anticipates the later original surveys of the second half of the eighteenth century. It was followed, in the next fifty years, by a paucity of new surveys. Notable among the few are John Warburton's maps of Yorkshire (1721), and Middlesex, Essex and Hertfordshire (1725).[41] These were at a smaller scale than Gascoyne's map of Cornwall, but William Williams continued the Gascoyne example by producing a one-inch map of Denbighshire and Flintshire, engraved by Senex, in about 1720.[42] Soon afterwards, Henry Beighton surveyed, and then published in 1727/8, a one-inch map of Warwickshire.[43] This was an exceptional map, far in advance of its contemporaries, and remained the standard cartographic source for the county until the new survey at the one-inch scale by William Yates's sons, William and George, between 1787 and 1789.

35 See Delano-Smith and Kain 1999 for a general account of mapping in England at this time.
36 For example, Howgego 1978; Moore 1996; Frostick 2002.
37 Bendall 1992; Fletcher 1995.
38 Bull 1977.
39 Harley 1972.
40 Ravenhill 1972.
41 Hodson 1984, 169–79.
42 Rodger 1972.
43 Harvey and Thorpe 1959, 19–36.

All this was to change after 1759. In that year, the Royal Society of Arts offered a premium of £100 for any original county survey drawn to a scale of one inch to a mile.[44] Compared with the actual cost of such an undertaking, this award was not overly generous in financial terms (for example, Benjamin Donn's map of Devon cost £2,000); yet, it undoubtedly influenced the increased production of original county surveys.[45] Between 1759 and 1801 – when the premium was last offered – thirty-seven English, eighteen Scottish and two Welsh counties had been surveyed at the scale of one inch to the mile or larger. Of these, only twenty-three were submitted for the award and only eleven (including Horwood's plan of London, 1792–9) actually won the society's premium and prestigious Gold Medal.

Such maps were made by provincial surveyors; in contrast, the London map-sellers rarely ventured into the field. Their influence lay in their control of the specialized end processes of engraving, printing and marketing – expertise in which was confined at this time to the capital. Thomas Jefferys was one of the few exceptions to this general rule. He had engraved the first premium-winning map – Benjamin Donn's Devonshire – published in 1765,[46] and between 1767 and 1771 engraved and published six of his own county surveys: Bedfordshire (1767), Huntingdonshire (1768), Oxfordshire (1769), Buckinghamshire (1770), Westmorland (1770) and Yorkshire (1771). The financial outlay required eventually bankrupted him, however. On the other hand, William Faden, who had revived the Jefferys business by 1773,[47] did make the business of subcontracting the survey work and then engraving and publishing county maps at his own expense a paying proposition, notably with Hodskinson's map of Suffolk (1783),[48] Gream's map of Sussex (1795),[49] and Donald and Milne's Norfolk (1797).[50]

Between 1690 and 1830, the whole of England, six Welsh counties, twenty-four Scottish counties and twenty-three Irish counties were surveyed and published by private enterprise.[51] These large-scale county surveys were often multi-sheet publications: Jefferys's *County of York* (1772), for example, was covered by twenty sheets. Faden had the advantage of being able to publish revised editions of Jefferys's earlier materal, as well as those of other surveyors,

44 Harley 1963–4.
45 The following account of Society of Arts mapping is taken from Harley 1963–4, 1965.
46 Ravenhill 1965.
47 Pedley 1996; Worms 2004.
48 Dymond 2003.
49 Kingsley 1982.
50 Barringer 1989.
51 Based on the entries in Rodger 1972.

but he also spotted the advantage of reducing this cumbersome material to a more manageable size, usually by halving the scale of the original. Faden thus issued reduced versions of Isaac Taylor's map of Dorset (1796), Donn's map of Devon (1799), Gream's Sussex (1799), Day and Masters's 1782 map of Somerset (1803), and Donald and Milne's map of Norfolk (1803).

The zenith of county map-making, however, was the partnership between private and public enterprise that resulted in the one-inch map of Kent engraved and published by Faden some time after 16 February 1801.[52] The survey had been undertaken by the Board of Ordnance with whom Faden enjoyed a close working relationship, first as engraver and printer, and then – once the Board of Ordnance had grasped the financial advantage of undertaking its own engraving and printing – as retailer of what became the official Ordnance Survey one-inch maps.[53] The final separation between official and private survey at the one-inch scale was to be protracted, just as the break between the county as the map production unit at the one-inch scale in favour of national uniform sheet lines was not immediate. The Ordnance Survey one-inch sheets covering the south of England were published, between 1805 and 1825, in ten parts, each covering the whole, or a substantial part, of a county – a direct echo of eighteenth-century publishing practice.

Perhaps even more reminiscent of the eighteenth century was the publication in 1825 of the Ordnance Survey one-inch sheets of Lincolnshire on the basis of subscription from landowners – a condition set by the Board of Ordnance on agreeing to survey the county out of turn. The official break with the tradition of the county unit was finally made on financial grounds. The dual pricing system of one tier of charges for the set of county sheets – the part – and another for individual sheets, introduced unnecessary complexity into the accounting system. When it was realized that the bulk of sales was of single sheets, publication in parts was discontinued and the obsolescence of the one-inch county cartographic unit in official circles was complete.[54]

The demise of the private county surveyor followed soon after, although the first three decades of the nineteenth century were characterized by a final flourishing of private-survey enterprise. In particular, the second decade of the nineteenth century saw the emergence of two surveyor/publishers, Christopher Greenwood (1786–1855) and A. Bryant (*fl.* 1820–35). From the end of the Napoleonic wars in 1815 up to 1832, Greenwood's mapping activity at the one-inch scale covered thirty-five counties. The stated objective was to

52 Hodson 1997b.
53 Harley and O'Donoghue 1975, vii–xxxvi; Seymour 1980, 67–73.
54 Harley 1987, xvi–xxvi.

complete England and Wales and produce, in effect, a national survey. Although this was not achieved by either surveyor, the Greenwood company, which included Christopher's brother John, did publish the surveys in reduced form, together with maps based on other source materials, in *Atlas of the counties of England* in 1834.[55]

In the ten years from 1820 to 1830, Bryant mapped and published thirteen counties at the scale of one inch to the mile or larger (1:63,360–1:42,240). Although Bryant's surveys were many fewer in number than Greenwood's, they were, in scale and content, more informative for the travelling public. Indeed, as a travelling map, they were superior to the Ordnance Survey one-inch map because they gave information on the quality of the route for driving purposes, a feature lacking from Ordnance Survey maps until the 1890s.[56]

Although this late county mapping was being undertaken side by side with the Ordnance Survey, analysis of the Bryant and Greenwood maps indicates that they owed little, if anything, to official cartography. One reason for this may be the aggressive action first taken in 1816 by the Board of Ordnance to protect its copyright in engraved one-inch maps. A warning notice, forbidding the trade from 'copying, reducing, or incorporating all or any of the Ordnance Maps of the Trigonometrical Survey'[57] appeared in several newspapers on 26 February 1816.[58] The effect of this salvo into the ranks of the trade remains to be explored, but if the Ordnance Survey maps were not immediately to be used as source materials, the existing county mapping of Britain provided ready compilation material for a range of maps of Ireland,[59] Scotland,[60] and England and Wales.[61] Perhaps the most important of these were the county atlases of the British Isles, especially those from the later eighteenth and early nineteenth centuries.

County atlases

In 1695, a new edition of Camden's *Britannia* (first published in Latin, 1586), revised by Dr Edmund Gibson – then Fellow of Queen's College, Oxford, and later Bishop of Lincoln and London – was published by Awnsham and John

55 Harley 1962; Hodson 2001, 132–3.
56 Hodson 2001, 133–4.
57 Ordnance Survey was known, until about 1810, as the Trigonometrical Survey: Hodson 1991.
58 For example, *The Times*, the *Morning Advertiser*, the *Courier*, and the *London Gazette*. Harley 1987, xxiv–xxv.
59 Andrews 1978, 1997; Bonar Law 1997.
60 I. Adams 1975a; Moir 1973–83; Moore 1991.
61 Shirley 1988.

Churchill.[62] The text was accompanied by fifty newly engraved maps by Robert Morden. These maps were larger and more detailed than most of those then available, and although they were edited redrawings of extant material, they were among the earliest to incorporate an attempt at the revision of English place-names, and to show roads – hitherto missing on many county maps.[63]

Morden died in 1703, but his Camden maps were to be reproduced, with corrections, in the revised editions of *Britannia* published as two-volume works between 1722 and 1772.[64] Another series of Morden county maps, like those of other map-makers, outlived their author, appearing in works such as *The new description and state of England* (1704). His maps for *Fifty six new and acurate* [*sic*] *maps of Great Britain, Ireland and Wales* (1708) were 'Perfected, Corrected and Enlarg'd by Mr Moll', and forty of these were included in *Magna Britannia et Hibernia* (1714–31). This six-volume work, originally published in ninety-two parts, was freely based on the 1695 edition of Camden's *Britannia* and was one of the earliest books to be published in parts.[65]

Herman Moll, described as an 'intellectual entrepreneur at the heart of the London map trade', and one of the most important British geographers and cartographers of the seventeenth and early eighteenth centuries, not only drew and engraved his own maps, but also frequently published them.[66] Moll based most of his maps for *A new description of England and Wales* (1724) on Morden's *Britannia* work. After Moll's death, most of his copperplates appear to have passed to the Bowles family, and the plates for this atlas, which persisted until about 1766, were revised by Emanuel Bowen.[67]

Up until 1760, the continuing pattern of reissuing old material persisted. For example, John Overton never possessed a complete set of county map plates and so he made up his stock by buying from outside sources, notably the Dutch cartographers Blaeu and Jansson. His son, Henry Overton, who had bought his father's business in 1707, in turn acquired Speed's plates in about 1713. These were incorporated in a succession of four atlases entitled *England fully described* ... between 1713 and 1743.[68] By 1754, most of Overton's plates of county maps were in the hands of William and Cluer Dicey, who sold them as loose sheets until at least 1782.[69] Even the sixteenth-century Saxton plates

62 Tyacke 1978, 66.
63 Harley 1972.
64 Hodson 1984, 98–112.
65 Hodson 1984, 9–31.
66 Reinhartz 1988, 1997.
67 Hodson 1984, 78–94.
68 Hodson 1984, 40–9.
69 Hodson 1984, 66–70.

were to experience a revival in the hands of George Willdey, who in 1732 issued *The shires of England and Wales*. The maps had been revised before 1700 by Philip Lea, who added roads and incorporated information from the surveys of Seller and Ogilby. Willdey had purchased these old Saxton plates at the Lea sale of 1730. Thomas Jefferys, who may have acquired the Saxton plates on the closure of the Willdey business in 1748, reissued *The shires of England and Wales* around 1749. By this time, Jefferys was promoting them as of antiquarian interest. Finally, the plates appear to have been purchased by the Diceys after Jefferys's death in November 1771, and were again sold as loose sheets, perhaps until 1782 or later.

There was, then, little in the way of innovation in the production of books and atlases of county maps until the publication by William Henry Toms in 1742 of *Chorographia Britanniae or a set of maps of all the counties in England and Wales*. The maps, drawn by Thomas Badeslade, were made, according to the title page, 'by Order and for the Use of his late Majesty King George I' and were based on Moll's work. While the content of the atlas may not have been new, the format certainly was. It was the first eighteenth-century atlas to be published in true pocket size: 170×110mm. This work immediately found a substantial and hitherto unexploited market and seems to have been a great success, becoming perhaps one of the two or three bestselling county atlases to be published before *Cary's new and correct English atlas* in 1787.

The next unquestionably successful commercial county atlas publishing venture, which began in 1749, was Emanuel Bowen and Thomas Kitchin's *Large English atlas*, printed and sold by T. Bowles, J. Bowles and Son, John Tinney and Robert Sayer. It was by far the most important English atlas to be published between 1695 and 1787. With few exceptions, the maps – issued between 1749 and 1760 – were based on the latest available surveys. Publication of the work was prolonged, and its completion was advertised in the *Public Advertiser* for 23 May 1760. New maps of Scotland and Ireland were inserted in *c.*1763. Like many eighteenth-century atlases, the maps could be bought bound or singly. The maps of the *Large English atlas* continued to be published by the partners and their successors, and then, without a new title page, by Laurie and Whittle until at least 1825.[70]

In an attempt to capitalize on the success of the *Large English atlas*, Bowen and Kitchin produced the maps in smaller format for the *Royal English atlas*. This was published in 1764 by Kitchin, Robert Sayer, Carington Bowles, Henry Overton, Henry Parker, John Bowles and John Ryall. It was not a

70 Hodson 1989, 125.

success, however. Its parent, although physically cumbersome, enjoyed pride of place on the gentleman's library table. The *Royal* (after the size of paper) scion was probably not sufficiently smaller in size, and although slightly easier to handle, was a commercial failure.[71] The same mistake was not made with Joseph Ellis's maps for *The new English atlas*, published a year later in 1765 by Robert Sayer and Carington Bowles. Ellis's atlas, being much smaller than either the *Large English* or the *Royal*, was a great success, going through many editions and remaining on sale until at least 1824. Promoted as a travelling atlas, it filled a true gap in the market for a small, portable county atlas.

Undoubtedly the highlight of county atlas publishing between 1695 and 1830 was *Cary's new and correct English atlas*, first published in 1787.[72] Large-scale surveys of many counties had been carried out since the publication of the *Large English atlas*, but this new information had not been incorporated into the subsequently published county atlases. The *New and correct* – by taking these primary cartographic sources as compilation material, and by adopting a plain, unadorned engraving style – became by far the bestselling atlas of the eighteenth century. It was a triumphant success. In this work, Cary also combined for the first time an itinerary with a comparatively reliable county atlas. Moreover, he carried out a regular programme of revision to the plates: the 1793 edition remained on sale for sixteen years, but by 1809 the plates were badly worn and he had a new set of maps engraved. There is no other example of a county atlas whose plates had to be completely replaced because of heavy wear. The 1809 edition continued on sale, much revised, until at least 1876.[73] An important feature of all Cary's British work was the attention that he paid to the road network. The road books and maps he and his firm published between 1784 and 1832 were arguably the most distinguished contribution to this popular genre of British cartography in the eighteenth and early nineteenth centuries.

Road books and maps

Ogilby's one-inch road book, *Britannia* (1675), was published thirty-five years after the introduction of the first stage-coach route between London and Oxford in 1640. Few road maps had existed before Ogilby's work; typographic itineraries were more common, and many were included as part of the contents

71 Harley and D. Hodson 1971, 7–15; this contains a facsimile of the maps. A more up-to-date account of the publication history of the atlas is Hodson 1997a, 3–18.

72 Burden 1991.

73 Hodson 1997a, 172–98.

of the thousands of almanacs published annually from 1571.[74] By 1830, the development of agriculture, trade and industry, going hand in hand with road and canal construction and road improvement, had transformed the cartography of communications. With this change, the publication of road books and maps – constantly revised to take account of the new turnpike roads and new roads set out under enclosure awards – became a flourishing concern.

Yet, the road map and atlas publishing business got off to a slow start.[75] Little was undertaken for nearly fifty years after *Britannia* appeared. Although John Ogilby and his kinsman William Morgan had very quickly published *Mr Ogilby's tables of his measur'd roads* (1676), this work lacked any maps and comprised only the written itineraries. It was not until the end of 1718 that Thomas Gardner's reduction of Ogilby's plates appeared, quickly followed by John Senex's similar work and, in 1720, by *Britannia depicta or Ogilby improv'd.* This 'Correct Coppy [*sic*] of Mr Ogilby's Actual Survey' was engraved by Emanuel Bowen, and published by Thomas Bowles.[76] Unlike its vast parent, this pretty little book of strip maps, with engraved accompanying text and small county maps, went through numerous printings between 1720 and 1764, and was still being advertised in a Bowles and Carver catalogue for 1795.

There were many more versions of Senex's reduction of Ogilby, such as Kitchin's *Post-chaise companion* (1767). Jefferys updated Senex's plates with the addition of thousands of roadside features for his *Itinerary; or travellers companion through England, Wales, and part of Scotland* (1775).[77] George Taylor and Andrew Skinner's atlases – *Survey & maps of the roads of North Britain or Scotland* (1776)[78] and *Maps of the roads of Ireland* (1778)[79] – also used Ogilby as a pattern. Numerous other guides and single-sheet road maps proliferated during the eighteenth century. Of all the producers of road maps, however, perhaps two stand out: Daniel Paterson and John Cary. The first of these, Daniel Paterson (1738–1825), was the author of many maps. A year after being commissioned into the army, he produced in 1766 a large sheet of *A scale of distances of the principal cities & towns of England*. This was followed, in 1771, by his famous *A new & accurate description of all the direct & principal cross roads in Great Britain*. This title went through at least eighteen editions, the final issue appearing around 1830. His two-volume *British itinerary* – dedicated to George III and

74 Hodson 2000. This is the only detailed analysis of early almanacs and road books in England and Wales.
75 The best general accounts of this genre of material are still Fordham 1916, 1924, but see also Carroll 1996, 361–410.
76 Harley 1970; Hodson 1984, 78–95.
77 Dickinson 1990.
78 Adams 1975a.
79 Andrews 1969.

first published by Carington Bowles in 1785 – contained, as well as the familiar strip maps, a letterpress description of the 'Direct roads of lesser note' and catered for a wealthier clientele. Paterson, who became Assistant Quarter-Master General, and Carington Bowles guarded their rights in his intellectual property with vigour. The second edition of his *Itinerary* (1796) contained the note 'Entered at Stationer's-Hall, and whoever pirates this work, or any part thereof, will be prosecuted.'

Three years later, in 1799, Paterson's publisher (now Francis Newbery) was himself being sued for plagiarism by the other great contemporary road-map maker, John Cary, who had, in 1798, just published his *New itinerary*, and claimed that the twelfth edition of Paterson's *New & accurate description* was 'a Piracy of a Publication of his own'. The initial judicial view was that Paterson's work was a 'most impudent plagiarism', but after three years in Chancery, and counter-accusations against Cary of editorial malpractice, Cary was to be awarded damages of only one shilling.[80] In 1784, Cary published the first of his many road books: *Cary's actual survey of the great post roads between London & Falmouth*. He had employed the young Aaron Arrowsmith on this work.[81] Ten years later, Cary was employed by the Post Office to make an official measurement of the kingdom's mail roads. This position gave to his road maps a stamp of authority that must have been a valuable commercial advantage. He was to publish, in that same year, his *New map of England & Wales, with part of Scotland*, showing all the 'Direct and principal cross roads'; Cary claimed that he had been 'materially assisted from Authentic Documents liberally supplied by the ... Post Masters General'. Printed in eighty-one small sheets at a scale of five miles to the inch (1:316,800), this work went through several revisions. In using the multi-sheet format favoured for the large-scale county maps, Cary produced the first true series map of England and Wales.[82]

In 1820, the Cary business began publishing the cartographic culmination of John Cary's career: the sixty-five-sheet *Improved map of England & Wales, with a considerable portion of Scotland*, first published between 1820 and 1832 by Cary's sons George (1787–1859) and John (1791–1852). In selecting the half-inch scale (1:126,720), Cary was following the example of Faden who had reduced the one-inch county surveys to this scale. On publication of the first sheet, the Board of Ordnance moved to suppress Cary's work on the grounds of plagiarism of the government survey.[83] The outcome is unknown, but any

80 Smith 1988.
81 Fordham 1925, 18.
82 For an explanation of series mapping, see Hodson 1999, 6.
83 Harley 1987, xxiv–xxv.

injunction that may have been served was clearly ineffectual as Cary went on to complete the map.

In fact, Cary could not have used Ordnance Survey mapping for the whole of this series because the official survey had covered less than half of England and Wales in published sheets by 1830. Although the primary purpose of the Ordnance Survey one-inch map was to serve as a general military map, it was soon acknowledged that its principal function was as a traveller's map. In this it was successful because it showed more routes than any map of Britain before it. It failed to distinguish between bridle roads and carriage roads, however, and to give any indication of width or surface quality. Such a classification system was not to be attempted by Ordnance Survey until 1886, and not fully introduced until 1919.[84]

One hundred years in advance of this development, Cary advertised in 1819 that his projected half-inch road map would show the 'whole of the Turnpike Roads ... as well as the Parish Roads; distinguishing the Carriage Roads from the Bye Roads, which has never yet been attempted in any Map of England'.[85] The use of colour was an integral part of the classification: 'Mail Roads' were hand-coloured in blue, turnpike roads in sepia, and 'Carriage Roads which are Parochial Roads' were coloured dark brown.[86] In using blue for the mail roads, Cary was continuing a practice he had used for his earlier *Traveller's companion, or, a delineation of the turnpike roads of England and Wales* (1790), in which the routes of the mail coaches were shown in blue. This delightful octavo volume was the smallest of Cary's sets of county maps and was an abridgement of the 1787 *New and correct* atlas.

Cary's *Improved map* was the most ambitious road map of its time, and, in its concept, was almost a century in advance of Ordnance Survey. It survived – its plates revised and embellished with railways – until the early twentieth century. Like all compilations, however, it was only as accurate as its sometimes-dubious source materials. The errors it contained, such as roads on the wrong alignment, would have been the cause of annoyance to travellers on land. Such mistakes in a sea chart were far more serious, and could cost lives; erroneous charts were cited as grounds for acquittal in naval courts martial at the beginning of the nineteenth century.[87] Just as important, therefore, as the survey of terrestrial roads was the charting of maritime roads – both the waters where ships lay at anchor off the coast and the wider oceans.

84 Hodson 1999, 127–37; 2000.
85 Fordham 1925, xx.
86 Hodson 2001, 131.
87 Fisher 2001, 25.

Hydrographic atlases and charts

Because Britain has a long sea-faring tradition, is traditionally dependent on a navy for national security, and has a long history of sea-borne commerce, it is surprising that the first truly British sea atlas was not published until 1693. John Sellers's *English pilot* (from 1671) in several volumes, covering the oceans and seas of the world, was the first major sea atlas to be produced in Britain, but it had been based on old Dutch plates, and owed little, if anything, to original hydrographic survey.[88] When Captain Greenvile Collins was appointed in 1681 by Charles II 'to make a survey of the sea coast of the Kingdom', the result was *Great Britain's coasting pilot* (1693), printed by Collins and sold by Richard Mount. It was to be reissued at least twelve times by a succession of combinations of the Mount and Page families and finally by the partnership of Mount and Davidson in 1792.[89] The publication of these two works marked the beginning of the English printed chart trade.[90]

The firm of Richard Mount, Thomas Page and their successors was to dominate English chart publishing for most of the eighteenth century. Their business in sea charts and atlases operated in much the same way as their terrestrial map counterparts – acquiring plates and republishing them, revised or not, under their own imprint. In this way, the plates of Samuel Thornton's magnificent *Sea atlas* (*c.*1702–15), which had incorporated many of the old Sellers plates, passed to the Mount and Page families.[91] Yet, while the business of eighteenth-century sea chart and atlas production was beset by plagiarism – in just the same way as topographical mapping – actual survey did take place increasingly towards the end of the eighteenth century. A handful of amateurs, few in number in the first half of the eighteenth century, but increasing as the century wore on, made original surveys of the coastal waters of Britain. Although he was perhaps no amateur (having been appointed by the Scottish Parliament for the purpose), John Adair undertook a hydrographic survey of the Scottish coast at the end of the seventeenth century. This resulted in the publication, in 1703, of his *Description of the sea-coast and islands of Scotland*.[92]

Encouraged by port officials, the surveyors C. Merit produced, in 1693, a chart of the approaches to the port of King's Lynn. Samuel Fearon and John Eyes's four-chart *Description of the sea coast of England and Wales, from Black-Comb*

88 Shirley 1995.
89 Much of this following section is based on Robinson 1962.
90 Fisher 2001, 3.
91 Hudson 1993.
92 Withers 2000; Moore 1985.

in Cumberland to the Point of Linus in Angelsea – published provincially in Liverpool by A. Sadler in 1738, but engraved in London by Emanuel Bowen – was the first to show Greenwich as the prime meridian. This survey had been financially underwritten by the 'gentlemen and merchants of the corporation and neighbouring county' of Liverpool. Elsewhere around Britain, numerous projects for coastal hydrographic surveying failed for lack of capital. Occasionally, private enterprise, such as that shown by Lewis Morris's *Cambria's coasting pilot* (1748), bore fruit. After prolonged negotiations with the Admiralty, it was eventually funded by subscription, attracting no fewer than 1,230 subscribers and becoming a popular work in great demand.

The surveys of Murdoch Mackenzie the elder of the Orkneys in 1747 to 1750 marked a new departure in survey technique: these were the first hydrographic charts to be based on triangulation. The resulting *Orcades, or a geographic and hydrographic survey of the Orkney and Lewis Islands*, engraved in London by Emanuel Bowen and published by the author in 1750, went into four editions, the last published in 1791. This work was followed in 1776 by the publication of his *Maritim* [*sic*] *survey of Ireland and the west coast of Great Britain*, undertaken by order of the Admiralty and, again, engraved by Emanuel Bowen and published by the author.[93] In foreign waters, the surveys of Des Barres in North American seas and the explorations of Captain James Cook, mainly in the South Pacific but also around Newfoundland, gave rise to numerous publications.[94]

In general, however, the need for up-to-date replacements for the hopelessly out-of-date charts of Sellers and Collins became so acute that the trade itself financed new surveys, in the same way that some topographical surveys had been funded after 1750. Robert Sayer and John Bennett, for example, commissioned Captain James Huddart to make a new survey of St George's Channel in 1777. By this time, Mount and Page were in decline and Sayer had moved into the field of chart publishing, having acquired Thomas Jefferys's chart copperplates after his death in 1771. This purchase, which included plates from the surveys of Captain James Cook, profoundly influenced the future direction of Sayer's business.[95] Sayer and Bennett reissued the *North American pilot* in 1775; within six years, they had published six new major chart atlases. By 1787, the year of John Bennett's death, Sayer's 49-page chart catalogue listed 25 pilots (books of charts and sailing directions) and 123 loose charts.

93 Withers 2002; see also David 2003 for Mackenzie's surveys of the southern English coast.
94 David 1988–97; Beaglehole 1974; Rutherford and Armstrong 2000.
95 Fisher 2001, 51.

The 1780s saw the establishment of new specialist chart publishers, who, with Robert Sayer, became the founding fathers of the companies that persisted throughout the nineteenth century. Their nautical stock-in-trade consisted not only of charts and sea atlases, but also of navigation and mathematical textbooks. The earliest competition to Sayer's business was the firm of David Steel, which began publishing coasting charts in 1778. By 1808, several Steel charts were thought good enough to be selected for supply to the fleet by the Admiralty Chart Committee, but the firm failed in the hands of Steel's final successors who were bankrupted in 1819. Another of Sayer's competitors was John Hamilton Moore (1738–1807, *fl.* 1781–1805). Moore's nautical textbooks, such as *The practical navigator and seaman's new daily assistant* (1772), were not distinguished by any attempt at accuracy, but the financial success of the *Practical navigator* allowed him to set up in business as a chart publisher. Moore employed as draughtsmen William Heather (1764–1812, *fl.* 1793–1812), who was to set up his own chart-selling business in 1793, and John Norie (1772–1843, *fl.* 1812–39) – who purchased Heather's firm for £9,500 on the latter's death in 1812, went into partnership with George Wilson in 1813, and acquired the stock-in-trade and copperplates of the Steel business in 1819.

Heather styled himself 'Chart Seller to the Admiralty, and to the Honourable the East India Company'. His 1804 catalogue listed ninety-two loose charts and eighteen bound pilots. Heather claimed that his *Marine atlas, or seaman's complete pilot*, containing about fifty charts covering the whole world, was the 'only publication of its kind in England'. He was noted for practical innovations in his chart-making; for example, he produced in 1796 a small-scale outline chart of the world on which the route of an entire voyage could be plotted. It became a popular and long-lived item.

The potentially lucrative market in chart publishing at the end of the eighteenth century is demonstrated not only by the fact that Sayer made £4,600 profit in 1781,[96] but also by the enormous sum of £10,000[97] for which he unsuccessfully sued Moore for breach of copyright in a chart of North America in 1784. When Sayer's assistants, Robert Laurie and James Whittle, acquired the Sayer business for a preferential price of £5,000 in 1794, the firm was the foremost of the British chart publishers and the only company able to offer worldwide coverage.

By 1795, it was clear, however, that the national hydrographic interest could not be safely served entirely by the products of private enterprise. Accordingly,

96 Fisher 2001, 10; worth £375,401 in 2002: McCusker 2001.
97 Worth £709,323 in 2002: McCusker 2001.

a government charting agency, the Hydrographic Office, was created, with Alexander Dalrymple, the East India Company's hydrographer, being appointed official hydrographer.[98] Nevertheless, Admiralty charts did not go on sale to the public until 1823, and, even then, the Royal Navy still relied, as it always had done, on charts bought from the London publishers. There was, then, no immediate threat to the private trade in the loose charts that were becoming increasingly commonplace in the chart-seller's stock-in-trade. More flexible than the bound sea atlases, sales of which fell towards the end of the eighteenth century, the separate charts produced by the private publishers were essential for plotting and were conveniently capable of being laid down on a table. From around 1760 they were strengthened by a backing of blue manilla paper, a practice adopted by Sayer, and by 1825 'blue-backing' was in almost universal use. These 'blue-back' charts, as they became known, were to be used by the merchant fleets throughout most of the nineteenth century in preference to the Admiralty chart which remained the specialist preserve of the Royal Navy.[99]

Conclusion

The 140 years between 1690 and 1830 had seen much change in the map, chart and atlas publishing trade in Britain. Cartographic output was prolific, if of variable quality, and covered the known world. In 1690, not a single county in Britain had been published at the one-inch scale. By 1830, private investment and enterprise in carrying out original survey work had resulted in the whole of England, and most of Scotland and Ireland, being covered in published mapping at this scale. By this time, however, the national topographic and hydrographic surveys – born of a need for complete coverage of land and sea at consistent standards of accuracy – had been in existence for forty and thirty-five years respectively. The immediate impact of the Trigonometrical Survey – as Ordnance Survey was first termed – was muted. Indeed, its first publication, the one-inch map of Kent in 1801, was a marriage between private and national interests. The triangulation itself had initially provided data for the private surveyors, but the advance from south to north of the published Ordnance Survey sheets of England and Scotland, and the production of larger-scale Ordnance Survey mapping of Ireland from 1824,[100] heralded the demise of the private county surveyor in Britain.

98 Cook 1999.
99 Fisher 1985, 2001.
100 Andrews 1974, 1978.

After one or two copyright altercations between Ordnance Survey and the trade at the beginning of the nineteenth century, an arrangement developed during the rest of the century whereby commercial map publishers were allowed, even encouraged, to use Ordnance Survey material as long as it was on a greatly reduced scale.[101] The official one-inch map, while signalling the end of the private topographical county surveyor, was, therefore, to provide the direct basis for most of the trade's general small-scale map publication of Britain during the rest of the nineteenth century. In a similar way, the data from the Hydrographic Office charts also became incorporated in private publications which were tailored to suit a wider section of the public.

To a limited extent, the established practice of acquiring the copperplates of former tradesmen persisted well into the nineteenth century. The prime example of this was the Cary half-inch plates that were to be augmented with railways by G.F. Cruchley (1796–1880), and from him were to pass to Gall & Inglis (founded 1810). The latter company was still issuing the maps, in a different format, at the beginning of the twentieth century.[102] Above all, by 1830, the technology of map publishing was on the threshold of change. Lithography had already been used, from 1808, for the production of maps by the War Office;[103] colour printing was in its infancy.[104] Moreover, the duplication of map copperplates by electrotyping was just seven years away,[105] and photography was to follow soon after.[106] This new technology, with all the accompanying innovation in cartographic design, was to be exploited to the full by new commercial map publishing dynasties such as W. and A.K. Johnston[107] and Bartholomew,[108] both founded in 1826, which were to continue into the twentieth century.

101 Y. Hodson 1999, 178–9.
102 Inglis 1960; Hodson 2001, 135–7.
103 Clark and Jones 1974.
104 Severud Cook 1995. Cf. Mosley, chap. 7, above.
105 Andrews 2002, 136–7.
106 Mumford 1972.
107 D. Smith 2000.
108 L. Gardiner 1976.

43

Enlarging the prospects of happiness: travel reading and travel writing

SHEF ROGERS

> He that would travel for the entertainment of others must remember that the great object of remark is human life. . . . He only is a useful traveler who brings home something by which his country may be benefited; who procures some supply of want or some mitigation of evil, which may enable his readers to compare their condition with that of others, to improve it whenever it is worse, and whenever it is better to enjoy it.
>
> Samuel Johnson, *Idler* no. 97, 23 February 1760

> One of the most distinguishing features in the literary history of our age and century, is the passion of the public for voyages and travels. Of the books that have lately been published, there are none, novels alone excepted, that, in point of number, bear any proportion to them.
>
> C. G. Worde, assistant librarian at the British Museum, 1795[1]

As these epigraphs reveal, informed contemporaries held firm opinions about the purpose and amount of travel writing produced in the eighteenth century. Although only a small proportion of the population had either the means or leisure to travel, those who could travel did so in ever-increasing numbers, especially to the Continent, and then wrote about their experiences. As the routes of the Grand Tour became ruts, affluent travellers focused on the emotional aspects of travel or explored farther afield, to Scandinavia and the Mediterranean. At the other end of the social spectrum, the buccaneers risked lives in hope of riches, and celebrated their adventures in accounts that fired the imaginations of readers for the next two centuries. Throughout the mid-eighteenth century an improving economy and peace at home enabled the government to fund so-called 'voyages of exploration', usually with secret orders to seek new trading opportunities. The American and French revolutions, followed by the Napoleonic wars, created new interest in domestic tourism (1780 sees the first use of 'tourist' in print), and new possibilities for

1 Moritz 1924, [3]: Matheson attributes the preface, from which this quotation comes, to Worde.

female authors such as Patricia Wakefield and Mariana Starke, who compiled significant predecessors to the formal guidebook (a compound word in its own right from 1818) later associated with the names of Murray and Baedeker. Such is the agreed trajectory of travel writing in the period.[2] Within that schema, this chapter attempts to indicate who was composing or compiling travel writing, how much of it was produced, who was reading it, and how travel writers, publishers and readers shaped British culture between 1695 and 1830.

The Restoration and return of the court from France intensified interest in travel, at least to the Continent, while William Dampier's *A new voyage round the world* (1697) renewed visions of riches from *Terra Australis*. Richard Lassells, in *The voyage of Italy*, first named the Grand Tour in 1670, and the Greenwich meridian, effectively placing London at the centre of the world, was first established as the basis for longitude measurements in 1675.[3] At the other end of the era, in 1830, the foundation of the Royal Geographical Society created an official distinction between the amateur traveller and the professional explorer, while the opening of the Liverpool–Manchester rail line heralded the possibility of tourism for a much broader proportion of society.

In this period of significant transition, ideas about exactly what constituted travel writing offered creative possibilities for writers of both fact and fiction.[4] The taste for travel clearly beguiled the major authors of this period, with notable works by Joseph Addison, Daniel Defoe, Jonathan Swift, Henry Fielding, Lady Mary Wortley Montagu, Tobias Smollett, Oliver Goldsmith (in verse), James Boswell (Corsica and Scotland), Laurence Sterne, Samuel Johnson, Hester Thrale Piozzi, Ann Radcliffe, Mary Wollstonecraft, William Wordsworth and Robert Southey. Addison's *Remarks on several parts of Italy* (1705) and Sterne's *Sentimental journey* (1768) particularly influenced subsequent travel narratives.

The engagement of so many talented writers with the genre helped make travel writing acceptable to a wide range of readers. A number of influential commentators stressed the innocence of the travel account relative to other genres, especially the novel, and agreed that armchair travel could provide the benefits of travel (reduction of prejudice, exposure to other political systems

2 For valuable discussions of the roles and styles of travel writing in this period, see Frantz 1934; Adams 1962, 1983; Batten 1978; Porter 1991.

3 The meridian was officially designated the zero meridian in 1884, but served unofficially on most maps, especially those available in Great Britain, from the late seventeenth century.

4 Differing definitions of travel writing also explain why Cox (1935) records more than 2,000 travel titles while *NCBEL* (also excluding the British Isles) lists only about 1,200 titles. Consequently, all statistics in this chapter are merely indicative of trends.

and social customs) without the expense, discomforts or possible corruptions of leaving home:

> Travel-writing was a staple of women's periodicals... Hannah More and Vicesimus Knox find travel-books 'very necessary', and Sarah Green recommends that a girl spend 'one morning a week' reading geography and travels... They were thought to provide 'peculiar Pleasure and Improvement' because in them 'no passion is strongly excited except wonder'.[5]

Maria Edgeworth and her brother Richard wrote in their 1798 work *Practical education* that 'There is a class of books which amuse the imagination of children without acting upon their feelings. We do not allude to fairy tales, for we apprehend that these are not now much read, but we mean voyages and travels; these interest young people universally.'[6] The reviewer of a 1777 anthology, *The modern traveller*, described it as 'well calculated for the million, but particularly for young persons: as no kind of reading is more pleasing, and at the same time more instructive. They may, therefore, with great propriety be given as presents to the younger readers of either sex.'[7] This consciousness of a moral role for travel writing may also have led to some judicious censorship by authors aiming at a general audience. The reviewer of Patricia Wakefield's *Family tour through the British empire* (1804) remarked that 'the "fair author" took care "to avoid every thing that might excite improper ideas" in the youths' minds'.[8] This didactic role was apparently appreciated by readers as well as reviewers: Anna Larpent, wife of the dramatic censor,

> used passages from Defoe's *Tour Through the Whole Island of Great Britain* to prepare her boys for a visit to Windsor Castle in 1792: 'I did it', she wrote, 'that they might have their observation raised when we carried them there. There is a great difference between *staring* and *seeing* – the one is merely Corporeal the other unites the mental to the bodily powers and lays in a stock of ideas.'[9]

The benefits of reading travel accounts, however, were not confined to childhood instruction. Both Bishop Hurd and Samuel Johnson advocated travel books as the best instruction for anyone not able to undertake journeys well beyond the beaten paths of France and Italy.[10]

5 Pearson 1999, 55. This advice regarding passion, from John Hawkesworth's *Adventurer* 4 (18 Nov. 1752), took on an ironic tone after Hawkesworth published his edition of Cook's voyages.

6 Edgeworth and Edgeworth 1974, I, 335–6.

7 Cited in Turner 2000, 23 from the *Monthly Review*, no. 56 (1777), 392. Cf. John Owen's similar remark that 'No taste is more prevailing than that for books of travels; none, perhaps, not professedly moral is less productive of mischief.' Owen 1796, I, vi, cited in Turner 2000, 131.

8 Cited in Dolan 2001, 53.

9 Brewer 1996, 241.

10 See Hurd 1764, 157–9 and Johnson, *Idler*, no. 97.

Travellers, too, were enthusiastic readers and frequently set out having already read the relevant travel accounts.[11] As a consequence, travel writing was probably the most self-consciously print-informed genre of the period; travellers often conceived of their travels as print-structured narratives. In October 1735 Walpole resorted to a parody of Addisonian style to depict for Thomas Gray the neglected sights between London and Cambridge.[12] During his own Grand Tour in 1740, Gray wrote in a similar vein to his close friend Thomas Warton. Gray ironically acknowledged his literary pretensions by proposing to print 'by subscription, in THIS LARGE LETTER The Travels of T: G: Gent:'.[13] These instances both reveal just how derivative a genre travel writing could be, and how few travellers in the period set off without well-known and respected models guiding their expectations.

Even the domestic traveller was well served. Accounts of travel within Great Britain and Ireland appeared in increasing numbers, resulting in more than three hundred published titles between 1695 and 1830.[14] Improvements in roads and transport services also made journeys easier, while the establishment of the Ordnance Survey in 1791 began to familiarize and regulate the English countryside. Even before steam, the speed of travel increased markedly, 'shortening the London–York run from five days in the seventeenth century to four days in 1706 and to thirty-one hours in 1790'.[15]

For the more exotic locales, a combination of scientific discovery, voyeurism and political competition, especially with Spain, served to motivate travellers and readers alike. The distinctions between travel accounts, botanical surveys and topographical records often blurred into one another, while a prescriptive text such as Berchtold's *An essay to direct and extend the inquiries of patriotic travellers* (1789) explicitly instructed readers to collect detailed information on prices, commodities and local practices, even providing blank tables for the reader to complete. Boswell's famous desire to see the South Seas was stimulated at least as much by a quest for carnal as for geographical knowledge. Merchants and monarchs sought faster or more predictable trade routes between, above

11 See Francis Garden's comments on various European travels, at the opening of his *Travelling memorandums, made in a tour upon the continent of Europe 1786–8*, I, 4–5 (3 vols., Edinburgh, 1791).

12 Gray 1935, I, 31.

13 Gray 1935, I, 138.

14 Matthews 1950 also records at least 325 British voyage and travel diaries, only about half of which have ever been published. The popularity of travel even came to be blamed for the amount of travel writing published. The reviewer of J. Hassell's *Tour of the Isle of Wight* (2 vols., 1790) asserts that 'Excursions are universally the fashion . . . That this passion is carried to a great extent, and pervades all ranks, may be inferred from the multitude of *Guides*, *Tours*, *Journeys*, *Excursions*, &c. which are continually published' (cited in Turner 2000, 37).

15 Ousby 1990, 10.

and below the Americas, along the coast of Africa, and eventually into its interior. These motives all enhanced readers' eagerness for new travel narratives, so that James Bruce's sixteen-year delay in publishing his *Travels to discover the source of the Nile, in the years 1768, 1769, 1770, 1771, 1772, and 1773* (1790) occasioned much public complaint.

The advent of the review periodicals also heightened public interest in travel literature by excerpting long passages of interesting encounters. Indeed, 'the influential attention which the review journals devoted to travel literature far exceeded their interest in fiction'.[16] Elizabeth Hagglund found that in its first decade (1749–58) the *Monthly Review* surveyed an average of thirty-eight travel publications per year,[17] while Wallace Cable Brown identified 'forty-six extensive reviews of Near East travel books, some of them continuing through several issues ... between 1805 and 1825'.[18] Of course, interest in these reviews, often extensive extracts rather than critical assessments, may also indicate that travel books were the type of publication about which readers wished to be informed rather than to read themselves.

Surrounded as they were by travel books and journalism, British citizens of the period were confident that they were great travellers, a pre-eminence granted by other European nations to their sea-girt neighbour. Abbé Le Blanc noted in his *Letters on the British Isles* (1747) that 'il est sûr que les Anglais sont le peuple de l'Europe qui voyage le plus',[19] a comment echoed by Dennis de Coetlogon almost verbatim a half-century later in the *Universal history of arts and sciences* (1795).[20] Publishing figures reinforce this view of England as the dominant producer of travel texts in this period. *NCBEL* lists slightly more than 1,500 travel items written or published between 1695 and 1800, of which about 90 are translated from originals in other languages: from French 55, German 11, Spanish 10, Latin 4, Dutch and Italian 3, Swedish 2, Danish, Portuguese and Russian 1 each. While the English were thus not insular in their views of travel, they were a net exporter of travel accounts, with nearly 200 English works translated almost immediately into other languages: into French 127, German 107, Dutch 28, Italian 11, Swedish 3, Polish 2, Latin, Russian, Danish, Spanish and Hungarian 1 each.

The majority of readers, of course, never left their firesides, but often journeyed much farther abroad. As Emily Dickinson was to note in her poem

16 Turner 2000, 11.
17 Hagglund 1998, 5.
18 Brown 1936, 74. For the Near East alone, Brown identified seventy separate titles published between 1775 and 1825, at least fifteen of which appeared in more than one edition (77–8).
19 Cited in Guerrero 1992, 1633, from page 60 of Le Blanc's original.
20 Cited in Batten 1990, 134.

'A book', 'There is no frigate like a book.' Indeed, titles relating to distant lands appear to have enjoyed some of the strongest demand. William Bowyer's ledgers reveal impressive print runs for George Anson's *Voyage round the world* (1748). Originally issued as a typically sumptuous quarto, Bowyer printed the first octavo edition that same year, in 2,000 copies, another 1,000 copies between 1756 and 1761, 2,000 copies of the duodecimo ninth edition in 1761, and at least another 3,000 in various formats through to the fifteenth edition in 1776. Most travel books did not possess such sustained selling power, but even Ulloa's *Voyage to South America* (1758), translated from Spanish, managed three editions totalling 2,500 copies in two volumes.[21]

Throughout these years, extensive collections of voyages and travels were issued frequently. At first glance, it is difficult to account for the eighty-five distinct collections of travels published between 1695 and 1830. Many of these are multi-volume sets, up to seventy-six volumes duodecimo, but averaging fifteen to twenty volumes. Because of their ambitious scope, such collections were frequently published serially.[22] The few cases for which the returns on publication can be calculated reveal that collections could be quite lucrative. Christine Ferdinand has computed the expenses and income for John Green's four-volume quarto *A new general collection of voyages and travels*, published and sold in parts from late 1743. The printer produced 12,000 proposals, then another 35,000 a month later. The print run decreased as initial enthusiasm diminished, settling to an average of about 1,500 copies per part, from which Thomas Astley, the publisher, realized a profit of about £6,000.[23] A half-century later E. D. Clarke 'cleared nearly £7000' for his six volumes of *Travels in Europe, Asia and Africa* (1810–23).[24]

Such figures may help account for the notoriously extravagant fee paid to John Hawkesworth for editing *An account of the voyages undertaken by the order of His present Majesty, for making discoveries in the southern hemisphere, and successively performed by Commodore Byron, Captain Wallis, Captain Carteret, and Captain Cook* (1773). This handsome three-volume quarto earned its compiler the unheard-of sum of £6,000. David Hume had received £1,940 for the first two volumes of his *History of England* (1754), Johnson had been paid £1,575 for his *Dictionary* (1755) and William Robertson had received £3,400 for his *Charles V* (1769). Tobias Smollett, however, had contracted with James Dodsley,

21 Maslen and Lancaster 1991. For Anson, see entries 3481, 5178, 4309, 4340, 4681, 4726, 4762, 5085. For Ulloa, see 4164, 4282, 4922. Other travel works printed by the Bowyers reveal print runs of 500–2,000.

22 Wiles 1957 includes every major pre-1750 collection except Daniel Coxe's 1741 three-volume quarto set.

23 Ferdinand 1999, 170–2.

24 Kirkpatrick 1916, 247.

Rivington and Strahan to produce his *Compendium of authentic and entertaining voyages* (7 vols. duodecimo, 1756) for a mere 150 guineas. Two years later Hawkesworth had still only been able to persuade Dodsley to part with 250–300 guineas to compile a *Compendium of the geography, natural history and antiquities of England*, a work that was never completed.[25] Thus his contract with William Strahan and Thomas Cadell was unprecedented, and ultimately proved unreasonable. As Strahan lamented to David Hume in a letter of 9 April 1774, 'the event of [this] purchase, if it does not cure Authors of their delirium, I am sure will have the proper effect upon booksellers'.[26] Apparently Strahan was correct about the effect: Edward Gibbon received only £490 for the first volume of *The decline and fall of the Roman empire* (1776) (though by 1788 he had realized £6,000 from a profit-sharing arrangement for the six volumes), and although Hester Thrale Piozzi received £500 from Cadell for her *Observations and reflections made in the course of a journey through France, Italy and Germany* (1789), Cadell was reported to have 'lost by the publication'.[27]

Even when sales were strong, however, many of these volumes were priced beyond the means of most readers. Certainly travel writings were not being purchased by the less well off, since only three travel titles are known to have been published as chapbooks – *Robinson Crusoe*, *Buccaneers in America* and a version of Anson's *Voyage* – and only the first of these enjoyed much popularity in that format. New England colonists apparently owned few travel accounts; none made the hundred most popular titles, though many owned Jedidiah Morse's *American universal geography*, the fourth most popular title.[28] Of Jan Fergus's admittedly small sample of servants in Daventry, Lutterworth and Rugby, none ordered or purchased on credit any travel writings.[29]

Among the major purchasers of these works, therefore, were the increasingly numerous circulating libraries. Even from the limited surviving records, it is clear that travel narratives were in demand and heavily borrowed. Between 1773 and 1784 the two most frequently borrowed titles in the Bristol Library were Hawkesworth's *Voyages* (201 loans) and Patrick Brydone's *Tour through Sicily and Malta* (1773) (192 loans).[30] A survey of eighteenth-century English libraries found that on average travel books made up 12 per cent of holdings. The category 'travels, voyages, histories and memoirs' was most often the second largest category, behind theology and sermons in the earlier period,

25 Dodsley 1988, 31, 517.
26 Abbott 1982, 147.
27 Farington 1923, I, 3–4.
28 Gilmor 1989, 64–7.
29 Fergus 1996.
30 Kaufman 1960, 122.

and behind novels after about 1760.[31] At Leeds, history and travel held second place to the more general 'belles-lettres' from at least 1768 to 1809,[32] and it is a rare auction or library catalogue that does not list among its notabilia either Churchill or Harris's *Collection*, *The world displayed*, or Cook's *Voyages*.

Thus, many readers in Britain must have availed themselves of the subscription libraries, particularly to obtain the more expensive quartos or volumes with plates, as confirmed by the case of Joseph Hunter, a fifteen-year-old Sheffield apprentice cutler whose 1798 reading diary survives. Hunter purchased mainly periodicals and newspapers, often used to inform his further reading of books, so that he was for the most part a reader of contemporary publications.[33] Hunter deserves praise for his honesty, because he freely admitted when he did not read a book. On 27 July he borrowed Campbell's *Journey overland to India* (1795) because 'we had a very high character given of it', filling five pages of his diary with transcription from the book. He then returned it for Pennant's *Outlines of the globe: the view of Hindoostan* (1798), but confessed, 'I have not read it but, Mr E[vans, his guardian] says it is very entertaining. There are some beautiful plates in it.'[34] The diary shows that Hunter's taste for travels was eclipsed only by his reading of books categorized as 'Moral and Miscellaneous', and equalled his borrowings for 'History and Antiquities', though he completed more of the travel volumes that he borrowed. Obtaining these multi-volume sets from libraries, however, could prove a frustrating business:

> he borrowed the second volume of Helen Maria Williams's *A Tour in Switzerland* (1798) on 22 October along with a copy of the *Gentleman's Magazine*, which needed to be returned after two nights. After making notes from the *Tour*, he returned it to the library on 24 October and replaced it with the first volume. ... Some texts, such as George Staunton's *An Authentic Account of an Embassy* (1797), which Hunter described as 'in universal demand,' were more difficult to complete. He returned volume 1 of this text after noting in the diary that he intended to read the second, but until it became available a few days later he had to content himself with Robert Townson's *Travels in Hungary* (1797).[35]

31 Kaufman 1967.

32 Beckwith 1947, 90.

33 Colclough 2000. I would like to thank Stephen Colclough for his generous assistance in identifying possible sources of contemporary comments on travel writing, drawing upon his own knowledge and the resources of the Reading Experience Database.

34 Colclough 2000, 36.

35 Colclough 2000, 31–2.

Thus Hunter's diary confirms the relative popularity of travel writing, demonstrates that accessibility depended to a great extent on loans rather than purchases, and highlights the attractions of these volumes for their contemporaneity and for their illustrations as well as their text.

Of course, not all readers read by themselves: Samuel Pepys and his wife often read together, as did Thomas Turner and his wife, and Anna Larpent and her husband. Turner's diary refers to Addison's *Remarks* and Defoe's *Tour*, but the only details of travel reading included in his abridged diary record his very leisurely perusal of Joseph Pitton de Tournefort's *A voyage into the Levant* (2 vols., 1718; 3 vols., 1741) throughout most of 1755.[36] In April 1792, Anna Larpent listened in the evening as her husband read to her from Captain David Sutherland's *A tour up the Straits, from Gibraltar to Constantinople* (1790).[37] Whether Turner's provincial abode accounts for his taste in older works is not clear, though provincial libraries' catalogues usually show their holdings to have been as current as those of their London counterparts.

If readers were so eager to learn about the latest journeys, what benefits were they expecting from all these accounts? Frantz argues convincingly that between 1660 and 1732 travel writing contributed significantly to the support of free-thinking.[38] Between 1695 and 1830 the catalogues of books for sale or loan reveal a notable increase in the number of travel accounts and a notable decrease in the number of religious works. Travel writing also gained a certain authority in learned discourse. As David Paxman has shown, John Locke resorted frequently to examples from travel writing to justify unconventional assertions in the *Essay concerning human understanding*. Travel and geography books constituted 'the fifth largest category in Locke's library', and 'citations to them occur more frequently than citations to other types of literature in the *Essay*'.[39] Margaret Hunt similarly notes that Adam Smith 'cited more than twenty' travel works in *The wealth of nations* (1776), and 'had in his personal library almost every major piece of published travel writing by a French or English travel writer of the seventeenth and eighteenth centuries'.[40] Thus it is tempting to argue that travel literature fostered significant new thinking in Britain, and in these two cases it clearly did.

Travel exempla were not universally accepted as authoritative, however. As Samuel Johnson complained of Montesquieu, 'who is really a fellow of genius

36 Turner 1984, 5–22 and appendix D.
37 Brewer 1996, 230–1.
38 Frantz 1934, 152–8.
39 Paxman 1995, 461.
40 M. Hunt 1993, 352.

too in many respects; whenever he wants to support a strange opinion, he quotes you the practice of Japan or of some other distant country, of which he knows nothing'.[41] In general, Johnsonian practicality and scepticism prevailed, and British travel writing served to 'confirm group values and knit individuals to their preferred community' rather than to challenge the status quo.[42] Nearly a century ago F. A. Kirkpatrick concluded his survey of travel publications by noting that 'this kind of writing, perhaps more than any other, both expresses and influences national predilections and national character'.[43] The travel writing of this period clearly excited readers, offering them expansive vistas that appealed at a distance but often failed to live up to expectations as the details became apparent. Familiarity in most cases bred contempt, or at least a certain smug satisfaction with home. As Carole Fabricant more eloquently puts it, in an argument that accounts for the popularity of travel writing even as it discounts its ultimate force,

> Foreign travel, along with the literature (both fiction and nonfiction) that recorded it, allowed the English to indulge their appetite for the bizarre and the primitive in a 'safe' manner, without its having any necessary effect upon the internal workings of English government and society; it encouraged the illusion of cultural diversity while permitting – indeed reinforcing – the continued ethnocentricity of English culture.[44]

England remained the measure against which all places were tested, just as Greenwich remained the source from which such global measurements began. Travel writing, by repeatedly confirming readers' own practices or by allowing them to pride themselves on freedom from prejudice whenever they conceded to another country or culture any admirable qualities, endorsed Englishness as the norm. In publishing these measures, Britons literally authorized their own sense of confidence and contributed to the cultural assumptions that would sustain the British empire through the nineteenth century.

41 14 Sep. 1773; Boswell 1934–50, v, 209.
42 M. Hunt 1993, 340. The controversy surrounding Hawkesworth's comments on Tahitian life and on the role of providence in Cook's first voyage highlighted the limits of readers' receptivity to non-traditional perspectives.
43 Kirkpatrick 1916, 255.
44 Fabricant 1987, 265–7.

44

Law books

WILFRID PREST

Definitions

In January 1786, as he prepared for a mid-life career change from Scots advocate to English barrister, James Boswell 'read in Blackstone for some days'.[1] Some years later another Edinburgh lawyer hoped that William Blackstone's *Commentaries on the laws of England* (Oxford, 1765–9), still regarded by English common lawyers as 'the magnum opus of the eighteenth century', might yield 'a certain degree of Information in the *English* Laws' to complement 'the best Books (though we have none nearly so good) on Scots Jurisprudence'.[2]

The title of this volume notwithstanding, there was – and arguably still is – no such thing as *British* law. While facilitating some cross-border traffic of cases and practitioners, the first Act of Union (6 Anne c. 11) preserved the autonomy of English common law and Scottish Roman or civilian legal institutions. Nor did the second union of 1800 incorporate Ireland's transplanted common-law jurisdiction (39 & 40 George III c. 67), although appeals from Dublin, as from Edinburgh, went henceforth to the House of Lords at Westminster. Irish courts and lawyers followed precedents and procedures laid down by English law books, many of which were reprinted in Dublin, like the pirated 1775 'sixth' edition of Blackstone's *Commentaries*, since no copyright legislation applied in Ireland until 1801 (41 George III c. 107).[3] Yet English and Irish law were not identical. The 1780s also saw the first printed volumes of Irish law reports since the early seventeenth century; these heralded 'a profusion of nominate Irish reports', while not immediately ending complaints about the fated oblivion of Irish

1 Lustig and Pottle 1986, 23.

2 Baker 2002b, 190; H. Mackenzie to Samuel Rose, 20 Mar. 1802, MS 3112, fol. 208, Department of Manuscripts, NLS.

3 Pollard 1989, 80–1. The best Blackstone bibliography is Eller 1938. Cf. Rose, chap. 4 and Benson, chap. 17, both above.

judicial decisions.[4] That eighteenth-century Irish law publishing involved more than merely reprints for export to England and its colonies is, however, indicated by the appearance of such works as Matthew Dutton's *Law of masters and servants in Ireland* (Dublin, 1723), 'the earliest textbook in English in the field of labour law'.[5]

Even within the common law's English (and Welsh) heartland, Roman law retained an academic beachhead at Oxford and Cambridge, whose bachelors and doctors of civil law dominated the ecclesiastical courts of the established church. Civil lawyers continued to publish major works on church law, including John Ayliffe's *Parergon juris canonici Anglicani: or, a commentary by way of supplement to the canons and constitutions of the church of England* (1726, 1734) and Thomas Oughton's two-volume *Ordo judiciorum; sive, methodus procedendi in negotiis et litibus in foro ecclesastico-civile Britannico et Hibernico* (1728, 1738), while Ayliffe's *A new pandect of Roman civil law* (1734) and George Harris's English translation of Justinian's *Institutes* (reprinted at Oxford in 1811 and Edinburgh in 1844)[6] demonstrate the continued vitality of English Roman law scholarship. So does Blackstone's *Commentaries*, the work of an Oxford doctor of civil law (DCL) and Middle Temple barrister who successfully adapted a Romanist structure to the task of expounding the disordered intricacies of English common law. Blackstone thereby fulfilled the earlier ambition of Thomas Wood (also an Oxford DCL, a barrister of Gray's Inn and subsequently a country clergyman), whose publications included both *A new institute of the imperial or civil law* (1704 and three subsequent editions) and the influential *An institute of the laws of England: or, the laws of England in their natural order, according to common use* (1720 and some nine subsequent editions).[7]

Even despite some continued intellectual cross-fertilization from the Roman and natural law traditions, English 'civilians' and their learning were increasingly overshadowed by the hegemonic common law. This brief survey accordingly concentrates on the vocational literature produced mainly for and by common lawyers, together with books on or about the law marketed to a lay audience. Criminal biography and accounts of criminal trials almost certainly constituted the largest body of law-related literature circulating in eighteenth- and early nineteenth-century England, but the bulk and typically non-legal preoccupations of this genre preclude its further consideration here.[8]

4 Vernon and Scriven 1787–9; Osborough 1993, 103; Ridgeway 1794, vii.
5 O'Higgins 1986, 94.
6 Hoeflich 1998, 424, n. 24; [G. Harris], *D. Justiniani institutionum libri quatuor … the four books of Justinian's institutions translated into English … by George Harris* (London, 1756).
7 Lobban 1991, 17–46; Robinson 1991.
8 Recent studies of this literature include Devereaux 1996; Bell 1991; and Linebaugh 1991.

Lawyers' books

Whereas the later sixteenth and early seventeenth centuries had seen unprecedented growth in the numbers of common lawyers and of lawsuits handled by the courts in which they practised, the late seventeenth to mid-eighteenth century was broadly an era of contraction, both for the legal profession and for litigation.[9] Thereafter lawyers' numbers and the volume of lawsuits steadily recovered, with strong growth continuing through and beyond the 1830s. Quantitative trends in eighteenth-century legal publishing, as recently tabulated by Michael Lobban, show a broadly congruent pattern. After little or no increase in the numbers of law books appearing annually between 1700 and 1780 (average annual production rose from 9.3 titles between 1701 and 1720 to 10.4 between 1761 and 1780, after a low point of 7.9 in the 1740s and 1750s), output moved rapidly ahead towards the end of the century, especially after 1790;[10] comparable figures for the first third of the nineteenth century have not been tabulated, but increased publication rates of both new and reissued law titles were undoubtedly sustained.

The common law's professional literature, and the manner of its production, exhibited a mixture of continuity and change throughout the eighteenth and early nineteenth centuries. Even as the bulk and variety of printed law books grew, lawyers continued to support a thriving manuscript culture, consulting not just handwritten documents but alphabetical abridgements, commonplace books, case notes and repertories of forms and precedents typically compiled by both students and younger practitioners.[11] Notes, reports and treatises written up by more established members of the profession also circulated widely. Thus Sir Matthew Hale's commentary on Coke's *First institutes*, copied for the use of Phillips Gybbon as a student at the Middle Temple from 1695, was later consulted by Sir Jeffrey Gilbert, Chief Baron of the Exchequer 1725–6, when compiling a series of texts on aspects of substantive law and jurisdiction, fourteen of which appeared in print posthumously, while others survive in manuscript.[12] An 'Index of Lord Chief Justice Hale's manuscripts' was borrowed by the veteran chief justice Sir William Lee in December 1747; Lee's own collection included a fair copy of the reading or lecture on land law delivered at New Inn by Serjeant Thomas Carthew (d. 1704) in the early

9 Brooks 1998, chaps. 3–5.

10 Lobban 1997, 72–3. For comment on the growth in the number of law booksellers and law stationers, see Turner, chap. 14 above.

11 See Baker 2002a, 475–6.

12 Macnair 1994, 258–60.

1690s, as well as copious extracts from a wide range of printed reports and legal treatises.[13] Blackstone claimed that the circulation of multiple copies of notes – 'in their nature imperfect, if not erronous' – taken at his Oxford lectures was his main motive for publishing the *Commentaries*.[14]

English common law was anything but a coherent body of rules derived from a small number of canonical texts, and its literature was correspondingly diverse and unsystematic. An early modern attorney's or barrister's working library, or law bookseller's stock, might have included some or all of the following: sets of parliamentary statutes and law reports, practice handbooks, treatises on particular aspects or topics of law, abridgements, dictionaries, overviews or 'institutional' works, and introductory student texts. Among new departures after 1750 were London-based periodical publications aimed at legal practitioners and frequently incorporating brief current law reports: for example, the *Lawyer's Magazine; or, Attorney's and Solicitor's Universal Library* (1761–2), the *Lawyers' and Magistrates' Magazine* (1790–4), and two similarly short-lived ventures of the erudite bookseller Samuel Paterson (d. 1802), *The Templar and Literary Gazette* (1773) and *The Templar: or, Monthly Register of Legal and Constitutional Knowledge* (1788–9). More durable were the *Law Magazine or, Quarterly Review of Jurisprudence* (1828–1915) and the weekly *Legal Observer, or Journal of Jurisprudence* (1832–), ancestor of the *Solicitor's Journal*. Another useful innovation was the professional directory, initiated by *Browne's General Law List* (1777–), which provided the names and addresses of legal practitioners throughout the country. In the interests of accuracy John Browne, 'Editor and Sole Proprietor', claimed to have spent £200 for 'a complete FOUNT of entire new TYPES, sufficiently extensive, and purposely cast to keep the whole book undisturbed' between successive reissues.[15] Finally, a growing sub-genre of professional anecdote, gossip and in-jokes emerged in print, including such anonymously published works as *The Causidicade* (1743),[16] *A northern circuit* (1751)[17] and the three-volume *Westminster Hall: or professional relics and anecdotes of the bar, bench and woolsack* (1825). The main categories of eighteenth- and early nineteenth-century common-law literature were otherwise entirely traditional, besides incorporating numerous reprints of earlier classics, such as the *Institutes* and *Reports* of Sir Edward Coke (d. 1633), *Doctor and student* by

13 Beinecke Library, Lee Papers, Box 18, folder 4; Holdsworth 1922–66, XII, 442.
14 Blackstone 1765–9, I, iii.
15 J. Browne, *Browne's general law list for the year 1800* (London, 1800), v.
16 The *ESTC* (T08929, T08930, T08931, T08932) attributes this work to Morgan McNamara (d. 1762).
17 By 'A Gentleman of the Middle Temple': *ESTC* T003998, T200754.

Christopher St German (d. 1540) and the *De laudibus legum Anglie* of Sir John Fortescue (d. 1479?).[18]

Yet alongside the persistence of such older texts, each major department of legal publishing also saw significant expansion and innovation. Reflecting the increased legislative tempo of Hanoverian parliaments, John Cay's *An abridgment of the publick statutes now in force* (1739, 1762) and Owen Ruffhead's *Statutes at large from magna charta to 1763* (1763–4) were among numerous retrospective collections of statutes to appear during the course of the eighteenth century. For pre-Hanoverian legislation the authority of all such works was superseded by the massive nine volumes of the *Statutes of the realm* (1810–25), compiled according to the best principles of contemporary legal-historical scholarship by a body of record commissioners appointed in 1800 on the recommendation of a House of Commons select committee.[19]

No comparable official initiative was taken to improve the coverage or contents of the published case law reports. Forty-six separate volumes of law reports appeared in the 1790s, a more than fourfold increase since the beginning of the century.[20] But as early as 1720 the anonymous preface to the third edition of the *Modern reports* claimed that its pages were 'more satisfactory and enlightening' than those of earlier reports, with their 'short and concise Way' of setting out judicial resolutions, whereby 'the Student is many Times at a Loss and left in the Dark': now at least some cases provided readers 'in a brief and summary Way what hath been offered by the Counsel Pro and Con, and the Debates of the Reverend Judges, as well as their ultimate Resolutions'.[21] This more expansive and informative mode of law reporting became the norm, with printed reports increasingly derived from manuscripts intended for publication, rather than notes originally taken for private use. A succession of reports by James Burrow (d. 1782), Henry Cowper (d. 1840) and Sylvester Douglas (d. 1823), published between the 1760s and 1830s, effectively codified the methodology of common-law case reporting, while those of William Peere Williams (d. 1736), covering the period 1695–1736, served as a model for subsequent Chancery reporters. From the 1780s onwards regular series of printed reports provided extensive up-to-date coverage of most superior common-law and equity jurisdictions, although the effects of unregulated

18 Lemmings 2000, 342.
19 Winfield 1925, 91–3.
20 Lobban 1997, 82–3.
21 *Modern reports: or select cases adjudged ... since the restoration of his majesty king Charles II* (1720), sig. a; cf. Cameron and Carroll 1966, item 2862.

competition between rival reporters brought growing criticism and eventual reform in the following century.[22]

Practice books, which sought to provide detailed and specific guidance to the form of legal documents and the 'course' or procedures of the courts, probably changed less than other departments of legal publishing. While the obsolescence of some older forms of action may have lessened the need for books of entries or compendia of writs, Anthony Fitzherbert's sixteenth-century formulary, the *New natura brevium*, was reprinted five times in London and once at Dublin during the eighteenth century. There was a seemingly insatiable demand for such frequently reissued works as [John Hawkins'] *The young clerk's tutor enlarged: being a most useful collection of the best precedents of recognizances, obligations, conditions, acquittances, bills of sale, warrants of attorney &c.*, which had first appeared in 1662. The seventeenth (1728) edition by 'Thomas Ollyff, Writing-Master, at the Hand and Pen in Fetter Lane' included a guide to Latin personal names, dates, titles and additions 'in their proper cases', directions for suing out various writs, and 'best Copies both of Court and Chancery Hand'.[23] At the other end of the market, texts on the abstruse learning of civil procedure and special pleading proliferated during the last half-century of our period, headed by the massive *Practice* (1790–4) of William Tidd (d. 1847) – a 'great fat book' which Dickens immortalized in *David Copperfield* – and H. J. Stephen's *Treatise on the principles of pleading* (1826).[24]

The later eighteenth century is generally regarded as opening a new era for monographic legal treatises, with the success of Blackstone's *Commentaries* encouraging 'more detailed studies of branches of the law that had been treated only in outline form by the master'.[25] While Charles Fearne's *Essay on the learning of contingent remainders and executory devises* (1772 and four further editions) and Sir William Jones's *Essay on the law of bailments* (1781 and three further editions) support this view, a substantial treatise literature existed decades earlier. Some examples include *The infants lawyer* (1697 and two further editions), which (as its title page averred) sought to expound 'the Law (Both Ancient and Modern) Relating to Infants', Samuel Carter's *Lex custumaria: or a treatise of copy-hold estates* (1696, 1701), the anonymous *Treatise of trover et conversion* (1696, 1721) and Matthew Bacon's *The compleat arbitrator* (1731 and two further editions), together with much of Gilbert's extensive œuvre.[26] If

22 Baker 2002b, 182–4; Holdsworth 1922–66, XII, 110–17; Wallace 1882, 501; Daniel 1884.
23 *ESTC* T108919.
24 Holdsworth 1922–66, XIII, 450–9; Baker 2002b, 89.
25 Simpson 1981, 658.
26 Lobban 1997, 85–8.

less analytical in structure or elegant in style than many (but hardly all) later treatises, their expository impulse and scope were not wholly dissimilar to those of such enduring, albeit much reworked, classics as William Woodfall's *The law of landlord and tenant* (1802, twenty-eighth edition 1978) or J.F. Archbold's text on criminal law, which first appeared in 1822 and reached its fifty-third edition in 2001.

A final broad and miscellaneous class of books offered readers access to the whole body of the law. Dictionaries that defined technical legal terms were already familiar works of reference; John Cowell's *The interpreter*, first published in 1607, continued to be reprinted into the eighteenth century.[27] It was only superseded by Giles Jacob's encyclopaedic and innovative *New law dictionary* (1729), the fruit of nine years' work and much legal publishing experience. By the time its eleventh edition came to be issued in 1797, Jacob's book had grown to fill two volumes, 'greatly enlarged and improved, by many material corrections and additions from the latest statutes, reports and other accurate publications', thanks to the labours of the Inner Temple barrister Thomas Edlyne Tomlins (d. 1841).[28] From the mid-seventeenth century onwards various authors had likewise attempted to expand the range of materials covered by alphabetically organized abridgements of legal sources. The most monumental achievement in this line was Charles Viner's self-published twenty-three-volume *General abridgment of law and equity, alphabetically arranged under proper titles; with notes and references to the whole* (1741–57), characterized by its somewhat self-important compiler (d. 1756) as 'an ingenious system or treatise of law'.[29] While for everyday use Viner's magnum opus never rivalled the handier abridgements by John Comyns (1762–7) and Matthew Bacon (1736–66), its author made a further signal contribution to legal learning by endowing from his profits the first ever university chair in English law.[30]

As Oxford's foundation Vinerian professor from 1758 to 1766, Blackstone continued to deliver the course of lectures on English law that he had launched as a private venture in 1753. Polished and revised over thirteen years, these formed the basis of his *Commentaries*, which first appeared in four volumes printed at Oxford University's Clarendon Press between 1765 and 1769, and then in a further eight English editions before its author's death in 1780. By the

27 *ESTC* T167098 (1701), T132902 (1708), T132904 (1727). Cf. F. Clay's advertisement in B. Langley, *A sure method of improving estates* (1728), prelims.
28 Holdsworth 1937, XII, 176–7.
29 Gibson and Holdsworth 1930, 251.
30 Holdsworth 1922–66, XII, 164–71; Baker 2002b, 186; Ibbetson 1999.

middle of the next century there had been twenty-three English and Irish editions, with nearly a hundred North American abridgements and editions produced by 1900.[31] Blackstone's unprecedented achievement was to encompass the common law's complexities in some two thousand clear, authoritative and well-written pages. While its standing has waxed and waned over the past two and a half centuries, Blackstone's *Commentaries* remains the most widely circulated and influential law book ever published in the English language.

The *Commentaries* had filled a long-standing need; Blackstone's was far from the first attempt at an introductory overview of English law for both law student and general reader. In the printed syllabus of his lectures, Blackstone gave qualified praise to the earlier efforts of Hale and Wood, as well as the work of Henry Finch, whose law-French *Nomotechnia* (1613) was characterized by its translator in 1759 as 'the first General Institute of the Laws of England'.[32] Yet despite its well-deserved popularity as an introductory work which had 'brought darkness to light, and reduced to system and method a farrago of legal knowledge',[33] the *Commentaries* did not meet every need of would-be practitioners and their parents seeking practical guidance on how best to learn the law and establish a legal career. Precisely to that end the indefatigable Giles Jacob had earlier introduced his *Student's companion: or the reason of the laws of England* (1725) with advice on books and modes of study, which was provided at greater length in J. Simpson's *Reflections on the natural and acquired endowments requisite for the study of the laws* (1764, 1765). Later works offering similar recommendations included Thomas Ruggles's *The barrister: or strictures on the education proper for the bar* (1792, 1818), the anonymous *A treatise on the study of the law* (1797), John Raithby's *The study and practice of the law considered* (1798, 1816), and R.W. Bridgman's *Reflections on the study of law* (1804).[34]

Lay law books

Even before the advent of students' books aimed at lawyers in the making, texts setting out the detailed legal powers and responsibilities of local governors were a law-publishing staple. In the eighteenth century leading examples included the civil-law trained clergyman Richard Burns's *Justice of the peace* (2 vols., 1755, 20th edition 1805) and Joseph Shaw's *Parish law* (which reached a

31 Eller 1938.

32 W. Blackstone, *An Analysis of the Laws of England* (Oxford, 1756), ii; [H. Finch], *A description of the common laws of England, according to the rules of art* (London, 1759), v.

33 T. Ruggles, *The barrister* (1792), 12.

34 See also Holdsworth 1937, XII, 417–29.

seventh edition in 1750). An even wider potential readership was solicited by Giles Jacob's *Every man his own lawyer: or, a summary of the laws of England in a new and instructive method* (1736, 10th edition 1788). Jacob here covered 'Actions and Remedies', courts and their officers, property real and personal, family law, 'the Liberty of the Subject', the Crown, government officers and criminal law: 'All of them so plainly treated of, that all Manner of Persons may be particularly acquainted with our Laws and Statutes, concerning Civil & Criminal Affairs, and know how to defend themselves, and their Estates and Fortunes, In all Cases whatsoever.' The eccentric John Rayner 'of the Inner Temple, Gentleman', later observed that although Jacob had been ridiculed by Pope as a 'Blunderbuss of Law', yet 'the profession are much obliged to him ... and I think no writer were better informed of the true method of drawing up a captivating title page ... pointing out those persons, to whom his book would be particularly useful, and they were generally pretty numerous ...'[35]

Jacob also published *Lex mercatoria; or the merchant's companion, containing all the laws and statutes relating to merchandise* (1718, 1729) and *Lex constitutionis: or, the gentleman's law* (1719), which provided basic constitutional and political information, plus 'An Introduction to the Common Law of England, with Respect to Tenure of Lands, Descents, Marriage-Contracts, Coverture &c'. Further guidance on the latter topics was given by *A treatise of feme coverts; or, lady's law* (1732, 1737), and more extensively in *The laws respecting women* (1777). Other authors purported to show 'How every Man, arrested or in Prison in the Counters, Marshalsea, White-Chapel, or other inferior Prisons, for Causes or Actions not arising within their respective Jurisdictions, may discharge himself', while a text also remarkable for its provincial origins offered horse-dealers 'a general idea of *The law respecting horses*'.[36] More useful to 'the general class of readers' was Thomas Edlyne Tomlins's *Law of wills* (first published 1785, seventh edition 1819), which claimed to have taken 'particular care ... to avoid the UNNECESSARY use of law terms', thereby benefiting 'such persons as are not acquainted with either the doctrines or the forms of law'.[37] If the institutional provision of legal education remained at a low ebb throughout our period, a ballooning body of printed self-help manuals provided legal advice and information – albeit of variable quality and utility – to a potentially huge non-professional readership.[38]

35 J. Rayner, *Observations on the statutes relating to the stamp duties* (London, 1786), xxxiv–xxxv.

36 T. Pearce, *The poor man's lawyer: or, laws relating to the inferior courts laid open* (London, 1755), t.p.; A. Stovin, *The law respecting horses* (Hull 1794), v.

37 T. Tomlins, *A familiar explanation of the law of wills and codicils* (1801), vi, x–xi.

38 Holdsworth 1937, XII, 99–101; Prest 2000, 303–13, 1801.

A second significant sub-genre of law books ostensibly directed at lay persons was concerned not to expound the law, but to expose its shortcomings and promote remedies for them. These works of complaint, protest and reform covered a wide range of issues. Thus authors offered *Animadversions upon the present laws of England; or, an essay to render them more useful and less expensive to all his majesty's subjects* (1750), *Considerations on various grievances in the practick part of our laws* (1756) and *Proposals ... to the parliament for remedying the great charge and delay of suits at law and in equity* (1707). One particularly influential early tract was Christopher Tancred's 250-page *Essay for the general regulation of the law* (1727), which possibly spurred a series of pro-reform petitions to Parliament in 1731; these calls for 'Englishing' all legal procedures prompted legislation to that effect later the same year.[39] Critiques and proposals relating to both civil and criminal justice also reinforced the campaigns for 'economical', parliamentary and penal reform, which gathered force during the closing decades of the eighteenth century. In the fourth volume of his *Commentaries*, which dealt with criminal law and appeared in 1769, Blackstone had himself commended the reformist principles of Cesare Beccaria, whose *Dei delitti e pene* (1764) did not appear in English translation until 1767.[40] A decade later the *Fragment on government; being an examination of ... the introduction to Sir William Blackstone's Commentaries* (1776) secured to Jeremy Bentham, Blackstone's former pupil and least forgiving critic, the intellectual leadership of what soon became a national law-reform movement.

Authors, readers, marketing, production

Law books were mostly written by lawyers, whose title page identification as such helped establish the authority and credibility of their books. Even critiques of the common law and its institutions were often penned by practitioners, although usually anonymously – Bentham himself had been called to the bar at Lincoln's Inn, although he never practised. Legal authorship, especially law reporting and treatise writing, was a recognized career option for younger barristers by the end of our period. Indeed the future Shakespearean scholar John Payne Collier helped blight his own professional prospects by censoriously observing that those who (like himself) had just 'mounted their wig and gown' often obtained work through 'the publication of some treatise upon a particular branch of law, or by a volume of reports of decided cases,

39 Prest 1993, 117–18.
40 *ESTC* T138985.

accompanied by a fulsome dedication to an individual, with the means of advancing them in their progress'.[41]

As distinct from one-book authors primarily seeking professional preferment, some practitioners evidently made a profitable sideline, perhaps even their main income, from editing and writing law books. Leading examples include the energetic and versatile Giles Jacob who, in addition to thirty-odd legal titles, published half as many literary works, and the shadowy J.F. Archbold, a barrister of Lincoln's Inn from 1814, about whom little more is known than his bibliography of more than forty legal publications.[42] For others the psychological rewards of authorship may have been paramount, as in the case of Joseph Chitty the elder (d. 1841), a successful special pleader and barrister who founded a legal dynasty and managed to continue producing practitioners' manuals for nearly four decades after his *Treatise on the law of bills of exchange* first appeared in 1799.[43] Something of a similar nature doubtless motivated such legal antiquaries as Daines Barrington (d. 1800), whose *Observations on the statutes* was first published anonymously in 1766, the King's Printer John Reeves (d. 1829), author of the first substantial *History of the English law* (1783–7), and Francis Hargrave (d. 1821), whose edited *Collection of tracts relative to the law of England* (1787) and *Collectanea juridica* (1791–2) drew on his extensive personal manuscript collection, now in the British Library. A few lawyer-authors also tried to use their books to advance personal causes or publicize grievances; thus John Rayner sought to vindicate his '*professional* Character' as a Commissioner of Bankrupts in the preface to his *Readings on statutes ... in the reign of ... George the Second* (1775).[44]

While there were many different motives for legal authorship, most law books brought their authors modest financial returns at best.[45] Blackstone's huge earnings from the *Commentaries* – totalling £12,488 between 1765 and 1772, when he sold the copyright to the printers William Strahan, Thomas Cadell and Daniel Prince for a further £2,000 (it earned them £7,147 more over the next fifteen years) – were entirely exceptional.[46] The point is borne out by the significantly lower range of prices Strahan paid for other law-book copyrights: an eighth share in Comyns's *Reports* cost him £1 10*s*. in 1762, while the

41 'Amicus Curiae' [J.P. Collier], *Criticisms on the bar; including strictures on the principal counsel* (London, 1819), 8.

42 Lobban 1997, 80; Simpson 1981, 664, n. 228. For further details of Jacob's career, see Matthew Kilburn's entry in *ODNB*.

43 Holdsworth 1952, 458–9, 481–2.

44 Cf. S. Brewster, *Ius feciale anglicanum: or a treatise of the laws of England relating to war and rebellion ... [with] an expostulary preface to the right honourable the Lord Parker* (London, 1725), i–xxiv.

45 Lobban 1997, 81–2.

46 London Metropolitan Archives, Clitherow Papers, ACC 1360/586/6; BL MS Add. 48807, fols. 1–12.

total value of Comyns's *Digest* in 1777 was rated at just over £600. Although in 1760 Jacob's *Law Dictionary* was valued as high as £800, its price had more than halved only seven years later.[47]

Quite apart from the intrinsic merits of his text, Blackstone's previous role in overhauling Oxford's university press had familiarized him with the economics of publishing.[48] In all respects his experience differed greatly from that of the attorney Richard Bridgman (d. 1820), who complained that his *Thesaurus juridicus* (1799–1800) had not achieved 'the reasonable expectation of a modest sale', forcing postponement of its final volume. Bridgman had evidently 'proposed a Subscription', but the response was 'limited'.[49] While not the commonest means of financing law books, subscription publishing was sometimes employed for more expensive and esoteric texts, such as John Ayliffe's edition of the Pandects, his colleague Thomas Oughton's *Ordo judiciorum* (1738), Viner's Abridgement, and the first American edition of Blackstone's *Commentaries*.[50]

As already noted, 'law books were not only for lawyers'.[51] When the leading bookseller of the cathedral city of Worcester advertised his wares in 1760, legal titles – including volumes of the statutes, Blackstone's antiquarian and occasional writings, three trial transcripts and Giles Jacob's *The complete parish officer* (1750) – made up the largest category among eighty-six stock items listed.[52] Law books also figured prominently in advertisements placed by London booksellers in the provincial press, as they did in metropolitan newspaper and journal advertising.[53] And if landholders, clergymen, merchants and parish officers constituted a sizeable secondary market for at least some categories of law books (in addition to those specifically directed at lay readers), practitioners were among the very broad audience targeted by such volumes as *The tradesman's lawyer and countrey-man's friend ... in contracts, bargains and agreements ... borrowing, lending and restoring ... goods pledged and pawned ... scandalous words ... leases ... landlord and tenant ... discharging and ending of actions ... statute laws, concerning labourers, trademen, artificers, apprentices, servants, petty chapmen, &c ... useful as well to professors of the law, as to tradesmen and others* (1703). Lawyers showed little concern that works such as these might reduce

47 British Library Add. MSS. 48806, fols. 3v, 9v.
48 Philip 1957.
49 Printed announcement dated 18 St James's Park, 5 Oct. 1801 and copies of author's correspondence with Francis Hargrave, 10 and 18 Nov. 1801 in copy of vol. 1 held by British Library at 512.c.17.
50 *Proposals for printing by subscription, A new pandect of the Roman civil law* (n.d.); Speck 1982, 63.
51 Feather 1985, 35–6.
52 Feather 1985, 75, 77.
53 Cooper 1997, 28; Ferdinand 1999, 164.

demand for their professional services. When a century later an attorney-author stated that the public had often been 'imposed upon by legal publications, whose title pages have promised much useful information', his aim was simply to discredit the competition and promote his own text, which claimed to cater for both lawyers and men of business.[54] On the other hand, it is also worth noting that non-routine common-law learning was not reserved for trainee barristers alone; according to his surviving commonplace book, Benjamin Smith read and commonplaced Blackstone, Wood's *Institutes*, Burrow's *Reports*, Bacon's *Abridgment* and Coke on Littleton, among numerous other texts, while apprenticed as an attorney to his father at Horbling, Lincolnshire, during the 1790s.[55]

Most eighteenth-century law books aimed primarily at a lay readership, like *The tradesman's lawyer*, included on their title page the imprint of the holder of the monopoly patent for law printing, or those to whom he had assigned that monopoly: in that particular case the 'assigns of Richard and Edward Atkins, for Thomas Beever at the Hand and Star within Temple Bar'. Such statements of provenance functioned as legitimizing testimony, validating the authenticity and authority of the text that followed.[56] Since 1556 only those holding a royal patent had been entitled to exercise the 'privilege of printing of all manner of law books, which any way relate to the common or statute law of England'.[57] Objections to this licensed monopoly from other booksellers and printers, and exceptions in favour of the two university presses and the King's Printer (who theoretically enjoyed sole right to print 'Statutes, Books, small Books, Acts of Parliament etc.'), provoked intermittent disputes and litigation until 1769.[58] William Strahan then effectively united the twin roles of King's Printer and law patentee, having originally acquired a half-share in the law patent from Samuel Richardson's widow for £1,250 in 1762.[59] By now the courts were more reluctant to endorse monopolies granted by royal prerogative. In the landmark copyright case of *Millar* v. *Taylor* (1769), Lord Mansfield held that the source of whatever authority the king exercised in relation to law printing derived from his copyright over certain legal and parliamentary materials, rather than from any inherent prerogative powers.[60] The immediate

54 G. Clark, *Memoranda legalis: or an alphabetical digest of the laws of England: adapted to the use of the lawyer, the merchant, and the trader* (1800), v. On professional resistance to disseminating legal knowledge, see Brooks 1998, 239–40; Ross 1998.

55 Schmidt 1996, 30–1, 37 nn. 28–9.

56 For the cultural and intellectual functions of patents and imprints, see Johns 1998, chap. 4 and *passim*.

57 Baker 2002b, 479–89; Sale 1950, 135 and chap. 8 *passim*.

58 See, for example, Melton 1985, 61–3.

59 Cochrane 1964, 123, 129–31; Eaves and Kimpel 1971, 507–9.

60 Lobban 1997, 76–7.

practical impact of this decision may have been limited (after William Strahan's death in 1781, his son Andrew Strahan and William Woodfall junior carried on business as 'Law Printers to the King's Most Excellent Majesty').[61] Yet it surely strengthened the trend noted by Dr Lobban, whereby from the middle of the eighteenth century 'a wider range of legal books ... did not bear the imprint of the law patentees'.[62]

If the publishing role of the law patent and its holders had become relatively insignificant by the 1830s, that of the specialist law bookseller-publisher was markedly augmented. As during the seventeenth century, so after 1700 several London booksellers brought out regular catalogues of law books, such as the successive issues of the *Bibliotheca legum* (1732–68) issued by John Worrall (d. 1771) from his shop 'in Bell-Yard, near Lincoln's Inn'. Like previous law bookseller's catalogues, Worrall's publication still provides a useful guide to prevailing prices, the general level of which does not appear to have risen for most of the century; as Worrall noted in 1753, while some scarce and out-of-print items had become more expensive, 'a much greater Number are lessened in their Value'.[63] On the publishing side, however, Worrall did not confine himself to law books, which indeed constituted fewer than half of all titles published under his imprint between the 1720s and early 1770s.[64]

Edward Brooke, Worrall's business successor, who continued the *Bibliotheca legum*, did publish mainly law books. Indeed by the early nineteenth century R.W. Bridgman claimed that the sheer bulk of legal material in print justified his own compilation of a full critical bibliography, rather than a mere bookseller's catalogue.[65] However, it was the printer, bookseller and stationer Samuel Brooke who became one of six founding members (along with Stephen Sweet, Alexander Maxwell and Steven and Sons, all of whom dealt in both new and second-hand stock from premises around and about the Inns of Court) of the 'Associated Law Booksellers'. This body was formed in 1822 'to print and publish New Term and Nisi Prius Reports and such other works in the different branches of the law, as may from time to time be considered by them'. Besides

61 Cf. F. Buller, *An introduction to the law relative to trials at nisi prius* (London, 1793), t.p.

62 Lobban 1997, 77, n. 46. The later history of the law patent is murky, possibly because its post-1781 holders effectively merged their theoretical monopoly rights with those of the King's Printer, who by 1831 was said to have 'the monopoly of printing law books': House of Commons, *Parliamentary papers, Select committee on King's Printers patent*, 1831–2, xviii.73.

63 J. Worrall, *Bibliotheca legum: or a new and compleat list of all the common and statute law books of this realm, and some others relating thereunto, from their first publication to Trinity term 1756* (London, 1756), t.p., sig. [a3v].

64 Lobban 1997, 77–8.

65 Lobban 1997, 78; Maxted 1977, 29. Later editions of the *Bibliotheca legum* were compiled by John Clarke (1806, 1808) and T.H. Horne (1819); see also J. and H. Butterworth, *A general catalogue of law books* (London, 1815); and Bridgman 1807, vii.

joining together to compile a *Catalogue of law books ancient and modern* (1825) issued under their individual names, the group's early enterprises included a new edition of Blackstone's *Commentaries*.[66] The one major London law bookseller and publisher not represented was Henry Butterworth who, after apprenticeship to his law bookseller uncle Joseph Butterworth, had begun business on his own account in 1818. The second (1820) edition of his *Catalogue of recent law publications* announced the imminent appearance of nine law titles 'printed for H. Butterworth'.[67] Thus by 1830 the 'great names in legal publishing' throughout the twentieth-century English and Commonwealth common-law worlds had already made their appearance.[68]

Parliamentary printing

The eighteenth and early nineteenth centuries saw massive increases in the volume of parliamentary transactions committed to print and major changes in the organization of that printing. While English law was increasingly shaped by parliamentary statute during the same period, only a brief sketch of these complex developments is possible here.

From 1680 the *Votes and proceedings* of the House of Commons had provided MPs, government officers and the public with a regular (albeit cryptic and formalized) printed record of parliamentary business. In 1742 the manuscript 'Journals' dating from 1547 began to be converted into print; from 1761 onwards these volumes were published after each annual parliamentary session. While the publication of current debates remained punishable as a breach of privilege, thinly disguised and largely non-verbatim newspaper and magazine reports of current proceedings compiled from a variety of sources gradually eroded sales of the *Votes and proceedings*.

In 1803 the journalist William Cobbett (d. 1835) began to publish his *Parliamentary debates*, a series taken over in 1812 by the printer T.C. Hansard (d. 1833), second son of Luke Hansard (d. 1828), who as printer to the House of Commons from 1774 was responsible for the *Journals* and most other parliamentary papers, including an ever-mounting body of bills, papers and reports. *Hansard's parliamentary debates*, as they were known from 1829, had as yet no official status, let alone a monopoly of parliamentary reporting. By contrast, his father Luke and younger brother Luke Graves Hansard (d. 1841), who also enjoyed the lucrative appointment of printer to the House by the Speaker's

66 Maxted 1977, 30; Maxwell 1974, 122–3; Birks 1960, 435–6.
67 Jones 1980, 7–15.
68 Munby and Norrie 1974, 264.

nomination, were closely involved with the conduct of parliamentary business. By 1817, when Luke Hansard wrote his fascinating 'Auto-Biography' as a present for two sons, he had built up the largest printing house in London, largely on the basis of 'the employment afforded by the House of Commons'.[69] Despite mounting attacks on their privileged status from reformers who saw them as symbols of a corrupt and inefficient patronage regime, the elder Hansards were justly proud of their skill at converting complex and disorderly manuscript into legible print, and otherwise facilitating access to the ever-expanding volume of printed parliamentary papers.[70]

69 Hansard 1991, 83 (the quotation comes from J. Rickman's testimony to the House of Commons Select Committee on Printing, July 1828).
70 Ford and Ford 1972; Hansard 1962; Lambert 1968; Bellot 1933.

45
Philosophical books

JOHN VALDIMIR PRICE

Three names dominate the trade in philosophy books in the period 1695–1830: John Locke, David Hume and Dugald Stewart. The triad familiar to undergraduates of Locke, Berkeley and Hume simply disappears when one considers the presence of their names on title pages up to the end of the eighteenth century: 229 times for Locke, 177 for Hume (including his *History of England*) and 55 for Berkeley. Locke's works provide an important exemplar for the historiography of philosophy, though not necessarily for the publishing of philosophy in the eighteenth century, while those of Dugald Stewart represent a transition from recondite inquiry to university textbook. Locke, Hume and Stewart were frequently reprinted in the nineteenth century, and in the case of Locke and Hume no end seems in sight.

Eighteenth-century publishers and readers had less restricted ideas about what constituted a philosophy book than philosophy departments in universities have at the beginning of the twenty-first century. In the eighteenth century, it is reasonably safe to say that a book is a philosophy book if its author thought it was philosophical, or if it had the words 'philosophy' or 'philosophical' in its title (surprisingly few of the best-known ones do), or if its topics are epistemology, or morality, or aesthetics, or theology with epistemological or moral overtones, suppositions or conditions. Many eighteenth-century readers would have regarded Alexander Pope's *Essay on man* (1733–4) and William Kenrick's *Epistles to Lorenzo* (1756) as philosophical, and they were intended as such by their authors, although they are written in verse.

John Locke's *Essay concerning human understanding* was the first overwhelmingly successful philosophical book to appear in Britain. First published by Thomas Basset in December 1689 (with title page dated 1690) in folio in two different issues, Locke's work, in an edition of 500–900 copies (the exact number is unknown), reached a second edition, this time published by Thomas Dring and Samuel Manship, in 1694 for the first issue, with the names of Locke's later publishers, Awnsham and John Churchill appearing on the title page for the first time in the second issue of the second edition. The Churchills published a third edition in 1695 and the greatly revised fourth edition of 1700 (the first for which we know definitely the price to a customer, 14*s*.), and later the first posthumous edition of 1706. These editions were all cumbersome folios. Not until the sixth edition of 1710 did the *Essay* appear in a more user-friendly octavo format, which was an edition, probably pirated, by Henry Hills; later issues have the Churchills as publishers on the title page. Locke's success as philosophical author was undoubtedly instrumental in making the publishing of philosophy in Britain a matter not merely of prestige, but of profit as well. Should anyone attempt a thorough census of the most frequently printed and reprinted philosophical book, Locke's *Essay* would surely come first. Awnsham Churchill made a considerable fortune as a publisher, and his success owed a good deal to his eye for a saleable philosophical treatise. Moreover, the popularity of the essay can be attributed to the clearness of Locke's prose (if not his ideas). Locke's payments were calculated in an equally clear fashion: he received 10*s*. for each 'sheet'.[1]

Locke's ideas were interesting enough for his work to find two other forms of publication, the first being John Wynne's *An abridgment of Mr Locke's Essay concerning human understanding*, which the Churchills published in March 1696, followed by a second edition in 1700, and several other editions in the eighteenth century. Wynne was a reasonably able expositor of Locke's ideas, though he forbore any exegesis of the first book, except for the introduction. Locke was to reach an even greater audience, however, when Joseph Addison decided, in the *Spectator*, no. 10 (12 March 1711) to bring philosophy out of the closet (so to speak) so that it could 'dwell' in coffee houses and at tea-tables. There seems to me little doubt that Addison not only helped popularize philosophy, but brought both joy to the hearts of philosophers and profits to the pockets of publishers. Wynne made most of Locke's ideas accessible in an octavo format, and Addison made Locke fashionable. Alexander Pope probably helped make Locke an accessory to female beauty, when he depicted Rufa studying Locke in the second of his *Moral essays* (1731–5), 'Epistle to a Lady' (line 23). Later, with periodicals and reviews,[2] authors, particularly those of philosophical books, could expect, with pleasure or dismay, to see large portions of their works quoted in the quality or serious journals. Locke's importance endures, despite David Hume's pronouncement in the first few pages of his *Enquiry concerning*

1 Yolton 1998, 69.
2 See Harris, chap. 20; Maidment, chap. 25; and Forster, chap. 33, all above.

human nature that 'ADDISON, perhaps, will be read with pleasure, when LOCKE shall be entirely forgotten.'

In almost every way an antithesis of Locke, George Berkeley achieved fame, or rather notoriety, in the eighteenth century with his immaterialist views. His first two important works, *An essay towards a new theory of vision* (1709) and *A treatise concerning the principles of human knowledge* (1710), were published in Dublin. Berkeley later incorporated *An essay* into his most successful book, *Alciphron*, published first by Jacob Tonson in London and later by Risk, Ewing and Smith in Dublin (with errors in the London edition corrected) in 1732. His *Treatise* was not published in London until 1734. The publication of *Alciphron* was something of a departure from the norm for Tonson (?1656–1736), who was more often associated with literary works, but the four further editions of *Alciphron* that he published give ample evidence that this enterprise was a commercial success.

Berkeley authored a number of other works, including a popular short work *Three dialogues between Hylas and Philonus* (1713), which used the dialogue form for philosophical issues more adroitly than any previous attempt in English. In later books, Berkeley wandered almost capriciously into other issues, such as Popery and the curative properties of tar-water, doing his reputation – with his contemporaries and with posterity – little good. Collected editions of his works were published in handsome quarto volumes in both London and Dublin in 1784, but they did little to breathe life into his reputation.

Perhaps the only eighteenth-century philosopher who seemed to take Berkeley seriously was David Hume, who in his *Treatise of human nature* (1739–40) paid tribute to him as a 'great philosopher', responsible for 'one of the greatest and most valuable discoveries that has been made of late years'.[3] Berkeley at least saw his early publications go into several editions: in his autobiography Hume noted that his *Treatise* 'fell dead-born from the Press'; it was not reprinted until 1817. The first two volumes of the *Treatise* were published anonymously by John Noon in late January or early February 1739. The third volume was published, also anonymously, in October 1740, but this time the publisher was Thomas Longman. David Norton has established, however, that the printer for all three volumes was the same, John Wilson.[4] Noon advertised the work as '*beautifully printed*', but, despite its many attractive features, the work did not sell well, and Noon may have declined to publish the third volume in 1740.

3 Hume 1739–40, I, 17.
4 Norton 1988.

Hume's contract with Noon is among the Hume papers now in the National Library of Scotland. He assigned all his rights to the first two volumes of the first edition of the *Treatise* to Noon for £50, the sum to be paid within six months of the date of the contract (26 September 1738); he was to receive twelve bound copies upon publication, and Noon was to publish 1,000 copies. The initial price for the two volumes was 10*s*. Noon may have regretted his purchase, since he had difficulty selling copies. Some nine years later, he published Moses Lowman's *Rational of the ritual of the Hebrew worship* in 1748, and the page of advertisements at the end includes volumes I and II of the *Treatise*; moreover, after Hume had attained great success with the first volume of his *History of England* in 1754, Noon advertised the *Treatise* on 7 and 9 December 1754 in the *Daily Advertiser*, promoting it as by the author of the *History of Great Britain*. Nevertheless, the work apparently continued to sell badly: both Noon and Longman advertised all three volumes in the *Daily Advertiser* for 26 January 1756 and again in the *London Evening Post* for 10 February 1756.[5]

Even if Hume had wanted to think about a second, revised edition of the *Treatise*, he would have had to buy from Noon all the unsold copies before a second edition could be published. Hume got around this difficulty, both philosophically and bibliographically, by ransacking the *Treatise* for its essential ideas and publishing them in the more digestible form of essays. The first essays appeared in Edinburgh in 1741–2, with a later edition in 1748; in 1751 Hume published his collected *Essays and treatises on several subjects*, which included both his *Enquiry concerning human nature* (1748) and his *Enquiry concerning the principles of morals* (1751). Six further editions followed during Hume's lifetime, and the sales of his works helped to make him rich and famous.

Locke, Berkeley and Hume have, of course, earned the respect and attention of academic philosophers and general readers for well over two centuries now. Even Hume's *Treatise* has enjoyed a revival of interest that would no doubt gratify its author. Yet none of these sustained a reputation during his lifetime like that of Dugald Stewart. As professor of moral philosophy at the University of Edinburgh from 1785 to his retirement in 1810, he had a great effect on a generation of students that spread from Edinburgh to the Continent and North America and, hence, had a profound effect on the Scottish Enlightenment. His first book, published in 1792, *Elements of the philosophy of the human mind*, formed part of a three-volume set; a second volume appeared in 1814, and a third in 1827. The first volume was not reprinted for ten years, but by that time he was

5 Mossner 1980, 328.

Britain's most important living philosopher.[6] His second book, *Outlines of moral philosophy. For the use of students in the University of Edinburgh* (1793), was not the first textbook specifically published for students of philosophy (Adam Ferguson's short pamphlet of 1755, revised in 1766 and published 1769 as *Institutes of moral philosophy*, was certainly the first to be used as a textbook during its author's tenure in a Scottish university), but it was reprinted and used throughout the nineteenth century in Britain, North America and continental Europe.

Some may rightly believe that Stewart's influence adversely affected Britain's nineteenth-century philosophers, who, with the exception of John Stuart Mill, did not shine as luminously as those from the eighteenth century. Yet, it must be admitted that Stewart had an effect on his students out of all proportion to his abilities as a philosopher. An American student attending his lectures wrote that he could not 'recollect, or mention ... the official exhibitions of Dugald Stewart ... without feelings of the most enthusiastic respect, and of the liveliest gratitude. I have never found any public speaker, in any situation, more eloquent in manner and language, and never have been made to feel more sensibly, by any orator, the dignity of human knowledge, – the beauty of human genius – or the elevation of human virtue.'[7] Stewart was but one of the Scottish literati whose works formed a significant part of university curricula here and abroad, and authors such as Archibald Alison, Thomas Reid, Henry Home, Lord Kames, William Campbell and Thomas Brown provided influential textbooks for several generations of university students.

Locke, Hume and Stewart are probably more important than Berkeley in terms of the sale and readership of philosophy books in this period, but there was also a great number of writers whose philosophical expositions found a ready public; and many whose works did not, but whose reputation has survived to the twenty-first century. A brief account of this subject can do no more than glance at some of the minor players; they remain in the background of the life of the mind in the eighteenth century, yet they provided a steady supply of books on 'philosophical' topics, and they often had insights into and reflections upon the major themes that found favour with the public.

Francis Hutcheson (1694–1746) is an obvious example of an author whose books were sought after by both readers and publishers – mostly in his lifetime

6 Perhaps this was not a great achievement: Francis Jeffrey, reviewing Stewart's *Philosophical essays* (1810), remarked 'The studies to which Mr Stewart has devoted himself have lately fallen out of favour with the English public ... [which] seems now to be almost without zeal or curiosity as to the progress of the Philosophy of Mind.' The review originally appeared in November 1810 and was reprinted in *Contributions to the Edinburgh Review* (London, 1846), II, 644–65.

7 Hook 1975, 86.

and part of the later eighteenth century – but thereafter hardly at all. While he was living, Hutcheson's works came out in octavos or duodecimos; only the posthumous *System of moral philosophy*, handsomely printed by the Foulis Press in 1755, was published in quarto. However attractive its format and production values, this important work was not popular with readers, and was not reprinted until the twentieth century. Hutcheson's first book, *An inquiry into the original of our ideas of beauty and virtue*, published anonymously in 1725 in both London and Dublin, appeared at least another six times in the eighteenth century under a variety of imprints. Often, as in the case of the fourth edition of 1738, the property was shared out among a number of booksellers. A later set, *An essay on the nature and conduct of the passions* (1728), was followed by another seven editions in the eighteenth century, again with a variety of booksellers appearing in their imprints as shares in the work were sold within the trade. Unlike Locke, Hutcheson was virtually unknown when his first work was published, but it and later works were important enough to lead him into the chair of moral philosophy at Glasgow University in 1729, when he was thirty-five. Both Adam Smith, his student at Glasgow, and David Hume, who sought his advice before seeking a publisher for his *Treatise*, acknowledged the quality of Hutcheson's writings, but Hutcheson seems to have been more of a favourite with 'professional' philosophers than with the educated reading public. In 1742, a Latin work, *Philosophiae moralis institutio compendiaria*, which may have formed the basis of his lectures to students at Glasgow, was published; it was translated into English in 1747, after his death, but seems unlikely to have served as a course outline for students.

One of the authors whom Hutcheson especially criticized in his works was Anthony Ashley Cooper, 3rd Earl of Shaftesbury, whose *Characteristicks, of men, manners, opinions, times* was first published in 1711 and reprinted eighteen times in the eighteenth century. Other than Lucretius' *De rerum natura*, it was the only philosophical work of fifty-six books in all that John Baskerville is known to have printed. For the most part, philosophical works did not find themselves candidates for fine printings, but Shaftesbury was as well known as Locke and probably more accessible to many readers. While most philosophical works published in the eighteenth century were printed in a variety of formats and volumes, Shaftesbury's work usually appeared in three octavo volumes. There were some curious exceptions, however: a four-volume edition in Glasgow in 1758 was almost certainly by Robert Urie, though no name of a printer or a publisher appears on the title page; the same is true for a similar four-volume edition in London the same year. In an earlier, anonymously published edition in London of 1733, in three duodecimo volumes, the publisher-printer (probably Thomas Johnson of The Hague[8]) gives a brief history of the early printing of Shaftesbury's pieces, and notes that 'five large Editions' have been sold. Lamenting the size and cost of these volumes, the publisher explains that in order to 'gratify the Publick in such a reasonable demand this pocket Edition is now made; & it is hoped [it] will give satisfaction, as well for its neatness & exactness, as for its price, which is less than half of the other'. The expensive engravings found in other editions said to be 'more for ornament than use' were not included, though Shaftesbury had put them to good pedagogical use. The publisher cleverly adjusted the registration so that the page numbers would 'answer every where those of the larger volumes. So that any passage or page quoted in this Work, or cited from it in any other, will answer as well to this as to any of the former Editions.'[9] So far as I can tell, no other philosophical work published in this period paid such particular attention to the ease of reference for putative readers.

Shaftesbury's work was discussed in many books and pamphlets, but it was forty years before a book devoted exclusively to the *Characteristicks* appeared: John Brown's *Essays on the Characteristicks* (1751). William Bowyer printed 750 copies of the first edition for the bookseller Charles Davis, and it appeared in April 1751 – followed by four other London editions, also printed by Bowyer, who supplied a copy for the two editions printed in Dublin in 1752.[10] The ready market for Brown's commentary on Shaftesbury almost certainly helped to promote sales of his later book, *Estimate on the manners and principles of the times*, first published in 1757, with a second volume in 1758.

In 1757 and 1758, Brown's *Estimate* was a bestseller (with six editions in the first year of its publication). Brown's bibliographer, Donald Eddy, suggests that 1,000 copies of each edition were printed, and there were another 1,000 copies printed of the seventh edition in 1758.[11] There also followed three Dublin editions, one Belfast edition, an American edition and a French translation. Emboldened by the success of this first volume, Bowyer printed 4,000 copies of the second volume, which was followed by Dublin editions and a French translation. It is not known what Brown was paid for the work, but there is little doubt that the publishers, L. Davis and C. Reymers, did rather better out of it than Brown did. The editions published in those two years were enough to saturate the market, and the work was not republished in the eighteenth century.

8 See Hoftijzer and Lankhorst, chap. 26, above.
9 Cooper 1732, I, [x].
10 Eddy 1971, 25–37.
11 Eddy 1971, 62–75.

Brown's natural successor is probably James Beattie, professor of moral philosophy at Marischal College, Aberdeen, who made an early reputation as a poet. It was his intense opposition to Hume and Hume's ideas, however, that led him to write his best-known book, *An essay on the nature and immutability of truth, in opposition to sophistry and scepticism* (1770). The story of its publication is an entertaining one. Beattie had a certain amount of diffidence about the book and left the arrangements about its publication to his friend Robert Arbuthnot and Sir William Forbes, Beattie's future biographer. Forbes writes in his life of Beattie that Beattie had entrusted to him and Arbuthnot the disposal of the manuscript 'as we should judge proper'. They applied 'to the bookseller, whom we thought most likely to publish it with advantage' and were 'mortified by his positive refusal to purchase the manuscript'. The bookseller offered, however, to publish it at Beattie's expense, an 'expedient' they knew that Beattie would never accede to. So they wrote to Beattie saying that they had accepted 50 guineas for the book, and Forbes sent him a bank draft for that sum, while he and Arbuthnot guaranteed the publisher, Alexander Kincaid and J. Bell in Edinburgh, against any losses. Beattie accepted these arrangements, though he confessed to Forbes that he was 'morally certain' that he and Arbuthnot had been responsible for underwriting the publication and seeing that he was paid. Happily for Beattie – and the publishers – the work proved to be far more popular than the Edinburgh booksellers thought it would be: the first edition sold out quickly and was followed by a second in 1771 and several other editions before the end of the century.

Beattie's popularity extended to Samuel Johnson (Hume's had not, of course), who allegedly said of the book that 'there is in it a depth of reasoning, and a splendor of language which make it one of the first rate productions of the age'.[12] Beattie was smugly satisfied, as well, and, on 16 May 1773, when he was dining with William Strahan, Hume's printer, Strahan had told him that his *Essay* 'has knocked up the sale of Mr David Hume's Essays'.[13] The truth of Strahan's remark notwithstanding, the critique of Hume evidently sold better than Hume's own text: by 1773, Beattie's *Essay* was in its fourth edition; Hume's *Essays and treatises* had been published in 1770 and 1772, but there were no further editions until the first posthumous edition of 1777. From the first edition of the *Essay on truth* in 1770 until about the middle of the nineteenth century, there were some fifteen separate editions of the work, and it

12 Recorded in Beattie's diary entry from his trip to London in 1773. His entry for 1 June 1773 details his conversation with Mr Garrick; see Forbes 1904, 79.

13 Forbes 1904, 76, 79. Beattie in fact is reporting what David Garrick had said to him of Johnson's opinion.

was included in collected editions of Beattie's works in 1776, with further editions in 1777 and 1778. Strahan had been responsible for an edition of Beattie's poetry in 1780, but not for the *Essay on truth*. He published Beattie's *Dissertations moral and critical* in 1783 and *Evidences of the Christian religion* in 1786, and his comment seems more likely to have been an appeal to authorial vanity. Some of Beattie's other works, for example his *Elements of moral science* (1790–3), were republished in the early part of the nineteenth century, but have otherwise dropped off the publishing map of philosophy as if they had never existed.

One can gain another perspective on the trade in and market for philosophical books by looking at just one concept that permeates eighteenth-century thought and virtually disappears by 1820, that of 'taste'. Addison made the idea popular before it became philosophical, and Hutcheson was the first to develop the concept rigorously. The topic was a popular one for essayists, letter-writers and even poets, but the first book-length treatment was that of John Gilbert Cooper, whose *Letters concerning taste* was published in 1755. Cooper designed the title page himself and insisted on having the book published anonymously. He asked Robert Dodsley for 25 guineas for the rights to the book, as well as a copy of Robert Woods's *Ruins of Palmyra* (1753). Tierney notes that Dodsley demurred at paying the asking price, and Cooper was offered £20 for the first edition and the copy of Woods's book as a gratuity for the second edition.[14] In fact, his receipt indicates that he accepted 'the value of Twenty pounds in books' for the copyright. Dodsley printed 750 copies of the first edition, which sold for 2*s*. each. The second edition has a cancel title page and a completely rewritten Editor's Advertisement; otherwise, the text is the same. Dodsley published a third edition in March 1757; this was printed by William Bowyer in an edition of 500 copies and on this occasion the price was 3*s*. 6*d*.[15]

Cooper's work, while philosophically lightweight, nevertheless answered reader interest in the concept of taste, and publishers not surprisingly found themselves happy to have treatises on the subject submitted to them.[16] In May 1759, Andrew Millar published Alexander Gerard's *Essay on taste*. As is well known, the book was seen through the press by one David Hume, whose association with Millar began in 1748, but not before Hume had tried his hand with several other publishers. The book was printed by William Bowyer

14 Dodsley 1988.

15 Maslen and Lancaster 1991, no. 4102.

16 Dickie 1996 does not mention Cooper, and as yet there is no systematic history of the concept of taste in the eighteenth century.

in an edition of 750 copies and delivered on 7 April 1759.[17] Bowyer's ledgers reveal that the title page was cancelled. The work was reprinted, with changes, in 1764 and 1780.

The next book to be devoted entirely to the concept was by James Usher (or Ussher), *Clio: or, a discourse on taste. Addressed to a young lady*. The first edition of 1767 was a small duodecimo, consisting of only 91 pages; when Usher brought out his second edition in 1769 (when it was priced at 2*s*. 6*d*.), he had expanded the work to 247 pages. A third edition followed in 1773. In each instance the bookseller was Thomas Davies, acting for himself alone. Davies was involved in publishing from about 1760 to 1785, and it was, of course, in his shop that Boswell was introduced to Johnson. He published virtually every kind of work, often acting in concert with other booksellers, but his exact arrangements with Usher are unknown.

Other philosophical works published in this period contained significant sections on taste, most notably Edmund Burke's *A philosophical enquiry into the origin of our ideas of the sublime and beautiful* and David Hume's *Four dissertations*, both published in 1757 – Burke's work priced at 3*s*. 6*d*. and Hume's at 3*s*. bound. Hume's essay 'Of the standard of taste' was one of the four dissertations, while the second edition of Burke's work, in 1759, contained a substantial introductory essay on taste, with the price now increased to 4*s*. 6*d*. Burke's *Sublime and beautiful* proved to be another philosophical bestseller; it was first published by the Dodsleys, and at least thirty separate editions appeared before 1830.

These various works by Cooper, Gerard, Hume and Burke had the effect of keeping the concept of taste as an aesthetic construct before the reading public throughout the second half of the eighteenth century. Not surprisingly, other philosophical authors – including Henry Home, Lord Kames, Hugh Blair and Thomas Reid – devoted substantial parts of their books to the concept. In 1790, Archibald Alison published his *Essays on the nature and principles of taste*, one of the last philosophical works in this period to be published in quarto. It was not reprinted until 1811, when it was dedicated to Dugald Stewart, whose own *Philosophical essays*, published in 1810, had a substantial section on taste. Having been more or less neglected for twenty-one years, Alison's work was then reprinted another five times in this period. Between the first and second edition of Alison's work, another book on taste excited critical attention, Richard Payne Knight's *Analytical inquiry into the principles of taste*, published in 1805 and three further editions in quick succession. The last relevant work

17 Maslen and Lancaster 1991, no. 4217.

in our period is that of Martin MacDermot, whose *Critical dissertation on the nature and principles of taste* appeared in 1822, and was reissued in 1823 with different prefatory material. Unlike previous eighteenth- and early nineteenth-century works on taste, this one seems to have dropped completely from sight, and thereafter publishers avoided similar publications.

Books and essays on taste thus document publishers' abilities to supply books on subjects that had the appeal of philosophical novelty for their readers and which sold surprisingly well. Taste proved, as Kazayuki Shimotani, has argued, a concept with a limited usefulness once its metaphorical limits had been reached, and that may account for the disappearance of books or essays devoted to it.[18] Publishers, like philosophers, want to move on, and the concept of taste, as an aesthetic principle, had little of the attraction for philosophers and readers in the nineteenth century that it had for those in the eighteenth century. In part, that is due to a different kind of interest in aesthetics in the nineteenth century; in part, it also appears that publishers found the market for multi-volume books on philosophy had diminished. Books and essays on taste, however, can serve as a general model for the changing nature of the market in philosophical books during the long eighteenth century. However difficult or remote the concept, authors of philosophical works required printers and booksellers to gain access to a large readership. Given that a large majority of philosophical books, not just ones on aesthetics but those on other philosophical topics, are not easy to read and sometimes contained ideas at variance with those of the book-buying public, the wonder is that there were so many, and so many that were financially successful, rather than so few.

18 Shimotani 2002, 4 and *passim*.

46

Scientific and medical books, 1695–1780

ALICE WALTERS

Eighteenth-century Britain witnessed both the rise of a consumer culture and the emergence among the public of an intense curiosity about the natural world and humankind's place in it. The intersection of these forces produced a flood of scientific and medical literature, including journals, pamphlets, broadsides and books. Recent scholarship has emphasized that the early modern scientific and medical book was the product of a messy, often contentious, process of negotiation among various parties – author, bookseller, printer, scientific or medical community, etc. – all of whom contributed in some way to the creation of an item that was at once a physical object, a text, a set of ideas (which might or might not be innovative, or even 'true'), the basis of an author's credibility and a bookseller's commodity.[1] Consumers bought books in order to gain access to one or more of these elements. Once purchased, a book could become something else to its owner, transforming (perhaps) into a scholar's obsession, a child's scrapbook, a lady's companion or just one of hundreds of elegantly bound tomes adorning the walls of a gentleman's library.

From among these myriad meanings we can tease out some generalizations about scientific and medical books. First, eighteenth-century scientific books – including texts on the physical and natural sciences, as well as mathematics and applied mathematics – were produced not just for practitioners, but also for gentlemen amateurs, curious ladies and middle-class schoolboys. Similarly, medical texts – including works in physiology, anatomy, pharmacy, and the various medical and surgical practices – made these disciplines more accessible and comprehensible to potential patients and at-home practitioners, as well as to the expanding community of medical practitioners. Within the bookselling community, certain firms came to be associated with both types of literature: thus, for example, scientific publishing was a speciality of John Nourse, William Innys, Andrew Millar, and the Longman and Rivington families,

1 Johns 1998; on the significance of this work to the history of the Enlightenment, see Sher 2000, 114–15.

while John Murray of London and Charles Elliot of Edinburgh were known for producing medical books.[2]

The commercial histories of scientific and medical books share some common characteristics, but their cultural roles tended to be quite different. More often than not, medical books were written by medical practitioners and read by students preparing for medical careers. The eighteenth-century British medical community, 'formally straight jacketed in its traditional, three-tiered, hierarchical structure' incorporating physicians, surgeons and apothecaries, offered would-be practitioners fairly well-defined educational programmes and professional identities.[3] Medical books, pamphlets and journal articles complemented the more formal educational experiences of the student (attendance at lectures and dissections, apprenticeship in hospitals, etc.), while their composition came to be associated by the end of the century with professional achievement in medicine.[4]

In contrast, writers of scientific books often earned their livings in occupations that typically had no direct relationship to the subject of their work, while their readers generally did not anticipate using the knowledge gained from their study to earn money.[5] One bibliography that lists the livelihoods of the writers of scientific and mathematical works published between 1700 and 1760 includes occupations such as ministers, drapers, bricklayers and farmers, as well as more predictable (and numerically more representative) occupations such as astronomer, instrument maker, engineer, teacher, surveyor and physician.[6] Similarly, a substantial number of scientific books produced during the century specifically targeted readers who would never be expected to earn their own livings, including women and gentlemen of leisure.[7]

Whether a book was intended for a student, practitioner or curious amateur, a key element in creating and maintaining a market for a scientific or medical work was accessibility – of both the text and the book. Thus, for example, the eighteenth century witnessed the beginning of a shift from Latin as the language of learning to the vernacular, and most eighteenth-century medical and scientific works followed this trend by appearing in English.[8] Even Newton's works were published in English translations; an English edition

2 For the publication of scientific books prior to 1760, see Wallis and Wallis 1986, 487–97; on John Murray, see Zachs 1998, especially 175–83.
3 Porter 1987, 27–30, (at 29).
4 Lawrence 1996, especially chaps. 6 and 7.
5 A similar contrast holds for medical v. scientific lecturing: see Porter 1995, 93.
6 Wallis and Wallis 1986, 482; see also Sher 2000, 128–9.
7 Walters 1997.
8 Zachs 1998, 176–8.

of his revolutionary *Philosophiae naturalis principia mathematica* (*Mathematical principles of natural philosophy*, 1687) was first published in 1729 by Benjamin Motte, brother of the translator Andrew Motte, while Newton's other major scientific text, the *Opticks*, was published first in English (in 1704) and then in Latin (in 1706).

Even after the *Principia* became available in English, however, would-be readers still faced the daunting task of wading through Newton's mathematics to conquer Newton's natural philosophy. The inability of most readers to do so successfully inspired the most important trend in the marketing of eighteenth-century books in the physical sciences: the promotion of works designed to present explanations of contemporary advances in natural philosophy unencumbered by mathematics. As a review of James Ferguson's book *Astronomy explained upon Sir Isaac Newton's Principles, and made easy to those who have not studied mathematics* noted, such works made accessible 'some general knowledge of this useful branch of science, to those who are unacquainted with mathematical calculations, and who have neither leisure nor capacity to tread the dry and intricate paths of Geometry'.[9]

The commercial success of Ferguson's work reveals the power of this approach. Ferguson published the first edition by subscription in 1756; the quarto volume sold for 15*s*. After publishing a second edition in 1757, he sold the copyright (and likely his remaining stock of books) to bookseller Andrew Millar for £300. Millar only published one edition before his death in 1769 – the third, also in quarto, which appeared in 1764 and sold for 18*s*. At Millar's death, the copyright to *Astronomy explained* was split into twelve parts and sold, fetching a total of £239. At this point, the proprietors seem to have decided to market the book to a new audience; the fourth edition (1770), of which 1,000 copies were printed, appeared in octavo, reducing the price to 9*s*. The publishers of the fifth edition (1772) produced another 1,000 octavo copies (again sold for 9*s*.) as well as 500 quarto copies (which still sold for 18*s*.). The sixth (1778) and seventh (1785) editions of the work enjoyed press runs of 1,500 copies, while 2,000 copies were published of the eighth (1790) and ninth (1794) editions – twice the usual press runs of 750–1,000 for books in the natural sciences.[10]

9 *Monthly Review*, 15 (1756), 236–44, at 236.

10 On the sale of Ferguson's copyright, see Millburn 1988, 93; on the sizes, press runs and prices of the various editions, see Wallis and Wallis 1986, 274–5; on the sale of Millar's copyright and press runs for the sixth to ninth editions, see the annotated catalogue (dated 13 June 1769) listing Millar's copies and quire stock, as well as the business ledger, Mar. 1776 to May 1796, p. 2, in the archives of the John Murray publishing house in the National Library of Scotland. See also Walters 1992, 27–39.

A similar story may be told for another book intended to make the wonders of the natural world more accessible – William Cheselden's *Anatomy of the humane body*. Cheselden first published the work in 1713 in an octavo edition, noting that it was 'design'd for the use of those who study Anatomy for their entertainment, or to qualify themselves for the knowledge of physick or surgery, and not for such as would be critically knowing in the minute parts etc.'. Cheselden's text enjoyed substantial success throughout the eighteenth century, to the benefit of the author. Apparently, Cheselden maintained ownership of at least part of the copyright until after the sixth edition was published in 1741; when Cheselden retired in 1749, he sold his copyright to Charles Hitch and Robert Dodsley for £200. Shares in Cheselden's *Anatomy* were bought and sold over the course of the century, and the book was republished through to the thirteenth edition, which appeared in 1792.[11]

Few authors were in a position to make as much money from a single publication as Ferguson and Cheselden did, as few works had the long-term staying power of these texts. Financial profit was probably not a major concern, however, for the majority of the writers who produced the scientific and medical books consumed by the eighteenth-century British public. Then as now, most scientific and medical authors made their livings in non-literary occupations, including technical, professional and medical practices and affiliated activities such as public, university and hospital lecturing and school teaching. A successful scientific lecturer, like J.T. Desaguliers, or a fashionable physician might make several hundred guineas a year or more from his labours; and, while schoolmasters, apothecaries and others who wrote scientific and medical works almost certainly made much less, they also probably earned enough to support themselves apart from their revenues as writers.[12] For most such authors, writing was a side-line, producing income that was likely of less importance than whatever contributions publication made to their larger scholarly or business interests, or (particularly in the case of medical practitioners) how it enhanced their professional identity.[13]

Consider, for example, *The microscope made easy*. Published in 1742 by Robert Dodsley, the work was the first scientific book by Henry Baker, then a recently elected Fellow of the Royal Society, teacher of the deaf, published poet and

11 On Cheselden's *Anatomy*, see Cope 1953, 6–8, at 6.

12 For a useful discussion of the finances of the eighteenth-century scientific practitioner, see Heilbron 1979, 153–4, 163–6; on the natural philosopher as entrepreneur, see Stewart 1992, esp. chaps. 4 and 5; on the income of physicians, see Porter 1987, 36.

13 Sher 2000, 129–30.

editor of a literary magazine, the *Universal Spectator*.[14] According to the contract for the sale of Baker's copyright, Dodsley agreed to pay Baker a guinea a sheet, plus twenty copies of the published book; half was to be paid at the time of publication, and half within two months. The contract also provided that Dodsley was to pay Baker another half guinea per sheet after the first edition of 1,000 copies was sold, and a half guinea per sheet if a second edition was printed within two years after the first sold out.[15] Under this contract, Baker probably made only about £35 for the first edition, and another £11 for the second edition of his book, published a year later. Since the contract made no provisions for more than two editions, it is not known whether Baker received any additional sums for the other three editions of the work Dodsley and his brother published through to 1769.

Sold for 5*s*., *The microscope made easy* turned out to be a very successful book. Dodsley issued two more editions in the following two years, and a fifth edition came from Tully's Head in 1769, some twenty-seven years after it first appeared. Moreover, it was combined into a single work with Baker's other major treatise on microscopy, *Employment for the microscope*, and published in 1758 and 1785. The work also gained a continental audience through a Dutch edition (1744) and a French edition (1754).[16] Though Baker may not have derived great financial profit from this success, it did enhance his value as an author in Dodsley's publishing business. Baker's second work, *The natural history of the polype*, netted Baker 2 guineas per sheet, plus twenty advance copies, and 5 guineas plus six copies for all future editions. In 1753, Baker received £88 11*s*. 6*d*. for his last work, *Employment for the microscope*, a payment of perhaps as much as 3 guineas per sheet.[17]

The non-financial profits derived from publication were likely of equal, if not greater, benefit to Baker. *The microscope made easy* established him as an important scientific writer, helping to expand his range of correspondents throughout Europe. From these correspondents, Baker acquired samples of, and information about, local natural objects – scientific knowledge that would have been difficult to acquire first hand, and that undoubtedly contributed to his status within the British scientific community.[18] The work also contributed to his social prestige by providing a medium through which he could act as

14 Biographical information on Baker is found in the *Dictionary of scientific biography*, and in G. L'E. Turner 1974.
15 Contract dated 3 June 1742, BL Egerton MS 738, fol. 3, cited in G. L'E. Turner 1974, 61.
16 Wallis and Wallis 1986, 258–9.
17 BL Egerton MS 738 fol. 5, cited in Dodsley 1988, 509; on the originality of *The natural history of the polype*, see G. L'E. Turner 1974, 62.
18 G. L'E. Turner 1974, 67–9.

patron for his own microscope maker, John Cuff. The newspaper advertisement announcing the publication of *The microscope made easy* made special mention of 'John Cuff, Optician, in Fleet Street'; the second and subsequent editions also listed Cuff's name, occupation and address in the imprint, and thereby provided a vehicle for the advertisement of his goods.[19] The first part of the book, in which Baker discussed the various types of microscopes available, focused on Cuff's microscopes.[20] Baker's correspondence supplemented this public association between *The microscope made easy* and Cuff's products with private endorsements. Many of Baker's correspondents originally contacted him to ask for his opinion about the best microscopes, and frequently also his assistance in purchasing them.[21] Baker always gave this business to Cuff. As one of Cuff's new clients wrote to Baker, 'Mr Cuff no doubt is sensible of the obligations he lyes under to you, I dare say your book has contributed not a little to the sale of his glasses.'[22]

The link between Baker's book and Cuff's microscopes illustrates a more general feature of the eighteenth-century scientific book trade: the commercial and conceptual relationship between scientific books and scientific instruments. Many eighteenth-century scientific publications were associated directly or indirectly to the products of the London scientific instrument trade. For example, texts 'on the use of the globes', which offered brief introductions to astronomy and geography illustrated by these popular pieces of library furniture, constitute one of the largest genres of scientific books published in the eighteenth century, with a new or republished title on the subject appearing almost yearly between 1750 and 1820. A few members of the instrument trade also wrote and published books illustrating and advertising their products, including perhaps the most prolific scientific author of the eighteenth century: lecturer and instrument retailer Benjamin Martin, who produced more than eighty works, ranging from single-sheet explanations of astronomical phenomena to multi-volume popularizations of Newtonian natural philosophy.[23] Martin's major competitor in the instrument business, George Adams senior, also wrote and published books and pamphlets illustrating his products, as did his son, George Adams junior; the latter's works were

19 *Daily Post*, 17 Nov. 1742.

20 G. L'E. Turner 1974, 61.

21 For examples, see the correspondence of Henry Baker in the John Rylands University Library of Manchester, esp. Robert Blair (Edinburgh) to Baker, 2 June 1743 (I, 252); Joseph Bruni (Turin) to Baker, 22 Mar. 1745, (II., 26); J. Mounsey (Riga) to Baker, 24 Feb. 1748 (III, 251).

22 Blair to Baker, 14 July 1743 (I, 212), in Baker Correspondence, the John Rylands University Library of Manchester .

23 On Martin, see Millburn 1976; Wallis and Wallis 1986, 211–19. On mathematical instrument makers in the Stationers' Company, see Turner, chap. 14, above.

republished well into the nineteenth century by the London instrument firm of W. and S. Jones.[24]

For the instrument maker, publication offered the opportunity to promote his products and expand his sales; for the lecturer, it provided the chance to reach an audience beyond the confines of his lecture halls, including students who might not be able (for reasons of distance, physical mobility, social propriety or other circumstances) to attend the lectures themselves. It is likely too that, enticed by the ideas they encountered in print, some attendees paid to see lectures given by their well-known scientific or medical authors. A few lecturers, concerned about losing their lecturing profits to their bookseller, limited their publication to course outlines, which could serve simultaneously as advertisements for potential students and aides-memoires for their alumni. In some cases, admiring students took it upon themselves to publish the lectures of their favourite teacher – with or without his consent.[25] The printing of a pirated copy of J.T. Desaguliers's lecture notes by one of his former pupils, which appeared under the title *Lectures of experimental philosophy* in 1719, prompted Desaguliers to rush out an 'authorized' edition of the work. Indeed, Desaguliers was haunted by piracy throughout his career; fifteen years after this incident, when he published his much-expanded *Course of experimental philosophy*, he vowed to sign each copy of his book if any bookseller issued a pirated edition.[26]

Piracy of scientific and medical books occasionally plagued booksellers, but plagiarism of these texts was rampant throughout the century. Among the best places to find stolen texts are the many eighteenth-century English encyclopaedias, which often made particular note of their scientific content, and which, like the first edition of the *Encyclopaedia Britannica*, were often mostly products of 'pastepot and scissors'.[27] Even Ephraim Chambers, editor of the venerable *Cyclopaedia*, admitted to 'purloining... other people's work'. He excused himself from censure, however, by pleading practical considerations:

> Dictionary writers, at least such as meddle with arts and science, seem in this case exempted from the common laws of meum and tuum;... their works are supposed, in great measure, compositions of other people; and whatever they take from others, they do it avowedly, and in the open sun. In effect, their quality gives them a title to every thing that may be for their purpose, wherever they find it; and if they rob, they do not do it any otherwise, than as the bee

24 On the Adams family, see Millburn 2000.

25 Sher 2000, 130–1; but see also Porter 1995, 94–5, on William Hunter's avoidance of publication.

26 Johns 1998, 181–2.

27 The description is that of William Smellie, editor of the first *Encyclopaedia Britannica*; Kerr 1811, I, 362–3; quoted in Kogan 1958, 14. On science and contemporary encyclopaedias, see Yeo 1991, 2000.

> does, for the public service. Their occupation is not pillaging, but collecting contributions; and if you ask them their authority, they will produce you the practice of their predecessors of all ages and nations.[28]

There were as many reasons to purchase and read scientific and medical books as there were to create them. Often the best evidence of the function that the book likely served is the book itself. Texts classified as 'scientific' included many types of books that were primarily reference works, including tables of foreign exchange, measurements and gauging, interest tables, trigonometric and logarithmic tables, and navigational tables; often, these kinds of books appeared in duodecimo, making them both cheap and portable. Texts intended for students, such as arithmetic books, also appeared in inexpensive 'handy' editions, which might be published in press runs of 2,000 or more; students (or their parents) could expect to pay around 2*s*. for this type of book. Taken together, reference and school-books undoubtedly represented the most numerous category of scientific and medical books published in the eighteenth century.

Books published to 'popularize' science for the elite and the middle classes offer a more interesting perspective on the cultural role of the scientific book. A large number of these types of works appeared as dialogues, following the example of the enormously popular *Entretiens sur la pluralité des mondes* by Bernard Fontenelle (1686). English versions of Fontenelle's *Conversations* were published and republished on a regular basis throughout the eighteenth century, inspiring British authors to pen their own dialogues. In turn, these works promoted science by associating it with politeness – a concept that largely defined the social interactions of the emerging middle classes. Shaped by these standards and agendas, the literature of polite science illustrated to young ladies and gentlemen the appeal of conversation spiced with a smidgen of science, and so served to relate science, and the reading of these works, to social interaction.[29] Thus, for example, the *Guardian* suggested in 1713 that women could pass the time while doing domestic chores by reading aloud to one another. To illustrate, the journal cited the example of Lady Lizard, who worked with her daughters making preserves while listening to one read Fontenelle: 'It was very entertaining to me to see them dividing their Speculations between Jellies and Stars, and making a sudden Transition from the Sun to an Apricot, or from the *Copernican* System to the figure of a

28 E. Chambers, *Cyclopedia*, 7th edn (London, 1751), 'Plagiary'.
29 On polite science literature, see Walters 1997.

Cheese-cake.'[30] Similarly, a book like *The Newtonian system of philosophy adapted to the capacities of young gentlemen and ladies* by 'Tom Telescope' – a dialogue on natural philosophy published in 1761 by John Newbery – could be read aloud to children by their parents or guardians.[31]

At the high end of the market for scientific and medical works were those books published in large format with multiple illustrations – works in natural history and botany, geography, anatomy, and other subjects, as well as encyclopaedias, which could cost as much as a guinea per volume. Similarly, purchasers might be expected to pay a premium price for highly technical works that were likely to have a very limited audience, such as books on higher mathematics or the latest publications of the medical faculty at the University of Edinburgh.[32]

Scientific and medical texts represented a small percentage of all titles published in eighteenth-century Britain. Yet, this literature contributed greatly to both the progress of the Enlightenment and the establishment of natural knowledge in British culture. By providing a means by which their authors could present their ideas, establish their identities and perhaps even earn some monetary rewards, such works contributed greatly to the advancement and the legitimization of scientific and medical disciplines, and to those who practised them.

30 *The Guardian*, no. 155 (8 Sept. 1713).
31 Secord 1985, 134. See also Fyfe 2000.
32 Sher 2000, 134–5.

47

Scientific and medical books, 1780–1830

JONATHAN R. TOPHAM

> The stirring up of the mind which took place during the French Revolution ... gave rise to the demand for more numerous and various publications, as well as for a superior quality in their character and contents ... Many more thought and read than formerly; and their thoughts were of a more original cast and bearing.
>
> *Blackwood's Edinburgh Magazine* (1824)[1]

> You begin ... with the attempt to *popularize* science: but you will only effect its *plebification*. It is folly to think of making all, or the many, philosophers, or even men of science and systematic knowledge.
>
> S.T. Coleridge (1830)[2]

The book trade of the late eighteenth and early nineteenth centuries underwent a massive expansion and diversification of its products. This was due in part to increasing commercialization following the ruling against perpetual copyright in 1774 and to the incremental introduction of mechanization after 1800. In addition, a rapid rise occurred in both literacy and reading, owing to such social and cultural changes as population growth, urbanization and the extension of elementary education. Consequently, new class-conscious reading audiences were formed. These transformations in print culture were accompanied by a related transformation in the natural and medical sciences. The natural sciences became increasingly divided into specialist disciplines, each with its own small cohort of expert practitioners who were increasingly separated from a wider, fragmenting public. Similarly, scientific societies proliferated, catering for local or specialist constituencies. Many existing fields, like chemistry and geology, were transformed by significant innovations, and new sciences, such as electro-chemistry, were introduced. At the same time, novel organizations such as the

1 [William Stevenson], 'On the reciprocal influence of the periodical publications and the intellectual progress of this country. No. 1', *Blackwood's Edinburgh Magazine*, 16 (1824), 518–28, at 521, 523.
2 Coleridge 1830, 82.

mechanics' institutes and the British Association for the Advancement of Science (founded 1831) were established to convey developments to wider audiences. A new word, 'scientist', was devised to describe the emerging specialists (although it was not widely used until later in the century) and a new notion of 'popularization' was used to describe their relationship with the proliferating audiences for science. These rapid developments were reflected in the very considerable changes which occurred in scientific and medical publications, ranging from the expansion of specialist scientific periodicals to the emergence of new genres of 'popular science' publishing for non-specialist audiences.[3]

One of the most striking expressions of the emerging specialization of the natural sciences and medicine was in the periodical literature.[4] The monthly miscellanies of the eighteenth century, typified by the *Gentleman's Magazine* (1731), had embodied Enlightenment ideals in their openness to readers' scientific observations and experiments, and the monthly review journals had likewise aimed at comprehensiveness. The new periodicals of the early nineteenth century, however, rapidly dispensed with these encyclopaedic ambitions. Following the lead of *Blackwood's Edinburgh Magazine* (1817), the fashionable monthlies abandoned the goal of forming a cumulative repository of universal information, jettisoned the associated sections, and increasingly relied on self-consciously literary articles contributed by well-paid men of letters. While the new quarterly reviews – the *Edinburgh* (1802), *Quarterly* (1809) and *Westminster* (1824) – continued to tackle scientific (and occasionally medical) works, their choice of topics was highly selective. Moreover, the specialist contributors now employed to review scientific books struggled to address specialist and non-specialist audiences simultaneously. At the same time, the new weekly literary journals, beginning with the *Literary Gazette* (1817), gave no room to original reports of scientific innovations, but instead reprinted news items extracted from specialist publications and published reports of scientific meetings.[5]

The reformulation of the general magazines and reviews was concomitant with the rapid development of specialist periodicals. Many of these were produced by the new learned societies, that symbolized the development of specialist disciplines and the increasing status and activity of cultural elites in Scotland, Ireland and the English provinces. During the last two decades of the eighteenth century, a number began to issue regular transactions – the Royal Irish Academy (in 1787), Royal Society of Edinburgh (in 1788),

3 Topham 2000a.
4 See Maidment, chap. 25 above.
5 Cantor *et al.* 2004, chap. 1.

Dublin Society (in 1799), and the newly formed Manchester Literary and Philosophical Society (in 1785). Among the specialist societies, the Society for the Encouragement of Arts, Manufactures and Commerce (founded 1754) issued the first volume of its *Transactions* in 1783, soon to be followed by similar publications from the Linnean Society (1791), Horticultural Society (1807), Geological Society (1811), Wernerian Natural History Society (1811), Royal Institution (1816), Royal Geological Society of Cornwall (1818) and Cambridge Philosophical Society (1821). This trend continued apace over succeeding decades, steadily increasing the extent to which scientific authority came to be associated with the specialist publications of the emerging scientific disciplines.

The increasing specialization of knowledge also offered new commercial opportunities in a periodical market that underwent rapid expansion and diversification. The monthly *Journal of Natural Philosophy, Chemistry and the Arts* (1797), produced as a commercial venture by the scientific writer and inventor William Nicholson, emulated a number of continental journals issued over the preceding two decades in publishing original contributions, translations and abstracts on the physical sciences. Men of science willingly published in Nicholson's *Journal*, knowing that their discoveries in such rapidly changing fields as electrochemistry would circulate within weeks, rather than the months or years typical of learned transactions. In addition, it provided men of science with a suitable forum for publishing more speculative research – anonymously, if necessary. Nicholson's *Journal* was well received, and its popularity soon encouraged a competitor, the *Philosophical Magazine* (1798), which was published by the newspaper proprietor and inventor Alexander Tilloch. In the decade following the end of the war with France, three further journals entered this crowded market. Such publications provided important editorial income for men of science, such as David Brewster, and also afforded valuable returns to several publishers, notably the printer Richard Taylor. However, the market was by no means sure, and by 1832 amalgamation had reduced the total number of such journals to two.[6]

Two other kinds of commercial science journal were produced at the turn of the century, and both gained competitors in the years after 1815. The growing concern with technology and industrialization was reflected in the *Repertory of Arts and Manufactures* (1794), which reported innovations in original articles, abstracts and reports. By the 1820s, the *Repertory* had to compete with other monthlies (the *London Journal of Arts* (1820) and the *Technical Repository*

6 Brock and Meadows 1998.

(1822)), as well as with a host of three-penny weeklies aimed at artisanal readers, including the *Mechanics' Magazine* (1823) and *Register of Arts* (1823). Another important late eighteenth-century market was in lavishly illustrated botanical books, often issued as part-works. William Curtis had capitalized on this market with the monthly *Botanical Magazine* (1787), containing botanical plates and accompanying text, but after 1797 Curtis's magazine had to compete with the *Botanist's Repository* as well as a further four magazines founded between 1815 and 1824.

The number and range of specialist titles in the sciences increased significantly in the 1820s; there were new periodicals devoted to natural history (*Zoological Journal* (1824) and *Magazine of Natural History* (1829)), to gardening (*Gardener's Magazine* (1826)), to agriculture (*Quarterly Journal of Agriculture* (1828)) and to veterinarianism (*Veterinarian* (1828) and *Farrier and Naturalist* (1828)). Medical periodicals also proliferated and diversified. Although a small number of such publications were issued in the eighteenth century, most of these were either transactions of learned and professional bodies (for example, *Medical Transactions Published by the Royal College of Physicians of London* (1768)) or the memoirs of less formal societies (for example, *Medical Observations and Inquiries* (1757)). However, the turn of the century saw a rash of new transactions (at least seven between 1780 and 1830) and many new commercial periodicals, particularly from the 1810s. Many of the latter were magazines and reviews, but the inception of the weekly *Lancet* (1823) initiated a new form of campaigning journalism which was to impact significantly on the organization of the medical profession.[7]

Although much scientific research appeared in the new specialist journals, and in the *Philosophical Transactions of the Royal Society of London*, it also continued to be published in book form. This was particularly evident in the natural historical sciences, where findings continued to be expressed in terms accessible to a non-specialist readership. To be commercially successful, however, original treatises had increasingly to be written to appeal to the widening range of reading audiences. Indeed, this was a consideration urged on scientific writers by the new entrepreneurial non-retailing publishers of the period, although it was one many were unable to satisfy. The fashionable John Murray published Charles Lyell's influential *Principles of geology* (3 vols., 1830–3), but considered that there were few 'who could write profound science and make a book readable'. Under Murray's careful management, the book sold well to a genteel readership in three costly volumes before being

7 Bynum, Lock and Porter 1992, chaps. 1–3.

reissued in four small 6*s*. volumes for a broader middle-class readership.[8] Murray's sense of the multiplicity of readerships for scientific books reflected developments over the preceding two decades, as radical publishers, small-time entrepreneurs, ideologically motivated societies and emerging highly capitalized fashionable publishing houses like Murray's own began to exploit new markets and new technologies.

During the war with France, the high price of labour and the increased cost of rags for paper manufacture, combined with the continued conservatism of the book trade, meant that new books were more expensive than ever before. After 1815, however, this situation began to change. The rapid sale of Cobbett's *Weekly Political Register* after 1816, when it was first published in a two-penny abridged edition, signalled the emergence of a working-class reading audience to both commercially and ideologically motivated publishers. One of the most successful was John Limbird, a minor entrepreneur in the Strand, whose two-penny weekly, the *Mirror of Literature, Amusement, and Instruction* (1822), sold tens of thousands of copies. The format of the *Mirror* was widely emulated in the 1820s, and within a decade, Limbird's use of stereotyping was supplemented by the use of steam presses in producing penny weeklies such as the *Penny Magazine*, which sold up to 200,000 copies.[9] The *Mirror* particularly inspired Henry Brougham, who in his *Practical observations upon the education of the people* (1825) asserted that its 'great circulation must prove highly beneficial to the bulk of the people' (p. 3). Brougham's *Practical observations* passed through at least nineteen editions in a year, and spurred the formation of the Society for the Diffusion of Useful Knowledge (SDUK). Urging rational education on working-class readers partly in order to stem political radicalism, the controversial activities of the SDUK marked an epoch in the history of scientific publishing.

The *Mirror* provided the model for the SDUK's earliest publications, the sixpenny parts of the *Library of useful knowledge*. This series included a number of treatises that addressed abstruse scientific subjects and were written by leading men of science, including George Airy on gravitation, Augustus De Morgan on calculus and John Lindley on plant physiology. Notwithstanding their abstruseness, most treatises had sold more than 20,000 copies by 1833, and the society's *Penny Magazine* was soon carrying similar material to even larger audiences. The publishing activities of the SDUK were complemented by the activities from the early 1820s of the new mechanics' institutes, which became

8 Quoted by J.A. Secord in Lyell 1997, xiv.
9 Cantor 2004, chap. 2; see also Altick 1998, 260–77.

a prominent part of British life. Often founded and run by bourgeois managers, mechanics' institutes generally stressed the importance of highly objectified scientific education in diverting working-class men from sensual pleasures and from radicalism. At a time when working men had access to few libraries beyond the largely religious collections often attached to chapels, the extensive provision of scientific books in mechanics' institutes constituted a significant innovation.[10]

The high-profile activities of the SDUK encouraged some of the new fashionable publishing houses to issue original works at cheaper prices by means of economies of scale and the technologies of mass production. This trend was led by Archibald Constable, whose 'Miscellany' (1827) offered non-fiction works in 1*s.* numbers (3*s.* 6*d.* per volume). John Murray soon followed with his 'Family Library' (1829) of 5*s.* volumes, which included David Brewster's *Life of Sir Isaac Newton* (1831) and *Letters on natural magic* (1832). Longmans also entered the field in 1829 with Dionysius Lardner's *Cabinet cyclopaedia*, consisting of 6*s.* treatises. By 1833, the Edinburgh printer and engraver William Lizars was issuing a more specialized 'Naturalist's Library' in 6*s.* volumes. These ventures enjoyed rather mixed financial fortunes, but they loudly proclaimed the emergence of an enlarged middle-class market for science books. Written by scientific specialists, who were often paid handsomely, such books were represented as contributions to a top-down form of 'popular science'. As James Secord has argued, these new forms of science writing often contained sweeping narratives of natural progress and majestic visions of all-encompassing natural laws, rather than merely the sober technicalities of specialist science.[11]

Scientific specialists were also increasingly well paid in writing for encyclopaedias. In the eighteenth century, the major British encyclopaedias – Ephraim Chambers's *Cyclopaedia* and the *Encyclopaedia Britannica* – had been assembled by compilers, and aimed at classifying universal knowledge. When Archibald Constable purchased the copyright and stock of the *Britannica* in 1812, however, his response to the expansion and specialization of scientific knowledge was to publish a *Supplement* (1815–24) consisting of commissioned articles from specialist contributors. Authors were offered princely sums – £1,000 each in the cases of Dugald Stewart and John Playfair, who prepared articles on the progress of philosophy and of mathematics and physics, respectively. This approach was adopted by other major ventures like David Brewster's *Edinburgh Encyclopaedia* (1808–30) and Coleridge's *Encyclopaedia metropolitana* (1817–45).[12]

10 Topham 1992.
11 Secord 2000, 41–76.
12 Yeo 2001, 246–76; Topham 2000a, 594.

Textbooks provided another growing market of financial importance to scientific writers. The opening of University College London in 1828, with its eschewal of religious tests, provided a new market for university textbooks across a range of scientific and medical subjects. Existing universities also fuelled demand. At Cambridge University, for instance, increasing student numbers, together with the introduction of more exacting examinations and of the analytical methods of continental mathematics, led to a growing market for mathematical textbooks. New specialist educational publishers, like John Deighton in Cambridge and George Byron Whittaker in London, capitalized on the reliable sales such publications attained. The growing market for elementary textbooks also offered substantial returns, and some of the new entrepreneurial publishers of the early nineteenth century made fortunes by publishing educational works. Thus, the one-time schoolmaster William Pinnock's nine-penny educational *Catechisms*, issued from 1812 and including many scientific subjects among their sixty-four titles, earned him thousands of pounds before ruinous financial speculations forced him to sell the copyrights around 1821.[13]

The changes in the sciences that took place in late eighteenth- and early nineteenth-century Britain – what has been called the 'second scientific revolution'[14] – were intimately interconnected with the revolution that took place in print culture. The diversification of reading audiences served to foster both the specialization of scientific knowledge and its removal into technical periodicals. Yet, neither men of science themselves, nor the new entrepreneurial publishers, were blind to the market for an increasing range of scientific publications addressed to non-specialists, including popular periodicals, introductory works, systematic treatises, encyclopaedias and textbooks. It was in negotiating these changed conditions of communication that the new notions of the scientific expert and of 'popular science', so characteristic of nineteenth-century science, began to be developed.

13 Topham 2000b; see also McKitterick 1998.
14 Brush 1988; see also Bellone 1980.

48

'Radical publishing'

MARCUS WOOD

When considering the effect of the popular movement for radical reform on English publishing and book production in the nineteenth century, the crucial time-frame runs from the beginning of the 1790s until the passage of the first great Reform Bill in 1832. It is almost impossible to outline and explain radical publishing in terms of its form, content and economics in the first three decades of the nineteenth century without indicating the revolutionary nature of developments in the early 1790s. In other words, British radical publishing was initially spawned by the French Revolution and by responses to the political and cultural outfall from that event in Britain.

What are the overall patterns and developments that might work towards a map of book and serial publishing directed at producing extreme social and political reform during the early nineteenth century? The first thing is to emphasize is that, like any broad-based political phenomenon which evolved over a long period, English radical publishing was not a stable phenomenon. Radical publishing enjoyed a series of rapid highs and lows during the last decade of the eighteenth century, and then again in the first two decades of the nineteenth century. In terms of the overall contours it is, however, fair to say that there were two periods when radical publishing was produced on a scale, and in innovative ways, which had a lasting impact upon both the British publishing industry and the formation of reading audiences. The first period ran from the outbreak of the French Revolution in 1789 to the end of the notorious 'Treason Trials' of 1794.[1] In 1790 Edmund Burke published *Reflections on the revolution in France*. The book constituted a loyalist touch-paper that set off one of the most remarkable pamphlet wars of English publishing history.[2] The so-called 'Revolution Debate' that resulted generated a mass of radical theory and loyalist counter-theory, but at its epicentre lay the

1 For the rhetoric and publishing strategies surrounding the Treason Trials, see Wood 1994, 96–154, and the magnificent Barrell 2000.

2 The best accounts of the so-called 'Revolution Debate' are Cobban 1960 and Butler 1984.

two parts of Thomas Paine's *The rights of man*. This blow-by-blow response to the *Reflections* was an unprecedented publishing phenomenon, which, as we shall see, in many ways set the rules for popular radical book production in the ensuing thirty years.

Radical support for the French Jacobins was widespread in the early 1790s, and indeed extended into the respectable arena of the Foxite Whigs. Yet, increasingly extreme mass criticism of the British electoral and economic systems, combined with the explosive course of events in France, led to a repressive paranoia among both the British power elite and Pitt's government, which represented their interests. Government reaction to the groundswell in radical anti-state propaganda, the dissemination of which was massively facilitated by the success of the radical 'corresponding societies' – and the London Corresponding Society (LCS) in particular – reached a head when leading members of the LCS, including Thomas Hardy, John Thelwall and John Horne Tooke, were publicly tried on charges of high treason in 1794. The absurd and protracted prosecutions failed dismally, and the accused were freed amid an unprecedented blaze of publicity, which was released into a popular audience beginning to develop a political consciousness of its own. During the two decades following the Treason Trials, radicalism generally, and radical publishing in particular, were dampened by sustained and periodically extreme state repression. Virtually every ultra-radical author of any importance was prosecuted for either sedition, libel or seditious blasphemy during this time. Several, most notoriously William Cobbett, periodically exiled themselves to America. Writers such as Thomas Spence, Daniel Isaac Eaton, Thomas Wooler, Richard Carlile and William Hone, who stayed at home to face the music, underwent multiple government prosecutions. All of the above named, with the exception of Hone, suffered debilitating prison sentences as a result of what they wrote and published. E.P. Thompson's *The making of the English working class*, still the highest authority on the social contexts for radical publishing, emphatically demonstrates that the books, pamphlets, prints and broadsides which form the focus for the following discussion were produced by remarkably brave people and at a very real human cost.[3] Although radicals managed to maintain a fitful production during the years following Pitt's notoriously repressive Two Acts and the popularly termed 'White Terror' which resulted, it was not until the French wars ended that radicalism really got back into its publishing stride. Consequently, the second great period of radical press experimentation ran from 1815 to 1822.

3 Thompson 1963; for a factual account of state prosecutions of radical publishers, see Aspinall 1949.

The initial resurgence in radical publishing reflected a national mood of anger, despair and very black humour. Successive crop failures, and the massive human and economic cost of the campaign against the French, placed the labouring poor of Britain in a desperate state following Napoleon's defeat at Waterloo. Britain was as close to possessing the right ingredients for genuine revolution as at any point in its history. As the radical reform movement re-established mass appeal and reached out to the great new urban centres of the industrial north, the London printers inaugurated a campaign of social criticism quite new in its scale, energy and diversity. The institutions of state power – the church, the law and the government – were ridiculed and interrogated with an unprecedented ferocity by radical intellectuals and satirists. Radical authors ranged from the intellectual elite, including William Godwin, Leigh Hunt and William Hazlitt, through populist authors, the most important being Thomas Paine and William Cobbett; yet radicalism also fed into a murky area of publishing entrepreneurs, scandal mongers and pornographers, who periodically fed off political events for their own ends. The ballad entrepreneur Jemmy Catnach of the notoriously seedy Seven Dials district of London is a fine example of such a figure: for thirty years he brought out popular ballads and chapbooks on radical themes when he thought they would sell.[4] The mini-renaissance of anti-state propaganda came of age in the furious public reaction to the 'Peterloo Massacre' of 1819, when a combination of local militia and government troops rode down a pro-reform crowd of 60,000–80,000 at St Peter's Fields, Manchester. Eleven men, women and children were killed, and more than five hundred seriously injured, many with sabre wounds. For the next three years the radicals never looked back. The resurgence ended in 1822 amid the uproarious outpourings of the radical free press that greeted the eventual coronation of George IV, and his earlier disastrous attempts to prosecute his estranged wife Queen Caroline for adultery. The 'Queen Caroline affair' was commandeered by the radical publicists in 1820 and by the end of 1821 had become a satiric feeding frenzy, a demonstration of the apparently unchecked freedoms that the radical free press had developed for itself.[5]

As stated earlier, radicalism was not stable, and the careers of those involved in the first waves of radical publishing, both in the early 1790s and in 1815–22, go through some remarkable and protean transformations involving extreme formal and conceptual developments. After 1822 it became increasingly

4 Wood 1994, 161–2, 176, 205, 215.

5 The fullest accounts of the development of popular radical rhetorics and publishing modes 1790–1822, and of their final efflorescence in the Queen Caroline affair, are Smith 1984, Wood 1994 and Dyer 1997.

difficult to remain, or indeed to become, a 'radical revolutionary' author. Although the old-style radical publishing did have a minor resurgence in the two years leading up to the great Reform Bill of 1832, it was effectively dead as both a political and publishing phenomenon. Even by the mid-1820s, Jacobin mimicry and Paineite contempt for the monarchy, for inherited privilege and for state religion were no longer options for writers or for publishers. The days of the Regency were long gone, and gone with them was the freedom openly to include pornographic imagery and Jacobin theory.[6] The charges of political apostasy levelled at Coleridge and Wordsworth as the nineteenth century developed are all too familiar, but the two great Romantics were simply finding their way as authors, just as all those radical writers who had worked in the heady days of 1789–1815 had to. Cobbett, singly the most influential radical journalist and book author working from 1780 to 1830, turned from the crushing head-on political collisions which typified works as different as *Advice to parsons*, *The protestant reformation* and the remarkably resilient *Political register*, and moved into a new type of book with *Rural rides*. The latter sold very well, and certainly still had a political agenda, though it was based in nostalgia for a lost agrarian past. Cobbett pioneered a new type of domestic travel book, with vast appeal to a diverse market, yet whether this still constitutes a radical form of publishing is open to debate.[7] Figures as different as William Hone, Thomas Evans, Samuel Bamford, Charles Neesom, Thomas Preston, William Benbow and the colourful ultra-radicals Robert Wedderburn and Samuel Waddington were forced to draw in their horns and try to shift into publishing areas which the new criteria of decency, nostalgia and self-improvement demanded. After 1832, old-style Jacobin authors and publishers simply do not exist in the United Kingdom; those with something still left to give were busy adapting both to new literary and political environments and, just as significantly, to the publishing revolution. The illustrated periodical press, which focused on the leisure industries and a new female readership, and the rise of the novel as the new mass entertainment publishing form, had changed reading audiences irrevocably.[8]

Having indicated the contours of a socio-economic map within which radical publishing functioned, we may now ask: what was the distinctive contribution of the British radical press to the production and consumption of books in England? To answer this question there is only one starting place: Thomas Paine. Part One

6 For a detailed assessment of the new morality of the ultra-radicals in the 1820s and 1830s, see McCalman 1988, 181–203.

7 By far the best assessment of Cobbett as a publishing phenomenon is Nattrass 1995.

8 See Suarez, Introduction, above.

of *The rights of man* came out early in 1791 and had sold 50,000 copies by the end of that year. In April 1792 Part Two was printed, along with Part One. E. P. Thompson estimates that the book, in all forms, sold 200,000 copies by 1793 in England and Ireland. In 1802 Paine reckoned the sale of *The rights of man*, Parts One and Two, in the range of 400,000–500,000; in 1809 he estimated the figure at one and a half million copies, including foreign translations.[9] Although these figures have been disputed, what is not in doubt is that the sales were vast and the audience at that time was unique in its scale. *The rights of man* initiated a new type of publishing: not merely a book, it was a radical press phenomenon. In the way it was written, the way it was marketed and the ways in which it was read, *The rights of man* was a new kind of text that transformed popular publishing in the first decades of the nineteenth century. Paine produced a work which, in its chimerical adaptability, tested the very limits of what a book – and what a market – might constitute. Indeed, the book changed the life of William Cobbett and Richard Carlile, both of whom talked of the manner in which it gave them a political consciousness for the first time; they thus essentialize the experience of hundreds of thousands of British people. The book not only taught radicals how to think politically, but also showed them how to package their political ideas for the people. *The rights of man* was extremely adaptable: from the beginning, it was modified and mass distributed via the corresponding societies. Although the first part was initially relatively expensive, once both parts had appeared the text was published in several cheap and simplified forms. It could be reduced to an aphoristic essence and sold in chapbook form; it was even reported by the government that Paine's lethal creation had been reduced to a mini-text, a few sentences of tiny print covering the paper for sweet wrappers.[10] Paine's work showed that once a text had seized the public imagination, it could infiltrate any number of related reproductive environments. In the dissemination of Paine's original pamphlet, we see one of the most decisive factors defining the radical free press during the first three decades of the nineteenth century – its formal variety. The physical packaging of a text is an integral part of how it is read and disseminated.[11]

When summing up the impact of radical publishing as it developed from 1789 to 1832 what stands out above all is its capacity for experimentation,

9 Figures for sales of *The rights of man* are debated in Smith 1984, 57–9. St Clair 2004, 257, questions the traditional estimates.

10 Smith 1984, 57–72 gives the fullest account of the processes of mass dissemination.

11 The best short assessment of Paine's impact on the thought and publishing of British radicals is Claeys 1989, 63–75; also Smith 1984, 68–108.

adaptation and parody. It is important to allude to the explosion of loyalist tract literature during the 1790s and its influence on certain branches of radical publishing, and I do so briefly below in the context of Hannah More. Yet, loyalist authors stopped short in terms of both their readiness and ability to infiltrate many of the newly expanding publishing environments of the early nineteenth century. Radical publishers felt no such timidity. Many of the leading figures were confident artisan autodidacts who were fascinated by the new forms of publishing, and were prepared to experiment with any and all of the developing areas of book and print production. The radical hunger for formal experimentation first emerged in the early 1790s in the wake of Paine's textual bomb. There were many figures who subsequently tried their hands at popular publishing, but Thomas Spence and Daniel Isaac Eaton should be singled out as publicists willing and able to exploit any area of the book and print trade. In terms of their impact on the formal experimentation of later radical publishing, they stand alone. Spence published journals, dictionaries, chapbooks, children's books, prints and conventional political pamphlets, and wrote political verse, fables, utopias and dialogues. Stylistically, he drew on millenarian discourse, exploiting the languages of popular enthusiasm and Old Testament prophecy. He could write for little children, or adopt a tone of satiric auteur reminiscent of the excoriating prose of Junius. Spence also brilliantly infiltrated the chapbook market with a string of titles that came out in the mid-1790s including *The end of oppression*, *The restorer of society to its natural state* and *The meridian sun of liberty*. For Spence, print technology could be harnessed in any area. Eaton was nearly as inventive as Spence in terms of the range of his publishing: his short-running but widely selling *Politics for the people, or a salmagundy for swine* (1793–5) was a complicated small octavo publication that drifted in a publishing hinterland somewhere between a commonplace book, a periodical, an anthology and a political journal. *Politics for the people* printed satires and parodies adapting high and low forms, which ranged from children's word games and rhymes, to fables, biblical models and showmen's notices. Much of the text consisted of short, brilliantly chosen and arranged selections from the classics and the great works of the English Civil War, which had previously set out the egalitarian and libertarian teachings now supported by the radicals. In this sense, it was a sort of cut-and-paste radical history book. Both Spence and Eaton were prosecuted for seditious libel for the illegal publishing of Paine's works, and subsequently set to producing published accounts of their own trials in book form, celebrating their judicial ordeals and sentences within the conventions of martyrology and gallows literature. Later radicals including William Hone, Thomas Wooler and

Richard Carlile were to follow Spence and Eaton's brilliant exploitation of trial literature in their own later political show trials.[12] Yet, despite their bold infiltration of a variety of book and publishing markets not normally associated with radicalism, the ultra-radical authors of the 1790s did not personally contribute to the radical revival after 1815. Both Eaton and Spence died in 1814; Paine died in America in 1809, ostracized largely as a result of his outrageous and often comical attacks on conventional Christian belief in *The age of reason*.

Finally, Spence's and Eaton's work is a testament to the way in which radical publishing broke out of conventional eighteenth-century styles of book production, to incorporate spectacular new developments in printing. Their work demonstrates the sheer satiric energy that defines the radical press from 1790 to 1830. This period also saw satiric verse, for example, undergo a phenomenal expansion as a direct result of the new formal experiments of radicals. Though there is room only to allude to this vital area of radical print production here, the extent of radical verse satire, and the manner in which radicals moved in and out of 'respectable' literary verse forms, comes out powerfully in Gary Dyer's meticulous and enormous select bibliography of British satirical verse from 1789 to 1832.[13] Similarly, the new visual and typographic conventions of advertising display, children's books, pornography and women's magazines were fed on hungrily. Given the creative dynamism with which radical pressmen approached their task as publicists, government attempts at restricting publishing activity often backfired. The newspaper stamp taxes, against which radical publishers were pitting their wits throughout this period, in many ways encouraged formal experimentation. Had it not been for the hated 'taxes on knowledge', Cobbett would never have been led into the production of his *Political register* in the new form of the notoriously wide-selling 'two-penny trash'. In 1816 Cobbett, infuriated that his sales were restricted by the expense of being able to publish only on very expensive officially 'stamped' paper, brought out the leading articles of the *Register* as a weekly pamphlet that cost 2*d*. Was Cobbett's new *Register* a newspaper, a periodical, a pamphlet or a book? Technically that is hard to answer; all that is certain is that it sold 40,000–60,000 copies a week and enjoyed a circulation several times larger than any other newspaper or periodical extant in the world at that date.[14]

12 For accounts of Spence and Eaton, see Thompson 1963, 180, 604–5, 613–15; Smith 1984, 88–9, 108–9, 96–109; McCalman 1988; Wood 1994, 56–95.

13 Dyer 1997, 210–51.

14 Nattrass 1995, 72–88, 90–118.

It could also be argued that it was the attempt to publish in forms not affected by the taxes that led all the leading radical pressmen, including Hone, Johnson, Cahuac, Fairburn, Dolby, Carlile and Wooler, to create their outlandish and hilarious parodies of a whole variety of popular forms of publishing. A brief survey of the major productions of William Hone, one of the major radical satirists of the first two decades of the nineteenth century, makes the point succinctly. By the time Hone stopped publishing extreme radical satire in 1822, he had managed to create a back list of phenomenally wide-selling publications which took in a huge formal range. Hone's *The political house that Jack built* of 1819 was a pamphlet which sold 100,000 copies within four months of publication, and which by 1822 had sold more copies than any other single radical publication, with the exception of *The rights of man*.[15] Yet it was brought out in the style of a new kind of illustrated children's book, which the innovative children's book publisher John Newbery had been perfecting during the previous decade.[16] While the nursery rhyme 'The house that Jack built' had been widely used in single-sheet print satire of the preceding two decades, Hone was the first to make the literalist move not merely of using a children's rhyme as the basis for satire, but of actually taking up the style of children's books. The advantages of such a form for political satire were massive. Incorporating the simple and dramatic style of woodcut imagery used in the books of Newbery and his imitators, the octavo parodic children's books brought out by Hone and his followers were funny and very easy to read. The simple language and the use of such models as nursery rhymes, board games, puzzles and abecedaries meant that they could appeal to a vast readership. Hone's work only had the impact it did because of his collaboration with George Cruikshank, then the leading print satirist of the day. Before the Hone and Cruikshank collaboration, single-sheet etched print satire and book production had operated predominantly as discreet publishing entities. Single-sheet, hand-coloured political satires were produced as works of art to stand on their own; they were looked at in coffee shops and print shop windows, or in the folios of collectors, as self-supporting entities. They were relatively expensive, and did not, certainly at the top end of the market, reach out to a very big readership. Although Cruikshank had undertaken a small amount of work for satirical journals before his work with Hone, this material had not broken with the conventions of the single-sheet etchings. So the elaborate hand-coloured prints which Cruikshank produced for issues of the *Scourge* and the

15 For sales figures and editions of all Hone's publications, see Bowden 1975.
16 Wood 1994, 215–35.

Satirist were long folding prints which were glued in as frontispieces to the periodical. The small woodcuts for the quarto-sized books and pamphlets of Hone were entirely different. Technically often crude and simplified in design, the woodcuts looked back to the chapbook and emblem traditions, as well as forward to the new styles of advertising and children's book illustration; this visual dimension in radical publishing was sensational. The impact of the radical exploitation of the wood engraving was probably the most emphatic and transformative technical legacy of radical book production. Hone himself looked back in the 1830s and concluded with some justification that, 'By showing what engraving on wood could effect in a popular way, and exciting a taste for art in the more humble ranks of life, [my illustrated political pamphlets] created a new era in the history of publication ... They are the parents to the present cheap literature, which extends to a sale of at least four hundred thousand copies every week.'[17] Hone's pamphlets did not single-handedly open the floodgates for cheap illustrated journalism, although their combination of type and woodblock in a single pamphlet page certainly provided a pattern for 'cheap literature' in the age of the steam press and machine-made paper. Hone's work did, however, exert a decided influence on the forms and methods of radical satire in the six years following Waterloo, and also led to a plethora of loyalist imitations.[18]

The distinguishing features of radical publication might finally be summarized as intellectual instability, economic promiscuity and formal variety; or then again intellectual variety, economic instability and formal promiscuity; or then again intellectual promiscuity, economic variety and formal instability. This discussion has necessarily been highly selective, but has maintained a focus on radical publishing activity that shifted the boundaries of the book and print markets. The analysis has foregrounded authors and works which reached large audiences and broke the publishing mould in terms of their novel forms. Yet, it needs to be emphasized that the sheer range of authors who might be categorized as radicals is almost limitless, and takes in many of the leading lights of Romanticism. Radicalism as a publishing phenomenon was wonderfully open, and it is consequently appropriate to end on a note of speculation, rather than closure. Accordingly, this overview concludes by thinking about how radicalism interacted with three vital growth areas in popular publishing – pornography, abolition and women's publishing. It is vital to understand that

17 Quoted in Wood 1994, 269.
18 Smith 1984, 165–70; Wood 1994, 258–63.

one explanation of the power and appeal of radical publishing lay in the ways in which it interfaced with a series of related revolutions in popular publishing.

Female contributions to ultra-radical book production in the nineteenth century were numerically limited, but there were a number of women authors who contributed to the dissemination of radical ideology in groundbreaking ways through their book production. Mary Wollstonecraft, by writing full-scale works of social analysis and political philosophy, as well as journalism and children's books, had of course demonstrated in the late eighteenth century that a radical female consciousness was capable of contributing to the most important political debates of the day. Wollstonecraft worked as editor and reader on the *Analytical Review*, a flagship radical paper produced by the most influential and pivotal of the popular radical publishers: Joseph Johnson. Through this powerful connection Wollstonecraft came into contact with the most significant radical artists, theorists and authors, including Thomas Paine, Henri Fuseli, William Blake and her future husband William Godwin. Wollstonecraft produced a series of books across a wide publishing range including political treatises, translations of foreign revolutionary literature, and even children's books. Her *Vindication of the rights of men* (1790), *Vindication of the rights of woman* (1792) and *History and moral view of the origin and progress of the French Revolution* (1794) were foundational texts, showing that women could write genuinely popular books on contemporary politics.[19]

Yet perhaps the biggest influence on subsequent women radical authors was not Wollstonecraft but the propagandist Hannah More. More's politics were anything but radical; in fact she was a leading propagandist for the loyalist cause during the French Revolution. Yet, as with Spence, it was not the content so much as the style and form of her publications which were to provide a model for subsequent liberal and radical women authors. More had shown herself adept at the production of anti-radical tract literature, which sold on a massive scale, and she had perfected a technique for presenting political arguments of some complexity in the form of simple dialogues, printed as short, inexpensive and large-print tracts. These *Cheap repository tracts* were mass produced and distributed by the Association for Preserving Liberty and Property against Republicans and Levellers (usually referred to as the Association). The Association had a nationwide distribution network and, as a propaganda machine, took publishing into a new dimension. The radicals attempted to combat its effects by channelling their own publications through the London Corresponding Society, but they had nothing like the resources of

19 The best accounts of Wollstonecraft as a radical author are Lorch 1990, 145–81; Todd 2000, 164–221.

the Association, and no single author as effective as More to spearhead the campaign. More undoubtedly acted as both an immediate catalyst and a lasting model for radical authors. It could even be argued that the efflorescence of radical pamphlet literature in the 1816–22 period was a spectacular reappropriation of a publishing space which had in many ways first been opened up by More and the loyalists two decades before. More also acted as a direct inspiration for several of the radical female pamphleteers of the 1820s and 1830s; several important women publicists of the period had cut their teeth writing as slavery abolitionists.[20] Abolition was a mass propaganda movement which had from the first invited in women as active contributors. Writing against slavery, women found themselves, for the first time, encouraged to produce polemical literature for a mass market. Their pamphlets and books, written in the forms of popular verse, children's books, dialogues and fables, reached out to a wide readership of both sexes. Consequently it is not surprising to see several women writers who began within abolition ranks moving out into publishing work that takes on women's rights and political reform. Elizabeth Heyrick is a good example of a figure who brilliantly combined her abolition views with a radical women's rights and reform agenda in a series of startling and wide-selling pamphlets.[21] More may also be seen as the formal inspiration for the early and utilitarian polemical publications of Harriet Martineau. Martineau was no radical reformer in any straightforward sense, but her constant commitment to social reform and her principled attacks on both outmoded agrarian labour systems and the ruinous effects of trade monopolies on the English colonies led her to produce the vastly influential series of bestsellers collected under the title *Illustrations of political economy*. Each volume in the series came out in tiny duodecimo format and sold in tens of thousands. They showed that there was a ready market in the early nineteenth century for liberal social theory that attacked conservative economic fiscal policy, argued against privilege and argued for the rights of the poor and the rights of women.[22]

Radical publishing did not develop in isolation, but existed alongside and in constant interaction with other publishing phenomena, of which the rising pornographic industry and the abolition movement are probably the most significant. Throughout the period 1790–1830, radicalism as a publishing phenomenon should also be seen as developing at precisely the same time as another mass propaganda movement – the campaign to abolish the slave trade

20 For More as propagandist, see Scheuermann 2002, 135–207; for More's influence on Martineau, see Wood 2002, 256–7.

21 For Heyrick's works, see Ferguson 1992.

22 Hunter 1995, 148–95; Webb 1960, 134–74.

and colonial slavery.[23] The formal and organizational impact of abolition publicity strategies upon the radical press is an under-researched but very important issue. Abolition was a transatlantic propaganda movement directed at mass audiences and drawing on a wide variety of contemporary publishing avenues. Like the radical reformers, abolitionists were prepared to absorb any publishing form that proved a useful host for their propagandas. In taking in travel literature, the political pamphlet, poetry, drama, the novel and the graphic arts, abolition had an impact on English book production in ways that run parallel with radicalism. While many reformers, including Henry Hunt, Francis Place and most spectacularly the negrophobe William Cobbett, were not sympathetic to abolition, several – including Tom Paine, Thomas Hardy, John Cartright and John Thelwall – did see freedom for the slave as aligned with the struggle for human rights in Britain. Thelwall was particularly successful in fusing his abolition theory with his radical ideas, and producing a universal liberation philosophy open to all races and sexes. Ex-slave, abolitionist and author of the first great slave autobiography, Olaudah Equiano was also a close associate of leading members of the London Corresponding Society. Equiano's *The interesting narrative* might be seen as a book that took radicalism into wider debates over freedom within the Diaspora. It is finally, however, not in the direct fusion of radical and abolition ideologies, but in the similarities they share as propaganda movements that anti-slavery and radical reform had their most central impact on publishing. Both movements were prepared to draw on any publishing resources from the highest to the lowest to get their messages across. Josiah Wedgwood cast the anti-slavery seal in tens of thousands of ceramic medallions, while the image was emblazoned on every form of abolition publishing. Thomas Spence cast trade tokens carrying radical texts and images in large numbers, while incorporating the aphorisms and imagery of these coins into a variety of his other publications. The impulse was the same: to saturate as many publishing modes as possible with an essentialized political message.

The interrelation of radicalism with the rapidly expanding pornographic industries constitutes one of the most fascinating demonstrations of the appropriative energy with which radicalism would colonize and subvert any emerging or established publishing area. The work of Lynn Hunt and her disciples has effectively demonstrated the extent to which radical French pre-revolutionary and revolutionary satire of the later eighteenth century drew on the recently developed pornographic industries and infiltrated the book and

23 For the interrelations of radical and abolition publishing, see Walvin 1977; Drescher 1982; for the complicated interplay of popular radical and elite pro-slavery responses to the passage of the Abolition Bill in the decade following 1807, see Drescher 1994; Hollis 1980.

print markets. The second half of the eighteenth century, the last three decades in particular, saw the growth of pornographic and libertine literatures in England and France. These literatures, while they certainly operated on a straightforwardly obscene and erotic level as popular entertainment, were also highly politicized.[24] The attitudes towards sexuality, and towards the corrupted sexuality of church and aristocracy which they privileged, provided them with an intensely destabilizing effect. Within England the sudden explosion of single-sheet print satire coincided with the development of a mass market for pornographic prints. Every leading political satirist working in England 1790–1820 produced work that used pornographic elements as part of the satiric vocabulary.

Pornography remains a badly neglected terrain in terms of its impact on nineteenth-century publishing and book production generally. When it comes to the interrelations of pornographic and radical publishing, the work of Iain McCalman remains the only detailed analysis. McCalman has demonstrated how many of the underworld ultra-radicals and hacks who operated in London during the great decades of radical publicity moved freely in and out of political and pornographic publishing.[25] Obscenity and bawdiness had long been elements within political satire. H. D. Symonds, who was one of Paine's earliest publishers, was also a pornographer. During the height of the Queen Caroline scandal, Benbow, Fairburn, Fores, Marks, Chubb and Wilson emerge as brilliant operators who delighted in drawing on their seedy experience as pornographers when producing satires based on personal defamation of character. The false memoirs, love poetry and confessions which they produced ridiculed leading statesmen, politicians and above all the Prince Regent and his mistresses, through the incorporation of ribald and often flagrantly pornographic and scatological materials. One of McCalman's original insights relates to the way he traces the extended careers of these figures into the expanding Victorian pornographic industries of the 1830s and 1840s. Radicalism may have gone out of fashion for good; pornography, as we know to our cost today, was here to stay. A series of shady figures, including Jack Mitford, John Benjamin Brookes, John Dugdale and John Duncombe, had all been involved in writing and reprinting mainstream radical publications during the Queen Caroline affair, and then began to specialize in pornography from the mid-1820s. William Dugdale, John's brother, who had opened his career as an ultra-radical revolutionary publishing William Watson's *Shamrock, thistle and rose*,

24 L. Hunt 1991, 1993; Darnton 1995.
25 McCalman 1984, 204–35; and for connections between abolition and pornography, see Wood 2002, 87–93.

was to become one of the dominant pornographic publishers of the nineteenth century. George Cannon shifted from radical pamphlet publication to a large-scale pornographic business and has the distinction of first publishing de Sade's work in Britain. Yet surveying the books and prints brought out by the ex-radicals indicates that they might still be seen to be using pornography to political ends. Sometimes this would take the form of reviving works by the French libertine *philosophes*, or related work by English libertine intellectuals. Hence, we find Peter Annet's *Social bliss* and John Wilkes's notorious *An essay on woman* reprinted by Richard Carlile and George Cannon. Even within the works written and published by the ex-radicals themselves, there is a continuous anti-clerical stance and a continual attack on the sexual depravity of the aristocracy, which maintained a radical inflection. William Dugdale's extremely dirty *Exquisite* was at one level appealing to an audience for erotica, but the unremitting focus on upper-class vice, with the professed desire of reforming the morals of the nation's elite, is typical of the moral confusions of radical pornography.

Yet despite these forays into the underworld of popular publishing, the radical free press went into decline after 1822, and never fully re-emerged. The second generation of radical publishers, the most significant of whom were Carlile, Benbow, Wooler, Hone, Fairburn, Johnson and Cobbett, were without exception formally ambitious authors with a radical heritage to which they were committed. Yet after 1822 they were presented with a new set of political conditions. Radicalism, because of its wide social base and its irreverent intellectual approach, had always flirted with lowness and unrespectability. From the outset, radical publishing, particularly as manifested in political satire, skirted the broadside, chapbook and print markets in ways that, as we have seen, drew on the anarchic humour and sensationalism of scandal, pornography and gallows literature. Radical publishers, who operated with seemingly no formal or moral limits during the Queen Caroline affair, found that the market for extreme anti-state publicity had all but dried up by the mid-1820s. Yet, in the years immediately preceding the passage of the great Reform Bill of 1832, there was something of a minor revival of radical publishing. The work of John Carpenter and C. J. Grant shows that there was a brief reignition of old radical values and publishing forms, not to mention a substantial revival of state prosecution of radical authors and booksellers. Cobbett and Carlile threw their journalistic skills into the fray and were both prosecuted yet again for their troubles. Yet, ironically, this served merely to emphasize how things had changed irrevocably.[26] If the old-style radical publishers were to survive they

26 The fullest account of the 1830s radical revival is Hollis 1970, 156–202.

had to adapt and reinvent their work for the new mainstream Victorian book markets, dominated by comparatively benign illustrated periodical journalism, by the arrival of the social novel and by new forms related to the leisure industries.[27]

27 James 1963, 1976; Anderson 1991.

49

Mining the archive: a guide to present and future book-historical research resources

MICHAEL F. SUAREZ, S.J.

Students of book history working in the period that this volume of *The Cambridge History of the Book in Britain* investigates - from the definitive end of the Printing Act (1695) to the more imprecise advent (*c*.1830) of the book as an industrial object produced and financed by specialist commercial publishers - are fortunate in the wealth of bibliographical and book-historical scholarship at their disposal. The more than 2,000 items comprising the bibliography of this history speak volumes about the richness and diversity of what has already been written, so that any scholar contributing so much as a photon to our illumination might say with Newton, 'If I have seen farther, it is by standing on the shoulders of giants.'[1] In this brief chapter, I would like to gesture toward some of the resources - primary in several senses - for the conduct of book history, 1695–1830, and to highlight some archival research projects that most need to be conducted. Such a highly attenuated survey, tendered in the hope of stimulating further undertakings, must perforce be indicative rather than exhaustive.[2]

Undoubtedly the most fundamentally important resource for bibliographical and book-historical research in the eighteenth century is *The English short-title catalogue* (*ESTC*).[3] *ESTC* is sometimes usefully supplemented by *The hand press book database*, produced by the Research Libraries Group (RLG) and the Consortium of European Research Libraries (CERL). As the sole extant online union catalogue for European hand-press books produced *c*.1455 to 1830, its reach into the early decades of the nineteenth century is especially welcome. Similarly, the broad scope and chronological range of *WorldCat*, the OCLC Online Union Catalog, makes it highly useful.[4] The *Nineteenth-century short-title*

1 See Merton 1965.
2 A variety of materials may be found, for example, at SHARP Web, www.sharpweb.org, and at Voice of the Shuttle, http://vos.ucsb.edu/browse.asp?id=2713#id3785. All URLs listed in this chapter were consulted in August 2007.
3 See http://estc.bl.uk. See Zeeman 1991; see also Crump and Harris 1983; and Snyder and Smith 2003.
4 See www.oclc.org/worldcat/introduction/default.htm.

catalogue (*NSTC*), which covers the years 1801 to 1919, has nothing like the bibliographical control of its earlier counterpart, the *ESTC*, perhaps understandably so, given the enormous increases in print production during the nineteenth century.[5] Among contemporary printed bibliographical sources, periodic listings of books – bearing such titles as *Bibliotheca Annua*, *Monthly Catalogue*, *Register of Books*, *Catalogue of All Books* and *Annual Catalogue* – as well as lists of books in periodicals (*viz.*, the *London Magazine*, the *Gentleman's Magazine*) should not be overlooked.[6] Robert Watt's *Bibliotheca Britannica* (4 vols., 1824) provides author and subject listings for more than 200,000 books, pamphlets and periodicals printed from 1450 to the early nineteenth century; a highly useful resource, it is particularly strong in eighteenth-century works.[7]

Eighteenth-century collections online (*ECCO*), which provides digital images of more than 150,000 books published in the eighteenth century, is a highly valuable resource.[8] The texts of many publications from 1695–1830 are available via Chadwyck-Healey's *Literature online* service (*LION*).[9] Whatever their source, substitutional formats (or 'surrogates') must be treated with caution, especially when used for book-historical research; they are generally unsuitable for bibliographical investigations.

Michael Turner has produced a remarkable database, *The London book trades: a biographical resource*, containing entries for more than 30,000 individuals active in the London book trades in various capacities from Caxton to *c.*1830.[10] It is useful not only for providing detailed biographical information about individuals, but also for establishing relationships (both personal and professional) among book-trade personnel.[11] Also helpful is the *British book trade index* (*BBTI*), which supplies brief biographical and professional details for men and women at work in the book trades in England and Wales from the

5 See http://nstc.chadwyck.com/marketing/about.jsp, consulted August 2007; on the explosion of print in nineteenth-century Britain, see Eliot 1994.

6 A number of such works are reprinted in the English Bibliographical Sources series by Gregg Press Ltd (London). See also Foxon 1963.

7 *Bibliotheca Britannica, or, a general index to British and foreign literature* was originally published serially, parts 1–4 between 1819 and 1820 in Glasgow, and parts 5–9 between 1821 and 1824 in Edinburgh.

8 See http://gale.cengage.com/EighteenthCentury.

9 See http://lion.chadwyck.co.uk/infoCentre/contents.jsp.

10 See http://sas-space.sas.ac.uk/dspace/handle/10065/224. Cf. I. Maxted's *The London book trades, 1735–1775: a checklist of members*, at http://bookhistory.blogspot.com/2007/01/london-1735-1755.html, and his *The British book trades 1710–1777*, at http://bookhistory.blogspot.com/2005/12/index.html. On membership in the book trades, see also Plomer 1922; Plomer, Bushnell and Dix 1932; Ramsden 1956; Todd 1972; Maxted 1977; McKenzie 1978; and Ferdinand 1992. See also I. Maxted, *The British book trades, 1710–1777: an index of masters and apprentices*, at http://bookhistory.blogspot.com/2007/01/apprentices-introduction.html. For Dublin, see Pollard 2000.

11 See Turner, chap. 14, above.

fifteenth century to 1850.[12] A similar resource, the *Scottish book trade index* (*SBTI*), is maintained by the National Library of Scotland.[13]

Mapping the print culture of eighteenth-century London (part of the London Book Trades Project) provides the locations of members of the London book trades from 1690 to 1820, with particular attention to the centre of book production and sales in Paternoster Row and St Paul's Churchyard.[14] Business directories, directories of towns and cities or counties – Pigot's being the best known – and street directories are especially useful for investigating provincial publishing.[15] Whether produced by entrepreneurial publishers wishing to capitalize on the eighteenth- and early nineteenth-century commercial revolution,[16] or by local registry offices, these resources can help book historians not only to construct local maps of print production and distribution, but also to trace commercial associations, deepening our understanding of print networks. Where available, tax records (for example, land tax and window tax assessments)[17] and commercial fire insurance archives are also valuable, documenting the location and ownership of business premises.[18] Like probate inventories, fire insurance information typically helps the investigator to gauge the commercial worth of a business.[19] Thus far (with a few exceptions), such archival data remain an insufficiently exploited resource.[20] In contrast, the records of the Stationers'

12 See www.bbti.bham.ac.uk.

13 See www.nls.uk/catalogues/resources/sbti/index.html.

14 See members.lycos.co.uk/bookhistory/index.html. On the locations of book-trades personnel in England, Scotland and Wales, see Turner, *The London book trades*; the *BBTI*; the *SBTI*; Plomer 1922; Plomer, Bushnell and Dix 1932; Maxted 1977, 1980. See also *The London Book trades 1775–1800: a topographical guide*, at http://bookhistory.blogspot.com/2007/01/streets-introduction.html. For Dublin, see Pollard 2000.

15 An excellent resource is the Historical Directories project run by the University of Leicester, 'a digital library of local and trade directories for England and Wales, from 1750 to 1919'; see www.historicaldirectories.org/hd/index.asp. For directories based in England and Wales, excluding London, Norton 1950 should also be consulted. The best guide to London directories remains Goss 1932.

16 See Suarez, Introduction, above.

17 Gibson and Medlycott 1983 provides the date and location (organized by county) of surviving land tax and window tax returns for England and Wales. Ginter 1992 usefully considers the possibilities and limitations of land tax records for historical analysis; Ward 1953 remains useful.

18 The best overview of fire insurance in England and Scotland from 1696 to 1850 is R. Pearson 2004; see 381–3 for a list of archival sources.

19 See, for example, Schwarz 1982, 65, reporting data from the Sun Fire Office and the Royal Exchange Assurance to assess the worth of London booksellers' businesses in the late 1770s. For a fine example of using probate inventories to document commercial development, see Mandelbrote 2003. Of course, the probate inventories of individuals not in the book trades have also proved useful in providing information about book ownership: see, for example, Leedham-Green 1986 and Garrigus 1997.

20 I. Maxted's *The British book trades 1775–1787: an index to insurance policies*, at http://bookhistory.blogspot.com/2007/01/insurance-introduction.html, provides a specialized index for a dozen years in the policy registers of the Sun and Royal Exchange, England's two largest insurers at that time. Further work of this kind is needed if insurance records are to become a more commonly exploited resource for book historians.

Company are well documented,[21] routinely used,[22] and widely available.[23] Moreover, a number of fine historical studies can assist the book historian in thinking about the multiple and changing roles of the Company during the period covered by this volume.[24]

We are also fortunate in the number and range of surviving business records available for study, many of them rich in ore yet to be mined. London printers are represented in part by two well-edited works: *The Bowyer Ledgers*, spanning more than 75 years (1699–1777);[25] and the *Ledger of Charles Ackers*, covering 1732 to 1748.[26] A document of related interest, the original Dawks-Bowyer-Nichols Notebook, held by the British Library of Political and Economic Science (the working Library of the London School of Economics and Political Science), contains 124 pages of printers' records (with some miscellaneous material) and an undated specimen *c.*1740 of William Bowyer's printing types. The notebook went missing around 1974; fortunately, the library has a copy, made by Keith Maslen.[27] A cache of records equal in historical value to the Bowyer hoard has yet to be edited: the printing ledgers and other business papers, beginning in 1738, of William Strahan and his successors are in the British Library (BL Add. MSS 48800–48918).[28] Four additional account books (supplementing Add. MSS 48804–48806, 48842, 48843, 48900 and 48901) are in the American Philosophical Society Library in Philadelphia (call number B St83), though only the fourth of these is particularly relevant.[29] The BL also holds the records of the Chiswick Press – a printing firm run by Charles Whittingham I (the uncle) and Charles Whittingham II (the nephew), best known for its relations with the bookseller William Pickering. The substantial archive (BL Add. MSS 41867–41960) documents its operations from July 1792 to December 1885.[30]

21 See R. Myers 1990.

22 D. F. McKenzie's three volumes documenting Stationers' Company apprentices from 1605 to 1800 are, for example, routinely cited in the *ODNB*. See McKenzie 1978 for the eighteenth-century apprentices.

23 A microfilm reproduction of all the surviving items in the Company's archive (from 1554 to 1920) – comprising 115 reels – was prepared by Robin Myers and published by Chadwyck-Healey in 1986. See also Arber 1875–94, 1906; and Eyre and Rivington 1913–14. Cf. Greg 1967.

24 See Turner, chap. 14, and Myers, chap. 39, both above; see also Blagden 1959, 1960a; Plant 1974; Ferdinand 1992; and Myers and Harris 1997.

25 Maslen and Lancaster 1991; see also Maslen 1993.

26 McKenzie and Ross 1968.

27 See Maslen 1992.

28 Of particular note are 48800–1, 48802A, 48802B, 48803, 48806–10 and 48887.

29 See Hernlund 1967, 1969. Although Hernlund 1967 is often used with regard to how printers' charges were determined, Philip 1957 is a better source. Maslen 1971 also provides a useful corrective to Hernlund.

30 See Plomer 1901; see also Warren 1896. BL Add. MS 41960 B, and Add. MSS 43975–43989, as well as Add. Ch. 70986–71003, should also be consulted.

In the north of England, the Cumbria Record Office preserves two daybooks of the Whitehaven printer John Ware, covering August 1799 to July 1802 and August 1802 to June 1805.[31] The account book of the printing office superintended by the Revd John Parry of Chester, spanning the years 1826–36, is important both for that region and for Welsh print culture, as Parry printed the monthly *Goleuad Cymru* (*The Illuminator of Wales*) between 1826 and 1830. The full accounts, with an introduction, are now in print.[32] Among the surviving records of Welsh printing, the sales book of Samuel Williams, printer in Aberystwyth, documents his activities between 1816 and 1820;[33] the accounts of the Wesleyan Printing Office at Llanfair Caereinion from June 1824 to May 1828 are found in the first part of the Welsh Methodist (Wesleyan) Archives (361D) in the National Library of Wales.[34]

Scotland, though rich in publishing and bookselling archives (see below), is less fortunate in its surviving materials pertaining to printing. The ledger of Thomas Ruddiman's printing office (NLS MS 763) documents this learned printer's work from 1710 to 1715.[35] The 'Case-Book' (1803–6) of the Ayrshire printer, bookseller and publisher John Wilson is likewise a valuable resource for the Scottish provincial book trade.[36] It was formerly in the possession of W.H. Dunlop, managing director of the *Ayr Advertiser*; I have been unable to determine its current location. In a different vein, Gaskell's bibliography of the Foulis Press (1740–76) will long remain a standard resource.[37]

The records of paper manufacturers are also of no small consequence for understanding production and consumption among the book trades. The most valuable of these, the Whatman and Balston MSS, now in the Kent County Archives (CKS-U289), include correspondence, accounts, business and legal papers – and detailed information about manufacturing techniques, ingredients and prices – for what was arguably the pre-eminent papermaking firm of its day.[38]

Printing and bookselling are as inseparable as Castor and Pollux in the archives of the Oxford University Press, which has a rich store of archival material covering both the learned and the bible presses – for example, in the

31 McKay 1996. See also McKay 2000, 2002.
32 Walters 1980–1.
33 See Rees 1984–7.
34 See Jones 1998.
35 See Duncan 1965.
36 See Thomson 1967; see also McKenzie 1969.
37 Gaskell 1986.
38 See T. Balston 1979 and J. N. Balston 1998. I am grateful to John Bidwell for bringing the Whatman and Balston papers to my attention.

Delegates' minutes and accounts from 1668 to 1756,[39] or the 'Bill Book' covering the years 1769–72 (OUP/PR/14/6/1).[40] The Cambridge University Press archives have, as of this writing, received greater scholarly attention,[41] although much of the material in McKenzie's 1966 study – *viz.*, 'The first Minute Book of the Curators of the Press', the 'Vice-Chancellor's Accounts', the 'Annual Press Accounts' and 'Vouchers' – awaits further analysis.[42]

The Society for Promoting Christian Knowledge (SPCK) archives, a substantial cache of materials on printing, publishing, financing and distributing printed matter from 1698, are held in the Cambridge University Library.[43] On loan to the same library are the archives of the British and Foreign Bible Society, dating from 1804, which chiefly provide information on the translation, production and distribution of bibles and, hence, shed light on the BFBS's ongoing engagement with the book trades.[44] Another substantial store of documents, the Nichols Family Archive,[45] contains a wealth of materials for book history and book-trade biography that extends far beyond the well-known documentation provided in John Nichols's *Literary anecdotes* and *Illustrations*.[46]

The commercial records of publishers and booksellers are deservedly prized for the evidence they provide. The business notebook of Thomas Bennett and Henry Clements, covering the years 1686 to 1719, is an invaluable resource, both because of the information it contains and because of the accompanying commentary of Hodgson and Blagden.[47] The extensive archives of the Longman Group, housed in the Reading University Library (RUL MS 1393), include materials from 1718 into the twentieth century.[48] Although some scholars have made excellent use of them, there is certainly more evidence to be gleaned from their study.[49] Regrettably, the 'memorandum book' (1695–1720) and *Monthly Mercury* ledger (1702–20) of the London bookseller

39 Gibson and Johnson 1943.

40 See Carter 1975; and Sutcliffe 1977. See also Gadd forthcoming; and Eliot forthcoming.

41 Works relevant to the period spanning the late seventeenth to the early nineteenth centuries include McKenzie 1966; and McKitterick 1992, 1998.

42 The Cambridge University Press archives (1696–1902) are available on microfilm (eleven reels), produced by Chadwyck-Healey in 1973. See also Leedham-Green 1973.

43 See McClure 1888; Clement 1952; and Mandlebrote, chap. 32, above.

44 See Mandlebrote, chap. 32, above, and www.lib.cam.ac.uk/deptserv/biblesociety.

45 See Pooley 2001, 2002. See also www.le.ac.uk/elh/resources/nichols/index.html.

46 Nichols 1812–16; and Nichols and Nichols 1817–58, respectively. Among other useful collections of book-trade biographies, see Bracken and Silver 1995.

47 Hodgson and Blagden 1956.

48 See http://www.reading.ac.uk/special-collections/collections/sc-longman.asp. See also the microfilm (73 reels), *Archives of the House of Longman, 1794–1914*, published by Chadwyck-Healey. See also Ingram 1981.

49 See Cox and Chandler 1925; Longman 1936; Owen 1954; Briggs 1974, 2008; and Wallis 1974.

and publisher Henry Rhodes in the National Archives of the United Kingdom – formerly the PRO – (PROB 49/4/1, 2) are in such poor condition that they can neither be photographed nor consulted.[50] More felicitously, extracts from the ledger of Henry Woodfall senior (1734–47) and of Henry Woodfall junior (1737–48) were preserved in the mid-nineteenth century by their publication in *Notes & Queries*.[51] The minute book of the partners in the *Grub Street Journal* furnishes a variety of evidence from August 1730 to August 1737.[52] Similarly, the minutes of the Committee of Partners in the *General Evening Post*, kept at Yale University's Lewis Walpole Library, document its operations between 1754 and 1786. Henry Sampson Woodfall's accounts (1765–71) for the *Public Advertiser* are in the British Library (BL Add. MSS 38,169).[53] Three ledgers from the London bookselling partnership of Thomas Hookham and James Carpenter (1791–98) are in the National Archives (PRO C104/75/1–3).[54] Understandably, the publishing archives of Cadell and Davies have already received some treatment,[55] though a full rendering of the firm's surviving papers – principally in the Beinecke Library (Gen: MSS 510, spanning the period 1767–1831; chiefly 1790–1820) – would nevertheless be highly desirable.[56]

The correspondence of Robert Dodsley has been widely consulted in James Tierney's exemplary edition,[57] but the letters and papers of Jacob Tonson and his son Jacob junior (chiefly found in BL Add. MSS 28,275), charting the progress of their business from 1710 to 1782, have yet to receive similar treatment.[58] Among many examples of such materials that might be very usefully edited is the letter book of Joseph Johnson, London bookseller and publisher – now in the Pforzheimer Collection of the New York Public Library (|Pforz A-RD 09) – consisting of some 240 missives from Johnson, sent between 1795 and 1810.[59] Another opportune project is the correspondence, mostly found in two letter-books in the Bodleian Library, of the bookseller John Bell (1735–1806).[60] Adam Budd's edition of Andrew Millar's business papers, *Bookseller of the Enlightenment: the correspondence, business ledgers, and*

50 See Blagden 1954, 1959. I am grateful to the staff at the National Archives for their help in attempting to rescue this important resource.
51 P., P.T. 1855a, 1855b.
52 See Turner 1978.
53 William Woodfall's diary (BL Add. MS 27,780) is also among the Woodfall papers. On Woodfall, father and son, and their influential newspaper, see Schweizer 2006.
54 See Fergus and Thaddeus 1987; Kurtz and Womer 2004; and Fergus 2006a, 284, 16–19.
55 See Besterman 1938.
56 See http://webtext.library.yale.edu/xml2html/beinecke.cadell.con.html#a9.
57 Dodsley 1988.
58 See also Papali 1968; Geduld 1969; and Lynch 1971.
59 See http://catnyp.nypl.org/record=b7086207.
60 Bodley MS Eng. Letters c.20 and c.21.

legal briefs of Andrew Millar, promises to be an important contribution to the field.[61]

Among the documents of English provincial booksellers and publishers, the day books and allied business records belonging to John and Thomas Clay (booksellers in Daventry, Rugby, Lutterworth and Warwick) from 1746 to 1792 may be consulted in the Northamptonshire Record Office.[62] Also valuable are four surviving ledgers (A–D, 1780–1807) of the Cirencester bookseller Timothy Stevens, housed at the Gloucestershire Record Office (D9125/7880).[63]

'The Edinburgh Day Book' (NLS MS Acc. 9800), recording the operations of an as yet unidentified Edinburgh bookseller from May 1715 to June 1717, is currently being edited by Richard Ovenden.[64] The John Murray Archive at the National Library of Scotland – which includes ledgers, journals and more than 150,000 letters from 1768 through to 1920 – houses many items of great interest for the history of the book.[65] The NLS holds another landmark resource in the business correspondence and financial papers of the Edinburgh booksellers and publishers Bell and Bradfute (1778–1941, though chiefly 1778–1844).[66]

Banking records, though rare, have proved useful in the past and will undoubtedly continue to do so. An important document of the Fleet Street bookseller-banker Robert Gosling – 'Gentleman's Ledger B' (1730–40) – is held at the Bodleian Library (MS Eng. Misc. C296).[67] The remaining Gosling's Bank documents, kept in the Barclays Group Archives in Wythenshawe, Manchester, provide particulars about the finances of booksellers, printers and authors.[68] Other banking firms, such as Baron Dimsdale and Company and C. Hoare and Co., have also left records that contain valuable information from the accounts of book-trade personnel.[69] Bankruptcies, an all-too-common fate among publishing booksellers,[70] almost invariably furnish the

61 Millar forthcoming.

62 See Fergus 2006a, 284, 28–32, *et infra*; see also Fergus 1984, 1996; Fergus and Portner 1987.

63 See Fergus 2006a, 284, 33–6.

64 See Ovenden in Brown and McDougall forthcoming.

65 See the catalogue at www.nls.uk/jma/mss/search/index.cfm.

66 See Zachs in Brown and McDougall forthcoming. For an inventory, see: www.hss.ed.ac.uk/chb/sbtai-db/PDFFiles/acc10662.pdf. Additional Bell and Bradfute material may be found in NLS (Dep 193 and 317, and Acc 8500); see also www.hss.ed.ac.uk/chb/sbtai-db/recordB.htm.

67 On Gosling and his brother Sir Francis, see Melton 1985; Joslin 1954, 177–8.

68 See Fleeman 1975. For other bookseller-bankers, and a discussion of the book trades' relations with bankers, see Suarez, Introduction, above.

69 The Dimsdale archives are held by the National Westminster Bank, London. On the Hoare ledgers, see Hoare 1955; Clay 1994.

70 See Suarez, Introduction, and Raven, chap. 3, both above. See also Hernlund 1994; Ferdinand 2001; Mandelbrote 2003; Harley 1966. On business risks and failures in eighteenth-century England, see Hoppit 1986, 1987; Duffy 1985; Marriner 1980.

book historian with detailed financial information about debts and assets, and can provide evidence of book-trade networks.[71]

Trade-sale catalogues are especially helpful in tracing the ownership of copies, typically of shares in copies. The Longman catalogues, which record trade sales in 1704 and from 1718 to 1768, are in the British Library. The Ward set of marked-up trade-sale catalogues (1718–52) is in the John Johnson Collection of Printed Ephemera in the Bodleian Library, as are the Rivington and Co. catalogues. The sales of John Murray and his successors are documented in the NLS's John Murray Archive.[72]

Records of publishing booksellers' copyright holdings are also useful, as are copyright assignments from authors.[73] A substantial body of such material is in MS (for example, BL Add. MSS 38,728–30, a 'collection of assignments of copyright between English authors and publishers', from 1 January 1703/4 to 12 April 1822) and awaits systematic investigation. In addition, a great deal of information on the ownership of copyrights, and on the culture of intellectual property, may be gleaned from legal cases.[74] The records of the Chancery and King's Bench, both in the National Archives, usually provide remarkably thorough documentation.[75] There are, in addition, scattered relevant materials in the State Papers Domestic (also in the National Archives; *viz.*, SP 35, 36 and 37, covering the reigns of George I, II and III, respectively), but these are perforce atypical as they invariably pertain to publications in which the state took a special interest.

Book-auction catalogues and booksellers' fixed-price catalogues may help historians gauge the commercial and cultural value of works; they are also sometimes useful for establishing provenance information.[76] The British Library, the Bodleian's John Johnson Collection and the University of Reading

71 See I. Maxted, *The British book trades 1731–1806: a checklist of bankrupts*, at http://bookhistory.blogspot.com/2007/01/bankrupts.html. C.Y. Ferdinand is currently working on a book-length study of eighteenth-century book-trade bankruptcies.

72 For a description and analysis of most of these materials, see Blagden 1951; Belanger 1970, 1975. See also http://www.bl.uk/reshelp/findhelprestype/prbooks/guidesalecat/salecatalogueguild.html. Cf. Coral 1974 and Coover 1987, 1988 on the sale of music copyrights at auction. On the purchase of copyrights in the Restoration, see G. Mandelbrote 1997.

73 See, for example, Dodsley 1988; Milhous and Hume 1999.

74 Particularly noteworthy studies include McDougall 1988, 1997; Deazley 2004. Perhaps understandably, legal records have attracted more studies on censorship than on copyright. To develop an understanding of press prosecutions in the eighteenth and nineteenth centuries, Thomas 1977 remains one of the best places to begin.

75 Horwitz 1995 is an excellent guide to the Chancery materials; see also Goulden 1982. *The English Reports*, published from 1220 to 1865 (178 volumes in the printed edition) – including opinions, heads of argument, pleadings and reports – and now available online (www.justis.com/Search.aspx), is an especially valuable resource.

76 See Pearson 1998; see also Suarez 1999a. For a catalogue of catalogues 1676–1900, see Munby and Coral 1977.

Library (to name but a few), all have noteworthy holdings of publishers' catalogues, prospectuses and announcements.[77] Although a great deal of work has been done on subscription publishing, the subject continues to hold promise for future inquiry,[78] especially in light of expanding notions of patronage and cultural capital.[79] The data already come to light on subscription lists and subscribers almost certainly merit further analysis and there are still prospectuses and subscription lists to be found, especially for works issuing from provincial presses. Plate subscriptions among cultural elites – for heavily illustrated books in natural history, classics, heraldry, philosophy, history and geography – were by no means limited to the Restoration.[80] In addition, we still know relatively little about trade subscription.

Domestic transactions most often leave no durable trace, but when books cross borders, official records of imports and exports usefully document the international trade. In some areas, port books (records of customs duties paid on overseas trade between 1565 and 1799) and Customs ledgers have already been put to good use,[81] but there is still a great deal of information in many such records that awaits careful study. Particularly relevant documents in the National Archives are: E 190 (Exchequer, Port Books, 1565–1799);[82] CUST 3 (consisting of 82 vols. of ledgers of imports and exports from 1697 to 1780);[83] CUST 14 (39 vols., but now available in microform only), comprising ledgers of imports and exports for Scotland, 1755–1827; and CUST 15 (140 vols.), ledgers of imports and exports for Ireland, 1698–1829.[84] In some cases, there are no port books documenting commercial activity in the later eighteenth century; the last book for Cardiff is dated 1736, for example, while the final ledger for Poole covers the year 1759–60. Moreover, all the London port books from 1697 to 1799 were destroyed in the 1890s because many were in poor condition. Researchers should also bear in mind that port books and Customs ledgers,

77 See http://www.bl.uk/reshelp/findhelprestype/prbooks/guidesalecat/salescatalogueguild.html and http://www.bodley.ox.ac.uk/johnson/.

78 Among many publications, Robinson and Wallis 1975; Cannon and Robinson 1995; Wallis 1996; and Amory 1995 are foundational for future study.

79 See, for example, Amory 1995; Griffin 1996; Brewer 1997.

80 See, for example, Ashworth 1981. Cf. Clapp 1933.

81 See, for example, Barber 1976, 1977, 1982; Cave 1987; Raven 1997b, 1999, 2000b. Cf. Gillespie 2005, 80–9, *et infra*, which makes judicious use of such materials for early modern book history. Other useful studies of eighteenth-century book imports and/or exports include: Paisey 1991; Fabian 1992a, 1992b; Kinane 1994; Fabian and Spieckermann 1995; Raven 1997a; Jefcoate 2004; Black 2004.

82 Some 20,000 survive, but many are in poor condition and there are significant lacunae in the record; see www.nationalarchives.gov.uk/catalogue/RdLeaflet.asp?sLeafletID=83&j=1. For helpful guides to the port books, see Williams 1955; Woodward 1970, 1973.

83 These ledgers provide information chiefly about the nature and quantity of goods imported and exported at the Port of London and the outports.

84 On the history and scholarly use of customs records, see Jarvis 1955–9; Carson 1977. Schumpeter 1960 provides a helpful overview of English overseas trade in the eighteenth century.

even when seemingly complete, can never produce a full reconstruction of international commercial trading (nor of coastal trade), because smuggling, fraud, evasion and corruption were not uncommon.[85] These gaps in the historical record notwithstanding, such documents, when used with appropriate judiciousness,[86] will continue to enlarge our understanding of the international trade in books.

The domestic trade, too, is also represented in these documents. In many cases, port books include coasting books, which record the issue and return of certificates for the transit of goods by coast from one English port to another. The use of canal, river and coastal shipping in the domestic distribution of paper and, especially, of printed matter is a topic ripe for further research.[87]

Bibliography and book history – endeavours that almost invariably benefit from being in close proximity to each other – are increasingly understood as mutually informing modes of historical inquiry. Both are undergoing a period of development that makes this an exciting time to be studying the book.[88] The many approaches and manifold sources available to the book historian, only some of which are mentioned here, engender the hope that readers of this volume will be enlivened to produce informative and thought-provoking chapters of their own.

85 See Cole 1958; Mui and Mui 1975.
86 Clark 1938; Andrews 1956; and Aström 1968 all offer salutary advice on the use and interpretation of these records.
87 See Suarez, Introduction, above.
88 See Suarez, 2003–4 (2006).

Abbreviations used in bibliography

Arber	Arber, E. (ed.) *A transcript of the registers of the Company of Stationers of London, 1554–1640*, 5 vols., London; rpt Gloucester, MA, 1967
BBTI	*The British book trade index* – currently accessed at www.bbti.bham.ac.uk
BC	*Book Collector*
BH	*Business History*
BIHR	*Bulletin of the Institute of Historical Research*
BL	British Library, London
Bodleian	Bodleian Library, Oxford
BSANZB	*Bibliographical Society of Australia & New Zealand Bulletin*
CBEL	Bateson, F.W. (ed.) *The Cambridge bibliography of English literature*, 5 vols., Cambridge, 1940–57
CERL	Consortium of European Research Libraries
CHBB II	Morgan, N. and Thomson, R.M. (eds.) *The Cambridge history of the book in Britain*, vol. II: *1100–1400*, Cambridge, 2008
CHBB III	Hellinga, L. and Trapp, J.B. (eds.) *The Cambridge history of the book in Britain*, vol. III: *1400–1557*, Cambridge, 1998
CHBB IV	Barnard, J. and McKenzie, D.F. with Bell, M. (eds.) *The Cambridge history of the book in Britain*, vol. IV: *1557–1695*, Cambridge, 2002
CJ	*Cartographic Journal*
CLRO	City of London Record Office
CRS	Catholic Record Society
CUL	Cambridge University Library
DJ	*Daily Journal*
DNB	*Dictionary of national biography*
EBST	*Edinburgh Bibliographical Society Transactions*
EcHR	*Economic History Review*

ECS	*Eighteenth-Century Studies*
EHR	*English Historical Review*
EP	*Evening Post*
ESTC	*English short-title catalogue* – currently accessed at http://estc.bl.uk
EUL	Edinburgh University Library
GA	*General Advertiser*
GM	*Gentleman's Magazine*
HBA I	Amory, H. and Hall, D. (eds.) *The history of the book in America*, vol. I: *The colonial book in the Atlantic world*, Cambridge, 2000
HBA II	Gross, R. A. and Kelly, M. (eds.) *The history of the book in America*, vol. II: *An extensive Republic: print culture and society in the new nation, 1790–1840*, Chapel Hill, NC, forthcoming
HBC I	Fleming, P. L., Gallichan, G. and Lamonde, Y. (eds.) *History of the book in Canada*, vol. I: *Beginnings to 1840*, Toronto, 2004
HJ	*Historical Journal*
HLB	*Harvard Library Bulletin*
HLQ	*Huntington Library Quarterly*
IM	*Imago Mundi*
JEcH	*Journal of Economic History*
JPHS	*Journal of the Printing Historical Society*
LBT	Turner, M. L. (ed.) *The London book trades: a biographical resource* – currently accessed at http://sasspace.sas.ac.uk/dspace/handle/10065/224
LC	*London Chronicle*
LEP	*London Evening Post*
LHD	*Library History Database* – currently accessed at www.r-alston.co.uk/library.htm
Library	*The Library: Transactions of the Bibliographical Society*
LJ	*London Journal*
MC	*Map Collector*
MChr	*Morning Chronicle*
MLQ	*Modern Language Quarterly*
MLR	*Modern Language Review*
MP	*Modern Philology*
MR	*Monthly Review*
N&Q	*Notes and Queries*
NCBEL	Watson, G. (ed.) *The new Cambridge bibliography of English literature*, 5 vols., Cambridge, 1969–77

NLI	National Library of Ireland
NLS	National Library of Scotland
NT	National Trust
OBS	Oxford Bibliographical Society
ODNB	*Oxford dictionary of national biography*
OED	*Oxford English dictionary*
P&P	*Past and Present*
PA	*Public Advertiser*
PBSA	*Papers of the Bibliographical Society of America*
PH	*Publishing History*
PL	*Private Library*
PMLA	*Publications of the Modern Language Associate of America*
PQ	*Philological Quarterly*
RES	*Review of English Studies*
QR	*Quarterly Review*
RUL	The University of Reading Library
SB	*Studies in Bibliography*
SBTI	*The Scottish book trade index* – currently accessed at www.nls.uk/catalogues/resources/sbti/index.html
SPCK	Society for Promoting Christian Knowledge
St.Co.	Stationers' Company
TC	*Term catalogues, 1668–1709 AD, with a number for Easter Term, 1711 AD*, ed. E. Arber, 3 vols., London, 1903–6
TCBS	Transaction of the Cambridge Bibiographical Society
TCD	Trinity College, Dublin
TRHS	*Transactions of the Royal Historical Society*
YULG	*Yale University Library Gazette*

Bibliography

Abbattista, B. 1985 'The business of Paternoster Row: towards a publishing history of the "Universal History" (1736–1765)', *PH*, 17, 5–38.

Abbey, J. R. 1952 *Scenery of Great Britain and Ireland in aquatint and lithography, 1770–1860*, London.

1953 *Life in England in aquatint and lithography, 1770–1860: architecture, drawing books, art collections, magazines, navy and army, panoramas, etc., from the library of J. R. Abbey; a bibliographical catalogue*, London.

1956–7 *Travel in aquatint and lithography, 1770–1860: from the library of J. R. Abbey; a bibliographical catalogue*, London.

Abbott, J. L. 1982 *John Hawkesworth: eighteenth-century man of letters*, Madison, WI.

Accardo, P. X. 1998 'Byron in America to 1830', *HLB*, n.s., 9, 2.

Adams, I. 1975a 'Economic process and the Scottish land surveyor', *IM*, 27, 13–18.

1975b 'George Taylor, a survey o'parts', *IM*, 27, 55–63.

Adams, J. R. R. 1987 *The printed word and the common man: popular culture in Ulster, 1700–1900*, Belfast.

Adams, P. G. 1962 *Travelers and travel liars, 1660–1800*, Berkeley, CA.

1983 *Travel literature and the evolution of the novel*, Lexington, KY.

Adams, T. R. 1993 'Mount and Page, publishers of eighteenth-century maritime books', in N. J. Barker 1993, 45–77.

Adams, T. R. and Barker, N. J. 1993 'A new model for the study of the book', in N. J. Barker 1993, 5–43.

Albert, W. 1972 *The turnpike road system in England, 1663–1840*, London.

1983 'The turnpike trusts', in Aldcroft and Freeman 1983, 31–63.

Aldcroft, D. H. and Freeman, M. J. (eds.) 1983 *Transport in the industrial revolution*, Manchester.

Alden, J. 1952 'Pills and publishing: some notes on the English book trade', *Library*, 5th ser., 7, 21–37.

Alderson, B. 1983 'Miniature libraries for the young', *PL*, 3rd ser., 6, 13–38.

1989 *The Ludford box and 'A Christmas-Box': their contribution to our knowledge of eighteenth-century children's literature*, Los Angeles, CA.

Alderson, B. and de Marez Oyens, F. 2006 *Be merry and wise: the origins of children's book publishing, 1650–1850*, New York.

Aldis, H. G. 1970 (1904) *A list of books printed in Scotland before 1700*, Edinburgh.

Alexander, D. 1993 *Affecting moments: prints of English literature made in the age of romantic sensibility, 1775–1800*, York.

Allen, B. 1987 *Francis Hayman*, New Haven, CT.

Allen, W. O. B. and McClure, E. 1898 *Two hundred years: the history of the Society for Promoting Christian Knowledge*, London.

Allnutt, W. H. 1878 'The first local newspaper', *N&Q*, 5th ser., 9, 12.

Alsop, J. D. 1986–7 'The circulation of the *London Gazette*', *Journal of Newspaper and Periodical History*, 3, 1, 23–6.

Alston, R. C. 1974 *A bibliography of the English language from the invention of printing to the year 1800: a corrected reprint of vols. I–X*, Ilkley.

(ed.) 1997 *Order and connexion: studies in bibliography and book history*, Cambridge, MA.

2004 'The history of *ESTC*', *Age of Johnson*, 14, 269–329.

Alston, R. C., Robinson, F. J. G. and Wadham, C. (eds.) 1983 *A check-list of eighteenth-century books containing lists of subscribers*, London.

Altholz, J. L. 1989 *The religious press in Britain, 1760–1900*, New York.

Altick, R. D. 1998 (1957) *The English common reader: a social history of the mass reading public, 1800–1900*, 2nd edn, Columbus, OH.

Amory, H. 1984 '"De facto copyright?": Fielding's works in partnership, 1768–1821', *Eighteenth Century Studies*, 17, 449–76.

1993a '"Proprietary illustration": the case of Cooke's *Tom Jones*', in Harvey, Kirsop and McMullin 1993, 137–47.

1993b 'Under the Exchange: the unprofitable business of Michael Perry, a seventeenth-century Boston bookseller', *Proceedings of the American Antiquarian Soceity*, 103, 31–60.

1995 'Virtual readers: the subscribers to Fielding's *Miscellanies* (1743)', *SB*, 48, 94–112.

2000a 'A note on statistics', in *HBA* I, 504–18.

2000b 'Printing and bookselling in New England', in *HBA* I, 83–116.

2001 'Pseudodoxia biblographica, or when is a book not a book? When it's a record', in *CERL Papers* II 2001, 1–14.

Amory, H. and Hall, D. D. 2000 *A history of the book in America*, vol. I, Cambridge.

Anderson, B. L. 1969 'Provincial aspects of the financial revolution in the eighteenth century', *BH*, 11, 2, 12–20.

1970 'Money and the structure of credit in the eighteenth century', *BH*, 12, 2, 87–100.

Anderson, P. J. 1991 *The printed image and the transformation of popular culture, 1790–1860*, Oxford.

Anderson, R. 1795 'Preface', in *The works of the British poets*, 14 vols., Edinburgh, I, 1–8.

André, P. and Heath, J. 1803 *Specimens of polyautography consisting of impressions taken from original drawings made purposely for this work*, London.

Andrews, J. H. 1956 'Two problems in the interpretation of the port books', *EcHR*, 2nd ser., 9, 119–22.

1969 'Introduction', in Taylor and Skinner 1969.

1974 *History in the Ordnance map: an introduction for Irish readers*, Dublin.

1978 *Irish maps*, Dublin.

1997 *Shapes of Ireland: maps and their makers, 1564–1839*, Dublin.

2002 *A paper landscape: the Ordnance Survey in nineteenth-century Ireland*, 2nd edn, Dublin.

Anon. 1735 *A letter from an author to a Member of Parliament Concerning the bill now depending in the House of Commons*, London.

Anon. 1747 *A general description of all trades, digested in alphabetical order: by which parents ... make choice of trades agreeable to the capacity, education, inclination, strength, and fortune of the youth under their care*, London.

Anon. 1750 *A dissertation on credit*, London.

Arber, E. (ed.), 1875–94 *A transcript of the registers of the Company of Stationers of London, 1554–1640*, 5 vols., London; rpt Gloucester, MA, 1967.

Arber, E. 1906 *The Term Catalogues, 1688–1709, with a number for Easter Term, 1711 AD*, London.

Armstrong, J. 1987 'The role of coastal shipping in UK transport: an estimate of traffic movements in 1910', *Journal of Transport History*, 8, 164–72.

Arnett, J. A. *pseud.* [John Hannett] 1837 *An inquiry into the nature and form of the books of the ancients; with a history of the art of bookbinding*, London.

Arnold, D. (ed.) 1998 *The Georgian country house: architecture, landscape and society*, Stroud.

Ashton, T. S. 1948 *The Industrial Revolution, 1760–1830*, Oxford.

1955 *An economic history of England: the 18th century*, London.

Ashworth, W. 1981 'John Bevis and his Uranographia (ca. 1750)', *Proceedings of the American Philosophical Society*, 125, 52–73.

Aspinall, A. 1948 'Statistical account of the London newspapers in the eighteenth century', *EHR*, 63, 201–32.

1949 *Politics and the press, c.1780–1850*, London.

Asquith, I. 1975 'Advertising in the press in the late eighteenth and early nineteenth centuries: James Perry and the *Morning Chronicle*', *HJ*, 18, 722–3.

1978 'The structure, ownership and control of the press, 1780–1855', in Boyce, Curran and Wingate (eds.) 1978, 98–116.

Astbury, R. 1978 'The renewal of the Licensing Act in 1693 and its lapse in 1695', *Library*, 5th ser., 33, 296–322.

Aström, S.-E. 1968 'The reliability of the English port books', *Scandinavian Economic History Review*, 16, 125–36.

Atkins, P. J. 1990 *The directories of London, 1677–1977*, London.

Austen, B. 1978 *English provincial posts, 1633–1840: a study based on Kent examples*, London.

Austen, J. 1995 *Jane Austen's letters*, 3rd edn, ed. D. Le Faye, Oxford.

Austen-Leigh, R. A. 1911 *The story of a printing house: a short account of the Strahans and the Spottiswoodes*, London.

Averley, G., assisted by J. G. B. Heal 1979 *Eighteenth-century British books: a subject catalogue*, 4 vols., Folkestone.

Avery, G. and Briggs, J. (eds.) 1989 *Children and their books: a celebration of the work of Iona and Peter Opie*, Oxford.

Babinski, M. 1998/2000 *Henry Popple's 1733 map of the British empire in America*, with addendum (2000), Garwood, NJ.

Backscheider, P. R. 1989 *Daniel Defoe: his life*, London.

(ed.) 2000 *Revising women: eighteenth-century 'women's fiction' and social engagement*, Baltimore, MD.

Bailyn, B. and Hench, J. B. (eds.) 1980 *The press and the American Revolution*, Worcester, MA.

Bain, I. 1966 'Thomas Ross & Son, copper- and steel-plate printers since 1833', *JPHS*, 2, 1–22.

1968 'James Moyes and his Temple Printing Office of 1825', *JPHS*, 4, 1–10.

Baker, F. 1939–40 'Wesley's printers and booksellers', *Proceedings of the Wesley Historical Society*, 22, 61–5, 97–101, 131–40, 164–8.

1941 'John Wesley and the "Imitatio Christi"', *London Quarterly and Holborn Review*, 166, 74–87.

1947 *A charge to keep: an introduction to the people called Methodists*, London.
1966 *A union catalogue of the publications of John and Charles Wesley*, Durham, NC.
Baker, J. H. 2002a 'English law books and legal publishing', in *CHBB* IV, 474–503.
2002b *An introduction to English legal history*, 4th edn, London.
Ball, D. 1985 *Victorian publishers' bindings*, London.
Ball, J. 1973 *William Caslon, 1693–1766: the ancestry, life and connections of England's foremost letter-engraver and type-founder*, Kineton.
Balston, J. N. 1998 *The Whatmans and wove paper: its invention and development in the west*, West Farleigh.
Balston, T. 1979 (1957) *James Whatman, father & son*, London.
Barbauld, A. L. 1820 'On the origin and progress of novel-writing', *The British novelists*, new edn, 50 vols., London.
Barber, G. G. 1960 'J. J. Tourneisen of Basle and the publication of English books on the Continent', *Library*, 5th ser., 15, 193–200.
1961 'Galignani's and the publication of English books in France from 1800 to 1852', *Library*, 5th ser., 16, 267–86.
1965 'Henry Saint John, viscount Bolingbroke, 1678–1751', *BC*, 14, 528–37.
1969 *French letterpress printing: a list of French printing manuals and other texts in French bearing on the technique of letterpress printing, 1567–1900*, Oxford.
1973 *Book making in Diderot's Encyclopédie: a facsimile reproduction of articles and plates*, Farnborough.
1976 'Books from the Old World and for the New: the British international trade in books in the eighteenth century', *Studies on Voltaire and the Eighteenth Century*, 151, 185–224.
1977 'Aspects of the booktrade between England and the Low Countries in the eighteenth century', *Documentatieblad van de Werkgroep 18e eeuw*, 34–5, 47–63.
1982 'Book imports and exports in the eighteenth century', in Myers and Harris 1982, 77–105.
1994 *Studies in the booktrade of the European Enlightenment*, London.
Barber, G. G. and Fabian, B. (eds.) 1981 *Buch und Buchhandel in Europa im achtzehnten Jahrhundert*, Wolfenbüttel.
Barber, P. 1990 'Necessary and ornamental: map use in England under the later Stuarts, 1660–1714', *Eighteenth Century Life*, 14, 3, 1–28.
Barker, H. 1998 *Newspapers, politics, and public opinion in late eighteenth-century England*, Oxford.
Barker, N. J. 1964 *The publications of the Roxburghe Club, 1814–1962*, Cambridge.
1978 *The Oxford University Press and the spread of learning, 1478–1978: an illustrated history*, Oxford.
1993 (ed.) *A potencie of life: books in society: the Clark lectures, 1986–1987*, London.
1994 'William Strahan and Laurence Sterne', in Brack 1994, 289–97.
1995 'John Evelyn in the British Library', *BC*, 44, 146–238.
1999 *Treasures from the libraries of National Trust country houses*, New York.
Barker, T. C. and Gerhold, D. 1993 *The rise and rise of road transport, 1700–1990*, Cambridge.
Barnard, F. A. 1820–9 *Bibliothecae Regiae catalogus*, 5 vols., London.
Barnard, J. 1963 'Dryden, Tonson, and subscriptions for the 1697 Virgil', *PBSA*, 67, 129–51.
1999 'The survival and loss rates of Psalms, ABCs, Psalter and Primers from the Stationers' Stock, 1660–1700', *Library*, 6th ser., 21, 148–50.

2000 'Dryden, Tonson, and the patrons of *The works of Virgil* (1697)', in Hammond and Hopkins 2000, 174–239.

Barnard, J. and Bell, M. 2002a 'Appendix I, Statistical tables', in *CHBB* IV, 779–93.

2002b 'The English provinces', in *CHBB* IV, 665–86.

Barnes, J. J. 1964 *Free trade in books: a study of the London book trade since 1800*, Oxford.

1970 'Gagliani and the publication of English books in France: a postscript', *Library*, 5th ser., 25, 294–312.

1983 'Depression and innovation in the British and American book trade, 1819–1939', in Carpenter 1983, 231–48.

Barnes, J. J. and Barnes, P. P. 2000 'Reassessing the reputation of Thomas Tegg, London publisher, 1776–1846', *Book History*, 3, 45–60.

Baron, S. A., Lindquist, E. N. and Shelvin, E. F. (eds.) 2007 *Agent of change: print culture studies after Elizabeth L. Eisenstein*, Amherst, MA.

Barrell, J. 2000 *Imagining the king's death: figurative treason, fantasies of regicide, 1793–96*, Oxford.

Barringer, J. C. 1989 'Introduction', in Faden 1989.

Barry, J. 1991 'The press and the politics of culture in Bristol, 1660–1775', in Black and Gregory 1991, 49–81.

1993 'Methodism and the press in Bristol, 1737–1775', *Wesley Historical Society, Bristol Branch Bulletin*, 64, 23.

2001 'Hell upon earth or the language of the playhouse', in Clark 2001, 139–58.

2003 'Communicating with authority: the uses of speech, script and print in Bristol, 1640–1714', in Crick and Walsham 2003, 191–208.

Barwick, G. F., Macfarlane, J. and Cotton, H. E. A. (eds.) 1908 (1789) *Hartly House, Calcutta: a novel of the days of Warren Hastings*, Calcutta.

Basker, J. G. 1988 *Thomas Smollett: critic and journalist*, Newark, DE.

Batten, C. L. 1978 *Pleasurable instruction: form and convention in eighteenth-century travel literature*, Berkeley, CA.

1990 'Literary responses to the eighteenth-century voyages', in Howse 1990, 128–59.

Battestin, M. C. and Battestin, R. R. 1977–8 'Fielding, Bedford, and the Westminster election of 1749', *ECS*, 11, 143–85.

1989 *Henry Fielding: a life*, London.

Battle of the reviews, 1760 *The battle of the reviews: [a satire]*, London.

Baxter, I. 1993 'The establishment of the first libraries for European soldiers in India', *South Asia Library Group Newsletter*, 40, 25–30.

Baxter, J. 1809 *The sister arts, or a concise and interesting view of the nature and history of paper-making, printing and bookbinding*, Lewes.

Baxter, W. T. 1945 *The house of Hancock: business in Boston, 1724–1775*, Cambridge, MA.

Beaglehole, J. C. 1974 *The life of Captain James Cook*, London.

Beales, R. W. and Green, J. N. 2000 'Libraries and their users', in *HBA* I, 399–403.

Beasley, J. C. *A check list of prose fiction published in England, 1740–1749*, Charlottesville, VA.

Beavan, I. 1987 'Bibliography of the Enlightenment: some supplementary notes on the Aberdeen booktrade', in Carter and Pittock 1987, 316–22.

2000 'Advertising judiciously: Scottish nineteenth-century publishers and the British market', in Isaac and McKay 2000, 69–78.

2001 ' "What constitutes the crime which it is your pleasure to punish so mercilessly?": Scottish booksellers' societies in the nineteenth century', in Isaac and McKay 2001, 71–82.

Beckford, W. 2000 *The consummate collector: William Beckford's letters to his bookseller*, ed. R. J. Gemmett, Norwich.

Beckwith, F. 1947 'The eighteenth-century proprietary library in England', *Journal of Documentation*, 3, 81–98.

Beetham, M. 1996 *A magazine of her own? Domesticity and desire in the woman's magazine, 1800–1914*, London.

Belanger, T. 1970 'Booksellers' sales of copyright: aspects of the London book trade, 1718–1768', unpub. thesis, Columbia University.

1975 'Booksellers' trade sales, 1718–1768', *Library*, 5th ser., 30, 281–302.

1978 'From bookseller to publisher: changes in the London book trade, 1750–1850', in Landon 1978, 7–16.

1982 'Publishers and writers in eighteenth-century England', in Rivers 1982a, 5–25.

Beljame, A. 1948 *Men of letters and the English public in the eighteenth century, 1660–1744: Dryden, Addison, Pope*, London.

Bell, B. 1998 ' "Pioneers of literature": the commercial traveller in the early nineteenth century', in Isaac and McKay 1998, 121–34.

Bell, I. A. 1991 *Literature and crime in Augustan England*, London.

Bell, J. 1783 *A chronological list of authors contained in Bell's beautiful edition of the Poets of Great Britain*, London.

Bell, M. 1988 'Mary Westwood: Quaker publisher', *PH*, 23, 5–66.

1989 'Hannah Allen and the development of a Puritan publishing business, 1646–51', *PH*, 26, 5–66.

1992 'Elizabeth Calvert and the "Confederates" ', *PH*, 32, 5–49.

2001 'A quantitative survey of British book production 1475–1700' in *The scholar and the database: papers presented on 4 November 1999 at the CERL conference hosted by the Royal Library, Brussels*, ed. L. Hellinga, 15–21. London.

Bell, M. and Barnard, J. 1992 'Provisional count of *STC* titles, 1475–1640', *PH*, 31, 47–64.

1998 'Provisional count of *Wing* titles, 1641–1700', *PH*, 44, 89–97.

Bell, M., Parfitt, G. A. E. and Shepherd, S. 1990 *A biographical dictionary of women writers, 1580–1720*, London.

Bell, M., Chew, S., Eliot, S. and Hunter, L. (eds.) 2001 *Re-constructing the book: literary texts in transmission*, Aldershot.

Bellamy, L. 1998 *Commerce, morality and the eighteenth-century novel*, Cambridge.

Bellone, E. 1980 *A world on paper: studies on the second scientific revolution*, Cambridge, MA.

Bellot, H. 1933 'Parliamentary printing, 1660–1837', *BIHR*, 11, 85–98.

Bendall, A. S. 1992 *Maps, land and society: a history, with a carto-bibliograpy, of Cambridgeshire estate maps, c.1660–1836*, Cambridge.

Benedict, B. M. 2000 'Jane Austen and the culture of circulating libraries: the construction of female literacy', in Backscheider 2000, 147–200.

Bennett, S. 2004 *Trade bookbinding in the British Isles, 1660–1800*, London.

Bentham, E. 1771 *Reflexions upon the study of divinity*, Oxford.

Bentley, G. E., Jr., 1964 *The early engravings of Flaxman's classical designs: a bibliographical study with a note on the duplicating of engravings by Richard J. Wolfe*, New York.

1977 *Blake books: annotated catalogues of William Blake's writings ... [etc.]*, Oxford.
1994 'Images of the word: separately published bible illustrations, 1539–1830', *SB*, 47, 103–28.
2001 *The stranger from paradise: a biography of William Blake*, New Haven, CT.
Bentley, G. E., Jr. and Weinglass, D. H. 1990 'F. J. Du Roveray, illustrated-book publisher, 1798–1806', *BSANZB*, 12, 1–49, 63–83, 97–146, 166–86.
Berg, J. van den and Hoftijzer, P. G. (eds.) 1991 *Church, change and revolution: transactions of the fourth Anglo-Dutch church history colloquium, Exeter, 1988*, Leiden.
Berg, J. van den and Nuttall, G. F. 1987 *Philip Doddridge (1702–1751) and the Netherlands*, Leiden.
Berkeley, G. 1948–57 *The works of George Berkeley, bishop of Cloyne*, ed. A.A. Luce and T. E. Jessop, 9 vols., London.
Berkvens-Stevelinck, C. M. G., Bots, H., Hoftijzer, P. G. and Lankhorst, O. S. (eds.) 1992 *Le magasin de l'univers: the Dutch Republic as the centre of the European book trade: papers presented at the international colloquium held at Wassenaar, 5–7 July 1990*, Leiden.
Bermingham, A. and Brewer, J. (eds.) 1995 *The consumption of culture, 1600–1800: image, object, text*, London.
Bernelle, A. (ed.) 1992 *Decantations: a tribute to Maurice Craig*, Dublin.
Berry, W. T. and Johnson, A. F. 1935 *Catalogue of specimens of printing types by English and Scottish printers and founders, 1665–1830*, London.
Berthiaud and Boitard, P. 1837 *Nouveau manuel complet des l'imprimeur en taille-douce*, Paris.
Bessemer, A. 1930 (1830) Specimen of printing types; reproduced in *JPHS*, 5, 99–132.
Besterman, T. (ed.) 1938 *The publishing firm of Cadell and Davies: select correspondence and accounts, 1793–1836*, London.
Bewick, T. 1975 *A memoir of Thomas Bewick written by himself*, ed. I. Bain, London.
Biba, O. and Wyn Jones, D. (eds.) 1996 *Studies in music history: presented to H. C. Robbins Landon on his seventieth birthday*, London.
Bidwell, J. 1990 *Early American papermaking: two treatises on manufacturing techniques reprinted from James Cutbush's 'American artist's manual' (1814)*, New Castle, DE.
1992 'The Brandywine paper mill and the Anglo-American book trade', unpub. thesis, University of Oxford.
2002a 'Designs by Mr. J. Baskerville for Six Poems by Mr T. Gray', *BC*, 51, 355–71.
2002b 'French paper in English books', in *CHBB* IV, 583–601.
Bigmore, E. C. and Wyman, C. W. H. 1880 *A bibliography of printing with notes and illustrations*, London.
Birks, M. 1960 'Stevens and Sons: 1810–1960', *The Law Society's Gazette*, July 1960, 435–7.
Birks, P. (ed.) 1993 *The life of the law: proceedings of the tenth British legal history conference, Oxford, 1991*, London.
Bishop, S. L. 1974 *Isaac Watts's 'Hymns and spiritual songs', 1707: a publishing history and a bibliography*, Ann Arbor, MI
Black, A. 1885 *Memoirs*, ed. A. Nicolson, Edinburgh.
Black, F. 2004 'Importation and book availability', in *HBC* I, 115–24.
Black, J. 2001 *The English press, 1621–1861*, Stroud.
Black, J. and Gregory, J. (eds.) 1991 *Culture, politics and society in Britain, 1660–1800*, Manchester.
Blackie, A. A. C. 1959 *Blackie and Son, 1809–1959: a short history of the firm*, London.
Blackstone, W. 1765–9 *Commentaries on the laws of England*, 4 vols., Oxford.
Blagden, C. 1949 *Fire more than water: notes for the story of a ship*, London.

1951 'Booksellers' trade sales, 1718–1768', *Library*, 5th ser., 5, 243–57.

1954 'The memorandum book of Henry Rhodes', *BC*, 3, no. 1, 28–38; 3, no. 2, 103–16.

1955 'The English Stock of the Stationers' Company: an account of its origins,' *Library*, 5th ser., 10, 163–85.

1957 'The English Stock of the Stationers' Company in the time of the Stuarts', *Library*, 5th ser., 12, 167–86.

1958 'The distribution of almanacks in the second half of the seventeenth century', *SB* 11, 107–16.

1959 'The Stationers' Company in the eighteenth century', *Guildhall Miscellany*, 1, no. 10, 36–53.

1960a *The Stationers' Company: a history, 1403–1959*, London.

1960b 'Thomas Carnan and the almanack monopoly', *SB*, 14, 23–41.

Blain, V., Clements, P. and Grundy, I. 1990 *The feminist companion to literature in English: women writers from the Middles Ages to the present*, New Haven, CT.

Blair, W. (ed.) 1813 *Correspondence on the formation, objects, and plan, of the Roman Catholic Bible Society*, London.

Blake, R. B. 1966 *Disraeli*, London.

Blakey, D. B. 1939 *The Minerva Press, 1790–1820*, London.

Blamires, D. 1996–7 'Chapbooks, fairytales and children's books in the writings of John Clare', *John Clare Society Journal*, 15, 27–53; 16, 43–70.

Bland, M. 1999 'The London book-trade in 1600', in Kastan 1999, 450–63.

Blanning, T. C. W. 2002 *The culture of power and the power of culture: old regime Europe, 1660–1789*, Oxford.

Blayney, P. W. M. 1990 *The bookshops in Paul's Cross churchyard*, London.

2007 'STC publication statistics: some caveats', *Library*, 7th ser., 8, 387–97.

Blinn, H. and Schmidt, W. G. 2003 *Shakespeare-deutsch: Bibliographie der Übersetzungen und Bearbeitungen*, Berlin.

Blom, F., Blom, J., Korsten, F. and Scott, G. (eds.) 1996 *English Catholic books, 1701–1800: a bibliography*, Aldershot.

2007 *The correspondence of Peter James Coghlan (1731–1800)*, Woodbridge.

Bloom, H. 1973 *The anxiety of influence: a theory of poetry*, Oxford.

Bloy, C. H. 1967 *A history of printing ink, balls and rollers, 1440–1850*, London.

Boghardt, M. 1983 'Der in der Buchdruckerei wohl unterrichtete Lehr-Jung: bibliographische Beshcreibung der im deutschsprachigen Raum zwischen 1608 und 1847 erschienenen typographischen Lehrbücher', *Philobiblon*, 27, 5–57.

Bolt, C. and Drescher, S. (eds.) 1980 *Anti-slavery, religion, and reform: essays in memory of Roger Anstey*, Folkestone.

Bonar Law, A. 1997 *The printed maps of Ireland, 1612–1850*, Dublin.

Bond, D. F. (ed.) 1965 *The Spectator*, 5 vols., Oxford.

1987 *The Tatler*, 3 vols., Oxford.

Bond, R. P. (ed.) 1957 *Studies in the early English periodical*, Chapel Hill, NC.

Bond, W. H. 1990 *Thomas Hollis of Lincoln's Inn: a whig and his books*, Cambridge.

Bonfield, L., Smith, R. M. and Wrightson, K. (eds.) 1986 *The world we have gained: histories of population and social structure: essays presented to Peter Laslett on his seventieth birthday*, Oxford.

Bonham-Carter, V. 1978 *Authors by profession*, vol. I: *From the introduction of printing until the Copyright Act 1911*, London.

Bonnant, G. 1999 *Le livre genevois sous l'ancien régime*, Geneva.

Bonnell, T. F. 1983 'The historical context of Johnson's "Lives of the poets": rival collections of English poetry, 1777–1810', unpub. thesis, University of Chicago.

1987 'John Bell's *Poets of Great Britain*: the "little trifling edition" revisited', *Modern Philology*, 85, 128–52.

1989 'Bookselling and canon-making: the trade rivalry over the English poets, 1776–1783', in Brown and Craddock 1989, 53–69.

1995 'Patchwork and piracy: John Bell's "connected system of biography" and the use of Johnson's *Prefaces*', *SB*, 48, 193–228.

1997 'Speaking of institutions and canonicity, don't forget publishers', *Eighteenth-Century Life*, 21, 97–9.

2004–5 (2008) 'When book history neglects bibliography: trouble with the "Old Canon" in *The Reading Nation*', *SB*, 57, 243–61.

2008 *The most disreputable trade: publishing the classics of English poetry, 1765–1810*, Oxford.

Borsay, P. 1977 'The English urban renaissance: the development of a provincial urban culture *c.*1680–*c.*1760', *Social History*, 2, 581–603.

Borsay, P. and McInnes, A. 1990 'Debate: leisure town or urban renaissance?', *P&P*, 126, 189–202.

Boscawen, W. 1798 *The progress of satire: an essay in verse*, London.

Bosse, A. 1645 *Traicté des manieres de graver en taille douce sur l'airin: par le moyen des eaux fortes, et des vernix durs et mols: ensemble de la façon d'en imprimer les planches et d'en construire la presse, et autres choses concernans lesdits arts*, Paris.

Boswell, J. 1774 *The decision of the Court of Session upon the question of literary property: in the cause of John Hinton ... against Alexander Donaldson and John Wood ...*, Edinburgh.

1791 *The life of Samuel Johnson, LLD*, 2 vols., London.

1934–50 *Boswell's Life of Johnson*, ed. G. B. Hill, rev. L. F. Powell, 2nd edn, 6 vols., Oxford.

1970 *Life of Johnson* (1791), ed. R. W. Chapman, corr. J. D. Fleeman, Oxford.

1989 *Boswell: the great biographer, 1789–1795* [diary], ed. M. K. Danziger and F. Brady, London.

Botein, S. 1983 'The Anglo-American book trade before 1776: personnel and strategies', in Joyce *et al.* 1983, 48–82.

Boud, R. C. 1975 'The early development of British geological maps', *IM*, 27, 73–96.

Bowden, A. 1975 'William Hone's political journalism, 1815–1821', unpub. thesis, University of Texas.

Bowden, R. 2001 'The English Stock and the Stationers' Company: the final years', in Myers 2001, 79–105.

Bowen, E. and Kitchin, T. 1971 *The Royal English atlas: eighteenth century county maps of England and Wales ...*, facs. plates, intro. J. B. Harley and D. Hodson, Newton Abbot.

Boyce, G., Curran, J. and Wingate, P. (eds.) 1978 *Newspaper history from the seventeenth century to the present day*, London.

Boyd, E. 1732 *The happy-unfortunate, or the female page: a novel*, London.

Brack, O M Jr. (ed.) 1994 *Writers, books and trade: an eighteenth-century miscellany for William B. Todd*, New York.

Bracken, J. K. and Silver, J. (eds.) 1995 *Dictionary of Literary Biography*, vol. CLIV: *The British literary book trade, 1700–1820*, Detroit, MI.

1996 *Dictionary of Literary Biography*, vol. CLXX: *The British literary book trade, 1475–1700*, Detroit, MI.

Bradley, C. J. and Coover, J. (eds.) 1987 *Richard S. Hill: tributes from friends*, Detroit, MI.

Braithwaite, H. 2003 *Romanticism, publishing and dissent: Joseph Johnson and the cause of liberty*, Basingstoke.

Brathwaite, R. 1631 *Whimzies: or a new cast of characters*, London.

Braudel, F. 1982 *Civilization & capitalism, 15th–18th century*, 3 vols., trans. S. Reynolds, London.

Brauer, A. 1979 'Deutsch-englische Buchhandelsbeziehungen vom 17. bis 19. Jahrhundert: Einige Streiflichter', *Buchhandelsgeschichte*, 2, 2, B65–B68.

Brewer, J. 1995 '"The most polite age and the most vicious": attitudes towards culture as a commodity, 1660–1880', in Bermingham and Brewer 1995, 341–61.

1996 'Reconstructing the reader: prescriptions, texts and stratgies in Anna Larpent's reading', in Raven, Small and Tadmor 1996, 226–45.

1997 *The pleasures of the imagination: English culture in the eighteenth century*, London.

Brewer, J. and Hellmuth, E. (eds.) 1999 *Rethinking Leviathan: the eighteenth-century state in Britain and Germany*, Oxford.

Bridgman, R. W. 1807 *A short view of legal bibliography: containing some critical observations on the authority of the reporters and other law writers; collected from the best authorities, and intended as a companion to the Author's Reflections on the study of law*, London.

Bridson, G. D. R. 1976 'The treatment of plates in bibliographical description', *Journal of the Society for the Bibliography of Natural History*, 7, 459–88.

Bridson, G. D. R. and Wakeman G. 1984 *Printmaking and picture printing: a bibliographical guide to artistic and industrial techniques in Britain, 1750–1900*, Oxford.

Briggs, A. (ed.) 1974 *Essays in the history of publishing in celebration of the 250th anniversary of the house of Longman, 1724–1974*, London.

2008 *A history of Longmans and their books, 1724–1990*, London.

Briggs, A. and Burke, P. 2002 *A social history of the media: from Gutenberg to the internet*, Cambridge.

Brissenden, R.F. (ed.) 1968 *Studies in the eighteenth century*, Canberra.

Britton, J. 1849–50 *The auto-biography of John Britton*, 3 pts, London.

Brock, W. H. and Meadows, A. J. 1998 *The lamp of learning: two centuries of publishing at Taylor and Francis*, 2nd edn, London.

Bronson, B. H. 1968 *Facets of the Enlightenment: studies in English literature and its contexts*, Berkeley, CA.

Brooks, C. W. 1998 *Lawyers, litigation and English society since 1450*, London.

Brooks, H. C. 1927 *Compendiosa bibliografia di edizioni Bodoniane*, Florence.

Broomhall, S. 2002 *Women and the book trade in sixteenth-century France*, Aldershot.

Brown, L. E. and Craddock, P. (eds.) 1989 *Studies in eighteenth-century culture*, vol. XIX, East Lansing, MI.

Brown, S., Clements, P. and Grundy, I. (eds.) 2006 *Orlando: women's writing in the British Isles from the beginnings to the present*, Cambridge: Cambridge University Press Online, http://orlando.cambridge.org.

Brown, S. W., Holmes, H. and McDougall, W. 2002 'The pen, the plough, and the publisher's purse', unpub. exhibition catalogue, Edinburgh University Library.

Brown, S. W. and McDougall, W. (eds.) (forthcoming) *The Edinburgh history of the book in Scotland*, vol. II: *Englightenment and expansion 1707–1800*, Edinburgh.

Brown, W. C. 1936 'The popularity of English travel books about the Near East, 1774–1825', *PQ*, 15, 70–80.

Brownrigg, L. L. and Smith, M. M. (eds.) 2000 *Interpreting and collecting fragments of medieval books*, Los Altos Hills, CA.

Brüggemann, L. W. 1797 *A view of the English editions, translations and illustrations of the ancient Greek and Latin authors: with remarks*, Stettin.

Bruland, K. and O'Brien, P. (eds.) 1998 *From family firms to corporate capitalism: essays in business and industrial history in honour of Peter Mathias*, Oxford.

Brunner, D. L. 1993 *Halle Pietists in England: Anthony William Boehm and the Society for Promoting Christian Knowledge*, Göttingen.

Bruntjen, S. H. A. 1985 *John Boydell, 1719–1804: a study of art patronage and publishing in Georgian London*, New York.

Brush, S. G. 1988 *The history of modern science: a guide to the second scientific revolution, 1800–1950*, Ames, IA.

Bryan, M. 1903–5 (1812) *A biographical and critical dictionary of painters and engravers, from the revival of the art under Cimabue . . . to the present time*, rev. G. C. Williamson, 5 vols., London.

Buchner, K. 1874 *Aus dem Verkehr einer deutschen Buchhandlung mit den Geschäftsgenossen*, 2nd edn, Beiträge zur Geschichte des deutschen Buchhandels, 2, Gießen.

Buckley, S. 1701 *A catalogue of books, in Greek, Latin, Italian, Spanish, English, and French. Collected chiefly from the libraries of John de Wit, Constantin Huygens, and Fredrick Spanheim . . . lately brought from France and Holland*, London.

1733 *A short state of the publick encouragement given to printing and bookselling in France, Holland, Germany, and at London. With reasons humbly offered to the Lords spiritual and temporal in Parliament assembled, for granting to S. Buckley such privilege for Thuanus in Latin, as is already granted to every British subject who is possessed of the copy of any book in English*, London.

Budd, A. 2002 '"Merit in distress": the troubled success of Mary Barber', *RES*, 53, 210, 204–27.

Bulatov, V. E., Delano Smith, C. and Herbert, F. 2001 'Andrew Dury's *Map of the present seat of war, between the Russians, Poles, and Turks* (1729)', *IM*, 53, 71–96.

Bull, G. B. G. 1977 *Thomas Milne's land use map of London and environs in 1800*, London.

Bullock, F. W. B. 1963 *Voluntary religious societies, 1520–1799*, St Leonards on Sea.

Burchell, J. 1996 *Polite or commercial concerts? Concert management and orchestral repertoire in Edinburgh, Bath, Oxford, Manchester, and Newcastle, 1730–1799*, New York.

Burden, E. 1991 'Cary's new and correct English atlas', *MC*, 57, 32–7.

Burdett, P. P. 1972 *A survey of the County Palatine of Chester* (1777), facs., intro. J. B. Harley and P. Laxton., London.

Burney, C. 1991 *The letters of Dr Charles Burney: 1751–1784*, vol. I, ed. A. Ribeiro, Oxford.

Burney, F. 1904 *Diary and letters of Madame D'Arblay*, as ed. by her niece C. Barrett, 6 vols., London.

Burnim, K. A. and Highfill, P. H. Jr. 1998 *John Bell: patron of British theatrical portraiture: a catalogue of the theatrical portraits in the edition of 'Bell's Shakespeare' and 'Bell's British theatre'*, Carbondale, IL.

Burrows, D. and Dunhill, R. 2002 *Music and theatre in Handel's world: the family papers of James Harris, 1732–1780*, Oxford.

Bush, J. A. and Wijffels, A. (eds.) 1999 *Learning the law: teaching and transmission of law in England, 1150–1999*, London.

Butler, D. 1899 *Henry Scougal and the Oxford Methodists: or, the influence of a religious teacher of the Scottish church*, Edinburgh.

Butler, M. B. 1972 *Maria Edgeworth: a literary biography*, Oxford.

1993 'Culture's medium: the role of the review', in Curran 1993, 120–47.

(ed.) 1984 *Burke, Paine, Godwin and the revolution controversy*, Cambridge.

Bynum, W. F., Lock, S. and Porter, R. (eds.) 1992 *Medical journals and medical knowledge: historical essays*, London.

Byrne, P. 1802 *Catalogue of the quire stock of books*, Philadelphia.

Cain, L. P. and Uselding, P. J. (eds.) 1973 *Business enterprise and economic change: essays in honor of Harold F. Williamson*, Kent, OH.

Cairncross, A. K. 1963 'Capital formation in the take-off', in Rostow 1963, 250–60.

Cameron, H. C. 1954 *Mr Guy's hospital*, Longman.

Cameron, R. E. (ed.) 1967 *Banking in the early stages of industrialization: a study in comparative economic history*, Oxford.

Cameron, W. 1888 *Hawkie: the autobiography of a gangrel*, ed. J. Strathesk, Glasgow.

Cameron, W. J. 1975 'John Bell (1745–1831): a case study of the use of advertisement lists as evidence in publishing history', *The Humanities Association Review*, 26, 3, 196–216.

Cameron, W. J. and Carroll, D. J. 1966 *Short title catalogue of books printed in the British Isles ... 1701–1800 held in the libraries of the Australian Capital Territory*, Canberra.

Campanini, Z. 1998 *Istruzioni pratiche ad un novello capo stampa, o sia regolamento per la direzione di una tipografia officina* (1789), ed. C. Fahy, Florence.

Campbell, R. 1747 *The London tradesman, a compendious view of all the trades now practised in London and Westminster*, London.

Camus, A. G. 1801 *Histoire et procédés du polytypage et de la stéréotypie*, Paris.

Cannon, J. and Robinson, F. (directors) 1995 *Biography database: 1680–1830* [CD-ROM], Newcastle upon Tyne.

Cannon, R. D. 1980 *A bibliography of bagpipe music*, Edinburgh.

Canton, W. 1904–10 *A history of the British and Foreign Bible Society*, 5 vols., London.

Cantor, G. N. (ed.) 2004 *Science in the nineteenth-century periodical: reading the magazine of nature*, Cambridge.

Capp, B. S. 1979 *English almanacs: astrology and the popular press, 1500–1800*, London.

Cardwell, J. 2004 'Fire insurance records and the eighteenth-century London book trade', unpub. paper.

Cardwell, R. (ed.) 2004 *The reception of Byron in Europe*, London.

Carlson, C. L. 1938 *The first magazine: a history of the Gentleman's Magazine*, Providence, RI.

Carnie, R. H. 1960 *Publishing in Perth before 1807*, Dundee.

1987 'Scholar-printers of the Scottish Enlightenment, 1740–1800', in Carter and Pittock 1987, 298–308.

Carpenter, K. E. (ed.) 1983 *Books and society in history*, New York.

Carretta, V. 1986 '"Images reflect from art to art"; Alexander Pope's collected works of 1717', in Fraistat 1986, 195–233.

Carroll, R. A. 1996 *The printed maps of Lincolnshire, 1576–1900: a carto-bibliography: with an appendix on road-books, 1675–1900*, Woodbridge.

Carson, E. 1977 'Customs records as a source for historical research', *Archives*, 12, 74–80.

Carswell, J. 1993 *The South Sea Bubble*, rev. edn, Stroud.

Carter, H. 1969 *A view of early typography up to about 1600*, Oxford.

1975 *A history of the Oxford University Press, vol. 1: To the year 1780: with an appendix listing the titles of books printed there, 1690–1780*, Oxford.

Carter, J. J. and Pittock, J. H. (eds.) 1987 *Aberdeen and the Enlightenment*, Aberdeen.

Carter, J. W. 1932 *Binding variants in English publishing, 1820–1900*, London.

1935 *Publishers' cloth: an outline history of publishers binding in England, 1820–1900*, New York.

1948 *Taste and technique in book collecting: a study of recent developments in Great Britain and the United States*, Cambridge.

1960 'William Ged and the invention of stereotype', *Library*, 5th ser., 15, 161–92.

Cartier, A. 1970 *Bibliographie des éditions des de Tournes: imprimeurs lyonnais*, Geneva.

Cash, A. H. 1986 *Laurence Sterne: the later years*, London.

Caslon, W. *A specimen of printing types by William Caslon* (1766), facs., ed. J. Mosley, *JPHS*, 16.

Castle, T. 2002 *Boss ladies, watch out! Essays on women, sex, and writing*, London.

Caulfield, R. (ed.) 1876 *The council book of the corporation of the city of Cork: from 1609 to 1643, and from 1690 to 1800*, Guildford.

(ed.) 1878 *The council book of the corporation of Youghal: from 1610 to 1659, from 1666 to 1687, and from 1690 to 1800*, Guildford.

Cave, R. 1987 *Printing and the book trade in the West Indies*, London.

CERL 2001 *The scholar and the database: papers presented on 4 November 1999 at the CERL conference hosted by the Royal Library, Brussels*, ed. L. Hellinga, London.

Chalaby, J. K. 1998 *The invention of journalism*, Basingstoke.

Challoner, R. 1755. *The garden of the soul: or, a manual of spiritual exercises and instructions for Christians who (living in the world) aspire to devotion*, London.

Chalmers, A. 1809 'Walker's British Classics', *The works of Peter Pindar, Esq.*, 4 vols., London.

1810 'Preface', in *The works of the English poets*, 21 vols., London.

Chambers, W. 1882 *Story of a long and busy life*, Edinburgh.

Chandler, J. H. and Dagnall, H. 1981 *The newspaper and almanac stamps of Great Britain and Ireland*, Saffron Walden.

Chapman, R. W. 1925–6 'Brooke's *Gustarus Vasa*', *RES*, 1, 460–1; 2, 99.

1931 'Eighteenth-century imprints', *Library*, 4th ser., 11, 503–4.

Chard, L. 1977 'Bookseller to publisher: Joseph Johnson and the English book trade, 1760 to 1810', *Library*, 5th ser., 32, 138–54.

Chartier, R. 1987 *The cultural uses of print in early modern France*, trans. L. G. Cochrane, Princeton, NJ.

(ed.) 1995 *Histoires de la lecture: un bilan des recherches*, Paris.

Chartres, J. A. 1977 'The capital's provincial eyes: London inns in the early eighteenth century', *LJ*, 3, 1, 24–39.

Chartres, J. A. and Hey, D. (eds.) 1990 *English rural society, 1500–1800: essays in honour of Joan Thirsk*, Cambridge.

Chatterton, T. 1971 *The complete works Thomas Chatterton*, ed. D. S. Taylor in association with B. B. Hoover, 2 vols. [continuously paginated], Oxford.

Chatto, W. A. and Jackson, J. 1861 *A treatise on wood engraving, historical and practical*; 2nd edn, London.

Checkland, S. G. 1975 *Scottish banking: a history, 1695–1973*, Glasgow.

Cheney, C.R., Cheney, J. and Cheney, W. G. 1936 *John Cheney and his descendants, printers in Banbury since 1767*, Banbury.

Chilton, C. W. 1982 *Early Hull printers and booksellers: an account of the printing, bookselling and allied trades from their beginnings to 1840*, Kingston-upon-Hull.

Christensen, J. 1987 *Practicing enlightenment: Hume and the formation of a literary career*, Madison, WI.

Christian, H. 1986 'A map collection to be sneezed at', *MC*, 37, 28–9.

Christianson, C. P. 1987 *Memorials of the book trade in medieval London: the archives of old London Bridge*, Cambridge.

1989 'Evidence for the study of London's late medieval manuscript-book trade', in Griffiths and Pearsall 1989, 87–108.

1999 'The rise of London's book-trade', in *CHBB* IV, 128–47.

Claeys, G. 1989 *Thomas Paine: social and political thought*, Boston, MA.

Clapham, J. 1944 *The Bank of England: a history, volume I: 1694–1796*, Cambridge.

Clapp, S. L. C. 1933 'The subscription enterprises of John Ogilby and Richard Blome', *MP*, 30, 365–79.

Clapperton, R. H. 1967 *The paper-making machine: its invention, evolution and development*, Oxford.

Clark, G. N. 1938 'Note on the port books', in his *Guide to English commercial statistics, 1696–1782*, London, 52–56.

Clark, P. 2000a *British clubs and societies, 1580–1800: the origins of an associational world*, Oxford.

2000b (ed.) *The Cambridge urban history of Britain*, vol. II: *1540–1840*, Cambridge.

Clark, P. and Jones, Y. 1974 'British military map-making in the Peninsular War', paper presented to the 7th International conference on cartography, Madrid (copy in British Library, Map Library).

Clark, S. 1683 *The Lives of Sundry Eminent Persons in this Later Age*, London.

Clark, S. (ed.) 2001 *Languages of witchcraft: narrative, ideology, and meaning in early modern culture*, Baskingstoke.

Clark, W. 1819 *Repertorium bibliographicum: or, some account of the most celebrated British libraries*, London.

Clarke, W. J. and Potter, W. A. 1953 *Early Nottingham printers and printing*, Nottingham.

Clarke, W. K. L. 1944 *Eighteenth century piety*, London.

Clay, C. G. A. 1994 'Henry Hoare, banker, his family and the Stourhead Estate', in Thompson 1994, 113–38.

Claydon, T. and McBride, I. (eds.) 1998 *Protestantism and national identity: Britain and Ireland, c.1650–c.1850*, Cambridge.

Clayton, T. 1992 'The print collection of George Clarke at Worcester College, Oxford', *Print Quarterly*, 9, 123–48.

1997 *The English print, 1688–1902*, New Haven.

1998 'Publishing houses: prints of country seats', in Arnold 1998, 46–8.

Clement, M. (ed.) 1952 *Correspondence and minutes of the SPCK relating to Wales, 1699–1740*, Cardiff.

1954 *The SPCK and Wales, 1699–1740*, London.

Cloonan, M. V. 1991 *Early bindings in paper: a brief history of European hand-made paper-covered books with a multilingual glossary*, London.

Cobban, A. (ed.) 1960 *The debate on the French Revolution, 1789–1800*, 2nd edn, London.

Cochrane, J. A. 1964 *Dr Johnson's printer: the life of William Strahan*, London.

Cockburn, H. 1856 *Memorials of his time*, Edinburgh.

Cohen, R. 1964 *The art of discrimination: Thomson's* The Seasons *and the language of criticism*, Berkeley, CA.

Colclough, S. M. 2000 'Procuring books and consuming tests: the reading experience of a Sheffield apprentice, 1798', *Book History*, 3, 21–44.

Cole, R. C. 1986 *Irish booksellers and English writers, 1740–1800*, London.

Cole, W. A. 1958 'Trends in eighteenth-century smuggling', *EcHR*, 2nd ser., 10, 395–410.

Coleman, D. C. 1975 (1958) *The British paper industry, 1495–1860: a study in industrial growth*, Westport, CT.

Coleridge, S. T. 1817 *Biographia literaria; or, biographical sketches of my literary life and opinions*, 2 vols., London.

1830 *On the constitution of church and state*, 2nd edn, London.

Collet, C. D. 1899 *History of the taxes on knowledge: their origin and repeal*, 2 vols., London.

Colley, L. 1994 *Britons: forging the nation, 1707–1837*, London.

Collins, A. S. 1928a *Authorship in the days of Johnson: being a study of the relation between author, patron, publisher, and public, 1726–1780*, London.

1928b *The profession of letters: a study of the relation of author to patron, publisher, and public, 1780–1832*, London.

Collins, M. 1990 *Money and banking in the UK: a history*, London.

Collinson, P., Hunt, A. and Walsham, A. 2002 'Religious publishing in England, 1557–1640', in *CHBB* IV, 29–66.

Collyer, J. 1761 *The parent's and guardian's directory, and the youth's guide, in the choice of a profession or trade*, London.

Colvin, H. M. 1964 *A catalogue of the architectural drawings of the eighteenth and nineteenth centuries in the library of Worcester College*, Oxford.

Congreve, W. 2009 *The works of William Congreve*, ed. D. F. McKenzie, prepared for publication by C. Y. Ferdinand, 3 vols., Oxford.

Connell, K. M. 1950 *The population of Ireland, 1750–1845*, Oxford.

Connell, P. 2000 'Bibliomania: book collecting, cultural politics, and the rise of literary heritage in romantic Britain', *Representations*, 71, 24–47.

Conolly, L. W. 1976 *The censorship of English drama, 1737–1824*, San Marino, CA.

Constable, T. 1873 *Archibald Constable and his literary correspondents: a memorial*, 3 vols., Edinburgh.

Constapel, B. 1998 *Der Musikverlag Johann André in Offenbach am Main*, Tutzing.

Contat, N. 1980 (1762) *Anecdotes typographiques: où l'on voit la description des coutumes moeurs et usage singuliers des compagnons imprimeurs*, ed. G. Barber, Oxford.

Cook, A. S. 1978 'Major James Rennel and *A Bengal atlas* (1780 and 1781)', *Indian Office Library and Records report for the year 1976*, 4–42.

1999 'Alexander Dalrymple and the Hydrographic Office', in Frost and Samson 1999, 53–68.

Cooke, R. 1987 *The palace of Westminster: Houses of Parliament*, London.

Cooper, A. A. C., 3rd earl of Shaftesbury 1732 *Characteristicks, of men, manners, opinions, times*, 3 vols., London.

1900 *Characteristics of men, manners, opinions, times*, ed. J. M. Robertson, 2 vols., London.

Cooper, B. 2002 'The Clementi–Beethoven contract of 1807: a reinvestigation', in Illiano, Sala and Sala 2002, 337–53.

Cooper, M. 1997 'The Worcester book-trade in the eighteenth-century', *Worcestershire Historical Society*, occasional publications, 8.

Cooper-Richet, D. 2001 'Les imprimés en langue anglaise en France au XIXe siècle: rayonnement intellectuel, circulation et modes de pénétration', in Michon and Mollier (eds.) 2001.

Coover, J. 1987 'The dispersal of engraved music plates and copyright in British auctions, 1831–1931', in Bradley and Coover 1987, 223–306.

1988 *Music at auction: Puttick and Simpson (of London), 1794–1971*, Warren, MI.

2001 *Private music collections: catalogs and cognate literature*, Warren, MI.

Cope, Z. 1953 *William Cheselden, 1688–1752*, Edinburgh.

Copinger, W. A. 1900 *On the English translations of the 'Imitatio Christi'*, Manchester.

Coral, L. 1974 'Music in English auction sales, 1676–1750', unpub. thesis, University of London.

Corfield, P. J. 1982 *The impact of English towns, 1700–1800*, Oxford.

1995 *Power and the professions in Britain, 1700–1850*, London.

Cotton, E. 1931 'A famous Calcutta firm: the history of Thacker Spink and Co.', *Bengall Past and Present*, 41, 159–64.

Cottrel, P. L. and Newton, L. 1999 'Banking liberalization in England and Wales, 1826–1844', in Sylla, Tilly and Tortella 1999, 75–117.

Couper, W. J. 1908 *The Edinburgh periodical press: being a bibliographical account of the newspapers, journals, and magazines issued in Edinburgh from the earliest times to 1800*, 2 vols., Stirling.

Cowan, B. W. 2005 *The social life of coffee: the emergence of the British coffeehouse*, London.

Cowell, N. 1994 'John Gamble and the St Neots paper mill', *The Quarterly: The Journal of the British Association of Paper Historians*, 12, 1–7.

Cowie, G. 1828 *The bookbinders' manual: containing a full description of leather and vellum binding*, London.

Cowley, J. D. 1924 'A century of law booksellers in London, 1650–1750', *Law Times*, 57, 347.

Cowper, E. 1828 *On the recent improvements in printing ... being the substance of a lecture delivered at the Royal Institution of Great Britain, Feb. 22, 1828*, London.

Cowper, W. 1904 *The correspondence of William Cowper*, ed. T. Wright, 4 vols., London.

1979 *Letters and prose writings*, ed. J. King and C. Ryskamp, 5 vols., Oxford.

Cox, E. G. 1935 *Reference guide to the literature of travel: including voyages, geographical descriptions, adventures, shipwrecks and expeditions*, 2 vols., Seattle.

Cox, H. and Chandler, J. E. 1925 *The house of Longman with a record of their bicentenary celebrations, 1724–1924*, London.

Crabbe, G. 1781 *The Library*, London.

Crafts, N. F. R. 1985 *British economic growth during the industrial revolution*, Oxford.

Craig, M. 1954 *Irish bookbindings, 1600–1800*, London.

Cranfield, G. A. 1962 *The development of the provincial newspaper, 1700–1760*, Oxford.

1978 *The press and society: from Caxton to Northcliffe*, London.

Crapulli, G. (ed.) 1985 *Trasmissione dei testi a stampa nel periodo moderno*, vol. II (II Seminario Internazionale), Rome.

Crawford, D. and Wagstaff, G. G. (eds.) 2002 *Encomium musicae: essays in memory of Robert J. Snow*, Hillsdale, NY.

Cressy, D. 1977 'Levels of illiteracy in England, 1530–1730', *HJ*, 20, 1–23.

1980 *Literacy and the social order: reading and writing in Tudor and Stuart England*, Cambridge.

Creswell, S. F. 1863 *Collections towards the history of printing in Nottinghamshire*, London.

Crick, J. and Walsham, A. (eds.) 2004 *The uses of script and print*, Cambridge.

Crocker, A. and Clarke, R. 2001 'Matthias Koops at Neckinger Mill, Bermondsey', *The Quarterly: The Journal of the British Association of Paper Historians*, 39, 15–22.

Crone, G. R. and Skelton, R. A. 1946 'English collections of voyages and travels', in Lynam 1946, 65–140.
Cropper, P. J. 1892 *Nottinghamshire printed chapbooks*, Nottingham.
Crouzet, F. M. J. (ed.) 1972 'Editor's introduction', in *Capital formation in the industrial revolution*, London, 1–69.
Crump, M. and Harris, M. (eds.) 1983 *Searching the eighteenth century*, London.
Cruse, A. 1930 *The Englishman and his books in the early nineteenth century*, London.
Crutchley, E. A. 1938 *A history and description of the Pitt Press*, Cambridge.
Cumberland, R. 1791 *Observer*, 5 vols., London.
Cumbers, F. 1956 *The Book Room: the story of the Methodist Publishing House and Epworth Press*, London.
Cunningham, H. and Innes, J. (eds.) 1998 *Charity, philanthropy and reform from the 1690s to 1850*, Baskingstoke.
Curran, S. (ed.) 1993 *The Cambridge companion to British Romanticism*, Cambridge.
Curtis, T. 1833 *The existing monopoly, an inadequate protection, of the authorised version of scripture*, London.
Curwen, H. 1873 *A history of booksellers: the old and the new*, London.
Dagnall, H. 1998a 'The size of newspapers', *The Quarterly: The Journal of the British Association of Paper Historians*, 28, 20–1.
1998b *The taxation of paper in Great Britain, 1643–1861: a history and documentation*, Edgware.
1998c 'The taxes on knowledge: excise duty on paper', *Library*, 6th ser., 20, 347–63.
Dale, B. 1906 *The good Lord Wharton*, London.
Dalton, R. and Hamer, S. H. 1910–18 *The provincial token-coinage of the 18th century*, London.
Daniel, W. T. S. 1884 *The history and origin of the law reports, together with a compilation of various documents shewing the progress and result of proceedings taken for their establishment, and the condition of the reports on the 31st December, 1883*, London.
Darlow, T. H. and Moule, H. F. 1903–11 *Historical catalogue of printed editions of the Holy Scripture in the library of the British and Foreign Bible Society*, 2 vols., London.
1968 *Historical catalogue of printed editions of the English Bible, 1525–1961*, rev. and expanded by A.S. Herbert, London.
Darnton, R. 1982 'What is the history of books?', *Daedalus*, Summer, 65–83.
1984 *The great cat massacre and other episodes in French cultural history*, New York.
1987 'Histoire du livre – Geschichte des Buchwesens: an agenda for comparative history', *PH*, 22, 33–41.
1990 *The kiss of Lamourette: reflections on cultural history*, New York.
1995 *Forbidden best-sellers of pre-revolutionary France*, New York.
Darton, F. J. H. 1999 *Children's books in England*, rev. B. Alderson, 3rd edn, London.
Darton, L. 2004 *The Dartons: an annotated check-list of children's books issued by two publishing houses, 1787–1876*, London.
Das Gupta, A. C. (ed.) 1959 *The days of John Company: selections from Calcutta Gazette, 1824–32*, Calcutta.
Daub, P. 1994 'Queen Caroline of England's music library', in Hunter 1994, 131–65.
Dauchy, S., Monballyu, J. and Wijffels, A. (eds.) 1997 *Auctoritates: law making and its authors*, Iuris scripta historica 13, Brussels.
Daultrey, S., Dickson, D. and Ó Gráda, C. 1981. 'Eighteenth-century Irish population: new perspectives from old sources', *JEcH*, 41, 601–28.

Daunton, M. J. 1995 *Progress and poverty: an economic and social history of Britain, 1700–1850*, Oxford.
(ed.) 1996 *Charity, self-interest and welfare in the English past*, London.
2005 *The organization of knowledge in Victorian Britain*, Oxford.
Davenport, C. 1904 'Bagford's notes on bookbindings: a paper read before the Bibliographical Society, Nov. 16 1903', *Library*, 7, 123–42.
David, A. 1988–97 *The charts and coastal views of Captain Cook's voyages*, 3 vols., London.
2003 'Lieutenant Murdoch Mackenzie and his survey of the Bristol Channel and the south coast of England', *CJ*, 40, 69–78.
Davidson, P. (ed.) 1992 *The book encompassed: studies in twentieth-century bibliography*, Cambridge.
Davies, G. L. H. 1983 *Sheets of many colours: the mapping of Ireland's rocks, 1750–1890*, Dublin.
Davies, T. 1780 *Memoirs of David Garrick*, 2 vols., London.
Davis, R. H. 1988 *Kendrew of York and his chapbooks for children: with a checklist*, Collingham.
Davison, L., Hitchcock, T., Keirn, T. and Shoemaker, R. B. (eds.) 1992 *Stilling the grumbling hive: the response to social and economic problems in England, 1689–1750*, Stroud.
Dawson, G. E. 1946 'The copyright of Shakespeare's dramatic works', in Prouty 1946, 11–35.
Day, A. *Admiralty Hydrographic Service, 1795–1919*, London.
Deazley, R. 2004 *On the origin of the right to copy: charting the movement of copyright law in eighteenth-century Britain (1695–1775)*, Oxford.
Deconinck-Brossard, F. 1993 'Eighteenth-century sermons and the age', in Jacobs and Yates 1993, 105–21.
Defoe, D. 1955 *The letters of Daniel Defoe*, ed. G. H. Healey, Oxford.
De Grazia, M. 1991 *Shakespeare verbatim: the reproduction of authenticity and the 1790 appartus*, Oxford.
Delano-Smith, C. and Kain, R. J. P. 1999 *English maps: a history*, London.
Demata, M. and Wu, D. (eds.) 2002 *British Romanticism and the Edinburgh review: bicentenary essays*, Basingstoke.
Dennis, J. 1939–43 *The critical works of John Dennis*, ed. E. N. Hooker, 2 vols., Baltimore, MD.
De Ricci, S. 1909 *A census of Caxtons*, London.
1930 *English collectors of books and manuscripts (1530–1930) and their marks of ownership*, Cambridge.
Derry, T. K. 1930 'The enforcement of a seven years apprenticeship under the Statute of Artificers', unpub. thesis, Oxford University.
De Saussure, C. 1995 *A foreign view of England in 1725–29: the letters of Monsieur César de Saussure to his family*, trans. and ed. Madame Van Muyden, London.
De Selincourt, E. (ed.) 1937 *The letters of William and Dorothy Wordsworth, the middle years*, 2 vols., Oxford.
Devereaux, S. 1996 'The City and the Sessions Paper: "public justice" in London, 1770–1800', *Journal of British Studies*, 33, 466–503.
Devine, T. M. 1978 'Social stability and agrarian change in the eastern Lowlands of Scotland, 1810–40', *Social History*, 3, 331–46.
1994 *The transformation of rural Scotland: social change and the agrarian economy, 1660–1815*, Edinburgh.
1995 'The golden age of tobacco', in Devine and Jackson 1995, 139–83.
1999 *The Scottish nation, 1700–2000*, London.
2000 'Scotland', in Clark 2000.

2004 'Scotland', in Floud and Johnson 2004, 388–416.
Devine, T. M. and Jackson, G. 1995 *Glasgow, vol. I: Beginnings to 1830*, Manchester.
Devine, T. M. and Mitchison, R. 1988 *People and society in Scotland: a social history of modern Scotland*, vol. I: *1760–1830*, Edinburgh.
De Vinne, T. L. 1900 *The practice of typography. A treatise on the processes of type-making, the point system, the names, sizes, styles and prices of plain printing types*. New York.
De Voogd, P. and Neubauer, J. (eds.) 2004 *The reception of Laurence Sterne in Europe*, London.
De Vries, J. 1984 *European urbanization, 1500–1800*, London.
Dibdin, T. F. 1811 *Bibliomania; or book madness; a bibliographical romance*, London.
1817 *The bibliographical decameron*, 3 vols., London.
1824 *The library companion*, 2 vols., London.
1836 *Reminiscences of a literary life*, 2 vols., London.
Dick, M. 1980 'The myth of the working-class Sunday school', *History of Education*, 9, 27–41.
Dickie, G. 1996 *The century of taste: the philosophical odyssey of taste in the eighteenth century*, Oxford.
Dickinson, G. 1990 'The deceit of Thomas Jefferys', *MC*, 50, 32–34.
Dickson, P. G. M. 1993 (1967) *The financial revolution in England: a study in the development of public credit, 1686–1756*, Aldershot.
D'Israeli, I. 1793 *Curiosities of literature*, vol. II, London.
1795 *An essay on the manners and genius of the literary character*, London.
1812 *Calamities of authors*, 2 vols., London.
Dix, E. R. McC. 1912 'List of all pamphlets, books etc. printed in Cork during the seventeenth century', *Proceedings of the Royal Irish Academy*, 30, sect. C, no. 3, 71–82.
1916 'Printing in the city of Waterford in the seventeenth century', *Proceedings of the Royal Irish Academy*, 32, sect. C, no. 21, 333–44.
Dixon, R. 2007 'The publishing of John Tillotson's collected works, 1695–1757', *Library*, 7th ser., 8, 154–81.
Dobson, A. 1916 'Fielding and Andrew Millar', *Library*, 3rd ser., 7, 177–90.
Doddridge, P. 1802–5 *The works of the Rev. P. Doddridge*, ed. E. Williams and E. Parsons, 10 vols., Leeds.
1829–31 *The correspondence and diary of Philip Doddridge, DD: illustrative of various particulars in his life hitherto unknown: with notices of many of his contemporaries; and a sketch of the ecclesiastical history of the times in which he lived*, ed. J. D. Humphreys, 5 vols., London.
Dodgshon, R. A. 1981 *Land and society in early Scotland*, Oxford.
Dodsley, R. 1988 *The correspondence of Robert Dodsley, 1733–1764*, ed. J. E. Tierney, Cambridge.
(ed.) 1997 *A collection of poems by several hands*, ed. M. F. Suarez, S.J., 6 vols., London.
D'Oench, E. 1999 *'Copper into gold': prints by John Raphael Smith, 1751–1812*, London.
Dolan, B. 2001 *Ladies of the grand tour*, London.
Donald, D. 1996 *The age of caricature: satirical prints in the reign of George III*, New Haven, CT.
Donne, B. 1965 *Benjamin Donn. A map of the county of Devon, 1765*, facs., intro. W. L. D. Ravenhill, London.
Donoghue, F. 1996 *The fame machine: book reviewing and eighteenth-century literary careers*, Stanford, CA.
Dossie, R. 1764 *The handmade to the arts*, 2nd edn, 2 vols., London.
Downie, J. A. 1979 *Robert Harley and the press: propaganda and public opinion in the age of Swift and Defoe*, Cambridge.

1981 'The growth of government tolerance of the press to 1790', in Myers and Harris 1981, 36–65.

Drescher, S. 1982 'Public opinion and the destruction of British colonial slavery', in Walvin 1982, 22–48.

1994 'Whose abolition? Popular pressure and the ending of the British slave trade', *Past and Present*, 142, 136–66.

Drotner, K. 1988 *English children and their magazines, 1751–1945*, New Haven, CT.

Dryden, J. 1942 *Letters of John Dryden: with letters addressed to him*, ed. C. E. Ward, Durham, NC.

Duckham, B. F. 1983 'Canals and river navigations', in Aldcroft and Freeman 1983, 100–41.

Dudin, R. M. 1977 (1772) *The art of the bookbinder and gilder*, trans. R. M. Atkinson, Leeds.

Duffy, E. (ed.) 1981 *Challoner and his church: a Catholic bishop in Georgian England*, London.

Duffy, I. P. H. 1985 *Bankruptcy and insolvency in London during the Industrial Revolution*, London.

Dugas, D.-J. 2001 'The London book trade in 1709', *PBSA*, 95, 23–58, 157–72.

Dunbabin, J. P. D. 1998 'Red lines on maps: the impact of cartographical errors on the border between the United States and British North America 1782–1842', *IM*, 50, 105–25.

Duncan, D. J. M. 1965 *Thomas Ruddiman: a study in Scottish scholarship of the early eighteenth century*, Edinburgh.

Dunlop, O. J. and Denman, R. D. 1912. *English apprenticeship and child labour. A history. With a supplementary section on the modern problem of juvenile labour*, London.

Dunton, J. 1699 *The Dublin scuffle*, London.

1705 *The life and errors of John Dunton*, London.

1818 *The life and errors of John Dunton*, ed. J. Nichols, 2 vols., London.

Durden, S. 1976 'A study of the first evangelical magazines, 1740–1748', *Journal of Ecclesiastical History*, 27, 255–75.

Durkacz, V. E. 1983 *The decline of the Celtic languages: a study of linguistic and cultural conflict in Scotland, Wales and Ireland from the Reformation to the twentieth century*, Edinburgh.

Dussinger, J. 2000 'Samuel Richardson's "Elegant disquisitions": anonymous writing in the *True Briton* and other journals?', *SB*, 53, 195–226.

Duval, G. 1992 'The Diceys revisited', *Factotum*, 35, 9–11.

1995 'More facts, afterthoughts and conjectures about the Diceys', *Factotum*, 40, 13–18.

Dye, I. 2001 'The Magnays, stationers and papermakers for four generations', *The Quarterly: The Journal of the British Association of Paper Historians*, 37, 11–19.

Dyer, G. 1997 *British satire and the politics of style, 1789–1832*, Cambridge.

Dymond, D. P. 2003 'Introduction', in Hodskinson 2003.

Dyson, A. 1983 'The rolling press: some aspects of its development from the seventeenth century to the nineteenth century', *JPHS*, 17, 1–30.

1984 *Pictures to print: the nineteenth century engraving trade*, London.

Eames, W. 1924 *Bibliographical essays* [by various authors.] *A tribute to Wilberforce Eames*, Cambridge, MA.

Earle, P. 1989 *The making of the English middle class: business, society and family life in London, 1660–1730*, London.

Eaves, T. C. D. 1950–1 'Graphic illustrations of the novels of Samuel Richardson, 1740–1810', *HLQ*, 14, 349–69.

Eaves, T. C. D. and Kimpel, B. D. 1971 *Samuel Richardson: a biography*, Oxford.

Eddy D. D. 1971 *A bibliography of John Brown*, New York.

Edgeworth, M. and Edgeworth, R. 1974 (1798) *Practical education*, 2 vols., New York.

Edinburgh Police Department 1839 *Regulations for the day-patrol and watchmen of the Edinburgh police establishment*, Edinburgh.

Edney, M. H. 1997 *Mapping an empire: the geographical construction of British India, 1765–1843*, London.

Edwards, M. M. 1967 *The growth of the British cotton trade, 1780–1815*, Manchester.

Ehrlich, C. 1990 *The piano: a history*, rev. edn, Oxford.

Eisenstein, E. L. 1979 *The printing press as an agent of change*, 2 vols., Cambridge.

Elbourne, E. 2002 *Blood ground: colonialism, missions, and the contest for Christianity in the Cape Colony and Britain, 1799–1853*, Montreal.

Eliot, S. 1994 *Some patterns and trends in British publishing, 1800–1919*, London.

1997–8 '*Patterns and trends* and the *NSTC*: some initial observations', *PH*, 42, 79–104; 43, 71–112.

2002 'Very necessary but not quite sufficient: a personal view of quantitative analysis in book history', *Book History*, 5, 283–93.

Eliot, S. (ed.) forthcoming *The history of Oxford University Press*, vol. II: *1780s–1910s*, Oxford.

Eller, C. S. 1938 *The William Blackstone Collection in the Yale Law Library: a bibliographical catalogue*, New Haven, CT.

Ellis, A. 1956 *The penny universities: a history of coffee-houses*, London.

Ellis, F. M. (ed.) 1970 *Poems on affairs of state: Augustan satirical verse*, vol. VI: *1697–1704*, New Haven, CT.

Ellis, J. 1998 'Risk, capital, and credit on Tyneside, circa 1690–1780', in Bruland and O'Brien 1998, 84–111.

Ellis, K. 1958 *The Post Office in the eighteenth century: a study in administrative history*, London.

Elphinston, J. 1783 *The hypercritic*, London.

Elwood, A. C. 1830 *Narrative of a journey overland from England ... to India*, 2 vols., London.

Engell, J. 1981 *The creative imagination: Enlightenment to Romanticism*, Cambridge, MA.

Engelsing, R. 1969 'Die Perioden der Lesergeschichte in der Neuzeit: Das statistische Ausmass und die soziokulturelle Bedeutung der Lektüre', *Archiv für Geschichte des Buchwesens*, 10, cols. 944–1002.

1971 *Der Bürger als Leser: Lesergeschichte in Deutschland, 1500–1800*, Stuttgart.

Enright,. B. J. 1955 'Richard Rawlinson: collector, antiquary, topographer', unpub. thesis, University of Oxford.

1990 '"I collect and I preserve": Richard Rawlinson, 1690–1755, and eighteenth-century book collecting', *BC*, 39, 27–54.

Erickson, L. 1996 *The economy of literary form: English literature and the industrialization of publishing, 1800–1850*, Baltimore, MD.

Ernesti, J. H. G. 1721 *Die wol-eingerichtete Buchdruckerey*, Nürnberg.

Essick, R. N. and Viscomi, J. 2001–2 'An inquiry into William Blake's method of color printing', *Blake: An Illustrated Quarterly*, 35, 3, 74.

2002 'Blake's method of color printing: some responses and further observations', *Blake: An Illustrated Quarterly*, 36, 2, 49.

Evans, D. W. 1982 *James Watson of Edinburgh printer and publisher*, EBST, 5, pt. 2, Edinburgh.

Evans, G. E. (n.d.) 'Selling bibles too cheaply, 1748', *Transactions of the Carmarthenshire Antiquarian Society and Field Club*, 17, 9–10.

Everitt, A. 1985 *Landscape and community in England*, London.

Ewing, G. and A. 1758 *A confutation of Mr George Faulkner's queries, published in his Journal of August 12, 1758*, Dublin.

Exman, E. 1965 *The brothers Harper*, New York.

Eyre, G. E. B. and Rivington, C. R. (eds.) 1913–14 *A transcript of the registers of the worshipful Company of Stationers; from 1640–1708 AD*, 5 vols., London.

Ezell, M. 1999 *Social authorship and the advent of print*, Baltimore, MD.

Fabian, B. 1976a 'English books and their eighteenth-century German readers', in Korshin 1976, 117–96; also in Fabian 1994.

1976b *Robert Wood, 'An essay on the original genius of Homer'*, Hildesheim.

1978a 'The correspondence between Edward Young and Johann Arnold Ebert', *Wolfenbütteler Beiträge*, 3, 129–34.

1978b 'Die erste englische Buchhandlung auf dem Kontinent', in Fabian 1978c, 122–44; also in Fabian 1994.

(ed.) 1978c *Festchrift für Rainer Gruenter*, Heidelberg.

1979a 'An eighteenth-century research collection: English books at Göttingen University library', *Library*, 6th ser., 1, 209–24; also in Fabian 1994.

1979b 'Die erste Bibliographie der englischen Literatur des achtzehnten Jahrhunderts: Jeremias David Reuß' *Gelehrtes England*', in *Das Buch und sein Haus . . .*, ed. R. Fuhlrott and B. Haller, Wiesbaden, vol. I, 16–43; also in Fabian 1994.

1982 'Die Meßkataloge und der Import englischer Bücher nach Deutschland im achtzehnten Jahrhundert', in Wittmann and Hack 1982, 154–68; also in Fabian 1994.

1983a 'The beginnings of English-language publishing in Germany in the eighteenth century', in Carpenter 1983, 115–43.

1983b *Friedrich Nicolai, 1733–1811: Essays zum 250. Geburstag*, Berlin.

1983c 'Nicolai und England', in Fabian 1983b, 174–97.

1985 'Englisch als neue Fremdsprache des 18. Jahrhunderts', in Kimpel 1985, 178–96.

1992a *The English book in eighteenth-century Germany*, London.

1992b 'The first English bookshop on the Continent', in Horden 1992, 47–64.

1994 *Selecta Anglicana: buchgeschichtliche Studien zur Aufnahme der englischen Literatur in Deutschland im achtzehnten Jahrhundert*, Wiesbaden.

Fabian, B. and Spieckermann, M.-L. 1980 'Deutsche Übersetzungen englischer humanmedizinischer Werke, 1680–1810: Eine vorläufige Bibliographie', *Medizinhistorisches Journal*, 15, 154–71 (addenda *ibid.*, 1984).

1995 'The house of Weidmann in Leipzig and the eighteenth-century importation of English books into Germany', in Flood and Kelly 1995, 299–317.

1997–9 'Swift in eighteenth-century Germany: a bibliographical essay', *Swift Studies*, 12, 5–35; 13 (1998), 5–26; 14 (1999).

2000–2 'Pope in eighteenth-century Germany: a bibliographical essay', *Swift Studies*, 15, 5–32; 16 (2001), 5–32; 17 (2002), 5–35.

Fabricant, C. 1987 'The literature of domestic tourism and the public consumption of private property', in Nussbaum and Brown 1987, 254–75.

Faden, W. 1989 *Faden's map of Norfolk*, intro. J. C. Barringer, facs. of 1797 edn, Dereham.

Fahy, C. 1986 'Descrizioni cinquecentesche della fabbricazione dei caratteri e del processo tipografico', *La bibliofilia*, 88, 47–86.

Fairer, D. 2003 *English poetry of the eighteenth century, 1700–1789*, London.

Farington, J. 1923 *The Farington diary*, ed. J. Grieg, 3rd edn, 2 vols., New York.

Fawcett, J. 1818 *An account of the life, ministry, and writings of the late Rev. John Fawcett ... comprehending many particulars relative to the revival and progress of religion in Yorkshire and Lancashire*, London.

Feather, J. 1980 'The book trade in politics: the making of the Copyright Act of 1710', *PH*, 8, 19–44.

1981 *The English provincial book trade before 1850, a checklist of secondary sources*, Oxford.

1982 'The English book trade and the law, 1695–1799', *PH*, 12, 51–75.

1983 'From censorship to copyright: aspects of the government's role in the English book trade, 1695–1775', in Carpenter 1983, 173–98.

1984 'John Clay of Daventry: the business of an eighteenth-century stationer', *SB*, 37, 198–209.

1985 *The provincial book trade in eighteenth-century England*, Cambridge.

1986 'British publishing in the eighteenth century: a preliminary subject analysis', *Library*, 6th ser., 8, 32–46.

1987 'The publishers and the pirates: British copyright law in theory and practice, 1710–1775', *PH*, 22, 5–32.

1988a *A history of British publishing*, London.

1988b 'Publishers and politicians: the remaking of the law of copyright in Britain, 1775–1842, part 1: Legal deposit and the battle of the library tax', *PH*, 24, 49–76.

1989 'Publishers and politicians: the remaking of the law of copyright in Britain 1775–1842, part 2: The rights of authors', *PH*, 25, 45–72.

1992 'English books in the Netherlands in the eighteenth century: reprints or piracies?', in Berkvens-Stevelinck *et al.* 1992, 143–54.

1994 *Publishing, piracy and politics: an historical study of copyright in Great Britain*, New York.

2004 'The history of the English provincial book trade: a research agenda', in McKay, Bell and Hinks 2004, 1–12.

Feinstein, C. H. 1981 'Capital accumulation and the Industrial Revolution', in Floud and McCloskey 1981, 128–42.

Feinstein, C. H. and Pollard, S. (eds.) 1988 *Studies in capital formation, 1750–1920*, Oxford.

Felton, H. 1713 *A dissertation on reading the classics, and forming a just style. Written in the year 1709*, London.

Fenwick, E. 1998 *Secresy, or the ruin on the rock*, ed. I. Grundy, 2nd edn, Peterborough, Ont.

Ferdinand, C. Y. 1990 'Local distribution networks in 18th-century England', in Myers and Harris 1990, 131–49.

1992 'Towards a demography of the Stationers' Company, 1601–1700', *PH*, 21, 51–69.

1997 *Benjamin Collins and the provincial newspaper trade in the eighteenth century*, Oxford.

1999 'Constructing the frameworks of desire: how newspapers sold books in the seventeenth and eighteenth centuries', in Raymond 1999a, 157–75.

2001 'The economics of the eighteenth-century provincial book trade: the case of Ward and Chandler', in Bell *et al.* 2001, 42–56.

Fergus, J. 1984 'Eighteenth-century readers in provincial England: the customers of Samuel Clay's circulating library and bookshop in Warwick 1771–72', *PBSA*, 78, 155–218.

1991 *Jane Austen: a literary life*, Basingstoke.

1996 'Provincial servants' reading in the late eighteenth century', in Raven, Small and Tadmor 1996, 202–25.

2000 'Women readers: a case study', in Jones 2000, 155–76.

2006a *Provincial readers in eighteenth-century England*, Oxford.

2006b 'Solace in books: reading trifling adventures at Rugby School', in Immel and Witmore 2006, 243–60.

Fergus, J. and Portner, R. 1987 'Provincial bookselling in eighteenth-century England: the case of John Clay reconsidered', *SB*, 40, 147–63.

Fergus, J. and Thaddeus, J. F. 1987 'Women, publishers, and money, 1790–1820', *Studies in Eighteenth-Century Culture*, 17, 191–207.

Ferguson, M. 1992 *Subject to others: British women writers and colonial slavery, 1670–1834*, London.

Ferriar, J. 2001 *The bibliomania*, ed. M. Vaulbert de Chantilly, London.

Fertel, M. D. 1723 *La science pratique de l'imprimerie*, St Omer.

Fielding, H. 1966 *The author's farce*, ed. C. B. Woods, Lincoln, NE.

1967 *Joseph Andrews*, ed. M. C. Battestin, Oxford.

1974a *The history of Tom Jones a foundling*, ed. F. Bowers with an introduction and commentary by M. C. Battestin, Oxford.

1974b *The Jacobite's journal and related writings*, ed. W. B. Coley, Oxford.

1983 *Amelia*, ed. M. C. Battestin, Oxford.

1989 *New essays by Henry Fielding: his contributions to the Craftsman, 1734–1739, and other early journalism; with a stylometric analysis by M. G. Farringdon*, commentary by M. C. Battestin, Charlottesville, VA.

Fielding, P. 2000 'Essay on the text', in Scott 2000a, 355–64.

Findlay, E. 2002 'Ralph Thoresby the diarist: the late seventeenth-century pious diary and its demise', *The Seventeenth Century*, 17, 108–30.

Finkelstein, D. 2002 *The house of Blackwood: author–publisher relations in the Victorian era*, University Park, PA.

Finn, M. C. 2003 *The character of credit: personal debt in English culture, 1740–1914*, Cambridge.

Fisher, S. 1985 'The "blueback" charts', *MC*, 31, 18–23.

2001 *The makers of the blueback charts: a history of Imray, Laurie, Norie & Wilson Ltd*, St Ives, Cambridgeshire.

Fitzgerald, E., Duchess of Leinster 1949–53 *The correspondence of Emily Fitzgerald, Duchess of Leinster, 1731–1814*, ed. B. Fitzgerald, 2 vols., Dublin.

Fitzpatrick, B. L. 1994 'Records of the establishment of the *London Daily Advertiser* in 1751', *Studies in Newspaper and Periodical History*, 2, 121–38.

1995 'The Rivingtons', in Bracken and Silver 1995, 238–47.

Fleeman, J. D. 1964 'William Somervile's "The chace", 1735', *PBSA*, 58, 1–7.

1975 'The revenue of a writer: Samuel Johnson's literary earnings', in Hunt, Philip and Roberts 1975, 211–30.

Fleming, P. L. 1988 *Upper Canadian imprints, 1801–1841: a bibliography*, Toronto.

2002 'Cultural crossroads: print and reading in eighteenth- and nineteenth-century English-speaking Montreal', *Proceedings of the American Antiquarian Society*, 112, no. 2, 231–67.

Fleming, P. L., Gallichan, G. and Lamonde, Y. (eds.) 2004 *History of the book in Canada*, vol. I: *Beginnings to 1840*, Toronto.

Fletcher, D. H. 1995 *The emergence of estate maps: Christ Church, Oxford, 1600 to 1840*, Oxford.

Fletcher, W. Y. 1902 *English book collectors*, London.

Flights of inflatus 1791 *Flights of inflatus; or, the sallies, stories, and adventures of a Wild-Goose philosopher*, by the author of the Trifles, 2 vols., London.

Flinn, M. W. 1970 *British population growth, 1700–1850*, London.
(ed.) 1977 *Scottish population history: from the 17th century to the 1930s*, Cambridge.
Flood, J. L. and Kelly, W. A. (eds.) 1995 *The German book, 1450–1750: studies presented to David L. Paisey*, London.
Floud, R. and Johnson, P. (eds.) 2004 *The Cambridge economic history of modern Britain*, vol. I: *Industrialisation, 1700–1860*, Cambridge.
Floud, R. and McCloskey, D. (eds.) 1981 *The economic history of Britain since 1700*, 2 vols., Cambridge.
1994 *The economic history of Britain since 1700*, 2nd rev. edn, Cambridge.
Fontaine, L., Postel Vinay, G., Rosenthal, P. L. and Servais, P. (eds.) 1997 *Des personnes aux institutions: réseaux et culture du credit du XVIe siècle au XXe siècle en Europe*, Louvain-la-Neuve.
Foot, M. M. 1984 'Some bookbinders' price lists of the seventeenth and eighteenth centuries', *De libris compactis miscellanea*, Brussels.
Forbes, M. 1904 *Beattie and his friends*, Westminster.
Ford, H. L. 1935 *Shakespeare, 1700–1740: a collation of the editions and separate plays, with some account of T. Johnson and R. Walker*, Oxford.
Ford, J. 1983 *Ackermann, 1783–1983: the business of art*, London.
Ford, P. and Ford, G. 1972 *A guide to parliamentary papers*, 3rd edn, Shannon, Co. Clare.
Ford, W. C. 1917 *The Boston book market, 1679–1700*, Boston, MA.
Fordham, H. G. 1916 *Road-books and itineraries bibliographically considered*, London.
1924 *The road-books and itineraries of Great Britain, 1570 to 1850: a catalogue with an introduction and a bibliography*, Cambridge.
1925 *John Cary, engraver, map, chart and print-seller and globe-maker, 1754 to 1835*, Cambridge.
Forster, A. 1990 *Index to book reviews in England, 1749–1774*, Carbondale, IL.
1997 *Index to book reviews in England, 1775–1800*, London.
2001 'Review journals and the reading public', in Rivers 2001, 171–90.
Forster, H. 1970–1 'Edward Young in translation', *BC*, 19, 481–500; 20, 47–67.
Foucault, M. 1977 *Language, counter-memory, practice: Selected essays and interviews*, ed. D. F. Bouchard, Oxford.
Foulis, R. 1774 *Memorial of the printers and booksellers of Glasgow, most humbly addressed to the honourable House of Commons, assembled in Parliament*, Glasgow.
Fournier, P. S. 1764–6 *Manuel typographique, utile aux gens de lettres, et à ceux qui exercent les différentes parties de l'art de l'imprimerie*, 2 vols., Paris.
1930 (1764–8) *Fournier on typefounding: the text of the 'Manuel typographique'*, trans. and ed. with notes by H. Carter, London.
1995 *Manuel typographique (1764–68): together with 'Fournier on typefounding' [by H. Carter]* (1930), ed. J. Mosley, 3 vols., Darmstadt.
Fowler, A. 1975 'The selection of literary constructs', *New Literary History*, 7, 39–55.
Foxon, D. F. 1963 'Monthly catalogues of books published', *Library*, 5th ser., 18, 223–8.
1975a *English verse, 1701–1750: a catalogue of separately printed poems with notes on contemporary collected editions*, 2 vols., Cambridge.
1975b 'Stitched books', *BC*, 24, 111–24.
1978 'The Stamp Act of 1712', unpublished Sandars Lectures, BL, Ac.2660M (32).
1991 *Pope and the early eighteenth-century book trade*, rev. and ed. J. McLaverty, Oxford.
Fraistat, N. (ed.) 1986 *Poems in their place: the intertextuality and order of poetic collections*, Chapel Hill, NC.

Francis, J. C. 1888 *John Francis, publisher of the Athenaeum: a literary chronicle of half a century*, London.

Francklin, R. (attrib.) 1744 *A new year's gift for the r[ight] h[onourabl]e, the E[arl] of B[ath]; in a letter from R[ichard] F[ranckli]n, B[ook]s[elle]r, to his L[ordshi]p*, London.

Franklin, B. 1961 *The papers of Benjamin Franklin*, vol. III: *January 1, 1745, through June 30, 1750*, ed. L. W. Labaree, New Haven, CT.

1986 *Benjamin Franklin's autobiography*, ed. J. A. L. Lemay and P. M. Zall, New York.

Frantz, R. W. 1934 *The English traveller and the movement of ideas, 1660–1732*, Lincoln, NE.

Frasca-Spada, M. and Jardine, N. (eds.) 2000 *Books and the sciences in history*, Cambridge.

Fraser, D. 1963 'The Nottingham press: 1800–1850', *Transactions of the Thoroton Society*, 67, 46–66.

Freeman, M. J. and Aldcroft, D. H. (eds.) 1988 *Transport in Victorian Britain*, Manchester.

Frost, A. and Samson, J. (eds.) 1999 *Pacific empires: essays in honour of Glyndwrs Williams*, Vancouver.

Frostick, R. 2002 *The printed plans of Norwich, 1558–1840: a carto-bibliography*, Norwich.

Funcke, J. M. 1998 (1740) *Kurtze Anleitung von Form- und Stahl-Schneiden*, facs. ed. J. Mosley, Darmstadt.

Furbank, P. N. and Owens, W. R. 1998 *A critical bibliography of Daniel Defoe*, London.

Fussell, G. E. 1935 *The exploration of England: a select bibliography of travel and topography: 1570–1815*, London.

Fussell, P. 1971 *Samuel Johnson and the life of writing*, New York.

Fyfe, A. 1999 'Copyrights and competition: producing and protecting children's books in the nineteenth century', *PH*, 45, 35–59.

2000 ' Young readers and the sciences', in Frasca-Spada and Jardine 2000, 276–90.

Gadd, I. (ed.) forthcoming *The history of Oxford University Press*, vol. I: *1478–1780s*, Oxford.

Gallagher, C. 1994 *'Nobody's story': the vanishing act of women writers in the marketplace, 1670–1820*, Oxford.

Gallaway, F. W. 1940 'The conservative attitude towards fiction, 1770–1830', *PMLA*, 55, 1041–59.

Gamble, W. 1923 *Music engraving and printing: historical and technical treatise*, London.

Gants, D. L. 2002 'A quantitative analysis of the London book trade, 1614–1618', *SB*, 55, 185–214.

Garbett, G. and Skelton, I. 1987 *The wreck of the Metta Katerina*, Pulla Cross.

Gardiner, L. 1976 *Bartholomew, 150 years*, Edinburgh.

Gardiner, R. A. 1976 'Thomas Jefferys' *American atlas*, 1776', *Geographical Journal*, 142, 2, 355–8.

Gardner, V. E. M. 2003 'John White and the development of advertising in the *Newcastle Courant*, 1711–1801', unpub. thesis, University of Newcastle upon Tyne.

Garrigus, C. E., Jr. 1997 'The reading habits of Maryland's planter gentry, 1718–1747', *Maryland Historical Magazine*, 92, 37–53.

Garside, P. 1983 'Rob's last raid: Scott and the publication of the Waverley novels', in Myers and Harris 1983, 88–118.

2000 'The English novel in the romantic era: consolidation and dispersal', in Garside, Raven and Schöwerling 2000, II, 15–103.

Garside, P., Raven, J. and Schöwerling, R. (eds.) 2000 *The English novel, 1770–1829: a bibliographical survey of prose fiction published in the British Isles*, 2 vols., Oxford.

Gaskell, P. 1952 'Printing the classics in the eighteenth century', *BC*, 1, 98–111.

1956a 'The decline of the common press', unpub. thesis, Cambridge University.
1956b 'The Strahan papers', *Times Literary Supplement*, 5 Oct, London.
1957 'Notes on eighteenth-century British Paper', *Library*, 5th ser., 12, 41.
1959 *John Baskerville: a bibliography*, Cambridge.
1965 'The bibliographical press movement', *JPHS*, 1, 1–13.
1970 'A census of wooden presses', *JPHS*, 6, 1–32.
1972 *A new introduction to bibliography*, Oxford.
1974 *A new introduction to bibliography*, 2nd edn, Oxford.
1986 *A bibliography of the Foulis Press*, 2nd edn, Winchester.

Gaskell, P., Barber, G. G. and Warrilow, G. 1968–71 'An annotated list of printers' manuals to 1850', *JPHS*, 4, 11–32; 'Addenda and corrigenda', *JPHS*, 7, 65–6.

Gaskell, R. 2004 'Printing house and engraving shop: a mysterious collaboration', *BC*, 53, 213–51.

Gaskill, H. (ed.) 2004 *The reception of Ossian in Europe*, London.

Gayer, A. D., Rostow, W. W. and Schwartz, A. J. 1953 *The growth and fluctuations of the British economy, 1790–1850*, 2 vols., Oxford.

Ged, W. 1781 *Biographical memoirs of William Ged; including a particular account of his progress in the art of block-printing*, London.

Geduld, H. M. 1969 *Prince of publishers: a study of the work and career of Jacob Tonson*, Bloomington, IL.

George, M. D. 1959 *English political caricature to 1792: a study of opinion and propaganda*, 2 vols., Oxford.

Gerhold, D. 1988 'The growth of the London carrying trade, 1681–1838', *EcHR*, 41, 392–410.
1996 'Productivity change in road transport before and after turnpiking, 1690–1840', *EcHR*, 49, 491–515.
1999 *Westminster Hall: nine hundred years of history*, London.

Germann, M. 1973 *Johann Jakob Thurneysen der Jüengere, 1754–1803, Verleger, Buchdrucker und Buchhäendler in Basel. Ein Beitrag zur Geschichte der Spaetaufklaerung in Basel und zur Geschichte des Eindringens der englischen und franzöesischen Aufkläerung im deutschen Sprachgebiet am Ende des 18. Jahrhunderts*. Basler Beiträege zur Geschichtswissenschaft, 128, ed. E. Bonjour and W. Kaegi, Basel and Stuttgart.

Gessner, C. F. and Hager, J. G. 1740–5 *Die so nöthing als nützliche Buchdruckerkunst und Schriftgiesserey*, 4 vols., Leipzig.

Gibbon, E. 1966 *Memoirs of my life*, ed. G. A. Bonnard, New York.

Gibbs, G. C. 1971 'The role of the Dutch Republic as the intellectual entrepôt of Europe in the seventeenth and eighteenth centuries', *Bijdragen en mededelingen betreffende de geschiedenis der Nederlanden*, 86, 323–49.

Gibson, A. J. S. and Smout, T. C. 1995 *Prices, food and wages in Scotland, 1550–1780*, Cambridge.

Gibson, J. and Medlycott, M. 1983 *Land and window tax assessments*, Birmingham.

Gibson, R. W. 1950 *Francis Bacon: a bibliography of his works and of Baconiana to the year 1750*, Oxford.

Gibson, S. and Holdsworth, W. S. 1930 'Charles Viner's *General abridgment of law and equity*', OBS, *Proceedings and Papers*, 2, 228–325.

Gibson, S. and Johnson, J. de M. (eds.) 1943 *The first minute book of the Delegates of Oxford University Press, 1668–1756*, Oxford.

Gifford, G. 2002 *A descriptive catalogue of the music collection at Burghley House, Stamford*, Aldershot.

Giles, P. 2001 *Transatlantic insurrections: British culture and the formation of American literature, 1730–1860*, Philadelphia, PA.

Gill, S. 1955 'Copyright and the publishing of Wordsworth, 1850–1900', in Jordan and Patten 1955, 74–92.

1998 *Wordsworth and the Victorians*, Oxford.

Gillespie, R. 2005 *Reading Ireland: print, reading and social change in early modern Ireland*, Manchester.

Gillespie, R. and Hadfield, A. (eds.) 2006 *The Oxford history of the Irish book*, vol. III: *The Irish book in English, 1550–1800*, Oxford.

Gillespie, R. A. 1990 'The Glasgow book trade to 1776', in McCarra and Whyte 1990, 53–63.

Gillespie, S. C. 1953 *A hundred years of progress: the record of the Scottish Typographical Association 1853 to 1952*, Glasgow.

Gillick, S. L. 1979 *A Chesterfield bibliography to 1800*, New York.

Gillow, J. 1885–1902 *A literary and biographical history, or bibliographical dictionary of the English Catholics, from the breach with Rome, in 1534, to the present time*, 5 vols., London.

Gilmartin, K. 1998 'Radical print culture in periodical form', in Rajan and Wright 1998, 35–63.

Gilmor, W. J. 1989 *Reading becomes a necessity of life: material and cultural life in rural New England, 1780–1835*, Knoxville, TN.

Gilson, D. G. 1997 *A bibliography of Jane Austen*, new edn, Winchester.

Ginarlis, J. and Pollard, S. 1988 'Roads and waterways, 1750–1850', in Feinstein and Pollard 1988, 208–12.

Gingerich, O. 2004 *The book nobody read: chasing the revolutions of Nicolaus Copernicus*, London.

Ginter, D. E. 1992 *A measure of wealth: the English land tax in historical analysis*, London.

Girdham, J. 1997 *English opera in late eighteenth-century London: Stephen Storace at Drury Lane*, Oxford.

Godwin, W. 1831 *Thoughts on man, his nature, productions, and discoveries. Interspersed with some particulars respecting the author*, London.

Goebel, T. 1906 (1883) *Friedrich Koenig und die Erfindung der Schnellpresse*, Stuttgart.

Goede, C. A. G. 1808 *Memorials of nature and art collected on a journey in Great Britain during the years 1802 and 1803*, 3 vols., London.

Goldgar, A. 1995 *Impolite learning: conduct and community in the Republic of letters, 1680–1750*, New Haven, CT.

Goldsmith, O. 1762 *The citizen of the world; or letters from a Chinese philosopher, residing in London, to his friends in the east*, London.

1966 *Collected works*, ed. A. Friedman, 5 vols., Oxford.

Gondris, J. (ed.) 1998 *Reading readings: essays on Shakespeare editing in the eighteenth century*, Madison, NJ.

Goody, J. (ed.) 1968 *Literacy in traditional societies*, Cambridge.

Gordon, G. (ed.) 1985 *Perspectives of the Scottish city*, Aberdeen.

Goss, C. W. F. 1932 *The London directories, 1677–1855*, London.

Goulden, R. J. 1982 *Some Chancery lawsuits, 1714–1758; an analytical list*, London.

1989 'The shadow limn'd: Matthias Koops', *IPH Information*, 23, 75–85.

Gourvish, T. R. 1988 'Railways 1830–70: the formative years', in Freeman and Aldcroft 1988, 57–91.

Graf, A. 1911 *L'Anglomania e l'influsso inglese in Italia nel secolo 18*, Turin.

Graff, H. 1987 *Legacies of literacy: continuities and contradictions in western culture and society*, Bloomington, IN.

Graham, M. 1813 *Journal of a residence in India*, 2nd edn, Edinburgh.

Graham, W. J. 1930 *English literary periodicals*, New York.

Grant, G. L. 2001 *English state lotteries, 1694–1826: a history and collectors guide to the tickets and shares*, London.

Gray, A. 1880 *Introduction to structural and systematic botany*, New York.

Gray, N. 1976 (1938) *Nineteenth century ornamented type faces*, new edn, London.

1981 'Slab-serif type design in England, 1815–1845', *JPHS*, 15, 1–35.

Gray, T. 1775 *The poems of Mr Gray, to which are prefixed memoirs of his life and writings by W. Mason*, York.

1935 *Correspondence of Thomas Gray*, ed. P. Toynbee and L. Whibley, 3 vols., Oxford.

Great Britain, Parliament, House of Commons 1774 *Memorial of the printers and booksellers of Glasgow, must humbly addressed to the honourable House of Commons, assembled in Parliament*, Glasgow.

1836 *The fifth report of the Commissioners appointed to inquire into the management of the Post-Office Department*, London.

Greaves, R. 1986 'Religion in the university, 1715–1800', in Sutherland and Mitchell 1986, 401–24.

Greaves, R. L. 2002 *Glimpses of glory: John Bunyan and English dissent*, Stanford, CA.

Green, I. 1996 *The Christian ABC: catechism and catechising in England, c.1530–1740*, Oxford.

2000 *Print and protestantism in early modern England*, Oxford.

Green, I. and Peters, K. 2002 'Religious publishing in England, 1640–1695', in *CHBB* IV, 67–93.

Green, J. N. 1987 'From printer to publisher: Mathew Carey and the origins of nineteenth-century book publishing', in Hackenberg 1987, 26–44.

2000 'English books and printing in the age of Franklin', *HBA* I, 248–98.

forthcoming 'The rise of book publishing', *HBA* II.

Green, R. 1906 *The works of John and Charles Wesley: a bibliography*, 2nd edn, London.

Greene, J. 1988 *Pursuits of happiness*, Chapel Hill, NC.

Greenland, M. and Day, R. E. 1991 *Compound-plate printing*, London.

Greenslade, S. L. 1963 'English versions of the Bible, 1525–1611', in *CHBB* II, 141–74.

Greenwood, J. 1971 *Newspapers and the Post Office, 1635–1834*, Reigate.

Greg, W. W. (ed.) 1903 *Catalogue of the books presented by Edward Capell to the library of Trinity College in Cambridge*, Cambridge.

(ed.) 1967 *A companion to Arber, being a calendar of documents in Edward Arber's 'Transcript of the registers of the Company of Stationers of London, 1554–1640', with text and calendar of supplementary documents*, Oxford.

Gregory, J. and Chamberlain, J. S. (eds.) 2003 *The national church in local perspective: the Church of England and the regions, 1660–1800*, Woodbridge.

Grenby, M. O. 2001 'Adults only? Children and children's books in British circulating libraries, 1748–1848', *Book History*, 5, 19–38.

Griffin, D. H. 1986 *Regaining paradise: Milton and the eighteenth century*, Cambridge.

1990 'The beginnings of modern authorship: Milton and Dryden', *Milton Quarterly*, 24, 1, 1–7.

1993 'Fictions of eighteenth-century authorship', *Essays in Criticism*, 43, 181–94.

1996 *Literary patronage in England, 1650–1800*, Cambridge.

2002 *Patriotism and poetry in eighteenth-century Britain*, Cambridge.
2005 'The social world of authorship, 1660–1714', in Richetti 2005, 37–60.
Griffiths, A. 1991 'The prints and drawings in the library of Consul Joseph Smith', *Print Quarterly*, 8, 127–39.
1993 'The Rogers Collection in the Cottonian Library, Plymouth', *Print Quarterly*, 10, 19–36.
1994 'Print collecting in the early eighteenth century in Rome, Paris and London', *Harvard University Art Museums Bulletin*, 2, 37–58.
2004 *Prints for books: book illustration in France, 1760–1800*, London.
Griffiths, D. 1990 *'A musical place of the first quality': a history of institutional music-making in York, c.1550–1989*, York.
Griffiths, D. N. 2002 *The bibliography of the Book of Common Prayer, 1549–1999*, London.
Griffiths, J. and Pearsall, D. (eds.) 1989 *Book production and publishing in Britain, 1375–1475*, Cambridge.
Griffiths, R. 1770 *The posthumous works of a late celebrated genius deceased*, 2 vols., London.
Griffiths, R. 1998 'Music publishing' in Jones and Rees 1998.
Groom, N. (ed.) 1999 *Thomas Chatterton and romantic culture*, London.
Gross, R. A. 2002 'Print and the public sphere in early America', in Stokes 2002, 245–64.
Grundy, I. 1988 'Sarah Gardner: "such trumpery" or "a lustre to her sex"', *Tulsa Studies in Women's Literature*, 7, 7–25.
1994 'Books and the woman: an eighteenth-century owner and her libraries', *English Studies in Canada*, 20, 1, 1–22.
1998 'Introduction', in Fenwick 1998.
Guedalla, P. 1931 *The duke*, London.
Guerrero, A. C. 1992 'British travellers in eighteenth-century Spain', *Studies on Voltaire and the eighteenth century*, 305, 1632–5.
Haas, W. 1790 *Beschreibung und Abrisse einer neuen Buchdruckerpresse erfunden in Basel im Jahre 1772*, Basel.
Habermas, J. 1989 *The structural transformation of the public sphere: an inquiry into a category of bourgeois society*, trans. T. Burger with the assistance of F. Lawrence, Cambridge, MA.
Hackenberg, M. (ed.) 1987 *Getting the books out: papers of the Chicago conference on the book in 19th century America*, Washington, DC.
Hadfield, A. 2004 'Editor as censor', Review of Sharpe and Zwicker 2003 in *Times Literary Supplement*, 20 Feb.
Hagglund, E. 1998 'Reviews of travel in the *Monthly Review*, 1749–1758: an introductory survey', *Studies in Travel Writing*, 2, 1–45.
Haig, R. L. 1960 *The Gazetteer, 1735–1797*, Carbondale, IL.
Haines, H. 1740 *Treachery, baseness and cruelty display'd to the full; in the hardships and sufferings of Mr H. Haines, late printer of the Country Journal, or Craftsman; ... now ... in close imprisonment ... for printing and publishing the Craftsman of Jul 2, 1737*, London.
Halsband, R. 1985 'The rococo in England: book illustrators, mainly Gravelot and Bentley', *Burlington Magazine*, 77, 870–80.
Hamlyn, H. 1947 'Eighteeenth-century circulating libraries in England', *Library*, 5th ser., 1, 197–218.
Hammelmann, H. and Boase, T. S. R. 1975 *Book illustrators in eighteenth-century England*, New Haven, CT.

Hammond, B. 1997 *Professional imaginative writing in England, 1670–1740*, Oxford.
Hammond, P. and Hopkins, D. (eds.) 2000 *John Dryden: tercentenary essays*, Oxford.
Handover, P. M. 1960 *Printing in London from 1476 to modern times: competitive practice and technical invention in the trade of book and bible printing, periodical production, jobbing &c.*, London.
Handrea, M. H. 1978 'Books in parts and the number trade', in Landon 1978, 34–51.
Hannett, John *pseud.* see Arnett 1837.
Hans, N. 1951 *New trends in education in the eighteenth century*, London.
Hansard, L. 1991 *The auto-biography of Luke Hansard, printer to the House, 1752–1828*, ed. R. Myers, London.
Hansard, L. G. 1962 *Luke Graves Hansard his diary, 1814–1841: a case study in the reform of patronage*, ed. by P. and G. Ford, Oxford.
Hansard, T. C. 1825 *Typographia: an historical sketch of the origin and progress of the art of printing*, London.
Hanson, L. W. 1936 *Government and the press, 1695–1763*, London.
1963 *Contemporary sources for British and Irish economic history, 1701–1750*, Cambridge.
Harlan, R. 1966 'David Hall's bookshop and its British sources of supply', in Kaser 1966, 1–24.
1976 'A colonial printer as bookseller in eighteenth-century Philadelphia: the case of David Hall', *Studies in Eighteenth-Century Culture*, 5, 355–70.
Harley, J. B. 1962 *Christopher Greenwood, county map-maker, and his Worcestershire map of 1822*, Worcester.
1963–4 'The Society of Arts and the survey of English counties, 1759–1809', *Journal of the Royal Society of Arts*, 112, 43–6, 119–23, 169–74, 538–43.
1965 'The re-mapping of England, 1750–1800', *IM*, 19, 56–67.
1966 'The bankruptcy of Thomas Jefferys: an episode in the economic history of eighteenth century map-making', *IM*, 20, 27–48.
1968 'Introduction', in Yates 1968, 7–21, 48.
(ed.) 1970 *Britannia Depicta, or Ogilby improved, by John Owen and Emanuel Bowen* (1720), Facsimile reprint, Newcaste upon Tyne.
1972 'Introduction', in Morden 1972, i–xii.
1987 'Introduction', in Ordnance Survey 1987, i–lvi.
Harley, J. B. and Hodson, D. (eds.) 1971 'Introduction', in Bowen and Kitchin 1971, 1–14.
Harley, J. B. and Laxton, P. 1974 'Introduction', in Burdett 1972, 1–36.
Harley, J. B. and O'Donoghue, Y. 1975 'Introduction', in Ordnance Survey 1975, i–xl.
1977 'Introduction', in Ordnance Survey 1977, i–xliv.
Harley, J. B. and Walters, G. 1978 'English map collecting, 1790–1840: a pilot survey of the evidence in Sotheby sale catalogues', *IM*, 30, 31–55.
Harmsen, T. 2000 *Antiquarianism in the Augustan age: Thomas Hearne, 1678–1735*, Oxford.
Harris, E. 1990 *British architectural books*, Cambridge.
Harris, E. M. 1967 'Sir William Congreve and his compound-plate printing', *United States National Museum Bulletin*, 252, *Contributions from the Museum of History and Technology*, paper 71, 71–87, Washington, DC.
1968–70 'Experimental graphic processes in England, 1800–1859', *JPHS*, 4, 33–86; 5, 41–80; 6, 53–89.
Harris, E. M. and Sisson, C. 1978 *The common press: being a record, description, and delineation of the early eighteenth-century handpress in the Smithsonian Institution*, Boston, MA.

Harris, F. and Hunter, M. C. W. 2003 *John Evelyn and his milieu*, London.
Harris, J. and Jackson-Stops, G. (eds.) 1984 *Britannia Illustrata*, Bungay.
Harris, M. 1970 'Figures relating to the printing and distribution of the *Craftsman*, 1726 to 1730', *BIHR*, 43, 233–42.
1975 'Newspaper distribution during Queen Anne's reign', in Hunt, Philip and Roberts 1975, 139–51.
1978a 'The management of the London newspaper press during the eighteenth century', *PH*, 4, 95–112.
1978b 'The structure, ownership and control of the press, 1620–1780', in Boyce, Curran and Wingate 1978, 82–117.
1980 'Astrology, almanacks and booksellers, a review article', *PH*, 8, 87–104.
1981 'Periodicals and the book trade', in Myers and Harris 1981, 66–94.
1987 *London newspapers in the age of Walpole: a study of the origins of the modern English press*, Rutherford, NJ.
1989 'Paper pirates: the alternative book trade in London in the mid-eighteenth century', in Myers and Harris 1989, 47–69.
1997 'Scratching the surface: engravers, printsellers and the London book trade in the mid-eighteenth century', in Hunt, Mandelbrote and Shell 1997, 95–114.
1999a 'Shipwrecks in print: representations of maritime disaster in the late seventeenth century', in Myers and Harris 1999, 39–63.
1999b 'Timely notices: the uses of advertising and its relationship to news during the late seventeenth century', in Raymond 1999a, 141–56.
2003 'Print in neighbourhood commerce: the case of Carter Lane', in Myers, Harris and Mandelbrote 2003, 45–69.
Harris, R. 1993 *A patriot press: national politics and the London press in the 1740s*, Oxford.
Harrison, D. F. 1992 'Bridges and economic development, 1300–1800', *EcHR*, 45, 240–61.
Harrison, F. M. 1936 'Some illustrators of *The pilgrim's progress* (part one): John Bunyan', *Library*, 4th ser., 17, 241–63.
1942 'Editions of *The pilgrim's progress*', *Library*, 4th ser., 22, 73–81.
Harrison, R., Woolven, G. B. and Duncan, R. (eds.) 1977 *The Warwick guide to British labour periodicals, 1790–1970*, Hassocks.
Hart, H. 1966 (1896) *Charles Earl Stanhope and the Oxford University Press*, reprint with notes by J. Mosley, London.
1970 (1900) *Notes on a century of typography at the University Press, Oxford, 1693–1794*, ed. H. Carter, Oxford.
Harvey, D. R., Kirsop, W. and McMullin, B. J. (eds.) 1993 *An index of civilisation: studies of printing and publishing history in honour of Keith Maslen*, Clayton.
Harvey, P. D. A. and Thorpe, H. 1959 *The printed maps of Warwickshire, 1576–1900*, Warwick.
Harvey, W. 1863 *London scenes and London people*, London.
Harvey, W. 1903 *Scottish chapbook literature*, Paisley.
Harwood, E. 1775 *A view of the various editions of Greek and Roman classics: with remarks*, London.
Hassall, W. O. 1959 'Portrait of a bibliophile. II. Thomas Coke, earl of Leicester, 1697–1759', *BC*, 8, 249–61.
Hatton, E. 1697 *The merchant's magazine: or, trade-man's treasury*, 2nd edn, London.
Havens, E. 2001 *Commonplace books: a history of manuscripts and printed books from antiquity to the twentieth century*, New Haven, CT.

Hawkins, J. 1961 *Life of Samuel Johnson LLD*, ed. H. Davis, New York.
Hay, D. and Rogers, N. 1997 *Eighteenth-century English society: shuttles and swords*, 2nd edn, Oxford.
Hayden, J. O. 1969 *The romantic reviewers, 1802–1824*, London.
Hazen, A. T. 1951 'One meaning of the imprint', *Library*, 5th ser., 6, 110–23.
Hazlitt, W. 1930–4 *The complete works of William Hazlitt*, ed. P. P. Howe, 21 vols., London.
Heal, A. 1968 (1925) *London tradesmen's cards of the xviii century: an account of their origin and use*, repr., New York.
Heber, R. 1829 *Narrative of a journey through the Upper Provinces of India*, 4th edn, 3 vols., London.
Heckrotte, W. 1987 'Aaron Arrowsmith's map of North America and the Lewis and Clark expedition', *MC*, 39, 16–20.
Heilbron, J. L. 1979 *Electricity in the seventeenth and eighteenth centuries*, Berkeley, CA.
Helgerson, R. 1983 *Self-crowned laureates: Spenser, Jonson, Milton, and the literary system*, Berkeley, CA.
Hellinga, L., Duke, A., Harskamp, J. and Hermans, T. (eds.) 2001 *The bookshop of the world: the role of the Low Countries in the book-trade, 1473–1941*, Goy-Houten.
Hellmuth, E. (ed.) 1990 *The transformation of political culture: England and Germany in the late eighteenth century*, Oxford.
Hemmeon, J. C. 1912 *The history of the British Post Office*, London.
Henderson, G. D. 1937 *Religious life in seventeenth-century Scotland*, Cambridge.
Hernlund, P. 1967 'William Strahan's ledgers: standard charges for printing, 1738–1785', *SB*, 20, 89–111.
1969 'William Strahan's ledgers II: charges for papers, 1738–1785', *SB*, 22, 179–95.
1994 'Three bankruptcies in the London book trade, 1746–61: Rivington, Knapton, and Osborne', in Brack 1994, 77–122.
Hetet, J. S. T. 1987 'A literary underground in Restoration England: printers and dissenters in the context of constraints, 1660–1689', unpub. thesis, University of Cambridge.
Hewitt, D. 1995 'Essay on the text', in Scott 1995, 357–64.
Hewlett, L. 1966 'James Rivington, Tory printer', in Kaser 1966, 165–93.
Heyd, M. 1995 *'Be sober and reasonable': the critique of enthusiasm in the seventeenth and early eighteenth centuries*, Leiden.
Heywood, O. 1881–5 *The Rev. Oliver Heywood, 1603–1702: his autobiography, diaries, anecdote and event books*, ed. J. H. Turner, 4 vols., Brighouse.
Higgs, H. 1935 *Bibliography of economics, 1751–1775*, Cambridge.
Hill, G. 1978 *Cartographical curiosities*, London.
Hill, J. 1999 'From provisional to permanent: books in boards, 1790–1840', *Library*, 6th ser., 21, 247–73.
Hills, R. L. 1988 *Papermaking in Britain, 1488–1988*, London.
2001 'The Chelsea mill of the Straw Paper Company', *The Quarterly: The Journal of the British Association of Paper Historians*, 39, 22–31.
Hillyard, B. 1984 'The Edinburgh Society's silver medals for printing', *PBSA*, 78, 3, 295–319.
Hindley, C. 1966 (1871) *Curiosities of street literature*, repr. with intro. by L. Shepard, London.
Hindmarsh, D. B. 1996 *John Newton and the English evangelical tradition: between the conversions of Wesley and Wilberforce*, Oxford.

Hinks, J. 2000 'Some radical printers and booksellers of Leicester, *c.*1790–1850', in Isaac and McKay 2000, 175–84.

2001 'The beginnings of the book trade in Leicester', in Isaac and McKay 2001, 27–38.

2002 'The history of the book trade in Leicester to *c.*1850', unpub. thesis, Loughborough University.

2004 'The book trade in its urban context, 1700–1850: evidence from the British Book Trade Index', unpublished paper given at the White Rose Book History Seminar, University of York, 2 June 2004.

Hinks, J. and Armstrong, C. (eds.) 2005 *Printing places: locations of book production and distribution since 1500*, Print Networks, New Castle, DE.

Hinks, J. and Bell, M. 2005 'The book trade in English provincial towns, 1700–1850: an evaluation of evidence from the *British Book Trade Index*', in *PH*, 57, 53–112.

Hoare, H. P. R. 1955 *Hoare's bank. A record, 1672–1955*, rev. edn, London.

Hobbs, M. 1993 'The Diceys revisited', *Factotum*, 36, 27.

Hobson, G. D. 1940 *English bindings 1490–1940 in the library of J. R. Abbey*, London.

Hodgart, M. 1978 'The subscription list for Pope's *Iliad*, 1715', in White 1978, 25–34.

Hodgson, N. and Blagden, C. 1956 *The notebook of Thomas Bennet and Henry Clements (1686–1719), with some aspects of book trade practice*, Oxford.

Hodgson, T. 1820 *An essay on the origin and progress of stereotype printing; including a description of the various processes*, Newcastle upon Tyne.

Hodnet, E. 1976 'Elisha Kirkall', *BC*, 25, 195–209.

Hodskinson, J. 2003 *Hodskinson's map of Suffolk in 1783*, facs., intro. D. P. Dymond, Dereham.

Hodson, D. 1984 *County atlases of the British Isles published after 1703: a bibliography*, vol. I: *Atlases published 1704–1742 and their subsequent editions*, Tewin.

1989 *County atlases of the British Isles published after 1703: a bibliography*, vol. II: *Atlases published 1743 to 1763 and their subsequent editions*, Tewin.

1997a *County atlases of the British Isles published after 1703: a bibliography*, vol. III: *Atlases published 1764–1789 and their subsequent editions*, London.

1997b 'On 1st January 1801 the first Ordnance Survey map was published and British cartography was never to be the same again', *Sheetlines*, 43, 3.

2000 'The early printed road books and itineraries of England and Wales', unpub. thesis, Exeter University.

Hodson, Y. 1988 'Prince William, royal map collector', *MC*, 44, 2–12.

1991 'Board of Ordnance surveys, 1683–1820', *Survey and Mapping Alliance*.

1999 *Popular maps: the Ordnance Survey popular edition one-inch map of England and Wales, 1919–1926*, London.

2000 'Roads on OS one-inch maps, 1801–1904', *Rights of Way Law Review*, Section 9.3, 119–27.

2001 'Nineteenth and early twentieth century non-OS maps', *Rights of Way Law Review*, Section 9.3, 129–38.

Hoeflich, M. H. 1998 'Legal history and the history of the book', *University of Kansas Law Review*, 46, 415–31.

Hofer, P. 1956 *Eighteenth-century book illustrations*, Los Angeles, CA.

Hoffman, P. *et al.* 2000 *Prices and real inequality in Europe since 1500*, Agricultural History Center working paper 102, Davis, CA.

2002 'Real inequality in Europe since 1500', *JEcH*, 62, 322–55.

Hofmann, T., Barker, N. J. and Hunter, M. C. W. 1995 *John Evelyn in the British Library*, London.

Hoftijzer, P. G. 1987 *Engelse boekverkopers bij de Beurs: de geschiedenis van de Amsterdamse boekhandels Bruyning en Swart, 1637–1725*, Amsterdam.

1991a 'Business and pleasure: a Leiden bookseller in England in 1772', in Roach 1991, 179–88.

1991b 'Religious and theological books in the Anglo-Dutch book trade at the time of the Glorious Revolution', in van den Berg and Hoftijzer 1991, 167–78.

1992 'The Leiden bookseller Pieter vander Aa (1659–1733) and the international book-trade', in Berkvens-Stevelinck *et al.* 1992, 169–84.

2002 'British books abroad: the Continent', in *CHBB* IV, 735–43.

Holdsworth, W. S. 1922–66 *A history of English law*, 2nd edn, 16 vols., London.

Hollis, P. 1970 *The pauper press: a study in working-class radicalism of the 1830s*, Oxford.

1980 'Anti-slavery and British working class radicalism in the years of reform', in Bolt and Drescher 1980, 294–315.

Holman, P. 2000 'The Colchester Partbooks', *Early Music*, 28, 577–95.

Holmes, G. 1982 *Augustan England: professions, state, and society, 1680–1730*, London.

Hook, A. 1975 *Scotland and America: a study of cultural relations, 1750–1835*, Glasgow.

Hoppit, J. 1986 'Financial crises in eighteenth-century England', *EcHR*, 39, 39–58.

1987 *Risk and failure in English business, 1700–1800*, Cambridge.

2000. *A land of liberty? England, 1689–1727*. Oxford.

Horden, J. (ed.) 1992 *Bibliographia: lectures 1975–1988 by recipients of the Marc Fitch Prize for Bibliography*, Oxford.

Horne, H. 1947 *A history of savings banks*, Oxford.

Horwitz, H. 1995 *Chancery equity records and proceedings: a guide to documents in the Public Record Office*, London.

Horwitz, R. and Finn, J. 1975 'Locke's Aesop's Fables', *Locke Newsletter*, 6, 71–88.

Hounslow, D. 1998 *The child subscribers to Thomas Boreman's 'Gigantick histories'*, Appleby-in-Westmorland.

2004 'From George III to Queen Victoria: a provincial family and their books', in McKay, Bell and Hinks 2004, 61–72.

Houston, R. A. 1982 'The literacy myth? Illiteracy in Scotland, 1630–1760', *P&P*, 96, 81–102.

1985 *Scottish literacy and the Scottish identity: illiteracy and society in Scotland and northern England, 1600–1800*, Cambridge.

1988 *Literacy in early modern Europe: culture and education, 1500–1800*, London.

Houston, R. A., and Whyte, I. D. (eds.) 1989 *Scottish society, 1500–1800*, Cambridge.

Howe, E. 1943 *Newspaper printing in the nineteenth century*, London.

1947 *The London compositor: documents relating to wages, working conditions and customs of the London printing trade, 1785–1900*, London.

1950a *A list of London bookbinders, 1648–1815*, London.

1950b *The London bookbinders, 1780–1806*, London.

1981 'The Stationers' Company almanacks: a late eighteenth century printing and publishing operation', *Wolfenbüttel symposium on the book and the book trade in eighteenth century Europe*, Hamburg, 195–209.

Howe, E. and Child, J. 1952 *The Society of London Bookbinders*, London.

Howell, B. E. 1973. 'The historical demography of Wales: some notes on sources', *Local Historian*, 10, n.p.

Howell, D. W. 2000. *The rural poor in eighteenth-century Wales*, Cardiff.

Howell, T. B. (ed.) 1816–26 *A complete collection of state trials: and proceedings for high treason and other crimes and misdemeanors from the earliest period to the year 1783* . . . , 33 vols., London.

Howgego, J. 1978 *Printed maps of London, circa 1553–1850*, 2nd edn, Folkestone.

Howsam, L. 1991 *Cheap bibles: nineteenth-century publishing and the British and Foreign Bible Society*, Cambridge.

Howse, D. (ed.) 1990 *Background to discovery: Pacific exploration from Dampier to Cook*, Berkeley, CA.

Howse, E. M. 1953 *Saints in politics*, London.

Huber, W. (ed.) 2004 *The Corvey Library and Anglo-German cultural exchange*, Munich.

Hudson, A. 1993 'The grand Samuel Thornton *Sea-Atlas*: a monument to the Thames School of Chartmakers', *MC*, 65, 2–6.

Hudson, P. 1986 *The genesis of industrial capital: a study of the West Riding wool textile industry, c.1750–1850*, Cambridge.

Hullmandel, C. 1824 *The art of drawing on stone*, London.

Hume, D. 1739–40 *A treatise of human nature*, 3 vols., London.

1879 *History of England*, 6 vols., New York.

Hume, R. D. 2006 'The economics of culture in London, 1660–1740', *HLQ*, 69, 487–533.

Hume, R. D. (ed.) 1980 *The London theatre world, 1660–1800*, Carbondale, IL.

Humphries, C. and Smith, W. C. 1970 *Music publishing in the British Isles from the beginning until the middle of the nineteenth century: a dictionary of engravers, printers, publishers, and music sellers, with a historical introduction*, 2nd edn, Oxford.

Hunnisett, B. 1980a *A dictionary of British steel engravers*, Leigh-on-Sea.

1980b *Steel-engraved book illustration in England*, London.

Hunt, A. 2001 'The sale of Richard Heber's library', in Myers, Harris and Mandelbrote 2001, 143–71.

Hunt, A., Mandelbrote, G. and Shell, A. (eds.) 1997 *The book trade and its customers, 1450–1900: historical essays for Robin Myers*, Winchester.

Hunt, C. J. 1975 *The book trade in Northumberland and Durham to 1860: a biographical dictionary of printers, engravers, lithographers, booksellers, stationers, publishers, mapsellers, printsellers, music-sellers, bookbinders, newsagents and owners of circulating libraries*, Newcastle upon Tyne.

Hunt, E. H. 1986 'Industrialization and regional inequality: wages in Britain, 1760–1914', *JEcH*, 46, 935–66.

Hunt, L. (ed.) 1991 *Eroticism and the body politic*, Baltimore, MD.

1993 *The invention of pornography: obscenity and the origins of modernity, 1500–1800*, New York.

Hunt, M. 1993 'Racism, imperialism, and the traveler's gaze in eighteenth-century England', *Journal of British Studies*, 32, 33–57.

Hunt, R. W., Philip, I. G. and Roberts, R. J. (eds.) 1975 *Studies in the book trade: in honour of Graham Pollard*, Oxford.

Hunter, D. 1986 'Music copyright in Britain to 1800', *Music and Letters*, 67, 269–82.

1987 'Copyright protection for engravings and maps in eighteenth-century Britain', *Library*, 6th ser., 9, 128–47.

1989 'The printing of opera and song books in England, 1703–1726', *Notes*, 46, 328–51.

1990 'English country psalmodists and their publications, 1700–1760', *Journal of the Royal Musical Association*, 115, 220–39.

1991 'The publishing of opera and song books in England, 1703–1726', *Notes*, 47, 647–85.

(ed.) 1994 *Music publishing and collecting: essays in honor of Donald W. Krummel*, Urbana, IL.

1997 *Opera and song books published in England, 1703–1726: a descriptive bibliography*, London.
2002 'George Frideric Handel as victim: composer–publisher relations and the discourse of musicology', in Crawford and Wagstaff 2002, 663–92.
Hunter, D. and Mason, R. 1999 'Supporting Handel through subscription to publications: the lists of *Rodelinda* and *Faramondo* compared', *Notes*, 56, 27–93.
Hunter, J. (ed.) 1832 *Letters of eminent men, addressed to Ralph Thoresby, FRS*, 2 vols., London.
Hunter, J. P. 1990 *Before novels: the cultural contexts of eighteenth-century English fiction*, London.
Hunter, R. J. 1988 'Chester and the Irish book trade, 1681', *Irish Economic and Social History*, 15, 89–97.
Hunter, S. 1995 *Harriet Martineau: the poetics of moralism*, Aldershot.
Hurd, R. 1764 *Dialogues on the uses of foreign travel; considered as a part of an English gentleman's education: between Lord Shaftesbury and Mr Locke*, 2nd edn, London.
Hutchins, H. C. 1925 *Robinson Crusoe and its printing, 1719–1731*, New York.
Ibbetson, D. 1999 'Charles Viner and his chair: legal education in eighteenth-century Oxford', in Bush and Wijffels 1999, 315–28.
Illiano, R., Sala, L. and Sala, M. (eds.) 2002 *Muzio Clementi: studies and prospects*, Bologna.
Immel, A. 1990 *Revolutionary reviewing: Sarah Trimmer's Guardian of Education and the cultural politics of juvenile literature: an index to The Guardian*, Los Angeles, CA.
2000 'James Pettit Andrews's "Books" (1790): the first critical survey of English children's literature', *Children's Literature*, 28, 147–63.
Immel, A. and Witmore, M. (eds.) 2006 *Childhood and children's books in early modern Europe, 1550–1800*, London.
Inglis, R. M. G. 1960 *Gall & Inglis, publishers, 1810–1960*, Edinburgh.
Ingram, A. 1981 *Index to the archives of the House of Longman, 1794–1914*, Cambridge.
Innes, J. 1990 'Politics and morals: the reformation of manners movement in later eighteenth-century England', in Hellmuth 1990, 57–118.
1996 'The "mixed economy of welfare" in early modern England: assessments of the options from Hale to Malthus (*c*.1683–1803)', in Daunton 1996, 139–80.
1999 'The state and the poor: eighteenth-century England in European perspective', in Brewer and Hellmuth 1999, 225–80.
Isaac, P. C. G. 1968 *William Davison of Alnwick: pharmacist and printer, 1781–1858*, Oxford.
(ed.) 1990 *Six centuries of the provincial book trade in Britain*, Winchester.
1997 *William Lubbock and other Newcastle bookbinders*, Newcastle upon Tyne.
2001 'The English provincial book trade: a northern mosaic', *PBSA*, 95.
2005 'John Murray II and Oliver & Boyd, his Edinburgh agents', in Hinks and Armstrong 2005, 131–46.
Isaac, P. C. G., and McKay, B. (eds.) 1997 *Images and texts: their production and distribution in the 18th and 19th centuries*, Print Networks, Winchester.
1998 *The reach of print: making, selling and using books*, Print Networks, Winchester.
2000 *The mighty engine: the printing press and its impact*, Print Networks, Winchester.
2001 *The moving market: continuity and change in the book trade*, Print Networks, New Castle, DE.
Jackman, W. T. 1916 *The development of transportation in modern England*, Cambridge.
Jackson, I. 2003 'Print in provincial England: Reading and Northampton, 1720–1800', unpub. thesis, University of Oxford.

Jackson, J. and Chatto, W. A. 1861 *A treatise on wood engraving historical and practical*, 2nd edn, London.

Jackson, M. V. 1989 *Engines of instruction, mischief and magic: children's literature in England from its beginnings to 1839*, Aldershot.

Jackson, W. A. 1965 *An annotated list of the publications of the Reverend Thomas Frognall Dibdin, DD, based mainly on those in the Harvard College Library, with notes of others*, Cambridge.

Jacobs, E. 2003 'Eighteenth-century British circulating libraries and cultural book history', *Book History*, 6, 1–22.

Jacobs, E. and Forster, A. 1995 ' "Lost books" and publishing history: two annotated lists of imprints for the fiction titles listed in the circulating library catalogs of Thomas Lowndes (1766) and M. Heavisides (1790), of which no known copies survive', *PBSA* 89, 260–97.

Jacobs, W. M., and Yates, N. (eds.) 1993 *Crown and mitre: religion and society in northern Europe since the Reformation*, Woodbridge.

James, E. 1702 *Mrs James's reasons that printing may not be a free-trade*, London.

James, L. 1963 *Fiction for the working man, 1830–1850: a study of the literature produced for the working classes in early Victorian urban England*, London.

(ed.) 1976 *English popular literature, 1819–1851*, New York.

Jamieson, E. 1972 *English embossed bindings, 1825–1850*, Cambridge.

Janssens, U. 1975 *Matthieu Maty and the 'Journal britannique', 1750–1755: a French view of English literature in the middle of the eighteenth century*, Amsterdam.

Janssens-Knorsch, U. 1993 'A remarkable collection of English books in the Netherlands: the Bibliotheca Scheurleeriana', *Lias*, 20, 278–320.

Jarvis, R. C. 1955–9 'The archival history of the customs records', *Journal of the Society of Archivists*, 1, 239–50.

Jarvis, S. 1995 *Scholars and gentlemen: Shakespearian textual criticism and representations of scholarly labour, 1725–1765*, Oxford.

Jebb, R. C. 1889 *Bentley*, 2nd edn, London.

Jefcoate, G. 1995 'Joseph Downing and the publication of Pietist literature in England, 1705–1734', in Flood and Kelly 1995, 319–32.

1996 'Wilhelm Philipp Best und der Londoner Buchhandel: Ein deutscher Diplomat im Dienst der Universitätsbibliothek im 18. Jahrhundert', *Leipziger Jahrbuch zur Buchgeschichte*, 6, 199–210.

2004 'Charles Heydinger: a German bookseller in eighteenth-century London, 1766–1784', in Huber 2004, 35–53.

Jefcoate, G. and Kloth, K. 1987 *A catalogue of English books printed before 1801 held by the University Library at Göttingen*, Hildesheim.

Jenkins, G. H. 1998 'The eighteenth century', in Jones and Rees 1998, 109–22.

Johns, A. 1998 *The nature of the book: print and knowledge in the making*, Chicago, IL.

Johnson, D. 1971 'An eighteenth-century Scottish music library', *Research Chronicle: Royal Musical Association*, 9, 90–5.

Johnson, Jane 2001 *A very pretty story: facsimile of a manuscript held in the Bodleian Library*, Oxford.

Johnson, John 1824 *Typographia, or the printer's instructor*, 2 vols., London.

Johnson, J. de M. 1937 'The development of printing, other than book-printing', *Library*, 4th ser., 17, 22–35.

Johnson, J. de M., and Gibson, S. 1946 *Print and privilege at Oxford to the year 1700*, London.
Johnson, R. 1794 *New duty on paper. The paper-maker and stationers assistant.* London.
Johnson, S. 1905 *Lives of the English poets*, ed. G. B. Hill, 3 vols., Oxford.
1964 *Poems*, ed. E. L. McAdam and G. Milne, New Haven, CT.
1968 *Johnson on Shakespeare*, ed. A. Sherbo, intro. B. H. Bronson, vols. VII and VIII of the Yale Works of Samuel Johnson (paginated continuously), New Haven, CT.
1992 *The letters of Samuel Johnson, vol. I: 1731–1772*, ed. B. Redford, Oxford.
2006 *The lives of the most eminent English poets; with critical observations on their works*, ed. R. Londsdale, 4 vols., Oxford.
Jolly, D. C. 1990 *Maps in British periodicals*, pt. 1: *Major monthlies before 1800*, Brookline, MA.
1991 *Maps in British periodicals*, pt. 2: *Annuals, scientific periodicals and miscellaneous magazines mostly before 1800*, Brookline, MA.
Jones, E. L. 1973 'Fashion manipulators: consumer tastes and British industries, 1660–1800', in Cain and Uselding 1973, 198–226.
Jones, H. K. 1980 *Butterworths: history of a publishing house*, London.
Jones, M. G. 1938 *The charity school movement: a study of eighteenth century Puritanism in action*, Cambridge.
1939 'Two accounts of the Welsh Trust, 1675 and 1678(?)', *Bulletin of the Board of Celtic Studies*, 9, 71–80.
1952 *Hannah More*, Cambridge.
Jones, P. E., and Reddaway, T. F. (eds.) 1962–7 *The survey of building sites in the City of London after the Great Fire of 1666 by Peter Mills and John Oliver*, 5 vols., London.
Jones, P. H. 1998 'The Welsh Wesleyan Bookroom, 1824–8: a new set of printing accounts', in Isaac and McKay 1998, 37–49.
Jones, P. H., and Rees, E. (eds.) 1998 *A nation and its books: a history of the book in Wales*, Aberystwyth.
Jones, R. F. 1919 *Lewis Theobald: his contribution to English scholarship*, New York.
Jones, V. (ed.) 1999 *Women and literature in Britain, 1700–1800*, Cambridge.
Jones, W. 1850 *The Jubilee Memorial of the Religious Tract Society: containing a record of its origin, proceedings, and results. AD 1799 to AD 1849*, London.
Jordan, J. O., and Patten, R. L. 1955 *Literature in the marketplace: nineteenth-century British publishing and reading practices*, Cambridge.
Joslin, D. M. 1954 'London private bankers, 1720–1785', *EcHR*, n.s., 7, 167–86.
Joyce, H. 1893 *The history of the Post Office from its establishment down to 1836*, London.
Joyce, W. L., Hall, D. D., Brown, R. D. and Hench J. B. (eds.) 1983 *Printing and society in early America*, Worcester, MA.
Juvenal, H. *pseud.* 1793 *Modern manners, a poem: in two cantos.* London.
Kabir, A. M. F. 1987 *The libraries of Bengal, 1700–1947*, London.
Kafker, F. A. (ed.) 1981 *Notable encyclopedias of the seventeenth and eighteenth centuries: nine predecessors of the Encyclopédie*, for the Voltaire Foundation, Oxford.
1994 *Notable encyclopedias of the late eighteenth century: eleven successors of the Encyclopédie*, for the Voltaire Foundation, Oxford.
Kaplan, B. 1967 *An unhurried view of copyright*, New York.
Kaser, D. 1957 *Messrs Carey & Lea of Philadelphia*, Philadelphia, PA.
1963 *The cost book of Carey & Lea, 1825–1838*, Philadelphia, PA.
(ed.) 1966 *Books in America's past: essays honoring Rudolph H. Gjelsness*, Charlottesville, VA.

Kassler, M. 2004 *Music entries at Stationers' Hall, 1710–1818*, Aldershot.

Kastan, D. S. 1999 *A companion to Shakespeare*, Oxford.

Katz, S. N. (ed.) 1971 'A New York mission to England: the London letters of Lewis Morris to James Alexander, 1735 to 1736', *William and Mary Quarterly*, 28, 450–64.

Kaufman, P. 1960 *Borrowings from the Bristol library, 1773–1784: a unique record of reading vogues*, Charlottesville, VA.

1964 'English book clubs and their role in social history', *Libri*, 14, 1–31.

1967 'The community library: a chapter in English social history', in *Transactions of the American Philosophical Society*, 57, pt. 7, 3–67.

Keene, D., Burns, A. and Saint, A. (eds.) 2004 *St Paul's: the cathedral church of London, 604–2004*, London.

Keener, F. M., and Lorsch, S. E. (eds.) 1988 *Eighteenth-century women and the arts*, New York.

Keir, D. E. 1952 *The house of Collins: the story of a Scottish family of publishers from 1789 to the present day*, London.

Kenney, E. J. 1974 *The classical text: aspects of editing in the age of the printed book*, Berkeley, CA.

Kenny, S. S. 1976 'Perennial favorites: Congreve, Vanbrugh, Cibber, Farquhar, and Steele', *MP*, 73 (supplement), 4–11.

1980 'The publication of plays', in Hume 1980, 309–36.

Kent, D. A. 1994 'Small businessmen and their credit transactions in early nineteenth-century Britain', *BH*, 36, 47–64.

Ker, N. R. 1983 *William Hunter as a collector of medieval manuscripts*, Glasgow.

Kernan, A. B. 1987 *Printing technology, letters and Samuel Johnson*, Princeton, NJ.

Kerr, R. 1811 *Memoirs of the life, writings, and correspondence of William Smellie*, 2 vols., Edinburgh.

Kerridge, E. 1988 *Trade and banking in early modern England*, Manchester.

Kewes, P. 1995 '"Give me the sociable pocket-books ...": Humphrey Mosely's serial publication of octavo play collections', *PH*, 38, 5–21.

Keymer, T. and Sabor, P. (eds.) 2001 *The Pamela controversy: criticisms and adaptations of Samuel Richardson's Pamela, 1740–1750*, 6 vols., London.

2005 *'Pamela' in the marketplace: literary controversy and print culture in eighteenth-century Britain and Ireland*, Cambridge.

Kidson, F. 1967 (1900) *British music publishers, printers, and engravers: London, provincial, Scottish, and Irish: from Queen Elizabeth's reign to George the Fourth's, with select bibliographical lists of musical works printed and published within that period*, New York.

Kiessling, N. K. 2002 *The library of Anthony Wood*, Oxford.

Kimpel, D. (ed.) 1985 *Mehrsprachigkeit in der deutschen Aufklärung*, Hamburg.

Kinane, V. 1994 '"Literary food" for the American market: Patrick Byrne's exports to Mathew Carey', *Proceedings of the American Antiquarian Society*, 104, 315–32.

King, A. H. 1963 *Some British collectors of music, c.1600–1900*, Cambridge.

Kingsley, D. 1982 *Printed maps of Sussex, 1575–1900*, Lewes.

Kingsley, D. and Mann, S. 1972 'Playing cards depicting maps of the British Isles and of English and Welsh counties', *Map Collectors' Series*, 9, no. 87.

Kinnell, M. 1988 'Childhood and children's literature: the case of M. J. Godwin and Co., 1805–1825', *PH*, 24, 77–99.

Kirchoff, A. 1894 'Der Zeitpunkt des Wegbleibens der Holländer von der Leipziger Messe', *Archiv für Geschichte des Deutschen Buchhandels*, 17, 363–5.

Kirkpatrick, F. A. 1916 'The literature of travel, 1700–1900', in Ward and Waller 1916, 240–56.

Kirsop, W. and Sherlock, M. (eds.) 2007 *The Commonwealth of books: essays and studies in honour of Ian Willison*, Melbourne.

Klancher, J. P. 1987 *The making of English reading audiences, 1790–1832*, Madison, WI.

Klein, L. 1995 'Politeness for plebes: consumption and social identity in early eighteenth-century England', in Bermingham and Brewer 1995, 362–82.

Kleinschmidt, J. R. 1948 *Les imprimeurs et libraires de la République de Genève, 1700–1798*, Geneva.

Klippel, F. 1994 *Englischlernen im 18. und 19. Jahrhundert: Die Geschichte der Lehrbücher und Unterrichtsmethoden*, Münster.

Knapp, L. M. 1932 'Smollett's works as printed by William Strahan, with an unpublished letter of Smollett to Strahan', *Library*, 4th ser., 13, 282–91.

1958 'Griffiths's "Monthly Review" as printed by Strahan', *N&Q*, n.s., 5, 216–17.

Knight, C. 1834 *The printing machine*, vol. I, London.

1854 *The old printer and the modern press*, London.

1864 *Passages of a working life during half a century*, 3 vols., London.

1865 *Shadows of the old booksellers*, London.

Knight, F. 1995 *The nineteenth-century church and English society*, Cambridge.

Knott, D. 1973–4 'Aspects of research into English provincial printing', *JPHS*, 9, 6–21.

Koenig, F. and Bauer, A. F. 1851 *The first printing machines constructed in London up to the year 1818 by Friedrich Koenig and Andreas Friedrich Bauer*, Leipzig.

Kogan, H. 1958 *The great EB: the story of the Encyclopaedia Britannica*, Chicago, IL.

Korshin, P. J. 1973–4 'Types of eighteenth-century literary patronage', *ECS*, 7, 453–73.

(ed.) 1976 *The widening circle: essays on the circulation of literature in eighteenth-century Europe*, Philadelphia, PA.

Koss, S. 1981 *The rise and fall of the political press in Britain*, vol. I: *The nineteenth century*, London.

Kossmann, E. F. 1935–6 'Haagsche uitgevers van de zeventiende en achttiende eeuw. III: Pierre Gosse senior', *Het Boek*, 23, 223–41.

1937 *De boekhandel te 's-Gravenhage tot het eind van de achttiende eeuw*, The Hague.

Kramnick, J. B. 1998 *Making the English canon: print capitalism and the cultural post, 1700–1770*, Cambridge.

Krill, J. 1987 *English artist's paper: Renaissance to Regency*, London.

2002 *English artists' paper: Renaissance to Regency*, 2nd edn, New Castle, DE.

Kruif, J. de. 1999 *Liefhebbers en gewoontelezers. Leescultuur in Den Haag in de achttiende eeuw*. Zutphen.

2001 'Classes of readers: owners of books in 18th-century The Hague', *Poetics* 28, 423–53.

Krummel, D. W. 1975 *English music printing, 1553–1700*, London.

1990 'Searching and sorting on the slippery slope: periodical publication of Victorian music', *Notes*, 46, 593–608.

1992 *The literature of music bibliography: an account of the writings on the history of music printing and publishing*, Berkeley, CA.

Krummel, D. W., and Sadie, S. (eds.) 1990 *Music printing and publishing*, Basingstoke.

Kunzle, D. 1990 *The history of the comic strip: the nineteenth century*, Berkeley, CA.

Kurtz, R. J. and Womer, J. L. 2004 'The novel as political marker: women writers and their female audiences in the Hookham and Carpenter Archives, 1791–1798', *Cardiff Corvey:*

Reading the Romantic Text, online journal, issue 13, www.cf.ac.uk/encap/corvey/articles/cc13_n02.html.

Lackington, J. 1792 *Memoirs of the first forty-five years of the life of James Lackington*, London.

Lady, A 1791 *Retaliation; or, the reviewers review'd. A satirical poem*, by a lady, London.

Laeven, A. H. 1992 'The Frankfurt and Leipzig bookfairs and the history of the Dutch booktrade in the seventeenth and eighteenth centuries', in Berkvens-Stevelinck *et al.* 1992, 185–98.

La Fontaine, A. H. J. 1797 *Clara Duplessis and Clairant: the history of a family of French emigrants. Translated from the German*, 3 vols., London.

Lambert, F. 1994 *Pedlar in divinity: George Whitefield and the transatlantic revivals, 1737–1770*, Princeton, NJ.

Lambert, J. A. 2001 *A nation of shopkeepers: trade ephemera from 1654 to the 1860s in the John Johnson collection*, exhibition catalogue, Oxford.

Lambert, S. 1968 'Printing for the House of Commons in the eighteenth century', *Library*, 5th ser., 23, 25–46.

Lancaster, W. T. (ed.) 1912 *Letters addressed to Ralph Thoresby, FRS*, Leeds.

Landon, R. G. (ed.) 1978 *Bookselling and book buying: aspects of the nineteenth century British and North American book trade*, Chicago, IL.

1995a 'The antiquarian book trade in Britain, 1695–1830', *PBSA*, 89, 409–17.

1995b 'The two Jameses: Edwards and Lackington', *Descant*, 91, 53–74.

2002 'The library of King George III', *Halcyon*, 29, 6–7.

Landseer, J. 1807 *Lectures on the art of engraving*, London.

Langford, P. 1989 *A polite and commercial people: England, 1727–1783*, Oxford.

1991 *Public life and the propertied Englishman, 1689–1798*, Oxford.

Langley, L. 1990 'The musical press in nineteenth-century England', *Notes*, 46, 583–92.

Langton, J. 2000 'Urban growth and economic change: from the late seventeenth century to 1841', in Palliser, Clark and Daunton 2001, II, 453–90.

Lankhorst, O. S. 1983 *Reinier Leers, 1654–1714, uitgever en boekverkoper te Rotterdam: een Europees 'libraire' en zijn fonds*, Amsterdam.

Laqueur, T. 1974 'Debate: literacy and social mobility in the Industrial Revolution in England', *P&P*, 64, 96–107.

1976 *Religion and respectability: Sunday schools and working class culture, 1780–1850*, New Haven, CT.

Larminie, V. 2002 'New *DNB* and early modern women's lives?', conference paper at *Early modern lives: biography and autobiography: Renaissance and seventeenth century*, London, 27 June.

Laugher, C. T. 1973 *Thomas Bray's grand design: libraries of the Church of England in America, 1695–1785*, Chicago, IL.

Lawrence, S. C. 1996 *Charitable knowledge; hospital pupils and practitioners in eighteenth-century London*, Cambridge.

Lawson, J. and Silver, H. 1973 *A social history of education in England*, London.

Ledsham, I. 1999 *A catalogue of the Shaw-Hellier collection in the music library, Barber Institute of Fine Arts, the University of Birmingham*, Aldershot.

Lee, A. J. 1976 *The origins of the popular press in England, 1855–1915*, London.

Lee, J. 1824 *Memorial for the Bible Societies in Scotland; containing remarks on the complaint of His Majesty's Printers against the Marquis of Huntly and others*, Edinburgh.

Leedham-Green, E. S. 1973 *A guide to the archives of the Cambridge University Press*, Bishops Stortford.

1986 *Books in Cambridge inventories: book-lists from the Vice-Chancellor's Court probate inventories in the Tudor and Stuart periods*, 2 vols., Cambridge.

Le Gal, S. 1952 'En marge de l'exposition du "livre anglais": l'Homère de Pope', *Bulletin du bibliophile*, n.s., 1, 49–54.

Legh, E. C., Baroness Newton 1925 *Lyme letters, 1660–1760*, London.

Legros, L. A., and Grant, J. C. 1916 *Typographical printing surfaces: the technology and mechanism of their production*, London.

Lemmings, D. 2000 *Professors of the law: barristers and English legal culture in the eighteenth century*, Oxford.

Lennon, C. 2006 'The print trade, 1700–1800', in Gillespie and Hadfield 2006, 74–87.

Lennox-Boyd, C. A. *et al.* 1994 *Theatre in the age of Garrick: English mezzotints from the collection of the Hon. Christopher Lennox-Boyd*, London.

Lessenich, R. P. 1972 *Elements of pulpit oratory in eighteenth-century England (1660–1800)*, Cologne.

Levine, J. M. 1991 *The battle of the books: history and literature in the Augustan age*, Ithaca, NY.

Lewine, J. 1969 (1898) *Bibliography of eighteenth century art and illustrated books: being a guide to collectors of illustrated works in English and French of the period*, London.

Lewis, J. 1739 *A complete history of the several translations of the Holy Bible, and New Testament, into English, both in MS and print: and of the most remarkable editions of them since the invention of printing*, 2nd edn, London.

Lewis, J. 1962 *Printed ephemera: the changing use of type and letterforms in English and American printing*, Ipswich.

Lewis, S. 1837 *A topographical dictionary of Ireland*, 2 vols., London.

Li, M.-H. 1963 *The great recoinage of 1696 to 1699*, London.

Lillywhite, B. 1963 *London coffee houses: a reference book of coffee houses of the seventeenth, eighteenth and nineteenth centuries*, London.

Linebaugh, P. 1991 *The London hanged: crime and civil society in the eighteenth century*, London.

Lipking, L. I. 1981 *The life of the poet: beginning and ending poetic careers*, Chicago, IL.

1998 *Samuel Johnson: the life of an author*, Cambridge, MA.

Lippincott, L. 1983 *Selling art in Georgian London: the rise of Arthur Pond*, New Haven, CT.

1988 'Arthur Pond's journal of receipts and expenses, 1734–1750', *Walpole Society*, 54.

Littlefield, G. E. 1900 *Early Boston booksellers, 1642–1711*, Boston, MA.

Lobban, M. 1991 *The common law and English jurisprudence 1760–1850*, Oxford.

1997 'The English legal treatise and English law in the eighteenth century', in Dauchy, Monballyu and Wijffels 1997, 69–88.

Locke, J. 1968 *The educational writings of John Locke*, ed. J. L. Axtell, Cambridge.

Lockyer, C. 1711 *An account of the trade in India*, London.

Lockyer, D. 1977 'The provision of books and libraries by the East India Company in India, 1611–1858', unpub. thesis, Library Association, London.

London Magazine 1732–66 *Monthly catalogues from the London Magazine 1732–66 with the index for 1732–58 compiled by Edward Kimber 1966*, English Bibliographical Sources series, London.

Long, J. 1848 *Hand-book of Bengal missions, in connexion with the Church of England*, London.

Longman, C. J. 1936 *The house of Longman, 1724–1800*, ed. by J. E. Chandler, London.

Lonsdale, R. 1961 'William Bewley and *The Monthly Review*: a problem of attribution', *PBSA*, 55, 309–18.
(ed.) 1969 *The poems of Gray, Collins and Goldsmith*, London.
Loonen, P. L. M. 1991 *For to learne to buye and sell: learning English in the Low Dutch area between 1500 and 1800: a critical survey*, Amsterdam.
Looney, J. J. 1983 'Advertising and society in England 1720–1820: a statistical analysis of Yorkshire newspaper advertisements', unpub. thesis, Princeton University.
Lorch, J. 1990 *Mary Wollstonecraft: the making of a radical feminist and the public sphere*, New York.
Loudon, J. H. 1980 *James Scott and William Scott, bookbinders*, London.
Love, H. 1993 *Scribal publication in seventeenth-century England*, Oxford.
2003 'Early modern print culture: assessing the models', *Parergon*, 20, 45–64.
Love, H. D. 1913 *Vestiges of old Madras, 1640–1800, from the East India Company records at Fort St George and the India Office, and from other source*, 4 vols., London.
Lubbers-Van Der Brugge, C. J. M. 1951 *Johnson and Baretti: some aspects of eighteenth-century literary life in England and Italy*, Groningen.
Luckett, R. 1981 'Bishop Challoner: the devotionary writer', in Duffy 1981, 71–89.
Luckombe, P. 1770 *A concise history of the origin and progress of printing; with practical instructions to the trade in general, compiled from those who have wrote on this curious art*, London.
Lustig, I. S., and Pottle, F. A. (eds.) 1986 *Boswell: the English experiment, 1785–1789*, London.
Lyell, Sir C. 1997 *Principles of geology*, ed. J. A. Secord, London.
Lyles, A. and Perkins, D. 1989 *Colour into line: Turner and the art of engraving*, London.
Lynam, E. (ed.) 1946 *Richard Hakluyt and his successors*, London.
Lynch, K. M. 1971 *Jacob Tonson: Kit-Cat publisher*, Knoxville, TN.
Lynch, M. 1989 'Continuity and change in urban society, 1500–1700', in Houston and Whyte 1989, 85–117.
MacAdam, R. I. 1858 'Six hundred Gaelic proverbs collected in Ulster', *Ulster Journal of Archaeology*, 1st ser., 6, 172–83.
McAnear, B. 1949 'William Bradford and the Book of Common Prayer', *PBSA*, 43, 101–10.
Macaulay, C. 1774 *A modest plea for the property of copyright*, Bath.
Macaulay, T. B. 1896–7 *Life and works of Lord Macaulay*, 10 vols., London.
McBurney, W. H. 1960 *A check list of English prose fiction, 1700–1739*, Cambridge, MA.
McCalman, I. D. 1984 'A radical underworld in early nineteenth century London: Thomas Evans, Robert Wedderburn, George Cannon and their circle, 1800–1835', unpub. thesis, Monash University.
1988 *Radical underworld: prophets, revolutionaries and pornographers in London, 1795–1840*, Cambridge.
McCarra, K. and Whyte, H. (eds.) 1990 *A Glasgow collection: essays in honour of Joe Fisher*, Glasgow.
McCarthy, W. 1997 'The celebrated academy at Palgrave: a documentary history of Anna Letitia Barbauld's school', *Age of Johnson*, 8, 279–392.
1999 'Mother of all discourses: Anna Barbauld's *Lessons for children*', *Princeton University Library Chronicle*, 60, 196–219.
McClure, E. (ed.) 1888 *A chapter in English church history: being the minutes of the Society for Promoting Christian Knowledge for the years 1698–1704*, London.

McCorison, M. A. 1991 'The Jayne Lecture. Humanists and byte-sized bibliography. Or, how to digest expanding sources of information', *Proceedings of the American Philosophical Society* 135, 61–72.

McCorkle, B. 1994 'The maps of Patrick Gordon's *Geography anatomiz'd*: an eighteenth-century success story', *MC*, 66, 10–15.

McCoy, R. E. 1968 *Freedom of the press: an annotated bibliography*, Carbondale, IL.

McCusker, J. J. 1985 *European bills of entry and marine lists: early commercial publications and the origins of the business press*, Cambridge, MA.

1986 'The business press in England before 1775', *Library*, 6th ser., 8, 205–31.

1991 'The early history of "Lloyd's List"', *Historical Research: The Bulletin of the Institute of Historical Research*, 64, October, 427–31.

1996 'The role of Antwerp in the emergence of commercial and financial newspapers in early modern Europe', in *La ville et la transmission des valeurs culturelles au bas Moyen Age et aux temps moderne* ..., Gemeentekrediet van België/Crédit Communal de Belgique, Collection Histoire, 96, 303–32, Brussels.

1997 *Essays in the economic history of the Atlantic world*, London.

2001a 'Comparing the purchasing power of money in Great Britain from 1264 to any other year including the present,' Economic History Services, www.eh.net/hmit/ppowerbp.

2001b *How much is that in real money? A historical price index for use as a deflator of money values in the economy of the United States*, 2nd edn., revised and enlarged, Worcester, MA.

2005 'The demise of distance: the business press and the origins of the information revolution in the early modern Atlantic world', *American Historical Review*, 105, 295–321.

McCusker, J. J., and Gravesteijn, C. 1991 *The beginnings of commercial and financial journalism: the commodity price currents, exchange rate currents, and money currents of early modern Europe*, Amsterdam.

McDougall, W. 1974 'Gavin Hamilton, John Balfour and Patrick Neill: a study of publishing in Edinburgh in the 18th century', unpub. thesis, Edinburgh University.

1978 'Gavin Hamilton, bookseller in Edinburgh', *British Journal for Eighteenth-Century Studies*, 1, 1–19.

1988 'Copyright litigation in the Court of Session, 1738–1749, and the rise of the Scottish book trade', *EBST*, 5, 2–31.

1990a 'A catalogue of Hamilton, Balfour and Neill publications, 1750–1762', in Myers and Harris 1990, 187–232.

1990b 'Scottish books for America in the mid-18th century', in Myers and Harris 1990, 21–46.

1997 'Smugglers, reprinters and hot pursuers: the Irish–Scottish book trade, and copyright prosecutions in the late eighteenth century', in Myers and Harris 1997, 151–83.

2002 'Charles Elliot's medical publications and the international book trade', in Withers and Wood 2002, 215–54.

2004 'Charles Elliot's book adventure in Philadelphia, and the trouble with Thomas Dobson', in Mckay, Bell and Hinks 2004, 197–212.

McDowell, P. 1998 *The women of Grub Street: press, politics and gender in the London literary marketplace, 1678–1730*, Oxford.

1999 'Women and the business of print', in Jones 1999, 135–54.

Mace, N. 1996 'Haydn and the London music sellers: Forster *v*. Longman & Broderip', *Music and Letters*, 77, 527–41.

1999 'Litigating the *Musical Magazine*: the definition of British music copyright in the 1780s', *Book History*, 2, 122–45.

McEwen, G. D. 1972 *The oracle of the coffee house: John Dunton's Athenian Mercury*, San Marino, CA.

McGann, Jerome J. 1991 *The textual condition*. Princeton, NJ.

MacGregor, A. 1994 *Sir Hans Sloane: collector, scientist, antiquary, founding father of the British Museum*, London.

McInnes, A. 1988 'The emergence of a leisure town: Shrewsbury, 1660–1760', *P & P*, 120, 53–87.

McIntosh, C. 1998 *The evolution of English prose, 1700–1800: style, politeness, and print culture*, Cambridge.

Mack, M. 1985 *Alexander Pope: a life*, New Haven, CT.

Mackarill, D. 2002 'George Gitton and George Robert Gitton, printers, Bridgnorth', *JPHS*, n.s., 4, 31–61.

McKay, B. 1996 'The daybooks of John Ware of Whitehaven', *Quadrat*, 4, 16–18.

2000 'John Ware, printer and bookseller of Whitehaven: a year from his day-books', in Isaac and McKay 2000, 163–74.

2002 'Books in eighteenth-century Whitehaven', in McKay, Bell and Hinks 2004, 51–60.

McKay, B., Bell, M. and Hinks, J. (eds.) 2004 *Light on the book trade: essays in honour of Peter Isaac*, Print Networks, New Castle, DE.

McKendrick, N. 1982 'Commercialization and the economy', in McKendrick, Brewer and Plumb 1982, 9–194.

McKendrick, N., Brewer, J. and Plumb, J. H. 1982 *The birth of a consumer society: the commercialisation of eighteenth-century England*, London.

McKenzie, D. F. 1966 *The Cambridge University Press, 1699–1712: a bibliographical study*, 2 vols., Cambridge.

1969 'Printers of the mind: some notes on bibliographical theories and printing-house practices', *SB*, 22, 1–75.

1974a 'The London book trade in 1668', *WORDS: Wai-te-ata Studies in Literature*, 4, 75–92.

1974b *Stationers' Company apprentices, 1641–1700*, Oxford.

1976 'The London book trade in the later seventeenth century', the Sanders Lectures 1975–6, unpub., copies in various libraries.

1978 *Stationers' Company apprentices, 1701–1800*, Oxford.

1984 'Stretching a point: or, the case of the spaced-out comps', in *SB*, 37, 106–21.

1988 'Bibliography and history: seventeenth-century England', the Lyell Lectures, University of Oxford, typescripts circulated privately.

1992 'The London book trade in 1644', in Horden 1992, 131–51.

McKenzie, D. F., and Ross, J. C. (eds.) 1968 *A ledger of Charles Ackers, printer of 'The London Magazine'*, Oxford.

McKenzie, E. C. 1997 *A catalog of British devotional and religious books in German translation from the Reformation to 1750*, Berlin.

McKeon, M. 1987 *The origins of the English novel, 1600–1740*, Baltimore, MD.

McKerrow, R. B. (ed.) 1910 *A dictionary of printers and booksellers in England, Scotland and Ireland, and of foreign printers of English books, 1557–1640*, London.

1928 *An introduction to bibliography for literary students*, 2nd edn, Oxford.

McKillop, A. D. 1936 *Samuel Richardson, printer and novelist*, Chapel Hill, NC.

Mackintosh, R. J. (ed.) 1836 *Memoirs of the life of the Right Honourable Sir James Mackintosh*, 2 vols., London.

McKitterick, D. 1986 *Cambridge University Library: a history. The eighteenth and nineteenth centuries*, Cambridge.

1992 *A history of Cambridge University Press*, vol. I: *Printing and the book trade in Cambridge, 1534–1698*, Cambridge.

1998 *A history of Cambridge University Press*, vol. II: *Scholarship and commerce, 1698–1872*, Cambridge.

2001 'Credit, cash and customers: Cornelius Crownfield and Anglo Dutch trade in the early eighteenth century', in Hellinga *et al.* 2001, 245–53.

2003 *Print, manuscript, and the search for order*, Cambridge.

Macky, J. 1714–22 *A journey through England*, 2 vols., London.

McLachlan, H. 1923 *The story of a nonconformist library*, Manchester.

1931 *English education under the Test Acts; being the history of the non-conformist academies, 1662–1820*, Manchester.

1934 *The Unitarian movement in the religious life of England: its contribution to thought and learning, 1700–1900*, London.

McLaverty, J. 1993 'The contract for Pope's translation of Homer's *Iliad*', *Library*, 6th ser., 15, 206–25.

2001 *Pope, print, and meaning*, Oxford.

McLean, H. A. 1914 *Robert Urie, printer in Glasgow c.1711–1771, with a handlist of books printed for him*, Glasgow.

McLeod, W. R., and McLeod, V. B. 1982 *A graphical directory of English newspapers and periodicals, 1702–1714*, Morgantown, WV.

McMullin, B. J. 1984 'The Vinegar Bible', *BC*, 33, 53–65.

1993 'T. Johnson, bookseller in The Hague', in Harvey, Kirsop and McMullin 1993, 99–112.

1996 'Extinguishing the fire at Dod's warehouse in 1762', *BC*, 45, 476–84.

1998 'Creating a good impression at the Oxford Bible Press in 1743', *SB*, 51, 205–12.

Macnair, M. 1994 'Sir Jeffrey Gilbert and his treatises', *Journal of Legal History*, 15, 252–68.

McNaughton, A. 1990 'A century of Saltmarket literature, 1790–1890', in Isaac 1990, 165–80.

Madden, L. (ed.) 1972 *Robert Southey, the critical heritage*, London.

Maddison, A. 1982 *Phases of capitalist development*, Oxford.

Madras Record Office 1911–70 *Despatches from England (Records of Fort St George)*, 61 vols., Madras.

Magnuson, P. 1998 *Reading public romanticism*, Princeton, NJ.

Mahony, R. and Rizzo, B. W. 1984 *Christopher Smart: an annotated bibliography, 1743–1983*, New York.

Maidment, B. 1992 *Into the 1830s: some origins of Victorian illustrated journalism*, Manchester.

Malcolm, J. P. 1810–11 *Anecdotes of the manners and customs of London during the eighteenth century*, 2nd edn, 3 vols., London.

Malthus, T. R. 1986 (1826) *The works of Thomas Robert Malthus*, vol. II: *An essay on the principle of population*, ed. E. A. Wrigley and D. Souden, London.

Mandal, A. A. 2006 'Making Austen mad: Benjamin Crosby and the non-publication of *Susan*', *RES*, 57, 507–25.

Mandelbrote, G. 1995 'From the warehouse to the counting-house: booksellers and bookshops in late 17th century London', in Myers and Harris 1995, 49–84.

1997 'Richard Bentley's copies: the ownership of copyrights in the late 17th century', in Hunt, Mandelbrote and Shell 1997, 55–94.

2001 'The organization of book auctions in late seventeenth-century London', in Myers, Harris and Mandelbrote 2001, 15–50.

2003 'Workplaces and living spaces: London book trade inventories of the late seventeenth century', in Myers, Harris and Mandelbrote 2003, 21–43.

Mandelbrote, S. 1997 'John Baskett, the Dublin booksellers, and the printing of the Bible, 1710–1724', in Hunt, Mandelbrote and Shell 1997, 115–31.

1998 'The Bible and national identity in the British Isles, *c.*1650–*c.*1750', in Claydon and McBride 1998, 157–81.

2001 'The English Bible and its readers in the eighteenth century', in Rivers 2001, 35–78.

Manguel, A. 1996 *A history of reading*, London.

Mann, A. J. 1998 'Book commerce, litigation and the art of monopoly: the case of Agnes Campbell, Royal Printer, 1676–1712', *Scottish Economic and Social History*, 18, 1, 132–56.

2000 *The Scottish book trade, 1500–1720: print commerce and print control in early modern Scotland*, East Linton.

2001 'The anatomy of the printed book in early modern Scotland', *The Scottish Historical Review* 80, 181–200.

Marishall, J. 1789 *A series of letters*, 2nd edn, 2 vols., London.

Marks, J. G. 1984 'Bookbinding in London about 1810: a German visitor's view', *BC*, 33, 449–56.

Marks, P. J. M. 1998 'The Edwards of Halifax bindery', *BLJ*, 24, 184–218.

Marotti, A. F. 1986 *John Donne, coterie poet*, Madison, WI.

Marr, G. S. 1924 *The periodical essayists of the eighteenth century*, London.

Marriner, S. 1980 'English bankruptcy records and statistics before 1850', *EcHR* 33, 351–66.

Marsh, J. 1998 *The John Marsh journals: the life and times of a gentleman composer (1752–1828)*, ed. B. Robins, Stuyvesant, NY.

Martin, P. 1995 *Edmond Malone: Shakespearean scholar, a literary biography*, Cambridge.

Maslen, K. I. D. 1969 'Edition quantities for *Robinson Crusoe*, 1719', *Library*, 5th ser., 145–50.

1971 'Printing charges: evidence and inference', *SB* 24, 91–98.

1972 'Printing for the author: from the Bowyer printing ledgers, 1710–1775', *Library*, 5th ser., 27, 302–9.

1992 'An editorial impasse: the Dawks–Bowyer–Nichols printers' notebooks', *BSANZB*, 16, 107–16.

1993 *An early London printing house at work: studies in the Bowyer Ledgers*, New York.

Maslen, K. I. D., and Lancaster, J. (eds.) 1991 *The Bowyer Ledgers: the printing accounts of William Bowyer, father and son, reproduced on microfiches: with a checklist of Bowyer printing, 1699–1777, a commentary, indexes, and appendixes*, London.

Mathias, P. 1969 *The first industrial nation: an economic history of Britain, 1700–1914*, London.

1979 *The transformation of England: essays in the economic and social history of England in the eighteenth century*, London.

1993 (1959) *The brewing industry in England, 1700–1830*, Aldershot.

Mathison, H. 1999 'Tropes of promotion and wellbeing: advertisement and the eighteenth-century Scottish periodical press', in Raymond 1999a, 206–25.

Matthews, W. 1950 *British diaries: an annotated bibliography of British diaries written between 1442 and 1942*, Berkeley, CA.

Maurer, M. 1987 *Aufklärung und Anglophilie in Deutschland*, Göttingen.

Maxted, I. 1977 *The London book trades, 1775–1800: a preliminary checklist of members*, Folkestone.

1980 *The London book trades, 1775–1800: a topographical guide, including a correction of major errors in the author's Preliminary checklist of members*, Exeter working papers in British book trade history 1, Exeter.

1996 *Newspaper readership in south west England: an analysis of the 'Flindell's Western Luminary' subscription list of 1815*, Exeter.

Maxwell, M. W. 1974 'The development of law publishing, 1799–1974', in Sweet and Maxwell 1974, 121–48.

Maxwell, W. H., and Maxwell, L. F. 1955 *A legal bibliography of the British commonwealth of nations*, vol. I: *English law to 1800*, 2nd edn, London.

May, A. 1996 'Making Moxon's mould', *JPHS*, 40, 15–23.

May, J. E. 1984 'On the inclusiveness of descriptive bibliographies: limitations of bibliographical catalogues like the *ESTC*', *Analytical and Enumerative Bibliography*, 8, 227–38.

1999 'Women as publishers, readers and writers', *East-Central Intelligencer*, 13, 45–8.

2001 'Who will edit the *ESTC*? (and have you checked OCLC lately?)', *Analytical and Enumerative Bibliography*, n.s., 12, 288–304.

Mayer, R. 1993–4 'Nathaniel Crouch, bookseller and historian: popular historiography and cultural power in the late 17th century', *ECS*, 27, 391–429.

Mayo, R. D. 1962 *The English novel in the magazines, 1740–1815; with a catalogue of 1375 magazine novels and novelettes*, Evanston, IL.

Melton, F. 1985 'Robert and Sir Francis Gosling: eighteenth-century bankers and stationers', in Myers and Harris 1985, 60–77.

Melton, J. van H. 2001 'The rise of the public in Enlightenment Europe', in *New approaches to European history*, Cambridge.

Memoirs of Literature 1722 *Memoirs of literature, containing a large account of many valuable books, letters and dissertations upon several subjects, miscellaneous overservations, &c.*, 8 vols., 2nd edn, London.

Mercer, M. 2001 'Dissenting academies and the education of the laity, 1750–1850', *History of Education*, 30, 35–58.

Mersey, Viscount C. C. B. 1928 *The Roxburghe Club, its history and its members, 1812–1927*, Oxford.

Merton, R. K. 1965 *On the shoulders of giants: a Shandean postscript*, New York.

Meyen, F. 1957 *Johann Joachim Eschenburg, 1743–1820, Professor am Collegium Carolinum zu Braunschweig: Kurzer Abriß seines Lebens und Schaffens nebst Bibliographie*, Braunschweiger Werkstücke: Veröffentlichungen aus Archiv, Biblothek und Museum der Stadt, 20, Braunschweig.

Michie, R. C. 1999 *The London Stock Exchange: a history*, Oxford.

Michon, J. and Mollier, J.-Y. (eds.) 2001 *Les mutations du livre et de l'édition dans le monde du XVIIIe siècle à l'an 2000*, Saint-Nicolas, Quebec.

Middleton, B. C. 1978 *A history of English craft bookbinding technique*, London.

1996 *A history of English craft bookbinding technique*, 4th edn, London.

Mijers, E. 2002 'Scotland and the United Provinces, c. 1680–1730: a study in intellectual and educational relations', unpub. thesis, University of St Andrews.

Miles, A. and Vincent, D. (eds.) 1993 *Building European society: occupational change and social mobility in Europe, 1840–1940*, Manchester.

Milhous, J., Dideriksen, D. and Hume, R. D. 2001 *Italian opera in late eighteenth-century London*, vol. II: *The Pantheon Opera and its aftermath*, Oxford.

Milhous, J. and Hume, R. D. 1994 'The Drury Lane Theatre library in 1768', *YULG*, 68, 116–34.

1999 'Playwrights' remuneration in eighteenth-century London', *HLB*, n.s., 10, nos. 2–3.

Millar, A. forthcoming *Bookseller of the Enlightenment: the correspondence, business ledgers, and legal briefs of Andrew Millar*, ed. by A. Budd, Oxford.

Millburn, J. R. 1976 *Benjamin Martin: author, instrument maker, and 'country showman'*, Leiden

1988 *Wheelwright of the heavens: the life and work of James Ferguson, FRS*, London.

2000 *Adams of Fleet Street: instrument makers to King George III*, Aldershot.

Miller, C. W. 1974 *Benjamin Franklin's Philadelphia printing*, Philadelphia, PA.

Miller, E. 1967 *Prince of librarians: the life and times of Antonio Panizzi of the British Museum*, Athens, OH.

Miller, E. H. 1959 *The professional writer in Elizabethan England: a study on nondramatic literature*, Cambridge, MA.

Millgate, J. 1984 *Walter Scott: the making of the novelist*, Toronto.

1987 *Scott's last edition: a study in publishing history*, Edinburgh.

1996 'Archibald Constable and the problem of London: "Quite the connection we have been looking for"', *Library*, 6th ser., 18, 110–23.

Milton, J. 1758 *Paradise lost*, Birmingham.

Mineka, F. E. 1944 *The dissidence of dissent: 'The Monthly Repository', 1806–1838 . . . with a chapter on religious periodicals, 1700–1825*, Chapel Hill, NC.

Mish, C. C. 1967 *English prose fiction, 1600–1700: a chronological checklist*, 3 parts, Charlottesville, VA.

Mitch, D. F. 1992 *The rise of popular literacy in Victorian England: the influence of private choice and public policy*, Philadelph, PA.

1993a '"Inequalities which every one may remove": occupational recruitment, endogamy, and the homogeneity of social origins in Victorian England', in Miles and Vincent 1993, 140–64.

1993b 'The role of human capital in the first Industrial Revolution', in Mokyr 1993, 267–307.

2004 'Education and skill of the British labour force', in Floud and Johnson 332–56.

Mitchell, B. R., and Deane, P. 1962 *Abstract of British historical statistics*, Cambridge.

Mitchell, C. J. 1985. 'The spread and fluctuation of eighteenth-century printing', *Studies on Voltaire and the Eighteenth Century*, 230, 305–21.

1987 'Provincial printing in eighteenth-century Britain', *PH*, 21, 5–25.

Mitchell, L. C. 2001 *Grammar wars: language as cultural battlefield in 17th- and 18th-century England*, Aldershot.

Mitchie, R. C. 1999 *The London Stock Exchange: a history*, Oxford.

Moir, D. G. 1973–83 'A history of Scottish maps', in Royal Scottish Geographical Society 1973–83, vol. I.

Mokyr, J. (ed.) 1993 *The British industrial revolution: an economic perspective*, Boulder, CO.

Momoro, A. F. 1793 *Traité élémentaire de l'imprimerie*, Paris.

Monk, R. C. 1966 *John Wesley: his puritan heritage*, London.

Monkman, K. 1970 'The bibliography of the early editions of Tristram Shandy', *Library*, 5th ser., 25, 11–39.

Montagu, Lady M. W. 1993 *Essays and poems and 'Simplicity', a comedy*, ed. R. Halsband and I. Grundy, 2nd edn, Oxford.

Montgomery, F. M. 1970 *Printed textiles: English and American cottons and linens, 1700–1850*, London.

Moon, M. 1990 *Benjamin Tabart's juvenile library: a bibliography of books for children published, written, edited and sold by Mr Tabart, 1801–1820*, Winchester.

1992 *John Harris's books for youth, 1801–1843*, rev. edn, Folkestone.

Moore, J. N. 1985 'Scotland's first sea atlas', *MC*, 30, 30–4.

1991 *The historical cartography of Scotland: a guide to the literature of Scottish maps and mapping prior to the Ordnance Survey*, 2nd rev. edn, Aberdeen.

1996 *The maps of Glasgow: a history and cartobibliography to 1865*, Glasgow.

Moore, T. 1825 *The private theatre of Kilkenny*, Dublin.

Moran, J. 1969 'The Columbian press', *JPHS*, 5, 1–23.

1973 *Printing presses: history and development from the fifteenth century to modern times*, London.

1975 *Stationers' Companies of the British Isles*, Newcastle upon Tyne.

Morden, R. 1972 *The county maps from William Camden's Britannia 1695 by Robert Morden*, facs., intro. J. B. Harley, Newton Abbot.

More, H. 2002 *Tales for the common people and other cheap repository tracts*, ed. C. MacDonald Shaw, Nottingham.

Moreau, C. 1825 *East India Company records . . . shewing a view of the past and present state of the British possessions in India as to their revenue, expenditure, debts, assets, trade, and navigation*, London.

Mores, E. R. 1961 (1778), *A dissertation upon English typographical founders and foundries* ed. H. Carter and C. Ricks, Oxford.

Morgan, F. (ed.) 1992 *The Female Tatler*, London.

Morgan, S. 1846 *The wild Irish girl*, 1846.

Morison, S. 1930 *John Bell, 1745–1831: bookseller, printer, publisher, type founder, journalist, &c.*, Cambridge.

1931 *Ichabod Dawks and his newsletter*, Cambridge.

1932 *The history of the English newspaper: one account of the physical development of journals printed in London between 1622 and the modern day*, Cambridge.

Morison, S., with Carter, H. 1967 *John Fell: the University Press and the 'Fell' types*, Oxford.

Moritz, C. P. 1924 (1795) *Travels of Carl Philipp Moritz in England in 1782*, intro. P. E. Matheson, London.

Morris, J. 1997 'Scottish ballads and chapbooks', in Isaac and McKay 1997, 89–111.

Moskal, J. 1991 'The picturesque and the affectionate in Wollstonecraft's *Letters from Norway*', *MLQ*, 52, 263.

Mosley, J. 1967 'The early career of William Caslon', *JPHS*, 3, 66–81.

1984 *British type specimens before 1831: a hand-list*, Oxford.

1991 'Illustrations of type founding engraved for the Description des Arts et Métiers of the Académie Royale des Sciences, 1694 to *c*.1700', *Matrix*, 111, 60–80.

Moss, G. 1990 'British copperplate-printed textiles', *Antiques*, 37, 940–50.

Mossner, E. C. 1980 *The life of David Hume*, 2nd edn, Oxford.

Most, G. W. 1997 'Classical scholarship and literary criticism', in Nisbet and Rawson 1997, 742–57.

Moxon, J. 1962 *Mechanick exercises on the whole art of printing (1683–4)*, ed. H. Davis and H. Carter, London.

Moyes, J. 1826 *Specimens of the types commonly used in the Temple Printing Office, Barverie Street*, London.

Mui, H. C., and Mui, L. H. 1975 'Trends in eighteenth-century smuggling reconsidered', *EcHR*, 2nd ser., 18, 28–42.

Mumby, F. A. 1930 *Publishing and bookselling: a history from the earliest times to the present day*, London.

Mumby, F. A., and Norrie, I. 1974 *Publishing and bookselling*, 5th edn, London.

Mumford, I. 1972 *Lithography, photography and photozincography in English map production before 1870*, London.

Munby, A. N. L. 1950 'Chirm's banded bindings', *TCBS*, 1, 180–5.

1953 'Collecting English signed bindings', *BC*, 2, 177–93.

Munby, A. N. L., and Coral, L. 1977 *British book sale catalogues, 1676–1800: a union list*, London.

Munter, R. 1967 *The history of the Irish newspaper, 1685–1760*, London.

Murray, D. 1913 *Robert and Andrew Foulis and the Glasgow press with some account of the Glasgow Academy of Fine Arts*, Glasgow.

Murray, H. 1805 *Morality of fiction: or, an inquiry into the tendency of fictitious narratives, with observations on some of the most eminent*, Edinburgh.

Murray, J. (ed.) 2001 *Mappa mundi: mapping culture/mapping the world*, Windsor, Ont.

Murray, L. 1826 *Memoirs of the life and works of Lindley Murray in a series of letters by himself*, York.

Musson, A. E. 1958 'Newspaper printing in the Industrial Revolution', *EHR*, n.s., 10, 411–26.

Myers, M. 1990 'Introduction', in Immel 1990, vii–xv.

1992 'Little girls lost: rewriting romantic childhood, righting gender and genre', in Sadler 1992, 131–43.

Myers, R. 1982 'Sale by auction: the rise of auctioneering exemplified', in Myers and Harris 1982, 126–63.

1983 *The English Stock of the Stationers' Company*, London.

(ed.) 1986 *Records of the Worshipful Company of Stationers, 1554–1920* (12 pts. on 115 microfilm reels), Cambridge.

1990 *The Stationers' Company archive: an account of the records, 1554–1984*, Winchester.

(ed.) 2001 *The Stationers' Company: a history of the later years, 1800–2000*, London.

Myers, R. and Harris, M. (eds.) 1981 *Development of the English book trade, 1700–1899*, Oxford.

1982 *Sale and distribution of books from 1700*, Oxford.

1983 *Author–publisher relations in the eighteenth and nineteenth centuries*, Oxford.

1985 *Economics of the British booktrade, 1605–1939*, Cambridge.

1987 *Aspects of printing from 1600*, Oxford.

1989 *Fakes and frauds: varieties of deception in print and manuscript*, Winchester.

1990 *Spreading the word: the distribution networks of print, 1550–1850*, Winchester.

1991 *Property of a gentleman: the formation, organization and dispersal of the private library, 1620–1920*, Winchester.

1994 *A millennium of the book: production, design and illustration in manuscript and print, 900–1900*, Winchester.

1995 *A genius for letters: booksellers and bookselling from the 16th to the 20th centuries*, Winchester.

1996 *Antiquaries, book collectors and the circles of learning*, Winchester.

1997 *The Stationers' Company and the book trade, 1550–1990*, Winchester.

1999 *Journeys through the market: travel, travellers and the book trade*, Winchester.

Myers, R., Harris, M. and Mandelbrote, G. (eds.) 2001 *Under the hammer: book auctions since the seventeenth century*, New Castle, DE.

2002 *Lives in print: biography and the book trade from the Middle Ages to the 21st century*, New Castle, DE.

2003 *London book trade: topographies of print in the metropolis from the sixteenth century*, New Castle, DE.

Nangle, B. C. 1934 *The Monthly Review, first series, 1749–1789: indexes of contributors and articles*, Oxford.

1955 *The Monthly Review, second series, 1790–1815: indexes of contributors and articles*, Oxford.

Nattrass, L. 1995 *William Cobbett: the politics of style*, Cambridge.

Neal, L. 1990 *The rise of financial capitalism: international capital markets in the Age of Reason*, Cambridge.

1994 'The finance of business during the Industrial Revolution', in Floud and McCloskey 1994, I, 151–81.

1998 'The financial crisis of 1825 and the restructuring of the British financial system', *Federal Reserve Bank of St Louis Review*, 80, 53–76.

2000 'How it all began: the monetary and financial architecture of Europe during the first global capital market, 1648–1815', *Financial History Review*, 7, 117–40.

Negus, S. 1724 *A compleat and private list of all the printing-houses in and about the cities of London and Westminster, &c*, in Nichols 1812–16, I, 288–312.

Nelsen, P. 1998 'Chedworth and the territoriality of the reader', in Gondris 1998, 140–63.

Nelson, C. and Seccombe, M. 1987 *British newspapers and periodicals, 1641–1700: a short-title catalogue of serials printed in England, Scotland, Ireland, and British America*, New York.

2002 'The creation of the periodical press, 1660–1695', in *CHBB* IV, 533–50.

Nelson, S. 1985 'Mould making, matrix fitting, hand casting', *Visible Language*, 19, 107–20.

Nenadic, S. 1988 'The rise of the urban middle classes', in Devine and Mitchison 1988, 109–26.

Neuburg, V. E. 1969 'The Diceys and the chapbook trade', *Library*, 5th ser., 24, 219–31.

1971 *Popular education in eighteenth century England*, London.

1972 *Chapbooks*, 2nd edn, London.

Newman, A. K. 1814–19 *Catalogue of A. K. Newman and Co.'s Circulating Library ... consisting of a general selection of books in every department of literature, and particularly embracing the whole of the modern publications*, 7 pts., London.

Newman, G. (ed.) 1997 *Britain in the Hanoverian age, 1714–1837: an encyclopedia*, New York.

Newth, J. D. 1957 *Adam and Charles Black, 1807–1957: some chapters in the history of a publishing house*, London.

Newton, D. and Smith, M. 1999 *The Stamford Mercury: three centuries of newspaper publishing*, Stamford.

Nicholas, S. J., and Nicholas, J. 1992 'Male literacy, "deskilling", and the Industrial Revolution', *Journal of Interdisciplinary History*, 23, 1–18.

Nichols, C. 1912 *Isaiah Thomas, printer, writer and collector: a paper read April 12, 1911, before the Club of Odd Volumes; with a bibliography of the books printed by Isaiah Thomas*, Boston, MA.
1924 'The literary fair in the United States', in Eames 1924, 83–92.
Nichols, J. 1812–16 *Literary anecdotes of the eighteenth century*, 9 vols., London.
Nichols, J. and Nichols, J. B. 1817–58 *Illustrations of the literary history of the eighteenth century*, 8 vols., London.
Nisbet , H. B., and Rawson, C. J. (eds.) 1997 *The Cambridge history of literary criticism*, vol. IV: *The eighteenth century*, Cambridge.
Nixon, H. M. 1970 'The memorandum book of James Coghlan: the stock of an 18th century printer and binder', *JPHS*, 6, 33–52.
1975 'Harleian bindings', in Hunt, Philip and Roberts 1975, 153–94.
1978 *Five centuries of English bookbinding*, London.
1984 *Catalogue of the Pepys Library at Magdalene College Cambridge*, vol. VI: Bindings, Woodbridge.
Nixon, H. M., and Foot, M. M. 1992 *The history of decorated bookbinding in England*, Oxford.
Noblett, W. 1972 'John Newbery, publisher extraordinary', *History Today*, 22, 265–71.
Noll, M. A., Bebbington, D. W. and Rawlyk, G. A. 1994 *Evangelicalism: comparative studies of popular Protestantism in North America, the British Isles, and beyond, 1700–1990*, Oxford.
Norman, W. 1693 *A catalogue of books in several faculties ... to be sold by way of auction on 23 November 1693, by William Norman*, Dublin.
Norton, D. 1988 'John Wilson, Hume's first printer', *The British Library Journal*, 14, 123–35.
Norton, J. E. 1940 *A bibliography of the works of Edward Gibbon*, Oxford.
1950 *Guide to the national and provincial directories of England and Wales, excluding London, published before 1856*, London.
Nowell-Smith, S. 1971 'Charles Manby Smith: his family and friends, his fantasies and fabrications', *JPHS*, 7, 1–28.
Nussbaum, F. and Brown, L. (eds.) 1987 *The new eighteenth century: theory, politics, English literature*, London.
Nuttall, G. F. 1977 *New College, London and its library*, London.
1979 *Calender of the correspondence of Philip Doddridge DD (1702–1751)*, London.
O'Brien, C. 1792–8 *A treatise on calico printing*, 2 vols., London.
O'Brien, K. 2001 'The history market in eighteenth-century England', in Rivers 2001, 105–34.
O'Brien, P. 1993 *Eyres' Press Warrington (1756–1803): an embryo university press*, Wigan.
O'Brien, S. 1986 'A transatlantic community of saints: the Great Awakening and the first evangelical network, 1735–1755', *The American Historical Review*, 9, 811–32.
1994 'Eighteenth-century publishing networks in the first years of transatlantic evangelicalism' in Noll, Bebbington and Rawlyk 1994, 38–57.
Ó Ciosáin, N. 1997 *Print and popular culture in Ireland, 1750–1850*, Basingstoke.
O'Connell, S. 1985 'Simon Gribelin, printmaker and metal-engraver', *Print Quarterly*, 2, 27–38.
2003 'The print trade in Hogarth's London', in Myers, Harris and Mandelbrote 2003, 71–88.
O'Day, R. 1982 *Education and society, 1500–1800: the social foundations of education in early modern Britain*, London.
O'Higgins, P. 1986 'Law printing in eighteenth-century Ireland', *Law Librarian*, 7, 93–4.

Ordnance Survey 1975 *The old series Ordnance Survey maps of England and Wales*, vol. I: *Kent, Essex, E. Sussex, and S. Suffolk*, intro. J. B. Harley and Y. O'Donoghue, Lympne Castle.

1977 *The old series Ordnance Survey maps of England and Wales*, vol. II: *Devon, Cornwall, and West Somerset*, intro. J. B. Harley and Y. O'Donoghue, Lympne Castle.

1987 *The old series Ordnance Survey maps of England and Wales*, vol. V: *Lincolnshire, Rutland and East Anglia (Lincs, Rutland, Norfolk and parts of Cambs, Hunts, Leics, Northants, Notts, Suffolk and Yorks)*, intro. J. B. Harley, Lympne Castle.

Orme, W. 1824 *Bibliotheca biblica: a select list of books on sacred literature; with notices biographical, critical, and bibliographical*, Edinburgh.

Ormes, I. 1997 *From rags to roms: a history of Spicers, 1796–1996*, Cambridge.

Osborough, W. N. 1993 'Puzzles from Irish reporting history', in Birks 1993, 89–111.

Ostman, H. 1983 *English fiction, poetry and drama in eighteenth century Sweden: 1765–1799 – a preliminary study*, Stockholm.

Ottley, H. 1866 *A biographical and critical dictionary of recent living painters and engravers, forming a supplement to Bryan's dictionary . . .*, London.

Ousby, I. 1990 *The Englishman's England: taste, travel and the rise of tourism*, Cambridge.

Owen, H. 1766 *Directions for young students in divinity: with regard to those attainments, which are necessary to qualify them for holy orders*, London.

Owen, J. 1796 *Travels into different parts of Europe*, 2 vols., London.

Owen, W. J. B. 1954 'Costs, sales and profits of Longman's editions of Wordsworth', *Library*, 5th ser., 93–107.

P., P. T. 1855a 'The ledger of Henry Woodfall, jun.', *N&Q*, 1st ser., 12, 217–19.

1855b 'Pope and Henry Woodfall', *N&Q*, 1st ser., 11, 377–78, 418–20.

Paintin, E. M. 1989 *The king's library*, London.

Paisey, D. 1991 'Printed books in English and Dutch in early printed catalogues of German university libraries', in Roach 1991, 127–48.

Palliser, D. M., Clark, P. and Daunton, M. (eds.) 2001 *The Cambridge urban history of Britain*, 3 vols., Cambridge.

Papali, G. F. 1968 *Jacob Tonson, publisher: his life and work (1656–1736)*, Auckland.

Papillon, J. M. 1985 (1766) *Traité historique et pratique de la gravure en bois*, facs., 2 vols., preface by M. Préaud, Paris.

Pardoe, F. E. 1975 *John Baskerville of Birmingham: letter-founder and printer*, London.

Parker, G. L. 1985 *The beginnings of the book trade in Canada*, Toronto.

Parker, H. 2000 *Literary magazines and British Romanticism*, Cambridge.

Parks, S. 1976 *John Dunton and the English book trade: a study of his career with a checklist of his publications*, New York.

Parnell, H. 1830 *On financial reform*, London.

Parry H. 1818 *The art of bookbinding: containing a description of the tools, forwarding, gilding and finishing, stationery binding, edge-colouring, marbling, sprinkling, &c. &c.*, London.

Parsons, I. 1974 'Copyright and society', in Briggs 1974, 29–60.

Paterson, S. 1772 *Joineriana: or the book of scraps*, 2 vols., London.

Patterson, L. R. 1968 *Copyright in historical perspective*, Nashville, TN.

Paulin, R. 1986 'Johann Joachim Eschenburg und die europäische Gelehrtenrepublik am Übergang von 18. zum 19. Jahrhundert', *Internationales Archiv für Sozialgeschichte der deutschen Literatur*, 11, 51–72.

Paulson, R. 1995 'Emulative consumption and literacy: the Harlot, Moll Flanders, and Mrs Slipslop', in Bermingham and Brewer 1995, 383–400.

Pawson, E. 1977 *Transport and economy: the turnpike roads of eighteenth century Britain*, London.

Paxman, D. B. 1995 '"Adam in a strange country": Locke's language theory and travel literature', *MP*, 92, 460–81.

Pearson, D. 1998 *Provenance research in book history*, London.

2004 *English bookbinding styles, 1450–1800: a handbook*, London.

Pearson, J. 1999 *Women's reading in Britain, 1750–1835: a dangerous recreation*, Cambridge.

Pearson, R. 2004 *Insuring the Industrial Revolution: fire insurance in Great Britain, 1700–1850*, Aldershot.

Peddie, R. A. 1943 '"Publishers' bindings", 1762–1850: a list of terms', *Library World*, 46, 20–1.

Pedley, M. S. 1996 'Maps, war and commerce: business correspondence with the London map firm of Thomas Jefferys and William Faden', *IM*, 48, 161–73.

2000 *The map trade in the late eighteenth century: letters to the London map sellers Jefferys & Faden*, Oxford.

Pelgen, S. 1996 'Zur Archäologie der Buchdruckletter: neue Funde zur Schriftgussgeschichte von (Kur-)Mainz', *Gutenberg Jahrbuch*, 182–208.

Pendred, J. 1955 *The earliest directory of the book trade by John Pendred (Vade mecum, 1785)*, ed. G. Pollard, London.

Perkin, M. R. (ed.) 1981 *The book trade in Liverpool to 1805: a directory*, Liverpool.

1984 'A note on the survival of books with Liverpool imprints', *Factotum*, occasional paper 3.

(ed.) 1987a *The book trade in Liverpool, 1806–50: a directory*, Liverpool.

1987b 'William Eyres and the Warrington Press', in Myers and Harris 1987, 69–89.

Peters, M. 1980 *Pitt and popularity: the patriot minister and London opinion during the Seven Years War*, Oxford.

Pfeiffer, R. 1968–76 *History of classical scholarship*, 2 vols., Oxford.

Philip, I. G. 1957 *William Blackstone and the reform of the Oxford University Press in the eighteenth century*, Oxford.

Phillips, J. W. 1998 *Printing and bookselling in Dublin, 1670–1800*, Dublin.

Phillipson, N. 1974 'Culture and society in the eighteenth century province: the case of Edinburgh and the Scottish Enlightenment', in Stone 1974, II, 407–48.

Pickering J. M. 1990 *Music in the British Isles, 1700 to 1800: a bibliography of literature*, Edinburgh.

Pickwood, N. 1994 'Onward and downward: how binders coped with the printing press before 1800', in Myers and Harris 1994, 61–106.

2005. 'Review of S. Bennett, *Trade Bookbinding in the British Isles, 1660–1800*', *Library*, 7th ser., 6, 4, 464–5.

Pienaar, W. J. B. 1929 *English influences in Dutch literature and Justus van Effen as intermediary*, Cambridge.

Piton, E. 1856 *Famille Firmin-Didot, imprimeurs, libraires, fondeurs, graveurs, papetiers, inventeurs et littérateurs*, Paris.

Plant, M. 1974 *The English book trade: an economic history of the making and sale of books*, 3rd edn, London.

Plomer, H. R. 1901 'A glance at the Whittingham Ledgers', *Library*, 2nd ser., 2, 147–63.

1905 'Westminster Hall and its booksellers', *Library*, 2nd ser., 6, 380–90.

1907 *A dictionary of the booksellers and printers who were at work in England, Scotland and Ireland from 1641 to 1667*, London.

1922 *A dictionary of the booksellers and printers who were at work in England, Scotland and Ireland from 1668 to 1725*, London.

Plomer, H. R., Bushnell, G. H. and Dix, E. R. McC. 1932 *A dictionary of the printers and booksellers who were at work in England, Scotland and Ireland from 1726 to 1775*, London.

Plumb, J. H. 1972 *The commercialisation of leisure in eighteenth-century England*, Stenton Lecture, Reading.

Pointon, M. R. 1970 *Milton and English art*, Manchester.

1986 *Mulready: a book with catalogue, published to accompany the exhibition William Mulready: 1786–1863 – Victoria and Albert Museum* ..., London.

1993 *Hanging the head: portraiture and social formation in eighteenth-century England*, New Haven and London.

Pollard, A. W. (ed.) 1915 *List of catalogues of English books sales, 1676–1900, now in the British Museum*, London.

Pollard, H. G. 1932 'Booksellers' binding', *Times Literary Supplement*, 10 Mar., 176.

1941 'Notes on the size of the sheet', *Library*, 4th ser., 22, 105–37.

1956 'Changes in the style of bookbinding, 1550–1830', *Library*, 5th ser., 11, 71–94.

1978 'The English market for printed books', The Sanders Lectures of 1949, repr. unrevised and uncorrected, *PH*, 4, 7–48.

Pollard, H. G., and Ehrman, A. 1965 *The distribution of books by catalogue from the invention of printing to AD 1800*, Cambridge.

Pollard, M. 1980 'Control of the press in Ireland through the King's Printer's Patent, 1600–1800', *Irish Booklore*, 4, 2, 79–95.

1989 *Dublin's trade in books, 1500–1800*, Oxford.

1992 'Plain calf for plain people – Dublin bookbinders' price lists', in Bernelle 1992, 177–86.

2000 *A dictionary of members of the Dublin book trade, 1550–1800, based on records of the Guild of St Luke the Evangelist*, London.

Pooley, J. 2001 'The papers of the Nichols family and business: new discoveries and the work of the Nichols Archive Project', *Library*, 7th ser., 2, 10–52.

2002 'Beyond the literary anecdotes: the Nichols family archive as a source for book trade biography', in Myers, Harris and Mandelbrote 2002, 119–50.

Pope, A. 1743 *The Dunciad, in four books*, London.

1797 *The works of Alexander Pope*, ed. J. Warton, 9 vols., London.

1935 *Pope's own miscellany. Being a reprint of 'Poems on several occasions,' 1717, containing new poems by Alexander Pope and others*, ed. N. Ault, London.

1936 *Prose works: the earlier works, 1711–1720*, ed. N. Ault, Oxford.

1939–69 *Poems*, ed. J. Butt *et al.*, 11 vols., New Haven, CT.

1956 *The correspondence of Alexander Pope*, ed. G. Sherburn, 5 vols., Oxford.

Porter, D. 1991 *Haunted journeys: desire and transgression in European travel writing*, Princeton, NJ.

Porter, R. 1987 *Disease, medicine, and society in England, 1550–1860*, Cambridge.

1995 'Medical lecturing in Georgian London', *British Journal for the History of Science*, 28, 91–9.

Potter, E. 1993 'The London bookbinding trade: from craft to industry', *Library*, 6th ser., 15, 259–80.

1997 'The changing role of the trade bookbinder, 1800–1900', in Hunt, Mandelbrote and Shell 1997, 161–74.
Pouchée, L. J. 1993 *Ornamented types; twenty-three alphabets from the Foundry of Louis John Pouchée: introduction James Mosley*. London.
Pratt, A. S. 1938 *Isaac Watts and his gifts of books to Yale College*, New Haven, CT.
Prescott, S. and Spencer, J. 2000 'Prattling, tattling and knowing everything: public authority and the female editorial persona in the early essay-periodical', *British Journal for Eighteenth-Century Studies*, 23, 43–57.
Pressnell, L. 1956 *Country banking in the Industrial Revolution*, Oxford.
Prest, W. R. (ed.) 1987 *The professions in early modern England*, Beckenham, Kent.
1993 'Law reform in eighteenth-century England', in Birks 1993, 113–23.
1998 *Albion ascendant: English history, 1660–1815*, Oxford
1999 'Lay legal knowledge in early modern England', in Bush and Wijffels, 1999, 303–13.
Preston, T. R. 1982 'Biblical criticism, literature, and the eighteenth-century reader', in Rivers 1982a, 97–126.
Preston, W. 1803 'Essay on the natural advantages of Ireland' *Transactions of the Royal Irish Academy*, 9, 161–428.
Price, C. 1989 'Italian opera and arson in late eighteenth-century London', *Journal of the American Musicological Society*, 42, 55–107.
1991 'Unity, originality, and the London Pasticcio', *HLB*, n.s., 2, 17–30.
Price, J. M. 1958 'A note on the circulation of the London press, 1704–1714', *BIHR*, 31, 215–19.
Price, L. 2004 'Reading: the state of the discipline', *Book History*, 7, 303–20.
Price, M. B. and Price, L. M. 1934 *The publication of English literature in Germany in the eighteenth century*, Berkeley, CA.
1955 *The publication of English humaniora in Germany in the eighteenth century*, Berkeley, CA.
Priestley, J. 1765 *An essay on a course of liberal education for civil and active life*, London.
Prouty, C. T. (ed.) 1946 *Studies in honor of A. H. R. Fairchild*, Columbia, MO.
Quaritch, B. (ed.) 1892–1921 *Contributions towards a dictionary of English book collectors*, London.
Quinlan, M. J. 1941 *Victorian prelude: a history of English manners, 1700–1830*, New York.
Quinn, S. 2004 'Money, finance and capital markets', in Floud and Johnson 2004, 147–74.
Rabin, R. and Zohn, S. 1995 'Arne, Handel, Walsh, and music as intellectual property: two eighteenth-century lawsuits', *Journal of the Royal Musical Association*, 120, 114–45.
Rack, H. D. 1989 *Reasonable enthusiast: John Wesley and the rise of Methodism*, London.
Rajan, T. and Wright, J. M. (eds.) 1998 *Romanticism, history and the possibilities of genre*, Cambridge.
Ralph, J. 1966 (1758) *The case of authors by profession or trade*, facs., intro. P. Stevick, Gainesville, FL.
Ram, T. H. 1999 *Magnitude in marginality: Edward Cave and the Gentleman's Magazine, 1731–1754*, Overveen, Netherlands.
Ramsden, C. 1956 *London bookbinders, 1780–1840*, London.
Ransom, H. 1938 'The rewards of authorship in the eighteenth century', *University of Texas Studies in English*, 18, 47–66.
Rau, F. 1980 *Zur Verbreitung und Nachahmung des 'Tatler' und 'Spectator'*, Heidelberg.

Rauch, A. 2001 *Useful knowledge: the Victorians, morality and the march of intellect*, Durham, NC.

Raven, J. 1987 *British fiction, 1750–1770: a chronological check-list of prose fiction printed in Britain and Ireland*, Newark, DE.

1988 'The commercialisation of literature in eighteenth-century Britain: an exercise in multi-variate statistical analysis', unpub. paper for the Voltaire Foundation, Oxford.

1990 'The Noble brothers and popular publishing, 1737–89', *Library*, 6th ser., 12, 293–345.

1992 *Judging new wealth: popular publishing and responses to commerce in England, 1750–1800*, Oxford.

1994 'Selling one's life: James Lackington, eighteenth-century booksellers and the design of autobiography', in Brack 1994, 1–24.

1997a 'Establishing and maintaining credit lines overseas: the case of the export book trade from London in the eighteenth century, mechanism and personnel' in Fontaine *et al.* 1997, 144–61.

1997b 'The export of books to colonial north America', *PH*, 42, 21–49.

1997c 'Memorializing a London bookscape: the mapping and reading of Paternoster Row and St Paul's churchyard, 1695–1814', in Alston 1997, 177–200.

1998 'New reading histories, print culture, and the identification of change: the case of eighteenth-century England', *Social History*, 23, 268–87.

2000a 'Historical introduction: the novel comes of age', in Garside, Raven and Schöwerling 2000, I, 15–121.

2000b 'The importation of books in the eighteenth century', in Amory and Hall 2000, 183–97.

2001a 'The book trades', in Rivers 2001, 1–34.

2001b 'British publishing and bookselling: constraints and developments', in Michon and Mollier 2000, 19–30.

2001c 'Constructing bookscapes: experiments in mapping the sites and activities of the London book trades of the eighteenth century', in Murray 2001, 35–59.

2002a 'The economic context', in *CHBB* IV, 568–82.

2002b *London booksellers and American customers: transatlantic literary community and the Charleston library society, 1748–1811*, Columbia, SC.

2003 'Location, size, and succession: the bookshops of Paternoster Row before 1800', in Myers, Harris and Mandelbrote 2003, 89–126.

2004 'St Paul's precinct and the book trade to *c.*1800', in Keene, Burns and Saint 2004, 430–8.

2007 *The business of books: booksellers and the English book trade, 1450–1850*, New Haven and London.

Raven, J., Small, H. and Tadmor, N. (eds.) 1996 *The practice and representation of reading in England*, Cambridge.

Ravenhill, W. L. D. 1965 'Introduction', in Donne 1965, 1–20.

1972 'Joel Gascoyne, a pioneer of large-scale county mapping', *IM*, 26, 60–70.

Raymond, J. (ed.) 1999a *News, newspapers, and society in early modern Britain*, London.

1999b 'The newspaper, public opinion, and the public sphere in the seventeenth century', in Raymond 1999a, 109–40.

Read, D. 1961 *Press and the people, 1790–1850: opinion in three English cities*, London.

Reader, W. J. 1966 *Professional men: the rise of the professional classes in nineteenth-century England*, London.

Real, H.-J. (ed.) 2005 *The reception of Jonathan Swift in Europe*, London.

Reay, B. 1991 'The context and meaning of popular literacy: some evidence from nineteenth-century rural England', *P&P*, 131, 89–121.

Reddick, A. H. 1990 *The making of Johnson's dicitionary, 1746–1773*, Cambridge.

Reed, T. B. 1952 (1887) *A history of the old English letter foundries*, new edn, rev. and enlarged by A. F. Johnson, London.

Reedy, G. 1985 *The Bible and reason: Anglicans and scripture in late seventeenth-century England*, Philadelphia, PA.

Rees, E. 1983–4 'Bookbinding in 18th century Wales', *Journal of the Welsh Bibliographical Society*, 51–66.

1984–7 'The sales-book of Samuel Williams, Aberystwyth printer', *Ceredigion*, 10, 255–67, 357–72.

1998 'The Welsh book trade from 1718 to 1820', in Jones and Rees 1998, 123–33.

Rees, T. and Britton, J. 1896 *Reminiscences of literary London from 1779 to 1853*, London.

Reilly, E. C. 1983 'The wages of piety: the Boston book trade of Jeremy Condy', in Joyce *et al.* 1983, 83–131.

Reilly, E. C., and Hall, D. 2000 'Customers and the market for books', in *HBA* I, 387–98.

Reinhartz, D. 1988 'Additions to the Gilf and Indies maps of Herman Moll', *MC*, 43, 27–30.

1997 *The cartographer and the literati: Herman Moll and his intellectual circle*, Lewiston, NY.

Reitinger, F. 1999 'Mapping relationships: allegory, gender and the cartographical image in eighteenth-century France and England', *IM*, 51, 106–29.

Remer, R. 1996 *Printers and men of capital: Philadelphia book publishers in the New Republic*, Philadelphia, PA.

Renier, A. 1964 *Friendship's offering: an essay on the annuals and gift books of the nineteenth century*, London.

Repertoire international des sources musicales 1964 Series B/2 *Recueils imprimes: XVIIIe siècle*, Munich.

1971–98 Series A/I *Einzeldrucke vor 1800*, 14 vols, Kassel.

Reynolds, L. D. and Wilson, N. G. 1991 *Scribes and scholars: a guide to the transmission of Greek and Latin literature*, 3rd edn, Oxford.

Rheinfurth, H. 1999 *Musikverlag Gombart: Basel, Augsburg (1789–1836)*, Tutzing.

Rich, E. E. and Wilson, C. H. (eds.) 1977 *The Cambridge economic history of Europe*, vol. v: *The economic organization of early modern Europe*, Cambridge.

Richardson, S. 1762 *The history of Sir Charles Grandison*, 4th edn, 7 vols., London.

1972 *The history of Sir Charles Grandison*, ed. J. Harris, Oxford.

Richetti, J. J. 1969 *Popular fiction before Richardson: narrative patterns, 1700–1739*, Oxford.

(ed.) 2005 *The Cambridge history of English literature, 1660–1780*, Cambridge.

Rickards, M. 1988 *Collecting printed ephemera*, Oxford.

2000 *The encyclopedia of ephemera: a guide to the fragmentary documents of everyday life for the collector, curator, and historian*, completed and ed. M. Twyman, with S. du Boscq de Beaumont and A. Tanner, London.

Ridgeway, W. 1794 *Reports of cases ... King's Bench and Chancery ... Lord Hardwicke ...*, London.

Riely, J. C. 1974 'Chesterfield, Mallet, and the publication of Bolingbroke's works', *RES*, n.s. 25, 61–5.

Rippon, J. 1804? *A discourse on the origin and progress of the Society for Promoting Religious Knowledge among the Poor, from its commencement in 1750, to the year 1802*, 2nd edn, London.

Ritvo, H. 1987 *The animal estate: the English and other creatures in the Victorian age*, Cambridge, MA.

Rivers, I. (ed.) 1982a *Books and their readers in eighteenth-century England*, Leicester.

1982b 'Dissenting and Methodist books of practical divinity', in Rivers 1982a, 127–64.

1991 *Reason, grace, and sentiment: a study of the language of religion and ethics in England, 1660–1780*, vol. I: *Whichcote to Wesley*, Cambridge.

2000 *Reason, grace, and sentiment: a study of the language of religion and ethics in England, 1660–1780*, vol. II: *Shaftesbury to Hume*, Cambridge.

(ed.) 2001 *Books and their readers in eighteenth-century England: new essays*, London.

2003 *The defence of truth through the knowledge of error: Philip Doddridge's academy lectures*, London.

2005 'Religion and literature', in Richetti 2005, 445–70.

2007 'The first evangelical tract society', *HJ*, 50, 1–22.

2012 *Vanity Fair and the Celestial City: dissenting, Methodist, and evangelical literary culture in England, 1720–1800*, Oxford.

Rivington, S. 1919 *The publishing family of Rivington*, London.

Roach, J. 1986 *A history of secondary education in England, 1800–1870*, London.

Roach, S. (ed.) 1991 *Across the narrow seas: studies in the history and bibliography of Britain and the Low Countries presented to Anna E. C. Simoni*, London.

Robberds, J. W. 1843 *A memoir of the life and writings of the late William Taylor of Norwich*, 2 vols., London.

Roberts, E. 1835 *Scenes and characteristics of Hindostan*, 3 vols., London.

Roberts, J. 2004 *George III and Queen Charlotte: patronage, collecting and court taste*, London.

Roberts, M. J. D. 1998 'Head versus heart? Voluntary associations and charity organization in England, c.1700–1850', in Cunningham and Innes 1998, 66–86.

Roberts, R. J. 2002 'The Latin trade', in *CHBB* IV 141–73.

Roberts, S. C. 1921 *A history of the Cambridge University Press, 1521–1921*, Cambridge.

Roberts, W. 1895 *The book-hunter in London: historical and other studies of collectors and collecting*, London.

Robinson, A. H. W. 1962 *Marine cartography in Britain*, Leicester.

Robinson, F. J. G. and Wallis, P. J. 1975 *Book subscription lists: a revised guide*, Newcastle upon Tyne.

Robinson, H. 1948 *The British Post Office*, Princeton, NJ.

Robinson, H. C. 1938 *Henry Crabb Robinson on books and their writers*, ed. E. J. Morley, 3 vols., London.

Robinson, M. 1792 *Vancenza; or, the dangers of credulity*, 2 vols., London.

Robinson, R. B. 1991, 'The two institutes of Thomas Wood: a study in eighteenth-century legal scholarship', *American Journal of Legal History*, 35, 432–58.

Rochedieu, C. A. E. 1948 *Bibliography of French translations of English works, 1700–1800*, Chicago, IL.

Rodger, E. M. 1972 *The large scale county maps of the British Isles, 1596–1850: a union list*, 2nd rev. edn, Oxford.

Rodger, R. 1985 'Employment, wages and poverty in Scottish cities, 1841–1914', appendix 1, in Gordon 1985.
Rogers, P. 1972 *Grub Street: studies in a subculture*, London.
1978 'Pope and his subscribers', *PH*, 3, 7–36.
1979 *Robinson Crusoe*, London.
1984 'Defoe's *Tour* (1742) and the chapbook trade', *Library*, 6th ser., 6, 275–9.
1985 *Literature and popular culture in eighteeth-century England*, Brighton.
Rogers, S. 2000 'The use of royal licences for printing in England, 1695–1760: a bibliography', *Library*, 7th ser., 1, 145–92.
Roper, D. 1955 'Smollett's "Four Gentlemen": the first contributors to the *Critical Review*', *RES*, n.s., 10, 38–44.
1961 'The politics of the "Critical Review", 1756–1817', *Durham University Journal*, 22, 117–22.
1978 *Reviewing before the 'Edinburgh', 1788–1802*, London.
Roscoe, S. 1973 *John Newbery and his successors, 1740–1814: a bibliography*, Wormley.
Roscoe, S. and Brimmell, R. A. 1981 *James Lumsden and Son of Glasgow: their juvenile books and chapbooks*, Pinner.
Rose, C. 1991 '"Seminarys of faction and rebellion": Jacobites, Whigs and the London charity schools, 1716–24', *HJ*, 34, 831–55.
1993 'The origins and ideals of the SPCK, 1699–1716', in Walsh, Haydon and Taylor 1993, 172–90.
Rose, M. 1993 *Authors and owners: the invention of copyright*, London.
Rosenberg, N. 1972–3 'Factors affecting the diffusion of technology', *Explorations in Economic History*, 10, 3–33.
Rosenthal, A. 1996 'The contract between Joseph Haydn and Frederick Augustus Hyde (1796)', in Biba and Wyn Jones 1996, 72–81.
Rosman, D. M. 1984 *Evangelicals and culture*, London.
Ross, R. 1998 'The commoning of the common law: the Renaissance debate over printing English law, 1520–1640', *University of Pennsylvania Law Review*, 146, 323–461.
Ross, T. 1992 'Copyright and the invention of tradition', *ECS*, 26, 1, 1–27.
Rostow, W. W. (ed.) 1963 *The economics of take-off into sustained growth. Proceedings of a conference held by the International Economic Association*, London.
Rothschild, N. M. V. 1947 *Two bindings by Roger Payne in the library of Lord Rothschild*, Cambridge.
Rousseau, G. S. 1982 'Science books and their readers in the eighteenth century', in Rivers 1982a, 197–255.
Roy, G. R. 1974 'Some notes on Scottish chapbooks', *Scottish Literary Journal*, 1, 50–60.
Royal Scottish Geographical Society 1973–83 *The early maps of Scotland to 1850 ... With a history of Scottish maps, by D. G. Moir*, 2 vols., 3rd rev. edn, Edinburgh.
Rubin, V. and Tuden, A. (eds.) 1977 *Comparative perspectives on slavery in New World plantation societies*, *Annals of the New York Academy of Sciences* 292, New York.
Russell, R. A. 1995 'Dramatists and the printed page: the social role of comedy from Richard Steele to Leigh Hunt', unpub. thesis, Oxford University.
Rutherford, J. and Armstrong, P. H. 2000 'James Cook RN, 1728–1779', *Geographers: Biobibliographical Essays*, 20, 9–23.
Sadleir, M. 1930 *The evolution of publishers' binding styles, 1770–1900*, London.
Sadler, G. E. (ed.) 1992 *Teaching children's literature: issues, pedagogy, resources*, New York.

Said, E. 1991 (1983) *The world, the text, and the critic*, London.
St Clair, W. 1989 'William Godwin as children's bookseller', in Avery and Briggs 1989, 165–80.
2004 *The reading nation in the romantic period*, Cambridge.
Sale, W. M. 1950 *Samuel Richardson: master printer*, Ithaca, NY.
Salter, J. L. 1978 'The books of an early eighteenth-century curate', *Library*, 5th ser., 33, 33–46.
Sambrook, J. 1991 *James Thomson, 1700–1748: a life*, Oxford.
Sandeman, H. D. 1868–9 *Selections from Calcutta Gazettes of the years 1784 [to 1823] ... showing the political and social condition of the English in India*, vols. IV–V, Calcutta.
Sanderson, M. 1972 'Literacy and social mobility in the Industrial Revolution in England', *P&P*, 56, 75–104.
Sandys, J. E. 1958 *A history of classical scholarship*, repr., 3 vols., New York.
Saunders, A. L. (ed.) 1997 *The Royal Exchange*, London.
Saunders, D. 1992 *Authorship and copyright*, London.
Saunders, D. and Hunter, I. 1991 'Lessons from the "Literatory": how to historicize authorship', *Critical Inquiry*, 17, 479–509.
Saunders, H. St G. 1951 *Westminster Hall*, London
Saunders, J. W. 1964 (1904) *The profession of English letters*, London.
Savage W. 1822 *Practical hints on decorative printing: with illustrations engraved on wood, and printed in colours at the type press*, London.
1841 *A dictionary of the art of printing*, London.
Savile, G. 1997 *Secret comment: the diaries of Gertrude Savile, 1721–1757*, ed. A. Saville, Kingsbridge.
Sayer, J. 1765 *The temple of Gnidus, a poem from the French prose of M. Sedondat, baron de Montsquieu*, London.
Sayer, R. and Bennett, J. 1970 *Sayer & Bennett's catalogue of prints for 1775*, facs. reprint, London.
Schellenberg, B. A. 2002 'Connecting the dots: plotting and reading the (woman) writer's career', *Canadian Society of Eighteenth-Century Studies conference*, Quebec, 24 Oct. 2002.
Scheuermann, M. 2002 *In praise of poverty: Hannah More counters Thomas Paine and the radical threat*, Lexington, KY.
Schmidt, A. J. 1996 'A career in the law: clerkship and the profession in late eighteenth-century Lincolnshire', *Lincolnshire History and Archaeology*, 31, 29–41.
Schmidt, R. 1902 (1979) *Deutsche Buchhändler, deutsche Buchdrucker: Beiträge zu einer Firmengeschichte des deutschen Buchgewerbes*, Hildesheim.
Schmidt, W. G. 2003 *'Homer des Nordens' und 'Mutter der Romantik': James Macphersons 'Ossian' und seine Rezeption in der deutschsprachigen Literatur*, 4 vols., Berlin.
Schofield, R. S. 1968 'The measurement of literacy in pre-industrial England', in Goody 1968, 311–25.
1973 'Dimensions of illiteracy, 1750–1850', *Explorations in Economic History*, 10, 437–54.
Schorr, J. L. 1982 *The life and works of Justus van Effen*, Laramie, WY.
Schöwerling, R. 1980 *Chapbooks: zur Literaturgeschichte einfachen Lesers: englische Konsumliterature 1680–1840*, Frankfurt am Main.
Schröder, K. 1975 *Lehrwerke für den Englischunterricht im deutschsprachigen Raum: 1665–1900*, Darmstadt.
1989 *Biographisches und bibliographisches Lexikon der Fremdsprachenlehrer des deutschsprachigen Raumes: Spätmittelalter bis 1800*, vol. II, Augsburg.

Schumpeter, E. B. 1960 *English overseas trade statistics, 1697–1808*, intro. T. S. Ashton, Oxford.

Schwarz, L. D. 1982 *London in the age of industrialization: entrepreneurs, labour force and living conditions, 1700–1850*, Cambridge.

Schweizer, K. W. 2006 'Newspapers, politics and public opinion in the later Hanoverian era', *Parliamentary History*, 25, Pt. 1, 32–48.

Scott, J. 1823 *The life of the Rev. Thomas Scott, Rector of Aston Sandford, Bucks; including a narrative drawn up by himself, and copious extracts of his letters*, 5th edn, London.

Scott, Sir W. 1890 *The journal of Sir Walter Scott*, 2 vols., Edinburgh.

1932–7 *The letters of Sir Walter Scott*, ed. H. J. C. Grierson *et al.*, 12 vols., Edinburgh.

1939 *The journal ... 1825–6*, ed. J. G. Tait, Edinburgh.

1972 *The journal of Sir Walter Scott*, ed. W. E. K. Anderson, Oxford.

1995 *The antiquary*, ed. D. Hewitt, Edinburgh.

2000a *The monastery*, ed. P. Fielding, Edinburgh.

2000b *The pirate*, ed. M. Weinstein and A. Lumsden, Edinburgh.

Seary, P. 1990 *Lewis Theobold and the editing of Shakespeare*, Oxford.

Secord, J. A. 1985 'Newton in the nursery: Tom Telescope and the philosophy of tops and balls, 1761–1838', *History of Science*, 23, 127–51.

2000 *Victorian sensation: the extraordinary publication, reception and secret authorship of 'Vestiges of the natural history of creation'*, Chicago, IL.

Selling, A. 1990 *Deutsche Gelehrten-Reisen nach England, 1660–1714*, Frankfurt am Main.

Seton-Karr, W. S. 1864–5 *Selections from Calcutta Gazette*, vols. I–II, Calcutta.

Severud Cook, K., 1995 'From false starts to firm beginnings: early colour printing of geological maps', *IM*, 47, 155–72.

Seville, C. 1999 *Literary copyright reform in early Victorian England: the framing of the 1842 Copyright Act*, Cambridge.

Seymour, W. A. (ed.) 1980 *A history of the Ordnance Survey*, Folkestone.

Shaaber, M. A. 1944 'The meaning of imprint in early printed books', *Library*, 4th ser., 24, 120–41.

Shaffer, E. (ed.) 2002 *The Athlone critical tradition series: the reception of British authors in Europe*, London.

Shankland, T. 1904–5 'Sir John Philipps; the SPCK; and the charity-school movement in Wales, 1699–1737', *Transactions of the Honourable Society of Cymmrodorion*, 74–216.

Sharpe, K. and Zwicker, S. N. (eds.) 2003 *Reading, society, and politics in early modern England*, Cambridge.

Shattock, J. 1989 *Politics and reviewers: the 'Edinburgh' and the 'Quarterly' in the early Victorian age*, Leicester.

Shaw, D. J. 2007 'Serialization of *Moll Flanders* in *The London Post* and *The Kentish Post*, 1722', *Library*, 7th ser., 8, 182–92.

Shaw, G. W. 1981 *Printing in Calcutta to 1800: a description and check list of printing in late 18th-century Calcutta*, London.

1987 *The South Asia and Burma retrospective bibliography (SABREB) Stage 1: 1556–1800*, London.

Shebbeare, J. 1757 *The occasional critic; or, the decrees of the Scotch tribunal in the Critical Review rejudged*, London.

Shefrin, J. 1999 *Neatly dissected for the instruction of young ladies and gentlemen in the knowledge of geography: John Spilsbury and early dissected puzzles*, Los Angeles, CA.

2003 *Such constant affectionate care: Lady Charlotte Finch, royal governess and the children of George III*, Los Angeles, CA.

Sher, R. B. 1998 'Corporatism and consensus in the late eighteenth-century book trade: the Edinburgh Booksellers' Society in comparative perspective', *Book History*, 1, 32–93.

2000 'Science and medicine in the Scottish Enlightenment: the lessons of book history', in Wood 2000, 99–156.

2006 *The Enlightenment and the book: Scottish authors and their publishers in eighteenth-century Britain, Ireland, and America*, Chicago.

Sher, R. B., and Amory, H. 2001 'From Scotland to the Strand: the genesis of Andrew Millar's bookselling career', in Isaac and McKay 2001, 51–70.

Sherburn, G. 1928 'Edward Young and book advertising', *RES*, 4, 414–17.

Shimotani, K. 2002 *The limits of the metaphorical concept of taste in eighteenth-century British aesthetics and criticism*, Tokyo.

Shipton, C. K. 1948 *Isaiah Thomas, printer, patriot and philanthropist, 1749–1831*, Rochester, NY.

Shirley, R. W. 1988 *Printed maps of the British Isles, 1650–1750*, London.

1995 'The maritime maps and atlases of Seller, Thornton, and Mount & Page', *MC*, 73, 2–9.

Shoemaker, R. B. 1992 'Reforming the City: the reformation of manners campaign in London, 1690–1738', in Davison *et al.* 1992, 99–120.

Shore, C. J. 1843 *Memoir of the life and correspondence of John Lord Teignmouth*, 2 vols., London.

Shorter, A. H. 1957 *Paper mills and paper makers in England, 1495–1800*, Hilversum.

1971 *Paper making in the British Isles: an historical and geographical study*, Newton Abbott.

Siebert, F. S. 1965 (1952) *Freedom of the press in England, 1476–1776: the rise and decline of government controls*, repr., Urbana, IL.

Silver, R. 1965 *Type founding in America, 1787–1825*, Charlottesville, VA.

Simon, B. (ed.) 1968 *Education in Leicestershire, 1540–1940: a regional study*, Leicester.

Simon, J. 1968 'Was there a charity school movement?', in B. Simon 1968, 55–100.

Simonton, D. 1998 *A history of European women's work: 1700 to the present*, London.

Simpson, A. W. B. 1981 'The rise and fall of the legal treatise: legal principles and the forms of legal literature', *University of Chicago Law Review*, 48, 632–79.

Siskin, C. 1998 *The work of writing: literature and social change in Britain, 1700–1830*, Baltimore, MD.

Slattery, W. C. (ed.) 1969 *The Richardson–Stinstra correspondence and Stinstra's prefaces to Clarissa*, Carbondale, IL.

Sledd, J. H., and Kolb, G. J. 1955 *Dr Johnson's dictionary: essays in the biography of a book*, Chicago, IL.

Smart, C. 1980 *Poetical works of Christopher Smart*, vol. I, ed. and intro. K. Williams, Oxford.

Smiles, S. 1884 *Men of invention and industry*, London.

1891 *A publisher and his friends: memoir and correspondence of the late John Murray, with an account of the origin and progress of the house, 1768–1843*, 2 vols., London.

Smith, C. M. 1967 (1857) *The working man's way in the world*, ed. E. Howe, London.

Smith, C. T. 2001 *Desmond*, ed. A. Blank and J. Todd, Peterborough, Ont.

Smith, D. 1988 'The Cary family', *MC*, 43, 40–7.

2000 'The business of "W. & A. K. Johnston", 1826–1901', *Journal of International Map Collectors' Society*, 82, 9–19.

Smith, G. 1738 *The laboratory or school of arts*, London.

1810 *The laboratory or school of arts*, 7th edn, 2 vols., London.

Smith, J. 1755 *The printer's grammer*, London.

1787 *The printer's grammar, chiefly collected from Smith's edition*, London.

Smith, J. 1867 *A descriptive catalogue of Friends' books, or books written by members of the Society of Friends, commonly called Quakers, from their first rise to the present time*, 2 vols., London.

Smith, M. 1994 *Religion in industrial society: Oldham and Saddleworth, 1740–1865*, Oxford.

Smith, M. M. 2000 'Fragments used for "servile purposes": the St Bride Library frisket for early red printing (with overview of later methods for red and black printing)', in Brownrigg and Smith 2000, 177–88.

Smith, N. 2008 *The literary manuscripts and letters of Hannah More*, Aldershot.

Smith, N. A., Adams, H. M. and Whiteley, D. P. (eds.) 1978 *Catalogue of the Pepys Library at Magdalene College, Cambridge*, vol. I: *Printed books*, Cambridge.

Smith, O. 1984 *The politics of language, 1791–1819*, Oxford.

Smollett, T. 2002 *The life and adventures of Sir Launcelot Greaves*, intro. and notes by R. Folkenflik, text ed. B. L. Fitzpatrick, Athens, GA.

Smout, T. C. 1963 *Scottish trade on the eve of the Union, 1660–1707*, Edinburgh.

1987 *A history of the Scottish people, 1560–1830*, London.

Snell, K. D. M. 1985 *Annals of the labouring poor: social change and agrarian England, 1660–1900*, Cambridge.

1999 'The Sunday-school movement in England and Wales', *P&P*, 164, 122–68.

Snell, K. D. M. and Ell, P. S. 2000 *Rival Jerusalems: the geography of Victorian religion*, Cambridge.

Snyder, H. L. 1968 'The circulation of newspapers in the reign of Queen Anne', *Library*, 5th ser., 23, 206–35.

Snyder, H. L. and Smith, M. S. (eds.) 2003 *The English short-title catalogue: past, present, future*, New York.

1976 'A further note', *Library*, 5th ser., 31, 387–9.

Solomon, H. R. 1996 *The rise of Robert Dodsley: creating the new age of print*, Carbondale, IL.

Sommerlad, M. J. 1967 *Scottish 'wheel' and 'herring-bone' bindings in the Bodleian Library*, Oxford.

Sommerville, C. J. 1996 *The news revolution in England: cultural dynamics of daily information*, New York.

Southey, R. 1819 'Inquiry into the Copyright Act', *QR*, 21, 196–213.

Spaeth, D. 2003 '"The enemy with": the failure of reform in the diocese of Salisbury in the eighteenth century', in Gregory and Chamberlain 2003, 121–44.

Spawn, W. and Kinsella, T. 1999 *Ticketed bookbindings from nineteenth-century Britain*, Bryn Mawr, PA.

Speck, W. A. 1982 'Politicians, peers and publication by subscription 1700–1750', in Rivers 1982a, 47–68.

Spector, R. D. 1966 *English literary periodicals and the climate of opinion during the Seven Years War*, The Hague.

Spence, J. 1966 *Observations, anecdotes, and characters of books and men*, ed. J. M. Osborn, 2 vols., Oxford.

Spencer, S. 1995 'Joseph Cottle', in Bracken and Silver 1995, 66–74.

Spicer, A. D. 1907 *The paper trade: a descriptive and historical survey of the paper trade from the commencement of the nineteenth century*, London.

Spieckermann, M.-L. 1979 'The English reprints of Richter in Altenburg: some notes and a list', *Factotum*, 7, 25.

Spinney, G. H. 1939 'Cheap repository tracts: Hazard and Marshall edition', *Library*, 4th ser., 20, 295–40.

Spufford, M. 1981 *Small books and pleasant histories: popular fiction and its readership in seventeeth-century England*, London.

1984 *The great reclothing of rural England: petty chapmen and their wares in the seventeenth century*, London.

1990 'The limitations of the probate inventory', in Chartres and Hey 1990, 139–74.

Staff, F. 1964 *The penny post, 1680–1918*, London.

Stallybrass, P. 2007 '"Little jobs": broadsides and the printing revolution', in Baron *et al.* 2007, 315–41.

Stanton, J. 1988 'Statistical profile of women writing in English from 1660 to 1800', in Keener and Lorsch 247–54.

Stationers' Company 1893 *A concise account of the origin and present position of the English Stock of the Stationers' Company*, London.

1985 *Records of the Worshipful Company of Stationers, 1554–1920*, ed. R. Myers, 115 reels of microfilm, Cambridge.

Stephens, F. G., and George, M. D. eds. 1870–1954 *Catalogue of political and personal satires preserved in the department of prints and drawings in the British Museum*, 11 vols., London.

Stephens, W. B. 1987 *Education, literacy, and society, 1830–70: the geography of diversity in provincial England*, Manchester.

1998 *Education in Britain, 1750–1914*, Basingstoke.

Stevens, W. 1824 'On the reciprocal influence of the periodical publications, and the intellectual progress of the country', *Blackwood's Edinburgh Magazine*, 16 Nov.

Stewart, L. 1992 *The rise of public science: rhetoric, technology and natural philosophy in Newtonian Britain, 1660–1750*, Cambridge.

Stewart-Brown, R. 1932 'The stationers, booksellers and printers of Chester to about 1800', *Transactions of the Historic Society of Lancashire and Cheshire*, 83, 101–52.

Stewart-Murphy, C. A. 1992 *A history of British circulating libraries: the book labels and ephemera of the Papantonio Collection*, Newtown, PA.

Stillinger, J. 1999 *Reading 'The Eve of St Agnes': the multiples of complex literary transaction*, Oxford.

Stiverson, C. Z., and Stiverson, G. A. 1983 'The colonial retail book trade: availability and affordability of reading material in mid-eighteenth-century Virgina', in Joyce *et al.* 1983, 132–73.

Stock, E. 1899–1916 *The history of the Church Missionary Society*, 4 vols., London.

Stoker, D. 1995 'The *Eighteenth-century short title catalogue* and provincial imprints', *JPHS*, 24, 9–35.

2004 'Freeman and Susannah Collins and the spread of English provincial printing', in McKay, Bell and Hinks 2004, 27–36.

Stokes, M. (ed.) 2002 *The state of American history*, Oxford.

Stokes, W. 1799 *Projects for establishing the internal peace and tranquillity of Ireland*, Dublin.

1806 *Observations on the necessity of publishing the scriptures in the Irish language*, Dublin.

Stone, L. 1969 'Literacy and education in England', *P&P*, 42, 69–139.

(ed.) 1974 *The university in society*, 2 vols., Princeton, NJ.

Stone, R. 1966/7 'The Albion press', *JPHS*, 2, 58–73; 'Addenda and corrigenda', *JPHS*, 3, 98–9.

Stott, A. 2003 *Hannah More: the first Victorian*, Oxford.

Stower, C. 1808a *The compositor's and pressman's guide to the art of printing*, London.

1808b *The printer's grammar; or introduction to the art of printing; containing a concise history of the art, with the improvements in the practice of printing for the last fifty years*, London.

Stranks, C. J. 1961 *Anglican devotion: studies in the spiritual life of the Church of England between the Reformation and the Oxford Movement*, London.

Straus, R. 1927 *The unspeakable Curll: being some account of Edmund Curll, bookseller; to which is added a full list of his books*, London.

1937 *Lloyd's: a historical sketch*, London.

Straus, R. and Dent, R. K. 1907 *John Baskerville a memoir*, London.

Streeter, H. W. 1970 *The eighteenth century English novel in French translation: a bibliographical study*, New York.

Strien, C. D. van and Ahsmann, M. 1992/3 'Scottish law students in Leiden at the end of the seventeenth century: the correspondence of John Clerk, 1694–1697', 2 parts, *Lias*, 19, 271–330; 20, 1–65.

Strutt, J. 1785–6 *A biographical dictionary; containing an historical account of all the engravers, from the earliest period of the art of engraving to the present time; and a short list of their most esteemed works . . .*, 2 vols., London.

Strype, J. 1720 *A survey of the cities of London and Westminster . . . , by John Stow*, 2 vols., London.

Stuart, D. 1838 'The late Mr Coleridge, poet', *Gentleman's Magazine*, n.s., 10, 2.

Stuart, J. and Revett, N. 1762–1816, *The Antiquities of Athens measured and delineated*, 4 vols., London.

Styles, M. and Arizpe, E. 2006 *Reading lessons from the eighteenth century: mothers, children and texts*, Lichfield.

Suarez, M. F., S.J. 1997 'The formation, transmission, and reception of Robert Dodsley's *Collection of poems by several hands*', in Dodsley 1997, I, 1–119.

1999a 'English book sale catalogues as bibliographical evidence: methodological considerations illustrated by a case study in the provenance and distribution of Dodsley's *Collection of poems*, 1750–1795', *Library*, 6th ser., 21, 321–60.

1999b '"This necessary knowledge": Thomas Chatterton and the ways of the London book trade', in Groom 1999, 96–118.

2000 'The business of literature: the book trade in England from Milton to Blake', in Womersley 2000, 131–47.

2001 'The production and consumption of the eighteenth-century poetic miscellany', in Rivers 2001, 217–51.

2002 'Uncertain proofs: Alexander Pope, Lewis Theobald, and questions of patronage', *PBSA*, 96, 404–34.

2003–4 (2006) 'Historiographical problems and possibilities in book history and national histories of the book', *SB*, 56, 141–70.

2007 '"The most blasphemous book that ever was publish'd": ridicule, reception, and censorship in eighteenth-century England', in Kirsop and Sherlock 2007, 48–77.

forthcoming *The poetic miscellany in Britain, 1701–1800: a bibliography with book-historical studies of eighteenth-century publishing practices, reading audiences, intellectual property, and canon formation*, Cambridge.

Suarez, M. F., S.J., and Zimmerman, S. M. 2006. 'John Clare's career and the early nineteenth-century English book trade', *Studies in Romanticism*, 45, 377–96.

Sullivan, A. (ed.) 1983a *British literary magazines: the Augustan age and the age of Johnson, 1698–1788*, Westport, CT.

1983b *British literary magazines: the Romantic age, 1789–1836*, Westport, CT.

Summers, M. 1938 *The gothic quest: a history of the gothic novel*, London.

Summerson, J. 1978 *Georgian London*, repr. edn, Harmondsworth.

Sunderland, J. 1988 'John Hamilton Mortimer: his life and works', *Walpole Society*, 52, 76–82.

Survey and Mapping Alliance 1991 *Ordnance Survey: past, present and future*, symposium proceedings, Chichester.

Sutcliffe, P. 1977 *The Oxford University Press: an informal history*, Oxford.

Sutherland, J. A. 1986 'Henry Colburn, publisher', *PH*, 19, 59–88.

1987 'The British book trade and the crash of 1826', *Library*, 6th ser., 9, 148–61.

1995 *The life of Walter Scott*, Oxford.

Sutherland, J. R. 1942 '*Polly* among the pirates', *MLR*, 37, 291–303.

Sutherland, K. 1987 'Fictional economies: Adam Smith, Walter Scott and the nineteenth-century novel', *English Literary History*, 54, 97–127.

1994 '"Events ... have made us a world of readers": reader relations, 1780–1830', in *Penguin history of literature*, vol. v: *The Romantic period*, ed. D. B. Pirie, 1994, 1–48.

Sutherland, L. S. and Mitchell, L. G. (eds.) 1986 *The history of the University of Oxford*, vol. v: *The eighteenth century*, Oxford.

Sweet, R. 1999 *The English town, 1680–1840: government, society and culture*, Harlow.

Sweet and Maxwell Limited 1974 *Then and now, 1799–1974: commemorating 175 years of law bookselling and publishing*, London.

Swift, A. K. 1985 'Sunderland bindings', unpub. chapter intended for thesis.

1986 'The formation of the library of Charles Spencer, 3rd earl of Sunderland (1674–1722): a study in the antiquarian book trade', unpub. thesis, University of Oxford.

1990 '"The French booksellers in the Strand": Huguenots in the London book trade, 1685–1730', *Proceedings of the Huguenot Society*, 25, 123–39.

1992 'Dutch penetration of the London market for books, *c.*1690–1730', in Berkvens-Stevelinck *et al.* 1992, 265–79.

Swift, J. 1939–68 *The prose works of Jonathan Swift*, ed. H. Davis, 14 vols., Oxford.

Sylla, R., Tilly, R. and Tortella, G. (eds.) 1999 *The state, the financial system and economic modernization*, Cambridge.

Tanselle, G. T. 1980 'Some statistics on American printing, 1764–1783', in Bailyn and Hench 1980, 315–63.

1995 'Printing history and other history', *SB*, 48, 269–89.

Tashjian, G. R., Tashjian, D. R. and Enright, B. J. 1990 *Richard Rawlinson: a tercentenary memorial*, Kalamazoo, MI.

Tattersfield, N. 1999 *Bookplates by Beilby and Bewick: a biographical dictionary of bookplates from the workshop of Ralph Beilby, Thomas Bewick and Robert Bewick, 1760–1849*, London.

2001 *John Bewick, engraver on wood, 1760–1795: an appreciation of his life together with an annotated catalogue of his illustrations and designs*, London.

Taylor, G. and Skinner, A. 1969 *Maps of the roads of Ireland*, facs. of the 2nd edn (1783), intro. J. H. Andrews, Shannon.

Taylor, J. T. 1943 *Early opposition to the English novel: the popular reaction from 1760 to 1830*, New York.

Taylor, R. 1847 'On the invention and first introduction of Mr Koenig's printing machine', *Philosophical Magazine*, 3rd ser., 208, 297–301.

Taylor, R. A. 1997 'Applegath and Cowper: their importance to the English letterpress printing industry in the nineteenth century', *JPHS*, 25, 47–69.

Tegg, T. 1870 *Memoir of the late Thomas Tegg: abridged from his autobiography by permission of his son, William Tegg*, for private circulation, London.

Temperley, N. 1998 *The hymn tune index: a census of English-language hymn tunes in printed sources from 1535 to 1820*, assisted by C. G. Manns and J. Herl, 4 vols., Oxford.

Tempesti, D. 1994 *Domenico Tempesti e I discorsi sopra l'intaglio ed ogni sorte d'intagliare in rame da lui provate e osservate dai più grand'huomini di tale professione*, ed. F. De Denaro, Florence.

Terrell, C. 1995 'A sequel to *The Atlantic Neptune* of J. F. W. DesBarres: the story of the copperplates', *MC*, 72, 2–9.

Terry, R. 2001 *Poetry and the making of the English literary past, 1660–1781*, Oxford.

Thomas, D. 1969 *A long time burning: the history of literary censorship in England*, London.

1977 'Press prosecutions of the eighteenth and nineteenth centuries: the evidence of King's Bench indictments', *Library*, 5th ser., 32, 315–32.

Thomas, I. 1810 *The history of printing in America*, Worcester, MA.

1970 (1810) *The history of printing in America*, ed. M. A. McCorison, New York.

Thompson, E. P. 1963 *The making of the English working class*, London.

Thompson, F. M. L. (ed.) 1994 *Landowners, capitalists and entrepreneurs: essays for Sir John Habakkuk*, Oxford.

Thompson, R. S. 1971 *Classics or charity?: the dilemma of the 18th century grammar school*, Manchester.

Thomson, A. G. 1974 *The paper industry in Scotland, 1590–1861*, Edinburgh.

Thomson, F. M. 1967 'John Wilson, an Ayrshire printer, publisher and bookseller' *The Bibliotheck* 5, no. 2, 41–61.

Thomson, J. 1981 *The seasons*, ed. J. Sambrook, Oxford.

Thoresby, R. 1830 *The diary of Ralph Thoresby, FRS*, ed. J. Hunter, 2 vols., 1830.

Tierney, J. E. 1973 '*The Museum* – the super-excellent magazine', *Studies in English Literature*, 13, 505–15.

1975 'The study of the eighteenth-century periodical: problems and progress', *PBSA*, 69, 165–86.

1995 'Book advertisements in mid-18th-century newspapers: the example of Robert Dodsley', in Myers and Harris 1995, 103–22.

2001 'Advertisement for books in London newspapers, 1760–1785', *Studies in Eighteenth-Century Culture*, 30 (Spring), 153–64.

The Times, 1935 *The history of The Times*, vol. I: *The Thunderer in the making, 1785–1841*, London.

Timperley, C. H. 1842 *Encyclopaedia of literary and typographical anecdote*, 2nd edn, London.

Todd, E. 1999 'The Transatlantic context: Walter Scott and nineteenth-century American literary history', unpub. thesis, University of Minnesota.

Todd, J. 2000 *Mary Wollstonecraft: a revolutionary life*, London.

Todd, W. B. 1952 'Concurrent printing: an analysis of Dodsley's *Collection of poems by several hands*', *PBSA*, 46, 45–57.

1972 *A directory of printers and others in allied trades, London and vicinity, 1800–1840*, London.

Todd, W. B., and Bowden, A. 1998 *Sir Walter Scott: a bibliographical history, 1796–1832*, New Castle, DE.

Topham, E. 1776 *Letters from Edinburgh written in the years 1774 and 1775, containing some observations on the diversions, customs, manners and laws of the Scotch nation*, London.

Topham, J. R. 1992 'Science and popular education in the 1830s: the role of the *Bridgewater Treatises*', *British Journal for the History of Science*, 25, 397–430.

2000a 'Scientific publishing and the reading of science in nineteenth-century Britain: a historiographical survey and guide to sources', *Studies in History and Philosophy of Science*, 31A, 559–612.

2000b 'A textbook revolution', in Frasca-Spada and Jardine 2000, 317–37.

Townsend, J. R. 1994 *John Newbury and his books*, Metuchen, NJ.

Treadwell, M. 1980 'London printers and printing houses in 1705', *PH*, 7, 5–44.

1981 'The Grover type foundry', *JPHS*, 15, 36–53.

1982a 'London trade publishers, 1675–1720', *Library*, 6th ser., 4, 99–134.

1982b 'Notes on London type founders, 1620–1720', unpub. paper delivered July 1982 to the Printing Historical Society in Oxford.

1989 'Of false and misleading imprints', in Myers and Harris 1989, 29–46.

1992 'Printers on the Court of the Stationers' Company in the seventeenth and eighteenth centuries', *JPHS*, 21, 29–42.

2003 'The Stationers and the Printing Acts at the end of the seventeenth century', in *CHBB*, IV, 755–79.

Tredrey, F. D. 1984 *The house of Blackwood, 1804–1954*, Edinburgh.

Tremaine, M. 1952 *A bibliography of Canadian imprints, 1751–1800*, Toronto.

Trollope, A. 1847 *The MacDermots of Ballycloran*, 3 vols., London.

Trusler, W. 1790 *The London adviser and guide*, 2nd edn, London.

Tuama, S. Ó. (ed.) 1981 *An Duanaire, 1600–1900: poems of the dispossessed*, Mountrath.

Tucoo-Chala, S. 1977 *Charles-Joseph Panckoucke et la librairie française*, Pau.

Turberville, A. S. 1957 *English men and manners in the eighteenth century: an illustrated narrative*, 2nd edn, Oxford.

Turbet, R. 1997 'Music deposited by Stationers' Hall at the library of the University and King's College of Aberdeen, 1753–96', *Research Chronicle: Royal Musical Association*, 30, 139–62.

Turnbull, G. 1951 *A history of the calico printing industry of Great Britain*, Altrincham.

Turner, C. 1992 *Living by the pen: women writers in the eighteenth century*, London.

Turner, G. L'E. 1974 'Henry Baker, FRS; founder of the Bakerian Lecture', *Royal Society Notes and Records*, 29, 53–79.

Turner, K. 2000 *British travel writers in Europe, 1750–1800: authorship, gender, and national identity*, Aldershot.

Turner, M. L. 1974 'Andrew Wilson, Lord Stanhope's stereotype printer: a preliminary report', *JPHS*, 9, 22–65.

(ed.) 1978 'The minute book of the partners in the *Grub Street Journal*', *PH*, 4, 49–94.

1985a 'The archives of the Stationers' Company as a source of biographical information on members of the English book trades, 1701–1830', in Crapulli 1985, 285–97.

1985b 'The personnel of the Stationers' Company, 1800–30: work in progress', in Myers and Harris 1985, 78–102.

Turner, S. 1999 'William Holland's satirical print catalogues, 1788–1794', *Print Quarterly*, 16, 127–36.

Turner, T. 1984 *The diary of Thomas Turner*, ed. D. G. Vaisey, Oxford.

Twining, T. 1893 *Travels in India a hundred years ago*, London.

1991 *A selection of Thomas Twining's letters, 1734–1804: the record of a tranquil life*, ed. R. S. Walker, 2 vols., Lewiston, NY.

Twyman, M. 1966 *John Soulby, printer, Ulverston, 1796–1827*, Reading.

1967 'The lithographic hand press 1796–1820', *JPHS*, 3, 3–50.

1970 *Lithography, 1800–1850: the techniques of drawing on stone in England and France and their application in works of topography*, London.

1976 *A directory of London lithographic printers, 1800–1850*, London.

1990 *Early lithographed books: a study of the design and production of improper books in the age of the hand press, with a catalogue*, London.

1996 *Early lithographed music: a study based on the H. Baron Collection*, London.

1998a *The British Library guide to printing: history and techniques*, London.

1998b (1970) *Printing, 1770–1970: an illustrated history of its development and uses in England*, London.

2001 *Breaking the mould: the first hundred years of lithography*, The Panizzi Lectures, 2000, London.

Tyacke, S. 1978 *London map-sellers, 1660–1720*, Tring.

Tyson, A. 1963 *The authentic English editions of Beethoven*, London.

Tyson, G. P. 1979 *Joseph Johnson: a liberal publisher*, Iowa City, IA.

Ullrich, H. 1977 (1898) *Robinson und Robinsonaden: Bibliographie, Geschichte, Kritik: ein Beitrag vergleichenden Litteraturgeschichte, im besonderen zur Geschichte des Romans und zur Geschichte der Jugendlitteratur* (1898), Weimar.

United Kingdom, Parliament 1822 *Third report of the commissioners of inquiry into the collection and management of the revenue arising in Ireland*, Parl. Papers, xiii.

1837–8 *First report from the select committee on postage*, Parl. Papers, xx.

1856 *The census of Ireland for the year 1851*, Parl. Papers, xxxi.

Unwin, R. W. 1984 *Charity schools and the defence of Anglicanism: James Talbot, rector of Spofforth, 1700–08*, York.

Updike, D. B. 1962 *Printing types, their history, forms and use: a study in survivals*, 2 vols., Cambridge, MA.

Utz, R. 2002 *Chaucer and the discourse of German philology: a history of reception and an annotated bibiliography of studies, 1793–1948*, Turnhout.

Vallancey, C. 1780 *The art of tanning and currying leather: with an account of all the different processes made use of in Europe and Asia, for dying leather red and yellow. Collected and published at the expence of the Dublin Society. To which are added Mr Phillip's method of dying the Turkey leather . . . also the new method of tanning: invented by the late David Macbride MD*, London.

Van Allen-Russell, A. 2002 '"For instruments not intended": the second J. C. Bach lawsuit', *Music and Letters*, 83, 3–29.

Vanderlint, J. 1734 *Money answers all things: or, an essay to make money sufficiently plentiful amongst all ranks of people: and increase our foreign and domestick trade*, London.

Van der Wee, H. 1977 'Monetary credit and banking systems', in Rich and Wilson 1977, 290–392.

van Eeghen, I. H. 1960–78 *De Amsterdamse boekhandel 1680–1725*, 5 vols., Amsterdam.

1966 'De befaamde drukkerij op de Herengracht over de Plantage, 1685–1755', *Jaarboek Amstelodamum*, 58, 82–100.

1982 'Europese "libraires": de gebroeders Huguetan in Amsterdam (1686–1705)', *Documentatieblad van de Werkgroep 18e Eeuw*, 53–4, 1–9.

Van Lennep, W., Avery, E. L., Scouten, A. H., Stone, G. W. and Hogan, C. B. (eds.) 1961–5 *The London stage, 1660–1800: a calendar of plays . . .* , 5 parts, Carbondale, IL.

Varey, S. 1993 'The *Craftsman*', *Prose Studies: History, Theory, Criticism*, 16, 58–77.

2001 'Revisiting a masterpiece: "Government and the press, 1695–1763" ', *Studies in the Literary Imagination*, 34, 49–61.

Varma, D. P. 1972 *The evergreen tree of diabolical knowledge*, Washington, DC.

Vernon, G. W. and Scriven, J. B. 1787–9 *Irish reports; or, reports of cases determined in the King's Courts, Dublin, with select cases in the House of Lords of Ireland.* 2 vols., Dublin.

Vertue, G. 1736 *The heads of the kings of England proper for Rapin's History . . .* London.

1933–4 'Vertue note books', III, Walpole Society, 22.

Veylit, A. 1994 'A statistical survey and evaluation of the "Eighteenth-century short-title catalog" ', unpub. thesis, University of California Riverside.

Ville, S. 2004 'Transport', in Floud and Johnson 2004, 295–331.

Vinz, C. 1969 'Das Verlagsverzeichnis der Waltherschen Hofbuchhandlung in Dresden vom Jahre 1833', *Archiv für Geschichte des Buchwesens*, 9, 89–206.

Viscomi, J. 1993 *Blake and the idea of the book*, Princeton, NJ.

Vliet, R. van 2002 'Nederlandse boekverkopers op de Buchmesse te Leipzig in echttiende eeuw', *Jaarboek voor Nederlandse boekgeschiedenis*, 9, 89–109.

Voltaire Foundation 1979 *Voltaire and the English: transactions of the Oxford Colloquium held at the Taylor Institution from 26 to 28 May 1978*, Oxford.

Wadsworth, K. W. 1987–92 'Philip, Lord Wharton – revolutionary aristocrat?', *Journal of the United Reformed Church History Society*, 4, 465–76.

Wakeman, G. and Pollard, H. G. 1993 *Functional developments in bookbinding*, New Castle, DE.

Waldron, M. 1996 *Lactilla, milkwoman of Clifton: the life and writings of Ann Yearsley, 1753–1806*, Athens, GA.

Walker, G. 1795 *The house of Tynian: a novel*, 4 vols., London.

Wallace, J. 1869 *The history of Blyth*, Blyth.

Wallace, J. W. 1882 *The reporters arranged and characterized with incidental remarks*, 4th edn, Edinburgh.

Wallis, P. 1974 *At the sign of the Ship: notes on the House of Longman, 1724–1974*, Harlow.

Wallis, P. J. 1996 *Book subscription lists: extended supplement to the revised guide by P. J. Wallis*, completed and edited by Ruth Wallis, Newcastle upon Tyne.

Wallis, R. V. and Wallis, P. J. 1986 *Biobibliography of British mathematics and its applications*, pt 2, *1701–1760*, Letchworth.

Walsh, J., Haydon, C. and Taylor, S. (eds.) 1993 *The Church of England, c.1689–c.1833*, Cambridge.

Walsh, M. 1997a 'Biblical scholarship and literary criticism', in Nisbet and Rawson 1997, 758–77.

1997b *Shakespeare, Milton and eighteenth-century literary editing: the beginnings of interpretative scholarship*, Cambridge.

2001 'Literary scholarship and the life of editing', in Rivers 2001, 190–215.

Walters, A. N. 1992 'Tools of Enlightenment: the material culture of science in eighteenth century Britain', unpub. thesis, University of California, Berkeley, CA.

1997 'Conversation pieces: science and politeness in eighteenth-century England', *History of Science*, 35, 121–54.

Walters, G. 1974 'The booksellers in 1759 and 1774: the battle for literary property', *Library*, 5th ser., 29, 287–311.

1980–1 'The account book, 1826–1836, of the Reverend John Parry, printer and publisher of Chester', *JPHS*, 15, 54–80.

Walton, J. 1968 'A survey of the printing trade and related occupations in Nottingham and Nottinghamshire to 1900', unpub. thesis, Library Association.

Walvin, J. 1977 'The impact of slavery on British radical politics, 1787–1838', in Rubin and Tuden 1977, 343–67.

(ed.) 1982 *Slavery and British society, 1776–1814*, London.

Warburton, J., Whitelaw, J. and Walsh, R. 1818 *History of the city of Dublin*, 2 vols., London.

Ward, A. W. and Waller, A. R. (eds.) 1916 *The Cambridge history of English literature*, vol. XIV, Cambridge.

Ward, W. R. 1953 *The English land tax in the eighteenth century*, Oxford.

Wardenaar, D. 1982 (1801) *Zetten en drukken in de achttiende eeuw: David Wardenaar's Beschrijving der boekdrukkunst*, ed. F. A. Janssen, Haarlem.

Warner, M. 1990 *The letters of the republic: publication and the public sphere in eighteenth-century America*, Cambridge, MA.

Warren, A. 1896 *The Charles Whittinghams, printers*, New York.

Watson, J. R. 1997 *The English hymn: a critical and historical study*, Oxford.

Watson, R. 1791 *A collection of theological tracts*, 2nd edn, 6 vols., London.

Watt, I. 1957 *The rise of the novel: studies in Defoe, Richardson and Fielding*, Berkeley, CA.

Watt, W. 1824 *Bibliotheca Britannica, or a general index to British and foreign literature*, 4 vols., Edinburgh.

Webb, R. K. 1955 *The British working class reader, 1790–1848: literacy and social tension*, London.

1960 *Harriet Martineau, a radical Victorian*, London.

Weedon, A. 2003 *Victorian publishing: the economics of book production for a mass market, 1836–1916*, Aldershot.

Weedon, M. J. P. 1949 *Richard Johnson and the successors to John Newbery*, London.

Weinstein, M. and Lumsden, A. 2000 'Essay on the text', in Scott 2000b, 293–4, 413–17.

Welch, R. 2002 'The book in Ireland from the Tudor re-conquest to the Battle of the Boyne', in *CHBB* IV, 701–18.

Welsh, C. 1885 *A bookseller of the last century: being some account of the life of John Newbery, and of the books he published, with a notice of the later Newberys*, London.

Welti, M. E. 1964 *Der Basler Buchdruck und Britannien: die Rezeption britischen Gedankenguts in den Basler Pressen von den Anfängen bis zum Beginn des 17. Jahrhunderts*, Basel.

Werkmeister, L. 1963 *The London daily press, 1772–1792*, Lincoln, NE.

Wesley, J. 1983 *A collection of hymns for the use of the people called Methodists*, in *The Oxford edition of the works of John Wesley*, vol. VII, ed. F. Hildebrandt, O. A. Beckerlegge and J. Dale, Oxford.

West, W. 1837 *Fifty years' recollections of an old bookseller*, London.

Wharton, R. 1738 *Historiae pueriles*, 2nd edn, London.

Whatley, C. A. 1997 *The Industrial Revolution in Scotland; prepared for the Economic History Society*, Cambridge.

White, C. 1970 *Women's magazines, 1693–1968*, London.

White, R. B. (ed.) 1978 *The dress of words*, Lawrence, KS.

Whitley, W. T. 1916–22 *A Baptist bibliography: being a register of the chief materials for Baptist history, whether in manuscript or in print, preserved in Great Britain, Ireland, and the colonies*, 2 vols., London.

Wiener, J. H. 1969 *The war of the unstamped: the movement to repeal the British newspaper tax, 1830–1836*, London.

1970 *A descriptive finding list of unstamped British periodicals, 1830–1836*, London.

Wiles, R. M. 1957 *Serial publication in England before 1750*, Cambridge.

1965 *Freshest advices: early provincial newspapers in England*, Columbus, OH.

1968 'Middle-class literacy in eighteenth-century England: fresh evidence', in Brissenden 1968, 49–66.

Wilford, J. (ed.) 1964 *The monthly catalogue: being an exact account of all books and pamphlets published in March M.DCC.XXIII. 1723–1730 (–Feb 1730. Collected by John Wilford)*, English bibliographical sources series 1, 2, London.

Wilkes, W. 1990 *Das Schriftgiessen: von Stempelschnitt, Matrizenfertigung und Letternguss: eine Dokumentation*, Stuttgart.

Willard, O. M. 1942 'The survival of English books printed before 1640: a theory and some illustrations', *Library*, 4th ser., 23, 171–90.

Williams, J. 1791 *Shrove Tuesday, a satiric rhapsody. By Anthony Pasquin, Esq.*, London.

Williams, J. A. 1968 *Catholic recusancy in Wiltshire, 1600–1791*, CRS monograph ser. 1, London.

1981 'Change or decay? The provincial laity, 1691–1781', in Duffy 1981, 27–54.

Williams, N. J. 1955 'The London port books', *Transactions of the London and Middlesex Archaeological Society*, 18, 13–26.

Williams, W. P. 1977 'Chetwin, Crooke, and the Jonson folios', *SB*, 30, 75–95.

Williams, W. P. and Baker, W. 2001 '*Caveat lector*: English book, 1475–1700 and the electronic age', *Analytical and Enumerative Bibliography*, n.s., 12, 1–29.

Wilson, F. J. F. and Grey, D. 1888 *A practical treatise upon modern printing machinery and letterpress printing*, London.

Wilson, P. 1982 'Classical poetry and the eighteenth-century reader', in Rivers, 1982a, 69–96.

Wilson, T. 1797 *The use of circulating libraries considered; with instructions for opening and conducting a library, either upon a large or small plan*, London.

Winchester, S. 2001 *The map that changed the world: the tale of William Smith and the birth of a science*, Harmondsworth.

Windle, J. and Pippin, K. 1999 *Thomas Frognall Dibdin, 1776–1847: a bibliography*, New Castle, DE.

Winfield, P. H. 1925 *The chief sources of English legal history*, Cambridge, MA.

Winkler, K. T. 1993 *Handwerk und Markt: Druckerhandwerk, Vertriebswesen und Tagesschrifttum in London 1695–1750*, Stuttgart.

Winton, C. 1980 'Dramatic censorship', in Hume 1980, 286–308.

1993 *John Gay and the London theatre*, Lexington, KY.

Withers, C. W. J. 1984 *Gaelic in Scotland, 1698–1891*, Edinburgh.

2000 'John Adair, 1660–1718', *Geographers: Biobibliographical Studies*, 20, 1–8.

2002 'The social nature of map making in the Scottish Enlightenment, *c.*1682–*c.*1832', *IM*, 54, 46–65.
Withers, C. W. J. and Wood, P. (eds.) 2002 *Science and medicine in the Scottish Enlightenment*, East Linton.
Withrington, D. 1988 'Schooling, literacy and society', in Devine and Mitchison 1988, 163–87.
Wittmann, R. and Hack, B. (eds.) 1982 *Buchhandel und Literatur: Festschrift für Herbert G. Göpfert*, Wiesbaden.
Wolf, E. 1974 *The library of James Logan of Philadelphia*, Philadelphia, PA.
1988 *The book culture of a colonial American city: Philadelphia books, bookmen, and booksellers*, Oxford.
Wolf, L. 1979 *Terminologische Untersuchungen zur Einführung des Buchdrucks im französischen Sprachgebiet*, Tübingen.
Wolff, J. 1981 *The social production of art*, London.
Wollenberg, S. 2001 *Music at Oxford in the eighteenth and nineteenth centuries*, Oxford.
Womersley, D. (ed.) 2000 *A companion to literature from Milton to Blake*, Oxford.
Wood, M. 1994 *Radical satire and print culture, 1790–1822*, Oxford.
2002 *Slavery, empathy and pornography*, Oxford.
Wood, P. (ed.) 2000 *The Scottish Enlightenment: essays in reinterpretation*, Rochester, NY.
Wood, R. 1976 *An essay on the original genius and writings of Homer*, ed. B. Fabian, Hildesheim.
Woodbridge, K. 1970 *Landscape and antiquity: aspects of English culture at Stourhead, 1718 to 1838*, Oxford.
Woodcroft, B. 1969 (1859) *Printing patents: abridgements of specifications relating to printing, 1617–1857*, ed. J. Harrison, London.
Woodfield, I. 2000 'John Bland: London retailer of the music of Haydn and Mozart', *Music and Letters*, 81, 210–44.
Woodmansee, M. 1984 'The genius and the copyright: economic and legal conditions of the "author"', *ECS*, 17, 425–48.
Woodmansee, M. and Jaszi, P. (eds.) 1994 *The construction of authorship: textual appropriation in law and literature*, Durham, NC.
Woodward, D. M. 1970 'Short guides to records: "Port Books"', *History*, 5th ser., 55, 207–10 (repr. 'Port Books', *Short Guides to Records* no. 22, 1994).
1973 'The port books of England and Wales', *Maritime History*, 3, 147–65.
Wordsworth, W. 1963 'Preface' to *Lyrical ballads*, 1802, in *Wordsworth and Coleridge: lyrical ballads*, ed. R. L. Breet and A. R. Jones, London.
Worms, L. 1986 'Mapsellers at the Royal Exchange, pt 2: 1660–1714', *MC*, 35, 16–20.
1993 'Thomas Kitchin's "Journey of Life": hydrographer to George III, mapmaker and engraver', 2 parts, *MC*, 62, 2–8; 63, 14–20.
1997 'The book trade at the Royal Exchange', in Saunders 1997, 209–26.
2000 'Location in the London map trade', *Journal of the International Map Collectors' Society*, 82, 33–42.
2004 'The maturing of British commercial cartography: William Faden (1749–1836) and the map trade', *CJ*, 41, 1, 5–11.
Wright, A. 1950 *Joseph Spence: a critical biography*, Chicago, IL.
Wrightson, K. 2002 *Earthly necessities: economic lives in early modern Britain, 1470–1750*, London.

Wrigley, E. A. 1986 'Men on the land and men in the countryside: employment in agriculture in early-nineteenth-century England', in Bonfield, Smith and Wrightson 1986, 295–336.

1987 *People, cities and wealth: the transformation of traditional society*, Oxford.

1988 *Continuity, chance and change: the character of the Industrial Revolution in England*, Cambridge.

1998 'Explaining the rise in marital fertility in England in the "long" eighteenth century', *EcHR*, 51, 435–64.

2000 'The divergence of England: the growth of the English economy in the seventeenth and eighteenth centuries', *TRHS*, 6th ser., 10, 117–41.

2004 *Poverty, progress, and population*, Cambridge.

Wrigley, E. A. and Schofield, R. S. 1981 *The population history of England, 1541–1871: a reconstruction*, Cambridge, MA; 2nd edn 1989.

Wrigley, E. A., Davies, R. S., Oeppen, J. E. and Schofield, R. S. 1997 *English population history from family reconstitution, 1580–1837*, Cambridge.

Wyn Jones, D. 1996 'From Artaria to Longman & Broderip: Mozart's music on sale in London', in Biba and Wyn Jones 1996, 105–14.

Yates, W. 1968 *A map of the county of Lancashire, 1786*, facs., intro. J. B. Harley, Liverpool.

Yeo, R. R. 1991 'Reading encyclopedias: science and the organization of knowledge in the British dictionaries of arts and sciences, 1730–1850', *Isis*, 82, 24–49.

2000 'Encyclopedic knowledge', in Frasca-Spada and Jardine 2000, 207–24.

2001 *Encyclopaedic visions: scientific dictionaries and Enlightenment culture*, Cambridge.

Yolton, J. 1998 *John Locke: a descriptive bibliography*, Bristol.

Zachs, W. 1998 *The first John Murray and the late eighteenth-century London book trade*, Oxford.

Zeeman, J. C. (ed.) 1991 *The eighteenth century short title catalogue: the cataloguing rules*, London.

Zionkowski, L. 2001 *Men's work: gender, class, and the professionalization of poetry, 1660–1784*, New York.

Zonca, V. 1607. *Novo teatro di machine et edificii per varie e secure operationi*, Padua.

Bibliography of URLs

'Anglo-American Cataloguing Rules', http://www.aacr2.org/index.html

Beinecke Staff, Yale University. 'Cadell & Davies Records', http://webtext.library.yale.edu/xml2html/beinecke.cadell.con.html#a9

'British Library, Guide to Sale Catalogues', http://www.bl.uk/reshelp/findhelprestype/prbooks/guidesalecat/salescatalogueguild.html

'Eighteenth Century Collections Online', http://gale.cengage.com/EighteenthCentury

English Short Title Catalogue, http://estc.bl.uk

Hall, N. and Raven, J. 2000 'Mapping the print culture of eighteenth-century London', http://members.lycos.co.uk/bookhistory Oxford.

'The Law Online', http://www.justis.com/Search.aspx, Justis Publishing.

'Literature Online: The Home of Literature and Criticism', http://lion.chadwyck.co.uk/infoCentre/contents.jsp

The London Book Trades Project. 'Researching the History of Eighteenth-Century London Book Production', http://members.lycos.co.uk/bookhistory/index.html

Maxted, Ian. 'The British book trades, 1710–1777', *Exeter Working Papers in Book Trade History*; 2, http://bookhistory.blogspot.com/2005/12/index.html

'The British book trades, 1710–1777: An Index of Masters and Apprentices. Introduction', *Exeter Working Papers in Book Trade History*; 2, http://bookhistory.blogspot.com/2007/01/apprentices-introduction.html

'The British book trades, 1731–1806: A Checklist of Bankrupts', *Exeter Working Papers in British Book Trade History*; 4, http://bookhistory.blogspot.com/2007/01/bankrupts.html.

'The British book trades 1775–1787: An Index to Insurance Policies. Introduction', *Exeter Working Papers in Book Trade History*; 8, http://bookhistory.blogspot.com/2007/01/insurance-introduction.html

'The London book trades, 1735–1775: A Checklist of Members in Trade Directories and in Musgrave's *Obituary*', *Exeter Working Papers in Book Trade History*; 3, http://bookhistory.blogspot.com/2007/01/london-1735-1775.html

'The London book trades 1775–1800: A Topographical Guide. Introduction,' *Exeter Working Papers in Book Trade History*; 1, http://bookhistory.blogspot.com/2007/01/streets-introduction.html

National Archives. 'Port Books, 1565–1799: Domestic Records Information 9: 1. Port Books, 1565–1799', http://www.nationalarchives.gov.uk/catalogue/RdLeaflet.asp?sLeafletID=83&j=1&j=1

National Library of Scotland. 'Inventory: Acc. 10662 Bell and Bradfute', http://www.hss.ed.ac.uk/chb/sbtai-db/PDFFiles/acc10662.pdf

'The John Murray Archive', http://www.nls.uk/jma/mss/search/index.cfm

New York Public Library. 'Record #b7086207', http://catnyp.nypl.org/record=b7086207

Nineteenth-Century Short Title Catalogue. 'About NSTC', http://nstc.chadwyck.com/marketing/about.jsp

OCLC. 'WorldCat at a Glance', http://www.oclc.org/worldcat/introduction/default.htm

'Orlando: women's writing in the British Isles from the beginnings to the present', http://orlando.cambridge.org; see Brown, Susan, Clements, P. and Grundy, I. (eds.) 2006–

School of Advanced Study. 'The London Book Trades: A Biographical Resource', http://sas-space.sas.ac.uk/dspace/handle/10065/224

'Society for the History of Authorship, Reading & Publishing', http://www.sharpweb.org/

University of Birmingham. 'The British Book Trade Index', http://www.bbti.bham.ac.uk

University of Cambridge. 'Cambridge University Library: Bible Society's library', http://www.lib.cam.ac.uk/deptserv/biblesociety/

University of Edinburgh. 'Scottish book trade archive inventory', http://www.hss.ed.ac.uk/chb/sbtai-db/recordB.htm

University of Leicester. 'Historical Directories', http://www.historicaldirectories.org/hd/index.asp

'The Nichols Archive Project', http://www.le.ac.uk/elh/resources/nichols/index.html

University of Reading. 'Special Collections: Records of the Longman Group', http://www.reading.ac.uk/special-collections/collections/sc-longman.asp

'Voice of the Shuttle', http://vos.ucsb.edu/browse.asp?id=2713#id3785

Index

2.1 Invitation to the funeral of Sir Arthur Shaen, County Roscommon, Ireland. Woodcut blocks with type inserted, completed by hand in 1725. 200×230mm.

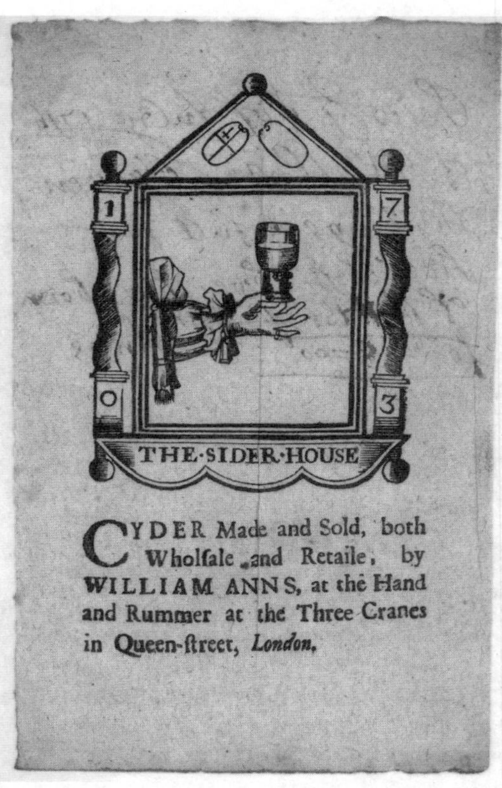

2.2 Trade card of William Anns, cider maker, Queen Street, London. Printed from type with woodcut illustration, 1703. 183×117mm.

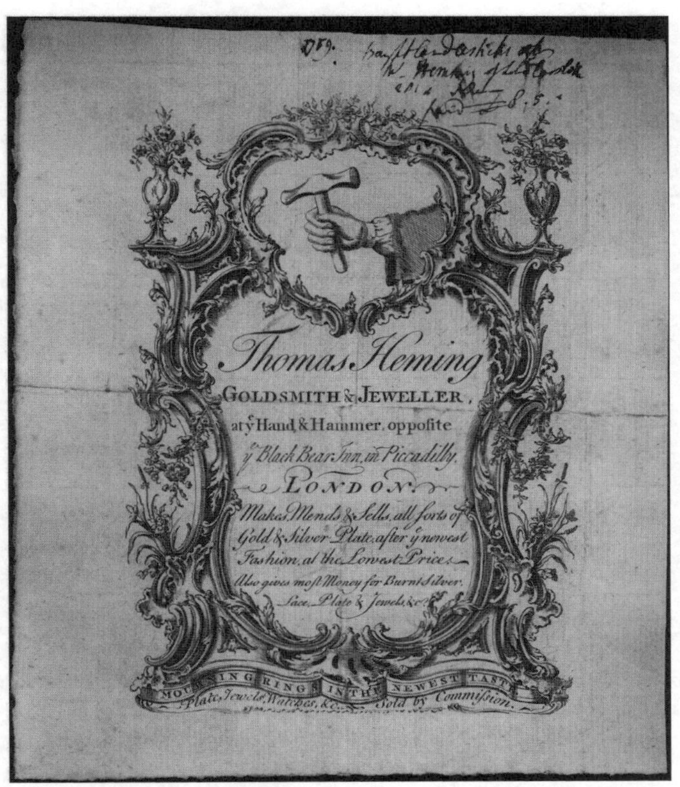

2.3 Trade card of Thomas Heming, goldsmith and jeweller, London. Printed intaglio, with manuscript note dated 1759. 195×163 mm.

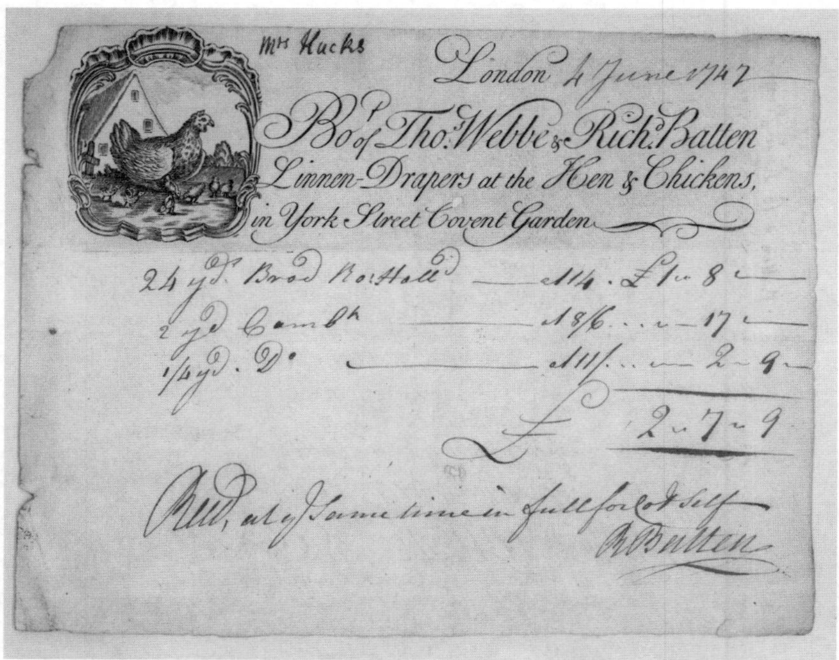

Mrs Hucks

London 4 June 1747

Bo.t of Tho.s Webbe & Rich.d Batten
Linnen-Drapers at the Hen & Chickens,
in York Street Covent Garden

24 yds Brod Ho: Holl.d	1/4	£1 " 8 "
2 yd Camb.k	8/6	" 17 "
1/4 yd. D.o	11/	" 2 " 9
	£	2 " 7 " 9

Rec.d at y.e Same time in full for o.d Self
R Batten

2.4 Invoice of Thomas Webbe and Richard Batten of Covent Garden, London. Printed intaglio and made out by hand on 4 June 1747. 170×214mm.

28th. February 1776.

Town – Houſe in STOCKTON,

At a General Meeting of the Juſtices of the Peace Acting within the Diviſion of STOCKTON WARD *in the County of Durham held here this Day.*

I T was R E S O L V E D

THAT no Licence be in future granted to any Ale-houſe Keeper or Innkeeper within the ſaid Ward, who ſhall knowingly ſuffer any Cock-Fighting, Card-Playing, or any Kind of Gaming in his or their Houſe, Out-houſe, Orchard, Garden, Yard, or Premiſes.

DARLINGTON: *Printed by* Meſſrs. DARNTON and SMITH.

2.5 Justices of the Peace notice concerning the licensing of ale houses in Stockton Ward, County of Durham. Letterpress, printed by Darnton and Smith, Darlington, 1776. 102×155 mm.

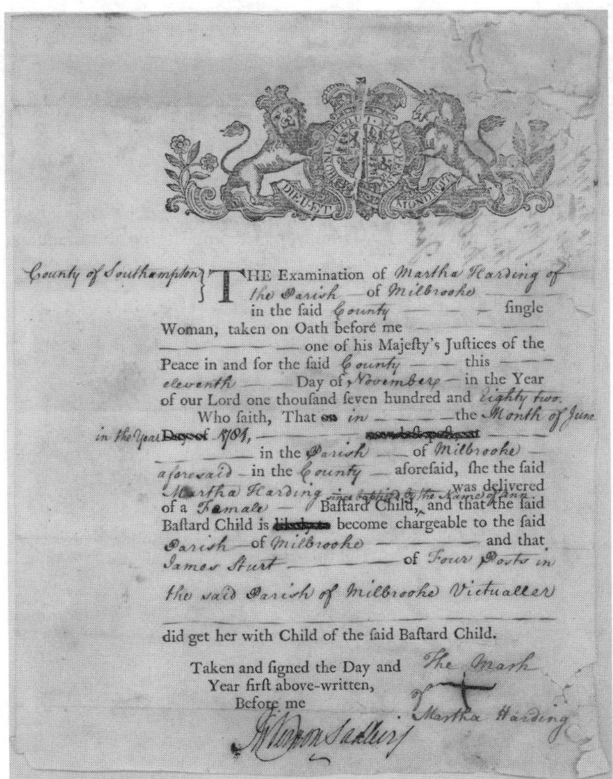

County of Southampton } THE Examination of Martha Harding of the Parish of Milbrooke in the said County single Woman, taken on Oath before me one of his Majeſty's Juſtices of the Peace in and for the ſaid County this eleventh Day of November in the Year of our Lord one thouſand ſeven hundred and Eighty two.

Who ſaith, That ~~on~~ in the Month of June in the Year ~~Day of~~ 1781, ~~[illegible]~~ in the Parish of Milbrooke aforesaid in the County aforeſaid, ſhe the ſaid Martha Harding was delivered of a Female Baſtard Child, since baptized by the Name of Ann and that the ſaid Baſtard Child is ~~[illegible]~~ become chargeable to the ſaid Parish of Milbrooke and that James Sturt of Four Posts in the said Parish of Milbrooke Victualler did get her with Child of the ſaid Baſtard Child.

Taken and ſigned the Day and Year firſt above-written, Before me [illegible] Sadleir

The Mark of Martha Harding

2.6 Bastardy form, printed from type with woodcut coat of arms. Completed in the parish of Milbrooke, County of Southampton, 1782. 250×190 mm.

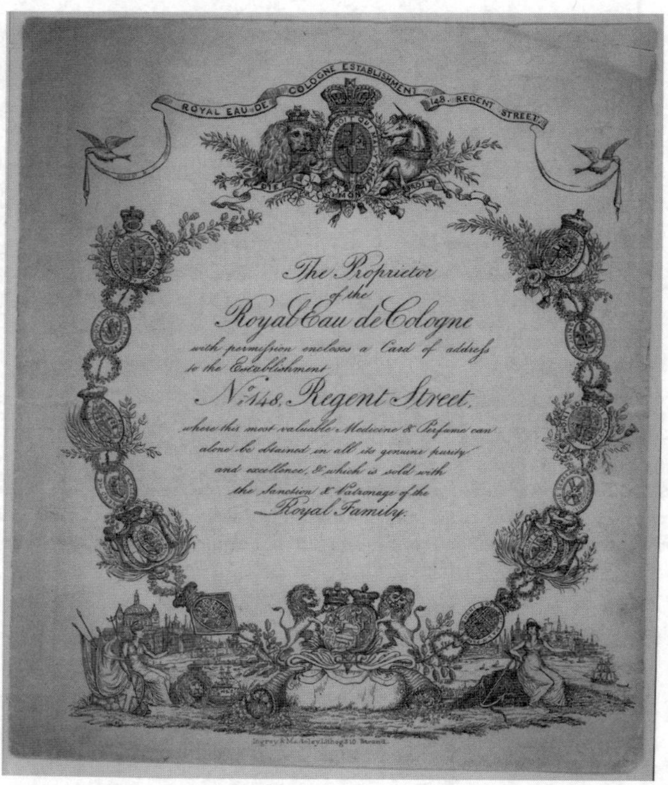

2.7 Advertising circular from the Proprietor of the Royal Eau de Cologne, Regent Street, London. Ink-drawn lithograph by G. E. Madeley, printed by Ingrey and Madeley, The Strand, late 1820s. 243×204mm.

2.8 Advertisement for Irish butter on sale at Woodburn & Jackson's, Ulverston. Letterpress, printed by John Soulby junior in a range of display types, 1826. 200×245 mm.

7.1 Printing at the rolling or copperplate press. From Abraham Bosse, *Traicté des manieres de graver en taille douce sur l'airin* (Paris, 1645), plate 16.

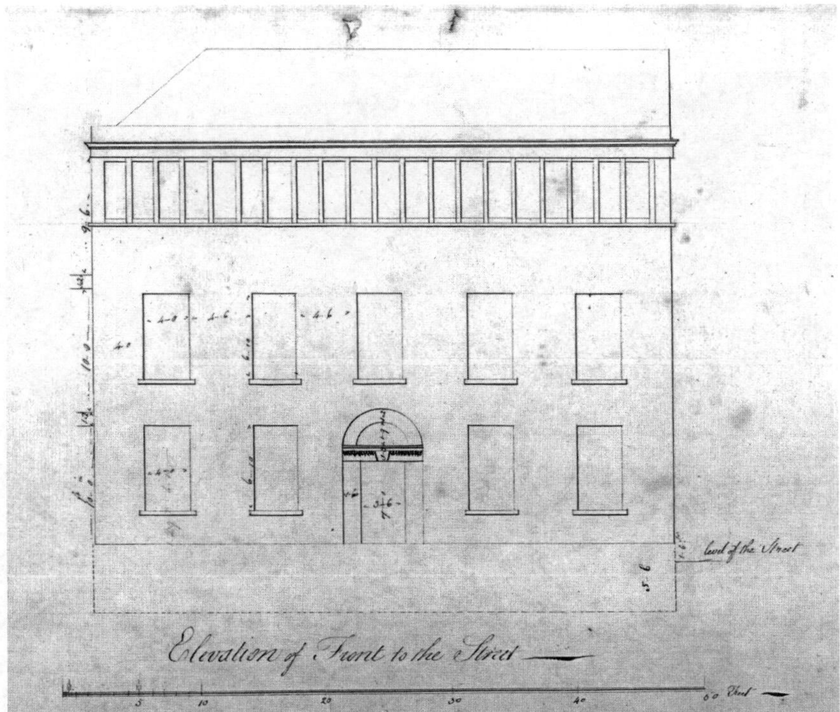

7.2 The King's Printing House, the printing office built in 1770 in East Harding Street, London, by the architect Robert Mylne (1734–1811) for the partnership of Eyre & Strahan.

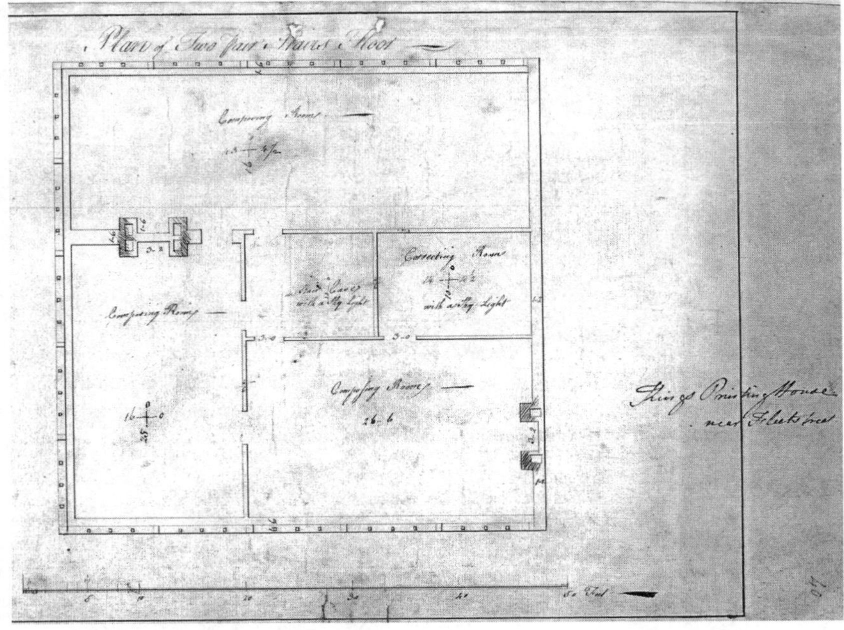

7.3 The King's Printing House, floor plan of the composing room on the top floor.

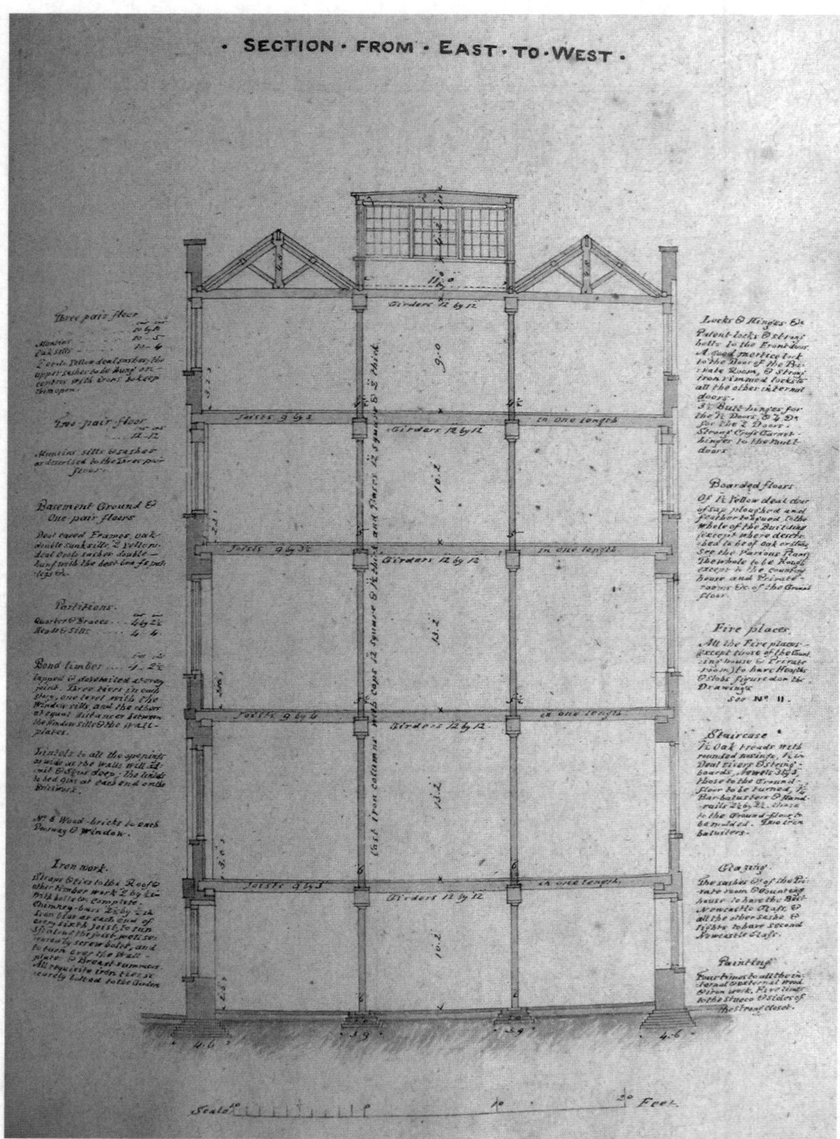

7.4 The Temple Printing Office, Bouverie Street, London, built by W. Pilkington for James Moyes, 1826. Section from the architect's 'Memoranda from the working drawings', 1824 showing the stone and iron construction. Drawing, ink and wash.

Interior of the Principal Composing Room.

7.5 The Temple Printing Office. Wood engraving showing the composing room on the top floor. From *Specimens of the types commonly used in the Temple Printing Office* (1826).

7.6 Stereotype workshop built for T.C. Hansard, from T.C. Hansard, *Typographia* (London, 1824). Wood engraving by J. Lee.

7.7 Printing office with compositors at their frames. A pressman using a roller is inking the forme on a Columbian press. In the centre foreground an octavo forme is being locked up with a mallet and shooting-stick on the imposing stone. In the background printed sheets are being hung up to dry. To the left of the printing press, paper damped for printing is held under a weighted board. Wood engraving by Thomas Kelly, *c.*1825.

DESCRIPTION.

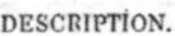

A Boy is represented as laying on

A. The sheet of white Paper.

B. The Cylinder which prints the first side of the Paper.

C. Drums over which the Paper travels to

D. The Cylinder which gives the final impression.

E. The Inking-Rollers under which the Form (*i. e.* the types) is in the act of passing.

F. The Reservoir of Ink from which the Inking-Rollers are supplied.

G. The Form receiving its last Inking before it goes under the Printing Cylinder.

H. A printed sheet is seen just being delivered into the hand of another Boy.

The Lines at the top of the Machine represent the Tapes which run round the Cylinders and secure the sheet.

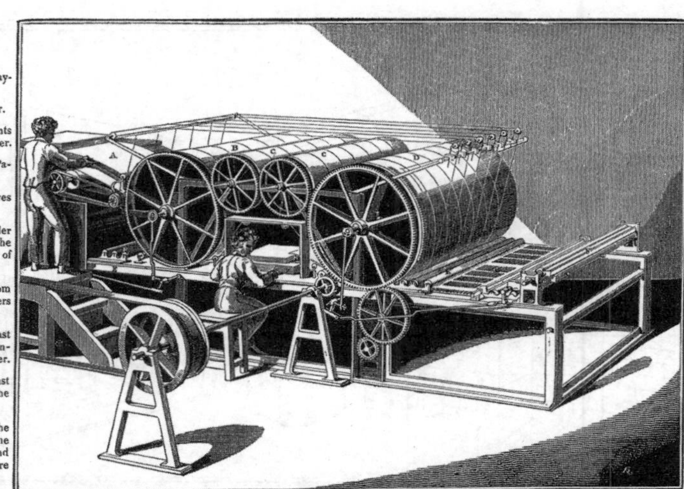

7.8 Cowper double printing machine, for delivering a sheet printed on two sides. From Edward Cowper, *On recent improvements in printing* (London, 1828).

THE

HERMIT.

Far in a wild, unknown to public view,
From youth to age a reverend Hermit grew;
The moss his bed, the cave his humble cell,
His food the fruits, his drink the crystal well:
Remote from men, with God he pass'd the days,
Prayer all his business, all his pleasure praise.
A life so sacred, such serene repose,
Seem'd heaven itself, till one suggestion rose;

11.1 *Poems by Goldsmith and Parnell* (London, William Bulmer, 1795).

THE
Hiſtory of the Rebellion, &c.
BOOK I.

Deut. IV. 7, 8, 9.

For what Nation is there ſo great, who hath God ſo nigh unto them, as the Lord our God is in all things that we call upon him for?

And what Nation is there ſo great that hath Statutes, and Judgments ſo righteous as all this Law, which I ſet before you this day?

Only take heed to thy ſelf, and keep thy ſoul diligently, leaſt thou forget the things which thine eyes have ſeen.

The Preface of the Author.

THAT Poſterity may not be Deceived by the proſperous Wickedneſs of thoſe times of which I write, into an Opinion, that nothing leſs than a general Combination, and univerſal Apoſtacy in the whole Nation from their Religion, and Allegiance, could, in ſo ſhort a time, have produced ſuch a total and prodigious Alteration, and Confuſion over the whole Kingdom; And that the Memory of thoſe, who, out of Duty and Conſcience, have oppoſed that Torrent, which did overwhelm them, may not looſe the recompence due to their Virtue, but having undergone the injuries and reproaches of this, may find a vindication in a better age: It will not be unuſeful for the information of the Judgement and Conſcience of men, to preſent to the world a full and clear Narration of the Grounds, Circumſtances, and Artifices of this Rebellion; not only from the time ſince the flame hath been viſible in a Civil war, but, looking farther back, from thoſe former paſſages and accidents, by which the Seed-plots were made and framed, from whence thoſe miſcheifs have ſucceſſively grown to the height, they have ſince arrived at.

AND in this enſuing Hiſtory, though the hand and judgement of God will be very viſible, in infatuating a People (as ripe and prepared for Deſtruction) into all the perverſe actions of Folly and Madneſs, making

11.2 Edward Hyde, 1st Earl of Clarendon, *The history of the rebellion* (Oxford, Clarendon Press, 1702).

Paſt. I. 1

Virgil's Paſtorals.

The Firſt Paſtoral.

OR,

Tityrus *and* Meliboeus.

The Argument.

The Occaſion of the Firſt Paſtoral was this. When Auguſtus *had ſetled himſelf in the* Roman *Empire, that he might reward his* Veteran *Troops for their paſt Service, he diſtributed among'em all the Lands that lay about* Cremona *and* Mantua: *turning out the right Owners for having ſided with his Enemies.* Virgil *was a Sufferer among the reſt; who afterwards recover'd his Eſtate by* Mecænas's *Interceſſion, and as an Inſtance of his Gratitude compos'd the following Paſtoral; where he ſets out his own Good Fortune in the Perſon of* Tityrus, *and the Calamities of his* Mantuan *Neighbours in the Character of* Melibæus.

MELIBOEUS.

Beneath the Shade which Beechen Boughs diffuſe,
You *Tity'rus* entertain your Silvan Muſe:
Round the wide World in Baniſhment we rome,
Forc'd from our pleaſing Fields and Native Home:
While ſtretch'd at Eaſe you ſing your happy loves:
And *Amarillis* fills the ſhady Groves.

TITYRUS.

These Bleſſings, Friend, a Deity beſtow'd:
For never can I deem him leſs than God.
The tender Firſtlings of my Woolly breed
Shall on his holy Altar often bleed.
He gave my Kine to graze the Flowry Plain:
And to my Pipe renew'd the Rural Strain.

B *MELIBOEUS,*

11.3 John Dryden, *The works of Virgil translated into English verse* (London, Jacob Tonson, 1697).

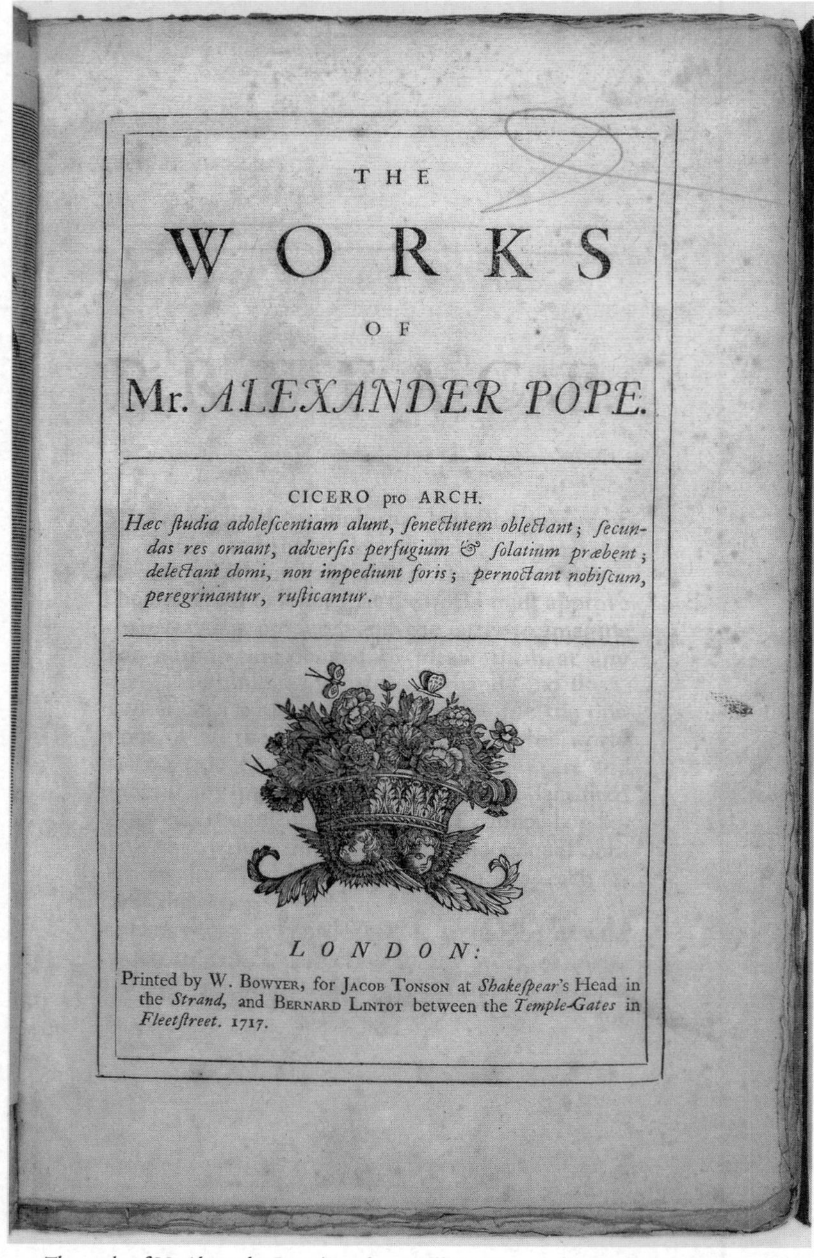

THE
WORKS
OF
Mr. ALEXANDER POPE.
CICERO pro ARCH.
Hæc ſtudia adoleſcentiam alunt, ſenectutem oblectant; ſecundas res ornant, adverſis perfugium & ſolatium præbent; delectant domi, non impediunt foris; pernoctant nobiſcum, peregrinantur, ruſticantur.
LONDON:
Printed by W. Bowyer, for Jacob Tonson at Shakeſpear's Head in the Strand, and Bernard Lintot between the Temple-Gates in Fleetſtreet. 1717.

11.4 *The works of Mr Alexander Pope* (London, William Bowyer for Jacob Tonson, 1717).

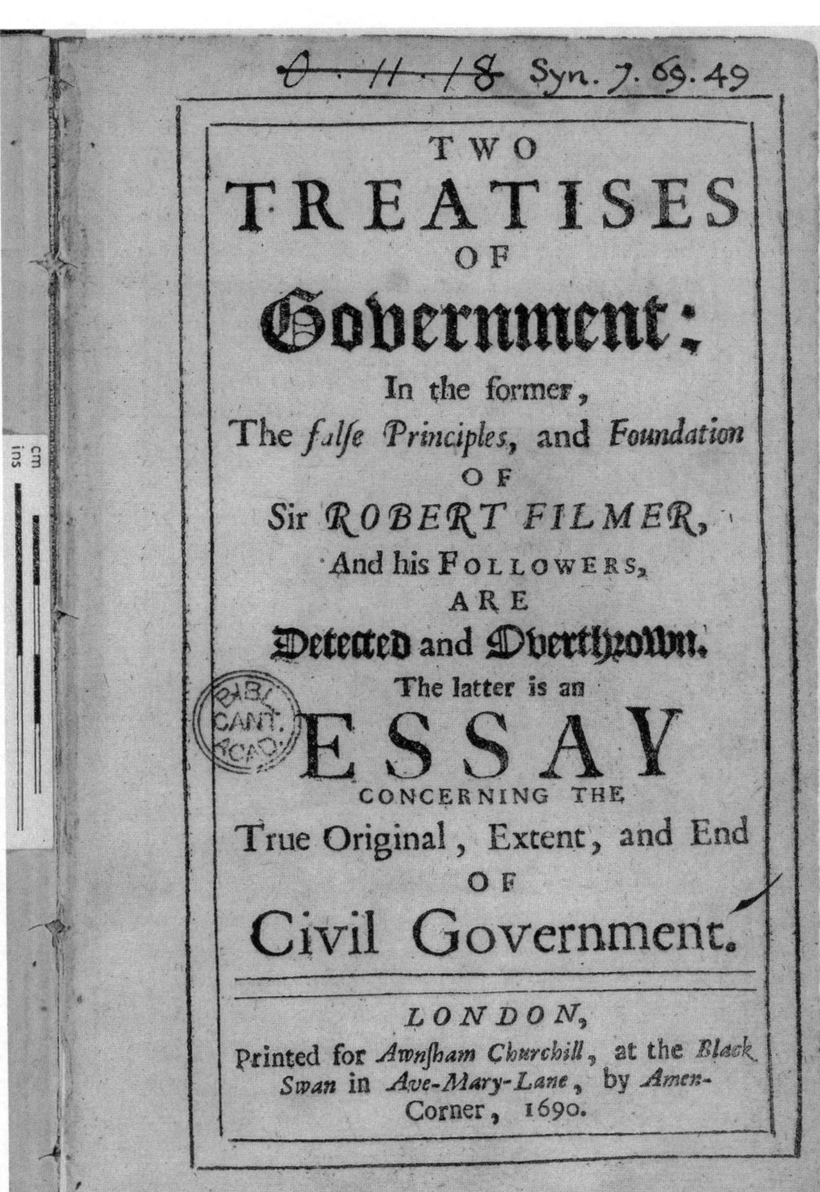

O. 11. 18 Syn. 7. 69. 49
TWO
TREATISES
OF
Government:
In the former,
The false Principles, and Foundation
OF
Sir ROBERT FILMER,
And his FOLLOWERS,
ARE
Detected and Overthrown.
The latter is an
ESSAY
CONCERNING THE
True Original, Extent, and End
OF
Civil Government.
LONDON,
Printed for Awnsham Churchill, at the Black
Swan in Ave-Mary-Lane, by Amen-
Corner, 1690.
BIBL. CANT. ACAD.

11.5 John Locke, *Two treatises of government* (London, Awnsham Churchill, 1690).

ALCIPHRON:

OR, THE

MINUTE PHILOSOPHER.

IN

SEVEN DIALOGUES.

Containing an APOLOGY *for the* Chriſtian Religion, *againſt thoſe who are called* Free-thinkers.

VOLUME *the* FIRST.

They have forſaken me the Fountain of living waters, and hewed them out ciſterns, broken ciſterns that can hold no water. Jerem. ii. 13.

Sin mortuus, ut quidam minuti Philoſophi cenſent, nihil ſentiam, non vereor ne hunc errorem meum mortui Philoſophi irrideant. Cicero.

LONDON:
Printed for J. TONSON in the *Strand*, 1732.

11.6 George Berkeley, *Alciphron: or, the minute philosopher* (London, Jacob Tonson, 1732).

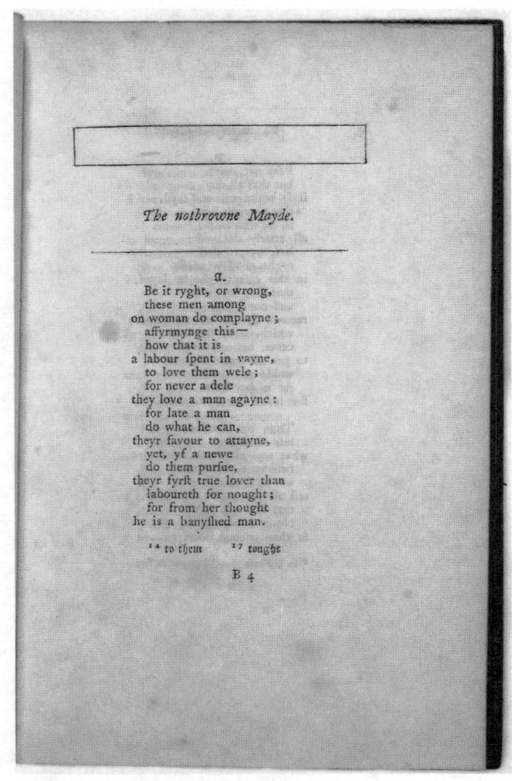

The notbrowne Mayde.

A.

Be it ryght, or wrong,
these men among
on woman do complayne ;
affyrmynge this —
how that it is
a labour ſpent in vayne,
to love them wele ;
for never a dele
they love a man agayne :
for late a man
do what he can,
theyr favour to attayne,
yet, yf a newe
do them purſue,
theyr fyrſt true lover than
laboureth for nought ;
for from her thought
he is a banyſhed man.

14 to them   17 tought

B 4

11.7 Edward Capell, *Prolusions* (London, J. and R. Tonson, 1760).

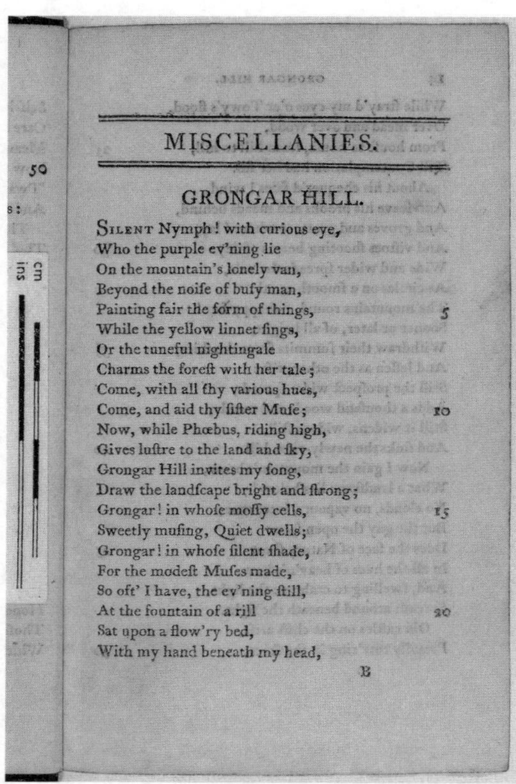

MISCELLANIES.

GRONGAR HILL.

Silent Nymph! with curious eye,
Who the purple ev'ning lie
On the mountain's lonely van,
Beyond the noiſe of buſy man,
Painting fair the form of things,
While the yellow linnet ſings,
Or the tuneful nightingale
Charms the foreſt with her tale;
Come, with all thy various hues,
Come, and aid thy ſiſter Muſe;
Now, while Phœbus, riding high,
Gives luſtre to the land and ſky,
Grongar Hill invites my ſong,
Draw the landſcape bright and ſtrong;
Grongar! in whoſe moſſy cells,
Sweetly muſing, Quiet dwells;
Grongar! in whoſe ſilent ſhade,
For the modeſt Muſes made,
So oft' I have, the ev'ning ſtill,
At the fountain of a rill
Sat upon a flow'ry bed,
With my hand beneath my head,

B

11.8 *The poems of John Dyer* (vol. LVIII of *The works of the English poets*, London, John Bell, 1790).

12.1 Pen and ink drawing of a London bookbinding workshop, *c.*1820, possibly that of Charles Lewis.

12.2 *Rider's British Merlin: For the Year of our Lord God 1748* (London, printed by R. Nutt for the Company of Stationers, 1748). Bound in boards with pockets inside the boards, prepared leaves for writing on, and covered in red, gold-tooled, tanned goatskin with a foredge flap and adjustable silver clasp.

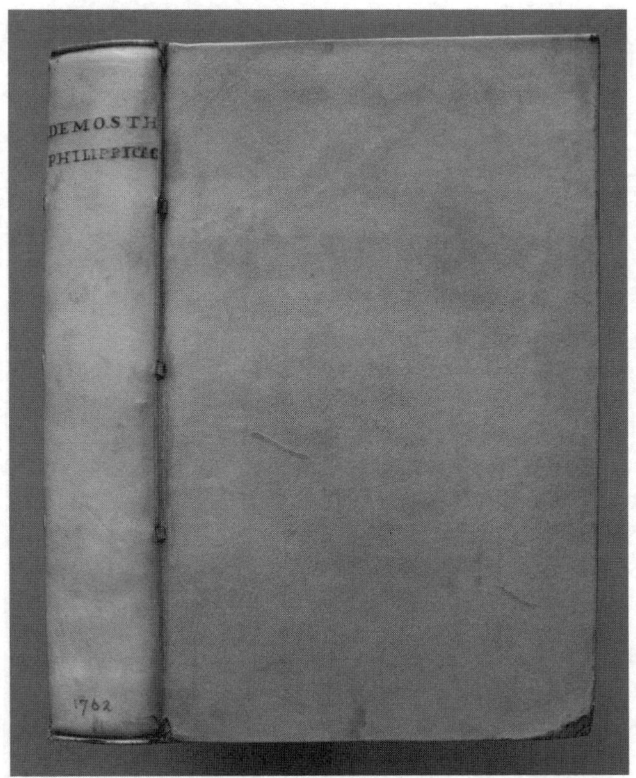

12.3 Demosthenes, *Orationes Philippicae duodecim* (Glasgow, Robert and Andrew Foulis, 1762). A 'dutch vellum' binding, a laced-case binding of plain vellum over boards, titled in ink.

12.4 A mid-eighteenth-century cash book, in a laced-case parchment binding over stiff boards, with a foredge flap and adjustable copper-alloy clasp.

12.5 *Novum Testamentum Græcum* (Oxford, E Theatro Sheldoniano, 1742). An Oxford binding with parchment 'front and back', and marbled paper on the sides.

12.6 [John Hill], *The Œconomy of Human Life, Part the Second* (London, M. Cooper, 1751). Bound in boards with *The Œconomy of a Winter's Day* (London, R. Griffiths, [1750?]) for the Earl of Orrery and covered in gold-tooled green-stained vellum.

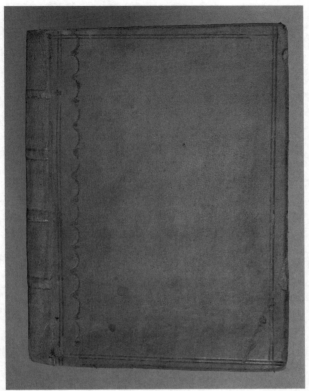

12.7 *Monita et præcepta Christiana, Editio Altera. In Usum Regiæ Scholæ Etonensis* (London, C. Dilly (Eton, T. Pote), 1787). Bound in boards and covered in tanned sheepskin with a blind-tooled roll run along the back edge of the boards.

12.8 William Sherlock, *A Practical Discourse concerning a Future Judgement ... The Eighth Edition* (London, printed by J.R. for D. Browne, J. Walthoe, B. Tooke, J. Pemberton and T. Ward, 1717). Bound in boards, covered in tanned calf with a blind-tooled single panel on each board, with sprinkled black pigment. The spine has been stained black as a foil to the gold tooling, which was possibly added later to an otherwise blind-tooled binding.

12.9 George Vertue, *A description of four ancient paintings, being historical portraitures of royal branches of the Crown of England* (London, 1740), bound with George Vertue, *A large Ancient Painting, representing King Edward VI* (London, 1750?) Contemporary binding in boards, covered in Russia calf and tooled in gold by Edwin Moore of Cambridge.

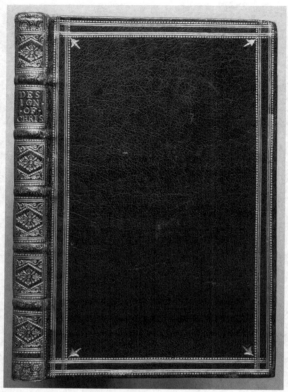

12.10 Edward Fowler, *The Design of Christianity*, 3rd edn (London, by J. H. for Luke Meredith, 1699). Contemporary binding in boards covered in gold-tooled dark blue tanned goatskin (turkey leather) by the Geometrical Compartment Binder.

12.11 *Gratulatio Academiæ Oxoniensis in nuptias auspicatissimas Illustriorum Principium Frederici Principis Walliæ et Agustæ Principissæ de Saxe-Gotha* (Oxford, E Typographeo Clarendoniano, 1736). Bound in boards, covered in gold-tooled tanned hairsheep (morocco leather).

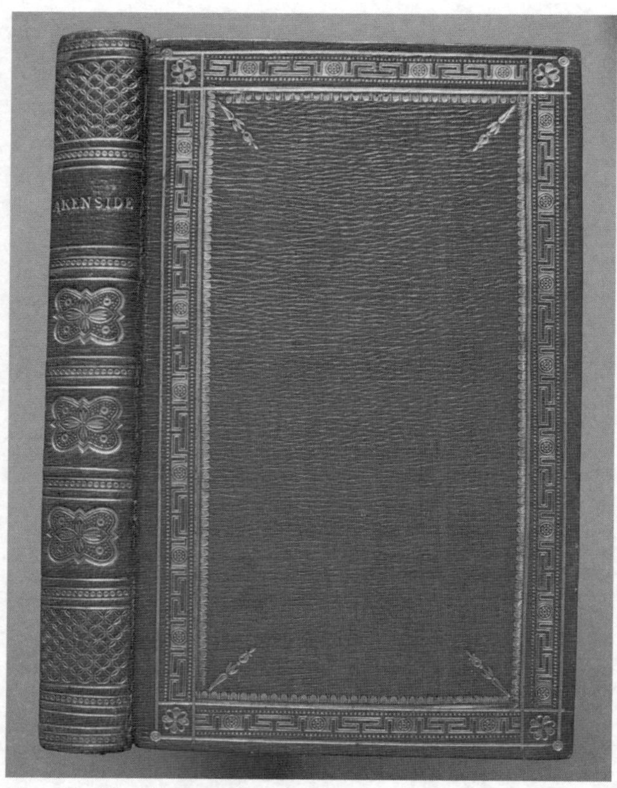

12.12 Mark Akenside, *The Pleasures of Imagination, A New Edition* (London, for T. Cadell and W. Davies, 1810). Bound by J. Price of Bath in boards with a smooth spine and covered in gold-tooled straight-grain red, tanned goatskin.

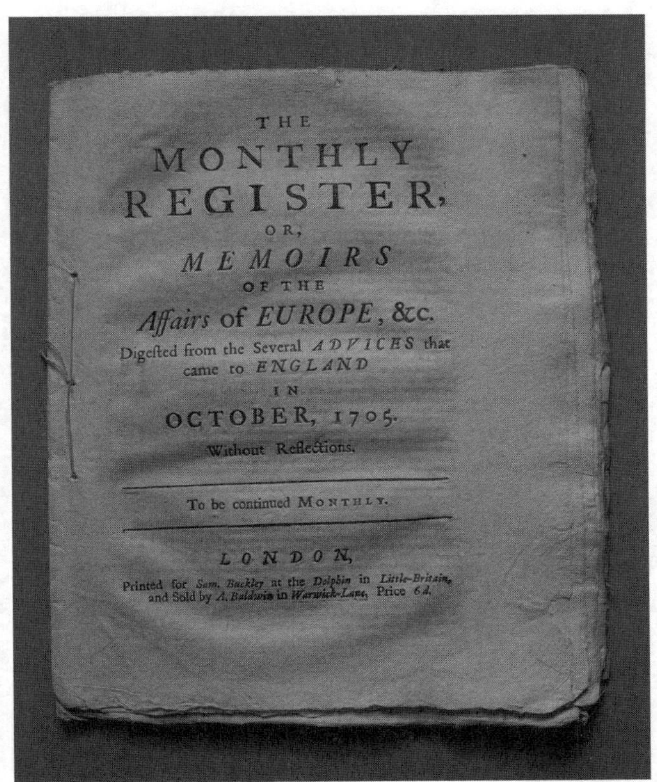

THE
MONTHLY
REGISTER,
OR,
MEMOIRS
OF THE
Affairs of *EUROPE*, &c.
Digested from the Several *ADVICES* that
came to *ENGLAND*
IN
OCTOBER, 1705.
Without Reflections.

To be continued MONTHLY.

LONDON,
Printed for *Sam. Buckley* at the *Dolphin* in *Little-Britain*,
and Sold by *A. Baldwin* in *Warwick-Lane*, Price 6 *d*.

12.13 *The Monthly Register, or, Memoirs of the Affairs of Europe ... in October, 1705* (London, for Samuel Buckley and sold by A. Baldwin, [1705]). Stitched through three holes with uncut edges.

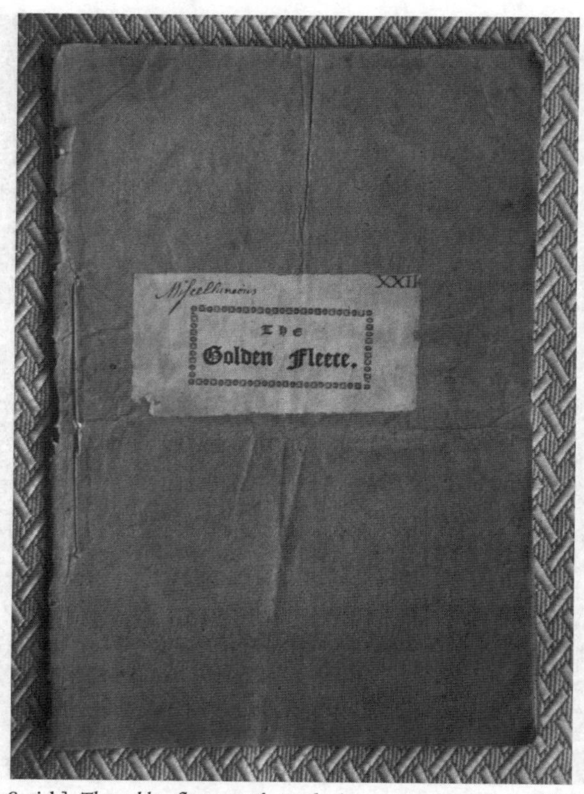

12.14 [Simon Smith], *The golden fleece: or the trade, interest, and well-being of Great Britain considered* (London, [*c.*1736]).

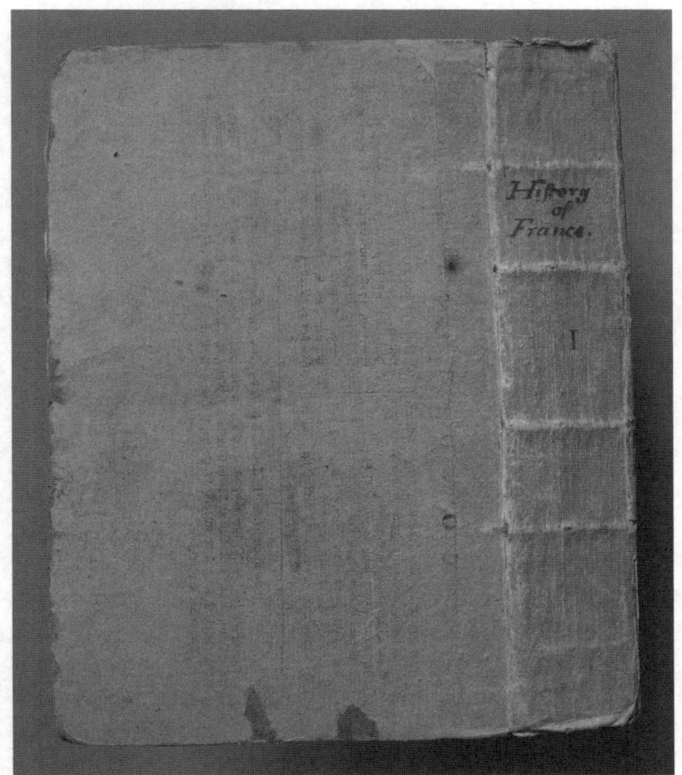

12.15 [Charles Hereford], *The History of France … in Three Volumes* (London, G. Kearsley, 1790). 'Bound in boards, sewn wide in the middle' and covered in white handmade laid paper on the spine and blue printed-waste paper on the boards.

12.16 *Æsopi fabulæ Græco-Latinæ* (Eton, J. Pote, 1769). Bound in the 'common manner' and covered in blind-tooled sheepskin.

12.17 *A short introduction to grammar* (London, by S. Buckley and T. Longman, 1768). Bound in the 'common manner' and covered in canvas.

12.18 R. Johnson, *A New History of the Grecian States ... designed for the use of young ladies and gentlemen* (London, E. Newbery, 1786). Case-bound in 'the vellum manner' with green parchment on the spine and marbled paper on the sides, with a printed paper label.

12.19 *Forget me not; a Christmas and New Year's Present for 1826* (London, R. Ackermann, 1828). Case-bound in a German-style three-piece case covered in glazed and printed green paper.

12.20 *The works of Samuel Johnson, LLD. In nine volumes* (Oxford, printed for William Pickering and Talboys and Wheeler, 1825). Volume VIII, case-bound, covered in rose-pink glazed calico with a printed label.

(1960) HARPTON COURT

London, Imported January 24, 1783. No. 18.

Oporto J Banks — 1 tun wine
Syms & Co — 10
T Whittington — 2
Mallett & Co — 5
T Prettyman — 8
D Shirley — 3
E Godsell — 3
Bennett & Co — 3
Page & Co — 2
H Bodicoate — 1
Andrews & Co 8
J M Chalie — 5
J Thompson & Co 4
T Dennis — 6
Johnston & Co — 4
Stewart & Co — 5
Guernsey Barclay & Co — 2
Lisbon Tulk and Co 5 tun wine
C Jackson 600l indigo
J Little 180 dozen fish skins
A Buller & Co 550l indigo

Cerella J & F Baring & Co 1500C raisins
Petersburgh Evan Pugh 230 quarters linseed
Altea G Turnbull & Co 1,00C raisins
Valentia G Turnbull & Co 2000C raisins
New York J Hyndman & Co 7200l tobacco
W Pitt 56000l tobacco
Murray & Co 7000l tobacco
St Kitts J Baillie 200C sugar
B Steane 12C sugar

S H I P S Entered Inwards

Iris, A Caldelugh, — New York
Fideon, R B Gibson, — Lisbon
Bavn Sucecss, D Farabcchie, Venice and Trieste
St Ann, J Anthony, — Gibraltar
Ann, D Shichan, — Cork
Venshal, A Jurgens, — Sevelle

GOODS EXPORTED, January 24.

India The United Company 1000 perpets, 700 long cloths, 365 qrs. wheat ground, 10 qrs. pease
R Twiss 80 bar. beef and pork
W Drummond 244 ps. glass
J Llewellen 5C playing cards
Lancaster, Bax & Ellill 170C lead
Johnston & Co 1132 ps. glass
T Day 104 bushel salt
J Middleditch 204l cochineal
W Benford 5120 ells sail cloth
T Brown 936 ps. glass
Hammond and Co 9726 ells sail cloth
Anderson and Co 4822 ditto
Edie and Co 2000 ditto
B Lane 20C copper
H & S F Freeman 110C lead

Oporto Smith and Co 20C cheese
Madeira D H Rucker 41 chaldron coals
Lisbou Hammond and Co 73C allom
Thomas Preston 162C lead
Newport Thellusson and Co 20C iron, 30 dozen hose, tin plates and colours at 180
Halifax H and S F Freeman 180C lead shot
Barbadoes S W Salte 250 ps. irish, 100 ps. british linen
St Thomas White and Co 30 ps brt. linen, british cottons 1180
Ostend C Sherwood 48C cheese
C R Puller 200 stuffs
T Baker 46C copperas at l12
John Ramsden mathematical instruments at l200
Thomas Preston 64C lead shot

GOODS EXPORTED by CERTIFICATE

India The United Company 30 ton beef
Drummond & Co 480 gallons wine, 370 gallons rum
North & Co 1C rice, 6C raisins, 1C currants, 2l spice, 8C ginger
J Middleditch 10C sugar, 5C raisins, 8C currants
Crawshay & Co 18 ton iron
G Johnston & Co 84 gallons wine
J Seaton 500 ditto
Africa Sargant & Co 775 callicoes
Cork Bennett & Co 316l pepper, 112l nutmegs
Dublin R Kennedy 1502l tea
Cazalet & Son 1171l thrown silk
E Gwillam 15200 ps. china
Ostend G French 600 bar. 9 tons beef
Osvald & Co 1500 hides
Goodchild and Co 394 bill hooks, 960 axes
R Vigne 756l bugles

Hambro B Elias 29900 rattans
Leghorne J A Pimental 149l rhubarb
Halifax Rashleigh and Co 10 ton iron, 25 bar. tar, 35 bar. pitch
Belfast R Kennedy 1451ol tea
St Thomas P Brown & Co 20 quarter oats
W Mills 100l pepper
Barbadoes J W Salte 113 callicoes, 61 lawns
J Slaughter 640l tea
Palmer & Co 2777l tea

S H I P S Cleared Outwards.

Maria, J Sheldrick, — Ostend
Vrow Alida, D Corbus, — Bremen
Active, R Moulton, — Jamaica
Savill, A Swan, — St Helena

N. B. Such Gentlemen as are desirous of taking the BILL OF ENTRY, are desired to apply to Mr. RICHARD AUSTIN Merchant, Numb. 1, Old-Bethlem, or to Mr. ROBERT SEYMOUR and Mr. PHILIP WICKS, in the Long-Room, at the Custom-House.

Printed by THOMAS PARKER, Number 4, Bull Head Court, Jewin Street.

22.1 London bills of entry: *London, Imported*, 24 Jan. 1783.

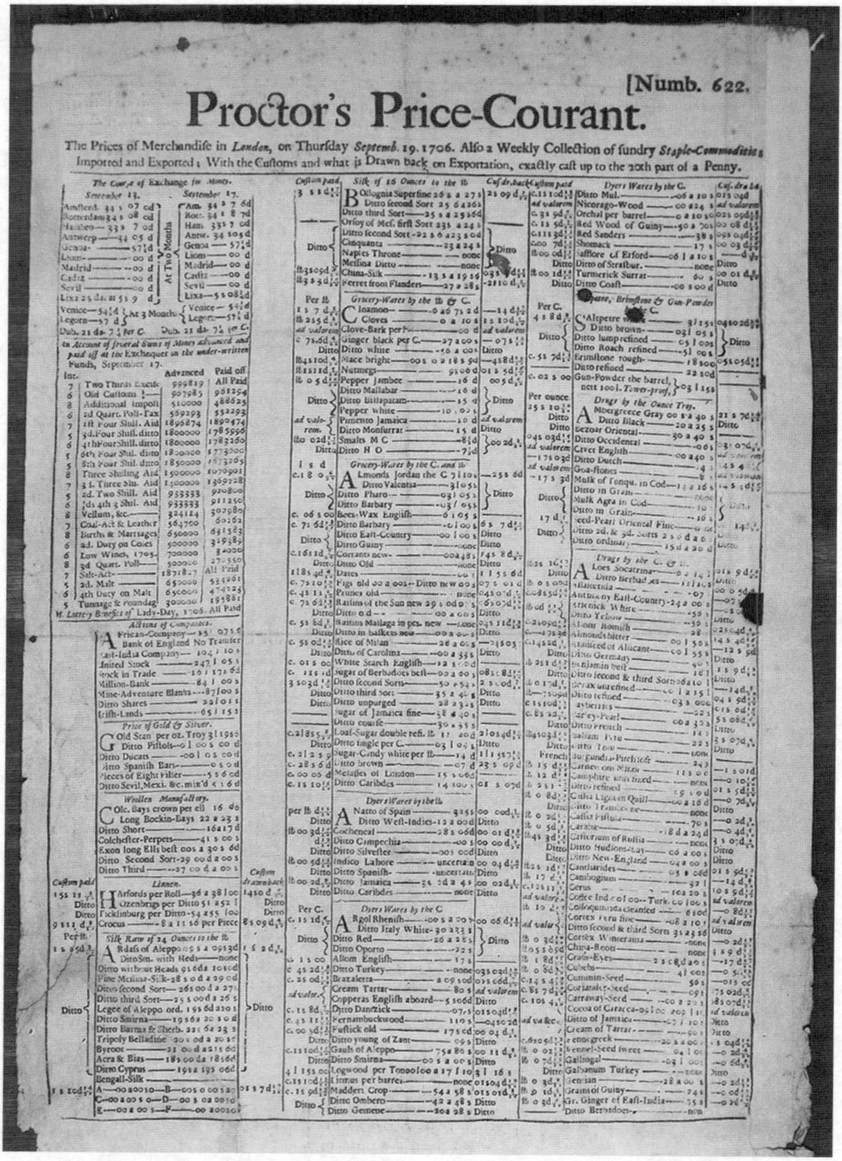

[Numb. 622.

Proctor's Price-Courant.

The Prices of Merchandise in *London*, on Thursday *Septemb.* 19. 1706. Also a Weekly Collection of sundry *Staple-Commodities* Imported and Exported; With the Customs and what is Drawn back on Exportation, exactly cast up to the 20th part of a Penny.

The Course of Exchange for Money.

An Account of several Sums of Money advanced and paid off at the Exchequer on the under-written Funds, September 17.

Actions of Companies.

Price of Gold & Silver.

Woollen Manufactory.

Linnen.

Silk Raw of 24 Ounces to the lb.

Silk of 16 Ounces to the lb.

Grocery-Wares by the lb & C.

Grocery-Wares by the C. and lb.

Dyers Wares by the lb.

Dyers Wares by the C.

Dyers Wares by the C.

Saltpetre, Brimstone & Gun-Powder by the C.

Drugs by the Ounce Troy.

Drugs by the C. & lb.

22.2 London commodity price current: *Proctor's Price-Courant*, 19 Sep. 1706 (recto and verso).

Custom paid	Drugs by the C. & l.	Price	Draw back
c 5 5 d	Gum Tragant	4l a 7l 10 s	—0 04d
c 12 s 0 d	Gum Sandrack	04 l 10 s	—10 s d
c 4 s 2 d	Gum Arabeck	65 s	03 s 06d
Ditto	Gum Senica	60 s	Ditto
lb 0 9d	Gum Elemnia	05 s 00 d	—00 2d
lb 0 5 d	Gum Shellack	07 l 05 s	—0 04d
Ditto	Ditto Seedlack	05 a 00 l	Ditto
— 01 d	Ditto Sticklack	42 a 65 s	—05 1d
c 13 s 1	Harts-Horn	50 a 00 l	10 s 9d
14 s 1 d	Looking-Glass the best	4 l 6	—12 s 9d
	Ditto 2d. & third Sorts	2 s 6d a 3 s 6d	Ditto
c 15 8d	Jallop	02 a 2 s 4	—0 17d
c 24 s 0	Ireos	52 s	—18 s 0d
02 s 05	Labdanum	55 s	—0 4
Ditto	Long Pepper	2 l 16 s	—
lb 0 8	Litharge-Gold	10 a 12 s	—01 s 05d
lb 0 5 d	Lapis Tutie	35 l	—00 4d
c 8 s 07d	Lead white	19 s 0d	—7 s 02d
c 7 2d	Ditto red	11 a 00 s	—6 s 0 d
—12 2d	Manna best	25 0d a 03 s 0	—10 d
—	Ditto 2d. & 3d. Sorts	2 s 0 s	Ditto
lb 0 17	Mastick	02 s 8d	—15 2d
lb 0 15	Myrrh	07 a 14 l	—01 s 01d
lb 0 12	Mechoacan	00 a 06 l	—10 d
lb 1 03d	Mercury Sublimate	6 s 0d	—00 12 d
lb 2 s	Ditto Præcipitate	7 s 6	02 s 4d
[illegible]	Opium	7 s 0d	—3 s 7d
[illegible]	Olibanum	50 a 60 s	—12 s 00d
c 14 1d	Opoponax	4 s 6	02 s 4d
lb 10	Oil Turpentine	36 s	—
ad valorem	Oil Bays	5 l 10 s	14 s 4d
c 17 s 0	Oil Anniseed	00 a 09 s	ad valorem
ad valorem	Oil Mace per Ex.	17 a 00 s	—02 1d
lb 02 s 0d	Oil Cloves	00 a 32 s	ad valorem
ad valorem	Quicksilver	5 s 00	—1 s 0d
lb 1 s 3 d	Rhubarb of Turkey	00 a 5 71	07 s 02d
lb 3 s 7d	Ditto Russia	00 a 03 s	Ditto
Ditto	Sarsaparilla	03 s	—1 s 2d
lb 1 5d	Sal Armoniack	7 l 15 s	—00 2d
lb 0 02	Salpetre Roach	4 l 10	—4 s 2d
c 4 s 03d	Ditto Lump	04 l 10 s	Ditto
Ditto	Scamony of Aleppo	16 a 00 s	07 s 02d
lb 8 7d	Ditto Smirna	14 a 00 s	Ditto
Ditto	Senna Alexandria	2 s 4d	—00 3d
—0 s 4d	Ditto Tripoly	none	Ditto
Ditto	Ditto Aleppo	none	Ditto
Ditto	Saffron English	22 a 24 s	—
lb 1 s 06d	Ditto Spanish	00 a 02 s	—01 8d
lb 1 s 05	Storax in Cake	03 s 00 d	—01 9
lb 2 s 1d	Sanders yellow	40 s	—00 8d
lb 10 d	Sanguis Draconis in Cakes	3 s 2 07 l	—00 4d
lb 0 5	Ditto in Drops	2 a 6 s	Ditto
Ditto	Sarsafrass	18 s	07 s 02d
c 8 s 07d	Semina Carti unrefined	05 s 2 00 s	2 s 09
c 34 s 0d	Ditto refined	18 s a 20 s	—1 s 9d
lb 2 s 1d	Spica Nardia	16 s	10 s 3d
c 18 s 3d	Succus Liquoritiæ	06 l 00 s	—1 s 2 1
lb 1 s 3d	Turmerick	3 l a 5 s	—00 1d
lb 0 1d	Tamerins	00 a 00 s	—00 3d
lb 00 4d	Turbith	none	—00 8d
lb 10 d	Turpentine Strasburgh	7 l 00 s	ad valorem
ad valorem	Ditto Venice	03 l 10 s	—
uncertain	Ditto common	20 s a 2 00 s	—00 7d
c 05 8	Tea fine	20 s	ad valorem, &c.
ad valorem, &c	Ditto 2d. & 3d. Sorts	12 s a 16 s	
	Verdigreece	0 s 18d a 0 s 20d	—
uncertain	Vitriol white	56 s	—
lb 0 5d	Ditto Roman	00 a 18 s	—00 4d
lb 04 3d	Venice-Treacle	4 s 6d	—3 s 7d
lb 1 0d	Vermillion whole	5 s 00	—10 d
Ditto	Ditto ground	06 s 00	Ditto
lb 0 17d	Wormseed Turkey in Soil	2 s 09	—14 d
Ditto	Ditto Garbled	04 s 00	Ditto
lb 0 17d	Zedoary	07 l 00 s	—14 d
	Tobacco by the lb		
lb 0 05d	York-River in parcel	10 a 11 d	—00 4d
Ditto	Ditto old	11 a 12 d	Ditto
Ditto	Bright for Ship. best aboard	8 a 9	Ditto
Ditto	Middling for Rappers	5½ a 6 d	Ditto
Ditto	Ordinary on board	4½ d a 5½ d	Ditto
Ditto	Antego	none	Ditto
Ditto	Rapphanack	10 a 11 d	Ditto
Ditto	Brown Spun here aboard	0 a 00 d	Ditto
Ditto	Ditto black sm. Twist aboard	07 d	Ditto
Ditto	Bermoodos	00 a 00 d	Ditto
ad valorem	Tobacco-Stalks	14 s a 17 s	ad valorem

Custom paid	Oil, Tallow, Pot-Ashes, Barilla, Soap & Whale-Fins.	Price	Custom draw back
8l 6 02	OIL of Genoa 236 gallons to the Tun	45 l 00	7l 12 s 0d
Ditto	Ditto Gallipoly	44 l 10 s	Ditto
Ditto	Ditto Sevil	00 l 00	Ditto
Ditto	Ditto Lisbon	44 l 00 s	Ditto
Ditto	Ditto Oporto	44 l 10 s	Ditto
Ditto	Ditto Majorca	none	Ditto
Ditto	Faro	42 a 00 l	Ditto
2 gal. 12 s	Oil in jars from Legorn	5 l 10 a 7 l 0	—10d
17 l 9 s 6	Linseed-Oil	37 a 00 l 00	15 l 16 s 3
ad valorem	Hempseed	32 l 00 s	ad valorem
Ditto	Ditto Rape	24 l 00 s	Ditto
uncertain	Oil of Greenland 252 gallons to the Tun	none	uncertain
Ditto	Ditto New-England	25 l	Ditto
Ditto	Ditto Newfoundland	27 l 00 s	Ditto
Ditto	Ditto Russia	none	Ditto
0 07 s 0d	Tallow of Russia	00 s	—6 s 08 d
Ditto	Ditto Irish	30 a 00 s	Ditto
Prohibited	Ditto English	29 a 30 s 0d	—
0 5 s 6d	Pot-Ashes of Russia	61 a 00 s	—5 s 2d
Ditto	Ditto Dantzick	38 a 44 s	Ditto
Ditto	Ditto Quinsboro	00 a 00 s	Ditto
Ditto	Ditto Riga	00 a 00 s	Ditto
Ditto	Pearl-Ashes	32 a 33 s	Ditto
0 3 s 09d	Barilla of Allicant	25 s 0	—3 s 06d
0 17 s 11	Soap of Allicant	00 l 00 s	—16 s 06d
Ditto	Ditto Genoa Marble best	48 s	Ditto
Ditto	Ditto Joppa	none	Ditto
c. 00 06d	Castle-Soap London make	00 a 56 s	—
uncertain	Whale-fins per Ton	00 a 230 l	
	Hemp, Pitch, Tar, Rosin, Timber, Deals & Pipe-Staves.		
	Lebou Rhine-Hemp	00 s	
c 02 s 6d	Ditto Riga-Rhine	23 s 6d	—2 s 2d
Ditto	Ditto Pass	18 s	Ditto
Ditto	Ditto Quinsboro Rhine	00 a 22 s 6d	Ditto
Ditto	Ditto Narve	00 a 00 s 0d	Ditto
Ditto	Ditto Russia	21 a 00 s 0	Ditto
uncertain	Pitch of Stockh. 12 barrels	none	uncertain
Ditto	Ditto Wybergh	00 l 00 s	Ditto
Ditto	Ditto Gottenburgh	18 l 00 s	Ditto
Ditto	English Stone-Pitch per C.	20 s 0d	Ditto
Ditto	Tar of Stockholm	16 s 00 s	Ditto
Ditto	Ditto Wiburg	00 l 00 s	Ditto
Ditto	Ditto Narve	none	Ditto
Ditto	Rosin black & yellow, Fr.	14 a 00 s	Ditto
Ditto	Ditto yellow & black, re.	20 a 00 s	Ditto
Ditto	Deal-Board the 1000	00 l a 00 l	Ditto
—9 s 7d	Pipe-Staves of Hambro 1000	17 l 00	08 s 00d
Ditto	Ditto Hogsheads	12 l 00 s	Ditto
24 s 09d	Ditto Barrels	08 l 10 s	—4 s
	Metals of sundry Sorts.		
—3 s 00d	TIN in Blocks the C.	80 s 00 d	
Ditto	Ditto in Bars aboard	82 s 0 d	
1 l 00 00	Lead of Darbyshire, the Fodder, 19 C.½	09 l 10 s	
Ditto	Ditto Yorkshire	09 l 05 s	—
	Ditto New-Castle	09 l 05 s	
ad valorem	Bilboa-Iron the C.	14 s a 15 s 00	ad valorem
—	Ditto St. Sebastian	15 a 16 s	—
Ditto	Swedeland	16 s 0d a 16 s 6d	Ditto
c 8 s 05d	Rose-Copper	none	—8 s 2d
Ditto	Copper-Plates Hambro thick	7 l 00 s	Ditto
Ditto	Ditto of Hungary	6 l 14 s	Ditto
c 13 s 1d	Ditto Square Tapers & Bottoms	16 d	12 s 10d
Ditto	Thatch Copper-Plates	08 l 01 s	Ditto
c 30 s 4d	Aken-Kettles in Sorts	07 l 12 s	—1 l 05 s
c. 15 s 09d	Shaven Lattin	09 l 10 s a 10 l	—14 s 2d
c 39 s 1d	Swedes Lattin-Wire	7 l 15 s a 08 l	35 s 12d
11 s 11	Tin-Plates of Hambro double per 100	57 a 58 s	11 s 3d
35 s 11d	Ditto single the 100	00 a 27 s 0d	—5 s 7d
c. 9 s 5 d	Steel Steer-Mark the Faggot	00 a 46 s	—8 s 09d
Ditto	Ditto English the Faggot	27 a 28 s	Ditto
Ditto	Ditto of Germany the C.	44 s a 46 s	Ditto
Ditto	Ditto of Venice the C.	00 a 00 s	Ditto
Ditto	Cullen Gad-Steel the barrel	00 l 00	Ditto
	Furrs, Wool, Hair & Yarn.		
—01 s 00	Coney-skins Engl. 120	06 a 40 s	—
per sk. 1 s 5	Bever Hudf. Bay-Parch.	0 s 00 d	—1 s 1d
Ditto	Ditto old Coat	6 s 0 d a 0 d	Ditto
Ditto	Bev. New-York Parchment	6 s 0 d	Ditto
Ditto	Ditto New-Engl. & Maryl.	5 s 0d	Ditto

Custom paid	Furrs, Wool, Hair & Yarn.	Price	Draw back
Free	Bever-Wool of Russia	0 a 0 s	—
per lb 3d	Ditto Wombs	11 a 12 s	00 s 03d
—0 03d	Coney-Wool—l.	7 a 0 s 6d	—
Free	Polish Wool the C.	05 a 07 l	—
lb 00 5d	Carmenia-Wool the l.	06 s	—00 5d
lb 00 0d	Cotton-Wool of Eastindia	00 d a 00	—0 d
Ditto	Cotton-Wool of Cyprus	9½ a 10 d	Ditto
Ditto	Ditto Acra	09 a 9½ d	Ditto
Ditto	Ditto fine Deroba a Smirna	8 a 8½ d	Ditto
Ditto	Ditto ordinary	7½ d	Ditto
Free	Cotton-Wool Berba. yel.	09 a 09½ d	Free
Free	Ditto white	10½ a 10¾ d	Free
Free	Sheeps Estridge the C.	00 a 00 s	Free
Free	Ditto Lambs	65 a 70 s	Free
Free	Segovia Felt-Wool per l.	09 d	Free
Free	Vigonia-Wool	08 a 09 d	Free
Free	St. Wool super. mar. R.	2 s 0d a 2 s 0 s	Free
Free	Ditto second Sort F	01 s 00 a 1 s 9 d	Free
Free	Ditto third Sort T	10 a 16 d	Free
lb 00 3d	Goats-Hair of Aleppo	none	—00 2d
Ditto	Ditto Smirna	none	—
—00 5d	Grogran-Yarn	00 s 0 d a 0 s 0d	—00 4d
c. 10 s 1d	Russia-Linnen Yarn	uncertain	—08 s 10d
lb 00 2d	Ditto Brumswick	6 s 6 d a 0 s 8 d	—00 1d
	Ditto Holland Heavy sort	8 s 6 a 8d	
	Ditto Light	8 s 3d	
—	Ditto Helverst. & Quidelb.	8 s a 06d	Ditto
—00 3d	Cott. Yarn —N°. 1, 2. — Ditto N°. 3 & 4. — Ditto N°. 5 & 8.	3 s 6 a 4	—00 3d
lb 00 2d	Cott. Yarn of Aleppo	13 a 14 d	—00 2d
Ditto	Ditto Beladine	14 a 15 d	Ditto
Ditto	Ditto Jerusalem	16 a 17 d	Ditto
Ditto	Smirna Cotton-Yarn fine	15 a 16 d	Ditto
Ditto	Ditto ordinary	00 a 15d	Ditto
	Brandy, English Spirits & Corn.		
ad valor	French Brandy 252 gall. to the Ton	10 s a 11 s l	ad valor
ad valor	Ditto Spanish	60 a 70 s	ad valor
ad valor	English Spirits of Melasses	40 a 42 l	ad valor
—	Ditto Sider-Spirits	00 l 00 l	—
—	Ditto Mault rectified	24 l 26 l	—
—	Mault-Spirits	20 a 22 l 00 s	—
—	Fruit-Spirits	42 a 44 l	—
	Wheat 8 bush. Quarter	20 a 23 s	
	Rye	12 s a 14 s	
	Barley	11 a 13 s 0d	
	Oats	10 s 0 d a 14 s 0d	
	Pease	20 s a 23 s	
	Beans	16 a 18 s	
	Mault Hartfordshire	20 a 00 s 0d	
	Ditto West-Country	17 s 0 a 19 s 0d	
	Ditto Norfolk, Suff. Kent	15 a 17 s 0d	
	Sundry Sorts of Merchandise.		
c. 01 s 06d	Hops English	3 l 00 a 3 l 10 s	—
c. 00 10d	Glew London-make	36 s	—
Ditto	Ditto Country	00 s	—
c. 2 s 00d	Hemp-Seed Norfolk Quarter	31 s	—
ad valorem	Flax-Seed	20 s	—
c. 3 s 00d	Rape-Seed	36 a 38 s	—
ad valorem	Canary-Seed	60 a 70 s	ad valorem
c. 00 06d	Mustard-Seed the bushel	06 s 08 s	
bar. 15 s	Anchovies the barrel new	uncertain	—14 d
c. 0 10 0d	Capers new the C.	uncertain	—0 10 d
lb 00 4d	Westphalia-Bacon the l.	11 d	—00 4
Free	Butter of Yorkshire	00 a 14 s	Ditto
Free	Ditto Suffolk	16 a 18 s 0d	Ditto
Free	Cheese of Cheshire old	28 a 30 s	Ditto
Free	Ditto new	20 a 26 s 00d	Ditto
Free	Ditto Warwickshire	22 a 23 s	Ditto
Free	Ditto Suffolk	10 a 15 s	Ditto
	Soap soft the barrel	4 l 04 s	
	Ditto second Sort	03 l 04 s	
	Ditto third	2 l 8 s	
	Coals the Chald. in the Pool	25 s 0	
01 s 7d	Cosh-Hides	00 a 00 d	01 s 06d
03 s 03d	Buff-Hid. dress.	0 s 10 d a 00 s 14 d	03 s 0d
01 s 03d	Russia-Hides 0 l & 0 l	00 a 00 d	01 s 01d
c. 4 s 02	Lignum Vitæ	00 s	—3 s 7d
ad valorem	Cowries	03 l 05 s	ad valorem
c. 18 s 10	Eleph. Teeth, 2 to the C.	14 l 00 s	—17 s 0
Ditto	Ditto 3 to the C.	12 l 00 s	Ditto
Ditto	Ditto 4 to the C.	00 l a 11 l 00 s	Ditto
Ditto	Ditto 5 & 6 to the C.	10 l 00	Ditto
Ditto	Ditto smallest	08 a 00 l	Ditto

CARGOE of the *Northumberland* from the Bay of *Bengal*, *Mountague* from *Bombay*, *Mary* and the *Seaford* from *Bengal*, for Account of the United *English Company* Trading to the *East-Indies*, Arriv'd 23d of *August*, 1706.

Pieces		Pieces		Peices	
Allibannees	901	Humhums	701	Tanjeebs	2086
Baftaes	1430	Luckhowries	1920	Taffaties	419
Byrampauts	4480	Mulmuls	3638		
Cossaes	3192	Neckcloths	1051		
Dorea's	2686	Niccanees	200		
Dimities	261	Photaes	400		
Dutty Soraguzzees	957	Ponsbaguzzees	451		
Dutty Doregusse	1000	Romals	2777		
Dutty Dolcar	183	Soofies	1225		
Gurrahs	1740	Sorts	87		

lb.	
48100	Cotton-Yarn
30400	Cassia Lignum
6000	Ginger
32900	Indico
17500	Long Pepper
40	Musk
11200	Nux Vomica
536700	Pepper
	Quicksilver, 24 bottles
11380	China raw Silk & 2 chests
3310	Bengal Ditto gr. lb.
33700	Redwood
157500	Saltpetre
3580	Seedlack
2900	Shellack
34600	Sugar

lb.
[illegible] Sugar-Candy
[illegible] Tincal
China-Ware — 16 chests
1090 Fans
[illegible]

Besides several Parcels of Goods, the Particulars whereof are not yet known.

For Account of the Old *East-India* Company.

35800 lb. Carmenia-Wool, 35500 lb. Pepper.

22.2 (cont.)

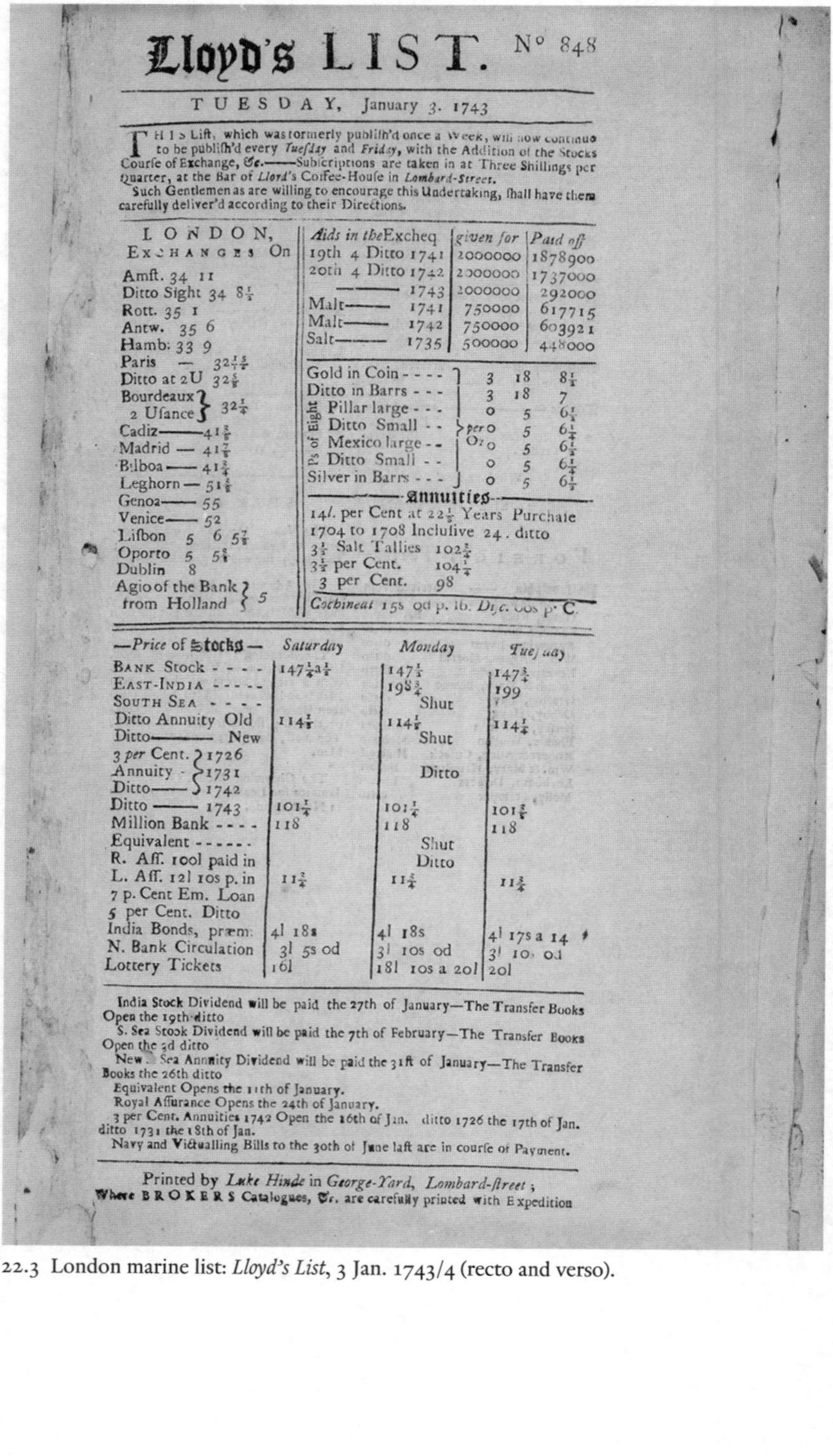

Lloyd's LIST. N° 848

TUESDAY, January 3. 1743

THIS List, which was formerly publish'd once a Week, will now continue to be publish'd every *Tuesday* and *Friday*, with the Addition of the Stocks Course of Exchange, *&c.*——Subscriptions are taken in at Three Shillings per Quarter, at the Bar of *Lloyd's* Coffee-House in *Lombard-Street*.

Such Gentlemen as are willing to encourage this Undertaking, shall have them carefully deliver'd according to their Directions.

LONDON,
EXCHANGES On

Amst.	34 11
Ditto Sight	34 $8\frac{1}{2}$
Rott.	35 1
Antw.	35 6
Hamb.	33 9
Paris —	$32\frac{1}{2}\frac{5}{8}$ [?]
Ditto at 2U	$32\frac{5}{8}$
Bourdeaux 2 Usance	$32\frac{1}{4}$
Cadiz——	$41\frac{3}{8}$
Madrid —	$41\frac{7}{8}$
Bilboa ——	$41\frac{3}{4}$
Leghorn —	$51\frac{3}{8}$
Genoa——	55
Venice——	52
Lisbon	5 6 $5\frac{7}{8}$
Oporto	5 $5\frac{5}{8}$
Dublin	8
Agio of the Bank from Holland	5

Aids in the Excheq		*given for*	*Paid off*
19th 4 Ditto	1741	2000000	1878900
20th 4 Ditto	1742	2000000	1737000
——	1743	2000000	292000
Malt——	1741	750000	617715
Malt——	1742	750000	603921
Salt——	1735	500000	448000

Gold in Coin - - - -	per Oz	3	18	$8\frac{1}{2}$
Ditto in Barrs - - -		3	18	7
Ps of Eight: Pillar large - - -		0	5	$6\frac{1}{2}$
Ps of Eight: Ditto Small - -		0	5	$6\frac{1}{4}$
Ps of Eight: Mexico large - -		0	5	$6\frac{1}{2}$
Ps of Eight: Ditto Small - -		0	5	$6\frac{1}{4}$
Silver in Barrs - - -		0	5	$6\frac{1}{2}$

Annuities

14*l.* per Cent at $22\frac{1}{2}$ Years Purchase
1704 to 1708 Inclusive 24. ditto
$3\frac{1}{2}$ Salt Tallies $102\frac{3}{4}$
$3\frac{1}{2}$ per Cent. $104\frac{1}{4}$
3 per Cent. 98

Cochineal 15s 0d p. lb. *Disc.* 00s [?] p. C.

—*Price* of **Stocks**—	*Saturday*	*Monday*	*Tuesday*
BANK Stock - - - -	$147\frac{1}{4}a\frac{1}{2}$	$147\frac{1}{2}$	$147\frac{3}{4}$
EAST-INDIA - - - -		$198\frac{3}{4}$ [?]	199
SOUTH SEA - - - -		Shut	
Ditto Annuity Old	$114\frac{1}{8}$	$114\frac{1}{8}$	$114\frac{1}{4}$
Ditto—— New		Shut	
3 *per* Cent. Annuity 1726			
Annuity 1731		Ditto	
Ditto—— 1742			
Ditto —— 1743	$101\frac{1}{4}$	$101\frac{1}{4}$	$101\frac{3}{8}$
Million Bank - - - -	118	118	118
Equivalent - - - - - -		Shut	
R. Aff. 100l paid in		Ditto	
L. Aff. 12l 10s p. in	$11\frac{3}{4}$	$11\frac{3}{4}$	$11\frac{3}{4}$
7 p. Cent Em. Loan			
5 per Cent. Ditto			
India Bonds, præm.	4l 18s	4l 18s	4l 17s a 14
N. Bank Circulation	3l 5s 0d	3l 10s 0d	3l 10s 0d
Lottery Tickets	16l	18l 10s a 20l	20l

India Stock Dividend will be paid the 27th of January—The Transfer Books Open the 19th ditto

S. Sea Stock Dividend will be paid the 7th of February—The Transfer Books Open the 3d ditto

New S. [?] Sea Annuity Dividend will be paid the 31st of January—The Transfer Books the 26th ditto

Equivalent Opens the 11th of January.

Royal Assurance Opens the 24th of January.

3 per Cent. Annuities 1742 Open the 16th of Jan. ditto 1726 the 17th of Jan. ditto 1731 the 18th of Jan.

Navy and Victualling Bills to the 30th of June last are in course of Payment.

Printed by *Luke Hinde* in *George-Yard*, *Lombard-street*; Where BROKERS Catalogues, *&c.* are carefully printed with Expedition

22.3 London marine list: *Lloyd's List*, 3 Jan. 1743/4 (recto and verso).

The MARINE List.

Gravesend —— arrived from
1 Jan. Good Intent, Hailes Norway

Hull —— arrived from
Nathaniel & John, Hailes Gottenb.

Bristol —— arrived from
31 Thomas & Rob. Taverner N.foundl.

Mountsbay —— arrived from
Hercules, Tayler St. Kitts

Southampton —— arrived from
31 4 Brothers, Ambrose Ostend

Downs —— arrived from
Remain for
2 Furnace Man of War, and the Ursula Tender.

Winds at Deal

30 NE 31 ENE 1st & 2d ENE.

New York —— arrived from
Rousby, Boyd Jamaica
Dolphin, Brown ditto
——, Latham ditto
——, Morgan ditto
——, Helm St. Kitts
——, Harris ditto

Boston —— arrived from
——, Hunter Lisbon

Leghorn N. S. arrived from
St. Francisca, Audibert Smyrna

Smyrna —— arrived from
5 Tuscany, Tanner London
Boston, Maverly ditto
Francis, Ashington ditto
Matilda, Wild ditto

FOREIGN Ports.

Philadelphia —— arrived from

St. Andrew, Brown	Cowes
Globe, Rees	Barbadoes
Eagle, Collins	ditto
Katherine, Evans	ditto
Wm. & Agnes, Morrill	ditto
Leverpool, Rowe	ditto
Joseph & Mary, Bowne	Jamaica
Grafton, Bay	ditto
Debby, Hogg	ditto
Betsey, Coleman	Antigua
Phenix, Willson	Mahone
Robert & Alice, Cusack	Holland
Wm. & Mary, Hamilton	Belfast
Leybourn, Dowers	Lisbon
Molly, Stamper	ditto

SHIP NEWS.

The Nancy, Marshall, from Londonderry for London, is stranded at Scilly; 'tis thought she will be got off again.

The Adventure, Sweetman, from Carolina for London, who was forc'd ashore in Margate Roads, is got off with Considerable Damage.

The Hercules, Tayler, from St. Kitts, last from St. Thomas's for London, met with a violent Storm off the Western Islands and was obliged to heave fourteen Hhds of Sugar and all her Guns overboard; she lost her Main-mast, Top-mast, Bowsprit, and several of her Men.

The Charming Molly, Goad, from Jamaica for London, is put into Boston in NewEngland.

22.3 (cont.)

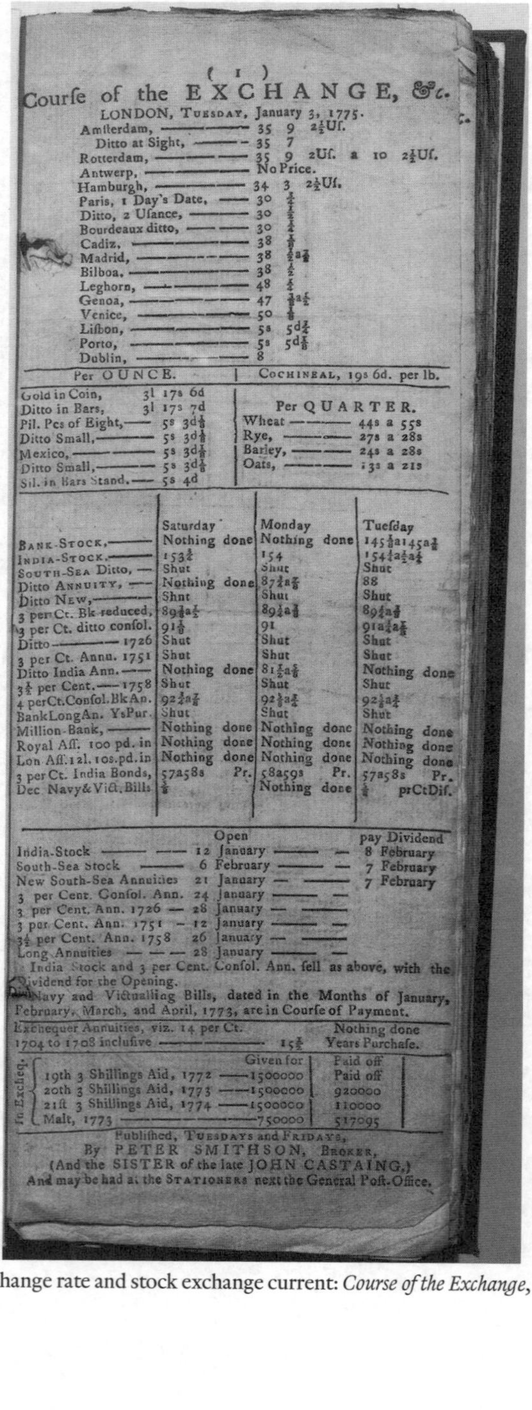

(1)

Course of the EXCHANGE, &c.

LONDON, Tuesday, January 3, 1775.

Amsterdam,	35 9 $2\frac{1}{2}$Us.
Ditto at Sight,	35 7
Rotterdam,	35 9 2Us. a 10 $2\frac{1}{2}$Us.
Antwerp,	No Price.
Hamburgh,	34 3 $2\frac{1}{2}$Us.
Paris, 1 Day's Date,	30 $\frac{3}{4}$
Ditto, 2 Usance,	30 $\frac{1}{2}$
Bourdeaux ditto,	30 $\frac{1}{4}$
Cadiz,	38 $\frac{1}{8}$
Madrid,	38 $\frac{1}{2}$a$\frac{5}{8}$
Bilboa,	38 $\frac{1}{2}$
Leghorn,	48 $\frac{1}{4}$
Genoa,	47 $\frac{3}{8}$a$\frac{1}{2}$
Venice,	50 $\frac{1}{8}$
Lisbon,	5s 5d$\frac{3}{4}$
Porto,	5s 5d$\frac{7}{8}$
Dublin,	8

Per OUNCE. | Cochineal, 19s 6d. per lb.

Per OUNCE	
Gold in Coin,	3l 17s 6d
Ditto in Bars,	3l 17s 7d
Pil. Pcs of Eight,	5s 3d$\frac{1}{8}$
Ditto Small,	5s 3d$\frac{1}{8}$
Mexico,	5s 3d$\frac{1}{8}$
Ditto Small,	5s 3d$\frac{1}{8}$
Sil. in Bars Stand.	5s 4d

Per QUARTER.

Wheat	44s a 55s
Rye,	27s a 28s
Barley,	24s a 28s
Oats,	13s a 21s

	Saturday	Monday	Tuesday
Bank-Stock,	Nothing done	Nothing done	145$\frac{3}{8}$a145a$\frac{1}{2}$
India-Stock,	153$\frac{3}{4}$	154	154$\frac{1}{4}$a$\frac{1}{2}$a$\frac{1}{4}$
South-Sea Ditto,	Shut	Shut	Shut
Ditto Annuity,	Nothing done	87$\frac{3}{4}$a$\frac{7}{8}$	88
Ditto New,	Shut	Shut	Shut
3 per Ct. Bk reduced,	89$\frac{3}{8}$a$\frac{1}{2}$	89$\frac{1}{4}$a$\frac{3}{8}$	89$\frac{1}{4}$a$\frac{3}{8}$
3 per Ct. ditto consol.	91$\frac{1}{8}$	91	91a$\frac{1}{4}$a$\frac{1}{8}$
Ditto 1726	Shut	Shut	Shut
3 per Ct. Annu. 1751	Shut	Shut	Shut
Ditto India Ann.	Nothing done	81$\frac{1}{2}$a$\frac{5}{8}$	Nothing done
$3\frac{1}{2}$ per Cent. 1758	Shut	Shut	Shut
4 perCt.Consol.BkAn.	92$\frac{3}{4}$a$\frac{7}{8}$	92$\frac{5}{8}$a$\frac{3}{4}$	92$\frac{5}{8}$a$\frac{3}{4}$
BankLongAn. YsPur.	Shut	Shut	Shut
Million-Bank,	Nothing done	Nothing done	Nothing done
Royal Ass. 100 pd. in	Nothing done	Nothing done	Nothing done
Lon Ass. 12l. 10s. pd. in	Nothing done	Nothing done	Nothing done
3 per Ct. India Bonds,	57a58s Pr.	58a59s Pr.	57a58s Pr.
Dec Navy & Vict. Bills	$\frac{5}{8}$	Nothing done	$\frac{5}{8}$ prCtDis.

	Open	pay Dividend
India-Stock	12 January	8 February
South-Sea Stock	6 February	7 February
New South-Sea Annuities	21 January	7 February
3 per Cent. Consol. Ann.	24 January	
3 per Cent. Ann. 1726	28 January	
3 per Cent. Ann. 1751	12 January	
$3\frac{1}{2}$ per Cent. Ann. 1758	26 January	
Long Annuities	28 January	

India Stock and 3 per Cent. Consol. Ann. fell as above, with the Dividend for the Opening.

Navy and Victualling Bills, dated in the Months of January, February, March, and April, 1773, are in Course of Payment.

Exchequer Annuities, viz. 14 per Ct. 1704 to 1708 inclusive — $15\frac{1}{2}$ Nothing done Years Purchase.

In Excheq.	Given for	Paid off
19th 3 Shillings Aid, 1772	1500000	Paid off
20th 3 Shillings Aid, 1773	1500000	920000
21st 3 Shillings Aid, 1774	1500000	110000
Malt, 1773	750000	517095

Published, Tuesdays and Fridays,
By PETER SMITHSON, Broker,
(And the SISTER of the late JOHN CASTAING,)
And may be had at the Stationers next the General Post-Office.

22.4 London exchange rate and stock exchange current: *Course of the Exchange, &c.*, 3 Jan. 1775.

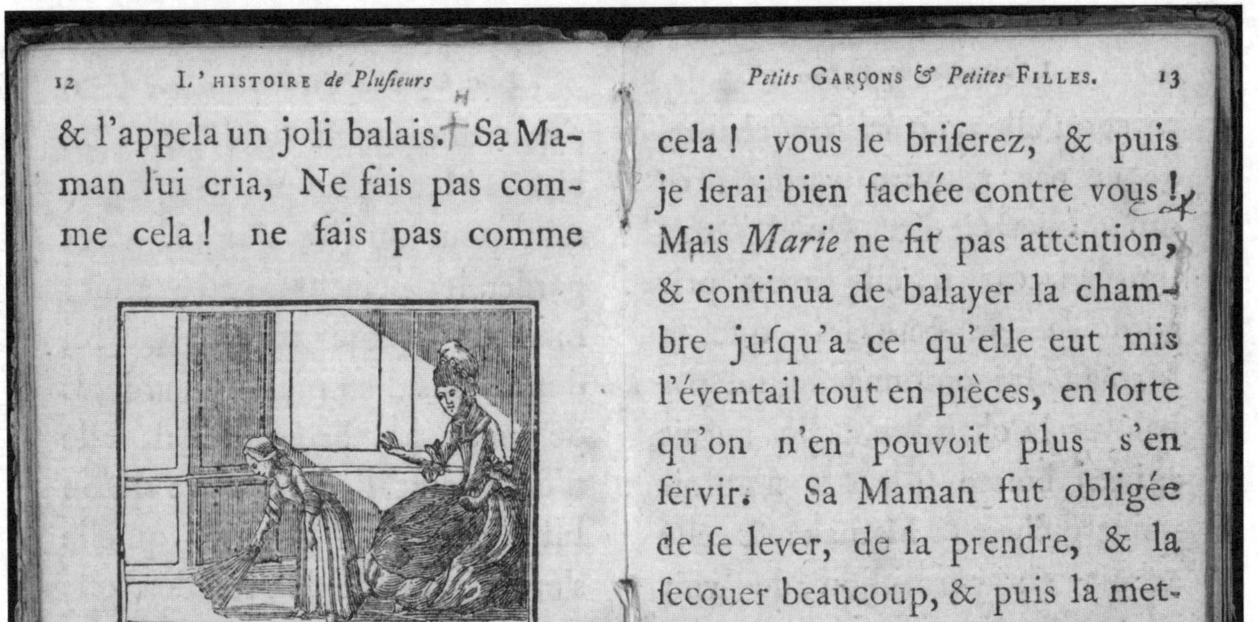

12 L'HISTOIRE *de Plufieurs*

& l'appela un joli balais. Sa Maman lui cria, Ne fais pas comme cela! ne fais pas comme

Petits GARÇONS & *Petites* FILLES. 13

cela! vous le briferez, & puis je ferai bien fachée contre vous! Mais *Marie* ne fit pas attention, & continua de balayer la chambre jufqu'a ce qu'elle eut mis l'éventail tout en pièces, en forte qu'on n'en pouvoit plus s'en fervir. Sa Maman fut obligée de fe lever, de la prendre, & la fecouer beaucoup, & puis la mettre dans un coin de la chambre,

40.1 The anonymous illustrator for Dorothy Kilner's children's books is notable for his sensitive and faithful interpretations of her text. This opening from the French translation of her *History of a great many little boys and girls* (London, John Marshall, *c.*1793?) has been marked up for lessons.

HARRIS'S JUVENILE LIBRARY.

THE FOLLOWING

LIST

OF

NEW AND USEFUL BOOKS

FOR

YOUNG PERSONS,

IS SUBMITTED TO THE NOTICE OF THE PUBLIC,

BY J. HARRIS,

(SUCCESSOR TO NEWBERY,)

At the Corner of St. Paul's Church-yard,

Who flatters himself, notwithstanding the boasting of his numerous Competitors, his ESTABLISHMENT still retains the consequence it has hitherto held, of being the first of its kind in ENGLAND. He begs farther to observe, that it is not merely his own Publications he has on Sale, but that he has an extensive Assortment of those produced by others; and the whole are to be found in Plain, or in Elegant Bindings, suitable for Presents.

It is almost needless to say, that Orders sent by the General or Threepenny Post, will be strictly attended to; and that a liberal allowance is always made to BOOKSELLERS, TOY SHOPS, SCHOOLS, &c.

40.2 Children's books publisher John Harris frequently used the covers of catalogues to ingratiate himself with the public, as well as to promote his full-service retail establishment in the vicinity of St Paul's.